ESSENTIALS OF EDUCATIONAL PSYCHOLOGY

BIG IDEAS TO GUIDE EFFECTIVE TEACHING

JEANNE ELLIS ORMROD
University of Northern Colorado, Emerita

BRETT D. JONES
Virginia Tech

FIFTH EDITION

330 Hudson Street, NY, NY 10013

Director and Portfolio Manager: *Kevin M. Davis*
Content Producer: *Janelle Rogers*
Development Editor: *Alicia Reilly*
Content Project Manager: *Pamela D. Bennett*
Media Project Manager: *Lauren Carlson*
Portfolio Management Assistant: *Anne McAlpine*
Executive Field Marketing Manager: *Krista Clark*
Executive Product Marketing Manager: *Christopher Berry*

Procurement Specialist: *Carol Melville*
Cover Designer: *Carie Keller*
Cover Photo: *Shutterstock/Suzanne Gipson*
Full-Service Project Management: *Norine Strang, Cenveo® Publisher Services*
Composition: *Cenveo® Publisher Services*
Printer/Binder: *LSC Communications/Owensville*
Cover Printer: *Phoenix Color/Hagerstown*
Text Font: *Garamond 3 LT Pro*

Cataloging-in-Publication Data is available on file at the Library of Congress.

ISBN 10:   0-13-489498-7
ISBN 13: 978-0-13-489498-0

1   18

To Olivia, Miles, and Jack Fox (from Jeanne)

and

To Mia and Jack Jones (from Brett)

About the Authors

JEANNE ELLIS ORMROD received her A.B. in psychology from Brown University and her M.S. and Ph.D. in educational psychology from The Pennsylvania State University. She earned licensure in school psychology through postdoctoral work at Temple University and the University of Colorado at Boulder and has worked as a middle school geography teacher and school psychologist. She was Professor of Educational Psychology at the University of Northern Colorado (UNC) until 1998 and is currently Professor Emerita in UNC's School of Psychological Sciences. She has published and presented extensively on cognition and memory, cognitive development, instruction, and related topics but is probably best known for this book and four others: *Human Learning* (currently in its 7th edition); *Educational Psychology: Developing Learners* (9th edition coauthored with Eric Anderman and Lynley Anderman); *Child Development and Education* (coauthored with Teresa McDevitt, currently in its 6th edition); and *Practical Research* (coauthored with Paul Leedy, currently in its 11th edition). After raising three children (two of whom have become teachers themselves), she now lives in New Hampshire with her husband, Richard. Within the past few years, she has had the good fortune to visit schools in diverse cultural settings, including Rwanda, Tanzania, Thailand, Malaysia, and Peru's Amazon region.

BRETT D. JONES is Professor of Educational Psychology in the School of Education at Virginia Tech (Virginia Polytechnic Institute and State University). He received his B.A.E. in architectural engineering from The Pennsylvania State University and his M.A. and Ph.D. in educational psychology from the University of North Carolina at Chapel Hill. He has held faculty positions as an educational psychologist at Duke University, the University of South Florida St. Petersburg, and Virginia Tech. He has taught over 20 different types of university courses related to motivation, cognition, and teaching strategies. Dr. Jones has also conducted workshops and invited presentations at several universities and has presented more than 100 research papers at conferences. His research, which includes examining instructional methods that support students' motivation and learning, has led to more than 70 articles, several book chapters, and two other books besides this book (*Motivating Students by Design: Practical Strategies for Professors* and *The Unintended Consequences of High-Stakes Testing*, the latter of which was coauthored with M. Gail Jones and Tracy Hargrove). He and his wife stay busy with their two children, who enjoy school, athletics, and cheering for the Hokies, Nittany Lions, and Tar Heels.

Preface

New to the Fifth Edition

Our knowledge about how children and adolescents learn and develop—and also about how best to *help* them learn and develop—grows by leaps and bounds every year. Throughout this fifth edition, we've made many changes to reflect new research findings and evidence-based classroom strategies. General changes include the following:

- **Reorganization of chapter sequence:** We have switched the order of "Complex Cognitive Processes" (now Chapter 3) and "Learning in Context" (now Chapter 4) to allow a smoother and more logical transition from "Learning, Cognition, and Memory" (Chapter 2). We have also switched the order of "Motivation and Affect" (now Chapter 5) and "Cognitive Development" (now Chapter 6) so that the latter chapter immediately precedes "Personal, Social, and Moral Development" (Chapter 7), and thus the two chapters about child and adolescent development are together in the book.

- **Explicit organization of chapter content to align with the book's Big Ideas:** As was true in the fourth edition, each chapter begins with three to six Big Ideas that summarize the chapter's content. In this edition, each major section of a chapter is explicitly tied to a Big Idea, with a Self-Check quiz and one or more relevant Application Exercises appearing at the end of the section.

- **New graphics to enhance readers' comprehension:** We have added new graphics in several chapters to visually summarize some of the concepts discussed in the text.

- **Many new online resources:** We have added many book-specific online resources, which can now all be accessed with a single click in the e-book. These resources include:

  - Many updated video examples of children and teachers in action

  - Animated Video Explanations that explain and illustrate certain key concepts and principles (users of the fourth edition may recognize these as short clips from that edition's lengthy interactive modules)

  - Interactive Application Exercises, many of which include classroom videos requiring analysis

  - Multiple-choice Self-Check quizzes (one connected to each Big Idea section)

  - Interactive exercises similar to those a preservice teacher might find on a licensure exam

More specific, chapter-by-chapter changes are the following additions and modifications:

- **Chapter 1:** Reorganization of the chapter content to move some ideas to other sections; minor revisions to the Ormrod's Own Psychological Survey; expanded discussion of educational psychology as a discipline; expanded discussion of principles and theories; reorganization of the principles within Big Idea 1.3; expanded discussion of strategies for learning and studying effectively; several new figures and illustrations related to educational psychology, organizations associated with educational psychology, knowledge needed by teachers, and the cyclical process of action research; new Application Exercises related to types of research, action research projects, and study strategies.

- **Chapter 2:** Reorganization to switch the order of Big Ideas 2.1 and 2.2; new title for Big Idea 2.1; new hotlinked Video Explanation that explains the basic structures of the brain; expanded discussion of working memory, with a revised figure consistent with the discussion; new discussion and associated figure to summarize the contents of long-term memory; reorganization of some of the meaningful learning strategies, with a new associated figure; new figure related to declarative and procedural knowledge; reorganization of the strategies provided in the *Encouraging Effective Long-Term Memory Storage Processes* section; new

Application Exercises related to misconceptions about the brain, active knowledge construction, the three-component model of memory, facilitating recall, and applying information processing strategies.

- **Chapter 3:** Reorganization to switch the order of the *Self-Regulation* and *Metacognition* sections and to include both sections in Big Idea 3.1; expanded discussion about the components and cycle of self-regulation, with a new associated figure; new See for Yourself exercise titled "Knowledge About Beliefs"; new examples of specific transfer; expanded discussion of well-defined and ill-defined problems; reorganization of subsections in the *Promoting Self-Regulation Skills and Metacognitive Development* section; new Application Exercises related to studying and remembering, transfer, problem solving and creativity, critical thinking, self-regulation, and instructional strategies associated with creative thinking.

- **Chapter 4:** New Big Idea to accompany the *Social Interaction as Context* section; new figure to show contexts that influence learning; four new art figures related to behavior, reinforcement, and punishment; expanded discussion of negative reinforcement; revision of table distinguishing among reinforcements and punishment; reorganization and revision of the *Technology and Media as Contexts* section; updated figures depicting environmental influences on learners; two new classroom strategies to address stereotypes and prejudice, with a new illustrative artifact; six new hotlinked Video Explanations that explain negative reinforcement, positive reinforcement, punishment, mediated learning experiences, cognitive tools, peer reinforcement, shaping, and intermittent reinforcement.

- **Chapter 5:** New entry titled "Interest theories" in the table related to theoretical perspectives; reorganization of the sections related to intrinsic and extrinsic motivation; change of the key term *personal interest* to *individual interest*; new figure related to self-efficacy; new Application Exercises related to the nature of motivation, psychological needs, cognitive factors influencing motivation, anxiety, and motivational teaching strategies.

- **Chapter 6:** Addition of *development* as a key term, with a new associated figure; new Think About It question related to growth; new figure showing the interplay among genes, the environment, and behavior; revision of the figure depicting neurons; three new figures related to working memory capacity, the development of knowledge, and intelligence; three new hotlinked Video Explanations that explain (a) mediated learning experiences and cognitive tools, (b) the zone of proximal development, and (c) apprenticeships and cognitive apprenticeships; new Application Exercises related to maturation, the zone of proximal development, Piaget's stages of conservation, dispositions and thinking, and scaffolding.

- **Chapter 7:** New discussion of peer relationships as an important factor influencing classroom climate; new discussion of how students' social motives influence the kinds of peer relationships they seek; expanded discussion of moral and prosocial development to reflect advancements in research findings; new section on providing support strategies and services for students who are homeless; new discussion of students who are recent refugees from war-torn countries; distinction between autism spectrum disorders and Asperger's syndrome (in line with some experts' current thinking about this issue); new Application Exercises related to temperament, social skills, and moral reasoning.

- **Chapter 8:** Revision of opening case study to incorporate the use of technology-based instructional strategies; emphasis on the importance of *evidence-based* strategies in this chapter as well as in Chapter 1; expanded discussion of standards that now includes the Next Generation Science Standards and ISTE standards for technological literacy, rebuttals to several common concerns regarding the Common Core, and the importance of enhancing students' literacy skills in *all* content domains; new section regarding the importance of planning lessons that enhance students' engagement; updated and expanded discussion of computer-based instruction (e.g., in intelligent tutoring programs); expanded discussion of students' independent online research to include webquests and teacher monitoring via a remote desktop feature; new section regarding the use of technology-based simulations and games; new section and Classroom Strategies box regarding modifying and/or supplementing instruction for English language learners; expanded discussion of differentiated instruction to include the importance of scaffolding note taking for students with disabilities and other historically low-achieving students.

- **Chapter 9:** Chapter title changed to "Strategies for Creating Effective Classroom and School Environments" (to more accurately reflect the chapter's content); introduction of *school climate* as a key term; new discussion regarding how poor teacher–student relationships can adversely affect teachers' as well as students' sense of relatedness and overall well-being; addition of "giving low grades" to the list of what *not* to use as a means of punishing students' misbehaviors; terms *positive behavior support* (PBS) and *schoolwide positive behavior support* changed to *positive behavioral interventions and supports* (PBIS) and *schoolwide positive behavioral interventions and supports* (SWPBIS), respectively, in line with current usage; new hotlinked Video Explanation that explains and illustrates the use of applied behavior analysis and functional analysis; new Application Exercises related to classroom arrangement, class rules, addressing behavior problems and student conflicts, and SWPBIS.

- **Chapter 10:** Increased emphasis on the use of a backward design; expanded discussion of rubrics, with a new illustrative example; updated and expanded discussions of how teachers might use technology in teacher assessments or student self-assessments; new discussion of how combining criterion-specific scores into a single criterion-referenced score can be problematic; expanded discussion of the downsides of basing final grades on improvement rather than on students' final achievement levels; new discussion of how computer technology can be used in standardized testing (e.g., via adaptive assessment); new discussion of the Every Student Succeeds Act (ESSA), which replaced the No Child Left Behind Act in late 2015; new section on the practice of using standardized achievement test results as possible indicators of teacher effectiveness (e.g., via value-added assessment); two new Video Explanations that (a) clarify and illustrate the difference between summative and formative assessments and (b) describe and illustrate formative assessment (e.g., via rubrics and checklists); new Application Exercises related to student feedback, good assessment practices, use of portfolios, high-stakes testing, and analysis of computer-generated reports of students' standardized achievement test results.

Our Rationale for This Book

The traditional approach to teaching and writing about educational psychology is to cover one theory at a time, explaining its assumptions and principles and then identifying implications for educational practice. But as we authors have gained increasing experience teaching educational psychology to college students, we've started to teach our courses differently, focusing more on commonalities than differences among theories. In fact, although researchers from different traditions have approached human cognition and behavior from many different angles, they sometimes arrive at more or less the same conclusions. The language they use to describe their observations is often different, to be sure, but beneath all the words are certain nuggets of truth that can be remarkably similar.

In this book, we've tried to bring educational psychology to the real world of children, teachers, and classrooms. We've also tried to integrate ideas from many theoretical perspectives into what is, for us, a general set of principles and strategies that psychology *as a whole* can offer beginning teachers. After a short introduction about the importance of research and study strategies (Chapter 1), we proceed to a discussion of the very essence of human experience: cognition (Chapter 2). From that foundation, we go in five different directions—to complex cognitive processes (Chapter 3), learning in various contexts (Chapter 4), motivation (Chapter 5), cognitive development (Chapter 6), and personal and social development (Chapter 7)—but always returning to basic cognitive processes that underlie various universal human phenomena. The last three chapters of the book build on the earlier ones to offer recommendations in instruction (Chapter 8), classroom management (Chapter 9), and assessment (Chapter 10).

Some of our colleagues in the field may be surprised to see our use of footnotes rather than APA style throughout the book. Our decision has been strictly a pedagogical one. Yes, students need to know that the principles and recommendations in this book are research-based. But we've found that APA style can be quite distracting for someone who is reading about psychology for the first time and trying to sort out what things are and are not important to learn and remember. Novice psychologists should be concerned more with the *ideas themselves* than with the people behind the ideas, and by putting most of the people in small print at the bottom of the page, we can help novices better focus their attention on what things truly are most important to know and understand.

MYEDUCATIONLAB®

The most visible change in the fifth edition (and certainly one of the most significant changes) is the expansion of the digital learning and assessment resources embedded in the etext. Designed to bring you more directly into the world of K–12 classrooms and to help you see the very real impact that educational psychology concepts have on learning and development, these digital learning and assessment resources also

- Provide you with practice using educational psychology concepts in teaching situations,
- Help you and your instructor see how well you understand the concepts presented in the book and the media resources,
- Help you more deeply think about and process educational psychology and how to use it as a teacher (and as a learner).

The online resources in the Enhanced Etext with MyEducationLab include:

- **Video Examples.** In almost all chapters, embedded videos provide illustrations of educational psychology principles or concepts in action. These video examples most often show students and teachers working in classrooms. Sometimes they show students or teachers describing their thinking or experiences.

- **Video Explanations.** Throughout the text, one of us authors (Jeanne Ormrod) provides video explanations of essential concepts. Excerpted from her series of longer educational psychology Study Modules, these brief lectures include animated slides and worked examples.

- **Self-Checks.** Throughout the chapters you will find MyEducationLab: Self-Check quizzes. There are three to six of these quizzes in each chapter, with one at the end of each Big Idea section. They are meant to help you assess how well you have mastered the concepts covered in the section you just read. These self-checks are made up of self-grading multiple-choice items that not only provide feedback on whether you answered the questions correctly or incorrectly, but also provide you with rationales for both correct and incorrect answers.

- **Application Exercises.** Also at the end of each Big Idea section, you can find one or two application exercises that can challenge you to use chapter content to reflect on teaching and learning in real classrooms. The questions you answer in these exercises are usually constructed-response items. Once you provide your own answers to the questions, you receive feedback in the form of model answers written by experts.

MyEdLab
Video Example 3.4.

In many content domains, one aspect of critical thinking is distinguishing between statements that are indisputable facts versus those that reflect personal opinions. What strategies does this sixth-grade teacher use to help students understand this distinction?

MyEdLab
Video Explanation 4.4.

This video illustrates the use of cognitive tools in a high school physics class.

In this chapter, you have learned about a wide variety of strategies for effectively planning and implementing instruction. In the hotlinked Self-Check quiz and Application Exercises that follow, you can check and apply your understandings related to Big Idea 8.4:

> *Different instructional strategies are appropriate for different instructional goals and objectives and for different students.*

MyEdLab Self-Check 8.4

MyEdLab Application Exercise 8.6. In this exercise, you can observe and analyze a bilingual lesson in high school history.

MyEdLab Application Exercise 8.7. In this exercise, you can apply what you have learned about planning and instruction to analyze an actual lesson plan.

- **Practice for Your Licensure Exam features.** Every chapter ends with an exercise that can give you an opportunity to apply the chapter's content while reading a case study and then answering multiple-choice and constructed-response questions similar to those that appear on many teacher licensure tests. By clicking on the MyEducationLab hotlink at the end of a Practice for Your Licensure Exam exercise, you can complete the activity online and get feedback about your answers.

PRACTICE FOR YOUR LICENSURE EXAM

Vision Unit

Ms. Kontos is teaching a unit on human vision to her fifth-grade class. She shows her students a diagram of the various parts of the human eye, such as the lens, cornea, pupil, retina, and optic nerve. She then explains that people can see objects because light from the sun or another light source bounces off those objects and into their eyes. To illustrate this idea, she shows them Picture A.

"Do you all understand how our eyes work?" she asks. Her students nod that they do.

The next day Ms. Kontos gives her students Picture B.

She asks students to draw one or more arrows on the picture to show how light enables the child to see the tree. More than half of the students draw arrows something like the one shown in Picture C.

1. **Constructed-response question**

   Obviously, most of Ms. Kontos's students have not learned what she thought she had taught them about human vision.

   A. Explain why many students believe the opposite of what Ms. Kontos has taught them. Base your response on contemporary principles and theories of learning and cognition.

   B. Describe two different ways in which you might improve on this lesson to help students gain a more accurate understanding of human vision. Base your strategies on contemporary principles and theories of learning and cognition.

2. **Multiple-choice question**

   Many elementary-age children think of human vision in the way that Ms. Kontos's fifth graders do—that is, as a process that originates in the eye and goes outward toward objects that are seen. When students revise their thinking to be more consistent with commonly accepted scientific explanations, they are said to be

   a. acquiring a new script.

   b. acquiring procedural knowledge.

   c. undergoing conceptual change.

   d. revising their worldview.

   MyEdLab **Licensure Exam 2.1**

- **Classroom Management Simulations.** In Chapter 9 and in the left-hand navigation bar of MyEducationLab, you will be able to access interactive simulations that engage you in decision making about classroom management strategies. These interactive cases focus on the classroom management issues teachers most frequently encounter on a daily basis. Each simulation presents a challenge scenario at the beginning and then offers a series of choices to solve each challenge. Along the way, you receive mentor feedback on your choices and have the opportunity to make better choices if necessary.

- **Study Modules.** In the left-hand navigation bar of MyEducationLab, you will also find a set of Study Modules. These interactive, application-oriented modules provide opportunities to learn foundational educational psychology concepts in ways other than reading about them. The modules present content through screen-capture videos that include animations, worked examples, and classroom videos. Each module consists of three parts. In the first part, begin with the Learn section that presents several key concepts and strategies. Then work through the problems in the Apply section. These will give you practice applying the concepts and principles to actual teaching and learning scenarios. The third part of each module is a multiple-choice test in the Assess section. This test includes higher-order questions that assess not only what you can remember about the module's content but also how well you can apply the concepts and strategies you've learned to real-life classroom situations.

- **Video Analysis Tool.** Our widely anticipated Video Analysis Tool is also available in the left-hand navigation bar of MyEducationLab. The Video Analysis Tool helps you build your skills in analyzing teaching. Exercises provide classroom videos and rubrics to scaffold your analysis. Timestamp and commenting tools allow you to easily annotate the video and connect your observations to educational psychology concepts you have learned in the text.

OTHER BOOK FEATURES

The book's 10 chapters have a variety of features that can help readers better understand, remember, and apply what they're reading. First, each chapter begins with three to six **Big Ideas**—overarching principles that provide a general organizational scheme for the chapter's content, Self-Check quizzes, Application Exercises, and end-of-chapter summary. Then, boldfaced **Guiding Principles** and **Key Strategies** throughout the chapter highlight key principles and concrete recommendations that can guide teachers in their decision making and classroom practices.

Immediately following the list of Big Ideas presented at the beginning of each chapter is a **case study** that introduces some of the ideas and issues we address in the chapter. Throughout each chapter, we periodically revisit the case to offer new insights and interpretations.

We often put readers themselves in the position of "learner" and ask them to engage in a short learning or thinking activity. Many of these **See for Yourself** exercises are similar to ones we've used in our own educational psychology classes. Our students have found them to be quite helpful in making concepts and principles more "real" for them—and hence more vivid, understandable, and memorable. An example of such an exercise follows.

SEE FOR YOURSELF
MARTIN'S PLIGHT

Imagine that you're in the ninth grade. You're walking quickly down the school corridor on your way to your math class when you see three boys from the so-called "popular" crowd cornering a small, socially awkward boy named Martin. The boys first make fun of Martin's thick glasses and unfashionable clothing, then they start taunting him with offensive names such as "fag" and "retard." What do you do?

a. You look the other way, pretending you haven't heard anything, and hurry on to class. If you were to stop to help, the boys might taunt you as well, and that will only make the situation worse.
b. You shoot Martin a sympathetic look and then head to class so that you won't be late. Afterward, you anonymously report the incident to the principal's office, because you know that the boys' behaviors have violated your school's antibullying policy.
c. You stop and say, "Hey, you jerks, cut it out! Martin's a really nice guy and doesn't deserve your insulting labels. Come on, Martin—let's go. We might be late for math class, so we need to hurry."

An additional feature comes in the form of **Think About It** questions in the margin that encourage readers to connect chapter content to their past experiences or current beliefs and in some cases also encourage readers to take concepts and principles in new directions.

If you quickly flip through the book, you'll see many classroom artifacts—that is, **examples of work created by actual students and teachers**. We use artifacts throughout the book to help readers connect concepts, principles, and strategies to students' behavior and to classroom practices.

> **think about it**
> Using what you've learned about attention, explain why texting on a phone while driving is illegal in many places. (For an explanation, click **here**.)

To a considerable degree, we talk about concepts and principles that apply to children and adolescents at all grade levels. Yet 1st graders often think and act very differently than 6th graders, and 6th graders can, in turn, be quite different from 11th graders. Chapters 2 through 10 each have one or more **Developmental Trends** tables that highlight and illustrate developmental differences that teachers are apt to see in grades K–2, 3–5, 6–8, and 9–12.

Chapters 2 through 10 also each have two or more **Classroom Strategies** boxes that offer concrete suggestions and examples of how teachers might apply a particular concept or principle. These features should provide yet another mechanism to help our readers apply educational psychology to actual classroom practices. And beginning in Chapter 3, each chapter has a **Cultural Considerations** feature that describes cultural differences in specific areas—for instance, in behavior, reasoning, or motivation.

Although our approach in this book is to integrate the concepts, principles, and educational strategies that diverse theoretical perspectives offer, it's also important for future teachers to have some familiarity with specific psychological theories and with a few prominent theorists who have had a significant influence on psychological thinking (e.g., Jean Piaget, Lev Vygotsky, B. F. Skinner). We occasionally mention these theories and theorists in the text discussion, but we also highlight them in **Theoretical Perspectives** tables in Chapters 2, 5, and 6.

Supplementary Materials

Many supplements to the textbook are available to enhance readers' learning and development as teachers.

Online Instructor's Manual.   Available to instructors for download at www.pearsonhighered .com/educator is an *Instructor's Manual* with suggestions for learning activities, supplementary lectures, group activities, and additional media resources. These have been carefully selected to provide opportunities to support, enrich, and expand on what students read in the textbook.

Online PowerPoint® Slides.   PowerPoint slides are available to instructors for download at www.pearsonhighered.com/educator. These slides include key concept summarizations and other graphic aids to help students understand, organize, and remember core concepts and ideas.

Online Test Bank.   The *Test Bank* that accompanies this text contains both multiple-choice and essay questions. Some items (lower-level questions) simply ask students to identify or explain concepts and principles they have learned. But many others (higher-level questions) ask students to apply those same concepts and principles to specific classroom situations—that is, to actual student behaviors and teaching strategies. The lower-level questions assess basic knowledge of educational psychology. But ultimately, it is the higher-level questions that can best assess students' ability to use principles of educational psychology in their own teaching practice.

TestGen.   TestGen is a powerful test generator available exclusively from Pearson Education publishers. Instructors install TestGen on a personal computer (Windows or Macintosh) and create their own tests for classroom testing and for other specialized delivery options, such as over a local area network or on the web. A test bank, which is also called a Test Item File (TIF), typically contains a large set of test items, organized by chapter and ready for your use in creating a test, based on the associated textbook material. Assessments—including equations, graphs, and scientific notation—can be created in either paper-and-pencil or online formats.

The tests can be downloaded in the following formats:

TestGen Testbank file—PC

TestGen Testbank file—MAC

TestGen Testbank—Blackboard 9 TIF

TestGen Testbank—Blackboard CE/Vista (WebCT) TIF

Angel Test Bank (zip)

D2L Test Bank (zip)

Moodle Test Bank

Sakai Test Bank (zip)

Artifact Case Studies: Interpreting Children's Work and Teachers' Classroom Strategies.   One of us authors, Jeanne Ormrod, has written *Artifact Case Studies* (ISBN 0-13-114671-8) as a supplement to the textbook. It's especially useful for helping students learn to apply psychological concepts and principles related to learning, motivation, development, instruction, and assessment. The case studies, or *artifact cases,* within this text offer work samples and instructional materials that cover a broad range of topics, including literacy, mathematics, science, social studies, and art. Every artifact case includes background information and questions to consider as readers examine and interpret the artifact. Instructors should contact their local Pearson Education sales representative to order a copy of this book and its accompanying Instructor's Manual.

Case Studies: Applying Educational Psychology.   With the assistance of Linda Pallock and Brian Harper, Jeanne Ormrod and Dinah Jackson McGuire have coauthored *Case Studies: Applying Educational Psychology* (2nd ed., ISBN 0-13-198046-7) to give students more in-depth practice in applying educational psychology to real children, teachers, and classrooms. The 48 cases in the book address many topics in educational psychology (learning and cognition, child and adolescent development, student diversity, motivation, instruction, classroom management, and assessment) across a variety of grade levels (preschool through high school). This book, too, is accompanied by an Instructor's Manual.

Acknowledgments

Although the title page lists us as the authors of this book, we've hardly written it alone. We're greatly indebted to the countless psychologists, educators, and other scholars whose insights and research findings we have pulled together in these pages. We also owe more thanks than we can possibly express to Kevin Davis, vice president and editor-in-chief at Pearson, who has guided our journey (in Jeanne's case, for more than 25 years) as we've tried to navigate through the myriad new topics, controversies, and technological changes that have encompassed both the field of educational psychology and the publishing world. And we are incredibly appreciative of the collective efforts of Alicia Reilly, Pam Bennett, Norine Strang, Lauren Carlson, and many others who have attended to the gazillion (and sometimes mysterious) details of turning this book into both concrete and virtual realities.

On the home front have been the many students and teachers whose examples, artifacts, and interviews illustrate some of the concepts, developmental trends, and classroom strategies we describe in the book: Aleph Altman-Mills, Andrew Belcher, Katie Belcher, Noah Davis, Shea Davis, Barbara Dee, Tina Ormrod Fox, Amaryth Gass, Anthony Gass, Ben Geraud, Darcy Geraud, Macy Gotthardt, Colin Hedges, Philip Hilbert, Erin Islo, Jesse Jensen, Sheila Johnson, Jack Jones, Mia Jones, Shelly Lamb, Michele Minichiello, Susan O'Byrne, Alex Ormrod, Jeff Ormrod, Isabelle Peters, Laura Riordan, Corey Ross, Ashton Russo, Alex Sheehan, Connor Sheehan, Matt Shump, Melinda Shump, Grace Tober, Ashleigh Utzinger, Grant Valentine, Caroline Wilson, Hannah Wilson, and Brian Zottoli.

Reviewers who helped shape this fifth edition were Vanessa Ewing, University of Northern Colorado and Metropolitan State University of Denver; Leah Johnson, Indiana University and Purdue University, Fort Wayne; Frank R. Lilly, California State University, Sacramento; and Karthigeyan Subramaniam, University of North Texas. We are greatly indebted to all of these individuals for their deep commitment to preparing future teachers and to getting the word out about the many things that the field of educational psychology has to offer.

We must also acknowledge the contributions of our professional colleagues around the country who've reviewed the first, second, third, and fourth editions of the book and offered many invaluable insights and suggestions: Lynley H. Anderman, University of Kentucky; Heidi Andrade, State University of New York at Albany; Bonnie Armbruster, University of Illinois at Urbana-Champaign; Ty Binfet, Loyola Marymount University; Bryan Bolea, Grand Valley State University; Kym Buchanan, University of Wisconsin–Stevens Point; Jessica Chittum, East Carolina University; Rhoda Cummings, University of Nevada at Reno; Emily de la Cruz, Portland State University; Karen A. Droms, Luzerne County Community College; Randi A. Engle, University of California, Berkeley; Robert B. Faux, University of Pittsburgh; William M. Gray,

University of Toledo; Robert L. Hohn, University of Kansas; Donna Jurich, Knox College; Adria Karle, Florida International University; Julita G. Lambating, California State University at Sacramento; Frank R. Lilly, California State University at Sacramento; Jenny Martin, Bridgewater College; Jeffrey Miller, California State University at Dominguez Hills; Anne Marie Rakip, South Carolina State University; Marla Reese-Weber, Illinois State University; Michelle Riconscente, University of Maryland at College Park; Cecil Robinson, University of Alabama; Analisa L. Smith, Nova Southeastern University; Beverly Snyder, University of Colorado at Colorado Springs; Karthigeyan Subramaniam, University of North Texas; Debi Switzer, Clemson University; Mark Szymanski, Pacific University; Kimberlee Taylor, Utah State University; Tenisha Tevis, American University; Michael P. Verdi, California State University at San Bernardino; Vickie Williams, University of Maryland, Baltimore County; Steven R. Wininger, Western Kentucky University; John Woods, Grand Valley State University; and Sharon Zumbrunn, Virginia Commonwealth University.

Finally, of course, Jeanne must thank her husband, Richard; her children, Tina, Alex, and Jeff; and her grandchildren, Olivia, Miles, and Jack. Meanwhile, Brett would like to thank his wife, Rebecca; his children, Mia and Jack; his parents, Carole and Jack; and his stepfather, Larry. Our families have shaped our lives—and so also this book—in ways too numerous to recall.

J. E. O.
B. D. J.

Brief Contents

Contents

5 Motivation and Affect 152

6 Cognitive Development 204

When administering the test, follow the directions closely and report any unusual circumstances. 428

Make appropriate accommodations for English language learners. 428

When interpreting test results, take students' ages and developmental levels into account. 429

If tests are being used to measure teacher or school effectiveness, advocate for a focus on students' improvement over time rather than on age-group averages. 429

Never use a single test score to make important decisions about students. 430

ESSENTIALS OF
EDUCATIONAL
PSYCHOLOGY

BIG IDEAS TO GUIDE EFFECTIVE TEACHING

Moodboard Premium/Glow Images

1

Introduction to Educational Psychology

Big Ideas to Master in this Chapter

1.1 Effective teachers use research findings and research-based theories to make decisions about instructional strategies, classroom management, and assessment practices.

1.2 Effective teachers continually work to enhance their professional knowledge and skills.

1.3 Learners read, study, and learn more efficiently when they plan appropriately and use effective strategies.

CASE STUDY: THE "NO D" POLICY

Anne Smith is a ninth-grade English teacher with 10 years of teaching experience, and by all accounts she's an excellent teacher. Even so, in previous years many of her students haven't invested much time or energy in their writing assignments and seemingly haven't been bothered by the Cs and Ds they've earned in her classes. In an effort to more fully engage this year's students in their schoolwork, Ms. Smith begins the school year by initiating two new policies. First, to pass her course, students must earn at least a C; she won't give anyone a final grade of D. Second, students will have multiple opportunities to revise and resubmit assignments. She'll give whatever feedback students need on the assignments—and, if necessary, one-on-one instruction—to help them improve their work. She solicits students' questions and concerns about the new policies, gains their agreement to "try something new," and engages them in a discussion of specific, concrete characteristics of A-quality, B-quality, and C-quality work. Then, as the school year progresses, she regularly administers brief surveys to get students' feedback about her innovations, asking such questions as "How is the 'no D' policy working for you?" "Do you think your grade is an accurate reflection of your learning?" and "Any suggestions?"

Students' responses on the surveys are overwhelmingly positive. Students mention noticeable improvements in the quality of their writing and increasingly report that they believe themselves to be in control of both their learning and their grades. Furthermore, they begin to see their teacher in a new light—"as one who will help them achieve their best work, not as one who just gives out grades . . . as a coach encouraging them along the long race of learning." Final course grades also confirm the value of the new policies: A much higher percentage of students earn grades of C or better than has been true in past years.[1]

- Effective teachers don't simply transmit new information and skills to students; they also work hard to help students *master* the information and skills. In the case study just presented, what strategies does Ms. Smith use to foster her students' writing development?

Teaching other people—especially teaching the generation that will follow you into the adult world—can be one of the most rewarding professions on the planet. It can also be a very challenging profession. Certainly effective teaching involves presenting a topic or skill in such a way that students can understand and master it. Yet it involves many other things as well. For instance, teachers must motivate students to *want* to learn the subject matter, must help students recognize what true mastery involves, and—to appropriately individualize instruction—must assess where each student currently is in his or her learning and development. And, in general, effective teachers create an environment in which students believe that if they work hard and have reasonable support, they can achieve at high levels. In the opening case study, Anne Smith does all of these things.

How children and adolescents think and learn, what knowledge and skills they have and haven't mastered, where they are in their developmental journeys, what their interests and

---

[1] Action research project described in A. K. Smith, 2009.

priorities are—all of these factors influence the effectiveness of various classroom strategies. Thus, the decisions *teachers* make in the classroom—decisions about what topics and skills to teach (*planning*), how to teach those topics and skills (*instruction*), how to keep students on task and supportive of one another's learning efforts (creating an effective *classroom environment*), and how best to determine what students have learned (*assessment*)—must ultimately depend on students' existing characteristics and behaviors.

Of course, as we saw from Anne Smith in the opening case study, teachers' classroom strategies also change what *students* know, think, and can do. Thus, the relationship between student characteristics and behaviors, on the one hand, and teacher strategies, on the other, is a two-way street. Furthermore, as you'll discover in later chapters, planning, instruction, the classroom environment, and assessment practices influence one another, as depicted in Figure 1.1. Notice how student characteristics and behaviors are at the center of the figure, because these must drive almost everything that teachers do in the classroom. Such an approach to teaching is sometimes known as **learner-centered instruction**.[2]

The purpose of this book is to help you understand children and adolescents—how they learn and develop, how they're likely to be similar to but also different from one another, what activities and assignments are apt to engage them in the classroom, and so on. It will also give you a toolbox of strategies for planning and carrying out instruction, creating an environment that keeps students motivated and on task, and assessing students' progress and achievement. Such topics are the domain of **educational psychology**, which is an academic discipline that (a) systematically studies the nature of human learning, development, motivation, and related topics and (b) applies its research findings to the identification and development of effective instructional practices. We begin by exploring how teachers can use different types of research findings to make instructional decisions.

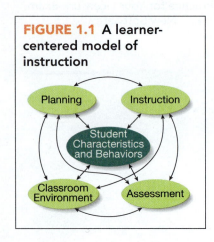

FIGURE 1.1 A learner-centered model of instruction

1.1 USING RESEARCH FINDINGS TO MAKE INSTRUCTIONAL DECISIONS

Big Idea 1.1 Effective teachers use research findings and research-based theories to make decisions about instructional strategies, classroom management, and assessment practices.

Teachers make instructional decisions based on their prior experiences, advice from others, knowledge and skills they learned in their formal schooling, and so on. Although many of these sources of information are potentially useful to teachers' instructional decisions, effective teachers rely on research findings and research-based theories to inform their practices. In the principles that follow, we discuss why teachers need to understand research, we examine the different types of research conducted by educational psychologists, and we explain how this research can be synthesized and organized to be helpful to teachers.

The effectiveness of various classroom practices can best be determined through systematic research.

You yourself have been a student for many years now, and you've undoubtedly learned a great deal about how individuals learn and develop and about how teachers can foster their learning and development. But exactly how much *do* you know? To help you find out, one of us authors has developed a short pretest titled *Ormrod's Own Psychological Survey (OOPS)*.

---

[2] For good general discussions of learner-centered instructional practices, see McCombs, 2005; National Research Council, 2000. You may also want to look at the American Psychological Association's (APA's) 14 *Learner-Centered Psychological Principles* on the APA website at www.apa.org; type "learner-centered principles" in the search box on APA's home page.

─────────────── **SEE FOR YOURSELF** ───────────────
ORMROD'S OWN PSYCHOLOGICAL SURVEY (OOPS)

Decide whether each of the following statements is *true* or *false.*

True/False

_____ 1. Some children are predominantly left-brain thinkers, whereas others are predominantly right-brain thinkers.

_____ 2. The best way to learn and remember a new fact is to repeat it over and over.

_____ 3. Students often misjudge how much they know about a topic.

_____ 4. Anxiety sometimes helps students learn and perform more successfully in the classroom.

_____ 5. Instruction is most effective when it is tailored to students' individual learning styles.

_____ 6. Children's personalities are largely the result of their home environments.

_____ 7. Playing video games can enhance children's cognitive development.

_____ 8. The ways in which teachers assess students' learning influence what and how students actually learn.

Now let's see how well you did on the OOPS. The answers, along with an explanation for each one, are as follows:

1. Some children are predominantly left-brain thinkers, whereas others are predominantly right-brain thinkers. FALSE—With the development of new medical technologies in recent years, researchers have learned a great deal about how the human brain works and which parts of it specialize in which aspects of human thinking. As we'll discover in Chapter 2, the two halves, or *hemispheres,* of the brain do seem to have somewhat different specialties, but they continually communicate and collaborate in tackling even the simplest of daily tasks. Practically speaking, there's no such thing as left-brain or right-brain thinking.[3]

2. The best way to learn and remember a new fact is to repeat it over and over. FALSE—Although repeating new information several times is better than doing nothing at all with it, repetition of specific facts is a relatively *in*effective way to learn. Students learn new information more easily and remember it longer when they connect it with things they already know. One especially effective strategy is **elaboration**: using prior knowledge to expand or embellish on a new idea in some way, perhaps by drawing inferences from a historical fact, identifying new examples of a scientific concept, or thinking of situations in which a mathematical procedure might be helpful. Chapter 2 describes several cognitive processes that help students learn and remember school subject matter effectively.

3. Students often misjudge how much they know about a topic. TRUE—Contrary to popular opinion, students are usually *not* the best judges of what they do and don't know. For example, many students think that if they've spent a long time studying a textbook chapter, they must know its contents very well. Yet if they've spent most of their study time inefficiently—perhaps by "reading" while thinking about something else altogether or by mindlessly copying definitions—they may know far less than they think they do. We'll consider this *illusion of knowing* further in Chapter 3.

4. Anxiety sometimes helps students learn and perform more successfully in the classroom. TRUE—Many people think that anxiety is always a bad thing. In fact, a little bit of anxiety can actually *improve* learning and performance, especially when students perceive a task to be something they can accomplish with reasonable effort. For instance, a small, manageable amount of anxiety can spur students to complete their work carefully and to study for tests. We'll explore the effects of anxiety and other emotions in Chapter 5.

5. Instruction is most effective when it is tailored to students' individual learning styles. FALSE—Contrary to a popular belief, most measures of supposed "learning styles" merely reflect students' self-reported *preferences,* and tailoring instruction to such preferences doesn't

─────────
[3] Schlegel, Alexander, & Tse, 2016.

noticeably enhance students' learning or academic achievement.[4] It is far more important that teachers base their instructional practices on knowledge of the cognitive processes that underlie how virtually *all* students think and learn. We'll learn more about students' preferences and *cognitive styles* in Chapter 6.

6. Children's personalities are largely the result of their home environments. FALSE—Certainly children's home environments shape their behaviors to some extent. But heredity also has a significant impact. From birth, infants are noticeably different in the extent to which they're calm or fussy, shy or outgoing, fearful or adventurous, and so on. As we'll see in Chapter 7, such differences in *temperament* appear to have their roots in biology and genetics, and they persist throughout the childhood years and into adulthood.

7. Playing video games can enhance children's cognitive development. TRUE or, more accurately, SOMETIMES TRUE—A great deal of time spent playing video games *instead of* reading, doing homework, and engaging in other school-related activities can definitely interfere with children's long-term academic success. But some video games can be powerful tools for promoting important cognitive abilities, such as spatial abilities and the flexible use of attention.[5] And educational technologists have increasingly been designing highly motivating video games that simulate real-world problems and foster complex problem-solving skills.[6] In upcoming chapters (especially Chapter 4 and Chapter 8), we'll examine many ways in which computer technologies can support students' learning and cognitive development.

8. The ways in which teachers assess students' learning influence what and how students actually learn. TRUE—What and how students learn depend, in part, on how they expect their learning to be assessed. For example, in the opening case study, Anne Smith's "No D" and multiple-submission policies encourage students to seek feedback about their work, benefit from their mistakes, and enhance their writing skills. In Chapter 10 we'll look more closely at the potential effects of classroom assessment practices on students' learning.

How many of the OOPS items did you answer correctly? Did some of the false items seem convincing enough that you marked them true? Did some of the true items contradict certain beliefs you had? If either of these was the case, you're hardly alone. College students often agree with statements that seem obvious but are, in fact, partially or completely incorrect.[7] Furthermore, many students in teacher education classes reject research findings when those findings appear to contradict their personal beliefs and experiences.[8]

It's easy to be persuaded by "common sense" and assume that what seems logical must be true. Yet common sense and logic don't always give us the real scoop about how people actually learn and develop, nor do they always give us appropriate guidance about how best to help students succeed in the classroom. Educational psychologists believe that knowledge about teaching and learning should come from a more objective source of information—that is, from systematic research. Increasingly, educators and policy makers alike are calling for **evidence-based practices**—the use of instructional methods and other classroom strategies that research has consistently shown to bring about significant gains in students' development and academic achievement.[9]

Educational psychologists focus on the scientific study of psychological principles that are relevant to education.

Integrating evidence-based practices into your teaching takes time and practice, of course. But it also takes knowledge of topics within the discipline of educational psychology, including knowledge of human learning and motivation, developmental trends, individual and group differences, classroom assessment and standardized testing, and effective classroom practices. Educational psychologists

---

[4] Kirschner & van Merriënboer, 2013; Kozhevnikov, Evans, & Kosslyn, 2014; Krätzig & Arbuthnott, 2006; Mayer & Massa, 2003.

[5] Green, 2014; Rothbart, 2011; Tobias & Fletcher, 2011.

[6] Blumberg, 2014; Squire, 2011.

[7] Gage, 1991; L. S. Goldstein & Lake, 2000; Woolfolk Hoy, Davis, & Pape, 2006.

[8] Gregoire, 2003; Holt-Reynolds, 1992; T. M. McDevitt & Ormrod, 2008; Patrick & Pintrich, 2001.

[9] Cook, Smith, & Tankersley, 2012. For example, see Darling-Hammond & Bransford, 2005; Waterhouse, 2006.

develop this knowledge by solving problems in the field of education through the use of rigorous scientific methods.[10] Topics in educational psychology are also studied by researchers in closely related disciplines, such as education, instructional design and technology, learning science, cognitive science, and other overlapping areas of psychology (e.g., behavioral, cognitive, developmental, social, and school psychology). In addition, neurologists, cognitive psychologists, and researchers from other disciplines are working together to discover how the *brain* influences people's behavior and learning and, conversely, how people's behavior and learning experiences can influence brain development. This rapidly expanding field, known as *cognitive neuroscience*, is making many noteworthy contributions to our understanding of human learning. As Figure 1.2 shows, educational psychology informs and is informed by many different disciplines.

One way that individuals contribute to the field of educational psychology is to publish their research findings in academic journals and books. Many educational psychologists also belong to regional, national, and international organizations to share their research and discuss ideas with others (see Figure 1.3 for examples). We authors synthesized much of this research in developing the Big Ideas presented in this book.

When educational psychologists write about and present their research, they identify the particular research articles, books, conference presentations, and other sources on which they base their claims. Most educational psychology publications and conferences require authors to follow **APA style**, guidelines prescribed by the American Psychological Association for identifying sources and preparing references.[11] In APA style, a source is cited by presenting the author(s) and date of publication in the body of the text. For example, this sentence from a prior paragraph would be cited as follows in APA style: College students often agree with statements that seem obvious but are, in fact, partially or completely incorrect (Gage, 1991; Goldstein & Lake, 2000; Woolfolk Hoy, Davis, & Pape, 2006). In this book, we've intentionally deviated from APA style by presenting the references in footnotes. We hope this style will help you focus on the *ideas* instead of on the names and dates provided in the references. But when you find some of the book's ideas especially interesting, exciting, or surprising, we urge you to read the footnoted sources firsthand by finding the detailed citations in the book's References list.

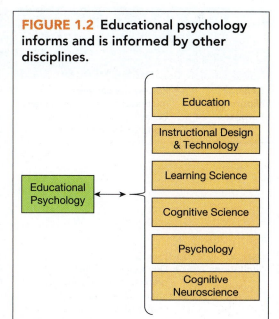

FIGURE 1.2 Educational psychology informs and is informed by other disciplines.

Educational Psychology ↔ Education · Instructional Design & Technology · Learning Science · Cognitive Science · Psychology · Cognitive Neuroscience

FIGURE 1.3 Examples of organizations that represent educational psychology

Organizations	Website URL
American Educational Research Association (AERA)	http://aera.net/
American Psychological Association (APA)	http://www.apa.org/
Association for Psychological Science (APS)	http://www.psychologicalscience.org/
International Society of the Learning Sciences (ISLS)	https://www.isls.org/

Research can provide quantitative information, qualitative information, or both.

Many research studies involve **quantitative research**: They yield numbers that reflect percentages, frequencies, or averages related to certain characteristics or phenomena. For example, a quantitative study might provide information about students' scores on achievement tests, students' responses to rating-scale questionnaires, or school district records of students' attendance and dropout rates.

Other studies involve **qualitative research**: They yield nonnumeric data—perhaps in the form of verbal reports, written documents, pictures, or maps—that capture many aspects of a complex situation. For example, a qualitative study might involve lengthy interviews in which students describe their hopes for the future, a detailed case study of interpersonal relationships within a tight-knit clique of adolescent girls, or in-depth observations of several teachers who create distinctly different psychological atmospheres in their classrooms.

---

[10] Harris, Graham, & Urdan, 2012; Reynolds & Miller, 2013.

[11] For more information on APA style, see its *Publication Manual* (APA, 2010) or visit www.apastyle.org

Table 1.1 • Contrasting Various Types of Research

	QUALITATIVE RESEARCH	QUANTITATIVE RESEARCH		
	Descriptive Studies	**Descriptive Studies**	**Correlational Studies**	**Experimental and Quasi-Experimental Studies**
General Nature and Purposes	• Portray the complex, multifaceted nature of human behavior, especially in real-world social settings	• Capture the current state of affairs regarding a real-world issue or problem	• Identify associations among characteristics, behaviors, and/or environmental conditions • Enable predictions about one variable, given knowledge of the degree or quantity of another variable • Provide an alternative when experimental manipulations are unethical or impossible	• Manipulate one (independent) variable in order to observe its possible effect on another (dependent) variable • Eliminate other plausible explanations for observed outcomes (especially in carefully controlled experimental studies) • Enable conclusions about cause-and-effect relationships
Limitations	• Don't enable either predictions or conclusions about cause-and-effect relationships	• Don't enable either (1) predictions about one variable based on another variable or (2) conclusions about cause-and-effect relationships	• Enable only imprecise predictions, with many exceptions to the general relationships observed • Don't enable conclusions about cause-and-effect relationships	• May not completely eliminate alternative explanations for observed outcomes (especially true for quasi-experimental studies) • In some cases, involve artificial laboratory conditions that don't resemble real-life learning environments (true for many tightly controlled experimental studies)
Examples of Questions That Might Be Addressed	• What things do high-achieving students say they do "in their heads" when they read and study their textbooks? • What distinct qualities characterize high schools in which members of various adolescent gangs interact congenially and respectfully? • In what ways do teachers' instructional practices change when their jobs and salaries depend on their students' scores on statewide or national achievement tests?	• How pervasive are gender stereotypes in popular children's literature? • What kinds of aggressive behaviors occur in schools, and with what frequencies? • How well have students performed on a recent national achievement test?	• Are better readers also better spellers? • Are students more likely to be aggressive at school if they often see violence at home or in their neighborhoods? • To what extent are students' class grades correlated with their scores on achievement tests?	• Which of two reading programs produces greater gains in reading comprehension? • Which method is most effective in reducing aggressive behavior—reinforcing appropriate behavior, punishing aggressive behavior, or a combination of both? • Do different kinds of tests (e.g., multiple-choice vs. essay tests) encourage students to study in different ways?

Ultimately educators gain a better understanding of students and effective classroom practices when they consider findings from *both* quantitative and qualitative research. Research that includes both quantitative and qualitative elements is called **mixed methods research**.[12] For example, in the research project described in the opening case study, Anne Smith tabulates students' responses to various survey questions and computes the percentages of various final class grades—all of which are quantitative information. But when she collects students' completed surveys, she also looks closely at their specific comments and suggestions, which provide qualitative information.

Different kinds of research lead to different kinds of conclusions.

In addition to yielding either quantitative or qualitative data (or both), research studies typically fall into one of four general categories: descriptive, correlational, experimental, or quasi-experimental. These various kinds of studies enable different kinds of conclusions and are appropriate for different types of research questions (see Table 1.1).

---

[12] Creswell, 2014.

A **descriptive study** does exactly what its name implies: It *describes* a situation. Descriptive studies might give us information about the characteristics of students, teachers, or schools. They might also provide information about how frequently certain events or behaviors occur. Descriptive studies allow us to draw conclusions about the way things are—the current state of affairs. Virtually all qualitative studies are primarily descriptive in nature, and some quantitative studies fall into the descriptive category as well.

A **correlational study** explores possible relationships among two or more variables. For example, it might tell us how closely various human characteristics are associated with each other, or it might give us information about the consistency with which certain human behaviors occur in conjunction with certain environmental conditions. In general, correlational studies enable us to draw conclusions about **correlation**: the extent to which two characteristics or phenomena tend to be found together or to change together. Two variables are correlated when one increases as the other increases (a *positive correlation*) or when one *decreases* as the other increases (a *negative correlation*) in a somewhat predictable manner. The bottom row of the fourth column in Table 1.1 presents three examples of possible correlational relationships: those between (1) reading and spelling ability, (2) aggressive behavior at school and violence at home, and (3) class grades and achievement test scores. Correlations are often described numerically with statistics known as *correlation coefficients*, described in Appendix A.

If a correlation exists between two variables, knowing the status of one variable allows us to make *predictions* about the other variable. For example, if we find a positive correlation between reading ability and spelling ability, we can predict that, on average, students who are proficient readers will also be good spellers. Our predictions will be imprecise at best, with exceptions to the general rule; for instance, we may occasionally see very good readers who are poor spellers. A more significant limitation of correlational studies is that although they may demonstrate that a relationship exists, they never tell us for certain *why* it exists. They don't tell us what specific factors—previous experiences, personality, motivation, or perhaps other things we haven't thought of—are the cause of the relationship we see. In other words, *correlation does not necessarily indicate causation.*

Descriptive and correlational studies describe things as they exist naturally in the environment. In contrast, an **experimental study**, or **experiment**, is a study in which the researcher somehow changes, or *manipulates,* one or more aspects of the environment (called *independent variables*) and then measures the effects of such changes on something else (called the *dependent variable*). In educational research the dependent variable is often some aspect of student behavior—perhaps end-of-year grades, skill in executing a complex physical movement, persistence in tackling difficult math problems, or ability to interact appropriately with peers.[13] In a good experiment a researcher *separates and controls variables,* testing the possible effects of one variable while keeping constant all other potentially influential variables. When carefully designed and conducted, experimental studies enable us to draw conclusions about causation—about what variables cause or influence certain other variables.

Often experimental studies involve two or more groups that are treated differently. Consider these examples:

- A researcher uses two different instructional methods to teach reading comprehension skills to two different groups of students. (Instructional method is the independent variable.) The researcher then assesses students' reading ability (the dependent variable) and compares the average reading-ability scores of the two groups.

- A researcher gives three different groups of students varying amounts of practice with woodworking skills. (Amount of practice is the independent variable.) The researcher subsequently scores the quality of each student's woodworking project (the dependent variable) and compares the average scores of the three groups.

- A researcher gives one group of students an intensive instructional program designed to improve their study skills. The researcher gives another group of students no instruction and gives a third group instruction in subject matter unrelated to study skills. (Presence

---

[13] You might think of the distinction this way: Student behavior (the dependent variable) *depends* on instructional practice or some other aspect of the environment (the independent variable).

or absence of instruction in study skills is the independent variable; the second and third groups did not receive instruction in study skills.) The researcher later (1) assesses the quality of students' study skills and (2) obtains their grade point averages (two dependent variables) to see whether the program had an effect.

Each of these examples includes **treatment groups** that are recipients of a particular intervention. The third example also includes two **control groups**: one that receives no intervention and another that receives a *placebo* intervention that's unlikely to affect the dependent variable(s) in question. In many experimental studies, participants are assigned to groups *randomly*—for instance, by drawing names out of a hat or having computer software randomly pick different participants for different groups. Such random assignment is apt to yield groups that are, on average, roughly equivalent on other variables (preexisting ability levels, personality characteristics, motivation, etc.) that might affect the dependent variable.

Random assignment to groups isn't always possible or practical, however, especially in research studies conducted in actual schools and classrooms. For example, when studying the potential benefits of a new teaching technique or therapeutic intervention, a researcher may not be able to completely control which students receive the experimental treatment and which do not, *or* a particular treatment or intervention may have important benefits for *all* students. In such situations, researchers often conduct a **quasi-experimental study**, in which they take into account, but don't completely control, other influential factors. The following are examples:

- A researcher implements a new after-school homework program at one high school and identifies a comparable high school without such a program to serve as a control group. The researcher obtains achievement test data for students at both schools both before and after the program's implementation. Ideally, to document the homework program's effectiveness, the average test scores for the two high schools should be the same *before* the program begins. Then, if differences exist at the end of the program, they may be attributed to the new homework program.

- A team of researchers wants to study the effects of safety instructions on children's behaviors on the playground. The researchers present the instructional intervention to first graders one week, second graders the following week, and kindergartners and third graders the week after that. The researchers monitor students' playground behavior before, during, and after the intervention to determine whether each grade-level group's risky playground behavior decreases immediately following the intervention.[14]

When researchers conduct such quasi-experimental studies, they don't control for all potentially influential variables and therefore can't completely rule out alternative explanations for the results they obtain. For instance, in the after-school homework program example, possibly the school getting the new homework program—but *only* that school—has simultaneously begun to use more effective instructional methods during the school day, and those methods are the reason for any increase in achievement scores. And in the playground safety example, perhaps certain other things coincidentally happened in the four classrooms during their respective safety-instructions weeks, and those things were the true causes of children's behavior improvements.

When carefully designed and conducted, experimental studies and, to a lesser degree, quasi-experimental studies enable us to draw conclusions about *causation*—about *why* behaviors occur. Yet for practical or ethical reasons, many important questions in education don't easily lend themselves to experimental manipulation and tight control of other potentially influential variables. For example, although we might find a correlation between children's aggression levels at school and the amount of violence in their home environments, it would be highly unethical to conduct an experimental study in which some children are intentionally placed in a violent environment. Consequently, some important educational questions can be addressed only with descriptive or correlational studies, even though such studies don't let us pin down precise cause-and-effect relationships.

---

[14] Here we're describing a study conducted by Heck, Collins, and Peterson (2001).

Drawing conclusions about cause-and-effect relationships requires that all other possible explanations for an outcome be eliminated.

Whenever we look at the results of a research study—regardless of who has conducted the study and regardless of whether it has been described in a professional journal or other credible media source—we mustn't be too hasty to draw conclusions about cause-and-effect relationships. As an example, imagine that Hometown School District wants to find out which of two new reading programs, *Reading Is Great* (RIG) or *Reading and You* (RAY), leads to better reading in third grade. The district asks each of its third-grade teachers to choose one of these two reading programs and use it throughout the school year. The district then compares the end-of-year achievement test scores of students in the RIG and RAY classrooms and finds that RIG students have gotten substantially higher reading comprehension scores than RAY students. We might quickly jump to the conclusion that RIG promotes better reading comprehension than RAY—in other words, that a cause-and-effect relationship exists between instructional method and reading comprehension. But is this really so?

Not necessarily. If we look at the study more closely, we realize that the school district hasn't eliminated all other possible explanations for the difference in students' reading comprehension scores. Remember, the third-grade teachers personally *chose* the instructional program they used. Why did some teachers choose RIG and others choose RAY? Were these two groups of teachers different in some way? Had RIG teachers taken more advanced courses in reading instruction, were they more open-minded and enthusiastic about using innovative methods, or did they devote more class time to reading instruction? Or, did the RIG teachers have students who were, on average, better readers to begin with? If the RIG and RAY classes were different from each other in any of these ways—or perhaps different in some other way we haven't thought of—then the district hasn't eliminated alternative explanations for why the RIG students have outperformed the RAY students. A better way to study the causal influence of reading program on reading comprehension would be to *randomly assign* third-grade classes to the RIG and RAY programs, thereby making the two groups similar (on average) in terms of student abilities and teacher characteristics.

Be careful that you don't jump to conclusions too quickly about what factors are affecting students' learning, development, and behavior in particular situations. You should scrutinize research reports carefully, always with these questions in mind: *Have the researchers separated and controlled variables that might have an influence on the outcome? Have they ruled out other possible explanations for their results?* Only when the answers to both of these questions are undeniably *yes* should you draw a conclusion about a cause-and-effect relationship.

think about it

What other possible differences between the RIG and RAY teachers might there be? (For one possible answer, click **here**.)

Principles and theories can help synthesize, explain, and apply research findings.

The large body of educational psychology research is more useful to teachers when it's organized into principles and theories. **Principles** describe the specific effects of certain factors on other factors or outcomes, such as those related to learning, development, and behavior. Consider this research-based principle: Students are likely to learn more when they are interested in what they are learning. The influential or "potentially causal" factor in this principle is *interest,* which has an effect on students' *learning.* Teachers at any grade level and subject area can use this principle in a variety of ways. For example, when teaching about a particular war—say, about the American Civil War or the French Revolution—a social studies teacher could select readings with interesting storylines about specific historical figures to pique students' interest as a way of enhancing their learning.

Whereas principles tell us *what* factors are important, theories tell us *why* these factors are important. A **theory** is an integrated set of concepts and principles developed to explain the underlying mechanisms of a phenomenon. Because human functioning is so complex, there is no one "mega-theory" in educational psychology to explain all of our thoughts, behaviors, and feelings. Instead, there are many smaller theories that explain various aspects of human functioning. For example, in Chapter 2 we'll discover that one prominent theory of how people learn—information processing theory—proposes that attention is an essential ingredient in the learning process. If a learner doesn't pay attention, information rapidly disappears from memory; in the words of a popular expression, the information goes "in one ear and out the other." The importance of attention in information processing theory suggests that strategies that capture and maintain students' attention are apt to enhance students' learning. Therefore, information processing theory could explain why students are likely to learn more when they're interested in what they're learning: they pay attention more closely to what they're supposed to be learning.

Sometimes people use the word *theory* to mean a guess, hunch, or an untested hypothesis. An example would be someone who says, "I have a theory about why he doesn't want to see her anymore." However, educational psychologists build theories over time based on evidence, not purely on speculation. Even so, theories continue to change as new research methods are devised, new research is conducted, and new research findings come to light. In contrast, principles tend to be fairly stable over time.

Although current theories may undergo modifications in the future, they can still be quite useful even in their unfinished forms. They help us integrate thousands of research studies into concise understandings of how children typically learn and develop, and they enable us to make reasonable estimates about how students are likely to perform and achieve in particular classroom contexts. In general, then, theories can help us both *explain* and *predict* human behavior, and so they give us numerous ideas about how best to help students achieve academic and social success at school. In fact, we have organized this book by grouping similar principles and theories together into *Big Ideas* to help you more easily understand the findings from many research studies.

Teachers need to use evidence-based practices that are consistent with effective teaching principles and theories, including those developed by educational psychologists. As teachers use research findings to inform their instructional decisions, they need to be critical consumers of research and examine the design of studies to ensure that the conclusions drawn are appropriate. In the hotlinked Self-Check quiz and Application Exercise that follow, you can check and apply your understandings related to Big Idea 1.1:

> *Effective teachers use research findings and research-based theories to make decisions about instructional strategies, classroom management, and assessment practices.*

MyEdLab Self-Check 1.1

MyEdLab Application Exercise 1.1. In this exercise, you can practice classifying different types of research studies and identifying the kinds of conclusions that might reasonably be drawn from the results of the studies.

1.2 DEVELOPING AS A TEACHER

Big Idea 1.2 Effective teachers continually work to enhance their professional knowledge and skills.

If you are currently enrolled in a teacher education program, you should think of your program as a good start on the road to becoming a skillful teacher.[15] It's *only* a start, however. True expertise in any profession, including teaching, takes many years of experience to acquire, although even a single year of teaching experience can make a significant difference.[16] So be patient with yourself, and recognize that occasionally feeling a bit unsure and making mistakes is not unusual. As you gain experience, you'll gradually become able to make decisions about routine situations and problems more quickly and efficiently, giving you time and energy to think creatively and flexibly about how best to teach classroom subject matter.[17] Here we offer several strategies to develop your knowledge and skills as a teacher—all of them based on research on teacher effectiveness.

---

[15] Bransford, Darling-Hammond, & LePage, 2005; Brouwer & Korthagen, 2005.

[16] P. A. Alexander, 2003; Berliner, 2001; Clotfelter, Ladd, & Vigdor, 2007; Henry, Bastian, & Fortner, 2011.

[17] Borko & Putnam, 1996; Bransford, Derry, Berliner, & Hammerness, 2005; Feldon, 2007.

Keep up to date on research findings and innovative evidence-based practices in education.

Occasional university coursework and in-service training sessions are two good ways to enhance teaching effectiveness.[18] Also, effective teachers typically subscribe to one or more professional journals, and as time allows, they attend professional conferences in their region. Many websites provide teachers with information and ideas about effective classroom practices, including the websites of professional organizations, such as the National Council of Teachers of Mathematics (www.nctm.org), the National Council for the Social Studies (www.socialstudies.org), the National Association for Music Education (www.nafme.org), the National Science Teachers Association (www.nsta.org), and the International Literacy Association (www.literacyworldwide.org).

Learn as much as you can about the subject matter you teach, about teaching strategies, and about learners and their development.

Effective teachers typically know their subject matter extremely well and can usually anticipate—and thus can also address—the difficulties students will have and the kinds of errors students will make in the process of mastering a certain skill or body of knowledge.[19] Effective teachers also know a variety of teaching strategies, including strategies for teaching particular topics and skills—strategies collectively known as **pedagogical content knowledge**.[20] In addition, effective teachers have knowledge of learners and their development in social contexts, which is why it's important for teachers to understand concepts related to educational psychology.[21]

With subject-matter knowledge, knowledge of teaching strategies, and knowledge of learners, teachers have the knowledge required to design and implement instruction that meets students' needs (see Figure 1.4). To meet the needs of *all* their students, teachers must be prepared to teach students with a wide variety of special needs in their classrooms. These **students with special needs** are different enough from their peers that they require specially adapted instructional materials or practices to help them maximize their learning and development. Many of these students are included in general education classrooms, a practice called **inclusion**. At several points in the book we'll consider students with particular kinds of special needs and identify strategies that may be especially useful in working with them.

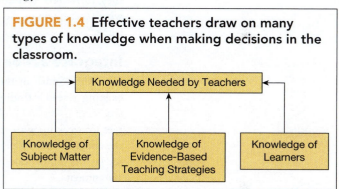

FIGURE 1.4 Effective teachers draw on many types of knowledge when making decisions in the classroom.

Learn as much as you can about the culture(s) of the community in which you are working.

In Cultural Considerations boxes throughout the book, you'll see numerous ways in which children from diverse cultural groups may think and behave differently than *you* did as a child. But a textbook can offer only a sampling of the many cultural differences you might encounter. You can become more informed about students' cultural beliefs and practices if you participate in local community activities and converse frequently with parents and other community members.[22]

Continually reflect on and critically examine your assumptions, inferences, and teaching practices.

In the opening case study, Anne Smith reflects on her students' performance in previous years and then institutes new assessment policies that might be more motivating and productive. Like Ms. Smith, effective teachers engage in **reflective teaching**: They continually examine and critique

---

[18] Desimone, 2009; Guskey & Sparks, 2002; Hamre et al., 2012; Hattie, 2009.

[19] Borko & Putnam, 1996; Cochran & Jones, 1998; H. C. Hill et al., 2008; D. C. Smith & Neale, 1991; Windschitl, 2002.

[20] Baumert et al., 2010; Cochran & Jones, 1998; Krauss et al., 2008; Shulman, 1986.

[21] Bransford, Darling-Hammond, & LePage, 2005.

[22] Castagno & Brayboy, 2008; McIntyre, 2010; Rogoff, 2003.

their assumptions, inferences, and instructional practices, and they regularly adjust their beliefs and strategies in light of new evidence.[23]

Communicate and collaborate with colleagues.

Good teachers rarely work in isolation. Instead they frequently communicate with colleagues in their own school district and across the nation—perhaps with colleagues in other countries as well—through face-to-face meetings, e-mail, regional or national conferences, and professional websites (e.g., www.oercommons.org). Ideally, teachers and administrators at a single school create a professional learning community, in which they share a common vision for students' learning and achievement, work collaboratively to achieve desired outcomes for all students, and regularly communicate with one another about their strategies and progress.[24] Most experienced teachers are happy to offer beginning teachers advice and support during challenging times. In fact, they're apt to be flattered to be asked!

Believe that you can make a difference in students' lives.

In Chapter 5 you'll discover the importance of having high self-efficacy—that is, of believing that you're capable of executing certain behaviors or reaching certain goals. Students are more likely to try to learn something if they believe they *can* learn it—in other words, if they have high self-efficacy. But teachers, too, must have high self-efficacy about what they can accomplish. Students who achieve at high levels are apt to be those whose teachers have confidence in what they, *as teachers,* can do—both individually and collectively—for their students.[25] Ultimately, what teachers do in the classroom *matters* for students, not only in the short term but for years to come.[26]

Integrate action research into your ongoing classroom practices.

Like Anne Smith in the opening case study, practicing teachers sometimes have questions that existing research findings don't fully answer. In action research, teachers conduct systematic studies of issues and problems in their own schools, with the goal of seeking more effective strategies for working with students. For example, an action research project might involve examining the effectiveness of a new teaching technique, seeking students' opinions on a new classroom policy (as Ms. Smith does), or ascertaining reasons why many students rarely complete homework assignments.

Action research studies typically involve the following steps:[27]

1. *Identify an area of focus.* The teacher-researcher begins with a problem and gathers preliminary information that might shed light on the problem, perhaps by reading relevant books or journal articles, searching the Internet, or discussing the issue with colleagues or students. The teacher-researcher then identifies one or more specific questions to address and develops a research plan for answering those questions (data-collection techniques, necessary resources, schedule, etc.). At this point, the teacher also seeks permission to conduct the study from school administrators and any other appropriate authorities. Depending on the nature of the study, parents' permission may be necessary.

2. *Collect data.* The teacher-researcher collects data relevant to the research questions. Such data might, for example, be obtained from questionnaires, interviews, achievement tests, students' journals or portfolios, existing school records (e.g., attendance patterns, school suspension rates), observations, or any combination of these.

3. *Analyze and interpret the data.* The teacher-researcher looks for patterns in the data. Sometimes the analysis involves computing particular statistics (e.g., percentages, averages, correlation coefficients), which would make it a quantitative study. At other times the analysis involves

[23] Hammerness, Darling-Hammond, & Bransford, 2005; T. Hogan, Rabinowitz, & Craven, 2003; Larrivee, 2006.
[24] DuFour, DuFour, & Eaker, 2008; P. Graham & Ferriter, 2009; Raudenbush, 2009.
[25] Holzberger, Philipp, & Kunter, 2013; J. A. Langer, 2000; Skaalvik & Skaalvik, 2008.
[26] Hattie, 2009; Konstantopoulos & Chung, 2011.
[27] Steps based on those recommended by Mills (2014).

an in-depth, nonnumeric inspection of the data, which would make it a qualitative study. Or, it could be a combination of both quantitative and qualitative data, which would make it a mixed methods study. The teacher-researcher then relates the findings to the original research questions.

4. *Develop and implement an action plan.* The final step distinguishes action research from the more traditional research studies described earlier. In particular, the teacher-researcher uses the information collected to *take action*—for instance, to change instructional strategies, school policies, or the classroom environment.

After the final step, a teacher-researcher may have all the information that he or she needs to work more effectively with students. Or, he or she may want to go through the process again by collecting more data, analyzing and interpreting the data, and developing and implementing another action plan. This cyclical process is shown in Figure 1.5 and could continue over and over.

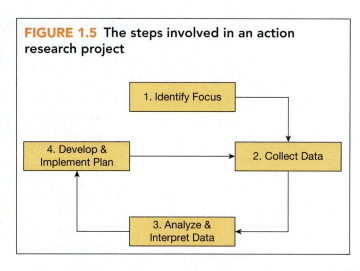

FIGURE 1.5 The steps involved in an action research project

Teachers can become more effective over time if they intentionally use strategies to increase their knowledge and skills. Teachers can develop their teaching skills by gaining knowledge, learning about students' cultures, reflecting on their beliefs and practices, communicating with colleagues, believing that they can influence students, and conducting action research. In the hotlinked Self-Check quiz and Application Exercise that follow, you can check and apply your understandings related to Big Idea 1.2:

> *Effective teachers continually work to enhance their professional knowledge and skills.*

MyEdLab **Self-Check 1.2**

MyEdLab **Application Exercise 1.2.** In this exercise, you will hear how a teacher selected an area of focus for her action research project. Then, you will describe the types of data that the teacher could collect to answer her research question.

1.3 STRATEGIES FOR LEARNING AND STUDYING EFFECTIVELY

Big Idea 1.3 Learners read, study, and learn more efficiently when they plan appropriately and use effective strategies.

This book includes many features that will, we hope, help you read about, study, and apply what researchers and experienced educators have learned about learning, development, motivation, and effective classroom practices. For example, each chapter begins with a few Big Ideas that capture the chapter's underlying themes. Each chapter also presents its major premises (guiding principles) and recommendations (key strategies) as boldfaced headings. In addition, the opening case studies and the figures, tables, exercises, concrete examples, margin questions, and application exercises interspersed throughout the book are all designed to enhance your understanding and memory of what you're reading.

Yet ultimately, how much you learn from the book is up to you. In upcoming chapters you'll learn a great deal about how human beings—including *you*—typically think about, learn, and remember new ideas. We're optimistic that you'll become a better student after reading those chapters, but in the meantime, here are some general strategies you can use as you read and study.[28]

---

[28] Ormrod, 2011.

Before you study, prepare for your study session.

When you're busy, it's tempting to rush into a study session without much planning. But you will find that you can make more effective use of your time if you plan your study sessions using these strategies:

- *Study at times when you're mentally alert.* Are you a "morning person"? A "night owl"? Identify the times you can most effectively study and then use these times for studying. You probably don't need to be as alert when you're running errands, checking social media, or doing your laundry, so save those tasks for when you're feeling less alert.

- *Select an appropriate environment for studying.* Don't underestimate the importance of selecting a place to study where you can concentrate. Find somewhere that's free of distractions. For example, you might need to leave your iPad in another room, turn off your phone, tell others not to disturb you, or go to a coffee shop if you can concentrate better there. Things that distract you might not distract others, so figure out what's best for you.

- *Be realistic about how much you can effectively learn and remember at any one time.* As you'll discover in Chapter 2, our brains only allow us to think about and learn a limited amount of information in a short amount of time. Plan ahead and divide lengthy learning activities into smaller chunks you can spread out over several days. And certainly don't leave an entire book chapter until the last minute!

- *Set goals for each study session.* Decide what you want to accomplish during a study session, and structure the session in a way that allows you to meet your goals. In Chapter 3, you will learn that setting goals can help you to monitor your learning and stay focused on what's important. Sometimes you won't meet all your goals for a study session because something you need to do takes longer than planned—that's not unusual. But with time and experience, you should become better able to set and accomplish realistic goals for each of your courses, which will allow you to plan your days, weeks, and even months more effectively.

During your study session, use effective study strategies.

Of course what you do *during* your study sessions significantly affects how much you will learn and remember. Here are some study strategies that can help you study more effectively:

- *Pay attention to what you're studying.* You need to be mentally active when you study if you want to remember what you're studying. If your mind starts to drift or you get sleepy, very little of what you are "studying" is likely to stay with you. If you're too tired, maybe you need to take a 5-minute break to do something that requires less attention. Or quit and come back again when you're more rested and less distracted.

- *Relate new information to your existing knowledge and prior experiences.* Think about how new ideas are consistent with your personal experiences, knowledge, and beliefs, as well as with things you've learned in other courses. You can even actively consider how some new information might contradict your existing experiences, knowledge, or beliefs. As the earlier OOPS test may have shown you, some of what you currently "know" and believe may be sort-of-but-not-quite accurate or even downright *in*accurate. People's existing beliefs can occasionally wreak havoc with new learning. For example, many students in teacher education classes adamantly reject research findings that appear to be inconsistent with their personal beliefs and experiences.[29] When you encounter puzzling or seemingly "wrong" ideas and findings, try to keep an open mind and consider how and why they might have some merit. Truly effective learners occasionally undergo *conceptual change*, revising their current understandings and beliefs in light of new and trustworthy evidence.

---

[29] Fives & Gill, 2015; Gregoire, 2003; Richardson, 2003.

- *Organize the new information.* Organizing information requires you to actively consider how various pieces of information are related. You can categorize related information together using outlines or diagrams. If the information includes cause-and-effect relationships, you can show these relationships, either through explanations or graphically using symbols and/or arrows.

- *Use visual imagery.* A picture may be worth 1,000 words. Form mental pictures of objects and ideas to aid in your memory of the information. You can also create pictures, diagrams, or other graphics to help you capture the meaning of the information.

- *Elaborate on what you read, going beyond it and adding to it.* As you learned earlier in this chapter, elaboration involves embellishing on new information in some way. So try to think *beyond* the things you read. Draw inferences from the ideas presented. Generate new examples of concepts. Identify your own educational applications of various principles of learning, development, and motivation. You will be more likely to understand and remember abstract information when you tie it to concrete objects and events. In this book, we try to help you do this by providing case studies and short examples that involve real children and teachers. We also include links to videos that depict classrooms in action and *See for Yourself* exercises such as the OOPS test—all of which can enhance your understanding and memory of new concepts and help you recognize them when you see them in your own work with children and adolescents.

think about it
How often do you elaborate while reading your textbooks? Do you learn and remember information more effectively when you elaborate on what you're reading?

- *Periodically check yourself to make sure you remember and understand what you have read.* To check your comprehension, try to summarize the material and ask yourself questions about it to ensure everything makes sense to you. Try to explain difficult concepts to someone who doesn't understand them.

After your study session, review what you studied.

What you do before and during your study sessions is important, but what you do *after* your study sessions can also help you to learn and remember information over the long term. Here are a couple suggestions:

- *Schedule time to review what you studied previously.* Research is clear on this point: Periodic review of previously learned material definitely helps students remember it more effectively and accurately. So make time in your schedule for review sessions in the days and weeks after your study sessions.

- *Quickly review what you learned previously.* The point of the review sessions is to review, not to redo what you did in your last study session; therefore, these sessions can be short. Simply remind yourself of the important points and clarify any misunderstandings. Review sessions can even occur immediately prior to a new study session and may help you better assimilate the new information with what you've already learned.

To study and learn most effectively, you need to prepare for your study sessions by ensuring that you're mentally alert and setting goals for yourself. During the study session, you should use effective study strategies, such as organizing information, using visual imagery, and elaborating on the information. And after your study session, you should have a plan for when you will review the information again. In the hotlinked Self-Check quiz and Application Exercise that follow, you can check and apply your understandings related to Big Idea 1.3:

> *Learners read, study, and learn more efficiently when they plan appropriately and use effective strategies.*

MyEdLab **Self-Check 1.3**

MyEdLab **Application Exercise 1.3.** In this exercise, you will read scenarios about students and make suggestions for strategies they can use to improve their learning.

1 SUMMARY

Each chapter in this book includes a summary organized around the Big Ideas listed at the beginning of the chapter. Following are the Big Ideas for Chapter 1.

■ **1.1: Effective teachers use research findings and research-based theories to make decisions about instructional strategies, classroom management, and assessment practices.** Effective teachers use practices that are *evidence-based*—that is, they encompass strategies that research has consistently shown to bring about significant gains in students' development, academic achievement, and personal well-being. Evidence-based practices are developed based on research conducted, in part, by educational psychologists who study the nature of human learning, development, motivation, and related topics. As researchers learn more and more about what various phenomena and events are like (descriptive studies), what variables are associated with one another (correlational studies), and what events cause what outcomes (experimental studies), they gradually develop and continually modify theories that integrate and explain their findings. Teachers can—and *should*—draw on research findings and well-supported theories about children's learning and development in their day-to-day and long-term instructional decision making.

■ **1.2: Effective teachers continually work to enhance their professional knowledge and skills.** As a teacher, you must think of yourself as a life-long learner who always has new things to discover about effective educational practices, the subject matter you teach, and the out-of-school environments and cultural groups in which your students live. Some of these things you can learn about through books, professional journals,

advanced coursework, the Internet, and collaboration with professional colleagues, but others may require immersing yourself in the local community or conducting action research. You must also be willing to reflect on and critically analyze your current assumptions, inferences, and instructional practices—good teachers acknowledge that they can sometimes be wrong, and they adjust their beliefs and strategies accordingly. One way you can analyze your instructional practices is to conduct your *own* action research to address specific questions you have about your students and classroom practices. Most importantly, you must remember that, as a teacher, the many little things you do every day can have a huge impact—either positive or negative—on students' academic and personal successes.

■ **1.3: Learners read, study, and learn more efficiently when they plan appropriately and use effective strategies.** You can use what you learn about thinking and learning not only to help children and adolescents be successful in the classroom but also to help *you* learn successfully. You should study at times when you're mentally alert and in places where you can concentrate fully. While you're studying, you should (1) pay close attention to what you're studying, (2) relate new information to your existing knowledge and prior experiences, (3) organize the information, (4) use visual imagery to form mental pictures of objects and ideas, (5) elaborate on what you're learning—for instance, by generating new examples and applications—and (5) occasionally stop to monitor your understandings of what you've read and studied. And after your study session, you should schedule some time in the future to briefly review what you've learned.

PRACTICE FOR YOUR LICENSURE EXAM

New Software

High school math teacher Mr. Gualtieri begins his class on Monday with an important announcement: "Our school has just purchased a new instructional software program that we can use on our classroom tablet computers. This program, called Problem-Excel, will give you practice in applying the mathematical concepts and procedures we'll be studying this year. I strongly encourage you to use it whenever you have free time so that you can get extra instruction and practice with things you might be having trouble with."

Mr. Gualtieri is firmly convinced that the new software will help his students better understand and apply certain concepts in his math curriculum this year. To test his hypothesis, he keeps a record of which students use the software and which students do not. He then looks at how well the two groups of students perform on his next classroom test. Much to his surprise, he discovers that, on average, the students who have used the software have earned

lower scores than those who have not used it. "How can this be?" he puzzles. "Is the software actually doing more harm than good?"

1. **Constructed-response question**

   Mr. Gualtieri wonders whether the instructional software is actually hurting, rather than helping, his students. Assume that the software has been carefully designed by an experienced educator. Assume, too, that Mr. Gualtieri's classroom test is a good measure of how well his students have learned the material they've been studying.

   A. Explain why Mr. Gualtieri cannot draw a conclusion about a cause-and-effect relationship from the evidence he has. Base your response on principles of educational research.

   B. Identify another plausible explanation for the results Mr. Gualtieri has obtained.

2. **Multiple-choice question**

   Which one of the following results would provide the most convincing evidence that the Problem-Excel software enhances students' mathematics achievement?

   a. Students at a high school are randomly assigned to two groups. One group works with Problem-Excel, and the other group works with a software program called Write-Away, designed to teach better writing skills. The Problem-Excel group scores higher than the Write-Away group on a subsequent mathematics achievement test.

   b. Ten high schools in New York City purchase Problem-Excel and make it available to their students. Students at these high schools get higher mathematics achievement test scores than students at 10 other high schools that have *not* purchased the software.

   c. A high school purchases Problem-Excel, but only four of the eight math teachers at the school decide to have their students use it. The students of these four teachers score at higher levels on a mathematics achievement test than the students of the other four teachers.

   d. All 10th graders at a large high school take a mathematics achievement test in September. At some point during the next 2 months, each student spends 20 hours working with Problem-Excel. The students all take the same math achievement test again in December and, on average, get substantially higher scores than they did in September.

   MyEdLab **Licensure Exam 1.1**

michaeljung/Fotolia

2

Learning, Cognition, and Memory

CASE STUDY: MAKING MOUNTAINS

Where do mountains come from? Seven-year-old Rob has an interesting take on the matter, as he reveals in the following conversation with an adult:

Adult: How were the mountains made?

Rob: Some dirt was taken from outside and it was put on the mountain and then mountains were made with it.

Adult: Who did that?

Rob: It takes a lot of men to make mountains—there must have been at least four. They gave them the dirt and then they made themselves all alone.

Adult: But if they wanted to make another mountain?

Rob: They pull one mountain down and then they could make a prettier one.[1]

- Rob's basic premise—that human beings are actively involved in mountain formation—is clearly incorrect. Nevertheless, his "knowledge" about mountains does have a few elements of truth. What things does Rob *correctly* know about mountains?
- What general principles about human learning might Rob's conception of mountain formation reveal?

Based on this conversation between Rob and the adult, it's hard to know exactly what Rob believes about mountains. He first talks about dirt being "put" on a mountain and about men "making" mountains. However, when he says, "they made themselves all alone," perhaps he's talking about the mountains *making themselves,* albeit with the assistance of a few men who "give" them dirt. Despite Rob's obviously naive notions, he has learned a few correct facts about mountains. In particular, he knows that (1) mountains are fairly big (requiring the work of "a lot of men"), (2) they're comprised of dirt (which is true, at least in part), and (3) they can be quite pretty to look at. To understand how children and adolescents acquire understandings about their physical and social worlds, about academic subject matter, and about themselves as human beings, we must first understand the nature of learning.

A good general definition of **learning** is: *a long-term change in mental representations or associations due to experience.* Let's divide this definition into its three parts. First, learning is a *long-term change,* in that it isn't just a brief, transitory use of information—such as remembering a phone number only long enough to make a phone call—but it doesn't necessarily last forever. Second, learning involves *mental representations or associations* and so presumably has its basis in the brain. Third, learning is a change *due to experience,* rather than the result of physiological maturation, fatigue, alcohol or drugs, or onset of mental illness.

Because the brain is the place where humans think about, make sense of, and learn from their environment, we begin this chapter by looking at the brain and some of its key characteristics. But much of what is known about the nature of learning and how to help students learn more effectively has been discovered by psychologists, not neuroscientists who study the brain. Therefore, the remainder of the chapter focuses on what psychologists have discovered about what goes on *inside* the learner during the learning process.

---

[1] Piaget, 1929, p. 348.

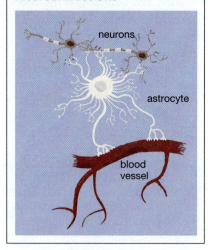

neurons

astrocyte

blood vessel

2.1 THINKING AND LEARNING IN THE BRAIN

Big Idea 2.1 The brain continues to change and learn over the course of a lifetime.

The brain is an incredibly complicated mechanism that includes several *trillion* cells. About 100 billion of them are nerve cells—**neurons**—that are microscopic in size and interconnected in countless ways. Some neurons receive information from the rest of the body, others synthesize and interpret the information, and still others send messages that tell the body how to respond to its present circumstances. Curiously, neurons don't actually touch one another. Instead, they use a variety of chemical substances to send messages across the tiny spaces—**synapses**—between them. Any single neuron may have synaptic connections with hundreds or even thousands of other neurons.[2]

Accompanying neurons are perhaps 1 to 5 trillion *glial cells,* which serve a variety of specialized functions. Some act as clean-up crew for unwanted garbage, others are "nutritionists" that control blood flow to neurons or "doctors" that tend to infections and injuries, and still others provide a substance known as *myelin* that enhances the efficiency of many neurons. And certain glial cells—star-shaped ones known as **astrocytes**—seem to be intimately involved in learning and memory (more about this point shortly).[3] Figure 2.1 can give you a sense of what neurons and astrocytes look like.

As you'll discover about cognitive development in Chapter 6, the brain changes in important ways over the course of childhood and adolescence. Yet four basic points about the brain are important to keep in mind as we explore cognition and learning in this chapter:

The various parts of the brain work closely with one another.

Groups of neurons and glial cells in different parts of the brain seem to specialize in different things. Structures in the lower and middle parts of the brain specialize in essential physiological processes (e.g., breathing, heart rate), body movements (e.g., walking, riding a bicycle), and basic perceptual skills (e.g., coordinating eye movements, diverting attention to potentially life-threatening stimuli). Complex thinking, learning, and knowledge are located primarily in the upper and outer parts of the brain collectively known as the **cortex**, which rests on the top and sides of the brain like a thick, bumpy toupee (see Figure 2.2). The portion of the cortex located near the forehead, known as the *prefrontal cortex,* is largely responsible for a wide variety of distinctly human activities, including sustained attention, reasoning, planning, decision making, coordinating complex activities, and preventing nonproductive thoughts and behaviors.[4] Other parts of the cortex are important as well, being actively involved in interpreting visual and auditory information, identifying the spatial characteristics of objects and events, and keeping track of general knowledge about the world.

To some degree, the left and right halves of the cortex—its two *hemispheres*—have different specialties.[5] For most people, the left hemisphere takes primary responsibility for language and logical thinking, whereas the right hemisphere is more dominant in visual and spatial tasks. Yet contrary to popular belief, people rarely, if ever, think exclusively in one hemisphere. There's no such thing as "left-brain" or "right-brain" thinking: The two hemispheres constantly collaborate in day-to-day tasks. In fact, learning or thinking about virtually anything tends to be *distributed* across many parts of the brain. A task as seemingly simple as identifying a particular word in speech or print involves numerous areas of the cortex.[6]

Most learning probably involves changes in neurons, astrocytes, and their interconnections.

From a physiological standpoint, how and where does learning occur? Until recently, the great majority of learning theorists believed that the physiological basis for most learning lies primarily in changes in the interconnections among neurons. In particular, learning may involve

---

[2] C. S. Goodman & Tessier-Lavigne, 1997; Lichtman, 2001; Mareschal et al., 2007.

[3] Koob, 2009; Oberheim et al., 2009; Verkhratsky & Butt, 2007.

[4] Otero & Barker, 2014; Verghese, Garner, Mattingley, & Dux, 2016.

[5] Byrnes, 2001; R. Ornstein, 1997; Siegel, 2012; M. S. C. Thomas & Johnson, 2008.

[6] Gonsalves & Cohen, 2010; Huey, Krueger, & Grafman, 2006; Jung & Haier, 2007; Pereira, Detre, & Botvinick, 2011; Posner & Rothbart, 2007; Schlegel, Alexander, & Tse, 2016.

strengthening existing synapses, forming new ones, or, in some cases, *eliminating* synapses. Eliminating synapses is important because effective learning requires not only that people think and do certain things, but also that they *not* think or do other things—in other words, that they inhibit tendencies to think or behave in particular ways.[7]

Within the past few years, some researchers have begun to speculate that astrocytes are just as important as neurons in learning and memory—possibly even more important. In humans, astrocytes outnumber neurons by at least 10 to 1—a ratio much larger than that for, say, mice and rats—and they have many chemically mediated connections with one another and with neurons. Astrocytes appear to have some control over what neurons do and don't do and how much neurons communicate with one another.[8]

Many new astrocytes form throughout our lifetimes.[9] Some new neurons form throughout life as well, especially in the *hippocampus* (a small, seahorse-shaped structure in the middle of the brain) and possibly also in certain areas of the cortex.[10] Learning experiences seem to stimulate the formation of new brain cells, although researchers don't yet know exactly how these new cells are related to learning and memory.

As for *where* learning occurs, the answer is: many places. The prefrontal cortex is active when people must pay attention to and think about new information and events, and all of the cortex may be active to a greater or lesser extent in interpreting new input in light of previously acquired knowledge. The hippocampus also seems to be a central figure in learning, in that it pulls together the information it simultaneously receives from various parts of the brain.[11]

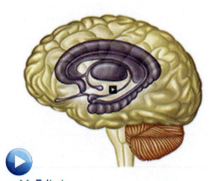

MyEdLab
2.1. Video Explanation

In this video, you can learn a little more about basic structures of the brain.

The brain functions in close collaboration with—rather than in relative isolation from—the rest of the body.

Obviously the brain can't function without the nutrition and health of the rest of the body, and it gets new information from the eyes, ears, and other sensory organs. But in addition, thinking and learning are often intimately intertwined with people's physical actions and reactions.[12] For example, when people think about throwing a baseball—even if they aren't actually throwing one—they activate parts of the brain that control arm and hand muscles involved in throwing.[13] And when people are pondering complex situations—perhaps math problems or perhaps the shapes and locations of various objects in space—gestures with their hands or arms can sometimes help them think and talk about the situations more effectively.[14]

Knowing how the brain functions and develops tells us only so much about learning and instruction.

As you'll see in upcoming sections of this chapter, recent research on the human brain has yielded helpful insights regarding human memory and effective instructional practices. It has also enhanced our knowledge about the typical course of cognitive development (see Chapter 6) and the neurological bases of certain disabilities (e.g., dyslexia, dyscalculia, autism spectrum disorders).[15]

Yet even as researchers determine how and where learning occurs, current knowledge of brain physiology doesn't begin to tell us everything we need to know about learning or how to foster it. For example, brain research can't tell us much about what information and skills are most important for people to have in a particular community and culture.[16] Nor does it provide

---

[7] Bruer & Greenough, 2001; Byrnes, 2001; Dempster, 1992; Haier, 2001; Merzenich, 2001; C. A. Nelson, Thomas, & de Haan, 2006.

[8] Koob, 2009; Oberheim et al., 2009; Scharfman & Binder, 2013; Szu & Binder, 2016; Verkhratsky & Butt, 2007.

[9] Han et al., 2013; Koob, 2009.

[10] Deng, Aimone, & Gage, 2010; Gould, Beylin, Tanapat, Reeves, & Shors, 1999; C. A. Nelson et al., 2006; Sapolsky, 1999.

[11] Bauer, 2002; Byrnes, 2001; Davachi & Dobbins, 2008; Huey et al., 2006.

[12] Abrahamson & Lindgren, 2014. The brain's reliance on other parts of the body to help it in its thinking processes is sometimes called *embodiment*.

[13] Spunt, Falk, & Lieberman, 2010.

[14] Alibali, Spencer, Knox, & Kita, 2011; Goldin-Meadow & Beilock, 2010.

[15] Butterworth & Varma, 2014; Tager-Flusberg, 2007; Varma, McCandliss, & Schwartz, 2008.

[16] L. Bloom & Tinker, 2001; Chalmers, 1996; Gardner, 2000b.

much specific guidance about how teachers can best help their students *acquire* such information and skills.[17] In fact, educators who speak of "using brain research" or "brain-based learning" are, in most instances, actually talking about what psychologists have learned from studies of human *behavior* rather than from studies of brain anatomy and physiology.

By and large, if we want to understand the nature of human learning and identify effective ways of helping children and adolescents learn more effectively, we must look primarily at what psychologists, rather than neurologists, have discovered. Hence, we continue our exploration of learning and cognitive processes by looking at what psychologists have discovered about human memory.

Learning involves changes in the interconnections among neurons and astrocytes in many areas of the brain. Although knowing about the physiological functioning of the brain can certainly be helpful, much of what is most useful to teachers about learning and teaching is based on what psychologists have discovered. In the hotlinked Self-Check quiz and Application Exercise that follow, you can check and apply your understandings related to Big Idea 2.1:

The brain continues to change and learn over the course of a lifetime.

MyEdLab **Self-Check 2.1**

MyEdLab **Application Exercise 2.1.** In this exercise, you can practice clarifying some of the misconceptions related to neurological and cognitive growth.

2.2 LEARNING AS ACTIVE CONSTRUCTION

Big Idea 2.2 Much of human learning involves a process of actively constructing knowledge, rather than passively absorbing it.

Psychologists have been studying the nature of learning for more than a century, and in the process they've taken a variety of theoretical perspectives. Table 2.1 summarizes four general viewpoints, listed largely in the order in which they've gained prominence in educational psychology. For the most part, these diverse perspectives complement rather than contradict one another, and together they can give us a rich, multifaceted picture of human learning. Accordingly, as you can see in the rightmost column of the table, they'll all contribute considerably to upcoming discussions of what learning involves and how teachers can better enhance students' classroom performance and long-term success.

Cognitive psychology is a theoretical perspective that focuses on the mental processes underlying learning and behavior, including perception, memory, and reasoning. Several basic principles, described in the following sections, are fundamental to what cognitive psychologists have discovered about learning.

By the time they reach school age, young learners are actively involved in much of their own learning.

Sometimes children learn from an experience without really giving the situation much thought. For example, as infants and toddlers acquire the basic vocabulary and syntax of their first language, they seem to do so without consciously trying to acquire these things or thinking about what they're learning. Much of this unconscious learning that occurs during infancy and toddlerhood is called *implicit learning,* and even older children and adults continue to learn some things about their environments in a nonintentional, "thoughtless" way.[18] But as children grow, they

MyEdLab **Content Extension 2.1.**
You can learn more about how theories of learning have evolved over time in this supplementary reading.

---

[17] D. M. Beck, 2010; Byrnes, 2007; G. A. Miller, 2010; Schenck, 2011.
[18] P. A. Alexander, Schallert, & Reynolds, 2009; S. W. Kelly, Burton, Kato, & Akamatsu, 2001; Kihlstrom, 2013; Siegel, 2012.

THEORETICAL PERSPECTIVES

Table 2.1 • General Theoretical Approaches to the Study of Learning

THEORETICAL PERSPECTIVE	GENERAL DESCRIPTION	EXAMPLES OF PROMINENT THEORISTS	WHERE YOU WILL SEE THIS PERSPECTIVE IN THE BOOK
Behaviorism	Early behaviorists argued that thought processes cannot be directly observed and thus cannot be studied objectively and scientifically. Accordingly, most behaviorists downplay the role of cognitive processes in learning and instead focus on two things researchers *can* observe and measure: people's behaviors (*responses*) and the environmental events (*stimuli*) that precede and follow those behaviors. Learning is viewed as a process of acquiring and modifying associations among stimuli and responses, largely through learners' direct interactions with the environment.	B. F. Skinner Edward Thorndike Ivan Pavlov MyEdLab: **Content Extension 2.2.** This supplementary reading provides more details about B. F. Skinner's foundational work in behaviorism.	We'll examine learning from a stimulus–response perspective early in Chapter 4 (see the first four principles in the section "Immediate Stimuli as Context"). We'll also draw from behaviorist ideas when we address classroom management in Chapter 9 (see the discussions of cueing, punishment, applied behavior analysis, functional analysis, and positive behavioral interventions and supports in the section "Reducing Unproductive Behaviors").
Social Cognitive Theory	Historically, social cognitive theorists have focused largely on the ways in which people learn from observing one another. Environmental stimuli affect behavior, but cognitive processes (e.g., *awareness* of stimulus–response relationships, *expectations* about future events) play a significant role as well. Often people learn through *modeling:* They watch and imitate what others do. Whether people learn and perform effectively is also a function of their *self-efficacy,* the extent to which they believe they can successfully accomplish a particular task or activity. As social cognitive theory has evolved over time, it has increasingly incorporated the concept of *self-regulation,* in which people take charge of and direct their own actions.	Albert Bandura Dale Schunk Barry Zimmerman	The social cognitive perspective will come into play in our discussion of self-regulation in Chapter 3, as well as in our discussions of modeling, vicarious consequences, incentives, and reciprocal causation in Chapter 4. Later, we'll sometimes draw from social cognitive theory as we examine motivation (and especially as we focus on self-efficacy and goals) in Chapter 5.
Cognitive Psychology	Although not denying that the environment plays a critical role in learning, information processing theorists concern themselves with what goes on *inside* learners, focusing on the cognitive processes involved in learning, memory, and performance. From observations of people's responses to various situations and tasks, these theorists draw inferences about how people may perceive, interpret, and mentally manipulate information they encounter in the environment. Many cognitive psychologists speculate about what internal mechanisms underlie human cognition (e.g., *working memory* and *long-term memory*) and about how people mentally process new information (e.g., through *elaboration* and *visual imagery*); this approach is called **information processing theory**. Other cognitive theorists focus on how individual learners create knowledge through their interactions with the environment; this approach is known as **individual constructivism**.	Richard Atkinson Richard Shiffrin Jean Piaget Jerome Bruner John Anderson John Bransford MyEdLab: **Content Extension 2.3.** This supplementary reading provides some key ideas about Jean Piaget's theory of cognitive development.	Cognitive psychology provides the basis for most of the discussion of learning and memory in this chapter. It will also be central to our discussion of complex cognitive processes in Chapter 3. It will be influential, too, in our discussions of cognitive factors influencing motivation in Chapter 5, cognitive development and intelligence in Chapter 6, social cognition in Chapter 7, and instructional strategies in Chapter 8.
Contextual Theories	Contextual theorists place considerable emphasis on the influence of learners' physical and social environments on cognition and learning. But rather than talk about specific stimuli (as behaviorists do), they focus on more general factors—physical, social, and cultural—that support "thoughtful" (i.e., cognition-based) learning. Some contextual theorists suggest that young learners initially use sophisticated thinking strategies in social interactions and gradually *internalize* these strategies for their own, personal use; this approach is known as **sociocultural theory**. Other contextual theorists emphasize that by working together, two or more people can often gain better understandings than anyone could gain alone; this approach is sometimes called **social constructivism**. Still other theorists propose that various ways of thinking are inextricably tied to particular physical or social circumstances; this approach goes by a variety of labels, including **situated learning** and **distributed cognition**.	Lev Vygotsky Jean Lave Barbara Rogoff Roy Pea Gavriel Salomon James Greeno MyEdLab: **Content Extension 2.4.** This supplementary reading provides more information about Lev Vygotsky's theory of cognitive development.	In Chapter 4, contextual theories will underlie our discussions of cultural and societal factors and technological advancements that significantly influence people's learning and thinking. Sociocultural theory will play a prominent role in our discussion of cognitive development in Chapter 6. We'll also bring contextual perspectives into play as we discuss complex cognitive process in Chapter 3, motivation in Chapter 5, instructional strategies in Chapter 8, and classroom management in Chapter 9. Furthermore, the "Cultural Considerations" boxes in Chapters 3 through 10 will continually remind us how students' cultural backgrounds are likely to influence their thoughts, perceptions, and behaviors.

increasingly engage in intentional, *explicit learning:* They consciously think about, interpret, and reconfigure what they see and hear in their environment. As a simple example, try the following exercise.

—————————————————— **SEE FOR YOURSELF** ——————————————————
TWELVE WORDS

Spend 30 seconds to memorize the following 12 words. Then look away and write down the words in the exact order in which they come to mind.

daisy	apple	dandelion
hammer	pear	wrench
tulip	pliers	watermelon
banana	rose	screwdriver

In what order did you remember the words? Did you recall them in their original order, or did you rearrange them somehow? If you're like most people, you grouped the words into three categories—flowers, fruit, and tools—and remembered one category at a time. In other words, you *organized* the words. As children get older, they're more likely to organize what they learn, and learners of all ages learn more effectively when they organize the subject matter at hand.

Cognitive processes influence what is learned.

You may have heard teachers, parents, employers, or others say that they want students to become better thinkers. But have you ever considered what's involved in *thinking?* Thinking is a broad term that can include many different **cognitive processes**—that is, the specific things individuals do mentally as they try to interpret and remember what they see, hear, and study. Cognitive processes are important because they have a profound effect on what people learn and remember. An example of a cognitive process is **encoding**, in which a learner changes or adds to incoming information in some way in order to remember it more easily. In the preceding "Twelve Words" exercise, sorting the words into categories was one possible encoding strategy. But perhaps, instead, you encoded the word list by creating a story or poem (e.g., "As *Daisy* and *Tulip* were walking, they ran across *Dandy* and *Rose* . . ."), or perhaps you formed a mental image of the 12 items in an elaborate, if not entirely edible, fruit salad (see Figure 2.3).

Cognitive psychologists have offered numerous explanations of how people mentally process and remember new information and events—explanations that fall into the general category of **information processing theory**. Many of their early explanations portrayed human thinking and learning as being similar to the ways computers operate. It has since become clear, however, that the computer analogy is too simple: People often think about and interpret information in ways that are difficult to explain in the one-thing-always-leads-to-another ways that characterize computers.[19]

Learners must be selective about what they focus on and learn.

People are constantly bombarded with information. Consider the many stimuli you're encountering at this very moment—the many letters in this text, the other objects you can see while you're reading, the various sounds reaching your ears, and the articles of clothing touching your skin, to name a few. You've probably been ignoring most of these stimuli until just now, when we specifically asked you to think about them. People can handle only so much information at any one time, and so they must be selective. Effective learners focus on what they think is important and ignore almost everything else.

FIGURE 2.3 A visual image for encoding a list of 12 words

---
[19] For example, see Hacker, Dunlosky, & Graesser, 2009a; G. Marcus, 2008; Minsky, 2006.

As an analogy, consider the hundreds of items you receive in the mail each year, not only in paper form via the post office but also in electronic form through e-mail. Do you open, examine, and respond to every piece of mail? Probably not. You may look closely at a few key items, inspect other items long enough to know that you don't need them, and discard others without even opening them.

Of course, people don't always make good choices about what to attend to. Just as they might overlook a small, inconspicuous rebate check while opening a colorful "You May Already Have Won . . ." sweepstakes announcement, so, too, might students fail to catch an important idea in a classroom lesson because they're focusing on trivial details in the lesson or on a classmate's attention-getting behavior across the room. An important job for teachers, then, is to help students understand what's most important to learn and what can reasonably be cast aside as "junk mail" or "e-mail spam."

Learners actively create—rather than passively absorb—much of what they know and believe about the world.

People learn some things simply by mindlessly "soaking up" certain regularities in their environment.[20] However, a good deal of human learning involves a process of **construction**: In an effort to make sense of their experiences, learners use many separate tidbits of information to create a general understanding, interpretation, or recollection of some aspect of their world.[21] As the conversation with 7-year-old Rob in the opening case study illustrates, learners are apt to construct their own, unique understandings of any given topic or situation, and these understandings may be accurate—or *not*—to varying degrees. Theories that focus primarily on the nature of constructive processes in learning are collectively known as **constructivism**, and a subset of these theories that addresses how learners idiosyncratically construct knowledge on their own (rather than in collaboration with other people) is known as **individual constructivism**.

In the following exercise, you'll almost certainly be able to see the process of construction in your own learning.

─────────────── **SEE FOR YOURSELF** ───────────────
ROCKY

Read the following passage *one time only:*

> Rocky slowly got up from the mat, planning his escape. He hesitated a moment and thought. Things were not going well. What bothered him most was being held, especially since the charge against him had been weak. He considered his present situation. The lock that held him was strong, but he thought he could break it. He knew, however, that his timing would have to be perfect. Rocky was aware that it was because of his early roughness that he had been penalized so severely—much too severely from his point of view.[22]

Now summarize what you've just read in two or three sentences.

Were you able to make sense of the passage? What did you think it was about? A prison escape? A wrestling match? Or something else altogether? The passage leaves a lot unsaid; for instance, it tells us nothing about where Rocky was, what kind of "lock" was holding him, or why timing was important. Yet you were probably able to use the information you were given to construct an overall understanding of Rocky's situation. Most people find meaning of one sort or another in the passage.

Active, constructive processes in learning—what theorists sometimes refer to as *meaning making*—are hardly limited to verbal material. For another example, try the following exercise.

─────────────

[20] For example, see Aslin & Newport, 2012.
[21] For two classic works on constructive processes in learning, see Bransford & Franks, 1971; Neisser, 1967.
[22] R. C. Anderson, Reynolds, Schallert, & Goetz, 1977, p. 372.

SEE FOR YOURSELF
THREE PICTURES

Look at the three pictures in Figure 2.4. What do you see in each one?

FIGURE 2.4 What do you see in these pictures?

Figures from "Age in the Development of Closure Ability in Children" by C. M. Mooney, 1957, *Canadian Journal of Psychology, 11*, p. 220. Copyright 1957 by Canadian Psychological Association. Reprinted with permission.

Most people perceive the picture on the left as being that of a woman, even though many of her features are missing. Enough features are visible—an eye and parts of her nose, mouth, chin, and hair—that you can construct a meaningful perception from them. Do the other two pictures provide enough information to enable you to construct two more faces? Constructing a face from the figure on the right may take you a while, but it can be done.

Objectively speaking, the three configurations of black splotches, and especially the two rightmost ones, leave a lot to the imagination. The woman in the middle is missing half of her face, and the man on the right is missing the top of his head. Yet knowing what human faces typically look like may have been enough to enable you to mentally add the missing pieces and perceive complete pictures. Curiously, once you've constructed faces from the figures, they then seem obvious. If you were to close this book now and not pick it up again for a week or more, you would probably see the faces almost immediately, even if you had had considerable trouble perceiving them originally.

Learners use what they already know and believe to help them make sense of new experiences.

In the "Rocky" and "Three Pictures" exercises you just completed, you were able to make sense of situations even though a lot of information was missing. Your prior knowledge—perhaps about typical prison escapes or wrestling matches and certainly about how human facial features are arranged—allowed you to fill in many missing details. Prior knowledge and beliefs usually play a major role in the meanings people construct.

When different learners construct different meanings from the same situation, it's often because they each bring unique prior experiences and knowledge to the situation. For instance, when the "Rocky" passage was used in an experiment with college students, physical education majors frequently interpreted it as a wrestling match, but music education majors (most of whom had little or no knowledge of wrestling) were more likely to think it was about a prison break.[23] Not only do learners bring different areas of expertise to a learning task, but they also bring different childhood experiences, cultural backgrounds, and general knowledge and assumptions about the world, and such differences are apt to have a significant impact on their meaning-making efforts. For example, we might reasonably guess that 7-year-old Rob had seen people moving large

think about it
Skillful readers typically skip some of the words on the page and yet accurately understand what they read. How is this possible? (For an explanation, click **here**.)

---
[23] R. C. Anderson et al., 1977.

mounds of dirt around—perhaps at construction sites—but he probably had no knowledge of the geological processes (e.g., erosion, plate tectonics) that underlie mountain formation.

> As students learn, they actively construct their knowledge, often using their existing knowledge to help them make sense of new experiences. In the hotlinked Self-Check quiz and Application Exercise that follow, you can check and apply your understandings related to Big Idea 2.2:
>
> > *Much of human learning involves a process of actively constructing knowledge, rather than passively absorbing it.*
>
> MyEdLab **Self-Check 2.2**
>
> MyEdLab **Application Exercise 2.2.** In this exercise, you can apply some principles of active knowledge construction to a first-grade lesson about the properties of air.

2.3 HOW HUMAN MEMORY OPERATES

Big Idea 2.3 Human memory is a complex, multifaceted information processing system that is, to a considerable degree, under a learner's control.

The term **memory** refers to a learner's ability to mentally "save" newly acquired information and behaviors. In some cases we'll use the term to refer to the actual process of saving knowledge or skills for a period of time. In other instances we'll use it to talk about particular "locations" where knowledge is held—for instance, in *working memory* or *long-term memory.*

The process of "putting" something into memory is called **storage**. In contrast, the process of remembering previously stored information—that is, "finding" it in memory—is **retrieval**. The following exercise illustrates the retrieval process.

— SEE FOR YOURSELF —
RETRIEVAL PRACTICE

How quickly can you answer each of the following questions?

1. What is your name?
2. What is the capital of France?
3. In what year did Christopher Columbus first sail across the Atlantic Ocean to reach the New World?
4. What did you have for dinner 3 years ago today?
5. When talking about serving appetizers at a party, people sometimes use a French term instead of the word *appetizer*. What is that French term, and how is it spelled?

As you probably noticed when you tried to answer these questions, retrieving some information from memory (e.g., your name) is an easy, effortless process. But other things can be retrieved only after some thought and effort. For example, it may have taken you a few seconds to recall that the capital of France is Paris and that Columbus first sailed across the Atlantic in 1492. Still other pieces of information—even though you certainly stored them in memory at one time—may be almost impossible to retrieve. Perhaps a dinner menu 3 years ago and the correct spelling of *hors d'oeuvre* fall into this category.

Human memory is a complex, multifaceted phenomenon that is still somewhat of a mystery. But many psychologists have found it helpful to think of the human memory system as having three general components that hold information for different lengths of time: sensory memory, working memory, and long-term memory (see Figure 2.5).[24] Oversimplified as this model undoubtedly is, we can use it in combination with countless research studies to derive some general principles about how human memory operates.[25]

---

[24] For example, see R. C. Atkinson & Shiffrin, 1968; Reisberg, 1997; Willingham, 2004.

[25] Findings from recent brain research reveal that the various components of memory depicted in Figure 2.5 aren't completely separate entities; for example, see Baddeley, 2001; Nee, Berman, Moore, & Jonides, 2008; Öztekin, Davachi, & McElree, 2010.

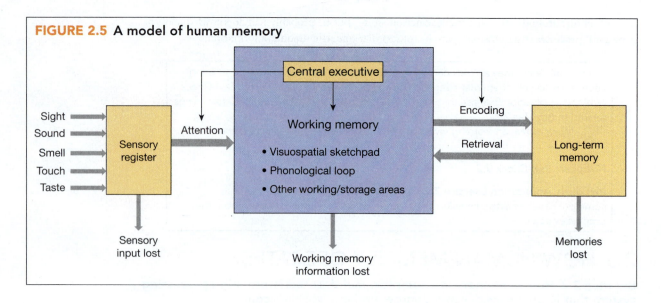

FIGURE 2.5 A model of human memory

Sensory input stays in a raw form only briefly.

If you've ever played at night with a sparkler—one of those metal sticks that, when lit, emits fiery sparks for a few minutes—you've seen the bright tail of light that follows it as it's waved around. If you've ever daydreamed in class, you may have noticed that when you tune back in to a lecture, you can still "hear" the three or four words that were spoken just *before* you started paying attention to your instructor again. The sparkler's tail and the words that linger aren't actually "out there" in the environment. Instead, they're recorded in your sensory register.

The **sensory register** is the component of memory that holds the information you receive from your senses—*input*—in more or less its original, *un*encoded form. Much of what your body sees, hears, smells, touches, or tastes is stored in the sensory register. In other words, the sensory register has a *large capacity:* It can hold a great deal of information at any one time.

That's the good news. The bad news is that information stored in the sensory register doesn't last very long.[26] Visual information (what you see) probably lasts for less than a second. For example, as a child, one of us authors, Jeanne, could never spell out her entire first name with a sparkler; the *J* had always faded before she got to the first *n,* no matter how quickly she wrote. Auditory information (what you hear) lasts slightly longer, perhaps for 2 or 3 seconds. To keep information for any time at all, then, learners need to move it to *working memory.*

Attention is essential for most learning and memory.

Recently received sensory information—such as a sparkler's glittery light—doesn't last very long no matter what we do. But we can preserve a memory of it in some minimal way—for instance, by perceiving alphabet letters or other familiar shapes in a sparkler's curlicue tail. In the model of memory presented in Figure 2.5, the first step in this process is **attention**: *Whatever a learner mentally pays attention to continues on to working memory.* If information in the sensory register doesn't get a learner's attention, it presumably disappears from the memory system, although it might be learned implicitly.[27]

Paying attention involves directing not only the appropriate sensory receptors (in the eyes, ears, fingertips, etc.) but also the *mind* toward whatever needs to be learned and remembered. Imagine yourself reading a textbook for one of your classes. Your eyes are moving down each page, but meanwhile you're thinking about something altogether different—a recent argument with a friend, a high-paying job advertised online, or your growling stomach. What will you remember from the textbook? Absolutely nothing. Even though your eyes were focused on the words in your book, you weren't *mentally* attending to the words.

---

[26] Cowan, 1995; Dahan, 2010; Darwin, Turvey, & Crowder, 1972; Sperling, 1960.

[27] Some nonattended-to information may remain, but without the learner's conscious awareness of it, it can be extremely difficult to recall, especially over the long run; for example, see Cowan, 2007.

Young children's attention often moves quickly from one thing to another and is easily drawn to objects and events unrelated to the task at hand. As children grow older, they become better able to focus their attention on a particular task and keep it there, and they're less distracted by irrelevant thoughts and events. Yet even adult learners can't keep their minds on a single task *all* the time.[28]

Even when learners *are* paying attention, they can attend to only a very small amount of information at any one time because attention has a *limited capacity*. For example, if you're reading your textbook and watching your favorite TV show, you can attend to your book or the TV, but you can't attend to both simultaneously. And if you're preoccupied in class with your instructor's ghastly taste in clothing and desperate need for a fashion makeover, you'll have a hard time paying attention to what your instructor is saying. Engaging in more than one task at the same time is sometimes called *multitasking,* although multitasking can be difficult and even impossible in some situations because of the limited capacity of our attention.

Exactly *how* limited is the capacity of human attention? People can often perform two or three well-learned, automatic tasks at once. For example, you can walk and chew gum at the same time, and you can probably drink a cup of coffee while you're driving a car. But when a stimulus or event is detailed and complex (as is true for reading a textbook) or when a task requires considerable thought and concentration (as is true for understanding a lecture in a college class or driving a car on a busy city street), then people can usually attend to only *one* thing at a time.[29]

Let's return to a point made earlier: Learners must be selective about what they focus on and learn. Now we see the reason why: Attention has a limited capacity, allowing only a very small amount of information stored in the sensory register to move on to working memory. The vast majority of the sensory input that the body initially receives is quickly lost from the memory system.

Working memory—where the action is in thinking and learning—has a short duration and limited capacity.

Working memory is the component of memory where attended-to information stays for a short time so that learners can make better sense of it. It "holds" what learners are conscious of at any moment in time and is where much of their active cognitive processing occurs. It's where they try to understand new concepts presented in a lecture, draw inferences from ideas encountered in a textbook passage, or solve a problem. Basically, this is the component that does most of the mental work of the memory system—hence its name *working* memory.

Rather than being a single entity, working memory seems to have several components for holding and working with different kinds of information, as shown in Figure 2.5.[30] For example, it appears to have a component specifically devoted to temporary storage of visual and spatial information; some theorists have called this a *visuospatial sketchpad*. It probably also has a component that enables very short-term retention of sounds, including spoken language; some theorists refer to this as a *phonological loop*. There may also be similar working and holding areas for input from the other senses, as well as a component that integrates multiple kinds of information.

Working memory also seems to include some sort of supervisory component—which many theorists call a **central executive**—that focuses attention, oversees the flow of information throughout the memory system, selects and controls complex voluntary behaviors, and inhibits counterproductive thoughts and actions.[31] Such processes—collectively known as *executive functions*—improve over the course of childhood and adolescence (largely as a result of brain maturation) and significantly enhance students' academic performance.[32]

Information stored in working memory doesn't last very long—perhaps 5 to 20 seconds at most—unless learners do something more with it.[33] Accordingly, it's sometimes called *short-term memory*. For example, imagine that you need to call to order a pizza for dinner, so you look up the restaurant's number on the Internet using your computer. Because you've paid attention to the

think about it
Using what you've just learned about attention, explain why texting on a phone while driving is illegal in many places. (For an explanation, click **here**.)

---

[28] Barron, Riby, Greer, & Smallwood, 2011; Dempster & Corkill, 1999; Reichle, Reineberg, & Schooler, 2010.

[29] J. R. Anderson, 2005; Cowan, 2007; Lien, Ruthruff, & Johnston, 2006; Oberauer & Hein, 2012.

[30] Baddeley, 2012.

[31] Alloway, Gathercole, Kirkwood, & Elliott, 2009; Aron, 2008; Banich, 2009; Cowan, Saults, & Morey, 2006; Logie, 2011; E. E. Smith, 2000; J. Wood, 2007.

[32] Atkins, Bunting, Bolger, & Dougherty, 2012; Best & Miller, 2010; Goldstein, Naglieri, Princiotta, & Otero, 2014; Masten et al., 2012.

[33] For example, see Baddeley, 2001; L. R. Peterson & Peterson, 1959; W. Zhang & Luck, 2009.

number, it's presumably in your working memory. But then you discover that you can't find your cell phone, nor do you have any paper and pencil handy. How might you remember the number until you can make the phone call? One common strategy is rehearsal—repeating it over and over—which can help you keep information in working memory until you need to use it. But once you stop talking to yourself, the information may quickly disappear.

For reasons that aren't entirely clear, the amount of information children can hold in working memory increases somewhat with age.[34] Yet even adults have only so much room to simultaneously hold and think about information. To see what we mean, put your working memory to work for a moment in the following exercise.

SEE FOR YOURSELF
A DIVISIVE SITUATION

Try computing the answer to this division problem *in your head*; put the numbers in your working memory and then close your eyes—*no peeking!*—as you try to calculate the answer:

$$59 \overline{)49{,}383}$$

Did you find yourself having trouble remembering some parts of the problem while you were dealing with other parts? Did you arrive at the correct answer of 837? Most people can't solve a division problem with this many digits unless they write it down, because working memory doesn't have enough space both to (1) hold all the numbers and (2) do all the math that the problem requires. Like attention, working memory has a *limited capacity*—perhaps just enough for a telephone number or very short grocery list.[35]

Sometimes students talk about putting class material in "short-term memory" so that they can do well on an upcoming exam. Such a statement reflects two common misconceptions: that (1) this component of memory lasts for several days, weeks, or months; and (2) it has a fair amount of "room." Now you know otherwise: Information stored in working (short-term) memory lasts less than 20 seconds unless it's processed further, and only a few things can be stored there at one time. Working (short-term) memory is definitely *not* the "place" to leave information you'll need for a class later today, let alone for an exam later in the week. For such memory tasks, storage in long-term memory is in order.

Long-term memory has a long duration and virtually limitless capacity.

Long-term memory is where learners store general knowledge and beliefs about the world, recollections of past experiences, and information learned in school. Such knowledge about *what and how things are* is known as declarative knowledge and includes items such as facts, figures, and events (e.g., Thomas Jefferson was the third president of the United States). Long-term memory is also where learners store knowledge about how to perform various behaviors, such as how to ride a bicycle, swing a baseball bat, or write a cursive letter *J*. Such knowledge about *how to do things* is known as procedural knowledge and includes procedures, strategies, and motor skills. *Procedures* refer to knowledge about how to carry out a series of steps, and *strategies* are plans to achieve a goal.[36] When procedural knowledge includes knowing how to respond differently under varying circumstances, it's sometimes called *conditional knowledge*.

Information stored in long-term lasts much longer than information stored in working memory—perhaps a day, a week, a month, a year, or a lifetime (more on the "lifetime" point later in the chapter). Even when it's there, however, learners can't always find and retrieve it when they need it. As we'll see in upcoming sections, the ability to retrieve previously learned information from long-term memory depends on both the way in which learners have initially encoded it and the context in which they're trying to remember it.

Long-term memory seems to be able to hold as much information as a learner needs to store there. There's probably no such thing as someone "running out of room." In fact, for reasons we'll

think about it
Did you have these misconceptions about short-term memory before you read this section? If so, have you now revised your understanding?

---

[34] Ben-Yehudah & Fiez, 2007; Kail, 2007.

[35] Cowan, 2010; Logie, 2011; G. A. Miller, 1956.

[36] Mayer, 2012.

discover shortly, the more information already stored in long-term memory, the easier it is to learn new things.

Information in long-term memory is interconnected and organized to some extent.

As you should recall from our earlier discussion of the brain, neurons have many, many synaptic connections with one another, and thinking about virtually any topic tends to involve many parts of the brain. It shouldn't surprise you to learn, then, that people's knowledge, beliefs, and skills tend to be interconnected in long-term memory. To get a glimpse of how ideas in your own long-term memory are interconnected and organized, try the following exercise.

SEE FOR YOURSELF
HORSE

What's the first word that comes to mind when you see the word *horse?* And what word does that second word remind you of? And what does the third word remind you of? Beginning with the word *horse,* follow your train of thought, letting each word remind you of a new word or short phrase, for a sequence of at least eight words or phrases. Write down the sequence of things as they come to mind.

You probably found yourself easily following a train of thought from the word *horse,* perhaps something like this route:

horse → cowboy → lasso → rope → knot → Girl Scouts → cookies → chocolate

The last word in your sequence might be one with little or no obvious relationship to horses. Yet you can probably see a logical connection between each word or phrase and the one that follows it. Related pieces of information tend to be associated with one another in long-term memory, perhaps in a network similar to the one depicted in Figure 2.6.

In the process of constructing knowledge, learners often create well-integrated entities that encompass particular ideas or groups of ideas. For instance, beginning in infancy, they form **concepts** that enable them to categorize objects and events.[37] Some concepts, such as *butterfly, chair,* and *backstroke,* encompass a fairly narrow range of objects or events. Others, such as *insect, furniture,* and *swimming,* have a broad scope and may subsume a number of more specific concepts, as illustrated by Noah's butterfly-is-an-insect drawing in Figure 2.7. Noah might, of course, associate *butterfly* with *swimming* as well as with *insect*—because one form of swimming is the butterfly stroke—in which case he could have a train of thought such as this:

horse → cowboy → lasso → rope → knot → Girl Scouts → camping → outdoors → nature → insect → butterfly → swimming

Learners often pull concepts together to construct general understandings of certain parts of their world. These understandings might take the form of **schemas**—tightly organized sets of facts related to particular concepts or phenomena.[38] For example, let's return to the concept *horse.* You know what horses look like, of course, and you can recognize one when you see one, so you obviously have a concept for these animals. But now think about the many things you know *about* horses. What do they eat? How do they spend their time? Where are you most likely to see them? No doubt you can easily retrieve many facts about horses, perhaps including their fondness for oats and carrots, their love of grazing and running, and their frequent appearance on farms and at racetracks. The various things you know about horses are closely interrelated in your long-term memory in the form of a "horse" schema.

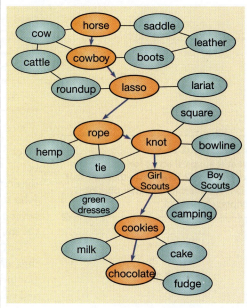

FIGURE 2.6 Related ideas are often associated with one another in long-term memory. Here you see one possible train of thought from *horse* to *chocolate.*

FIGURE 2.7 Eight-year-old Noah depicts organized knowledge related to the concepts *butterfly* and *insect.*

---
[37] J. M. Mandler, 2007; Quinn, 2002.
[38] For example, see Rumelhart & Ortony, 1977; Kalyuga, 2010; Schraw, 2006.

People have schemas not only about objects but also about events. When a schema involves a predictable sequence of events related to a particular activity, it's sometimes called a **script**.[39] The next exercise provides an example.

SEE FOR YOURSELF
JOHN

Read the following passage *one time only.*

> John was feeling bad today so he decided to go see the family doctor. He checked in with the doctor's receptionist, and then looked through several medical magazines that were on the table by his chair. Finally the nurse came and asked him to take off his clothes. The doctor was very nice to him. He eventually prescribed some pills for John. Then John left the doctor's office and headed home.[40]

---

think about it

What is a typical script for a trip to the grocery store? To a movie theater? To a fast-food restaurant? (For possible scripts, click **here**.)

You probably had no trouble making sense of the passage because you've been to a doctor's office yourself and have a schema for how those visits usually unfold. You can therefore fill in a number of details that the passage doesn't tell you. For example, you probably inferred that John *went* to the doctor's office, although the story omits this essential step. Likewise, you probably concluded that John took off his clothes in the examination room, *not* in the waiting room, even though the story never makes it clear where John did his striptease. When critical information is missing, as is true in the story about John, schemas and scripts often enable learners to fill in the gaps in a reasonable way.

On a much larger scale, humans—young children included—construct general understandings and belief systems, or **theories**, about how the world operates.[41] Such self-constructed theories include many concepts and the relationships among them, such as correlational relationships and cause-and-effect relationships. Theories constructed by individuals are similar to the theories developed by researchers in that they include sets of concepts and principles developed to explain a particular phenomenon (as explained in Chapter 1). Yet, individuals' self-constructed theories are a little different from the ones developed by researchers because individuals develop their theories based on their knowledge, beliefs, and experiences that may or may not be based on scientific evidence. To see what some of your own theories are like, try the next exercise.

SEE FOR YOURSELF
COFFEEPOTS AND RACCOONS

Consider each of the following situations:

1. People took a coffeepot that looked like Drawing A. They removed the handle, sealed the top, took off the top knob, sealed the opening to the spout, and removed the spout. They also sliced off the base and attached a flat piece of metal. They attached a little stick, cut out a window, and filled the metal container with birdseed. When they were done, it looked like Drawing B. Was the object now a coffeepot or a bird feeder?

A

2. Doctors took the raccoon in Drawing C and shaved away some of its fur. They dyed what was left black. Then they bleached a single stripe all white down the center of the animal's back. Then, with surgery, they put in its body a sac of super-smelly odor, just like the smell a skunk has. After they were all done, the animal looked like Drawing D. At this point, was the animal a skunk or a raccoon?[42]

B

C

D

---

[39] Sometimes the term *script* is used in reference to knowing a specific set of steps for doing something, in which case it might be better classified as *procedural* knowledge than as declarative knowledge.

[40] G. H. Bower, Black, & Turner, 1979, p. 190.

[41] Gelman, 2003; Keil & Newman, 2008; Wellman & Gelman, 1998.

[42] Both scenarios based on Keil, 1989, p. 184.

You probably concluded that the coffeepot had been transformed into a bird feeder but that the raccoon was still a raccoon despite its cosmetic makeover and stinky surgery. How is it possible that the coffeepot could be made into something entirely different, whereas the raccoon could not? Even young children seem to make a basic distinction between human-made objects (e.g., coffeepots, bird feeders) and biological entities (e.g., raccoons, skunks).[43] For instance, human-made objects are defined largely by the *functions* they serve (e.g., brewing coffee, feeding birds), whereas biological entities are defined primarily by their origins (e.g., the parents who brought them into being, their DNA).[44] Thus, when a coffeepot begins to hold birdseed rather than coffee, it becomes a bird feeder because its function has changed. But when a raccoon is cosmetically and surgically altered to look and smell like a skunk, it still has raccoon parents and raccoon DNA and so can't possibly *be* a skunk.

By the time children reach school age, they've constructed basic theories about their physical, biological, and social worlds.[45] For example, in the opening case study, we get a glimpse of 7-year-old Rob's theory about the earth's topography—a theory in which human beings apparently play a critical role. By school age, children have also constructed preliminary theories about the nature of their own and other people's thinking. For instance, they realize that people's inner thoughts are distinct from external reality, and they understand that the people in their lives have thoughts, emotions, and motives that drive much of what they do (see Chapter 7). In general, self-constructed theories help children make sense of and remember personal experiences, classroom subject matter, and other new information.[46] Yet because children's theories often evolve with little or no guidance from more knowledgeable individuals, they sometimes include erroneous beliefs about the world that can wreak havoc with new learning (more about this point a bit later).

Although it's difficult to easily represent how long-term memory is organized, Figure 2.8 includes some of the long-term memory items we've presented so far. Declarative knowledge is composed of discrete facts that group together into concepts, which comprise schemas/scripts, theories, and beliefs. Procedural knowledge consists of procedures about how to do things, strategies for how to achieve goals, and conditional knowledge about when to use particular strategies. How well long-term memory is integrated and the ways in which it's integrated are to some degree the result of how learners first store information in long-term memory, as we'll see in our explanation of the next principle.

Some long-term memory storage processes are more effective than others.

Intentionally storing new information in long-term memory involves encoding the information to move it from working memory into long-term memory (see Figure 2.5). However, effectively storing new information in long-term memory usually involves connecting it to relevant

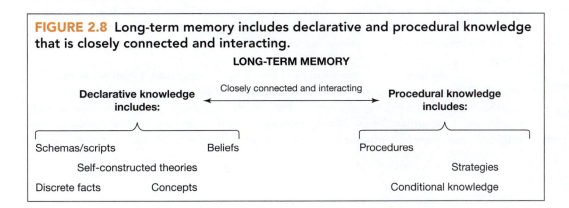

FIGURE 2.8 Long-term memory includes declarative and procedural knowledge that is closely connected and interacting.

LONG-TERM MEMORY

Declarative knowledge includes: Closely connected and interacting   Procedural knowledge includes:

Schemas/scripts   Beliefs   Procedures
Self-constructed theories   Strategies
Discrete facts   Concepts   Conditional knowledge

[43] Gelman & Kalish, 2006; Inagaki & Hatano, 2006; Keil, 1986, 1989.
[44] Greif, Kemler Nelson, Keil, & Gutierrez, 2006; Inagaki & Hatano, 2006; Keil, 1987, 1989.
[45] Geary, 2005; Torney-Purta, 1994; Wellman & Gelman, 1998.
[46] Gelman, 2003; Reiner, Slotta, Chi, & Resnick, 2000; Wellman & Gelman, 1998.

information that's *already* in long-term memory—a process that requires bringing the "old" information back into working memory.[47] The next exercise illustrates this point.

SEE FOR YOURSELF
LETTERS AND A PICTURE
---

1. Study each of the following strings of letters until you can remember them perfectly:

   AIIRODFMLAWRS   FAMILIARWORDS

2. Study the line drawing shown here until you can reproduce it accurately from memory.

No doubt you found the second letter string easier to remember because you could relate it to something you already knew: the words *familiar words*. How easily were you able to learn and remember the picture? Do you think you could draw it from memory a week from now? Do you think you could remember it more easily if it had the title "Bird's Eye View of a Cowboy Riding a Bicycle"? The answer to the last question is almost certainly yes, because the title would help you relate the picture to familiar shapes, such as those of a bicycle and a cowboy hat.[48]

With the preceding exercise in mind, let's distinguish between two basic types of learning: rote learning and meaningful learning (e.g., see Table 2.2). Learners engage in **rote learning** when they try to learn and remember something without attaching much meaning to it. For example, you'd be engaging in rote learning if you tried to remember the letter string FAMILIARWORDS simply as a list of isolated letters or if you tried to remember the cowboy/bicycle drawing as a collection of random, unrelated lines and curves.

One common form of rote learning is *rehearsal,* repeating something over and over within a short time frame (typically a few minutes or less), either by saying it aloud or by continuously thinking about it in an unaltered, verbatim fashion. We've previously seen that rehearsal can help learners keep information in working memory indefinitely. Contrary to what many students think, however, rehearsal is *not* a very effective way of storing information in *long-term* memory. If learners repeat something often enough, it might eventually "stick," but the process is slow and tedious. Furthermore, for reasons we'll identify later, people who use rehearsal and other forms of rote learning often have trouble remembering what they've learned.[49]

In contrast to rote learning, **meaningful learning** involves recognizing a relationship between new information and something previously stored in long-term memory. Seeing the words *familiar words* in the letter string FAMILIARWORDS and seeing a bicycle-riding cowboy in a line drawing are two examples. Similarly, a first grader might connect subtraction facts to previously learned addition facts in the same "family" (e.g., $5 - 3 = 2$ is the reverse of $2 + 3 = 5$), and a high school history student might see parallels between the "ethnic cleansing" in eastern Europe in the 1990s and the Nazis' belief in White supremacy in the 1930s and 1940s. In the vast majority of cases, meaningful learning is more effective than rote learning for storing information in long-term memory.[50] It's especially effective when learners relate ideas to *themselves* as human beings.[51]

Meaningful learning can take a variety of forms, and in many cases it involves adding to or restructuring information in some way. For instance, in **organization**, learners pull new information together into an integrated, logical structure. For example, they might group information into categories (recall the earlier "Twelve Words" exercise with *daisy, apple,* etc.). Alternatively, learners might identify interrelationships among various pieces of information. As an illustration, students

think about it

In your own experiences as a student, how often have classroom assessments encouraged you to memorize information word for word rather than to learn it meaningfully?

---

[47] For a good discussion of this point, see Kirschner, Sweller, & Clark, 2006.
[48] G. H. Bower, Karlin, & Dueck, 1975.
[49] J. R. Anderson, 2005; Ausubel, Novak, & Hanesian, 1978; Craik & Watkins, 1973.
[50] Ausubel et al., 1978; Ghetti & Angelini, 2008; Marley, Szabo, Levin, & Glenberg, 2008; R. E. Mayer, 2010b; Wittrock, 1974.
[51] Heatherton, Macrae, & Kelley, 2004; Kesebir & Oishi, 2010; T. B. Rogers, Kuiper, & Kirker, 1977.

Table 2.2 • Long-Term Memory Storage Processes

PROCESS	DEFINITION	EXAMPLE	EFFECTIVENESS
Rote learning: Learning primarily through repetition and practice, with little or no attempt to make sense of what is being learned			
Rehearsal	Repeating information verbatim, either mentally or aloud	Word-for-word repetition of a formula or definition	Relatively ineffective: Storage is slow, and later retrieval is difficult
Meaningful learning: Making connections between new information and prior knowledge			
Organization	Making connections among various pieces of new information	Thinking about how one's lines in a play relate to the play's overall story line	Effective if organizational structure is legitimate and consists of more than just a list of separate facts
Visual imagery	Forming a mental picture of something, either by actually seeing it or by envisioning how it might look	Imagining how various characters and events in a novel might have looked	Individual differences in effectiveness; especially beneficial when used in combination with elaboration or organization
Elaboration	Embellishing on new information based on what one already knows	Generating possible reasons that historical figures made the decisions they did	Effective if associations and additions made are appropriate and productive

in a physics class might learn that *velocity* is the product of *acceleration* and *time* ($v = a \times t$) and that an object's *force* is determined by both the object's *mass* and its *acceleration* ($f = m \times a$). The goal here isn't simply to memorize the formulas (that would be rote learning) but rather to make sense of the relationships the formulas represent. In most instances, learners who learn an organized body of information remember it better—and they can use it more effectively later on—than would be the case if they tried to learn the same information as a list of separate, isolated facts.[52]

Another effective long-term memory storage process is **visual imagery**, forming a mental picture of objects or ideas. To discover firsthand how effective visual imagery can be, try learning a bit of Mandarin Chinese in the next exercise.

——— SEE FOR YOURSELF ———
FIVE CHINESE WORDS

Try learning these five Chinese words by forming the visual images described (don't worry about learning the tone marks over the words).

Chinese Word	English Meaning	Image
fáng	house	Picture a *house* with *fangs* growing on its roof and walls.
mén	door	Picture a restroom *door* with the word *MEN* painted on it.
kè	guest	Picture a person giving someone else (the *guest*) a *key* to the house.
fàn	food	Picture a plate of *food* being cooled by a *fan*.
shū	book	Picture a *shoe* with a *book* sticking out of it.

Now find something else to do for a couple of minutes. Stand up and stretch, get a glass of water, or use the restroom. But be sure to come back to your reading in just a minute or two. . . .

Now that you're back, cover the list above of Chinese words, English meanings, and visual images. Try to remember what each word means:

kè   fàn   mén   fáng   shū

---

[52] Bjorklund, Schneider, Cassel, & Ashley, 1994; Haugwitz, Sumfleth, & Sandmann, 2010; Nesbit & Adesope, 2006; P. A. Ornstein, Grammer, & Coffman, 2010.

FIGURE 2.9 You can use the acronym MOVE to remember that Meaningful learning involves Organization, Visual imagery, and Elaboration to "move" information from working memory to long-term memory.

```
┌──────────────┐  MOVE  ┌──────────────┐
│ Information in│ ─────▶ │  Long-Term   │
│   Working    │        │    Memory    │
│   Memory     │        │              │
└──────────────┘        └──────────────┘
```

MyEdLab

Video Example 2.1.

What strategies does 16-year-old Hilary use to remember Spanish vocabulary words, the U.S. Constitution's Second Amendment, and other facts?

think about it

Learning something to automaticity is *not* the same thing as rote learning. In what important way are these two processes different? (For an explanation, click **here**.)

Did the Chinese words remind you of the visual images you stored? Did the images, in turn, help you remember the English meanings? You may have easily remembered all five words, or you may have remembered only one or two. People differ in their ability to use visual imagery: Some form images quickly and easily, whereas others form them only slowly and with difficulty. Especially for people in the former category, visual imagery can be a powerful means of storing information in long-term memory.[53]

Still another form of meaningful learning is **elaboration**, in which learners use their prior knowledge to embellish on a new idea, thereby storing *more* information than was actually presented. For example, a student who reads that some species of dinosaurs had powerful jaws and sharp teeth might correctly deduce that those species were meat eaters. Similarly, if a student learns that the crew on Columbus's first trip across the Atlantic threatened to revolt and turn the ships back toward Europe, the student might speculate, "I'll bet the men were really scared when they continued to travel west day after day without ever seeing signs of land."[54] And to use elaboration to help you remember these strategies for encoding information into long-term memory, you could use the acronym MOVE to remember that Meaningful learning involves Organization, Visual imagery, and Elaboration to "move" information from working memory to long term memory (see Figure 2.9).

The three forms of meaningful learning just described—organization, visual imagery, elaboration—are clearly *constructive* in nature: They all involve combining several pieces of information into a meaningful whole. When you organize information, you give it a logical structure (categories, cause-and-effect relationships, etc.). When you use visual imagery, you create mental pictures (perhaps a house with fangs or a restroom door labeled *MEN*) based on how certain objects typically look. And when you elaborate on new information, you combine it with things you already know to help you make better sense of it.

Practice makes knowledge more automatic and durable.

Storing something in long-term memory on one occasion is hardly the end of the learning process. When people continue to practice the information and skills they acquire—and especially when they do so in a variety of situations and contexts—they gradually become able to use what they've learned quickly, effortlessly, and automatically. In other words, people eventually achieve **automaticity** for well-practiced knowledge and skills.[55]

As noted earlier, rehearsal—repeating information over and over within the course of a few seconds or minutes—is a relatively *in*effective way of getting information into long-term memory. But when we talk about acquiring automaticity, we're talking about repetition over the long run: reviewing and practicing information and procedures at periodic intervals over the course of a few weeks, months, or years. When practice is spread out in this manner, people learn things better and remember them longer.[56]

Practice is especially important for gaining procedural knowledge. Procedural knowledge ranges from relatively simple actions (e.g., correctly holding a pencil or gripping a tennis racket) to far more complex skills, such as writing in cursive or hitting a forehand stroke in tennis. These complex skills are acquired slowly over a period of time, often only with a lot of practice.[57] People who show exceptional ability in a particular skill domain—say, in figure skating or playing the piano—typically practice a great deal, often a minimum of 3 to 4 hours a day over a period of 10 years or more.[58]

---

[53] Behrmann, 2000; Johnson-Glenberg, 2000; Konkle, Brady, Alvarez, & Oliva, 2010; Sadoski & Paivio, 2001; Urgolites & Wood, 2013; R. F. Williams, 2012.

[54] Notice that we're using the term *elaboration* to describe something that *learners* do, not something that teachers do. Elaboration as a *cognitive process* occurs inside rather than outside the learner. However, teachers can certainly help students engage in elaboration, as you'll discover later in the chapter.

[55] J. R. Anderson, 2005; P. W. Cheng, 1985; Graham, Harris, & Fink, 2000; R. W. Proctor & Dutta, 1995; Semb & Ellis, 1994.

[56] Cepeda, Vul, Rohrer, Wixted, & Pashler, 2008; Ennis & Chen, 2011; R. W. Proctor & Dutta, 1995; Rohrer & Pashler, 2007.

[57] Ericsson, 2003; Macnamara, Hambrick, & Oswald, 2014; Proctor & Dutta, 1995.

[58] Ericsson, 1996; Horn, 2008.

Many complex procedures begin largely as explicit, declarative knowledge—in other words, as *information* about how to execute a procedure rather than as the actual *ability* to execute it. For example, hitting a forehand stroke in tennis may involve the following basic declarative knowledge: (1) turning sideways, (2) bending knees slightly, (3) bringing the tennis racket back to a hitting position, and (4) following through with the stroke after contacting the ball. When learners use declarative knowledge to guide them as they carry out a new procedure, their performance is slow and laborious and requires a lot of concentration and mental effort. At this point, teachers or coaches may need to remind learners about the steps involved in the procedure, and learners may need to talk themselves through their actions (e.g., "bring the racket back and then follow through"). But as they continue to practice the activity, their declarative knowledge gradually evolves into procedural knowledge. This knowledge becomes fine-tuned over time and eventually allows learners to perform an activity quickly and efficiently—that is, with automaticity (see Figure 2.10).[59]

With age and experience, children acquire more effective learning strategies.

Sometimes learners engage in effective long-term memory storage processes without intentionally trying to do so. For example, if one of us authors said, "*I used to live in Colorado,*" you might immediately deduce that she lived in or near the Rocky Mountains, and you might even picture snow-capped mountains in your head. In this case you're automatically engaging in elaboration and visual imagery: The statement made no mention of the Rockies, so you supplied this information from your own long-term memory.

At other times learners deliberately use certain cognitive processes in their efforts to learn and remember information. For example, in the "Twelve Words" exercise near the beginning of the chapter, you may have quickly noticed the categorical nature of the words in the list and intentionally used the categories *flowers, fruit,* and *tools* to organize them. Similarly, in the "Five Chinese Words" exercise, you intentionally formed visual images in accordance with the instructions. When learners *intentionally* engage in certain cognitive processes to help them reach their goal of learning and remembering something, they're using a **learning strategy**.

A general inclination to relate new information to prior knowledge—meaningful learning—occurs in one form or another at virtually all age levels.[60] More specific and intentional learning strategies (e.g., rehearsal, organization, visual imagery) are fairly limited in the early elementary years but increase in both frequency and effectiveness over the course of childhood and adolescence. The frequency of elaboration—especially as a process that learners *intentionally* use to help them remember something—picks up a bit later, often not until adolescence, and is more common in high-achieving students. Table 2.3 summarizes developmental trends in learning strategies across the grade levels.

Prior knowledge and beliefs affect new learning, usually for the better but sometimes for the worse.

What learners already know provides a **knowledge base** on which new learning—especially *meaningful* learning—can build. For example, when you read the passage about John's visit to the doctor's office earlier in the chapter, you could make sense of the passage only if you've visited a doctor many times and know how such visits typically go. Generally speaking, people who already know something about a topic learn new information about the topic more effectively than people who have little relevant background.[61]

Occasionally, however, prior knowledge *interferes* with new learning. In some cases it may do so because learners make inappropriate connections. For example, when a fourth grader named Rita was asked why America was once called the "New World," she responded that some of the early European explorers "wanted to get to China 'cause China had some things they wanted.

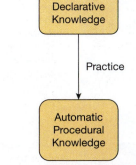

FIGURE 2.10 Complex procedures can begin as declarative knowledge and then gradually become automatic procedural knowledge over time with practice.

Declarative Knowledge

Practice

Automatic Procedural Knowledge

MyEdLab
Video Example 2.2.

With age and experience, children become increasingly strategic in their efforts to remember new information. What strategies do 6-year-old Brent, 12-year-old Colin, and 16-year-old Hilary say they use to remember a list?

---

[59] J. R. Anderson, 1983, 1987; Baroody, Eiland, Purpura, & Reid, 2013; Beilock & Carr, 2003.
[60] G. Mandler, 2011; Pressley & Hilden, 2006; Siegler & Alibali, 2005; R. F. Williams, 2012.
[61] P. A. Alexander, Kulikowich, & Schulze, 1994; Cromley & Azevedo, 2007; Hutchinson, Pak, & Turk-Browne, 2016; Kintsch, 2009; Schneider, 1993; Shapiro, 2004.

DEVELOPMENTAL TRENDS

Table 2.3 • Typical Learning Strategies at Different Grade Levels

GRADE LEVEL	AGE-TYPICAL CHARACTERISTICS	EXAMPLE	SUGGESTED STRATEGIES
Grades K–2	• Organization of physical objects as a way to remember them • Occasional rehearsal to remember verbal material; used infrequently and relatively ineffectively • Emerging ability to use visual imagery to enhance memory, especially with adult prompting • Few intentional efforts to learn new information; learning and memory are a byproduct of other things children do (creating things, talking about events, etc.)	At the end of the school day, a first-grade teacher reminds students that they need to bring three things to school tomorrow: an object that begins with the letter *W* (for a phonics lesson), a signed permission slip for a field trip to a local historic site, and a warm jacket to wear on the field trip. Six-year-old Cassie briefly mumbles "jacket" to herself a couple of times and naively assumes she'll remember all three items without further mental effort.	• Get students actively involved in topics, perhaps through hands-on activities, engaging reading materials, or fantasy play. • Relate new topics to students' prior experiences. • Model rehearsal as a strategy for remembering things over the short run. • Provide pictures that illustrate verbal material. • Give students concrete mechanisms for remembering to do things (see upcoming discussions of *retrieval cues*).
Grades 3–5	• Spontaneous, intentional, and increasingly effective use of rehearsal to remember things for a short time period • Increasing use of organization as an intentional learning strategy for verbal information • Increasing effectiveness in use of visual imagery as a learning strategy	As 10-year-old Jonathan studies for an upcoming quiz on clouds, he looks at photos of four kinds of clouds in his science book and says each one's name aloud. Then he repeats the four cloud types several times: "Cumulus, cumulonimbus, cirrus, stratus. Cumulus, cumulonimbus, cirrus, stratus. . . ."	• Emphasize the importance of making sense of information. • Encourage students to organize what they're learning; suggest possible organizational structures. • Provide visual aids to facilitate visual imagery, and suggest that students create their own drawings or visual images of things they need to remember.
Grades 6–8	• Predominance of rehearsal as a learning strategy • Greater abstractness and flexibility in categories used to organize information • Emergence of elaboration as an intentional learning strategy	Raj and Owen are studying for a middle school science quiz on kinds of rocks. "Let's group them somehow," Raj says. Owen suggests grouping them by color (gray, reddish, etc.). But after further discussion, the boys agree that sorting them into *sedimentary*, *igneous*, and *metamorphic* would be a better approach.	• Suggest questions that students might ask themselves as they study; emphasize questions that promote elaboration (e.g., "Why would ___ do that?" "How is ___ different from ___?"). • Assess true understanding rather than rote memorization in assignments and quizzes.
Grades 9–12	• Continuing reliance on rehearsal as an intentional learning strategy, especially by low-achieving students • Increasing use of elaboration and organization to learn new material, especially by high-achieving students	In a high school history class, Kate focuses her studying on memorizing names, dates, and places. In contrast, Janika likes to speculate about the personalities and motives of such historical characters as Alexander the Great, Napoleon Bonaparte, and Adolf Hitler.	• Ask thought-provoking questions that engage students' interest and help students see the relevance of topics to their own lives. • Have students work in mixed-ability cooperative groups, in which high-achieving students can model effective learning strategies for low-achieving students.

Sources: Bjorklund & Coyle, 1995; Bjorklund & Jacobs, 1985; Bjorklund et al., 1994; Cowan et al., 2006; DeLoache & Todd, 1988; Gaskins & Pressley, 2007; Gathercole & Hitch, 1993; Kosslyn, Margolis, Barrett, Goldknopf, & Daly, 1990; Kunzinger, 1985; Lehmann & Hasselhorn, 2007; Lucariello, Kyratzis, & Nelson, 1992; Marley et al., 2008; L. S. Newman, 1990; P. A. Ornstein et al., 2010; Plumert, 1994; Pressley, 1982; Pressley & Hilden, 2006; Schneider & Pressley, 1989; Schwamborn, Mayer, Thillmann, Leopold, & Leutner, 2010.

They had some cups or whatever—no, they had furs."[62] Rita apparently associated the word *China* with dinnerware—including cups—and also knew that some early explorers sought exotic animal furs. In fact, the early explorers who were seeking a quick route to China wanted to get certain spices and other commodities unavailable at home—*not* cups or furs.

At other times learners' prior knowledge is either insufficient or incorrect. For example, imagine a group of children who think the earth is flat. This idea might be consistent with their early experiences, especially if they live in, say, Illinois or Kansas. You now tell them that the

---

[62] VanSledright & Brophy, 1992, p. 849.

world is actually round. Rather than replacing the *flat* idea with a *round* one, they might pull both ideas together and conclude that the earth is shaped something like a pancake, which is flat *and* round. Alternatively, they might envision a hollow-sphere version of the earth, with people living on a flat surface within it (see Figure 2.11).[63]

As you can see, then, learners sometimes construct **misconceptions**—beliefs that are inconsistent with widely accepted and well-validated explanations of certain phenomena or events. Figure 2.12 presents examples of misconceptions that children and adolescents may bring with them to the classroom. Especially when such misconceptions are embedded in learners' general theories about the world, instruction intended to correct them may have little impact.[64] Instead, thanks to the process of elaboration—a process that usually facilitates learning—learners may interpret or distort the new information to be consistent with what they already "know" and thus continue to believe what they've always believed. For example, one 11th-grade physics class was studying the idea that an object's mass and weight do *not*, by themselves, affect the speed at which the object falls. Students were asked to build egg containers that would keep eggs from breaking when dropped from a third-floor window. They were told that on the day of the egg drop, they would

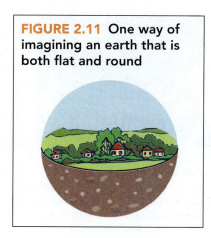

FIGURE 2.11 One way of imagining an earth that is both flat and round

---

FIGURE 2.12 Common student misconceptions

ASTRONOMY

Fact: The earth revolves around the sun.
Misconception: The sun revolves around the earth. It "rises" in the morning and "sets" in the evening, at which point it "goes" to the other side of the earth.

Fact: The earth is shaped more or less like a sphere.
Misconception: The earth is shaped like a round, flat disk *or* the earth is a hollow sphere with people living on a flat surface inside.

Fact: The four seasons are the result of the angle at which the sun's rays hit different parts of the earth's surface; distance from the sun is a largely irrelevant factor.
Misconception: The seasons are the result of the earth's distance from the sun; the earth is closer to the sun in the summer, farther away in the winter.

BIOLOGY

Fact: A living thing is something that carries on such life processes as metabolism, growth, and reproduction.
Misconception: A living thing is something that moves and/or grows. The sun, wind, clouds, and fire are living things.

Fact: A plant is a living thing that produces its own food.
Misconception: A plant takes in food from the ground. It grows in a garden and is relatively small.

PHYSICS

Fact: An object remains in uniform motion until a force acts on it; a force is needed only to *change* speed or direction.
Misconception: Any moving object has a force acting on it. For example, a ball thrown in the air continues to be pushed upward by the force of the throw until it begins its descent.

Fact: Light objects and heavy objects fall at the same rate unless other forces (e.g., air resistance) differentially affect the objects

(e.g., feathers tend to fall slowly because they encounter significant air resistance relative to their mass).
Misconception: Heavy objects fall faster than light objects.

HISTORY AND GEOGRAPHY

Fact: Dinosaurs had long been extinct at the time that early human beings appeared on the earth.
Misconception: Dinosaurs and early humans inhabited the earth at the same time.

Fact: Maps and globes typically include a lot of human-constructed information that isn't evident on the physical earth.
Misconception: The lines separating countries or states are marked on the earth.

Fact: Erosion is an ongoing process.
Misconception: Erosion is largely something that happened in the past; for example, the Grand Canyon is no longer eroding.

Fact: Rivers run from higher elevation to lower elevation.
Misconception: Rivers run from north to south (going "down" on a map). For example, rivers can run from Canada into the United States, but not vice versa.

MATHEMATICS

Fact: Multiplication and division can lead to either larger or smaller numbers (e.g., 5 divided by ½ is 10, a number larger than 5).
Misconception: Multiplication always leads to a larger number, and division always leads to a smaller number.

Fact: The size of a fraction is a function of the proportion of the top number relative to the bottom number.
Misconception: Fractions with large numbers indicate larger amounts than fractions with small numbers (e.g., the erroneous conclusion that $^4/_{35}$ must be larger than $^4/_5$).

Sources: W. F. Brewer, 2008; Brophy, Alleman, & Knighton, 2009; S. Carey, 1986; Hynd, 1998a; Kyle & Shymansky, 1989; V. R. Lee, 2010; Liben & Myers, 2007; M. C. Linn & Eylon, 2011; Maria, 1998; Martínez, Bannan-Ritland, Kitsantas, & Baek, 2008; J. Nussbaum, 1985; K. J. Roth & Anderson, 1988; Sneider & Pulos, 1983; Vosniadou, 1994; Vosniadou & Brewer, 1987; Vosniadou et al., 2008; "rivers" misconception courtesy of R. K. Ormrod.

---

[63] W. F. Brewer, 2008; Vosniadou, Vamvakoussi, & Skopeliti, 2008.
[64] Derry, 1996; P. K. Murphy & Mason, 2006; Sinatra & Pintrich, 2003; C. L. Smith, Maclin, Grosslight, & Davis, 1997.

MyEdLab
Video Example 2.3.
Novice researchers often "prove" what they expect to find, a phenomenon known as *confirmation bias*. As you watch this video, notice how three students conclude that *weight* determines how fast a pendulum swings, whereas the fourth student concludes that *length* is the critical factor. Up to this point, the students have failed to *separate and control variables,* so neither conclusion is warranted from the group's data. (Recall the discussion of separating and controlling variables in Chapter 1.)

record the time it took for the eggs to reach the ground. Convinced that heavier objects fall faster, a student named Barry added several nails to his egg's container. Yet when he dropped it, classmates timed its fall at 1.49 seconds—a time very similar to that for other students' lighter containers. Rather than acknowledge that light and heavy objects fall at the same rate, Barry explained the result by rationalizing that "the people weren't timing real good."[65]

This tendency to look for what one thinks is true and to ignore evidence to the contrary is known as **confirmation bias**. For example, when students in a science lab observe results that are inconsistent with their expectations, many are apt to discredit the results, perhaps complaining that "our equipment isn't working right" or "I can never do science anyway."[66] Similarly, when students in a history class read accounts of a historical event that conflict with prior, not-quite-accurate beliefs about the event—especially if those beliefs are widely held in their cultural group—they may stick with their initial understandings.[67]

As you can see, then, although prior knowledge and beliefs about a topic are usually a blessing, they can sometimes be a curse.

Learners differ in the factors that influence their ability to learn and remember.

Children and adolescents differ considerably in the various factors that influence their ability to learn and remember in the classroom, including their attention spans, working memory capabilities, long-term memory storage processes, and prior knowledge. For example, on average, girls have a slight edge over boys in keeping their attention focused on classroom activities and in performing certain kinds of memory tasks, such as remembering lists and specific life events.[68] And students of both genders vary in their general ability to think about, encode, and respond to new events and ideas quickly and easily. Some of this variability is the result of differences in working memory capacity and executive functioning. Students with a smaller overall capacity and minimal ability to mentally control what they're thinking about often have trouble remembering instructions, tackling complex tasks, and keeping their minds on a task at hand—all of which adversely affect their academic achievement levels.[69] Working memory and executive functioning difficulties are especially common in children who have grown up in chronically stressful living conditions, often as a result of living in extreme poverty.[70]

Students' prior knowledge can also vary significantly because each student has been exposed to a unique set of experiences, interpersonal relationships, and cultural practices and beliefs. Thus, students from diverse backgrounds may come to school with somewhat different knowledge—different concepts, schemas, scripts, self-constructed theories, and so on—that they'll use to make sense of any new situation.[71] To see what we mean, try the next exercise.

——————————— **SEE FOR YOURSELF** ———————————
THE WAR OF THE GHOSTS

Read the following story *one time only:*

> One night two young men from Egulac went down to the river to hunt seals, and while they were there it became foggy and calm. Then they heard war-cries, and they thought, "Maybe this is a war-party." They escaped to the shore, and hid behind a log. Now canoes came up, and they heard the noise of paddles, and saw one canoe coming up to them. There were five men in the canoe, and they said:
> "What do you think? We wish to take you along. We are going up the river to make war on the people."
> One of the young men said: "I have no arrows."
> "Arrows are in the canoe," they said.

---

[65] Hynd, 1998a, p. 34.
[66] Minstrell & Stimpson, 1996, p. 192.
[67] Levstik, 2011; Porat, 2004.
[68] Das, Naglieri, & Kirby, 1994; Halpern, 2006; Halpern & LaMay, 2000.
[69] Alloway, Gathercole, Kirkwood, & Elliott, 2009; DeMarie & López, 2014; Miyake & Friedman, 2012.
[70] Evans & Schamberg, 2009; Masten et al., 2012; Noble, McCandliss, & Farah, 2007.
[71] Berti, Toneatti, & Rosati, 2010; E. Fox, 2009; Levstik, 2011; Pritchard, 1990.

"I will not go along. I might be killed. My relatives do not know where I have gone. But you," he said, turning to the other, "may go with them."

So one of the young men went, but the other returned home.

And the warriors went on up the river to a town on the other side of Kalama. The people came down to the water, and they began to fight, and many were killed. But presently the young man heard one of the warriors say, "Quick, let us go home: that Indian has been hit." Now he thought: "Oh, they are ghosts." He did not feel sick, but they said he had been shot.

So the canoes went back to Egulac, and the young man went ashore to his house, and made a fire. And he told everybody and said, "Behold I accompanied the ghosts, and we went to fight. Many of our fellows were killed, and many of those who attacked us were killed. They said I was hit, and I did not feel sick."

He told it all, and then he became quiet. When the sun rose he fell down. Something black came out of his mouth. His face became contorted. The people jumped up and cried. He was dead.[72]

Now cover the story, and write down as much of it as you can remember.

Compare your own rendition of the story with the original. What differences do you notice? Your version is almost certainly the shorter of the two, and you probably left out many details. But did you also find yourself distorting certain parts of the story so that it made more sense to you?

A Native American ghost story, "The War of the Ghosts" may be inconsistent with some of the schemas and scripts you've acquired from your own experiences, especially if you were raised in a non–Native American culture. In an early study of long-term memory, students at England's Cambridge University were asked to read the story twice and then to recall it at various times later on. Students' recollections of the story often included additions and distortions that made the story more consistent with English culture. For example, people in England rarely go "to the river to hunt seals" because seals are saltwater animals and most rivers have freshwater. Students might therefore say that the men went to the river to *fish*. Similarly, the ghostly aspect of the story didn't fit comfortably with most students' religious beliefs and so was often modified. When one student was asked to recall the story 6 months after he had read it, he provided the following account:

Four men came down to the water. They were told to get into a boat and to take arms with them. They inquired, "What arms?" and were answered "Arms for battle." When they came to the battlefield they heard a great noise and shouting, and a voice said: "The black man is dead." And he was brought to the place where they were, and laid on the ground. And he foamed at the mouth.[73]

Notice how the student's version of the story leaves out many of its more puzzling aspects—puzzling, at least, from his own cultural perspective. This finding demonstrates that learners' prior knowledge can affect how they understand new situations and provides another example of how learners actively construct their knowledge.

Students are more likely to remember information when they store it in their long-term memory using effective meaningful learning strategies such as organization, visual imagery, and elaboration. Students' prior knowledge and beliefs affect students' learning, sometimes for the better and sometimes for the worse. In the hotlinked Self-Check quiz and Application Exercise that follow, you can check and apply your understandings related to Big Idea 2.3:

Human memory is a complex, multifaceted information processing system that is, to a considerable degree, under a learner's control.

MyEdLab **Self-Check 2.3**

MyEdLab **Application Exercise 2.3.** In this exercise, you can practice applying the three-component model of memory to classroom examples.

---

[72] Bartlett, 1932, pp. 71–72.
[73] Bartlett, 1932, p. 65.

2.4 WHY LEARNERS MAY OR MAY NOT REMEMBER WHAT THEY HAVE LEARNED

Big Idea 2.4 Human memory is fallible: Learners don't remember everything they learn, and sometimes they *mis*remember what they've learned.

As we've seen, a great deal of the environmental input a learner receives never reaches long-term memory (as shown by the arrows labeled "lost" in Figure 2.5). Perhaps the learner didn't pay attention in the first place, so the information never went beyond the sensory register. Or perhaps after attending to it, the learner didn't continue to process it, so it went no further than working memory. Even when information does reach long-term memory, it needs considerable time—often several hours or longer—to completely "firm up," or *consolidate,* in the brain. Anything that interferes with this **consolidation** process—even something as seemingly "minor" as not getting a good night's sleep—adversely affects long-term memory of new information.[74]

But let's assume that new information of some sort *has* had the time and conditions it needs to consolidate in the brain. Under such circumstances, it may or may not be easy to retrieve, as reflected in the following general principles.

How easily something is recalled depends on how it was initially learned.

Retrieving information from long-term memory appears to involve following a pathway of associations. Almost literally, it's a process of going down Memory Lane. One idea reminds you of another idea—that is, one idea *activates* another—the second idea reminds you of a third idea, and so forth, in a manner similar to what happened when you followed a train of thought from the word *horse* earlier in the chapter. If the pathway of associations eventually leads you to what you're trying to remember, you do indeed remember it. If the path takes you in other directions, you're out of luck.[75]

To be memorable, then, a new piece of information must be connected with other things already in long-term memory. Ideally, the new and the old have a logical relationship. To illustrate this idea, let's return once again to all that mail you routinely get in your mail and e-mail boxes. Imagine that, on average, you receive five important items—five things you really want to save—every day. That adds up to more than 1,800 items a year. Over the course of 15 years, you'd have more than 27,000 important things stashed somewhere in your home, on your computer, or in cloud storage.

Now imagine that one day you hear that stock in a clothing company (Mod Bod Jeans) has tripled in value. You recall that your wealthy Uncle Fred bought you some Mod Bod stock for your birthday several years ago, and you presumably decided that the paperwork documenting the purchase was important enough to save. But where did you put it? How easily you find it—in fact, whether you find it at all—depends on how you've been storing your mail as you've accumulated it. If you've been storing it in a logical, organized fashion—for instance, all the bills you've paid by regular mail on a closet shelf, all banking and investment paperwork in alphabetical order in a file drawer, and all electronic documents from family and friends in labeled folders on your computer—you should quickly locate your uncle's gift. But if you simply tossed each day's mail and e-mail randomly about, you might search for a long, long time without ever finding it.

Like a home with 15 years' worth of mail, long-term memory contains a great deal of information. And like your search for the Mod Bod paperwork, the ease with which information is retrieved from long-term memory depends somewhat on whether the information has been stored in a logical place—that is, whether it's connected to related ideas. By making connections to existing knowledge—that is, by engaging in meaningful learning—learners know where to look for information when they need it. Otherwise, they may never retrieve it again.

Learners are especially likely to retrieve information when they have *many* possible pathways to it—in other words, when they've associated the information with many other things they know and with many different contexts in which they might use it. Making multiple connections is like using cross-references in your mail storage system. You may have filed the Mod Bod

think about it

Think of an exam you've recently taken. Which student would have gotten a higher score: one who had studied course material verbatim or one who had engaged in meaningful learning?

---

[74] Payne & Kensinger, 2010; Rasch & Born, 2008; Wixted, 2005.

[75] As an example of such *interference* in long-term memory retrieval, see Healey, Campbell, Hasher, & Osher, 2010.

paperwork in the banking/investments file drawer, but you may also have written its location on notes-to-self you've put in other places—perhaps with your birth certificate (because you received the stock on your birthday) and in a computer folder of family documents and photos (because a family member gave you the stock). By looking in one of these logical places, you'll discover where to find the Mod Bod documentation.

Remembering depends on the context.

Sometimes learners acquire and practice certain behaviors and ways of thinking in a very limited set of environments—say, in their science or foreign language classes. When this happens, the learners may associate those behaviors and ways of thinking *only* with those particular environments and thus fail to retrieve what they've learned when they're in other contexts. This tendency for some responses and cognitive processes to be associated with and retrieved only in some contexts but not others—or more easily retrieved in certain physical or social contexts—is often called **situated learning** or **situated cognition**.[76] For example, if students associate principles of geometry only with math classes, they may not retrieve those principles at times when geometry would come in handy—say, when trying to determine whether a 10-inch pizza that costs $8.00 is a better value than an 8-inch pizza that costs $6.00.[77]

In general, learners are more likely to retrieve previously acquired knowledge and skills in a new context if that context provides one or more **retrieval cues** that trigger "travel" along potentially helpful pathways in long-term memory.[78] You can see what we mean in the next exercise.

SEE FOR YOURSELF
THE GREAT LAKES

1. If you went to school in North America, at one time or another you probably learned the names of the five Great Lakes. See if you can recall all of them in the next 15 seconds before you read any further.
2. If you had trouble remembering all five lakes within that short time, here's a hint: The first letters of the Great Lakes spell the word *HOMES*. Now can you recall all five lakes?

If you did poorly at Step 1, the word *HOMES* probably helped you at Step 2 because it gave you some ideas about where to "look" in your long-term memory. For example, if you couldn't initially remember Lake Michigan, *HOMES* told you that one of the lakes begins with the letter *M*, leading you to brainstorm *M* words until, possibly, you stumbled on "Michigan." The letters in *HOMES* acted as retrieval cues that started your search of long-term memory in the right directions.

Fortunately, not all school learning is "stuck" in a particular classroom. People use many of the skills they've learned at school—reading, writing, arithmetic, map interpretation, and so on—in a variety of everyday situations in the outside world.[79] Nevertheless, people don't use what they've learned in the classroom as often as they might. We'll explore this issue further in discussions of *transfer* in Chapter 3.

How easily something is recalled and used depends on how often it has been recalled and used in the past.

Practice doesn't necessarily make perfect, but as we've seen, it does make knowledge more durable and automatic. Practice also makes knowledge easier to "find" later when it's needed.[80] When we use information and skills frequently, we essentially "pave" the pathways we must travel to find them, in some cases creating superhighways.

think about it

What types of retrieval cues are available when you take a multiple-choice test compared with when you take a test that requires you to provide short answers to items (for example, "Define the word *democracy*")? (For an explanation, click **here**.)

---

[76] For classic works related to this topic, see J. S. Brown, Collins, & Duguid, 1989; Greeno, Collins, & Resnick, 1996; Light & Butterworth, 1993; Säljö & Wyndhamn, 1992.

[77] Sometimes the terms *situated learning* and *situated cognition* refer to circumstances in which it's simply *easier* to learn, think, or behave in a certain physical or social context or with certain culturally created physical or cognitive tools (e.g., Greeno & Engeström, 2014; Hickey, 2011; van de Sande & Greeno, 2012).

[78] Balch, Bowman, & Mohler, 1992; Holland, Hendriks, & Aarts, 2005; Tulving & Thomson, 1973.

[79] J. R. Anderson, Reder, & Simon, 1996.

[80] Finn & Roediger, 2011; Pyc & Rawson, 2009.

Knowledge that has been learned to automaticity has another advantage as well. Remember, working memory has a limited capacity: The active, "thinking" part of the human memory system can handle only so much at a time. Thus, when much of its capacity must be used for recalling single facts or carrying out simple procedures, little room remains for addressing the more complex aspects of a task. One key reason for learning some facts and procedures to automaticity, then, is to free up working memory capacity for complex tasks and problems that require those facts and procedures.[81] For example, fourth graders who encounter the multiplication problem

$$87$$
$$\times 59$$

can solve it more easily if they can quickly retrieve such basic facts as $9 \times 8 = 72$ and $5 \times 7 = 35$. High school chemistry students can more easily interpret Na_2CO_3 (sodium carbonate) if they don't have to stop to think about what the symbols Na, C, and O represent. And eighth graders can spend more time focusing on the content and structure of their essays as they write if they have automatized basic spelling, grammar, and handwriting or keyboarding skills.[82]

Recall often involves construction or reconstruction.

Have you ever remembered an event very differently than a friend did, even though the two of you had participated actively and equally in the event? Were you and your friend both certain of the accuracy of your own memories and therefore convinced that the other person remembered the situation incorrectly? Like storage, retrieval has a constructive side, which can explain your differing recollections.

Retrieving something from long-term memory isn't necessarily an all-or-none phenomenon. Sometimes people retrieve only certain parts of something they've previously learned. In such situations they may construct their "memory" of an event by combining the tidbits they can recall with their general knowledge and assumptions about the world.[83] The following exercise illustrates this point.

—————————————— **SEE FOR YOURSELF** ——————————————
MISSING LETTERS

Fill in the missing letters of the following words:

1. exist-nce
2. adole---nce
3. perc--ve
4. gesundh--t

Could you retrieve the missing letters from your long-term memory? If not, you may have found yourself making guesses using either your knowledge of how the words are pronounced or your knowledge of how words in the English language are typically spelled. Perhaps you used the "*i* before *e* except after *c*" rule for Word 3; if so, you correctly reconstructed *perceive*. Perhaps you also recalled the *-escence* spelling pattern in such words as *obsolescence* and *effervescence*, in which case you would have spelled *adolescence* correctly. But if you applied the common spelling pattern *-ance* to Word 1, you misspelled *existence*. Neither pronunciation nor typical English spelling patterns would have helped you with *gesundheit*, a German word often used after someone sneezes.

When people fill in gaps in what they can recall based on what seems logical, they often make mistakes—a phenomenon known as **reconstruction error**. Sometimes, of course, they never learned the missing information to begin with, and so their constructions are merely "best guesses" about the facts. Such is undoubtedly the case for 7-year-old Rob when he explains mountain formation in the opening case study. Regardless of how accurate a "retrieved" memory is, however,

---

[81] De La Paz & McCutchen, 2011; R. W. Proctor & Dutta, 1995; L. B. Resnick, 1989; Walczyk et al., 2007.
[82] Limpo & Alves, 2013.
[83] Brainerd & Reyna, 2005; Ranganath, 2010; Roediger & McDermott, 2000.

the very process of thinking or rethinking about it promotes further consolidation—in many instances *reconsolidation*—that strengthens whatever a person previously knew or decided must be true.[84]

Long-term memory isn't necessarily forever.

People certainly don't need to remember everything. For example, you might have no reason to remember the phone number of a classmate you called yesterday, the plot of last week's rerun of *The Big Bang Theory,* or the due date of an assignment you turned in last semester. Much of the information you encounter is, like junk mail, not worth keeping for the long haul.

Unfortunately, people sometimes forget important things as well as inconsequential ones. Some instances of forgetting may reflect **retrieval failure**: A person simply isn't looking in the right "place" in long-term memory.[85] Perhaps the forgetful person hasn't learned the information in a meaningful way, or perhaps the person doesn't have a good retrieval cue. But other instances of forgetting may be the result of **decay**: Knowledge stored in long-term memory may gradually weaken over time and eventually disappear altogether, especially if it isn't used very often.[86] To some degree, then, the expression "Use it or lose it" may apply to human memory.

Regardless of whether forgetting is due to retrieval failure or to decay, human beings don't always remember the things they've learned. However, teachers can do many things to increase the odds that their students *do* remember academic subject matter, as we'll see in the next section.

Students' memory and retrieval are affected by a variety of factors, such as how something was initially learned, the context in which it was learned, and how often it's been recalled in the past. In the hotlinked Self-Check quiz and Application Exercise that follow, you can check and apply your understandings related to Big Idea 2.4:

> *Human memory is fallible: Learners don't remember everything they learn, and sometimes they misremember what they've learned.*

MyEdLab **Self-Check 2.4**

MyEdLab **Application Exercise 2.4.** In this exercise, you can analyze how a ninth-grade teacher tries to facilitate students' future recall by helping them to make connections among pieces of information.

2.5 PROMOTING EFFECTIVE COGNITIVE PROCESSES

Big Idea 2.5 Effective teachers help students mentally process new information and skills in ways that facilitate long-term memory storage and retrieval.

Given the selective and constructive nature of human learning and memory, the things students learn in instructional settings are rarely complete and precise reproductions of what a teacher or textbook has presented. A teacher's goal, then, should not—and *cannot*—be that students absorb all the information they're given. A more achievable goal is that students construct appropriate and useful understandings of academic subject matter—that they make reasonable *sense* of it.

How effectively students make sense and meaning from what they're studying depends in large part on the cognitive processes in which they engage. Although students are ultimately the ones in control of their own thinking and learning, a teacher can certainly help them think and learn more effectively. The teacher strategies in this section are organized into five general categories: supporting optimal brain functioning, remembering the limitations of attention and working memory, encouraging effective long-term memory storage processes, facilitating retrieval, and monitoring students' progress.

---

[84] Monfils, Cowansage, Klann, & LeDoux, 2009; Schiller et al., 2010.
[85] Einstein & McDaniel, 2005; Loftus & Loftus, 1980.
[86] Altmann & Gray, 2002; J. R. Anderson, 2005; Schacter, 1999.

Supporting Optimal Brain Functioning

We urge you to be cautious when you read books, articles, and websites about promoting "brain-based learning," because many of them are speculative at best. Following are three recommendations that have a solid foundation in brain research.

Provide ongoing intellectual stimulation, but don't overdo it.

New challenges and learning opportunities—age-appropriate ones, of course—seem to enhance brain functioning, in part by nourishing existing neurons, synapses, and astrocytes and in part by stimulating the growth of new ones.[87] At the same time, teachers shouldn't inundate students with nonstop challenging tasks and assignments, to the point that students have little or no time for mental "relaxation." Human beings seem to benefit from a certain amount of mental downtime—enough that they have a chance to reflect on their academic and personal experiences, identify new interconnections among things they've learned, and identify future plans and goals for their performance.[88]

Providing an occasional opportunity for mental downtime *doesn't* mean giving students lots of time in which they have nothing to do. Instead, such an opportunity might take the form of a reflective essay or small-group discussion about a topic or issue related to the day's lessons. When students have *nothing* to do in the classroom, many of them may have insufficient self-regulation skills to use the time productively, and thus they may engage in behaviors that interfere with their own and their classmates' learning (more on this point in Chapter 9).

Encourage physical exercise.

Physical exercise appears to be beneficial for brain health, especially if it includes aerobic activities that keep the cardiovascular system in good working order. A particular benefit is that it enhances the functioning of the central executive—the component of working memory that helps learners keep their minds productively engaged in the task at hand.[89]

Encourage students to get plenty of sleep.

As you well know, a good night's sleep improves mental alertness and can help people ward off germs that can make them sick. But in addition, sleep supports the brain's efforts to consolidate new memories, rendering them more memorable over the long run.[90]

Unfortunately, typical school schedules, especially their early-morning starting times, are poor matches with the sleeping patterns of many high school students. But teachers can support good sleeping habits in another way—in particular, by minimizing the likelihood that students will "pull an all-nighter" to prepare for a test or complete a complex assignment. For example, teachers might give numerous short quizzes—each on a small amount of classroom subject matter—rather than giving two or three comprehensive tests that each cover a large body of material (more on this point in Chapter 10). Teachers might also break a 10-page paper into several small pieces, each of which is due on a different date, to help students plan their work out over time. And more generally, teachers can be reasonable about the amount of homework that they assign by considering students' other out-of-school activities.

Remembering the Limitations of Attention and Working Memory

The model of human memory we've examined in this chapter tells us that attention is critical for moving information into working memory and that working memory has a short duration (less than half a minute) and limited capacity. These two points have several implications for classroom practice.

MyEdLab
Video Example 2.4.

As you listen to 16-year-old Josh in this video, think about how his teachers might help him juggle his homework obligations with his brain's need for sleep.

---

[87] Koob, 2009; C. A. Nelson et al., 2006.

[88] Immordino-Yang, Christodoulou, & Singh, 2012.

[89] Castelli, Hillman, Buck, & Erwin, 2007; G. D. Cohen, 2005; Tomporowski, Davis, Miller, & Naglieri, 2008.

[90] Dinges & Rogers, 2008; Kirby, Maggi, & D'Angiulli, 2011; Payne & Kensinger, 2010; Rasch & Born, 2008.

CLASSROOM STRATEGIES

Getting and Keeping Students' Attention

- **Create stimulating lessons in which students *want* to pay attention.**
  In a unit on nutrition, a high school biology teacher has students determine the nutritional value of various menu items at a popular local fast-food restaurant.

- **Get students physically involved with the subject matter.**
  A middle school history teacher schedules a day late in the school year when all of his classes "go back in time" to the American Civil War. In preparation for the event, the students spend several weeks learning about the Battle of Gettysburg, researching typical dress and meals of the era, gathering appropriate clothing and equipment, and preparing snacks and lunches. On the day of the "battle," students assume various roles, such as Union and Confederate soldiers, government officials, journalists, merchants, housewives, doctors, and nurses.

- **Incorporate a variety of instructional methods into lessons.**
  After explaining how to calculate the areas of squares and rectangles, a fourth-grade teacher has students practice calculating area in a series of increasingly challenging word problems. She then breaks the class into three- and four-member cooperative groups, gives each group a tape measure and calculator, and asks the students to calculate the area of their irregularly shaped classroom floor. To complete the task, the students must divide the room into several smaller rectangles, compute the area of each rectangle separately, and add the subareas together.

- **Provide frequent breaks from quiet, sedentary activities, especially when working with students in the elementary grades.**
  To provide practice with the alphabet, a kindergarten teacher occasionally has students make letters with their bodies. For example, one child stands with arms extended up and out to make a *Y* and two other children bend over and join hands to form an *M*.

- **In the middle school and high school grades, encourage students to take notes.**
  In a middle school science class, different cooperative groups have been specializing in and researching various endangered animal species. As each group gives an oral report about its species to the rest of the class, the teacher asks students in the audience to jot down questions about things they would like to know about the animal. At the end of their oral report, members of the presenting group address their classmates' questions.

- **Minimize distractions when students must work quietly and independently.**
  The windows of two third-grade classrooms in an elementary school overlook the school's playground area, and students in those rooms are often distracted when children in other classes are playing outside. Hence, in preparation for an upcoming statewide assessment, arrangements are made for children in other classes to play group games in the gymnasium during their recess periods.

Sources: Some strategies based on Di Vesta & Gray, 1972; Kiewra, 1989; Ku, Chan, Wu, & Chen, 2008; Pellegrini & Bjorklund, 1997; Posner & Rothbart, 2007.

Grab and hold students' attention.

What teachers do in the classroom can have a huge impact on the extent to which students pay attention to the subject matter at hand. For example, teachers can pique students' curiosity about a topic, perhaps by presenting unusual or puzzling phenomena or modeling their own enthusiastic interest. Incorporating a wide variety of instructional methods into the weekly schedule—discovery learning sessions, debates about controversial issues, cooperative problem-solving activities, and so on—also helps keep students actively attentive to and engaged in mastering new information and skills. The Classroom Strategies box "Getting and Keeping Students' Attention" offers and illustrates several additional suggestions.

MyEdLab
Video Example 2.5.
What specific phrases and behaviors does this teacher use to grab and hold students' attention?

Keep the limited capacity of working memory in mind.

Virtually any learning activity imposes a **cognitive load**—a certain amount of information that learners must simultaneously think about, along with certain *ways* that they must think about it, in order to make sense of and remember what they're studying.[91] When teachers design and conduct lessons, then, they must consider just how much of a load students' working memories can reasonably handle at any given time. For example, they should pace their presentation of important information slowly enough that students have time to effectively process what they're seeing and hearing. They might repeat the same idea several times (perhaps rewording it each time), stop to write important points on the board, and provide numerous examples and illustrations. And in many instances, tablets, laptop computers, or other technological devices can provide external

[91] R. E. Mayer, 2011; Plass, Moreno, & Brünken, 2010; Sweller, 1988, 2008.

memory aids that help students keep track of the ideas they generate—perhaps key points to include in a persuasive essay or alternative research designs for a science project.

Even with such strategies, however, the amount of new information presented in a typical classroom is much more than students can reasonably learn and remember, and students aren't always the best judges of what things are most important to focus on.[92] Teachers must help students zero in on the things that truly matter—for example, by emphasizing main ideas, offering guidelines on what and how to study, providing written or audio materials that students can access later as they study, and omitting irrelevant information and unnecessary details from explanations and lectures.

Encouraging Effective Long-Term Memory Storage Processes

Students who are paying attention and not overloaded with information are ready to actively *think about* what they're studying. To do so, they need to consciously and intentionally engage in effective meaningful learning strategies, such as organization, visual imagery, and elaboration. The following suggestions should promote active, effective learning.

Relate new ideas to students' prior knowledge and experiences.

Students can more effectively learn and remember classroom subject matter if they connect it to many other things they already know. Yet students don't always make such connections on their own, and as a result they're likely to resort to rote learning. Teachers can promote more meaningful learning by encouraging students to relate new material to one or more of the following:

- Concepts and ideas in the same subject area—for example, recognizing that multiplication in arithmetic is simply a variation of addition
- Concepts and ideas in other subject areas—for example, considering how advances in atomic physics have affected historical events
- Students' general knowledge of the world—for example, relating the concept of *inertia* to how passengers are affected when an automobile quickly turns a sharp corner
- Students' personal experiences—for example, identifying similarities between the family feud in *Romeo and Juliet* and students' own group conflicts
- Students' current activities and needs outside of the classroom—for example, applying persuasive writing skills in crafting a personal essay for a college application
- Students' sense of place—for example, connecting themes in novels to local people and places[93]

Ideally, teachers should use students' existing knowledge as a starting point whenever they introduce a new topic—a strategy known as **prior knowledge activation**. For example, in a first-grade classroom, teachers might begin a unit on plants by asking students to describe what their parents do to keep flowers or vegetable gardens growing. Or, in a secondary English literature class, teachers might introduce Sir Walter Scott's *Ivanhoe* (in which Robin Hood is a major character) by asking students to tell the tale of Robin Hood as they know it.

Take advantage of students' diverse background knowledge in designing instruction.

Some students from low-income families—but *only* some of them—may lag behind their classmates in such basic academic skills as reading, writing, and computation.[94] Yet they're apt to bring many strengths to the classroom. They may have a wealth of knowledge about pop culture, such as rap music lyrics, dialogues from popular films, and so on.[95] They're often quite clever at improvising with everyday objects.[96] If they work part time, they may have a good understanding of the working

---

[92] P. A. Alexander & Jetton, 1996; Broekkamp, Van Hout-Wolters, Rijlaarsdam, & van den Bergh, 2002; Gathercole, Lamont, & Alloway, 2006.

[93] Azano, 2011.

[94] Farkas, 2008; Goldenberg, 2001; Serpell, Baker, & Sonnenschein, 2005; Siegler, 2009.

[95] Alim, 2007; Freedom Writers, 1999.

[96] Torrance, 1995.

world. If financial resources have been particularly scarce, they may have a special appreciation for basic human needs and true empathy for victims of war or famine around the world. In some domains, then, students who've grown up in poverty have more knowledge and skills than their economically advantaged peers.

Teachers can take advantage of these diverse backgrounds when designing instruction. For example, teachers can ensure that students with diverse backgrounds participate in class discussions to share their perspectives. And during activities when students work together in groups, teachers can place students with different backgrounds in the same group. Then, as students work on activities in their group, they can share their unique perspectives and knowledge, as well as help their peers understand ideas from different perspectives.[97]

Provide experiences on which students can build.

In some instances, of course, students simply don't have the background knowledge they need to understand a new topic. In such cases, teachers can provide concrete experiences that provide a foundation for classroom lessons. For example, students can better understand how large some dinosaurs were if they see a life-size dinosaur skeleton at a natural history museum. They can more easily understand the events of an important battle if they visit the battlefield. Often teachers can create foundational experiences at school, perhaps by offering opportunities to work with physical objects and living creatures (e.g., timing the fall of light versus heavy objects, caring for a class pet), providing computer software that simulates complex activities (e.g., running a lemonade stand, dissecting a frog), or conducting in-class activities similar to those in the adult world (e.g., trying a mock courtroom case, conducting a political campaign).

Help students organize ideas by making connections among them.

At all grade levels, many students focus on learning isolated facts, without gaining an understanding of how the facts fit together.[98] Yet the more interrelationships students identify within the subject matter they're learning—in other words, the better they *organize* it—the more easily they can remember and apply it later on. When students form many logical connections within the specific concepts and ideas of a topic, they gain a **conceptual understanding** of the topic. For example, rather than simply memorize basic mathematical computation procedures, students should learn how those procedures reflect underlying principles of mathematics. And rather than learn historical facts as a list of unrelated people, places, and dates, students should put those facts within the context of major social and religious trends, economic considerations, human personality characteristics, and so on.

One strategy for helping students find interrelationships within a content area is to organize instructional units around a few core ideas and themes, always relating specific ideas back to this core.[99] (For example, two core ideas in this chapter are the *constructive nature of learning and memory* and the *importance of meaningful learning*.) Another strategy is to have students create charts or drawings that require them to pull together what they've been learning, as 9-year-old Trisha has done in her drawing of the water cycle in Figure 2.13.[100] Still another is to ask students to teach what they've learned to others—a task that may encourage them to focus on main ideas and pull these ideas together in a way that makes sense.[101] But ultimately, students are most likely to gain a

FIGURE 2.13 In this drawing, 9-year-old Trisha effectively integrates what she has learned about the water cycle.

[97] Miyake & Kirschner, 2014.

[98] M. Carr, 2010; De Corte, Op't Eynde, Depaepe, & Verschaffel, 2010; Lesgold, 2001; M. C. Linn & Eylon, 2011; Paxton, 1999.

[99] Brophy, Alleman, & Knighton, 2009; Prawat, 1993; J. J. White & Rumsey, 1994.

[100] van der Veen, 2012.

[101] Hatano & Inagaki, 2003; McCaslin & Good, 1996; Roscoe & Chi, 2007.

conceptual understanding of a topic if they explore it in depth—for instance, by considering many examples, examining cause-and-effect relationships, and discovering how specific details relate to general principles. Accordingly, many educators advocate the principle *Less is more: Less* material studied more thoroughly is learned *more* completely and with greater understanding.[102]

Facilitate visual imagery.

Because we are all visual learners, visual imagery can be a highly effective way to learn and remember information. Teachers can promote students' use of visual imagery in a variety of ways. For example, they can ask students to imagine how certain events in literature or history might have looked. They can provide visual materials (pictures, charts, videos, three-dimensional models, computer animations, etc.) that illustrate or graphically organize important ideas. And they can ask students to create their *own* pictures, diagrams, or models of things they're learning, as Trisha has done in her drawing of the water cycle.[103]

Often teachers better help students remember new ideas when they encourage students to encode classroom subject matter *both* verbally and visually.[104] In Figure 2.14, 9-year-old Nicholas uses both words and a picture to describe his findings from a third-grade science experiment, in which he observed what happened when he dropped small, heavy objects into a glass of water. Nick has difficulties with written language that qualify him for special educational services. Notice how he misspells many words and, in his second sentence, writes *up* from the bottom of the page. Perhaps by writing upward rather than in the normal top-down fashion, Nick is thinking about how the water traveled up and out of the glass as blocks were dropped into it.

Present questions and tasks that encourage elaboration.

The more students elaborate on new material—the more they mentally expand on what they're learning—the more effectively they're apt to understand and remember it. The Classroom Strategies box "Encouraging Elaboration of Classroom Topics" describes and illustrates several ways teachers might help students effectively embellish on classroom topics.

Suggest mnemonics for hard-to-remember facts.

Some things are hard to make sense of—hard to learn meaningfully. For instance, why do bones in the human body have such names as *humerus, fibula,* and *ulna?* Why is *fáng* the Chinese word for house? Why is Augusta the capital of Maine? For all practical purposes, there's no rhyme or reason to such facts.

When students are likely to have trouble making connections between new material and their prior knowledge, or when a body of information has an organizational structure with no obvious underlying logic (e.g., as is true for many lists), special memory tricks known as **mnemonics** (pronounced ne-mon-iks) can help them learn classroom material more effectively.[105] Three commonly used mnemonics are described in Figure 2.15.

Give students time to think.

We've talked about the importance of having students find personal meaning in, organize, visualize, and elaborate on classroom subject matter. Such processes require thought, and thought requires time. Yet some teachers are impatient, giving students very little time—in some cases *less*

FIGURE 2.14 With both words and a picture, 9-year-old Nicholas describes his findings from a science experiment. His second sentence begins at the bottom of the page and goes upward. (Translation: "We poured so many cubes [that] the cup overflowed. The blocks took up all the room.")

MyEdLab
Video Example 2.6.

What mnemonic strategies are used by the students and teacher to remember seemingly arbitrary facts?

---

[102] Brophy et al., 2009; Marshall, 1992; Sizer, 1992, 2004.

[103] R. K. Atkinson et al., 1999; Carlson, Chandler, & Sweller, 2003; Edens & Potter, 2001; R. E. Mayer, 2010a; Sadoski & Paivio, 2001; Schwamborn et al., 2010; Van Meter, 2001; Van Meter & Garner, 2005; Verdi, Kulhavy, Stock, Rittschof, & Johnson, 1996.

[104] R. E. Mayer, 2011; Moreno, 2006; Sadoski & Paivio, 2001; Winn, 1991.

[105] Bulgren, Schumaker, & Deshler, 1994; M. S. Jones, Levin, Levin, & Beitzel, 2000; Pressley, Levin, & Delaney, 1982; Scruggs & Mastropieri, 1989.

FIGURE 2.15 Common mnemonic techniques

VERBAL MEDIATION

A **verbal mediator** is a word or phrase that creates a logical connection, or "bridge," between two pieces of information. Verbal mediators can be used for such paired pieces of information as foreign-language words and their English meanings, countries and their capitals, chemical elements and their symbols, and words and their spellings. Following are examples:

Information to Be Learned	**Verbal Mediator**
Handschuh is German for "glove."	A glove is a *shoe* for the *hand*.
Quito is the capital of Ecuador.	Mosquitoes are at the *equator*.
Au is the symbol for gold.	'*Ay, you* stole my *gold* watch!
The word *principal* ends with the letters *pal* (not *ple*).	The *principal* is my *pal*.
The *humerus* bone is the large arm bone above the elbow.	The *humorous* bone is just above the *funny* bone.

KEYWORD METHOD

Like verbal mediation, the **keyword method** aids memory by making a connection between two things. This technique is especially helpful when there is no logical verbal mediator to fill the gap—for example, when there is no obvious sentence or phrase to relate a foreign-language word to its English meaning. The keyword method involves two steps, which can be illustrated using the Spanish word *amor* and its English meaning, "love":

1. Identify a concrete object to represent each piece of information. The object may be either a commonly used symbol (e.g., a heart to symbolize love) or a sound-alike word (e.g., a suit of armor to represent *amor*). Such objects are *keywords*.

2. Form a mental image of the two objects together. To remember that *amor* means "love," you might picture a knight in a suit of armor with a huge red heart painted on his chest.

You used the keyword method when you learned the meanings of *fáng, mén, kè, fàn,* and *shū* in the "Five Chinese Words" exercise earlier in the chapter. Following are additional examples:

Information to Be Learned	**Visual Image**
Das Pferd is German for "horse."	Picture a *horse* driving a *Ford*.
Augusta is the capital of Maine.	Picture a *gust of* wind blowing through a horse's *mane*.
Tchaikovsky composed "Swan Lake."	Picture a *swan* swimming on a *lake*, wearing a *tie* and *coughing*.

SUPERIMPOSED MEANINGFUL STRUCTURE

A larger body of information, such as a list of items, can often be learned by superimposing a meaningful organization—a familiar shape, word, sentence, rhythm, poem, or story—on the information. Following are examples of such **superimposed meaningful structures**:

Information to Be Learned	**Superimposed Meaningful Structure**
The shape of Italy	A "boot"
The Great Lakes (Huron, Ontario, Michigan, Erie, Superior)	HOMES
Strings on a guitar (E A D G B E)	Edgar ate dynamite. Good-bye, Edgar.
The number of days in each month	Thirty days has September. . . .
How to turn a screw (clockwise to tighten it; counterclockwise to loosen it)	Righty, tighty; lefty, loosey.
How to multiply in a mathematical expression of the form $(ax + b)(cx + d)$	FOIL: multiply the *First* terms within each set of parentheses, then the two *Outer* terms, then the two *Inner* terms, and finally the *Last* terms

than a second—to respond to questions. If students don't respond in that short time, the teachers speak again—perhaps by asking a different question or answering a question themselves. Some teachers are equally reluctant to let much time lapse after students answer questions or make comments in class—once again, they may allow 1 second or less of silence—before responding to a statement or asking another question.[106] The problem here is one of insufficient **wait time**.

When teachers instead allow at least *3 seconds* to elapse after their own questions and after students' comments, dramatic changes can occur in students' behaviors. More students (especially

---

[106] Jegede & Olajide, 1995; M. B. Rowe, 1974, 1987.

CLASSROOM STRATEGIES

Encouraging Elaboration of Classroom Topics

- **Communicate the belief that students can and should make sense of what they're studying.**

  A middle school language arts teacher tells his class that he doesn't expect students to memorize the definitions he gives them for new vocabulary words. "Always put definitions in your own words," he says, "and practice using your new words in sentences. For example, one of the new words in this week's list is *garish*. Look at the definition I just gave you. In what situations might you use *garish*?"

- **Ask questions that require students to draw inferences from what they're learning.**

  Students in a high school first-aid class have learned that when people suffer from traumatic shock, many normal bodily functions are depressed because less blood is circulating through the body. The teacher asks, "Given what you've learned about traumatic shock, why do experts recommend that if we find a person in shock, we *have the person lie down* and *keep him or her warm but not hot*?"

- **Have students apply what they've learned to new situations and problems.**

  To give her class practice in creating and interpreting bar graphs, a second-grade teacher asks children to write their favorite kind of pet on a self-stick note she has given each of them. "Let's make a graph that can tell us how many children like different kinds of pets," she says. On the board the teacher draws a horizontal line and a vertical line to make the graph's x-axis and y-axis. "Let's begin by making a

  column for dogs," she continues. "How many of you wrote *dog* as your favorite pet? Seven of you? OK, put your sticky notes on the graph where I've written *dog*. We'll put them one above another to make a bar." After the dog lovers have attached their notes to the graph, the teacher follows the same procedure for cats, birds, fish, and so on.

- **Focus on an in-depth understanding of a few general principles—the *big ideas* within a discipline— instead of covering many topics superficially.**

  In planning his geography curriculum for the coming school year, a fourth-grade teacher realizes that his students may gain little from studying facts and figures about numerous countries around the globe. Instead, he chooses six countries with very different cultures— Italy, Japan, Morocco, New Zealand, Peru, and Tanzania—that the class will focus on during the year. Through an in-depth study of these countries, the teacher plans to help his students discover how different climates, topographies, cultures, and religions lead to different lifestyles and economies.

- **Create opportunities for small-group or whole-class discussions in which students can freely exchange their views.**

  In a unit on World War II, a high school history teacher has students meet in small groups to speculate about the problems the Japanese people must have faced after atomic bombs were dropped on Hiroshima and Nagasaki.

Sources: Some strategies based on Brophy et al., 2009; Croninger & Valli, 2009; Middleton & Midgley, 2002; Slavin, Hurley, & Chamberlain, 2003; N. M. Webb et al., 2008.

more females and minority students) participate in class, and students begin to respond to one another's comments and questions. Students are more likely to support their reasoning with evidence or logic and more likely to speculate when they don't know an answer. Furthermore, students are more motivated to learn classroom subject matter, are better behaved in class, and actually learn more. Such changes are in part due to the fact that with increased wait time, *teachers'* behaviors change as well. Teachers ask fewer simplistic questions (e.g., those requiring recall of facts) and more thought-provoking ones (e.g., those requiring elaboration). They modify the direction of a discussion to accommodate students' comments and questions, and they allow their classes to pursue a topic in greater depth than they had originally planned. And their expectations for many students, especially previously low-achieving ones, begin to improve.[107]

Facilitating Retrieval

Even when students engage in meaningful learning, they don't necessarily retrieve important information when they need it. Remember, retrieval involves following a pathway of mental associations, and students sometimes travel down the wrong path. The next two recommendations can enhance students' ability to retrieve what they've learned.

---

[107] Castagno & Brayboy, 2008; Giaconia, 1988; Mohatt & Erickson, 1981; M. B. Rowe, 1974, 1987; Tharp, 1989; Tobin, 1987.

Provide many opportunities to practice important knowledge and skills.

Some information and skills are so fundamental that students must become able to retrieve and use them quickly and effortlessly—that is, with automaticity. For example, to read well, students must be able to recognize most of the words on the page without having to sound them out or look them up in the dictionary. To solve mathematical word problems, students should have such number facts as $2 + 4 = 6$ and $5 \times 9 = 45$ on the tips of their tongues. And to write well, students should be able to form letters and words without having to stop and think about how to make an uppercase *G* or spell *the*. Unless such knowledge and skills are learned to automaticity, a student may use so much working memory capacity retrieving and using them that there's little "room" to do anything more complex.[108]

Ultimately, students can learn basic information and skills to automaticity only by using and practicing them repeatedly over time.[109] This is *not* to say that teachers should fill each day with endless drill-and-practice exercises involving isolated facts and procedures (e.g., see Figure 2.16). Automaticity can occur just as readily when the basics are embedded in a variety of stimulating and challenging activities. Furthermore, students should practice new skills within the context of instruction and guidance that help them *improve* those skills. The Classroom Strategies box "Helping Students Acquire New Skills" provides examples of instructional strategies that can help students more effectively acquire procedural knowledge.

At the same time, teachers must be aware that automaticity has a downside.[110] In particular, students may quickly recall certain ideas or perform certain procedures when other, less automatic ideas or procedures are more useful. Students can be more flexible—and thus more likely to identify unique approaches to situations or creative solutions to problems—if they aren't automatically "locked in" to a particular response. We'll revisit this issue in our discussion of *mental set* in Chapter 3.

Give hints that help students recall or reconstruct what they've learned.

Sometimes forgetting is simply a matter of retrieval difficulty: Students either can't "find" knowledge that's in long-term memory or else neglect to "look" for it altogether. In such situations retrieval cues are often helpful and appropriate. For example, if a student asks how the word *liquidation* is spelled, a teacher might say, "*Liquidation* means to make something liquid. How do you spell *liquid?*" Another example comes from one of the author's (Jeanne's) former teacher interns, Jesse Jensen. A student in her eighth-grade history class had been writing about the Battle of New Orleans, a decisive victory for the United States in the War of 1812. The following exchange took place:

> *Student:* Why was the Battle of New Orleans important?
>
> *Jesse:* Look at the map. Where is New Orleans?
>
> (The student points to New Orleans.)
>
> *Jesse:* Why is it important?
>
> *Student:* Oh! It's near the mouth of the Mississippi. It was important for controlling transportation up and down the river.

In the early grades teachers typically provide many retrieval cues: They remind students about the tasks they need to do and when to do them ("I hear the fire alarm. Remember, we all walk quietly during a fire drill"; or "It's time to go home. Do you all have the field trip permission slip to take to your parents?"). But as students grow older, they must develop greater

FIGURE 2.16 Occasional rote practice of numerals and letters can be helpful in promoting automaticity, but too much conveys the idea that learning basic skills is boring and tedious. Here 5-year-old Gunnar has practiced writing numerals 1 through 9, although he practiced writing 9 *backward!*

---

[108] De La Paz & McCutchen, 2011; R. E. Mayer & Wittrock, 1996; Sweller, 1994; Walczyk et al., 2007.

[109] Karpicke, 2012; R. W. Proctor & Dutta, 1995; Rohrer & Pashler, 2010.

[110] Killeen, 2001; E. J. Langer, 2000; LeFevre, Bisanz, & Mrkonjic, 1988.

CLASSROOM STRATEGIES

Helping Students Acquire New Skills

- **Help students understand the logic behind the procedures they're learning.**

  As a teacher demonstrates the correct way to swing a tennis racket, he asks his students, "Why is it important to have your feet shoulder-width apart rather than together? Why is it important to follow through with your swing after you hit the ball?"

- **When skills are especially complex, break them into simpler tasks that students can practice one at a time.**

  Knowing how overwhelming the task of driving a car can be initially, a driver education teacher begins behind-the-wheel instruction by having students practice steering and braking in an empty school parking lot. Only later, after students have mastered these skills, does she have them drive in traffic on city streets.

- **Provide mnemonics that can help students remember a sequence of steps.**

  A math teacher presents this equation:

  $$y = \frac{3\,(x + 6)^2}{2} + 5$$

"When x equals 4, what does y equal?" she asks. She gives students a mnemonic, *Please excuse my dear Aunt Sally,* that they can use to help them remember how to solve problems involving such complex algebraic expressions. First, you simplify things within parentheses (this is the *P* in *Please*). Then, you simplify anything with an exponent (this is the *e* in *excuse*). Then, you do any necessary multiplication and division (these are the *m* and *d* in *my dear*). Finally, you do any remaining addition and subtraction (these are the *A* and *S* in *Aunt Sally*).

- **Give students many opportunities to practice new skills, and provide the feedback they need to help them improve.**

  A science teacher asks his students to write lab reports after each week's lab activity. Because many of his students have had little or no previous experience in scientific writing, he writes numerous comments when he grades the reports. Some comments describe the strengths he sees, and others provide suggestions for making the reports more objective, precise, or clear.

Sources: P. A. Alexander & Judy, 1988; J. R. Anderson et al., 1996; Beilock & Carr, 2004; Ennis & Chen, 2011; Hattie & Timperley, 2007; Hecht, Close, & Santisi, 2003; R. W. Proctor & Dutta, 1995; Shute, 2008; van Merriënboer & Kester, 2008.

independence, relying more on themselves and less on their teachers for certain things they need to remember. At all grade levels, teachers can teach students ways of providing retrieval cues for *themselves*. For example, if second-grade teachers expect children to bring signed permission slips to school the following day, they might ask the children to write a reminder on a piece of masking tape that they attach to their jackets or backpacks. If middle school teachers give students a major assignment due several weeks later, they might suggest that students help themselves remember the due date by taping a note to their bedside table or typing a reminder in their cell phone calendars. In such instances teachers are fostering *self-regulation*, a topic we'll explore in Chapter 3.

Monitoring Students' Progress

As you'll learn in Chapter 10, some classroom assessments—such as listening to what students say in class and watching their body language—are spontaneous, informal ones. Others—such as in-class quizzes and assigned projects—are more systematic, formal ones that require advance planning. Both informal and formal assessments are important for promoting effective cognitive processes, as the following recommendations reveal.

Regularly assess students' understandings.

Teachers must continually keep in mind that students will each interpret classroom subject matter in their own idiosyncratic ways, and occasionally they may construct *mis*information, as Rob does in the opening case study. They may also interpret nonacademic interactions in ways their teachers didn't anticipate. For example, the first day that 8-year-old Darcy attended third grade at a new school, she accidentally got egg in her hair. Her teacher, Mrs. Whaley, took her to the nurse's office to have the egg washed out. As revealed in the journal entries in Figure 2.17, Darcy initially misinterpreted Mrs. Whaley's comment as unflattering criticism. Not until 5 days later did she learn Mrs. Whaley's intended meaning.

It's essential, then, that teachers regularly monitor students' understandings about both academic topics and nonacademic issues. Asking questions, encouraging dialogue, listening carefully to students' ideas and explanations—all of these strategies can help teachers get a handle on the "realities" students have constructed for themselves.

Identify and address students' misconceptions.

Teachers often present new information with the expectation that it will correct students' erroneous beliefs. Yet students of all ages can hold on quite stubbornly to their existing misconceptions about the world, even after considerable instruction that explicitly contradicts them.[111] In some cases students never make the connection between what they're learning and what they already believe, perhaps because they're engaging in rote learning as they study academic subject matter. In other instances students truly try to make sense of classroom material, but—thanks to the process of elaboration—they interpret new information in light of what they already "know" about the topic, and they may reject or discredit something that doesn't fit. (Recall the earlier discussion of *confirmation bias*.)

When students hold scientifically inaccurate or in other ways counterproductive beliefs about the world, teachers must work actively and vigorously to help them revise their thinking. That is, teachers must encourage **conceptual change**. The Classroom Strategies box "Promoting Conceptual Change" presents and illustrates several potentially useful techniques.

FIGURE 2.17 As you can see from her journal entries, 8-year-old Darcy initially interpreted a casual remark to the school nurse in a way very different from the teacher's intended meaning. Fortunately, the teacher corrected the misunderstanding a few days later.

> *October 22nd*
>
> *I went to a new school today. My teacher's name is Mrs. Whaley. I accidentally cracked an egg on my head. Mrs. Whaley told the nurse that I was a show off and a nuisance. I got really sad and wanted to run away from school, but I didn't leave.*
>
> . . .
>
> *October 27th*
>
> *We presented our book reports today. I was the last one to present my book report. Whenever I did my book report, they laughed at me, but the teacher said they were laughing with me. I asked the teacher why she had called me a nuisance the first day. And she said, "Darcy, I didn't call you a nuisance. I was saying to Mrs. Larson that it was a nuisance to try to wash egg out of your hair." I was so happy. I decided to like Mrs. Whaley again.*

Focus assessments on meaningful learning rather than rote learning.

As students get older, they increasingly encounter assignments, exams, and other formal assessments that teachers use to determine final class grades. Unfortunately, many teachers' classroom assessment practices tend to encourage students to learn school subjects in a rote rather than meaningful manner (e.g., see Figure 2.18). When students discover that assignments and exams focus primarily on recall of unrelated facts—rather than on understanding and application of an integrated body of knowledge—they may rely on rote learning, believing that this approach will yield a higher score and that meaningful learning would be counterproductive.[112] Ultimately, teachers must communicate in every way possible—including in their classroom assessments—that it's more important to *make sense* of classroom material than to memorize it. In Chapter 10 we'll identify numerous strategies for assessing meaningful learning.

FIGURE 2.18 Seventh-grade science students complete these and other fill-in-the-blank questions while they watch a video about dinosaurs. Although the questions probably help students pay attention to the video, they encourage rote rather than meaningful learning.

> 1) One of the coolest things about dinosaurs is that of all the millions there were, we only know about a few ___thousand___ of them.
> 2) The word "fossil" comes from the Latin word meaning ___dug up___.
> 3) What four things can fossils tell us about dinosaurs?
>   1 ate   3 what they died w/ young
>   2 look like   4. size/weight
> 4) Two steps in the process of fossilization are:
>   -need to die   -then are covered in layers of sediment
> 5) One of the processes which forms a fossil is ___re-mineralized___ This means that minerals replace the bones of the dinosaur.
> 6) The evidence that dinosaurs once lived is found in discovering ___fossils___.
> 7) Scientists can learn about dinosaurs by observing ___where___ their fossils are buried, how ___deep___ the fossils are, and what is buried ___nearby___ the dinosaur fossils.
> 8) Dinosaurs lived on earth for about ___160___ million years.
> 9) Dinosaurs died out about ___65___ million years ago.
> 10) One reason dinosaurs may have become extinct is ___a meteorite___.

Be on the lookout for students who have unusual difficulty with certain cognitive processes.

Some students may show ongoing difficulties in processing and learning from academic lessons or social interactions. Students with **learning disabilities** have significant deficits in one or more specific cognitive processes. For instance, they may have trouble remembering verbal instructions,

think about it

What kinds of assessment tasks are likely to encourage automaticity for basic knowledge and skills? (For possible tasks, click **here**.)

---

[111] Chambliss, 1994; Chinn & Brewer, 1993; Hynd, 1998b; M. C. Linn & Eylon, 2011; Strike & Posner, 1992; Vosniadou, 2008.

[112] Crooks, 1988; Newstead, 2004.

CLASSROOM STRATEGIES

Promoting Conceptual Change

- **Probe for misconceptions that may lead students to interpret new information incorrectly.**

  When a third-grade teacher asks, "What is gravity?" one student replies that it's "something that pulls you down." The teacher points to Australia on a globe and asks, "What do you mean by *down*? What do you think would happen if we traveled to Australia? Would gravity pull us off the earth and make us fall into space?"

- **Provide information and experiences that explicitly contradict students' misunderstandings.**

  In a lesson about air, a first-grade teacher addresses the common misconception that air has no substance. She asks students to predict what will happen when she submerges an upside-down glass in a large bowl of water, and the children have differing opinions about whether the "empty" glass will fill with water. The teacher stuffs the glass with a crumpled paper towel, turns it upside down, and pushes it straight down into the water. The paper towel remains dry, leading the class to a discussion of how air takes up space.

- **Ask questions that challenge students' misconceptions.**

  A high school physics teacher has just begun a unit on inertia. Some students assert that when a baseball is thrown in the air, a force continues to act on the ball, pushing it upward for a short while. The teacher asks, "What force in the air could possibly be pushing that ball upward after it has left the thrower's hand?" The students offer several possibilities but acknowledge that none of them provides a satisfactory explanation.

- **Show students how an alternative explanation is more plausible and useful—how it makes more sense—than their original belief.**

  The same physics teacher points out that the baseball continues to move upward even though no force pushes it in that direction. He brings in the concept of *inertia*: The ball needs a force only to get it *started* in a particular direction. Once the force has been exerted, other forces (gravity and air resistance) alter the ball's speed and direction.

- **Give students corrective feedback about responses that reflect misunderstanding.**

  Students in a fourth-grade class have just completed a small-group lab activity in which they observe the reactions of earthworms to varying conditions. Their teacher asks them, "What happens if an earthworm dries out?" One student responds, "They like water; they like to splash around in it . . . if they're in the hot sun they can die because they'll dry up . . . their cells will get hard." The teacher acknowledges that the student is right about the preference for moist conditions while also gently refining the student's explanation: "Absolutely right, good. I don't think they usually like to splash around in water so much, but they like to stay where it's moist."

- **Build on any kernels of truth in students' existing understandings.**

  When asked "What is rain?" a sixth grader says that it's "water that falls out of a cloud when the clouds evaporate . . . it comes down at little times like a salt shaker when you turn it upside down . . . there's little holes [in the cloud] and it just comes out." The teacher identifies two accurate understandings in the student's explanation: (1) clouds have water, and (2) evaporation is involved in the water cycle. She uses this knowledge as starting points for further instruction; for instance, she clarifies where in the water cycle evaporation is involved (i.e., in cloud formation) and how a cloud actually *is* water, not a shaker-like water container.

- **When pointing out misconceptions, do so in a way that maintains students' self-esteem.**

  A fourth-grade teacher begins a lesson on plants by asking, "Where do plants get their food?" Various students suggest that plants get their food from dirt, water, or fertilizer. The teacher responds, "You know, many children think exactly what you think. It's a very logical way to think. But actually, plants *make* their food, using sunlight, water, and things in the soil." The teacher then introduces the process of photosynthesis.

- **Engage students in discussions of the pros and cons of various explanations.**

  After students express the stereotypical belief that new immigrants to the country are "lazy," a middle school social studies teacher invites several recent immigrants to visit the class and describe their efforts to adjust to their new environment. The following day, he asks students to reflect on what the guest speakers told them: "Several of you have expressed the opinion that many immigrants are lazy. Do you think the people you met yesterday were lazy? Why or why not?" In the ensuing discussion the students begin to realize that most immigrants probably work very hard to adapt to and succeed in their new society and its culture.

- **Ask students to apply their revised understandings to new situations and problems.**

  When several students express the belief that rivers always run from north to south, a middle school geography teacher reminds them that water travels from higher elevations to lower elevations, not vice versa. She then pulls out a map of Africa. "Let's look at the Nile River," she says. "One end of the Nile is here [she points to a spot on Egypt's Mediterranean coast] and the other end is here [she points to a spot in Uganda]. In which direction must the Nile be flowing?"

MyEdLab
Video Example 2.7.

This video shows the lesson about earthworms.

Sources: C. Chan, Burtis, & Bereiter, 1997; Chinn & Samarapungavan, 2009; D. B. Clark, 2006; diSessa, 2006; Hattie & Timperley, 2007; M. C. Linn & Eylon, 2011; Mason, Gava, & Boldrin, 2008; P. K. Murphy & Mason, 2006; Pine & Messer, 2000; Pintrich, Marx, & Boyle, 1993; Putnam, 1992; Slusher & Anderson, 1996; C. L. Smith, 2007; Stepans, 1991, p. 94 (salt shaker example); Vosniadou, 2008; Zohar & Aharon-Kraversky, 2005.

recognizing words in print (*dyslexia*), or thinking about and remembering information involving numbers (*dyscalculia*). Students with **attention-deficit hyperactivity disorder (ADHD)** may show marked deficits in attention, have trouble inhibiting inappropriate thoughts and behaviors, or both. Most experts believe that learning disabilities and ADHD have a biological basis, sometimes as a result of genetic inheritance and sometimes as a result of adverse environmental conditions (e.g., exposure to toxic substances) during early brain development.[113]

When students have been officially identified as having a learning disability or ADHD, specialists are often called on to assist them in their learning. Even so, most of these students are in general education classrooms for much or all of the school day. Strategies for working effectively with them include the following:[114]

- Identify and capitalize on the times of day when students learn best.
- Minimize distractions (e.g., provide a quiet work location or headphones that block distracting noises).
- Explicitly present the information students need to learn; also be explicit about how various ideas are organized and interrelated.
- Use multiple modalities to present information (e.g., supplement verbal explanations with pictures or simple diagrams).
- Assertively address students' areas of weakness (e.g., in reading or math).
- Provide technological aids that can enhance students' performance (e.g., text-to-speech software for poor readers, spell-checkers for poor spellers).
- Teach mnemonics for important facts and procedures.
- Help students organize and use their time effectively.
- Teach general learning and memory strategies.
- Provide a structure to guide students' learning efforts (e.g., present a partially filled-in outline for taking notes; suggest questions to answer while reading a textbook chapter; break large projects into small, manageable steps).
- Keep study sessions short; provide frequent breaks so that students can release pent-up energy.
- Regularly monitor students' recall and understanding of classroom material.

Some of these strategies should look familiar because you've seen them at earlier points in the chapter. We'll revisit others when we discuss metacognition and self-regulation in Chapter 3. By and large, the most effective strategies for students with special educational needs are the same ones that are especially effective with *any* learner. Clearly, then, effective instruction involves a lot more than simply telling students what they need to learn.

Teachers can do many things to help students remember and learn information, including supporting optimal brain functioning, understanding the limitations of attention and working memory, encouraging effective long-term memory storage processes, and monitoring students' progress. In the hotlinked Self-Check quiz and Application Exercise that follow, you can check and apply your understandings related to Big Idea 2.5:

Effective teachers help students mentally process new information and skills in ways that facilitate long-term memory storage and retrieval.

MyEdLab **Self-Check 2.5**

MyEdLab **Application Exercise 2.5.** The items in this exercise ask you to identify strategies that teachers might use to effectively teach topics or skills in various content domains.

---

[113] Barkley, 2010; Nigg, 2010; Rosen, Wang, Fiondella, & LoTurco, 2009; Shaywitz, Mody, & Shaywitz, 2006.

[114] Barkley, 2006; Brigham & Scruggs, 1995; Eilam, 2001; E. S. Ellis & Friend, 1991; J. M. Fletcher, Lyon, Fuchs, & Barnes, 2007; N. Gregg, 2009; Meltzer, 2007; Pellegrini & Bohn, 2005; Wilder & Williams, 2001.

2 SUMMARY

As a way of summarizing the contents of the chapter, let's return to the Big Ideas presented at the beginning of the chapter.

■ **2.1: The brain continues to change and learn over the course of a lifetime.** At the most basic level, learning probably involves changes in neurons, astrocytes, and their interconnections in the brain. Different parts of the brain specialize in different tasks, but many parts of the brain in both hemispheres tend to work closely together in everyday tasks. Although brain research provides useful insights into cognitive development and the neurological bases of certain disabilities, by and large teachers must look elsewhere—in particular, to psychological and educational research—for guidance about how best to help students learn.

■ **2.2: Much of human learning involves a process of actively constructing knowledge, rather than passively absorbing it.** Learning isn't simply a process of "soaking up" information from the environment. Rather, it's a process of *creating meanings* from both informal experiences and formal instruction. In their attempts to make sense of the world, learners combine some (but not all) of what they observe with their existing knowledge and beliefs to create ever-expanding and distinctly unique understandings of the world.

■ **2.3: Human memory is a complex, multifaceted information-processing system that is, to a considerable degree, under a learner's control.** A somewhat oversimplified model of human memory—but a very useful one nevertheless—has three distinct components. One component, the *sensory register*, holds incoming sensory information for 2 or 3 seconds at most. What a learner pays attention to moves on to *working memory*, where it's held for a somewhat longer period while the learner actively thinks about, manipulates, and interprets it. Yet working memory can hold only a small amount of information at one time, and information that isn't being actively thought about tends to disappear quickly (typically in less than half a minute) unless the learner processes it sufficiently to store it in long-term memory.

Long-term memory appears to have as much capacity as human beings could ever need. In fact, the more information learners already have there, the more easily they can store new facts and ideas. Effective storage typically involves *meaningful learning*—that is, connecting new information with existing knowledge and beliefs. By making such connections, learners make better sense of their experiences, retrieve what they've learned more easily, and create an increasingly organized and integrated body of knowledge that helps them interpret new experiences. As children grow older, they gradually take charge of their own learning, and most of them increasingly use effective learning strategies to remember classroom subject matter. Sometimes, however, learners of all ages distort new information, such that they construct inaccurate and potentially counterproductive understandings.

■ **2.4: Human memory is fallible: Learners don't remember everything they learn, and sometimes they misremember what they've learned.** Learners are more likely to remember new information over the long run if they stored it effectively to begin with—for instance, if they organized it, formed visual images of it, or elaborated on it—and if they've learned it to a level of automaticity. Yet retrieval is also somewhat context dependent: Learners are more likely to remember something if their environment provides retrieval cues that get them "looking" in the right "places" in long-term memory. Retrieval is often a constructive or reconstructive process: Learners recall only part of what they've learned or experienced and then fill in the gaps—perhaps correctly, perhaps not—based on their existing knowledge and beliefs about the world.

■ **2.5: Effective teachers help students mentally process new information and skills in ways that facilitate long-term memory storage and retrieval.** One way to enhance students' learning and academic achievement is, of course, to encourage healthful personal habits, such as sleeping well and getting regular physical exercise. But in addition, teachers must use instructional strategies that take into account the general nature of human learning and the strengths and limitations of the human memory system. In particular, teachers must continually emphasize the importance of *understanding* classroom subject matter—making sense of it, drawing inferences from it, seeing how it all ties together, and so forth—rather than simply memorizing it in a rote, "thoughtless" manner. Such an emphasis must be reflected not only in teachers' words but also in their instructional activities, assignments, and assessment practices. For example, rather than merely presenting important ideas in classroom lectures and asking students to take notes, teachers might ask thought-provoking questions that require students to evaluate, synthesize, or apply what they're learning. As an alternative to asking students to memorize procedures for adding two-digit numbers, teachers might ask them to devise at least three different ways they might solve problems such as $15 + 45$ or $29 + 68$ and to justify their reasoning. Rather than assessing students' knowledge of history by asking them to recite names, places, and dates, teachers might ask them to explain why certain historical events happened and how those events altered the course of subsequent history. At the same time, teachers must also be alert to students' misconceptions about academic topics and work hard to promote *conceptual change.*

PRACTICE FOR YOUR LICENSURE EXAM

Vision Unit

Ms. Kontos is teaching a unit on human vision to her fifth-grade class. She shows her students a diagram of the various parts of the human eye, such as the lens, cornea, pupil, retina, and optic nerve. She then explains that people can see objects because light from the sun or another light source bounces off those objects and into their eyes. To illustrate this idea, she shows them Picture A.

"Do you all understand how our eyes work?" she asks. Her students nod that they do.

The next day Ms. Kontos gives her students Picture B.

She asks students to draw one or more arrows on the picture to show how light enables the child to see the tree. More than half of the students draw arrows something like the one shown in Picture C.

A

B

C

1. Constructed-response question

Obviously, most of Ms. Kontos's students have not learned what she thought she had taught them about human vision.

A. Explain why many students believe the opposite of what Ms. Kontos has taught them. Base your response on contemporary principles and theories of learning and cognition.

B. Describe two different ways in which you might improve on this lesson to help students gain a more accurate understanding of human vision. Base your strategies on contemporary principles and theories of learning and cognition.

2. Multiple-choice question

Many elementary-age children think of human vision in the way that Ms. Kontos's fifth graders do—that is, as a process that originates in the eye and goes outward toward objects that are seen. When students revise their thinking to be more consistent with commonly accepted scientific explanations, they are said to be

a. acquiring a new script.

b. acquiring procedural knowledge.

c. undergoing conceptual change.

d. revising their worldview.

MyEdLab **Licensure Exam 2.1**

Monkey Business/Fotolia

3

Complex Cognitive Processes

CASE STUDY: TAKING OVER

When an eighth-grade math teacher goes on maternity leave midway through the school year, substitute teacher Ms. Gaunt takes over her classes. In accordance with Massachusetts state standards, the students are expected to master numerous mathematical concepts and procedures, including working with exponents and irrational numbers, graphing linear equations, and applying the Pythagorean theorem. Yet many students haven't yet mastered more basic concepts and operations, such as percentages, negative numbers, and long division. A few haven't even learned basic number facts.

Before long, Ms. Gaunt discovers that many students have beliefs and attitudes that also impede their learning progress. For instance, some think that a teacher's job is to present material in such a way that they "get it" immediately and will remember it forever. Thus they neither work hard to understand the material nor take notes during her explanations. And most students are concerned only with getting the right answer as quickly as possible. They depend on calculators to do their mathematical thinking for them and complain when Ms. Gaunt insists that they solve a problem with pencil and paper rather than a calculator. Students rarely check to see whether their solutions make logical sense. For example, in a problem such as this one:

> Raj can type 35 words a minute. He needs to type a final copy of his English composition, which is 4,200 words long. How long will it take Raj to type his paper?

a student might submit an answer of 147,000 minutes—an answer that translates into more than 100 days of around-the-clock typing—and not give the outlandishness of the solution a second thought. (It would actually take Raj 2 hours to type the paper.)

In mid-April, Ms. Gaunt begins moving through lessons more rapidly so that she can cover the mandated eighth-grade math curriculum before the upcoming statewide math competency exam. "Students can't do well on the exam if they haven't even been exposed to some of the required concepts and procedures," she reasons. "Mastery probably isn't possible at this point, but I should at least *present* what students need to know. Maybe this will help a few of them with some of the test items."[1]

- Why are the students having trouble mastering the eighth-grade math curriculum? Can you identify at least three different factors that appear to be interfering with students' learning?

One factor impeding students' learning is their lack of prerequisite knowledge and skills on which the eighth-grade curriculum depends. For instance, if students haven't learned basic number facts—let alone achieved automaticity for them—even simple word problems may exceed their working memory capacity. But students' beliefs about learning and problem solving are also coming into play. In their minds, learning should come quickly and easily if the teacher does her job. They don't seem to realize that understanding classroom subject matter is an active, constructive

---

[1] We thank a friend (who wishes to remain anonymous) for sharing this case.

process involving considerable effort on their part and that certain strategies (e.g., taking notes) can enhance their learning. And they view mathematical problem solving as a quick, mindless enterprise that involves plugging numbers into a calculator and writing down the result, rather than a step-by-step process that requires logical reasoning and frequent self-checking.

Study skills and problem solving are examples of **complex cognitive processes**, processes in which learners go far beyond the specific information they're studying, perhaps to apply it to a new situation, use it to solve a problem or create a product, or critically evaluate it. Mastering basic facts and skills is important, but learners gain little if they can't also *do something* with what they've learned. In this chapter, we'll look at a variety of complex cognitive processes, including self-regulation, metacognition, transfer, problem solving, creativity, and critical thinking.

3.1 SELF-REGULATION AND METACOGNITION

Big Idea 3.1 Effective learners regularly plan for their learning, monitor it, reflect on it, and strive to improve it.

Effective Self-Regulated Learning

Truly effective learning requires learners to actively and consciously engage in activities directed specifically at thinking about and learning something. Effective learners make decisions about, direct, monitor, and evaluate their own learning and behavior—in other words, they engage in some degree of *self-regulated learning, self-regulated behavior,* and, more generally, **self-regulation**.[2] To get a sense of how self-regulating *you* are, test yourself in the following exercise.

───────────────── **SEE FOR YOURSELF** ─────────────────
SELF-REFLECTION ABOUT SELF-REGULATION

For each of the following situations, choose the alternative that most accurately describes your attitudes, thoughts, and behaviors as a college student. Only *you* will see your answers, so be honest!

1. With respect to my final course grades, I'm trying very hard to
   a. earn all As.
   b. earn all As and Bs.
   c. keep my overall grade point average at or above the minimally acceptable level at my college.
2. As I read or study a textbook, I
   a. often notice when my attention is wandering, and I immediately try to get my mind back on my work.
   b. sometimes notice when my attention is wandering, but not always.
   c. often get so lost in daydreams that I waste a lot of time.
3. Whenever I finish a study session, I
   a. write down how much time I've spent on my schoolwork.
   b. make a mental note of how much time I've spent on my schoolwork.
   c. don't really think much about the time I've spent.
4. When I turn in an assignment, I
   a. usually have a good idea of the grade I'll get on it.
   b. am often surprised by the grade I get.
   c. don't think much about the quality of what I've done.
5. When I do exceptionally well on an assignment, I
   a. feel good about my performance and might reward myself in some way.
   b. feel good about my performance but don't do anything special for myself afterward.
   c. don't feel much different than I had before I received my grade.

Regardless of how you answered Item 1, you could probably identify a particular goal toward which you're striving. Your response to Item 2 should give you an idea of how much you monitor and try to control your thoughts when you're studying. Your responses to Items 3 and 4 tell you something about how frequently and accurately you evaluate your performance. And your response to Item 5 indicates whether you're likely to reinforce yourself for desired behaviors.

───────────
[2] Good general references on this topic include Bandura, 1986, 1989; Zimmerman & Moylan, 2009; Zimmerman & Schunk, 2004.

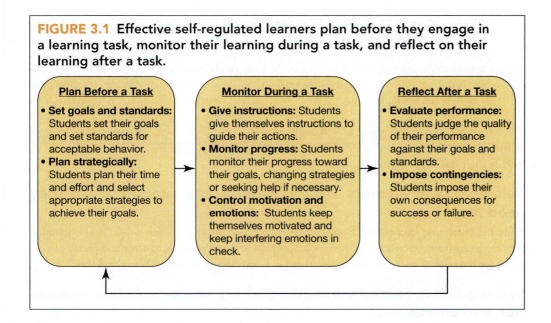

FIGURE 3.1 Effective self-regulated learners plan before they engage in a learning task, monitor their learning during a task, and reflect on their learning after a task.

It can be helpful to categorize the different aspects of self-regulation into those that occur before a learning task (such as reading or studying), during a task, and after a task, as shown in Figure 3.1. The following general principles further illustrate these components of self-regulation.

Self-regulating learners establish goals for their performance and plan their actions accordingly.

Self-regulating learners know what they want to accomplish when they read and study—perhaps to learn specific facts, gain a good conceptual understanding of a topic, or simply do well on an upcoming test. Often their immediate goals are tied to longer-term goals and aspirations, such as getting a college scholarship, exhibiting their work in a prestigious art show, or becoming a veterinarian. With such short- and long-term goals in mind, they make conscious decisions about how much time and effort to put into a learning task and select strategies that will help them achieve their goals.[3]

To a considerable degree, learners' goals reflect self-imposed general standards for performance, and these standards vary from one learner to the next. For example, one student may perceive high classroom achievement to be very important and may strive for straight As, whereas another might be satisfied with mediocre performance and be content with Cs.[4] Often learners' goals and standards are modeled after those they see other people adopt.[5] For instance, at the high school one of us authors attended, many students wanted to go to the best college or university possible, and such lofty ambitions were contagious. But at a different high school, getting a job after graduation—or perhaps *instead* of graduation—might be the aspiration more commonly modeled by a student's classmates.

Self-regulating learners control and monitor their processes and progress during a learning task.

Self-regulating learners intentionally engage in processes that will enhance their learning.[6] They try to focus their attention on the subject matter at hand and to clear their minds of potentially distracting thoughts. They may also employable **self-instructions** that help them direct their efforts.

[3] Bandura, 2008; Gaskins, Satlow, & Pressley, 2007; R. B. Miller & Brickman, 2004; Muis, 2007; Winne & Hadwin, 1998; Zimmerman & Schunk, 2004.

[4] Corker & Donnellan, 2012; Pajares, 2009.

[5] Bandura, 1986; Fitzsimmons & Finkel, 2010.

[6] Harnishfeger, 1995; Winne, 1995; Zimmerman & Moylan, 2009.

As an example, one formerly impulsive child has learned to talk himself through matching tasks in which he needs to find two identical pictures among several very similar ones:

> I have to remember to go slowly to get it right. Look carefully at this one, now look at these carefully. Is this one different? Yes, it has an extra leaf. Good, I can eliminate this one. . . . Good, I'm going slow and carefully.[7]

Another important aspect of self-regulation is **self-monitoring**: Self-regulating learners continually check their progress toward their goals, and they change their learning strategies or modify their goals if necessary.[8]

Self-regulating learners seek assistance and support when they need it.

Truly self-regulating learners don't necessarily try to do everything on their own. On the contrary, they recognize occasions when they need other people's help and seek it out. They're especially likely to ask for the kind of help that will enable them to work more independently in the future.[9]

Self-regulating learners monitor and try to control their motivation and emotions.

Self-regulating learners use a variety of strategies to keep themselves on task—perhaps embellishing on an assignment to make it more fun, reminding themselves of the importance of doing well, or promising themselves a reward after they finish.[10] For example, a middle school student named Jamaal regularly gives himself a pep talk as he works on math problems:

> I'll be, like, "Come on." I'll be thinking about different ways to solve problems and stuff like that. I'll be saying, "Come on, Jamaal, you can do this," and stuff like that . . . I don't know what it does, but it's just like extra comfort to me.[11]

Self-regulating learners also try to keep in check any emotions (anxiety, anger, etc.) that might interfere with their performance (more about such *emotion regulation* in Chapter 5).[12]

Self-regulating learners evaluate the final outcomes of their efforts.

Both at home and in school, children's and adolescents' behaviors and achievements are often judged by others—their parents, teachers, classmates, and so on. But as young people become increasingly self-regulating, they also begin to engage in **self-evaluation**, judging their own performance with respect to the goals and standards they've set for themselves. Their ability to evaluate themselves with some degree of objectivity and accuracy will ultimately be critical for their learning and achievement over the long run.[13]

Self-regulating learners self-impose consequences for their performance.

How do you feel when you accomplish a difficult task—for instance, when you earn an A in a challenging course or make a 3-point shot in a basketball game? How do you feel when you fail in your endeavors—for instance, when you get a D on an exam or thoughtlessly hurt a friend's feelings?

When you accomplish a challenging task, you might feel quite proud of yourself and give yourself a mental pat on the back. In contrast, when you fail to accomplish something you've set

---

[7] Meichenbaum & Goodman, 1971, p. 121.

[8] D. L. Butler & Winne, 1995; Greene & Azevedo, 2009; Schneider, 2010.

[9] R. Butler, 1998b; J. Lee & Shute, 2010; A. M. Ryan, Pintrich, & Midgley, 2001; Zusho & Barnett, 2011.

[10] Pajares, 2009; Usher, 2009; Wolters, 2003.

[11] Usher, 2009, p. 295.

[12] Bronson, 2000; Buckley & Saarni, 2009; K. L. Fletcher & Cassady, 2010; Winne, 1995.

[13] Andrade, 2010; Dunning et al., 2004; Gaskins et al., 2007; Pajares, 2009; Schraw & Moshman, 1995.

out to do, you're probably unhappy with your performance, and you might also feel guilty, regretful, or ashamed. Likewise, as children and adolescents become increasingly self-regulating, they begin to reinforce themselves when they accomplish their goals—perhaps by engaging in a favorite activity or perhaps simply by feeling proud or telling themselves they did a good job. And they may punish themselves when they do something that doesn't meet their personal standards—at a minimum, by feeling sorry, guilty, or ashamed.[14] Such self-reinforcement and self-punishment are **self-imposed contingencies**. Melinda's poem about horseback riding presented in Figure 3.2 clearly shows both self-punishment ("Now I'm feeling guilty because I'm making the horse work harder") and self-reinforcement ("Good job! . . . Now I feel warm inside and proud").

Students' self-evaluations and self-imposed contingencies can then affect their goals, standards, plans, and motivation when they begin their next task (as depicted by the arrow at the bottom of Figure 3.1 leading from "Reflecting After a Task" to "Planning Before a Task").[15] For example, if Melinda has a positive self-evaluation and believes that her time practicing horseback riding has allowed her to meet her goals, she may set similar goals next time and use similar strategies to meet them. But if she is unhappy with her performance or if she doesn't meet her goals, she may readjust her goals and standards or plan to use different strategies to help her achieve her goals in the future.

FIGURE 3.2 In this poem about horseback riding, 16-year-old Melinda reveals two forms of a self-imposed contingency: guilt and pride.

"Sit up,
　　shoulders back,
　　　　drop your right shoulder."
Now I feel guilty because I'm making the horse work harder.
"Heels down,
　　elbows at your sides,
　　　　lower leg back,
　　　　　　drop your right shoulder down and back."
Now I feel like I have no talent and like I'm hurting the horse.
"More impulsion from the left hind leg!
　　Send him into the rein more!"
Now I'm thinking, "This is so complicated!"
"Good job!
　　Walk when you're ready and give him the rein.
　　　　Did you feel that?"
"Yeah!"
"Good! That was really good!
　　You've accomplished so much with him and your position."
Now I feel warm inside and proud. All this time has paid off
　　and I realize that's why I love horseback riding so much!

Most learners become increasingly self-regulating over the course of childhood and adolescence, partly as a result of maturation in key areas of the brain.

Let's return now to the three-component model of memory introduced in Chapter 2 (see Figure 2.5). The mental "headquarters" of self-regulation is in the *central executive*—the subcomponent of working memory that oversees executive functions such as focusing attention, monitoring the flow of information throughout the memory system, selecting and controlling complex voluntary behaviors, and inhibiting counterproductive thoughts and actions. To a considerable degree, learners' central-executive abilities depend on areas in the front part of the brain that continue to develop throughout childhood, adolescence, and early adulthood.[16] Thus learners' self-regulation skills are apt to emerge only slowly as they grow older.[17]

Table 3.1 presents typical advancements in self-regulation in the elementary and secondary school years. As you can see in the table, a few elements of self-regulation (e.g., setting self-chosen goals, self-evaluation of behavior) are evident in the primary grades. Additional aspects (e.g., conscious attempts to focus attention, ability to complete short learning tasks at home) tend to appear in the upper elementary grades. Still others (e.g., planning, self-motivation) emerge in the middle school and high school years. One aspect of self-regulation—seeking help when needed—may actually *decline,* however, especially if students consistently struggle with their academic work but want to hide their difficulties and they perceive their teachers to be aloof and nonsupportive.[18]

---

[14] Harter, 1999; R. B. Miller & Brickman, 2004; K. R. Harris, Santangelo, & Graham, 2010; Zimmerman & Moylan, 2009.

[15] Zimmerman & Cleary, 2009.

[16] Two especially important areas are the *prefrontal cortex* and *anterior cingulate cortex;* for example, see Munakata, Snyder, & Chatham, 2012; Posner & Rothbart, 2007; Velanova, Wheeler, & Luna, 2008.

[17] Demetriou, Christou, Spanoudis, & Platsidou, 2002; Fischer & Daley, 2007; Luciana, Conklin, Hooper, & Yarger, 2005; Rothbart, 2011; Steinberg, 2009.

[18] Marchand & Skinner, 2007.

DEVELOPMENTAL TRENDS
TABLE 3.1 • Self-Regulation at Different Grade Levels

GRADE LEVEL	AGE-TYPICAL CHARACTERISTICS	EXAMPLE	SUGGESTED STRATEGIES
Grades K–2	• Some internalization of adults' standards for behavior • Emerging ability to set self-chosen goals for learning and achievement • Some use of self-instructions to guide behavior • Some self-evaluation of effectiveness and appropriateness of actions; feelings of guilt about wrongdoings • Individual differences in self-control of impulses, emotions, and attention; amount of self-control in these areas affects peer relationships and classroom performance	Most of the children in a kindergarten class can sit quietly and listen when their teacher reads a storybook. But a few of them squirm restlessly and occasionally poke or otherwise distract their classmates.	• Discuss rationales for class rules for behavior. • Show students how some behaviors can help them reach their goals and how other behaviors interfere with goal attainment. • Organize the classroom so that students can carry out some activities on their own (e.g., have reading centers where children can listen to audiobooks). • When students show impulsiveness or poor emotion control, provide guidelines and consistent consequences for behavior.
Grades 3–5	• Improving ability to self-assess performance and progress • Guilt and shame about unsatisfactory performance and moral transgressions • Emerging self-regulating learning strategies (e.g., conscious attempts to focus attention, ability to do short assignments independently at home) • Increasing ability to allocate study time appropriately for the learning task at hand • Persistent difficulties with self-control for some students	Every Thursday evening, 8-year-old Logan studies for the weekly spelling test his teacher will give his class the following day. Sometimes he asks his father or older brother to test him on especially difficult words.	• Have students set specific, concrete goals for their learning. • Encourage students to assess their own performance; provide criteria they can use to evaluate their work. • Ask students to engage in simple, self-regulated learning tasks (e.g., small-group learning activities, short homework assignments); provide some structure to guide students' efforts. • Encourage students to use their peers as resources when they need help. • If students have continuing difficulty with self-control, teach self-instructions that can help them control their behavior.
Grades 6–8	• Increasing ability to plan future actions, due in part to increased capacity for abstract thought • Increasing mastery of some self-regulating learning strategies, especially those that involve overt behaviors (e.g., keeping a calendar of assignments and due dates) • Self-motivational strategies (e.g., minimizing distractions, devising ways to make a boring task more enjoyable, reminding oneself about the importance of doing well) • Decrease in help-seeking behaviors during times of confusion, especially if teachers appear to be aloof and nonsupportive	For fear of appearing to be "stupid" in her math class, 13-year-old Katherine rarely asks questions when she doesn't understand a new concept or procedure.	• Assign homework and other tasks that require independent learning. • Provide concrete strategies for keeping track of learning tasks and assignments (e.g., provide monthly calendars in which students can write due dates). • Provide concrete guidance about how to learn and study effectively (e.g., using self-imposed contingencies, such as not playing a video game until after one has read an assigned textbook chapter). • Give students frequent opportunities to assess their own learning; have them compare your evaluations with their own.
Grades 9–12	• More long-range goal setting • Increasing ability to accurately self-evaluate learning and achievement • Wide variation in ability to self-regulate learning, especially when out-of-school assignments conflict with attractive leisure activities; few self-regulating learning strategies among many low-achieving high school students • For a small number of older adolescents, persistent difficulties in self-control that can adversely affect classroom behavior and peer relationships	After moving from fairly small middle schools to a much larger, consolidated high school, some students diligently complete their homework each night. But many others are easily enticed into more enjoyable activities with friends—hanging out at a local fast-food restaurant, instant-messaging on cell phones, and so on—and their grades decline significantly as a result.	• Relate classroom learning tasks to students' long-range personal and professional goals. • Assign complex independent learning tasks, providing the necessary structure and guidance for students who are not yet self-regulating learners. • Have high-achieving students describe their strategies for resisting attractive alternatives and keeping themselves on task when doing homework.

Sources: Blair, 2002; Bronson, 2000; Damon, 1988; Dunning et al., 2004; Eccles, Wigfield, & Schiefele, 1998; Fries, Dietz, & Schmid, 2008; Hampson, 2008; M. Hofer, 2010; M. H. Jones, Estell, & Alexander, 2008; Kochanska, Gross, Lin, & Nichols, 2002; Liew, McTigue, Barrois, & Hughes, 2008; Marchand & Skinner, 2007; J. S. Matthews, Ponitz, & Morrison, 2009; Meichenbaum & Goodman, 1971; Meltzer et al., 2007; S. D. Miller, Heafner, Massey, & Strahan, 2003; Paris & Paris, 2001; Posner & Rothbart, 2007; Schneider, 2010; Valiente, Lemery-Calfant, Swanson, & Reiser, 2008; Wolters & Rosenthal, 2000.

When children and adolescents are self-regulating, they set more ambitious academic goals for themselves, learn more effectively, and achieve at higher levels in the classroom.[19] Self-regulation becomes increasingly important in adolescence and adulthood, when many learning activities—reading, doing homework, finding information on the Internet—occur in isolation from other people and therefore require considerable self-direction.[20] Unfortunately, not all adolescents acquire a high level of self-regulation, perhaps in part because traditional instructional practices do little to foster it.[21] For example, consider a student named Anna, whose grades declined markedly after she left her small neighborhood K–8 school for a large city high school. Anna was overwhelmed by the demands of her ninth-grade classes, and her first-semester final grades included several Ds and an F. Anna explained her low grades this way:

> In geography, "he said the reason why I got a lower grade is 'cause I missed one assignment and I had to do a report, and I forgot that one." In English, "I got a C . . . 'cause we were supposed to keep a journal, and I keep on forgetting it 'cause I don't have a locker. Well I do, but my locker partner she lets her cousins use it, and I lost my two books there. . . . I would forget to buy a notebook, and then I would have them on separate pieces of paper, and I would lose them." And, in biology, "the reason I failed was because I lost my folder . . . it had everything I needed, and I had to do it again, and, by the time I had to turn in the new folder, I did, but he said it was too late . . . ."[22]

To some extent, self-regulated learning probably develops from opportunities to engage in age-appropriate independent learning activities.[23] But self-regulated learning also has roots in socially regulated learning.[24] At first, an adult (e.g., a teacher or parent) might help children learn by setting goals for a learning activity, keeping children's attention focused on the learning task, suggesting effective strategies, monitoring progress, and so on. Then, in **co-regulated learning**, the adult and children share responsibility for directing various aspects of the learning process.[25] The adult initially provides considerable metacognitive support for children's learning efforts but gradually removes it as the children become more self-regulating. Some instructional software programs provide the same kind of support, suggesting learning strategies, assisting with comprehension monitoring, and so forth as needed.[26] Alternatively, several learners of *equal ability* might collectively regulate a learning task, perhaps in a cooperative group activity.[27] In such a situation, different learners can take on different responsibilities and monitor one another's progress.

The Roles of Metacognition

As you've probably gleaned from our description so far, effective self-regulation requires learners to possess a variety of mental abilities, as well as dispositions to use them productively. In this section, we'll explain some of these mental abilities in more detail, starting with **metacognition**, which literally means "thinking about thinking." Metacognition includes learners' knowledge and beliefs about their own cognitive processes, as well as their conscious attempts to engage in behaviors and thought processes that enhance learning and memory. For example, you've undoubtedly learned by now that you can acquire only so much information so fast—you can't possibly absorb the contents of an entire textbook in an hour. You've also discovered that you can learn information more quickly and recall it more easily if you put it into some sort of organizational framework. And perhaps you've taken to heart one of the recommendations in Chapter 1: You periodically check yourself to make sure you remember and understand what you've read.

---

[19] D. L. Butler & Winne, 1995; Corno et al., 2002; Duckworth & Seligman, 2005; Valiente, Lemery-Chalfant, & Swanson, 2010; Zimmerman & Kitsantas, 2005.

[20] Azevedo, 2005b; Meltzer et al., 2007; Winne, 1995; Winters, Greene, & Costich, 2008.

[21] Meltzer, 2007; Paris & Ayres, 1994; Zimmerman & Risemberg, 1997.

[22] Roderick & Camburn, 1999, p. 305.

[23] Corno & Mandinach, 2004; Paris & Paris, 2001; Vye et al., 1998; Zimmerman, 2004.

[24] Stright, Neitzel, Sears, & Hoke-Sinex, 2001; Vygotsky, 1962; Zimmerman, 1998.

[25] McCaslin & Good, 1996; McCaslin & Hickey, 2001; C. Quintana, Zhang, & Krajcik, 2005; Zimmerman, 2004.

[26] Azevedo, 2005a.

[27] DiDonato, 2011; Hickey, 2011; Volet, Vaura, & Salonen, 2009.

The more learners know about thinking and learning—that is, the greater their metacognitive knowledge—the better their learning and academic achievement will be, in part because they can use this knowledge as they engage in self-regulation.[28] Because *strategies* are critical to both metacognition and self-regulation, the next two principles relate to effective study strategies. These principles are followed by a third principle about how children and adolescents' metacognition develops over time and a fourth principle related to the important role of learners' *beliefs* in their learning processes.

Some effective study strategies are easily seen in learners' behaviors.

Some study strategies are **overt strategies**—ones that are readily apparent in what learners do in their efforts to master new topics and skills. For instance, effective learners allocate specific times to study and find a quiet place to work. When they have to learn and remember a large body of information—say, for a major exam—they might spread their studying over several days or weeks.

Another easily observable study strategy is taking notes. In general, learners who take more notes learn and remember more. The *quality* of the notes is equally important: Good notes reflect the main ideas of a lesson or reading assignment.[29] Ideally, too, students should be *making sense* of the information they're writing down—perhaps elaborating on it in some way—rather than just copying it in a rote, word-for-word manner.[30] Figure 3.3 shows the notes that two seventh graders took about King Midas in a unit on Greek mythology. Both sets were taken using a note-taking form their teacher provided. Notice how the notes on the left provide a good overall synopsis of the King Midas story and might reasonably help the student remember the story fairly accurately. In contrast, the notes on the right are probably too brief and disjointed to be useful.

FIGURE 3.3 Good class notes involve both quantity and quality, as seen in the notes on the left but not those on the right. Both sets were taken during a seventh-grade lesson on Greek mythology.

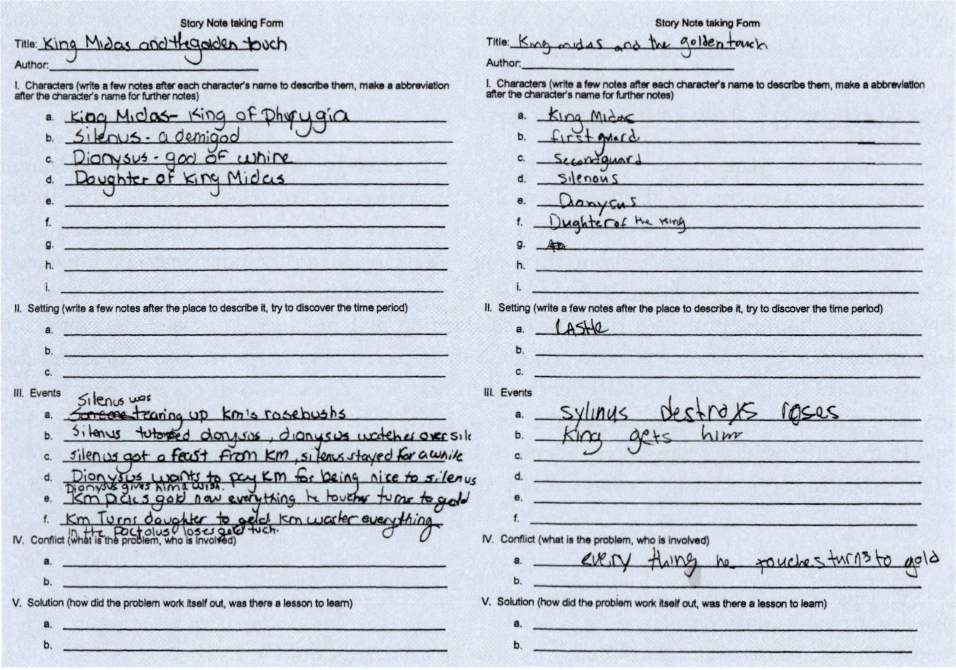

Story Note taking Form

Title: King Midas and the golden touch

Author:

I. Characters (write a few notes after each character's name to describe them, make a abbreviation after the character's name for further notes)

a. King Midas- King of Phrygia
b. Silenus - a demigod
c. Dionysus - god of whine
d. Daughter of King Midas
e.
f.
g.
h.
i.

II. Setting (write a few notes after the place to describe it, try to discover the time period)

a.
b.
c.

III. Events

a. ~~Someone~~ Silenus was tearing up km's rosebushs
b. Silenus tutored dionysus, dionysus watches over silk
c. silenus got a feast from km, silenus stayed for awhile
d. Dionysus wants to pay km for being nice to silenus Dionysus gives him a wish.
e. Km picks gold now everything he touches turns to gold
f. Km Turns daughter to gold km washes everything in the Pactolus loses gold tuch.

IV. Conflict (what is the problem, who is involved)

a.
b.

V. Solution (how did the problem work itself out, was there a lesson to learn)

a.
b.

Story Note taking Form

Title: King midas and the golden touch

Author:

I. Characters (write a few notes after each character's name to describe them, make a abbreviation after the character's name for further notes)

a. King Midas
b. first guard
c. Second guard
d. Silenous
e. Dionysus
f. Dughter of the king
g.
h.
i.

II. Setting (write a few notes after the place to describe it, try to discover the time period)

a. CASHe
b.
c.

III. Events

a. sylinus destroys roses
b. King gets him
c.
d.
e.
f.

IV. Conflict (what is the problem, who is involved)

a. every thing he touches turns to gold
b.

V. Solution (how did the problem work itself out, was there a lesson to learn)

a.
b.

[28] B. K. Hofer & Pintrich, 2002; J. Lee & Shute, 2010; Meltzer, 2007.

[29] A. L. Brown, Campione, & Day, 1981; Kiewra, 1985; J. Lee & Shute, 2010; Peverly, Brobst, Graham, & Shaw, 2003.

[30] Mueller & Oppenheimer, 2014.

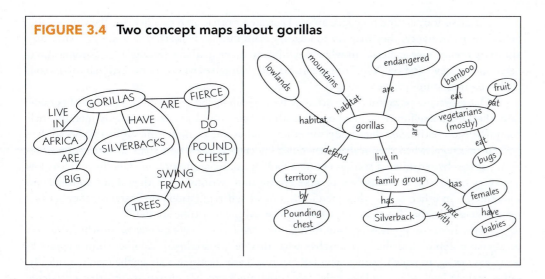

FIGURE 3.4 Two concept maps about gorillas

Still another effective overt strategy is organizing information in an explicit, concrete manner.[31] One way of organizing material is *outlining* it, which can be especially helpful for low-achieving students.[32] A second approach is creating a **concept map**, a diagram that depicts the concepts of a unit and their interrelationships.[33] Figure 3.4 shows concept maps that two different students might construct after a lesson about gorillas. The concepts themselves are circled, and their interrelationships are indicated by lines with words or short phrases. Several concept-mapping software programs are available for creating and modifying concept maps quickly and easily (e.g., Kidspiration, MindMapper Jr.). Concept mapping certainly doesn't have to be high-tech, however. For example, even nonreading preschoolers can make simple concept maps using pictures of objects and pieces of yarn.[34]

Not only can self-constructed organizational structures help students learn more effectively, but they can also help teachers *assess* students' learning. For example, the concept map on the left side of Figure 3.4 reveals only spotty, fragmented knowledge about gorillas. Furthermore, the student who created the map has two ideas that need correction. First, contrary to a common stereotype, gorillas don't regularly swing from trees, although young ones may occasionally climb a tree to escape danger. Second, gorillas aren't especially "fierce" creatures. For the most part, they live a peaceful existence within their family group; they get nasty (e.g., by beating their chests) only when a human being, non-family-member gorilla, or other potential encroacher threatens their territory.

Study strategies are effective only to the extent that they involve productive cognitive processes.

Strategies such as taking notes and constructing concept maps are helpful, in large part, because they require the kinds of cognitive processes described in Chapter 2. For example, to take notes, learners must *pay attention* to and *encode* information (possibly through organizing information, creating a visual image, and/or rehearsing the information at least once more), thus facilitating effective storage in long-term memory. To construct a concept map, learners must engage in *meaningful learning* by thinking about how key concepts relate to one another and to what they already know. They must also *organize* the information on the map, which results in a physical map that can be encoded as a *visual image*. Thus, class notes and concept maps can provide a means to help learners encode information by requiring them to use **covert strategies**—mental strategies we can't directly see—that are ultimately responsible for successful learning.[35]

---

[31] M. A. McDaniel & Einstein, 1989; Hattie, 2009; Mintzes, Wandersee, & Novak, 1997; Nesbit & Adesope, 2006.

[32] L. Baker, 1989; M. A. McDaniel & Einstein, 1989; Wade, 1992.

[33] Hattie, 2009; Haugwitz, Sumfleth, & Sandmann, 2010; Nesbit & Adesope, 2006; Novak, 1998.

[34] Stephanie Wehry, personal communication, April 8, 2011.

[35] Di Vesta & Gray, 1972; Kardash & Amlund, 1991; Katayama & Robinson, 2000; Kiewra, 1989; Rawson & Kintsch, 2005; Veenman, 2011.

MyEdLab
Video Example 3.1.

What do these teachers do or explain to help students improve their comprehension-monitoring strategies?

think about it

As you read a textbook, when is the information in working memory? In long-term memory? With your answers in mind, explain why students should monitor their comprehension both as they read and also at a later time. (For an explanation, click **here**.)

Effective learners often engage in study strategies that aren't evident in their observable behaviors. For instance, they may try to identify main ideas in what they're reading.[36] They may also try to relate new material to what they already know, perhaps finding logical connections between the "new" and the "old," or perhaps asking themselves whether new material might contradict their existing beliefs.[37]

One especially powerful covert strategy is **comprehension monitoring**, a process of periodically checking oneself for recall and understanding. Successful learners continually monitor their comprehension both *while* they study something and at one or more times *after* they've studied it.[38] Furthermore, when they realize they don't understand, they take steps to correct the situation, perhaps by rereading a section of a textbook or asking a question in class. In contrast, low achievers rarely check themselves or take appropriate actions when they don't comprehend something—in other words, they aren't effective at self-regulation. For instance, they seldom reread paragraphs they haven't completely understood the first time around.[39]

Sometimes comprehension monitoring takes the form of *self-explanation,* in which learners occasionally stop to describe to themselves what they've just studied.[40] Another similar approach is *self-questioning,* in which learners regularly stop and ask themselves about the material. Ideally, self-questions include not only simple, fact-based questions but also questions that encourage elaboration (e.g., "What might happen if _____?" "How is _____ different from _____?").[41] Yet another comprehension-monitoring strategy is *summarizing* a body of information, either mentally or on paper.[42]

Metacognitive knowledge and skills gradually improve with age.

As children grow older, they become increasingly aware of their own thinking and learning processes and increasingly realistic about what they can learn and remember in a given time period (see Table 3.2). With this growing self-awareness come more effective study strategies.

Truly effective strategies emerge quite slowly, however, especially if young learners don't get guidance from teachers, parents, or other adults about how to study.[43] For instance, unless specifically instructed to take notes, many young adolescents take few or no notes to help them remember class material. And even when they do take notes, they're apt to use superficial strategies in choosing what to focus on—perhaps focusing on definitions and formulas in a textbook or writing down only the things their teacher writes on the board—and miss critical ideas as a result.[44]

Furthermore, many children and adolescents engage in little or no comprehension monitoring.[45] When they don't monitor their learning and comprehension, they don't know what they know and what they don't know, and so they may think they've mastered something when they really haven't. This **illusion of knowing** is seen in learners at all levels, even college students.[46]

Comprehension monitoring isn't just an important study strategy in its own right—it also plays a pivotal role in the development of *other* study strategies.[47] Learners will acquire and use new, more effective strategies only if they realize that their prior strategies have been *in*effective in helping them learn. If, instead, they mistakenly believe that they're successfully mastering school topics, they'll have little reason to abandon ineffective strategies (such as rote memorization) for more sophisticated ones.

---

[36] Afflerbach & Cho, 2010; Eason, Goldberg, Young, Geist, & Cutting, 2012; Dole, Duffy, Roehler, & Pearson, 1991.

[37] Ausubel, Novak, & Hanesian, 1978; P. K. Murphy & Mason, 2006; Sinatra & Pintrich, 2003.

[38] Hacker, Dunlosky, & Graesser, 2009b.

[39] L. Baker & Brown, 1984; Haller, Child, & Walberg, 1988; N. J. Stone, 2000; Veenman, 2011.

[40] Fonseca & Chi, 2011; McNamara & Magliano, 2009; Renkl, 2011; Siegler & Lin, 2010.

[41] De La Paz, 2005; A. King, 1992; Dunning, Heath, & Suls, 2004; Wong, 1985.

[42] A. King, 1992; R. E. Mayer, 2010b; Shanahan, 2004; Wade-Stein & Kintsch, 2004.

[43] J. E. Barnett, 2001; Rawson & Kintsch, 2005; Schommer, 1994a; Schneider, 2010; Veenman, 2011.

[44] Dee-Lucas & Larkin, 1991; Dole et al., 1991; R. E. Reynolds & Shirey, 1988.

[45] Dole et al., 1991; McKeown & Beck, 2009; Nokes & Dole, 2004.

[46] L. Baker, 1989; D. L. Butler & Winne, 1995; Dunlosky & Lipko, 2007; Hacker & Bol, 2004; N. J. Stone, 2000.

[47] Kuhn, Garcia-Mila, Zohar, & Andersen, 1995; Lodico, Ghatala, Levin, Pressley, & Bell, 1983; Loranger, 1994.

DEVELOPMENTAL TRENDS

TABLE 3.2 • Metacognition at Different Grade Levels

GRADE LEVEL	AGE-TYPICAL CHARACTERISTICS	EXAMPLE	SUGGESTED STRATEGIES
Grades K–2	• Awareness of thought in oneself and others, albeit in a simplistic form; limited ability to reflect on the specific nature of one's own thought processes • Considerable overestimation of what has been learned and how much can be remembered • Belief that learning is a relatively passive activity • Belief that the absolute truth about any topic is "out there" somewhere, waiting to be discovered	An adult tells 6-year-old Brent that she will read him a list of 12 words; she then asks him to predict how many he'll be able to remember. Brent predicts "about 8 or 9 . . . maybe all of them," but in fact he recalls only 6. Later, when the adult asks him what he did to try to remember the words, he says only, "Think" and "Holded it, hold it in my brain." **MyEdLab:** Video Example 3.2. You can observe Brent's explanation here.	• Talk often about thinking processes (e.g., "I *wonder* if . . ." "How might you *remember* to . . .?"). • Provide opportunities for students to "experiment" with their memories (e.g., playing "I'm going on a trip and am going to pack ___," in which each student repeats items previously mentioned and then adds another item to the list). • Introduce simple learning strategies (e.g., rehearsal of spelling words, repeated practice of motor skills).
Grades 3–5	• Increasing ability to reflect on the nature of one's own thought processes • Some overestimation of memory capabilities • Emerging realization that learning is an active, constructive process and that people may misinterpret what they observe • Continuing belief in an absolute truth "out there"	After reading several explanations of how ancient humans migrated from Asia to North America, a cooperative learning group in a combined fifth- and sixth-grade classroom includes the following points in its summary of what the group has learned: "The more that we learn, the more we get confused about which is fact and which is fiction . . . We have made [our] own theories using information we found and trying to make sense of it."	• Provide simple techniques (e.g., self-test questions) that enable students to monitor their learning progress. • Examine scientific phenomena through hands-on activities and experimentation; ask students to make predictions about what will happen and to debate competing explanations for what they observe.
Grades 6–8	• Few and relatively ineffective study strategies (e.g., poor note-taking skills, little or no comprehension monitoring) • Belief that "knowledge" about a topic consists largely of a collection of discrete facts • Increasing realization that knowledge can be subjective and that conflicting perspectives may each have some validity (e.g., "people have a right to form their own opinions") • Increasing differentiation among the underlying natures of various content domains (e.g., thinking that math involves right vs. wrong answers, whereas social studies allows for diverse opinions)	The students in Ms. Gaunt's eighth-grade math class rarely take notes to help them remember new concepts and procedures, and most are more concerned about getting correct answers than about making sense of mathematical operations (see the opening case study).	• Teach and model effective strategies within the context of various subject areas. • Scaffold students' studying efforts (e.g., provide a structure for note taking, give students questions to answer as they study). • Introduce multiple perspectives about topics (e.g., asking whether Christopher Columbus was a brave scientist in search of new knowledge or, instead, an entrepreneur in search of personal wealth). • Explicitly ask students to reflect on their beliefs about the nature of various academic disciplines (e.g., "Can a math problem sometimes have two *different* right answers?").
Grades 9–12	• Growing (but incomplete) knowledge of which study strategies are effective in different situations; persistent use of rote memorization by some students • Increasing mastery of covert learning strategies (e.g., intentional elaboration, comprehension monitoring) • Increasing recognition that knowledge involves understanding interrelationships among ideas • Increasing recognition that mastering a topic or skill takes time and practice (rather than happening quickly as a result of innate ability) • Emerging understanding that conflicting perspectives should be evaluated on the basis of evidence and logic (seen in a small minority of high school students)	When 16-year-old Hilary is asked to describe the things she does to help her remember school subject matter, she says, "When I'm trying to study for tests, I try to associate the things I'm trying to learn with familiar things . . . if I have a Spanish vocabulary test, I'll try to . . . with the Spanish words, I'll try to think of the English word that it sounds like . . . sometimes if I can't find any rule, then I just have to memorize it, just try to remember it, just go over it a lot." **MyEdLab:** Video Example 3.3. You can observe Hilary's explanation here. 	• Continue to teach and model effective learning strategies; ask students to describe their strategies to one another. • Develop classroom assignments and assessments that emphasize understanding, integration, and application, rather than recall of discrete facts. • Present various subject areas as dynamic entities that continue to evolve with new discoveries and theories. • Have students weigh pros and cons of various explanations and documents using objective criteria (e.g., hard evidence, logical reasoning processes).

Sources: Andre & Windschitl, 2003; Astington & Pelletier, 1996; J. E. Barnett, 2001; Bendixen & Feucht, 2010; Buehl & Alexander, 2006; Chandler, Hallett, & Sokol, 2002; Elder, 2002; Flavell, Friedrichs, & Hoyt, 1970; Flavell, Miller, & Miller, 2002; Hatano & Inagaki, 2003; Hewitt, Brett, Scardamalia, Frecker, & Webb, 1995, p. 7 (migration example); P. M. King & Kitchener, 2002; Ku, Chan, Wu, & Chen, 2008; Kuhn, 2009; Kuhn, Garcia-Mila, Zohar, & Andersen, 1995; Kuhn & Park, 2005; Kuhn & Weinstock, 2002; Lovett & Flavell, 1990; McCrudden & Schraw, 2007; Meltzer, Pollica, & Barzillai, 2007; Muis, Bendixen, & Haerle, 2006; P. A. Ornstein, Grammer, & Coffman, 2010; Schneider, 2010; Schommer, 1994a, 1997; Short, Schatschneider, & Friebert, 1993; J. W. Thomas, 1993; vanSledright & Limón, 2006; Wellman, 1985, 1990; J. P. Williams, Stafford, Lauer, Hall, & Pollini, 2009.

Learners' beliefs about the nature of knowledge and learning influence their approaches to learning tasks.

One of us authors once had a conversation with her son Jeff, then an 11th grader, about the Canadian Studies program a local university had just added to its curriculum. Jeff's comments revealed a very simplistic view of what "history" is:

Jeff: The Canadians don't have as much history as we [Americans] do.

Mom: Of course they do.

Jeff: No, they don't. They haven't had as many wars.

Mom: History's more than wars.

Jeff: Yeah, but the rest of that stuff is really boring.

Once Jeff reached college, he discovered that history is a lot more than wars and other, "really boring" stuff. In fact, he majored in history and now, as a middle school teacher, actually *teaches* history. But it's unfortunate that he had to wait until college to discover the true nature of knowledge in history.

The following exercise will encourage you to reflect on your own beliefs about the nature of knowledge.

─────── **SEE FOR YOURSELF** ───────
BELIEFS ABOUT KNOWLEDGE

Rate your beliefs for each of the following items on a scale from 1 to 5. A rating of 1 indicates that you strongly agree with the statement to the *left* of the five-point scale and a rating of 5 indicates that you strongly agree with the statement to the *right* of the scale.

	1	2	3	4	5	
A. Knowledge can be learned quickly and easily.	1	2	3	4	5	Knowledge is acquired gradually with time and effort.
B. Knowledge is fixed and known.	1	2	3	4	5	Knowledge is fluid and continues to evolve.
C. Knowledge is simple, discrete bits of information.	1	2	3	4	5	Knowledge is complex and involves interconnected ideas.
D. Knowledge exists outside the learner and can be transmitted from an authority.	1	2	3	4	5	Knowledge is constructed by the learner in interaction with more knowledgeable people or sources.
E. Knowledge from an authority can be accepted unquestioned.	1	2	3	4	5	Knowledge must be supported with credible evidence.

Your answers to the items in this exercise tell you something about your beliefs about knowledge and learning, which are collectively known as **epistemic beliefs** (you may also see the term *epistemological* beliefs or epistemic *cognition*). Students' epistemic beliefs are important because they often influence their studying, learning, and motivation.[48] For example, when learners believe that learning happens quickly with little or no effort on their part—as Ms. Gaunt's students apparently do in the opening case study—they're apt to believe they've mastered something before they really have. Furthermore, they tend to give up quickly in the face of failure and express discouragement or dislike regarding the topic they're studying. In contrast, when learners believe that learning is a gradual process that often takes time and effort, they're likely to use a wide variety of learning strategies as they study and to persist until they've made sense of the material.[49]

---

[48] Bendixen & Feucht, 2010; B. K. Hofer & Bendixen, 2012; B. K. Hofer & Pintrich, 1997; Muis, 2007.

[49] D. L. Butler & Winne, 1995; Kardash & Howell, 2000; Muis, 2007; Schommer, 1990, 1994b.

As another example, some students believe that when they read a textbook, they're passively soaking up many separate pieces of information from the page. Similarly, Ms. Gaunt's students think that mathematics consists simply of a bunch of procedures that yield single right answers but don't necessarily have to make sense.[50] More effective learners recognize that learning requires them to construct their own meanings by actively interpreting, organizing, and applying new information. The latter individuals are more likely to engage in meaningful learning as they read and study and more likely to undergo conceptual change when they encounter ideas that contradict existing understandings.[51]

Epistemic beliefs tend to evolve over the course of childhood and adolescence, as reflected in some of the entries in Table 3.2.[52] Children in the elementary grades typically believe in the certainty of knowledge: They think that for any topic there's an absolute truth "out there" somewhere. As they reach high school, some of them—and *only* some—begin to realize that knowledge is a subjective entity and that different perspectives on a topic can occasionally be equally valid. Additional changes can occur during the high school grades. For example, 12th graders are more likely than 9th graders to believe that knowledge consists of complex interrelationships rather than discrete facts and that learning happens slowly rather than quickly. And throughout adolescence, students' epistemic beliefs become increasingly specific to particular content domains.[53] For instance, students may believe that in math, answers are always either right or wrong (again recall Ms. Gaunt's students) but that in social studies, conflicting perspectives might all have some validity.

As you can see, then, higher ratings on the items in the preceding "Beliefs About Knowledge" exercise are generally more productive because learners with those beliefs tend to be more motivated to persist at a task and to use more effective learning strategies.

Effective learners self-regulate their learning by setting goals and standards, planning strategically, monitoring their progress, controlling their motivation and emotions, evaluating their performance, and imposing their own consequences for success or failure. With age, learners become better at self-regulating their learning, and their metacognitive knowledge and skills improve. In the hotlinked Self-Check quiz and Application Exercise that follow, you can check and apply your understandings related to Big Idea 3.1:

> *Effective learners regularly plan for their learning, monitor it, reflect on it, and strive to improve it.*

MyEdLab **Self-Check 3.1**

MyEdLab **Application Exercise 3.1.** In this exercise, you will analyze 12-year-old Colin's description of how he studies and remembers information that he learns in school.

3.2 TRANSFER

Big Idea 3.2 Specific facts don't always have much applicability to the outside world, but many general principles, strategies, and attitudes acquired at school are potentially applicable to a wide variety of situations.

How students think about and study school subject matter has implications not only for how well they can understand and remember it, but also for how effectively they can *use and apply* it later on. Here we're talking about **transfer**: a phenomenon in which something a person has learned at one time affects how the person learns or performs in a later situation. Following are examples:

- Elena speaks both English and Spanish fluently. When she begins a French course in high school, she immediately recognizes many similarities between French and Spanish. "Aha," she thinks, "what I know about Spanish will help me learn French."

---

[50] Such beliefs about math are common; see Muis, 2004.

[51] Mason, 2010; Muis, 2007; Schommer-Aikins, 2002; Sinatra & Pintrich, 2003.

[52] Kuhn & Park, 2005; Muis et al., 2006; Schommer, Calvert, Gariglietti, & Bajaj, 1997.

[53] Buehl & Alexander, 2006; Muis et al., 2006.

- In her middle school history class, Stella discovers that she does better on quizzes when she takes more notes. She decides to take more notes in her science class as well, and once again the strategy pays off.

- Ted's fifth-grade class has been working with decimals for several weeks. His teacher asks, "Which number is larger, 4.4 or 4.14?" Ted recalls something he knows about whole numbers: Numbers with three digits are larger than numbers with only two digits. He mistakenly concludes that the larger number is 4.14 because it has three digits and 4.4 only has two digits.

In most cases, prior learning *helps* learning or performance in another situation. Such **positive transfer** takes place when Elena's Spanish helps her learn French and when Stella's practice with note taking in history class improves her performance in science class. In some instances, however, existing knowledge or skills *hinder* later learning. Such **negative transfer** is the case for Ted, who transfers a principle related to whole numbers to a situation where it doesn't apply: comparing decimals.

Positive transfer to real-world tasks and problems should, of course, be a major goal for students at all grade levels. Unfortunately, however, learners often *don't* apply school subject matter to out-of-school situations because they don't retrieve it from long-term memory when it might be useful.[54] The principles in this section capture many research findings regarding when transfer is and isn't likely to occur.

think about it
Can you think of a recent situation in which you exhibited positive transfer? Can you think of one in which you exhibited negative transfer?

Meaningful learning and conceptual understanding increase the probability of transfer.

Learners are much more likely to apply new knowledge and skills when they engage in meaningful rather than rote learning.[55] Ideally, learners should acquire *conceptual understanding* of a topic, such that many concepts and procedures are interrelated in a cohesive, logical whole (recall our discussion of this concept in Chapter 2). When knowledge and skills are appropriately interconnected in long-term memory, learners are more likely to retrieve them in relevant situations.

In general, then, the *less-is-more* principle introduced in Chapter 2 applies here: Learners are more likely to transfer new knowledge and skills to new situations—including those in the outside world—when they study a few things in depth and learn them *well,* rather than studying many topics superficially.[56] In-depth instruction is especially effective when learners see many examples of concepts and have many opportunities to apply skills to diverse situations. In such cases learners can connect their new knowledge to a wide variety of contexts, increasing the odds that they'll retrieve it later when they need it.[57]

The less-is-more principle is clearly being violated in the opening case study. Ms. Gaunt decides that she must move fairly quickly if she is to cover the entire eighth-grade math curriculum, even if it means that few students will master any particular topic or procedure. Given the upcoming statewide math exam, she may feel that she has few alternatives, but her students are unlikely to *use* what they're learning on future occasions.

Both positive and negative transfer are more common when a new situation appears to be similar to a previous one.

Transfer from one situation to another is more likely to occur when the two situations overlap in some way, in large part because the new situation provides retrieval cues that remind learners of relevant things they learned in the previous situation.[58] Consider Elena, the student fluent in Spanish who is now taking French. When Elena first encounters French number words (*un, deux, trois),* they should quickly trigger recall of similar-sounding Spanish words (*uno, dos, tres).*

---

[54] Levstik, 2011; R. E. Mayer & Wittrock, 1996; D. N. Perkins & Salomon, 2012; Renkl, Mandl, & Gruber, 1996.

[55] Bereiter, 1995; Brooks & Dansereau, 1987; R. E. Mayer & Wittrock, 1996; Pugh & Bergin, 2006.

[56] Haskell, 2001; M. C. Linn, 2008; R. A. Schmidt & Bjork, 1992.

[57] Cox, 1997; M. C. Linn, 2008; D. N. Perkins & Salomon, 2012; R. A. Schmidt & Bjork, 1992.

[58] Bassok, 2003; Day & Goldstone, 2012; Haskell, 2001.

Specific transfer occurs when the original learning task and the transfer task overlap in some way, such as in their content or underlying structure. For example, consider the following three problems:

1. An automotive engineer has designed a car that can reach a speed of 15 miles per hour within 5 seconds. What is the car's rate of acceleration?

2. A car salesperson tells a customer that a particular model of car can reach a speed of 40 miles per hour within 8 seconds. What is the car's acceleration rate?

3. A zoologist reports that a cheetah can increase its speed by 6 kilometers per hour each second. How long will it take the cheetah to reach a running speed of 60 kilometers per hour?

Let's pretend that Joey's teacher just taught him how to solve Problem 1 in class by using the formula $v = a \times t$ (velocity = acceleration $\times$ time elapsed) and then gave him Problem 2 for homework. Would Joey be able to solve Problem 2? Well, probably, because Problems 1 and 2 have similar content (both involve cars) and similar underlying structures (both involve the relationship among velocity, acceleration, and time). Given that these problems overlap in content and structure, it's likely that specific transfer will occur.

If Joey is also given Problem 3 for homework, will he be able to solve it after he correctly solves Problem 2? Problem 3 involves specific transfer because it has the same general structure as Problems 1 and 2 (the $v = a \times t$ formula can be used to solve it). However, several things are different about Problem 3: the content topic switched from cars to cheetahs, the units of measurement switched from miles per hour to kilometers per hour, and the variable that needs to be calculated in the formula changed from acceleration rate to time. Given these differences, solving Problem 3 may be more difficult for Joey than solving Problems 1 or 2. But he should be able to solve it because the underlying structure is similar to that of Problems 1 and 2, even though the content and some other factors have changed.

All three of these problems can be solved if Joey recognizes that they involve the same underlying principle: velocity = acceleration $\times$ time elapsed. On average, general principles, rules, and theoretical explanations are more widely applicable than specific facts and information (e.g., knowing what $2 + 3$ equals).[59] For example, in solving computational problems requiring division, it's helpful to keep in mind that dividing positive numbers leads to a smaller amount *only* when the divisor is a number greater than 1. And in making sense of various historical and current events, it's helpful to know that a country's citizens sometimes revolt when government officials act unjustly. Of course, some facts are indispensable, but by themselves, facts have limited usefulness in new situations.

Knowledge and skills can be transferred to very different situations.

So far, we've seen that specific transfer occurs when the original learning task and the transfer task overlap in content or structure. But it's also possible for transfer to occur when the original learning task and the transfer task differ in both content and structure—a situation that's called **general transfer**. Remember Stella, who discovered that she does better on her history quizzes when she takes more notes? Well, she also decided to take notes as she watched a YouTube video about how to play her favorite song on the guitar. She believed that taking notes would help her to remember how to play the chords in the song. In this case, her history class and playing the song don't overlap much in content (history versus music) or structure (a formal school class versus an informal video), so it's an instance of general transfer.

Especially as they get older, some learners acquire an ability to apply broad principles to topics quite different from those they've previously studied. For example, in one research study, fifth graders and college students were asked to develop a plan for increasing the population of bald eagles, an endangered species in their state.[60] None of the students in either age-group had previously studied strategies for eagle preservation, and the plans that both groups developed were largely inadequate. Yet in the process of developing their plans, the college students addressed more sophisticated

---

[59] S. M. Barnett & Ceci, 2002; Bransford & Schwartz, 1999; Haskell, 2001; M. Perry, 1991.
[60] Bransford & Schwartz, 1999.

questions than the fifth graders did. In particular, the fifth graders focused on the eagles themselves (e.g., How big are they? What do they eat?), whereas the college students looked at the larger picture (e.g., What type of ecosystem supports eagles? What about predators of eagles and eagle babies?).[61] Thus the college students were drawing on an important principle they had acquired in their many years of science study: Living creatures are more likely to survive and thrive when their habitat supports rather than threatens them.

Identifying the extent to which the content and structure of problems overlap is not a precise science. Sometimes it can be difficult to determine whether a problem involves mostly specific transfer or mostly general transfer, especially when the content and structure overlap to some extent but not very much. Nonetheless, the distinction between specific and general transfer is a useful one to consider in that, on average, specific transfer is easier for students than general transfer.[62]

Learning strategies, general beliefs, and attitudes can also transfer to new situations.

Many learning and study strategies, such as note taking, have wide applicability: When learners acquire effective strategies within the context of one content domain, they often apply the strategies in a very different domain.[63] In addition, the general beliefs and attitudes that learners acquire about learning and thinking—for instance, confidence in their ability to master school subject matter, recognition that learning often takes hard work, and willingness to consider multiple viewpoints on controversial issues—can have a profound impact on later learning and achievement across multiple domains and so clearly illustrate general transfer at work.[64]

Transfer increases when the learning environment encourages it.

We return once again to the concepts *situated learning* and *situated cognition*, which we previously discussed in Chapter 2. As we noted in those discussions, learners often exhibit a phenomenon known as *situated learning* or *situated cognition*—that is, they associate particular behaviors and ways of thinking only with certain contexts and so they don't use what they've learned in other relevant contexts. Situated learning and cognition, then, can sometimes interfere with positive and general transfer.

In informal, real-world learning activities, learners typically know that they'll need to apply what they're learning to new tasks and problems, the happy result being that they *do* apply it when they need it. In many formal school settings, however, teachers encourage students to learn academic subject matter for mysterious purposes—for example, "You'll need to know this in college" or "It will come in handy later in life." Teachers are more likely to promote transfer when, instead, they create a **culture of transfer**—a learning environment in which applying school subject matter to diverse situations and topics is both the expectation and the norm.[65] In such classrooms, teachers often encourage students to ask themselves *How might I use this information?* as they listen, read, and study. And they regularly present tasks and problems in which students *must* apply what they're learning to real-world contexts.

For tonight's homework assignment, memorize all 50 states in the U.S.A. in reverse alphabetical order.

Rote memorization tasks such as this one have little or no benefit because neither the information to be learned nor the "mental exercise" involved is likely to transfer to future situations. Furthermore, such tasks communicate the message that schoolwork is a waste of time.

[61] Bransford & Schwartz, 1999, p. 67.

[62] S. M. Barnett & Ceci, 2002; Bassok, 2003.

[63] J. M. Alexander, Johnson, Scott, & Meyer, 2008; Bransford et al., 2006; Brooks & Dansereau, 1987; D. N. Perkins, 1995.

[64] Bransford & Schwartz, 1999; Dai & Sternberg, 2004; De Corte, 2003; Pugh, Bergin, & Rocks, 2003.

[65] Engle, 2006; Engle, Lam, Meyer, & Nix, 2012; Gresalfi & Lester, 2009; Haskell, 2001; M. C. Linn, 2008; Pea, 1987.

An important goal of schooling is to help students transfer the knowledge and skills they learn in school to other situations outside of school. Students are more likely to transfer new knowledge and skills to new situations when they study topics in depth and when the new situation is similar to a previous one. In the hotlinked Self-Check quiz and Application Exercise that follow, you can check and apply your understandings related to Big Idea 3.2:

> *Specific facts don't always have much applicability to the outside world, but many general principles, strategies, and attitudes acquired at school are potentially applicable to a wide variety of situations.*

MyEdLab **Self-Check 3.2**

MyEdLab **Application Exercise 3.2.** In this activity, you can practice identifying whether or not transfer is likely to occur in a variety of scenarios.

3.3 PROBLEM SOLVING AND CREATIVITY

Big Idea 3.3 Learners tend to be more effective problem solvers and more creative thinkers if they have considerable knowledge from which to draw and if they can think flexibly about new tasks and problems.

Both problem solving and creativity involve applying—that is, transferring—previously learned knowledge or skills to a new situation. The world presents many, many problems that differ widely in content, scope, and amount of creativity needed, as illustrated in the next exercise.

––––––––––––––––––––––––– **SEE FOR YOURSELF** –––––––––––––––––––––––––
FOUR PROBLEMS

Take a few minutes to solve each of the following problems:

1. You buy two apples for 25¢ each and one pear for 40¢. How much change will you get back from a dollar bill?
2. You have a rectangle with a width of 8 meters and a height of 6 meters, as shown here. How long is the diagonal line?
3. What improvements can be made to the wagon shown here to make it more fun to play with?
4. What are some possible uses of a brick? Generate as many different and unusual uses as you can.[66]

All of these problems involve **problem solving** because they require you to use your existing knowledge and skills to address an unanswered question or puzzling situation. If you had already solved these exact problems before, then they would no longer be problems for you, although they may be problems for someone else. All problems have at least three components: the givens, the operations, and the goal.[67] The *givens* are pieces of information given when the problem is presented, the *operations* are actions that can be performed to approach or reach the goal, and the *goal* is what the solution to the problem will accomplish. Problems differ considerably in the extent to which they're clearly specified and structured. At one end of this clarity-and-structure continuum is the **well-defined problem,** in which the goal is clearly stated, all information needed to solve the problem is present, and only one correct solution exists. Calculating correct change after a

––––––––––––

[66] Problems 3 and 4 modeled after Torrance, 1970.
[67] Glass, Holyoak, & Santa, 1979; Wickelgren, 1974.

purchase (Problem 1 in the previous exercise) and determining the length of the diagonal for the rectangle (Problem 2) are well-defined problems.

At the other end of the continuum is the **ill-defined problem**, in which the desired goal is unclear, information needed to solve the problem is missing, or several possible solutions may exist. Improving the design of a wagon (Problem 3) is somewhat ill-defined: Many different types of improvements might make it more fun to play with, yet some improvements might make it more fun than others. The brick problem (Problem 4) is even less defined—the goal is simply to identify uses of a brick—so, clearly, there's no single correct solution. On average, ill-defined problems are harder to solve than well-defined ones.

Problem solving requires students to engage in varying degrees of creativity, depending on the scope of the problem and on students' existing knowledge and skills. Psychologists have diverse opinions about the nature of **creativity**, but it generally involves new and original behavior yielding a product appropriate for—and in some way valued in—one's culture.[68] To successfully tackle a

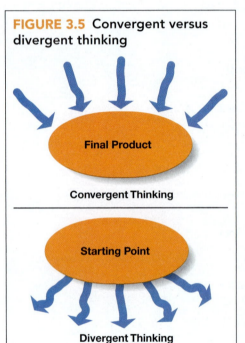

FIGURE 3.5 Convergent versus divergent thinking

Final Product

Convergent Thinking

Starting Point

Divergent Thinking

problem, people typically pull together two or more pieces of information into some sort of "whole" that resolves the problem. This combining of information into a single idea or product is known as **convergent thinking**, which may require some creativity in how the information is combined. In contrast, **divergent thinking** is the process of generating many different ideas from a single starting point (see Figure 3.5). Divergent thinking involves creativity when students begin with a single idea and take it in a variety of directions, at least one of which leads to something that's new, original, and culturally appropriate.

As illustrations of the difference between convergent and divergent thinking, let's return to the "Four Problems" exercise you completed earlier. To answer Problem 1, you must pull together at least four facts ($2 \times 25 = 50$, $50 + 40 = 90$, 1 dollar = 100 cents, and $100 - 90 = 10$) to arrive at the solution "10¢." To answer Question 2, you must use the Pythagorean theorem (the square of the hypotenuse equals the sum of the squares of the other two sides) plus at least four number facts ($6^2 = 36$, $8^2 = 64$, $36 + 64 = 100$, $\sqrt{100} = 10$) to arrive at the solution of 10 meters. Both Problems 1 and 2, then, involve convergent thinking. In contrast, Questions 3 and 4 require you to think in many different ways about a single object—you must consider how different parts of the wagon might be embellished and how a brick might be used in different contexts—with some of your responses being novel and unique. For example, perhaps you thought a brick might make an interesting base for a table lamp, or maybe you fastened a hobby horse to the wagon's handle to make it look like a horse and buggy. Questions 3 and 4, then, involve divergent thinking.

In general, you should think of problem solving and creativity as overlapping processes: Solving problems often involves thinking creatively, and being creative typically requires solving one or more problems. In the wagon problem, for example, although you ultimately need only a single solution, you must engage in divergent thinking to generate a variety of options before you select your final solution that you believe will make the wagon the most fun.

The general principles in this section apply to both problem solving and creativity.

The depth of learners' knowledge influences their ability to solve problems and think creatively.

Successful problem solvers and creative thinkers usually have considerable knowledge and conceptual understanding of the topic in question.[69] Especially in the case of creativity, such knowledge may also involve mental associations among very different ideas and subject areas.[70]

When learners have limited knowledge about a topic and little conceptual understanding of it, they're apt to choose problem-solving strategies on the basis of superficial problem characteristics.[71] For example, when one of us authors was in elementary school, one of her teachers suggested

[68] For example, see Beghetto & Kaufman, 2010.

[69] M. Carr, 2010; Hecht & Vagi, 2010; Lubart & Mouchiroud, 2003; Mayer, 2013; Mayer & Wittrock, 2006; Simonton, 2000; Sweller, 2009a.

[70] Runco & Chand, 1995.

[71] Chi, Feltovich, & Glaser, 1981; Schoenfeld & Hermann, 1982; Walkington, Sherman, & Petrosino, 2012.

that the word *left* in a word problem calls for subtraction. Interpreting a "left" problem as a subtraction problem works well in some instances but not others. Consider these two problems:

- Tim has 7 apples. He gives 3 apples to Sarah. How many apples does he have left?
- At the grocery store, Tim buys some apples for $2.00. When he leaves the store, he has $1.50 left. How much money did Tim have before he bought the apples?

The second problem requires addition, not subtraction.

Both convergent and divergent thinking are constrained by working memory capacity.

You may recall from an exercise in Chapter 2 just how difficult it can be to solve a long division problem in your head. Remember, working memory has a limited capacity: It can hold only a few pieces of information and accommodate only so much cognitive processing at a time. If a problem or task requires a person to handle a great deal of information at once, to manipulate information in a very complex way, or to generate a wide variety of new ideas, working memory capacity may be insufficient for arriving at an accurate or creative result.[72]

Learners can overcome the limits of working memory in at least two ways. One obvious approach is to create an external record of needed information—for example, by putting it on paper or on an electronic device. Another approach is to learn some skills to automaticity—in other words, to learn them to a point where they can be retrieved quickly and easily.[73] Yet in the case of automaticity, it's possible to have too much of a good thing, as you'll see shortly.

How learners represent a problem or situation influences their strategies and eventual success.

Any particular problem or situation might be represented in working memory in a variety of ways. As an example, see whether you can solve the problem in the following exercise.

--- **SEE FOR YOURSELF** ---
PIGS AND CHICKENS

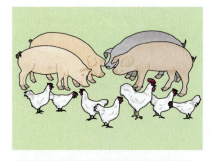

Old MacDonald has a barnyard full of pigs and chickens. In total, there are 21 heads and 60 legs in the barnyard (not counting MacDonald's own head and legs). How many pigs and how many chickens are in the barnyard?

Try to solve this problem before you read any further. Did you solve it? If you're having trouble, try thinking about the problem this way:

Imagine that the pigs are standing upright on their two hind legs, with their front two legs raised over their heads. All the animals, then, are standing on two legs. Figure out how many legs are on the ground and how many must be in the air. From this information, can you determine the number of pigs and chickens in the barnyard?

Because there are 21 heads, there must be 21 animals. Thus there must be 42 legs on the ground (21×2), which leaves 18 pigs' legs in the air ($60 - 42$). There must, therefore, be 9 pigs ($18 \div 2$) and 12 chickens ($21 - 9$).

If you're a proficient mathematician, you may simply have used algebra to represent and solve the problem, perhaps using x for the number of pigs and y for the number of chickens and then solving for these variables in the equations $x + y = 21$ and $4x + 2y = 60$. Algebra provides many helpful procedures for solving problems involving unknown quantities. In our own experiences, however, we've found that most college students display *situated cognition* (as we described in Chapter 2) and rarely use algebra to solve problems outside of a math class. At all grade levels, students often have trouble solving word problems because they don't know how to translate the problems into procedures or operations they've learned at school.[74]

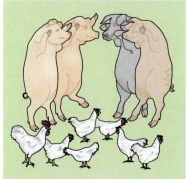

Some ways of representing a problem promote more successful problem solving than others.

---

[72] Hambrick & Engle, 2003; K. Lee, Ng, & Ng, 2009; Sweller, 2009a.

[73] N. Frederiksen, 1984a; R. E. Mayer & Wittrock, 2006; Sweller, 1994.

[74] K. Lee et al., 2009; R. E. Mayer & Wittrock, 2006; L. B. Resnick, 1989; Walkington et al., 2012.

Sometimes learners represent a problem or situation in a seemingly logical way that nevertheless fails to yield a workable result. As an example, take a stab at the next problem.

— **SEE FOR YOURSELF** —
CANDLE PROBLEM

How might you stand a candle upright in front of a bulletin board that is attached to the wall? You don't want the candle to touch the bulletin board because the flame might singe the board. Instead, you need to place the candle about a centimeter away from the board. How can you accomplish the task using some or all of the following materials: a small candle (birthday cake size), a metal knitting needle, matches, a box of thumbtacks, and a 12-inch plastic ruler?[75]

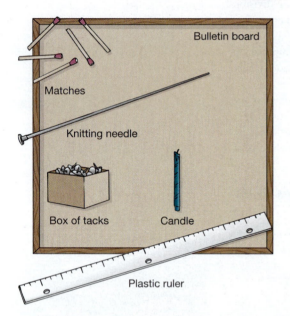

Bulletin board

Matches

Knitting needle

Box of tacks   Candle

Plastic ruler

As it turns out, the ruler and knitting needle are useless here. Piercing the candle with the knitting needle will probably break the candle, and you're unlikely to have much luck balancing the ruler on a few tacks. (We speak from experience here, as our own students have unsuccessfully tried both strategies.) The easiest solution is to fasten the thumbtack box to the bulletin board with tacks and then attach the candle to the top of the box with either a tack or some melted wax. Many people don't consider this possibility because they represent the box only as a *container of tacks,* and so they overlook its potential use as a candle stand. When people represent a problem or situation in a way that excludes potential solutions, they're victims of a **mental set**.

Mental sets sometimes emerge when learners practice solving a particular kind of problem (e.g., doing subtraction problems in math or applying the formula $E = mc^2$ in physics) without practicing other kinds of problems at the same time.[76] In general, repetitive practice can lead learners to represent problems and situations in a particular way without really thinking about them—that is, it can lead to automaticity in representation. Although automaticity in the basic information and skills needed for problem solving and creative thinking is often an advantage (it frees up working memory capacity), automaticity in mentally *representing* problems and situations can yield incorrect solutions or inappropriate products, in part because it may lead learners down a counterproductive path of associations in long-term memory.[77]

Problem solving and creativity often involve heuristics that facilitate but don't guarantee successful outcomes.

Some problems can be successfully solved with an **algorithm**, a specific sequence of steps that guarantees a correct solution. For example, perhaps you've successfully put together a new bookcase by following the "Directions for Assembly" that came with all the pieces. And in the opening case study, Ms. Gaunt's students can correctly determine that Raj needs 120 minutes (2 hours) to type his paper if they use the standard procedure for paper-and-pencil long division.

Yet the world presents many problems for which no algorithms exist. And creativity, by its very nature, requires original, nonalgorithmic approaches to situations. Furthermore, algorithms are few and far between outside the domains of math and science. There are no rules we can follow to design a fun wagon, address ongoing ethnic and religious conflicts in the Middle East, or reduce global climate change—a problem that involves economics, political science, and psychology as much as physics, meteorology, and climate science.

In the absence of an algorithm, learners must instead use a **heuristic**, a general approach that may or may not yield a successful outcome. Some heuristics are specific to particular content domains. Others, such as the following, can be useful in a variety of contexts:[78]

- **Identify subgoals.** Break a large, complex task into two or more specific subtasks that can be more easily addressed.

[75] Problem based on one described by Duncker, 1945.
[76] E. J. Langer, 2000; Luchins, 1942.
[77] Lubart & Mouchiroud, 2003; Rohrer & Pashler, 2010; D. L. Schwartz, Chase, & Bransford, 2012.
[78] Baer & Garrett, 2010; J. E. Davidson & Sternberg, 2003; De Corte, Op't Eynde, Depaepe, & Verschaffel, 2010; Zhong, Dijksterhuis, & Galinsky, 2008.

- **Represent parts of the situation on paper or on an electronic device.** Make a diagram, list a problem's components, or jot down potential solutions or approaches.
- **Draw an analogy.** Identify a situation analogous to the problem situation, and derive potential solutions from the analogy.
- **Brainstorm.** Generate a wide variety of possible approaches or solutions—perhaps including some that seem outlandish or absurd—without initially evaluating any of them. After creating a lengthy list, evaluate each item for its potential relevance and usefulness.
- **"Incubate" the situation.** Let a problem remain unresolved for a few hours or days, thereby allowing mental sets to dissipate and enabling a broad search of long-term memory for potentially productive approaches.

think about it
Can you think of times in your life when you've used these heuristics to solve problems?

Effective problem solving and creativity require self-regulation and metacognition.

Self-regulation and metacognition play an important role not only in effective learning and studying but also in problem solving and creativity. For example, effective problem solvers and creative thinkers tend to do the following:[79]

- Identify one or more specific goals toward which to strive.
- Break a complex problem or task into two or more simpler components.
- Plan a systematic, sequential approach to addressing these components.
- Continually monitor and evaluate their progress toward their goal(s).
- Identify and address obstacles that may be impeding their progress.
- Change to new strategies if the current ones aren't working.
- Apply high standards in evaluating final results.

Such metacognitive processes enable learners to use creative problem-solving strategies flexibly, to apply those strategies to more complex situations, and to know when particular strategies are and are not appropriate.

In the opening case study, many of Ms. Gaunt's students rarely critique their problem solutions for logical sense—for instance, they don't recognize that typing a 4,200-word paper is unlikely to take 100 days. Essentially the students engage in little or no self-evaluation of their problem solutions. Truly successful learners evaluate not only their own work but also the ideas and work of others. In other words, they engage in critical thinking, our next topic.

Students engage in solving many different types of problems in school and out of school. Effective problem solving involves a variety of knowledge, skills, creativity, self-regulation, and metacognition, depending on the scope of the problem and the knowledge and skills of the problem solver. In the hotlinked Self-Check quiz and Application Exercise that follow, you can check and apply your understandings related to Big Idea 3.3:

> *Learners tend to be more effective problem solvers and more creative thinkers if they have considerable knowledge from which to draw and if they can think flexibly about new tasks and problems.*

MyEdLab **Self-Check 3.3**

MyEdLab **Application Exercise 3.3.** In this exercise, you can apply your knowledge of problem solving and creativity.

---

[79] M. Carr, 2010; Csikszentmihalyi, 1996; J. E. Davidson & Sternberg, 1998; De Corte et al., 2010; Dominowski, 1998; Glover, Ronning, & Reynolds, 1989; Minsky, 2006; Runco & Chand, 1995.

3.4 CRITICAL THINKING

Big Idea 3.4 Critical thinking requires both a sophisticated view of the nature of knowledge and a general disposition to carefully scrutinize and evaluate new information and ideas.

Critical thinking involves evaluating the accuracy, credibility, and worth of information and lines of reasoning.[80] It can take a variety of forms, depending on the context. The following exercise presents four possibilities.

SEE FOR YOURSELF

COLDS, CARS, CHANCE, AND CHEER

Read and respond to each of the following situations.

1. It's autumn, and the days are becoming increasingly chilly. You see the following advertisement:

   > Aren't you tired of sniffles and runny noses all winter? Tired of always feeling less than your best? Get through a whole winter without colds. Take Eradicold Pills as directed.[81]

   Should you go buy a box of Eradicold Pills?

2. You have a beat-up old car and have invested several thousand dollars to get it in working order. You can sell the car in its present condition for $1,500, or you can invest $2,000 more on repairs and then sell it for $3,000. What should you do?[82]

3. You've been rolling a typical six-sided die (i.e., one member of a pair of dice). You know that the die isn't heavier on one side than another, and yet in the past 30 rolls, you haven't rolled a number 4 even once. What are the odds that you'll get a 4 on the next roll?

4. This research finding was presented by Dr. Edmund Emmer at an annual conference of the American Educational Research Association:

   > Teachers who feel happy when they teach are more likely to have well-behaved students.[83]

   If you're a teacher, do such results indicate that you should try to feel happy when you enter the classroom each morning?

In each of these situations, you had to evaluate information and make some sort of judgment. In Item 1, we hope you weren't tempted to buy Eradicold Pills, because the advertisement provided no proof that they reduce cold symptoms. It simply included the suggestion to "Take Eradicold Pills as directed" within the context of a discussion of undesirable symptoms—a common ploy in persuasive advertising.

As for Item 2, it makes more sense to sell the car now. If you sell the car for $3,000 after making $2,000 worth of repairs, you'll make $500 less than you would otherwise. Many people mistakenly believe that their past investments justify making additional ones, when in fact, past investments are irrelevant to the present circumstances.[84]

In Item 3, the chance of rolling a 4 on an evenly balanced die is—as always—one in six. The outcomes of previous rolls are irrelevant because each roll is independent of the others. But when a 4 hasn't shown up even once in 30 rolls, many people believe that a 4 is long overdue and so greatly overestimate its probability.

Now what about Item 4, making sure you're happy each time you enter the classroom? One common mistake people make in interpreting research results is to think that an association between two things—a *correlation*—means that one of those things must definitely *cause* the other. As noted in Chapter 1, however, correlation doesn't necessarily indicate a cause-and-effect relationship. Perhaps teacher happiness directly influences students' classroom behavior, but there are other possible explanations for the correlation as well. For instance, perhaps good

---

[80] Beyer, 1985; Heyman, 2008; J. Moon, 2008.
[81] R. J. Harris, 1977, p. 605.
[82] Modeled after Halpern, 1998.
[83] Emmer, 1994.
[84] Halpern, 1998.

student behavior makes teachers feel happy (rather than vice versa), or maybe teachers who are feeling upbeat use more effective teaching techniques and keep students on task as a result of using those techniques.[85]

The four situations presented in the exercise illustrate several forms that critical thinking might take:[86]

- **Verbal reasoning:** Understanding and evaluating persuasive techniques found in oral and written language (e.g., deductive and inductive logic). You engaged in verbal reasoning when deciding whether to purchase Eradicold Pills.
- **Argument analysis:** Discriminating between reasons that do and don't support a conclusion. You engaged in argument analysis when you considered possible pros and cons of investing an additional $2,000 in car repairs.
- **Probabilistic reasoning:** Determining the likelihood and uncertainties associated with various events. You engaged in probabilistic reasoning when you determined the probability of rolling a 4 on the die.
- **Hypothesis testing:** Judging the value of data and research results in terms of the methods used to obtain them and their potential relevance to certain conclusions. When hypothesis testing includes critical thinking, it involves considering questions such as these:
  - Was an appropriate method used to measure a particular outcome?
  - Have other possible explanations or conclusions been eliminated?
  - Can the results obtained in one situation be reasonably generalized to other situations?

You engaged in hypothesis testing when you evaluated Dr. Emmer's findings about teacher happiness.

The specific cognitive processes involved can differ quite a bit depending on the content domain. In writing, critical thinking might involve reading the first draft of a persuasive essay to look for errors in logical reasoning or for situations in which opinions haven't been sufficiently justified. In science, it may involve revising existing theories or beliefs to account for new evidence—that is, it may involve conceptual change. In history, it might involve drawing inferences from historical documents, attempting to determine whether things *definitely* happened a particular way or only *maybe* happened that way. And in many fields, including educational psychology, it involves evaluating the quality of research findings on which assertions are made—hence the footnoted references we've provided for you throughout this book.

As you might guess, critical thinking abilities emerge gradually over the course of childhood and adolescence.[87] Yet all too often, learners at all grade levels—and even many well-educated adults—take the information they see in textbooks, news reports, on the Internet, and elsewhere at face value. In other words, they engage in little or no critical thinking as they consider the accuracy, credibility, and worth of the information they encounter.[88]

The following two principles can help us understand why critical thinking tends to be the exception rather than the rule.

Critical thinking requires sophisticated epistemic beliefs.

Learners are more likely to look analytically and critically at new information if they believe that even experts' understandings of a topic continue to evolve as new evidence accumulates. They're *less* likely to engage in critical thinking if they believe that "knowledge" is an absolute, unchanging entity.[89] In other words, learners' *epistemic beliefs* enter into the critical thinking process.

MyEdLab
Video Example 3.4.

In many content domains, one aspect of critical thinking is distinguishing between statements that are indisputable facts versus those that reflect personal opinions. What strategies does this sixth-grade teacher use to help students understand this distinction?

---

[85] Emmer, 1994.
[86] Halpern, 1997, 1998, 2008; E. M. Nussbaum, 2008.
[87] Amsterlaw, 2006; P. M. King & Kitchener, 2002; Kuhn & Franklin, 2006; Pillow, 2002.
[88] Kuhn, 2009; G. Marcus, 2008; M. J. Metzger, Flanagin, & Zwarun, 2003; Sinatra, Kienhues, & Hofer, 2014.
[89] Bråten, Britt, Strømsø, & Rouet, 2011; Bromme, Kienhues, & Porsch, 2010; Kuhn, 2001a; Schommer-Aikis, 2002.

Critical thinking is a disposition as much as a cognitive process.

By **disposition**, we mean a general inclination to approach and think about learning and problem-solving situations in a particular way—perhaps in a thoughtful, analytical, evaluative manner, on the one hand, or in a thought*less,* unquestioning way, on the other. Some learners clearly have a general disposition to think critically about the subject matter they read and study.[90] Those who do show more advanced reasoning capabilities and are more likely to undergo conceptual change when it's warranted.[91]

Researchers don't yet have a good understanding of why some learners are more predisposed to think critically than others. The larger culture and society in which learners live certainly have an effect, as can be seen in the Cultural Considerations box "Influences of Culture and Community on Complex Cognitive Processes." And quite possibly, teachers' actions in the classroom—for instance, whether they encourage exploration, risk taking, and critical thinking with respect to classroom topics—make a difference.[92] In the following classroom interaction, a teacher actually seems to *discourage* any disposition to think analytically and critically about classroom material:

> *Teacher:* Write this on your paper . . . it's simply memorizing this pattern. We have meters, centimeters, and millimeters. Let's say . . . write millimeters, centimeters, and meters. We want to make sure that our metric measurement is the same. If I gave you this decimal, let's say .234 m (yes, write that). In order to come up with .234 m in centimeters, the only thing that is necessary is that you move the decimal. How do we move the decimal? You move it to the right two places. (Jason, sit up please.) If I move it to the right two places, what should .234 m look like, Daniel, in centimeters? What does it look like, Ashley?
>
> *Ashley:* 23.4 cm.
>
> *Teacher:* Twenty-three point four. Simple stuff. In order to find meters, we're still moving that decimal to the right, but this time, boys and girls, we're only going to move it one place. So, if I move this decimal one place, what is my answer for millimeters?[93]

Undoubtedly, this teacher means well: She wants her students to understand how to convert from one unit of measurement to another. But notice the attitude she engenders: "Write this . . . it's simply memorizing this pattern."

Critical thinking and other complex cognitive processes will obviously enhance learners' long-term success both in higher education and in the outside world. We now look at various ways in which teachers might encourage such processes.

Critical thinking requires students to critically evaluate evidence and logic. It can take several different forms, including verbal and probabilistic reasoning, argument analysis, and hypothesis testing. In the hotlinked Self-Check quiz and Application Exercise that follow, you can check and apply your understandings related to Big Idea 3.4:
> *Critical thinking requires both a sophisticated view of the nature of knowledge and a general disposition to carefully scrutinize and evaluate new information and ideas.*

MyEdLab **Self-Check 3.4**

MyEdLab **Application Exercise 3.4.** In this exercise, you can test your knowledge of some of the different forms of critical thinking.

---

[90] Halpern, 2008; D. N. Perkins, Tishman, Ritchhart, Donis, & Andrade, 2000; R. F. West, Toplak, & Stanovich, 2008.

[91] Southerland & Sinatra, 2003; Stanovich, 1999.

[92] Flum & Kaplan, 2006; Kuhn, 2001b, 2006; J. Moon, 2008.

[93] Dialogue from J. C. Turner, Meyer, et al., 1998, p. 741.

CULTURAL CONSIDERATIONS

Influences of Culture and Community on Complex Cognitive Processes

Learners' experiences at home and in their general community and culture can have a significant effect on the development of complex cognitive processes. Following are several areas in which researchers have observed cultural diversity.

EPISTEMIC BELIEFS. People from various cultural groups don't completely agree on what it means to *learn* something. From the perspective of mainstream Western culture, learning is largely a mental enterprise: People learn in order to understand the world and acquire new skills and abilities. But for many Chinese, learning also has moral and social dimensions: It enables a person to become increasingly virtuous and honorable and to contribute in significant ways to society's general welfare. Furthermore, from a traditional East Asian perspective, true mastery of a topic comes only with a great deal of diligence, concentration, and perseverance—a position that stands in stark contrast to the American students in the chapter's opening case study.[a]

LEARNING STRATEGIES. Consistent with a belief that learning requires diligence and perseverance, many East Asian parents and teachers encourage frequent use of rehearsal and rote memorization as learning strategies.[b] Rehearsal and memorization are also common in cultures that value committing oral histories or verbatim passages of sacred text (e.g., the Bible, the Koran) to memory.[c] In contrast, many schools in mainstream Western culture are increasingly conducting lessons and encouraging strategies that foster meaningful learning. Even so, Western schools typically insist that students learn certain things—such as multiplication tables and word spellings—by heart.[d]

SELF-REGULATED LEARNING. Also consistent with the importance placed on diligence

and persistence, East Asian parents and teachers are apt to encourage considerable self-discipline and stick-to-it-iveness as children tackle new projects. In doing so, they foster self-regulation.[e] Self-regulation is less common when young learners have few role models for effective study habits and self-regulation skills. This may be the case for some (but *only* some) children and adolescents who attend schools in low-socioeconomic neighborhoods. Although these students may hope to graduate, go on to college, and eventually become successful professionals, they may have little idea about how to accomplish such things.[f] The following interview with a middle school student in inner-city Philadelphia illustrates the problem:

> *Adult:* Are you on track to meet your goals?
> *Student:* No. I need to study more.
> *Adult:* How do you know that?
> *Student:* I just know by some of my grades. [mostly Cs]
> *Adult:* Why do you think you will be more inclined to do it in high school?
> *Student:* I don't want to get let back. I want to go to college.
> *Adult:* What will you need to do to get better grades?
> *Student:* Just do more and more work. I can rest when the school year is over.[g]

The student wants to get a college education, but to do so he understands only that he needs to "study more" and "do more and more work." Motivation and effort are important, to be sure, but so are planning, time management, regular self-monitoring and self-evaluation, and appropriate help-seeking—things about which this student seems to have little knowledge. Some learners, then, may need considerable guidance and support to acquire the learning and

self-regulation strategies that will serve them well in college and the outside world.

CRITICAL THINKING. Critical thinking is another complex cognitive process that seems to depend somewhat on students' cultural backgrounds. Some cultures place high value on respecting one's elders or certain religious leaders; in doing so, they may foster the epistemic belief that "truth" is a cut-and-dried entity that is best gained from authority figures.[h] In addition, a cultural emphasis on maintaining group harmony may discourage children from hashing out differences in perspectives, which critical thinking often entails.[i] Perhaps as a result of such factors, critical thinking may be less common in some groups (e.g., in some traditional Asian and Native American communities and in some fundamentalist religious groups) than in others.[j] In some situations, then, teachers must walk a fine line between teaching students to critically evaluate persuasive arguments and scientific evidence, on the one hand, and to show appropriate respect and strive for group harmony in their community and culture, on the other.

[a] Dahlin & Watkins, 2000; H. Grant & Dweck, 2001; J. Li, 2005; J. Li & Fischer, 2004.
[b] Dahlin & Watkins, 2000; D. Y. F. Ho, 1994; Purdie & Hattie, 1996.
[c] MacDonald, Uesiliana, & Hayne, 2000; Rogoff et al., 2007; Q. Wang & Ross, 2007.
[d] Q. Wang & Ross, 2007.
[e] Morelli & Rothbaum, 2007.
[f] Belfiore & Hornyak, 1998; B. L. Wilson & Corbett, 2001.
[g] Dialogue from *Listening to Urban Kids: School Reform and the Teachers They Want* by Bruce L. Wilson and Dick Corbett, p. 23. Copyright © 2001 by the State University of New York Press. State University of New York. Reprinted with permission. All rights reserved.
[h] Losh, 2003; Qian & Pan, 2002; Tyler et al., 2008.
[i] Heyman, 2008; Kağitçibaşi, 2007; Kuhn & Park, 2005.
[j] Kuhn, Daniels, & Krishnan, 2003; Kuhn & Park, 2005; Tyler et al., 2008.

3.5 PROMOTING SELF-REGULATION SKILLS AND METACOGNITIVE DEVELOPMENT

Big Idea 3.5 Effective teachers foster students' self-regulation skills and metacognitive development in age-appropriate ways.

As we've seen, self-regulation skills and metacognitive awareness tend to improve in significant ways throughout the elementary and secondary school years. Yet many students at all grade levels have little knowledge about effective learning strategies—for example, they may think that

CLASSROOM STRATEGIES

Fostering Self-Regulation

- **Have students observe and record their own behavior.**
  A student with attention-deficit hyperactivity disorder frequently tips his chair back to the point where he might topple over. Concerned for the student's safety, his teacher asks him to record each instance of chair-tipping behavior on a sheet of graph paper. Both student and teacher notice how quickly the behavior disappears once the student has become aware of his bad habit.

- **Teach students instructions they can give themselves to remind them of what they need to do.**
  To help students remember the new dance steps they're learning, their teacher instructs them to say such things as "One, two, gallop, gallop" and "One leg, other leg, turn, and turn" while performing the steps.

- **Provide the guidance students need to evaluate their own performance.**
  A science teacher gives students a list of criteria to evaluate the lab reports they've just written. In assigning grades, she considers not only what students have written in their reports but also how accurately students have evaluated their own reports.

- **Use video technology to enhance students' self-monitoring and self-evaluation abilities.**
  Charles is a highly intelligent fifth grader whose classroom behaviors—aggression, temper tantrums, refusals to do schoolwork—have his parents and teachers totally exasperated.

Nothing has worked with him—not traditional behaviorist techniques (e.g., praise, time-outs), counseling, or paper-and-pencil self-monitoring sheets. But when his special education teacher begins videotaping and then showing him his behaviors in math class, he's appalled at what he sees: "Do I really look like that?" "Did I really say that?" "Turn it off!" Charles expresses a strong desire to be "normal," becomes more obedient and respectful in class, and begins to appreciate the praise and other reinforcers he has previously rejected.

- **Teach students to reinforce themselves for appropriate behavior.**
  A teacher helps students develop more regular study habits by encouraging them to make a favorite activity—for example, practicing basketball, watching a movie, or texting a friend—contingent on completing their homework first.

- **Give students age-appropriate opportunities to engage in learning tasks with little or no help from their teacher.**
  A middle school social studies teacher distributes various magazine articles related to current events in the Middle East, making sure that each student receives an article appropriate for his or her reading level. He asks students to read their articles over the weekend and prepare a one-paragraph summary to share with other class members. He also provides guidelines about what information students should include in their summaries.

Sources: Andrade, 2010; Bear, Torgerson, & Dubois-Gerchak, 2010, p. 83 (Charles example); Mace, Belfiore, & Hutchinson, 2001; Hatzigeorgiadis, Zourbanos, Galanis, & Theodorakis, 2011; McMillan, 2010; Reid, Trout, & Schartz, 2005; Vintere, Hemmes, Brown, & Poulson, 2004, p. 309 (dancing self-instructions example); Zimmerman, 2004.

studying involves memorizing facts—and they aren't always able to keep themselves focused on productive learning activities.[94] With these points and a growing body of research findings in mind, we offer a few recommendations.

MyEdLab
Video Example 3.5.

What strategies does this elementary school teacher use to encourage students to self-regulate their learning and behavior?

Guide and support self-regulated learning and behavior.

If students are to become productive and successful adults who work well independently, they must become increasingly self-regulating over the course of childhood and adolescence. Some students acquire self-regulation skills largely on their own, but many others need considerable guidance and support. For example, students with a history of academic failure acquire better study habits when they're given explicit instruction in self-regulation strategies.[95]

Consistent with the concept of *co-regulation* introduced earlier, teachers can probably best foster self-regulation skills by initially providing considerable support and then gradually giving students more control as they become more self-directed. The right-hand column in Table 3.1, presented earlier in the chapter, offers suggestions that are apt to be appropriate at different grade levels. The Classroom Strategies box "Fostering Self-Regulation" offers several more specific ideas.

Of the many self-regulation strategies students might acquire, perhaps most important are strategies with which students can monitor and evaluate their own learning and behavior. Following are several things teachers might do to encourage self-monitoring and self-evaluation:[96]

- Have students set specific goals for their learning and then self-reflect on their achievements relative to those goals.

---

[94] J. E. Barnett, 2001; M. C. Linn & Eylon, 2011; Pintrich & De Groot, 1990; Schommer, 1994a.

[95] Cosden, Morrison, Albanese, & Macias, 2001; Eilam, 2001; Graham & Harris, 1996; Meltzer, 2007; N. E. Perry, 1998.

[96] Belfiore & Hornyak, 1998; Brunstein & Glaser, 2011; Dunning et al., 2004; Eilam, 2001; McCaslin & Good, 1996; McMillan, 2010; Meltzer, 2007; Paris & Paris, 2001; N. E. Perry, 1998.

FIGURE 3.6 After a cooperative group activity with three classmates, Rochelle and her teacher used the same criteria to rate Rochelle's performance and that of her group. With the two sets of ratings side by side, Rochelle can evaluate the accuracy of her self-assessments.

Project description ___Travel Guide___

Evaluate with a 1 for weak, a 2 for fair, a 3 for good, a 4 for very good, and a 5 for excellent.

Student	Teacher	
4	4	1. The task was a major amount of work in keeping with a whole month of effort.
5	4	2. We used class time quite well.
4	5	3. The workload was quite evenly divided. I did a fair proportion.
4	5	4. I showed commitment to the group and to a quality project.
5	4	5. My report went into depth; it didn't just give the obvious, commonly known information.
5	5	6. The project made a point: a reader (or viewer) could figure out how all of the details fitted together to help form a conclusion.
5	5	7. The project was neat, attractive, well assembled. I was proud of the outcome.
4	5	8. We kept our work organized; we made copies; we didn't lose things or end up having to redo work that was lost.
5	4	9. The work had a lot of original thinking or other creative work.
4	4	10. The project demonstrated mastery of basic language skills—composition, planning, oral communication, writing.
45	45	Total

Comments:

46 group average   (A)ᴳ   (A)ᴵ

- Provide specific criteria students can use to judge their performance; have them compare their self-evaluations with teacher evaluations (e.g., see Figure 3.6).
- To check for long-term retention of reading material, suggest questions that students can ask themselves to assess their understanding after a significant time delay.
- Ask students to keep ongoing records of their performance and to reflect on their learning in writing assignments, journals, or portfolios.

To be successful over the long run, students must actively monitor their behavior as well as their academic performance. Yet children and adolescents aren't always aware of how frequently they do something inappropriately or of how *in*frequently they do something well. To help students attend to the things they do and don't do, teachers can have them observe and record their own behavior in a concrete manner. For example, if Gavin talks out of turn too often, his teacher can help him become aware of the problem by asking him to make a checkmark on a recording sheet every time he catches himself speaking out of turn. If Lizzie has trouble staying on task during assigned activities, her teacher might give her an electronic beeper and ask her to record what she has just been doing every time she hears a beep. Such

MyEdLab
Video Example 3.6.

Many technological aids are available to help students acquire self-regulation skills. What aids does Brandon use in this video?

self-focused record keeping helps students stay on task and complete assignments, and their disruptive behaviors tend to diminish.[97]

Even kindergartners and first graders can be encouraged to reflect on their performance and progress, perhaps through questions such as "What were we doing that we're proud of?" and "What can we do that we didn't do before?"[98] By regularly engaging in self-monitoring and self-evaluation of classroom assignments, students should eventually develop appropriate standards for their performance and routinely apply those standards to the things they accomplish—true hallmarks of a self-regulating learner.

Encourage metacognitive self-reflection.

Metacognition lies at the heart of effective school learning: Students must regularly *think about their thinking.* To encourage metacognitive self-reflection, a teacher might:

- Ask students to explain what they're doing and why they're doing it while they work on a problem.[99]

- Give students questions to ask *themselves* as they work on a problem—questions such as "Am I getting closer to my goal?" and "Why is this strategy most appropriate?"[100]

- Have students keep *learning journals* in which they explain the main ideas of lessons, generate their own examples of new concepts, and identify strategies for overcoming gaps in their understandings.[101]

- Conduct *strategy share* discussions in which various class members explain their techniques for learning and remembering specific classroom topics.[102]

The right-hand column of Table 3.2, presented earlier in the chapter, offers additional suggestions.

Explicitly teach effective learning strategies.

We have previously described numerous learning strategies in this book, most notably in the section "Strategies for Learning and Studying Effectively" at the end of Chapter 1 and in the section "Encouraging Effective Long-Term Memory Storage Processes" in Chapter 2. Explicit training in reading and study strategies—preferably integrated into everyday instruction about academic topics—can definitely enhance students' learning and achievement and is especially important for students who have a history of academic difficulties.[103] Ideally, students should learn many different learning strategies and the situations in which each one is appropriate. For instance, trying to *make sense* of new ideas—meaningful learning—is essential for learning general principles within a discipline, whereas mnemonics are often more useful for learning hard-to-remember pairs and lists. And different organizational techniques—outlines, concept maps, two-dimensional comparison tables, and so on—are more or less suitable for different situations.[104] Students should have opportunities to practice each new strategy with a variety of learning tasks over a period of time. Effective strategy instruction is clearly *not* a one-shot deal.

When teaching learning strategies, teachers must be sure to include covert strategies—elaboration, comprehension monitoring, and so on—as well as overt ones. One effective way to teach covert mental processes is to model them by thinking aloud about classroom topics.[105] For example, in a high school history lesson on Napoleon, a teacher might say, "Hmm . . . it seems to me that Napoleon's military tactics were similar to those of the ancient Assyrians. Let's briefly recall the things

MyEdLab
Video Example 3.7.

How does this second-grade teacher explicitly teach her students a reading strategy?

---

[97] K. D. Allen, 1998; Belfiore & Hornyak, 1998; K. R. Harris, 1986; Reid, Trout, & Schartz, 2005; Webber, Scheuermann, McCall, & Coleman, 1993.

[98] N. E. Perry, VandeKamp, Mercer, & Nordby, 2002, p. 10.

[99] Siegler & Lin, 2010; Dominowski, 1998; Johanning, D'Agostino, Steele, & Shumow, 1999.

[100] M. Carr, 2010; A. King, 1999, p. 101; Kramarski & Mevarech, 2003, p. 286.

[101] Glogger, Schwonke, Holzäpfel, Nückles, & Renkl, 2012.

[102] Meltzer et al., 2007.

[103] Eason et al., 2012; Hattie, Biggs, & Purdie, 1996; Meltzer & Krishnan, 2007; Nokes & Dole, 2004; Veenman, 2011.

[104] R. K. Atkinson et al., 1999; D. H. Robinson & Kiewra, 1995.

[105] Brophy, Alleman, & Knighton, 2009; A. L. Brown & Palincsar, 1987; Pressley, El-Dinary, Marks, Brown, & Stein, 1992.

the Assyrians did." When assigning a textbook chapter for homework, a teacher might say, "Whenever I read a textbook chapter, I begin by looking at the headings and subheadings in the chapter. I then think about questions that the chapter will probably address, and I try to find the answers as I read. Let me show you how *I* might tackle the chapter I've asked you to read tonight. . . ."

Yet students are likely to use new study strategies only if they discover for themselves that the strategies are truly helpful.[106] For instance, one of us authors occasionally does little "experiments" in her classes, presenting information that's hard to make sense of and giving about half of the students a specific mnemonic for remembering it. Then, after giving the students a mock "test" on the information, she writes students' "test scores" on the board, putting the scores of the mnemonic and no-mnemonic students in separate columns. The performance of the two groups is usually so dramatically different that the students readily acknowledge the usefulness of the strategy she has taught them.

Students often need considerable support in their early efforts to use new strategies. For example, to help students identify the most important information in a lesson, a teacher might provide a list of objectives for the lesson, write key concepts and principles on the board, or ask questions that focus students' attention on central ideas.[107] To help students elaborate on what they read, teachers can provide examples of questions for students to answer (e.g., "Explain why . . ." or "What is a new example of . . .?").[108] And to help students in their early note-taking efforts, teachers might provide a structure to fill in during a lesson. An example of such a structure for a lesson on muscles is presented in Figure 3.7. You can find another example in the two sets of notes on Greek mythology presented earlier in Figure 3.3.

Some instructional software programs also give guidance in developing and using metacognitive skills—for instance, by occasionally asking students to relate new ideas to things they've

---

FIGURE 3.7 Example of a partially filled-in outline that can guide students' note taking

MUSCLES

A. **Number of Muscles**
   1. There are approximately _____ muscles in the human body.

B. **How Muscles Work**
   1. Muscles work in two ways:
      a. They _____ , or shorten.
      b. They _____, or lengthen.

C. **Kinds of Muscles**
   1. _____ muscles are attached to the bones by _____ .
      a. These muscles are _____ (voluntary/involuntary).
      b. The purpose of these muscles is to _____

         _____ .

   2. _____ muscles line some of the body's _____ .
      a. These muscles are _____ (voluntary/involuntary).
      b. The purpose of these muscles is to _____

         _____ .

   3. The _____ muscle is the only one of its kind.
      a. This muscle is _____ (voluntary/involuntary).
      b. The purpose of this muscle is to _____

         _____ .

---

[106] Paris & Paris, 2001; Pressley & Hilden, 2006; Veenman, 2011.

[107] Bulgren, Marquis, Lenz, Deshler, & Schumaker, 2011; Ku et al., 2008; McCrudden & Schraw, 2007; R. E. Reynolds & Shirey, 1988; Veenman, 2011.

[108] Questions from A. King, 1992, p. 309.

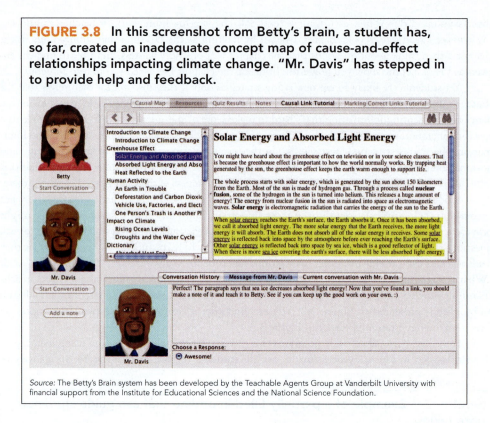

FIGURE 3.8 In this screenshot from Betty's Brain, a student has, so far, created an inadequate concept map of cause-and-effect relationships impacting climate change. "Mr. Davis" has stepped in to provide help and feedback.

Source: The Betty's Brain system has been developed by the Teachable Agents Group at Vanderbilt University with financial support from the Institute for Educational Sciences and the National Science Foundation.

previously learned or to self-check their understandings of particular concepts they've recently been asked to learn.[109] An example is Betty's Brain, a computer-based learning environment in which students read several resources about a topic such as thermodynamics or climate change and then create a concept map representing the cause-and-effect relationships they discover in the resources. Students are told that a "child" named Betty will learn about the topic through the map they create and that, as Betty's "teacher," they should periodically assess her understandings with questions or a quiz. If Betty doesn't perform well, students must work to improve her understandings, and in the process, they learn a great deal about the topic themselves. For example, Figure 3.8 shows an in-progress unit on climate change. The student/teacher has made some inappropriate causal links in her concept map, leading computer-based Betty to perform poorly on assessments. A virtual "mentor" (Mr. Davis) has stepped in to provide guidance about how to identify cause-and-effect relationships in a small section of text. Here the student has just correctly identified a *sea ice decreases absorbed light energy* relationship, and Mr. Davis has suggested her next course of action.[110]

Communicate that acquiring knowledge is a dynamic, ongoing process—that one never completely knows something.

Epistemic beliefs about particular academic disciplines, as well as about knowledge and learning more generally, have a significant impact on how students study, what they learn, how readily they apply classroom subject matter, and how often they critically evaluate it. Instruction in study strategies alone won't necessarily change those beliefs.[111]

One possible way to change students' epistemic beliefs is to talk specifically about the nature of knowledge and learning—for instance, to describe learning as an active, ongoing process of finding interconnections among ideas and constructing increasingly complex understandings.[112] But

---

[109] Azevedo & Witherspoon, 2009; Koedinger, Aleven, Roll, & Baker, 2009.

[110] For more information about *Betty's Brain,* see Leelawong & Biswas, 2008; Segedy, Kinnebrew, & Biswas, 2013; also go to teachableagents.org

[111] Schraw & Moshman, 1995.

[112] Gaskins & Pressley, 2007; Muis et al., 2006; Schommer, 1994b.

probably a more effective approach is to provide classroom experiences that lead students to discover that knowledge must necessarily be a dynamic, rather than static, entity and to realize that successful learning sometimes occurs only through effort and persistence. For example, teachers can have students address complex issues and problems that have no clear-cut right or wrong answers.[113] They can teach strategies for gathering data and testing competing hypotheses.[114] Teachers can ask students to compare several explanations of a particular phenomenon or event and consider the validity and strength of evidence supporting each one.[115] And they can show students, perhaps by presenting puzzling phenomena, that their own current understandings, and in some cases even those of experts in the field, don't yet adequately explain all of human experience.[116]

MyEdLab
Video Example 3.8.

What strategies does this teacher use to communicate to students that acquiring knowledge is a dynamic, ongoing process?

Teachers play an important role in promoting students' self-regulation skills and metacognitive development. Teachers can do so in a variety of ways, including modeling effective self-regulation and metacognitive strategies and designing instructional activities that allow students to practice these strategies. In the hotlinked Self-Check quiz and Application Exercise that follow, you can check and apply your understandings related to Big Idea 3.5:

> *Effective teachers foster students' self-regulation skills and metacognitive development in age-appropriate ways.*

MyEdLab **Self-Check 3.5**

MyEdLab **Application Exercise 3.5.** This exercise allows you to examine a teacher's approach to helping students become more self-regulated.

3.6 CREATING A CLASSROOM ENVIRONMENT THAT NURTURES COMPLEX PROCESSES

Big Idea 3.6 Effective teachers create conditions that encourage students to engage in transfer, creative problem solving, and critical thinking related to classroom subject matter.

In the opening case study, the upcoming state competency exam puts pressure on Ms. Gaunt to move quickly through the eighth-grade math curriculum. Unfortunately, such *high-stakes tests* lead many teachers to emphasize basic facts, concepts, and procedures, with little regard for what students might *do* with these things (we'll talk more about high-stakes tests in Chapter 10).[117] If teachers focus classroom activities on the learning of isolated facts, and if they also use assessment techniques that emphasize knowledge of those facts, students will naturally begin to believe that school learning involves nothing more than mindlessly absorbing information and regurgitating it later on. But if teachers instead focus activities on *doing things with* information—applying it to new situations, using it to solve problems, critically evaluating it, and so on—then students should acquire many thinking skills that will serve them well in the outside world. The following instructional practices are apt to promote a variety of complex cognitive processes simultaneously.

Create an atmosphere in which transfer, creative problem solving, and critical thinking are both expected and valued.

If students are to apply classroom subject matter to new situations and problems and to think creatively and critically about it, they must see classroom topics as things they can actually use—as things that in some way *matter* to them. Furthermore, students must believe that they can express conflicting opinions, occasionally think "outside the box," and make mistakes without fear of

---

[113] Feucht, 2010; P. M. King & Kitchener, 2002; Schommer-Aikins, Bird, & Bakken, 2010; Yang & Tsai, 2010.

[114] Andre & Windschitl, 2003; P. M. King & Kitchener, 2002; C. L. Smith, Maclin, Houghton, & Hennessey, 2000.

[115] Andre & Windschitl, 2003; Chinn, 2006; P. M. King & Kitchener, 2002; Rule & Bendixen, 2010; vanSledright & Limón, 2006.

[116] Rule & Bendixen, 2010; Vosniadou, 1991; Yang & Tsai, 2010.

[117] Baer & Garrett, 2010; Hursh, 2007; Jacob, 2003; Jones, Jones, & Hargrove, 2003; R. M. Ryan & Brown, 2005.

censure or embarrassment. Here we're talking about the overall psychological atmosphere—the classroom climate—in which learning takes place. Following are more specific suggestions:[118]

- Conduct some activities in which students know that their work won't be evaluated.
- Welcome unusual ideas, even those that might fly in the face of conventional ways of thinking.
- Insist that all students try to understand and be respectful of diverse perspectives.
- Consistently communicate that mistakes and failures are inevitable in any challenging activity.
- Give students several opportunities to get constructive feedback before turning in a final product.

Teach complex thinking skills within the context of specific topics and content domains.

Teachers occasionally run across packaged curricular programs designed to teach study skills, problem solving, creativity, or critical thinking. As a general rule, however, teachers should teach complex cognitive processes *not* as separate entities, but instead within the context of day-to-day academic topics. For example, they might teach critical thinking and problem-solving skills during science lessons or teach creative thinking during writing instruction.[119] And to help students become truly effective learners, teachers should teach study strategies in *every* academic discipline.[120] For example, when presenting new information in class, a teacher might (1) suggest how students can organize their notes, (2) describe mnemonics for facts and procedures that are hard to remember, and (3) ask various students to summarize the main points of a lesson. When assigning textbook pages to be read at home, a teacher might (4) suggest that students think about what they already know about a topic before beginning to read, (5) provide questions for students to ask themselves as they read, and (6) have students create concept maps interrelating key ideas.

Pursue topics in depth rather than superficially.

Students can't just study the material on one occasion if they'll be expected to apply classroom subject matter to real-world situations and problems, use it flexibly and creatively, and think critically about it. Instead, students must *master* the material. Ultimately, students should gain a thorough, conceptual understanding of topics that can help them make better sense of their world and function more effectively in adult society. This less-is-more principle applies across the board: Teaching a few topics in depth is almost invariably more effective than skimming over the surface of a great many.[121]

Provide numerous and varied opportunities to apply classroom subject matter to new situations and authentic problems.

The more that students practice using what they've learned to address new tasks and problems—and the more *diverse* those tasks and problems are—the greater the probability that they'll apply school subject matter in future situations, including contexts outside of school.[122] For example, a teacher might show students how human digestion processes have implications for nutrition and physical well-being, how physics concepts apply to automobile engines and home construction, or how principles of economics have an impact on global climate change.

One widely recommended approach is to use authentic activities, activities similar or identical to those that students might encounter in real-world contexts. For example, students acquire better writing skills when they write stories and essays for a real audience—perhaps classmates or peers on the Internet—rather than completing traditional workbook exercises.[123] They gain a more complete understanding of how to use and interpret maps when they construct their *own* maps rather

[118] Beghetto & Kaufman, 2010; Engle, 2006; Lubart & Mouchiroud, 2003; D. N. Perkins & Ritchhart, 2004; Rule & Bendixen, 2010.

[119] Abrami et al., 2008; Beal, Arroyo, & Cohen, 2009; Bonney & Sternberg, 2011; Desoete, Roeyers, & De Clercq, 2003.

[120] Hattie et al., 1996; Meltzer et al., 2007; Paris & Paris, 2001; Veenman, 2011.

[121] Amabile & Hennessey, 1992; Brophy et al., 2009; N. Frederiksen, 1984a; M. C. Linn, 2008; D. N. Perkins, 1990; Prawat, 1989; Rittle-Johnson, Siegler, & Alibali, 2001.

[122] Gijbels, Dochy, Van den Bossche, & Segers, 2005; Gresalfi & Lester, 2009; M. C. Linn, 2008; J. R. Stone, Alfeld, & Pearson, 2008; J. F. Wagner, 2010.

[123] Benton, 1997; Graham, 2006; E. H. Hiebert & Fisher, 1992.

than answering workbook questions about maps (e.g., see Figure 3.9).[124] And they're more likely to check their solutions to math problems—in particular, to make sure their solutions make logical sense—when they use math for real-life tasks.[125]

Authentic activities can also be highly motivating.[126] As an example, consider one high school student's recollection of a ninth-grade moon-tracking activity:

> It was the first time I can remember in school doing something that wasn't in the textbook . . . like we were real scientists or something. We had to keep data sheets, measure the time and angle of the moonrise every day for a month. It drove my mom nuts because sometimes we'd be eating dinner, and I'd look at my watch and race out the door! We had to measure the river near us to see how it was affected by the moon . . . I went down to the river more than I have in my whole life, I think. Then we had to do the calculations, that was another step, and we had to chart our findings. The test was to analyze your findings and tell what they meant about the relationship of the tides and the moon. . . . I felt that I did something real, and I could see the benefit of it.[127]

By placing classroom activities in real-world contexts, teachers help students discover the reasons that they're learning academic subject matter. Accordingly, authentic activities may be especially valuable in working with students who are at risk for academic failure.[128]

Authentic activities can be developed for virtually any area of the curriculum. For example, teachers might have students:

- Write an editorial
- Participate in a debate
- Create a class website
- Converse in a foreign language
- Make a video
- Perform in a concert
- Plan a personal budget
- Design an electrical circuit

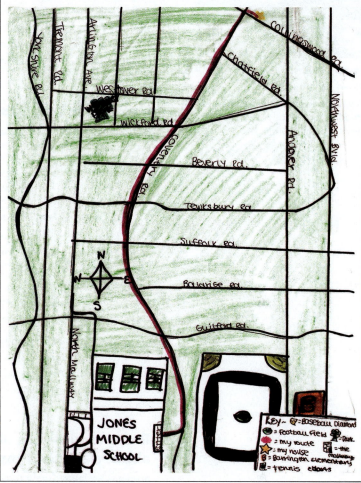

FIGURE 3.9 In an authentic mapping activity, 12-year-old Mary Lynn constructed this map of the area between her home and school.

Some authentic activities take the form of **problem-based** or **project-based learning**, in which students acquire new knowledge and skills as they work on complex problems or projects similar to those they might find in the outside world.[129] Occasionally authentic activities may also involve **service learning**—that is, they involve projects that directly or indirectly enhance the quality of life in the outside community. To be truly effective in enhancing students' learning—rather than sources of frustration and failure—most authentic activities require considerable teacher support.[130] Furthermore, they should be sufficiently simple that they don't impose an unmanageable cognitive load.[131]

It probably isn't a good idea to fill the entire school day with complex, authentic tasks, however, for two reasons. First, students can sometimes achieve automaticity for basic skills more

think about it
What authentic activities might you use to facilitate students' transfer of the discipline(s) you hope to teach?

---

[124] Gregg & Leinhardt, 1994.

[125] Cognition and Technology Group at Vanderbilt, 1993; J. R. Stone et al., 2008.

[126] M. Barnett, 2005; Marks, 2000; Wirkala & Kuhn, 2011.

[127] Wasley, Hampel, & Clark, 1997, pp. 117–118.

[128] L. W. Anderson & Pellicer, 1998; Christenson & Thurlow, 2004; Tate, 1995.

[129] Hmelo-Silver, 2004, 2006; Hung, Jonassen, & Liu, 2008; Mergendoller, Markham, Ravitz, & Larmer, 2006; Polman, 2004; Wirkala & Kuhn, 2011.

[130] Hmelo-Silver, Duncan, & Chinn, 2007; Krajcik & Blumenfeld, 2006; Mergendoller et al., 2006; Spiro & DeSchryver, 2009.

[131] Kester, Paas, & van Merriënboer, 2010; Plass, Kalyuga, & Leutner, 2010.

MyEdLab
Video Example 3.9.

In what authentic activities are the students engaged for this high school service learning project?

quickly when they practice them in relative isolation from other activities. For example, when learning to play the violin, students need to master their fingering before they join an orchestra, and when learning to play soccer, they need to practice dribbling and passing before they can effectively play a game.[132] Second, some authentic activities may be too expensive and time-consuming to warrant regular use in the classroom.[133] In these cases, after-school programs can provide a time for students to engage in more authentic tasks.[134] Teachers' highest priority should be to encourage learning processes that enhance long-term retention and transfer of classroom subject matter—organization, elaboration, comprehension monitoring, and so on—through whatever kinds of tasks achieve that end.[135]

Use technology to simulate real-world-like tasks and problems.

Some simulations promote complex cognitive processes within seemingly authentic contexts—in some cases in the form of video or computer games that students play alone or with peers. Following are examples:

- *Civilization.* Learners begin "living" several thousand years ago and, over many centuries, build an increasingly complex society. In an effort to survive and thrive, they must make decisions about food, natural resources, government, emerging technologies, and interactions with other social and cultural groups (www.civilization.com).

- *StockTrak.* Learners "invest" in various stocks in the stock market and track profits and losses in their virtual "portfolios" over time (www.stocktrak.com).

- *Extreme Event.* During a disaster simulation, learners respond to disasters and build community resilience by working together to make decisions and solve problems (https://www .koshland-science-museum.org/explore-the-science/extreme-event).

Simulations are often both motivating and challenging—thereby keeping students on task for extended periods—and can significantly enhance students' critical thinking and problem-solving skills.[136] A particular advantage is that they can be designed in ways that keep students' cognitive load within reasonable bounds and appropriately structure and guide students' efforts.[137]

Present questions and tasks that require students to think flexibly about classroom topics.

Students are more likely to think creatively when their teacher poses questions and tasks that require them to use previously learned information in new and unusual ways—in other words, to engage in divergent thinking.[138] Here are two examples in the domain of history:

- "In the 12th century, the Khmer people in Southeast Asia created Angkor Wat, a huge stone temple more than 200 feet high. The stones were extremely heavy, and the people had no cement. How might they have built the temple?"[139]

- "In the 1860s, Americans used the Pony Express to send messages quickly across the country. In what other ways might people have sent long-distance messages at that time?"[140]

It's also helpful to encourage students to encode situations and problems in multiple ways so that they don't get locked into mental sets that exclude potentially effective approaches and solutions. For example, a teacher might ask students to work in cooperative groups to identify several different ways of representing a single problem on paper—perhaps as a formula, a table,

---

[132] J. R. Anderson, Reder, & Simon, 1996; Bransford et al., 2006.

[133] M. M. Griffin & Griffin, 1994.

[134] Schnittka, Brandt, Jones, & Evans, 2012.

[135] J. R. Anderson et al., 1996.

[136] Barab, Gresalfi, & Ingram-Goble, 2010; Black, Khan, & Huang, 2014; de Jong, 2011; Kuhn & Pease, 2008; Squire, 2011; Zohar & Aharon-Kraversky, 2005.

[137] de Jong, 2011; Kuhn & Pease, 2010; Sarama & Clements, 2009.

[138] Bransford et al., 2009; D. N. Perkins, 1990; Sternberg, 2010.

[139] Question courtesy of Jeff Ormrod.

[140] Feldhusen & Treffinger, 1980.

and a graph.[141] Alternatively, a teacher might have students explore potential ways of solving a problem *before* teaching them the concepts or procedures an expert would use to solve it.[142] And certainly, a teacher should mix the kinds of problems that students tackle in any single practice session. Mixing problem types requires students to think carefully about which problem-solving procedures are appropriate for each one so that they don't fall into a particular mental set and simply apply the same procedures over and over again mindlessly.[143]

Encourage critical evaluation of information and ideas presented in printed materials and online.

To become effective life-long learners, students must learn that not all sources of information can be trusted—that some messages presented through various media are misleading or blatantly wrong. In our current era of ever-expanding information technology, taking a critical stance toward new information is now more important than ever. For example, although entries in the popular website Wikipedia are generally accurate, they occasionally include inaccuracies added by nonexperts. Furthermore, virtually anyone can post personal beliefs and opinions somewhere on the Internet (e.g., blogs)—often presenting these things as irrefutable "facts"—and it's quite easy for readers to be fooled. Many students at all grade levels—even many college students—naively assume that almost everything they read on the Internet is fact.[144]

Critical thinking encompasses a diverse set of skills, and so strategies for encouraging it are many and varied. Here are several suggestions:

- Encourage some intellectual skepticism—for instance, by urging students to question and challenge the ideas they read and hear—and communicate the epistemic belief that people's knowledge and understanding of any single topic might continue to change over time.[145]

- Model critical thinking—for instance, by thinking aloud while analyzing a persuasive argument or scientific report.[146]

- Give students many opportunities to practice critical thinking—for instance, by identifying flaws in the arguments of persuasive essays, evaluating the quality and usefulness of scientific findings, and using evidence and logic to support particular viewpoints.[147]

- Ask questions such as these to encourage critical thinking:
  - Who produced this document? What biases or predispositions did the author or authors have?
  - What persuasive technique is the author using? Is it valid, or is it designed to mislead the reader?
  - What assumptions underlie the assertions and arguments presented?
  - What information contradicts information in other documents?
  - What reasons support the conclusion? What reasons *don't* support it?
  - What actions might I take to improve the design of this study?[148]

- Have students debate controversial issues from several perspectives, and occasionally ask them to take a perspective quite different from their own.[149]

- Embed critical thinking skills within the context of authentic activities as a way of helping students retrieve those skills later on, both in the workplace and in other aspects of adult life.[150]

The Classroom Strategies box "Fostering Critical Thinking" presents examples of what teachers might do in language arts, social studies, and science.

MyEdLab
Video Example 3.10.

What strategies does this middle school teacher use to teach students critical thinking skills in a lesson about persuasive writing?

---

[141] Brenner et al., 1997; J. C. Turner, Meyer, et al., 1998.

[142] Niu & Zhou, 2010; D. L. Schwartz et al., 2012.

[143] Dunlosky, 2013; E. J. Langer, 2000; Mayfield & Chase, 2002.

[144] Manning, Lawless, Goldman, & Braasch, 2011; M. J. Metzger et al., 2003; Wiley et al., 2009.

[145] Afflerbach & Cho, 2010; Kardash & Scholes, 1996; Kuhn, 2001a.

[146] J. Moon, 2008; Onosko & Newmann, 1994.

[147] Halpern, 1998; Kuhn & Crowell, 2011; Monte-Sano, 2008; Yang & Tsai, 2010.

[148] Questions based on De La Paz & Felton, 2010, p. 182; Halpern, 1998, p. 454; S. A. Stahl & Shanahan, 2004, pp. 110–111.

[149] E. M. Nussbaum, 2008; E. M. Nussbaum & Edwards, 2011; Reiter, 1994.

[150] Derry et al., 1998; Halpern, 1998; Muis & Duffy, 2013; Sandoval, Sodian, Koerber, & Wong, 2014.

CLASSROOM STRATEGIES

Fostering Critical Thinking

- **Teach elements of critical thinking.**
  In a unit on persuasion and argumentation, a middle school language arts teacher explains that a sound argument meets three criteria: (1) The evidence presented to justify the argument is accurate and consistent; (2) the evidence is relevant to and provides sufficient support for the conclusion; and (3) little or no information has been omitted that, if present, would lead to a contradictory conclusion. The teacher then has students practice applying these criteria to a variety of persuasive and argumentative essays.

- **Foster epistemic beliefs that encourage critical thinking.**
  Rather than teach history as a collection of facts to be memorized, a high school teacher portrays the discipline as an attempt by informed but inevitably biased scholars to interpret and make sense of historical events. On several occasions, he asks students to read two or three different historians' accounts of the same incident and to look for evidence of personal bias in each one.

- **Embed critical thinking skills within the context of authentic activities.**
  In a unit on statistical and scientific reasoning, an eighth-grade science class studies concepts related to probability, correlation, and experimental control. Then, as part of a simulated legislative hearing, the students work in small groups to develop arguments for or against a legislative bill concerning the marketing and use of vitamins and other dietary supplements. To find evidence to support their arguments, the students apply what they've learned about statistics and experimentation as they read and analyze journal articles and government reports about the possible benefits and drawbacks of nutritional supplements.

- **Teach students how to evaluate the accuracy of information posted on Internet websites.**
  On a teacher-created educational website called "All About Explorers" (allaboutexplorers.com), elementary students practice distinguishing between credible and questionable information while searching for facts about well-known early explorers. For example, as students look for information about Christopher Columbus, they visit a bogus "website" that describes Columbus as having been born in 1951 but dying in 1906—a timeline that obviously makes no sense—and asserts that the king and queen of Spain called Columbus on his toll-free number.

Sources: Derry, Levin, Osana, & Jones, 1998 (statistics example based on this study); Halpern, 1997 (criteria for a sound argument); Paxton, 1999 (bias in history example).

Support complex cognitive processes through group discussions and projects.

Group discussions and activities can help students gain a better understanding of a topic and promote complex cognitive processes, especially when structured and scaffolded to some degree.[151] When students talk with one another, they must verbalize—and therefore become more metacognitively aware of—what and how they themselves are thinking. They also hear other (possibly better) study strategies, problem-solving techniques, and critical analyses. And by working together, students can often accomplish more difficult tasks than they would accomplish on their own.

One effective approach is to teach students to ask one another, and then answer, thought-provoking questions about the material they're studying—for instance, *Why is it that such-and-such is true?*[152] In the following dialogue, fifth graders Katie and Janelle are working together to study class material about tide pools. Katie's job is to ask Janelle questions that encourage elaboration:

> *Katie:* How are the upper tide zone and the lower tide zone different?
>
> *Janelle:* They have different animals in them. Animals in the upper tide zone and splash zone can handle being exposed—have to be able to use the rain and sand and wind and sun—and they don't need that much water and the lower tide animals do.
>
> *Katie:* And they can be softer 'cause they don't have to get hit on the rocks.
>
> *Janelle:* Also predators. In the spray zone it's because there's predators like us people and all different kinds of stuff that can kill the animals and they won't survive, but the lower tide zone has not as many predators.
>
> *Katie:* But wait! Why do the animals in the splash zone have to survive?[153]

---

[151] Jadallah et al., 2011; E. M. Nussbaum, 2008; A. M. O'Donnell, Hmelo-Silver, & Erkens, 2006; Vaughn et al., 2011; Wentzel & Watkins, 2011.

[152] Kahl & Woloshyn, 1994; A. King, 1994, 1999; Rosenshine, Meister, & Chapman, 1996; E. Wood et al., 1999.

[153] A. King, 1999, p. 97.

Notice how the two girls are continually relating the animals' characteristics to survival in different tide zones, and eventually, Katie asks why animals in the splash zone even *need* to survive—a question that clearly reflects critical thinking.

Incorporate complex cognitive processes into assessment activities.

It can be fairly easy to construct assignments and tests that assess knowledge of basic facts and procedures. But it's ultimately more important that teachers assess what students can *do* with what they've learned.[154] As an illustration, Figure 3.10 presents an assessment task that asks students to apply their knowledge of geographic principles to a new situation. By consistently incorporating application of classroom topics into assessment tasks and problems, teachers clearly communicate that academic subject matter can and should be flexibly and creatively used in many different contexts.

FIGURE 3.10 Example of an assessment activity that asks students to apply what they have learned in geography to a new situation

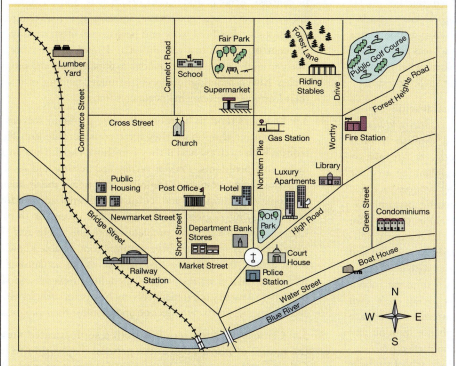

Here is a map of a small city named Riverdale. Apply principles of geography to answer the following questions. In each case, explain your reasoning.

1. Where in the city would you be most likely to find a steel mill?
2. Where would you be most likely to find upper-income, single-family homes?
3. Which area of the city appears to be undergoing urban renewal?
4. Where in the city would you expect traffic to be heaviest?

Answer Key: (1) between the river and the railroad tracks, where both water and transportation are easily accessible; (2) near the riding stables and golf course, as horseback riding and golf are popular but expensive forms of recreation; (3) the southeastern part of the city, as evidenced by the luxury apartments and condominiums; (4) in the south central area, which appears to be the central business district.

---

[154] For example, see M. C. Linn & Eylon, 2011; Shepard, Hammerness, Darling-Hammond, & Rust, 2005.

Teachers can implement many different strategies to help students transfer their knowledge and skills and support their problem solving, creativity, and critical thinking. These strategies include those that affect the overall classroom climate, as well as those that lead to the design of effective assignments and assessments. In the hotlinked Self-Check quiz and Application Exercise that follow, you can check and apply your understandings related to Big Idea 3.6:

Effective teachers create conditions that encourage students to engage in transfer, creative problem solving, and critical thinking related to classroom subject matter.

MyEdLab **Self-Check 3.6**

MyEdLab **Application Exercise 3.6.**   In this exercise, you will identify instructional strategies that a teacher uses to encourage students to think creatively as they complete an assignment.

3 SUMMARY

Complex cognitive processes are those in which learners go far beyond the information they've learned, perhaps to better understand it, apply it to a new situation, use it to solve a problem or create a product, or critically evaluate it. The Big Ideas presented at the beginning of the chapter can help us summarize what researchers and experienced educators have learned about such processes.

■ **3.1: Effective learners regularly plan for their learning, monitor it, reflect on it, and strive to improve it.** *Self-regulation*—the process of directing, monitoring, and evaluating one's own performance—affects students' learning. Self-regulation includes establishing goals for performance, planning a course of action, giving self-instructions, monitoring progress, actively controlling motivation and emotions, evaluating performance, and self-imposing consequences (either internal or external) for success and failure. Most learners become increasingly self-regulating with age, in part as a result of brain maturation and in part through co-regulated learning activities with adults.

Metacognition—which literally means "thinking about thinking"—includes knowledge and beliefs about one's own cognitive processes, along with conscious attempts to engage in behaviors and cognitive processes that enhance learning and memory. Although metacognitive awareness and effective learning strategies improve with age, even many high school students are quite naive about how they can best study and learn classroom subject matter. To some degree, learners' *epistemic beliefs* regarding the nature of knowledge and learning affect the study strategies they use. For example, students who realize that reading is a constructive process are more likely to engage in meaningful learning as they read and more likely to undergo conceptual change when they encounter ideas that contradict what they currently believe.

■ **3.2: Specific facts don't always have much applicability to the outside world, but many general principles, strategies, and attitudes acquired at school are potentially applicable to a wide variety of situations.** When learners apply something they've learned in one context to a new context, *transfer* is occurring. Transfer of specific facts is most common when a new situation appears to be similar to a previous one in which certain knowledge and skills have come into play (e.g., knowing how to count in French can help someone learn how to count in Spanish).

In contrast, general study strategies, beliefs, and attitudes (e.g., knowing how to take good notes, realizing that mastering classroom topics takes hard work and persistence) often transfer from one content domain to a very different domain. Learners are most likely to apply school subject matter to outside tasks and problems if they have a meaningful conceptual understanding of it and if their learning environment encourages transfer.

■ **3.3: Learners tend to be more effective problem solvers and more creative thinkers if they have considerable knowledge from which to draw and if they can think flexibly about new tasks and problems.** *Problem solving*—addressing and resolving an unanswered question or troubling situation—and *creativity*—developing an original and culturally appropriate product—involve varying degrees of convergent and divergent thinking. Learners can usually solve problems more effectively and think more creatively when they have acquired considerable knowledge about a topic, have automatized basic skills but *not* automatized particular ways of representing challenging problems and situations, have a variety of problem-solving heuristics at their disposal, and can metacognitively reflect on and monitor their progress.

■ **3.4: Critical thinking requires both a sophisticated view of the nature of knowledge and a general disposition to carefully scrutinize and evaluate new information and ideas.** *Critical thinking* involves evaluating the accuracy, credibility, and worth of information and lines of reasoning. It takes a variety of forms, such as analyzing persuasive arguments, identifying statements that do and don't support a particular conclusion, and judging the value of data collected through different research methods. When learners have sophisticated epistemic beliefs (e.g., a realization that one's understanding of a topic continues to evolve over time) and are generally predisposed to question and evaluate new information, they're more likely to think critically about what they read and hear.

■ **3.5: Effective teachers foster students' self-regulation skills and metacognitive development in age-appropriate ways.** Many learners at all grade levels benefit from explicit instruction and support in how to self-regulate their behaviors and cognitive processes. For example, teachers might ask students to set specific goals for their learning or provide concrete criteria by which students can evaluate their accomplishments. Teachers can foster students' metacognitive development by (1) encouraging self-reflection about study techniques and problem-solving strategies, (2) teaching specific strategies for studying and remembering academic subject matter, and (3) providing classroom experiences that reveal the dynamic nature of knowledge and the effortful persistence that true mastery requires.

■ **3.6: Effective teachers create conditions that encourage students to engage in transfer, creative problem solving, and critical thinking related to classroom subject matter.**

Students are more likely to engage in complex cognitive processes if these processes are integrated into the ongoing curriculum in diverse content domains and if they feel psychologically safe to take risks and make mistakes. Opportunities to apply new topics and skills should be commonplace, as should group discussions that enable students to critique and build on one another's ideas. Ultimately, transfer, creative problem solving, critical thinking, and other complex cognitive processes should be the expectation and norm in the classroom, not only in lessons but also in assessment activities.

PRACTICE FOR YOUR LICENSURE EXAM

Interview with Charlie

Seventeen-year-old Charlie has been earning As in his high school classes; now, at the end of his 11th-grade year, he has a 4.0 grade point average. He has particular interests in science and technology; in fact, in addition to challenging coursework at school, Charlie has taken several computer courses at a local community college. His mother says, "He invests a lot of time in projects (writing papers, reports, etc.) but doesn't crack open a book to read or study often."

One afternoon Charlie has the following discussion with an adult:

Adult: Why do you think your grades have been so good?

Charlie: I do the homework, and I do well on the tests. I don't really study—I just make sure to focus on the homework and make sure it makes sense to me. . . . What I do depends on the circumstances. For math and chemistry, just doing homework and going over it with friends during lunch or something helps. That's about all I do for studying.

Adult: What do you mean, "make sure it makes sense"?

Charlie: If I look at the problem and I know the process of how to do it, like in math and chemistry.

Adult: Let's say that a teacher assigns a textbook chapter for you to read sometime in the next three days. What things would you do—in your head, that is—when you read the chapter?

Charlie: Depends on the book and the class. Probably just skim it. Is the teacher just telling us to read it, or are there questions with it? I think about those things. We have a textbook in my computer programming class. I go through the chapter, look at examples and the [computer] code. I don't look at the other stuff.

Adult: I haven't heard you talk about trying to memorize anything.

Charlie: We do have to memorize. If I write it down once—a formula or something—and can use it in a few problems, I get it.

Adult: Do you ever use flashcards?

Charlie: Flashcards wouldn't work for what I do.

Adult: How do you know when you've really learned something—I mean, *really* learned it—and will remember it for a long time?

Charlie: When I do a couple of problems and they don't seem as hard . . . when I can get the right answer every time.

Adult: Your teachers probably expect you to do a lot of things outside of class, right? How do you make sure you get them all done?

Charlie: Making lists is really helpful, of everything that's due.

Adult: So what do you do with the lists?

Charlie: I either do things as soon as possible or else procrastinate, do it the night before. Sometimes I have a free block at the end of the day to do it. Or I go home and do my chemistry right away. Or I might wait until the last minute. It depends on whether I'm hanging out with friends.

1. **Multiple-choice question**

   Charlie says, "I don't really study—I just make sure to focus on the homework and make sure it makes sense to me." Which one of the following terms most accurately describes the nature of this statement?

   a. Algorithm

   b. Metacognition

   c. Critical thinking

   d. Divergent thinking

2. **Multiple-choice question**

   Which one of the following statements is the best example of *comprehension monitoring?*

   a. "Depends on the book and the class. Probably just skim it."

   b. "I go through the chapter, look at examples and the [computer] code. I don't look at the other stuff."

   c. "When I do a couple of problems and they don't seem as hard . . . when I can get the right answer every time."

   d. "I either do things as soon as possible or else procrastinate, do it the night before. Sometimes I have a free block at the end of the day to do it."

3. **Constructed-response question**

   Would you characterize Charlie's learning strategies as involving *rote learning* or *meaningful learning?* Use excerpts from the interview to support your answer.

   MyEdLab **Licensure Exam 3.1**

Ian Shaw/Alamy

4

Learning in Context

Big Ideas to Master in this Chapter

4.1 Learners' behaviors and cognitive processes are influenced by the specific stimuli and consequences in their immediate environment.

4.2 Learners co-construct their knowledge with individuals whose abilities are similar to or greater than their own.

4.3 The cultural, societal, and technological contexts in which learners grow up also influence their behaviors and cognitive processes, as do the academic domains that learners study in school and elsewhere.

4.4 Although various environmental contexts influence learners and their development, so, too, do learners influence the environments in which they live and grow.

4.5 Effective teachers create a classroom environment that encourages and supports productive behaviors and ways of thinking.

4.6 Effective teachers adapt instruction to the broader cultural and socioeconomic contexts in which students live.

CASE STUDY: WHY JACK WASN'T IN SCHOOL

Jack was a Native American seventh grader who lived in the Navajo Nation in the American Southwest. Although he enjoyed school, worked hard in his studies, and got along well with classmates, he'd been absent from school all week. In fact, he'd been absent from home as well, and his family (which didn't have a telephone) wasn't sure exactly where he was. Jack's English teacher described the situation to Donna Deyhle, an educator who had known Jack for many years:

> That seventh grader was away from home for 5 days, and his parents don't care! . . . Almost one-third of my Navajo students were absent this week. Their parents just don't support their education. How can I teach when they are not in my classes?

A few days later, Jack's sister explained why her parents had eventually begun to look for Jack:

> He went to see [the film] *Rambo II* with friends and never came home. If he was in trouble we would know. But now the family needs him to herd sheep tomorrow.

It was spring—time for the family to plant crops and shear the sheep—and all family members needed to help out. Jack's whereabouts were soon discovered, and the family stopped by Donna's house to share the news:

> Jack's dad said, "We found him." His mother turned in his direction and said teasingly, "Now maybe school will look easy!" Jack stayed at home for several days, helping with the irrigation of the corn field, before he decided to return to school.[1]

- Did you interpret Jack's absence from school in the same way his English teacher did, concluding that "his parents don't care" about his education? If so, how might your own cultural background have influenced your conclusion?
- Like most parents, Jack's mother and father cared deeply about his school achievement and general well-being. What alternative explanations might account for their behaviors in this situation?

Quite possibly you concluded that Jack and his parents don't place much value on formal education. If so, your conclusion might have been based on two widely held beliefs in your culture: (1) School should take priority over most activities at home and elsewhere, and (2) responsible parents insist that their children attend school. In reality, most Navajo children and adults appreciate the importance of a good education. To fully understand what transpired in Jack's family, we need to know a couple of things about Navajo culture. First, Navajo people place high value on individual autonomy: Even children must be self-sufficient and make their own decisions.[2] From this perspective, good parenting doesn't mean demanding that children do certain things or behave in certain ways; instead, Navajo parents offer suggestions and guidance, perhaps in the form of gentle teasing ("Now maybe school will look easy!"), that nudge children toward productive choices. But in addition to individual autonomy, Navajos value cooperation

---

[1] Three excerpts from Deyhle & LeCompte, 1999, pp. 127–128.
[2] Deyhle & LeCompte, 1999.

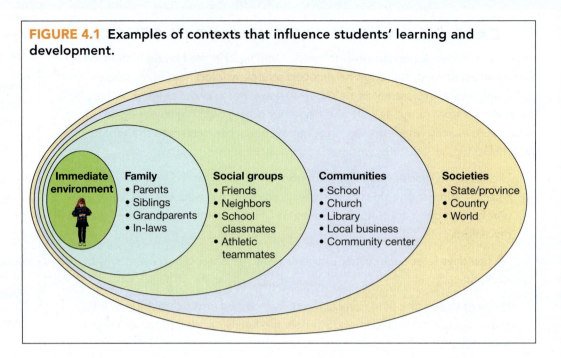

FIGURE 4.1 Examples of contexts that influence students' learning and development.

and interdependence, believing that community members should work together for the common good; hence Jack's highest priority was helping his family during planting season. Such respect for both individual decision making and cooperative interdependence is seen in many other Native American communities as well.[3]

Learning always takes place within particular *contexts*—not only within the immediate environment, but also within families, social groups, communities, and societies, as shown in Figure 4.1. Such contexts are the subject of this chapter. We'll begin by looking at the effects of learners' immediate surroundings—that is, the objects and events they encounter at any given time. Then, we'll gradually expand our field of vision to examine both the general contexts in which learners live—for example, their families, social groups, and communities—as well as the technological and academic legacies their society has bestowed upon them. Early in the chapter, we'll draw heavily from **behaviorism** and **social cognitive theory**, but as we proceed, contemporary **contextual theories** will increasingly guide our discussion. If you need a brief refresher on these perspectives, refer back to Table 2.1 in Chapter 2.

4.1 IMMEDIATE STIMULI AS CONTEXT

Big Idea 4.1 Learners' behaviors and cognitive processes are influenced by the specific stimuli and consequences in their immediate environment.

To some degree, learners' behaviors (also called **responses**) are influenced by the objects and events (called **stimuli**, which is plural for **stimulus**) in their immediate surroundings. For example, in the opening case study, Jack is enticed to see a movie with his friends and then, later, to help out with his family's farming chores. Several general principles sum up much of what researchers have discovered about how stimuli in a learner's immediate environment can influence the learner's behaviors—sometimes for the long run.

Some stimuli tend to elicit certain kinds of responses.

Certain stimuli in our lives naturally lead us to respond in particular ways. A friend's invitation to watch an action-packed adventure film might be hard to pass up. A highly biased newspaper editorial might make us angry and lead us to write a letter to the editor. Different pieces of music

---

[3] Chisholm, 1996; M. L. Manning & Baruth, 2009; Rogoff, 2003; Tyler et al., 2008.

evoke different moods and behavioral states, perhaps exciting or agitating us, perhaps provoking us to tap our feet or get on the dance floor, or perhaps helping us relax and "keep calm." A stimulus that precedes and evokes a particular response is known as an **antecedent stimulus**.

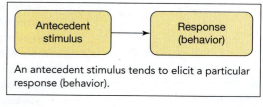

An antecedent stimulus tends to elicit a particular response (behavior).

In school settings, a variety of environmental conditions have been shown to bring about particular behaviors, sometimes for the better and sometimes for the worse. For example, preschoolers are more likely to interact with their peers if they have a relatively small area in which to play and the available toys (e.g., balls, puppets) encourage cooperation and group activity.[4] The kinds of games older children are asked to play influence their interpersonal behavior: Cooperative games promote cooperative behavior, whereas competitive games promote aggressive behavior.[5] The nature of academic assignments influences students' on-task behavior in the classroom. For instance, students are more likely to behave appropriately in class when they have some confidence that they'll be able to complete assigned tasks successfully.[6]

Learners are more likely to acquire behaviors that lead to desired consequences.

Learners often learn and perform new behaviors specifically because those behaviors lead to certain end results. Following are examples:

- Laura studies hard for her French vocabulary quiz. She gets an A on the quiz.
- Linda copies her answers to the French quiz from Laura's paper. She, too, gets an A.
- Julian changes the way he holds a basketball before shooting it toward the basket. He now makes more baskets than he used to.
- James throws paper clips at the girl beside him and discovers that this is a good way to get her attention.

To get something they want, then, learners can acquire either productive behaviors (e.g., studying, trying a new basketball strategy) or nonproductive ones (e.g., cheating, throwing paper clips).

When we talk about the effects of desired consequences on learners' behaviors, we're talking about **operant conditioning**, a form of learning described by many behaviorists and most notably by B. F. Skinner.[7] The central principle of operant conditioning is a simple one:

A response that is followed by a reinforcing stimulus (a reinforcer) is more likely to occur again.

When behaviors are consistently followed by desired consequences, they tend to increase in frequency. When behaviors don't produce results, they usually decrease and may disappear altogether.

Teachers often talk about giving students rewards for academic achievement and appropriate classroom behavior. But as you may have noticed, we haven't used the term *reward* in our description of operant conditioning, and for a very important reason. The word *reward* brings to mind things we'd all agree are pleasant and desirable—perhaps praise, money, or special privileges. But some individuals increase their behavior for consequences that others wouldn't find very appealing. A **reinforcer** is *any consequence that increases the frequency of a particular behavior,* whether or not other people would find that consequence desirable. The act of following a particular response with a reinforcer is known as **reinforcement**.

MyEdLab Content Extension 4.1. For our readers who haven't yet learned about B. F. Skinner's operant conditioning, this supplementary reading describes and illustrates some of his key ideas.

Reinforcers can take various forms, and different ones are effective for different learners. Some are **primary**

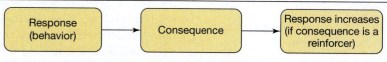

A response (behavior) may lead to a particular consequence. If the consequence then *increases* the response in the future, it's called a *reinforcer*.

---

[4] W. H. Brown, Fox, & Brady, 1987; Frost, Shin, & Jacobs, 1998; S. S. Martin, Brady, & Williams, 1991.

[5] Bay-Hinitz, Peterson, & Quilitch, 1994.

[6] Mac Iver, Reuman, & Main, 1995; Moore & Edwards, 2003; Mueller, Nkosi, & Hine, 2011; S. L. Robinson & Griesemer, 2006.

[7] For example, see B. F. Skinner, 1953, 1954, 1968. Some behaviorists instead use the term *instrumental conditioning*.

reinforcers, in that they serve a basic biological or psychological need. Food, water, sources of warmth, and oxygen are all primary reinforcers. To some extent, physical affection and cuddling seem to address built-in needs as well, and for an adolescent addicted to an illegal substance, the next "fix" is also a primary reinforcer.[8]

In contrast, **secondary reinforcers** don't satisfy any biological or psychological need; praise, money, good grades, and trophies are examples. Such stimuli may become reinforcing over time through their association with other stimuli that already have a reinforcing effect. For example, if praise is occasionally associated with a special candy treat from Mother, and if money often comes with a hug from Dad, the praise and money eventually become reinforcing in and of themselves.

All the examples mentioned so far are instances of **positive reinforcement**. Whenever a particular stimulus is *presented* after a behavior and the behavior increases as a result, positive reinforcement has occurred. Don't be misled by the word *positive,* which in this case has nothing to do with the pleasantness or general desirability of the stimulus being presented. Positive reinforcement can occur even when the presented stimulus is one that others might think is *un*pleasant or *un*desirable. Instead, *positive* simply means *adding* something to the situation. Although many students will behave in ways that earn teacher praise, others may behave to get themselves *any* form of teacher attention, even a scolding.[9] Most students will work for A-level grades, but a few may actually prefer Cs or even Fs. (As a school psychologist, one of us authors worked with a high school student who used Fs as a way to get revenge on his overly controlling parents.) Depending on the individual, any one of these stimuli—praise, a scolding, an A, or an F—can be a positive reinforcer. Following are examples of the forms positive reinforcement might take:

- A *concrete reinforcer* is an actual object—something that can be touched (e.g., a sticker, eraser, or toy).
- A *social reinforcer* is a gesture or sign (e.g., a smile, attention, praise, or "thank you") that one person gives another, usually to communicate positive regard.
- An *activity reinforcer* is an opportunity to engage in a favorite pastime. Learners will often do one thing, even something they don't like to do, if completing the task enables them to do something they enjoy.[10]
- Sometimes the simple message that an answer is correct or that a task has been done well—*positive feedback*—is reinforcement enough. Positive feedback is most effective when it tells learners in explicit terms what they're doing well and what they can do to improve their performance even further (see Figure 4.2).[11]

think about it
Can you think of other examples of secondary reinforcers? (For some examples, click **here**.)

Teachers' and peers' attention is often a *positive* reinforcer—that is, it *increases* the behavior it follows—even if the messages being communicated are intended to discourage the behavior.

The reinforcers just listed are **extrinsic reinforcers**, those provided by the external environment (often by other people). Yet some positive reinforcers are **intrinsic reinforcers**, those that come from learners themselves or are inherent in tasks being performed. Learners engage in some activities simply because they enjoy the activities or like to feel competent and successful. When people perform certain behaviors in the absence of any external reinforcers—when they read an entire book without putting it down, do extra classwork without being asked, or practice with a neighborhood rock band into the early hours of the morning—they're probably working for the intrinsic reinforcers that such activities yield.

As you can see in Table 4.1, children's preferences for various kinds of reinforcers tend to change over the course of development. A second developmental trend is evident in the table as

[8] Harlow & Zimmerman, 1959; Lejuez, Schaal, & O'Donnell, 1998; Vollmer & Hackenberg, 2001.
[9] Dolezal & Kurtz, 2010; Mueller et al., 2011.
[10] Premack, 1959, 1963.
[11] Hattie & Gan, 2011; Narciss, 2008; Shute, 2008.

well: As children grow older, they become better able to handle **delay of gratification**. That is, they can forgo small, immediate reinforcers for the larger reinforcers their long-term efforts may bring down the road.[12] Whereas a preschooler or kindergartner is apt to choose a small reinforcer she can have *now* over a larger and more attractive reinforcer she can't get until tomorrow, an 8-year-old may be willing to wait a day or two for the more appealing item. Delay of gratification appears to peak in late adolescence, and some adolescents can delay gratification for several weeks or even longer.[13]

Learners are also likely to acquire behaviors that help them avoid or escape unpleasant circumstances.

Sometimes learners behave not to *get* something, but instead to *get rid of* something. On such occasions, negative reinforcement rather than positive reinforcement is at work. Whereas positive reinforcement involves the presentation of a stimulus, **negative reinforcement** brings about the increase of a behavior through the *removal* of a stimulus—typically an unpleasant one, at least from the learner's perspective. The word *negative* here isn't a value judgment. It simply refers to the act of *taking away* (rather than adding) a stimulus. To remember this, think of how positive and negative are used in mathematics: a positive sign is used to add and a negative sign is used to subtract. Following are examples of negative reinforcement, all of which lead to an increase in behavior by removing a stimulus:

- Reuben must read Charles Dickens's *A Tale of Two Cities* for his English literature class. He doesn't like having the assignment hanging over his head—he doesn't like worrying about it—so he finishes the book a week early. After he's done, the annoying *worry* feeling disappears. If he completes more assignments early, then the frequency of his behavior increases because the response takes away the worry feeling.

- Rhonda is in the same literature class. Each time she sits down at home to read *A Tale of Two Cities,* she finds it confusing and hard to understand. She quickly ends her study sessions by finding other things she "needs" to do, such as texting or playing basketball with neighbors. In other words, the *unpleasant feelings* disappear, at least for the time being. If she continues to avoid difficult assignments, then the frequency of her behavior increases because the response temporarily removes her unpleasant feelings.

- Some students in this literature class complain loudly and vigorously about having to read a book written by "some dead guy" instead of, say, *Hunger Games* or another novel popular with their peer group. In an emotional response to the students' resistance, their teacher explodes: "Stop it, *STOP IT*, **STOP IT!**" The students immediately quiet down. Through his action, the teacher terminates a *noisy and unpleasant situation*. If the students continue to quiet down when the teacher yells, then the frequency of his yelling behavior increases because it takes away the noisy and unpleasant situation.

In these examples, notice how negative reinforcement sometimes promotes desirable behaviors (such as completing an assignment early and quieting boisterous students) and at other times promotes undesirable behaviors (such as procrastination). Notice, as well, how students aren't the only ones who respond to negative reinforcement in the classroom: the teacher was reinforced for yelling when his class was overly loud. The teacher's emotional outbursts won't necessarily be productive over the long run, however, especially if he doesn't proactively address reasons why some students are having trouble making sense of Dickens's novel.

FIGURE 4.2 In commenting on Matt's book project, a middle school teacher is explicit about what Matt can do to improve but vague about what he has done well. Knowing what *specific* things made his summary and project description "very good" would help Matt repeat these things in the future.

> Science Fiction Book Project
> Name Matt
> Title 20,000 Leagues under The Sea
> Author Jules Verne
> Type of project:
> Comic strip
> Presentation:
> Very good summary and description of your project.
>   A
>
> Project:
> Excellent drawings, Matt!
> Captions in a strip should tell more of the story, though. You don't show how/why these places are connected.   A-

Negative reinforcement

NOT THE SAME AS PUNISHMENT

MyEdLab
Video Explanation 4.1.

This animated explanation can help you understand the nature of negative reinforcement.

[12] Atance, 2008; L. Green et al., 1994; Steinberg, Graham, et al., 2009.

[13] Achterberg, Peper, van Duijvenvoorde, Mandl, & Crone, 2016.

DEVELOPMENTAL TRENDS

Table 4.1 • Effective Reinforcers at Different Grade Levels

GRADE LEVEL	AGE-TYPICAL CHARACTERISTICS	EXAMPLE	SUGGESTED STRATEGIES
Grades K–2	• Preference for small, immediate reinforcers over larger, delayed ones • Examples of effective reinforcers: • Concrete reinforcers (e.g., stickers, crayons, small trinkets) • Teacher approval (e.g., smiles, praise) • Privileges (e.g., going to lunch first) • "Grown-up" responsibilities (e.g., taking absentee forms to the office)	When a kindergarten teacher asks children to choose between a small snack before morning recess or a larger one after recess, most of them clamor for the smaller, immediate snack.	• Give immediate praise for appropriate behavior. • Describe enjoyable consequences that may come later as a result of students' present behaviors. • Use colorful stickers to indicate a job well done; choose stickers that match students' interests (e.g., use favorite cartoon characters). • Have students line up for recess, lunch, or dismissal based on desired behaviors (e.g., "Table 2 is the quietest and can line up first"). • Rotate opportunities to perform classroom duties (e.g., feeding the goldfish, watering plants); make such duties contingent on appropriate behavior.
Grades 3–5	• Increasing ability to delay gratification (i.e., to put off small reinforcers in order to gain larger ones later on) • Examples of effective reinforcers: • Concrete reinforcers (e.g., snacks, pencils, small toys) • Teacher approval and positive feedback • "Good citizen" certificates • Free time (e.g., to draw or play games)	Nine-year-old Li-Mei glows with pride when her teacher praises her for helping a classmate with a challenging writing assignment.	• Use concrete reinforcers only occasionally, perhaps to add novelty to a classroom activity. • Award a certificate to a "citizen of the week," explicitly identifying things the recipient has done especially well; be sure that every student gets at least one certificate during the school year. • Plan a field trip for students with good attendance records (especially useful for students at risk for academic failure).
Grades 6–8	• Increasing desire to have social time with peers • Examples of effective reinforcers: • Free time with friends • Acceptance by and approval of peers • Teacher approval and emotional support (especially critical after the transition to middle school or junior high) • Specific positive feedback about academic performance (preferably given in private)	Students in a sixth-grade science class work diligently on an assigned lab activity, knowing that if they complete it before the end of class, they can have a few minutes to talk with friends.	• Make short periods of free time with peers (e.g., 5 minutes) contingent on accomplishing assigned tasks. • Spend one-on-one time with students, especially those who appear to be socially isolated. • Provide explicit feedback about what things students have done well (e.g., their use of colorful language in an essay or their prosocial behavior with classmates).
Grades 9–12	• Increasing ability to postpone immediate pleasures in order to gain desired long-term outcomes • Concern about getting good grades (especially for students who are applying to selective colleges) • Examples of effective reinforcers: • Opportunities to interact with friends • Specific positive feedback about academic performance • Public recognition for group performance (e.g., newspaper articles about a school club's public service work) • Positions of responsibility (e.g., being student representative to Faculty Senate)	When 16-year-old Deon's friends ask him to go to the movies on a Thursday evening, he declines. "I have to study for tomorrow's history test," he says. "If I keep my grades up, I'll have a better chance of getting a good college scholarship."	• Acknowledge students' concern about earning good grades, but focus their attention on the value of learning school subject matter for its own sake (see the discussion of achievement goals in Chapter 5). • Take precautions to ensure that cheating and plagiarism are *not* reinforced. • Publicize accomplishments of extracurricular groups and athletic teams in local news media. • Provide opportunities for independent decision making and responsibility, especially when students show an ability to make wise decisions.

Sources: E. M. Anderman & Mueller, 2010; L. H. Anderman, Patrick, Hruda, & Linnenbrink, 2002; Atance, 2008; Cizek, 2003; Fowler & Baer, 1981; L. Green, Fry, & Myerson, 1994; Hine & Fraser, 2002; Krumboltz & Krumboltz, 1972; M. G. Sanders, 1996; Shute, 2008; Steinberg, Graham, et al., 2009; M.-T. Wang & Holcombe, 2010.

Negative reinforcement often comes into play when students face especially difficult academic tasks.[14] The following explanation reveals what one student with a learning disability learned to do:

> When it comes time for reading I do everything under the sun I can to get out of it because it's my worst nightmare to read. I'll say I have to go to the bathroom or that I'm sick and I have to go to the nurse right now. My teacher doesn't know that I'll be walking around campus. She thinks I am going to the bathroom or whatever my lame excuse is. All I really want to do is get out of having to read.[15]

Learners tend to steer clear of behaviors that lead to unpleasant consequences.

Over the years, we authors have heard many people incorrectly use the term *negative reinforcement* when they plan to impose unpleasant consequences to reduce someone's inappropriate behavior. In reality, they're talking about administering punishment, *not* negative reinforcement. Whereas negative reinforcement increases the frequency of a response, **punishment** is a consequence that *decreases* the frequency of the response it follows.

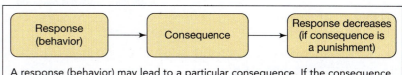

A response (behavior) may lead to a particular consequence. If the consequence then *decreases* the response in the future, it's called a *punishment*.

All punishing consequences fall into one of two categories. **Presentation punishment** involves presenting a new stimulus, presumably something a learner finds unpleasant and doesn't want. Scoldings and teacher scowls, *if* they lead to a reduction in the behavior they follow, are instances of presentation punishment. **Removal punishment** involves removing an existing stimulus or state of affairs, presumably one a learner finds desirable and doesn't want to lose. Loss of a privilege, a fine or penalty (involving the loss of money or previously earned points), and "grounding" (when certain pleasurable outside activities are missed) are all examples of removal punishment.

To systematically determine whether a consequence is a reinforcer or punishment, follow these steps: (1) identify the response (behavior) that seems to be having an effect, (2) determine whether the response increases or decreases, and (3) determine whether something is presented/added or removed/subtracted. Table 4.2 organizes these ideas and provides examples of each type of reinforcement and punishment.

Certain forms of punishment, especially those that are mild in nature and cause no physical or psychological harm, can be quite effective in reducing inappropriate behaviors. Indirectly, then, they can help children and adolescents acquire more productive behaviors.[16] But without proper precautions, the use of punishment in the classroom—even something as seemingly "minor" as yelling at students, as the English literature teacher does in the earlier example—can be counterproductive and is generally less effective than reinforcement.[17] In our discussion of classroom management strategies in Chapter 9, we'll look at effective punishments and guidelines for their use.

MyEdLab
Video Explanation 4.2.

This animated explanation can help you learn to distinguish among positive reinforcement, negative reinforcement, and punishment.

Learners acquire many behaviors by observing other people's actions.

People learn some new behaviors simply by experimenting with various actions and seeing which ones lead to reinforcement and which ones lead to punishment—largely a trial-and-error approach. But they probably learn many more behaviors by observing and imitating the behaviors of other individuals. In fact, the human brain seems to be specially equipped for imitation. Certain neurons in the brain, appropriately called **mirror neurons**, become active either (1) when learners observe others engaging in a particular behavior or (2) when learners engage in that same behavior themselves. It appears, then, that the brain is prewired to make connections between observing

---

[14] Dolezal & Kurtz, 2010; McComas, Thompson, & Johnson, 2003; Van Camp et al., 2000.

[15] Zambo & Brem, 2004, p. 5.

[16] Conyers et al., 2004; R. V. Hall et al., 1971; Landrum & Kauffman, 2006; Walters & Grusec, 1977.

[17] For example, see J. Ellis, Fitzsimmons, & Small-McGinley, 2010.

Table 4.2 • Distinguishing Among Positive Reinforcement, Negative Reinforcement, and Punishment

	CONSEQUENCE	EFFECT	EXAMPLES
Reinforcement (response increases)	Positive reinforcement (stimulus presented)	Response *increases* after a new stimulus (presumably one the learner finds desirable) is *presented*.	• A student *is praised* for writing an assignment in cursive. She begins to write other assignments in cursive as well. (Cursive writing increases after praise is presented.) • A student *gets lunch money* by bullying a girl into surrendering hers. He begins bullying his classmates more frequently. (Bullying increases after money is presented/received.)
	Negative reinforcement (stimulus removed)	Response *increases* after a previously existing stimulus (presumably one the learner finds undesirable) is *removed*.	• A student *no longer has to worry* about a research paper he has completed several days before the due date. He begins to do his assignments ahead of time whenever possible. (Working ahead of time increases after worrying is removed.) • A student *escapes the principal's wrath* by lying about her role in a recent incident of school vandalism. She begins lying to school faculty members whenever she wants to avoid a punishment. (Lying increases after punishment is removed/avoided.)
Punishment (response decreases)	Presentation punishment (stimulus presented)	Response *decreases* after a new stimulus (presumably one the learner finds undesirable) is *presented*.	• A student *is scolded* for taunting other students. She taunts others less frequently after that. (Taunting decreases after scolding is presented.) • A student *is laughed at by classmates* for asking a "stupid" question during a lecture. He stops asking questions in class. (Questioning decreases after the laughing is presented.)
	Removal punishment (stimulus removed)	Response *decreases* after a previously existing stimulus (presumably one the learner finds desirable) is *removed*.	• A student *is not allowed to play on her softball team for three games* for showing poor sportsmanship. She rarely shows poor sportsmanship in future games. (Poor sportsmanship decreases after playing time is removed.) • A student *loses points on a test* for answering a question in a creative but unusual way. He takes fewer risks on future tests. (Creative answers decrease after points are removed.)

think about it

After studying Table 4.2, can you explain in your own words how negative reinforcement is *not* the same as punishment?

and doing, thus enhancing learners' ability to acquire new skills from their social and cultural surroundings.[18]

When one person demonstrates a behavior and another person imitates it, **modeling** is occurring. Consistent with how the term is used both in everyday speech and in social cognitive theory, we'll sometimes use *modeling* to describe what the model does (i.e., demonstrate a behavior) and at other times to describe what the observer does (i.e., imitate that behavior). To minimize confusion, we'll often use the verb *imitate* rather than *model* when referring to what the observer does.

In general, a **model** can take one of three forms.[19] One type, of course, is a *live model*—an actual person demonstrating a behavior. But people can also learn from a *symbolic model*—a person or character portrayed in a book, film, television show, video game, or other media. For example, children and adolescents can learn valuable lessons by studying the behaviors of important figures in history or reading stories about people who accomplish great things in the face of adversity. Finally, people can learn from *verbal instructions*—descriptions of how to successfully execute certain behaviors—without another human being, either live or symbolic, being anywhere in sight.

Learners acquire a wide variety of physical skills—for instance, complex dance steps and gymnastic skills—in part by watching other people do them first.[20] They can also gain many

---

[18] Arbib, 2005; Decety & Cacioppo, 2010; Gallese, Gernsbacher, Heyes, Hickok, & Iacoboni, 2011; Nielsen & Tomaselli, 2010.

[19] Bandura, 1977, 1986.

[20] Boyer, Miltenberger, Batsche, & Fogel, 2009; Magill, 1993; Vintere, Hemmes, Brown, & Poulson, 2004.

academic skills—for instance, in writing, art, and mathematical problem solving—by observing what others do.[21] Modeling of such skills can be especially effective when the model demonstrates not only how to *do* a task but also how to *think about* the task.[22] As an example, consider how a teacher might model the thinking processes involved in the long-division problem in the margin:

$$4\overline{)276}$$

First I have to decide what number to divide 4 into. I take 276, start on the left and move toward the right until I have a number the same as or larger than 4. Is 2 larger than 4? No. Is 27 larger than 4? Yes. So my first division will be 4 into 27. Now I need to multiply 4 by a number that will give an answer the same as or slightly smaller than 27. How about 5? $5 \times 4 = 20$. No, too small. Let's try 6. $6 \times 4 = 24$. Maybe. Let's try 7. $7 \times 4 = 28$. No, too large. So 6 is correct.[23]

By observing and imitating others, learners acquire many interpersonal behaviors as well. For instance, they often learn **prosocial behaviors**—showing compassion, sharing possessions, and, in general, putting others' needs and well-being before their own—when they see models that exhibit prosocial behavior. In contrast, they're more likely to be aggressive and violent when they witness aggression and violence in their personal lives or in the media.[24] And when they hear a model say one thing and do the opposite, they're more likely to imitate what the model *does* than what the model *says*.[25] To be truly effective, models must practice what they preach.

Under what circumstances are learners most likely to model other people's behaviors? The next exercise should help you discover the answer.

SEE FOR YOURSELF
FIVE PEOPLE

Write down the names of five people whom you admire and whose behaviors you'd like to imitate in some way. Then, beside each name, write one or more reasons *why* you admire these people.

Chances are, the five people you chose have one or more of the following characteristics:[26]

- **Competence.** Learners typically try to imitate people who do something well, not those who do it poorly.

- **Prestige and power.** Learners often imitate people who are famous or powerful, either at a national or international level (e.g., a renowned athlete, a popular rock star) or on the local scene (e.g., a head cheerleader, the captain of the school hockey team, a gang leader).

- **"Gender-appropriate" behavior.** Learners are more likely to adopt behaviors they believe are appropriate for their gender (with different learners defining *gender-appropriate* somewhat idiosyncratically).

- **Behavior relevant to one's own situation.** Learners are most likely to imitate behaviors they believe will help them in their own lives and circumstances.

The last of these—behavior relevant to one's own situation—leads us to the next general principle.

---

[21] Braaksma, Rijlaarsdam, & van den Bergh, 2002; Geiger, LeBlanc, Dillon, & Bates, 2010; K. R. Harris, Santangelo, & Graham, 2010; Schunk & Hanson, 1985; Schunk & Swartz, 1993.

[22] R. J. Sawyer, Graham, & Harris, 1992; Schunk, 1981, 1998; Schunk & Swartz, 1993; Zimmerman & Kitsantas, 1999.

[23] Schunk, 1998, p. 146.

[24] C. A. Anderson et al., 2003; Carnagey, Anderson, & Bartholow, 2007; N. E. Goldstein, Arnold, Rosenberg, Stowe, & Ortiz, 2001; Guerra, Huesmann, & Spindler, 2003; Hearold, 1986; Rushton, 1980.

[25] Bryan, 1975.

[26] Bandura, 1986; Grace, David, & Ryan, 2008; C. L. Martin & Ruble, 2004; Powers, Sowers, & Stevens, 1995; Sasso & Rude, 1987.

Learners learn what behaviors are acceptable and effective by observing what happens to people whom they perceive to be similar to themselves.

When one of us authors was in third grade, she entered a Halloween costume contest dressed as "Happy Tooth," a character in several toothpaste commercials at the time. She didn't win the contest; a "witch" won first prize. So the following year she entered the same contest dressed as a witch, figuring she was a shoo-in for first place. Her dressing-as-a-witch behavior increased not because she was reinforced for such behavior, but rather because she saw someone *else* being reinforced for it.

Learners sometimes experience reinforcement and punishment *vicariously*—that is, by observing the consequences of other people's behaviors. Learners who observe someone else being reinforced for a particular behavior tend to exhibit that behavior more frequently themselves—a phenomenon known as **vicarious reinforcement**. For example, by taking note of consequences their classmates experience, students might learn that studying hard leads to good grades, that being elected to class office brings status and popularity, or that neatness counts.

Conversely, when learners see someone else get punished for a certain behavior, they're *less* likely to behave that way themselves—a phenomenon known as **vicarious punishment**. For example, when a coach benches a basketball player for unsportsmanlike conduct, other players are unlikely to behave similarly. Unfortunately, vicarious punishment can suppress desirable behaviors as well as undesirable ones. For instance, when a teacher belittles a student's question by calling it "silly," other students may be reluctant to ask questions of their own.

By seeing what happens to themselves and others, learners form expectations about the probable outcomes of various actions.

So far we've been focusing largely on what learners *do*. But the consequences of their own and others' behaviors also affect what learners *think*. In particular, learners begin to see patterns in the consequences that follow various responses, leading them to form expectations that certain responses will lead to desirable results and other responses won't. These expectations, in turn, affect what learners do and don't do in future situations.[27] To understand how this principle might play out in your own life, try the next exercise.

─────────────────── **SEE FOR YOURSELF** ───────────────────
DR. X

Think about a class you're taking now or have taken recently—not an online class but one that involves an instructor and students regularly convening in a single room. How many of the following questions can you answer about your instructor, whom we'll call "Dr. X"?

1. Is Dr. X right-handed or left-handed?
2. Is Dr. X a flashy dresser or a more conservative one?
3. What kind of shoes does Dr. X wear to class?
4. Does Dr. X wear a wedding ring?
5. Does Dr. X bring a laptop computer to class each day?

───

If you've attended class regularly, you can probably answer at least two of these questions and possibly all five. But it's likely that you've never mentioned what you've learned to anyone else because you've had no reason to believe that demonstrating your knowledge about such matters would be reinforced. When learners *do* expect reinforcement for such knowledge, it suddenly surfaces. For example, when one of us authors teaches an educational psychology class, she often takes a minute sometime during the semester to hide her feet behind the podium and ask her students what her shoes look like. Students first look at her as if she has two heads, but after a few seconds of awkward silence, at least a half dozen of them (usually those sitting in the first two rows) begin to describe her shoes, right down to the rippled soles, scuffed leather, and beige stitching.

[27] Bandura, 1986, 2008.

Students learn many things in the classroom. They learn facts and figures, they learn ways of getting their teacher's attention, and they may even learn which classmate stores M&Ms in his desk or what kind of shoes their teacher wears to class. Of all the things they learn, they're most likely to demonstrate the things they think will bring reinforcement.

When learners choose to behave in a way that might bring future reinforcement, they're working for an **incentive**. Incentives are never guaranteed—for instance, people never know for sure that they're going to get an A on a test when they study for it or that they're going to win a Halloween costume contest when they enter it. It will influence learners' behaviors only if they think that, by working hard, they can actually obtain it. For example, in a classroom of 30 children, a competition in which one prize will be awarded for the highest test score is apt to motivate just a handful of students who regularly achieve at high levels (more on this point in Chapter 5).

What happens when learners' expectations aren't met—for instance, when expected reinforcement never comes? When, as a fourth grader, one of us authors entered the Halloween costume contest as a witch, she lost once again. (First prize went to a girl wearing a metal colander on her head and claiming to be *Sputnik,* the first satellite launched into space by what was then the Soviet Union.) That was the last time she entered a Halloween contest because she had expected reinforcement and felt cheated because she didn't get it by winning. When learners think that a certain response is going to be reinforced, yet the response *isn't* reinforced, they're less likely to exhibit that response in the future. In other words, the *non*occurrence of expected reinforcement is a form of punishment.[28]

Just as the nonoccurrence of reinforcement is a form of punishment, the nonoccurrence of punishment is a form of reinforcement.[29] Perhaps you can think of a time when you broke a rule, expecting to be punished, but got away with your crime. Or perhaps you can remember seeing someone else break a rule without being caught. When nothing bad happens after a forbidden behavior, people may actually feel as if they've been reinforced for the behavior.

With the preceding points in mind, let's return to the opening case study. After going to a movie with friends, Jack was gone for 5 days without telling his family where he was. In some families, such behavior would be totally unacceptable, and a child would reasonably expect to be punished for it. But in Jack's family and within the context of his local cultural environment, the behavior was within acceptable bounds. In this situation, the lack of punishment wasn't necessarily reinforcing for Jack because he wasn't *expecting* any punishment.

Acquired knowledge and skills are often tied to a limited set of activities and environments.

We return now to the concepts of **situated learning** and **situated cognition**, which we introduced in Chapter 2. When learners acquire new information, behaviors, and ways of thinking in a particular activity or particular kind of environment, they may use the things they've learned *only* when they're in the same context once again.[30] Thus, in the lingo of contemporary contextual theories, some learned knowledge and skills are apt to be *situated* in certain contexts.

Thanks to situated learning and cognition—or maybe we should say "*no* thanks"—students may abandon the knowledge and skills they've learned in one class once they're in another class. For example, in one research study,[31] high school students were asked to figure out how much postage they should put on an envelope of a particular weight, and they were given a table of postage rates that would enable them to determine the correct amount. When students in a social studies class were given the task, most of them used the postage table to find the answer. But when students in a math class were given the task, most of them ignored the postage table and tried to *calculate* the postage in some manner, sometimes figuring it to several decimal places. Thus the students in the social studies class were more likely to solve the problem correctly, probably because they were well accustomed to looking for information in tables and charts in that

think about it
Can you think of a personal experience in which not receiving expected reinforcement felt like punishment?

---

[28] Bandura, 1986.
[29] Bandura, 1986.
[30] J. S. Brown, Collins, & Duguid, 1989; Greeno, Collins, & Resnick, 1996; Lave & Wenger, 1991; Light & Butterworth, 1993; Robbins & Aydede, 2009.
[31] Säljö & Wyndhamn, 1992.

class. In contrast, many of the students in the math class drew on strategies they associated with mathematics (using formulas and performing calculations) and overlooked the more efficient and accurate approach.

Learners often think and perform more effectively when they can offload some of the cognitive burden onto something or someone else.

As you should recall from Chapter 2, active cognitive processing takes place in working memory, which—*by itself*—can handle only a small amount of information at any one time. For complex, multifaceted tasks, then, it's helpful to shift some of the cognitive load elsewhere—an idea that's sometimes referred to as **distributed cognition**.[32] One way to "distribute" the cognitive load is to use one or more physical objects—*tools*—our culture has developed in order to make daily living easier and more productive. For example, when struggling with a challenging problem, many people make the task easier to handle by writing parts of it on paper or using a calculator or computer to carry out multistep computations. Perhaps you've never thought of paper as being a "tool," but that is, in fact, what it is. Paper helps us record and remember our thoughts and activities, both as individuals and as a society, in ways that our brains could never do on their own. To make good use of either paper or more high-tech tools, however, people must also rely on the various symbol systems their culture has developed, such as a writing system, diagrams, and maps. We'll examine such *cognitive tools* a bit later, in the "Culture as Context" section.

Another way to distribute the cognitive load is to share it with other individuals. When learners spread a challenging task or problem across many minds, they can draw on multiple perspectives, knowledge bases, and talents, and they can rely on others' assistance with especially challenging activities. Social interaction, then, is another important context for learning, as we'll see now.

Learners behave in ways that lead to desired consequences and avoid unpleasant ones. As a result, it's possible for teachers to change students' behaviors by using consequences such as rewards and punishments. Students also learn by observing teachers and students, as well as by observing what happens to students when they behave in certain ways. In the hotlinked Self-Check quiz and Application Exercise that follow, you can check and apply your understandings related to Big Idea 4.1:

> *Learners' behaviors and cognitive processes are influenced by the specific stimuli and consequences in their immediate environment.*

MyEdLab Self-Check 4.1

MyEdLab Application Exercise 4.1. In this exercise, you'll apply what you've learned about reinforcement by reading and analyzing concrete examples of students and teachers in action.

4.2 SOCIAL INTERACTION AS CONTEXT

Big Idea 4.2 Learners co-construct their knowledge with individuals whose abilities are similar to or greater than their own.

In the preceding section, we discussed things that other people might do *to* or *for* a learner, including providing consequences and modeling behavior. Yet contemporary contextual theories, especially **social constructivism** and **sociocultural theory**, alert us to the fact that many effective learning contexts involve ongoing *interaction* among two or more individuals. The next three principles reflect such social interaction.

---

[32] For example, see Pea, 1993; Salomon, 1993; E. R. Smith & Conrey, 2009. A related concept is *distributed intelligence* (see Chapter 6).

Learners sometimes co-construct new understandings with more experienced individuals.

Adults and other more experienced individuals often help children and adolescents make sense of the world through joint discussion and *co-construction of meaning* regarding a phenomenon or event they are experiencing or have recently experienced together.[33] Such an interaction, sometimes called a **mediated learning experience**, encourages a young learner to think about the phenomenon or event in particular ways: to attach labels to it, recognize concepts and principles that underlie it, draw certain inferences and conclusions from it, and so on.

As an example, consider the following exchange, in which a 5-year-old boy and his mother are talking about a prehistoric animal exhibit at a natural history museum:

Boy: Cool. Wow, look. Look giant teeth. Mom, look at his giant teeth.

Mom: He looks like a saber tooth. Do you think he eats meat or plants?

Boy: Mom, look at his giant little tooth, look at his teeth in his mouth, so big.

Mom: He looks like a saber tooth, doesn't he. Do you think he eats plants or meat?

Boy: Ouch, ouch, ouch, ouch. (referring to sharp tooth)

Mom: Do you think he eats plants or meat?

Boy: Meat.

Mom: How come?

Boy: Because he has sharp teeth. (growling noises)[34]

Even without his mother's assistance, the boy would probably learn something about the characteristics of saber-toothed tigers from his museum visit. Yet his mom helps him make better sense of the experience than he might have done on his own—for instance, by using the label *saber tooth* and helping him connect tooth characteristics to eating preferences. Notice how persistent his mom is in asking him to make the tooth–food connection. She continues to ask her question about meat versus plants until he finally infers, correctly, that saber-toothed tigers must have been meat eaters.

When children talk with parents, teachers, and other adults about past and present experiences, their memory for those experiences is better as a result.[35] Furthermore, through such discussions, children gradually incorporate into their own thinking the ways in which the people around them talk about and interpret the world.[36]

MyEdLab
Video Explanation 4.3.

This video shows an example of a mediated learning experience in which a teacher helps students make sense of their observations of goldfish.

Learners also co-construct knowledge and understandings with peers who have ability levels similar to or greater than their own.

Adults usually have more knowledge than children's peers do, and they tend to be more skillful teachers. Accordingly, they're often the partners of choice when children are trying to master complex new subject matter and skills.[37] Yet peers, too, have an important role to play in learning. For example, look once again at Figure 2.4 (the three black-and-white faces) in Chapter 2. Did you initially have trouble seeing the man on the right side of the figure? If so, perhaps you enlisted the assistance of friends or classmates to help you identify the top of the man's head, locations of the eyes and an ear, and other details. Think, too, about times when you've worked cooperatively with classmates to make sense of confusing class material. Quite possibly, by sharing various interpretations, your group jointly constructed a better understanding of the material than any one of you could have constructed on your own.

Learners often talk with one another to help them make better sense of their experiences—for instance, by exploring, discussing, explaining, and debating certain topics in study groups or classroom discussions. When learners work together in such a manner, they are, in essence,

---

[33] Costa, 2008; Feuerstein, Feuerstein, & Falik, 2010; John-Steiner & Mahn, 1996; P. K. Murphy, Wilkinson, & Soter, 2011.

[34] Ash, 2002, p. 378.

[35] Haden, Ornstein, Eckerman, & Didow, 2001; Hemphill & Snow, 1996; K. Nelson, 1993; Tessler & Nelson, 1994.

[36] Liben & Myers, 2007; Markus & Hamedani, 2007; K. Nelson, 1996; Vygotsky, 1962, 1978.

[37] Gauvain, 2001; Radziszewska & Rogoff, 1988.

engaging in distributed cognition: They spread the learning task across many minds and can draw on multiple knowledge bases and ideas.[38] There's certainly some truth to the adage "Two heads are better than one."

As an example of distributed cognition, let's look in on Ms. Lombard's fourth-grade class, which has been studying fractions. The students have learned how to add and subtract fractions but not yet studied how to divide by fractions. Nevertheless, they're working in small groups to tackle the following problem, which requires dividing 20 by $\frac{3}{4}$:[39]

> Mom makes small apple tarts, using three-quarters of an apple for each small tart. She has 20 apples. How many small apple tarts can she make?[40]

One group has already agreed that Mom can use three-fourths of each apple to make 20 tarts, with one-fourth of each apple being left to make additional tarts.

> *Liz:* So you've got twenty quarters *left.*
>
> *Jeanette:* Yes, . . . and twenty quarters is equal to five apples, . . . so five apples divided by—
>
> *Liz:* Six, seven, eight.
>
> *Jeanette:* But three-quarters equals three.
>
> *Kerri:* But she can't make only three apple tarts!
>
> *Jeanette:* No, you've still got twenty.
>
> *Liz:* But you've got twenty quarters, if you've got twenty quarters you might be right.
>
> *Jeanette:* I'll show you.
>
> *Liz:* No, I've drawn them all here.
>
> *Kerri:* How many quarters have you got? Twenty?
>
> *Liz:* Yes, one quarter makes five apples and out of five apples she can make five tarts which will make that twenty-five tarts and then she will have, wait, one, two, three, four, five quarters, she'll have one, two, three, four, five quarters. . . .[41]

Eventually, the group arrives at the correct answer: Mom can make 26 tarts and will have half an apple left over.

When learners share their ideas and perspectives with one another, they can enhance their understanding of a topic in numerous ways:

- They must clarify and organize their thoughts well enough to explain and justify them to others.
- They tend to elaborate on what they've learned—for example, by drawing inferences, generating hypotheses, and formulating new questions.
- They're exposed to the views of others, who may have more accurate understandings or culturally different—yet equally valid—perspectives.
- They may discover flaws and inconsistencies in their own thinking.
- They can model effective ways of thinking about and studying academic subject matter for one another.

---

[38] Fonseca & Chi, 2011; Hewitt & Scardamalia, 1998; Palincsar & Herrenkohl, 1999; Salomon, 1993; Wiley & Bailey, 2006.

[39] In case your memory of how to divide by a fraction is rusty, you can approach the problem $20 \div \frac{3}{4}$ by inverting the fraction and multiplying, like so: $20 \times \frac{4}{3} = \frac{80}{3} = 26\frac{2}{3}$. In the problem Ms. Lombard presents, Mom can make 26 tarts and have enough apple to make two-thirds of another tart. If Mom has two-thirds of the three-fourths of an apple she needs to make another whole tart, then she has half an apple left over ($\frac{2}{3} \times \frac{3}{4} = \frac{1}{2}$).

[40] J. Hiebert et al., 1997, p. 118.

[41] J. Hiebert et al., 1997, p. 121.

- They gain practice in the argumentation skills that experts in various disciplines use to advance the frontiers of knowledge—for instance, presenting evidence in support of conclusions and examining the strengths and weaknesses of various explanations.

- In the process of debating controversial material, they may gain a more sophisticated view of the nature of knowledge and learning. For example, they may begin to realize that (1) acquiring "knowledge" involves acquiring an integrated set of ideas about a topic and (2) such knowledge is likely to evolve only gradually over time (this point should remind you of the discussion of *epistemic beliefs* in Chapter 3).[42]

It's important to keep in mind, too, that as our 21st-century world becomes more and more complex—with research and knowledge about various topics expanding at a mind-boggling rate—such collaborative sense-making efforts are increasingly becoming the norm rather than the exception in the adult world.

Joint meaning making with peers doesn't necessarily have to occur in a single learning session, however. Social construction of meaning may proceed gradually over the course of several days or weeks or even longer. For example, teenagers who share an interest in computers may communicate regularly in order to help one another acquire sophisticated computer programming skills.[43] And if we look at human beings' interpretations of their experiences on a much grander scale, the evolution of such diverse academic disciplines as mathematics, science, history, and psychology reflects co-construction of knowledge and understandings stretched out over the course of many decades or centuries.

Other people sometimes provide the support learners need to take on challenging new tasks.

The world presents many complex, challenging tasks that young learners can't tackle on their own, especially at first. Often, however, learners *can* tackle these tasks when others guide and support them in some way; that is, when others provide scaffolding.[44] **Scaffolding** is a support mechanism that helps a learner successfully perform a challenging task. For example, a parent or teacher might provide helpful *hints* on how to effectively execute a new procedure or break a multifaceted task into several smaller, more accomplishable ones. Also, when learners collaborate in a group activity, they often provide scaffolding for one another by divvying up various aspects of the activity and giving one another suggestions and guidance based on their individual talents and areas of expertise. We'll explore the concept of scaffolding in greater depth in the discussion of cognitive development in Chapter 6.

Scaffolding sometimes takes the form of one or more physical cues. Here the scaffold is a blue circle drawn on the pavement to help a 6-year-old practice executing layup shots; the circle indicates the spot from which the boy should jump and shoot.

Students learn by interacting with others and co-constructing their knowledge. Teachers can facilitate the co-construction of knowledge by providing learning experiences that allow students to engage in activities with the teacher and other students. In the hotlinked Self-Check quiz and Application Exercise that follow, you can check and apply your understandings related to Big Idea 4.2:

Learners co-construct their knowledge with individuals whose abilities are similar to or greater than their own.

MyEdLab **Self-Check 4.2**

MyEdLab **Application Exercise 4.2.** In this exercise, you can identify some ways in which presenting ideas to others can help the presenter better understand the ideas.

---

[42] Andriessen, 2006; Bendixen & Rule, 2004; Chinn, 2006; Hatano & Inagaki, 2003; K. Hogan, Nastasi, & Pressley, 2000; D. W. Johnson & Johnson, 2009b; A. King, 1999; Kuhn, 2015; Kuhn & Crowell, 2011; E. M. Nussbaum, 2008; Reznitskaya & Gregory, 2013; Schwarz, Neuman, & Biezuner, 2000; Sinatra & Pintrich, 2003; N. M. Webb & Palincsar, 1996; Wentzel & Watkins, 2011.
[43] Barron, 2006.
[44] The classic reference for this concept is D. Wood, Bruner, & Ross, 1976.

4.3 CULTURE, SOCIETY, TECHNOLOGY, AND ACADEMIC DOMAINS AS CONTEXTS

Big Idea 4.3 The cultural, societal, and technological contexts in which learners grow up also influence their behaviors and cognitive processes, as do the academic domains that learners study in school and elsewhere.

Almost any long-standing social group develops some sort of **culture**, which includes both behaviors and beliefs that are passed from old members to new ones, from generation to generation. Through its culture, a human social group ensures that each new generation acquires and benefits from the wisdom that preceding generations have accumulated. By passing along this collective knowledge base, a cultural group increases the chances that it will survive and thrive over the long run.

Culture is a pervasive part of any learning environment—it permeates people's social interactions, as well as the books, toys, websites, and other human-made objects and media that people encounter. But culture is an inside-the-head thing as well as an out-there-in-the-world thing, in that it provides an overall framework by which people determine what things are normal and abnormal, true and not true, rational and irrational, good and bad (see Figure 4.3).[45] A learner's cultural background influences the perspectives and values the learner acquires, the skills the learner masters and finds important, and the long-term goals toward which the learner strives. For example, in the opening case study, Jack stayed home from school for several days so that he could help out with spring planting activities. Such a cooperative, *everyone-pitches-in* attitude would be essential for any family whose livelihood depends on a good harvest.

Cultures aren't static entities. Instead, they continue to change over time as they incorporate new ideas, practices, and ways of thinking, and especially as they come into contact with other cultural groups.[46] Furthermore, considerable variation exists in people's beliefs and behaviors within a particular culture, in that individual members may adopt some cultural values and practices but reject others.[47]

FIGURE 4.3 As an assignment for his Spanish class, 14-year-old Bernie created a burlap-and-yarn eagle inspired by Mexican designs. But the true essence of a cultural group isn't found in its art, music, clothing, holiday celebrations, and other observable customs. Rather, it comprises the assumptions, beliefs, and values that underlie its members' behaviors and interpretations of the world, as revealed in excerpts from 13-year-old Melinda's essay about Shinto gods.

Shinto gods are called Kami. It is believed that these spirits are found in the basic forces of fire, wind, and water. Most influence agriculture and this of course was how the earliest people survived. They relied on what they grew to live. So the gods had to help them grow their crops or they died. It seems natural for people to worship things that will help them survive, and worshiping forces that affect what you grow was the common practice in early history. These basic forces even affect the survival of modern people. We all still need agriculture to live and forces of nature really determine whether crops grow or not.

Shintoists never developed strong doctrines, such as the belief in life after death that many other religions have. However they have developed some moral standards such as devotion, sincerity, and purity. . . .

All Shintoists have a very good and simple set of rules or practice. They want to be honorable, have feelings for others, support the government, and keep their families safe and healthy. I think these are good principles for all people, whether they practice a religion or not. . . .

---

[45] M. Cole, 2006; Goodnow, 2010; Kağitçibaşi, 2007.
[46] Kitayama, Duffy, & Uchida, 2007; Rogoff, 2003.
[47] A. B. Cohen, 2009; Goodnow, 2010; Matute-Bianchi, 2008.

Sometimes the word *culture* is used to refer to behaviors and beliefs that are widely shared over a large geographic area. As an example, *mainstream Western culture* encompasses behaviors, beliefs, and values shared by many people in North American and western European societies. Among other things, members of this culture generally value self-reliance, democratic decision making, and academic achievement.[48] Other cultures are more local and self-contained. For instance, a culture might be specific to a particular island in the South Pacific. Still others may be *subcultures* that reside within but are in some ways different from a more widespread and dominant culture.

Although countries in North America and western Europe share a common mainstream culture, most also have many distinct cultural groups within them. For example, the United States is a nation comprised largely of immigrants and their descendants; only Native Americans lived on U.S. soil before the 1500s. People with a heritage from a particular country or region often form an **ethnic group**—a group of individuals with a common culture and the following characteristics:[49]

- Its roots either precede the creation of or are external to the country in which it currently resides. For example, it may be composed of people of the same race, national origin, or religious background.

- Its members share a sense of interdependence—a sense that their lives are intertwined.

However, we can't determine people's ethnicity strictly based on physical characteristics (e.g., race) or birthplace. For instance, one of us authors has a daughter who was born in Colombia and has Hispanic and Native American biological ancestors, but because she was raised by two European American parents, ethnically she is more European American than anything else. In general, we can get the best sense of students' cultural backgrounds and ethnic group memberships by learning the extent to which they have participated and continue to participate in various cultural and ethnic-group activities.[50] Furthermore, some individuals participate actively in two or more cultures or ethnic groups, perhaps because their parents came from distinctly different racial or ethnic backgrounds or perhaps because they encounter new perspectives and ways of doing things as they move from one community or country to another.[51]

Culture as Context

The cultures in which learners participate have significant effects on their learning and development, as revealed in the following general principles.

Any cultural group encourages and models certain behaviors and actively discourages certain other behaviors.

Most members of a cultural group work hard to help growing children adopt the behaviors and beliefs that the group holds dear. Beginning early in life, children learn that there are some things they can or should do and other things they definitely should *not* do. They also acquire a cultural "lens" for viewing social situations and tasks. This process of molding behavior and beliefs so that children fit in with their cultural group is called **socialization**.

Sometimes adults' socialization efforts are obvious. For instance, when an adult tells Jenna, "It's not nice to hit other children," and puts Jenna in a time-out situation for her aggressive behavior, the message is crystal clear. At other times socialization is more subtle. For example, adults communicate cultural values and beliefs by encouraging and modeling certain activities ("Let's give some of our clothes and toys to the homeless shelter") and discouraging others ("Stay away from that neighborhood; there are drug dealers on every corner"). In the opening case study, note the subtle, teasing approach Jack's mother used to convey the importance of school: "Now maybe school will look easy!"

---

[48] Hollins, 1996; Tamis-Lemonda & McFadden, 2010.
[49] NCSS Task Force on Ethnic Studies Curriculum Guidelines, 1992.
[50] Gutiérrez & Rogoff, 2003.
[51] A. M. Lopez, 2003; Mohan, 2009; Root, 1999.

Children typically learn their earliest lessons about their culture's standards and expectations from parents and other family members, who teach them such things as personal hygiene and rudimentary interpersonal skills (e.g., saying "please" and "thank you"). Yet once children begin school, teachers become equally important socialization agents.[52] For instance, many first-grade teachers ask their students to sit quietly rather than interrupt when an adult is speaking, middle school teachers engage students in cooperative learning activities, and high school teachers expect students to turn in homework assignments on time. In doing such things, these teachers communicate important cultural beliefs: that children should defer to and show respect for adults, that cooperation with peers can enhance learning and productivity, and that punctuality is essential for succeeding in life.

To the extent that a society includes a variety of cultures and ethnic groups, different families socialize different behaviors and ways of looking at the world. The Cultural Considerations boxes in Chapters 3 through 10 of the book can give you a taste of the diversity that teachers are apt to see in school-age children. But as you read these boxes, please keep in mind a point made earlier: *Considerable variation exists in the beliefs and behaviors found within a single cultural group.*[53]

Every culture passes along many cognitive tools that enhance learners' thinking capabilities.

We see obvious effects of culture in many of children's everyday activities; for example, in the books they read, the jokes they tell, the roles they enact in pretend play, and the extracurricular activities they pursue. Yet culture permeates children's thinking processes as well, for instance by providing a variety of **cognitive tools**—including concepts, symbols, and problem-solving strategies—that make the "raw data" of any complex situation more manageable and thus help children effectively deal with many of the tasks and problems they face.[54]

One of the most universal and basic cultural creations—language—provides many cognitive tools that shape growing children's thinking processes. For instance, preschoolers learn to categorize some people as "girls" and others as "boys," and they begin to associate certain behaviors with one sex or the other. Over time, the many words and concepts children acquire—for instance, *snow, yucky, birthday party, bully*—help them make sense of and respond to their physical and social experiences in generally adaptive ways.

Some cognitive tools are almost entirely mental and symbolic in nature. For example, members of most cultures use a systematic counting system (1, 2, 3. . .) and certain units of measurement (e.g., inches, kilograms) to help them organize and make sense of the various quantities—the *amounts* of things—they encounter in their environment. Other cognitive tools must, by nature, have both physical and symbolic components. For example, a student might use a *calendar* to keep track of upcoming school activities, assignments, and due dates. And students in a science class might draw a *line graph* to see if a particular region's average annual rainfall has substantially increased or decreased over the past few decades. But it's important to remember that all these tools are *cultural creations*—hence they're part of the particular social and cultural contexts in which learners grow up—and so not all learners are familiar with them.

Every culture instills certain worldviews that color people's interpretations of events.

Recall that our definition of culture includes *beliefs* as well as behaviors. When people's beliefs are related to specific physical, biological, social, or mental phenomena, they're known as *theories* (see Chapter 2). In contrast, a **worldview** is a general set of beliefs and assumptions about reality—about "how things are and should be"—that influences learners' interpretations and understandings of a wide variety of phenomena.

MyEdLab
Video Explanation 4.4.

This video illustrates the use of cognitive tools in a high school physics class.

---

[52] Helton & Oakland, 1977; Hess & Holloway, 1984; Wentzel & Looney, 2007.

[53] Markus and Hamedani (2007) point out that it's easier to use a label such as "East Asians" than to say "people participating in the ideas and practices that are pervasive in East Asian cultural contexts" (p. 11). If we're not careful, however, such simple labels can lead us to inaccurately overgeneralize about people from any geographic location or cultural background.

[54] Pea, 1993; Salomon, 1993; E. R. Smith & Conrey, 2009.

CULTURAL CONSIDERATIONS

Examples of How Various Cultural and Ethnic Groups May Socialize Children Differently

Various cultural and ethnic groups can instill distinctly different values, priorities, and social behaviors in growing children. Following are a few examples that researchers have often observed. As you read the examples, be careful that you don't form hard-and-fast stereotypes about any of the groups mentioned here. We authors can't stress this point enough: People in any single cultural and ethnic group are apt to be quite different from one another in their general priorities, habits, and behaviors.

INDIVIDUAL VERSUS COOPERATIVE EFFORTS. In a traditional classroom in mainstream Western culture, learning is often a solitary, individual endeavor: Students receive praise, colorful stickers, or good grades when they personally perform at high levels. Sometimes teachers add a competitive element to personal achievement; for instance, they may grade exams "on a curve" or post "best" papers on the bulletin board. Yet many Native American, Mexican American, African, East Asian, and Pacific Island cultural groups value *group* achievement over individual success. Students from such cultures are often more accustomed to working cooperatively and for the benefit of the community, rather than for themselves.[a] The Zulu word *ubuntu,*[b] reflecting the belief that people attain their "humanness" largely through relationships with others and have a responsibility to work for the common good, epitomizes this cooperative spirit.

EYE CONTACT. For many of us, looking someone in the eye is a way to show that we're trying to communicate or are listening intently to what the person is saying. But in many Native American, African American, Mexican American, and Puerto Rican communities, a child who looks an adult in the eye is showing disrespect. In these communities, children are taught to look *down* in the presence of adults.[c]

PERSONAL SPACE. In some cultures, such as in some African American and Hispanic communities, people stand close together when they talk, and they may touch one another frequently.[d] In contrast, European Americans and Japanese Americans tend to keep a fair distance from one another—they maintain some **personal space**—especially if they don't know one another very well.[e]

PUBLIC VERSUS PRIVATE PERFORMANCE. In many classrooms learning is a public enterprise: Individual students are often expected to answer questions or demonstrate skills in full view of their classmates, and they're encouraged to ask questions themselves when they don't understand. Such practices, which many teachers take for granted, may confuse or even alienate students of some ethnic groups.[f] For example, many Native American children are accustomed to practicing a skill privately at first, performing in front of a group only after they've attained a reasonable level of mastery.[g] And children in some Native American and Hawaiian communities may feel more comfortable responding to an adult's questions as a group rather than interacting with an adult one-on-one.[h]

FAMILY RELATIONSHIPS AND EXPECTATIONS. In some groups—for example, in many Native American, Hispanic, Arab American, and Asian groups, as well as in some rural European American communities—family bonds and relationships are especially important, and extended family members often live nearby. Children growing up in these cultural groups are likely to feel responsibility for their family's well-being, to have a strong sense of loyalty to other family members, and to go to great lengths to please their elders. It isn't unusual for students in such cultures to leave school when their help is needed at home, as Jack does in the opening case study.[i]

In most cultures school achievement is highly valued, and parents encourage their children to do well in school.[j] But some cultural groups place even higher priority on other accomplishments. For example, when preparing young children for school, many Hispanic families place particular emphasis on instilling appropriate social behaviors—for instance, showing respect for adults and cooperating with peers.[k] And in some African American and Native American families, early pregnancies are cause for joy even if the mothers-to-be haven't yet completed high school.[l]

CONCEPTIONS OF TIME. Many people regulate their lives by the clock: Being on time to appointments, social engagements, and the dinner table is important. This emphasis on punctuality isn't characteristic of all cultures, however. For example, many Native American cultures—and some Hispanic cultures as well—don't observe strict schedules and timelines.[m] Not surprisingly, children from these cultural backgrounds may sometimes be late for school and may have trouble understanding the need to complete school tasks within a certain time frame.

[a] X. Chen & Wang, 2010; Mejía-Arauz, Rogoff, Dexter, & Najafi, 2007; Paradise & Robles, 2016; Tyler et al., 2008; Varnum, Grossmann, Kitayama, & Nisbett, 2010.
[b] On a professional trip to South Africa in 2005, one of us authors was struck by how often this word was used in daily conversation.
[c] Jiang, 2010; McCarthy, Lee, Itakura, & Muir, 2006; Tyler et al., 2008.
[d] Slonim, 1991; Trawick-Smith, 2003; Ward, Bochner, & Furnham, 2001.
[e] Irujo, 1988; Trawick-Smith, 2003.
[f] Eriks-Brophy & Crago, 1994; Garcia, 1994; Lomawaima, 1995; Tyler et al., 2008.
[g] Castagno & Brayboy, 2008; Suina & Smolkin, 1994.
[h] K. H. Au, 1980; L. S. Miller, 1995.
[i] Banks & Banks, 1995; Deyhle & LeCompte, 1999; Fuligni, 1998; Kağitçibaşi, 2007; McIntyre, 2010; Tyler et al., 2008.
[j] Monzó, 2010; Pearce, 2006; Spera, 2005.
[k] Greenfield et al., 2006; Tyler et al., 2008.
[l] Deyhle & Margonis, 1995; Stack & Burton, 1993.
[m] Tyler et al., 2008; Ward et al., 2001.

The following exercise should enable you to reflect on some beliefs and assumptions that your own worldview might encompass.[55]

––––––––––––––––––––––––– **SEE FOR YOURSELF** –––––––––––––––––––––––––
CONSIDERING THE BIG PICTURE

For each of the following six general topics, choose the option that best matches your personal beliefs and assumptions.

1. Life and the universe came into being
   a. through random acts of nature.
   b. as part of a divine plan and purpose.
2. Objects in nature (rocks, trees, etc.)
   a. have some degree of consciousness.
   b. are incapable of conscious thought.
3. People are most likely to enhance their well-being by
   a. relying on scientific principles and logical reasoning processes.
   b. seeking guidance from authority figures.
4. The human world is
   a. fair and just—good deeds ultimately bring rewards, and misdeeds are eventually punished.
   b. is not necessarily fair and just.
5. Human beings
   a. are at the mercy of the forces of nature.
   b. should strive to master the forces of nature.
   c. must learn to live in harmony with nature.
6. People's successes and failures in life are the result of
   a. their own actions.
   b. divine intervention.
   c. fate.
   d. random occurrences.

Have you ever explicitly thought about such issues before? Quite possibly you haven't. Worldviews are often such an integral part of everyday thinking that learners take them for granted and usually aren't consciously aware of them. To a considerable degree, the beliefs and assumptions they encompass are culturally transmitted, with different cultures communicating somewhat different beliefs and assumptions either explicitly through their words or implicitly through their actions.[56] As a result, worldviews are not always acquired consciously; thus, they reflect *implicit* rather than explicit learning. Nevertheless, they influence learners' interpretations of current events and classroom subject matter. For example, if students believe that the world and its inhabitants are guided and protected by an omniscient and benevolent Greater Being, they're not as likely to believe that global climate change is real or poses a significant threat to human society.[57] And if students' culture consistently emphasizes the importance of accepting and living in harmony with nature as it is, they might struggle with a science curriculum that explores how human beings might manipulate and gain control over natural events.[58]

Every culture has certain ways of doing things, and these, too, are passed from generation to generation.

Any cultural group passes along not only certain ways of interpreting the world but also certain ways of *doing things*. In other words, different cultures foster somewhat different kinds of *procedural knowledge*. Some procedural knowledge is task- or topic-specific and is conveyed directly and explicitly—for example, "Here's how to write a cursive *A*," and "Let me show you how to do long division." But cultures also pass along a good deal of procedural knowledge within the context of **communities of practice**—groups of people who share common interests and goals and regularly

–––––––––––––––––––––––

[55] M. Cole & Hatano, 2007; E. M. Evans, 2008; Furnham, 2003; Keil & Newman, 2008; Kelemen, 2004; Koltko-Rivera, 2004; Medin, 2005.

[56] Astuti, Solomon, & Carey, 2004; Berti, Toneatti, & Rosati, 2010; M. Cole & Hatano, 2007; Kitayama, 2002; Losh, 2003.

[57] Feinberg & Willer, 2011.

[58] Atran, Medin, & Ross, 2005; Medin, 2005.

interact and coordinate their efforts in pursuit of those interests and goals.[59] Communities of practice tend to adhere to certain standards for action and interaction—standards that are often unwritten understandings rather than explicitly stated rules. For example, in the adult world of mainstream Western culture, people in various professions—medicine, law, education, scientific research—tend to communicate regularly with one another and to support one another in particular ways. In most cases, new members of a community of practice learn the acceptable ways of doing things primarily by actively participating in the group. Often a learner begins by participating only at the fringe of the group, perhaps by doing menial chores or by assisting or apprenticing with a more experienced group member. In other words, a novice is gradually introduced to the ways of the group through **legitimate peripheral participation**.[60] Participation is *legitimate* in the sense that the novice contributes in genuine, authentic ways to the group's overall effort. It's *peripheral* in that it involves only small tasks at the outer edge, or periphery, of the action.

Communities of practice are hardly limited to adult professional groups. For example, volunteer organizations (e.g., the American Red Cross) and organized youth groups (e.g., Girl Scouts and Boy Scouts) are essentially communities of practice as well. Schools, too, are communities of practice, in that they have certain prescribed ways of doing things in order to accomplish particular goals—for example, following schedules, completing assignments, and meeting deadlines.

Inconsistencies between home and school cultures can interfere with school learning and performance.

For most children, expectations for behavior are different at school than at home. For instance, at home, children may be accustomed to speaking whenever they have something to say, but at school, there are times when silence is golden. Or at home, children may be able to choose what they want to do and when to do it, but the school day typically involves a series of tasks that all children must complete at certain times. To the extent that behaviors expected at school differ from those allowed or expected at home, children may experience some confusion, or **culture shock**, when they begin school.

Culture shock is more intense for some children than for others. Most schools in North America and western Europe are based largely on mainstream Western culture, and so children with this cultural background often adjust easily to the school environment. But students who come from other cultural backgrounds, especially those with very different views about acceptable behavior, may initially find school a confusing and unsettling place. For example, recent immigrants from faraway places may not know what to expect from other people in their new country or what behaviors other people expect *of them*. Children raised in a culture where gender roles are clearly differentiated—where males and females are socialized to behave very differently—may have difficulty adjusting to a school in which similar expectations are held for both sexes.[61] Any such **cultural mismatch** between home and school cultures can interfere with students' adjustment to the school setting and ultimately with their academic achievement as well.[62]

Often children from diverse cultural backgrounds try desperately to fit in at school yet find the inconsistencies between home and school hard to resolve. For instance, children from devout Muslim families frequently have trouble finding the time and place they need to pray during the school day, and they may have little energy for school activities during the month-long fasting period of Ramadan. And thoughtless classmates might ask Muslim girls who wear headscarves, "Are you bald? Is there something wrong with your hair?" or taunt them by calling them names.[63]

Cultural mismatch is compounded when teachers misinterpret behaviors that reflect students' cultural and ethnic backgrounds. The following exercise provides an example.

---

[59] Barab & Dodge, 2008; Lave, 1991; Nolen, 2011; R. K. Sawyer & Greeno, 2009; Wenger, 1998.
[60] Lave & Wenger, 1991.
[61] Kirschenbaum, 1989; Sirin & Ryce, 2010; Vasquez, 1988.
[62] Phalet, Andriessen, & Lens, 2004; S. J. Schwartz, Unger, Zamboanga, & Szapocznik, 2010; Tyler et al., 2008; Ward et al., 2001.
[63] Igoa, 1995; McBrien, 2005, p. 86; Sirin & Ryce, 2010.

Imagine that, as a new teacher, you're approaching the school building on the first day of school. You see seven or eight boys standing in a cluster just outside the front door. Two of them are engaged in a heated argument, and the others are watching and listening with apparent delight. Here are just a few of the many insults you hear being hurled back and forth:

"Your momma so fat her driver's license says, 'Picture continued on other side'!"
"Yeah? Well, your momma so fat she got to iron her pants on the driveway!"
"That ain't nothin'. Your momma so fat her cereal bowl comes with a lifeguard!"
"Hey, man, your momma so fat she got smaller fat women orbitin' around her!"

The argument seems to be escalating, with the insults about the two boys' mothers becoming more and more outrageous. Should you intervene?

The incident you've just witnessed is probably an example of *sounding* or *playing the dozens,* a friendly exchange of insults common among male youth in some African American communities.[64] Some boys engage in such exchanges to achieve status among their peers—those who concoct the biggest, most creative insults are the winners—whereas others do it simply for amusement. But people unfamiliar with African American culture might misinterpret them as being potentially serious and worrisome.

As students gain experience with the culture of their school, they become increasingly aware of their teachers' and peers' expectations for behavior and ways of thinking. Many eventually become adept at switching their cultural vantage point as they move from home to school and back again.[65] One Mexican American student's recollection provides an example:

> At home with my parents and grandparents the only acceptable language was Spanish; actually that's all they really understood. Everything was really Mexican, but at the same time they wanted me to speak good English.... But at school, I felt really different because everyone was American, including me. Then I would go home in the afternoon and be Mexican again.[66]

think about it
Can you think of ways in which your own school environment was mismatched with the culture in which you were raised?

But not all students make such an easy adjustment. Some actively resist adapting to the existing school culture, perhaps because they view it as being inconsistent with—even contradictory to—their own cultural background and identity.[67] And let's face it: Traditional classrooms don't always encourage behaviors that are in students' long-term best interests. For example, a classroom that encourages students to compete with one another for grades—rather than fostering the cooperation that many cultural groups value—may engender an unhealthy one-upmanship that interferes with congenial peer relationships both in and outside the classroom.

Society as Context

A concept related to culture, but also somewhat distinct from it, is **society**: a very large, enduring social group that is socially and economically organized and has collective institutions and activities. For instance, virtually any nation is a society, in that it has a government that regulates some of its activities, a set of laws that identify permissible and unacceptable behaviors, a monetary system that allows members to exchange goods and services, and so on.

A society influences its members' learning in a variety of ways, including through the resources it provides, the activities it supports, and the general messages it communicates. For example, a society's infrastructure—such as its roads, power plants, and telephone and cable

---

[64] Adger, Wolfram, & Christian, 2007; R. E. Reynolds, Taylor, Steffensen, Shirey, & Anderson, 1982; Smitherman, 1998; you may also see the terms *joaning, signifying,* or *snapping.*

[65] Y. Hong, Morris, Chiu, & Benet-Martínez, 2000; LaFromboise, Coleman, & Gerton, 1993; Phalet et al., 2004; Phelan, Davidson, & Cao, 1994.

[66] Padilla, 1994, p. 30.

[67] Cross, Strauss, & Fhagen-Smith, 1999; Kumar, Gheen, & Kaplan, 2002; Ogbu, 2008a; S. J. Schwartz, Unger, Zamboanga, & Szapocznik, 2010.

lines—enables the movement of people and goods over great distances and regular collaboration among its residents. Various media (newspapers, television, the Internet, etc.) convey information, ideas, opinions, and messages (often subtle ones) about desired behaviors and group stereotypes. And, of course, schools provide formal structures through which children and adults alike acquire knowledge and skills that will presumably enhance their personal and professional success.

The next three principles reflect characteristics of societies that are especially relevant to learners' classroom performance and long-term social and professional success.

Any large society has multiple layers that all affect children's learning and development either directly or indirectly.

A key characteristic of any society is that it has small organized structures nested within other, larger ones (see Figure 4.4).[68] For many children, the most basic level is the *family,* which can potentially support learning in a number of ways—for example, by providing good nutrition and medical care, engaging children in stimulating educational activities, setting certain expectations for behavior, and providing social and emotional support. Surrounding the family is another layer, the *social groups* in which children learn how to interact with peers, engage in fun recreational activities (e.g., games, playing with toys), and receive social and emotional support. Another layer, the *community,* can offer educational experiences (e.g., school education, preschool and after-school programs, library and museum programs, local business internships), recreational opportunities (e.g., playgrounds, sports clubs), and social and emotional support (e.g., helpful neighbors, church and synagogue resources). At a still broader level, the *societies* (e.g., state, province, country) in which children reside influence children's development through legislation that governs school policy, tax dollars that flow back to local schools, agencies and professional groups that offer information and training in new teaching strategies, online resources, and so on. Permeating all of these layers are general *cultural beliefs* about how people should think and behave.

MyEdLab
Video Example 4.1.

What strategies does this elementary school teacher use to teach children about some of the roles that their society plays in their personal lives?

MyEdLab Content Extension 4.2.
Learn more about society's multiple layers—and especially about Urie Bronfenbrenner's concept of *ecological systems*—in this supplementary reading.

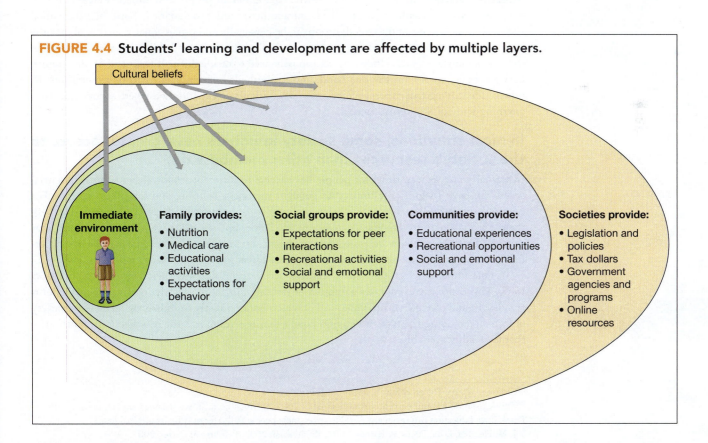

FIGURE 4.4 Students' learning and development are affected by multiple layers.

Cultural beliefs

Immediate environment

Family provides:
- Nutrition
- Medical care
- Educational activities
- Expectations for behavior

Social groups provide:
- Expectations for peer interactions
- Recreational activities
- Social and emotional support

Communities provide:
- Educational experiences
- Recreational opportunities
- Social and emotional support

Societies provide:
- Legislation and policies
- Tax dollars
- Government agencies and programs
- Online resources

---

[68] Much of the discussion in this paragraph is based on Urie Bronfenbrenner's *ecological systems theory* and *bioecological model;* for instance, see Bronfenbrenner, 1989, 2005; Bronfenbrenner & Morris, 1998; C. D. Lee, 2010.

A society's various layers interact with one another and with children's existing characteristics as they influence children's development; in the process, they also *change* one another. For example, a temperamentally hyperactive child might initially elicit stringent disciplinary actions at school (within the communities layer), but concerned parents (within the family layer) might seek out teachers and suggest alternative strategies that effectively channel the child's behavior into productive activities. And government agencies (within the societies layer) might provide websites that help both parents and teachers better foster children's cognitive development. In general, societies are *dynamic systems* encompassing mutually influencing variables that are constantly in flux.[69]

In the United States, the **Individuals with Disabilities Education Act (IDEA)** provides an example of how national policy can indirectly affect learning.[70] This legislation guarantees that children with disabilities have access to appropriate interventions and services designed to enhance their physical and cognitive development. It also mandates that once these children reach school age they must be educated in neighborhood schools with nondisabled peers to the fullest extent possible—a practice known as *inclusion*. Early intervention clearly *is* effective in enhancing the development of children with a wide variety of special educational needs.[71] Furthermore, many children with mild disabilities achieve at higher levels if they remain in general education classrooms rather than being segregated into "special" classes or schools—something that often happened prior to IDEA's initial enactment in 1975. Placement in regular classes is most successful when instructional materials and practices are tailored to students' specific educational needs and academic levels.[72]

MyEdLab Content Extension 4.3.
Learn more about IDEA in this supplementary reading.

Different members of a society have different specialties, and they call on one another's areas of expertise as needed.

In an earlier discussion of distributed cognition, we noted that people sometimes work together to tackle a challenging task, with each of them potentially contributing unique ideas and talents to the project. We can apply this notion of *distribution* on a much larger scale as well. In particular, a society is characterized by **distributed knowledge**: Different people have different areas of expertise, and so society members must rely on one another in order to maximize both their individual success and the success of the overall group. To be personally and professionally successful over the long run, then, children and adolescents must gain the knowledge and skills that will enable them to (1) seek out the expertise they may occasionally need to tackle difficult tasks and (2) distinguish between true experts, on the one hand, and individuals who only *claim* to be experts, on the other.[73] Identifying true experts can be especially difficult on the Internet, where anyone can claim anything without any verification.

In most situations, some society members have greater access to the society's resources than other members do.

In virtually any society, different people have access to different resources, and this differential access can have a significant impact on younger members' learning and long-term success. For example, some children, but not all, have a quiet place at home to study and parents who can help them with challenging homework assignments. Some, but not all, have a home computer that provides Internet access, word processing programs, and other tools that enhance classroom performance. Some, but not all, live near or can easily travel to public libraries, museums, and zoos.

One important factor affecting learners' access to resources is their **socioeconomic status (SES)**. This concept encompasses a number of variables, including family income, parents' education levels, and parents' occupations—all of which either directly or indirectly influence a variety of factors, including the type of neighborhood a family lives in and the educational opportunities that are readily available.

[69] C. D. Lee, 2010; Thelen & Smith, 1998.

[70] This legislation was most recently reauthorized in 2004, at which point it was renamed the Individuals with Disabilities Education Improvement Act. However, most people still refer to it by its original name.

[71] J. M. Fletcher, Lyon, Fuchs, & Barnes, 2007; Kağitçibaşi, 2007; Pelphrey & Carter, 2007.

[72] P. Hunt & Goetz, 1997; Scruggs & Mastropieri, 1994; Slavin, 1987; Soodak & McCarthy, 2006; Stainback & Stainback, 1992.

[73] Bromme, Kienhues, & Porsch, 2010.

Children's and adolescents' socioeconomic status is correlated with their school performance: Higher-SES students tend to have higher academic achievement, and lower-SES students tend to be at greater risk for dropping out of school. As students from lower-SES families move through the grade levels, many of them fall further and further behind their higher-SES peers. When researchers find achievement differences among students from different ethnic groups, the differences in the students' socioeconomic status, *not* their cultural differences per se, seem to be largely to blame.[74]

Children and adolescents from low-SES families are a diverse group. Some live in inner-city neighborhoods, others live in rural areas, and some live in modest apartments or homes in wealthy suburban towns. Regardless of where they live, some of these learners may face one or more of the following challenges:

- **Poor nutrition and health care.** Poor nutrition in early childhood is associated with poorer attention and memory and impaired learning ability. Poor nutrition can influence school achievement both directly—for instance, by hampering early brain development—and indirectly—for instance, by leaving children listless and inattentive in class. And inadequate health care means that some conditions that interfere with school attendance and performance, such as asthma and hearing problems, go unaddressed.[75]

- **Inadequate housing and frequent moves.** Many low-SES families live in tight quarters, perhaps sharing only one or two rooms with other family members. In old, poorly maintained apartment buildings, children may be exposed to lead in the dust from deteriorating paint, and such lead can cause brain damage. In addition, if children move frequently from one rental apartment to another, they must often change schools as well. In the process, they lose existing social support networks and may miss lessons on important academic skills.[76]

- **Unhealthy social environments.** On average, low-SES neighborhoods and communities have higher frequencies of violence and vandalism, greater prevalence of alcoholism and drug abuse, and greater numbers of antisocial peers. Furthermore, there are fewer productive outlets for leisure time—for instance, libraries, recreation centers, and sports leagues—and fewer positive adult role models. Such factors appear to be partly responsible for the lower academic achievement of students who live in poverty.[77]

- **Lower-quality schools.** Unfortunately, children who most need good schools are often least likely to have them. On average, schools in low-SES neighborhoods and communities tend to receive less funding and, as a result, are often poorly equipped and maintained. Teacher turnover rates are high. Furthermore, some teachers at these schools have low expectations for students, offer a less challenging curriculum, assign less homework, and provide fewer opportunities to develop advanced thinking skills than do teachers in wealthier school districts.[78]

Children who face only one or two of these challenges often do quite well in school, but those who face most or all of them are at high risk for academic failure.[79] Especially when poverty is an ongoing way of life rather than a temporary situation, children may feel considerable emotional stress about their life circumstances,[80] and as you'll discover in Chapter 5, students learn

---

[74] Byrnes, 2003; Farkas, 2008; N. E. Hill, Bush, & Roosa, 2003; J.-S. Lee & Bowen, 2006; McLoyd, 1998; Murdock, 2000; Rumberger, 2011; Sirin, 2005.

[75] Ashiabi & O'Neal, 2008; Berliner, 2005; Benton, 2008; Noble, Tottenham, & Casey, 2005; Sigman & Whaley, 1998; R. A. Thompson & Nelson, 2001.

[76] Croninger & Valli, 2009; Dilworth & Moore, 2006; Gruman, Harachi, Abbott, Catalano, & Fleming, 2008; Hattie, 2009; Hernandez, Denton, & Macartney, 2008; Hubbs-Tait, Nation, Krebs, & Bellinger, 2005; Mantzicopoulos & Knutson, 2000; P. M. Miller, 2011.

[77] Aikens & Barbarin, 2008; Duncan & Magnuson, 2005; Nettles, Caughy, & O'Campo, 2008; Tamis-Lemonda & McFadden, 2010; Yoshikawa, Aber, & Beardslee, 2012.

[78] G. W. Evans, 2004; McLoyd, 1998; Pianta & Hamre, 2009; Raudenbush, 2009.

[79] Becker & Luthar, 2002; Gerard & Buehler, 2004; Grissmer, Williamson, Kirby, & Berends, 1998.

[80] Brooks-Gunn, Linver, & Fauth, 2005; G. W. Evans & Kim, 2007; Gershoff, Aber, Raver, & Lennon, 2007; Yoshikawa et al., 2012.

and perform less effectively when they're highly anxious. Not all low-SES children live in chronically stressful conditions, of course, and those whose families provide consistent support, guidance, and discipline generally enjoy good mental health.[81]

Technology and Media as Contexts

Strictly speaking, *technology* includes any human-made application of scientific knowledge for a practical purpose, such as a pencil, lightbulb, or iPad. And the term *media* (which is plural for *medium*) refers to the various means through which people communicate across space and time. Some common media are radio, television, books, and music. Our focus here will be on *digital technologies* and *digital media*—those that enable us to electronically store, manipulate, and transmit information. (The word *digital* refers to the fact that the information is stored as many, many 0s and 1s, collectively known as *bits.*) Computer hardware and software, cell phones, video cameras, video game systems, and the Internet are all examples.

As digital technologies have become more widely available and affordable, they've also become more pervasive in modern-day societies. Furthermore, they enable learners to electronically "travel" well beyond their immediate physical and social surroundings, as reflected in the next two principles.

Mobile devices allow learners to connect to a wide variety of people and resources.

Many students are proficient in using mobile devices (e.g., cell phones, smartphones, and tablets) to make calls, send text messages, take and send photographs, play games, and post opinions and photos on social networking sites such as Facebook and Twitter. For most adolescents, the primary motive for using cell phones and other new technologies is to initiate and maintain social relationships, especially with peers.[82]

But in school, these mobile devices allow learners to connect with individuals who are more knowledgeable than them about particular content areas. When used in this manner, mobile technologies enable learners to access that *distributed knowledge* described earlier, including facts and data. Learners can gain needed information about almost any subject area—and sometimes they gain *mis*information—by using an Internet search engine such as Google or Bing. Mobile devices also allow learners to bring their out-of-class experiences into the classroom. As an example, in a lesson on healthy eating, students might take pictures of what they eat each day, log the content of their meals, and create a bar chart of its nutritional value.[83]

However, these types of technologies certainly have their downsides. For example, ever-present mobile devices can be a source of distraction for students who should be focusing on their schoolwork, and some video games communicate the message that aggression and violence are perfectly acceptable—perhaps even desirable—in today's society. Nonetheless, these technologies have opened doors to many new and exciting ways of educating young people, as we'll see later in this chapter and in subsequent ones.

Some media create "virtual" contexts that simulate real-world-like environments and events.

Digital technologies enable people to be active participants in a simulated environment. For example, in video game systems such as PlayStation, Wii, and Xbox, children and adolescents can "run" and "jump" their way through various physical challenges in search of coins or other prizes, "fight" and "kill" bad guys in exotic locations, or "play" tennis or football on a digital "court" or "field." Some simulated environments are called *virtual worlds* because they allow participants to represent themselves as avatars and to have realistic experiences somewhere other than where they are physically located. Teachers have used virtual worlds to allow students to participate in activities that simulate real-world activities that would otherwise be difficult to access from where they

---

[81] N. E. Hill et al., 2003; M. O. Wright & Masten, 2006.

[82] Ito et al., 2009; Valkenburg & Peter, 2009; Warschauer, 2011.

[83] Sharples & Pea, 2014.

are physically located. As you'll discover in Chapter 8, educational technologists have created a variety of online virtual worlds that can help students develop skills in science, math, and social studies. When such software programs require students to interact with one another, they can also enhance students' skills in negotiation, collaboration, and leadership.

Academic Content Domains as Contexts

In the early millennia of human civilization, cultures and societies focused largely on teaching children knowledge and skills related to basic survival (hunting, growing crops, cooking, etc.), and experts in such areas as woodworking, metalwork, and medicine often taught their knowledge to new generations through one-on-one apprenticeships. But as cultural groups developed writing systems and constructed increasingly complex understandings of their physical, biological, and social worlds, they began to establish formal schools that could more efficiently pass their cultural creations on to future generations. One way in which schools made the ever-expanding knowledge base more manageable for instruction was to subdivide it into various academic disciplines, such as reading, mathematics, science, social studies, music, and art.

Because different disciplines focus on different phenomena—and thus on different kinds of tasks and problems—they also require somewhat different thinking skills. For example, effective reading requires automatic retrieval of the meanings of thousands of words, whereas mathematical problem solving requires precisely thinking about quantities and flexibly manipulating symbols that represent them. Furthermore, various subject areas may depend more or less heavily on different areas of the brain.[84]

In a very real way, then, different content domains are additional *contexts* in which students learn, and strategies for effectively teaching the subject matter can vary significantly from one domain to another. Following are two general principles to keep in mind about these domain-specific contexts.

Each academic discipline provides many cognitive tools that enhance thinking and problem solving.

Virtually every academic content domain offers many discipline-specific concepts, symbols, and ways of thinking that can help learners more effectively interpret and deal with the various situations and problems that daily life presents. Let's begin with mathematics, as reflected in the following exercise.

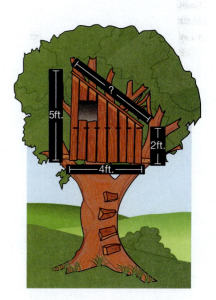

———————————— **SEE FOR YOURSELF** ————————————
BUILDING A TREEHOUSE

Imagine that you're building a treehouse that has a floor 4 feet across, a side wall 2 feet high, and an opposite wall 5 feet high, as shown here. You need to buy planks for a slanted roof that will reach from the taller wall to the shorter one. How long must the roof planks be to reach from one wall to the other?

———

One way to address the problem would be to measure the side walls and floor in the drawing and determine whether the drawing has been created using a particular scale. If so, you could apply the same scale in estimating the length of the necessary roof planks. A second approach involves geometry and algebra. If you've studied geometry, you've probably learned the Pythagorean theorem: In any right triangle, the square of the hypotenuse (the longest side) equals the sum of the squares of the other two sides. Looking at the top part of the treehouse (from the dotted line upward) as a triangle, we can find the length for the roof planks (x) this way:

$$(\text{slanted side})^2 = (\text{horizontal side})^2 + (\text{vertical side})^2$$
$$x^2 = 4^2 + (5 - 2)^2$$
$$x^2 = 16 + 9$$
$$x^2 = 25$$
$$x = 5$$

———————————————

[84] Dehaene, 2007; Katzir & Paré-Blagoev, 2006; Norton, Kovelman, & Pettito, 2007; Plumert & Spencer, 2007; Posner & Rothbart, 2007.

Regardless of which approach you took, you would have used several cognitive tools of mathematics, perhaps (1) the concepts of *measurement, inches, feet,* and *scale,* or (2) the *Pythagorean theorem,* the concept of *variable (x),* and algebraic procedures.

Other academic disciplines offer cognitive tools suited for other kinds of tasks and problems. For example, people often become better musicians when they can interpret musical notation, understand what *chords* and *thirds* are, and think about particular musical pieces using such concepts. People can make better sense of certain physical phenomena when they understand and apply scientific concepts such as *force, gravity,* and *chemical reaction.* They can write more compelling essays and poems if they make use of *metaphors* or *onomatopoeia.* And they can more easily find their way to faraway places when they can interpret maps and common map-making conventions, such as the use of lines to represent roads, dots to represent towns and cities, and a mathematical *scale* to convey relative distances.

think about it
Think about the academic discipline in which you are majoring. What cognitive tools does it provide to help you tackle new tasks and problems?

Different content domains require somewhat different cognitive processes and, as a result, somewhat different ways of learning.

In your many years as a student, you may have found some subject areas to be easier to understand and master than others. Maybe you struggled a bit with mathematics. (If so, did you take one look at the preceding treehouse exercise and decide to *skip* it?) Alternatively, if you did well in math, did you instead have trouble with spelling, history, or studio art?

Different subject areas call for different mental processes. Math, of course, requires reasoning about quantities, and at more advanced levels it also requires mental manipulation of abstract symbols that can be hard to connect to concrete reality. In contrast, reading and writing proficiency involve not only mastering specific letter–sound and word–sound correspondences but also employing multiple meaning-making strategies (for reading) and verbal communication techniques (for writing). Proficiency in science requires systematic observations and data collection (e.g., through separation and control of variables), objective analysis of findings, and an ability to distinguish between valid and invalid conclusions. In social studies, learners must look at human events and problems from the perspectives of people living in societies and time periods very different from their own. And studio art requires paying close attention to the physical world and representing it in visually compelling ways. It shouldn't surprise you to learn, then, that "best" instructional practices in one discipline are often quite different from those in another discipline.

Teachers are part of a school culture that socializes students in certain ways—both explicitly and implicitly. Teachers may share cognitive tools with students explicitly, yet may implicitly share their worldviews through their actions. Cultural beliefs are also passed along to students through their families, other social groups, their communities, and the society in which they live. Digital technologies and media can also provide contexts for learning, as can academic content domains. Thus, students are influenced by a variety of cultural legacies as they participate in school activities. In the hotlinked Self-Check quiz and Application Exercise that follow, you can check and apply your understandings related to Big Idea 4.3:

> *The cultural, societal, and technological contexts in which learners grow up also influence their behaviors and cognitive processes, as do the academic domains that learners study in school and elsewhere.*

MyEdLab **Self-Check 4.3**

MyEdLab **Application Exercise 4.3.** In this exercise, you can analyze scenarios in which students have trouble reconciling beliefs they've previously acquired at home with information and expectations they encounter at school.

4.4 HOW LEARNERS MODIFY THEIR ENVIRONMENTS

Big Idea 4.4 Although various environmental contexts influence learners and their development, so, too, do learners influence the environments in which they live and grow.

In the preceding sections, we've seen various ways in which people's environments—especially their social and cultural ones—affect their behavior and learning. But the reverse is true as well: Learners influence their environments, sometimes unintentionally and sometimes quite deliberately, as the next two principles reveal.

Learners alter their current environment through both their behaviors and such internal variables as beliefs, mental processes, feelings, and personality traits.

To some degree, learners' specific behaviors change their environments. For example, a student who misbehaves while participating in a classroom activity might be removed from the activity and told to just sit on the side and watch. Personal, internal variables—beliefs, mental processes, feelings, personality traits, knowledge, and so on—can also affect learners' environments. For instance, learners can pay attention (an internal variable) to only a few aspects of their environment because of the limited capacity of attention and working memory (see Chapter 2). In fact, all three of the items just described—*internal variables, the environment,* and *behavior*—influence one another. This interdependence among internal variables, the environment, and behavior is known as **reciprocal causation** because one item can affect the others and vice versa.[85] Figure 4.5 illustrates this concept, and Table 4.3 presents several examples of the three-way interplay in its "General Examples" column.

As a concrete illustration of how internal variables, the environment, and behavior are continually intertwined, let's consider Scene 1 in the case of a student named Lori:

> Scene 1
>
> Lori often comes late to Mr. Broderick's seventh-grade social studies class, and she's usually not prepared for the day's activities. In class, she spends more time interacting with friends (e.g., whispering, passing notes) than engaging in assigned tasks. Lori's performance on most exams and assignments is unsatisfactory—when she turns in her work at all.
>
> In mid-October, Mr. Broderick takes Lori aside to express concern about her lack of classroom effort. He suggests that she could do better if she paid more attention in class. He also offers to work with her after school twice a week to help her understand class material. Lori isn't optimistic, describing herself as "not smart enough to learn this stuff."
>
> Over the next few days Lori buckles down and exerts more effort, but she never stays after school for extra help. And before long she's back to her old habits. Mr. Broderick eventually concludes that Lori is a lost cause and decides to devote his time and effort to helping more motivated students.

Lori's low expectations for academic achievement (an internal variable) may partly explain why she spends so much time in task-irrelevant activities (behaviors). The fact that she devotes her attention (another internal variable) to her classmates, rather than to her teacher, affects the particular stimuli she experiences (her environment). Lori's poor study habits and resulting poor performance on assignments and exams (her behaviors) adversely affect both her expectations for future academic success (an internal variable) and Mr. Broderick's treatment of her (her environment). By eventually concluding that Lori is a lost cause, Mr. Broderick begins to ignore Lori (which changes her environment), contributing to her further failure (her behavior) and even lower self-confidence (an internal variable). You can see some of these interactive effects in the Scene 1 column in Table 4.3. Clearly, Lori is showing signs of being at risk for long-term academic failure.

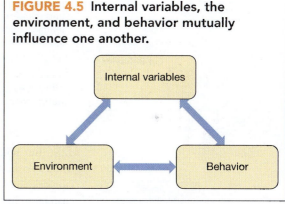

FIGURE 4.5 Internal variables, the environment, and behavior mutually influence one another.

Internal variables

Environment

Behavior

---

[85] Bandura, 1989, 2006, 2008; T. Williams & Williams, 2010.

Table 4.3 • Mutual Influences (Reciprocal Causation) Among Environment, Behavior, and Internal Variables

		GENERAL EXAMPLES	EXAMPLES IN LORI'S CASE: SCENE 1	EXAMPLES IN LORI'S CASE: SCENE 2
Effect of Environment	On Behavior	Reinforcement and punishment affect future behavior.	The teacher's decision to spend most of his time with other students leads to Lori's continuing classroom failure.	New instructional methods lead to Lori's improved academic performance.
	On Internal Variables	Feedback from others affects the learner's expectations (either positively or negatively) about future performance.	The teacher's lack of time and effort with Lori perpetuates her low self-confidence about classroom tasks.	New instructional methods capture Lori's interest and attention.
Effect of Behavior	On Environment	Specific behaviors affect the amount of reinforcement and punishment received.	Lori's poor classroom performance initially leads her teacher to meet privately with her and then eventually to ignore her.	Lori's improved learning strategies and academic performance lead to more frequent reinforcement.
	On Internal Variables	Current successes and failures affect expectations for future performance.	Lori's current poor classroom performance leads to her low expectations about future performance.	Lori's improved learning strategies and academic performance boost her self-confidence about future classroom performance.
Effect of Internal Variables	On Environment	Expectations about future performance in various domains affect the specific activities the learner chooses to engage in and therefore also affect the learning opportunities the learner encounters.	Lori's attention to classmates during instructional activities causes her peers to be more influential stimuli than her teacher.	Lori's increased attention to classroom activities enhances the effectiveness of the teacher's instruction.
	On Behavior	Attention, learning strategies, and other cognitive processes affect the learner's classroom performance.	Lori's attention to classmates rather than to instruction leads to academic failure.	Lori's greater self-confidence and increased motivation lead to more regular and effective study habits.

But now imagine that after reading several research articles about how to work with students at risk, Mr. Broderick develops greater optimism that he can break the vicious cycle of reciprocal causation for students such as Lori. Midway through the school year, he makes several changes in his teaching:

- He communicates clearly and consistently that he expects all students to succeed in his classroom.
- He incorporates students' personal experiences and interests into the study of social studies.
- He identifies specific, concrete goals that students will accomplish each week and provides the structure and guidance students need to meet them.
- After consulting with the school's reading specialist and school psychologist, he helps students develop more effective reading and learning strategies.
- He gives a quiz each Friday so that students can see that they're making regular progress.

Let's see what happens next, as we consider Scene 2:

Scene 2

By incorporating students' personal experiences and interests into daily lessons, Mr. Broderick begins to capture Lori's attention. She starts to realize that social studies has implications for her own life and so she becomes more involved in class activities. With the more structured assignments, increased guidance about how to study, and frequent quizzes, Lori finds herself succeeding in a subject at which she previously experienced only failure. Mr. Broderick frequently communicates his pleasure about her progress through his facial expressions, verbal feedback, and willingness to provide help whenever she needs it.

By the end of the school year, Lori is studying course material more effectively and completing her assignments regularly. She's looking forward to next year's social studies class, confident that she'll continue to do well.

Once again, we see the interplay among environment, behavior, and internal variables. Mr. Broderick's new instructional methods (Lori's environment) engage Lori's attention (an internal variable), and they foster better study habits and enhance academic performance (her behaviors). Lori's improved classroom performance, in turn, influences Mr. Broderick's treatment of her (her environment) and her own self-confidence (an internal variable). And her improved self-confidence, her greater attention to classroom activities, and her increased motivation to succeed (all internal variables) affect her ability to benefit from Mr. Broderick's instruction (her environment) and thus also affect her classroom success (her behavior). The Scene 2 column in Table 4.3 presents examples of these new interactions.

Learners actively seek out environments that are a good fit with their existing characteristics and behaviors.

As children get older, they can increasingly *choose* and thereby control their environments. With such choice and control, they're apt to seek out situations in which they feel comfortable—situations that match their existing abilities, interests, and needs and that allow them to engage in preferred activities (more on this point in Chapter 5). This tendency to seek out environmental conditions that are a good match with existing characteristics and skills—a phenomenon known as **niche-picking**—can significantly increase existing differences among learners.[86]

For example, as children move through the grade levels, they gain a wider choice of peers with whom they can spend time, and they increasingly affiliate with peers who share their interests and activities. As they reach middle school or junior high school, and even more so as they reach high school, they select some of the courses they take—thus, they begin to focus on the subject matter they enjoy and may steer clear of the subject matter they've consistently found to be frustrating. As they master public transportation systems or learn how to drive, they have increasing access to environments beyond home and the immediate neighborhood. Some of these environments, such as a library, gymnasium, or music studio, can help them acquire valuable new knowledge and skills. Other environments, such as a gathering place for antisocial peers or an all-night party where illegal drugs are readily available, can be harmful to their cognitive and social development.

Although children and adolescents influence and control their own environments to some degree, teachers, too, have considerable control over an environment that is a big part of youngsters' daily lives: school. We turn now to strategies for making the school environment one that fosters young people's learning, academic achievement, and social success.

think about it

Can you explain reciprocal causation in your own words? Can you provide an example from your own experience?

think about it

Look once again at the boldfaced concepts presented in the section "Developing as a Teacher" in Chapter 1. Which concept does Mr. Broderick's actions best illustrate? (For the answer, click **here**.)

> Students learn in a dynamic environment in which their internal variables (e.g., beliefs, mental processes, feelings) affect and are affected by the environment and their behaviors. Changes to any one of these items—internal variables, the environment, or behavior—can produce changes in the other items. Teachers need to be aware of how the interplay among these items may be affecting students' learning and behavior. In the hotlinked Self-Check quiz and Application Exercise that follow, you can check and apply your understandings related to Big Idea 4.4:
>
> *Although various environmental contexts influence learners and their development, so, too, do learners influence the environments in which they live and grow.*
>
> MyEdLab **Self-Check 4.4**
>
> MyEdLab **Application Exercise 4.4.** In this exercise, you will analyze a student's behavior and apply the concept of reciprocal causation to a situation.

[86] O. S. P. Davis, Haworth, & Plomin, 2009; Flynn, 2003; Halpern & LaMay, 2000; Scarr & McCartney, 1983.

4.5 PROVIDING SUPPORTIVE CONTEXTS FOR LEARNING

Big Idea 4.5 Effective teachers create a classroom environment that encourages and supports productive behaviors and ways of thinking.

The various layers of the environment—from the specific stimuli learners encounter in their immediate circumstances to the general cultures and societies in which learners are continually immersed—have numerous implications for classroom practice. The strategies offered in this section fall into two general categories: encouraging productive behaviors and providing physical, social, and technological support for effective cognitive processes.

Encouraging Productive Behaviors

The concepts of *antecedent stimulus*, *reinforcement*, and *modeling* can be quite helpful in promoting productive learner behaviors, as the following recommendations reveal.

Create conditions that elicit desired responses.

Early in the chapter, we saw how certain stimulus conditions—for instance, cooperative games and classroom assignments appropriate for students' ability levels—tend to evoke productive behaviors. Furthermore, a general classroom climate in which students feel accepted and respected by teachers and classmates alike tends to bring out the best in almost everyone (more on this point in Chapter 5 and Chapter 9).

Sometimes teachers provide explicit reminders about desirable and undesirable behaviors—a strategy known as **cueing**. In some instances, cueing involves a nonverbal signal, such as ringing a bell or flicking an overhead light switch to remind children to talk quietly rather than loudly. At other times, it involves a verbal reminder, either direct or indirect, about what children should be doing—for example, "Remember to use your *indoor* voices as you talk" and "I see some art supplies that need to be put away." Such statements are examples of the *retrieval cues* discussed in Chapter 2, although in this case they remind students about appropriate classroom behavior rather than about academic subject matter.

Make sure that productive behaviors are reinforced and that unproductive behaviors are *not* reinforced.

Teachers should be sure to regularly reinforce desirable behaviors, such as reading frequently, constructing a well-researched science fair poster, and working cooperatively with classmates. This idea is summarized nicely by the phrase "Catch students being good." When students aren't motivated to engage in classroom tasks and activities, reinforcers tailored to students' developmental levels and individual interests—such as stickers, special privileges, and free time to engage in favorite activities—can keep students on task as they work to master important information and skills. And under certain conditions, positive feedback (and sometimes even *negative* feedback) can be a very powerful reinforcer. The Classroom Strategies box "Using Feedback to Improve Learning and Behavior" offers suggestions for maximizing feedback's effectiveness.

In some cases, teachers can let students *choose* their reinforcers and perhaps even choose different reinforcers on different occasions.[87] One useful strategy is a **token economy**, in which students who exhibit desired behaviors receive *tokens* (e.g., poker chips or specially marked pieces of colored paper) that they can later use to "purchase" a variety of *backup reinforcers*—perhaps small treats, free time in the reading center, or a prime position in the lunch line. By and large, however, teachers should stay away from concrete reinforcers such as small toys and trinkets, which can distract students' attention away from their schoolwork.

Regardless of the form reinforcement takes, *some* kind of reinforcer should follow desired behaviors. Otherwise, those behaviors might decrease and eventually disappear—a phenomenon

MyEdLab
Video Example 4.2.

How is a token reinforcer being used in this special education classroom?

---
[87] Berg et al., 2007; Bowman, Piazza, Fisher, Hagopian, & Kogan, 1997; Fisher & Mazur, 1997; Ulke-Kurcuoglu & Kircaali-Iftar, 2010.

CLASSROOM STRATEGIES

Using Feedback to Improve Learning and Behavior

- **Be explicit about what students are doing well—ideally, at the time they are doing it.**
  When praising her students for appropriate classroom behavior, a second-grade teacher is quite specific about the actions for which she is commending them. For example, she says, "I like the way you're working quietly" and "Thank you, Ricky, for not disturbing the rest of the class."

- **Give concrete guidance about how students can improve their performance.**
  A high school physical education teacher tells a student, "Your time in the 100-meter dash wasn't as fast as it could have been. It's early in the season, though, and if you work on your endurance, I know you'll improve. Also, I think you might get a faster start if you stay low when you first come out of the starting blocks."

- **Communicate optimism that students *can* improve.**
  When a student in a middle school geography class gives an oral report on Mexico, she bores her classmates with a lengthy description of her family's recent trip to Puerto Vallarta. Many students begin to communicate their displeasure through body language and occasional whispers across the aisle. At the end of class, the student is devastated that her report has been so poorly received. Her teacher takes her aside and gently says, "You included many interesting facts in your report, Julie, and your many pictures and artifacts really helped us understand Mexican culture. But you know how young teenagers are—they can have a pretty short attention span at times. I'll be assigning oral reports again in a couple months. Before you give yours, let's sit down and plan it so that your classmates will think, 'Wow, this is really interesting!'"

- **Don't overwhelm students with too much feedback; tell them only what they can reasonably attend to and remember at the time.**
  As a kindergarten teacher watches one of his students practice writing several alphabet letters, he helps the student hold her pencil in a way that gives her better control. He doesn't mention that she's writing her *B*s and *D*s backward; he'll save this information for a later time, after she has mastered her pencil grip.

- **Minimize feedback when students already know exactly what they've done well or poorly.**
  A high school student has been getting poor grades in his math class largely as a result of insufficient effort. When he begins to try harder and do his homework regularly, his quiz scores improve tremendously. As his teacher hands him his first quiz after his newfound diligence—a quiz on which he's earned a score of 96%—she says nothing, but she smiles and gives him a thumbs-up.

- **Teach students strategies for appropriately asking for feedback.**
  A fourth-grade teacher has three students with intellectual disabilities in her class. She knows that these students may need more frequent feedback than their classmates. She teaches them three steps to take when they need her assistance: (1) They should raise their hands or walk quietly to her desk; (2) they should wait patiently until she has time to speak with them; and (3) they should make their needs known (e.g., "How am I doing?" "What do I do next?").

Sources: Boyanton, 2010; D. L. Butler & Winne, 1995; M. A. Craft, Alberg, & Heward, 1998, p. 402 (fourth-grade example); Feltz, Chase, Moritz, & Sullivan, 1999; Hattie & Gan, 2011; Hattie & Timperley, 2007; K. A. Meyer, 1999; Shute, 2008; Stokes, Luiselli, Reed, & Fleming, 2010; Tunstall & Gipps, 1996; Wise & O'Neill, 2009.

known as **extinction**. Initially, to increase the frequency of a desired response, reinforcement should be *continuous,* occurring every time the response occurs. Once a student makes the response frequently, reinforcement can be *intermittent*—that is, given on some occasions but not others—so that the response doesn't extinguish.

Meanwhile, teachers must be careful that they don't inadvertently reinforce behaviors that will interfere with learners' success over the long run. For example, if a teacher repeatedly allows Carol to turn in assignments late because she says she forgot her homework, and if that teacher often lets Caleb get his way by bullying classmates, the teacher is reinforcing—and hence increasing—Carol's irresponsibility and Caleb's aggressiveness.

Make response–reinforcement contingencies clear.

Whenever teachers use reinforcement in the classroom, they should explicitly describe the cause-and-effect relationships, or **contingencies**, between responses and reinforcers. For example, kindergarten students are more likely to respond appropriately if they're told, "The quietest group can be first in line for lunch." Ninth graders are more likely to complete their Spanish assignments if they know that by doing so they'll be able to go on a field trip to a local Cinco de Mayo festival.

One concrete way of communicating both behavioral expectations and response–reinforcement contingencies is a **contingency contract**. To develop such a contract, the teacher meets with a student to discuss a problem behavior (e.g., talking to friends during independent seatwork or

think about it
Which form of reinforcement—continuous or intermittent—would you use to encourage students to persist at difficult tasks? (For the answer, click **here**.)

MyEdLab
Video Explanation 4.5.

This video can help you identify instances of teacher and peer reinforcement in real classrooms.

speaking disrespectfully to classmates). The teacher and student then identify and agree on desired behaviors that the student will demonstrate (e.g., completing seatwork assignments within a certain time frame; speaking with classmates in a friendly, respectful manner). The two also agree on one or more reinforcers for those behaviors (e.g., a certain amount of free time, or points earned toward a particular privilege). Together the teacher and student write and sign a contract that describes the desired behaviors and contingent reinforcers. Contingency contracts can be a highly effective means of improving a wide variety of academic and social behaviors.[88]

As an alternative to punishment, reinforce productive behaviors that are incompatible with unproductive ones.

Some occasions clearly call for punishment, as you'll discover in Chapter 9. But at other times a teacher can reduce the frequency of an unproductive behavior simply by reinforcing a *different* behavior. Ideally, the two behaviors are incompatible behaviors, in that they can't be performed simultaneously. For example, try the following exercise.

SEE FOR YOURSELF
ASLEEP ON YOUR FEET

Have you ever tried to sleep while standing up? Horses can do it, but most humans really can't. In fact, there are many pairs of actions that are impossible to perform simultaneously. Take a minute to identify something you can't possibly do when you perform each of these activities:

When you. . .	You can't simultaneously. . .
Sit down	_____
Eat crackers	_____
Take a walk	_____

Obviously, there are many possible right answers. For instance, sitting is incompatible with standing. Eating crackers is incompatible with singing—or at least with singing *well*. Taking a walk is incompatible with taking a nap. In each case it's physically impossible to perform both activities at exactly the same time.

To apply the concept of incompatible behaviors in the classroom, a teacher might, for example, reinforce a hyperactive student for sitting down, because sitting is incompatible with getting-out-of-seat and roaming-around-the-room behaviors. Similarly, a teacher might discourage off-task responses by reinforcing *on*-task responses or discourage verbally aggressive behavior by reinforcing socially appropriate actions. And consider how one school dealt with a chronic litterbug:

> Walt often leaves banana peels, sunflower seed shells, and other garbage in and outside the school building. When the school faculty establishes an Anti-Litter Committee, it puts Walt on the committee, and the committee eventually elects him as its chairman. Under Walt's leadership, the committee institutes an anti-litter campaign, complete with posters and lunchroom monitors, and Walt receives considerable recognition for the campaign's success. Subsequently, school personnel no longer find Walt's garbage littering the building and school grounds.[89]

Model desired behaviors.

Teachers teach not only by what they say but also by what they do, so it's critical that teachers model appropriate behaviors and *not* model inappropriate ones. Do they model enthusiasm and excitement about the subject matter or merely tolerance for a dreary topic the class must somehow muddle through? Do they model fairness to all students or favoritism to a small few? Do they expound on the virtues of innovation and creativity yet use the same curriculum materials year after year? Their actions often speak louder than their words.

---

[88] K. L. Lane, Menzies, Bruhn, & Crnobori, 2011; D. L. Miller & Kelley, 1994.
[89] Krumboltz & Krumboltz, 1972.

Four conditions help students learn effectively from models:[90]

- **Attention.** Attention is critical for getting information into working memory (see Chapter 2). To learn effectively, then, students must pay attention to the model and especially to critical aspects of the modeled behavior.

- **Retention.** The learner must remember what the model does—in particular, by storing it in long-term memory. Students are more likely to remember information if they encode it in more than one way, perhaps as both a visual image and a verbal message (again see Chapter 2). For instance, teachers might describe what they're doing while they demonstrate a particular skill. They might also attach descriptive labels to complex behaviors that would otherwise be difficult to remember.[91] For example, when teaching swimming, an easy way to help students remember the sequence of arm positions in the elementary backstroke is to teach them the labels *chicken, airplane,* and *soldier* (see Figure 4.6).

FIGURE 4.6 Students can often more easily remember a complex behavior, such as the arm movements for the elementary backstroke, when those behaviors have verbal labels.

"Chicken"   "Airplane"   "Soldier"

- **Motor reproduction.** The learner must be physically capable of reproducing the behavior being demonstrated. When students lack this ability, motor reproduction obviously can't occur; for example, 6-year-olds who watch an adult throw a softball don't have the muscular coordination to mimic a good throw. It's often useful to have students imitate a desired behavior immediately after they see it, enabling their teacher to give individually tailored suggestions for improvement. Yet teachers must keep in mind a point made in the earlier Cultural Considerations box: Students from some ethnic groups may prefer to practice new behaviors in private at first and to demonstrate what they've learned only after they've achieved some degree of competence.

- **Motivation.** Finally, the learner must be motivated to demonstrate the modeled behavior. The next principle can be helpful in enhancing learners' motivation to imitate productive behaviors.

Provide a variety of role models.

In addition to modeling desired behaviors themselves, teachers should expose students to other models whom students are likely to perceive as competent and prestigious. For example, teachers might invite respected professionals (e.g., police officers, nurses, journalists) to demonstrate skills within particular areas of expertise. They might also have students read about or observe positive role models in books, videos, and other media.

Furthermore, students can benefit from observing the final products of a model's efforts. Art students might gain useful strategies by studying the works of masters such as Vincent Van Gogh and Pablo Picasso, and music students can acquire new strategies by listening to skillful musicians with diverse musical styles. In one seventh-grade language arts class, students found examples of figurative writing in favorite books (see Figure 4.7), and such examples served as models for their own writing efforts.

Recall that one of the characteristics of effective models listed earlier is *behavior relevant to one's own situation*. Students are less likely to perceive a model's behaviors as relevant to their own circumstances if the model is different from them in some obvious way. For instance,

FIGURE 4.7 Students in Barbara Dee's seventh-grade language arts class chose these models of effective figurative writing from books they were reading.

"The blackness of the night came in, like snakes around the ankles."
—Caroline Cooney, *Wanted,* p. 176

"Flirtatious waves made passes at the primly pebbled beach."
—Lilian Jackson Braun, *The Cat Who Saw Stars,* p. 120

"Water boiled up white and frothy, like a milkshake."
—Lurlene McDaniel, *For Better, for Worse, Forever,* p. 60

"I try to swallow the snowball in my throat."
—Laurie Halse Anderson, *Speak,* p. 72

---

[90] Bandura, 1986.
[91] Gerst, 1971; T. L. Rosenthal, Alford, & Rasp, 1972; Vintere et al., 2004.

students from a lower-SES neighborhood or ethnic-minority group won't necessarily see the actions of a middle-income European American as being useful for themselves. Similarly, students with disabilities may believe they're incapable of accomplishing the things a nondisabled teacher demonstrates. So it's important that teachers include individuals from low-SES backgrounds and minority-group cultures, as well as individuals with disabilities, in the models they present to students. Such models can give students cause for optimism that they, too, can achieve lofty goals.[92]

Shape complex behaviors gradually over time.

When dramatic changes are necessary, it's unreasonable to expect students to make them overnight. In such a situation, a process known as **shaping** can be effective. To shape a desired behavior, a teacher takes the following steps:

1. First reinforce any response that in some way resembles the desired behavior.
2. Then reinforce a response that more closely approximates the desired behavior (while no longer reinforcing the previously reinforced response).
3. Then reinforce a response that resembles the desired behavior even more closely.
4. Continue reinforcing closer and closer approximations to the desired behavior.
5. Finally, reinforce only the desired behavior.

Each response in the sequence is reinforced every time it occurs until the student exhibits it regularly; only at that point does the teacher increase the expectation for performance. For example, imagine that a student, Miranda, can't seem to sit still long enough to get much of anything done. Her teacher would ultimately like her to sit still for 20-minute periods. However, the teacher may first have to reinforce her for staying in her seat for just *2* minutes. As Miranda makes progress, her teacher can gradually increase the sitting time required for reinforcement.

Teachers can often use shaping to help students acquire complex physical and psychomotor skills. As an example, in the early elementary grades teachers gradually shape students' handwriting skills—for instance, expecting increasingly small and well-shaped letters (see Figure 4.8). And in secondary schools, physical education teachers and coaches teach and expect increasingly proficient athletic skills.[93]

In much the same way, teachers can (and often do) gradually shape students' ability to work independently on assignments. They begin by giving first graders structured tasks that may take

FIGURE 4.8 As Jeff moved through the elementary grades, gradual changes in his writing paper required him to write smaller and, eventually, with only a single line to guide him.

Grade 1

I like to riyt.

Grade 2

One day Lonely was eating his brefisk

Grade 4

When we left Greeley I didnt want to goOn the same day we stoped at a restrant. Then we went on In the ernen.

---

[92] Evans-Winters & Ivie, 2009; Kincheloe, 2009; Powers et al., 1995.
[93] Harrison & Pyles, 2013; Stokes, Luiselli, & Reed, 2010.

only 5 to 10 minutes to complete. As students move through the elementary school years, their teachers expect them to work independently for longer periods and give them increasingly complex assignments to do at home. By the time students reach high school, they have extended study halls and complete lengthy tasks on their own after school hours. In the college years, student assignments require a great deal of independence and self-direction.

Have students practice new behaviors and skills in a variety of contexts—ideally including real-world settings outside of school.

As noted earlier, learning and cognition are sometimes *situated* in particular contexts. For example, students may recall the Pythagorean theory *only* in a math class and neglect to use it when it might come in handy while building a treehouse at home. And they may apply what they've learned about persuasive writing only in writing essays in a language arts class, rather than also using it to evaluate political campaign brochures and newspaper editorials. If teachers want students to use what they've learned in many situations both in and out of school, they should give students practice using the subject matter with a variety of stimulus materials and in a variety of contexts, including some contexts outside of school. For example, teachers might assign homework that involves interviewing family members or neighbors about cultural beliefs or political concerns, or they might present complex problems in realistic computer-simulated environments. Community service projects and part-time internships with local businesses can provide opportunities for legitimate peripheral participation in society's various communities of practice.

Providing Physical, Social, and Technological Support for Effective Cognitive Processes

Environmental contexts, both past and present, affect not only students' behaviors but also their thinking processes, as reflected in the next set of recommendations.

Provide physical and cognitive tools that can help students work and think more effectively.

When you think of tools, you're apt to think of scissors, screwdrivers, and other physical objects. But keep in mind that many human tools—for instance, concepts, mathematical formulas, and specific study strategies—are entirely cognitive in nature. And still others—such as dictionaries, calculators, and flowcharts—are both physical and cognitive, in that they're physical manifestations of concepts, formulas, thought processes, and other forms of human cognition. All of these tools can greatly enhance students' ability to make sense of school subject matter, solve problems, communicate with others, and, more generally, thrive and prosper.

Modern technologies offer many cognitive tools that enable students to tackle challenging learning tasks while also keeping the cognitive load within reasonable limits. For example, students can record and organize a complex set of new ideas using *concept-mapping* software, and they can use computer spreadsheets and graphing software to explore and examine the effects of different values of x in an algebraic equation. Ultimately, technology can provide an electronic "playground" in which students can experiment with and expand on ideas.[94]

Technological innovations collectively known as **assistive technology** can be especially helpful for students who have physical or cognitive disabilities. For example, software programs that translate printed materials into spoken language can be invaluable tools for students who have a visual impairment (e.g., blindness), dyslexia, or intellectual disability. And specially adapted joysticks and voice recognition systems can supplement or replace computer keyboards for students who have limited muscle control due to a spinal cord injury or cerebral palsy. Such tools provide the scaffolding that some students need to participate successfully in a regular school curriculum with nondisabled classmates.

In some cases, teachers and students can work *together* to create effective tools for making better sense of classroom subject matter. For example, in the elementary grades, a teacher and his

think about it

How might you use shaping to teach an 8-year-old to swing a baseball bat? How might you use it to teach an aggressive high school student to behave prosocially? (For possible shaping-based strategies, click **here**.)

[94] J. A. Langer, 2011; Spiro & DeSchryver, 2009.

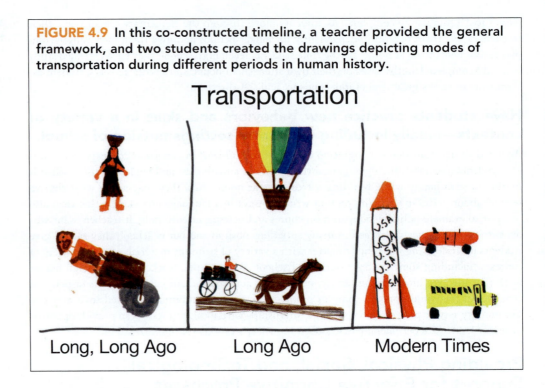

FIGURE 4.9 In this co-constructed timeline, a teacher provided the general framework, and two students created the drawings depicting modes of transportation during different periods in human history.

Transportation

Long, Long Ago   Long Ago   Modern Times

students might co-construct a timeline depicting forms of transportation during different time periods in history (see Figure 4.9).[95] In the secondary grades, a teacher and her students might collaboratively create a two-dimensional table to help them compare and contrast what they're learning about the climate, geography, and economic resources of various states or countries.

Equip students with the literacy skills they need to effectively use and learn from various technologies and media.

The word *literacy* has two distinct meanings. In its narrower sense, it refers to one's reading and writing abilities. Here, we'll be using it in its broader sense: a general ability to understand and communicate meanings using the various concepts and symbols of a particular content domain or community of practice. Our focus will be on two forms of literacy essential for making effective use of computer technology and the Internet: technological literacy and information literacy.

Technological literacy encompasses the knowledge and skills a person needs to effectively use digital technologies and media, including smartphones, laptops, tablet computers (e.g., iPads and Kindles), and digital cameras. For example, it includes:

* Use of common functions, such as "open," "cut," "paste," and "save"
* Use of device-specific operating systems—for instance, how to take a picture on a smartphone and how to create a new folder on a computer's virtual "desktop"
* Use of specific computer applications, such as software programs for e-mail, word processing, graphics design, photo editing, and multimedia presentations

Meanwhile, the increasingly *distributed* nature of society's collective knowledge base requires **information literacy**: the knowledge and skills a person needs to effectively find, evaluate, organize and use information about a particular topic. For instance, it includes:

* Use of an Internet search engine (e.g., Google, Bing) to find relevant websites—for instance, how to identify effective keywords and how to choose among the many links a search might yield
* Critical evaluation of various websites to determine the likely validity of their content
* Synthesis of information from multiple sources into an integrated, organized whole

---

[95] Brophy, Alleman, & Knighton, 2009.

Perhaps through past experiences with smartphones, video games, or home computers, many students come to school with some of these skills. But other students may not have the basics, such as knowing how to turn a particular device on and off.

Yet even students who seem to be technologically sophisticated may lack all the cognitive skills they need to *learn* effectively from technology. Learning from Internet websites can be especially difficult, for several reasons. First, students may have trouble sorting through the thousands of sites that an Internet search yields in order to determine which ones are truly relevant to their questions and needs. Second, they may not have the knowledge and skills they need to discriminate between sites that present objective information, on the one hand, and those that convincingly offer biased social or political propaganda, on the other. Third, they may not know how to organize and synthesize the separate bits of information they've found on various sites. Finally, they may not have the self-motivating "stick-to-it-iveness" that lengthy and occasionally frustrating Internet searches can involve.[96]

Some of the skills just listed involve *critical thinking* or *self-regulation*—two topics we explored in Chapter 3. Following are more general suggestions for enhancing students' technological literacy and information literacy skills:

- Use a database or search engine that restricts the websites to which students have access (e.g., EBSCO Information Services' "Searchasaurus" search engine).
- Provide specific questions students should try to answer as they read a website's content.
- Ask students to write summaries of what they've learned from multiple websites, perhaps in collaboration with classmates.[97]

One widely used, more comprehensive approach to teaching technological and information literacy skills is known as the Big6 (pronounced "big six," see big6.com). This approach involves teaching the following skills and subskills:[98]

1. Task definition
   - Defining the problem to be solved, identifying the questions to be answered
   - Identifying the information needed to solve the problem and answer the questions
2. Information-seeking strategies
   - Brainstorming all possible sources
   - Evaluating the sources and choosing the best options
3. Location and access
   - Finding the selected sources
   - Finding the needed information within those sources
4. Use of information
   - Engaging with (e.g., reading, hearing, or touching) the information
   - Extracting relevant information
5. Synthesis
   - Organizing information from the selected sources
   - Creating a product or performance, presenting the results
6. Evaluation
   - Judging the product or performance (in terms of its effectiveness)
   - Judging the process undertaken (in terms of its efficiency)

Learners who effectively find and use information in various media typically apply all these skills, in some instances taking them in sequential order and in other instances moving flexibly back and forth among them.

Many school computer systems now include a *remote desktop* feature that can help teachers both guide and monitor students' use of the Internet. With this feature, a teacher can share his or her own computer screen with students and demonstrate how to use a search engine, explore

---

[96] Afflerbach & Cho, 2010; K. Hartley & Bendixen, 2001; Leu, O'Byrne, Zawilinski, McVerry, & Everett-Cacopardo, 2009; F. H. Manning, Lawless, Goldman, & Braasch, 2011.

[97] Gil, Bråten, Vidal-Abarca, & Strømsø, 2010; F. H. Manning et al., 2011; Wiley et al., 2009.

[98] M. B. Eisenberg & Berkowitz, 2011; Jansen, 2007, 2009; also see www.big6.com.

various websites, and so on. The feature also allows the teacher to view every student's computer screen from afar. If a particular student goes astray, the teacher can lock the student's screen and send appropriate feedback.

Encourage student dialogue and collaboration.

We've previously identified many advantages to having learners talk with one another about classroom topics. Accordingly, many theorists recommend that group discussions be a regular feature of classroom instruction. For example, in a lesson on Nathaniel Hawthorne's *The Scarlet Letter,* high school English teacher Sue Southam wants students to construct an understanding of the character Arthur Dimmesdale. She reads a description of Dimmesdale in the novel and says:

> Jot down some of the important characteristics of that description. What's the diction that strikes you as being essential to understanding Dimmesdale's character? How do you see him? If you were going to draw a portrait of him, what would you make sure he had? . . . Just write some things, or draw a picture if you'd like.

Ms. Southam walks around the room, monitoring what students are doing until they appear to have finished writing. She then initiates a class discussion of Dimmesdale's nature:

Ms. Southam: What pictures do you have in your minds of this man . . . if you were directing a film of *The Scarlet Letter?*

Mike: I don't have a person in mind, just characteristics. About five-foot-ten, short, well-groomed hair, well dressed. He looks really nervous and inexperienced. Guilty look on his face. Always nervous, shaking a lot.

Ms. Southam: He's got a guilty look on his face. His lips always trembling, always shaking.

Mike: He's very unsure about himself.

Matt: Sweating really bad. Always going like this. (He shows how Dimmesdale might be wiping his forehead.) He does . . . he has his hanky. . . .

Ms. Southam: Actually, we don't see him mopping his brow, but we do see him doing what? What's the action? Do you remember? If you go to the text, he's holding his hand over his heart, as though he's somehow suffering some pain.

Another student: Wire-framed glasses. . . . I don't know why. He's like. . . .

Mike: He's kind of like a nerd-type guy. . . . Short pants. . . .

Ms. Southam: But at the same time . . . I don't know if it was somebody in this class or somebody in another class . . . he said, "Well, she was sure *worth* it." Worth risking your immortal soul for, you know? . . . Obviously she's sinned, but so has he, right? And if she was worth it, don't we also have to see him as somehow having been worthy of her risking *her* soul for this?

By hearing such diverse ideas, students can gain an increasingly complex, multifaceted understanding of Dimmesdale that probably includes both verbal concepts (e.g., *unsure, nerd*) and visual images. (You'll see this dialogue again in Chapter 7, but at that point, you'll look at it from a very different angle.)

In the lesson just presented, the teacher is actively involved in facilitating student discussion. Yet students can also co-construct understandings without teacher assistance, as we saw earlier in a small-group discussion of a math problem involving apple tarts. With or without teacher assistance, classroom dialogues can help students master classroom subject matter, perhaps by helping them acquire more sophisticated interpretations of literature or a greater conceptual understanding of what it means to divide by a fraction.[99] Classroom dialogues have an important benefit for teachers as well: By carefully monitoring students' comments and questions, teachers

MyEdLab
Video Example 4.4.

Observe more of this class discussion about *The Scarlet Letter* in this video.

---

[99] E. H. Hiebert & Raphael, 1996; J. Hiebert et al., 1997; Lampert, Rittenhouse, & Crumbaugh, 1996; P. K. Murphy, Wilkinson, Soter, Hennessey, & Alexander, 2009; Schank & Abelson, 1995; C. L. Smith, 2007; Walshaw & Anthony, 2008.

can identify and address any misconceptions that might interfere with students' ability to acquire new knowledge and skills.

Use computer technology to support both within-class and across-class communication.

Computer technology can certainly enhance students' communication and collaboration within a single classroom. For example, course management systems such as Blackboard and Moodle provide electronic discussion boards and chat rooms through which all members of a class can regularly interact at school and elsewhere. Another good resource is Google Apps for Education, through which schools can create a separate e-mail account for every student, post school and classroom calendars with scheduled activities and due dates, and upload documents to which teachers and students alike can contribute.

Thanks to the Internet, individual students or entire classes can also communicate and collaborate with students or classes in other locations—even in other nations (e.g., see www.iearn .org). One simple vehicle for doing so is Skype (www.skype.com), through which people at two different locations can both see and hear one another on any computer, tablet, or smartphone that has a built-in video camera and microphone.

Create a community of learners.

Imagine a class that is studying the theme *changing populations*. Students are divided into small groups to study one of five different subtopics: *extinct, endangered, artificial, assisted,* and *urbanized.* Each group conducts research and prepares teaching materials related to its subtopic. The class then reassembles into new groups that include at least one representative from each of the previous groups. Within these new groups, students teach one another what they've learned.[100]

The scenario just described illustrates one way in which teachers can encourage student dialogue and thereby facilitate co-construction of meaning. In particular, the scenario is an example of a **community of learners**, a class in which teachers and students collaborate to build a body of knowledge and help one another learn about it.[101] Following are other characteristics of a typical community of learners:

- All students are active participants in class activities.
- The primary goal is to acquire a body of knowledge on a specific topic, with students contributing to and building on one another's efforts.
- Students draw on many resources—textbooks, the school library, the Internet, and one another—in their efforts to learn about the topic.
- Discussion and collaboration among two or more students are common occurrences and play a key role in learning.
- Diversity in students' interests and rates of progress is expected and respected.
- Students and teacher coordinate their efforts in helping one another learn; no one has exclusive responsibility for teaching others.
- Everyone is a potential resource for others; different individuals are likely to serve as resources on different occasions, depending on the topics and tasks at hand. In some cases, individual students focus on particular topics and become local experts on them. Occasionally people outside the classroom share their expertise as well.
- The teacher provides some guidance and direction for activities, but students also offer guidance and direction.
- Mechanisms are in place through which students can share what they've learned with others; students regularly critique one another's work.
- The process of learning is emphasized as much as, and sometimes more than, the finished product.

MyEdLab
Video Example 4.5.

In this technology-based interaction, high school students in Hawaii and New Hampshire learn from one another about the histories of their respective states. The discussion shown here occurs after the students have already communicated via an electronic discussion board. What benefits might students gain from this real-time interaction?

---

[100] A. L. Brown & Campione, 1994; this approach, in which students learn about various topics in small groups and then teach what they've learned to a few peers in a second round of small groups, is known as a *jigsaw technique.*

[101] Bielaczyc & Collins, 2006; A. L. Brown & Campione, 1994; Campione, Shapiro, & Brown, 1995; A. Collins, 2006; Engle, 2006; Rogoff, Matusov, & White, 1996.

Computer networks can also be used to promote a community of learners.[102] In electronic environments such as Google Docs and Office Online, students can create a variety of documents—perhaps brief notes, lengthy reports, problem solutions, diagrams, or short stories—and post their work as computer files that their classmates can read, react to, and possibly modify or build on. Students can also interact in an ongoing web-based chat room or forum in which they present questions or issues to which their classmates respond. For example, students might jointly wrestle with the fact that heat melts some solids but burns others, or they might critique various theories about how human beings first migrated to and then spread throughout North and South America.[103]

Alternatively, teachers and their students can jointly create class-specific *wikis,* websites on which individual class members can add to, edit, or rearrange material previously contributed by other members. Popular wiki-creation websites include pbworks.com, wikisineducation .wikifoundry.com, and wikispaces.com.

A class organized as a community of learners tends to be highly motivating for students and can promote fairly complex thinking processes for extended time periods.[104] It can also give students a sense of the strategies scientists and other scholars use to advance the frontiers of knowledge: conducting individual and collaborative research, sharing ideas, building on one another's findings, and the like. In addition to its motivational and cognitive benefits, a community of learners can foster productive peer relationships and create a *sense of community* in the classroom—a sense that teachers and students have shared goals, are mutually respectful and supportive of one another's efforts, and believe that everyone makes an important contribution to classroom learning (more on this concept in Chapter 9).

A community of learners can be especially worthwhile when a classroom includes students from diverse cultural and socioeconomic backgrounds.[105] Such a community values the contributions of all students and draws on everyone's individual backgrounds, cultural perspectives, and unique abilities to enhance the overall performance of the class. It also provides a context in which students can form friendships across the lines of ethnicity, gender, socioeconomic status, and disability.

However, you should also keep in mind some potential weaknesses of communities of learners, as well as of group discussions in general.[106] Some students may dominate interactions, and others—such as recent immigrants who have limited proficiency in English—may participate little or not at all. Furthermore, what students learn is inevitably limited to the knowledge they personally acquire and share with one another, and students may occasionally pass along their biases, misconceptions, and ineffective strategies. Obviously, then, when teachers conduct classroom discussions or structure classrooms as communities of learners, they must carefully monitor student conversations to make sure that students ultimately acquire *accurate* understandings of the topics they're studying.

Teachers can often encourage students to engage in productive behaviors and ways of thinking by capitalizing on principles and research findings related to reinforcement and modeling. They can also use different technologies to support learning and provide opportunities for discussion and collaboration among students. In the hotlinked Self-Check quiz and Application Exercise that follow, you can check and apply your understandings related to Big Idea 4.5:

> *Effective teachers create a classroom environment that encourages and supports productive behaviors and ways of thinking.*

MyEdLab Self-Check 4.5

MyEdLab Application Exercise 4.5. In this exercise, you can practice evaluating teachers' behaviors to determine whether they effectively use cueing, extinction, reinforcement, punishment, or shaping to decrease or eliminate students' unproductive behaviors.

---

[102] Bereiter & Scardamalia, 2006; Scardamalia & Bereiter, 2006; G. Stahl, Koschmann, & Suthers, 2006; J. Zhang, Scardamalia, Reeve, & Messina, 2009.
[103] Hewitt, Brett, Scardamalia, Frecker, & Webb, 1995; Hewitt & Scardamalia, 1998.
[104] A. L. Brown & Campione, 1994; Engle, 2006; Engle & Conant, 2002; Rogoff, 1994; Scardamalia & Bereiter, 2006; Turkanis, 2001.
[105] Kincheloe, 2009; Ladson-Billings, 1995b; Rothstein-Fisch & Trumbull, 2008.
[106] A. L. Brown & Campione, 1994; Hynd, 1998b; E. R. Smith & Conrey, 2009; Walshaw & Anthony, 2008; T. White & Pea, 2011.

4.6 TAKING STUDENTS' BROADER CULTURAL AND SOCIOECONOMIC CONTEXTS INTO ACCOUNT

Big Idea 4.6 Effective teachers adapt instruction to the broader cultural and socioeconomic contexts in which students live.

Although students' learning and classroom achievement are influenced by what goes on inside the classroom, it is also influenced by what goes on *outside* the classroom by students' cultural groups, neighborhoods, and so on. Our recommendations in this section take this fact into account.

Learn as much as you can about students' cultural backgrounds, and come to grips with your own cultural lens.

In the opening case study, Jack's English teacher complained that "his parents don't care" and that, in general, the parents of Navajo students "just don't support their [children's] education."[107] When people act in accordance with beliefs, values, and social conventions very different from our own, it's all too easy for us to write them off as being "odd," "unmotivated," or "negligent." The assumptions and worldviews we've acquired in our own culture—perhaps including an assumption that good parents actively direct and control their children's behaviors—are often so pervasive in our lives that we tend to treat them as common sense, or even as facts, rather than as the beliefs they really are. These beliefs become a *cultural lens* through which we view events—a lens that may lead us to perceive other cultures' practices as somehow irrational and inferior to our own.[108]

Teachers can most effectively work with students from diverse backgrounds when they understand the fundamental assumptions and beliefs that underlie students' and families' behaviors—not only by reading about various cultures in books, in journals, and on websites, but also by participating in local community activities and conversing regularly with community members.[109] Furthermore, effective teachers are keenly aware that their own cultural beliefs are just that—*beliefs*. And they make a concerted effort *not* to pass judgment on cultural practices and beliefs very different from their own, but rather to try to understand why people of other cultural groups think and act as they do.[110]

MyEdLab
Video Example 4.6.

What suggestions do these students have for their teachers to help students feel more comfortable in the classroom?

Remember that membership in a particular cultural or ethnic group is not an either-or situation but, instead, a more-or-less phenomenon.

As noted earlier in the chapter, individuals vary considerably in how much they *participate* in various cultural and ethnic-group activities. The extent of their participation inevitably affects the strengths of their culture-specific behaviors and beliefs. For example, some Mexican American students live in small, close-knit communities where Spanish is spoken and traditional Mexican practices and beliefs permeate everyday life, but others live in more culturally heterogeneous communities in which Mexican traditions are often cast aside. Likewise, some students who have recently emigrated from another country hold steadfastly to the customs and values of their homeland, whereas others eagerly adopt many customs and habits of their new school and community.[111]

Incorporate the perspectives and traditions of many cultures into the curriculum.

True **multicultural education** isn't limited to cooking ethnic foods, celebrating Cinco de Mayo, or studying famous African Americans during Black History Month. Rather, it integrates the perspectives and experiences of numerous cultural groups throughout the curriculum and gives all students reasons for pride in their cultural heritages. Students from diverse backgrounds are more

---

[107] Deyhle & LeCompte, 1999, p. 127.

[108] Gollnick & Chinn, 2009; van den Bergh, Denessen, Hornstra, Voeten, & Holland, 2010.

[109] Castagno & Brayboy, 2008; Moje & Hinchman, 2004; H. L. Smith, 1998.

[110] Banks et al., 2005; Brophy et al., 2009; Rogoff, 2003.

[111] Bornstein & Cote, 2010; S. M. Quintana et al., 2006.

MyEdLab
Video Example 4.7.

American history classes have traditionally presented only a European American view of historical events. What concerns does this Native American educator raise about such a curriculum?

likely to be motivated to do well in school—and to *actually* do well there—when they perceive the school curriculum to be relevant to their own cultures.[112]

Teachers can incorporate content from diverse cultures into many aspects of the school curriculum. Following are examples:[113]

- In language arts, study the work of authors and poets from a variety of ethnic groups (e.g., study the lyrics of popular hip-hop songs).
- In math and science, draw on students' experiences with their community's farming, hunting, cooking, and building construction practices.
- In history, look at wars and other major events from diverse perspectives (e.g., the Native American perspective on European settlers' westward migration, the Spanish perspective on the Spanish–American War, the Japanese perspective on World War II).
- In both history and current events, consider such issues as discrimination and oppression.

Multicultural education involves learning about commonalities as well as differences. For example, in the elementary grades, students might learn that many cultural groups formally celebrate children's transition to adulthood—perhaps with *bar mitzvahs* and *bot mitzvahs* (for Jewish boys and girls), *quinceañeras* (for girls in certain Latin American cultures), or *Seijin no hi* (for 20-year-old Japanese youth). In the secondary grades, students might examine issues that adolescents of all cultures face: gaining the respect of elders, forming trusting relationships with peers, and finding a meaningful place in society. One important goal of multicultural education should be to communicate that, underneath it all, people are more alike than different.[114]

Students should be encouraged to contribute to the multicultural curriculum—for example, by bringing in photographs and favorite foods from home and by expressing their varying experiences and perspectives without fear of ridicule or censure.[115] Ultimately, teachers must help students realize that diverse cultural groups have much to learn from one another. For example, students may be surprised to learn that several key practices underlying many democratic governments—such as sending delegates to represent particular groups at a central location, allowing only one person in a governing council to speak at a time, and keeping government and military bodies separate—were adopted from Native American governing practices (those of the Iroquois League) in the 1700s.[116]

Fostering appreciation for diverse perspectives doesn't necessarily mean portraying all cultural practices as equally acceptable, however. Rather, it means that teachers and students should try to understand another cultural group's behaviors within the context of that group's beliefs and assumptions. Teachers certainly must *not* embrace a culture that blatantly violates some people's basic human rights.

Be sensitive to cultural differences in behaviors and beliefs, and when appropriate, adapt instructional methods to students' preferred ways of learning and behaving.

If students are to be successful at school and in mainstream Western culture, their teachers must gently and patiently encourage certain behaviors—such as being punctual and working independently—that will make such success possible. Yet many cultural differences in behavior are simply that—*differences*—and have no adverse effect on students' short- and long-term achievement. In working with students from diverse backgrounds, effective teachers engage in **culturally responsive teaching**: They use strategies that build on students' existing knowledge and skills and accommodate students' accustomed ways of behaving and learning. For example, if students'

[112] Banks & Banks, 1995; Brayboy & Searle, 2007; Moje & Hinchman, 2004; Paradise & Robles, 2016; Tatum, 1997; Tyler et al., 2008.
[113] J. M. Hughes, Bigler, & Levy, 2007; J. Kim, 2011; Lipka, Yanez, Andrew-Ihrke, & Adam, 2009; McIntyre, 2010; NCSS Task Force on Ethnic Studies Curriculum Guidelines, 1992; K. Schultz, Buck, & Niesz, 2000.
[114] Brophy et al., 2009; Ulichny, 1996.
[115] Gollnick & Chinn, 2009; Jiang, 2010.
[116] Rogoff, 2003; Weatherford, 1988.

cultures stress the importance of cooperation with others, teachers can enhance their learning by making frequent use of cooperative group activities.[117] And if students' home environments are high-energy ones in which several activities may take place simultaneously—as is sometimes true in African American and Hispanic families—teachers might create a similarly high-energy, multi-activity classroom environment.[118] Even the simple act of looking students in the eye (or not) can make a significant difference, as one teacher revealed in the following anecdote:

> A teacher [described a Native American] student who would never say a word, nor even answer when she greeted him. Then one day when he came in she looked in the other direction and said, "Hello, Jimmy." He answered enthusiastically, "Why hello Miss Jacobs." She found that he would always talk if she looked at a book or at the wall, but when she looked at him, he appeared frightened.[119]

Culturally responsive teaching means taking students' worldviews into account as well. For example, when discussing topics such as ecology and global climate change with Native American students, science teachers can build on a widely shared Native American conviction that people should live in harmony with nature rather than try to control it.[120] In some cases, academic subject matter may conflict with students' most core beliefs; occasionally it may conflict with the very essence of who they are as individuals. For instance, students who strongly believe in the divine creation of human beings may readily dismiss any suggestion that the human race has evolved from more primitive species.[121] And students whose cultures view certain historical battles as involving good guys triumphing over bad guys—or vice versa—may disregard more balanced perspectives in which each side of a controversy had legitimate needs and concerns.[122] Under such circumstances, a more achievable goal may be to help students *understand* (rather than *accept*) academic scholars' explanations and lines of reasoning.[123]

MyEdLab
Video Example 4.8.
How could the issues raised by this Native American educator be used by teachers to reconsider some of their worldviews?

Be sensitive to the culture shock that recent immigrants might be experiencing.

In recent years, immigration has become a highly politicized topic in the United States and elsewhere. Whatever teachers' own political views might be on the topic, they must realize that *all* children deserve guidance and support in their efforts to acquire the knowledge and skills they will need to be successful in the adult world. For recent immigrants, such guidance and support might include not only extra academic assistance but also explicit instruction in the typical practices and customs—"how things are done"—of their new culture.[124] Also, some students may require accommodations for their religious beliefs; for instance, teachers might discreetly give devout Muslim students a private place for early afternoon prayer and might excuse them from vigorous physical exercise when they're fasting during Ramadan.[125]

Work hard to break down rigid stereotypes of particular cultural and ethnic groups.

Although teachers and students should certainly be sensitive to real differences among people from various backgrounds, it's counterproductive to hold a **stereotype**—a rigid, simplistic, and inevitably inaccurate caricature—of any particular group. Sometimes people acquire stereotypes from the prejudicial remarks and practices of friends or family members.[126] In other cases, a

---

[117] Castagno & Brayboy, 2008; Ladson-Billings, 1995a.
[118] Tyler et al., 2008.
[119] Gilliland, 1988, p. 26.
[120] Atran et al., 2005.
[121] E. M. Evans, 2008; Southerland & Sinatra, 2003.
[122] Levstik, 2011; Porat, 2004.
[123] Feinberg & Willer, 2011; Southerland & Sinatra, 2003.
[124] Vang, 2010; Ward et al., 2001.
[125] Sirin & Ryce, 2010.
[126] Branch, 1999; Nesdale, Maass, Durkin, & Griffiths, 2005; Theobald & Herley, 2009.

history of conflict and animosity between two groups may lead people to conclude that people in the opposing group have undesirable qualities.[127] Occasionally stereotypes appear in curriculum materials and classroom instruction—as happens, for instance, when American children role-play the first Thanksgiving by dressing in paper-bag "animal skins," painting their faces, and wearing feathers on their heads.[128] And in many instances, students simply have little or no experience with a cultural group very different from their own.

At a minimum, unflattering stereotypes lead to misunderstandings among members of diverse cultural groups. When left uncorrected, they can also lead to overtly discriminatory and malicious behaviors—including ethnic jokes, racial taunts, and social exclusion—that can affect the victims' physical and mental health.[129] Teachers must work hard (sometimes *very* hard) to correct students' inaccurate and demeaning cultural and ethnic stereotypes, and they must vigorously address any acts of prejudice and discrimination witnessed in the classroom and elsewhere. The Classroom Strategies box "Addressing Students' Stereotypes and Prejudices" offers several concrete strategies.

Multicultural understanding also comes from interacting regularly and productively with people from diverse cultural, ethnic, and racial groups. When students from diverse groups interact regularly—and especially when they come together as equals, work toward common goals, and see themselves as members of the same "team"—they're more apt to accept and, better still, *value* one another's differences.[130] In the discussion of peer relationships in Chapter 7, we offer several strategies for promoting productive interactions and friendships among students from diverse backgrounds. By learning to appreciate multicultural differences within a single classroom, students take an important step toward appreciating the multicultural nature of the world at large.

Identify and, if possible, provide missing resources and experiences important for successful learning.

Some students from very poor families lack basic essentials that will be important for their school success, such as nutritious meals, adequate health care, warm clothes, and school supplies. Many government programs and community agencies can help to provide these things. School districts offer free and reduced-cost meal programs for children from low-income families. Many communities have low-cost health clinics. Some charitable organizations distribute warm winter jackets, and some office supply stores donate school supplies to children who need them. Indeed, most communities can provide a variety of resources for students who have limited financial means.

In addition to connecting low-income students and families with community resources, teachers should identify basic experiences that students haven't had and try to provide some of them, such as field trips to zoos, aquariums, natural history museums, farms, the mountains, or the ocean. And, of course, teachers should identify and teach any basic skills—perhaps in storybook reading or computer literacy—that most of their classmates have acquired at home. When teachers do so, they're likely to see significant improvements in students' classroom performance.[131]

Yet teachers must also remember that students who have grown up in poverty may, in some respects, have more knowledge and skills than their economically more advantaged peers (see Chapter 2). Such knowledge and skills can often provide a basis for teaching classroom subject matter. Furthermore, students who are willing to talk about the challenges they've faced can sensitize classmates to the serious inequities that currently exist in society. In general, research gives us cause for optimism that students from low-income backgrounds can achieve at high levels if their teachers are committed to helping them do so and give them a strong academic program that supports their learning efforts.[132]

---

[127] Pitner, Astor, Benbenishty, Haj-Yahia, & Zeira, 2003.

[128] Bigler & Liben, 2007; Brayboy & Searle, 2007.

[129] Allison, 1998; G. H. Brody et al., 2006; Killen, 2007; J. H. Pfeifer, Brown, & Juvonen, 2007; Sirin & Ryce, 2010.

[130] Dovidio & Gaertner, 1999; Oskamp, 2000; J. H. Pfeifer et al., 2007.

[131] S. A. Griffin, Case, & Capodilupo, 1995; Jordan, Glutting, Dyson, Hassinger-Das, & Irwin, 2012; G. Phillips, McNaughton, & MacDonald, 2004; Siegler, 2009; Warschauer, 2011.

[132] Becker & Luthar, 2002; Goldenberg, 2001; Long, Conger, & Iatarole, 2012; G. Phillips et al., 2004.

CLASSROOM STRATEGIES

Addressing Students' Stereotypes and Prejudices

- **Use curriculum materials that represent all cultures and ethnic groups as competent, legitimate participants in mainstream society, rather than as exotic curiosities who live in a separate world.**

  A history teacher peruses a history textbook to make sure that it portrays members of all ethnic groups in a nonstereotypical manner. He supplements the text with readings that highlight the important roles that members of various ethnic groups have played in history.

- **Assign literature depicting peers from diverse cultural backgrounds.**

  As part of a research project in England, several elementary school teachers read to students a series of stories involving close friendships between English children and refugees from other countries. Following this experimental intervention, the students express more positive attitudes toward refugee children than do control-group students who haven't heard the stories.

- **Conduct class discussions about prejudice and racism that exist in the school and local community.**

  A middle school in a suburban community creates a number of mixed-race focus groups in which students regularly convene to share their views about interracial relations at the school. Although some students of European American ancestry initially feel uncomfortable talking about this topic with their minority-group peers, once the ice has been broken, greater cross-cultural understanding and communication result.

- **Expose students to successful role models from various ethnic backgrounds.**

  A teacher invites several successful professionals from minority groups to speak with her class about their careers. When some students seem especially interested in one or more of these careers, she arranges for the students to spend time with the professionals in their workplaces.

- **Ask students to draw a picture of a professional in a particular job setting and use the drawings to discuss stereotypes students may have about particular professions.**

  A teacher asks students to draw a scientist and to list some characteristics of a scientist; one drawing by a fifth-grade student is shown to the right. Then, students place their drawing on a large table in the classroom. As the students look at the drawings, the teacher asks them to identify patterns among the drawings. Based on students' responses, the teacher asks them further questions, such as: "Why do you think that many of you drew the scientist as a man?" and "Are all scientists men?" Through her questioning, the teacher forces students to confront some of their stereotypes. She hopes that by raising students' awareness of their stereotypes, they will be more likely to question and change their own inaccurate beliefs.

- **Ask students to identify biases against particular cultural groups in TV show clips, commercials, and film trailers.**

  A high school social studies teacher organizes students into groups of four and asks them to identify biases against cultural groups in a few preselected YouTube videos of TV show clips, commercials, or film trailers. For example, students look for biases against Latina women in TV show clips from *Modern Family* and *Family Guy*. The teacher also asks students to identify perspectives that are not included in the ways in which the biased groups are represented.

- **Assign small-group cooperative projects in which students from diverse backgrounds must combine their unique talents to achieve a common goal.**

  A fourth-grade teacher has small cooperative groups design and conduct schoolwide surveys soliciting other students' opinions on various topics (e.g., ideas for school fundraisers, preferences for cafeteria menu items). The teacher intentionally creates groups that are culturally heterogeneous, knowing that the group members will draw on diverse friendship networks in seeking volunteers to take the surveys. In addition, he makes sure that every group member has something unique to offer in survey design or data analysis—perhaps knowledge of word processing software, artistic talent, or math skills.

- **Emphasize that some people affiliate with two or more cultural groups and that individual members of any single group are often very different from one another in behaviors, beliefs, and values.**

  In a geography unit on major world religions, a middle school teacher regularly points out that members of any single religion often have very different customs. "For example," he says, "some Muslim women dress in much the same way that women in this country do; others wear headscarves in addition to regular, modern clothes; and still others dress in a burqa that covers everything except their hands and shoes. Usually, the women wear a scarf or burqa to show modesty about their bodies. In fact, some Jewish women also wear headscarves as a sign of modesty, but many others don't."

When asked to draw a scientist and list some characteristics of scientists, a fifth-grade girl produced this drawing.

Sources: Adger et al., 2007; Barbarin, Mercado, & Jigjidsuren, 2010; Bondy & Pennington, 2016 (example of students identifying biases in videos); Boutte & McCormick, 1992; L. Cameron, Rutland, Brown, & Douch, 2006 (refugee stories example); Dovidio & Gaertner, 1999; Gutiérrez & Rogoff, 2003; Mohan, 2009; Oskamp, 2000; J. H. Pfeifer et al., 2007; Schultz, Buck, & Niesz, 2000 (focus groups example); Tatum, 1997.

While they're at school, students are active participants in the school's overall culture. However, they also remain active participants in one or more other cultures in their lives—some of which may be similar to their school's culture and others of which may be quite different. One important way in which teachers create a comfortable and productive learning environment for students is by being aware of and sensitive to the variety of cultural perspectives that both their students and they themselves hold; teachers must also be vigilant about how various cultures are represented in classroom lessons and activities. In the hotlinked Self-Check quiz and Application Exercise that follow, you can check and apply your understandings related to Big Idea 4.6:

Effective teachers adapt instruction to the broader cultural and socioeconomic contexts in which students live.

MyEdLab **Self-Check 4.6**

MyEdLab **Application Exercise 4.6.** This exercise provides you with the opportunity to think more about culturally responsive teaching.

4 SUMMARY

Our focus in this chapter has been on the many contexts that shape human learning and development. The Big Ideas presented at the beginning of the chapter sum up much of the chapter's content, and so we return to them now.

■ **4.1: Learners' behaviors and cognitive processes are influenced by the specific stimuli and consequences in their immediate environment.** Human learning takes place within many contexts that operate at a variety of levels. Learners' most local and immediate learning contexts consist of stimuli and events in the here-and-now—both those that elicit certain behaviors and those that are the consequences of learners' behaviors. Some especially influential factors are the people in learners' lives who model various ways of performing and thinking about everyday tasks.

A good deal of the knowledge and skills that learners acquire are tied to specific activities and environments. To some degree, this *situated* nature of learning is the result of the fact that learners mentally connect the new things they learn with some things—but not with other things—already in their long-term memories (see Chapter 2). But in addition, some activities and environments—but not others—provide the tools and social support systems learners need to keep their cognitive load at a manageable level during challenging tasks.

■ **4.2: Learners co-construct their knowledge with individuals whose abilities are similar to or greater than their own.** Learners acquire knowledge and skills not only from the things that environmental events and other people do *to* or *for* them but also from the things that other people do *with* them. Learners often co-construct knowledge with other people, sometimes with adults and other more experienced individuals and sometimes with peers whose ability levels are similar to their own. Social interaction has many benefits. For instance, it introduces learners to ways in which their culture interprets and responds to everyday experiences and problems, and it encourages learners to elaborate on prior knowledge and examine existing beliefs for possible gaps

in understanding. Also, other people can often provide the support and guidance—the *scaffolding*—learners need to successfully tackle new challenges.

■ **4.3: The cultural, societal, and technological contexts in which learners grow up also influence their behaviors and cognitive processes, as do the academic domains that learners study in school and elsewhere.** Culture is a largely human phenomenon that defines appropriate and inappropriate behaviors and beliefs and enables the transmission of knowledge and skills from one generation to the next. Any culture provides a wide variety of physical and cognitive tools that help learners survive and thrive in their physical and social worlds. Inconsistencies between cultures at home and at school can wreak havoc with school success, however, and teachers must bring the two contexts into alignment to the extent possible.

The society within which learners live is an additional context that can affect learning either directly or indirectly—for instance, through government policies that mandate certain instructional practices and through community groups and institutions that offer topic-specific expertise, learning opportunities, and support services. Yet not every member of a society has equal access to its resources. For example, many students in lower socioeconomic families and neighborhoods have substandard housing, poor health care, and low-quality schools—factors that in one way or another can negatively impact students' long-term academic and social success.

An especially noteworthy aspect of 21st-century societies is the increasing availability of digital technologies and media. These high-tech resources enable regular cross-communication and cross-fertilization of ideas. Furthermore, they give learners easy access to society's distributed knowledge and expertise—and, unfortunately, also to a good deal of misinformation and propaganda. Some technologies (e.g., many video game systems) can create virtual "environments" in which learners can mentally immerse themselves for hours at a time.

One final context to keep in mind is the various academic content domains that modern-day societies have created to compartmentalize human beings' accumulating knowledge about their physical, biological, and social worlds. Although these content domains certainly overlap to some degree, each of them offers unique sets of cognitive tools that may require somewhat different instructional strategies.

■ **4.4: Although various environmental contexts influence learners and their development, so, too, do learners influence the environments in which they live and grow.** Learners' characteristics and behaviors affect the consequences they experience, the ways in which other people treat them, and the resources to which they have access. And especially as they get older and more independent, learners may actively seek out environments that are a good match with their existing characteristics and behaviors. Such niche-picking tends to increase differences among learners' ability levels in various subject areas.

■ **4.5: Effective teachers create a classroom environment that encourages and supports productive behaviors and ways of thinking.** Teachers can do many things to create supportive learning contexts for students. For example, they can make sure that productive behaviors lead to desirable consequences (reinforcement) and that counterproductive behaviors do not. They can provide role models to illustrate effective ways of handling life's various personal and professional challenges. They can also provide many physical and cognitive tools—including reference materials, digital technologies, discipline-specific ways of interpreting and analyzing various physical and social phenomena—that enable students to think about and respond to everyday situations and problems effectively. And they can conduct dialogues and cooperative activities that enable students to learn from one another.

■ **4.6: Effective teachers adapt instruction to the broader cultural and socioeconomic contexts in which students live.** Teachers can better promote students' learning and development when they understand and accommodate students' culture-specific behaviors and beliefs and when they also take into account the unique strengths and needs of students from lower-income families. Furthermore, by providing a truly *multicultural* education—one that incorporates the perspectives and experiences of numerous cultural and ethnic groups into the curriculum—and working hard to break down inaccurate stereotypes of particular groups, teachers can better equip students for participating in a multicultural world.

PRACTICE FOR YOUR LICENSURE EXAM

Adam

Thirteen-year-old Adam seems to cause problems wherever he goes. In his sixth-grade classroom, he is rude and defiant. On a typical school day, he comes to class late, slouches in his seat, rests his feet on his desk, yells obscenities at classmates and his teacher, and stubbornly refuses to participate in classroom activities. Not surprisingly, his grades are very low, just as they have been for most of his school career.

Away from his teacher's watchful eye, Adam's behavior is even worse. He shoves and pushes students in the hall, steals lunches from smaller boys in the cafeteria, and frequently initiates physical fights on the school grounds.

For obvious reasons, no one at school likes Adam very much. His classmates say he's a bully, and their parents describe him as a "bad apple," rotten to the core. Even his teacher, who tries to find the best in all of her students, has seen few redeeming qualities in Adam and is beginning to write him off as a lost cause.

Adam doesn't seem to be bothered by the hostile feelings he generates. Already he's counting the days until he can legally drop out of school.

1. **Constructed-response question**

Adam is the type of student whom educators often refer to as a *student at risk:* He has a high probability of failing to acquire the minimal academic skills he will need to be successful in the adult world.

A. It is entirely possible that factors in his home and neighborhood are encouraging Adam's inappropriate behaviors. Yet factors at school may also be contributing to these behaviors. Drawing from concepts and principles of learning related to *operant conditioning,* identify two possible school-based causes for Adam's behaviors at school.

B. Again drawing on operant conditioning concepts and principles, describe two different strategies you might use to help Adam develop more appropriate and productive behaviors.

2. **Multiple-choice question**

Social cognitive theorists suggest that learning environments are ultimately the result of *reciprocal causation.* Which one of the following alternatives best reflects this concept?

a. Adam's defiant behaviors may be his way of escaping assignments he doesn't think he can complete successfully.

b. Adam's behaviors alienate his teacher, whose subsequent actions reduce his learning opportunities and class performance.

c. One of Adam's classmates decides that aggression is appropriate classroom behavior and acts accordingly.

d. Many parents complain to the principal that Adam is adversely affecting the quality of their children's education.

MyEdLab **Licensure Exam 4.1**

Greatstock Photographic Library/Alamy

5

Motivation and Affect

CASE STUDY: PASSING ALGEBRA

Fourteen-year-old Michael has been getting failing grades in his eighth-grade algebra class, prompting his family to ask graduate student Valerie Tucker to tutor him. In his initial tutoring session, Michael tells Ms. Tucker that he has no hope of passing algebra because he's not very good at math and his teacher doesn't teach the subject matter very well. In his mind, he's powerless to change either his own ability or his teacher's instructional strategies, making continuing failure inevitable.

As Ms. Tucker works with Michael over the next several weeks, she encourages him to think more about what *he* can do to master algebra and less about what his teacher may or may not be doing to help him. She points out that he did well in math in earlier years and so certainly has the ability to learn algebra if he puts his mind to it. She also teaches him a number of strategies for understanding and applying algebraic principles. Michael takes a giant step forward when he finally realizes that his own efforts play a role in his classroom success:

> Maybe I can try a little harder. . . . The teacher is still bad, but maybe some of this other stuff can work.[1]

When Michael sees gradual improvement on his algebra assignments and quizzes, he becomes increasingly aware that the specific strategies he uses are just as important as his effort:

> I learned that I need to understand information before I can hold it in my mind. . . . Now I do things in math step by step and listen to each step. I realize now that even if I don't like the teacher or don't think he is a good teacher, it is my responsibility to listen. I listen better now and ask questions more.[2]

As Michael's performance in algebra continues to improve in later weeks, he gains greater confidence that he can master algebra after all, and he comes to realize that his classroom success is ultimately up to him:

> The teacher does most of his part, but it's no use to me unless I do my part. . . . Now I try and comprehend, ask questions and figure out how he got the answer. . . . I used to just listen and not even take notes. I always told myself I would remember but I always seemed to forget. Now I take notes and I study at home every day except Friday, even if I don't have homework. Now I study so that I know that I have it. I don't just hope I'll remember.[3]

- On what factors does Michael initially blame his failure? To what factors does he later attribute his success? How do his changing beliefs affect his learning strategies?
- What inferences about motivation might you draw from the case study? How might learners' cognitive processes influence their motivation? How might teachers' behaviors also have an impact?

---

[1] Tucker & Anderman, 1999, p. 5.
[2] Tucker & Anderman, 1999, p. 5.
[3] Tucker & Anderman, 1999, p. 6.

Michael initially believes he's failing algebra because of two things he can't control, his own low ability and his teacher's poor instruction. As a result, he doesn't listen very attentively or take notes in class. With Ms. Tucker's guidance, however, Michael gains a better understanding of algebra and learns how to use it to solve mathematical problems. He also discovers that increased effort and better strategies—for instance, taking notes and asking questions—*do* affect his classroom performance. Suddenly Michael himself—not his teacher and not some genetically predetermined inability that lurks within him—is in control of the situation. As a result, his confidence skyrockets, and he works hard to master algebra.

In our discussions of learning and development in previous chapters, we've focused primarily on the question "What can children and adolescents do and learn?" As we turn to motivation in this chapter, we focus on a very different question: "How *likely* are children and adolescents to do what they're capable of doing and to learn what they're capable of learning?" Even when learners have the capabilities and prior experiences necessary to do something, their *motivation* affects whether they intend to do it and then whether they follow through to actually do it.

In the upcoming pages, we'll identify a variety of factors that influence motivation. We'll also look at the feelings, emotions, and general moods that learners bring to bear on a task—things that psychologists collectively refer to as **affect**. Later we'll translate what we've learned about both topics into effective instructional strategies.

5.1 THE NATURE OF MOTIVATION

Big Idea 5.1 Teachers play a major role in motivating students by designing effective learning environments and supporting students' motivation-related beliefs over time.

Motivation is an inner state that energizes, directs, and sustains behavior. It's a sense of *intending to* that directs people's actions toward particular goals. As Figure 5.1 illustrates, motivation is affected both by *internal factors* that are inside people—such as their needs, cognition, and affect—and by *external factors* that are outside of them, such as their teachers' instructional strategies. Together, these internal and external factors motivate people to get moving in a particular direction and to *keep* moving toward—and ideally accomplish—their goals.[4]

Humans seem to be purposeful by nature: They set goals for themselves and initiate courses of action they think will help them achieve those goals. For school-age children and adolescents, some goals (e.g., "I want to finish reading my dinosaur book") are short term and transitory. Other goals (e.g., "I want to be a paleontologist") are apt to be long term and relatively enduring. Thus motivation affects the choices learners make—for instance, whether to enroll in physics or studio art and whether to spend an evening playing video games with friends or, instead, completing a challenging homework assignment.

Motivation influences the activities that learners choose, as well as the degree to which they engage in those activities. Although teachers can't see students' motivation, they *can* see some of its effects by observing aspects of students' **academic engagement**—their level of behavioral, cognitive, and emotional involvement in an academic activity—as follows:[5]

- **Behavioral engagement.** *Motivation increases the amount of effort and persistence in activities directly related to learners' needs and goals.*[6] It determines whether learners pursue a task enthusiastically and wholeheartedly or apathetically

FIGURE 5.1 The cyclical nature of academic motivation

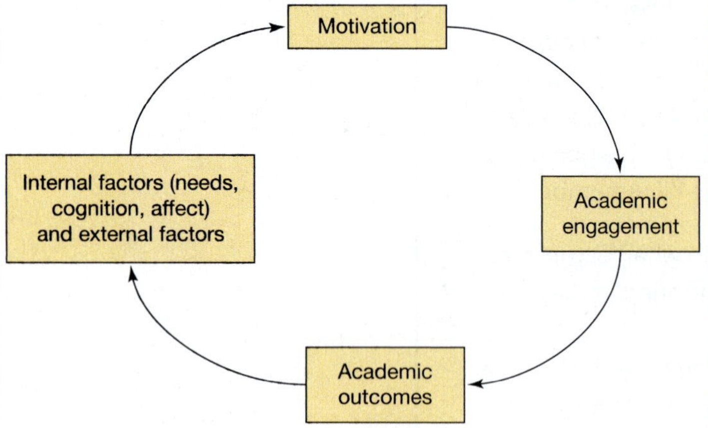

Motivation → Academic engagement → Academic outcomes → Internal factors (needs, cognition, affect) and external factors → Motivation

Sources: Based on Osborne & Jones, 2011; Reeve, 2009a; E. A. Skinner & Pitzer, 2012.

---

[4] M. E. Ford & Smith, 2007; Gollwitzer & Bargh, 2005; Rovee-Collier, 1999.
[5] Christenson, Reschly, & Wylie, 2012; Fredricks, Blumenfeld, & Paris, 2004.
[6] Csikszentmihalyi & Nakamura, 1989; Maehr, 1984; Pintrich, Marx, & Boyle, 1993.

and lackadaisically. Further, motivated learners are more likely to persist at a task until they've completed it, even if they're occasionally interrupted or frustrated in the process. In general, then, motivation increases learners' *time on task,* an important factor affecting their learning and achievement.[7]

- **Cognitive engagement.** *Motivation influences what learners pay attention to and how actively they mentally process information.*[8] Motivated learners are more likely to pay attention, and as we discovered in Chapter 2, attention is critical for getting information into working memory. Motivated learners also try to understand and elaborate on material—to learn it meaningfully—rather than simply "go through the motions" of learning in a superficial, rote manner. We see this principle at work in the opening case study. As Michael's confidence and motivation increases, he begins to pay attention, take notes, and ask questions in class.

- **Emotional engagement.** *Motivation influences learners' feelings and general affect about activities.*[9] Learners who are motivated to pursue a learning activity generally have good feelings about it, such as being excited about learning and enjoying the activity. Those who are less motivated usually have unpleasant feelings about the activity and may be bored, sad, frustrated, or anxious. As we'll discover later in the chapter, learners who are emotionally engaged in activities also tend to be more behaviorally and cognitively engaged in the activities.

Because of the effects of motivation on learners' behavioral, cognitive, and emotional engagement, motivation often leads to improved *academic outcomes* such as learning and achievement (see Figure 5.1). For instance, the learners who are most motivated to learn and excel in classroom activities tend to be the highest achievers.[10] Conversely, the learners who are least motivated to master academic subject matter are at high risk for dropping out before they graduate from high school.[11]

As you can see in Figure 5.1, students' academic outcomes can affect the internal and external factors that, in turn, affect their motivation. For example, in the opening case study, Michael's poor performance in math (an academic outcome) led him to low-ability beliefs (an internal factor), which led to low motivation and little engagement (e.g., he didn't take notes), which perpetuated his poor achievement. Fortunately, Ms. Tucker (an external factor) broke the cycle by working hard to change his ability beliefs and teaching him new learning strategies. His more optimistic beliefs and better strategies led to higher achievement, which, in turn, led to increased motivation and more engagement (e.g., asking questions and taking notes), which led to still further improvements in his learning and achievement.

Psychologists have developed a variety of theories to explain the nature of human motivation. Because no single theory can fully capture a learner's motives, different theories provide different pieces of the motivation "puzzle." Table 5.1 describes two early perspectives of motivation and several contemporary cognitive perspectives that will guide much of our discussion in this chapter. If you look closely at the descriptions in the table, you might notice that some of these theories overlap to some extent. For example, the concepts of *competence* (self-determination theory), *self-worth* (self-worth theory), *expectancy* (expectancy–value theory), and *self-efficacy* (social cognitive theory) all reflect two general ideas: (1) People like to believe they can perform an activity competently, and (2) their self-confidence (or lack thereof) regarding that activity affects their behavior. In this chapter, we aim to synthesize, rather than identify differences among, current theories of motivation, and in doing so, certain terms (e.g., *self-worth, self-efficacy*) will be used more than others.

---

[7] Larson, 2000; E. Skinner, Furrer, Marchand, & Kindermann, 2008; Wigfield, 1994.

[8] Blumenfeld, Kempler, & Krajcik, 2006; Hidi & Renninger, 2006; Sins, van Joolingen, Savelsbergh, & van Hout-Wolters, 2008; Voss & Schauble, 1992.

[9] Pekrun, 2006; Renninger & Hidi, 2011.

[10] Gottfried, 1990; Hidi & Harackiewicz, 2000; L. H. Meyer, Weir, McClure, & Walkey, 2008.

[11] Brayboy & Searle, 2007; Hardré & Reeve, 2003; Vallerand, Fortier, & Guay, 1997.

THEORETICAL PERSPECTIVES

Table 5.1 • Theoretical Approaches to the Study of Motivation

THEORETICAL PERSPECTIVE	GENERAL DESCRIPTION	EXAMPLES OF PROMINENT THEORISTS	WHERE YOU WILL SEE THIS PERSPECTIVE IN THE BOOK
EARLY PERSPECTIVES			
Behaviorism	From a behaviorist perspective, motivation is often the result of *drives,* internal states caused by a lack of something necessary for optimal functioning. Consequences of behavior (reinforcement, punishment) are effective only to the extent that they either increase or decrease a learner's drive state. In recent years some behaviorists have added a *purposeful* element to the behaviorist perspective: They suggest that learners intentionally behave in order to achieve certain end results.	Clark Hull B. F. Skinner Dorothea Lerman Jack Michael MyEdLab: **Content Extension 5.1.** This supplementary reading provides more details about B. F. Skinner's foundational work in behaviorism.	We previously examined the effects of reinforcement and punishment in Chapter 4. In this chapter, we draw on behaviorist ideas primarily in our discussions of extrinsic motivation. The purposeful element of behaviorism will be useful in our discussions of functional analysis and positive behavior support in Chapter 9.
Humanism	Historically, humanists have objected to behaviorists' depiction of people's behaviors as being largely the result of external environmental factors. In the humanist view, people have within themselves a tremendous potential for psychological growth, and they continually strive to fulfill that potential. When given a caring and supportive environment, people strive to understand themselves, to enhance their abilities, and to behave in ways that benefit both themselves and others. Because early humanist ideas were grounded more in philosophy than in research findings, many contemporary motivation theorists have largely left them by the wayside. However, one contemporary perspective, positive psychology (see the final row of this table) has some roots in the humanist perspective.	Carl Rogers Abraham Maslow MyEdLab: **Content Extension 5.2.** This supplementary reading explains Abraham Maslow's hierarchy of needs.	Because humanists conducted little research to substantiate their ideas, we don't specifically look at them in this book. However, the humanist focus on internal, growth-producing motives has clearly influenced the contemporary cognitive perspectives we *do* consider.
CONTEMPORARY PERSPECTIVES			
Self-determination theory	Self-determination theorists propose that people have three basic needs: a need to be effective in dealing with the environment (*competence*), a need to control the course of their lives (*autonomy*), and a need to have close, affectionate relationships with others (*relatedness*). Learners are more motivated to learn school subject matter when these three needs are met.	Edward Deci Richard Ryan Johnmarshall Reeve	Self-determination theory guides much of our discussion of basic human needs early in the chapter, and recommendations related to these needs are presented in the chapter's final section. The discussion of internalized values is also based on self-determination theory.
Self-worth theory	Self-worth theorists believe that protecting one's own sense of competence—that is, one's sense of *self-worth*—is a high priority for human beings. One way to maintain and possibly enhance self-worth is to be successful in daily activities. But curiously, when learners suspect that they may fail at an activity, they sometimes do things that make failure even more likely (e.g., procrastinating until the last minute). Although such *self-handicapping* decreases the probability of success, it also enables people to justify their failure, both to themselves and to others, and so enables them to maintain their self-worth.	Martin Covington	Self-worth theory is clearly evident in the chapter's discussion of basic human needs. Also, when we look at self-handicapping midway through the chapter, we identify a variety of counterproductive behaviors through which students may try to maintain their sense of self-worth in the face of seemingly insurmountable challenges.
Expectancy–value theory	Expectancy–value theorists propose that motivation for performing a particular task is primarily a function of two variables. First, learners must believe they can succeed. In other words, they must have a high expectation, or *expectancy,* for their task performance. Second, learners must believe that they will gain direct or indirect benefits for performing a task. That is, they must place *value* on the task itself or on the outcomes that are likely to result.	Jacquelynne Eccles Allan Wigfield	Expectancy-value theorists' findings related to the effects of learners' expectancies are incorporated into the discussion of self-efficacy. Their findings related to the effects of learners' values are presented midway through the chapter. *(continued)*

THEORETICAL PERSPECTIVE	GENERAL DESCRIPTION	EXAMPLES OF PROMINENT THEORISTS	WHERE YOU WILL SEE THIS PERSPECTIVE IN THE BOOK
Social cognitive theory	Social cognitive theorists emphasize the importance of *self-efficacy*—the extent to which one believes oneself to be capable of successfully performing certain behaviors or reaching certain goals—in motivation. Social cognitive theorists also point out that human behavior is typically goal directed, thereby providing a foundation for *goal theory* (described separately in the next row).	Albert Bandura Dale Schunk Barry Zimmerman Frank Pajares	We discover concepts related to social cognitive theory in the *cognitive factors* section of the chapter.
Goal theory	Goal theorists focus on the kinds of outcomes (goals) toward which learners direct their behavior. Learners are apt to have goals in a variety of areas, including but not limited to academic performance, social relationships, careers, financial gain, and physical and psychological well-being. In recent years many goal theorists have focused on students' goals related to learning in academic settings, which they refer to as achievement goals.	Carol Dweck Carol Ames Paul Pintrich Edwin Locke Gary Latham Martin Ford	The goal-directed nature of human motivation is evident early in the chapter. Later, we look at the effects of various kinds of goals, with a particular focus on mastery goals (reflecting a desire to gain new knowledge and skills) and performance goals (reflecting a desire to look competent in the eyes of others).
Attribution theory	Attribution theorists look at learners' beliefs about why various things happen to them—for instance, about why learners think they are doing well or poorly on academic tasks. These beliefs, known as *attributions*, influence learners' optimism about future success and about the actions they might take to bring about such success. For example, learners are more likely to work hard on classroom tasks if they believe that their ultimate success depends on something they themselves do—that is, if they attribute classroom success to internal and controllable factors.	Bernard Weiner Carol Dweck Sandra Graham	Midway through the chapter, we look closely at the nature and effects of attributions. We also discover that over time, many learners acquire a general attributional style, either a realistically optimistic one (a mastery orientation) or an overly pessimistic one (learned helplessness).
Interest theories	Interest theorists examine the factors that affect and that are affected by short-term *situational interests* and longer-term *individual interests*. Environmental factors that attract learners' attention and elicit positive emotions can lead students to become interested for the short term. But other factors, such as knowledge, value, and continued positive feelings, are needed to foster an individual interest that endures over time.	Ann Renninger Suzanne Hidi Mary Ainley Andreas Krapp Ulrich Schiefele	We discuss interest primarily in the *cognitive factors* section of the chapter as we explore situational and individual interests.
Positive psychology	Positive psychology embraces early humanists' belief that people have many uniquely human qualities propelling them to engage in productive, worthwhile activities. But like other contemporary motivation theories, it bases its views on research findings rather than philosophical speculations. As a distinct perspective of motivation, positive psychology emerged on the scene only in the late 1990s, and in its current form it is better characterized as a collection of ideas than as a full-fledged, well-integrated theory.	Martin Seligman Mihaly Csikszentmihalyi Christopher Peterson	The influence of positive psychology can best be seen in the discussions of flow (an intense form of intrinsic motivation), optimism (incorporated into sections on self-efficacy and attributions), and emotion regulation.

Furthermore, many of the same principles underlie different theoretical perspectives, as will be evident after you complete the following exercise.

———————————— **SEE FOR YOURSELF** ————————————
REFLECTING ON YOUR BELIEFS ABOUT MOTIVATION

Decide whether each of the following statements is *true* or *false*.

True/False

_____ 1. Some students have little or no motivation.

_____ 2. If students aren't motivated to learn certain classroom topics, there's not much a teacher can do to motivate them.

_____ 3. Students can turn their motivation "on" and "off" quickly and easily.

Now let's see how your answers compare to the following three general principles that researchers have found to be true about motivation:

1. *All children and adolescents are motivated.* One common misconception is that some students are motivated but others are not. In reality, all students have basic needs and desires—that is, they're all motivated. However, some may strive to satisfy these needs and desires in ways that don't contribute to their academic achievement; for example, they may be more interested in playing sports or video games, texting friends, or using social media. One key strategy for motivating students to engage actively and productively in classroom learning activities, then, is to capitalize on their *existing* motives.

2. *Conditions in the classroom have a significant impact on students' motivation to learn and achieve.* Another common misconception is that motivation is something students "carry around" inside of them. In fact, a good deal of motivation is **situated motivation**—that is, it emerges from conditions in a learner's immediate environment.[12] As you'll discover, there are many, *many* things teachers can do in the classroom environment to enhance students' motivation to learn and master classroom subject matter.[13]

3. *Motivation to do well in school is grounded in a variety of cognitive and sociocultural factors that evolve over time.* Yet a third misconception is that students can turn their motivation "on" or "off" at will, much as one would flip a light switch. Although teachers can create situations that capture students' interests and get them immediately engaged in learning activities, students' motivation to achieve—or *not* achieve—in school is also the result of many factors that don't easily change overnight. Internal factors, such as students' thoughts, beliefs, and goals, often take time to change. In the opening case study, Michael's confidence for mastering math improves, but only *gradually* as he discovers that by applying effort and good strategies, he can be successful in the class.

Some external factors may also change only slowly, perhaps because they're integral parts of students' outside lives. For example, parents may believe that math is inherently easier for boys than girls and thus communicate the message that their sons are more likely than their daughters to succeed in math-related careers.[14] Such gender stereotypes about math ability—which are largely unfounded—can affect students' motivation to study math and to persist in their efforts to understand challenging mathematical concepts.[15]

In the upcoming pages we'll identify a variety of internal factors (i.e., needs, cognition, and affect) that influence students' motivation—factors that we'll later translate into strategies for promoting motivation and productive affect in instructional settings. We'll begin by identifying several of human beings' most basic psychological needs.

think about it

How is *situated motivation* similar to the *situated learning* and *situated cognition* concepts in Chapter 4?

Teachers can motivate students by designing instruction that takes into consideration students' needs, cognition, and affect. When students are more motivated, they're more likely to engage in learning activities and meet the objectives of the instruction. In the hotlinked Self-Check quiz and Application Exercise that follow, you can check and apply your understandings related to Big Idea 5.1:

> Teachers play a major role in motivating students by designing effective learning environments and supporting students' motivation-related beliefs over time.

MyEdLab **Self-Check 5.1**

MyEdLab **Application Exercise 5.1.** In this exercise, you can examine the cyclical nature of motivation as a teacher gives students feedback during a math problem.

---

[12] Nolen, Horn, & Ward, 2015.

[13] Boaler, 2002; Paris & Turner, 1994; Rueda & Moll, 1994; J. C. Turner & Patrick, 2008.

[14] Eccles, Jacobs, & Harold, 1990; Gunderson, Ramirez, Levine, & Beilock, 2012.

[15] Jacobs, 1991.

5.2 BASIC HUMAN NEEDS

Big Idea 5.2 Learners are more motivated to learn and achieve at high levels when their basic psychological needs are being met.

Psychologists have speculated that people have a wide variety of needs. Some needs—such as for oxygen, food, water, and warmth—are related to physical well-being, and these needs undoubtedly take high priority when physical survival is in jeopardy.[16] Other needs are more closely related to *psychological* well-being—that is, to feeling comfortable and content in day-to-day activities. In the following principles, we explore several basic psychological needs that can have a significant effect on learners' motivation and psychological well-being.[17]

Learners have a basic need for arousal.

Several classic studies conducted in the 1950s and 1960s suggest that humans have a basic need for stimulation—that is, a **need for arousal**.[18] As an example, try the following exercise.

SEE FOR YOURSELF
DOING NOTHING

For the next 5 minutes, you're going to be a student who has nothing to do. *Remain exactly where you are*, put your book aside, and *do nothing*. Time yourself so that you spend exactly 5 minutes on this "task." Let's see what happens.

What kinds of responses did you make during your 5-minute break? Did you fidget a bit, perhaps wiggling tired body parts or scratching newly detected itches? Did you interact in some way with something or someone else, perhaps tapping on a table or talking to another person in the room? Did you get out of your seat altogether—something you were specifically asked *not* to do? Hopefully, the exercise has shown you that you tend to feel better when you're doing something—even something quite trivial—rather than nothing at all. It may have also reminded you of one of the three general principles about motivation presented earlier: All learners are motivated.

Some theorists have suggested that not only do people have a basic need for arousal but they also strive for a certain *optimal level* of arousal at which they feel best.[19] Too little stimulation is unpleasant, but so is too much. For example, you may enjoy watching a television reality show or listening to music, but you would probably rather not try to listen to a live band, watch television, and listen to an iPod all at once. Different people have different optimal levels, and they may prefer different kinds of stimulation. For instance, some children and adolescents are *sensation seekers* who thrive on physically thrilling and possibly dangerous experiences.[20] Others prefer a lot of cognitive stimulation—eagerly tackling challenging puzzles, reading about intriguing new ideas, arguing with peers about controversial issues, and so on—reflecting a *need for cognition*, which we will discuss further in Chapter 6.[21]

The need for arousal explains some of the things students do in the classroom. For example, it explains why many students happily pull out a favorite book and read it if they finish in-class assignments before their classmates. But it also explains why students sometimes engage in off-task behaviors—for instance, passing notes or playing practical jokes—during boring lessons. Obviously, students are most likely to stay *on* task when classroom activities keep them sufficiently aroused that they have little need to look elsewhere for stimulation.

MyEdLab **Content Extension 5.3.** One early theorist, Abraham Maslow, suggested that people's various needs form a hierarchy, such that certain kinds of needs typically take precedence over others. Learn more about Maslow's hierarchy of needs in this supplementary reading.

---

[16] Maslow, 1973, 1987.

[17] The second, third, fourth, and fifth principles are based loosely on Deci and Ryan's self-determination theory; for example, see Deci & Moller, 2005; Deci & Ryan, 1985, 1992, 2012; Reeve, Deci, & Ryan, 2004; R. M. Ryan & Deci, 2000.

[18] For example, see Berlyne, 1960; Heron, 1957; also see E. M. Anderman, Noar, Zimmerman, & Donohew, 2004, for a more contemporary discussion of this need.

[19] E. M. Anderman et al., 2004; Berlyne, 1960; Labouvie-Vief & González, 2004.

[20] Cleveland, Gibbons, Gerrard, Pomery, & Brody, 2005; V. F. Reyna & Farley, 2006.

[21] Cacioppo, Petty, Feinstein, & Jarvis, 1996; Raine, Reynolds, & Venables, 2002.

Learners want to believe they are competent and have self-worth.

The 2-year-old child of one of us authors said, "I'm going to do some great dance maneuvers, and then you can clap for me." Why would she say this? Or consider a middle school student who tells his parents that he doesn't want their help with his homework because he can do it himself. What do these two children have in common? Well, underlying both of these statements may be a basic **need for competence**—a need for people to believe that they can deal effectively with their environment.[22] The 2-year-old seems to want her father to clap to acknowledge that she is a competent dancer. And the middle school student seems to want to prove to himself and others that he is competent at completing his homework by himself. People of all ages need to feel competent. In fact, some evidence indicates that *protecting* this sense of competence, which is sometimes known as **self-worth**, is one of people's highest priorities.[23]

Other people's judgments and approval play a key role in the development of a sense of competence and self-worth.[24] Regularly achieving success in new and challenging activities—as Michael eventually does in math in the opening case study—is another important way of maintaining or enhancing perceptions of competence. But consistent success isn't always possible, particularly when learners must undertake especially difficult tasks. In the face of such tasks, an alternative way to maintain self-worth is to *avoid failure* because failure gives the impression of low ability.[25] Failure avoidance manifests itself in a variety of ways. Learners might refuse to engage in a task, minimize the task's importance, or set exceedingly low expectations for their performance.[26] They might also hold tightly to their current beliefs despite considerable evidence to the contrary.[27] The need to protect self-worth, then, may be one reason why learners are reluctant to undergo conceptual change.

Learners want to determine the course of their lives to some degree.

Humans have a basic **need for autonomy** in that they want control over the things they do and the paths their lives take.[28] For instance, when we think "I *want* to do this" or "This is *my* choice," we have a high sense of autonomy. In contrast, when we think "I *have to*" or "I *should*," we're telling ourselves that someone or something else is making decisions for us. As an example of the latter situation, try the following exercise.

———————————————— **SEE FOR YOURSELF** ————————————————
PAINTING BETWEEN THE LINES

Imagine that a teacher gives you a set of watercolor paints, a paintbrush, two sheets of paper (a fairly small one glued on top of a larger one), and some paper towels. He asks you to paint a picture of your home and then gives you the following instructions:

> You have to keep the paints clean. You can paint only on this small sheet of paper, so don't spill any paint on the big sheet. And you must wash out your brush and wipe it with a paper towel before you switch to a new color of paint so that you don't get the colors all mixed up. In general, don't make a mess with the paints.[29]

How much fun do you think your task would be? After reading these rules, how eager are you to begin painting?

These rules about painting are restrictive: They make it clear that the teacher is in charge of the situation and that you, as the artist, have few choices about how to complete your task. You aren't given much *empowerment*—that is, you don't have much freedom to control your actions.[30]

---

[22] Boggiano & Pittman, 1992; Elliot & Dweck, 2005b; Reeve et al., 2004; White, 1959.

[23] Covington, 1992; Hattie, 2008; Rhodewalt & Vohs, 2005; Sedikides & Gregg, 2008.

[24] Harter, 1999; Rudolph, Caldwell, & Conley, 2005; Weiner, 2005.

[25] Covington & Müeller, 2001; Elliot & Dweck, 2005a; Urdan & Midgley, 2001.

[26] Covington, 1992; Martin, Marsh, & Debus, 2001; Rhodewalt & Vohs, 2005.

[27] Sherman & Cohen, 2002; Sinatra & Mason, 2008.

[28] d'Ailly, 2003; deCharms, 1972; Deci & Moller, 2005; Kağitçibaşi, 2007; Deci & Ryan, 2012.

[29] Koestner, Ryan, Bernieri, & Holt, 1984, p. 239.

[30] B. D. Jones, 2009, 2015.

With more empowerment, it's likely that you would have more desire to paint the picture and express more creativity.[31]

Even preschoolers and kindergartners seem to prefer classroom activities of their own choosing, and their perceptions of autonomy versus control are often seen in their notions of "play" or "work."[32] For example, when students in Ms. Paley's kindergarten class are asked whether activities at the class painting table are "work" or "play," two of them respond as follows:

> *Clarice:* If you paint a real picture, it's work, but if you splatter or pour into an egg carton, then it's play.
>
> *Charlotte:* It's mostly work, because that's where the teacher tells you how to do stuff.[33]

Learners want to feel connected to other people.

To some extent we're all social creatures: We live, work, and play with our fellow human beings. It appears that most people of all ages have a fundamental need to feel socially connected and to secure the love and respect of others. In other words, they have a **need for relatedness**.[34]

Warm and caring interpersonal relationships are typically among students' highest priorities.[35] Students are more likely to be academically motivated and successful—and more likely to stay in school rather than drop out—when they believe that their teachers and peers like and respect them and when they feel that they truly "belong" in the classroom community.[36]

The need for relatedness manifests itself in a variety of behaviors at school. Many children and adolescents place high priority on interacting with friends, often at the expense of getting their schoolwork done.[37] They may also be concerned about projecting a favorable public image—that is, by looking smart, popular, athletic, or cool. By looking good in the eyes of others, they not only satisfy their need for relatedness but also enhance their need for competence and sense of self-worth.[38] Still another way to address the need for relatedness is to work for the betterment of others, such as by helping peers who are struggling with classroom assignments.[39]

The need for relatedness seems to be especially high in early adolescence.[40] Young adolescents tend to be quite concerned about what their classmates think of them, often prefer to hang out in tight-knit groups, and are especially susceptible to peer influence (e.g., see Figure 5.2; more on these points in Chapter 7).

Learners experience greater enjoyment and interest in school activities when their basic psychological needs are met.

When school activities allow learners to meet one or more of the basic psychological needs identified earlier (e.g., need for competence, autonomy), they are more likely to enjoy and show interest in their school activities—that is, they exhibit **intrinsic motivation**.[41] For intrinsically motivated learners, participating in an activity is its own reward. Learners may also participate in an activity because it leads to a desired reward or consequence, in

MyEdLab
Video Example 5.1.

As 12-year-old Claudia describes what she likes about school, notice how the things she lists probably meet her needs for competence, autonomy, and relatedness.

FIGURE 5.2 Interacting with peers—in this case, by passing a note during class—is a high priority for many students.

[31] Amabile & Hennessey, 1992; Deci, 1992; Koestner et al., 1984; Peterson, 2006; Reeve, 2006.

[32] E. J. Langer, 1997; Paley, 1984; Schmidt, Hanley, & Layer, 2009.

[33] Paley, 1984, p. 31.

[34] Connell & Wellborn, 1991; Kağitçibaşi, 2007; Martin & Dowson, 2009; Deci & Ryan, 2012.

[35] Dowson & McInerney, 2001; Juvonen, 2006.

[36] Furrer & Skinner, 2003; Goodenow, 1993; Hughes, Luo, Kwok, & Loyd, 2008; Hymel, Comfort, Schonert-Reichl, & McDougall, 1996; A. M. Ryan & Patrick, 2001.

[37] Dowson & McInerney, 2001; Doyle, 1986; Wigfield, Eccles, Mac Iver, Reuman, & Midgley, 1991.

[38] Harter, 1999; Juvonen, 2000; Rudolph et al., 2005.

[39] Dowson & McInerney, 2001; M. E. Ford & Smith, 2007.

[40] Brown, Eicher, & Petrie, 1986; Juvonen, 2000; A. M. Ryan & Patrick, 2001.

[41] Cacioppo et al., 1996; Deci & Ryan, 2012; Reeve, 2006; R. M. Ryan & Deci, 2000.

which case they exhibit **extrinsic motivation**. Extrinsically motivated learners may want the good grades, money, or recognition that particular activities and accomplishments bring when the activities are completed. Essentially they're motivated to perform an activity as a means to an end.

think about it
Extrinsic and intrinsic motivation are similar to the concepts of extrinsic and intrinsic reinforcers described in Chapter 4. In what key ways are these motivation concepts different from extrinsic and intrinsic reinforcers?

Learners may exhibit primarily intrinsic or extrinsic motivation for given activity. But in many cases, learners are simultaneously motivated by both intrinsic and extrinsic factors.[42] For example, a high school student who enjoys her writing course exhibits intrinsic motivation. However, she may also be motivated by the fact that she knows a good grade will help her get a scholarship at her favorite university; and thus, she also exhibits extrinsic motivation because she wants to receive a good grade.

Intrinsically motivated learners are eager to learn classroom topics, willingly tackle assigned tasks, are more likely to process information in effective ways (e.g., by engaging in meaningful learning), and are more likely to achieve at high levels.[43] Some learners with high levels of intrinsic motivation become so focused on and absorbed in an activity that they lose track of time and completely ignore other tasks—a phenomenon known as **flow**.[44] In contrast, extrinsically motivated learners may have to be enticed or prodded, may process information only superficially, and are often interested in performing only easy tasks and meeting minimal classroom requirements.[45] However, the use of extrinsic motivators can be effective when students won't otherwise engage in a particular activity, as we discussed in Chapter 4. Also, students' intrinsic motivation can wane a bit over the course of the school day or school year—especially during lengthy activities and assignments—and extrinsic motivators can keep them on task during the interim. And over time, activities that are initially not enjoyable or interesting can become more so, as we'll discover in our discussion of *values* later in the chapter.

In the early elementary grades, most students are eager and excited to learn new things at school. But sometime between grades 3 and 9, their intrinsic motivation to learn and master school subject matter declines.[46] This decline is probably the result of several factors. As learners get older, they are more frequently reminded of the importance of good grades (extrinsic motivators) for promotion, graduation, and college admission, and many begin to realize that they aren't necessarily "at the top of the heap" in comparison with their peers.[47] Furthermore, they become more cognitively able to think about and strive for long-term goals, and they begin to evaluate school subjects in terms of their relevance to such goals, rather than in terms of any intrinsic appeal.[48] Also, students may grow increasingly impatient with the overly structured, repetitive, and boring activities they often encounter at school.[49]

Although students have many needs, the needs for arousal, competence, autonomy, and relatedness have been shown to be especially important to students' motivation and achievement in educational settings. In the hotlinked Self-Check quiz and Application Exercise that follow, you can check and apply your understandings related to Big Idea 5.2:

> Learners are more motivated to learn and achieve at high levels when their basic psychological needs are being met.

MyEdLab **Self-Check 5.2**

MyEdLab **Application Exercise 5.2.** In this exercise, you can examine how the characteristics of an active learning classroom can help to meet students' basic psychological needs.

---

[42] Cameron, 2001; Covington, 2000; Hayenga & Corpus, 2010; Lepper et al., 2005.

[43] Hayenga & Corpus, 2010; Lepper, Corpus, & Iyengar, 2005.

[44] Csikszentmihalyi, 1990; Csikszentmihalyi, Abuhamdeh, & Nakamura, 2005.

[45] Larson, 2000; Reeve, 2006; Schiefele, 1991; Tobias, 1994; Voss & Schauble, 1992.

[46] Corpus, McClintic-Gilbert, & Hayenga, 2009; Covington & Müeller, 2001; Lepper et al., 2005; Otis, Grouzet, & Pelletier, 2005.

[47] Covington & Müeller, 2001; Harter, 1992; Wigfield, Byrnes, & Eccles, 2006.

[48] Lepper et al., 2005.

[49] Battistich, Solomon, Kim, Watson, & Schaps, 1995; Larson, 2000.

5.3 COGNITIVE FACTORS IN MOTIVATION

Big Idea 5.3 Learners' thoughts and beliefs about themselves and about classroom subject matter can influence their motivation to learn in the classroom.

A variety of mental entities and processes—including learners' thoughts, beliefs, and goals—are internal factors that affect motivation. Conversely, learners' motives influence their cognitive processes—perhaps by increasing their attention and cognitive engagement in a task and by enhancing meaningful learning and complex cognitive processes. The following principles describe a number of cognitive factors that influence learners' motivation, sometimes for the short run and sometimes for the long haul.

Learners find some topics inherently interesting.

When we say that people have **interest** in a particular topic or activity, we mean that they find the topic or activity intriguing and engaging. Learners who are interested in what they're doing or studying experience cognitive arousal, and they feel emotions such as enjoyment and excitement.[50] Interest, then, has both cognitive and affective components.

Take a minute to consider your own interests in the following exercise.

SEE FOR YOURSELF
THE DOCTOR'S OFFICE

You have just arrived at the doctor's office for your annual checkup. The receptionist tells you that the doctor is running late and that you'll probably have to wait an hour before you can be seen. As you sit down in the waiting room, you notice six magazines on the table beside you: *Better Homes and Gardens, National Geographic, Time, People, Popular Mechanics,* and *Sports Illustrated.*

1. Rate each of these magazines in terms of how *interesting* you think its articles would be to you:

	Not at All Interesting	Somewhat Interesting	Very Interesting
Better Homes and Gardens	_____	_____	_____
National Geographic	_____	_____	_____
Time	_____	_____	_____
People	_____	_____	_____
Popular Mechanics	_____	_____	_____
Sports Illustrated	_____	_____	_____

2. Even though you think some of the magazines will be more interesting than others, you decide to spend 10 minutes reading each one. Estimate how much you think you might *remember* from what you read in each of the six magazines:

	Hardly Anything	A Moderate Amount	Quite a Bit
Better Homes and Gardens	_____	_____	_____
National Geographic	_____	_____	_____
Time	_____	_____	_____
People	_____	_____	_____
Popular Mechanics	_____	_____	_____
Sports Illustrated	_____	_____	_____

---

[50] Ainley & Ainley, 2011; Hofer, 2010; Renninger, 2009; Renninger, Nieswandt, & Hidi, 2015.

Now compare your two sets of ratings. Chances are that the magazines you rated most interesting are also the magazines from which you'll learn and remember the most.

Learners who are interested in a particular topic devote more attention to it and become more cognitively engaged in it.[51] They're also apt to learn it in a more meaningful and elaborative fashion—for instance, by relating it to prior knowledge, interconnecting ideas, drawing inferences, forming visual images, generating examples, and identifying potential applications.[52] And unless they're emotionally attached to their current beliefs, interested learners are more likely to undergo conceptual change when they encounter information that contradicts their existing understandings.[53] As you might guess, then, learners who are interested in what they study show higher academic achievement and are more likely to remember the subject matter over the long run.[54]

Psychologists distinguish between two general types of interest. **Situational interest** is evoked by something in the immediate environment. Things that are new, different, unexpected, or especially vivid often generate situational interest, as do things with a high activity level or intense emotions.[55] Learners also tend to be intrigued by topics related to people and culture (e.g., disease, violence, holidays), nature (e.g., dinosaurs, weather, the sea), and current events (e.g., television shows, popular music, substance abuse, gangs).[56] Works of fiction (novels, short stories, movies, and so on) are more interesting and engaging when they include themes and characters with which readers can personally identify.[57] And nonfiction is more interesting when it is easy to understand and relationships among ideas are clear.[58]

Learners also tend to have personal preferences about the topics they pursue and the activities in which they engage. Because such **individual interests** are relatively stable over time, we see a consistent pattern in the choices learners make (e.g., see Figure 5.3). Some individual interests probably come from learners' prior experiences with various activities and topics. Often interest and knowledge perpetuate each other: Individual interest in a topic fuels a quest to learn more about the topic, and the increased knowledge gained, in turn, promotes greater interest.[59]

MyEdLab
Video Example 5.2.

In this video, children act out how various animals move and then watch several snails moving in a transparent container. Which of the children's behaviors suggest that the lesson is eliciting situational interest?

FIGURE 5.3 Many children and adolescents have individual interests that pervade much of what they do. Here we see an example of Matt's passion for soccer during the high school years. He created this art—a heart gradually morphing into a soccer ball in a crowd—to accompany an essay about soccer in his language arts portfolio. Matt's interest in soccer was evident many years earlier, as you'll see in excerpts from his first-grade journal in Chapter 9.

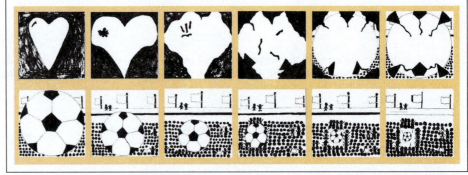

[51] Hidi & Renninger, 2006; E. Skinner et al., 2008.

[52] Hidi & Renninger, 2006; Pintrich & Schrauben, 1992; Schraw & Lehman, 2001; Tobias, 1994.

[53] Andre & Windschitl, 2003; Linnenbrink & Pintrich, 2003; Mason, Gava, & Boldrin, 2008.

[54] Garner, Brown, Sanders, & Menke, 1992; Hidi & Harackiewicz, 2000; Mason et al., 2008; Renninger, Hidi, & Krapp, 1992.

[55] Hidi & Renninger, 2006; Mitchell, 1993; Renninger et al., 1992; Schank, 1979.

[56] Zahorik, 1994.

[57] Hidi & Harackiewicz, 2000; Schank, 1979; Wade, 1992.

[58] Schraw & Lehman, 2001; Wade, 1992.

[59] P. A. Alexander, 1997; Hidi & McLaren, 1990; Tobias, 1994.

Even in the early elementary grades, many children have specific interests—perhaps in reptiles, ballet, or outer space—that persist over time and lead to consistent patterns in the choices made.[60] By and large, learners form interests in activities that they can do well in and that are stereotypically appropriate for their gender and socioeconomic group.[61] Individual interests are ultimately more beneficial than situational interests because they sustain engagement, effective cognitive processing, and improvement over the long run. Yet situational interest is important as well because it captures learners' attention and emotion and can provide a seed from which an individual interest might grow.[62]

To engage voluntarily in activities, learners want their chances of success to be reasonably good.

In our earlier discussion of self-worth, we discovered that people have a general need to feel competent in their environment. Yet people also realize that they have both strengths and weaknesses. In other words, their beliefs about their competence can vary across activities and subject areas. The following exercise illustrates this point.

--- **SEE FOR YOURSELF** ---

SELF-APPRAISAL

Take a moment to answer the following questions:

1. Do you believe you'll be able to understand and apply educational psychology by reading this book and thinking carefully about its content? Or do you believe you're going to have trouble with the material regardless of how much you read and study it?
2. Do you think you could learn to execute a reasonably good overhand serve in volleyball if you were shown how to do it and given time to practice? Or do you think you're so uncoordinated that no amount of training and practice would help?
3. Do you think you could walk barefoot over 50 yards of hot coals unscathed? Or do you think the soles of your feet would burn to a crisp?

Your responses say something about your self-efficacy for the tasks about which you were just asked. In general, **self-efficacy** is a learner's self-constructed judgment about his or her ability to execute specific behaviors or reach specific goals; thus, it affects the learner's expectations for future performance. For example, we hope you have high self-efficacy for learning educational psychology—a belief that with careful thought about what you're reading, you'll be able to understand and apply the ideas in this book. You may or may not have high self-efficacy about learning to execute a good overhand volleyball serve. You probably have low self-efficacy about your ability to walk barefoot over 50 yards of hot coals.

Learners are more likely to choose and persist in activities for which they have high self-efficacy.[63] High self-efficacy also leads them to engage in effective cognitive and metacognitive processes (paying attention, elaborating, effectively managing study time, etc.) that help them learn and achieve at higher levels (see Figure 5.4).[64]

To a considerable degree, self-efficacy for a particular task or activity arises out of past experiences. Learners feel more confident that they can succeed at a task—that is, they have higher self-efficacy—when they've previously succeeded at

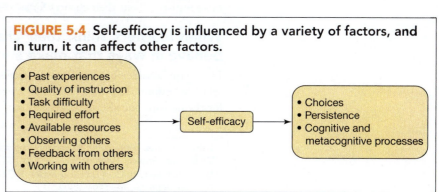

FIGURE 5.4 Self-efficacy is influenced by a variety of factors, and in turn, it can affect other factors.

- Past experiences
- Quality of instruction
- Task difficulty
- Required effort
- Available resources
- Observing others
- Feedback from others
- Working with others

→ Self-efficacy →

- Choices
- Persistence
- Cognitive and metacognitive processes

---

[60] J. M. Alexander, Johnson, Leibham, & Kelley, 2008; Nolen, 2007; Y.-M. Tsai, Kunter, Lüdtke, Trautwein, & Ryan, 2008.

[61] J. M. Alexander et al., 2008; Hidi, Renninger, & Krapp, 2004; Nolen, 2007; Wigfield, 1994.

[62] Ainley & Ainely, 2015; A. A. Alexander, Kulikowich, & Schulze, 1994; Durik & Harackiewicz, 2007; Hidi & Renninger, 2006; Reed, Schallert, Beth, & Woodruff, 2004.

[63] Bandura, 1997, 2000, 2006; Schunk & Pajares, 2005; Schunk & Usher, 2012; Wigfield & Eccles, 2002.

[64] Bembenutty & Karabenick, 2004; Bong & Skaalvik, 2003; R. Klassen, 2002; Pajares, 2005; Shores & Shannon, 2007.

that task or at similar ones.[65] In the opening case study, Michael has been getting Fs in his algebra class, and so his expectations for passing the class are initially at rock-bottom. But as he sees himself improve with effort and new strategies, his self-efficacy increases and he begins to show signs of motivation to master algebra. He starts listening carefully and taking notes in class, and says he studies "every day except Friday, even if I don't have homework."[66]

Recall how Michael's initial pessimism about his math class is based not only on his self-assessment of his math ability but also on his teacher's poor instruction. When learners form expectations about the likelihood of future success, they consider not only their own past successes but other factors as well (see Figure 5.4). The quality of instruction, the perceived difficulty of a task, the amount of effort that will be needed, and the availability of resources and support will all influence their predictions.[67] Under ideal circumstances, learners identify personal strengths on which they can depend, tried-and-true strategies they can use, and environmental support systems that can help them surmount any difficulties they may encounter—a combination that gives them hope and optimism about their chances for success.[68]

Social factors, too, play a role in the development of self-efficacy. Seeing other people achieve success at an activity—especially seeing successful peers similar to themselves—enhances learners' own self-efficacy for the activity.[69] Words of encouragement (e.g., "I bet Judy will play with you if you just ask her") and suggestions about how to improve (e.g., "I know that you can write a better essay, and here are some suggestions how") can also enhance self-efficacy, at least for the short run.[70] In addition, learners often have higher self-efficacy about accomplishing a task successfully when they work in a group rather than alone. Such **collective self-efficacy** depends not only on learners' perceptions of their own and other group members' capabilities but also on their perceptions of how effectively they can work together and coordinate their roles and responsibilities.[71]

Once learners have developed a high sense of self-efficacy in a particular content domain, an occasional failure is unlikely to dampen their optimism much. In fact, when these learners encounter small setbacks on the way to achieving success, they learn that sustained effort and perseverance are key ingredients of that success. In other words, they develop **resilient self-efficacy**.[72] The key word here is *occasional* failure. If students *consistently* fail at an activity, they gain little confidence about their chances of future success. For instance, students with learning disabilities, who may have encountered failure after failure in classroom activities, often have low self-efficacy for mastering school subject matter.[73]

Most 4- to 6-year-olds are quite confident about their ability to perform various tasks. In fact, they may overestimate what they're capable of doing.[74] As they progress through the elementary grades, however, they can better recall their past successes and failures, and they become increasingly aware that their performance doesn't always compare favorably with that of their peers.[75] Presumably as a result of these changes, they become less confident, although usually more realistic, about their chances for success in specific academic domains.[76]

When learners think their chances of success are slim, they may behave in ways that make success even *less* likely.

Even with considerable persistence, learners can't always be successful at certain tasks they're asked to perform. Repeated failures in a particular domain may lower not only their self-efficacy for the domain but also their general sense of competence and self-worth. When learners can't

---

[65] Usher & Pajares, 2008, 2009; Valentine, Cooper, Bettencourt, & DuBois, 2002; T. Williams & Williams, 2010.
[66] Tucker & Anderman, 1999, p. 6.
[67] Dweck & Elliott, 1983; Wigfield & Eccles, 1992, 2000, 2002; Zimmerman, Bandura, & Martinez-Pons, 1992.
[68] Peterson, 2006; Snyder, 1994, 2002.
[69] Dijkstra, Kuyper, van der Werf, Buunk, & van der Zee, 2008; Schunk, 1983; Schunk & Pajares, 2005; Usher, 2009; Usher & Pajares, 2009.
[70] Usher, 2009; Usher & Pajares, 2008; Zeldin & Pajares, 2000.
[71] Bandura, 1997, 2000.
[72] Bandura, 1994, 2008; Dweck, 2000.
[73] R. M. Klassen & Lynch, 2007; Lackaye & Margalit, 2006.
[74] R. Butler, 2008; Eccles, Wigfield, & Schiefele, 1998; Lockhart, Chang, & Story, 2002.
[75] Butler, 2008; Davis-Kean et al., 2008; Dijkstra et al., 2008.
[76] Bandura, 1986; Schunk & Zimmerman, 2006; Wigfield et al., 2006.

avoid tasks at which they think they'll do poorly, they have alternative strategies at their disposal. Occasionally they make excuses that seemingly justify their poor performance.[77] They may also engage in **self-handicapping**—that is, doing things that actually *undermine* their chances of success. Self-handicapping takes a variety of forms, including the following:[78]

- **Reducing effort:** Putting forth an obviously insufficient amount of effort to succeed
- **Misbehaving:** Engaging in off-task behaviors in class
- **Setting unattainably high goals:** Working toward goals that even the most capable individuals couldn't achieve
- **Taking on too much:** Assuming so many responsibilities that no one could possibly accomplish them all
- **Procrastinating:** Putting off a task until success is virtually impossible
- **Cheating:** Presenting others' work as one's own
- **Using alcohol or drugs:** Taking substances that will inevitably reduce performance

It might seem paradoxical that learners who want to be successful would actually try to undermine their own success. But if they believe they're unlikely to succeed no matter what they do—and especially if failure will reflect poorly on their intelligence and ability—they increase their chances of *justifying* the failure and thereby protecting their self-worth.[79] In the following interview, a student named Christine explains why she sometimes doesn't work very hard on her assignments:

> *Interviewer:* What if you don't do so well?
>
> *Christine:* Then you've got an excuse. . . . It's just easier to cope with if you think you haven't put as much work into it.
>
> *Interviewer:* What's easier to cope with?
>
> *Christine:* From feeling like a failure because you're not good at it. It's easier to say, "I failed because I didn't put enough work into it" than "I failed because I'm not good at it."[80]

Curiously, some learners are more likely to perform at their best and less likely to display self-handicapping behaviors when outside, uncontrollable circumstances seemingly minimize their chances of success. In such cases, failure doesn't indicate low ability and so it doesn't threaten their sense of self-worth.[81]

Learners are more likely to devote time to activities that have value for them.

Another cognitive factor influencing motivation is **value**: Learners must believe there are direct or indirect benefits in performing a task. Their appraisal of the value of various tasks affects the subject matter and activities they pursue in their free time, the courses they choose in junior high and high school, and many other choices they make.[82]

Learners value activities that are intriguing and enjoyable—in other words, activities that are *interesting*.[83] Activities that are viewed as *important* also tend to be valued. As an example, a ninth-grade boy who sees himself as a musician and as a future high school band teacher would likely place a high value on success in activities related to music. Still other activities have high

---

[77] Covington, 1992; Urdan & Midgley, 2001.
[78] Anderman, Griesinger, & Westerfield, 1998; Covington, 1992; D. Y. Ford, 1996; Hattie, 2008; E. E. Jones & Berglas, 1978; Riggs, 1992; Urdan, Ryan, Anderman, & Gheen, 2002.
[79] Covington, 1992; Rhodewalt & Vohs, 2005; Sedikides & Gregg, 2008.
[80] Martin, Marsh, Williamson, & Debus, 2003, p. 621.
[81] Covington, 1992.
[82] Durik, Vida, & Eccles, 2006; Jacobs, Davis-Kean, Bleeker, Eccles, & Malanchuk, 2005; Mac Iver, Stipek, & Daniels, 1991; Wigfield & Eccles, 2002.
[83] Eccles and Wigfield have suggested four possible reasons why value might be high or low: interest, importance, utility (usefulness), and cost; see Eccles, 2005, 2009; Wigfield & Eccles, 1992, 2000.

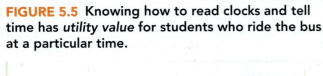

FIGURE 5.5 Knowing how to read clocks and tell time has *utility value* for students who ride the bus at a particular time.

I go to the bus stop at __8 : 20__.

value because they're seen as a means to a desired goal; that is, they have *utility* (e.g., see Figure 5.5). For example, although the daughter of one of us authors found mathematics confusing and frustrating, she struggled through 4 years of high school math classes simply because many colleges require that much math background. In other words, the math courses were useful in helping her to achieve her goal of attending college.

In contrast, learners tend *not* to value activities that require more time or effort than they're worth—activities that essentially *cost* too much. For example, you could probably become an expert on some little-known topic (e.g., animal-eating plants of Borneo, the nature of rats' dreams), but you probably have more important things to which to devote your time and energy right now. Other activities may have a significant emotional cost because they're associated with bad feelings. For example, if learners become frustrated often enough in their efforts to understand science, they may eventually begin to steer clear of science whenever they can. And anything likely to threaten a learner's sense of competence or self-worth is likely to be avoided.

In the early elementary years, children often pursue activities they find interesting and enjoyable, regardless of their expectations for success.[84] As they get older, however, they increasingly attach value to activities for which they have high expectations for success and to activities they think will help them meet long-term goals, and they begin to *de*value activities at which they expect to do poorly.[85]

Learners' social and cultural environments influence the things they value as well. As children grow older, they tend to adopt many of the priorities and values of the people around them. Values can develop gradually over the course of childhood and adolescence, perhaps in the sequence depicted in Figure 5.6.[86] Although learners engage in activities for a variety of reasons, sometimes they engage in activities initially because of the external consequences that result—in other words, they're extrinsically motivated. For instance, students may do schoolwork to earn praise or to avoid being punished for poor grades. If students internalize the "pressure" to perform the activities and begin to see the activities as important in their own right, their *external regulation* can gradually evolve into the *introjection*, *identification*, and *integration* shown in Figure 5.6.

The more learners have internalized the value of academic subject matter, the more engaged they become in the subject matter and the better their overall learning is likely to be.[87] Appreciation of an activity's value also fosters self-regulated learning—a general work ethic in which learners spontaneously engage in activities that, although not always fun or immediately gratifying, are essential for reaching long-term goals.[88] Such internalization of values is most likely to occur if adults (parents, teachers, etc.) who espouse those values provide a warm, supportive, and structured environment that offers learners some autonomy in decision making. All too often, such conditions *aren't* present when it comes to learning academic subject matter. Accordingly, the value students find in many school subjects (e.g., math, English, music, sports) declines markedly over the school years.[89]

---

[84] Wigfield, 1994.

[85] Jacobs, Lanza, Osgood, Eccles, & Wigfield, 2002; Osborne & Jones, 2011; Wigfield, 1994.

[86] Deci & Moller, 2005; Deci & Ryan, 1995, 2012; R. M. Ryan & Deci, 2000.

[87] Assor, Vansteenkiste, & Kaplan, 2009; B. D. Jones, Ruff, & Osborne, 2015; La Guardia, 2009; Lens, Simons, & Dewitte, 2002; Osborne & Jones, 2011; R. M. Ryan & Deci, 2000.

[88] Harter, 1992; McCombs, 1996; R. M. Ryan, Connell, & Grolnick, 1992; Stipek, 2002.

[89] Deci & Moller, 2005; Eccles et al., 1998; Jacobs et al., 2002; La Guardia, 2009; Watt, 2004; Wigfield et al., 1991.

Learners typically form goals related to their academic achievement; the specific nature of these goals influences learners' cognitive processes and behaviors.

As noted earlier, much of human behavior is directed toward particular goals. For school-age children and adolescents, some of these goals are apt to relate to school learning and performance. Let's consider what three different boys might be thinking during the first day of a basketball unit in Mr. Wesolowski's physical education class:

Tim: This is my chance to show all the guys what a great basketball player I am. If I stay near the basket, Travis and Tony will keep passing to me, and I'll score a lot of points. I can really impress Mr. Wesolowski and my friends.

Travis: I hope I don't screw this up. If I shoot at the basket and miss, I'll look like a real loser. Maybe I should just stay outside the 3-point line and keep passing to Tim and Tony.

Tony: I really want to become a better basketball player. I can't figure out why I don't get more of my shots into the basket. I'll ask Mr. Wesolowski to give me feedback about how I can improve my game. Maybe some of my friends will have suggestions, too.

All three boys want to play basketball well. That is, they all have *achievement goals.* But they have different reasons for wanting to play well. Tim is concerned mostly about looking good in front of his teacher and classmates and so wants to maximize opportunities to demonstrate his skill on the court. Travis, too, is concerned about the impression he'll make, but he just wants to make sure he *doesn't look bad.* Unlike Tim and Travis, Tony isn't thinking about how his performance will appear to others. Instead, he's interested mainly in developing his basketball skills and doesn't expect immediate success. For Tony, making mistakes is an inevitable part of learning a new skill, not a source of embarrassment or humiliation.

Tony's approach to basketball illustrates a **mastery goal**, a desire to acquire additional knowledge or master new skills (i.e., to *develop* competence).[90] Tim and Travis each have a **performance goal**, a desire to present themselves as competent in the eyes of others (i.e., to *demonstrate* competence). More specifically, Tim has a **performance-approach goal**: He wants to look good and receive favorable judgments from others. In contrast, Travis has a **performance-avoidance goal**: He wants to avoid looking bad and receiving unfavorable judgments. Achievement goals often have an element of social comparison, in that learners are concerned about how their accomplishments compare to those of their peers.[91]

Mastery goals, performance-approach goals, and performance-avoidance goals aren't necessarily mutually exclusive. Learners may simultaneously have two kinds, or even all three.[92] For example, returning to our basketball example, we could imagine a fourth boy, Trey, who wants to improve his basketball skills *and* look good in front of his classmates *and* not come across as uncoordinated.

In most instances, having mastery goals is the optimal situation. As Table 5.2 reveals, learners with mastery goals tend to engage in the activities that will help them learn. They pay attention, process information in ways that promote effective long-term memory storage, and learn from their mistakes. Learners with mastery goals also have a healthy perspective about learning, effort, and failure. They realize that learning is a process of trying hard and continuing to

FIGURE 5.6 Sequence in which values can become internalized as part of a learner's identity

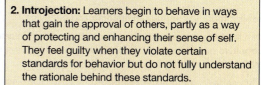

1. **External regulation:** Learners are initially motivated to behave in certain ways, based primarily on the external consequences that will follow the behaviors; that is, the learners are extrinsically motivated.

2. **Introjection:** Learners begin to behave in ways that gain the approval of others, partly as a way of protecting and enhancing their sense of self. They feel guilty when they violate certain standards for behavior but do not fully understand the rationale behind these standards.

3. **Identification:** Learners now see some behaviors and activities as being personally important or valuable for them.

4. **Integration:** Learners integrate certain behaviors and activities into their overall system of motives and values. In essence, these behaviors become a central part of their identity and general sense of self.

---

[90] Some theorists distinguish between *mastery-approach* and *mastery-avoidance goals.* Our focus here is on mastery-approach goals. Mastery-avoidance goals—that is, wanting to avoid possible failure in a new learning task—seem to have effects similar to those of performance-avoidance goals (e.g., see Elliot, 2005; Elliot & McGregor, 2000; Witkow & Fuligni, 2007).

[91] Elliot, 2005; Midgley et al., 1998; Régner, Escribe, & Dupeyrat, 2007.

[92] Covington & Müeller, 2001; Hidi & Harackiewicz, 2000; Liem, 2016; Meece & Holt, 1993; Schwinger & Wild, 2012.

Table 5.2 • Typical Differences Between Learners with Mastery Goals and Learners with Performance Goals

LEARNERS WITH MASTERY GOALS	LEARNERS WITH PERFORMANCE GOALS (ESPECIALLY THOSE WITH PERFORMANCE-AVOIDANCE GOALS)
Are more likely to be actively engaged in classroom activities and intrinsically motivated to learn classroom subject matter	Are more likely to be extrinsically motivated (i.e., motivated by expectations of external reinforcement and punishment) and more likely to cheat to obtain good grades
Believe that competence develops over time through practice and effort; persist in the face of difficulty	Believe that competence is a stable characteristic (people either have talent or they don't); think that competent people shouldn't have to try very hard; give up quickly when facing difficulty
Exhibit more self-regulated learning and behavior	Exhibit less self-regulation
Use learning strategies that promote true comprehension and complex cognitive processes (e.g., elaboration, comprehension monitoring, transfer)	Use learning strategies that promote only rote learning (e.g., repetition, copying, word-for-word memorization); may procrastinate on assignments
Choose tasks that maximize opportunities for learning; seek out challenges	Choose tasks that maximize opportunities for demonstrating competence; avoid tasks and actions (e.g., asking for help) that make them look incompetent
Are more likely to undergo conceptual change when confronted with convincing evidence that contradicts current beliefs	Are less likely to undergo conceptual change, in part because they are less likely to notice the discrepancies between new information and existing beliefs
React to easy tasks with feelings of boredom or disappointment	React to success on easy tasks with feelings of pride or relief
Seek feedback that accurately describes their ability and helps them improve	Seek feedback that flatters them
Willingly collaborate with peers when doing so is likely to enhance learning	Collaborate with peers primarily when doing so can help them look competent or enhance social status
Evaluate their own performance in terms of the progress they make	Evaluate their own performance in terms of how they compare with others
Interpret failure as a sign that they need to exert more effort	Interpret failure as a sign of low ability and therefore predictive of future failures
View errors as a normal and useful part of the learning process; use errors to improve performance	View errors as a sign of failure and incompetence; engage in self-handicapping to provide apparent justification for errors and failures
Are satisfied with their performance if they try hard and make progress	Are satisfied with their performance only when they succeed; are apt to feel ashamed and depressed when they fail
View a teacher as a resource and guide to help them learn	View a teacher as a judge and as a rewarder or punisher
Remain relatively calm during tests and classroom assignments	Are often quite anxious about tests and other assessments
Are more likely to be enthusiastic about, and become actively involved in, school activities	Are more likely to distance themselves from the school environment

Sources: C. Ames & Archer, 1988; R. Ames, 1983; E. M. Anderman, Griesinger, & Westerfield, 1998; E. M. Anderman & Maehr, 1994; Corpus et al., 2009; Dweck, 1986; Dweck, Mangels, & Good, 2004; L. S. Fuchs et al., 1997; Gabriele, 2007; Graham & Weiner, 1996; Hardré, Crowson, DeBacker, & White, 2007; Jagacinski & Nicholls, 1984, 1987; Kaplan & Midgley, 1999; Lau & Nie, 2008; Liem, Lau, & Nie, 2008; Linnenbrink & Pintrich, 2002, 2003; Locke & Latham, 2006; McCombs, 1988; McGregor & Elliot, 2002; Middleton & Midgley, 1997; Murphy & Alexander, 2000; Newman & Schwager, 1995; Nolen, 1996; Pekrun, Elliot, & Maier, 2006; Pugh & Bergin, 2006; Rawsthorne & Elliot, 1999; A. M. Ryan, Pintrich, & Midgley, 2001; Schiefele, 1991, 1992; Schunk, Meece, & Pintrich, 2014; Sideridis, 2005; Sinatra & Mason, 2008; Sins et al., 2008; Skaalvik, 1997; Southerland & Sinatra, 2003; Stipek, 2002; Urdan & Midgley, 2001; Urdan, Midgley, & Anderman, 1998.

persevere even in the face of temporary setbacks. Consequently, these learners are the ones who are most likely to stay on task and who benefit the most from their classroom experiences.[93]

In contrast, learners with performance goals—especially those with performance-*avoidance* goals—may stay away from the challenging tasks that could help them master new skills. Furthermore, these learners tend to process information in a rote, relatively "thoughtless" manner. Performance-*approach* goals are a mixed bag. They sometimes have very positive effects, spurring learners on to achieve at high levels, especially in adolescence and especially in combination with mastery goals.[94] Yet by themselves, performance-approach goals may be less beneficial than

---

[93] Kumar et al., 2002; Shim, Ryan, & Anderson, 2008; Sins et al., 2008; Wentzel & Wigfield, 1998.

[94] Hidi & Harackiewicz, 2000; Linnenbrink, 2005; McNeil & Alibali, 2000; Rawsthorne & Elliot, 1999; Urdan, 1997.

mastery goals. To accomplish them, learners may exert only the minimal effort required, use relatively superficial learning strategies, and possibly cheat on classroom assessments.[95] Performance-approach goals appear to be most detrimental when learners are fairly young (e.g., in the elementary grades) and have low self-efficacy for classroom tasks.[96]

Most young children focus primarily on mastery goals.[97] But once they're in school, they're regularly surrounded by peers with whom they can compare their performance, and so they begin to view success as doing as well as or better than classmates. In addition, they may have trouble evaluating their progress on the complex cognitive skills they're learning (reading, writing, math, etc.) and so they must rely on others (e.g., teachers) to make judgments about their competence and progress. For such reasons, performance goals become increasingly prevalent as children progress through the elementary and secondary school grades.[98] Most academically motivated high school students are primarily concerned about getting good grades, and they prefer short, easy tasks to lengthier, more challenging ones. Performance goals are also common in team sports, where the focus is often more on winning and gaining public recognition than on developing new skills and seeing improvement over time.[99]

Learners must juggle their achievement goals with their many other goals.

Children and adolescents typically have a wide variety of goals.[100] Not only might they want to do well in school, but they also want to have a good time, be healthy and safe, earn money, and eventually embark on a rewarding career. Many of their goals are apt to be **social goals** that can help them meet their need for relatedness. For example, they may want to gain the approval of adults, be liked and respected by peers, belong to a supportive social group, and contribute to other people's welfare.[101] When a sixth-grade student found out that she wasn't going to be in a math class with her best friends the following year in seventh grade, she exclaimed, "My life is ruined!" This comment shows that social goals are very important for some students.

Among learners' many goals are certain **core goals** that drive much of what they do.[102] For instance, learners who attain high levels of academic achievement typically make classroom learning a high priority, whereas learners who achieve at lower levels are often more concerned with social relationships.[103] Some students seem to demonstrate high levels of perseverance and passion for their long-term goals, a stable disposition that has been called *grit*.[104] Researchers are still trying to figure out why some students exhibit higher levels of grit than others.

Learners use several strategies to juggle their many goals.[105] Sometimes they find activities that allow them to address two or more goals simultaneously. For instance, they can address both achievement goals and social goals by forming a study group to prepare for a test. Sometimes they modify their ideas of what it means to achieve particular goals. For instance, an ambitious high school student who initially hopes to earn all As in three challenging classes may eventually decide that earning Bs in two of them is more realistic. And sometimes learners entirely abandon one

needds

Surgeon
I want to be a surgeon
because I can help people
if the get sick and can
treat them they will feel better.
And can save ther lives. I will
study hard for lots of years.

Career aspirations are often among learners' many goals. Here 7-year-old Ashton explains why he wants to be a surgeon. Notice how his career goal also has a social-goal component: "I can help people if [they] get sick."

[95] E. M. Anderman, Griesinger, & Westerfield, 1998; Brophy, 1987; L. H. Meyer et al., 2008; Midgley, Kaplan, & Middleton, 2001.

[96] Hidi & Harackiewicz, 2000; Kaplan, 1998; Kaplan & Midgley, 1997; Midgley et al., 2001.

[97] Bong, 2009; Dweck & Elliott, 1983.

[98] Bong, 2009; Dweck & Elliott, 1983; Elliot, 2005; Elliot & McGregor, 2000; Harter, 1992; Régner et al., 2007.

[99] Roberts, Treasure, & Kavussanu, 1997.

[100] M. E. Ford & Smith, 2007; Schutz, 1994.

[101] H. A. Davis, 2003; Dowson & McInerney, 2001; M. E. Ford & Smith, 2007; Patrick, Anderman, & Ryan, 2002; Wentzel, Filisetti, & Looney, 2007.

[102] Boekaerts, de Koning, & Vedder, 2006; Schutz, 1994.

[103] Wentzel & Wigfield, 1998; Wigfield, Eccles, & Pintrich, 1996.

[104] Duckworth, Peterson, Matthews, & Kelly, 2007.

[105] Covington, 2000; Dodge, Asher, & Parkhurst, 1989; Phelan, Yu, & Davidson, 1994; Urdan & Maehr, 1995.

goal in order to satisfy another. For example, they may find that the multiple demands of school co-erce them into focusing on performance goals (e.g., getting good grades) rather than studying the subject matter as thoroughly as they'd like. Brian, a junior high school student, expresses his regret about leaving mastery goals behind as he strives for performance goals:

> I sit here and I say, "Hey, I did this assignment in five minutes and I still got an A+ on it." I still have a feeling that I could do better, and it was kind of cheap that I didn't do my best and I still got this A. . . . I think probably it might lower my standards eventually, which I'm not looking forward to at all. . . . I'll always know, though, that I have it in me. It's just that I won't express it that much.[106]

Because most learners have a strong need for relatedness, their social goals often influence their classroom behavior and the priority they give to various achievement goals. If learners want to gain their teacher's attention and approval, they're apt to strive for good grades and in other ways shoot for performance goals.[107] If they seek friendly relationships with classmates or are concerned about others' welfare, they may eagerly engage in such activities as cooperative learning and peer tutoring.[108] A desire for close relationships with others may also lead them to ask peers for help, but if they want to impress peers with their high ability—a performance goal—they probably *won't* ask for help.[109] If they want to gain the approval of *low-achieving* peers, they may exert little effort in their studies and possibly even avoid classroom tasks altogether.[110]

Learners identify what are, in their minds, the likely causes of their successes and failures.

As we've seen in previous chapters, learners actively try to make sense of their experiences. Such sense-making sometimes involves identifying reasons for success or failure in particular situations. To gain insight into the kinds of explanations you yourself might identify, try the following exercise.

SEE FOR YOURSELF
CARBERRY AND SEVILLE

1. Professor Josiah S. Carberry has just returned the first set of exams, scored and graded, in your advanced psychoceramics class. You discover that you've gotten one of the few high test grades in the class, an A–. Why did you do so well when most of your classmates did poorly? Jot down several possible explanations for why you might have received a high grade in Dr. Carberry's class.
2. An hour later, you get the results of the first test in Professor Barbara F. Seville's sociocosmetology class, and you learn that you *failed* it! Why did you do so poorly? Jot down several possible reasons for your F on Dr. Seville's test.

The reasons you just wrote down are called attributions. **Attributions** are learners' beliefs about what behaviors and other factors influence events in their lives. Learners form attributions for many events in their daily lives—why they do well or poorly on tests and assignments, why they're popular or unpopular with peers, why they're skilled athletes or totally uncoordinated, and so on. Are the attributions you wrote for your grades in Professor Carberry and Seville's courses similar to those shown in Figure 5.7? Obviously, these examples are only some of many attributions you could have made. Notice that the attributions in Figure 5.7 are categorized in three ways:[111]

- **Locus ("place"): Internal versus external.** Learners sometimes attribute the causes of events to *internal* factors within themselves. Thinking that a good grade is due to your own hard work and believing that a poor grade is due to your lack of ability are examples

---

[106] Thomas & Oldfather, 1997, p. 119.
[107] Hinkley, McInerney, & Marsh, 2001; Urdan & Mestas, 2006.
[108] L. H. Anderman & Anderman, 1999; Dowson & McInerney, 2001.
[109] A. M. Ryan, Hicks, & Midgley, 1997.
[110] Brown, 1990; M. E. Ford & Nichols, 1991; Schultheiss & Brunstein, 2005.
[111] Weiner, 1986, 2000, 2010.

FIGURE 5.7 Possible attributions for the good test grade in Dr. Carberry's class (the "a" responses) and the bad test grade in Dr. Seville's class (the "b" responses)

	Internal Locus		External Locus	
	Controllable	**Uncontrollable**	**Controllable**	**Uncontrollable**
Stable	1a. "I take school seriously and always make studying a high priority." 1b. "I really don't care about college—never will!"	2a. "I'm really intelligent!" 2b. "I don't have much natural talent in sociocosmetology."	3a. "Dr. Carberry was lenient in grading me because I'm friendly in class." 3b. "Professor Seville doesn't like me because I always argue with her in class."	4a. "Professor Carberry is known around campus for his easy tests." 4b. "Dr. Seville is a really bad instructor; she has no clue how to teach."
Unstable	5a. "I studied a lot for the test." 5b. "I didn't go to class for 2 weeks because I was too busy blogging."	6a. "I was in a good mood, and so I was able to concentrate on the questions." 6b. "I had the flu all week, and I was still tired when I took the test."	7a. "A tutor at the college learning center helped me study the right things." 7b. "I couldn't convince my friends to study for the test with me."	8a. "I was lucky that Dr. Carberry asked only questions about things I'd studied." 8b. "The student next to me was constantly distracting me with his coughing."

of internal attributions. At other times learners attribute events to *external* factors outside themselves. Concluding that you received a scholarship because you "lucked out" and interpreting a classmate's scowl as a sign of her bad mood (rather than as something you might have done to upset her) are examples of external attributions.

- **Stability: Stable versus unstable.** Sometimes learners believe that events are due to *stable* factors—to things that probably won't change much in the near future. For example, if you believe that you do well in science because of your innate intelligence or that you have trouble making friends because you're unattractive, you're attributing events to stable, relatively long-term causes. But sometimes learners instead believe that events result from *unstable* factors—things that can change from one time to the next. Thinking that winning a tennis game because of a lucky shot and believing you got a bad test grade because you were exhausted when you took the test are examples of attributions involving unstable factors.

- **Controllability: Controllable versus uncontrollable.** On some occasions, learners attribute events to *controllable* factors—to things they can influence and change. For example, if you think a classmate invited you to a party because you often smile and say nice things to him, and if you think you failed a test simply because you didn't study the right things, you're attributing these events to controllable factors. On other occasions, learners attribute events to *uncontrollable* factors—to things over which they have no influence. If you think that you were chosen for the lead in the school play only because you look "right" for the part or that you played a lousy game of basketball because you were sick, you're attributing these events to uncontrollable factors.

It's important to remember that attributions are constructed by learners in their minds; therefore, their attributions may not reflect the *real* causes of an outcome. For instance, a student may blame a low test grade on a "tricky" test or an "unfair" teacher when the real cause was the student's own lack of effort or ineffective study strategies. In general, learners tend to attribute their successes to internal causes (e.g., high ability, hard work) and their failures to external causes (e.g., luck, other people's behaviors) to maintain their sense of self-worth.[112] Yet when learners *consistently* fail at tasks, and especially when they see their peers succeeding at those same tasks,

think about it

In Chapter 3 we discovered that learners who don't carefully monitor their comprehension may have an *illusion of knowing*, thinking they've learned something they actually *haven't* learned. If learners who have an illusion of knowing fail an exam, to what would they likely attribute their failure? (For an explanation, click **here**.)

---

[112] Hattie, 2008; Paris & Byrnes, 1989; Rhodewalt & Vohs, 2005; Whitley & Frieze, 1985.

they're apt to put the blame on a stable and seemingly uncontrollable internal factor: their own low ability.[113] Such an attribution is counterproductive, of course, because it doesn't spur learners to engage in successful strategies. Instead, they might engage in self-handicapping, which can lead to behaviors that make failure even *more* likely.

Learners' attributions for past successes and failures affect their future performance.

Let's return to those two fictional exams you considered in the "Carberry and Seville" exercise—the psychoceramics exam (on which you got an A–) and the sociocosmetology exam (on which you got an F). Imagine that you'll be taking a second exam in both psychoceramics and sociocosmetology in about 3 weeks' time. How much time will you spend studying for each exam?

The amount of time you spend studying for your upcoming exams will depend somewhat on your attributions for your earlier test grades. Let's first consider your A– on Professor Carberry's exam. If you think you did well because you studied hard for this test (1a and 5a in Figure 5.7), you'll probably spend a lot of time studying for the second test because effort is controllable. If you think you did well because you're smart or a natural whiz at psychoceramics (2a in the figure), you may not study quite as much, especially if you think of academic ability as an inherited, uncontrollable, talent. If you think the A– reflects how much Carberry likes you because of your friendly disposition (3a in the figure), you may decide that time spent talking to him after class is more important than time spent studying. And if you believe your success was because he gives easy tests (4a in the figure), you may hardly study at all.

Now let's consider your failing grade on Professor Seville's exam. Once again, the way in which you interpret the grade will influence the ways in which you prepare for the second exam—if, in fact, you prepare at all. If you believe you didn't study enough or prepare appropriately (5b in the figure), you may spend more time studying the next time because your effort and strategies are controllable. If you think your poor grade was due to a temporary situation—perhaps you weren't feeling well (6b in the figure), or perhaps you couldn't concentrate during the exam (8b in the figure)—you may study in much the same way as you did before, because these unfortunate events were uncontrollable and unstable. If you believe your failure was due to your low aptitude for sociocosmetology (2b in the figure) or to the fact that Seville is a poor instructor (4b in the figure), you may study even less than you did the first time. After all, what good will it do to study when your poor test performance is due to something uncontrollable and stable?

As you can see, your future effort and performance in these courses depend on your attributions. One especially important attribution is whether you believe that your innate intelligence is controllable or uncontrollable. As we will discover in Chapter 6, psychologists disagree about the extent to which intelligence is the result of the environment (and thus controllable and able to be increased with instruction and practice) or inherited genetics (and thus stable and uncontrollable). Even children and adolescents have differing opinions on the matter.[114] Those with an **incremental view of intelligence** believe that intelligence can and does improve with effort and practice. In contrast, those with an **entity view of intelligence** believe that intelligence is a distinct ability that is built-in and relatively permanent.[115] A student named Sarah clearly reveals an entity view in her explanation of why she has trouble in math:

> My dad is very good at math, and my brother, I, and my mom aren't good at math at all, we inherited the "not good at math gene" from my mom and I am good in English but I am not good in math.[116]

Students with an incremental view of intelligence and specific academic abilities are likely to adopt mastery goals in the classroom, to work hard at their studies, and to earn increasingly high grades. In contrast, students with an entity view (like Sarah) adopt performance goals,

---

[113] Covington, 1987; Hong, Chiu, & Dweck, 1995; Schunk, 1990; Weiner, 1984.

[114] Dweck, 2000; Dweck et al., 2004; Dweck & Leggett, 1988; B. D. Jones, Byrd, & Lusk, 2009.

[115] These implicit theories about the changeability of intelligence are sometimes called *mindsets;* Dweck, 2006; Yeager & Dweck, 2012.

[116] K. E. Ryan, Ryan, Arbuthnot, & Samuels, 2007, p. 5.

quickly lose interest in topics that don't come easily to them, self-handicap in the face of failure, and earn lower grades over time.[117]

Learners' attributions also influence a number of other factors that either directly or indirectly affect their future performance:

- **Emotional reactions to success and failure.** Naturally, learners are happy when they succeed and sad when they fail. But attributions bring other emotions into the mix as well. Learners are apt to feel proud about their successes and guilty and ashamed about their failures only if they attribute these outcomes to internal causes—for instance, to things they themselves have done. If instead, learners think someone else was to blame for an undesirable outcome, they're apt to be angry—an emotion that's unlikely to lead to productive follow-up behaviors.[118]

- **Expectations for future success or failure.** When learners attribute their successes and failures to stable factors (e.g., innate ability or the lack of it), they expect their future performance to be similar to their current performance. In contrast, when they attribute their successes and failures to *un*stable factors (e.g., effort or luck), their current success rate will have little influence on their expectation for future success, and a few failures won't put much of a dent in their self-efficacy. The most optimistic learners—those with the highest expectations for future success—are the ones who attribute their successes to internal, stable factors such as an enduring work ethic and innate intelligence or ability and attribute their failures to unstable factors such as lack of effort or inappropriate strategies.[119]

- **Effort and persistence.** Learners who believe their failures result from their own lack of effort (an internal, controllable cause) are apt to try harder and persist in the face of difficulty. Learners who, instead, attribute failure to a lack of innate ability (an internal, uncontrollable cause) give up easily and sometimes can't even perform tasks they've previously done successfully.[120]

- **Learning strategies.** Learners who expect to succeed in the classroom and believe that academic success is a result of their own doing are more likely to apply effective learning strategies—especially when they're *taught* these strategies. These learners are also more apt to be self-regulating learners and to seek help when they need it. In contrast, learners who expect failure and believe their academic performance is largely out of their hands often reject effective learning strategies in favor of rote-learning approaches.[121]

Given all of these effects, it shouldn't surprise you to learn that students with internal, controllable attributions for classroom success (rather than external ones they can't control) are more likely to achieve at high levels and graduate from high school.[122]

In the opening case study, Michael initially attributes his failure in algebra to two uncontrollable, stable factors: low math ability and poor instruction. These factors probably make him feel a combination of shame (due to his low ability) and anger (due to the poor instruction). Because the perceived causes of his failure are both stable and out of his control, he expects future failure no matter what he does and thus has little reason to exert much effort (e.g., he doesn't take notes). But as he acquires new study strategies and gains a better understanding of algebraic concepts and procedures, he experiences success in class. This leads him to attribute his performance to two unstable, internal factors he *can* control—effort and better strategies:

> I realize now that even if I don't like the teacher or don't think he is a good teacher, it is my responsibility to listen. . . . The teacher does most of his part, but it's no use to me unless I do my part. . . . Now I try and comprehend, ask questions and figure out how he got the answer.[123]

[117] Blackwell, Trzesniewski, & Dweck, 2007; Dweck & Leggett, 1988; Dweck & Molden, 2005; B. D. Jones, Wilkins, Long, & Wang, 2012.
[118] Hareli & Weiner, 2002; Pekrun, 2006.
[119] Dweck, 2000; Eccles, 2009; Pomerantz & Saxon, 2001; Schunk, 1990; Weiner, 2005.
[120] Blackwell, Trzesniewski, & Dweck, 2007; Dweck, 1978, 2000; Feather, 1982; Weiner, 1984.
[121] R. Ames, 1983; Dweck, Mangels, & Good, 2004; Mangels, 2004; D. J. Palmer & Goetz, 1988; Pressley, Borkowski, & Schneider, 1987; Zimmerman, 1998.
[122] L. E. Davis, Ajzen, Saunders, & Williams, 2002; Dweck et al., 2004; Pintrich, 2003.
[123] Tucker & Anderman, 1999, pp. 5–6.

Learners' attributions are affected by their teachers' attributions and resulting expectations for students' performance.

Teachers form opinions about their students' strengths, weaknesses, and potential for academic success. In many instances, teachers size up their students fairly accurately. They know which ones need help with reading skills, which ones have short attention spans, which ones have trouble working together in a cooperative group, and so on, and they can adapt their instruction and assistance accordingly.[124] Yet even the best teachers sometimes make errors in their judgments, perhaps underestimating students who are members of ethnic minority groups or come from low socioeconomic backgrounds.[125] Furthermore, many teachers have an entity view of intelligence, and so they perceive students' ability levels to be relatively fixed and stable.[126] Their attributions regarding these "stable" abilities affect their expectations for students' performance, which in turn, lead them to treat students differently. When teachers have high expectations for students, they present challenging tasks, interact with students frequently, persist in their efforts to help students understand, and give a lot of positive feedback. In contrast, when teachers have low expectations for certain students, they present easy tasks, offer few opportunities for speaking in class, and give little feedback about students' responses.[127]

Teachers' beliefs about students' abilities also affect their attributions for students' successes and failures.[128] Consider the following interpretations of a student's success:

- "You did it! You're so smart!"
- "That's wonderful. Your hard work has really paid off, hasn't it?"
- "You've done very well. It's clear that you really know how to study."
- "Terrific! This is certainly your lucky day!"

And now consider these interpretations of a student's failure:

- "Hmmm, maybe this just isn't something you're good at. Perhaps we should try a different activity."
- "Why don't you practice a little more and then try again?"
- "Let's see if we can come up with some study strategies that might work better for you."
- "Maybe you're just having a bad day."

All of these comments are presumably intended to make a student feel good. But notice the different attributions they imply—in some cases to uncontrollable abilities (being smart or not "good at" something), in other cases to controllable and therefore changeable behaviors (hard work, lack of practice, effective or ineffective study strategies), and in still other cases to external, uncontrollable causes (a lucky break, a bad day).

Teachers communicate their attributions for students' performance not only through what they say, but also through the emotions they convey.[129] As an example, let's return to the opening case study, in which Michael is initially doing poorly in his eighth-grade algebra class. Imagine that you're Michael's teacher. Imagine, too, that you believe Michael has low mathematical ability: He just doesn't have a "gift" for math. When you see him consistently getting Ds and Fs on assignments and quizzes, you might reasonably conclude that his poor performance is beyond his control, and so you communicate pity and sympathy. But now imagine, instead, that you believe Michael has *high* math ability: He definitely has what it takes to do well in your class. When you see his poor marks on assignments and quizzes, you naturally assume he isn't trying very hard. In your eyes, Michael has complete control over the amount of effort he exerts, and so you might express anger or annoyance when he doesn't do well. Some teachers might even punish him for his poor performance.[130]

---

[124] Dweck & Molden, 2005; Goldenberg, 1992–1993.

[125] Banks & Banks, 1995; McLoyd, 1998.

[126] Oakes & Guiton, 1995; C. Reyna, 2000.

[127] Babad, 1993; Brophy, 2006; T. L. Good & Brophy, 1994; Graham, 1990; Rosenthal, 1994.

[128] Weiner, 2000, 2005.

[129] C. Reyna & Weiner, 2001; Weiner, 2005.

[130] C. Reyna & Weiner, 2001; Weiner, 2005.

Most children and adolescents are well aware of their teachers' differential behaviors toward different students and use such behaviors to draw inferences about their own and others' abilities.[131] When they can't figure out why they're doing well or poorly, they may eagerly seek out information to help them explain their performance.[132] If teachers repeatedly give them low-ability messages, they may begin to see themselves as their teachers see them, and their behavior may mirror their self-perceptions.[133] In some cases, then, teachers' expectations and attributions may become **self-fulfilling prophecies**: What teachers expect students to achieve becomes what students actually *do* achieve.[134] Self-fulfilling prophecies occur most frequently when students are making a significant transition in their schooling (e.g., when they enter first grade or begin junior high school), and they're more common for girls and for students from ethnic minority groups.[135]

With age, learners increasingly attribute their successes and failures to ability rather than to effort.

As children grow older, they become increasingly able to distinguish among the various possible causes of their successes and failures: effort, ability, luck, task difficulty, and so on.[136] In the early elementary school grades, children think of effort and ability as positively correlated: People who try harder are more competent. Thus, they tend to attribute their successes to hard work and are usually optimistic about their chances for future success as long as they try hard. Sometime around age 9, children begin to understand that effort and ability often compensate for each other and that people with less ability may need to exert greater effort. At about the same time, many also begin to attribute their successes and failures to an inherited ability—for instance, to something they call "intelligence"—which they perceive to be fairly stable and uncontrollable. If they're usually successful at school tasks, they will have high self-efficacy for such tasks. But if they often fail, their self-efficacy can plummet.[137]

Over time, learners acquire a general attributional style.

Consider these two girls, who have the *same* ability:

- Jane is an enthusiastic, energetic learner. She works hard at school activities and takes obvious pleasure in doing well. She likes challenges, especially the brainteaser problems her teacher assigns as extra-credit work each day. She can't always solve the problems, but she takes failure in stride and is eager for more problems the following day.

- Julie is an anxious, fidgety student who doesn't have much confidence in her ability to accomplish school tasks successfully. In fact, she often underestimates what she can do: Even when she has succeeded, she doubts that she can do it again. She prefers filling out drill-and-practice worksheets that help her practice skills she's already mastered, rather than attempting new tasks and problems. As for those daily brainteasers Jane likes so much, Julie sometimes takes a stab at them but gives up quickly if the answer isn't obvious.

Over time, some learners, like Jane, develop an "I can do it" attitude known as a **mastery orientation**—a general sense of optimism that they can master new tasks and succeed in a variety of endeavors. Other learners, like Julie, develop an "I *can't* do it" attitude known as **learned helplessness**—a general sense of futility about their chances for future success. You might think of this distinction, which really reflects a continuum rather than an either–or dichotomy, as a difference between *optimists* and *pessimists*.[138]

---

[131] R. Butler, 1994; T. L. Good & Nichols, 2001; Weinstein, 2002.

[132] Weiner, 2000.

[133] Marachi, Friedel, & Midgley, 2001; Murdock, 1999.

[134] For a classic study of the self-fulfilling prophecy, see Rosenthal & Jacobson, 1968.

[135] Graham, 1990; Hinnant, O'Brien, & Ghazarian, 2009; Jussim, Eccles, & Madon, 1996; Kuklinski & Weinstein, 2001; Raudenbush, 1984.

[136] Dweck & Elliott, 1983; Eccles et al., 1998; Nicholls, 1990.

[137] Dweck, 1986; Eccles [Parsons] et al., 1983; Nicholls, 1990; Schunk, 1990.

[138] Peterson, 1990, 2006; Scheier & Carver, 1992; Seligman, 1991.

Even when learners with a mastery orientation and those with learned helplessness have equal ability initially, those with a mastery orientation behave in ways that lead to higher achievement over the long run. They set ambitious goals, seek challenging situations, and persist in the face of failure. Learners with learned helplessness behave quite differently. Because they underestimate their ability, they set goals they can easily accomplish, avoid the challenges that are likely to maximize their learning and cognitive growth, and respond to failure in counterproductive ways (e.g., giving up quickly) that almost guarantee future failure.[139]

By age 5 or 6, some children begin to show a consistent tendency either to persist at a task and express confidence they can master it, or, instead, to abandon a task quickly and believe they don't have the ability to do it.[140] As a general rule, however, children younger than age 8 rarely exhibit extreme forms of learned helplessness, perhaps because they still believe that success is due largely to their own efforts.[141] In early adolescence, a general sense of helplessness becomes more common. Some middle schoolers believe they can't control the things that happen to them (e.g., they're apt to have an entity view of intelligence) and are at a loss for strategies about how to avert future failures.[142] In the opening case study, Michael's initial pessimism about his chances of future success in algebra suggests some degree of learned helplessness, at least about mathematics.

Table 5.3 draws from developmental trends in attributions and other cognitive factors in motivation to describe common motivational characteristics of students in the elementary, middle, and high school grades.

DEVELOPMENTAL TRENDS
Table 5.3 • Motivation at Different Grade Levels

GRADE LEVEL	AGE-TYPICAL CHARACTERISTICS	EXAMPLE	SUGGESTED STRATEGIES
Grades K–2	• Tendency to define teacher-chosen activities as "work" and self-chosen activities as "play" • Rapidly changing interests for many students; more stable interests for others • Pursuit of interesting and enjoyable activities regardless of expectation for success • Tendency to attribute success to hard work and practice, leading to optimism about what can be accomplished	Six-year-old Alex loves learning about lizards. He often draws lizards during his free time, and when he goes to the school library, he invariably looks for books about lizards and other reptiles. One day, with his teacher's permission, he brings his pet iguana to class and explains the things he must do to keep it healthy.	• Engage students' interest in classroom topics through hands-on, playlike activities. • Entice students into reading, writing, and other basic skills through high-interest books and subject matter (e.g., animals, superheroes, princes and princesses). • Show students how they've improved over time; point out how their effort and practice have contributed to their improvement.
Grades 3–5	• Emergence of fairly stable individual interests • Increasing tendency to observe peers' performance as a criterion for judging one's own performance, resulting in a gradual decline in expectancies for overall academic performance • Increasing focus on performance goals • Increasing belief in innate ability as a significant and uncontrollable factor affecting learning and achievement	During a gymnastics unit in physical education, 9-year-old Marta watches her peers as they perform forward and backward rolls, handstands, and cartwheels. She willingly executes the rolls, but when she has trouble getting her legs up for a handstand, she quickly gives up, saying, "I can't do handstands and cartwheels—not like Jessie and Sharonda can."	• Allow students to pursue individual interests in independent reading and writing tasks. • Teach students strategies for tracking their own progress over time. • Demonstrate your own fascination and enthusiasm about classroom topics; communicate that many topics are worth learning about for their own sake. • Identify strengths in every student; provide sufficient support to enable students to gain proficiency in areas of weakness.

(continued)

---

[139] Dweck, 2000; Graham, 1989; Peterson, 1990, 2006; Seligman, 1991.

[140] Burhans & Dweck, 1995; Ziegert, Kistner, Castro, & Robertson, 2001.

[141] Eccles et al., 1998; Lockhart, Chang, & Story, 2002; Paris & Cunningham, 1996.

[142] Dweck, 2000; Paris & Cunningham, 1996; Peterson, Maier, & Seligman, 1993.

GRADE LEVEL	AGE-TYPICAL CHARACTERISTICS	EXAMPLE	SUGGESTED STRATEGIES
Grades 6–8	• Increasing interest in activities that are stereotypically "gender-appropriate"; decrease in activities considered to be "gender-inappropriate" • Noticeable decline in perceptions of competence and intrinsic motivation for mastering academic subject matter • Increasing tendency to value activities associated with long-term goals and high expectations for success • Decline in perceived value of many content domains (e.g., English, math, music, sports) • Increasing focus on social goals (e.g., interacting with peers, making a good impression)	Thirteen-year-old Regina has always liked math. But now that she's in an advanced eighth-grade math class, she's starting to worry that her peers might think she's a "math geek." She diligently does her math homework every night and earns high grades on assignments and quizzes, but she rarely raises her hand in class to ask or answer questions. And when her friends ask her about the class, she rolls her eyes and says that she's in the class only because "Dad made me take it."	• Promote interest in classroom topics by presenting puzzling phenomena and building on students' individual interests. • Focus students' attention on their improvement; minimize opportunities for them to compare their own performance to that of classmates. • Relate classroom subject matter to students' long-term goals (e.g., through authentic activities). • Provide opportunities for social interaction as students study and learn (e.g., through role-playing activities, classroom debates, cooperative learning projects).
Grades 9–12	• Increasing integration of certain interests, values, and behaviors into one's *sense of self* (i.e., one's overall beliefs about who one is as a person; see Chapter 7) • Continuing decline in intrinsic motivation to master academic subject matter • Prevalence of performance goals (e.g., getting good grades) rather than mastery goals for most students • Increase in cheating as a means of accomplishing performance goals • Increasing focus on postgraduation goals (e.g., college, careers); for some students, inadequate self-regulation strategies for achieving these goals	Sixteen-year-old Randall wants to become a pediatric oncologist—"a cancer doctor for kids," he tells people, "so I can help kids with leukemia, like my sister had." He knows he needs good grades in order to get into a prestigious college, which, in turn, can help him get into medical school. Yet he has trouble saying no when his friends ask him to go to a basketball game the night before an important biology test. And when he gets home after the game, he spends an hour playing video games instead of studying.	• Provide opportunities to pursue interests and values through out-of-class projects and extracurricular activities (e.g., community service work). • Make it possible for students to attain good grades through reasonable effort and effective strategies (e.g., minimize competitive grading practices, such as grading on a curve). • Discourage cheating (e.g., by giving individualized assignments and monitoring behavior during in-class assessments), and impose appropriate consequences when cheating occurs. • Teach self-regulation strategies that can help students reach their long-term goals (see Chapter 3).

Sources: J. M. Alexander et al., 2008; Blumenfeld et al., 2006; Bong, 2009; Brophy, 2008; Cizek, 2003; Corpus et al., 2009; Covington, 1992; Dijkstra et al., 2008; Dotterer, McHale, & Crouter, 2009; Eccles et al., 1998; Hidi et al., 2004; Jacobs et al., 2005; Jacobs et al., 2002; Lepper et al., 2005; Nolen, 2007; Otis et al., 2005; Paley, 1984; Patrick et al., 2002; Renninger, 2009; Schunk & Zimmerman, 2006; Shute, 2008; Watt, 2004; Wigfield, 1994; Wigfield et al., 2006; Wigfield et al., 1991; Wigfield & Wagner, 2005; Wilson & Corbett, 2001; Youniss & Yates, 1999.

Culture influences the cognitive factors underlying motivation.

Virtually all the cognitive factors underlying motivation are influenced by learners' environments. Some of them—for instance, values, goals, and attributions—seem to be especially susceptible to cultural influence. The Cultural Considerations box "Cultural and Ethnic Differences in Motivation" describes numerous influences that culture is apt to have, not only on how learners prioritize various activities, form goals for themselves, and interpret consequences, but also on the specific ways in which learners satisfy their basic psychological needs.

> Students' motivation is affected by several cognitive factors, including their interest, self-efficacy, values, goals, attributions, and beliefs about whether intelligence is changeable or fixed. Students' motivation is also affected by their teachers' attributions and expectations for students' performance. In the hotlinked Self-Check quiz and Application Exercise that follow, you can check and apply your understandings related to Big Idea 5.3:
> *Learners' thoughts and beliefs about themselves and about classroom subject matter can influence their motivation to learn in the classroom.*
>
> MyEdLab **Self-Check 5.3**
>
> MyEdLab **Application Exercise 5.3.** This exercise will allow you to apply your knowledge of cognitive factors that can influence students' motivation, such as goals, self-efficacy, attributions, and views of intelligence.

Cultural and Ethnic Differences in Motivation

Virtually all children and adolescents have the basic needs we've identified in this chapter. However, the means by which they satisfy their needs, the particular goals they set for themselves, and the attributions they form for their successes and failures vary considerably, depending, in part, on the behaviors and values that their culture and society model and encourage. Following are several areas in which researchers have found cultural and ethnic differences.

ACHIEVING A SENSE OF SELF-WORTH. In mainstream Western culture, achieving a sense of self-worth often involves *being good at* certain things and also *thinking* that one is good at these things. In such a context, learners are likely to engage in self-handicapping as a means of justifying poor performance. But not all cultures stress the importance of positive self-evaluations. For instance, many people in East Asian cultures place greater importance on how well other people view an individual as living up to society's standards for behavior. In such cultures the focus is more likely to be on correcting existing weaknesses—that is, on *self-improvement*—than on demonstrating current strengths.[a]

ACHIEVING A SENSE OF AUTONOMY. Children and adolescents around the world want some autonomy, but the amount of autonomy and the forms that it takes may differ considerably from group to group.[b] For example, adults in some Native American groups (e.g., those living in the Navajo Nation in the southwestern United States) give children more autonomy and control over decision making, and do so at an earlier age, than do many adults in mainstream Western culture.[c] (Recall the opening case study "Why Jack Wasn't in School" in Chapter 4.) In contrast, many Asian and African American parents give children *less* autonomy than other American adults, in some cases as a way of ensuring children's safety in potentially hostile environments.[d]

Cultural differences have also been observed in one important aspect of autonomy: opportunities to make choices. Although young people around the world find choice-making opportunities highly motivating, those from Asian cultures often prefer that people they trust (e.g., parents, teachers, respected peers) make choices for them.[e] Perhaps Asian children see trusted others as people who can make *wise* choices, which will ultimately lead to higher levels of learning and competence.

ADDRESSING THE NEED FOR RELATEDNESS. In comparison to other groups, Asian children tend to spend less time socializing with peers and place greater importance on gaining teachers' attention and approval.[f] Furthermore, whereas Asian students are likely to have friends who encourage academic achievement, some students from certain other ethnic groups (boys especially) may feel considerable peer pressure *not* to achieve at high levels, perhaps because high achievement reflects conformity to mainstream Western culture (more on this point in Chapter 7).

Additionally, children and adolescents from many cultural and ethnic groups (e.g., those from many Native American, Hispanic, and Asian communities, as well as those in some rural European American communities) have especially strong loyalties to family and may have been raised to achieve for their respective communities, rather than just for themselves as individuals. Motivating statements such as "Think how proud your family will be!" and "If you go to college and get a good education, you can really help your community!" are likely to be especially effective for such learners.[g]

The need for relatedness can sometimes be at odds with the need for autonomy. In particular, achieving relatedness can involve doing what *others* want one to do, whereas achieving autonomy involves doing what one *personally* wants to do. Many East Asians resolve this apparent conflict by willingly agreeing to adjust personal behaviors and goals to meet social demands and maintain overall group harmony.[h]

VALUES AND GOALS. Most cultural and ethnic groups place high value on getting a good education.[i] But researchers have observed differences in more specific values related to school learning. For example, many Asian cultures (e.g., in China, Japan, and Russia) emphasize learning for learning's sake: With knowledge comes personal growth, better understanding of the world, and greater potential to contribute to society. Important for these cultures, too, are hard work and persistence in academic studies, even when the content isn't intrinsically enjoyable.[j] Students from European American backgrounds are less likely to be diligent when classroom topics have little intrinsic appeal, but they often find value in academic subject matter that piques their curiosity and in assignments that require creativity, independent thinking, or critical analysis.[k]

Learners from diverse cultural backgrounds may also define academic success differently and, as a result, may set different achievement goals. For example, on average, Asian American students aim for higher grades than do students from other ethnic groups, in part to win the approval of their parents and in part to bring honor to their families.[l] Even so, Asian American students—and African American students as well—tend to focus more on mastery goals (i.e., truly understanding what they are studying) than European American students do.[m] And students brought up in cultures that value group achievement over individual achievement (e.g., many Asian, Native American, Mexican American, and Pacific Islander cultures) tend to focus their mastery goals not on how much they alone can improve but instead on how much they *and their peers* can improve—or in some instances on how much their own actions can contribute to the betterment of the larger social group or society.[n]

ATTRIBUTIONS. Learners' cultural and ethnic backgrounds influence their attributions as well. For instance, students from families with traditional Asian cultural beliefs are more likely than students from mainstream Western culture to attribute classroom success and failure to unstable factors—effort in the case of academic achievement, and temporary situational factors in the case of appropriate or inappropriate behaviors.[o] Also, some researchers have found a greater tendency for African American students to develop a sense of learned helplessness about their ability to achieve academic success.[p] To some extent, racial prejudice may contribute to their learned helplessness: Students may begin to believe that because of the color of their skin, they have little chance of success no matter what they do.[q]

---

[a] Heine, 2007; Li, 2005; Sedikides & Gregg, 2008.
[b] d'Ailly, 2003; Deyhle & LeCompte, 1999; Fiske & Fiske, 2007; Rogoff, 2003.
[c] Deyhle & LeCompte, 1999.
[d] McLoyd, 1998; Qin, Pomerantz, & Wang, 2009; Tamis-Lemonda & McFadden, 2010.
[e] Bao & Lam, 2008; Hufton, Elliott, & Illushin, 2002; Iyengar & Lepper, 1999; Vansteenkiste, Zhou, Lens, & Soenens, 2005.
[f] Dien, 1998; Steinberg, 1996.
[g] Chiu & Hong, 2005; Fiske & Fiske, 2007; Kağitçibaşi, 2007; Suina & Smolkin, 1994; Timm & Borman, 1997.
[h] Heine, 2007; Iyengar & Lepper, 1999; Kağitçibaşi, 2007; Li & Fischer, 2004.
[i] Cook & Ludwig, 2008; Fuligni & Hardway, 2004; Phalet, Andriessen, & Lens, 2004; Spera, 2005.
[j] Chiu & Hong, 2005; Hufton et al., 2002; Li, 2006; Morelli & Rothbaum, 2007.
[k] Hess & Azuma, 1991; Kuhn & Park, 2005; Nisbett, 2009.
[l] Nisbett, 2009; Steinberg, 1996.
[m] Freeman, Gutman, & Midgley, 2002; Qian & Pan, 2002; Shim & Ryan, 2006.
[n] Chiu & Hong, 2005; Kağitçibaşi, 2007; Li, 2005, 2006.
[o] Grant & Dweck, 2001; Hess, Chih-Mei, & McDevitt, 1987; Li & Fischer, 2004; Weiner, 2004.
[p] Graham, 1989; Holliday, 1985.
[q] Sue & Chin, 1983; van Laar, 2000.

5.4 AFFECT AND ITS EFFECTS ON MOTIVATION AND LEARNING

Big Idea 5.4 Learners' affect (their feelings, emotions, and moods) influences and is influenced by both their motives and their cognitive processes.

At the beginning of the opening case, Michael probably feels quite frustrated and doesn't like algebra very much. After learning effective strategies and improving his performance, however, he studies every day except Friday. At this point, we might suspect, Michael takes pride in his performance and perhaps even enjoys working on his algebra assignments. Emotions, moods, and other forms of affect permeate many aspects of learners' lives—and not surprisingly, affect is closely related to their motivation and learning, as reflected in the following principles.

Affect and motivation are interrelated.

Without a doubt, people's automatic emotional reactions to certain events—for instance, a quick, fearful retreat from a person wielding a gun or knife—increase their chances of physical survival.[143] But affect also plays a significant role in the more intentional, goal-directed aspects of human motivation. As a general rule, people act in ways they think will help them feel happy and comfortable rather than sad, confused, or angry—feelings that depend, in part, on whether they're satisfying their basic needs and accomplishing their goals.[144]

Some emotions, such as pride, guilt, and shame—collectively known as **self-conscious emotions**—are closely tied to people's self-evaluations and thus affect their sense of self-worth.[145] When people evaluate their behaviors and accomplishments as being consistent with their culture's standards for appropriate and desirable behavior, they're apt to feel proud. In contrast, when they see themselves as failing to live up to those standards—for instance, when they thoughtlessly cause harm to someone else—they're apt to feel guilty and ashamed.

Affect and motivation are interrelated in other ways, too. When learners pursue a task they find interesting, they experience considerable positive affect (e.g., pleasure, enjoyment, excitement).[146] Positive affect comes with high self-efficacy as well. Furthermore, learners' reactions to the outcomes of events depend on how they *interpret* those outcomes—in particular, whether they hold themselves, other people, environmental circumstances, or something else responsible for what has happened (recall the earlier discussion of attributions).[147]

Affect is closely tied to learning and cognition.

Affect is often an integral part of learning and cognition.[148] For example, while learning how to perform a task, learners simultaneously learn whether or not they like doing it.[149] Learners can think more creatively and solve problems more effectively when they enjoy the topic they're working with, and their academic successes often result in feelings of excitement, pleasure, and pride.[150] In contrast, learners may feel frustrated and anxious when they must struggle to master new material (as Michael does in the opening case study), and they may develop a dislike for the subject matter.[151]

---

[143] Damasio, 1994; Öhman & Mineka, 2003.

[144] Ackerman, Izard, Kobak, Brown, & Smith, 2007; E. M. Anderman & Wolters, 2006; Mellers & McGraw, 2001; J. L. Tsai, 2007.

[145] Hidi & Renninger, 2006; Pekrun, 2006; Pekrun, Goetz, Titz, & Perry, 2002; Schiefele, 1998.

[146] Lewis & Sullivan, 2005; Pekrun, 2006.

[147] Hareli & Weiner, 2002; Harter, 1999; J. E. Turner, Husman, & Schallert, 2002.

[148] A certain structure in the brain, the *amygdala,* is especially important in making affect–cognition connections, in that it enables learners to associate particular emotions with particular stimuli or memories; for example, see Adolphs & Damasio, 2001; Kuhbandner, Spitzer, & Pekrun, 2011; Phelps & Sharot, 2008; Posner & Rothbart, 2007.

[149] Zajonc, 1980.

[150] E. M. Anderman & Wolters, 2006; Fredrickson, 2009; McLeod & Adams, 1989; Pekrun, 2006; Snow, Corno, & Jackson, 1996.

[151] Carver & Scheier, 1990; Goetz, Frenzel, Hall, & Pekrun, 2008; Stodolsky, Salk, & Glaessner, 1991.

Additionally, specific facts and ideas can occasionally evoke emotional reactions, as you'll discover in the following exercise.

─────────────── **SEE FOR YOURSELF** ───────────────
FLYING HIGH

As you read each of the following statements, decide whether it evokes positive feelings (e.g., happiness, excitement), negative feelings (e.g., sadness, anger), or no feelings whatsoever. Check the appropriate blank in each case.

	Positive Feelings	Negative Feelings	No Feelings
1. The city of Denver opened DIA, its new international airport, in 1995.	_____	_____	_____
2. In a recent commercial airline crash, 90 passengers and 8 crew members lost their lives.	_____	_____	_____
3. A dozen people survived that crash, including a 3-month-old infant found in the rear of the plane.	_____	_____	_____
4. The area of an airplane in which food is prepared is called the *galley*.	_____	_____	_____
5. Several major airlines are offering $129 round-trip fares to a beach resort in Mexico.	_____	_____	_____
6. Those $129 fares apply only to flights leaving at 5:30 in the morning.	_____	_____	_____
7. Some flights between North America and Europe now include two full-course meals.	_____	_____	_____

You probably had little or no emotional reaction to Statements 1 (the opening of DIA) and 4 (the definition of *galley*). In contrast, you may have had pleasant feelings when you read Statements 3 (the surviving infant) and 5 (the low fares to Mexico) and unpleasant feelings when you read Statements 2 (the high number of deaths) and 6 (the dreadful departure time for those Mexico flights). Your response to Statement 7 (the two full-course meals) may have been positive, negative, or neutral, depending on your previous experiences with airline cuisine.

As learners think about, learn, or retrieve something, their very thoughts and memories may become emotionally charged—a phenomenon known as **hot cognition**. For example, learners might get excited when they read about advances in science that could lead to effective treatments for spinal cord injuries, cancer, or mental illness. They may feel sad when they read about living conditions in certain parts of the world. They will likely get angry when they learn about the atrocities committed against African American slaves in the pre–Civil War days of the United States or against millions of Jewish people and members of other minority groups in Europe during World War II.

When information is emotionally charged, learners are more apt to pay attention to it, continue to think about it over a period of time, and repeatedly elaborate on it.[152] And encountering information that conflicts with what they currently know or believe can cause learners considerable mental discomfort, something that Piaget called *disequilibrium* but that many contemporary theorists call **cognitive dissonance**. Such dissonance typically leads learners to try to resolve the inconsistency in some way, perhaps by undergoing conceptual change or perhaps by finding fault with the new information (recall the discussion of *confirmation bias* in Chapter 2).[153] Later on, learners can usually retrieve material with high emotional content more easily than they can recall relatively nonemotional information.[154] It appears that learners' affective

MyEdLab
Video Example 5.3.

When children see something they don't expect to see, they can experience cognitive dissonance—a feeling of mental discomfort that may motivate them to learn more about a topic. How does the teacher in this video create cognitive dissonance?

[152] G. H. Bower, 1994; Heuer & Reisberg, 1992; Schacter, 1999; Zeelenberg, Wagenmakers, & Rotteveel, 2006.
[153] Harmon-Jones, 2001; Marcus, 2008; Sinatra & Mason, 2008.
[154] Barkley, 1996; McGaugh, 2015; Phelps & Sharot, 2008; Reisberg & Heuer, 1992. Occasionally people have trouble retrieving highly anxiety-arousing memories. This phenomenon, known as *repression*, may occasionally occur with very traumatic personal events but is unlikely to be a factor in the retrieval of academic subject matter (e.g., see Goodman et al., 2003; McNally & Geraerts, 2009).

reactions to classroom subject matter become integral parts of their network of associations in long-term memory.[155]

Productive affect can trigger effective learning strategies.

How effectively learners think about and make sense of new information depends, in part, on their general mood while they're studying. In general, positive affect, such as feelings of pleasure and excitement, leads learners to attend actively to the subject matter at hand, to work hard to make sense of it, to think creatively and open-mindedly about it, and to use self-regulating learning strategies to keep themselves on task. In contrast, if learners feel generally sad or frustrated—or if they're bored with the subject matter—they're likely to process new information in more superficial, inflexible ways (e.g., by using rehearsal).[156]

Affect can also trigger certain behaviors.

Learners' emotions often lead them to behave in certain ways. For example, feeling guilty or ashamed about something they've done can lead children and adolescents to make amends for their wrongdoings (more about this point in Chapter 7). Feeling frustrated during unsuccessful attempts to reach important goals can lead them to lash out at others or withdraw from classroom activities.[157] Feeling anxious about an upcoming event can be especially powerful in its influence on behavior, as the next principle reveals.

Some anxiety is helpful, but a lot is often a hindrance.

Imagine you're enrolled in Professor Josiah S. Carberry's course in advanced psychoceramics. Today is your day to give a half-hour presentation on the topic of psychoceramic califractions. You've read several books and numerous articles on your topic and undoubtedly know more about it than anyone else in the room. Furthermore, you've meticulously prepared a set of note cards to guide you during your presentation. As you sit in class waiting for your turn to speak, you should be feeling calm and confident. Instead, you're a nervous wreck: Your heart is pounding wildly, your palms are sweaty, and your stomach is in a knot. When Professor Carberry calls you to the front of the room and you begin to speak, you have trouble remembering what you wanted to say, and you can barely read your note cards because your hands are shaking so much.

It's not as if you *want* to be nervous about speaking in front of your psychoceramics class. Furthermore, you can't think of a single reason why you *should* be nervous. After all, you're an expert on your topic, you're not having a bad-hair day, and your classmates aren't likely to laugh at you or make fun of you on social media if you make a mistake. So what happened to the self-assured student who stood practicing in front of the mirror last night? You're a victim of **anxiety**: You have an uncontrollable feeling of uneasiness and apprehension about an event because you're not sure what its outcome will be. This feeling is accompanied by a variety of physiological symptoms, including a rapid heartbeat, increased perspiration, and muscular tension (e.g., a "knot" or "butterflies" in the stomach).

Just as learners have an optimal level of arousal, so, too, do they have an optimal level of anxiety. A small amount of anxiety often improves performance. When it does so, it's called **facilitating anxiety**. A little anxiety spurs learners into action—for instance, they go to class, complete assignments, and study for exams (see Figure 5.8).[158] However, a great deal of anxiety usually interferes with effective performance.[159] When it has this counterproductive effect, it's known as **debilitating anxiety**.

FIGURE 5.8 This writing sample, by 14-year-old Loretta, illustrates how anxiety can sometimes improve learning and achievement.

A Stressful Situation

Once I had a science test that the teacher told us about two days ahead of time. Of course I hadn't thought to read the chapter yet so I had to read it and study. I got nervous and started throwing a fit. I was saying that I couldn't do it over and over again.

Finally I took a deep breath and study as much as I could. The next day I took the test and I got, something like a 96. I was so surprised, and relieved.

---

[155] G. H. Bower & Forgas, 2001.

[156] Ahmed, Werf, Kuyper, & Minnaert, 2013; G. H. Bower, 1994; Fredrickson, 2009; Linnenbrink & Pintrich, 2004; Pekrun, 2006; Pekrun et al., 2002; Snow et al., 1996.

[157] Berkowitz, 1989; E. Skinner et al., 2008; Wisner Fries & Pollak, 2007.

[158] Preckel, Holling, & Vock, 2006; Shipman & Shipman, 1985.

[159] Young & Young, 2015.

At what point does anxiety stop facilitating and begin debilitating performance? Very easy tasks—things that learners can do almost without thinking (e.g., running)—are typically facilitated by high levels of anxiety. But more difficult tasks—those that require considerable thought and mental effort—are best performed with only a small or moderate level of anxiety.[160] A lot of anxiety in difficult situations can interfere with several processes critical for successful learning and performance:[161]

- Paying attention to what needs to be learned
- Processing information effectively (e.g., by organizing or elaborating on it)
- Retrieving and using information and skills that have previously been learned

Anxiety is especially likely to interfere with such processes when a task places heavy demands on working memory or long-term memory—for instance, when a task involves problem solving or creativity. In such situations, learners may be so preoccupied with doing poorly that they can't get their minds on what they need to accomplish.[162]

In general, learners are more likely to experience debilitating anxiety when they face a *threat,* a situation in which they believe they have little or no chance of succeeding. Facilitating anxiety is more common when learners face a *challenge,* a situation in which they believe they can probably achieve success with a significant yet reasonable amount of effort.[163]

Children and adolescents are apt to have some degree of anxiety, either facilitating or debilitating, in many of the following circumstances:[164]

think about it
Did you previously believe that *any* amount of anxiety is detrimental? If so, have you now revised your thinking about anxiety's effects?

- A *situation in which physical safety is at risk*—for example, being regularly exposed to violence at school or in the neighborhood
- A *situation in which self-worth is threatened*—for example, hearing unflattering remarks about one's race or gender
- *Physical appearance*—for example, feeling too fat or thin, or reaching puberty either earlier or later than peers
- A *new situation*—for example, moving from one school district to another midway through the school year
- *Judgment or evaluation by others*—for example, receiving a low grade from a teacher or being disliked or excluded by peers
- *Frustrating subject matter*—for example, having a history of difficulty with one or more content domains (as is true for many students with learning disabilities)
- *Excessive classroom demands*—for example, being expected to learn a great deal of material in a very short time
- *Classroom tests*—for example, facing a high-stakes test that affects one's chances for promotion or graduation
- *The future*—for example, not knowing how to make a living after high school graduation

Learners' particular concerns change somewhat as they grow older. Table 5.4 describes developmental trends in anxiety, as well as in affect more generally, across childhood and adolescence.

Different cultures nurture different emotional responses.

Many emotions—especially joy, sadness, fear, anger, disgust, and surprise—are seen even in young infants and thus are almost certainly part of our genetic heritage.[165] Nevertheless, various cultural groups have different views about what kinds of emotions and emotional reactions are

---

[160] Kirkland, 1971; Landers, 2007; Zeidner & Matthews, 2005.

[161] Cassady, 2004; Eysenck, 1992; Zeidner & Matthews, 2005.

[162] Ashcraft, 2002; Beilock, 2008; Matthews, Zeidner, & Roberts, 2006; J. C. Turner, Thorpe, & Meyer, 1998.

[163] Combs, Richards, & Richards, 1976; Deci & Ryan, 1992; Zeidner & Matthews, 2005.

[164] Ashcraft, 2002; Cassady, 2004; Chabrán, 2003; Covington, 1992; DuBois, Burk-Braxton, Swenson, Tevendale, & Hardesty, 2002; Harter, 1992; Hembree, 1988; King & Ollendick, 1989; Phelan et al., 1994; Sarason, 1980; Stipek, 2002; Stodolsky et al., 1991; Wigfield & Meece, 1988; K. M. Williams, 2001a; Zeidner & Matthews, 2005.

[165] Collins, 2005.

DEVELOPMENTAL TRENDS

Table 5.4 • Anxiety and Other Forms of Affect at Different Grade Levels

GRADE LEVEL	AGE-TYPICAL CHARACTERISTICS	EXAMPLE	SUGGESTED STRATEGIES
Grades K–2	• Possible culture shock and intense anxiety upon beginning school, especially if students have had few or no preschool experiences • Possible separation anxiety when parents first leave the classroom (especially in the first few days of kindergarten) • Reduced anxiety when teachers and other adults are warm and supportive • Only limited control of overt emotional behaviors (e.g., may cry easily if distressed or act impulsively if frustrated)	Although Jeff has attended preschool since the age of 2, he's quite nervous about going to kindergarten. On his first day at the "big kids' school," he's reluctant to say good-bye to his mother. When Mom finally tells him she has to leave, he bursts into tears—a reaction that some of his classmates will taunt him about for several years.	• Ask parents about routines followed at home; when appropriate, incorporate these routines into classroom procedures. • If possible, provide an opportunity for students to meet you a few days or weeks before school begins. • Be warm, caring, and supportive with all students (but check school policies about hugs and other forms of physical affection). • Address inappropriate behaviors gently but firmly (see Chapter 9).
Grades 3–5	• Increasing control of overt emotional behaviors • Emergence of math anxiety for some students, especially if they receive little or no assistance with math tasks • Tendency for close friends (especially girls) to talk about and dwell on negative emotional events; continues into adolescence • Possible anxiety and stress as a result of others' racist and sexist behaviors (e.g., racial slurs, unkind remarks about emerging sexual characteristics); continues into adolescence	For 9-year-old Tina, basic arithmetic procedures with whole numbers (addition, multiplication, etc.) are easy to understand. But she can make no sense of the new procedures she's learning for fractions—how to find common denominators, divide one fraction by another, and so on—and becomes increasingly frustrated when her attempts to solve fraction problems yield incorrect answers. Her aversion to math soon leads her to avoid the subject whenever possible, both in and outside of school.	• Monitor students' behaviors for subtle signs of serious anxiety or depression; talk with students privately if they seem anxious or upset, and consult with the school counselor if necessary. • Ensure that students master basic concepts and procedures before proceeding to more complex material (especially important in teaching math, a subject area in which advanced knowledge and skills build on more basic concepts and skills). • Insist on respect for all class members' characteristics, feelings, and backgrounds; don't tolerate racist or sexist actions.
Grades 6–8	• General decline in positive, upbeat emotions; extreme mood swings, partly as a result of hormonal changes accompanying puberty • Increased anxiety and potential depression accompanying the transition to middle school or junior high school • Decrease in enjoyment of school (especially for boys) • Increasing anxiety about how one appears to others (*imaginary audience*; see Chapter 7)	At the beginning of seventh grade, 12-year-old Jeannie moves from a small, close-knit elementary school to a large junior high school. At her new school, she knows only a few students in each class, and her teachers present themselves as cold, no-nonsense disciplinarians. Jeannie struggles in her efforts to make new friends and feels awkward when she must occasionally sit by herself in the cafeteria. Before long, she regularly complains of stomachaches so that she can stay home from school.	• Expect mood swings, but monitor students' behavior for signs of long-term depression. • Make a personal connection with every student; express confidence that students can succeed with effort, and offer support to facilitate success. • Design activities that capture students' interest in the subject matter; relate topics to students' personal lives and goals. • Provide opportunities for students to form friendships with classmates (e.g., cooperative group projects).
Grades 9–12	• Continuing emotional volatility (especially in grades 9 and 10) • Increasing ability to reflect on and control extreme emotional reactions, due in part to ongoing brain maturation • Considerable anxiety about school if transition to a secondary school format has been delayed until high school • Susceptibility to serious depression in the face of significant stress • Increasing prevalence of debilitating anxiety regarding tests, especially high-stakes tests • Feelings of uncertainty about life after graduation	In a text message to a classmate, 15-year-old Jonathan reveals his crush on a popular cheerleader. The classmate thinks the message is amusing ("I can't believe that loser thinks he has a chance with the head cheerleader!") and forwards it to more than 50 members of the sophomore class. Jonathan is at a loss about how to cope with his humiliation and contemplates suicide as the only solution to the problem. (*Teachers should immediately report any suspicions of planned student suicides*; see Chapter 7.)	• Be especially supportive if students have just made the transition from an elementary school format (e.g., show personal interest in students' welfare, teach effective study skills). • Take seriously any signs that a student may be considering suicide (e.g., overt or veiled threats, such as "I won't be around much longer"; actions that indicate "putting one's affairs in order," such as giving away prized possessions). • Give frequent classroom assessments so that no single test score is a "fatal" one; help students prepare for high-stakes tests. • Present multiple options for postgraduation career paths.

Sources: Arnett, 1999; Ashcraft, 2002; Benes, 2007; Benner & Graham, 2009; Chabrán, 2003; DuBois et al., 2002; Eccles & Midgley, 1989; Elkind, 1981; Gentry, Gable, & Rizza, 2002; Hill & Sarason, 1966; Hine & Fraser, 2002; Kerns & Lieberman, 1993; Kuhl & Kraska, 1989; Lapsley, 1993; Larson & Brown, 2007; Larson, Moneta, Richards, & Wilson, 2002; D. K. Meyer & Turner, 2006; Midgley, Middleton, Gheen, & Kumar, 2002; Roderick & Camburn, 1999; Rose, 2002; Rudolph, Lambert, Clark, & Kurlakowsky, 2001; Snow et al., 1996; Spear, 2000; Wiles & Bondi, 2001.

appropriate, leading to differences in how they socialize growing children. The Cultural Considerations box "Cultural and Ethnic Differences in Affect" describes the kinds of cultural diversity researchers have observed. We turn our attention now to how one very important aspect of our own society and culture—*school*—can have positive influences on children's and adolescents' motivation and affect.

CULTURAL CONSIDERATIONS

Cultural and Ethnic Differences in Affect

Researchers have seen consistent cultural differences in several aspects of affect: emotional expressiveness, views about appropriate emotions, the extent to which cognitive dissonance occurs, and sources of anxiety.

EMOTIONAL EXPRESSIVENESS. On average, cultural groups differ in the degree to which they show their feelings in their behaviors and facial expressions. For example, whereas Americans and Mexicans are often quite expressive, people from East Asian cultures tend to be more reserved and may be reluctant to confide in other people in times of sadness or distress.[a] Considerable variability exists in any large society, of course. For instance, in one study with Americans, people of Irish ancestry were more apt to reveal their feelings in their facial expressions than were people of Scandinavian ancestry.[b]

The emotion for which cultural differences are most prevalent is anger. Mainstream Western culture encourages children to act and speak up if someone infringes on their rights and needs, and expressing anger in a nonviolent way is considered quite acceptable. In many southeast Asian cultures, however, any expression of anger is viewed as potentially undermining adults' authority or disrupting social harmony.[c]

VIEWS ABOUT APPROPRIATE WAYS TO FEEL. Children brought up in some cultural groups, including many Buddhist groups and certain Native American and Pacific Islander communities, are encouraged not even to *feel* anger.[d] As an illustration, if a child growing up in the Tamang culture of Nepal is unfairly embarrassed or accused, he or she might respond, "Tilda bomo khaba?" ("Why be angry?"). After all, the event has already occurred, and being angry about it serves no purpose.[e]

Even seemingly "positive" emotions are not always viewed favorably. Some cultures that place high priority on social harmony discourage children from feeling pride about personal accomplishments because such an emotion focuses attention on an individual rather than on the overall group.[f] And for some cultural groups, joy and happiness can often be too much of a good thing. For instance, many Chinese and Japanese advocate striving for contentment and serenity—relatively calm emotions—rather than joy, excitement, and other intense emotions.[g]

COGNITIVE DISSONANCE AS A MOTIVATOR. For many learners, encountering two conflicting, seemingly opposite ideas causes what Piaget called *disequilibrium* and what contemporary motivation theorists call *cognitive dissonance*—a form of mental discomfort that spurs learners to resolve the discrepancy in some way. Not all cultural groups are bothered by logical conflicts, however. When one of us was in China a few years ago, she was struck by how often people described something as being both one thing and also its opposite. Researchers report that many East Asians are quite tolerant and accepting of logical contradictions.[h]

SOURCES OF ANXIETY. Learners from different cultural backgrounds may have somewhat different sources of anxiety. For instance, some children and adolescents from Asian American families may feel so much family pressure to perform well in school that they regularly experience debilitating test anxiety.[i] And young people who are recent immigrants to a new country are often anxious about a variety of things: how to behave, how to interpret others' behaviors, how to make friends, and, more generally, how to make sense of the strange new culture in which they now find themselves (recall the discussion of *cultural mismatch* in Chapter 4).[j]

Anxiety may be at the root of a phenomenon known as **stereotype threat**, which can lead students from stereotypically low-achieving groups to perform more poorly on assessments than they would otherwise perform simply because they're aware that their group traditionally *does* do poorly (e.g., African Americans on statewide standardized tests; girls on math tests).[k] When students are aware of the unflattering stereotype—and especially when they believe that the task they're performing reflects their ability in an important domain—their heart rates and other physiological correlates of anxiety go up, and their performance goes down.[l] The negative effects of stereotype threat are more common when students interpret their performance on a task as an evaluation of their competence or overall self-worth.[m] Furthermore, stereotype threat is more likely to arise when students have an entity view of ability—a belief that ability is relatively fixed and permanent—rather than an incremental view.[n]

[a] Camras, Chen, Bakeman, Norris, & Cain, 2006; Cole & Tan, 2007; Kim, Sherman, & Taylor, 2008; Morelli & Rothbaum, 2007; Tyler et al., 2008.

[b] Camras et al., 2006; Cole, Tamang, & Shrestha, 2006; Tsai & Chentsova-Dutton, 2003.

[c] Mesquita & Leu, 2007; Morelli & Rothbaum, 2007; Zahn-Waxler, Friedman, Cole, Mizuta, & Hiruma, 1996.

[d] Cole, Bruschi, & Tamang, 2002; Cole et al., 2006; Solomon, 1984.

[e] Cole et al., 2002, p. 992.

[f] Eid & Diener, 2001.

[g] Cole & Tan, 2007; Kagan, 2010; Mesquita & Leu, 2007.

[h] Heine, 2007; Norenzayan, Choi, & Peng, 2007; Peng & Nisbett, 1999.

[i] Pang, 1995.

[j] Cole & Tan, 2007; Dien, 1998; Igoa, 1995.

[k] K. E. Ryan & Ryan, 2005; Smith, 2004; Steele, 1997.

[l] Aronson et al., 1999; Aronson & Steele, 2005; McKown & Weinstein, 2003; Osborne, 2007.

[m] Davies & Spencer, 2005; Huguet & Régner, 2007; McKown & Weinstein, 2003; Walton & Spencer, 2009.

[n] Ben-Zeev et al., 2005; Dweck et al., 2004; C. Good, Aronson, & Inzlicht, 2003.

Emotions, moods, and other forms of affect play an important role in students' motivation and learning. In the hotlinked Self-Check quiz and Application Exercise that follow, you can check and apply your understandings related to Big Idea 5.4:

> *Learners' affect (their feelings, emotions, and moods) influences and is influenced by both their motives and their cognitive processes.*

MyEdLab **Self-Check 5.4**

MyEdLab **Application Exercise 5.4.** In this exercise, you can identify some teacher behaviors and beliefs that can help to reduce students' debilitating anxiety in the classroom.

5.5 PROMOTING MOTIVATION AND PRODUCTIVE AFFECT

Big Idea 5.5 Effective teachers create conditions that support learners' needs, cognition, and affect.

Early in the chapter, Figure 5.1 gave you a general idea of how internal and external factors, motivation, academic engagement, and academic outcomes influence one another in a cyclical manner. Figure 5.9 is an expanded version of that figure; it provides details about what each component in the cycle involves and thus can help us summarize many of the key principles we've identified about motivation and affect. But you should note another important feature of the figure: The internal and external factors on the left side of the figure don't just influence motivation, they can also influence *each other*. For example, a teacher who engages students in hands-on, thought-provoking science experiments (an external factor) might lead students to believe that science is fun and to aspire to possible careers as scientists (internal factors). Meanwhile, a student who shows obvious interest in a certain topic or activity (an internal factor) might lead parents or teachers to provide learning opportunities (external factors) through which the student can further pursue that interest area. (Recall the discussion of how learners modify their environments in Chapter 4.)

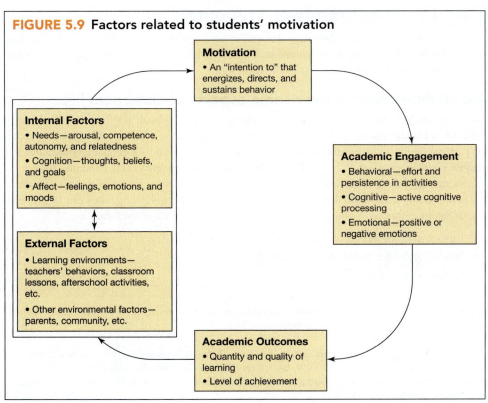

FIGURE 5.9 Factors related to students' motivation

Sources: Based on Osborne & Jones, 2011; Reeve, 2009a; E. A. Skinner & Pitzer, 2012.

MUSIC acronym	Students are more motivated when they believe that:	Strategies to motivate students	These strategies can support students':
M	They are eMpowered	**Empower** students by giving them reasonable control and choices.	Need for autonomy
U	The content is Useful	Demonstrate the **usefulness** of activities for students' lives and goals.	Values
S	They can be Successful	Help students believe they can **succeed** at classroom tasks.	Need for competence, self-worth, self-efficacy, mastery- and performance-approach goals, productive attributions, incremental views of intelligence, and mastery orientation **Can minimize students'** self-handicapping, learned helplessness, entity views of intelligence, performance-avoidance goals, and debilitating anxiety
I	The content is Interesting	Stimulate **interest** in curriculum topics.	Situational and individual interests; need for arousal, affect, chances for flow, and facilitating anxiety
C	They have Caring relationships	Show and promote **caring** within the classroom community.	Need for relatedness

FIGURE 5.10 Strategies to motivate students can be organized using the acronym MUSIC.

Source: Based on B. D. Jones, 2009, 2015.

In this final section of the chapter, we'll focus on *external* factors—in particular, on many specific strategies teachers can use to foster productive motivation and affect in children and adolescents. We can use the acronym MUSIC to organize many specific strategies into five more general strategies: Teachers should *eMpower* students, demonstrate the U*sefulness* of teaching activities, ensure that students believe they can S*ucceed*, stimulate I*nterest,* and show and promote C*aring* (see Figure 5.10).[166] After examining strategies related to each component of the MUSIC acronym, we'll identify strategies more directly aimed at facilitating productive affect.

Strategies That Empower Students

Students are more motivated when they feel empowered—that is, when they believe they have some control over their learning environment.[167] The first four suggestions can empower students by supporting their sense of autonomy in the classroom.

Give students control over some aspects of classroom life.

When students have some sense of autonomy about events at school, they're more likely to be motivated to engage in academic and extracurricular activities, use effective self-regulation strategies, perform better academically, use skills acquired at school in out-of-school settings, and stay in school until graduation.[168] Naturally, teachers can't give students total freedom about what they can and can't do at school. Nevertheless, teachers can do several things to enhance students' sense of autonomy about school-related tasks and activities. For one thing, they can let students make decisions, either individually or as a group, about some or all of the following:[169]

- Rules and procedures to make a class run more smoothly
- Specific topics for research or writing projects
- Specific works of literature to be read

---

[166] The MUSIC® acronym and associated approach to motivating students are part of the MUSIC® Model of Motivation (theMUSICmodel.com); B. D. Jones, 2009, 2015, 2016.

[167] B. D. Jones, 2009, 2015.

[168] Chittum & Jones, 2015; Hagger, Chatzisarantis, Barkoukis, Wang, & Baranowski, 2005; Hardré & Reeve, 2003; Jang, Kim, & Reeve, 2012; E. J. Langer, 1997; Reeve, Bolt, & Cai, 1999; Shernoff, Knauth, & Makris, 2000; Soenens, Sierens, Vansteenkiste, Dochy, & Goossens, 2011; Standage, Duda, & Ntoumani, 2003; Wijnia, Loyens, Derous, & Schmidt, 2015.

[169] Lane, Falk, & Wehby, 2006; Larson, 2000; Meece, 1994; Parkes, Jones, & Wilkins, 2015; Reed et al., 2004; Stipek, 2002.

- Due dates for some assignments
- The order in which specific tasks are completed
- Ways of achieving mastery of a particular skill or of demonstrating that it has been mastered (e.g., see Figure 5.11)
- The criteria by which some assignments will be evaluated
- The method by which they can learn the material assigned for homework
- Specific activities and procedures in extracurricular activities (school clubs, community service projects, etc.)

To the extent that students can make choices about such matters, they're more likely to be interested in what they're doing, to work diligently and persistently, and to take pride in their work.[170] Furthermore, students who are given choices—even students with serious behavior problems—are less likely to misbehave in class.[171]

In some situations, students' choices can be almost limitless. For example, in a unit on expository writing, a wide variety of student-selected research topics might be equally appropriate. In other situations, teachers may need to impose certain limits on the choices students make. For example, if a teacher allows a class to set its own due dates for certain assignments, it might be with the stipulation that the schedule evenly distributes the student and teacher workload over a reasonable time period.

FIGURE 5.11 By offering several options for demonstrating understanding of a science fiction book, a sixth-grade language arts teacher enhances students' sense of autonomy.

Choose One!

SCIENCE FICTION BOOK PROJECTS

_____ Write a "Dear Abby" letter from one of the main characters, in which he or she asks for advice on solving his or her main problem. Then answer the letter.

_____ Draw a time line of the main events of the book.

_____ Create a comic book or a comic strip page that features a major scene from the book in each box.

_____ Make a collage of objects and printed words from newspapers and magazines that give the viewer a feeling for the mood of the book.

_____ Your book probably takes place in an unusual or exotic setting, so illustrate and write a travel brochure describing that location.

_____ Imagine yourself as a scientist who has been asked to explain the unusual events in the book. Write up a report in scientific style.

_____ With other students who have read the same book, plan a bulletin board display. Write a plot summary; character and setting descriptions; discussions of special passages. Each group member must contribute one artistic piece—for example, new book cover, bookmark, poster, banner, some of the ideas listed above. Arrange the writing and artwork under a colorful heading announcing the book.

Evaluate students' performance in a noncontrolling manner.

In most classrooms, teachers have the final word in evaluating students' performance. Unfortunately, such external evaluation can undermine students' sense of autonomy and intrinsic motivation, especially if communicated in a controlling manner. Ideally, teachers should present evaluations of students' work not as "judgments" that remind students how they _should_ perform but as information that can help them improve their knowledge and skills.[172] For instance, rather than saying, "You didn't follow my instructions for writing a persuasive essay" (which can be perceived as controlling), a teacher might say, "You make some good points, but your essay could be more convincing if you also include and rebut counterarguments to your point of view" (which can be perceived as informational feedback).

Use extrinsic reinforcers when necessary, but do so in ways that preserve students' sense of autonomy.

Teachers can motivate students through praise, stickers, free time, good grades, and other extrinsic reinforcers. However, a potential problem with using extrinsic reinforcers is that they may undermine intrinsic motivation, especially if students perceive them to be limiting their choices, controlling their behavior, or in other ways undermining their sense of autonomy.[173] Extrinsic reinforcers may also communicate the message that classroom tasks are unpleasant "chores" (why else would a reinforcer be necessary?) rather than activities to be carried out and enjoyed for their own sake.[174]

MyEdLab
Video Example 5.4.

What strategies does this AP Calculus teacher use to give students control over their learning?

---

[170] Deci & Ryan, 1992; Patall, Cooper, & Wynn, 2010; Reeve, 2006; Ross, 1988; J. C. Turner, 1995.

[171] Dunlap et al., 1994; Lane et al., 2006; Powell & Nelson, 1997; Vaughn & Horner, 1997.

[172] Deci & Moller, 2005; Reeve et al., 2004; Stipek, 2002.

[173] Deci, 1992; Deci, Koestner, & Ryan, 1999, 2001; Lepper & Hodell, 1989; Pulfrey, Darnon, & Butera, 2013; Reeve, 2006.

[174] Hennessey, 1995; Stipek, 1993.

Extrinsic reinforcers appear to have no adverse effects when they're unexpected (e.g., when students get special recognition for a public service project in the local community) or when they're not contingent on specific behaviors (e.g., when they're used simply to make an activity more enjoyable).[175] They can even be beneficial if used to encourage students not only to do something but also to do it *well*.[176] And if they communicate that students *have* done something well (as a high grade might) or have made considerable improvement, they can enhance students' sense of self-efficacy and competence and focus students' attention on mastering the subject matter.[177]

Sometimes students may initially find a new topic or skill boring or frustrating and therefore need external encouragement to continue.[178] So how can teachers use extrinsic reinforcers and still empower students? One strategy is to praise students in a manner that communicates information but doesn't show an intent to control behavior.[179] Consider these statements as examples:

- "Your description of the main character in your short story makes her come alive."
- "I think you've finally mastered the rolling *R* sound in Spanish."
- "This poster clearly states the hypothesis, method, results, and conclusions of your science project. Your use of a bar graph makes the differences between your treatment and control groups easy to see and interpret."

Another strategy is to teach students to reinforce *themselves* for their accomplishments, a practice that clearly keeps control in students' hands (see the discussion of *self-imposed contingencies* in Chapter 3).

Ask students to set some personal goals for learning and performance.

Students typically work harder toward *self-chosen* goals than toward goals that others have chosen for them, possibly because self-chosen goals help them maintain a sense of autonomy and possibly also because students are more likely to think of self-chosen goals as being relevant to their own lives and needs—and hence as being useful and having *value*.[180] Although teachers should certainly encourage students to develop long-term goals (e.g., going to college, becoming an environmental scientist), such goals are sometimes too general and abstract to guide immediate behavior.[181] Self-chosen goals are especially motivating when they're specific ("I want to learn how to do a cartwheel"), challenging ("Writing a limerick looks difficult, but I'm sure I can do it"), and short-term ("I'm going to learn to count to one hundred in French by the end of the month").[182] By setting and working for a series of short-term, concrete goals—sometimes called **proximal goals**—students get regular feedback about the progress they're making; and if they succeed in achieving their goals, they may develop a greater sense of self-efficacy that they can master school subject matter and achieve at higher levels.[183] Figure 5.12 shows a handout that one middle school teacher used to encourage students to identify and commit to short-term goals for their learning. Such goals, accompanied by regular *achievement* of them, may be especially important for students with a history of academic failure.[184] Students' goals should, of course, be compatible with their teachers' goals for student achievement—an issue we'll address in Chapter 8.

FIGURE 5.12 With this handout, a middle school information technology teacher asks students to reflect on their current strengths and identify specific goals for improvement. This handout is for girls; boys get one that shows a silhouette with shorter hair.

---

[175] Cameron, 2001; Deci et al., 2001; Reeve, 2006.

[176] Cameron, 2001.

[177] Cameron, 2001; Deci & Moller, 2005; Hynd, 2003; Reeve, 2006.

[178] Cameron, 2001; Deci et al., 2001; Hidi & Harackiewicz, 2000.

[179] Deci, 1992; R. M. Ryan, Mims, & Koestner, 1983.

[180] Reeve, 2009b; Tabachnick, Miller, & Relyea, 2008; Wentzel, 1999; Wigfield & Eccles, 2000.

[181] Bandura, 1997; Husman & Freeman, 1999.

[182] Alderman, 1990; Brophy, 2004; Locke & Latham, 2006.

[183] Bandura, 1997; Locke & Latham, 2002; Page-Voth & Graham, 1999; Schunk & Pajares, 2005.

[184] E. S. Alexander, 2006.

Strategies That Demonstrate the Usefulness of Activities

A frequent question in any teacher's mind should be "Do students understand and appreciate why they're doing this?" and the answer should always be *yes.* Students' values and goals are especially relevant to the "U" component of the MUSIC acronym—usefulness—as reflected in the next two recommendations.[185]

Explicitly relate class activities to students' existing values and goals.

On some occasions, teachers can foster motivation for learning certain topics and skills by capitalizing on students' current values and goals. For instance, teachers might demonstrate how a new skill might enhance their ability to help their family or neighborhood or to achieve their career goals. And in general, teachers can convey how classroom subject matter can help students make better sense of the world around them.[186] This approach is consistent with our discussion of authentic activities in Chapter 4.

Create conditions that foster internalization of values essential for students' long-term academic and professional success.

No matter how much teachers try to make classroom topics and tasks interesting and engaging, some of them may have little appeal to students. In such situations, students will pursue classroom assignments more energetically and persistently if they truly appreciate the importance of classroom learning and achievement—*in general*—to their long-term goals. The more students have internalized the value of learning and academic success, the more they'll be cognitively engaged in school subject matter and the better their overall classroom performance is likely to be.[187] Values are also an important aspect of self-regulated learning: They underlie a general work ethic in which learners spontaneously engage in activities that, although not always fun or immediately gratifying, are essential for reaching long-term goals.[188]

Strategies That Foster Success

Students are more motivated when they perceive they can be successful in the classroom and in the school environment in general. Following are several key strategies for enhancing students' optimism about being successful—the "S" component of the MUSIC acronym.

Protect and enhance students' self-efficacy and overall sense of competence and self-worth.

Simply telling students they're "good" or "smart" or "nice" is unlikely to boost a low sense of self-worth.[189] Furthermore, vague, abstract statements such as "You're special" have little meaning in the concrete realities of young children.[190] A more effective approach is to enhance students' self-efficacy for specific activities and tasks. As students become increasingly confident about their ability to succeed in particular domains, they may also gain a greater sense of competence and general self-worth.[191]

As noted earlier, learners' own past successes in an activity enhance their self-efficacy for the activity. Their previous successes are most likely to increase their self-efficacy when they realize that *they themselves* have been responsible for their successes—that is, when they attribute their

[185] Brophy, 2008; Deci & Moller, 2005; Eccles, 2007; Jacobs et al., 2005; Reeve, 2009b.

[186] P. A. Alexander et al., 1994; C. Ames, 1992; Blumenfeld et al., 2006; Brophy, Alleman, & Knighton, 2009; Ferrari & Elik, 2003.

[187] Brophy, 2008; La Guardia, 2009; Otis et al., 2005; Ratelle, Guay, Vallerand, Larose, & Senécal, 2007; R. M. Ryan & Deci, 2000; Walls & Little, 2005.

[188] Harter, 1992; McCombs, 1996; R. M. Ryan et al., 1992.

[189] Crocker & Knight, 2005; Katz, 1993; Marsh & Craven, 1997.

[190] McMillan, Singh, & Simonetta, 1994.

[191] Bong & Skaalvik, 2003; Harter, 1999; Osborne & Jones, 2011; Swann, Chang-Schneider, & McClarty, 2007.

performance to their own effort and ability.[192] Teachers can play a role here by drawing students' attention to specific, concrete successes—including significant improvements—that students may not have noticed on their own.

But how do students acquire self-efficacy for a task they've never tried? As mentioned earlier, words of encouragement ("You can do it, I *know* you can!") can sometimes be helpful over the short run. But a more powerful approach is to show students that peers very similar to them have successfully mastered the task at hand.[193]

Ideally, learners should have a reasonably accurate sense of what they can and cannot accomplish, putting them in a good position to capitalize on their strengths, address their weaknesses, and set realistic goals.[194] Yet a tad of overconfidence can be beneficial, in that it entices learners to take on challenging activities that will help them develop new skills and abilities.[195] Within this context, it's often useful to distinguish between *self-efficacy for learning* ("I can master this if I put my mind to it") and *self-efficacy for performance* ("I already know how to do this").[196] Self-efficacy for learning (for what one can *eventually* do with effort) should be on the optimistic side, whereas self-efficacy for performance should be more in line with current ability levels.

The Classroom Strategies box "Enhancing Self-Efficacy and Self-Worth" provides several examples of how teachers can help students feel successful and boost their self-efficacy for specific topics and skills, as well as their more general beliefs about competence. Teachers should keep in mind, however, that academic achievement isn't necessarily the most important thing affecting students' sense of self-worth. For many children and adolescents, such factors as physical appearance, peer approval, and social success are more influential.[197] Ideally, then, teachers should help students achieve success in the nonacademic as well as academic aspects of their lives.

Present challenges that students can realistically accomplish.

Challenges can promote cognitive development (see Chapter 6), but in addition, students who take on and master challenges gain a greater sense of self-efficacy and experience considerable satisfaction and pride in their accomplishments.[198] The artifact in Figure 5.13 reveals 8-year-old Anthony's pride about finishing his first 100-page book.

Challenges can have another benefit as well: They heighten students' interest in the subject matter.[199] When students are interested in learning about and mastering a topic, they often pursue further challenges of their own accord. They also exhibit considerable persistence in the face of difficulty—in part because earlier successes have led to greater self-efficacy—and they continue to remain interested even when they make frequent errors.[200] As you can see, then, challenges, self-efficacy, and interest mutually enhance one another, leading to a "vicious" cycle of the most desirable sort.

When are learners most likely to take on new and potentially risky challenges? Conditions such as the following appear to be optimal:[201]

FIGURE 5.13 In writing about "A Book That Changed Me," 8-year-old Anthony expresses pride in reading his first book of more than 100 pages. Also notice Anthony's personal interest in sports. One book (*At the Plate*) involves baseball; the other (*On the Court*) involves basketball.

> A Book That canged me
>
> The Book that canged me was At The Plat With Ken Jriffey Jr. This Book canged me becouse it was my first book that had over onehondred pagis after that I read On The Cort With Mikeol Jordon. I asow liked it becouse it was by Matt Crister the Frst spotswiter for Kids.

---

[192] Dweck, 2009; Lam, Yim, & Ng, 2008; Schunk, Meece, & Pintrich, 2014.

[193] Dijkstra et al., 2008; Schunk & Pajares, 2005.

[194] Försterling & Morgenstern, 2002; Martin, 2008; Wang & Lin, 2005.

[195] Assor & Connell, 1992; Lockhart et al., 2002; Pajares, 2005.

[196] Lodewyk & Winne, 2005; Schunk & Pajares, 2004; Zimmerman & Kitsantas, 2005.

[197] Eccles et al., 1998; Rudolph et al., 2005.

[198] Clifford, 1990; Csikszentmihalyi & Nakamura, 1989; Deci & Ryan, 1992; Shernoff et al., 2000; J. C. Turner, 1995.

[199] Deci & Ryan, 1992; Miller & Meece, 1997; Perry, Turner, & Meyer, 2006; J. C. Turner, 1995.

[200] Covington, 1992; Csikszentmihalyi et al., 2005; Deci, 1992; Harter, 1992.

[201] Brophy & Alleman, 1992; Clifford, 1990; Corno & Rohrkemper, 1985; Deci & Ryan, 1985; Dweck & Elliott, 1983; Stipek, 1993.

CLASSROOM STRATEGIES

Enhancing Self-Efficacy and Self-Worth

- **Teach basic knowledge and skills to mastery.**
  A high school biology teacher makes sure all students clearly understand the basic structure of DNA before moving to mitosis and meiosis, two topics that require knowledge of DNA structure.

- **Define success in terms of task accomplishment or improvement, not in terms of performance relative to others.**
  A second-grade teacher and one of her students meet to discuss items in the student's end-of-year portfolio. They identify several ways in which the student's writing has improved during the past year.

- **Assure students that they can be successful at challenging tasks, and point out that others like them have succeeded before them.**
  Early in the school year, many students in beginning band express frustration about learning to play their instruments. Their teacher reminds them that students in last year's beginning band also started out with little skill but eventually gained considerable proficiency. A few weeks later, the beginning band class attends a concert at which the school's advanced band (last year's beginning band class) plays a medley from the Broadway musical *The Lion King*.

- **Assign large, complex tasks as small-group activities.**
  A middle school teacher has students work in groups of three or four to write research papers about early colonial life in North

America. The teacher makes sure that the students in each group collectively have the skills in library research, writing, word processing, and art necessary to complete the task. She also makes sure that every student has unique skills to contribute to the group effort.

- **Help students track their progress.**
  As first graders are learning how to weave on small circular looms, one student approaches her teacher in tears, frustrated that her first few rows are full of mistakes. The teacher responds, "Look, Dorothy, this is the history, your own history, of learning to weave. You can look at this and say, 'Why, I can see how I began, here I didn't know how very well, I went over two instead of one; but I learned, and then—it is perfect all the way to the end!'" The student returns to her seat, very much comforted, and finishes her piece. She follows it with another, flawless one and proudly shows it to her teacher.

- **When negative feedback is necessary, present it in a way that communicates competence and the ability to improve.**
  A third-grade teacher tells a student, "I can see from the past few assignments that you're having trouble with long division. I think I know what the problem is. Here, let me show you what you need to do differently."

Sources: Bandura, 1997, 2000; Butler, 1998a; Covington, 1992; Deci & Ryan, 1985; Graham & Golen, 1991; Hawkins, 1997, p. 332 (weaving example); Pintrich & Schunk, 2002; Schunk, 1983; Shute, 2008; Urdan & Turner, 2005.

- Standards for success are realistic for each individual.
- Scaffolding is sufficient to make success possible.
- There are few, if any, penalties for errors.
- The same rewards cannot be obtained by engaging in easier tasks, *or* rewards are greater for challenging tasks than for easy ones.
- Learners attribute their success to their own ability, effort, and strategies.

Teachers should keep in mind, however, that the school day shouldn't necessarily be one challenge after another. Such a state of affairs would be absolutely exhausting and probably quite discouraging. Instead, teachers should strike a balance between relatively easy tasks, which will boost students' self-efficacy over the short run, and the challenging tasks so critical for longer-term competence and self-worth.[202]

Form and communicate optimistic expectations and attributions.

Students are more likely to perceive that they can succeed when their teachers hold optimistic expectations for their performance (within realistic limits, of course) and when their teachers attribute students' successes and failures to things over which either students or teachers have control (*students'* effort, *teachers'* instructional methods, etc.). The Classroom Strategies box "Forming Productive Expectations and Attributions" offers several strategies that can benefit teachers and students alike. The final strategy in the box—*Remember that teachers can definitely make a difference*—is probably the most important one. Teachers must keep in mind an important point about intelligence presented earlier: Ability can and does change over time, especially when environmental conditions are conducive to such change. For this reason, teachers should take an *incremental view*

MyEdLab
Video Example 5.5.

What strategies does this teacher use to communicate optimistic expectations for students' achievement?

---

[202] Spaulding, 1992; Stipek, 1993, 1996.

of students' abilities and continually reassess and modify their expectations and attributions for student achievement as new evidence presents itself.

Minimize competition.

Competition is widespread in mainstream Western societies, not only in adult activities (e.g., in business and politics) but also in elementary and secondary schools. Schools compare students in a variety of ways. When teachers post "best work" on a bulletin board, they indirectly communicate that other papers aren't as good. When teachers grade "on the curve," their grades reflect how students stack up against one another, and only those at the top of the stack are identified as being successful. When students take college aptitude tests, their test scores reflect not what they know and can do but how their performance compares with that of their peers (more on this point in the

---

CLASSROOM STRATEGIES

Forming Productive Expectations and Attributions

- **Look for strengths in every student.**
  A 9-year-old boy who lives in a homeless shelter seems to have learned almost nothing about rules for punctuation and capitalization, and his spelling is more typical of a first grader than a fourth grader. Nonetheless, the stories he writes often have unusual plot twists and creative endings. His teacher suspects that his frequent moves from one school district to another have left big gaps in his knowledge of written language, so the teacher finds a parent volunteer who can work with him on his writing several times a week.

- **Consider multiple possible explanations for students' low achievement and classroom misbehaviors.**
  Several seventh-grade teachers confer regarding their experiences with a student who, at age 8, suffered a traumatic brain injury when he fell off a kitchen counter and landed on his head. His art and music teachers describe him as very disruptive in class and believe that he intentionally misbehaves in order to draw attention to himself. In contrast, his math and science teachers have found that he can easily stay on task—and can achieve at average to above-average levels—as long as they provide reasonable structure for assignments and classroom behavior. These two teachers point out that some children with brain injuries have trouble inhibiting inappropriate behaviors through no fault of their own.

- **Communicate optimism about what students can accomplish.**
  In September, a high school teacher tells his class, "Next spring I'll ask you to write a 15-page research paper. That may seem like a lot now, but in the next few months we'll work on the various skills you'll need to research and write your paper. By April, 15 pages won't seem like a big deal at all!"

- **Objectively assess students' progress, and be open to evidence that contradicts your initial assessments of students' abilities.**
  A kindergarten teacher initially has low expectations for the daughter of migrant workers, a girl named Lupita who has previously had little access to books, toys, and other educational resources. When a video camera captures Lupita's strong leadership ability and her skill in assembling puzzles, the teacher realizes that Lupita has considerable potential and works hard to help her acquire the math and literacy skills she'll need to be successful in first grade. (See the opening case study "Hidden Treasure" in Chapter 6.)

- **Attribute students' successes to a combination of high ability and such controllable factors as effort and learning strategies.**
  In a unit on basketball, a middle school physical education teacher tells students, "From what I've seen so far, you all have the capability to play a good game of basketball. And it appears that many of you have been regularly practicing after school."

- **Attribute students' failures to factors that are controllable and easily changed.**
  A high school student seeks his teacher's advice about how he might improve his performance in her class. "I know you can do better than you have been, Frank," the teacher replies. "I wonder if part of the problem might be that with your part-time job and all of your extracurricular activities, you just don't have enough time to study. Let's sit down before school tomorrow and look at what and how much you're doing to prepare for class."

- **When students fail despite obvious effort, attribute their failures to a lack of effective strategies and help them acquire such strategies.**
  A student in an advanced science class is having difficulty on the teacher's challenging weekly quizzes. The student works diligently on her science every night and attends the after-school help sessions her teacher offers on Thursdays, yet to no avail. The teacher observes that the student is trying to learn the material by rote—an ineffective strategy for answering questions that involve applying scientific principles to new situations—and so teaches her strategies that promote more meaningful learning.

- **Remember that teachers can definitely make a difference.**
  The teachers at a historically low-achieving middle school in a low-income, inner-city neighborhood meet once a month to learn about teaching strategies that are especially effective with children from low-income families. They're encouraged by the many research studies indicating that children at all socioeconomic levels can achieve at high levels when instruction takes their existing skills into account and when teachers provide reasonable guidance and support. They experiment with various strategies in their own classrooms and share especially effective ones at their group meetings.

Sources: Some ideas based on Brophy, 2006; Carrasco, 1981 (Lupita example); Curtis, 1992; Dweck, 2000, 2009; Hattie, 2009; Hawley, 2005 (brain injury example); J. A. Langer, 2000; Pressley et al., 1987; Roeser, Marachi, & Gehlbach, 2002; Skaalvik & Skaalvik, 2008; Weinstein, Madison, & Kuklinski, 1995.

discussion of *norm-referenced scores* in Chapter 10). Participation in school sports is also competitive, especially at the high school level, in that only students with the best athletic skills can join a team, and only the best of the best achieve starting-player status.

Students are apt to be motivated by competition *if* they believe they have a reasonable chance of succeeding, which is often evidenced by winning.[203] But competition can have several negative side effects of which you should be aware:[204]

- It promotes performance goals rather than mastery goals.
- It can lead to undesirable or counterproductive behaviors, such as cheating or preventing classmates from getting needed resources for assignments.
- For students who expect to lose, it can lead to self-handicapping.
- For the students who *actually* lose, it can lead to a sense of low self-efficacy and self-worth.
- Because it makes differences among students more obvious, it encourages attributions to ability rather than to effort.

For such reasons, competition ultimately leads to lower achievement for many students. When classroom success is judged on the basis of how well students perform relative to one another rather than on the basis of how much improvement they make, most students earn lower grades, show less creativity, and develop more negative attitudes toward school.[205] Competitive classroom environments may be especially disadvantageous to female students and to students from ethnic minority groups.[206]

Focus students' attention more on mastery goals than on performance goals.

To some degree, performance goals are inevitable in today's schools and in society at large.[207] Ultimately, however, mastery goals are the ones most likely to lead to effective learning and performance over the long run.[208] Focusing attention on mastery goals, especially when these goals relate to students' own lives, may especially benefit students from diverse ethnic backgrounds and students at risk for academic failure.[209]

Sometimes mastery goals come from within, especially when students have high interest in, and high self-efficacy for, learning something.[210] Yet classroom practices can also encourage mastery goals.[211] For instance, teachers can do the following:[212]

- Help students succeed by giving specific suggestions about how students can improve.
- Insist that students *understand,* rather than simply memorize, classroom material.
- Present subject matter that students find valuable in and of itself.
- Show how topics and skills are relevant to students' future personal and professional goals.
- Encourage students to use their peers not as a reference point for their own progress, but rather as a source of ideas and help.

Some motivation theorists have suggested that mastery goal strategies can be organized using the acronym "TARGETS," which stands for Task, Autonomy, Recognition, Grouping, Evaluation, Time, and Social support.[213] This multifaceted TARGETS approach to fostering mastery goals is presented in Table 5.5.

---

[203] Deci & Ryan, 1992; Johnson & Johnson, 2009; Linnenbrink, 2005.
[204] C. Ames, 1984; Deci & Moller, 2005; Hattie, 2008; Martin et al., 2003; Nicholls, 1984; Pekrun, 2006; Stipek, 1996; Thorndike-Christ, 2008.
[205] Amabile & Hennessey, 1992; Covington, 1992; Graham & Golen, 1991; Krampen, 1987.
[206] Inglehart, Brown, & Vida, 1994; Tyler et al., 2008.
[207] Butler, 1989; Elliot & McGregor, 2000.
[208] For example, see Elliot, Shell, Henry, & Maier, 2005; Gabriele, 2007; Vansteenkiste, Lens, & Deci, 2006.
[209] S. D. Miller & Meece, 1997; Wlodkowski & Ginsberg, 1995.
[210] Bandura, 1997; Murphy & Alexander, 2000; Schiefele, 1992.
[211] Church, Elliot, & Gable, 2001; Midgley, 2002.
[212] C. Ames, 1992; E. M. Anderman & Maehr, 1994; Bong, 2001; Brophy, 2004, 2008; Danner, 2008, Graham & Weiner, 1996; Meece, 1994; Middleton & Midgley, 2002; J. C. Turner, Meyer, et al., 1998; Urdan et al., 2002.
[213] C. Ames, 1992; L. H. Anderman & Anderman, 2009; Epstein, 1989; Maehr & Anderman. 1993.

Table 5.5 • Seven "TARGETS" Principles That Support Mastery Goals

PRINCIPLE	EDUCATIONAL IMPLICATIONS	EXAMPLE
Classroom **tasks** affect motivation.	• Present new topics through tasks that students find interesting, engaging, and perhaps emotionally charged. • Encourage meaningful rather than rote learning. • Relate activities to students' lives and goals. • Provide sufficient support to enable students to be successful.	Ask students to conduct a scientific investigation about an issue that concerns them.
The amount of **autonomy** students have affects motivation, especially intrinsic motivation.	• Give students some choice about what and how they learn. • Teach self-regulation strategies. • Solicit students' opinions about classroom practices and policies. • Have students take leadership roles in some activities.	Let students choose among several ways of accomplishing an instructional objective, being sure that each choice offers sufficient scaffolding to make success likely.
The amount and nature of the **recognition** students receive affect motivation.	• Acknowledge not only academic successes but also personal and social successes. • Commend students for improvement as well as for mastery. • Provide concrete reinforcers for achievement only when students are not already motivated to learn. • Show students how their own efforts and strategies are directly responsible for their successes.	Commend students for a successful community service project.
The **grouping** procedures in the classroom affect motivation.	• Provide frequent opportunities for students to interact (e.g., cooperative learning activities, peer tutoring). • Plan small-group activities in which all students can make significant contributions. • Teach the social skills that students need to interact effectively with peers. • Create an atmosphere of mutual caring, respect, and support.	Have students work in small groups to tackle a challenging issue or problem for which there are two or more legitimate solutions.
The forms of **evaluation** in the classroom affect motivation.	• Make evaluation criteria clear; specify them in advance. • Minimize or eliminate competition for grades (e.g., don't grade "on a curve"). • Give specific feedback about what students are doing well. • Give concrete suggestions for how students can improve. • Teach students how to evaluate their own work.	Give students concrete criteria with which they can evaluate the quality of their own writing.
How teachers schedule **time** affects motivation.	• Give students enough time to gain mastery of important topics and skills. • Let students' interests dictate some activities. • Include variety in the school day (e.g., intersperse high-energy activities among more sedentary ones). • Include opportunities for independent learning during the school day.	After explaining a new concept, engage students in a hands-on activity that lets them see the concept in action.
The amount of **social support** students believe they have in the classroom affects motivation.	• Create a general atmosphere of mutual caring, respect, and support among all class members. • Convey affection and respect for every student, along with a genuine eagerness to help every student succeed. • Create situations in which all students feel comfortable participating actively in classroom activities (including students who are excessively shy, students who have limited academic skills, students who have physical disabilities, etc.).	When working with students who seem chronically disengaged from classroom lessons, identify their specific areas of strengths and provide opportunities for them to showcase their expertise in the classroom.

Sources: L. H. Anderman & Anderman, 2009; L. H. Anderman, Andrzejewski, & Allen, 2011; L. H. Anderman, Patrick, Hruda, & Linnenbrink, 2002; Epstein, 1989; Maehr & Anderman, 1993; Patrick et al., 1997. Historically, the "A" in the TARGETS acronym has stood for *authority,* but in our view *autonomy* better captures the essence of this principle.

Strategies That Stimulate Interest

Students are more motivated when they're interested in the class activities—the "I" in the MUSIC acronym. Remember that interest can be thought of as a transitory, situational interest or a longer-term, individual interest, as reflected in the next two recommendations.

Conduct interest-arousing lessons and activities.

One essential strategy for keeping students interested and engaged in learning is to conduct lessons that address students' basic need for arousal. Educational psychologists have identified numerous ways of provoking situational interest in classroom subject matter, and many of them work by satisfying students' need for either cognitive or physical stimulation. For instance, teachers can do the following:[214]

---

[214] Ainley, 2006; Andre & Windschitl, 2003; Beike & Zentall, 2012; Brophy et al., 2009; Chinn, 2006; Flum & Kaplan, 2006; Frenzel, Goetz, Lüdtke, Pekrun, & Sutton, 2009; Hidi & Renninger, 2006; Patrick, Mantzicopoulos, & Samarapungavan, 2009; Zahorik, 1994.

FIGURE 5.14 Examples of how teachers might generate situational interest in various content domains.

Art: Have students make a mosaic from items they've found on a scavenger hunt around the school building.

Biology: Have class members debate the ethical implications of conducting medical research on animals.

Creative writing: Ask students to write newspaper-like restaurant reviews of the school cafeteria or neighborhood fast-food restaurants.

Geography: Present household objects not found locally, and ask students to guess where they might be from.

Health education: In a lesson about alcoholic beverages, have students role-play being at a party and being tempted to have a beer or wine cooler.

History: Have students read children's perspectives of historical events (e.g., Anne Frank's diary during World War II, Zlata Filipovic's diary during the Bosnian War).

Language Arts: Examine lyrics in popular hip-hop music, looking for grammatical patterns and literary themes.

Mathematics: Have students play computer games to improve their automaticity for number facts.

Music: In a unit on musical instruments, let students experiment with a variety of simple instruments.

Physical education: Incorporate steps from hip-hop, swing, or country line dancing into an aerobics workout.

Physical science: Have each student make several paper airplanes and then fly them to see which design travels farthest.

Reading: Turn a short story into a play, with each student taking a part.

Spelling: Occasionally depart from standard word lists, instead asking students to learn how to spell the names of favorite television shows or classmates' surnames.

Sources: Some ideas derived from Alim, 2007; Brophy, 1986; Lepper & Hodell, 1989; McCourt, 2005; Spaulding, 1992; Stipek, 1993; Wlodkowski, 1978.

- Model curiosity and enthusiasm about classroom topics.
- Occasionally incorporate novelty, variety, fantasy, or mystery into lessons and procedures.
- Encourage students to identify with historical figures or fictional characters and to imagine what these people might have been thinking or feeling.
- Present dramatic stories with novel characters and unusual endings.
- Provide opportunities for students to respond actively to the subject matter, perhaps by manipulating physical objects, creating new inventions, debating controversial issues, or teaching something they've learned to peers.

Figure 5.14 presents examples of how teachers might generate situational interest in a variety of content domains.

Relate activities to students' individual interests.

To design instruction with consideration for students' individual interests, teachers first need to *identify* students' interests, because these interests often vary.[215] Through observations, teachers can pay attention to what students do in their free time. For example, teachers might notice the types of books students read, games they play, or websites they visit when they have choices. Teachers can also talk to students informally before or after class about their interests and hobbies. More formally, teachers can briefly interview or survey students about their interests. A survey given to students at the beginning of the school year might include questions such as, "What do you like to do in your spare time?" "What are some of your interests?" or "What types of careers are you considering?" Teachers can also give assignments and activities that provide students with choices so that *students* can select topics that interest them (e.g., see Figure 5.15).[216]

---

[215] Kerger, Martin, & Brunner, 2011.
[216] A. W. Williams, 2013.

FIGURE 5.15 Teachers can capitalize on students' individual interests by allowing flexibility in the topics students explore as they work on basic skills. Twelve-year-old Connor gained practice in basic research and graphing skills by surveying fellow students about his favorite topic: cars. His findings are shown here.

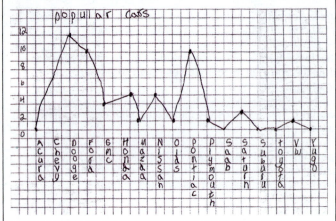

Strategies That Show and Promote Caring

Students are more motivated to do well in school when they believe that their teacher and peers *care* about their academic success and general well-being.[217] The following strategies are relevant to this "C" component of the MUSIC acronym.

Show students that you like them and are concerned about their well-being.

Teachers can communicate fondness for students in a variety of ways.[218] For example, they can express interest in students' outside activities and accomplishments and, when needed, provide extra assistance or a sympathetic ear in times of trouble. Teachers can also demonstrate caring by attending to students' *academic* needs—for instance, by being well prepared for each lesson, holding high expectations for students' achievement, and tailoring instructional strategies to students' current knowledge and ability levels.[219] Such caring messages may be especially important for low-achieving students, students from low-income families, and students from culturally different backgrounds.[220]

Provide regular opportunities for students to interact productively with one another.

For many students, school is, first and foremost, a place where they can see their friends every day—a place where they can meet their need for relatedness. When planning daily lessons and classroom activities, then, teachers should include opportunities for students to have productive, satisfying interactions with their peers, ideally enabling students to learn academic subject matter *and* address their need for relatedness simultaneously.[221] Although some instructional goals can best be accomplished when students work independently, others can be accomplished just as easily (perhaps even more easily) when students work together. Group-based activities, such as discussions, debates, role-playing, cooperative learning tasks, and competitions among two or more teams of equal ability, all provide the means through which students can satisfy their need for relatedness while simultaneously acquiring (and possibly co-constructing) new knowledge and skills.[222] Most effective are activities in which all students have something unique to contribute and so can in some way "shine" and gain the admiration of peers.

The Classroom Strategies box "Showing and Promoting Caring" presents several strategies for enhancing social relationships in the classroom.

Strategies That Generate Productive Affect for Learning

Students learn at high levels not only when they're genuinely motivated to master academic subject matter but also when their emotional states are conducive to productive cognitive processes and behaviors. Following are four recommendations for fostering feelings and emotions that can enhance students' learning.

Get students emotionally involved in the subject matter.

Academic subject matter certainly doesn't need to be dry and emotionless. On the contrary, students will often remember more if they have strong feelings about what they're studying, perhaps getting very excited about a scientific discovery or quite angry about past or present social

[217] Raufelder, Sahabandu, Martínez, & Escobar, 2015; Rimm-Kaufman, Baroody, Larsen, Curby, & Abry, 2014.

[218] Juvonen, 2006; Pianta, Belsky, Vandergrift, Houts, & Morrison, 2008; Reyes, Brackett, Rivers, White, & Salovey, 2012; Roorda, Koomen, Spilt, & Oort, 2011.

[219] C. Bergin & Bergin, 2009; Reeve, 2006; Wentzel, 1997.

[220] Bergin & Bergin, 2009; Meehan, Hughes, & Cavell, 2003; Milner, 2006; Phelan, Davidson, & Cao, 1991.

[221] Wentzel & Wigfield, 1998.

[222] Blumenfeld et al., 2006; Brophy, 1987; Linnenbrink, 2005; Urdan & Maehr, 1995.

CLASSROOM STRATEGIES

Showing and Promoting Caring

- **Have students work together on some learning tasks.**
  A high school history teacher incorporates classroom debates, small-group discussions, and cooperative learning tasks into every month's activities.

- **Continually communicate the message that you like and respect your students.**
  A middle school teacher tells one of his students that he saw her dancing troupe's performance at the local shopping mall over the weekend. "I had no idea you were so talented," he says. "How many years have you been studying dance?"

- **Praise students privately when being a high achiever is not sanctioned by peers.**
  While reading a stack of short stories his students have written, a high school English teacher discovers that one of his students,

Brigitta, has written an especially good story. Knowing that Brigitta is eager to maintain her popularity with low-achieving classmates, he writes his comments on the second page of her story, where others won't be able to see them. There he writes, "Great work, Brigitta! I think it's good enough to enter into the state writing contest. I'd like to meet with you before or after school some day this week to talk more about the contest."

- **Create a classroom culture in which respect for *everyone's* needs and well-being is paramount.**
  When a second-grade teacher overhears two boys making fun of a fellow student who stutters, she discretely pulls them aside, explains that the classmate is extremely self-conscious about his speech and is working hard to improve it, and tactfully reminds the boys that they, too, have imperfections as well as strengths.

---

injustices. In addition to presenting subject matter that evokes emotional reactions, teachers can promote hot cognition by revealing their own feelings about a topic. For instance, they might bring in newspaper articles and other outside materials about which they're excited, present material in an enthusiastic or impassioned fashion, and share the particular questions and issues about which they themselves are concerned.[223] And although teachers don't necessarily want to give the impression that schoolwork is all fun and games, they can occasionally incorporate a few game-like features into classroom tasks and activities.[224] For example, they might assign simple crossword puzzles to introduce new spelling words or use a television game show format for a class history review (the game show strategy also addresses students' need for relatedness).

Foster emotion regulation.

As indicated in the chapter's second Cultural Considerations box ("Cultural and Ethnic Differences in Affect"), various cultural groups differ in the extent to which they encourage emotional expressiveness or restraint. Even so, all children and adolescents function better at school when they engage in **emotion regulation**—that is, when they keep emotional reactions to events (e.g., excitement, sadness, anger) within socially acceptable limits.[225]

Certainly, teachers should refer students with severe emotional difficulties to school counselors and other specially trained professionals. But a few simple strategies can help many students cope with the everyday disappointments and frustrations of life:[226]

- Help students identify strategies for minimizing the damage that certain events may have caused.

- Encourage students to find potential benefits in an unfortunate event—for instance, to treat it as a "wake-up call" or look for the "silver lining."

- Teach students strategies that can help them prevent similar unfortunate events in the future.

Through such coping strategies, students may learn that although they can't always control everything that happens to them, they can control how they *think* about what happens, enabling them to maintain at least some sense of autonomy.[227]

MyEdLab
Video Example 5.6.

What strategies does this first-grade teacher use to help a student regulate her emotions and to prevent a similar unfortunate situation in the future?

---

[223] Brophy, 2004; Brophy et al., 2009; Pekrun, 2006.

[224] Brophy, 2004.

[225] Labouvie-Vief & González, 2004; Wisner Fries & Pollak, 2007.

[226] J. E. Bower, Moskowitz, & Epel, 2009; Hall, Goetz, Haynes, Stupnisky, & Chipperfield, 2006; Pekrun, 2006; Peterson, 2006; Richards, 2004.

[227] This phenomenon is known as *secondary control;* see Rothbaum, Weisz, & Snyder, 1982.

Keep anxiety at a low to moderate level.

As noted earlier in the chapter, learners work most effectively and productively when they're a little bit anxious—enough to spur them into action—but not overly so. Teachers can address students' concerns about social matters (e.g., worries about peer acceptance and respect) by teaching social skills and by planning activities that foster productive peer interactions. Teachers can address students' concerns about their uncertain futures by teaching skills that will be marketable in the adult world and by providing assistance with college applications. But perhaps most importantly, teachers must take steps to ensure that students don't become overly anxious about classroom tasks and subject matter.

Because anxiety (like all emotions) is largely beyond students' immediate control, simply telling them to "Relax" or "Calm down" is not likely to be effective. The key here is to *prevent* rather than "cure" debilitating anxiety. Following are several strategies that should keep students' anxiety at a facilitative level:[228]

- Communicate clear, concrete, and realistic expectations for performance.
- Match instruction to students' cognitive levels and capabilities (e.g., use concrete materials to teach mathematics to students not yet capable of understanding abstract mathematical symbols).
- Provide supplementary sources of support for learning challenging topics and skills until mastery is attained (e.g., additional practice, individual tutoring, a structure for taking notes).
- Teach strategies that enhance learning and performance (e.g., effective study skills).
- Assess students' performance independently of how well their classmates are doing, and encourage students to assess their own performance in a similar manner.
- Provide feedback about specific behaviors, rather than global evaluations of classroom performance.
- Allow students to correct errors, so that no single mistake is ever a "fatal" one.

As students make the transition to middle school or high school, make an extra effort to minimize their anxiety and address their need for relatedness.

Elementary school classrooms are often very warm, nurturing ones in which teachers and students get to know one another quite well. But somewhere around fifth to seventh grade, many students move from elementary school to a middle school or junior high school and encounter several changes in the nature of their schooling:[229]

- The school is larger and has more students.
- Students have several teachers at a time, and each teacher has many students. As a result, teacher–student relationships tend to be more superficial and less personal than in elementary school, and teachers have less awareness of how well individual students are understanding and mastering classroom subject matter.
- There is more whole-class instruction, with less individualized instruction that takes into account each student's academic needs.
- Classes are less socially cohesive. Students may not know their classmates very well and may be reluctant to ask peers for assistance.
- Students have fewer opportunities to make choices about the topics they pursue and the tasks they complete. At the same time, they have more independence and responsibility regarding their learning. For example, they may have relatively unstructured assignments to be accomplished over a two- or three-week period, and they must take the initiative to seek help when they're struggling.
- Teachers place greater emphasis on demonstrating (rather than acquiring) competence. Thus mistakes are more costly for students. (This change reflects a shift from *mastery goals* to *performance goals*.)
- Standards for assigning grades are more rigorous, so students may earn lower grades than they did in elementary school. Grades are often assigned on a comparative and competitive basis, with only the highest-achieving students getting As and Bs.

[228] Brophy, 1986; Hattie & Timperley, 2007; Pekrun, 2006; Shute, 2008; Stipek, 1993; Zeidner, 1998.
[229] H. A. Davis, 2003; Dijkstra et al., 2008; Eccles & Midgley, 1989; Hine & Fraser, 2002; Midgley et al., 2002; Rolland, 2012; Wentzel & Wigfield, 1998; Wigfield et al., 2006.

CLASSROOM STRATEGIES

Easing the Transition to Middle and Secondary School

- **Provide a means through which every student can feel part of a small, close-knit group.**
  During the first week of school, a ninth-grade math teacher forms *base groups* of three or four students who provide support and assistance for one another throughout the school year. At the beginning or end of every class period, the teacher gives group members 5 minutes to help one another with questions and concerns about daily lessons and homework assignments.

- **Address students' personal and social needs as well as their academic needs.**
  Early in the school year, while his classes are working on a variety of cooperative learning activities, a middle school social studies teacher schedules individual appointments with each of his students. In these meetings, he searches for interests that he and his students share and encourages the students to seek him out whenever they need help with academic or personal problems. Throughout the semester, he continues to touch base with individual students (often during lunch or before or after school) to see how they're doing.

- **Teach students the skills they need to be successful independent learners.**
  After discovering that few of her students know how to take effective class notes, a high school science teacher distributes a daily "notes skeleton" that guides them through the note-taking process. The skeleton might include headings such as "Topic of the Lesson," "Definitions," Important Ideas," and "Examples." As students' class notes improve over the course of the school year, the teacher gradually reduces the amount of structure she provides.

- **Assign grades based on mastery (not on comparisons with peers), and provide reasonable opportunities for improvement.**
  A middle school language arts teacher requires students to submit two drafts of every essay and short story he assigns; he gives students the option of submitting additional drafts as well. He judges the compositions on several criteria, including quality of ideas, organization and cohesiveness, word usage, grammar, and spelling. He explains and illustrates each of these criteria and gives ample feedback on every draft that students turn in.

- High-stakes tests (e.g., tests that affect promotion to the next grade level) become increasingly common.

Furthermore, previously formed friendships can be disrupted as students move to new (and perhaps differing) schools.[230] And, of course, students may find the physiological changes that accompany puberty and adolescence unsettling. This combination of changes often leads to decreased confidence, a lower sense of self-worth, less intrinsic motivation, and considerable anxiety. Focus on social relationships increases, academic achievement drops, and some students become emotionally disengaged from the school environment—a disengagement that may eventually result in dropping out of school.[231]

If students remain in an elementary school in early adolescence (e.g., up to eighth grade), rather than move to a middle school or junior high environment, their attitudes and motivation are more likely to remain positive and productive.[232] By the time they reach ninth grade, however, they almost inevitably make the transition to a secondary school format, where they will experience many of the changes that their peers in other school districts experienced a few grades earlier.[233] Students in lower-income, inner-city school districts are especially at risk for making a rough transition from an elementary to a secondary school format.[234]

Students who make a smooth transition to secondary school are more likely to be academically successful and, as a result, more likely to graduate from high school.[235] The Classroom Strategies box "Easing the Transition to Middle and Secondary School" offers several strategies for teachers at the middle school and high school levels.

Up to this point, we've touched only briefly on those peer relationships that can make such a difference in students' successful transitions to middle schools and high schools. As we turn to personal and social development in the next chapter, we'll look at such relationships more closely. We'll also identify factors that help or hinder young people in their efforts to establish productive relationships with kids their age.

---

[230] Pellegrini & Long, 2004; Wentzel, 1999.

[231] Cohen & Garcia, 2008; Eccles & Midgley, 1989; Gentry, Gable, & Rizza, 2002; Lam et al., 2016; Urdan & Maehr, 1995.

[232] Midgley et al., 2002; Rudolph et al., 2001.

[233] Benner & Graham, 2009; Hine & Fraser, 2002; Midgley et al., 2002; Otis et al., 2005; Tomback, Williams, & Wentzel, 2005.

[234] Ogbu, 2003; Roderick & Camburn, 1999.

[235] Otis et al., 2005; Roderick & Camburn, 1999; Wigfield et al., 1996.

Teachers have control over many of the external factors that can affect students' motivation in school. To create a learning environment that promotes students' motivation and productive affect, teachers can empower students, show them how the learning activities are useful to their lives, ensure that they believe they can succeed if they put forth the required effort, stimulate their interest, and promote a caring culture in the classroom. In the hotlinked Self-Check quiz and Application Exercise that follow, you can check and apply your understandings related to Big Idea 5.5:

> *Effective teachers create conditions that support learners' needs, cognition, and affect.*

MyEdLab **Self-Check 5.5**

MyEdLab **Application Exercise 5.5.** In this exercise, you can apply the MUSIC strategies to a problem-based mathematics lesson.

5 SUMMARY

Motivation, affect, and learning always go hand in hand, with each playing a crucial role in the development of the others. We can get a big-picture view of the interplay among motivation, affect, and learning by returning to the Big Ideas presented at the beginning of the chapter.

■ **5.1: Teachers play a major role in motivating students by designing effective learning environments and supporting students' motivation-related beliefs over time.** Motivation is an "intention to" condition that energizes, directs, and sustains behavior. The specific nature of students' motives can impact their behavioral, cognitive, and emotional engagement in classroom activities. Motivation is influenced by *internal* factors, such as by students' basic psychological needs, cognitive processes, and affect. Furthermore, both motivation and these internal factors can be influenced by factors *external* to students, such as teachers' instructional strategies, ongoing classroom events and activities, and circumstances beyond school walls.

In general, motivation is an integral part of a larger cycle that includes not only these internal and external factors but also academic engagement and academic outcomes, with each one either directly or indirectly influencing the others. Teachers can potentially enhance students' motivation to learn and achieve in the classroom by intervening at any point in the cycle. For instance, a teacher might foster high motivation in low-achieving students by (1) teaching them new study strategies that enable them to succeed on classroom tasks (thus increasing academic outcomes) or (2) helping them interpret their successes as evidence of their own efforts and strategies and thus altering their attributions (which are internal factors).

■ **5.2: Learners are more motivated to learn and achieve at high levels when their basic psychological needs are being met.** Virtually all people appear to share certain fundamental needs. In addition to basic physical needs for food, water, oxygen, and other substances essential for life, people seem to have psychological needs, such as a need for some degree of physical and cognitive stimulation (a need for arousal); a need to believe that they can deal effectively with their environment (a need for competence); a need to believe that they are generally good, capable individuals (a need for self-worth); a need to direct the course of their life events

to some extent (a need for autonomy); and a need to feel socially connected to other people and to gain others' love and respect (a need for relatedness). Students are more likely to enjoy and show interest in school activities—that is, be intrinsically motivated—when one or more of their basic psychological needs are met. However, when learners have little or no intrinsic motivation to acquire important knowledge and skills, then extrinsic reinforcers can help to keep them on the road to academic success.

■ **5.3: Learners' thoughts and beliefs about themselves and about classroom subject matter can influence their motivation to learn in the classroom.** Motivation depends on several cognitive factors—including interests, self-efficacy, values, goals, and attributions—that typically emerge and evolve gradually over time. Among the most important of these is self-efficacy: Learners are apt to be motivated to perform particular tasks and activities when they're confident that they can accomplish those tasks and activities successfully. But in addition, learners' motivation in the classroom depends on the extent to which assignments are a good match with their interests, values, and goals. Learners must also interpret events in productive ways—for instance, by attributing both their successes and their failures to things over which they have control (e.g., effort, effective learning strategies).

■ **5.4: Learners' affect (their feelings, emotions, and moods) influences and is influenced by both their motives and their cognitive processes.** Motivation and learning are closely intertwined with affect, including both the emotions that learners bring to the learning situation and the feelings that instructional materials elicit. On average, topics that evoke strong feelings (excitement, anger, etc.) tend to be more memorable than neutral topics. However, it's possible to have too much of a good thing. For instance, situations that arouse a lot of anxiety often interfere with effective information processing and memory.

■ **5.5: Effective teachers create conditions that support learners' needs, cognition, and affect.** Many teaching strategies can be organized into five broad MUSIC principles for effectively motivating students: Teachers should e**M**power students, demonstrate the **U**sefulness of teaching activities, help students perceive that they can **S**ucceed, stimulate **I**nterest, and show and promote **C**aring. Teachers can *empower* students by giving them control over some aspects of their learning environment, providing them with feedback in a noncontrolling manner, minimizing the use of extrinsic reinforcers, and allowing them to choose some short-term goals for their learning. It's also important for students to understand the *usefulness* of school activities—and the value of academic success more generally—for their own personal goals.

Age-appropriate teacher guidance and support in particular content domains can enhance students' *success* rates in those domains, thereby bolstering students' domain-specific self-efficacy and more general sense of competence and self-worth. By focusing students' attention on mastery goals—that is, on truly mastering a task or topic rather than simply attaining high test scores and grades—teachers increase the odds that students will engage in meaningful rather than rote learning. And by portraying students' successes and failures as being within students' power to control (e.g., through reasonable effort and use of good strategies), teachers can foster an optimistic, I-can-do-it attitude toward future learning activities.

High-*interest,* stimulating activities can satisfy students' need for arousal and keep them cognitively and affectively engaged in classroom activities. Additionally, teachers can build on students' more enduring individual interests. Designing instruction that incorporates students' interests is also a way for teachers to demonstrate that they *care* about students. Other ways to show caring include planning and implementing well-designed instructional activities and showing genuine concern for students' academic and personal well-being. For instance, small-group and whole-class activities (cooperative learning projects, class debates, etc.) allow students to interact with one another in ways that can allow students to have satisfying relationships with their classmates.

In addition to fostering productive motivation through the five general MUSIC strategies, it's important that teachers engender productive emotions and minimize counterproductive ones. Ideally, teachers should promote hot cognition—that is, they should help students engage emotionally as well as cognitively with classroom topics. Furthermore, teachers can help students keep excess anxiety in check by matching instruction to students' current ability levels, communicating clear expectations for students' performance, and giving students some wiggle room to make errors without penalty. And many students are likely to need teachers' assistance in regulating intense emotional reactions to unsettling circumstances and in making the often anxiety-arousing transitions to middle school and high school.

PRACTICE FOR YOUR LICENSURE EXAM

Praising Students' Writing

Mrs. Gaskill's second graders are just beginning to learn how to write the letters of the alphabet in cursive. Every day Mrs. Gaskill introduces a new cursive letter and shows her students how to write it correctly. She also shows them some common errors in writing the letter—for instance, claiming that she's going to make the "perfect *f*" and then making it much too short and crossing the lines in the wrong place—and the children delight in finding her mistakes. After the class explores each letter's shape, Mrs. Gaskill asks her students to practice it, first by writing it in the air using large arm movements and then by writing it numerous times on lined paper.

Meanwhile, Mrs. Gaskill has decided to compare the effects of two kinds of praise on the children's performance. She has placed a small colored sticker on each child's desk to indicate membership in one of two groups. When children in Group 1 write a letter with good form, she gives them a happy-face token, says "Great" or "Perfect!" and either smiles or gives them a pat on the back. When children in Group 2 write a letter with good form at least once, she gives them a happy-face token and says something like "You sure are working hard," "You can write beautifully in cursive," or "You're a natural at this." When children in either group fail to meet her standards for cursive writing, she gives them whatever corrective feedback they need.

Therefore, the only way in which Mrs. Gaskill treats the two groups differently is in what she says to them when they do well, either giving them fairly cryptic feedback (for Group 1) or telling them that they are trying hard or have high ability (for Group 2). Despite such a minor difference, Mrs. Gaskill finds that the children in Group 2 say they enjoy cursive writing more, and they use it more frequently in their spelling tests and other writing tasks. Curiously, too, the children in Group 1 often seem disappointed when they receive their seemingly positive feedback. For instance, on one occasion a girl who writes beautifully but has the misfortune of being in Group 1 asks, "Am *I* a natural at this?" Although the girl consistently gets a grade of "+" for her cursive writing, she never writes in cursive voluntarily throughout the 3-week period in which Mrs. Gaskill conducts her experiment.[236]

1. **Constructed-response question**

   Mrs. Gaskill praises all of her students for their performance, yet some kinds of praise seem to be more effective than others.

   A. Identify two sources of evidence to support the claim that students who receive lengthy, specific feedback (Group 2) enjoy writing in cursive more than students who receive brief, general feedback (Group 1).

   B. Explain why the praise given to Group 2 might be more motivating than the praise given to Group 1. Base your explanation on contemporary principles and theories of motivation.

2. **Multiple-choice question**

   Which one of the following teacher behaviors in the case is an example of an *attribution?*

   a. Amusing the students by intentionally writing the letter *f* incorrectly

   b. Commenting that "You sure are working hard"

   c. Awarding happy-face tokens for good writing

   d. Giving students a pat on the back for good work

   MyEdLab **Licensure Exam 5.1**

---

[236] Study described by Gaskill, 2001.

Losevsky Photo and Video/Shutterstock

6

Cognitive Development

CASE STUDY: HIDDEN TREASURE

Six-year-old Lupita has spent most of her life in Mexico with her grandmother, but she recently joined her migrant-worker parents in the United States and is now a quiet, well-behaved student in Ms. Padilla's kindergarten class. Ms. Padilla rarely calls on her because of her apparent lack of academic skills and is thinking about holding her back for a second year of kindergarten. Yet a researcher's video camera captures a side of Lupita her teacher hasn't noticed. On one occasion Lupita is quick to finish her Spanish assignment and starts to work on a puzzle during her free time. A classmate approaches, and he and Lupita begin playing with a box of toys. A teacher aide asks the boy whether he has finished his Spanish assignment, implying that he should return to his seat to complete it, but the boy doesn't understand the aide's subtle message. Lupita gently persuades the boy to finish his schoolwork and then returns to her puzzle. Two classmates having trouble with their own puzzles request Lupita's assistance, and she patiently shows them how to work cooperatively to assemble the pieces.

Ms. Padilla is amazed when she views the video. She readily admits, "I had written her off—her and three others. They had met my expectations and I just wasn't looking for anything else." Ms. Padilla and her aides begin working closely with Lupita on academic skills and often allow her to take a leadership role in group activities. At the end of the school year, Lupita earns achievement test scores indicating exceptional competence in language and math, and she is promoted to first grade.[1]

- Why might Ms. Padilla initially underestimate Lupita's academic potential?
- What clues in the case study suggest that Lupita is, in fact, an intelligent child?

Over the years, Ms. Padilla has almost certainly had students who lacked basic knowledge and skills (color and shape names, counting, the alphabet, etc.), and many of them undoubtedly struggled with the kindergarten curriculum as a result. And in Ms. Padilla's experience, children usually speak up or raise their hands if they have useful contributions to class discussions, but Lupita is quiet and reserved. With such things in mind, it might be all too easy to conclude that Lupita needs a second year in kindergarten. Yet the speed with which Lupita finishes her assignment and her behavior during free time—her facility with puzzles, her correct interpretation of an aide's subtle message, and her skill in guiding peers—suggest that she learns quickly and has considerable social know-how.

From preschool to high school and beyond, individuals change in many ways. The orderly, enduring changes that occur over the life span are called **development**. Recall from Chapter 2 that long-term changes due to *experience* are called *learning*. However, students also develop due to their genetic heritage—the characteristics and predispositions they're born with—and these genetic factors interact with students' experiences in dynamic and complex ways to affect their development.[2] Although the focus of this chapter is on **cognitive development**—developmental changes in thinking, reasoning, and language—many other aspects of development have also been studied, including the following: personal development (changes in one's personality), social development (changes in how one relates to others), moral development (changes in standards regarding right and wrong behaviors), physical development (changes in one's body), and

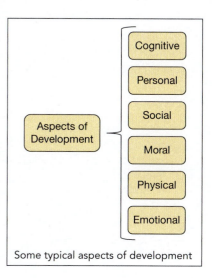

Some typical aspects of development

---

[1] Based on case described by Carrasco, 1981.
[2] Lerner, Liben, & Mueller, 2015; Zelazo, 2013.

emotional development (changes in how one understands, expresses, and regulates his or her emotions). We've seen a few developmental changes in previous chapters, especially changes in learning strategies (Chapter 2) and self-regulation (Chapter 3). In this chapter, we'll examine child and adolescent development more closely, and we'll continue to consider developmental trends in future chapters.

Table 6.1 describes six theoretical perspectives from which we'll draw in upcoming discussions. Keep in mind that, for the most part, these various perspectives aren't mutually exclusive. For example, some developmental theorists have incorporated both the cognitive-developmental and information processing perspectives in their work on cognitive development (notice how theorists Robbie Case and Kurt Fischer appear in two places in Table 6.1). Keep in mind, too, that the perspectives presented in the table aren't the only ones psychologists have used in studying child development. Behaviorism, social cognitive theory, and other perspectives, although not as dominant, have made significant contributions to developmental psychology as well.

The ideas of two early developmental theorists, Jean Piaget and Lev Vygotsky, have been especially influential in the study of cognitive development and so play key roles in this chapter. Piaget, who was Swiss, developed many ingenious tasks to probe children's and adolescents' thinking and reasoning.[3] He observed that young learners acquire self-constructed understandings of physical and social phenomena that change in qualitatively distinct ways over time. Hence Piaget was a cognitive-developmental theorist. Meanwhile, Vygotsky, who was Russian, proposed mechanisms through which children's social and cultural environments influence their development, and his work provided the groundwork for sociocultural theory.[4] Some of Vygotsky's ideas—especially mediated learning, cognitive tools, and the importance of culture—appeared in Chapter 4. However, because Vygotsky was, first and foremost, concerned about children's cognitive development, we'll continue to look at his ideas in the pages ahead.

Our initial focus in this chapter will be on general processes and trends that characterize the development of the great majority of children and adolescents. Later, we'll look at the variability in cognitive abilities we're likely to see among children in any single group—variability that is sometimes referred to as *intelligence*.

6.1 GENERAL PRINCIPLES OF DEVELOPMENT

Big Idea 6.1 As a result of ongoing interactions between biological and environmental influences, children show some similar patterns but also considerable diversity in their developmental pathways.

Virtually any aspect of development is characterized by several general principles.

The sequence of development is somewhat predictable.

Researchers have observed many **universals** in development—similar patterns in how children change over time despite considerable differences in their environments. Some of this universality is marked by the acquisition of **developmental milestones**—new, developmentally more advanced behaviors—in predictable sequences. For example, children usually learn to walk only after they've learned to sit up and crawl. And they become concerned about what other people think of them only after they realize that other people *do* think about them.

Children develop at different rates.

Many descriptive studies tell us the average ages at which children and adolescents reach various developmental milestones. For example, the average child can hold a pencil and scribble at age 1½, starts using rehearsal as a way of remembering information somewhere between ages 5 and 7, and enters puberty at age 10 (for girls) or 11½ (for boys).[5] But not all children reach

---

[3] For example, see Piaget, 1928, 1952b, 1959, 1970, 1980; Inhelder & Piaget, 1958.

[4] For example, see Vygotsky, 1962, 1978, 1987, 1997. Vygotsky died in 1934, but many of his works weren't translated into English until considerably later.

[5] T. M. McDevitt & Ormrod, 2016; McLane & McNamee, 1990.

THEORETICAL PERSPECTIVES

Table 6.1 • General Theoretical Approaches to the Study of Child and Adolescent Development

THEORETICAL PERSPECTIVE	GENERAL DESCRIPTION	EXAMPLES OF PROMINENT THEORISTS	WHERE YOU WILL SEE THIS PERSPECTIVE IN THE BOOK
Cognitive-Developmental Theory	Cognitive-developmental theorists propose that one or more aspects of development can be characterized by a predictable sequence of stages. Each stage builds on acquisitions from any preceding stages and yet has a structure that's qualitatively different from the structure(s) of the prior stages. Most cognitive-developmental theories also reflect individual constructivism, in that they portray children as actively trying to make sense of their world and constructing increasingly complex understandings and abilities with which to interpret and respond to experiences.	Jean Piaget Jerome Bruner Robbie Case Kurt Fischer Lawrence Kohlberg MyEdLab: Content Extension 6.1. This supplementary reading provides some key ideas about Jean Piaget's Theory of Cognitive Development. MyEdLab: Content Extension 6.2. This supplementary reading explains Lawrence Kohlberg's Theory of Moral Development.	The ideas of Piaget and other cognitive-developmental theorists appear frequently in this chapter's discussions of developmental processes and trends (e.g., see the discussions of assimilation, accommodation, and equilibration, as well as Table 6.2 and some entries in Table 6.3). We'll look at Kohlberg's cognitive-developmental theory in the discussion of moral development in Chapter 7.
Nativism	Some behaviors are biologically built in. A few of these behaviors (e.g., sucking on a nipple) are evident at birth. Others (e.g., walking) emerge gradually, usually in a predictable order, as genetic instructions propel increasing physical *maturation* of the brain and body. Nativists suggest that in addition to genetically preprogrammed behaviors, some knowledge, skills, and predispositions—or at least the basic "seeds" from which such things will grow—are also biologically built in.	Renee Baillargeon Elizabeth Spelke Noam Chomsky	The influence of nativism is most obvious in this chapter's discussions of heredity, maturation, sensitive periods, brain development, and intelligence. It is also reflected in the discussions of temperament both in this chapter and in Chapter 7.
Sociocultural Theory	Sociocultural theorists emphasize the role of social interaction and children's cultural heritage in directing the course of development. Parents, teachers, and peers are especially instrumental, in that they pass along culturally prescribed ways of thinking about and responding to objects and events. As children gain practice in certain behaviors and cognitive processes within the context of social interactions, they gradually adopt and adapt these behaviors and processes as their own.	Lev Vygotsky Barbara Rogoff Jean Lave Mary Gauvain MyEdLab: Content Extension 6.3. This supplementary reading briefly explains Lev Vygotsky's theory of cognitive development.	We've previously made use of sociocultural theory in Chapter 4. Vygotsky's theory and other sociocultural perspectives come into play in this chapter whenever we discuss the influence of social interaction on cognitive development (e.g., see the discussions of internalization, zone of proximal development, cultural differences, and distributed intelligence). In addition, sociocultural theory underlies many of the chapter's recommendations for fostering cognitive development (e.g., see the discussions of play activities, reciprocal teaching, scaffolding, and apprenticeships). It will also help us understand the effectiveness of peer mediation in Chapter 7.
Information Processing Theory	Developmental psychologists who take an information processing approach focus on how memory capabilities and specific cognitive processes change with age. For example, some examine how an expanding working memory capacity enables more complex thought. Others consider how increasingly sophisticated metacognitive knowledge and beliefs spur more advanced and effective learning strategies. Still others explore the cognitive processes involved in children's social interactions with peers.	John Flavell Robert Siegler Deanna Kuhn Robbie Case Kurt Fischer Nicki Crick Kenneth Dodge	We first encountered this perspective in Chapter 2. Information processing theory provides the foundation for this chapter's discussions of developmental trends in working memory and knowledge base, as well as for the chapter's discussions of cognitive processes in intelligence and related abilities. In Chapter 7, we'll draw on this perspective in the discussion of social information processing.

(continued)

THEORETICAL PERSPECTIVE	GENERAL DESCRIPTION	EXAMPLES OF PROMINENT THEORISTS	WHERE YOU WILL SEE THIS PERSPECTIVE IN THE BOOK
Ecological Systems Theory	Ecological systems theorists point out that to fully understand and explain children's development, we must consider the various environmental contexts in which children grow up—not only the immediate contexts with which children have everyday contact (e.g., home and school) but also the broader environments within which these immediate contexts exist (e.g., the community and its resources, the federal government and its laws and policies). These various layers of context interact with and affect one another in myriad ways (e.g., community employment opportunities affect a family's ability to provide nourishing food and stimulating activities for children).	Urie Bronfenbrenner Carol Lee **MyEdLab: Content Extension 6.4.** This supplementary reading highlights ecological systems perspectives of child development.	Ecological systems theory provides a basis for the discussion of "layers" of context in Chapter 4. It also highlights the importance of considering the cultural groups in which children grow up, as evidenced in the Cultural Considerations boxes in Chapters 3 through 10.
Psychodynamic Theory	By and large, psychodynamic theorists focus on personality development, and sometimes on abnormal development as well. They propose that a child's early experiences can have significant effects on a child's later development, even when those experiences are buried in a child's *unconscious* and thus unavailable for recall and self-reflection. Some psychoanalytic theorists also propose that children go through qualitatively distinct stages in their development. One key concept in many psychodynamic theories is *identity*, one's self-constructed definition of who one currently is and hopes to become in the future.	Sigmund Freud Erik Erikson **MyEdLab: Content Extension 6.5.** This supplementary reading notes some main ideas from Erik Erikson's theory of psychosocial development.	Identity formation will be an important topic in our discussion of sense of self in Chapter 7. In that discussion, we'll draw on research by James Marcia (a psychologist who built on Erik Erikson's theory) to identify the various paths that adolescents might take in their search for identity.

developmental milestones at the average age—some reach them earlier, some later—leading to considerable variability at any age and grade level. Thus, we must never jump to conclusions about what a particular learner can and cannot do based on age alone.

Development is often marked by spurts and plateaus.

Development doesn't necessarily proceed at a constant rate. Instead, periods of relatively rapid growth (*spurts*) may appear between periods of slower growth (*plateaus*). For example, toddlers may speak with a limited vocabulary and one-word "sentences" for several months, yet sometime around their second birthday their vocabulary expands rapidly and their sentences become longer and longer within just a few weeks' time. Years later, after seemingly stalling out height-wise, many children undergo an adolescent growth spurt, shooting up several inches within a year or so. Occasionally children even take a temporary step *backward*, apparently because they're in the process of overhauling a particular physical or cognitive skill and are about to make a major leap forward.[6]

think about it

Can you think of times in your cognitive or physical development (or other type of development) when you experienced rapid or slower growth?

Development involves both quantitative and qualitative changes.

In some cases, development simply means acquiring *more* of something—for instance, more height, more knowledge, and more friends. Yet in many respects children tend to think and behave in qualitatively different ways at different ages. For example, in the early elementary grades, children rely largely on rehearsal when they're trying to remember something, with more sophisticated strategies such as organization and elaboration emerging in the middle and high school years (see Chapter 2). And in high school, some students' epistemic beliefs may gradually shift from a *knowledge-as-discrete-facts* view to a *knowledge-as-integrated-understanding* view (see Chapter 3).

Some theorists (especially cognitive-developmental theorists) suggest that patterns of uneven growth and qualitative change reflect distinctly different periods in children's development. In a **stage theory**, development is characterized as progressing through a predictable sequence of stages, with earlier stages providing a foundation on which later, more advanced ones build. For example, as we'll discover shortly, Piaget characterized the development of logical reasoning skills

---

[6]Gershkoff-Stowe & Thelen, 2004; Morra, Gobbo, Marini, & Sheese, 2008.

as having four distinct stages, and another prominent cognitive-developmental theorist, Lawrence Kohlberg, proposed that moral development also has a stagelike nature (see Chapter 7).

In recent years, many developmental psychologists have begun to believe that most aspects of development can be better characterized as reflecting general *trends* rather than discrete stages. Even so, developmental changes often do occur in a predictable sequence, with some acquisitions occurring before—and possibly being prerequisites for—later ones.

Heredity and environment interact in their effects on development.

Virtually all aspects of development are affected either directly or indirectly by children's inherited genetic profiles.[7] If you've taken a biology course, you should recall that all of our genetic information is stored in *genes* that are comprised of deoxyribonucleic acid (DNA). This DNA, which is present in every cell in our bodies, is what drives our development and makes us all unique individuals. For example, soon after birth children begin to show genetic inclinations, or *temperaments,* that predispose them to respond to physical and social events in certain ways—perhaps to be calm or irritable, outgoing or shy, cheerful or fearful (more on temperament in Chapter 7). And throughout childhood and adolescence, genes continue to guide children's growth through the process of **maturation**, a gradual, genetically driven acquisition of more advanced physical and neurological capabilities over the course of childhood and adolescence. Even such seemingly simple skills as walking, running, and jumping emerge primarily as a result of genetically controlled advancements in the brain and in muscular strength and control.[8]

Yet genes have their effects only as they interact with conditions in their environment.[9] Thus, environmental factors also make substantial contributions to children's development. For example, genes require certain "supplies" and outside influences—in the forms of oxygen, nutrients, and environmental stimulation—to carry out their work. Thus, as we learned in Chapter 4, poor nutrition can hamper brain development. Also, basic motor skills appear only after brain and muscle maturation make them possible, exercise and practice (environmental influences) affect how fast children can run and how far they can jump. And although children's behaviors are partly the result of genetically based temperaments, the ways in which their local environment and broader culture socialize them to behave—through reinforcement, punishment, modeling, and so on—are just as influential.

The effects of both genes and the environment are well documented, but psychologists disagree about how *much* each contributes to development—an issue known as *nature versus nurture.* In fact, inherited genes (nature) and the environment (nurture) typically *interact* in their effects, such that we can probably never disentangle their unique influences on development.[10] In some cases the interaction between genes and the environment takes the form of a **sensitive period**, a biologically predetermined point in development during which a child is especially susceptible to environmental conditions. For example, the quality of nutrition has a greater impact on cognitive development in the early years, when children's brains are rapidly maturing, than in middle childhood or adolescence.[11] There may also be sensitive periods for some aspects of language development. In particular, children have an easier time mastering a language's grammatical subtleties and learning how to pronounce words flawlessly if they're immersed in the language within the first 5 to 10 years of life.[12] However, there's *no* evidence to indicate that sensitive periods exist for traditional academic subjects such as reading, writing, or mathematics.[13]

Children's own behaviors also influence their development.

Not only do children's genes interact with their environment, but so, too, do children's day-to-day *behaviors* interact with environmental factors. Furthermore, some of their behaviors are a result of genetic characteristics. Ultimately, then, we have a three-way interplay among genes, the

---

[7] Moore, 2013; Zelazo, 2013.
[8] Kovas, Malykh, & Petrill, 2014.
[9] Lickliter, 2013.
[10] Belsky, Bakermans-Kranenburg, & van IJzendoorn, 2007; S. W. Cole, 2009; W. Johnson, 2010; Spencer et al., 2009.
[11] Sigman & Whaley, 1998.
[12] Bialystok, 1994; Bortfeld & Whitehurst, 2001; M. S. C. Thomas & Johnson, 2008.
[13] Bruer, 1999; Geary, 1998, 2008; Wolf, Gottwald, Galante, Norton, & Miller, 2009.

FIGURE 6.1 Internal variables (such as genetic inclinations), the environment, and behavior mutually influence one another.

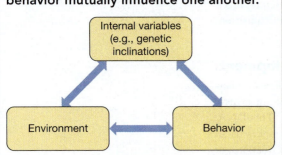

Internal variables (e.g., genetic inclinations)

Environment

Behavior

think about it

What kinds of extracurricular activities have you deliberately sought out? Would you say that they have strengthened abilities you already had to some degree?

environment, and behavior, as shown in Figure 6.1.[14] This three-way interplay should look familiar to you because it's the same relationships shown in Figure 4.5 in Chapter 4. The relationships among internal variables, the environment, and behavior are reflected in two principles previously presented in Chapter 4:

- **Learners alter their current environment through both their behaviors and their internal variables, such as genes, traits, and mental processes.** For example, in the opening case study, Lupita behaves in a quiet, reserved manner, possibly reflecting an inherited temperament to be calm and shy (i.e., inherited genetics affect her behavior). Because her behavior is so easy to overlook, Ms. Padilla gives her very little time and attention in class (i.e., behavior affects the environment). Had a researcher's video camera not captured some of her strengths, Lupita might have spent a second year in kindergarten.

- **Learners actively seek out environments that are a good fit with their existing behaviors and internal variables.** In the opening case study, Lupita voluntarily chooses to work on a puzzle during her free time. Thus, she actively seeks out a task that will nurture her interests and abilities (i.e., internal variables affect her environment).

Research based on various theoretical perspectives has yielded several universals in development that can be helpful to teachers. Yet, teachers must remember that students don't all reach developmental milestones at exactly the same age. In the hotlinked Self-Check quiz and Application Exercise that follow, you can check and apply your understandings related to Big Idea 6.1:

> As a result of ongoing interactions between biological and environmental influences, children show some similar patterns but also considerable diversity in their developmental pathways.

MyEdLab **Self-Check 6.1**

MyEdLab **Application Exercise 6.1.** In this exercise, you will examine the effects that a teenager's early maturation had on his environment, and consequently, on him.

6.2 DEVELOPMENTAL PROCESSES

Big Idea 6.2 Cognitive development depends not only on brain maturation but also on stimulating physical, social, and cultural experiences and on children's natural inclinations to organize and try to make sense of those experiences.

Inherited genes, the environment, and children's own behaviors all nudge children toward increasingly complex and sophisticated ways of thinking and behaving. The means by which they do so are reflected in the following principles.

The brain continues to develop throughout childhood, adolescence, and adulthood.

When babies are born, their brains have all of the basic parts but are hardly finished products. Genetically driven maturational processes bring about many important changes in the brain during the first 20 or 30 years of life. The prefrontal cortex—the part of the brain responsible for planning, decision making, and many other advanced reasoning processes—is especially slow to mature and doesn't take on a truly adultlike form until individuals reach their early 20s.[15] (Figure 2.2 in Chapter 2 shows the prefrontal cortex.)

As we discovered in Chapter 2, two kinds of brain cells—neurons and astrocytes—appear to play a significant role in learning and development, and some parts of the brain continue to form new ones (especially new astrocytes) throughout a person's lifetime.[16] But to fully understand

---

[14] O. S. P. Davis, Haworth, & Plomin, 2009; Mareschal et al., 2007; Plomin & Spinath, 2004; Scarr & McCartney, 1983.

[15] Otero & Barker, 2014.

[16] Deng, Aimone, & Gage, 2010.

developmental changes in the brain, we need to know a bit more about neurons and their three primary components: the cell body, the dendrites, and the axon (see Figure 6.2). Like all cells in living creatures, every neuron has a *cell body,* which contains its nucleus and is responsible for its general well-being. In addition, a neuron has many branchlike structures, called *dendrites,* which receive messages from other neurons. A neuron also has an *axon,* a long, arm-like structure that transmits information to other neurons. Figure 6.2 shows six neurons and some interconnections, or *synapses,* among them. Keep in mind, that neurons don't actually touch one another. Instead, the synapses that connect them consist of tiny spaces across which various chemical messages are sent.

Neurons begin to form synapses with one another long before a child is born, but shortly after birth the rate of synapse formation increases dramatically. Much of this early **synaptogenesis** appears to be driven primarily by genetic programming rather than by learning experiences. Thanks to synaptogenesis, children in the elementary grades have many more synapses than adults do. As children encounter a wide variety of stimuli and experiences in their daily lives, some synapses come in quite handy and become stronger because they are used repeatedly. Other synapses are largely irrelevant and useless, and these gradually fade away through a process known as **synaptic pruning**. In some parts of the brain, intensive

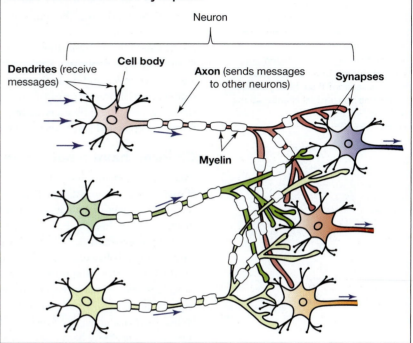

FIGURE 6.2 Neurons consist of a cell body, dendrites, and axons. Messages (depicted by arrows in this figure) are received by dendrites and transmitted through the axon to other neurons via the synapses.

synaptic pruning occurs fairly early (e.g., in the preschool or early elementary years). In other parts, it begins later and continues until well into adolescence.[17]

Why do growing brains create a great many synapses, only to eliminate a sizable proportion of them later on? In the case of synapses, more isn't necessarily better.[18] Experts speculate that by generating more synapses than will ever be needed, human beings have the potential to adapt to a wide variety of conditions and circumstances. As children encounter certain regularities in their environment, some synapses are actually a nuisance because they're inconsistent with typical environmental events and behavior patterns. Synaptic pruning, then, may be Mother Nature's way of making the brain more efficient.

Another developmental process that enhances the brain's efficiency over time is **myelination**: Many neurons gradually acquire a white, fatty coating known as *myelin.* A detailed discussion of myelin is beyond the scope of this book, but we should note that its arrival means that neurons can transmit messages much faster than they could previously. A few neurons (especially those involved in basic survival skills) become myelinated before birth, but most of them don't acquire myelin until well after birth, with different areas becoming myelinated in a predictable sequence.[19]

In the cortex—and especially the prefrontal cortex—synaptic pruning continues into the middle childhood and adolescent years, a second wave of synaptogenesis occurs at puberty, and myelination continues into early adulthood.[20] And several parts of the brain, especially those that are heavily involved in thinking and learning, continue to increase in size and interconnections until late adolescence or early adulthood.[21] In addition, the beginning of puberty is marked by significant changes in hormone levels, which affect the continuing maturation of brain structures

---

[17] Bruer, 1999; Huttenlocher & Dabholkar, 1997; M. H. Johnson & de Haan, 2001; Steinberg, 2009.

[18] Bruer & Greenough, 2001; Bryck & Fisher, 2012; Byrnes, 2001; Spear, 2007.

[19] Byrnes, 2001; M. Diamond & Hopson, 1998.

[20] Blakemore & Choudhury, 2006; Giedd et al., 2012; M. H. Johnson & de Haan, 2001; Lenroot & Giedd, 2007; Paus et al., 1999.

[21] Giedd et al., 1999; Pribram, 1997; Sowell & Jernigan, 1998; Sowell, Thompson, Holmes, Jernigan, & Toga, 1999; E. F. Walker, 2002.

and possibly also affect the production and effectiveness of the chemical substances used in synapses.[22] This combination of changes may affect and possibly limit adolescents' functioning in a variety of areas, including attention, planning, and impulse control.[23] We'll return to this point in our discussion of adolescent risk taking in Chapter 7.

One widespread myth about the brain is that it does all its "maturing" within the first few years of life and that its development can best be nurtured by bombarding it with as much stimulation as possible—reading instruction, violin lessons, art classes, and so on—before its owner ever reaches kindergarten. But as we've just seen, nothing could be further from the truth. In fact, young brains probably aren't able to benefit from some kinds of experiences, especially those that are fairly complex and multifaceted.[24] And from a physiological standpoint, the brain's ability to reorganize itself in order to adapt to changing circumstances—its **plasticity**—persists throughout the life span.[25] The early years are important for development, to be sure, but so are the later years. For most topics and skills, there isn't a single "best" or "only" time to learn.[26]

Children have a natural tendency to organize their experiences.

Even as young infants, human beings seem to be predisposed to categorize their world.[27] In his theory of cognitive development, Jean Piaget proposed that the things children learn and do are organized as **schemes**—groups of similar actions or thoughts that are repeatedly used in response to the environment. (Don't confuse these with the *schemas*—tightly organized sets of facts related to particular concepts or phenomena—described in Chapter 2.[28]) Initially, Piaget suggested, schemes are based largely on sensory and behavioral responses to objects. For example, an infant may have a putting-things-in-mouth scheme that he applies to a variety of objects, including his thumb, cookies, and toys. Over time, however, mental schemes—many of which are essentially categories or concepts—emerge as well. For instance, a 7-year-old may have a scheme for identifying snakes that includes their long, thin bodies, their lack of legs, and their slithery nature. A 13-year-old may have a scheme for what constitutes *fashion,* enabling her to classify various peers as being either very cool or "total losers."

Children are naturally inclined to make sense of and adapt to their environment.

Mother Nature also seems to endow children with a natural curiosity about their world. Accordingly, they actively seek out information to help them understand and make sense of it. For example, young children often experiment with new objects, manipulating them and observing the effects of their actions. And they may ask a seemingly endless series of questions in their efforts to understand the things they observe around them.[29] For example, as we authors know from our own experiences, they're apt to ask questions such as: "How did the whole world start?" "How does the television work?" "How do babies get in mommy's tummies?"

Piaget proposed that underlying children's curiosity is a desire to adapt to and be successful in their environment. Such adaptation occurs through two complementary processes, assimilation and accommodation. **Assimilation** entails responding to and possibly interpreting an object or event in a way that's consistent with an existing scheme. For example, an infant may assimilate a new teddy bear into his putting-things-in-the-mouth scheme. A 7-year-old may quickly identify a new slithery object in the garden as a snake. And a 13-year-old may readily label a classmate's clothing as being either quite fashionable or "soooo yesterday."

But sometimes children can't easily relate to a new object or event using existing schemes. In these situations, one of two forms of **accommodation** occurs: Children either (1) modify an existing scheme to account for the new object or event or (2) form a new scheme to deal with it.

think about it

Did you have this early-enrichment belief about the brain before you read this section? If so, have you now undergone conceptual change about the issue?

MyEdLab

Video Example 6.1.

Young children are naturally curious about objects in their environment. In what ways does 2-year-old Maddie explore the properties of her new toy?

---

[22] Steinberg, 2009; E. F. Walker, 2002.

[23] Blakemore & Choudhury, 2006; Kuhn & Franklin, 2006; Steinberg, 2009; Shen et al., 2010; Spear, 2007.

[24] C. A. Nelson, Thomas, & de Haan, 2006.

[25] Chein & Schneider, 2012; Kolb, Gibb, & Robinson, 2003; C. A. Nelson et al., 2006.

[26] Bruer, 1999; Byrnes & Fox, 1998; Geary, 1998, 2008.

[27] Gelman, 2003; Mandler, 2007; Quinn, 2007.

[28] Piaget distinguished between *schemes* and *schemas* (e.g., see Piaget, 1970, translator's footnote on p. 705), but neither concept is identical to the *schemas* about which contemporary theorists speak.

[29] Frazier, Gelman, & Wellman, 2009; Kemler Nelson, Egan, & Holt, 2004.

For example, an infant may have to open his mouth wider than usual to accommodate a teddy bear's fat paw. A 7-year-old who encounters a long, slithery creature with four legs can't apply the *snake* scheme (snakes don't have legs) and thus, after talking to his parents, may acquire a new scheme—*salamander.* And a 13-year-old may have to revise her existing scheme of fashion according to changes in what's hot and what's not.

Assimilation and accommodation typically work hand in hand as children develop their knowledge and understanding of the world. Children interpret each new event within the context of their existing knowledge (assimilation) but at the same time may modify their knowledge as a result of the new event (accommodation). Accommodation rarely happens without assimilation: Children can benefit from (accommodate to) new experiences only when they can relate those experiences to their current knowledge and beliefs.

Development builds on prior acquisitions.

We've just seen how children can typically accommodate to new stimuli and events only when they can also assimilate those new stimuli and events into their existing understandings. We previously encountered this idea—albeit using different terminology—in the discussion of *rote* versus *meaningful learning* in Chapter 2: Children learn more effectively when they can relate new information and experiences to what they already know. Furthermore, the idea underlies the notion of *stage theory* mentioned earlier in this chapter: Later stages build on the accomplishments of preceding ones.

In general, then, children rarely start from scratch. Instead, virtually all aspects of their development involve a continual process of refining, building on, and occasionally reconfiguring previous abilities and achievements. In the opening case study, Ms. Padilla is concerned about Lupita's lack of basic academic skills. Although she mistakenly assumes that Lupita isn't capable of acquiring these skills in a single school year, she's on target in one respect: The skills will be essential for Lupita's success in first grade and beyond.

Observations of the physical environment—and, ideally, frequent interactions with it—promote development.

Piaget believed that active experimentation with the physical world is essential for cognitive growth. By exploring and manipulating physical objects—for instance, fiddling with sand and water, playing games with balls and bats, and conducting science experiments—children see the effects of erosion, discover principles related to force and gravity, and so on. When interaction with the physical environment isn't possible, children must at least be able to *observe* various cause-and-effect relationships in their physical environment.[30] Alternatively, children can learn a great deal from observing and perhaps experimenting with various "objects" in a computer-simulated environment, as we noted in our discussion of virtual worlds in Chapter 4.[31]

Language development facilitates cognitive development.

Cognitive development is, of course, essential for the development of language: Children can talk only about things that they can in some way first *think* about. But language is equally important for children's cognitive development.[32] From Piaget's perspective, it provides a set of entities (*symbols*) through which humans can mentally represent external events and internal schemes. We often think by using specific words that our language provides; for instance, when we think about pets, our thoughts are apt to include such words as *dog* and *cat.*

In Lev Vygotsky's theory of cognitive development, thought and language are separate functions for infants and young toddlers. In these early years, thinking occurs independently of language, and when language appears, it's first used primarily as a means of communication rather than as a mechanism of thought. But sometime around age 2, thought and language become intertwined: Children begin to express their thoughts when they speak, and they begin to think in words. Their rapidly expanding vocabularies at this age enable them to represent and think about a wide variety of objects and events.

---

[30] Bebko, Burke, Craven, & Sarlo, 1992; Brainerd, 2003.

[31] de Jong, 2011; Sarama & Clements, 2009.

[32] For recent discussions of language's roles in learning and cognitive development, see Ganea, Shutts, Spelke, & DeLoache, 2007; K. Nelson & Fivush, 2004; Pinker, 2007; Q. Wang & Ross, 2007.

think about it

What aspect of *self-regulation* do self-talk and inner speech remind you of? (Review the discussion of self-regulation in Chapter 3 and then click **here** for the answer.)

MyEdLab
Video Explanation 6.1.

This video describes and illustrates mediated learning experiences and cognitive tools.

When thought and language first merge, children often talk to themselves—a phenomenon known as **self-talk**. Vygotsky suggested that self-talk plays an important role in cognitive development. By talking to themselves, children learn to guide and direct their own behaviors through difficult tasks and complex maneuvers in much the same way that adults may have previously guided them. With time and experience, self-talk gradually evolves into **inner speech**, in which children "talk" to themselves mentally rather than aloud. They continue to direct themselves verbally through tasks and activities, but others can no longer see and hear them do it.[33]

Self-talk is hardly unique to young children, of course. As you undoubtedly know from your own experiences, even adults occasionally talk to themselves when they face new challenges (e.g., "OK, first I need to do this and then I can . . .").

Interactions with other people promote development.

Language facilitates cognitive development in another way as well: It enables children to exchange ideas with adults and peers. Both Piaget and Vygotsky suggested that social interaction is critical for cognitive development. In Piaget's view, exchanging ideas with others helps children realize that other individuals see things differently than they themselves do and that their own perspectives aren't necessarily completely accurate or logical ones. For example, a 9-year-old may recognize the logical inconsistencies in what she says only after someone else points them out. And through discussions with peers or adults about social and political issues, a high school student may modify some initially abstract and idealistic notions about how the world "should" be to reflect constraints that the real world imposes.

For Vygotsky, social interactions are even more important, in that they provide the very foundations for cognitive development. Two concepts introduced in Chapter 4 are, in fact, key ideas in Vygotsky's theory. One is the notion of *mediated learning experiences:* As adults interact with children, they often share the general meanings and interpretations they attach to objects, events, and human experience in general. The second is *cognitive tools:* Not only do adults help children interpret new experiences, but they also share concepts, procedures, and strategies that enable children to deal effectively with complex tasks and problems. To the extent that specific cultures pass along unique interpretations, beliefs, concepts, ideas, procedures, strategies, and so on, children in different cultures will acquire somewhat different knowledge, skills, and ways of thinking.

In addition, Vygotsky proposed that social activities provide the seeds from which complex cognitive processes can grow. Essentially, children use complex processes first in interactions with other people and gradually become able to use them independently in their own thinking. Vygotsky called this phenomenon **internalization**. The progression from self-talk to inner speech just described is an example: Over time, children gradually internalize adults' directions so that they're eventually giving *themselves* directions. Yet keep in mind that children don't necessarily internalize *exactly* what they see and hear in social contexts. Rather, internalization often involves transforming ideas and processes to make them uniquely one's own.[34]

Not all mental processes evolve as children interact with adults; some instead develop as children interact with peers. For example, children frequently argue with one another about a variety of matters—how best to carry out an activity, what games to play, who did what to whom, and so on. Childhood arguments can help children discover that there are often several ways to view the same situation. Eventually, children internalize the arguing process, developing the ability to look at a situation from several different angles *on their own.*[35]

Formal schooling promotes development.

Informal conversations are one common method through which adults pass along culturally relevant ways of interpreting situations. But from the perspective of sociocultural theorists, contemporary cognitive-developmental theorists, and information processing theorists, formal education is just as important, perhaps even more so. (Recall how much progress Lupita makes once Ms. Padilla and her aides begin to work hard to help her master basic academic skills.) Through formal, preplanned lessons, teachers systematically impart the ideas, concepts, and procedures used

---

[33] Also see Berk, 1994; Winsler & Naglieri, 2003.

[34] Thus, Vygotsky's theory, although primarily sociocultural in nature, also has a constructivist element to it.

[35] Vygotsky, 1978.

in various academic disciplines. In this way, rather than having to reinvent the wheel (both literally and figuratively), each generation can benefit from the discoveries, understandings, and problem-solving strategies of previous generations.[36]

Inconsistencies between existing understandings and new events promote development.

Earlier we noted that children are naturally inclined to make sense of their environment. When children can comfortably address new events using what they've previously learned about the world, they're in a state that Piaget called **equilibrium**. But as children grow older and expand their horizons, they sometimes encounter situations for which their current knowledge and skills aren't helpful. Such situations create **disequilibrium**, a sort of mental "discomfort" that spurs them to reexamine their current understandings. By replacing, reorganizing, or better integrating certain schemes—in other words, through accommodation—children can better understand and address previously puzzling events. The movement from equilibrium to disequilibrium and back to equilibrium again is known as **equilibration**. Piaget suggested that equilibration and children's desire to achieve equilibrium promote the development of more complex levels of thought and knowledge.

To better understand how thinking changes with age and discover the circumstances under which children might revise their thinking in light of new experiences, Piaget developed a variety of tasks that would reveal children's reasoning processes and in some cases create disequilibrium. As an example of such a task, try the following exercise.

——————————— **SEE FOR YOURSELF** ———————————
WOODEN BEADS

In the margin are 12 wooden beads—some brown and some white. Are there more wooden beads or more brown beads?

A ridiculously easy question, you might think. But in fact, young children often answer incorrectly, responding that there are more *brown* beads than wooden ones. Consider the following dialogue between a 6-year-old, whom we'll call "Brian,"[37] and an adult about a similar set of brown and white wooden beads:

Adult: Are there more wooden beads or more brown beads?

Brian: More brown ones, because there are two white ones.

Adult: Are the white ones made of wood?

Brian: Yes.

Adult: And the brown ones?

Brian: Yes.

Adult: Then are there more brown ones or more wooden ones?

Brian: More brown ones.[38]

During further questioning, Brian continues to assert that the brown beads outnumber the wooden beads. In an effort to help him see otherwise, the adult asks him to draw two necklaces, one made of the brown beads and another made of the wooden beads. Brian draws a series of black rings for the brown-beads necklace; he draws a series of black rings plus two white rings for the wooden-beads necklace.

Adult: Good. Now which will be longer, the one with the brown beads or the one with the wooden beads?

Brian: The one with the brown beads.[39]

---

[36] Case & Okamoto, 1996; M. Cole, 2006; Karpov & Haywood, 1998; Raudenbush, 2009; Vygotsky, 1962.

[37] Piaget identified children in his studies by abbreviations, in this case by the letters *BRI*.

[38] Dialogue from Piaget, 1952a, pp. 163–164.

[39] Dialogue from Piaget, 1952a, p. 164.

Notice how the adult continues to probe Brian's reasoning to be sure he realizes that all the beads are wooden, but only some are brown. Even so, Brian responds that there are more brown beads than wooden ones. Piaget suggested that young children such as Brian have trouble with **class inclusion** tasks in which they must simultaneously think of an object as belonging to two categories—in this case, thinking of a bead as being both *brown* and *wooden* at the same time.

Notice, too, how the adult asks Brian to draw two necklaces, one made with the wooden beads and one made with the brown beads. The adult hopes that after Brian draws a brown-and-white necklace that's longer than an all-brown necklace, he'll notice that his drawings are inconsistent with his statement that there are more brown beads. The inconsistency might lead Brian to experience disequilibrium, perhaps to the point that he'll reevaluate his conclusion and realize that, logically, there *must* be more wooden beads than brown ones. In this case, however, Brian is apparently oblivious to the inconsistency, remains in equilibrium, and thus has no need to revise his thinking.

Challenging tasks promote development.

Children can typically do more difficult things in collaboration with adults or other, more advanced individuals than they can do on their own.[40] The range of tasks children cannot yet perform independently but *can* perform with other people's help and guidance is, in Vygotsky's terminology, the **zone of proximal development (ZPD)** (see Figure 6.3). We see an example in the opening case study: Two of Lupita's classmates can assemble puzzles only when Lupita provides assistance.

A child's zone of proximal development includes learning and problem-solving abilities that are just beginning to emerge. Naturally, children's ZPDs change over time: As some tasks are mastered, other, more complex ones appear on the horizon to take their place. Furthermore, ZPDs can vary considerably in "width": With assistance, some children may be able to stretch their existing abilities considerably, whereas others may be able to handle tasks that are only slightly more difficult than those they can currently do on their own.

Vygotsky proposed that children develop very little from repeating tasks they can already do independently. Rather, they develop primarily from taking on challenges that require support—that is, tasks within their zones of proximal development. But children's ZPDs also set upper limits on what they're cognitively capable of doing and learning. Impossible tasks—those that children can't complete even with considerable structure and guidance—are of no benefit whatsoever.

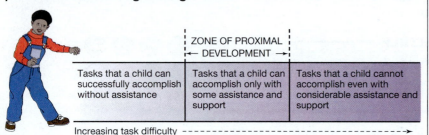

FIGURE 6.3 Tasks in a child's zone of proximal development (ZPD) promote maximal cognitive growth.

ZONE OF PROXIMAL
← DEVELOPMENT →

| Tasks that a child can successfully accomplish without assistance | Tasks that a child can accomplish only with some assistance and support | Tasks that a child cannot accomplish even with considerable assistance and support |

Increasing task difficulty - →

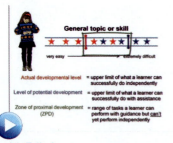

General topic or skill

★ ★ ★ ★ ★ ★ ★ ★ ★ ★

very easy   extremely difficult

Actual developmental level	= upper limit of what a learner can successfully do independently
Level of potential development	= upper limit of what a learner can successfully do with assistance
Zone of proximal development (ZPD)	= range of tasks a learner can perform with guidance but can't yet perform independently

▶

MyEdLab
Video Explanation 6.2.

This video illustrates the zone of proximal development and its change over time.

Children spend a considerable amount of time trying to understand the world as they experience it through their various senses; for example, they manipulate physical objects and eagerly seek out adults' explanations of puzzling phenomena and events. And they try to make sense of their experiences by organizing them into more general ideas, and they continue to revise and expand on these ideas over time as new information becomes available through newer experiences. To promote students' development, teachers can challenge them in ways that allow them to stretch their existing abilities. In the hotlinked Self-Check quiz and Application Exercise that follow, you can check and apply your understandings related to Big Idea 6.2:

> *Cognitive development depends not only on brain maturation but also on stimulating physical, social, and cultural experiences and on children's natural inclinations to organize and try to make sense of those experiences.*

MyEdLab **Self-Check 6.2**

MyEdLab **Application Exercise 6.2.** In this exercise, you can determine whether or not students in the scenarios are working within their zones of proximal development.

---

[40] Fischer & Immordino-Yang, 2002; Vygotsky, 1978.

6.3 TRENDS IN COGNITIVE DEVELOPMENT

Big Idea 6.3 Children continually build on existing knowledge and skills to develop more advanced thinking and reasoning abilities.

In our discussions of learning and cognition in previous chapters, we've already identified three noteworthy trends in cognitive development:

- With age and experience, children acquire more effective learning strategies (Chapter 2).
- Most learners become increasingly self-regulating over the course of childhood and adolescence (Chapter 3).
- Metacognitive knowledge and skills gradually improve with age (Chapter 3).

We now pull from the research of information processing theorists and cognitive-developmental theorists (including both Piaget and more contemporary researchers) to identify the following additional trends.

Children's growing working memory capacity enables them to handle increasingly complex cognitive tasks.

As you should recall from Chapter 2, working memory has a very limited capacity and learners can think about only so much at once. In fact, children ages 5 to 8 seem to have only about half of the working memory capacity that adults have.[41] Fortunately, as children grow older, their working memory capacity increases, and they can gradually handle bigger and more complex thinking and learning tasks. Some of this increase in capacity is likely due to an increase in the physical capacity of the working memory. But as children grow, they also acquire more knowledge and strategies that allow them to process information more effectively, so it frees up more available "space."[42] As an analogy, if you think of working memory as a "box," two things happen as children get older: The box gets a little bigger, and children can "pack" it more effectively (see Figure 6.4).

Children's growing knowledge base enhances their ability to learn new things.

One key reason children use increasingly effective learning strategies with age is that they acquire an ever-expanding body of knowledge that can help them interpret, organize, and elaborate on new experiences. In cases where children have more knowledge than adults, the children are often the more effective learners.[43] For example, when one of us authors used to read books about lizards together with her son, her son always remembered more than she did because, even as a 6-year-old, he knew a great deal about reptiles, whereas his mom knew very little.

Children's knowledge, beliefs, and thinking processes become increasingly integrated.

Through such processes as knowledge construction, organization, and elaboration, children increasingly pull together what they know and believe about the world into cohesive wholes (e.g., recall the discussion of children's *theories* in Chapter 2). Whereas the knowledge base of young children is apt to consist of many separate, isolated facts, the knowledge base of older children and adolescents typically includes many interconnections among concepts and ideas.[44]

FIGURE 6.4 This "box" analogy might help you understand why working memory capacity seems to increase over the course of development: Compared to Box 1 (reflecting the stage of affairs for young children), Box 2 is larger and more efficiently packed, allowing more "items" to fit.

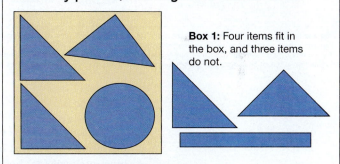

Box 1: Four items fit in the box, and three items do not.

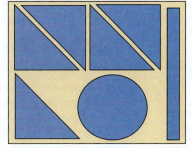

Box 2: All seven items now fit in the box because the box is bigger and more efficiently packed.

---

[41] Cowan, Ricker, Clark, Hinrichs, & Glass, 2015; Kharitonova, Winter, & Sheridan, 2015.

[42] Ben-Yehudah & Fiez, 2007; Cowan et al., 2015; Kail, 2007; Van Leijenhorst, Crone, & Van der Molen, 2007.

[43] Chi, 1978; Rabinowitz & Glaser, 1985.

[44] J. M. Alexander, Johnson, Albano, Freygang, & Scott, 2006; Bjorklund, 1987; Fischer & Immordino-Yang, 2002; Flavell, Miller, & Miller, 2002.

Table 6.2 • Piaget's Four Stages of Cognitive Development			
STAGE	**PROPOSED AGE RANGE**[a]	**GENERAL DESCRIPTION**	**EXAMPLES OF ABILITIES ACQUIRED**
Sensorimotor	Begins at birth	Schemes are based largely on behaviors and perceptions. Especially in the early part of this stage, children cannot think about things that are not immediately in front of them, and so they focus on what they are doing and seeing at the moment.	• *Trial-and-error experimentation with physical objects:* Exploration and manipulation of objects to determine their properties • *Object permanence:* Realization that objects continue to exist even when removed from view • *Symbolic thought:* Representation of physical objects and events as mental entities (*symbols*)
Preoperational	Emerges at about age 2	Thanks in part to their rapidly developing language and the symbolic thought it enables, children can now think and talk about things beyond their immediate experience. However, they do not yet reason in logical, adultlike ways.	• *Language:* Rapid expansion of vocabulary and grammatical structures • *Intuitive thought:* Some logical thinking based on hunches and intuition rather than on conscious awareness of logical principles (especially after age 4)
Concrete Operations	Emerges at about age 6 or 7	Adultlike logic appears but is limited to reasoning about concrete, real-life situations.	• *Class inclusion:* Ability to classify objects as belonging to two or more categories simultaneously • *Conservation:* Realization that amount stays the same if nothing is added or taken away, regardless of alterations in shape or arrangement
Formal Operations	Emerges at about age 11 or 12[b]	Logical reasoning processes are applied to abstract ideas as well as to concrete objects and situations. Many capabilities essential for advanced reasoning in science and mathematics appear.	• *Reasoning about hypothetical ideas:* Ability to draw logical deductions about situations that have no basis in physical reality • *Proportional reasoning:* Conceptual understanding of fractions, percentages, decimals, and ratios • *Separation and control of variables:* Ability to test hypotheses by manipulating one variable while holding other variables constant

[a]The age ranges presented in the table are *averages*; some children reach more advanced stages a bit earlier, others a bit later. Also, some children may be in *transition* from one stage to the next, displaying characteristics of two adjacent stages at the same time.
[b]Recent researchers have found much variability in when adolescents begin to show reasoning processes consistent with Piaget's formal operations stage. Furthermore, not all cultures value or nurture formal operational logic, perhaps because it is largely irrelevant to people's daily lives and tasks (see the Cultural Considerations box later in this chapter).

Piaget suggested that not only children's knowledge but also their *thought processes* become increasingly integrated over time. In particular, their many "thinking" schemes gradually combine into well-coordinated systems of mental processes. These systems—which Piaget called *operations*—allow children to think in increasingly logical ways, as will be evident in the next three developmental trends.[45]

Thinking becomes increasingly logical during the elementary school years.

Piaget proposed that cognitive development proceeds through four distinct stages, which are summarized in Table 6.2. Children's thinking during the school years reflects characteristics of three of these stages—the preoperational, concrete operations, and formal operations stages—and so will be relevant to our discussion here. Yet keep in mind that children's reasoning abilities appear to emerge more gradually than Piaget's stage theory might lead us to believe. Furthermore,

---

[45] For a more recent, neo-Piagetian perspective on how thinking processes might become integrated, see Kurt Fischer's discussions of *multiple, parallel strands* (e.g., Fischer & Immordino-Yang, 2002; Fischer, Knight, & Van Parys, 1993).

many contemporary theorists believe—and Piaget himself acknowledged—that the four stages better describe how children and adolescents *can* think, rather than how they always *do* think, at any particular age.[46]

In Piaget's view, reasoning in the **preoperational stage** is somewhat illogical. As an example, recall 6-year-old Brian's insistence that in a set of 12 wooden beads, including 10 brown ones and 2 white ones, there are more brown beads than wooden ones. And consider the following situation:

> Five-year-old Nathan is shown the three "before" glasses depicted in Figure 6.5. He is asked whether Glasses A and B contain the same amount of water, and he replies confidently that they do. Then, the water is poured from Glass B into Glass C, and he is asked whether A and C have the same amount (depicted as the "after" glasses in Figure 6.5). Nathan replies, "No, Glass A has more because it's taller."

Nathan's response reflects lack of **conservation**: He doesn't realize that the amount of water in the two glasses must be equivalent because nothing has been added or taken away. Young children such as Nathan often confuse changes in appearance with changes in amount.

Piaget found that children as young as age 4 or 5 occasionally draw logically correct conclusions about class inclusion and conservation problems. However, he suggested that their reasoning is based on hunches and intuition rather than on any conscious awareness of underlying logical principles, and so they can't yet explain *why* their conclusions are correct. More recently, researchers have discovered that how logically young children think depends partly on situational factors, such as how task materials are presented, how questions are worded, and whether adults provide guidance about how to think about a problem.[47]

In any event, most children have mastered simple logical thinking tasks, such as those involving class inclusion and simple forms of conservation, by age 6 or 7—an age at which, in Piaget's view, they're now in the **concrete operations stage**. They continue to refine their newly acquired logical thinking capabilities for several years. For example, some simple forms of conservation, such as the conservation-of-liquid problem presented in Figure 6.5, appear at age 6 or 7. Others don't emerge until later. Consider the problem in Figure 6.6. Using a balance scale, an adult shows a child that two balls of clay have the same weight. One ball is removed from the scale and smashed into a pancake shape. Does the pancake weigh the same as the unsmashed ball, or are the weights different? Not until around age 9 do children realize that the flattened pancake must weigh the same as the round ball it was previously.[48] And some conservation-of-weight tasks are difficult even for young adolescents. For instance, although most eighth graders would acknowledge that a large block of Styrofoam has weight, they may claim that a tiny piece torn from the block has no weight at all.[49]

Thinking becomes increasingly abstract in the middle school and secondary school years.

In Piaget's theory, children in the concrete operations stage can reason only about concrete objects and events, and especially about things they can actually see. Once they acquire abilities that characterize the **formal operations stage**—perhaps at around age 11 or 12, Piaget suggested—they're capable of abstract thought and so can think about concepts and ideas that have little or no basis in everyday concrete reality. For example, in mathematics, they should have an easier time understanding such concepts as *negative number, pi* (π), and *infinity*. And in science, they should be able to think about *molecules* and *atoms* and understand how it's possible for temperatures to go below zero.

In Piaget's theory, formal operational thought also involves *hypothetical reasoning,* thinking logically about things that may or may not be true. In some instances, such reasoning involves things that are definitely *false.* As an example, try the following exercise.

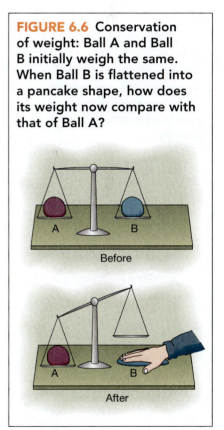

FIGURE 6.5 Conservation of liquid: Do Glasses A and C contain the same amount of water?

FIGURE 6.6 Conservation of weight: Ball A and Ball B initially weigh the same. When Ball B is flattened into a pancake shape, how does its weight now compare with that of Ball A?

---

[46] Flavell, 1994; Halford & Andrews, 2006; Klaczynski, 2001; Morra et al., 2008; Tanner & Inhelder, 1960.

[47] Halford & Andrews, 2006; Morra et al., 2008; Siegler & Svetina, 2006.

[48] Morra et al., 2008; Sroufe, Cooper, DeHart, & Bronfenbrenner, 1992.

[49] C. L. Smith, Maclin, Grosslight, & Davis, 1997; Wiser & Smith, 2008.

Take a moment to answer these two questions:

1. If all children are human beings,
   And if all human beings are living creatures,
   Then must all children be living creatures?
2. If all children are basketballs,
   And if all basketballs are jellybeans,
   Then must all children be jellybeans?

You probably responded fairly quickly that, yes, all children must be living creatures. The second question is trickier. It follows the same line of reasoning as the first but the conclusion it leads to—all children must be jellybeans—contradicts what's true in reality.

Abstract and hypothetical reasoning processes seem to emerge earlier and more gradually than Piaget proposed. Children in the elementary grades occasionally show an ability to reason abstractly and hypothetically about certain topics.[50] And yet once children reach puberty, they may continue to struggle with some abstract subject matter. For instance, although many can understand some abstract scientific and mathematical concepts in early adolescence, they're apt to have trouble understanding abstract concepts in history and geography until well into the high school years.[51] In fact, some adolescents never do show much evidence of formal operational thinking, especially if their culture and schooling do little to encourage it.[52]

Once learners become capable of abstract thought, they're able to look beyond the literal meanings of messages. Children in the early elementary grades often take the words they hear at face value—for instance, interpreting the expression "Your eyes are bigger than your stomach" quite literally (see Figure 6.7). And they have little success determining the underlying meanings of such proverbs as "Look before you leap" and "Don't put the cart before the horse." Students' ability to interpret proverbs in a generalized, abstract fashion continues to improve even in the high school years.[53]

Another outcome of abstract and hypothetical thinking is the ability to envision how the world might be different from the way it actually is. In some cases, adolescents envision a world much *better* than the one they live in, and they exhibit considerable concern and idealism about social and political issues. Some secondary school students devote a great deal of energy to local or global problems, such as water pollution or animal rights. However, they may offer recommendations for change that aren't practical in today's world. For example, a teenager might argue that "all you need is love" to overcome racism or suggest that a nation should eliminate its weapons and armed forces as a way of moving toward world peace. Piaget proposed that adolescent idealism reflects an inability to separate one's own logical abstractions from the perspectives of others and from practical considerations. Only through experience do adolescents eventually begin to temper their optimism with some realism about what's possible with limited resources and the idiosyncrasies of human nature.

Several logical thinking processes important for mathematical and scientific reasoning improve considerably during adolescence.

In Piaget's view, several additional abilities accompany the advancement to the formal operations stage. One is *proportional reasoning,* the ability to understand and think logically about such proportions as fractions, decimals, percentages, and ratios. For example, if you can quickly and easily recognize that the following statement is true

$$\frac{2}{8} = \frac{6}{24} = 0.25 = 25\%$$

then you've mastered proportional reasoning to some degree.

FIGURE 6.7 In this drawing, 8-year-old Jeff interprets the expression "Your eyes are bigger than your stomach" quite literally.

---

[50] S. R. Beck, Robinson, Carroll, & Apperly, 2006; S. Carey, 1985; McNeil & Uttal, 2009; Metz, 1995.

[51] Kuhn & Franklin, 2006; Lovell, 1979; Tamburrini, 1982.

[52] Flieller, 1999; Lerner, 2002; Rogoff, 2003.

[53] Owens, 1996; Winner, 1988.

Scientific reasoning skills also improve in adolescence. Two of them—*formulating and testing hypotheses* and *separating and controlling variables*—together enable learners to use the scientific method, in which several possible explanations for an observed phenomenon are proposed and tested in a systematic manner. As an example, consider the pendulum problem in the next exercise.

SEE FOR YOURSELF
PENDULUM PROBLEM

In the absence of other forces, an object suspended by a rope or string—a pendulum—swings at a constant rate. (A yo-yo and a playground swing are two everyday examples.) Some pendulums swing back and forth rather slowly, others more quickly. What characteristics of a pendulum determine how fast it swings? Jot down at least three hypotheses about the variable(s) that might affect a pendulum's oscillation rate.

Now gather several small objects or varying weights (e.g., a paperclip, a house key, a heavy bolt) and a piece of string. Tie one of the objects to one end of the string, and set your pendulum in motion. Conduct one or more experiments to test each of your hypotheses.

What can you conclude? What variable or variables affect the rate at which a pendulum swings?

What hypotheses did you generate? Four common ones involve the weight of the object, the length of the string, the force with which the object is pushed, and the height from which the object is released. Did you test each of your hypotheses in a systematic fashion? A person capable of formal operational thinking separates and controls variables, testing one at a time while holding all others constant. (This strategy should remind you of our discussion of *experimental studies* in Chapter 1.) For example, if you were testing the hypothesis that weight makes a difference, you might have tried objects of different weights while keeping constant the length of the string, the force with which you pushed each object, and the height from which you dropped or pushed it. Similarly, if you hypothesized that length was a critical factor, you might have varied the string length while continuing to use the same object and setting the pendulum in motion in a consistent manner. If you carefully separated and controlled variables, you should have come to the correct conclusion: Only *length* affects a pendulum's oscillation rate.

As early as first or second grade, children show signs that they can think about simple proportions.[54] And by the upper elementary grades, some can separate and control variables, especially if given guidance about the importance of controlling all variables except the one they're currently testing.[55] But by and large, the mathematical and scientific reasoning abilities just described don't really take wing until puberty, and they continue to develop throughout adolescence.[56]

The progression of logical reasoning processes shown in Table 6.3 draws on both Piaget's early work and more recent research findings. It also presents examples of teaching strategies that take these processes into account.

Children can think more logically and abstractly about tasks and topics they know well.

The ability to think logically about a situation or topic depends to some degree on learners' background knowledge and educational experiences. For example, 5-year-olds are more likely to solve class inclusion problems—such as whether a picture of three cats and six dogs has more animals than it has dogs—if an adult helps them think logically about such problems.[57] Children in the elementary grades can better understand fractions if they work with familiar concrete objects.[58] Young adolescents become increasingly able to separate and control variables

---

[54] Empson, 1999; Van Dooren, De Bock, Hessels, Janssens, & Verschaffel, 2005.

[55] Barchfeld, Sodian, Thoermer, & Bullock, 2005; Kuhn & Pease, 2008; Lorch et al., 2010.

[56] Barchfeld et al., 2005; Byrnes, 1988; Kuhn, Garcia-Mila, Zohar, & Andersen, 1995; Tourniaire & Pulos, 1985; Van Dooren et al., 2005; Zohar & Aharon-Kraversky, 2005.

[57] Siegler & Svetina, 2006.

[58] Empson, 1999; Fujimura, 2001.

DEVELOPMENTAL TRENDS

TABLE 6.3 • Logical Thinking Abilities at Different Grade Levels

GRADE LEVEL	AGE-TYPICAL CHARACTERISTICS	EXAMPLE	SUGGESTED STRATEGIES
Grades K–2	• Emergence of class inclusion • Emergence of conservation in simple tasks • Increasing ability to explain and justify conclusions about logical reasoning tasks	Five-year-old Lucinda confidently and accurately declares that two rows of quarters each have five coins. But when an adult spreads the quarters in one row far apart, she declares that the longer row has more quarters because it's "like more far away . . . bigger."	• Use concrete manipulatives and experiences to illustrate new ideas. • Have students classify objects in multiple ways (e.g., by color, then by size). • Ask students whether a set of objects you've just rearranged has more or fewer objects than it did before. Also ask them to (1) explain their reasoning and (2) explain why someone else might think the amount hasn't changed.
Grades 3–5	• Emergence of conservation in more challenging tasks (e.g., conservation of weight); full development of conservation continuing into adolescence • Ability to understand simple fractions (e.g., $\frac{1}{3}$, $\frac{1}{5}$, $\frac{1}{8}$) that can be related to concrete objects and everyday events • Occasional abstract and hypothetical thinking	When fourth graders are shown a pizza that's been cut into 12 slices, they easily identify one-half of the pizza (6 slices) and one-third of the pizza (4 slices). But when the lesson moves from concrete depictions of fractions to strictly symbolic representations, many begin to have trouble understanding.	• Supplement verbal explanations with concrete examples, pictures, and hands-on activities. • Introduce simple fractions by relating them to everyday objects (e.g., pizza slices, kitchen measuring cups). • Have students engage in simple scientific investigations, focusing on familiar objects and phenomena.
Grades 6–8	• Increasing ability to reason logically about abstract, hypothetical, and contrary-to-fact situations • Some ability to test hypotheses and to separate and control variables, especially with scaffolding; conclusions sometimes reflect *confirmation bias* (see Chapter 2) • Increasing ability to understand and work with proportions • Some ability to interpret figurative language (e.g., proverbs, figures of speech)	A seventh-grade science teacher asks students to conduct experiments to determine which one or more of three variables—weight, length, and height of initial drop—affects a pendulum's oscillation rate. One group of four students consistently varies both weight and length in its experiments and ultimately concludes (erroneously) that a pendulum's weight is the deciding factor.	• Make abstract concepts concrete in some way (e.g., relate *gravity* to everyday experiences, show a diagram of an *atom*). • Ask students to speculate on the meanings of well-known proverbs (e.g., "Two heads are better than one"). • Assign problems that require the use of simple fractions, ratios, or decimals. • Have students conduct simple experiments to answer specific questions about cause–and–effect.
Grades 9–12	• Increasing proficiency in the scientific method (e.g., formulation and testing of hypotheses, separation and control of variables); effects of confirmation bias still evident • Greater proficiency in interpreting figurative language • Idealistic (but not always realistic) views about how various aspects of society might be improved	When 14-year-old Alicia is asked to explain the proverb "A rolling stone gathers no moss," she offers an interpretation that goes beyond its literal meaning: "Maybe when you go through things too fast, you don't . . . collect anything from it." **MyEdLab: Video Example 6.2.** You can contrast Alicia's response with 10-year-old Kent's response here. 	• Study particular topics in depth; introduce complex and abstract explanations and theories. • Ask students to speculate on the meanings of unfamiliar proverbs (e.g., "Discretion is the better part of valor"). • Have students design some of their own experiments in science labs and science fair projects. • Encourage discussions about social, political, and ethical issues; elicit multiple perspectives on these issues.

Sources: Barchfeld et al., 2005; M. Donaldson, 1978; Elkind, 1981; Empson, 1999; Flavell, 1963; Fujimura, 2001; Halford & Andrews, 2006; Inhelder & Piaget, 1958; Karplus, Pulos, & Stage, 1983; Kuhn & Franklin, 2006; Lorch et al., 2010; Metz, 1995; Morra et al., 2008; Newcombe & Huttenlocher, 1992; Owens, 1996; Piaget, 1928, 1952b, 1959; Rosser, 1994; Siegler & Alibali, 2005; Siegler & Lin, 2010; Van Dooren et al., 2005; Wiser & Smith, 2008; Zohar & Aharon-Kraversky, 2005.

if they have many experiences that require them to do so.[59] Middle school and high school students (and adults as well) often apply formal operational reasoning processes to topics about which they have a great deal of knowledge and yet think concretely about topics with which they're unfamiliar.[60]

As an illustration of how knowledge affects scientific reasoning processes, consider the fishing pond in Figure 6.8. In one study[61] 13-year-olds were shown a similar picture and told, "These four children go fishing every week, and one child, Herb, always catches the most fish. The other children wonder why." If you look at the picture, it's clear that several variables might be involved, including the child's location, the kind of bait, and the length of fishing rod. Adolescents who were avid fishermen more effectively separated and controlled variables for this situation than they did for the pendulum problem described earlier, whereas the reverse was true for nonfishermen.

True expertise comes only after many years of study and practice.

Some learners eventually acquire a great deal of information about a particular topic—say, lizards, World War II, auto mechanics, or computer programming—to the point that they're *experts*. Not only do experts know more than their peers, but their knowledge is also qualitatively different from that of others. In particular, their knowledge tends to be tightly organized, with many interrelationships among ideas and many abstract generalizations unifying more specific, concrete details.[62] Such qualities enable experts to retrieve the things they need more easily, to find parallels between seemingly diverse situations, and to interpret and solve problems more creatively.[63] Ideally, then, expertise is *adaptive:* It combines considerable knowledge and skills with open-mindedness and innovation.[64]

There may be three somewhat distinct stages in the development of knowledge related to a particular topic, as illustrated in Figure 6.9.[65] At the first stage, *acclimation,* learners familiarize themselves with a new content domain, much as someone might do by taking an introductory course in biology, European history, or economics. At this point, learners pick up a lot of facts that they tend to store in relative isolation from one another. As a result of such fragmented learning, they're likely to hold on to many misconceptions that they may have acquired before they started studying the subject systematically.

At the second stage, *competence,* learners acquire considerably more information about the subject matter, and they also acquire some general principles that help tie the information together. People develop competence only after studying a particular subject in depth, perhaps by taking several biology courses or reading a great many books about World War II. Because learners at the competence stage make numerous interconnections among the things they learn, they're likely to correct some of their earlier misconceptions.

At the final stage, **expertise**, learners have truly mastered their field. They know a great deal about the subject matter, and they've pulled much of their knowledge together—including,

FIGURE 6.8 What are some possible reasons that Herb is catching more fish than the others?

Source: Based on Pulos & Linn, 1981.

MyEdLab
Video Example 6.3.

Knowledge about a particular content domain enhances children's ability to separate and control variables in that domain. For example, notice how a child with fishing experience (10-year-old Kent) identifies more variables in the fishing problem than does an older child who has never fished (14-year-old Alicia).

---

[59] Kuhn & Pease, 2010; Lorch et al., 2010; Schauble, 1990.

[60] Girotto & Light, 1993; M. C. Linn, Clement, Pulos, & Sullivan, 1989; Schliemann & Carraher, 1993.

[61] Pulos & Linn, 1981.

[62] J. M. Alexander, Johnson, Leibham, & Kelley, 2008; P. A. Alexander & Judy, 1988; Bédard & Chi, 1992; Horn, 2008; R. W. Proctor & Dutta, 1995.

[63] Chi, Glaser, & Rees, 1982; De Corte, Greer, & Verschaffel, 1996; Horn, 2008; Rabinowitz & Glaser, 1985; Voss, Greene, Post, & Penner, 1983.

[64] Bransford et al., 2009.

[65] The stages described here are based on the work of P. A. Alexander, 1997, 1998, 2004.

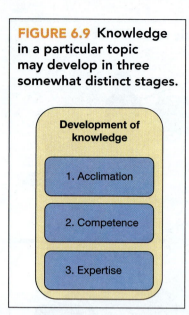

FIGURE 6.9 Knowledge in a particular topic may develop in three somewhat distinct stages.

Development of knowledge

1. Acclimation

2. Competence

3. Expertise

perhaps, a few persistent misconceptions—into a tightly integrated whole. At this point, they're helping to lead the way in terms of conducting research, proposing new ways of looking at things, solving problems, and, in general, making new knowledge. Expertise comes only after many years of study and practice in a particular field.[66] As a result, few learners ever reach this stage, and we're unlikely to see it before late adolescence or adulthood.

> Researchers have identified trends in how children and adolescents develop over time. For example, we see increases in students' working memory capacity and general knowledge about the world. And thinking processes become more integrated, logical, and abstract, which allows mathematical and scientific reasoning to improve. Teachers need to keep such trends in mind as they develop age-appropriate lessons and activities for students at different grade levels. In the hotlinked Self-Check quiz and Application Exercise that follow, you can check and apply your understandings related to Big Idea 6.3:
>
> *Children continually build on existing knowledge and skills to develop more advanced thinking and reasoning abilities.*
>
> **MyEdLab** Self-Check 6.3
>
> **MyEdLab** Application Exercise 6.3. In this exercise, you will apply your knowledge of Piaget's stages of conservation to three girls engaged in conservation tasks.

6.4 INTELLIGENCE

Big Idea 6.4 Although children in any age-group differ somewhat in intelligence, cognitive styles, and dispositions, appropriately supportive environments can significantly enhance these abilities and characteristics.

What kinds of behaviors lead you to believe that a person is intelligent? Is intelligence a general ability that contributes to success in many different domains? Or is it possible for someone to be intelligent in one domain yet not in another? What exactly *is* intelligence?

Psychologists haven't reached consensus on the answers to these questions. Virtually all of them agree, however, that children in any single age-group differ in how quickly they acquire new knowledge and skills. Most psychologists also agree that intelligence has several distinctive qualities:

- It's *adaptive:* It involves modifying and adjusting one's behaviors to accomplish new tasks successfully.

- It's related to *learning ability:* Intelligent people learn information more quickly and easily than less intelligent people.

- It involves the *use of prior knowledge* to analyze and understand new situations effectively.

- It also involves the complex interaction and coordination of *many different thinking and reasoning processes.*

- It's *culture specific:* "Intelligent" behaviors in one culture aren't necessarily intelligent behaviors in another culture.

With these qualities in mind, we offer an intentionally broad definition of **intelligence**: the ability to apply prior knowledge and experiences flexibly to accomplish challenging new tasks.

Regardless of the forms intelligence might take, most psychologists think of it as being somewhat distinct from what a child has actually learned (e.g., as reflected in school achievement). At the same time, intelligent thinking and intelligent behavior *depend* on prior learning. The more young learners know about the world in general and about the tasks they need to perform, the more intelligently they can behave. Intelligence, then, isn't necessarily a permanent characteristic that learners either "have" or "don't have." Instead, intelligence can change—and often *does* change—through experience, learning, and environmental support.

The following general principles summarize much of what researchers have learned about intelligence.

---

[66] P. A. Alexander, 1997, 1998, 2004; Ericsson, 2003; Horn, 2008.

Intelligence can be measured only imprecisely at best.

Curiously, although psychologists can't pin down exactly what intelligence is, they've been trying to measure it for more than a century. In 1904, government officials in France asked Alfred Binet to develop a means of identifying students who were unlikely to benefit from regular school instruction and therefore needed special educational services. Binet devised a test that measured general knowledge, vocabulary, perception, memory, and abstract thought. In doing so, he designed the earliest general measure of cognitive functioning—something we now call an **intelligence test**.

To get a sense of what intelligence tests are like, try the following exercise.

SEE FOR YOURSELF
MOCK INTELLIGENCE TEST

Answer each of these questions:

1. What does the word *penitence* mean?
2. How are a goat and a beetle alike?
3. What should you do if you get separated from your family in a large department store?
4. What do people mean when they say, "A rolling stone gathers no moss"?
5. Complete the following analogy: ▽ is to ▼ as ◯● is to:

   a. ●●   b. ●◯   c. (vertical ●/◯)   d. ▷◁

These test items are modeled after items on many contemporary intelligence tests. Although intelligence tests have evolved considerably since Binet's time, they continue to measure many of the same abilities—such as general knowledge, vocabulary, and abstract thinking—that Binet's original test did.

Scores on intelligence tests were originally calculated using a formula that involves division. Hence they were called "intelligence quotient" scores, or **IQ scores**. Although we still use the term *IQ*, intelligence test scores are no longer based on the old formula. Instead, they're determined by comparing a child's performance on a test with the performance of others in the same age-group. A score of 100 indicates average performance: Children with this score have performed better than half of their age-mates on the test and not as well as the other half. Scores well below 100 indicate below-average performance on the test. Scores well above 100 indicate above-average performance.

Figure 6.10 shows the percentage of individuals getting scores at different points along the scale (e.g., 12.9% of individuals get scores between 100 and 105).[67] Notice how the curve is high in the middle and low at both ends, indicating that scores close to 100 are far more common than scores considerably higher or lower than 100. For example, if we add up the percentages in different parts of Figure 6.10, we find that approximately two-thirds of children (68%) score within 15 points of 100 (i.e., between 85 and 115). In contrast, only 2.3% of children score as low as 70, and only 2.3% score as high as 130. This symmetric and predictable distribution of scores happens by design rather than by chance: Psychologists have created a method of scoring intelligence test performance that intentionally yields such a distribution. You can learn more about the nature of IQ scores in the discussion of *standard scores* in Appendix B, "Understanding and Interpreting Standardized Test Results."

Modern intelligence tests have been designed, in part, with Binet's original purpose in mind: to predict how well students are likely to perform in school.

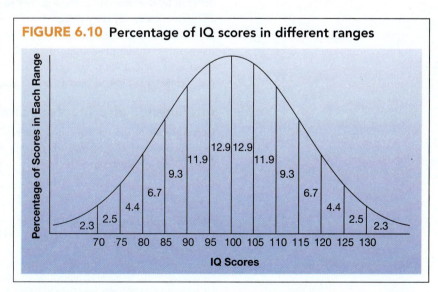

FIGURE 6.10 Percentage of IQ scores in different ranges

(Chart: Percentage of Scores in Each Range vs. IQ Scores; values along the curve: 2.3, 2.5, 4.4, 6.7, 9.3, 11.9, 12.9, 12.9, 11.9, 9.3, 6.7, 4.4, 2.5, 2.3; x-axis marks at 70, 75, 80, 85, 90, 95, 100, 105, 110, 115, 120, 125, 130)

---

[67] If you have some background in descriptive statistics, it may help you to know that most intelligence tests have a mean of 100 and a standard deviation of 15.

Studies repeatedly show that performance on intelligence tests is correlated with school achievement.[68] On average, children with higher IQ scores do better on standardized achievement tests, earn higher course grades, and complete more years of education. In other words, IQ scores often *do* predict school achievement, albeit imprecisely. As a result, school psychologists and other specialists frequently use intelligence tests to help them identify students who have disabilities or other special needs that require individualized education programs.

It's important to keep three points in mind about this IQ–achievement relationship. First, intelligence doesn't necessarily *cause* achievement; it's simply *correlated* with achievement. Even though students with high IQ scores typically perform well in school, we can't say conclusively that their high achievement is actually the result of their intelligence. Intelligence probably does play an important role in school achievement, but many other factors are also involved—factors such as motivation, quality of instruction, family and neighborhood resources, and peer-group expectations. Second, the relationship between IQ scores and achievement is an imperfect one, with many exceptions to the rule. For a variety of reasons, some students with high IQ scores don't perform well in school, and others achieve at higher levels than we'd predict from their IQ scores alone. Third and most important, we must remember that an IQ score simply reflects a child's performance on a particular test at a particular time—it's *not* a permanent characteristic etched in stone—and that some change is to be expected over time.

■

think about it

Did you have the misconception that IQ is a permanent number? If so, have you undergone conceptual change about the nature of IQ scores?

■

To some degree, intelligence reflects the general speed, efficiency, and control of cognitive processing.

Whenever we use a single IQ score as an estimate of a learner's cognitive ability, we're buying into the notion that intelligence is a single, general ability that affects performance on many different tasks. Historically, considerable evidence has supported this idea. Although different intelligence tests yield somewhat different scores—especially when they have different kinds of content—people who score high on one test tend to score high on others as well.[69] One early psychologist, Charles Spearman, called this single "intelligence" entity a *general factor,* or **g**.[70] (You may sometimes see the term *Spearman's g.*)

Recall how, in the opening case study, Lupita finishes an assignment more quickly than many of her classmates. Some contemporary information processing theorists believe that underlying g may be a general ability to process information quickly and efficiently.[71] Other contemporary theorists suggest that effective use of working memory—especially its central executive component—and metacognitive abilities are also key factors in general intelligence.[72]

Several decades after Spearman introduced the concept of g, psychologist Raymond Cattell found evidence for two distinctly different components of general intelligence.[73] First, learners differ in **fluid intelligence**, their ability to acquire knowledge quickly and adapt to new situations effectively. Second, they differ in **crystallized intelligence**, the knowledge and skills they've accumulated from their personal experiences, formal schooling, and culture. Fluid intelligence is more important for new, unfamiliar tasks, especially those that require rapid decision making and involve nonverbal content. Crystallized intelligence is more important for familiar tasks, especially those that depend heavily on language and prior knowledge.

Intelligence also involves numerous specific processes and abilities.

Certainly, intelligence isn't just a matter of doing something quickly and efficiently. It also requires a variety of specific abilities that might be relevant to some tasks and activities but not to others.[74] As an illustration, let's return to the "Mock Intelligence Test" exercise presented earlier.

---

[68] N. Brody, 1997; Deary, Strand, Smith, & Fernandez, 2007; Gustafsson & Undheim, 1996; Nisbett et al., 2012.

[69] McGrew, Flanagan, Zeith, & Vanderwood, 1997; Neisser et al., 1996; Spearman, 1927.

[70] Spearman, 1904, 1927.

[71] N. Brody, 2008; Bornstein et al., 2006; Coyle, Pillow, Snyder, & Kochunov, 2011; Haier, 2003.

[72] Cornoldi, 2010; Meinz & Hambrick, 2010; Nisbett et al., 2012; H. L. Swanson, 2008.

[73] Cattell, 1963, 1987; also see Nisbett, 2009.

[74] P. L. Ackerman & Lohman, 2006; Carroll, 2003; McGrew et al., 1997; Neisser et al., 1996; Spearman, 1927; Thurstone, 1938.

Defining words such as *penitence* (Item 1) requires good verbal skills and considerable knowledge of English vocabulary. In contrast, finding analogies among geometric figures (Item 5) involves reasoning about nonverbal entities.

Some theorists have built on Cattell's distinction between fluid and crystallized intelligence to suggest that intelligence has three layers, or *strata*[75] (see Figure 6.11). In the *Cattell–Horn–Carroll theory of cognitive abilities*, the top stratum is general intelligence, or *g*. Underlying it in the middle stratum are 9 or 10 specific abilities—processing speed, general reasoning ability, general world knowledge, ability to process visual input, and so on—that encompass fluid and/or crystallized intelligence to varying degrees. And underlying these abilities in the bottom stratum are more than 70 very specific abilities, such as reading speed, mechanical knowledge, and number and richness of associations in memory—all of which a particular child might have to varying degrees. With its large number of specific abilities, the Cattell–Horn–Carroll theory is too complex to describe in detail here, but you should be aware that psychologists are increasingly finding it useful in predicting and understanding students' achievement in various content domains.[76] Consequently, many modern intelligence tests include measures of the cognitive abilities identified in the Cattell–Horn–Carroll theory.[77]

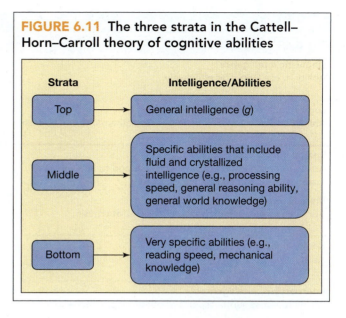

FIGURE 6.11 The three strata in the Cattell–Horn–Carroll theory of cognitive abilities

Strata	Intelligence/Abilities
Top	General intelligence (g)
Middle	Specific abilities that include fluid and crystallized intelligence (e.g., processing speed, general reasoning ability, general world knowledge)
Bottom	Very specific abilities (e.g., reading speed, mechanical knowledge)

Learners may be more intelligent in some domains than in others.

In contrast to a multi-layer view of intelligence is a **multiple intelligences theory**—one in which people can be more or less intelligent in distinctly different ways. For example, psychologist Robert Sternberg has proposed a *triarchic* model of intelligence in which people vary with respect to three relatively independent types of thinking. *Analytical intelligence* involves making sense of, analyzing, contrasting, and evaluating the kinds of information and problems often seen in academic settings and on intelligence tests. *Creative intelligence* involves imagination, invention, and synthesis of ideas within the context of new situations (recall the discussion of creativity in Chapter 3). *Practical intelligence* involves applying knowledge and skills effectively to manage and respond to everyday problems and social situations.[78]

Another multiple intelligences theory is that of Howard Gardner, who suggests that humans can differ with respect to eight distinct abilities.[79] Because of this theory's popularity with educators, we've summarized Gardner's eight intelligences in Table 6.4. (Gardner suggests that there may also be a ninth, *existential* intelligence dedicated to philosophical and spiritual issues, but he acknowledges that he's found only limited evidence for it,[80] and so the table doesn't include it.) Gardner's theory gives us optimism that most learners might be fairly intelligent in at least one area, perhaps showing exceptional promise in language, math, music, or athletics. In the opening case study, Lupita reveals an ability that Gardner would identify as *interpersonal intelligence:* She correctly interprets an adult's subtle message, persuades one classmate to finish his work, and skillfully assists two others as they struggle with puzzles.

Gardner presents some evidence to support the existence of multiple intelligences. For example, he describes people who are quite skilled in one domain (e.g., composing music) and yet have seemingly average abilities in other domains. Also, people who suffer brain damage may lose abilities related to only one intelligence (e.g., they lose only their language skills). However, some psychologists don't believe that Gardner's evidence is sufficiently compelling to support the notion of eight truly independent abilities, in part because of all the existing evidence for a *g* factor

[75] P. L. Ackerman & Lohman, 2006; Carroll, 1993, 2003; D. P. Flanagan & Ortiz, 2001; Horn, 2008.

[76] J. J. Evans, Floyd, McGrew, & Leforgee, 2001; L. Phelps, McGrew, Knopik, & Ford, 2005; B. E. Proctor, Floyd, & Shaver, 2005.

[77] Roberts & Lipnevich, 2012.

[78] Sternberg, 1998, 2004; Sternberg et al., 2000.

[79] Gardner, 1983, 1998, 1999.

[80] Gardner, 2000a, 2003.

Table 6.4 • Gardner's Multiple Intelligences

TYPE OF INTELLIGENCE	EXAMPLES OF RELEVANT BEHAVIORS
Linguistic intelligence: Ability to use language effectively	• Making persuasive arguments • Writing poetry • Noticing subtle nuances in word meanings
Logical-mathematical intelligence: Ability to reason logically, especially in mathematics and science	• Solving mathematical problems quickly • Generating mathematical proofs • Formulating and testing hypotheses about observed phenomena[a]
Spatial intelligence: Ability to notice details of what one sees and to imagine and manipulate visual objects in one's mind	• Conjuring up mental images • Drawing a visual likeness of an object • Seeing subtle differences among visually similar objects
Musical intelligence: Ability to create, comprehend, and appreciate music	• Playing a musical instrument • Composing a musical work • Identifying the underlying structure of music
Bodily-kinesthetic intelligence: Ability to use one's body skillfully	• Dancing • Playing basketball • Performing pantomime
Interpersonal intelligence: Ability to notice subtle aspects of other people's behaviors	• Reading other people's moods • Detecting other people's underlying intentions and desires • Using knowledge of others to influence their thoughts and behaviors
Intrapersonal intelligence: Awareness of one's own feelings, motives, and desires	• Discriminating among such similar emotions as sadness and regret • Identifying the motives guiding one's own behavior • Using self-knowledge to interact more effectively with others
Naturalist intelligence: Ability to recognize patterns in nature and differences among various life-forms and natural objects	• Identifying members of particular plant or animal species • Classifying natural forms (e.g., rocks, types of mountains) • Applying one's knowledge of nature in such activities as farming, landscaping, or animal training

[a]This example may remind you of Piaget's theory of cognitive development. Many of the stage-specific characteristics that Piaget described fall within the realm of logical-mathematical intelligence.
Sources: Gardner, 1983, 1999.

Close attention to detail in 10-year-old Luther's drawing of a plant suggests some talent in what Gardner calls *naturalist* intelligence.

in intelligence.[81] Other psychologists agree that people might have a variety of relatively independent abilities but argue for different distinctions than those Gardner makes (e.g., recall the second-stratum abilities in the Cattell–Horn–Carroll theory). Still others reject the idea that abilities in certain domains, such as music or body movement, are really "intelligences" per se.[82]

Regardless of the exact structure of intelligence—if, in fact, a precise structure could ever be pinned down—two things are clear. First, intelligence is a very complex, multifaceted entity. And second, any single learner is likely to be more intelligent in some ways than in others.

Intelligence is a product of both inherited characteristics and environmental influences.

At least as it's measured by IQ tests, intelligence does appear to have some basis in the brain.[83] For example, compared with their average-IQ peers, children with high IQ scores show a prolonged period of development in the cortex. A high level of intelligence also seems to involve ongoing, efficient interactions among numerous brain regions. It's highly likely that these differences are partly the result of heredity and the maturational changes that genetics drives.[84] However, children don't inherit a single "IQ gene" that determines their intellectual ability. Instead, they inherit a variety of characteristics that in one way or another affect their cognitive development and intellectual abilities.[85]

[81] N. Brody, 1992; Corno et al., 2002; Kail, 1998; Waterhouse, 2006.

[82] Bracken, McCallum, & Shaughnessy, 1999; Sattler, 2001.

[83] Burgaleta, Johnson, Waber, Colom, & Karama, 2014; Yokota et al., 2015.

[84] Jung & Haier, 2007; Kovas, Malykh, & Petrill, 2014; Rizzi & Posthuma, 2013; Shaw et al., 2006.

[85] Kovas, Petrill, & Plomin, 2007; Kovas & Plomin, 2007; Meinz & Hambrick, 2010; Shaw et al., 2006.

Environmental factors influence intelligence as well, sometimes for the better and sometimes for the worse. Poor nutrition in the early years of development (including the months between conception and birth) leads to lower IQ scores, as does a mother's excessive use of alcohol during pregnancy.[86] Attending school has a consistently positive effect on IQ scores.[87] Moving a child from a neglectful, impoverished home environment to a more nurturing, stimulating one (e.g., through adoption or foster parenting) can result in IQ gains of 15 points or more.[88] Furthermore, researchers are finding that, worldwide, there has been a slow but steady increase in people's performance on intelligence tests—a trend that's probably the result of better nutrition, smaller family sizes, better schooling, increasing cognitive stimulation (through increased access to television, reading materials, etc.), and other improvements in people's environments.[89]

How *much* of a role do heredity and environment each play in the development of intelligence? In previous decades this nature-versus-nurture question has been a source of considerable controversy. But in fact, as noted earlier in the chapter, genetic and environmental factors interact in their influences on cognitive development and intelligence in ways that are virtually impossible to separate. For example, as you should recall, genes require reasonable environmental support to do their work. In an extremely impoverished environment—one with a lack of adequate nutrition and stimulation—heredity may have little to say about children's intellectual growth, but under better circumstances, it can have a significant influence.[90]

Intelligence may take different forms at different age levels.

Some psychologists working in the area of giftedness have suggested that not only is intelligence somewhat specific to particular domains but also that its basic nature changes with age and experience. From their perspective, the developmental course of exceptional abilities and talents might be as follows:[91]

1. Initially (typically in childhood), people show exceptional *potential* in a certain domain, perhaps in reading, math, or music.

2. With appropriate instruction, guidance, and practice opportunities, people show exceptional *achievement* in the domain.

3. If people continue to pursue the domain and practice domain-specific tasks over a lengthy time period (typically into adulthood), they may eventually gain considerable *expertise and eminence*, to the point that their accomplishments are widely recognized.

Here, then, we see a very dynamic view of intelligence: Although its roots may be in certain natural endowments, over the long run, intelligence requires both environmental nurturance and personal perseverance.[92]

Learners may have specific cognitive styles and dispositions that predispose them to think and act in more or less intelligent ways.

Most measures of intelligence focus on specific things that a person *can* do, with little consideration of what a person is *likely* to do. For instance, intelligence tests don't evaluate the extent to which learners are motivated to accomplish certain goals or willing to actively take charge of and self-regulate their own learning. Yet such inclinations are sometimes just as important as intellectual ability in determining success in academic and real-world tasks, as you will remember from Chapter 3 and Chapter 5.[93]

---

[86] Benton, 2008; D'Amato, Chitooran, & Whitten, 1992; Neisser et al., 1996; Ricciuti, 1993.

[87] Ceci, 2003; Gustafsson, 2008; Nisbett et al., 2012.

[88] Duyme, Dumaret, & Tomkiewicz, 1999; Nisbett et al., 2012; Scarr & Weinberg, 1976; van IJzendoorn, Juffer, & Klein Poelhuis, 2005.

[89] Daley, Whaley, Sigman, Espinosa, & Neumann, 2003; Flynn, 2003, 2007; E. Hunt, 2008; Neisser, 1998b; Nisbett et al., 2012.

[90] Ceci, 2003; Nisbett et al., 2012; Turkheimer, Haley, Waldron, D'Onofrio, & Gottesman, 2003.

[91] Dai, 2010; Subotnik, Olszewski-Kubilus, & Worrell, 2011.

[92] Dai, 2010; Subotnik et al., 2011.

[93] Duckworth & Seligman, 2005; Kuhn, 2006; Luciana, Conklin, Hooper, & Yarger, 2005; D. N. Perkins, Tishman, Ritchhart, Donis, & Andrade, 2000.

Students with the same intelligence levels often approach classroom tasks and think about classroom topics differently. Some of these individual differences are **cognitive styles**—characteristic ways in which people tend to think about a task and process new information—over which learners have little or no conscious control. Other individual differences are **dispositions**—general inclinations to approach and think about learning and problem-solving tasks in a particular way—that students intentionally bring to bear on their efforts to master school subject matter. You don't need to agonize over the distinction between these two concepts because their meanings overlap considerably. Both involve not only specific cognitive tendencies but also personality characteristics. However, dispositions also have a motivational component—an I-*want*-to-do-it-this-way quality.[94]

Over the years, psychologists and educators have examined a variety of cognitive styles (some have used the term *learning styles*) and dispositions. The traits they've identified and the instruments they've developed to assess these traits don't always hold up under the scrutiny of other researchers.[95] Furthermore, tailoring particular instructional strategies to students' self-reported styles—which in some cases are nothing more than students' *preferences*—doesn't necessarily enhance academic achievement.[96]

A dimension of cognitive style worthy of attention, however, is a distinction between analytic and holistic thinking.[97] In *analytic* thinking, learners tend to break new stimuli and tasks into their component parts and to see these parts somewhat independently of their context (this style should remind you of Sternberg's analytical intelligence). In contrast, *holistic* thinking involves perceiving situations as integrated, indivisible wholes that are closely tied to their context. One way of thinking isn't necessarily better than the other; instead, the two cognitive styles are likely to be adaptive in different situations. Researchers have observed that cultures differ somewhat in their focus on analytic versus holistic thinking, as you can see in the Cultural Considerations box "Cultural Differences in Reasoning Skills, Intelligence, and Cognitive Style."

Meanwhile, researchers have found that certain dispositions are clearly beneficial for classroom learning:[98]

think about it
Which of these dispositions characterize your own behaviors and thinking?

- **Stimulation seeking:** Eagerly interacting with one's physical and social environment in order to gain new experiences and information
- **Need for cognition:** Frequently seeking and engaging in challenging cognitive tasks
- **Conscientiousness:** Consistently addressing assigned tasks in a careful, focused, and responsible manner
- **Critical thinking:** Regularly evaluating information or arguments in terms of their accuracy, credibility, and worth, rather than accepting them at face value (recall how Chapter 3 describes critical thinking as a disposition as well as a cognitive process)
- **Open-mindedness:** Flexibly considering alternative perspectives and multiple sources of evidence and suspending judgment for a time, rather than leaping to immediate conclusions

Such dispositions are often positively correlated with students' learning and achievement, and many theorists have suggested that they play a causal role in what and how much students learn. In fact, dispositions sometimes "overrule" intelligence in their influence on long-term achievement.[99] For example, learners with a high need for cognition learn more from what they read, are more likely to base conclusions on sound evidence and logical reasoning, and are more likely to undergo conceptual change when it's warranted.[100] And learners who critically evaluate new

---

[94] Kuhn, 2001a Messick, 1994b; D. N. Perkins & Ritchhart, 2004; Stanovich, 1999; L.-F. Zhang & Sternberg, 2006.

[95] Cassidy, 2004; Krätzig & Arbuthnott, 2006; Messick, 1994b.

[96] Curry, 1990; R. E. Mayer & Massa, 2003; Nieto & Bode, 2008; Pashler, McDaniel, Rohrer, & Bjork, 2009.

[97] Norenzayan, Choi, & Peng, 2007; Riding & Cheema, 1991; L.-F. Zhang & Sternberg, 2006.

[98] Cacioppo, Petty, Feinstein, & Jarvis, 1996; DeBacker & Crowson, 2009; Halpern, 2008; Hampson, 2008; Kardash & Scholes, 1996; P. M. King & Kitchener, 2002; G. Matthews, Zeidner, & Roberts, 2006; Raine, Reynolds, & Venables, 2002; Southerland & Sinatra, 2003; Trautwein, Lüdtke, Schnyder, & Niggli, 2006; R. F. West, Toplak, & Stanovich, 2008.

[99] Dai & Sternberg, 2004; Kuhn & Franklin, 2006; D. N. Perkins & Ritchhart, 2004.

[100] Cacioppo et al., 1996; Dai & Wang, 2007; P. K. Murphy & Mason, 2006.

CULTURAL CONSIDERATIONS

Cultural Differences in Reasoning Skills, Intelligence, and Cognitive Style

Researchers have found that the acquisition of at least one key aspect of concrete operational thinking—conservation—and several aspects of formal operational thinking depend partly on whether a cultural group nurtures them. Furthermore, cultures differ somewhat in their views of what it means to be an "intelligent" person and in their tendencies to think analytically or holistically.

CONSERVATION. Imagine two equal-sized balls of clay, as shown here.

You change the shape of one ball, perhaps flattening it into a pancake or rolling it into a sausage shape. Rather than asking a child if the two pieces of clay *weigh* the same (this would be the conservation-of-weight task shown in Figure 6.6), you simply ask whether the two pieces have the same *amount*. On average, school children in Europe and North America master such *conservation of substance* with clay at around age 7. In one classic study, however, Mexican children whose families regularly made pottery mastered this task by age 6.[a] Apparently, making pottery requires children to make frequent judgments about needed quantities of clay, and these judgments must be fairly accurate regardless of the clay's specific shape. Yet in other cultures, especially in those where children neither attend school nor work at activities that require keeping track of quantity, conservation may appear several years later than it does in mainstream Western societies.[b]

FORMAL OPERATIONAL REASONING SKILLS. In some cultures, formal operational thinking skills have little relevance to people's daily lives and activities.[c] For example, let's return to the second problem in the earlier "Beings and Basketballs" exercise:

If all children are basketballs,
And if all basketballs are jellybeans,
Then must all children be jellybeans?

Following rules of formal logic—that is, if we assume the first two premises to be true—the answer is *yes*. Such reasoning

about hypothetical and perhaps contrary-to-fact ideas is taught and encouraged in many schools in mainstream Western societies, especially within the context of math and science instruction. But in numerous other cultures, including many modern Asian societies, logical reasoning tends to be rooted in people's everyday, concrete realities. Adults in these cultures may find little purpose in hypothetical and contrary-to-fact reasoning and so don't always nurture it in their schools or elsewhere.[d]

In some cultures, aspects of formal operational thought conflict with people's worldviews.[e] For instance, whereas most people in mainstream Western culture place great value on the scientific method—forming hypotheses, collecting evidence to test them, separating and controlling variables, and so on—people in certain other cultures tend to depend on other sources of information, perhaps authority figures, holy scriptures, or general cultural folklore as a more trusted means of determining what is "truth."

VIEWS AND MANIFESTATIONS OF INTELLIGENCE. In North America and western Europe, intelligence is thought of primarily as an ability that influences children's academic achievement and adults' professional success. But this view is hardly universal. Many Hispanic, African, Asian, and Native American cultures think of intelligence as involving social as well as academic skills—maintaining harmonious interpersonal relationships, working effectively with others to accomplish challenging tasks, and so on.[f] And in Buddhist and Confucian societies in the Far East (e.g., China, Taiwan), intelligence also involves acquiring strong moral values and making meaningful contributions to society.[g]

Cultural groups differ, too, in the behaviors they believe reflect intelligence. For instance, on many traditional intelligence tests, speed is valued: Children score higher if they answer questions quickly as well as correctly. Yet people in some cultures tend to value thoroughness over speed and may even be suspicious of tasks completed very quickly.[h] As another example, many people in mainstream Western culture consider

strong verbal skills to be a sign of high intelligence. In contrast, many Japanese and many Inuit people of northern Quebec interpret excessive chattiness as a sign of immaturity or low intelligence.[i] One researcher working at an Inuit school in northern Quebec asked a teacher about a boy whose language seemed unusually advanced for his age-group. The teacher replied:

> Do you think he might have a learning problem? Some of these children who don't have such high intelligence have trouble stopping themselves. They don't know when to stop talking.[j]

Later in the chapter, we'll identify reasons why intelligence tests are, at best, only imperfect measures of *any* learner's intellectual abilities, and so teachers must be extremely cautious in interpreting the scores these tests yield. Clearly, extra caution is warranted when children come from diverse cultural backgrounds.

ANALYTIC VERSUS HOLISTIC THINKING. On average, people from mainstream Western culture tend to be analytic thinkers, whereas people from East Asian cultures think more holistically.[k] Certainly logical and scientific reasoning requires analytic thinking, but holistic thinking can help learners identify associations and relationships among seemingly very different phenomena. For example, holistically minded Chinese scientists identified the underlying cause of the ocean's tides—the moon's gravitational pull on any large body of water—many centuries before more narrowly focused, earth-centered European scientists did.[l]

[a] Price-Williams, Gordon, & Ramirez, 1969.
[b] Fahrmeier, 1978; Morra et al., 2008.
[c] M. Cole, 1990; J. G. Miller, 1997.
[d] Norenzayan et al., 2007.
[e] Kağitçibaşi, 2007; Losh, 2003; Norenzayan et al., 2007.
[f] Greenfield et al., 2006; J. Li & Fischer, 2004; Sternberg, 2004, 2007.
[g] J. Li & Fischer, 2004; Sternberg, 2003.
[h] Sternberg, 2007.
[i] Crago, 1988; Minami & McCabe, 1996; Sternberg, 2003.
[j] Crago, 1988, p. 219.
[k] Norenzayan et al., 2007; Park & Huang, 2010; Varnum, Grossmann, Kitayama, & Nisbett, 2010.
[l] Nisbett, 2009.

evidence and are open-minded about diverse perspectives show more advanced reasoning capabilities and achieve at higher levels.[101]

Researchers don't yet have a good understanding of how various cognitive styles and dispositions originate. Perhaps inherited temperamental differences (e.g., in stimulation seeking) are involved.[102] Epistemic beliefs about the underlying nature of knowledge—for instance, the belief that knowledge is fixed and unchanging, on the one hand, or dynamic and continually evolving, on the other—may also play a role.[103] And almost certainly teachers' actions and the general classroom atmosphere they create—for example, whether students are encouraged to pursue intriguing topics, take risks, and think critically—make a difference.[104]

Learners act more intelligently when they have physical or social support for their efforts.

Implicit in our discussion so far has been the assumption that intelligent behavior is something that individuals engage in with little or no help from the objects or people around them. But let's return to the concept of *distributed cognition,* discussed previously in Chapter 4: Learners can think and perform more effectively when they can offload, or *distribute,* part of their cognitive load onto something or someone else. Some psychologists instead use the term **distributed intelligence** to refer to this idea; in many respects, the two terms are synonymous.[105] More specifically, learners can "distribute" a challenging task in at least three ways. First, they can use physical tools, especially technology (e.g., calculators, computers), to handle and manipulate large amounts of information. Second, they can mentally encode and manipulate the situations they encounter using various symbolic systems—words, charts, diagrams, mathematical equations, and so on—and other cognitive tools their culture provides. And third, they can work with other people to explore ideas and solve problems. When learners work together on complex, challenging tasks and problems, they often think more intelligently than any one of them could think alone. In fact, learners sometimes teach one another strategies and ways of thinking that can help each of them to think even *more* intelligently on future occasions.[106]

From a distributed-intelligence perspective, intelligence isn't an immutable characteristic that learners "carry around" with them, nor is it something that can be easily measured and then summarized with one or more test scores. Instead, it's a highly variable, context-specific ability that increases when appropriate environmental, cultural, and social supports are available.

> Although it's difficult to define intelligence precisely, psychologists have identified several characteristics of intelligence, including that it's adaptive and culture specific, and that it involves the use of prior knowledge and many different cognitive processes. Intelligence isn't necessarily a single, general entity that students "have" in varying degrees; instead, students may perform more intelligently in some domains than in others. Furthermore, children's and adolescents' intelligence levels (and IQ scores) are clearly impacted by environmental conditions—a fact that should give teachers cause for optimism about the impact they can have on their students' intellectual growth. In the hotlinked Self-Check quiz and Application Exercise that follow, you can check and apply your understandings related to Big Idea 6.4:
>
> *Although children in any age-group differ somewhat in intelligence, cognitive styles, and dispositions, appropriately supportive environments can significantly enhance these abilities and characteristics.*
>
> MyEdLab **Self-Check 6.4**
>
> MyEdLab **Application Exercise 6.4.** In this exercise, you will identify some teaching strategies that a teacher uses to promote productive dispositions and thinking.

---

[101] DeBacker & Crowson, 2009; G. Matthews et al., 2006; Stanovich, 1999.
[102] Raine et al., 2002; Rothbart, 2007.
[103] P. M. King & Kitchener, 2002; Kuhn, 2001b; Mason, 2003.
[104] Flum & Kaplan, 2006; Gresalfi, 2009; Kuhn, 2001b, 2006.
[105] Barab & Plucker, 2002; Hutchins, 1995; T. Martin, 2009; Pea, 1993; D. N. Perkins, 1995; B. Rhodes, 2008; Salomon, 1993.
[106] Applebee, Langer, Nystrand, & Gamoran, 2003; A.-M. Clark et al., 2003; Salomon, 1993; Spörer & Brunstein, 2009.

6.5 ADDRESSING STUDENTS' DEVELOPMENTAL NEEDS

Big Idea 6.5 As effective teachers plan and implement instruction, they accommodate students' developmental differences and diversity, with the ultimate goal of promoting all students' cognitive and intellectual development.

As we've examined principles of cognitive development and intelligence, we've discovered that learners of different ages—and to some degree learners of the *same* age—have different thinking and reasoning capabilities. We've also discovered that environmental factors can definitely impact learners' thinking and reasoning capabilities for the better. In this final section of the chapter, we look at (1) how to accommodate developmental differences and diversity in the classroom and (2) how to foster cognitive development in *all* children and adolescents.

Accommodating Developmental Differences and Diversity

Think, for a moment, about your own experiences in the early elementary grades. What topics did you study, and what instructional strategies did your teachers use to teach those topics? Now think about your high school years. In what ways were the subject matter and instructional methods different from those in elementary school? Certainly, many differences come to mind. For example, in the early elementary grades you probably focused on basic knowledge and skills, such as letter–sound correspondences, short-story reading, capitalization and punctuation, and addition and subtraction of two-digit numbers. Your teachers probably provided a lot of structure and guidance, giving you many concrete tasks through which you could practice and eventually master certain information and procedures. By high school, however, you were studying complex topics—biological classification systems, historical events, symbolism in literature and poetry, manipulation of algebraic equations, and so on—that were abstract and multifaceted, and your teachers put much of the burden of mastering those topics on *you*.

Such differences reflect the fact that classroom instruction must be *developmentally appropriate:* It must take into account the characteristics and abilities that learners of a particular age-group are likely to have. Yet as we've discovered, learners develop at different rates, and so instruction must also allow for considerable diversity at any single grade level. The following recommendations can help teachers in their efforts to accommodate developmental and individual differences in the classroom.

Explore students' reasoning with problem-solving tasks and probing questions.

In his work with children and adolescents, Piaget pioneered a technique known as the **clinical method**. In particular, he would give a child a problem and probe the child's reasoning about it through a series of individually tailored follow-up questions. We saw an example of the clinical method in the interview with 6-year-old Brian presented earlier. An adult asked Brian whether a set of 12 wooden beads—some brown, some white—had more wooden beads or more brown beads. When Brian responded, "More brown ones," the adult continued to press Brian (e.g., by asking him to draw a brown-beads necklace and a wooden-beads necklace) to be sure Brian truly believed there were more brown beads and possibly also to create disequilibrium.

By presenting a variety of Piagetian tasks involving either concrete or formal operational thinking skills—for instance, tasks involving class inclusion, conservation, separation and control of variables, or proportional reasoning—teachers can gain valuable insights into how students think and reason. Typically, when teachers use the clinical method for assessment purposes, they don't give feedback about right and wrong answers. Instead, they simply ask a variety of questions to determine how a child interprets a situation. Sometimes they also ask the child to respond to alternative interpretations.[107] For example, if a child says that a tall, thin glass and a short, wider one contain the same amounts of water, a teacher might say:

> The other day a student told me that the tall glass contains more water because the water in that one is higher than it is in the short glass. What do you think about that?

---

[107] diSessa, 2007.

Formulating follow-up questions that effectively probe a child's reasoning often comes only with considerable experience, however. Figure 6.12 presents a procedure that a novice interviewer might use in probing students' reasoning related to *conservation of displaced volume,* a fairly advanced form of conservation that, in Piaget's theory, emerges sometime around puberty.

The clinical method isn't limited to traditional Piagetian reasoning tasks, however. On the contrary, it can be used for a wide variety of topics and skills. For example, a teacher might present various kinds of maps (e.g., a road map of Arizona, a bus-route map for Chicago, a three-dimensional relief map of a mountainous area) and ask students to interpret what they see. Children in the primary grades (especially kindergartners and first graders) are apt to interpret many map symbols in a concrete fashion, perhaps thinking that roads depicted in red are *actually* red. They

---

FIGURE 6.12 Conservation of displaced volume: An example of how a teacher might probe a student's reasoning using Piaget's clinical method

Materials

2 glasses containing equal amounts of water
2 balls of clay equal in size and smaller in diameter than the water glasses
2 rubber bands
1 plastic knife

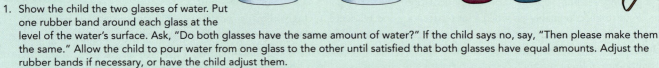

Procedure

1. Show the child the two glasses of water. Put one rubber band around each glass at the level of the water's surface. Ask, "Do both glasses have the same amount of water?" If the child says no, say, "Then please make them the same." Allow the child to pour water from one glass to the other until satisfied that both glasses have equal amounts. Adjust the rubber bands if necessary, or have the child adjust them.
2. Show the child the two balls of clay. Ask, "Are these balls of clay the same size?" If the child says no, say, "Then please make them the same size." Allow the child to add to or subtract from one or both of the balls until satisfied that the two are equal.
3. Being sure that the child is watching, place one ball of clay in one of the glasses of water. Say, "See how the water went up when I did that. Let's move the rubber band to the place where the surface of the water is." Move the rubber band appropriately.
4. Take the other ball of clay and other glass of water. Say, "I'm going to cut this ball of clay into several pieces." Use the plastic knife to cut the ball into four or five pieces. Ask, "How much do you think the water will rise when I drop all this clay into the glass? Move the rubber band to the level where you think the water's surface will be." Allow the child to adjust the rubber band until satisfied with its location. If the child moves the rubber band to the same level as the other rubber band, proceed with Steps 5a–7a. If the child moves it to a higher or lower level than the other rubber band, proceed with Steps 5b–6b.

If the child has predicted an equal rise in height:

5a. Say, "Tell me why you think the water will rise to that spot." Examples of possible responses are
   • "It's the same amount of clay."
   • "I don't know. I just guessed."
6a. Drop all the pieces of clay into the water. Say, "You were right. Are you surprised?" Examples of possible responses are
   • "Not surprised. Even though you cut the clay up, there's still the same amount."
   • "Surprised, because I wasn't really sure it would go there."
7a. If the child was surprised, ask, "Why do you think it rose to that level?" Listen to determine whether the child now understands that the same amount of clay should, regardless of the number of pieces, displace the same amount of water.

If the child has predicted an unequal rise in height:

5b. Say, "Tell me why you think the water will rise to that spot." Examples of possible responses are
   • "There's less clay."
   • "There are more pieces."
   • "I don't know. I just guessed."
6b. Drop all the pieces of clay into the water. Say, "You weren't quite right. Look, it rose the same amount of water as in the other glass. Why do you think it rose to that level?" Examples of possible responses are
   • "Even though you cut the clay up, there's still the same amount as in the other ball."
   • "It doesn't make sense because the smaller pieces should take up less room in the glass."
   • "I don't know."

Interpretation

Children who have fully achieved conservation of displaced volume should (1) predict that the water in the second glass will rise to the same level as that in the first glass and (2) justify the prediction by saying that both the water and clay in the two glasses will be the same. Children who are on the verge of achieving conservation of displaced volume might either (1) predict the correct level without initially being able to justify it or (2) initially make an incorrect prediction. In either case, however, they should be able to explain the final result by acknowledging that, despite differences in appearance, the clay in the two glasses displaces the same amount of water. Children who can neither make a correct prediction nor explain the final result are not yet able to reason correctly about problems involving conservation of displaced volume.

might also have difficulty with the scale of a map, perhaps thinking that a line can't be a road because "it's not fat enough for two cars to go on" or that a mountain depicted by a bump on a relief map isn't really a mountain because "it's not high enough."[108] Understanding the concept of the *scale* of a map requires proportional reasoning—an ability that students don't fully acquire until adolescence—and so it's hardly surprising that young children would be confused by it.

Interpret intelligence test results cautiously.

As we've seen, intelligence tests are simply collections of questions and tasks that psychologists have developed and continue to revise over the years to get a handle on how well children and adolescents think, reason, and learn. These tests predict school achievement to some extent, but they're hardly magical instruments that can mysteriously determine a learner's true intelligence—if, in fact, such a thing as "true" intelligence even exists. Whenever teachers are aware of IQ scores that have been obtained for particular students, they should keep the following points in mind:[109]

- Different kinds of intelligence tests may yield somewhat different scores.
- A student's performance on any test is inevitably affected by temporary factors present at the time the test is taken—general health, mood, motivation, time of day, distracting circumstances, and so on. Such factors are especially influential for young children, who are apt to have high energy levels, short attention spans, and little interest in sitting still for more than a few minutes. (Here we're talking about a test's *reliability,* a concept we'll consider in Chapter 10.)
- Test items typically focus on skills that are important in mainstream Western culture, especially in school settings. The items don't necessarily tap into skills that might be more highly valued in other contexts or cultures.
- Some students may be unfamiliar with the content or types of tasks involved in particular test items and, as a result, perform poorly on those items.
- Students with limited English proficiency (e.g., recent immigrants) are at an obvious disadvantage when an intelligence test is administered in English.
- Some students (e.g., students of color who want to avoid being perceived as conforming to "White" culture) may not be motivated to perform at their best.
- IQ scores have a limited "shelf life." They predict school achievement over the short run (e.g., over the next two to three years) but not necessarily over the long run, especially when the scores are obtained during the preschool or early elementary years.

Used within the context of other information, IQ scores can, in many cases, give a general idea of a student's current cognitive functioning. But as you can see from the limitations just listed, teachers should always maintain a healthy degree of skepticism about the accuracy of IQ scores, especially when students come from diverse cultural backgrounds, have acquired only limited proficiency in English, or were fairly young when the scores were obtained.

Look for signs of exceptional abilities and talents.

Earlier we discovered that a learner benefits most from tasks he or she can accomplish only with assistance—tasks that are in the learner's *zone of proximal development.* Because different students are at different points in their cognitive development, they're apt to have different ZPDs, and almost any classroom is likely to have one or more students whose ability levels far surpass those of their peers. Although experts disagree about how such **giftedness** should be defined and identified, it's probably the result of both genetic and environmental factors.[110]

Students who are gifted tend to be among our schools' greatest underachievers. When required to progress at the same rate as their nongifted peers, they achieve at levels far short of their capabilities. Furthermore, many students with special gifts and talents become bored or frustrated

---

[108] Liben & Myers, 2007, p. 202.

[109] Bartholomew, 2004; Hayslip, 1994; Neisser et al., 1996; Ogbu, 1994; D. N. Perkins, 1995; Sattler, 2001; Stanovich, 2009; Sternberg, 2005, 2007; Zigler & Finn-Stevenson, 1992.

[110] Dai, 2010; Renzulli, 2002; Simonton, 2001; Winner, 2000b.

when school assignments don't challenge them, and others become so accustomed to the "easy A" that they have trouble coping with the mistakes they're likely to make when they venture into new areas.[111]

The traditional approach to identifying giftedness is to use IQ scores, perhaps with 125 or 130 as a cutoff point. Yet some students may be gifted in only one domain—say, in science or creative writing—and tests of general intelligence might not be especially helpful in identifying these students.[112] And for a variety of reasons, students from some minority-group backgrounds don't perform as well on intelligence tests as students raised in mainstream Western culture.[113] Students from some cultures may have had little experience with common intelligence test items, such as reasoning about self-contained logical problems (recall the children–basketballs–jellybeans problem) or finding patterns in geometric figures.[114] Other students may try to hide their talents in order to avoid ridicule by classmates who don't value academic achievement.[115]

It's critical, then, that educators not rely solely on intelligence tests to identify students who may need a more challenging curriculum than their peers. The following are examples of traits teachers might look for:[116]

- Advanced vocabulary, language, and reading skills
- Extensive general knowledge about the world
- Ability to learn more quickly, easily, and independently than peers
- Advanced and efficient cognitive processes and learning strategies
- Flexibility, originality, and resourcefulness in thinking and problem solving
- Ability to apply concepts and ideas to new, seemingly unrelated situations
- High standards for performance (sometimes to the point of unrealistic perfectionism)
- High motivation to accomplish challenging tasks; boredom during easy tasks
- Above-average social development and emotional adjustment (although a few extremely gifted students may have difficulties because they're so *very* different from their peers)

Researchers and expert teachers have found a variety of instructional strategies to be effective for students who are gifted. Common suggestions are presented and illustrated in the Classroom Strategies box "Working with Students Who Have Exceptional Abilities and Talents."

Consult with specialists if children show significant delays in development.

Whereas some children and adolescents show exceptionally advanced development, others show unusual *delays* in development. When delays appear only in a specific aspect of cognitive functioning, perhaps learners haven't had sufficient experience to develop it or perhaps a *learning disability* is present. In contrast, learners with a general **intellectual disability**—occasionally referred to as *mental retardation*—show developmental delays in most aspects of their academic and social functioning.[117] More specifically, these learners exhibit *both* of the following characteristics:[118]

- **Significantly below-average general intelligence:** They have intelligence test scores that are quite low—usually no higher than 70, reflecting performance in the bottom 2% of their age-group. In addition, they learn slowly and show consistently poor achievement in virtually all academic subject areas.

---

[111] Dai, 2010; Mendaglio, 2010; Parker, 1997.

[112] D. J. Matthews, 2009; Moran & Gardner, 2006.

[113] McLoyd, 1998; Neisser, 1998a; Walton & Spencer, 2009.

[114] Nisbett, 2009; Rogoff, 2003; Sternberg, 2005.

[115] Dweck, 2009; Ogbu, 2008a.

[116] Cornell et al., 1990; Dai, 2010; Mendaglio, 2010; Parker, 1997; Shavinina & Ferrari, 2004; Steiner & Carr, 2003; Subotnik et al., 2011; Winner, 2000a, 2000b.

[117] Many special educators now prefer the term *intellectual disability* over the term *mental retardation* (e.g., Luckasson et al., 2002), and in 2007 the American Association on Mental Retardation changed its name to the American Association on Intellectual and Developmental Disabilities.

[118] Luckasson et al., 2002.

CLASSROOM STRATEGIES

Working with Students Who Have Exceptional Abilities and Talents

- **Individualize instruction in accordance with students' specific talents.**
  A middle school student with exceptional reading skills and an interest in Shakespeare is assigned several Shakespearean plays. After reading each play, he discusses it with his class's teaching intern, who is an English major at a nearby university.

- **Form study groups of students who have similar abilities and interests.**
  A music teacher provides weekly instruction to a quartet of exceptionally talented music students.

- **Teach complex cognitive skills within the context of specific school topics rather than separately from the regular school curriculum.**
  A teacher has an advanced science study group conduct a series of experiments related to a single topic. To promote scientific reasoning and critical thinking, the teacher gives the students several questions they should ask themselves as they conduct these experiments—questions that encourage them to separate and control variables, critically evaluate conclusions, and so on.

- **Provide opportunities for independent study.**
  A second-grade teacher finds educational software through which a mathematically gifted 8-year-old can study decimals, exponents, square roots, and other concepts she appears to be ready to master.

- **Engage students in challenging, multifaceted public service projects (i.e., *service learning*).**
  Three high school students collaborate to identify and collect information about several historical buildings and monuments in their community. They create a flyer that will be used by the local historical society and share it with their classmates as they lead them on a walking tour of these structures.

- **Encourage students to set high goals for themselves.**
  A teacher encourages a student from a lower socioeconomic background to consider going to college and helps the student explore possible sources of financial assistance for higher education.

- **Seek outside resources to help students develop their exceptional talents.**
  A student with an exceptional aptitude for learning foreign languages studies Russian at a local university.

- **Ask students to prepare part of a lesson.**
  A middle school teacher asks a high-ability student to prepare a presentation related to an upcoming class topic.

MyEdLab
Video Example 6.4.

In this video, a teacher discusses some of the ways in which she engages a high-ability student in her class.

Sources: Ambrose, Allen, & Huntley, 1994; Dai, 2010; Hattie, 2009; J. A. Kulik & Kulik, 1997; Lubinski & Bleske-Rechek, 2008; Lupart, 1995; Piirto, 1999; Terry, 2003, 2008 (walking tour example).

- **Deficits in adaptive behavior:** They typically behave in ways that would be expected of much younger children. Their deficits in *adaptive behavior* include limitations in practical intelligence—that is, managing the ordinary activities of daily living—and social intelligence—that is, behaving in culturally appropriate ways in social situations.

The preceding characteristics must be evident in childhood. Thus, a learner who shows them beginning at age 16, perhaps as the result of a serious head injury, would *not* be classified as having an intellectual disability.

Intellectual disabilities are often caused by genetic conditions. For example, they are common in children with Down syndrome, an inherited condition marked by distinctive facial features, shorter-than-average arms and legs, and poor muscle tone. Other intellectual disabilities are due to biological but noninherited causes, such as severe malnutrition or excessive alcohol consumption during the mother's pregnancy or prolonged oxygen deprivation during a difficult birth.[119] In still other situations, environmental factors, such as parental neglect or an extremely

---

[119] Dorris, 1989; Keogh & MacMillan, 1996.

CLASSROOM STRATEGIES

Working with Students Who Have Significant Delays in Cognitive Development

- **Introduce new material at a slower pace, and provide many opportunities for practice.**

  An elementary teacher gives a student only two new addition facts a week because any more than two seem to overwhelm him. Every day, the teacher has the student practice writing the new facts and review the facts learned in preceding weeks.

- **Explain tasks and expected behaviors concretely and in very specific language.**

  An art teacher gives a student explicit training in the steps he needs to take at the end of each painting session: (1) Rinse the paintbrush out at the sink, (2) put the brush and watercolor paints on the shelf in the back room, and (3) put the painting on the counter by the window to dry. Initially, the teacher needs to remind the student of every step in the process. But with time and practice, the student eventually carries out the process independently.

- **Give students explicit guidance about how to study.**

  An elementary teacher tells a student, "When you study a new spelling word, it helps if you repeat the letters out loud while you practice writing the word. Let's try it with *house*, the word you're learning this morning. Watch how I repeat the letters—H…O…U…S…E—as I write the word. Now you try doing what I just did."

- **Encourage independence.**

  A middle school teacher teaches a student how to use her calculator to figure out what she needs to pay for lunch every day. The teacher also gives the student considerable practice in identifying the correct bills and coins to use when paying various amounts.

- **Provide technology that can enhance students' self-reliance.**

  Using a task organizer app on a smartphone (e.g., Visules, Picture Scheduler), a high school life skills teacher creates a sequence of step-by-step pictures that can help a student learn and remember how to cook a hard-boiled egg.

Sources: Feuerstein, Feuerstein, & Falik, 2010; K. L. Fletcher & Bray, 1995; Heward, 2009; Patton, Blackbourn, & Fad, 1996; Prout, 2009; Turnbull et al., 2010.

MyEdLab

Video Example 6.5.

Although students with intellectual disabilities experience difficulties in most or all parts of the curriculum and exhibit deficits in adaptive behavior, many of these students are sociable and eager to fit in at school. What factors in Trista's school and home environments might have facilitated her social success in high school?

impoverished and unstimulating home environment, may be at fault.[120] Although usually a long-term condition, an intellectual disability isn't necessarily a lifelong disability, especially when its cause is environmental rather than genetic.[121]

Severe intellectual disabilities are usually identified long before children begin kindergarten or first grade. However, mild cases can go undetected until school age. Teachers who suspect that a student has significant delays in cognitive development and adaptive behavior should definitely consult with specialists trained in identifying and working with children who have special educational needs.

Some students with mild intellectual disabilities spend part or all of the school day in general education classrooms. They're apt to have poor reading and language skills, less general knowledge about the world, poor memory for new information, difficulty with abstract ideas, and few (if any) metacognitive skills.[122] Nevertheless, they can make considerable academic progress when instruction is appropriately paced and provides a lot of guidance and support. The Classroom Strategies box "Working with Students Who Have Significant Delays in Cognitive Development" offers suggestions for working effectively with these students.

Fostering Cognitive Development in All Students

The findings of Vygotsky, Piaget, and contemporary developmental researchers yield numerous strategies for fostering children's and adolescents' cognitive development. The following recommendations summarize many of these strategies.

Encourage play activities.

Vygotsky suggested that play is hardly the frivolous activity it appears to be. Quite the contrary, play enables children to stretch their abilities in new ways.[123] For example, as a kindergartner, the son of one of us authors often played "restaurant" with his friend Scott. In a corner of the

---

[120] Batshaw & Shapiro, 2002; D. A. Chapman, Scott, & Mason, 2002; A. A. Baumeister, 1989.

[121] Hallahan, Kauffman, & Pullen, 2009; Landesman & Ramey, 1989; Ormrod & McGuire, 2007.

[122] Beirne-Smith, Ittenbach, & Patton, 2002; Butterfield & Ferretti, 1987; Heward, 2009; Kail, 1990; Turnbull, Turnbull, & Wehmeyer, 2010.

[123] Vygotsky, 1978; also see Pellegrini, 2009.

basement, the boys created a restaurant "kitchen" with a toy sink and stove and stocked it with plastic dishes, cooking utensils, and "food" items. They created a separate dining area with child-sized tables and chairs and made menus for their customers. On one occasion they invited both sets of parents to "dine" at the restaurant, taking orders, serving "meals," and eventually leaving the bills. Fortunately, they seemed quite happy with the few pennies they were paid.

In their restaurant play, the two boys took on several adult roles (restaurant manager, waiter, cook) and practiced a variety of adultlike behaviors. In real life, such a scenario would, of course, be impossible: Very few 5-year-olds have the skills necessary to run a restaurant. Yet the element of make-believe brought these tasks within the boys' reach.

Furthermore, as children play, their behaviors must conform to certain standards or expectations. In the preschool and early elementary school years, children often act in accordance with how a father, teacher, or waiter would behave. In the organized group games and sports that come later, children must follow a specific set of rules. By adhering to such restrictions on their behavior, children learn to plan ahead, to think before they act, and to engage in self-restraint—skills critical for successful participation in the adult world.[124]

Play, then, is hardly a waste of time. Instead, it provides a valuable training ground for adult life, and perhaps for this reason, it's seen in virtually all cultures worldwide.

Share the wisdom of previous generations.

We now return to a point about culture made in Chapter 4, because it's an important one: *Through its culture, a human social group ensures that each new generation acquires and benefits from the wisdom that preceding generations have accumulated.* Thanks to its culture, then, any social group becomes collectively more intelligent over time.

Some aspects of a culture are transmitted through informal conversations between adults and children, but many others are passed along through formal education in various academic disciplines. Each discipline includes numerous concepts, procedures, and other cognitive tools that can help students better understand and work effectively in their physical and social worlds.

Instruction in useful cognitive tools typically begins quite early. For example, in mainstream Western culture, many children learn color and shape names, counting, and the alphabet in the preschool years. For those who don't, acquiring such basic tools must be a high priority in kindergarten or first grade.[125] For example, Figure 6.13 shows an excerpt from a kindergartner's "Caterpillar Number Book," in which she practices representing the number 4.

Rely heavily on concrete objects and activities, especially in the early elementary grades.

As Piaget and many other researchers have discovered, children in the elementary grades often have trouble thinking and reasoning about ideas that are abstract, hypothetical, or contrary to fact. It's important, then, that elementary school teachers make classroom subject matter concrete for students. For example, in the primary grades teachers might have students use *manipulatives*—physical objects such as blocks, beads, and pennies—to acquire conservation of number and make sense of basic addition and subtraction facts.[126] In the middle elementary grades, paper- or computer-based illustrations can replace concrete objects to some extent, provided that mathematical concepts are still depicted in concrete terms—for instance, as pictures or diagrams.[127]

Virtually any academic discipline has its share of abstract ideas, and elementary teachers should either translate those ideas into concrete terms or else, if possible, postpone discussion of them until the upper elementary grades at the earliest. For example, in history, the very idea of historical *time*—whether it be a particular year (e.g., 1492) or a certain lengthy time span (e.g., 100 years)—is far beyond children's immediate experience. Accordingly, elementary school teachers conducting history lessons should probably minimize the extent to which they talk about specific

FIGURE 6.13 On this page of 5-year-old Luisa's "Caterpillar Number Book," she represents the number 4 in three ways: as a numeral, as segments of a caterpillar's body, and as caterpillar bites in a leaf.

---

[124] Coplan & Arbeau, 2009; A. Diamond, Barnett, Thomas, & Munro, 2007.

[125] Siegler, 2009; Slavin, Lake, Chambers, Cheung, & Davis, 2009.

[126] Ginsburg, Cannon, Eisenband, & Pappas, 2006; T. Martin, 2009; Sherman & Bisanz, 2009.

[127] Sarama & Clements, 2009.

MyEdLab
Video Example 6.6.

In what specific ways does this fourth-grade teacher use concrete materials to help his students understand how to add fractions with different denominators?

years before the recent past.[128] Instead, especially in the primary grades, teachers might focus on important events in their nation's history—for example, having children reenact an early Thanksgiving celebration or showing photographs of covered wagons crossing the North American prairie—without much regard for the sequence of events over a long period. Such lessons may lead to a disjointed knowledge of history, but they provide a concrete foundation on which more abstract and integrated history lessons can later build.

Present abstract ideas more frequently in the middle school and high school grades, but tie them to concrete objects and events.

Many of the concepts, symbols, and other useful cognitive tools that previous generations have passed along to us are fairly abstract. Yet as we've seen, abstract thinking emerges only gradually over the course of childhood and adolescence. Accordingly, abstract ideas should be introduced slowly at first, especially in the upper elementary and middle school grades, and they should be accompanied by concrete activities and illustrations as often as possible. Even in high school, actually *seeing* an abstract concept or principle in action can help students encode and remember it more effectively (recall the discussion of *visual imagery* in Chapter 2).

At all grade levels teachers can occasionally have students engage in **discovery learning**, in which students interact with their environment to derive new concepts and principles *for themselves*. Teachers might also conduct **inquiry learning** activities, which typically have the goal of helping students acquire more effective *reasoning processes* either instead of or in addition to acquiring new ideas. For example, to help students learn to separate and control variables in scientific investigations, a teacher might have them design and conduct experiments related to, say, factors affecting how fast a pendulum swings or how far a ball travels after rolling down an incline.[129] Such activities can often promote more advanced reasoning skills, especially when combined with appropriate instruction and guidance.[130]

Although discovery and inquiry activities have considerable value, teachers should also keep in mind three potential downsides.[131] First, students don't always have sufficient metacognitive skills to effectively direct their explorations and monitor their findings. Second, students may be overwhelmed by the many facets and subfacets of what they're observing—so much so that they can't adequately think about and sort through all the data available to them.[132] And third, students may "discover" evidence that supports their existing misconceptions and ignore evidence that contradicts those misconceptions, reflecting *confirmation bias* (see Chapter 2). The Classroom Strategies box "Conducting Effective Discovery and Inquiry Learning Activities" offers several guidelines that can help to minimize such problems. Probably the most important of its suggestions is to *structure and guide* the activity to some degree—for example, by posing specific questions students should try to answer or helping them identify variables that might be relevant to their investigation.[133]

Initially introduce sophisticated reasoning processes within the context of familiar situations and group work.

Piaget proposed, and other researchers have since confirmed, that sophisticated mathematical and scientific reasoning processes—for instance, proportional reasoning, formulating and testing hypotheses, and separating and controlling variables—don't fully emerge until adolescence. And even then, students are more likely to use these processes when they're dealing with topics they know well. For example, a science teacher might initially ask students to separate and control variables related to a commonplace activity, perhaps fishing, growing sunflowers, or teaching new tricks to a family pet. A social studies teacher might ask students to use proportional reasoning to compute distances on a local city map drawn to a particular scale. A physical education teacher might ask students to formulate and test various hypotheses about the most effective way to throw a softball.

---

[128] Barton & Levstik, 1996.

[129] Lorch et al., 2010.

[130] Alfieri, Brooks, Aldrich, & Tenenbaum, 2011; Eysink et al., 2009; Lorch et al., 2010; Monte-Sano, 2008.

[131] de Jong, 2011; Plass, Kalyuga, & Leutner, 2010; B. White, Frederiksen, & Collins, 2009.

[132] M. C. Linn & Eylon, 2011; Sweller, 2010.

[133] M. C. Brown, McNeil, & Glenberg, 2009; Hardy, Jonen, Möller, & Stern, 2006; M. C. Linn & Eylon, 2011; B. Y. White & Frederiksen, 1998.

CLASSROOM STRATEGIES

Conducting Effective Discovery and Inquiry Learning Activities

- **Identify a concept or principle about which students can learn something significant through interaction with their physical or social environment.**

  In a unit on erosion, a sixth-grade teacher sets a 4-foot-long tray at a slight incline at the front of the classroom. The tray contains quite a bit of sand at its higher end. In a series of experiments, students pour water into the tray's higher end and look at how varying water pressures and quantities differentially affect sand movement.

- **Make sure students have the necessary prior knowledge to make sense of what they observe.**

  A high school physics class studies basic principles of velocity, acceleration, and force. In a follow-up lab activity, students place metal balls of various weights and sizes at the top of an inclined plane and observe each ball's progress as it rolls down the slope. A computer attached to the plane enables the students to measure the rate of acceleration for each ball, thereby also enabling them to determine whether either weight or size influences acceleration. From the data, the students can draw conclusions about the effects of gravity.

- **Show puzzling results to create disequilibrium and arouse curiosity.**

  A fifth-grade science teacher shows her class two glasses of water. In one glass, an egg floats at the water's surface; in the other glass, an egg rests on the bottom. The students hypothesize that one egg has more air inside and is lighter as a result. But then the teacher switches the eggs into opposite glasses. The egg that the students believe to be heavier now floats, and the supposedly lighter egg sinks to the bottom. The students are quite surprised and demand to know what's going on. (Ordinarily, water is less dense than an egg, so an egg placed in it will quickly sink. But in this situation, one glass contains saltwater—a mixture denser than an egg and so capable of keeping it afloat.)

- **Structure and guide a discovery session so that students proceed logically toward discoveries you want them to make.**

  A seventh-grade science teacher asks students to speculate about variables that might influence the rate at which a pendulum swings. His students offer three possibilities: the length of the pendulum, the weight of the object at the bottom, and the angle at which the pendulum is initially dropped. The students work in small groups to test each of these hypotheses. When one group fails to separate and control variables, the teacher asks its members to look closely at their data: "What did you change between test one and test two? . . . Which caused the higher frequency [oscillation rate]? . . . Why can't you all come to a conclusion by looking at the numbers?" He continues to ask questions until the students realize they have simultaneously varied both length and weight in their experimentation.

- **Have students record their findings.**

  Students in a high school biology class collect data from a local stream and use handheld wireless computer-networking devices to send their findings to a central class computer. Once back in the classroom, the students consolidate and graph the data and look for general patterns and trends.

- **Help students relate their findings to concepts and principles in the academic discipline they're studying.**

  After students in a high school social studies class have collected data on average incomes and voting patterns in different counties within their state, their teacher asks, "How can we interpret these data given what we've learned about the relative wealth of members of the two major political parties?"

Sources: Boxerman, 2009 (erosion example); M. C. Brown et al., 2009; Bruner, 1966; de Jong & van Joolingen, 1998; N. Frederiksen, 1984a; Hardy et al., 2006; Kirschner, Sweller, & Clark, 2006; Klahr, 2009; Leach & Scott, 2008; M. C. Linn & Eylon, 2011; Lorch et al., 2010; Minstrell & Stimpson, 1996; Monte-Sano, 2008; Moreno, 2006; E. L. Palmer, 1965 (egg example); Pea & Maldonado, 2006 (stream example); D. L. Schwartz & Martin, 2004; B. Y. White & Frederiksen, 1998, 2005.

Allowing students to work together in groups—a strategy consistent with Vygotsky's concept of *internalization*—can be an effective means to nurture advanced reasoning processes. Vygotsky proposed that many complex cognitive processes have their roots in social interactions, in that processes that children initially used in interactions with others gradually become internalized so that they can be used independently. We see an example of this idea in **reciprocal teaching**, an approach to teaching reading and listening comprehension strategies in which students learn to ask one another questions about textbook passages or children's literature.[134] Several students and their teacher meet in a group to read a piece of text, occasionally stopping to discuss and process the text aloud. Initially, the teacher leads and models the discussion, asking questions about the text to promote elaboration, comprehension monitoring, and other effective reading strategies. Gradually, he or she turns the role of "teacher" over to different students, who then take charge of the discussion and ask one another the kinds of questions their teacher has modeled. Eventually, students can read and discuss a text almost independently of their teacher. They work together to construct meaning and check one another for comprehension and possible misunderstandings, and they become increasingly flexible in how they apply their newly acquired strategies.

In most instances of reciprocal teaching, students take turns reading sections of the text being discussed. Sometimes, however, the teacher reads the text, especially when working with

---

[134] A. L. Brown & Palincsar, 1987; Palincsar & Brown, 1984, 1989; Palincsar & Herrenkohl, 1999.

novice readers. As an illustration, let's look at a reciprocal teaching session in which six first graders and their teacher are discussing a text about snowshoe rabbits. The teacher has just read a description of a mother rabbit giving birth to and caring for several babies. In the discussion that follows, a student named Kam takes the role of "teacher."

Kam: When was the babies born?

Teacher: That's a good question to ask. Call on someone to answer that question.

Kam: Robby? Milly?

Milly: Summer.

Teacher: What would happen if the babies were born in the winter? Let's think.

[Several children make a number of responses, including: "The baby would be very cold." "They would need food." "They don't have no fur when they are just born."]

Kam: I have another question. How does she get the babies safe?

Kris: She hides them.

Kam: That's right but something else. . . .

Teacher: There is something very unusual about how she hides them that surprised me. I didn't know this.

Travis: They are all in a different place.

Teacher: Why do you think she does this?

Milly: Probably because I heard another story, and when they're babies they usually eat each other or fight with each other.

Teacher: That could be! And what about when that lynx comes?

[Several children comment that that would be the end of all the babies.]

Travis: If I was the mother, I would hide mine. I would keep them all together.

Kris: If the babies are hidden and the mom wants to go and look at them, how can she remember where they are?

Teacher: Good question. Because she does have to find them again. Why? What does she bring them?

Milly: She needs to bring food. She probably leaves a twig or something.

Teacher: Do you think she puts out a twig like we mark a trail?

[Several children disagree and suggest that she uses her sense of smell. One child, recalling that the snowshoe rabbit is not all white in the winter, suggests that the mother might be able to tell her babies apart by their coloring.]

Teacher: So we agree that the mother rabbit uses her senses to find her babies after she hides them. Kam, can you summarize for us now?

Kam: The babies are born in the summer. . . .

Teacher: The mother . . .

Kam: The mother hides the babies in different places.

Teacher: And she visits them . . .

Kam: To bring them food.

Travis: She keeps them safe.

Teacher: Any predictions?

Milly: What she teaches her babies . . . like how to hop.

Kris: They know how to hop already.

Teacher: Well, let's read and see.[135]

---

[135] Lesson courtesy of Annmarie Palincsar. Copyright © by Annemarie Palincsar. Reprinted with permission of the author.

In this lesson the teacher models elaborative questions and connections to prior knowledge ("What would happen if the babies were born in the winter?" "Do you think she puts out a twig like we mark a trail?") and provides general guidance and occasional hints about how students should process the passage about snowshoe rabbits ("Kam, can you summarize for us now?" "And she visits them . . ."). Also notice in the dialogue how students support one another in their efforts to process what they are reading. Consider this exchange as an example:

> *Kam:* I have another question. How does she get the babies safe?
>
> *Kris:* She hides them.
>
> *Kam:* That's right but something else. . . .

Reciprocal teaching has been used successfully with a wide variety of students, ranging from first graders to college students, to teach effective reading and listening comprehension skills.[136] In a classic early study of this approach,[137] six seventh-grade students with a history of poor reading comprehension participated in 20 reciprocal teaching sessions, each lasting about 30 minutes. Despite the relatively short intervention, students showed remarkable improvement in their reading comprehension skills. They became increasingly able to process reading material in an effective manner and to do so independently of their classroom teacher. Furthermore, they generalized their new reading strategies to other classes, sometimes even surpassing the achievement of their classmates.[138]

Scaffold students' early efforts at challenging tasks and assignments.

In the eyes of Vygotsky and many contemporary developmental psychologists, growing children gain the most from those tasks they can accomplish only with the guidance and support of others—that is, tasks within their zone of proximal development. Other people's guidance and support are known as **scaffolding**, a concept first presented in Chapter 4.

Now that we can see the importance of scaffolding from a developmental perspective, let's look more closely at what it might entail. Following are some forms scaffolding might take:[139]

- Help students develop a plan for accomplishing a complex new task.
- Demonstrate proper performance in a manner students can easily imitate.
- Divide a multifaceted task into several smaller, simpler tasks.
- Give specific guidelines for accomplishing the task (e.g., see Figure 6.14).
- Ask questions that encourage students to think about the topic or task in productive ways.
- Provide a calculator, computer software (word processing program, spreadsheet, etc.), or other technology that makes some aspects of the task easier.
- Remind students of what their goals are in performing the task (e.g., what a problem solution should look like).
- Give frequent feedback about how students are progressing.

Depending on their particular knowledge and ability levels, different students at any single grade level may need different kinds of scaffolding to support their success. As students become more adept at performing a new task, scaffolding is ideally modified to nurture newly emerging skills. And over time the scaffolding is gradually phased out—a process known as *fading*—until students can complete the task entirely on their own. In fact, providing *too much* scaffolding— more than a learner needs—can be an unwanted distraction.[140]

Scaffolding can come from other students as well as from teachers. In the opening case study, Lupita scaffolds two classmates' attempts at assembling puzzles. Furthermore, when several students work together on a difficult task, they may be able to accomplish something that none of

MyEdLab
Video Example 6.7.

In what specific ways does the third-grade teacher scaffold Luis's understanding of how leopards in this video interact with their environments?

---

[136] Alfassi, 2004; E. R. Hart & Speece, 1998; Johnson-Glenberg, 2000; K. D. McGee, Knight, & Boudah, 2001; Palincsar & Brown, 1989; Reinking & Leu, 2008; Rosenshine & Meister, 1994; Slater, 2004.

[137] Palincsar & Brown, 1984.

[138] A. L. Brown & Palincsar, 1987; Palincsar & Brown, 1984.

[139] A. Collins, 2006; Hmelo-Silver, 2006; Lajoie & Derry, 1993; Lodewyk & Winne, 2005; Merrill et al., 1996; Rogoff, 1990; Rosenshine & Meister, 1992; D. Wood, Bruner, & Ross, 1976.

[140] van Merriënboer & Sweller, 2005.

FIGURE 6.14 A checklist to scaffold ninth graders' efforts to write a five-paragraph essay

Essay Checklist

Use the following checklist each time you write an essay to make sure that you have completed the steps and have every part you need.

Introduction
- ☐ My first sentence is a Hook sentence.
- ☐ I have a clear Thesis sentence that answers the question of the assignment.
- ☐ I have a List sentence that introduces my three main body paragraphs.
- ☐ I have a Transition sentence at the end.

Main Body Paragraphs
- ☐ Each of my main body paragraphs talks about one main idea or point.
- ☐ Each of my main body paragraphs gives information that supports this point.

Conclusion
- ☐ My conclusion paragraph restates my List sentence in a different way.
- ☐ My conclusion paragraph restates my Thesis sentence.
- ☐ My conclusion paragraph connects my essay to me or to the world.

Source: Checklist by Jeffrey Ormrod. Copyright © by Jeffrey Ormrod. Reprinted with permission of the author.

them could accomplish on their own (recall our earlier discussions of *distributed cognition* and *distributed intelligence*). Cross-grade tutoring is yet another possibility, and students at both the giving and receiving ends of the instruction are likely to benefit. For example, when older children tutor younger ones in such basic subjects as writing and math, the "teachers" gradually *internalize* the suggestions they give their "students" (e.g., "Make sure every sentence has a period," "Now carry that 1 to the tens column") and so are more likely to use those suggestions themselves.[141]

Involve students in age-appropriate ways in adult activities.

When you were a young child, did you sometimes help your mother, father, or an older sibling bake things in the kitchen? Did the cook let you pour, measure, and mix ingredients once you were old enough to do so? Did the cook also give you directions or suggestions as you performed these tasks?

Older family members often allow young children to perform household tasks (e.g., cooking, cleaning, or painting) while providing guidance about how to do the tasks appropriately. Likewise, teachers should introduce students to common adult activities within a structured and supportive context. For instance, students might take active roles in school fund-raisers, such as chili dinners or multifamily garage sales. They might assist with costume design and scenery construction for a school play. Or they might communicate with scientists or government officials through e-mail or teleconferences. When teachers get students actively involved in adult activities, they're engaging students in **guided participation** in the world of adults and, often, in those specific *communities of practice* described in Chapter 4.[142]

In some instances, adults work with children and adolescents in formal or informal **apprenticeships,** one-on-one mentorships in which the adults teach the youngsters new skills, guide their initial efforts, and present increasingly difficult tasks as proficiency improves and the zone of proximal development changes. Many cultures use apprenticeships as a way of gradually introducing children to particular skills and trades—perhaps sewing, weaving, or playing a musical instrument.[143]

When the expert in an apprenticeship not only guides the novice in how to perform a task but also guides him or her in how to *think about* the task, it's sometimes called a **cognitive apprenticeship.**[144] For instance, a student and a teacher might work together to accomplish a challenging task or solve a difficult problem (perhaps collecting data samples in biology fieldwork,

MyEdLab
Video Explanation 6.3.

This video describes apprenticeships and cognitive apprenticeships.

---

[141] Biemiller, Shany, Inglis, & Meichenbaum, 1998; Graesser, D'Mello, & Cade, 2011.

[142] Rogoff, 2003.

[143] A. Collins, 2006; D. J. Elliott, 1995; Lave & Wenger, 1991; Rogoff, 1990, 1991.

[144] A. Collins, 2006; J. S. Brown, Collins, & Duguid, 1989; Dennen & Burner, 2008; W. Roth & Bowen, 1995.

solving a mathematical brainteaser, or translating a difficult passage from German to English). In the process of talking about various aspects of the task or problem, the teacher and student together analyze the situation and develop the best approach to take, and the teacher models effective ways of thinking about and mentally processing the situation.

Although apprenticeships differ widely from one context to another, they typically have many or all of these features:[145]

- **Modeling:** The teacher demonstrates the task and simultaneously thinks aloud about the process while the student observes and listens.
- **Coaching:** As the student performs the task, the teacher gives frequent suggestions, hints, and feedback.
- **Scaffolding:** The teacher provides various forms of support for the student, perhaps by simplifying the task, breaking it into smaller and more manageable components, or providing less complicated equipment.
- **Articulation:** The student explains what he or she is doing and why, allowing the teacher to examine the student's knowledge, reasoning, and problem-solving strategies.
- **Reflection:** The teacher asks the student to compare his or her performance with that of experts or perhaps with an ideal model of how the task should be done.
- **Increasing complexity and diversity of tasks:** As the student gains greater proficiency, the teacher presents more complex, challenging, and varied tasks to complete, often within real-world contexts.
- **Exploration:** The teacher encourages the student to frame questions and problems on his or her own and thereby expand and refine acquired skills.

Be optimistic that with appropriate guidance and support, all students can perform more intelligently.

Contemporary views of intelligence give us reason to be optimistic about what children and adolescents can accomplish, especially when teachers actively nurture and support their cognitive growth. If intelligence is as multifaceted as some psychologists believe, then scores from any single IQ test can't possibly provide a complete picture of students' intelligence levels. In fact, teachers are likely to see intelligent behavior in many of their students—quite possibly in *all* of them—in one way or another. One student may show promise in mathematics, another may be an exceptionally gifted writer, and a third may show talent in art or music. Furthermore, intelligent behavior draws on a variety of cognitive processes that can definitely improve over time with experience and practice. And the notion of distributed intelligence suggests that intelligent behavior should be relatively commonplace when students have the right tools, symbolic systems, and social groups with which to work.

Teachers must also remember that to the extent that intelligence is dependent on culture, intelligent behavior is apt to take different forms in students from different backgrounds.[146] In mainstream Western culture, children's intelligence may be reflected in their ability to deal with complex problems and abstract ideas. Among students who've been raised in predominantly African American communities, it may be reflected in oral language, such as in colorful speech, creative storytelling, or humor. In Native American cultures, it may be reflected in interpersonal skills or exceptional craftsmanship. Teachers must be careful not to limit their conception of intelligence only to students' ability to succeed at traditional academic tasks.

It's important, too, that teachers nurture the kinds of dispositions that will predispose students to think and act intelligently on a regular basis. Teachers can get students off to a good start by encouraging and modeling productive ways of thinking about classroom subject matter—for instance, by asking students to evaluate the quality of scientific evidence and consistently demonstrating open-mindedness about diverse perspectives.[147] The Classroom Strategies box "Promoting Productive Dispositions" presents examples of what teachers might do.

---

[145] A. Collins, 2006; A. Collins, Brown, & Newman, 1989; Hmelo-Silver, 2006.
[146] Dai, 2010; Haywood & Lidz, 2007; Maker & Schiever, 1989; Nisbett, 2009; H. L. Smith, 1998; Sternberg, 2005.
[147] Halpern, 1998; Kuhn, 2001b; D. N. Perkins & Ritchhart, 2004.

CLASSROOM STRATEGIES

Promoting Productive Dispositions

- **Communicate your own enthusiasm for learning about new topics.**

  In a unit on poetry, a middle school English teacher says, "In our culture, we're accustomed to poems that rhyme and have a steady beat. But many centuries ago, the Japanese developed a very different form of poetry. This form, called *haiku*, is really cool. I'll give you some of my favorite examples, and then as a class, we'll create some new haiku."

- **Model open-mindedness about diverse viewpoints and a willingness to suspend judgment until all the facts are in.**

  In a hands-on activity, students in a second-grade class experiment with particles of different sizes—pouring them, piling them, trying to bury things with them, and so on. Then, in a whole-class discussion, their teacher solicits students' varying observations and conclusions about the nature of particles, all the while communicating respect for students' ideas.

  MyEdLab
  Video Example 6.8.
  The video shows students in the second-grade class experimenting with particles.

- **Conduct learning activities in which students collaborate to address intriguing, multifaceted issues.**

  A few weeks before a national presidential election, a high school social studies teacher says, "Many of the campaign ads we see on television now are harshly criticizing opposing candidates, and some of them may be misrepresenting the facts. In your cooperative groups today, you'll be looking at transcripts of three political ads, one each from a different candidate's campaign. Each group has at least two laptops or tablets with Wi-Fi. Your job is to be fact checkers—to search the Internet for credible websites that can either confirm or disconfirm what the candidates are saying about their own records or those of their opponents. Tomorrow, we'll compare the findings of various groups."

- **Ask students to evaluate the quality of scientific evidence, and scaffold their efforts sufficiently that they can reach appropriate conclusions.**

  Working in pairs, fifth graders conduct "experiments" in a computer program that simulates the effects of various factors (amount of rainfall, rate of snowmelt, type of soil, etc.) on local flooding. To guide students' investigations, the program asks them to form and then test specific hypotheses, and it occasionally asks them if a particular series of tests has controlled for other potentially influential factors.

Sources: Strategies based on discussions by de Jong, 2011; Gresalfi, 2009; Halpern, 1998; Kuhn, 2001b; D. N. Perkins & Ritchhart, 2004; vanSledright & Limón, 2006.

Ultimately, intelligent behavior depends not only on students' own thought processes but also on the supportive contexts in which students work. Therefore, rather than asking the question, "How intelligent are my students?" teachers should instead ask themselves, "How can I help my students think as intelligently as possible? What physical and cognitive tools and what social support systems can I provide?"

A wide variety of instructional strategies have been shown to enhance students' cognitive development. Some of these strategies are appropriate for students at particular age levels or for students with exceptional abilities, but many of them are applicable for students of all ages and ability levels. In the hotlinked Self-Check quiz and Application Exercise that follow, you can check and apply your understandings related to Big Idea 6.5:

> As effective teachers plan and implement instruction, they accommodate students' developmental differences and diversity, with the ultimate goal of promoting all students' cognitive and intellectual development.

MyEdLab Self-Check 6.5.

MyEdLab Application Exercise 6.5. In this exercise, you can practice applying concepts related to scaffolding to various classroom situations.

6 SUMMARY

With our discussions of cognitive development and intelligence in mind, we can now summarize issues related to the Big Ideas presented at the beginning of the chapter.

■ **6.1: As a result of ongoing interactions between biological and environmental influences, children show some similar patterns but also considerable diversity in their developmental pathways.** Children and adolescents reach various developmental milestones in a somewhat predictable sequence, although the ages at which they reach these milestones vary considerably from one individual to the next. The course of development is often uneven, marked by dramatic changes or qualitative shifts at some points and by slower, more gradual changes at others. Both genetic and environmental factors influence development, but because they interact in their effects and also because children's own behaviors also influence the development of various characteristics, the relative contributions of genetics and environment are often impossible to determine.

■ **6.2: Cognitive development depends not only on brain maturation but also on stimulating physical, social, and cultural experiences and on children's natural inclinations to organize and try to make sense of those experiences.** Although the brain changes in dramatic ways in the first few years of life, it continues to mature even after the teenage years. Developmental changes in the brain enable increasingly complex thought processes throughout childhood, adolescence, and early adulthood. The brain retains some plasticity throughout life, enabling people of all ages to acquire new knowledge and skills in most domains.

Young learners seem naturally inclined to learn about, organize, and adapt to their world, and they actively seek interactions both with their physical environment and with other people. Adults and other more advanced individuals foster children's cognitive development by providing labels for experiences, modeling procedures for tackling problems, and in other ways passing along culturally appropriate interpretations and behaviors. Social interaction has an additional benefit as well: Children gradually internalize the processes they initially use with others and can eventually use those processes on their own. Ultimately, young learners benefit most from challenges, both those that call into question existing beliefs (those that create disequilibrium) and those that require the use of newly emerging abilities (those that lie within learners' zones of proximal development).

■ **6.3: Children continually build on existing knowledge and skills to develop more advanced thinking and reasoning abilities.** Thanks in part to increases in working memory capacity and to an ever-expanding and better-integrated knowledge base, young learners become increasingly capable of logical and abstract thinking over the course of childhood and adolescence. In adolescence, several abilities emerge that enhance thinking about science and math, including logical reasoning about contrary-to-fact situations, separating and controlling variables, and proportional reasoning. Advanced reasoning processes continue to develop during the high school years, especially if a learner's culture encourages them, but true expertise in any field comes only after many years of study and practice.

■ **6.4: Although children in any age-group differ somewhat in intelligence, cognitive styles, and dispositions, appropriately supportive environments can significantly enhance these abilities and characteristics.** Virtually all children and adolescents continue to gain new cognitive abilities and skills with age, but learners in any single age-group differ considerably in their general ability levels. Most psychologists call this individual difference variable *intelligence.* Psychologists disagree, however, about the extent to which intelligence is a single entity that influences a wide variety of tasks, on the one hand, or a collection of distinct, semi-independent abilities, on the other. Intelligence tests provide a rough idea of how a child's general cognitive ability compares to that of his or her peer group, but they're imprecise measures at best, and the IQ scores they yield are apt to change somewhat over time. Furthermore, intelligent behavior depends on environmental factors, both those that may have nurtured or impeded a child's cognitive development in the past and those that may support or hinder a child's performance at present. Intelligent behavior also depends on cognitive styles and dispositions—analytic and holistic processing, critical thinking, open-mindedness, and so on—that predispose learners to think about new ideas and events in insightful and productive ways.

■ **6.5: As effective teachers plan and implement instruction, they accommodate students' developmental differences and diversity, with the ultimate goal of promoting all students' cognitive and intellectual development.** When considered within the context of other information, IQ scores can often give teachers a general sense of students' current cognitive functioning. But equally helpful are problems and questions that reveal how students think and reason about various situations and topics. Through such information and through careful observation of students' day-to-day behaviors, teachers may discover that some students have exceptional abilities and talents begging to be nurtured and that other students have developmental delays requiring the attention of specialists and special instructional accommodations.

Not only must teachers ascertain where students are currently "at" in their thinking and reasoning, but they must also take active steps to help every student make advancements in important cognitive abilities and skills. One important strategy is providing opportunities for pretend play, organized games and sports, and other play activities in which students practice adult-like skills and learn how to plan ahead and abide by certain rules for behavior. Another important (in fact *essential*) strategy is to pass along the collective wisdom of the culture—the many concepts, procedures, and other cognitive tools that previous generations have found to be helpful in making sense of and dealing with the world. Instruction should rely heavily on concrete objects and activities in the early years but increasingly introduce abstract ideas and encourage sophisticated reasoning processes as students move through adolescence. Teachers should structure and guide—that is, *scaffold*—students' early attempts at challenging tasks, gradually removing the scaffolding as students gain proficiency. And as ability levels improve, students should participate in meaningful ways in adult activities. In general, teachers should remember that with appropriate guidance and support, virtually all students can learn to think and act in increasingly complex, intelligent ways.

PRACTICE FOR YOUR LICENSURE EXAM

A Floating Stone

After lunch one day, first-grade teacher Mr. Fox calls his students to the carpet area so that he can show them a "curious thing." Once the children are all seated and attentive, he puts a large fishbowl in front of them and fills it with water. Then, out of his jacket pocket, he pulls a piece of granite a little smaller than a golf ball and holds the stone over the bowl.

"What's going to happen when I drop this stone into the water?" he asks the children. "Do you think it will float like a boat does?"

Several of the children shout, "No, it's gonna sink!" Mr. Fox drops the stone into the water, and, sure enough, it sinks.

"You were right," Mr. Fox says. "Hmm, I have another stone in my pocket." He pulls out a much larger one—in this case, a piece of pumice (cooled lava) that is filled with tiny air pockets. "When I was traveling last summer, I found this at the bottom of an old volcano. Do you think this one will sink like the other one did?"

The children declare that it will definitely sink. Mr. Fox drops it into the fishbowl, where it momentarily submerges and then floats to the surface. "Hmm, what just happened?" he says as he looks inquisitively at his class.

Many of the children gasp with surprise. When a girl named Cora insists, "You didn't do it right!" Mr. Fox retrieves the pumice and drops it in the water again, with the same result. "No, no, that's impossible!" Cora yells. "Stones always sink—*always!*" She rubs and shakes her head, almost as if she's a bit upset. (Case based on similar lesson described by Hennessey & Beeth, 1993.)

1. **Constructed-response question**

   Cora is noticeably surprised and possibly upset when she sees the pumice stone float.

   A. Use one or more concepts from Jean Piaget's theory of cognitive development to explain why Cora reacts as strongly as she does to the floating pumice.

   B. Again drawing on Piaget's theory, explain why Mr. Fox intentionally presents a phenomenon that will surprise the children.

2. **Multiple-choice question**

   Imagine that you perform the same demonstration with high school students rather than first graders. If you were to make use of Vygotsky's theory of cognitive development, which one of the following approaches would you be most likely to take in helping the students understand the floating pumice?

   a. Before performing the demonstration, ask students to draw a picture of the fishbowl and two stones.

   b. Drop several light objects (e.g., a feather, a piece of paper, a small sponge) into the fishbowl before dropping either stone into it.

   c. Praise students who correctly predict that the larger stone will float, even if they initially give an incorrect explanation about why it will float.

   d. Teach the concept of *density,* and explain that an object's average density relative to water determines whether it floats or sinks.

   MyEdLab **Licensure Exam 6.1**

Monkey Business/Fotolia

7

Personal, Social, and Moral Development

Big Ideas to Master in this Chapter

7.1 Children's behaviors are the results of inherited traits, environmental conditions and contexts, and maturational changes in the brain, all of which gradually shape children's personalities and sense of self.

7.2 In order to benefit fully from their interactions with peers, children must have good social skills and be able to interpret and respond to various social situations and problems in productive ways.

7.3 Some signs of moral reasoning and prosocial behavior emerge early in life, but key components of morality continue to evolve over the course of childhood and adolescence.

7.4 Effective teachers accommodate individual differences in students' temperaments and personalities, help students acquire a healthy sense of self, and foster students' ongoing social and moral development.

7.5 Students who most need teachers' guidance and support are those who face exceptional personal or social challenges.

CASE STUDY: THE SCHOOL PLAY

The eighth graders at Fairview Middle School are sharply divided into two groups, the "popular" ones and the "unpopular" ones. The popular students have little time or tolerance for their low-status peers, and a few of them regularly pick on a small, friendless boy named William, usually by ridiculing him but occasionally by physically poking or shoving him.

Justifiably concerned about students' disrespectful behaviors toward certain classmates—and especially concerned about the bullying—members of Fairview's English department suggest that the annual eighth-grade play take a different form this year. Rather than holding tryouts and selecting only a handful of students as cast members (as has been done in previous years), all 103 eighth graders will participate in some way, perhaps in the cast or perhaps in scenery construction, costume design, lighting, or marketing.

A humorous, two-act melodrama is selected, complete with a handsome but clueless hero, a resourceful heroine, a dastardly villain, and several other central characters, along with a 10-member chorus that will provide the occasional cheering and booing any good melodrama requires. The often-bullied William is chosen to play Lucifer Nastybuns, the dastardly villain.

The students and many of their teachers work on the production throughout late winter and early spring. The sheer ambitiousness of the project and the fact that the class's efforts will be on public display on opening night instill a cohesiveness and class spirit that the faculty hasn't seen before. William surprises everyone with his spirited portrayal of Lucifer, and on opening night, his classmates give him rave reviews: "Who knew William was so cool?" "OMG, Will wuz fabulous!" "FOFL!!!"[1]

- Middle school students often divide themselves into different social groups, with some groups having higher social status than others. Why might social groups be so important for young adolescents?
- What benefits might the all-class school play have? Why does it pull the class together?

For many students, early adolescence can be a time of considerable anxiety. Students must grapple not only with the physiological changes of puberty, but also with disruptions of long-standing childhood friendships, more superficial interactions with teachers, and higher expectations for academic performance. Self-confidence may plummet, at least temporarily, and students are apt to look to their peers for emotional and moral support. Being in a high-status, "popular" group can be a source of comfort, but students can have high status only if some of their peers have *low* status. With the all-class school play, everything changes. Suddenly the students have a common goal, and only by working cooperatively with *all* of their classmates can any of them look good.

School isn't just a place where children and adolescents acquire thinking skills and master academic subject matter. It's also a place where they acquire beliefs about themselves and strategies for getting along with other people. In other words, school provides a critical social and cultural context in which young people grow personally and socially as well as academically.

---

[1] Based on a case described by M. Thompson & Grace, 2001. "OMG" and "FOFL" are text-messaging shorthand for "Oh my God" and "Fall on (the) floor laughing," respectively.

As we consider personal, social, and moral development in this chapter, we'll draw from all six of the theoretical perspectives of child and adolescent development identified in Table 6.1 in Chapter 6. And we'll discover that with age and experience, young learners construct increasingly sophisticated beliefs about themselves, other people, and society as a whole. Thus children's and adolescents' personal, social, and moral understandings are, like their understandings of the physical world, very much *self-constructions*.

7.1 PERSONALITY AND SENSE OF SELF

Big Idea 7.1 Children's behaviors are the results of inherited traits, environmental conditions and contexts, and maturational changes in the brain, all of which gradually shape children's personalities and sense of self.

All of us have unique qualities that make us different from the people around us. In the following exercise, take a minute to reflect on the qualities that make *you* unique.

SEE FOR YOURSELF
DESCRIBING YOURSELF

Using either pen and paper or a note-writing app on your smartphone or computer, write at least 10 words or phrases that describe the kind of person you are.

How did you describe yourself? For example, did you say that you're friendly? smart? funny? moody? uncoordinated? open-minded? Your list tells you something about your **sense of self**— your perceptions, beliefs, judgments, and feelings about who you are as a person. If you were able to be relatively objective, your answers also tell you something about your **personality**—your distinctive ways of behaving, thinking, and feeling.

Children's and adolescents' personalities and sense of self have a significant influence on their adjustment at school and elsewhere. For example, at a typical middle school, students who are outgoing and self-assured may quickly converge to form an "in-crowd," whereas those who are shy and lack self-confidence may keep to themselves or regularly interact with just one or two friends. Students who have a flair for the dramatic may delight in performing for an audience (as William apparently does), whereas those who are more reserved and reticent may prefer to stay out of the spotlight.

The following principles describe the nature, origins, and effects of human personalities and sense of self.

Heredity and environment interact to shape personality.

A child's **temperament** is his or her general tendency to respond to and deal with environmental stimuli and events in particular ways. Children seem to have distinct temperaments almost from birth. For example, some are quiet and subdued, whereas others are more active and energetic. Researchers have identified many temperamental styles that emerge early in life and are relatively enduring, including general activity level, adaptability, persistence, adventurousness, shyness, fearfulness, irritability, and distractibility. Most psychologists agree that such temperamental differences have genetic, biological origins and often persist into adolescence and adulthood.[2]

Genetic differences in temperament are only *predispositions* to behave in certain ways, however, and environmental conditions can point different children with the same predispositions in somewhat different directions.[3] One influential environmental factor is the parenting style that mothers, fathers, and other primary caregivers use in raising children. In mainstream Western culture, the ideal situation seems to be **authoritative parenting**, which combines affection and respect for children with reasonable restrictions on behavior. Authoritative parents provide a loving and supportive home, communicate high standards for performance, explain why certain behaviors are unacceptable, enforce household rules consistently, involve children in decision

MyEdLab
Video Example 7.1.

Even when all students are productively engaged in a classroom activity, they show temperamental differences in such traits as general energy level and assertiveness. For example, notice how some boys dominate this small-group activity in which several students experiment with a small water wheel.

---

[2] Bates & Pettit, 2007; Kagan, 2010; Kagan, Snidman, Kahn, & Towsley, 2007; M. Pfeifer, Goldsmith, Davidson, & Rickman, 2002; Rothbart, 2011; A. Thomas & Chess, 1977.
[3] Hollenstein & Lougheed, 2013; Keogh, 2003; Rothbart, 2011.

making, and provide age-appropriate opportunities for autonomy. Children from authoritative homes tend to be self-confident, energetic, socially skillful, and compassionate. They listen respectfully to others, follow reasonable rules for behavior, are relatively independent and self-regulating, and strive for academic achievement.[4] For the most part, such characteristics are consistent with the values espoused by mainstream Western culture.

Authoritative parenting isn't universally "best," however. Certain other parenting styles may be better suited to particular cultures and environments. For instance, in **authoritarian parenting**, parents expect complete and immediate compliance; they neither negotiate expectations nor provide reasons for their requests. In many African American, Asian American, and Hispanic families, high demands for obedience are made within the context of close, supportive parent–child relationships. Underlying the "control" message is a more important message: "I love you and want you to do well, but it's equally important that you act for the good of the family and community."[5] Authoritarian parenting is also more common in impoverished economic environments. When families live in low-income, inner-city neighborhoods where danger potentially lurks around every corner, parents may better serve their children by being very strict and directive about activities.[6] In any case, keep in mind that parenting styles have, at most, only a *moderate* influence on children's personalities.[7] Many children and adolescents thrive despite their caregivers' diverse parenting styles, provided that the caregivers aren't severely neglectful or abusive.[8]

A child's cultural environment also influences personality development more directly by encouraging (i.e., *socializing*) certain kinds of behaviors.[9] For example, as noted in Chapter 5, cultures vary considerably in the extent to which they encourage children to show or hide their feelings. Cultures vary, too, in the extent to which they nurture shyness, outgoingness, and assertiveness, as we'll see in a Cultural Considerations box later in the chapter.

Nature and nurture interact in many ways to shape children's personalities. For example, children who are temperamentally energetic and adventuresome are likely to seek out a wider variety of experiences than those who are quiet and restrained (e.g., recall the discussion of *niche-picking* in Chapter 4). Children who are naturally vivacious and outgoing typically have more opportunities than shy children to learn social skills and establish rewarding interpersonal relationships. And when children have temperaments that clash with cultural norms or parental expectations, they're apt to evoke negative reactions in others and lead parents to use a more controlling, authoritarian parenting style.[10]

Despite some relatively stable personality traits, children often behave somewhat differently in different contexts.

As children grow older, the many interactions among their inherited temperaments and environmental circumstances lead to unique and fairly stable personality profiles. Research with both children and adults has yielded five general personality traits—known as the "Big Five" traits—that are relatively independent of one another.[11] You can remember them using the word *OCEAN*:

- **Openness:** The extent to which one is curious about the world and receptive to new ideas and experiences
- **Conscientiousness:** The extent to which one is careful, organized, self-disciplined, and likely to follow through on plans and commitments
- **Extraversion:** The extent to which one is socially outgoing and seeks excitement

> **think about it**
> The words *authoritative* and *authoritarian* differ only in their last four letters, but the two terms refer to very different parenting styles. In what important ways are these two styles different? (For an explanation, click **here**.)

> **think about it**
> A quick review from Chapter 2: What purpose does the word OCEAN serve here? (For an explanation, click **here**.)

---

[4] Barber, Stolz, & Olsen, 2005; Baumrind, 1989, 1991; M. R. Gray & Steinberg, 1999; Stright, Gallagher, & Kelley, 2008; J. M. T. Walker & Hoover-Dempsey, 2006; Zhou et al., 2008.

[5] Bornstein & Lansford, 2010; X. Chen & Wang, 2010; Halgunseth, Ispa, & Rudy, 2006; McLoyd, 1998; Rothbaum & Trommsdorff, 2007.

[6] McLoyd, 1998.

[7] W. A. Collins, Maccoby, Steinberg, Hetherington, & Bornstein, 2000; Weiss & Schwarz, 1996.

[8] Belsky & Pluess, 2009; J. R. Harris, 1998; Scarr, 1992.

[9] For a good theoretical discussion of this issue, see Mendoza-Denton & Mischel, 2007.

[10] Bates & Pettit, 2007; N. A. Fox, Henderson, Rubin, Calkins, & Schmidt, 2001; J. R. Harris, 1998; Keogh, 2003; Maccoby, 2007; Rothbart, 2011; Scarr, 1993.

[11] Caspi, 1998; DeYoung et al., 2010; G. Matthews, Zeidner, & Roberts, 2006; Saarni, Campos, Camras, & Witherington, 2006.

- **Agreeableness:** The extent to which one is pleasant, kind, and cooperative in social situations
- **Neuroticism:** The extent to which one is prone to negative emotions (e.g., anxiety, anger, depression)

Such traits lead to some consistency—but not *total* consistency—in children's behaviors across situations.[12] Variability is especially common when children move from one environment to a very different one. For example, a student might be quite outgoing and sociable with his close friends but shy and withdrawn with people he doesn't know very well. And a student is more likely to be conscientious about completing schoolwork if her teacher helps her understand that academic ability improves with effort and practice—thus conveying an *incremental* view of intelligence (see Chapter 5)—and gives her guidance about how to organize assignments in a "to-do" list.[13]

Behaviors related to self-control are at least partly the result of brain development.

Beginning quite early in life, children show differences in their ability to regulate their behaviors. Some of this variability is the result of differences in an aspect of temperament known as **effortful control**, which appears to have its basis in the brain. In particular, some children are better able than others to consciously restrain themselves from making impulsive responses when other, less dominant responses might be more productive.[14] As children grow older, those who show high levels of effortful control can better plan ahead, focus their attention where they need to, and keep inappropriate emotional reactions in check. Such children also tend to be better behaved in class and to achieve at higher levels than their classmates with less self-control.[15]

Effortful control is a critical ingredient in the effective functioning of the *central executive*—the take-charge component of working memory introduced in Chapter 2. Accordingly, its biological underpinnings appear to be in the prefrontal cortex, the area of the brain located right behind the forehead (see Figure 7.1 for a reminder). As noted in Chapter 6, the prefrontal cortex doesn't fully mature until early adulthood—well after the teenage years. But long before this—beginning with the onset of puberty—certain other changes occur both in the brain and in hormone levels that can heighten young people's desires for enjoyable activities and immediate rewards. The unfortunate result is that many adolescents have trouble planning ahead and controlling their impulses.[16] Furthermore, they tend to make choices based on emotions ("This will be fun") or faulty assumptions ("This will make me look grown-up") rather than on logic and sound judgment ("There's a high probability of a bad outcome").[17] As you might guess, adolescent risk taking is most common in social contexts, where having fun is typically a high priority and it's easy to get swept away by what peers are doing or suggesting.[18]

Even though adolescents look and behave like adults in so many ways, then, it's important to remember that in one very important respect they're still children: They have trouble saying "No" to enticing opportunities that aren't necessarily in their long-term best interests. Hence, many middle school and high school students need considerable structure and prompting related to homework completion and other independent learning activities. And they're more likely to steer clear of potentially dangerous activities if they can find just as much pleasure in safer, more prudent ones.

As children grow older, they construct increasingly multifaceted understandings of who they are as people.

Some psychologists distinguish between two aspects of a person's sense of self. One aspect is *self-concept,* which includes general assessments of one's own characteristics, strengths, and weaknesses (e.g., "I'm a high-achieving student," "My nose is a bit crooked"). The other aspect is *self-esteem,*

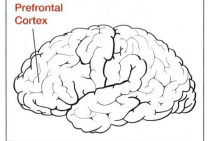

FIGURE 7.1 The biological basis for self-control resides largely in the prefrontal cortex, which continues to mature throughout childhood, adolescence, and early adulthood.

Prefrontal Cortex

[12] Hampson, 2008; Mendoza-Denton & Mischel, 2007.

[13] Belfiore & Hornyak, 1998; Dweck, 2008.

[14] Bates & Pettit, 2007; Rothbart, 2011; Rothbart, Sheese, & Posner, 2007.

[15] Blair & Razza, 2007; Liew, McTigue, Barrois, & Hughes, 2008; Valiente, Lemery-Calfant, Swanson, & Reiser, 2008.

[16] Figner & Weber, 2011; Shulman et al., 2016; Somerville, Jones, & Casey, 2010; Steinberg, 2009.

[17] Luna, Paulsen, Padmanabhan, & Geier, 2013; V. F. Reyna, Chapman, Dougherty, & Confrey, 2012; Shulman et al., 2016.

[18] Albert, Chein, & Steinberg, 2013; Galván, 2012; Knoll, Magis-Weinberg, Speekenbrink, & Blakemore, 2015.

which includes judgments and feelings about one's own value and worth (e.g., "I'm *proud* of my academic record," "I *hate* my crooked nose!"). We've encountered related ideas before, albeit under different names. In Chapter 5 we noted that human beings seem to have a basic need to feel competent and worthy (recall the discussion of *self-worth*). We also noted that people realize they're more likely to be successful in some activities than others—that is, they have higher *self-efficacy* for certain activities.

So how are these four terms—self-concept, self-esteem, self-worth, and self-efficacy—different from one another? In general, *self-concept* addresses the question "*Who* am I?" The terms *self-esteem* and *self-worth* both address the question "*How good* am I as a person?" Please don't agonize over the subtle distinctions among these three terms, because their meanings overlap considerably, and thus they're often used interchangeably.[19]

In contrast to the other three terms, *self-efficacy* addresses the question "*How well can I do such-and-such?*" In other words, it refers to people's beliefs about their competence, not in general, but in a specific domain or activity. To some extent, however, people's specific self-efficacies for various tasks and activities contribute to their more general sense of self.[20]

In their overall self-assessments, young children tend to make distinctions between two general domains: how competent they are at day-to-day tasks (including schoolwork) and how well they are liked by family and friends. As they grow older, children make finer and finer distinctions—for instance, they realize that they may be more or less competent or "good" in various academic subjects, athletic activities, peer relationships, and physical attractiveness.[21] Each of these domains may have a greater or lesser influence on students' overall sense of self. For some, academic achievement may be the overriding factor, whereas for others, physical attractiveness or popularity with peers may be more important.[22]

With age, self-perceptions become more realistic, abstract, and stable.

In the preschool and early elementary school years, children tend to think of themselves in terms of concrete, easily observable characteristics and behaviors—for instance, they may talk about their age, gender, and favorite activities.[23] At this point in their development, most of them have a generally positive sense of self.[24] Often they believe they're more capable than they really *are* and that they can easily overcome initial failures. Such optimism is probably due to their tendency to base self-assessments on their continuing improvements in "big boy" and "big girl" tasks. But as children have more opportunities to compare themselves with peers during the elementary school years—and also become cognitively more able to *make* such comparisons—their self-assessments become increasingly realistic.[25] They also start to pull together their many self-observations into generalizations about the kinds of people they are (e.g., "friendly," "good at sports," "smart," "dumb"), and, for good or for bad, such generalizations lead to increasingly stable self-concepts.[26]

As children reach adolescence and gain greater capability for abstract thought, they're even more likely to think of themselves in terms of general, fairly stable traits. Consider 12-year-old Tina's self-description when she was in sixth grade:

> I'm cool. I'm awesome. I'm way cool. I'm 12. I'm boy crazy. I go to Brentwood Middle School. I'm popular with my fans. I play viola. My best friend is Lindsay. I have a gerbil named Taj. I'm adopted. I'm beautiful.

As children get older, they increasingly include abstract qualities in their self-descriptions. Here 12-year-old Melinda identifies several abstract characteristics—musical, lovable, imaginative, noble, and animal-lover—in spelling her name.

---

[19] Bracken, 2009; Byrne, 2002; McInerney, Marsh, & Craven, 2008.
[20] Bong & Skaalvik, 2003; McInerney et al., 2008; Schunk & Pajares, 2004.
[21] Arens, Yeung, Craven, & Hasselhorn, 2011; Bracken, 2009; Davis-Kean & Sandler, 2001; Harter, 1999; Yun, Farran, Lipsey, & Bilbrey, 2010.
[22] Crocker & Knight, 2005; D. Hart, 1988; Harter, 1999.
[23] D. Hart, 1988; Harter, 1983.
[24] Harter, 1999; Lockhart, Chang, & Story, 2002; Robins & Trzesniewski, 2005.
[25] R. Butler, 2008; J. W. Chapman, Tunmer, & Prochnow, 2000; Davis-Kean et al., 2008.
[26] D. A. Cole et al., 2001; Harter, 1999.

Although Tina listed a few concrete characteristics (e.g., her musical instrument and best friend), she had clearly developed a fairly abstract self-perception. Tina's focus on coolness, popularity, and beauty, rather than on intelligence or academic achievement (or, we might add, modesty), is fairly typical: Social acceptance and physical appearance are far more important to most young adolescents than academic competence.[27] In girls especially, dissatisfaction with one's physical appearance can have a significant negative impact on self-esteem and lead to bouts of depression.[28]

Adolescents increasingly reflect on their characteristics and abilities and begin to struggle with seeming inconsistencies in their self-perceptions, perhaps wondering, "Who is the *real* me?" Eventually (perhaps around 11th grade), they integrate their various self-perceptions into a complex, multifaceted self-concept that reconciles apparent contradictions. For instance, they may realize that diverse emotions mean that they're "moody" and that their inconsistent behaviors on different occasions mean that they're "flexible."[29]

As adolescents pull their numerous self-perceptions together, many begin to form a general sense of **identity**: a self-constructed definition of who they are, what things they find important, and what goals they want to accomplish in life. In their ongoing search for a long-term identity, they may initially take on temporary identities, aligning themselves with a particular peer group, insisting on a certain mode of dress, or overhauling their self-descriptions on Facebook.[30] They may also have somewhat different identities in different contexts, depending on the traditional roles they've played in each context.[31] For example, a student might be a "loser" at school but a "star" in an out-of-school activity or a "leader" in a neighborhood gang.

One developmental psychologist has described four distinct patterns that might characterize adolescents' search for identity:[32]

- **Identity diffusion:** The individual has made no commitment to a particular career path or ideological belief system. Some haphazard experimentation with particular roles or beliefs may have taken place, but the individual hasn't yet embarked on a serious exploration of issues related to self-definition.
- **Foreclosure:** The individual has made a firm commitment to an occupation, a particular set of beliefs, or both. The choices have been based largely on what other people (especially parents) have prescribed, without an earnest exploration of other possibilities.
- **Moratorium:** The individual has no strong commitment to a particular career or set of beliefs but is actively exploring and considering a variety of professions and ideologies. In essence, the individual is undergoing an identity crisis.
- **Identity achievement:** After going through a period of moratorium, the individual has emerged with a clear choice of occupation, a commitment to particular political or religious beliefs, or both.

For most young people, the ideal situation seems to be to proceed through a period of moratorium—an exploration that is likely to continue into adulthood—before finally settling on a clear identity.[33] Foreclosure—identity choice *without* prior exploration—rules out potentially more productive alternatives, and identity diffusion leaves young people without a clear sense of direction in life.

As children reach puberty, they understand that they are unique individuals, but they may overestimate their uniqueness.

Young teenagers often believe themselves to be unlike anyone else—a phenomenon known as the **personal fable**.[34] They may think their own feelings are completely unique—those around them have never experienced such emotions—and so no one else, least of all parents and teachers, can

MyEdLab Content Extension 7.1. One early theorist, Erik Erikson, suggested that identity formation is a major preoccupation for adolescents. You can learn more about Erikson's theory in this supplementary reading.

think about it
Which of these four terms best describes your current status in your identity development?

---

[27] D. Hart, 1988; Harter, 1999.
[28] C. G. Campbell, Parker, & Kollat, 2007; Stice, 2003; E. J. Wright, 2007.
[29] Harter, 1999.
[30] Alemán & Vartman, 2009; Greenhow, Robelia, & Hughes, 2009; Seaton, Scottham, & Sellers, 2006.
[31] Eccles, 2009; Faircloth, 2012; Vadeboncoeur, Vellos, & Goessling, 2011.
[32] Marcia, 1980, 1991; also see Berzonsky & Kuk, 2000; Seaton et al., 2006.
[33] Kroger, 2007; Luyckx et al., 2008; Seaton et al., 2006; Sinai, Kaplan, & Flum, 2012.
[34] Elkind, 1981; Lapsley, 1993.

possibly know how they feel. For some adolescents, the personal fable can include a sense of invulnerability and immortality, leading them to believe themselves immune to the normal dangers of life and exacerbating any risk-taking tendencies. When warned of potentially dire consequences of experimenting with drugs and alcohol, having unprotected sexual intercourse, or driving at high speeds, they're apt to think, "It won't happen to me."[35]

The personal fable and risk-taking behaviors both decline in the later adolescent years, but they don't entirely disappear.[36] Hence they are—and must be—a source of concern to parents and teachers of older adolescents as well as younger ones.

Self-perceptions influence children's behaviors, and vice versa.

Children and adolescents tend to behave in ways that mirror their beliefs about themselves. For example, if they see themselves as good students, they're more likely to pay attention in class, follow directions, persist at complex math problems, and enroll in challenging courses. If they see themselves as friendly and socially desirable, they're more likely to seek the company of their classmates and perhaps run for a position in student government. If they see themselves as physically competent, they'll more eagerly pursue extracurricular athletics.

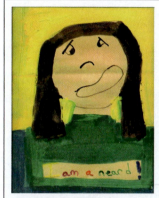

In this self-portrait, 10-year-old Sarah characterizes herself as a nerd. Her incorrect spelling may reflect her knowledge of how the similar-sounding word *heard* is spelled.

If learners assess themselves fairly accurately, they're in a good position to choose age-appropriate activities and work toward realistic goals.[37] A slightly inflated self-assessment can be beneficial as well, because it may give learners the self-confidence they need to take on new challenges.[38] However, self-concepts that are *too* inflated may give some students an unwarranted sense of superiority over classmates and lead them to bully or in other ways act aggressively toward peers.[39] And as you might guess, significant *under*estimates lead learners to avoid the many challenges that are apt to enhance their cognitive, social, and physical growth.[40]

In general, learners who have positive self-perceptions are more likely to succeed academically, socially, and physically, and such successes serve to maintain or enhance those positive self-perceptions.[41] But an interplay between self-perceptions and behavior exists for less flattering self-perceptions as well, creating a vicious cycle: A poor sense of self leads to less productive behavior, which leads to fewer successes, which perpetuates the poor sense of self.[42]

Other people's behaviors affect children's sense of self.

Children's personal successes and failures aren't the only things affecting their sense of self. A second important factor is their social context—more specifically, *other people's behaviors*—which influences their self-perceptions in at least two ways. For one thing, as children get older—and especially as they reach adolescence—how they evaluate themselves depends partly on how their own performance compares to that of their peers.[43] Those who see themselves achieving at higher levels than others are apt to develop a more positive sense of self than those who consistently find themselves falling short. Thus, comparisons with peers can dampen high-ability students' sense of self when they attend classes made up largely of students who have similarly high ability.[44]

In addition, learners' self-perceptions are affected by how other people behave *toward* them, which indirectly sends messages about strengths and weaknesses.[45] For example, adults influence

---

[35] DeRidder, 1993; Dodge et al., 2009; Jacobs & Klaczynski, 2002; B. Mills, Reyna, & Estrada, 2008; Nell, 2002.

[36] Frankenberger, 2000; Nell, 2002; V. F. Reyna & Farley, 2006.

[37] R. F. Baumeister, Campbell, Krueger, & Vohs, 2003; Harter, 1999.

[38] Assor & Connell, 1992; Lockhart et al., 2002; Pajares, 2009.

[39] R. F. Baumeister et al., 2003; Menon et al., 2007; Thomaes, Bushman, Stegge, & Olthof, 2008.

[40] Marsh & O'Mara, 2008; Schunk & Pajares, 2004; Steuer & Dresel, 2011; Zimmerman & Moylan, 2009.

[41] Arens et al., 2011; M. S. Caldwell, Rudolph, Troop-Gordon, & Kim, 2004; Marsh, Gerlach, Trautwein, Lüdtke, & Brettschneider, 2007; Valentine, DuBois, & Cooper, 2004; T. Williams & Williams, 2010.

[42] M. S. Caldwell et al., 2004; Ma & Kishor, 1997; Marsh & Craven, 2006; Thomaes, Reijntjes, Orobio de Castro, & Bushman, 2009; Valentine, Cooper, Bettencourt, & DuBois, 2002.

[43] Dijkstra, Kuyper, van der Werf, Buunk, & van der Zee, 2008; Seaton, Marsh, & Craven, 2009; Trautwein, Gerlach, & Lüdtke, 2008.

[44] Chiu, 2012; Köller, Zeinz, & Trautwein, 2008; Liem, Marsh, Martin, McInerney, & Yeung, 2013.

[45] Bukowski, Brendgen, & Vitaro, 2007; M. S. Caldwell et al., 2004; Crosnoe, 2011; Dweck, 2000; M. J. Harris & Rosenthal, 1985; Rudolph, Caldwell, & Conley, 2005; Pajares, 2009.

children's sense of self by holding high or low expectations for academic performance and by drawing attention to the various things that children do well or poorly. Meanwhile, peers communicate information about social and athletic competence, perhaps by seeking out a child's companionship or ridiculing the child in front of others. In the opening case study, when William initially has trouble making friends and the allegedly "popular" students pick on him, he may understandably have low self-esteem. Fortunately, the school play allows him to showcase one of his talents, and his classmates see him in a new light. Suddenly he's "fabulous" and "FOFL," or "fall-on-floor-laughing"—in other words, a really funny guy. Such reactions from his classmates, if they continue for any length of time, should enhance his social self-confidence.

In early adolescence, many students have a heightened concern about what others think of them. They may initially go to extremes, thinking that in any social situation, everyone else's attention is focused squarely on them—a phenomenon known as the **imaginary audience**.[46] Because they believe themselves to be the center of attention, young teenagers (especially girls) are often preoccupied with their physical appearance and can be quite self-critical. To some degree, this heightened concern about what other people might think of them appears to be linked to maturational changes in certain areas of the brain, including in areas that underlie self-focused emotions such as shame and embarrassment.[47]

Table 7.1 summarizes developmental trends in children's and adolescents' sense of self. It also offers ideas for how teachers can enhance students' sense of self at different grade levels.

Group memberships also affect children's sense of self.

Membership in one or more groups can impact learners' sense of self as well.[48] If you think back to your own school years, perhaps you can recall taking pride in something your entire class accomplished or feeling good about a community service project completed through an extracurricular club. Group membership isn't necessarily voluntary, however. For example, in the opening case study, some of the allegedly "unpopular" students would probably have preferred to belong to the "popular" group. In general, learners are more likely to have high self-esteem if they're members of a successful or prestigious group.

School groups aren't the only important ones in children's lives, of course. For instance, in racially and culturally diverse communities—where different skin colors, languages, customs, and so on are obvious—children's membership in a particular racial or ethnic group may be a significant aspect of their sense of self. We'll look at the importance of this *ethnic identity* more closely in a Cultural Considerations box later in the chapter.

Gender plays a significant role in most children's sense of self.

As young children become increasingly aware of the typical characteristics and behaviors of boys, girls, men, and women, they gradually pull together their knowledge into self-constructed understandings, or **gender schemas**, of how males and females are different. These gender schemas, in turn, become part of their sense of self and provide guidance about how to behave, such as how to dress, what toys to play with, and what interests and academic content domains to pursue.[49] For example, some boys believe that working hard at school is a "girl" thing, and their motivation to do well in academic tasks suffers as a result.[50]

Because gender schemas are self-constructed, their contents are apt to vary considerably from one individual to another.[51] For example, some adolescent girls incorporate into their "female" schema the unrealistic standards for beauty presented in popular media (films, fashion magazines, etc.). As they compare themselves to these standards, they almost invariably come up short, their self-assessments of their physical attractiveness decline, and some fall victim to

In this self-portrait drawn at age 7, Tina showed her awareness of physical features consistent with her Hispanic and Native American genetic heritage. Notice how her classmates in the background all have lighter skin and blonde hair.

---

[46] Elkind, 1981; R. M. Ryan & Kuczkowski, 1994; Somerville, 2013.

[47] Somerville et al., 2013.

[48] Brewer & Yuki, 2007; B. B. Brown, Herman, Hamm, & Heck, 2008; Eccles, 2009; Harter, 1999; Thorkildsen, Golant, & Cambray-Engstrom, 2008; Wigfield, Byrnes, & Eccles, 2006.

[49] Bem, 1981; Eccles, 2009; Leaper & Friedman, 2007; Ruble, Martin, & Berenbaum, 2006.

[50] Elmore & Oyserman, 2012.

[51] Crouter, Whiteman, McHale, & Osgood, 2007; Liben & Bigler, 2002.

DEVELOPMENTAL TRENDS

TABLE 7.1 • Sense of Self at Different Grade Levels

GRADE LEVEL	AGE-TYPICAL CHARACTERISTICS	EXAMPLE	SUGGESTED STRATEGIES
Grades K–2	• Self-descriptions largely limited to concrete, easily observable characteristics • Some tendency to overestimate abilities and chances of future success, especially in domains in which one has little or no prior experience	When 6-year-old Jeff is asked to describe himself, he says, "I like animals. I like making things. I do good in school. I'm happy. Blue eyes, yellow hair, light skin." He mentions nothing about his shyness, sense of humor, and ability to work and play independently—characteristics that would require considerable self-reflection and abstract thought to identify.	• Encourage students to stretch their abilities by tackling the challenging tasks they think they can accomplish. • Provide sufficient scaffolding to make success possible in various domains. • Praise students for the things they do well; be specific about the behaviors you're praising.
Grades 3–5	• Increasing awareness of and differentiation among particular strengths and weaknesses • Association of such emotions as pride and shame with various self-perceptions	When Kellen begins fifth grade at his neighborhood middle school, his class work rapidly deteriorates, despite individualized instruction in reading and spelling. At home one day his mother finds him curled in a ball under his desk, crying and saying, "I can't do this anymore!" Alarmed, Mom takes him to a series of specialists, who diagnose severe dyslexia. Kellen's parents eventually find a school that provides considerable structure and scaffolding for students with learning disabilities. There Kellen shows dramatic improvement in virtually every area of the curriculum, and his self-esteem skyrockets.	• Focus students' attention on their improvement over time. • Encourage pride in individual and group achievements, but be aware that students from some ethnic groups may prefer that recognition be given only for group achievements. • Provide opportunities for students to look at one another's work only when *everyone* has something to be proud of.
Grades 6–8	• Increasingly abstract self-conceptions • For many, a decline in self-esteem after the transition to middle or junior high school (especially for girls) • Excessive belief in one's own uniqueness, sometimes accompanied by risk taking and a sense of invulnerability to normal dangers (personal fable) • Heightened concern about others' perceptions and judgments of oneself (imaginary audience)	Meghan describes a recent event in her eighth-grade algebra class: "I had to cough but I knew if I did everyone would stare at me and think I was stupid, hacking away. So I held my breath until I turned red and tears ran down my face and finally I coughed anyway and everyone *really* noticed then. It was horrible."	• After students make the transition to middle school or junior high, be especially supportive and optimistic about their abilities and potential for success. • Provide safe outlets for risk-taking behavior; show no tolerance for potentially dangerous behaviors on school grounds. • Be patient when students show exceptional self-consciousness; give them strategies for presenting themselves well to others.
Grades 9–12	• Search for the "real me" and an adult identity; experimentation with a variety of possible identities • Increasing integration of diverse self-perceptions into an overall, multifaceted sense of self • Gradual increase in self-esteem • Continuing risk-taking behavior (especially for boys)	Sixteen-year-old Kayla often revises her profile on Facebook and regularly changes the photo that appears at the top of her profile. Sometimes she displays a happy Kayla, at other times a more sullen one; an early photo shows her in her basketball uniform, but a later one shows her in a skimpy party dress.	• Give students opportunities to examine and try out a variety of adultlike roles. • Encourage students to explore and take pride in their cultural and ethnic heritages, but *without* communicating the message that their own heritages are somehow superior to those of others. • When discussing the potential consequences of risky behaviors, present the facts but don't make students so anxious or upset that they can't effectively learn and remember the information (e.g., avoid scare tactics).

Sources: Bracken, 2009; R. Butler, 2008; Davis-Kean et al., 2008; Dweck, 2000; Elkind, 1981; Figner & Weber, 2011; Greenhow, Robelia, & Hughes, 2009; Harter, 1999; Liem, Marsh, Martin, McInerney, & Yeung, 2013; Lockhart et al., 2002; Marcia, 1980, 1991; T. M. McDevitt & Ormrod, 2007 (Kellen example); Nell, 2002; Nuemi, 2008; O'Mara, Marsh, Craven, & Debus, 2006; Orenstein, 1994, p. 47 (Meghan example); Pajares, 2009; Robins & Trzesniewski, 2005; Seaton et al., 2006; Sinai et al., 2012; Somerville et al., 2013; Spear, 2007; Tatum, 1997; Whitesell, Mitchell, Kaufman, Spicer, & the Voices of Indian Teens Project Team, 2006.

MyEdLab
Video Example 7.2.

Especially in the teenage years, an obsession with physical appearance can sometimes lead to eating disorders, as 16-year-old Josh explains.

eating disorders in an effort to achieve the super-thin bodies they believe to be ideal.[52] Meanwhile, some teenage boys go out of their way to meet self-constructed "macho" standards for male behavior by putting on a tough-guy act at school and bragging (perhaps accurately, but more often not) about their sexual conquests.[53] Fortunately, many adolescents' gender schemas become more flexible in the high school years, allowing greater freedom in behavior choices.[54]

Some researchers have found gender differences in overall self-esteem—especially in adolescence—with boys rating themselves more favorably than girls. This gender difference appears to be partly due to boys' tendency to *over*estimate their abilities and possibly also to girls' tendency to *under*estimate theirs.[55] Most adolescent boys' and girls' self-perceptions tend to be consistent with stereotypes about what males and females are "good at." Even when actual ability levels are the same—and for academic topics, ability levels usually *are* quite similar—on average, boys rate themselves more highly in mathematics, whereas girls rate themselves more highly in reading and social studies. On average, too, adolescent boys rate their athletic ability and physical appearance more positively than girls do.[56]

Despite the influence of others, growing children define and socialize *themselves* to a considerable degree.

Young people get many messages—sometimes consistent, sometimes not—from parents, teachers, peers, and others about who they are, what they should think, and how they should behave. But rarely do they passively adopt others' ideas and opinions as their own. Instead, they evaluate the information they get, choose some role models over others, weigh the pros and cons of going along with the crowd, and gradually develop their own views about what their strengths and weaknesses are and which behaviors are and are not appropriate for themselves. Before long, much of the pressure to behave in particular ways comes from within rather than from outside—a phenomenon called **self-socialization**.[57]

The decisions young people make about which individuals and sources of information to take seriously depend on their developmental levels and life experiences.[58] Parents are dominating forces in the lives of most children in the primary grades, and most parents continue to be influential with respect to core beliefs and values throughout their children's middle school and secondary school years. Nevertheless, growing children increasingly look to their peers for ideas about how to behave—for instance, what music to listen to, how to spend leisure time, and whether bullying and other forms of aggression are acceptable. We turn to the nature of peer relationships next.

As a teacher, you'll find that the things you've just learned about personality and sense of self can be quite helpful in your efforts to nurture students' academic and personal growth. In the hotlinked Self-Check quiz and Application Exercises that follow, you can check and apply your understandings related to Big Idea 7.1:

Children's behaviors are the results of inherited traits, environmental conditions and contexts, and maturational changes in the brain, all of which gradually shape children's personalities and sense of self.

MyEdLab **Self-Check 7.1.**

MyEdLab **Application Exercise 7.1.** In this interactive exercise, you can practice applying what you have learned about temperament and goodness of fit.

MyEdLab **Application Exercise 7.2.** In this exercise, you can examine two student artifacts and form a few hypotheses about each student's sense of self.

---

[52] S. Moore & Rosenthal, 2006; Stice, 2003; Weichold, Silbereisen, & Schmitt-Rodermund, 2003.

[53] Pollack, 2006; K. M. Williams, 2001a.

[54] Eccles, 2009; Elmore & Oyserman, 2012; M. Rhodes & Gelman, 2008.

[55] Hyde, 2007; Lundeberg & Mohan, 2009; Pajares, 2005.

[56] D. A. Cole et al., 2001; Hattie, 2009; Herbert & Stipek, 2005; Hyde, Lindberg, Linn, Ellis, & Williams, 2008; Köller et al., 2008; Stice, 2003; Wigfield et al., 2006.

[57] B. B. Brown, 1990; Crosnoe, 2011; Nuemi, 2008; Prinstein & Dodge, 2008b.

[58] Bukowski, Velasquez, & Brendgen, 2008; Cauce, Mason, Gonzales, Hiraga, & Liu, 1994; Furman & Buhrmester, 1992; Galambos, Barker, & Almeida, 2003; Nestemann & Hurrelmann, 1994.

7.2 PEER RELATIONSHIPS

Big Idea 7.2 In order to benefit fully from their interactions with peers, children must have good social skills and be able to interpret and respond to various social situations and problems in productive ways.

For many students, interacting with and gaining the acceptance of peers—in some way *fitting in*—are more important than classroom learning and achievement.[59] Yet social success and academic success aren't an either-or situation. In fact, students who enjoy good relationships with their peers at school are *more* likely to achieve at high levels. And, as you might guess, these students also have higher self-esteem and fewer emotional problems.[60]

In any classroom, the general quality of peer relationships can have a major impact on the overall psychological atmosphere, or **classroom climate**, in which students are studying and learning. Are students respectful of one another, and do they work cooperatively to help one another learn? Or do some students continually snub, belittle, or harass certain classmates based on, say, perceived "stupidity" or lack of "coolness"? Teachers cannot ignore the nature of students' interpersonal relationships; instead, they must work hard to nurture relationships that support every class member's academic and personal growth.

The following principles can summarize much of what researchers have learned about peer relationships in childhood and adolescence.

Peer relationships promote personal, social, and academic development in ways that adult–child relationships often cannot.

Peer relationships, especially friendships, serve several important functions in children's and adolescents' personal and social development.[61] For one thing, they provide an arena for learning and practicing a variety of social skills, including cooperation, negotiation, emotion regulation, and conflict resolution. They can also provide academic support—for instance, by helping one another with challenging academic tasks. In addition, peers—especially good friends—can provide companionship, safety, and emotional support: They become a group with whom to eat lunch, a safe haven from playground bullies, and shoulders to cry on in times of confusion or trouble. Think of poor William in the opening case study, who is initially picked on by other students and has no friends to come to his assistance.

Many adolescents (especially girls) reveal their innermost thoughts and feelings to their friends.[62] Friends often understand a teenager's perspective—the preoccupation with physical appearance, concerns about the opposite sex, and so on—in a world of seemingly "clueless" adults. By sharing their thoughts and feelings with one another, teens may discover that they aren't as unique as they once thought, and thus the personal fable mentioned earlier may slowly fade from the scene.[63]

Exactly *what* young people gain from their interactions with peers depends to some degree on their motives—that is, on what they hope to gain from the interactions. Those who are looking for companionship and ongoing emotional support are apt to work toward developing their social skills and enhancing the quality of their friendships. Those who are more interested in gaining social prestige—for instance, by becoming one of the "popular kids"—tend to be more concerned about making a good impression on socially powerful peers than on building mutually supportive relationships. Sadly, some youngsters, perhaps because they feel socially awkward and anxious, tend to withdraw from social situations as much as possible as a way of minimizing the chances of being labeled a "loser" or "geek."[64]

friends o ur for you when
you are lonely and sad.
they play with you,
they are nice, they are
mean, they tell stors
And the things they Do.
they walk you to the
nursce,

In this writing sample, 7-year-old Andrew sees friends largely as companions and sources of entertainment (they're for "when you are lonely," "they play with you," "they tell stories"). Yet he also recognizes that friends can occasionally be a source of support ("they walk you to the nursce").

MyEdLab
Video Example 7.3.

Good friendships can offer many benefits. What benefits does 13-year-old Ryan describe?

[59] Crosnoe, 2011; Dowson & McInerney, 2001; LaFontana & Cillessen, 2010.

[60] Bukowski, Motzoi, & Meyer, 2009; Gest, Domitrovich, & Welsh, 2005; A. J. Martin & Dowson, 2009; Wentzel, 2009.

[61] Bukowski et al., 2009; Granic, Lobel, & Engels, 2014; Ladd, Kochenderfer-Ladd, Visconti, & Ettekal, 2012; Laursen, Bukowski, Aunola, & Nurmi, 2007; Wentzel, Baker, & Russell, 2009.

[62] Levitt, Guacci-Franco, & Levitt, 1993; A. J. Rose & Smith, 2009.

[63] Elkind, 1981.

[64] A. M. Ryan, Jamison, Shin, & Thompson, 2012; A. M. Ryan & Shim, 2008.

Peers help define "appropriate" ways of behaving.

Not only do peers provide social and emotional support but they can also be powerful socialization agents who both directly and indirectly encourage certain ways of behaving.[65] Peers define options for leisure time, perhaps forming study groups, playing video games, or smoking cigarettes behind the school building. They serve as role models and provide standards for acceptable behavior, showing what's possible, what's admirable, what's cool. And they sanction one another for stepping beyond acceptable bounds, perhaps through ridicule, gossip, or ostracism.

Traditionally such influences have been known as *peer pressure,* but many of them are better described as **peer contagion**, in which certain behaviors "spread" from one child or adolescent to another through a variety of means.[66] Although overt peer pressure can definitely have an impact, a good deal of peer contagion is the result of self-imposed pressure—*self-socialization* at work. Twelve-year-old Mariel described this phenomenon well as she explained what happened when students from two different elementary schools transitioned to the same middle school in fifth grade:

> When you get to middle school the other school comes in. You're like, "Oh no, what if they don't like me?" So you try to be cool and stuff. But you never seem to get there. They're always one step ahead of you.

A common misconception is that peer influences are invariably a bad thing, but in fact, they're a mixed bag. Many peers encourage such desirable qualities as working hard in school, treating people kindly, and engaging in community service. Others, however, encourage cutting class, bullying certain students, consuming alcohol or drugs, or in other ways engaging in counterproductive behaviors.[67]

Although peers' behaviors and values certainly have an impact, their effects have probably been overrated. Most children and adolescents acquire a strong set of values and behavioral standards from their families, and they don't necessarily discard these values and standards in the company of peers.[68] Furthermore, they tend to choose friends who are similar to themselves in motives, styles of behavior, academic achievement, and leisure-time activities, and they may gradually distance themselves from friends who are very different from them socially and academically.[69] In some cases, students lead "double lives" that enable them to attain academic success while maintaining peer acceptance. For example, although they attend class and do their homework faithfully, they may feign disinterest in scholarly activities, disrupt class with jokes or goofy behaviors, and express surprise at receiving high grades.[70] In addition, they may act tough when they're in public, saving their softer sides for more private circumstances, as one sixth grader's explanation reveals:

> You'd still have to have your bad attitude. You have to act—it's just like a movie. You have to act. And then at home you're a regular kind of guy, you don't act mean or nothing. But when you're around your friends you have to be sharp and stuff like that, like push everybody around.[71]

On average, boys and girls interact with peers in distinctly different ways.

Most children and young adolescents affiliate primarily with peers of the same sex.[72] Boys' and girls' play groups and friendships are different in key ways that affect their personal and social development. Boys tend to hang out in relatively large groups that engage in rough-and-tumble

---

[65] Rubin, Cheah, & Menzer, 2010; A. M. Ryan, 2000; M. F. H. Schmidt & Tomasello, 2012; Wentzel & Watkins, 2011.

[66] Altermatt, 2012; B. B. Brown, Bakken, Ameringer, & Mahon, 2008; Sandstrom, 2011.

[67] Hamm, Hoffman, & Farmer, 2012; Mayeux, Houser, & Dyches, 2011; Prinstein & Dodge, 2008b; Spinrad & Eisenberg, 2009.

[68] B. B. Brown, 1990; W. A. Collins et al., 2000; Galambos et al., 2003; Gniewosz & Noack, 2012.

[69] Hartl, Laursen, & Cillessen, 2015; Kindermann, McCollam, & Gibson, 1996; Prinstein & Dodge, 2008a; A. M. Ryan, 2001.

[70] B. B. Brown, 1993; Grimes, 2002; Juvonen, 2006.

[71] Juvonen & Cadigan, 2002, p. 282.

[72] Best, 2010; A. J. Rose & Smith, 2009.

play, organized group games, and physical risk-taking activities.[73] They enjoy competition and can be fairly assertive in their efforts to achieve individual and group goals.[74] Especially as they get older, many prefer keeping some personal and emotional distance between themselves and their friends—perhaps as a way of showing their "manliness"—and often try to hide their true emotions in social situations.[75]

Whereas boys tend to be competitive, girls are more affiliative and cooperative. Girls seem to be more attuned to other people's mental states and exhibit greater sensitivity to the subtle, nonverbal messages—the body language—that others communicate.[76] They spend much of their leisure time with only a few close friends, with whom they may share certain secrets and confidences.[77] Although girls can certainly be assertive at times, they also tend to be concerned about maintaining group harmony, and so they may occasionally subordinate their own wishes to those of others.[78] And they're more concerned about resolving interpersonal conflicts than boys are, as 17-year-old Paul explains:

> Normally with, like, my guy friends, we just get over it. There's no working it out, you just sit . . . like, "Fine, whatever," you know? And we get over it. Girl friends, you gotta talk to them and work it out slowly. Apologize for doing whatever you did wrong. There's a whole process.

Social groups become increasingly important in adolescence.

Most children establish friendships with one or more peers even before they reach school age. As they move through the elementary grades, some of them form larger social groups that often get together. Once children gel as a group, they prefer members of their group over nonmembers, and they may in some instances develop feelings of hostility and rivalry toward members of other groups.[79] Even in the early elementary grades, children are aware that social groups can vary considerably in social status, and hence their associations with one group or another can affect their self-esteem.[80]

As youngsters reach puberty, larger groups become an especially prominent feature of their social worlds. Researchers have identified several distinct types of groups during the adolescent years: cliques, crowds, subcultures, and gangs. **Cliques** are moderately stable friendship groups of perhaps four to eight individuals, and such groups provide the setting for most voluntary social interactions. Clique boundaries tend to be fairly rigid and exclusive (some people are "in"; others are "out"), and memberships in various cliques often affect social status.[81] Here is 14-year-old Courtney's description of an especially exclusive "popular" clique in her eighth-grade class:

> There are table groups at lunch. My group gave them all names. The popular ones, we call them the Sardines. They are in their little box, they don't let anyone into their box, they're so close together. You'll never see one of them by themselves. Like one of them's a TV and the other ones are like little remotes following her.

Crowds are considerably larger than cliques and don't have the tight-knit cohesiveness and carefully drawn boundaries of a clique. In fact, group members don't necessarily even interact much with one another. Nevertheless, they tend to share common interests, attitudes about academic achievement, and (occasionally) ethnic background. Students often assign labels to these various groups—not only the "popular" students mentioned in the opening case study but perhaps also the "brains," "jocks," "druggies," "goths," or "nerds"—and view some groups more favorably than others.[82]

MyEdLab
Video Example 7.4.
In this video, a seventh grader and her mother talk about the social cliques at the local middle school. Are the cliques they describe similar to or different from the cliques in your own middle school and high school experiences?

think about it
What distinct group labels did students at your high school identify?

[73] Best, 2010; Maccoby, 2002; Pellegrini, Kato, Blatchford, & Baines, 2002.

[74] Benenson et al., 2002; Jonkmann, Trautwein, & Lüdtke, 2009; Leaper & Friedman, 2007; Maccoby, 2002.

[75] Best, 2010; N. Eisenberg, Martin, & Fabes, 1996; Lippa, 2002; K. M. Williams, 2001a.

[76] Bosacki, 2000; Deaux, 1984.

[77] Block, 1983; N. Eisenberg et al., 1996; A. J. Rose, 2002.

[78] Benenson et al., 2002; Leaper & Friedman, 2007; Maccoby, 2002.

[79] Bigler, Brown, & Markell, 2001; Dunham, Baron, & Banaji, 2006; J. R. Harris, 1998; Nesdale, Maass, Durkin, & Griffiths, 2005.

[80] B. B. Brown et al., 2008; Dunham et al., 2006; Nesdale et al., 2005.

[81] Aikins & Litwack, 2011; B. B. Brown, 2011; Goodwin, 2006; Kindermann et al., 1996.

[82] Crosnoe, 2011; Juvonen & Galván, 2008; D. Schwartz & Gorman, 2011.

Sometimes a crowd takes the form of a subculture, a group that resists a powerful dominant culture by adopting a significantly different way of life.[83] Some subcultures are relatively benign; for example, as one of us authors knows firsthand, some boys become baggy-pants "skaters" who spend much of their free time riding skateboards and addressing almost everyone (including their mothers) as "dude." Other subcultures are more worrisome, such as those that endorse racist and anti-Semitic behaviors (e.g., "skinheads") and those that practice Satanic worship and rituals. Adolescents are more likely to affiliate with troublesome subcultures if they feel alienated from the dominant culture—perhaps that of their school or that of society more generally—and want to distinguish themselves from it in some way.[84]

A gang is a cohesive social group characterized by initiation rites, distinctive colors and symbols, ownership of a specific "territory," and feuds with one or more rival groups. Typically, gangs are governed by strict rules for behavior, with stiff penalties for rule violations. Adolescents (and occasionally also younger children) affiliate with gangs for a variety of reasons.[85] Some do so as a way of demonstrating loyalty to their family, friends, or neighborhood. Some seek the status and prestige—and occasionally also the physical protection—that gang membership brings. Some have poor academic records and perceive gang activity as an alternative means of gaining recognition for accomplishments. Many members of gangs have troubled relationships with their families or have been consistently rejected by peers, and so they turn to gangs to get the emotional support they can find nowhere else.

In the upper secondary school grades, a greater capacity for abstract thought allows many adolescents to think of other people more as unique individuals and less as members of specific categories. They gain new awareness of the characteristics they share with people from diverse backgrounds. Perhaps as a result, ties to specific peer groups tend to dissipate, hostilities between groups soften, and young people become more flexible about the peers with whom they associate.[86]

Romantic relationships in adolescence can provide valuable practice for the intimate relationships of adulthood.

Even in the primary grades, many children talk of having boyfriends or girlfriends, and the opposite sex is a subject of interest throughout the elementary school years. But with the onset of adolescence, the biological changes of puberty bring on new, often unsettling feelings and sexual desires. Not surprisingly, then, romance is a frequent topic of thought and conversation in the middle and high school grades.[87] Young adolescents' romances tend to exist more in their minds than in reality; for instance, two students might be identified as "going out" even if they never actually date. Their romantic thoughts may also involve crushes on people who are out of reach—perhaps favorite teachers or movie stars.[88]

Eventually, many adolescents begin to date, especially if their friends are also dating. Early choices in dating partners are often based on physical attractiveness or social status, and dates may involve only limited and superficial interaction.[89] As adolescents move into the high school grades, some form more intense, affectionate, and long-term relationships with members of the opposite sex, and these relationships often (but by no means always) lead to sexual intimacy.[90] The age of first sexual intercourse has decreased steadily during the last few decades, perhaps in part because the media often communicate the message that sexual activity among unmarried partners is acceptable.[91]

From a developmental standpoint, romantic relationships have definite benefits: They can address young people's needs for companionship, affection, and security, and they provide an

For many children, thoughts of romance emerge early. Here is just one of many notes 5-year-old Isabelle wrote about a classmate named Will.

---

[83] J. S. Epstein, 1998.

[84] Crosnoe, 2011; J. R. Harris, 1998.

[85] Dishion, Piehler, & Myers, 2008; Kodluboy, 2004; Petersen, 2004; Simons, Whitbeck, Conger, & Conger, 1991.

[86] Furman & Collins, 2009; Gavin & Fuhrman, 1989; Kinney, 1993.

[87] B. B. Brown, Feiring, & Furman, 1999; Furman & Simon, 2008.

[88] B. B. Brown, 1999; Eckert, 1989; B. C. Miller & Benson, 1999.

[89] B. B. Brown, 2011; Furman, Brown, & Feiring, 1999; Pellegrini, 2002.

[90] J. Connolly & Goldberg, 1999; Furman & Collins, 2009.

[91] Brooks-Gunn & Paikoff, 1993; S. Moore & Rosenthal, 2006; Zimmer-Gembeck & Helfand, 2008.

opportunity to experiment with new social skills and interpersonal behaviors. At the same time, romance can wreak havoc with adolescents' emotions. Adolescents have more extreme mood swings than younger children or adults, and for many of them, this instability may be partly due to the excitement and frustrations of being romantically involved or *not* involved.[92]

As students reach high school (occasionally earlier), a significant minority of them find themselves attracted to their own sex either instead of or in addition to the opposite sex. Adolescence can be a particularly confusing time for gay, lesbian, and bisexual individuals. Some struggle to make sense of their sexual orientation and may experience considerable peer rejection and depression. Yet many others enjoy good mental health, especially if their home and school environments communicate acceptance of diverse sexual orientations.[93]

Teenagers often have mixed feelings about their early sexual experiences, and those around them—parents, teachers, peers—are often uncertain about how to handle the topic.[94] When parents and teachers do broach the topic of sexuality, they often raise it in conjunction with *problems,* such as irresponsible behavior, substance abuse, disease, and unwanted pregnancy. And they rarely raise the issue of gay, lesbian, and bisexual orientations except within the context of acquired immune deficiency syndrome (AIDS) and other risks.[95]

Truly popular children have good social skills.

When the daughter of one of us authors was in junior high school, she sometimes said, "No one likes the popular kids." As self-contradictory as her remark might have been—and Mom always told her that it was—it's consistent with research findings. When students are asked to identify their most "popular" classmates, they identify peers who have dominant social status at school (perhaps those who belong to a prestigious social group) but in many cases are aggressive or stuck-up.[96] Fourteen-year-old Courtney's description of allegedly popular students at her school provides a good illustration:

> Nobody likes the popular kids. We all think they're bratty, they're mean. The only reason they're popular is because they'll make out with guys at the back of the bus. . . . They don't include anyone. They have their own parties that consist only of themselves. They can't branch out.

Contrary to Courtney's description, *truly* **popular students**—those whom many classmates select as people they'd like to do things with—may or may not hold high-status positions, but they're kind, trustworthy, and socially skillful. They also tend to show genuine concern for others—for instance, by sharing, cooperating, and empathizing with peers.[97]

In contrast to popular students, **rejected students** are those whom classmates select as being their *least* preferred social companions. Students with few social skills—for example, those who are impulsive or aggressive and those who continually try to draw attention to themselves—typically experience peer rejection.[98] Students who are noticeably overweight and those who, on the surface, appear to be gay or lesbian are also frequent targets of ridicule, harassment, and rejection.[99] And in many schools, students from racial and ethnic minority groups can be regular objects of derogatory remarks and other forms of racism and discrimination, as can students from low-income families.[100] Especially when peer rejection and exclusion continue over a lengthy period, rejected students are at high risk for emotional problems, low school achievement, and poor school attendance.[101]

---

[92] Davila, 2008; Furman & Collins, 2009; Larson, Clore, & Wood, 1999; B. C. Miller & Benson, 1999.

[93] Darwich, Hymel, & Waterhouse, 2012; Konishi, Saewyc, & Smith, 2011; J. P. Robinson & Espelage, 2011; Savin-Williams, 2008.

[94] Alapack, 1991; Katchadourian, 1990; Zimmer-Gembeck & Helfand, 2008.

[95] Filax, 2007; M. B. Harris, 1997.

[96] Cillessen & van den Berg, 2012; W. E. Ellis & Zarbatany, 2007; Hawley, 2014; Rodkin, Espelage, & Hanish, 2015.

[97] Asher & McDonald, 2009; Cillessen & Rose, 2005; Mayeux et al., 2011.

[98] Asher & McDonald, 2009; Pedersen, Vitaro, Barker, & Borge, 2007; Rubin et al., 2010.

[99] Swearer, Espelage, Vaillancourt, & Hymel, 2010.

[100] Banks & Banks, 1995; Graham & Hudley, 2005; McBrien, 2005; Phelan, Yu, & Davidson, 1994.

[101] Bellmore, 2011; Cillessen & van den Berg, 2012; Ladd et al., 2012.

A third group, **controversial students**, elicit diverse reactions, in that some peers really like these students and others really *dis*like them. Controversial students can, like rejected students, be quite aggressive, but they also have sufficiently good social skills that they maintain close relationships with certain peers.[102] Many students whom classmates refer to as "popular" actually fall into this category.

Researchers have described another category as well.[103] **Neglected students** are those whom peers rarely identify as someone they would either most like or least like to do something with. Some neglected students prefer to be alone, others are quite shy or don't know how to go about initiating interaction, and still others are content with having only one or two close friends.[104] For some of these students, "neglected" status is a relatively temporary situation. Others are totally friendless for extended periods—such is often the case for recent immigrants and for students with disabilities—and these students are at higher-than-average risk for depression.[105]

In recent decades, digital technologies have provided new mechanisms for interacting with peers.

Thanks to wireless technologies (e.g., cell phones) and the Internet, many young people now communicate quite frequently—daily, sometimes almost hourly—with some of their peers.[106] For example, e-mail and instant messaging (i.e., "texting") allow quick and easy ways of asking classmates about homework assignments, making plans for social activities, and seeking friends' advice and emotional support. Social networking sites (e.g., Facebook, Instagram) provide means of sharing personal information, maintaining and enhancing friendships, and potentially finding like-minded age-mates. Internet chat rooms allow group discussions about virtually any topic. Judicious use of such mechanisms can enhance students' self-esteem, connectedness with peers, social problem solving, and general psychological well-being.[107]

Unfortunately, however, some students use these technologies in ways that can do a good deal of social and psychological harm. For example, they may voluntarily share sexually explicit photographs or other X-rated material by using "hidden apps" that, on the surface, look like something innocent (such as a calculator) to parents, teachers, and other unsuspecting adults. And as we'll see shortly, they may harass or humiliate one or more of their peers through *cyberbullying*.

Whether children and adolescents interact face to face or at a distance through various technologies, their ability to interact effectively with peers requires developmental advancements in social cognition—a topic we explore now.

Social Cognition

To be truly effective in interpersonal relationships, children and adolescents must engage in **social cognition**: They must consider how people around them are likely to think about, behave in, and react to various situations. By and large, those who regularly think about other people's thoughts and feelings tend to be socially skillful and make friends easily.[108] Some psychologists propose that social cognition is a distinctly human ability—which they call *emotional intelligence*—whereas others believe that it's simply an integral part of people's general intellectual and social functioning.[109]

To some degree, the human brain may be "prewired" for social cognition—in particular, through the **mirror neurons** described earlier in Chapter 4. Mirror neurons fire either when a person is performing a particular behavior or when the person watches *someone else* perform that behavior, and hence they enable quick identification of what another person is doing. Some mirror

---

[102] Asher & McDonald, 2009; Bukowski et al., 2007; Cillessen, Schwartz, & Mayeux, 2011.

[103] Altogether, researchers have identified five groups of students. The fifth group, *average students,* are liked by some peers and disliked by others, but without the intensity of feelings that characterize controversial students.

[104] Asher & Renshaw, 1981; Gazelle & Ladd, 2003; Guay, Boivin, & Hodges, 1999; McElhaney, Antonishak, & Allen, 2008.

[105] Asher & Paquette, 2003; Gazelle & Ladd, 2003; Igoa, 2007; Laursen et al., 2007; Yuker, 1988.

[106] N. Carr, 2011; Crosnoe, 2011; Greenhow et al., 2009; Valkenburg & Peter, 2009.

[107] Ellison, Steinfield, & Lampe, 2007; Greenhow et al., 2009; Gross, 2009; Gross, Juvonen, & Gable, 2002; Valkenburg & Peter, 2009; Yang & Brown, 2013.

[108] Bosacki, 2000; P. L. Harris, 2006; Izard et al., 2001; Cillessen & van den Berg, 2012.

[109] J. D. Mayer, Salovey, & Caruso, 2008; Waterhouse, 2006; Zeidner, Roberts, & Matthews, 2002.

neurons are specifically involved in facial expressions associated with emotions such as anguish and disgust, enabling rapid detection of those emotions in others. However, competent social cognition also requires involvement of the prefrontal cortex—probably the most "thoughtful" part of the brain—in order to draw reasonable inferences about *why* other individuals are behaving and feeling in certain ways.[110]

The following principles describe how social cognition influences children's and adolescents' interpersonal effectiveness.

As children get older, they become increasingly aware of other people's thoughts and feelings.

One important element of social cognition is **perspective taking**, looking at the world from other people's viewpoints. The following situation provides an example.

--- **SEE FOR YOURSELF** ---
LAST PICKED

Consider the following scenario:

> Kenny and Mark are co-captains of the soccer team. They have one person left to choose for the team. Without saying anything, Mark winks at Kenny and looks at Tom, who is one of the remaining children left to be chosen for the team. Mark looks back at Kenny and smiles. Kenny nods and chooses Tom to be on their team. Tom sees Mark and Kenny winking and smiling at each other. Tom, who is usually one of the last to be picked for team sports, wonders why Kenny wants him to be on his team. . . .

- Why did Mark smile at Kenny?
- Why did Kenny nod?
- Why did Kenny choose Tom to be on the team? How do you know this?
- Do you think that Tom has any idea of why Kenny chose him to be on the team? How do you know this? . . .
- How do you think Tom feels?[111]

To answer these questions, you must look at the situation from the perspectives of the three children involved. For instance, if you put yourself in Tom's shoes, you might suspect that he has mixed feelings. If he enjoys soccer, he may be happy to have a chance to play, but he may also be wondering whether the other boys' nonverbal signals indicate malicious intentions to make him look foolish on the soccer field. And, of course, Tom may feel embarrassed or demoralized at consistently being one of the last children picked for a team. (Accordingly, asking some students to choose others for their teams, as might be done in a physical education class, is generally *not* recommended.)

As you should recall from Chapter 3, metacognition improves over the course of development: With age and experience, children become increasingly aware of their own thought processes. In fact, as children learn more about their own thinking, they also become more adept at drawing inferences about what other people might be thinking. More generally, children develop a **theory of mind** that encompasses increasingly complex understandings of human mental and psychological states, including people's thoughts, beliefs, feelings, and motives. A reasonably accurate theory of mind enables children to interpret and predict the behaviors of the important people in their lives and, as a result, to interact effectively with those individuals.[112]

Consistent with what Jean Piaget and other researchers have found to be true for cognitive development, young children tend to focus on other people's concrete, observable characteristics and behaviors. However, they do have some awareness of other people's inner worlds. As early as age 4 or 5, they realize that what *they* know might be different from what *others* know, and they have some ability to draw inferences about other people's mental and emotional states.[113] As they

MyEdLab
Video Example 7.5.

What examples of perspective taking can you identify in this interview with 13-year-old Crystal?

---

[110] Gallese, Gernsbacher, Heyes, Hickok, & Iacoboni, 2011; Liu, Sabbagh, Gehring, & Wellman, 2009; Rizzolatti & Sinigaglia, 2008; Spunt & Lieberman, 2013.

[111] Bosacki, 2000, p. 711, format adapted.

[112] Flavell, 2000; Gopnik & Meltzoff, 1997; Wellman & Gelman, 1998.

[113] P. L. Harris, 2006; Schult, 2002; Wellman, Phillips, & Rodriguez, 2000.

progress through the elementary grades, they begin to realize that people's actions don't always reflect their thoughts and feelings—for instance, someone who looks happy might actually feel sad.[114] They also begin to understand that people don't just observe events but also *interpret* events, and thus others might view a situation differently than they themselves do.[115] In other words, children increasingly understand that thinking and learning are active, constructive processes.

By early adolescence, children realize that people can have mixed feelings about events and other individuals.[116] And courtesy of their expanding cognitive abilities, memory capacity, and social awareness, they become capable of **recursive thinking**.[117] That is, they can think about what other people might be thinking about them and eventually can reflect on other people's thoughts about themselves through multiple iterations (e.g., "You think that I think that you think . . ."). Adolescents don't always engage in such thinking, however (nor do adults, for that matter). As noted in the earlier description of the *imaginary audience,* focusing primarily on one's *own* perspective—without a realistic assessment of what others' perspectives are likely to be—is a common phenomenon in early adolescence.[118]

In the high school years, teenagers can draw on a rich body of knowledge derived from their many social experiences and, as a result, become ever more skillful at drawing inferences about people's psychological characteristics, intentions, and needs.[119] In addition, they're more attuned to the complex dynamics that influence behavior—not only thoughts, feelings, and present circumstances but also past experiences.[120] What we see emerging in the high school years, then, is a budding psychologist: an individual who can be quite astute in deciphering and explaining the motives and actions of others.

Children's cognitive processes in social situations influence their behaviors toward others.

Children and adolescents have a lot to think about when they consider what other people are thinking, feeling, and doing. Such **social information processing**—the mental processes involved in making sense of and responding to social events—is simply a more socially oriented version of the cognitive processes described in Chapter 2. Among other things, social information processing involves paying *attention* to certain behaviors in a social situation and trying to interpret and make sense of them through *elaboration.* For example, when children interact with peers, they might focus on certain remarks, facial expressions, and body language and try to figure out what a peer really means by, say, a thoughtless comment or sheepish grin. Children also consider one or more *goals* they hope to achieve during an interaction—perhaps preserving a friendship, on the one hand, or teaching somebody a "lesson," on the other. Then, taking into account both their interpretations and their goals, they draw on their previous knowledge and experiences to *retrieve* a number of possible responses and choose what is, in their eyes, a productive course of action.[121]

The behaviors young people attend to, the ways in which they interpret those behaviors, and the particular goals they have for their social interactions have a considerable impact on how effectively they interact with others. This point will become clear as we discuss the next principle.

Aggressive behavior is often the result of counterproductive cognitive processes.

When we see or hear the word *aggression,* we're most likely to think about **physical aggression**, which can potentially cause bodily injury. For example, in the opening case study, a few of the "popular" (i.e., high-status) students occasionally poke or shove poor William. But more often the allegedly popular students ridicule William, perhaps by calling him derogatory names or making

---

[114] Flavell, Miller, & Miller, 2002; Gnepp, 1989.

[115] Flavell, Green, & Flavell, 1995; Flavel, Miller, & Miller, 2002; Wellman, 1990.

[116] S. K. Donaldson & Westerman, 1986; Flavell & Miller, 1998; Harter & Whitesell, 1989.

[117] Flavell et al., 2002; Oppenheimer, 1986; Perner & Wimmer, 1985.

[118] Tsethlikai & Greenhoot, 2006; Tsethlikai, Guthrie-Fulbright, & Loera, 2007.

[119] N. Eisenberg, Carlo, Murphy, & Van Court, 1995; Paget, Kritt, & Bergemann, 1984.

[120] C. A. Flanagan & Tucker, 1999; Selman, 1980.

[121] Arsenio & Lemerise, 2004; Cillessen & van den Berg, 2012; Crick & Dodge, 1996; Dodge, 1986; Greenhoot, Tsethlikai, & Wagoner, 2006; E. R. Smith & Semin, 2007.

fun of certain things that he does. Such ridicule constitutes **psychological aggression**, an action intended to cause mental anguish or reduce self-esteem. In some cases, psychological aggression is specifically aimed at undermining friendships and other interpersonal relationships—perhaps by spreading unkind rumors or ostracizing someone from a valued social group—in which case it's also called *relational aggression*. Boys are more prone to physical aggression than girls are, but girls can be quite adept at psychological aggression, especially in the middle school and high school years.[122]

Researchers have identified two distinct groups of aggressive children and adolescents.[123] Those who engage in **proactive aggression** deliberately initiate aggressive actions as a means of obtaining desired goals. In contrast, those who engage in **reactive aggression** behave aggressively primarily in response to frustration or provocation. Members of the former group who direct considerable aggression toward particular individuals—whether it be physical or psychological aggression—are known as **bullies**. Students who are immature, anxious, and socially isolated are frequent victims of bullies, as are students with nontraditional sexual orientations and students with disabilities.[124]

Bullying certainly isn't limited to face-to-face interactions. Wireless technologies and the Internet provide vehicles for **cyberbullying**—electronically transmitting hostile messages, broadcasting personally embarrassing information, or in other ways causing someone significant psychological distress. For example, a student might upload humiliating video footage on YouTube, post unflattering (and possibly false) gossip on Facebook, or set up a website on which classmates can "vote" for their class's "biggest loser" or "easiest slut."[125] Cyberbullying can be more harmful than face-to-face bullying, in part because the perpetrators often remain anonymous (and thus can't be confronted) and in part because highly defamatory material can spread like wildfire through a large peer group.[126]

Some children and adolescents are genetically more predisposed to aggression than their peers, and others may exhibit heightened aggression as a result of neurological abnormalities.[127] Yet several cognitive and motivational factors also play a role in aggressive behavior:

- **Poor perspective-taking ability:** Many highly aggressive children have limited ability to look at situations from other people's perspectives or to empathize with their victims.[128]
- **Misinterpretation of social cues:** Children who are either physically or psychologically aggressive toward peers tend to interpret others' behaviors as reflecting hostile intentions, especially when those behaviors have ambiguous meanings. This **hostile attributional bias** is especially prevalent in children who are prone to *reactive* aggression.[129]
- **Prevalence of self-serving goals:** For most children and adolescents, establishing and maintaining interpersonal relationships are a high priority. For aggressive youngsters, however, more self-serving goals—perhaps maintaining an inflated self-image, seeking revenge, or gaining power and dominance—often take precedence.[130]
- **Ineffective social problem-solving strategies:** Aggressive individuals often have little knowledge of how to persuade, negotiate, or compromise, and so they resort to hitting, shoving, barging into play activities, and other ineffective strategies.[131]
- **Beliefs about the appropriateness and effectiveness of aggression:** Many aggressive children and adolescents believe that violence and other forms of aggression are acceptable ways of resolving conflicts and retaliating against others' misdeeds. Those who display high

> Jerry sez he did it with u last nite
>
> Not a surprise. U dressed like a slut!
>
> Yeah, SLUT!!! :-(
>
> Not true. Jerry wuz lying!
> Delivered
>
> Leave us alone!
>
> We all hate u!
>
> Go away!!!

Unfortunately, cell phones and other digital technologies make bullying entirely too easy.

[122] Card, Stucky, Sawalani, & Little, 2008; Crick, Grotpeter, & Bigbee, 2002; Goodwin, 2006; Pellegrini, 2011; A. J. Rose & Smith, 2009.

[123] Crick & Dodge, 1996; Poulin & Boivin, 1999; Vitaro, Gendreau, Tremblay, & Oligny, 1998.

[124] Hamovitch, 2007; McDougall & Vaillancourt, 2015; J. P. Robinson & Espelage, 2012; M. W. Watson, Andreas, Fischer, & Smith, 2005.

[125] Shariff, 2008; Valkenburg & Peter, 2009; Willard, 2007.

[126] Kowalski & Limber, 2007; Rivers, Chesney, & Coyne, 2011.

[127] Brendgen et al., 2008; Raine, 2008; van Goozen, Fairchild, & Harold, 2008.

[128] Coie & Dodge, 1998; Damon & Hart, 1988; R. F. Marcus, 1980.

[129] E. Chen, Langer, Raphaelson, & Matthews, 2004; Crick et al., 2002; Dodge et al., 2003; Rodkin et al., 2015.

[130] R. F. Baumeister, Smart, & Boden, 1996; Menon et al., 2007; Pellegrini, Roseth, Van Ryzin, & Solberg, 2011; Rodkin et al., 2015.

[131] Neel, Jenkins, & Meadows, 1990; D. Schwartz et al., 1998; Troop-Gordon & Asher, 2005.

rates of *proactive* aggression are also apt to believe that aggressive action will yield positive results—for instance, that it will enhance social status at school or restore "honor" to one's family or social group. Not surprisingly, aggressive individuals tend to associate with one another, thereby confirming one another's beliefs that aggression is appropriate.[132]

Unless adults actively intervene, some aggressive children show a continuing pattern of aggression as they grow older, almost guaranteeing long-term maladjustment and difficulties with peers.[133] The victims of aggression certainly suffer as well. Children who are frequent targets of bullying become anxious and depressed—sometimes suicidal—and their classroom performance can deteriorate as a result.[134] They may fear retaliation if they alert adults to their plight, and so they have little optimism that things will improve.[135] As one junior high school student put it, telling a teacher about bullying incidents "only gets me in more trouble from the bullies because they pick on me, they hit me, they call me names. . . They call me 'stink bomb,' 'stinky,' 'dirty boy,' and stuff like that."[136]

Even children who simply *observe* peer-on-peer aggression can suffer considerable psychological distress, especially if they don't intervene on the victim's behalf. Perhaps they feel guilty that they didn't come to the victim's assistance, or perhaps they worry that they themselves might soon be victimized. Furthermore, if they see bullying and other aggressive behaviors going unpunished, some may come to believe that such actions are perfectly acceptable.[137]

We'll consider strategies for addressing bullying and other forms of chronic aggression later in the chapter. For now, we should note that young people's decisions to act aggressively (or not) reflect their general beliefs about right and wrong—and thus are one indicator of their moral and prosocial development.

Students' social skills play a key role in their ability to establish and maintain productive relationships with their classmates and other peers—which, in turn, can have a major impact both on their psychological well-being and on their ability to successfully learn and achieve at school. In the hotlinked Self-Check quiz and Application Exercise that follow, you can check and apply your understandings related to Big Idea 7.2:

> *In order to benefit fully from their interactions with peers, children must have good social skills and be able to interpret and respond to various social situations and problems in productive ways.*

MyEdLab **Self-Check 7.2**

MyEdLab **Application Exercise 7.3.** In this activity, you can apply what you have learned about children's social development to a second-grade writing activity.

7.3 MORAL AND PROSOCIAL DEVELOPMENT

Big Idea 7.3 Some signs of moral reasoning and prosocial behavior emerge early in life, but key components of morality continue to evolve over the course of childhood and adolescence.

Some interpersonal behaviors, such as sharing, helping, and comforting, are aimed at benefiting others more than oneself. These **prosocial behaviors**, plus such traits as honesty, fairness, and concern for other people's needs and rights, fall into the domain of **morality**. By and large, children and

---

[132] R. P. Brown, Osterman, & Barnes, 2009; Crick, Murray-Close, Marks, & Mohajeri-Nelson, 2009; Dishion et al., 2008; Fontaine, Yang, Dodge, Bates, & Pettit, 2008; Mayeux et al., 2011; Paciello, Fida, Tramontano, Lupinetti, & Caprara, 2008; Pellegrini & Bartini, 2000; M. W. Watson et al., 2005.

[133] Crick et al., 2009; Dodge et al., 2003; Hampson, 2008; Pepler, Jiang, Craig, & Connolly, 2008; Swearer et al., 2010.

[134] Hoglund, 2007; Ladd et al., 2012; McDougall & Vaillancourt, 2015; P. K. Smith, 2011; Swearer et al., 2010.

[135] Holt & Keyes, 2004; R. S. Newman & Murray, 2005.

[136] Bergamo & Evans, 2005, p. 17.

[137] L. M. Jones, Mitchell, & Turner, 2015; M. J. Mayer & Furlong, 2010; E. J. Meyer, 2009; Rivers, Poteat, Noret, & Ashurst, 2009.

adolescents who think and behave in moral and prosocial ways gain more support from their teachers and peers and, as a result, achieve greater academic and social success over the long run.[138]

Morality and prosocial behavior are complex entities that appear to involve multiple parts of the brain. Certainly mirror neurons are involved, in that they partially underlie children's perspective-taking abilities. But moral and prosocial actions also require certain emotions and reasoning capabilities, and these reside in distinctly different brain regions.[139]

Several general principles describe the nature of moral and prosocial development over the course of childhood and adolescence.

> Something I Would Vote For
>
> I would vote for No more hurting whales & dolphins. I think it is important to save them because they were here before us. Also some speices are already exctinct like the chinese river dolphin. That is what I would vote for.

A strong moral code often encompasses a concern for the welfare of many animal species, as shown in 9-year-old Mia's response to the topic "Something I Would Vote For."

Children begin applying internal standards for behavior at a very early age.

Well before their first birthday, children show that they value prosocial behavior over antisocial behavior, and by age 3 they have some understanding that behaviors causing physical or psychological harm are inappropriate.[140] By age 4 most children understand that causing another person harm is wrong regardless of what authority figures might tell them and regardless of what consequences certain behaviors may or may not bring.[141]

Children increasingly distinguish between moral and conventional transgressions.

Virtually every culture discourages some behaviors—moral transgressions—because they cause damage or harm, violate human rights, or run counter to basic principles of equality, freedom, or justice. A culture typically discourages other behaviors—conventional transgressions—that, although not unethical, violate widely held agreements about how people should act (e.g., children shouldn't talk back to adults or burp at meals). Whereas many moral transgressions are universal across cultures, conventional transgressions are usually specific to a particular culture.[142] For example, although burping is frowned on in mainstream Western culture, people in some cultures burp as a compliment to the cook. Occasionally, certain conventions do have moral overtones, as you can see in the Cultural Considerations box "Cultural and Ethnic Diversity in Personal, Social, and Moral Development."

Children's awareness of social conventions emerges in infancy and increases throughout the preschool, elementary, and secondary school years.[143] But especially as children reach adolescence, they don't always agree with adults about which behaviors constitute moral transgressions, which ones fall into the conventional domain, and which ones are simply a matter of personal choice. For example, many adolescents resist rules they think are infringements on their personal freedoms—for instance, rules about clothing, hair style, and talking in class.[144]

Children's capacity to respond emotionally to other people's misfortunes and distress increases throughout the school years.

Within the first 2 or 3 years of life, two emotions important for moral development emerge.[145] First, children occasionally show guilt—a feeling of discomfort when they know they've inflicted damage or caused someone else pain or distress. They also feel shame—a feeling of embarrassment or humiliation when they fail to meet their own or other people's standards for moral behavior.

---

[138] Caprara, Barbaranelli, Pastorelli, Bandura, & Zimbardo, 2000; Ladd et al., 2012; Spinrad & Eisenberg, 2009.

[139] Decety & Cowell, 2014; Gallese, Gernbacher, Heyes, Hickok, & Iacoboni, 2011; Moll et al., 2007; Young & Saxe, 2009.

[140] Hamlin, 2013; Hamlin & Wynn, 2011; Helwig, Zelazo, & Wilson, 2001.

[141] Laupa & Turiel, 1995; Smetana, 1981; Tisak, 1993.

[142] Nucci, 2009; Smetana, 2006; Turiel, 2002.

[143] Helwig & Jasiobedzka, 2001; Laupa & Turiel, 1995; Nucci, 2001; Nucci & Nucci, 1982; E. Robbins & Rochat, 2011; M. F. H. Schmidt & Tomasello, 2012.

[144] Nucci, 2009; Smetana, 2005.

[145] Kochanska, Gross, Lin, & Nichols, 2002; M. Lewis & Sullivan, 2005.

Cultural and Ethnic Diversity in Personal, Social, and Moral Development

Researchers have observed cultural and ethnic differences in many aspects of personal, social, and moral development. Following are especially noteworthy ones. As you read about them, however, keep in mind that such characteristics (a) are only *average* group differences and (b) can change significantly from one generation to the next if families move to a very different cultural environment—for example, if they move from the Far East to North America.[a]

PERSONALITY. Although children's personalities are partly the result of temperamental differences, culture also plays a significant role in molding their personality characteristics. For example, many Asian children are raised to be shy and reserved, whereas many children in North America and some European countries are raised to be outgoing, assertive, and independent. Furthermore, some cultural groups explicitly nurture different characteristics in males and females. For instance, some Hispanic groups encourage boys to be strong and assertive (*machismo*) while urging girls to be demure and nurturing (*marianismo*).[b]

SENSE OF SELF. As noted earlier in the chapter, young people's group memberships affect their sense of self. In some cultures, children see their group membership and connections with other individuals as central parts of who they are as human beings; for example, this is the case in many Middle Eastern and Far Eastern countries, in Māori communities in New Zealand, and in many Native American communities in the Western Hemisphere.[c] Such cultural groups encourage children to take pride in accomplishments that contribute to the greater good of the family or larger community as well as, or perhaps *instead of*, their own accomplishments.[d]

In addition, many young people have a strong **ethnic identity**: They're both aware and proud of their ethnic group and willingly adopt some of the group's behaviors. Occasionally a strong ethnic identity can lead them to reject mainstream Western values; for instance, students of color may accuse high-achieving students of *acting White*, a label that essentially means "you're not one of us."[e] For the most part, however, students with a strong and positive ethnic identity do *well* in school both academically and socially.[f] Furthermore, pride in one's ethnic heritage can serve as an emotional buffer against other people's prejudicial insults and discrimination.[g] The following statement by an African American high school student provides an example:

I'm proud to be black and everything. But, um, I'm aware of, you know, racist acts and racist things that are happening in the world, but I use that as no excuse, you know. I feel as though I can succeed. . . . I just know that I'm not gonna let [racism] stop me.[h]

Not all children and adolescents from minority groups affiliate strongly with their cultural and ethnic groups. Some young people (especially those with multiple racial or cultural heritages) fluctuate in the strength of their ethnic identity depending on the context and situation.[i] In addition, older adolescents may experiment with varying forms of an ethnic identity—perhaps initially adopting an intense, inflexible, and hostile one before eventually settling into a more relaxed, open-minded, and productive one.[j]

SOCIAL SKILLS AND RELATIONSHIPS. Interpersonal behaviors vary from culture to culture as well. For instance, some cultural groups (e.g., some groups in northern Canada and in the South Pacific) regularly use seemingly antisocial behaviors—especially teasing and ridicule—to teach children to remain calm and handle criticism.[k] In contrast, many Native Americans, many people of Hispanic heritage, and certain African American communities place particular emphasis on group harmony, and many Asian groups strongly discourage physical and psychological aggression. Children from these backgrounds may be especially adept at negotiation and peace making.[l]

Most children and adolescents of all cultures value the company of age-mates, but the extent to which they actually spend time with their peers is partly a function of their cultural group. For example, on average, Asian Americans spend less leisure time with friends than young people from other groups, and they're more likely to choose friends who value academic achievement.[m] Language differences also come into play here: Children who have recently immigrated from a non-English-speaking country to an English-speaking one may have relatively little interaction with peers because of their limited ability to communicate.[n]

MORALITY AND PROSOCIAL BEHAVIOR. Conceptions of moral and immoral behavior vary as a function of cultural background as well. Virtually all cultures espouse the importance of both individual rights and fairness (i.e., an *ethic of justice*) and compassion for others (i.e., an *ethic of caring*). In addition,

some cultural groups see such things as *group loyalty, respect for authority figures,* and *reverence and devotion to certain individuals or objects* as being essential elements of personal morality.[o] Various cultural groups place greater or lesser emphasis on each of these potential aspects of moral behavior.[p] For example, in much of North America, helping others (or not) is considered to be a voluntary choice, but in some societies (e.g., in many Asian and Arab countries) it is one's *duty* to help others. Such a sense of duty, which is often coupled with strong ties to family and the community, can lead to considerable prosocial behavior.[q]

Some diversity is also seen in the behaviors that cultural groups view as moral transgressions versus those they see as conventional transgressions.[r] For example, in some cultures telling lies to avoid punishment for inappropriate behavior is considered morally wrong, but in certain other cultures, it's a legitimate way of saving face.[s] And whereas in mainstream Western culture, how one dresses is largely a matter of convention and personal choice, in some deeply religious groups, certain forms of dress (e.g., head coverings) are viewed as moral imperatives.

---

[a] L. Chang et al., 2011.

[b] L. Chang et al., 2011; X. Chen, Chung, & Hsiao, 2009; Goldston et al., 2008; Huntsinger & Jose, 2006; Rothbart, 2011; Rubin et al., 2010; Tamis-Lemonda & McFadden, 2010.

[c] Kağitçibaşi, 2007; Macfarlane, Webber, Cookson-Cox, & McRae, 2014; M. Ross & Wang, 2010; Whitesell, Mitchell, Kaufman, Spicer, & the Voices of Indian Teens Project Team, 2006.

[d] Banks & Banks, 1995; P. M. Cole & Tan, 2007.

[e] Bergin & Cooks, 2008; O'Connor, Mueller, Lewis, Rivas-Drake, & Rosenberg, 2011; Ogbu, 2008a.

[f] Altschul, Oyserman, & Bybee, 2006; Chavous et al., 2003; Mandara, Gaylord-Harden, Richards, & Ragsdale, 2009; Nasir, McLaughlin, & Jones, 2009; Smokowski, Buchanan, & Bacalleo, 2009.

[g] L. Allen & Aber, 2006; P. J. Cook & Ludwig, 2008; Goodnow, 2010; Pahl & Way, 2006.

[h] Way, 1998, p. 257.

[i] Hitlin, Brown, & Elder, 2006; Y. Hong, Wan, No, & Chiu, 2007; Yip & Fuligni, 2002.

[j] Cross, Strauss, & Fhagen-Smith, 1999; Nasir et al., 2009; Seaton et al., 2006.

[k] Rogoff, 2003.

[l] X. Chen & Wang, 2010; Gardiner & Kosmitzki, 2008; Guthrie, 2001; Halgunseth et al., 2006; Rubin et al., 2010; Xu, Farver, Chang, Yu, & Zhang, 2006.

[m] Rubin et al., 2010; Steinberg, 1996.

[n] Ahn, 2005; Igoa, 2007.

[o] Haidt, 2012; J. G. Miller, 2007.

[p] J. G. Miller, 2007; Snarey, 1995; Turiel, 2002.

[q] X. Chen et al., 2009; J. G. Miller, 2007; Greenfield, 1994; Rubin et al., 2010; Triandis, 1995.

[r] Nucci, 2001, 2009.

[s] Triandis, 1995.

Both guilt and shame, although unpleasant emotions, are good signs that children are developing a sense of right and wrong and will work hard to correct their misdeeds.[146]

Guilt and shame are the result of doing something perceived to be wrong. In contrast, empathy—experiencing the same feelings as someone in unfortunate circumstances—appears in the absence of personal wrongdoing. The ability to empathize emerges in the preschool years and continues to develop throughout childhood and adolescence (e.g., see Figure 7.2).[147] Truly prosocial children—those who help others even in the absence of their own wrongdoing—typically have a considerable capacity for perspective taking and empathy.[148] Empathy is especially likely to spur prosocial behavior when it leads to sympathy, whereby children not only assume another person's feelings but also have concerns for the individual's well-being.[149]

With age, reasoning about moral issues becomes increasingly abstract and flexible.

To probe people's reasoning about moral issues, researchers sometimes present moral dilemmas, situations in which two or more people's rights or needs may be at odds and for which there are no clear-cut right or wrong solutions. The following exercise is an example.

─────────── **SEE FOR YOURSELF** ───────────
MARTIN'S PLIGHT

Imagine that you're in the ninth grade. You're walking quickly down the school corridor on your way to your math class when you see three boys from the so-called "popular" crowd cornering a small, socially awkward boy named Martin. The boys first make fun of Martin's thick glasses and unfashionable clothing, then they start taunting him with offensive names such as "fag" and "retard." What do you do?

a. You look the other way, pretending you haven't heard anything, and hurry on to class. If you were to stop to help, the boys might taunt you as well, and that will only make the situation worse.

b. You shoot Martin a sympathetic look and then head to class so that you won't be late. Afterward, you anonymously report the incident to the principal's office, because you know that the boys' behaviors have violated your school's antibullying policy.

c. You stop and say, "Hey, you jerks, cut it out! Martin's a really nice guy and doesn't deserve your insulting labels. Come on, Martin—let's go. We might be late for math class, so we need to hurry."

───

Looking for the moral high ground in this situation, you might very well have chosen Alternative *c*. But if you were a ninth grader—someone who might still be working hard to fit in with your peer group—is that *really* what you would do?

In his groundbreaking early research on moral development, Lawrence Kohlberg gave children and adults a variety of moral dilemmas and asked them both what they would do and why they would do it. Based on the hundreds of responses he obtained, Kohlberg proposed that as children grow older, they construct increasingly complex views of morality. In Kohlberg's view, the development of moral reasoning is characterized by a sequence of six stages grouped into three general *levels* of morality: preconventional, conventional, and postconventional (see Table 7.2). Children with preconventional morality haven't yet adopted or internalized society's conventions regarding what things are right and wrong but instead focus largely on external consequences that certain actions might bring to themselves, as illustrated in Alternative *a* in the exercise. Kohlberg's second level, conventional morality, is characterized by general, often unquestioning obedience either to an authority figure's dictates or to established rules and norms, even when there are no consequences for disobedience. Alternative *b* in the exercise is an example: You report a violation of school rules to school authorities, but you don't want to be late to class—that would violate another school rule—and through your actions, you don't jeopardize any good relationships you might have with the supposedly "popular" boys.

[146] N. Eisenberg, 1995; Harter, 1999; Narváez & Rest, 1995.

[147] N. Eisenberg et al., 1995; Spinrad & Eisenberg, 2009.

[148] Damon, 1988; Decety & Cowell, 2014; N. Eisenberg, Zhou, & Koller, 2001; Hoffman, 1991.

[149] Batson, 1991; Decety & Cowell, 2014 (who use the term *empathic concern*); N. Eisenberg & Fabes, 1998; Malti, Gummerum, Keller, & Buchman, 2009; Turiel, 1998.

think about it
How do you feel when you inadvertently inconvenience someone else? when you hurt someone else's feelings? when a friend unexpectedly loses a close family member? Do such feelings as guilt, shame, and sympathy come to mind?

FIGURE 7.2 In this poem about the Holocaust, Matthew, a middle school student, expresses empathy for its victims.

hopes
goals
dreams
happiness
  broken
   destroyed
    eliminated
     exterminated
no steps forward
no evolution
no prosperity
no hope
But
maybe
perhaps
except
if we
help
together
we stand
a chance.

Table 7.2 • The Three Levels and Six Stages of Moral Reasoning in Kohlberg's Theory of Moral Development

LEVEL	PROPOSED AGE RANGE	STAGE	NATURE OF MORAL REASONING
Level I: Preconventional morality	Seen in preschool children, most elementary school students, some junior high school students, and a few high school students	Stage 1: Punishment-avoidance and obedience	People make decisions based on what is best for themselves, without regard for others' needs or feelings. They obey rules only if established by more powerful individuals; they may disobey if they aren't likely to get caught. "Wrong" behaviors are those that will be punished.
		Stage 2: Exchange of favors	People recognize that others also have needs. They may try to satisfy others' needs if their own needs are also met ("You scratch my back, and I'll scratch yours"). They continue to define right and wrong primarily in terms of consequences to themselves.
Level II: Conventional morality	Seen in a few older elementary school students, some junior high school students, and many high school students (Stage 4 usually doesn't appear before high school)	Stage 3: Good boy/good girl	People make decisions based on what actions will please others, especially authority figures (e.g., teachers, popular peers). They're concerned about maintaining relationships through sharing, trust, and loyalty, and they consider other people's perspectives and intentions when making decisions.
		Stage 4: Law and order	People look to society as a whole for guidelines about right and wrong. They know that rules are necessary for keeping society running smoothly and believe that it's their duty to obey them. However, they perceive rules to be inflexible; they don't necessarily recognize that as society's needs change, rules should change as well.
Level III: Postconventional morality	Rarely seen before college (Stage 6 is extremely rare even in adults)	Stage 5: Social contract	People recognize that rules represent agreements among many individuals about appropriate behavior. Rules are seen as useful mechanisms that maintain the general social order and protect individual rights, rather than as absolute dictates that must be obeyed simply because they are the law. People also recognize the flexibility of rules; rules that no longer serve society's best interests can and should be changed.
		Stage 6: Universal ethical principle	Stage 6 is a hypothetical, ideal stage that few people ever reach. People in this stage adhere to a few abstract, universal principles (e.g., equality of all people, respect for human dignity, commitment to justice) that transcend specific norms and rules. They answer to a strong inner conscience and willingly disobey laws that violate their own ethical principles.

Sources: Colby & Kohlberg, 1984; Colby, Kohlberg, Gibbs, & Lieberman, 1983; Kohlberg, 1976, 1984, 1986; Reimer, Paolitto, & Hersh, 1983; Snarey, 1995.

MyEdLab Content Extension 7.2.
You can learn more about Kohlberg's theory in this supplementary reading.

In contrast to the somewhat rigid nature of conventional morality, people at Kohlberg's third level, **postconventional morality**, view rules as useful but changeable mechanisms that ideally can maintain the general social order and protect human rights; rules aren't absolute decrees that must be obeyed without question. These people live by their own abstract principles about right and wrong and may disobey rules inconsistent with these principles. Alternative *c* has an element of postconventional reasoning: You're more concerned about protecting Martin's physical and psychological safety than you are about getting to class on time.

Considerable research on moral reasoning has followed on the heels of Kohlberg's work. Some of it supports Kohlberg's proposed sequence: Generally speaking, people seem to make advancements in the order Kohlberg described.[150] And as Kohlberg suggested, moral development emerges out of children's own, self-constructed beliefs—beliefs they often revisit and revise. Nevertheless, his theory has weaknesses. For one thing, Kohlberg underestimated young children, who, as we discovered earlier, acquire some internal standards of right and wrong long before they reach school age. Also, his stages encompassed a mixture of moral issues (e.g., causing harm) and social conventions (e.g., having rules to help society run smoothly), but as we've seen, children distinguish between these two domains, and their views about each domain may change differently over time.[151] A third weakness is that Kohlberg's theory pays little attention to one very

---

[150]Boom, Brugman, & van der Heijden, 2001; Colby & Kohlberg, 1984; Snarey, 1995; Stewart & Pascual-Leone, 1992.

[151]Nucci, 2001, 2009.

important aspect of morality: *showing compassion and helping* other people.[152] Finally, Kohlberg overlooked motives, social benefits, and other situational factors that children and adolescents consider when deciding what actions are morally right and wrong.[153] For example, they're more apt to think of lying as immoral if it causes someone else harm than if it apparently has no adverse effect—that is, if it's just a "white lie" or enables them to escape from what they believe to be unreasonable restrictions on their behavior.[154]

Many contemporary developmental psychologists believe that moral reasoning involves general *trends* rather than distinct stages. It appears that children and adolescents gradually construct several different standards that guide their moral reasoning and decision making in various situations. Such standards include the need to address one's own personal interests, consideration of other people's needs and motives, a desire to abide by society's rules and conventions, and, perhaps eventually, an appreciation for abstract ideals regarding human rights and society's overall needs.[155] With age, young people increasingly apply more advanced standards, but even a fairly primitive one—satisfying one's own needs without regard for others—may occasionally take priority.[156]

Table 7.3 describes the forms that moral reasoning and other aspects of morality are apt to take at various grade levels. As you look at the suggested strategies in the right-hand column of the table, notice how several of them are consistent with the *authoritative parenting* style described earlier in the chapter.

Challenges to current moral perspectives can promote advancement toward more sophisticated reasoning.

Kohlberg drew on Piaget's concept of *disequilibrium* to explain how learners progress to more advanced moral reasoning. (As you may recall from Chapter 5, some contemporary motivation theorists instead use the term *cognitive dissonance.*) In particular, children and adolescents occasionally encounter dilemmas and persuasive arguments that they can't adequately respond to using their current moral perspectives. Over time they become increasingly aware of weaknesses in their thinking, especially if their judgments are challenged by people who reason at one stage above their own. For example, a Stage 3 student who agrees to let a popular cheerleader copy his homework may begin to question his decision if a Stage 4 student argues that the cheerleader would learn more by doing her own homework. By struggling with such challenges, Kohlberg suggested, children and adolescents may begin to revise their own thoughts about morality and gradually move from one stage to the next.

Although most contemporary psychologists reject Kohlberg's idea of discrete stages, researchers have confirmed his view that disequilibrium spurs moral development. For instance, classroom discussions of controversial topics and moral issues appear to promote increased perspective taking and the transition to more advanced reasoning.[157] Implicit in this finding is a very important point: Children's moral reasoning does *not* result simply from adults dogmatically passing along particular moral values and preachings.[158] Instead, it emerges out of children's own, personally constructed beliefs—beliefs they often revisit and revise over time.

Cognition, affect, and motivation all influence moral and prosocial behavior.

Most children behave more morally and prosocially as they grow older, and their increasingly moral behavior is due, in part, to more advanced moral reasoning.[159] However, the correlation between moral reasoning and moral behavior isn't an especially strong one. As mentioned earlier, affective factors—guilt, shame, empathy, and sympathy—also enter into the picture. For instance, when children feel guilty about damage or distress they've caused, they may work hard to repair

---

[152] Gilligan, 1982, 1987; P. L. Hill & Roberts, 2010; J. G. Miller, 2007.

[153] Aikins & Litwack, 2011; Helwig et al., 2001; Killen & Smetana, 2008; Nucci, 2009; Piaget, 1932/1960; Thorkildsen, 1995; Turiel, 1998.

[154] S. A. Perkins & Turiel, 2007; Turiel, Smetana, & Killen, 1991.

[155] Killen & Smetana, 2008; Krebs, 2008; Nucci, 2009; Rest, Narvaez, Bebeau, & Thoma, 1999.

[156] Rest et al., 1999; Turiel, 1998.

[157] DeVries & Zan, 1996; Power, Higgins, & Kohlberg, 1989; Schlaefli, Rest, & Thoma, 1985.

[158] Damon, 1988; Higgins, 1995; N. Park & Peterson, 2009; Turiel, 1998.

[159] Blasi, 1980; N. Eisenberg, Zhou, et al., 2001; Paciello et al., 2008.

DEVELOPMENTAL TRENDS

TABLE 7.3 • Moral Reasoning and Prosocial Behavior at Different Grade Levels

GRADE LEVEL	AGE-TYPICAL CHARACTERISTICS	EXAMPLE	SUGGESTED STRATEGIES
Grades K–2	• Some awareness that behaviors causing physical or psychological harm are morally wrong • Ability to distinguish between behaviors that violate human rights and dignity versus those that violate social conventions • Guilt and shame about misbehaviors that cause obvious harm or damage • Some empathy for, as well as attempts to comfort, people in distress • Appreciation for the need to be fair; fairness seen as strict equality in how a desired commodity is divided	When Jake pushes Otis off the ladder of a playground slide, several of the boys' kindergarten classmates are horrified. One child shouts, "That's wrong!" and several others rush to Otis's side to make sure he's not hurt.	• Make standards for behavior very clear. • When students misbehave, give reasons that such behaviors are unacceptable, focusing on the harm and distress they have caused for others (i.e., use *induction*, a strategy described later in the chapter). • Encourage students to comfort others in times of distress. • Model sympathetic responses; explain what you're doing and why you're doing it. • Keep in mind that some selfish behavior is typical for the age-group; when it occurs, encourage perspective taking and prosocial behavior.
Grades 3–5	• Knowledge of social conventions for appropriate behavior • Growing realization that fairness doesn't necessarily mean equality—that some people (e.g., peers with disabilities) may need more of a desired commodity than others • Increasing empathy for unknown individuals who are suffering or needy • Recognition that one should strive to meet others' needs as well as one's own; growing appreciation for cooperation and compromise • Increased desire to help others as an objective in and of itself	At the suggestion of his third-grade teacher, 8-year-old Jeff acts as a "special friend" to Evan, a boy with severe physical and cognitive disabilities who joins the class two or three days a week. Evan can't speak, but Jeff gives him things to feel and manipulate and talks to him whenever class activities allow conversation. And the two boys regularly sit together at lunch. Jeff comments, "Doing things that make Evan happy make me happy, too."	• Make prosocial behaviors (e.g., giving, sharing, caring for others) a high priority in the classroom. • Explain how students can often meet their own needs while helping others (e.g., when asking students to be "reading buddies" for younger children, explain that doing so will help them become better readers themselves). • Use prosocial adjectives (e.g., *kind, helpful*) when praising altruistic behaviors.
Grades 6–8	• Growing awareness that some rules and conventions are arbitrary; in some cases accompanied by resistance to these rules and conventions • Interest in pleasing and helping others, but with a tendency to oversimplify what "helping" requires • Tendency to believe that people in dire circumstances (e.g., homeless people) are entirely responsible for their own fate	After the midwinter break, 13-year-old Brooke returns to school with several large nose rings and her hair styled into long, vertical spikes above her head. The school principal tells her that her appearance is inappropriate and insists that she go home to make herself more presentable. Brooke resists, claiming, "I have a right to express myself however I want!"	• Talk about how rules enable classrooms and other groups to run more smoothly. • Involve students in group projects that will benefit their school or community. • When imposing discipline for moral transgressions, accompany it with explanations about the harm that has been caused (i.e., use *induction*), especially when working with students who have deficits in empathy and moral reasoning.
Grades 9–12	• Increasing concern about doing one's duty and abiding by the rules of society as a whole, rather than simply pleasing certain authority figures • Realization that most rules and conventions serve useful purposes • Genuine empathy for people in distress • Belief that society has an obligation to help people in need	Several high school students propose and establish a school chapter of Amnesty International, an organization dedicated to the preservation of human rights around the world. The group invites knowledgeable guest speakers from various countries and conducts several fundraisers to help combat abusive practices against women.	• Explore moral issues in social studies, science, and literature. • Encourage community service as a way of engendering feelings of commitment to helping others. Ask students to reflect on their experiences through group discussions or written essays. • Have students read autobiographies and other literature that depict heroic figures who have actively worked to help people in need.

Sources: N. Eisenberg, 1982; N. Eisenberg & Fabes, 1998; Farver & Branstetter, 1994; C. A. Flanagan & Faison, 2001; Gibbs, 1995; Gummerum, Keller, Takezawa, & Mata, 2008; D. Hart & Fegley, 1995; Hastings, Utendale, & Sullivan, 2007; Helwig & Jasiobedzka, 2001; Helwig et al., 2001; Hoffman, 2000; Kohlberg, 1984; Krebs & Van Hesteren, 1994; Kurtines, Berman, Ittel, & Williamson, 1995; Laupa & Turiel, 1995; M. Lewis & Sullivan, 2005; Nucci, 2009; Nucci & Weber, 1995; Rothbart, 2011; Rushton, 1980; Smetana & Braeges, 1990; Spinrad & Eisenberg, 2009; Turiel, 1983, 1998; Wainryb, Brehl, & Matwin, 2005; Yates & Youniss, 1996; Yau & Smetana, 2003; Youniss & Yates, 1999; Zahn-Waxler, Radke-Yarrow, Wagner, & Chapman, 1992.

the damage, soothe hurt feelings, and in other respects "make things right."[160] And when they can empathize and sympathize with people in dire circumstances, they're apt to show considerable caring and compassion even in the absence of their own wrongdoing.

Nevertheless, children's own needs and goals often come into play as well. For instance, although children may want to do the right thing, they may also be concerned about whether others will approve of their actions and about what positive or negative consequences might result. Children are more apt to behave in accordance with their moral standards if the benefits are high (e.g., they gain others' approval or respect) and the personal costs are low (e.g., an act of altruism involves little sacrifice).[161] They're also more likely to behave prosocially if the recipients have helped them in the past or might be able to help them in the future.[162] As it turns out, young people often help themselves when they help others: Many children who engage in altruistic behaviors enhance not only other people's well-being but also their *own* sense of well-being.[163]

Moral values become an important part of some young people's sense of self.

Some adolescents incorporate a commitment to moral values into their overall sense of identity: They think of themselves as generally caring individuals who are concerned about the rights and well-being of others.[164] Their acts of altruism and compassion aren't limited to their friends and acquaintances but also extend to the community at large. For example, in one study, researchers conducted in-depth interviews with inner-city Hispanic and African American teenagers who showed an exceptional commitment to helping others (by volunteering many hours at Special Olympics, a neighborhood political organization, a nursing home, etc.). These teens didn't necessarily display more advanced moral reasoning than their peers (as defined by Kohlberg's stages), but they were more likely to describe themselves in terms of moral traits and goals (e.g., helping others) and to mention certain ideals toward which they were striving.[165]

As you can see, then, morality and sense of self are interrelated. In fact, the various topics we've discussed in this chapter—personality, sense of self, peer relationships, social cognition, and moral and prosocial development—are all interconnected. For example, moral beliefs influence the interpersonal behaviors that learners believe to be appropriate (social cognition). Those interpersonal behaviors influence the quality of peer relationships, which, in turn, influences learners' self-concepts and self-esteem. This ripple effect works in other directions as well. For instance, learners' sense of self is apt to influence their interpretations of other people's behaviors toward them (social cognition again) and so will also influence their responses and overall social effectiveness (e.g., recall the discussion of hostile attributional bias). And the general patterns observed in individual learners' social and moral behaviors are all part of that general characteristic we call "personality."

think about it

Given these situational factors affecting moral and prosocial behavior, under what conditions is a student most likely to choose Alternative c in the "Martin's Plight" dilemma presented earlier? (For possible answers, click **here**.)

In order to effectively foster students' moral and prosocial development, teachers must first understand the general nature of such development. In the hotlinked Self-Check quiz and Application Exercise that follow, you can check and apply your understandings related to Big Idea 7.3:

Some signs of moral reasoning and prosocial behavior emerge early in life, but key components of morality continue to evolve over the course of childhood and adolescence.

MyEdLab **Self-Check 7.3**

MyEdLab **Application Exercise 7.4.** In this activity, you can practice discerning the logic underlying various children's moral reasoning about academic cheating.

---

[160] N. Eisenberg, 1995; Harter, 1999; Malti et al., 2009.

[161] Batson & Thompson, 2001; Cillessen et al., 2011; Hawley, 2014; Narváez & Rest, 1995; Wentzel, Filisetti, & Looney, 2007.

[162] A. Martin & Olson, 2015.

[163] J. G. Miller, Kahle, & Hastings, 2015.

[164] Arnold, 2000; Blasi, 1995; Hastings, Utendale, & Sullivan, 2007; McFarland, Brown, & Webb, 2013; Thorkildsen et al., 2008; Youniss & Yates, 1999.

[165] D. Hart & Fegley, 1995.

7.4 PROMOTING PERSONAL, SOCIAL, AND MORAL DEVELOPMENT

Big Idea 7.4 Effective teachers accommodate individual differences in students' temperaments and personalities, help students acquire a healthy sense of self, and foster students' ongoing social and moral development.

The things we've discovered about personal, social, and moral development have many implications for classroom practice. Recommendations in this section of the chapter are divided into three subsections, one each for the personal, social, and moral aspects of development. In a subsequent section, we'll consider additional strategies in the three domains that can be especially beneficial for students who face exceptional personal or social challenges. It's important to note, however, that advancements in the three domains are closely intertwined—thus, fostering young people's development in one area is likely to enhance their development in other areas as well.

Fostering Personal Development

The characteristics students bring with them to school—including their distinct temperaments and personalities and their beliefs about who they are as individuals—are apt to have a significant influence on their classroom performance. The following strategies for fostering students' personal development should enhance their academic and social success in the classroom.

Accommodate students' diverse temperaments.

To some degree, students' typical ways of behaving—for instance, their energy levels, attentiveness, sociability, and ability to keep impulses in check—reflect temperamental differences that aren't entirely within their control. Many temperamental variables affect how students engage in and respond to classroom activities and so also affect students' learning and achievement.[166] Yet there's no single "best" temperament that maximizes classroom success. Instead, children are more likely to succeed at school when there's a **goodness of fit**, rather than a mismatch, between their natural inclinations and typical behaviors, on the one hand, and classroom expectations, on the other.[167] For example, highly energetic, outgoing children often shine—but quieter students might feel anxious or intimidated—when teachers want students to participate actively in group discussions and projects. Quieter children do better—and some energetic children may be viewed as disruptive—when teachers require a lot of independent seatwork. The Classroom Strategies box "Accommodating Students' Diverse Temperaments" presents several examples of how teachers can translate this goodness-of-fit idea into effective classroom practices.

Keep in mind that although temperamental differences are, by definition, *genetic* predispositions to behave in particular ways, various cultural groups may encourage some ways of behaving and actively *dis*courage other kinds of behaviors. For example, as noted in the earlier Cultural Considerations box, students from Asian backgrounds are more likely to be shy and reserved—but only *on average*—than students of European descent. Teachers are most effective when they take such cultural differences into account in their daily instructional and classroom-management strategies.

Help students get a handle on who they are and who they want to become.

Students who have a healthy sense of self believe both that (a) they can successfully tackle certain challenging tasks (reflecting high self-efficacy) and (b) in general, they are good and capable people (reflecting high overall self-worth). We identified several ways of enhancing students' sense of self-efficacy and self-worth in Chapter 5, and many additional ones appear earlier in this chapter in the right-most column of Table 7.1. Undoubtedly, the most effective strategy is to *help students be successful,* not only at academic tasks but also in social situations.

Yet equally important for enhancing students' sense of self is to help them gain an understanding of who they are as people—their strengths and weaknesses, likes and dislikes, hopes and

---

[166] Keogh, 2003; Rothbart, 2007; Saudino & Plomin, 2007.
[167] Keogh, 2003; Rothbart, 2011; A. Thomas & Chess, 1977.

CLASSROOM STRATEGIES

Accommodating Students' Diverse Temperaments

- **Minimize downtime for students with high energy levels.**
  As a way of letting a chronically restless third grader release pent-up energy throughout the school day, his teacher gives him small chores to do (e.g., erasing the board, sharpening pencils, cleaning art supplies) and shows him how to complete the chores quietly so as not to disturb classmates.

- **Provide regular opportunities for highly sociable students to interact with classmates.**
  In a unit on colonial America, a fifth-grade teacher assigns a project in which students must depict a typical colonial village in some way (e.g., by writing a research paper, drawing a map on poster board, or creating a miniature three-dimensional model). The students can choose to work on the project alone or with one or two classmates, with the stipulation that students who work with peers must undertake more complex projects than students who work alone.

- **Be especially warm and attentive with very shy students, and identify contexts in which they feel comfortable interacting with peers and openly expressing their ideas.**
  A ninth-grade teacher has a new student join one of his classes midway through the school year. The student comes to class alone each day and doesn't join in conversations with peers before or after class. When the teacher sees her eating lunch by herself in the cafeteria one day, he sits beside her and engages her in conversation about her previous school and community. The following day in class, he assigns a small-group, cooperative learning project that students will work on periodically over the next 2 weeks. He forms cooperative groups of three or four students each, making sure to place the new girl with two students who he knows will be friendly and helpful.

- **When students have trouble adapting to new circumstances, give them advance notice of unusual activities and provide extra structure and reassurance.**
  A kindergarten teacher has discovered that two children in his class do well when the school day is orderly and predictable but often become anxious or upset whenever the class departs from its usual routine. To prepare the children for a field trip to the fire station on Friday, the teacher begins talking about the trip on Monday, explaining what the class will do and see during the visit. He also recruits the father of one of the anxiety-prone children to serve as a parent assistant that day.

- **If students seem to be overwhelmed by noisy or chaotic situations, locate or create a more calm and peaceful environment for them.**
  Several middle school students find the school cafeteria loud and unsettling. Their math teacher offers her classroom as a place where they can occasionally eat instead. On some days she eats with them. At other times she sits at her desk and grades papers, but the students know that she'll gladly stop to talk if they have a question or concern.

- **Teach self-regulation strategies to students who act impulsively.**
  A high school student often shouts out comments and opinions in her history class. One day the student's teacher takes her aside after school and gently explains that her lack of restraint is interfering with classmates' ability to participate in discussions. To sensitize the student to the extent of the problem, the teacher asks her to keep a daily tally of how many times she talks without first raising her hand. A week later the two meet again, and the teacher suggests a self-talk strategy that can help the student actively participate without dominating discussions.

Sources: Some strategies based on suggestions by M.-L. Chang & Davis, 2009; Keogh, 2003.

fears, and so on—and who they might ultimately want to become.[168] Not all students can achieve at superior levels in the classroom, nor can they all be superstars on the athletic field. Students are more likely to have a positive sense of self if they find one or more activities—perhaps singing, student government, or competitive jump-roping—in which they can shine.[169] And when students have long-standing difficulties in certain domains, discovering that their failures are due to a previously undiagnosed disability (e.g., dyslexia or attention-deficit hyperactivity disorder) can help repair some of the damage to self-esteem.[170] Such a discovery helps students make sense of *why* they haven't been able to perform certain tasks as well as their peers. It can also spur them and their teachers to identify effective coping strategies. In the following reflection, one student reveals how, in coming to terms with his dyslexia, he's acquired a healthy sense of self despite his disability:

> Dyslexia is your brain's wired differently and there's brick walls for some things and you just have to work either around it or break it. I'm dyslexic at reading that means I need a little bit more help. If you have dyslexia the thing you have to find is how to get over the hump, the wall. Basically you either go around it and just don't read and get along in life without it or you break down the wall.[171]

---

[168] Sinai et al., 2012; Thorkildsen et al., 2008.

[169] Bracken, 2009; Harter, 1999; Jenlink, 1994.

[170] MacMaster, Donovan, & MacIntyre, 2002; Zambo, 2003.

[171] Zambo, 2003, p. 10.

Notice that the student doesn't resign himself to inevitable failure—instead, he talks about *getting over the hump, the wall*. This phrase should remind you of the discussion of *attributions* in Chapter 5: He's attributing his difficulties to controllable factors such as effort and new strategies, leading to an optimistic, *incremental view* of his reading ability.[172]

Create a warm, supportive environment with clear standards for behavior and explanations of why some behaviors are unacceptable.

An *authoritative* environment—one that combines affection and respect for children with reasonable restrictions on their behavior—seems to be important not only in parenting but also in teaching.[173] Warm teacher–student relationships can help students meet their need for relatedness, and positive feedback about students' strengths and successes can enhance their sense of self. At the same time, teachers must let students know in no uncertain terms which behaviors are and are not acceptable in the classroom. Behaviors that jeopardize the rights, safety, or psychological well-being of others—such as stealing, aggression, and comments that ridicule a particular individual, gender, or ethnic group—must be immediately addressed and suppressed.

In upcoming sections of this chapter, we'll identify effective strategies for establishing good teacher–student relationships and addressing inappropriate behaviors; many additional strategies will follow in Chapter 9. But for now, we should note that any disciplinary action for unacceptable behavior is most likely to foster students' long-term personal, social, and moral development when it's accompanied by **induction**—that is, by an explanation of *why* a behavior is unacceptable.[174] For example, a teacher might describe how a behavior harms another student either physically ("Having your hair pulled the way you just pulled Mai's can really be painful") or emotionally ("You hurt John's feelings when you call him names like that"). Alternatively, a teacher might explain how an action has caused someone else inconvenience ("Because you ruined Marie's jacket, her parents are making her do extra chores to earn the money for a new one"). Still another approach is to explain someone else's perspective, intention, or motive ("This science project you've just ridiculed may not be as fancy as yours, but I know that Cameron spent many hours working on it and is quite proud of what he's done").

Induction is victim centered: It helps students focus on the distress of others and recognize that they themselves have been the cause. The consistent use of induction in disciplining children, especially when accompanied by *mild* punishment for misbehavior, appears to promote cooperation with rules and foster the development of prosocial behavior.[175]

Channel adolescents' risk-taking tendencies into safe activities.

Especially at the middle school and high school levels, teachers must be aware of adolescents' propensity to engage in dangerous, high-risk behaviors. Yet scare tactics—perhaps talking about peers who have died from drug overdoses or been killed in high-speed chases—typically have little effect on teenagers' behavior. Nor do rational explanations of probabilities—such as the likelihood of getting pregnant in a single sexual encounter—make much of a difference. When adolescents get together in recreational activities, common sense and reason seem to go out the window. Teachers, administrators, parents, and other community members must all work together to keep adolescent risk taking in check. For instance, many communities now hold all-night after-prom parties in the school building or other supervised location as a way of keeping students from drinking and driving. Another strategy is to provide outlets for *reasonable* risk taking, such as climbing walls, skateboard parks, and small-group, supervised wilderness trips.[176]

Sometimes adolescents engage in risky behaviors in an attempt to project an adultlike image, to be "cool" and "with it."[177] There are much healthier ways to show one's coolness and

---

[172] For example, see Yeager & Dweck, 2012.

[173] For example, see J. M. T. Walker & Hoover-Dempsey, 2006.

[174] Hoffman, 2000; Rothbart, 2011.

[175] G. H. Brody & Shaffer, 1982; Hoffman, 2000; Nucci, 2001; Spinrad & Eisenberg, 2009; Turiel, 2006.

[176] Spear, 2007; Steinberg, 2005.

[177] J. P. Allen & Antonishak, 2008; Blanton & Burkley, 2008; Crosnoe, 2011.

withit-ness, some of which teachers can encourage at school. Gaining competence and prestige in rock music, athletics, and community service are just a few of the many possibilities.

Encouraging Effective Social Cognition and Interpersonal Skills

Teachers are in an excellent position to foster productive ways of thinking about social situations and to help students interact effectively with others. The following recommendations are based on research findings related to social cognition, social skills, and peer relationships.

Foster perspective taking and empathy.

Virtually any classroom offers many opportunities for perspective taking and empathy. One strategy is to talk frequently about people's thoughts, feelings, and motives, as is done in induction.[178] In doing so, teachers must, of course, use age-appropriate language—for instance, kindergarten teachers might use words such as *think, want,* and *sad,* whereas fifth-grade teachers could use words such as *misunderstanding, frustration,* and *mixed feelings.* Most high school students have the cognitive and social reasoning capabilities to understand fairly abstract and complex psychological terms, such as *being passive-aggressive* and *having an inner moral compass.*

Another, related strategy is to ask students to take an opposing party's perspective—that is, to put themselves in someone else's shoes—in times of disagreement or conflict.[179] An example is the use of **peer mediation**, in which students help one another solve interpersonal problems. In this approach, students learn how to mediate conflicts among classmates by asking opposing sides to express their differing viewpoints and then work together to devise a reasonable resolution.[180] In one research study involving several second- through fifth-grade classrooms,[181] students were trained to help peers resolve interpersonal conflicts by asking the opposing sides to do the following:

1. Define the conflict (the problem).
2. Explain their own perspectives and needs.
3. Explain the other person's perspectives and needs.
4. Identify at least three possible solutions to the conflict.
5. Reach an agreement that addresses the needs of both parties.

Students took turns serving as mediator for their classmates, such that everyone had experience resolving the conflicts of others. As a result, the students more frequently resolved their *own* interpersonal conflicts in ways that addressed the needs of all involved parties, and they were less likely to ask for adult intervention than were students in an untrained control group.

The benefits of peer mediation provide an example of Lev Vygotsky's proposal that sophisticated cognitive processes often have their roots in social interactions. In a peer mediation session, students model effective conflict resolution skills for one another, and they may eventually internalize the skills they use in solving others' problems to solve their *own* problems. Peer mediation is most effective when students of diverse ethnic backgrounds, socioeconomic groups, and achievement levels all serve as mediators. It's appropriate primarily for small, short-term interpersonal problems, such as hurt feelings or conflicts over use of limited resources. In comparison, even the most proficient of peer mediators may be ill prepared to handle conflicts that reflect deep-seated and emotionally charged attitudes and behaviors—for instance, conflicts that involve sexual harassment or homophobia.[182]

Opportunities for perspective taking and empathy may also arise in lessons about academic subject matter. For example, in discussions of current events, teachers might have different students—or, using the Internet, different classrooms—take different countries' perspectives as they explore significant world problems, such as climate change or arms control.[183] In history

---

[178] Ruffman, Slade, & Crowe, 2002; Woolfe, Want, & Siegal, 2002.

[179] Adalbjarnardottir & Selman, 1997; Gehlbach, Brinkworth, & Harris, 2012.

[180] Deutsch, 1993; D. W. Johnson & Johnson, 1996, 2006.

[181] D. W. Johnson, Johnson, Dudley, Ward, & Magnuson, 1995.

[182] Casella, 2001a; K. M. Williams, 2001b.

[183] Gehlbach et al., 2008.

FIGURE 7.3 Two examples of perspective taking in history assignments

> Roots II ON THE BOAT TO AMERICA
>
> I could feel the pain Kunta-Kinte was having. Once I had a paper cut and when in the ocean it hurt more than a wasp sting, and that was just paper cut! I can't even imagine the pain or fright that Kunta-Kinte had being taken from his family and home. Or his parents' hurt finding out that first son was being taken to be a slave, their son that had just become a man.
>
> I also am horrified about how they treated women. Beely-warmers! The makes angre!

> My Diary
>
> July 1, 1700
> Dear Diary - Today was a scorcher. I could not stand it and I was not even working. The slaves looked so hot. I even felt for them. And it is affecting my tobacco. It's too hot too early in the season. The tobacco plants are not growing quickly enough. I can only hope that it rains. Also today Robert Smith invited me to a ball at his house in two days. In 5 days I am going to have my masked ball. We mailed out the invitations two days ago. My wife, Beth, and I thought of a great idea of a masked ball. We will hire our own band.
>
> July 2, 1700
> Dear Diary - It was another scorcher. I wish it would cool down. I don't think the slaves can handle it. It looked like some of them would faint. I had them drink more water. Later in the day a nice breeze came up. Then I gave them the rest of the day off. Also today we planned a trip to Richmond. . . .
>
> July 5, 1700
> Dear Diary - Today we had to wake up before the sun had risen. After a breakfast of hot cakes, eggs, and sausage, we headed back home. We got there at the end of the morning. When I got back it was very, very hot. One of the slaves fainted so I gave them the rest of the day off, fearing revolt. I also gave them extra food and water. It makes me think that they are only people too. I know that this is unheard of but it really makes me think.

lessons, teachers can ask students to imagine people's feelings or role-play events during particularly traumatic and stressful times.[184] Figure 7.3 shows two writing samples created during history lessons about slavery in the pre–Civil War United States. The reaction paper on the left was written by 10-year-old Charmaine, whose fifth-grade class had been watching *Roots,* a television miniseries about a young African man (Kunta Kinte) who is captured and brought to America to be a slave. Charmaine acknowledges that she can't fully grasp Kunta Kinte's physical pain (her own experience with pain has been limited to having a paper cut in saltwater). Even so, she talks about his "pain" and "fright" and about his parents' "hurt" at losing their firstborn son, and she is incensed by some colonists' view of African women as little more than "beeby {baby} warmers." The diary entries on the right were written by 14-year-old Craig, whose ninth-grade history teacher asked his class to write journal entries that might capture the life of a southern plantation owner. Notice that Craig tries to imagine someone else (a plantation owner) taking *other people's* perspectives (those of slaves). Such two-tiered perspective taking is similar to recursive thinking but in this case involves thinking "I think that you think that someone else thinks. . . ." Notice, too, that Craig has the plantation owner engage in some minimal prosocial behavior: giving the slaves time off on hot summer days and providing extra food and water. It may not surprise you to learn that Charmaine and Craig, now young adults, are both actively involved in public service.

Talk with students about what it *really* means to be popular.

Especially in the middle school and high school grades, some students do things that aren't in their own or others' best interests in order to be part of the "popular" crowd.[185] For example, they may ridicule and bully peers whom they perceive to be odd or nerdy—a situation we saw in the

---

[184] Brophy, Alleman, & Knighton, 2009; M. Davison, 2011; P. Lee & Ashby, 2001.
[185] Cillessen et al., 2011; Cillessen & van den Berg, 2012.

opening case study. And they may abruptly abandon friendships that could undermine their image of "coolness," as 14-year-old Courtney explained when describing something that happened in a close-knit group of five girls:

> The five of us would hang out, sit at the same lunch table. Then Jamie became good friends with another group. They had parties, became the popular group, so Jamie left us. She had been Maggie's best friend, so Maggie was devastated. Jamie wouldn't talk to us, wouldn't even wave at us in the hallway.

One way teachers might discourage such behaviors is to act as *myth busters,* explicitly opening up conversations about what true popularity involves. For example, a teacher might begin by having students think of a few peers they genuinely like and then of a few peers they really *don't* like. These mental lists must remain only in students' own heads—*no names should be mentioned*—but by asking students to reflect on such questions as "What characteristics do people on your first list have in common?" and "Why don't you like the people on your second list?" qualities such as "kind" and "trustworthy" (for the first list) and "stuck-up" and "mean" (for the second list) might come to light. And to the extent that students are willing to share their perceptions and experiences related to the school's social-status hierarchy—again, *without naming names* or in some other way finger-pointing— they provide yet another opportunity for classmates to engage in perspective taking and empathy.

Provide frequent opportunities for social interaction and cooperation.

Schools and classrooms invariably involve complex social situations in which students can learn and practice new social skills. For instance, students' play activities— whether the fantasy play of preschoolers and kindergartners or the rule-based games of older children and adolescents—can promote cooperation, sharing, perspective taking, and conflict resolution skills.[186] Assignments and activities that require students to cooperate with one another to achieve a common goal (as the school play does in the opening case study) can foster leadership skills and a willingness to both help and get help from peers.[187] Simply changing assigned seating arrangements on a regular basis enables students can get to know certain classmates better and perhaps discover common interests or similar senses of humor.[188] And extracurricular activities provide additional opportunities for students to interact and work cooperatively with a wide range of peers.[189]

Explicitly teach social skills to students who have trouble interacting effectively with others.

Because of their social isolation, rejected and neglected students have few opportunities to develop the good social skills that many of them desperately need.[190] When they do interact with peers, their behaviors may be counterproductive, leaving them more isolated than ever. Consider the plight of a seventh grader named Michelle:

> Michelle is an extremely bright student whose academic accomplishments have earned much teacher praise over the years. But despite her many scholastic successes, Michelle has few friends. To draw attention to herself, she talks incessantly about her academic achievements. Her classmates interpret such bragging as a sign of undeserved arrogance and insult her frequently as a way of knocking her down a peg or two. In self-defense, Michelle begins hurling insults at her classmates as soon as she sees them—beating them to the punch, so to speak.

Extracurricular activities can foster productive peer relationships and a general "team spirit." They can also be a source of success for students who struggle with academic tasks. Here 7-year-old Danny, who has a learning disability, expresses his love of baseball.

[186] Coplan & Arbeau, 2009; Creasey, Jarvis, & Berk, 1998; Gottman, 1986; Pellegrini & Bohn, 2005; Rubin, 1982.

[187] Certo, 2011; Y. Li et al., 2007; Webb & Farivar, 1994.

[188] van den Berg, Seters, & Cillessen, 2012.

[189] Feldman & Matjasko, 2005; Genova & Walberg, 1984; Mahoney, Cairns, & Farmer, 2003; A. J. Martin & Dowson, 2009.

[190] Bukowski et al., 2007; Coie & Cillessen, 1993; McElhaney et al., 2008.

When students routinely offend or alienate others (as Michelle does), their peers seldom give them constructive feedback that might help them improve their behavior on future occasions, and so it may be up to teachers and other adults to give them that guidance.

Teachers and other school personnel can teach students appropriate ways of interacting with others both through explicit verbal instructions and through modeling desired behaviors. Such instruction is especially effective when students also have an opportunity to practice their newly learned social skills (perhaps through role-playing) and get concrete feedback about how well they're doing.[191]

Teaching social problem-solving skills can be helpful as well. Some students lack productive ways of solving social problems; for example, they might rudely snatch classroom materials that a classmate has been monopolizing or barge into a playground game without asking first. One effective approach in working with such students is to teach them a series of mental steps, as follows:[192]

1. Define the problem.
2. Identify several possible solutions.
3. Predict the likely consequences of each solution.
4. Choose the best solution.
5. Identify the steps required to carry out the solution.
6. Carry out the steps.
7. Evaluate the results.

Such steps—which you may recognize as involving *social cognition*—often help students with a history of interpersonal problems to develop more effective social skills.[193]

Explain what bullying is and why it cannot be tolerated.

Students and teachers alike often have misconceptions about bullying. Many think it involves only physical aggression, even though psychological aggression—for instance, name calling, deliberate social exclusion, and defamatory Internet postings—constitutes bullying as well. Another common misconception is that the victims of bullies somehow deserve what they get, perhaps because they display immature behaviors or need to "toughen up" and learn to defend themselves. Thus many students condone bullying and act as a supportive audience for the perpetrators.[194]

Certainly, a recommendation offered earlier—*foster perspective taking and empathy*—can go part of the way toward discouraging bullying. But in addition, all students must learn about the various forms bullying can take and the truly harmful effects it can have on its victims. Researchers and experienced educators have found the following schoolwide strategies to be helpful:[195]

- Explain that bullying doesn't necessarily involve physical aggression—that it can instead involve actions intended to cause psychological distress: taunts, threats, sexual harassment, unkind rumors, social exclusion, humiliating Internet postings, and the like.
- Use the mnemonic PIC to help students remember that bullying is:
  - Purposeful behavior ("He meant to do it")
  - Imbalanced ("That's not fair; he's bigger")
  - Continual ("I'm afraid to enter the classroom because she's always picking on me")
- Explicitly forbid name calling, including derogatory labels for a particular sex, ethnic group, sexual orientation, or disability.
- Explain that even seemingly mild forms of bullying can have long-term adverse effects on students' personal and emotional well-being.

---

[191] Bierman & Powers, 2009; S. N. Elliott & Busse, 1991; K. L. Lane, Menzies, Bruhn, & Crnobori, 2011; Themann & Goldstein, 2001; S. Vaughn, 1991; D. E. Watkins & Wentzel, 2008.

[192] S. N. Elliott & Busse, 1991; Meichenbaum, 1977; Shure & Aberson, 2006; Weissberg, 1985; Yell, Robinson, & Drasgow, 2001.

[193] K. R. Harris, 1982; Meichenbaum, 1977; Yell et al., 2001.

[194] Salmivalli & Peets, 2009; Swearer et al., 2010.

[195] Ansary, Elias, Greene, & Green, 2015; Bradshaw, 2015; D. J. Connor & Baglieri, 2009; Frey, Hirschstein, Edstrom, & Snell, 2009; Horne, Orpinas, Newman-Carlson, & Bartolomucci, 2004, pp. 298–299; Juvonen & Galván, 2008; E. J. Meyer, 2009; Parada, Craven, & Marsh, 2008; S. W. Ross & Horner, 2009; Swearer et al., 2010; Willard, 2007; Yeager & Dweck, 2012.

- Communicate that stopping bullying isn't only a school expectation but also a moral imperative—that students must safeguard other people's physical and psychological well-being as well as their own.

- Also communicate optimism that *all* students—including chronic bullies and their victims—have the potential to change for the better. In other words, promote an *incremental view* of personality development—a view in which other people's personality traits *aren't* necessarily stable, "built-in" characteristics that will inevitably persist throughout their lifetimes.

- Recruit well-respected students (e.g., student council members, members of school sports teams) to keep a lookout for bullying in stairways, washrooms, and other places where school faculty members might not be present.

- Teach students effective skills for discouraging bullying incidents among peers (e.g., saying "Stop, you're being disrespectful" and escorting the victim from the scene).

- Prominently post a general code of conduct for student behavior throughout the school building.

As we'll discover in Chapter 9, mutual respect for one another's welfare and well-being both on and off campus is a key ingredient in the *sense of community* so important for students' school success.

Teachers can find some of the strategies just listed—and many others as well—at the U.S. government website www.stopbullying.gov. But despite such strategies, some bullying is likely to occur, and students may fear retaliation if they try to stand up to the bullies or inform a faculty member about the bullying.[196] It's important, then, that students have a mechanism through which they can report bullying incidents with anonymity.

Be alert for incidents of bullying and other forms of aggression, and take appropriate actions with both the victims and the perpetrators.

School faculty members *must* intervene when they see some students victimize others, and they must keep alert for other possible incidents of bullying.[197] Regular victims of bullies need social and emotional support from both their teachers and their classmates. Some may also need one or more sessions with a school counselor, perhaps to address feelings of vulnerability and depression or perhaps to learn social skills and help-seeking strategies that can minimize future victimization incidents.[198] One successful school program provided regular "lunch buddies" (college-student volunteers) who joined chronically bullied students in the cafeteria twice a week, indirectly conveying to peers the message that these students had many positive qualities.[199]

The perpetrators of aggression require intervention as well. They must be given appropriate consequences for their actions, of course, but they should also be helped to behave more productively. Specific strategies should be tailored to the thoughts and motives that underlie their aggression. Such strategies as encouraging perspective taking, helping students interpret social situations more productively, and teaching effective social problem-solving skills are all potentially useful in reducing aggression and other disruptive behaviors.[200] Putting students in situations where they must explicitly *help*, rather than harm, others—for instance, asking them to tutor younger children—can also be beneficial.[201]

Yet even when an aggressive student shows dramatic improvements in behavior, classmates may continue to steer clear, perhaps thinking "Once a bully, always a bully."[202] So when teachers and other adults work to improve the behaviors of aggressive students, they must work to improve the students' reputations as well. For example, teachers might encourage active involvement in

MyEdLab
Interactive Case 7.1.

Teachers must intervene whenever the students are either the perpetrators or victims of aggression. In this activity, you can gain practice with potentially effective intervention strategies.

---

[196] L. M. Jones et al., 2015; R. S. Newman & Murray, 2005; Salmivalli & Peets, 2009.

[197] In the United States, taking action to address many forms of bullying is mandated by a 1999 Supreme Court decision; see *Davis v. Monroe County Board of Education,* 526 U.S. 629.

[198] Espelage & Swearer, 2004; Frey et al., 2009; R. S. Newman, 2008; Yeung & Leadbeater, 2007.

[199] Newgent, Cavell, Johnson, & Stegman, 2008.

[200] Cunningham & Cunningham, 2006; Dodge, Godwin, & The Conduct Problems Prevention Research Group, 2013; Frey et al., 2009; Hudley & Graham, 1993.

[201] J. R. Sullivan & Conoley, 2004.

[202] Bierman, Miller, & Stabb, 1987; Caprara, Dodge, Pastorelli, & Zelli, 2007; Juvonen & Weiner, 1993.

extracurricular groups or conduct cooperative learning activities in which students can exhibit their newly developed social skills. Teachers should also demonstrate through words and actions that *they* like and appreciate every student, including formerly antisocial ones. When teachers do so, their attitudes are apt to be contagious.[203]

Ultimately, interventions with aggressive students are most likely to be effective if schools communicate the importance of acting kindly and respectfully toward all members of the school community—teachers and students alike.[204] Furthermore, the overall school climate must be a relatively peaceful one. At some schools, violence and aggression are commonplace, and students may believe that acting aggressively is the only way to ensure that they don't become victims of *someone else's* aggression. Unfortunately, they may be right: Putting on a tough, seemingly invulnerable appearance (sometimes known as "frontin' it") can be critical for their well-being.[205] Such a situation is, of course, hardly conducive to effective learning and academic achievement. We'll look at strategies for addressing schoolwide aggression and violence in Chapter 9.

Explicitly discourage inappropriate communications and postings via cell phones and the Internet.

As we've seen, cyberbullying can be especially devastating. Threatening text messages can be sent at all hours of the day or night. And humiliating postings on social networking sites can be quickly "liked" by dozens of peers and "shared" with hundreds or thousands of others. Many school districts now have policies that prohibit student-to-student cyberbullying. Although cyberbullying often occurs beyond school walls, in many cases it's easily documented, perhaps by a victim who saves a harassing text message or by a concerned classmate who alerts school personnel to a disrespectful Facebook post. Furthermore, students who bully their peers in cyberspace tend to be the same ones who bully their peers at school, and students who are electronically bullied tend to be the same ones who are bullied in face-to-face interactions.[206] In any event, schools *must* address incidents of cyberbullying in the same ways they address on-site bullying, intervening on behalf of the victims and administering appropriate consequences to the perpetrators.[207]

Wireless technologies and the Internet can threaten students' well-being in a second way as well: They provide vehicles for unscrupulous individuals (usually adults) to misrepresent themselves in chat rooms or elsewhere in an attempt to prey on naive and potentially vulnerable young people.[208] Certainly, teachers must warn students about such predators whenever they have an appropriate opportunity to do so, but they should also keep in mind that students are less likely to wander through cyberspace in search of new friendships when they have supportive peer relationships at school.

Promote understanding, communication, and interaction among diverse groups.

Even when they're in the same building with a large number of peers, students frequently congregate in small groups or cliques with whom they spend much of their time, and a few students remain socially isolated (recall William's isolation before his breakout role in the school play). Immigrant students rarely interact with long-term residents, and newcomers to a school are often socially isolated. Many students with disabilities are neglected or rejected by their classmates.[209]

Often students divide themselves along racial or ethnic lines when they eat lunch and interact in the school yard. In fact, such self-imposed segregation *increases* once students reach the middle school grades. As young adolescents from racial and ethnic minority groups begin to look closely and introspectively at issues of racism and ethnic identity, they often find it helpful to compare experiences and perspectives with other group members.[210] Furthermore, commonly held

[203] L. Chang, 2003; L. Chang et al., 2004.

[204] Espelage & Swearer, 2004; E. J. Meyer, 2009; Parada et al., 2008; S. W. Ross & Horner, 2009.

[205] K. M. Williams, 2001a.

[206] E. J. Meyer, 2009; Raskauskas, 2010.

[207] In the United States, a recent ruling by the Fourth Circuit Court of Appeals supports a school's right to punish off-campus student-to-student bullying; see *Kowalski v. Berkeley County Schools,* 652 F. 3d 565 (2011).

[208] Wolak, Finkelhor, Mitchell, & Ybarra, 2008.

[209] Hymel, 1986; Juvonen & Hiner, 1991; Olneck, 1995; Pérez, 1998; Schofield, 1995; Yuker, 1988.

[210] B. B. Brown et al., 2008; Schofield, 1995; Tatum, 1997.

stereotypes and prejudices (either real or presumed) can exacerbate any apparent boundaries between diverse social groups.[211] And in some cases, students simply have little or no knowledge about a cultural group very different from their own.

To promote intergroup interaction, then, a necessary first step is to help students understand the customs, perspectives, and needs of their classmates from diverse backgrounds. Especially as students get older and become cognitively capable of reflecting on their own and others' thoughts and feelings, they often benefit from heart-to-heart discussions about prejudice and racism in their own community and school. Some students from mainstream Western culture may initially feel uncomfortable talking about this topic with their minority-group peers, but once the ice is broken, greater cross-cultural understanding and communication can result.[212] And students are more likely to be accepting of classmates with disabilities if they understand the nature of those disabilities, *provided that* the students and their parents have given permission to share what might otherwise be confidential information.

It's equally important that schools give students many opportunities to form productive cross-group relationships. Teachers and school administrators can take a variety of proactive steps to broaden the base of students' social interactions. Several possibilities are presented in the Classroom Strategies box "Encouraging Productive Interactions Among Diverse Individuals and Groups," and additional strategies aimed specifically at reducing gang-related hostilities are presented in Chapter 9. When students from diverse groups interact regularly—and especially when they come together as equals, work toward a common goal, and see themselves as members of the same "team"—they're more apt to accept and possibly even *value* one another's differences.[213]

Promoting Moral Reasoning and Prosocial Behavior

Some of the recommendations in the preceding sections should promote moral and prosocial development as well as other aspects of personal and social development. For example, the use of induction—explaining *why* certain behaviors won't be tolerated—can help students acquire more prosocial attitudes toward their classmates. And by encouraging perspective taking and empathy, teachers foster advancements in moral reasoning and altruistic behavior as well as in social skills. Following are four additional recommendations.

Expose students to numerous models of moral and prosocial behavior.

Children and adolescents are more likely to exhibit moral and prosocial behavior when they see other people (including their teachers!) behaving in moral rather than immoral ways. For instance, when they see adults or peers being generous and showing concern for others, they tend to do likewise.[214] Good models can be found in various media as well—for example, in carefully selected and age-appropriate literature, in prosocial song lyrics, and, yes, even in some video games.[215]

Engage students in discussions of social and moral issues.

As noted earlier, the disequilibrium (cognitive dissonance) that students experience when they wrestle with moral dilemmas can often promote more advanced moral reasoning. Social and moral dilemmas often arise within the school curriculum. Following are examples:

- Is military retaliation for acts of terrorism acceptable if it involves killing innocent people?
- Should laboratory rats be used to study the effects of cancer-producing agents?
- Was Hamlet justified in killing Claudius to avenge the murder of his father?

Students typically have a variety of opinions about social and moral issues, and they often get emotionally as well as cognitively involved in the subject matter (recall the discussion of *hot cognition*

---

[211] Black-Gutman & Hickson, 1996; G. L. Cohen & Garcia, 2008; Ogbu, 2008b.

[212] Schultz, Buck, & Niesz, 2000; Tatum, 1997.

[213] Dovidio & Gaertner, 1999; Oskamp, 2000; J. H. Pfeifer, Brown, & Juvonen, 2007; Ramiah & Hewstone, 2013.

[214] Hoffman, 2000; Rushton, 1980; Spinrad & Eisenberg, 2009.

[215] Dubow, Huesmann, & Greenwood, 2007; Greitemeyer, 2011; K. Lee et al., 2014; Nucci, 2001; Tobias, Fletcher, Dai, & Wind, 2011.

CLASSROOM STRATEGIES

Encouraging Productive Interactions among Diverse Individuals and Groups

- **Set up situations in which students can form cross-group friendships.**
  To help students get to know a greater number of their peers, a junior high school science teacher gives them assigned seats in her classroom and changes the seating chart once a month. She also decides how students will be paired for weekly lab activities.

- **Minimize or eliminate barriers to social interaction.**
  Students in a third-grade class learn basic words and phrases in American Sign Language so that they can work and play with a classmate who is deaf.

- **Encourage and facilitate participation in extracurricular activities, and take steps to ensure that no single group dominates in membership or leadership in any particular activity.**
  When recruiting members for the scenery committee for the eighth grade's annual school play, the committee's teacher–adviser encourages both "popular" and lower-status students to participate. Later he divides the workload in such a way that students who don't know one another very well must work closely and cooperatively.

- **Conduct class discussions about the negative consequences of intergroup hostilities.**
  A high school English teacher in a low-income, inner-city school district uses a lesson on Shakespeare's *Romeo and Juliet* to start

a discussion about an ongoing conflict between two rival ethnic-group gangs in the community. "Don't you think this family feud is stupid?" she asks, referring to Shakespeare's play. When students agree, she continues, "The Capulets are like the Latino gang, and the Montagues are like the Asian gang. . . Don't you think it's stupid that the Latino gang and the Asian gang are killing each other?" The students immediately protest, but when she presses them to justify their thinking, they gradually begin to acknowledge the pointlessness of a long-standing neighborhood rivalry whose origins they can't even recall.

- **Develop nondisabled students' understanding of students with disabilities, *provided that* the students and their parents give permission to share what might otherwise be confidential information.**
  In a widely publicized case, Ryan White, a boy who had contracted AIDS from a blood transfusion, met considerable resistance against his return to his neighborhood school because parents and students thought he might infect others. After Ryan's family moved to a different school district, school personnel actively educated the community about the fact that AIDS doesn't spread through casual day-to-day contact. Ryan's reception at his new school was overwhelmingly positive. Later Ryan described his first day at school: "When I walked into classrooms or the cafeteria, several kids called out at once, 'Hey, Ryan! Sit with me!'"

Sources: D. J. Connor & Baglieri, 2009; Dilg, 2010; Feddes, Noack, & Rutland, 2009; Feldman & Matjasko, 2005; *Freedom Writers*, 1999, p. 33 (Shakespeare example); Mahoney, Cairns, & Farmer, 2003; A. J. Martin & Dowson, 2009; Schofield, 1995; Schultz et al., 2000; Sleeter & Grant, 1999; Tatum, 1997; van den Berg et al., 2012; R. White & Cunningham, 1991, p. 149 (Ryan White example).

in Chapter 5). To facilitate productive discussions about such issues, teachers must create a trusting and nonthreatening classroom atmosphere in which students can express ideas without fear of censure or embarrassment. Teachers should also help students identify all aspects of a dilemma, including the needs and perspectives of the various individuals involved. The most fruitful discussions occur when teachers encourage students to explore their reasons for thinking as they do—that is, to clarify and reflect on the moral principles on which they're basing their judgments.[216]

Discourage all forms of cheating.

Another behavior teachers must explicitly and consistently discourage is *cheating* in its various forms, whether it be submitting a research paper downloaded from the Internet (i.e., plagiarism), copying other students' responses to quizzes or homework, or giving friends unfair advance notice of test questions. The prevalence of cheating increases as students get older, and by high school, the great majority of students are apt to cheat at one time or another.[217]

Students cheat for a variety of reasons. Some may be more interested in doing well on an assessment than in actually learning the subject matter; for them, performance goals predominate over mastery goals. Others may believe that teachers' or parents' expectations for their performance are so high as to be unattainable and that success is out of reach unless they *do* cheat. In addition, students may perceive certain assessments (tests especially) to be poorly constructed,

---

[216] Nucci, 2001, 2006; Reimer et al., 1983.
[217] Cizek, 2003.

arbitrarily graded, or in some other way a poor reflection of what they've learned. Often, too, peers may communicate through words or actions that cheating is common and justifiable.[218]

Unfortunately, students don't always see cheating as being a violation of moral standards.[219] Perhaps they're trying to help a friend, they say, or perhaps they see an assignment as being a waste of time or hopelessly beyond their ability levels. Not only does cheating hinder students' classroom learning—students gain very little from copying other people's work—but it's also dishonest and therefore immoral. Several strategies can potentially discourage cheating:[220]

- Explain in clear, concrete terms what cheating is—for example, that it includes not only representing another person's work as one's own but also giving certain classmates an unfair advantage over others.

- Contrast cheating with legitimate collaboration, in which everyone learns something and the submitted work is honestly represented as a joint effort.

- Independently verify suspected instances of cheating (e.g., by searching the Internet for a document that you think a student might have copied word for word).

- Provide enough guidance and support that students can reasonably accomplish assigned tasks without cheating.

Get students actively involved in community service.

Earlier in the chapter, we discovered that adolescents are more likely to act in moral and prosocial ways if they have integrated a commitment to moral ideals into their overall sense of identity. Regular community service—ideally beginning well before adolescence—can facilitate this aspect of identity development. Through ongoing community service activities (e.g., food and clothing drives, visits to homes for the elderly, community cleanup efforts), elementary and secondary students alike learn that they have the skills and the responsibility for helping those less fortunate than themselves and in other ways making the world a better place in which to live. In the process, they also begin to think of themselves as concerned, compassionate, and moral citizens.[221] And when high school students participate in community service projects, they gain a sense that their school activities can actually *make a difference* in other people's lives, increasing their desire to stay in school rather than drop out.[222]

You've just read about many potentially effective strategies for promoting students' personal, social, and moral development. In the hotlinked Self-Check quiz and Application Exercises that follow, you can check and apply some of your understandings related to Big Idea 7.4:

> *Effective teachers accommodate individual differences in students' temperaments and personalities, help students acquire a healthy sense of self, and foster students' ongoing social and moral development.*

MyEdLab Self-Check 7.4.

MyEdLab Application Exercise 7.5. In this exercise, you can listen to a teenager talk about what it's like to be a member of a racial and ethnic minority-group member in the United States. You can then reflect on implications of her comments for good teaching strategies.

MyEdLab Application Exercise 7.6. In this exercise, you can apply what you have learned in the preceding section as you identify age-appropriate strategies for enhancing students' moral and prosocial development.

---

[218] E. M. Anderman, Griesinger, & Westerfield, 1998; Cizek, 2003; F. Danner, 2008; E. D. Evans & Craig, 1990; Lenski, Husemann, Trautwein, & Lüdtke, 2010; Murdock & Anderman, 2006; Murdock, Miller, & Kohlhardt, 2004.
[219] L. H. Anderman, Freeman, & Mueller, 2007; Honz, Kiewra, & Yang, 2010.
[220] L. H. Anderman et al., 2007; Bellanca & Stirling, 2011; Honz et al., 2010; Lenski et al., 2010.
[221] J. P. Allen & Antonishak, 2008; Celio, Durlak, & Dymnicki, 2011; Kahne & Sporte, 2008; W.-M. Roth, 2011; Thorkildsen et al., 2008; Youniss & Yates, 1999.
[222] Eccles, 2007.

7.5 SUPPORTING STUDENTS WHO FACE EXCEPTIONAL PERSONAL OR SOCIAL CHALLENGES

Big Idea 7.5 Students who most need teachers' guidance and support are those who face exceptional personal or social challenges.

All students need a certain amount of teacher support in order to reach their full potential, but some students need considerably more support than others. In this section, we'll focus on **students at risk**—those who are on a path toward poor long-term developmental outcomes. Traditionally educators have used the term *at risk* primarily in reference to students who have a high probability of dropping out of school before they earn their high school diplomas. Here, however, we'll use the term more broadly to include students with significant social or emotional problems as well.

With research about students who face exceptional personal or social challenges in mind, we offer the following recommendations.

Be on the lookout for exceptional challenges that students may have previously faced or are currently facing at home.

Ideally, families provide the guidance, encouragement, emotional support, and resources that students need to succeed at school and in the outside world. Unfortunately, not all families provide nurturing environments for their children. Some parents have such limited financial resources that they can't afford adequate food, housing, or medical care. Other parents are so overwhelmed by personal crises (e.g., marital conflict, loss of employment, or a life-threatening illness) that they have little time or energy to devote to anyone else. Still others suffer from mental illness or have serious substance abuse problems. And in some cases, parents have learned only ineffective parenting strategies from their *own* parents.[223] Such challenges increase the likelihood that children will have emotional problems (e.g., anxiety or depression), ineffective social skills (e.g., aggression), and poor classroom behavior (e.g., chronic disruptiveness). The more challenges children have previously faced or currently face at home, the more vulnerable they are.[224]

Often among those young people who have previously faced and continue to face exceptional life challenges are recent refugees from war-torn countries. Such students may have experienced or witnessed exceptional violence in their home countries, lost parents or other close family members, and been homeless and hungry for many months on end. Understandably, then, they may suffer from bouts of depression, debilitating anxiety, anger, and (in some cases) posttraumatic stress disorder. Compounding these very significant personal problems may be uncertainty both about their future livelihoods and living accommodations and about the norms and expectations of a new culture very different from the one in which they've grown up.[225]

Obviously, teachers and other school staff members must be especially attuned to the personal, emotional, and academic needs of students whose life circumstances have been so challenging as to be almost beyond comprehension. In addition to providing whatever support systems are possible at school, faculty members can certainly help to connect students and their families to government programs and local agencies that provide meals, warm clothing, physical and mental health care, and other basic necessities.

Also, if poor parenting practices have been a significant factor affecting students' current functioning, teachers can serve as valuable resources to parents about possible strategies for promoting children's personal and social development, perhaps through newsletters, parent–teacher conferences, and parent discussion groups (we'll identify specific mechanisms for

---

[223] R. H. Bradley, 2010; Cummings, Schermerhorn, Davies, Goeke-Morey, & Cummings, 2006; Hemmings, 2004; Serbin & Karp, 2003; R. A. Thompson & Wyatt, 1999.

[224] Brooks-Gunn, Linver, & Fauth, 2005; P. T. Davies & Woitach, 2008; El-Sheikh et al., 2009; G. W. Evans & Kim, 2007; Jaffee, Hanscombe, Haworth, Davis, & Plomin, 2012; Maikovich, Jaffee, Odgers, & Gallop, 2008.

[225] A. L. Sullivan & Simonson, 2016.

communicating with parents in Chapter 9). The important thing is to communicate information *without* pointing fingers or being judgmental about parenting practices. As noted in the discussion of authoritative and authoritarian parenting styles early in the chapter, how parents treat their children is sometimes the *result,* rather than the cause, of how their children behave. If children are quick to comply with reasonable requests, parents may have no reason to be overly strict disciplinarians. If, instead, children are temperamentally hyperactive or impulsive, parents may have to impose more restrictions on behavior and administer more severe consequences for misbehaviors. Teachers must be careful that they don't always place total credit or blame on parents for their parenting styles.

At the same time, teachers must be alert for signs of possible child maltreatment. In some cases, parents and other primary caregivers neglect children: They fail to provide nutritious meals, adequate clothing, and other essential items. In other cases, they abuse their children physically, sexually, or emotionally. Possible indicators of neglect or abuse are chronic hunger, lack of warm clothing in cold weather, untreated medical needs, frequent or serious physical injuries (e.g., bruises, burns, broken bones), and exceptional knowledge about sexual matters.[226]

Parental neglect and abuse can have significant adverse effects on children's personal and social development.[227] On average, children who have been routinely neglected or abused have low self-esteem, poorly developed social skills, and low school achievement. Many are angry, aggressive, and defiant. Others can be depressed, anxious, socially withdrawn, and occasionally suicidal. Teachers are both morally and legally obligated to report any cases of suspected child abuse or neglect to the proper authorities (e.g., the school principal or child protective services). Two helpful resources are the National Child Abuse Hotline (1-800-4-A-CHILD, or 1-800-422-4453) and the website for Childhelp (www.childhelp.org).

Fortunately, many children and adolescents do well in school despite exceptional hardships on the home front. Some are **resilient students** who acquire characteristics and coping skills that help them rise above their adverse circumstances. As a group, resilient students have easygoing temperaments, likable personalities, positive self-concepts, and high yet realistic goals. They believe that success comes with hard work—for example, they have an *incremental view* of their abilities—and their bad experiences serve as constant reminders of the importance of getting a good education.[228]

Resilient students usually have one or more individuals in their lives whom they trust and can turn to in difficult times. Such individuals might be family members, neighbors, close friends, adult volunteer mentors in the local community, or school staff members. For example, resilient students often mention teachers who have taken a personal interest in them and been instrumental in their school success. Teachers are most likely to foster resilience in students by demonstrating true affection and respect for students, being available and willing to listen when students have concerns, holding high expectations for students' performance, and providing the encouragement and support students need to succeed both inside and outside the classroom.[229]

Identify additional supportive strategies and services for students who are homeless.

Children of homeless families typically face major challenges in their daily lives. Many have chronic physical problems, limited social support networks, significant mental health issues, and inappropriate behaviors. Some may be reluctant to come to school because they lack bathing facilities and suitable clothing. And some may have moved so frequently from one school to another that they have large gaps in their academic skills.[230]

think about it
Were you an easy or difficult child to raise? How much might the parenting style in your childhood home have been the result of your particular temperament?

---

[226] Crosson-Tower, 2010; Turnbull, Turnbull, & Wehmeyer, 2010.

[227] Bates & Pettit, 2007; Crosson-Tower, 2010; J. Kim & Cicchetti, 2006; R. A. Thompson & Wyatt, 1999.

[228] S. Goldstein & Brooks, 2006; Kim-Cohen & Gold, 2009; Martinez-Torteya, Bogat, von Eye, & Levendosky, 2009; Rothbart, 2011; Schoon, 2006; Werner & Smith, 2001; Yeager & Dweck, 2012.

[229] Bukowski et al., 2009; E. Chen, 2012; DuBois, Portillo, Rhodes, Silverthorn, & Valentine, 2011; Masten & Coatsworth, 1998; D. A. O'Donnell, Schwab-Stone, & Muyeed, 2002.

[230] Fantuzzo, LeBoeuf, Chen, Rouse, & Culhane, 2012; Herbers et al., 2012; McLoyd, 1998; P. M. Miller, 2011; Polakow, 2007.

When students either live in a homeless shelter or else regularly move from one temporary location to another, strategies such as the following can support their efforts to achieve academic and social success at school:[231]

- Pair new students with classmates who can provide guidance and assistance—for example, by explaining school procedures and making introductions to other students.
- Provide a notebook, clipboard, or other portable "desk" on which students can do their homework outside of school.
- Find adult or teenage volunteers to serve as tutors outside of school.
- Meet with students' parents at their homeless shelter or other temporary residence rather than at school.
- Share copies of homework assignments, school calendars, and newsletters with shelter officials.

When teachers use such strategies, however, they must keep in mind that students and their families are apt to feel embarrassed about their homeless status.[232] Accordingly, showing respect for their privacy and self-esteem must be a high priority.

Also be on the lookout for students who appear to be social outcasts.

Recall the earlier discussions of *rejected students* and *neglected students*. Both groups tend to hover at the very fringes of a school's social life. Like William in the opening case study, they have few, if any, friends, and hence get little or no social and emotional support from their peers. Having no one to talk to or play with during recess, sitting alone at lunch day after day, perhaps even being told "You can't sit here!"—we authors are guessing that all of our readers have been in such situations at one time or another and can empathize a bit with these students.

Social exclusion by age-mates over a lengthy period—psychologists call it *social marginalization*—can cause students considerable psychological distress and shame. To cope with such feelings and try to preserve their sense of self-worth, students may psychologically disengage from school life, jeopardizing their academic achievement as well as their social development and emotional well-being. Some marginalized teenagers begin to associate with a few equally marginalized peers, who may or may not encourage attitudes and behaviors that are in teens' long-term best interests.[233]

Certainly, some of the strategies presented earlier in the chapter can help integrate marginalized students into their school's social activities (e.g., look once again at the sections on bullying and the Classroom Strategies box "Encouraging Productive Interactions among Diverse Individuals and Groups"). But in addition, teachers should explicitly reach out to these students, providing emotional support and ideally helping them find one or two prosocial age-mates who share similar interests.[234] Another potentially effective strategy is to help them reinterpret some of their unpleasant social experiences in ways that aren't so demoralizing and debilitating (e.g., "Some kids make fun of other kids to make themselves look 'tough,' when underneath they don't feel tough at all").[235]

Provide extra support and guidance for students who have disabilities that affect their personal or social functioning.

Some students show enduring patterns of social, emotional, or behavioral difficulties that significantly interfere with their classroom performance and interpersonal relationships. Symptoms of such **emotional and behavioral disorders** typically fall into one of two broad categories. **Externalizing behaviors** have direct or indirect effects on other people; examples are aggression, defiance, lying, stealing, and general lack of self-control. **Internalizing behaviors** primarily affect the student with the disorder; examples are extreme adverse emotions (e.g., severe anxiety or depression, exaggerated mood swings), withdrawal from social interaction, and eating disorders. Some emotional and behavioral disorders result from environmental factors, such as stressful living conditions, inconsistent parenting practices, child maltreatment, or family alcohol or drug abuse. But

---

[231] Pawlas, 1994.

[232] Polakow, 2007.

[233] Crosnoe, 2011; Loose, Régner, Morin, & Dumas, 2012.

[234] Crosnoe, 2011.

[235] For a related intervention that shows considerable promise, see Yeager et al., 2014.

biological causes, such as inherited predispositions, chemical imbalances, and brain injuries, may also be involved.[236]

Other disabilities that adversely affect students' social functioning—and sometimes their academic learning as well—are collectively known as **autism spectrum disorders**, which are probably caused by abnormalities in the brain. Common to all of these disorders are marked impairments in social cognition (e.g., perspective taking), social skills, and social interaction. Students with autism spectrum disorders differ considerably in the severity of their condition. Some have exceptional talents in one or more specific areas, such as math, engineering, computer science, art, or poetry, as illustrated by the poignant poem presented in Figure 7.4. But in severe cases, children have major delays in cognitive development and language and exhibit certain bizarre behaviors—perhaps constantly rocking or waving fingers, continually repeating what someone else has said, or showing unusual fascination with a very narrow category of objects or topics.[237]

Until recently, a condition known as *Asperger syndrome* was considered to be a mild form of autism, in that people with the disorder have normal language skills and average or above-average intelligence but display some of the behaviors that characterize the autism spectrum (e.g., poor social skills, exceptional repetitiveness, and highly focused interests). Some experts now believe, however, that Asperger syndrome might be a separate category with neurological bases somewhat different from those for autism spectrum disorders.[238]

Professional intervention is called for whenever students are identified as having an emotional or behavior disorder, an autism spectrum disorder, or Asperger syndrome. Nevertheless, many students with these disabilities are in general education classrooms for much or all of the school day. Strategies for working effectively with them include the following:[239]

- Communicate a genuine interest in students' well-being.
- Explicitly teach and scaffold productive social cognition and effective interpersonal skills.
- Stick to a consistent and predictable weekly schedule (especially for students with autism spectrum disorders).
- Make classroom activities relevant to students' interests.
- Consistently communicate the need for appropriate classroom behavior.
- Expect gradual improvement rather than overnight success.

Know the warning signs of severe depression and possible suicide.

Serious depression can be the result of biology (e.g., hormonal imbalances), life circumstances (e.g., a romantic breakup, chronic peer rejection or bullying, exceptional stress at home), or a combination of the two.[240] Some seriously depressed students think about taking their own lives. Warning signs include:[241]

- Sudden withdrawal from social relationships
- Increasing disregard for personal appearance
- Dramatic personality change (e.g., sudden elevation in mood)
- Preoccupation with death and morbid themes
- Overt or veiled threats (e.g., "I won't be around much longer")
- Actions that indicate "putting one's affairs in order" (e.g., giving away prized possessions)

FIGURE 7.4 In this masterful poem, 15-year-old Aleph describes what it feels like to have autism. Copyright © by Aleph Altman-Mills. Reprinted with permission of the author.

On Not Looking Disabled

It's great to be one of the *good* special ed kids
and get restrained less than your friends do!

"You don't look disabled," you tell me,
but this is what disabled looks like.

"You don't look disabled."
You tell me it's a compliment.
You tell me my brain and my body are insults.

We know that our brains and our bodies are insults.
We know that we're supposed to be Indistinguishable
From Typically Developing Peers.
We know our parents want to lose us in a crowd.

I've spent too long
trying to have quiet hands,
trying to sit so still my heart stops beating,
trying to look at your eyes,
when I know you will never see me;
you'll either see a girl without a disability,
or a disability without a girl.

"You don't look disabled!"
and I feel like a spy among the real people
in a costume so tight it shrinks my lungs to capsules,
mask glazed on so you can almost pretend it is my face.

I have learned not to look disabled
through years of pills and hands and cruel guttered laughs
and I wish to god that looking disabled was safe.

[236] Angold, Worthman, & Costello, 2003; P. T. Davies & Woitach, 2008; El-Sheikh et al., 2009; D. Glaser, 2000; H. C. Johnson & Friesen, 1993; Martinez-Torteya et al., 2009.

[237] Gallese et al., 2011; Hobson, 2004; Lord, 2010; Pelphrey & Carter, 2007; Tager-Flusberg, 2007.

[238] For example, see Duffy, Shankardass, McAnulty, & Als, 2013.

[239] J. M. Chan & O'Reilly, 2008; Clarke et al., 1995; Dalrymple, 1995; Evertson & Weinstein, 2006; Hertel & Mathews, 2011; Leaf et al., 2012; Myles & Simpson, 2001; Wentzel, Donlan, Morrison, Russell, & Baker, 2009.

[240] Champagne & Mashoodh, 2009; Dodge, 2009; Furman & Collins, 2009; Goldston et al., 2008; Hyman et al., 2006; Leadbeater & Hoglund, 2009.

[241] Kerns & Lieberman, 1993; Wiles & Bondi, 2001.

Teachers must take any of these warning signs seriously and seek help from trained professionals, such as a school psychologist or counselor, *immediately*.

Intervene early and often with students who are at risk for dropping out of school.

Some students have personal circumstances or negative school experiences that lead them to drop out of school before high school graduation, and a subset of these students leave without basic skills in reading or math.[242] Many school dropouts, then, are ill-equipped to make productive contributions to their families, communities, or society at large.

Students at risk for dropping out of school typically have some or all of the following characteristics:

- **A history of academic failure:** On average, students who drop out have less effective study skills, achieve at lower levels, and are more likely to have repeated a grade than their classmates who graduate.[243]

- **Emotional and behavioral problems:** Potential dropouts tend to have lower self-esteem than their more successful classmates, and they're more likely to exhibit serious behavioral problems (e.g., fighting, substance abuse) both in and out of school. Often their close friends are low-achieving and, in some cases, antisocial peers.[244]

- **Lack of psychological attachment to school:** Students at risk for academic failure are less likely to identify with their school or to believe that they are valued members of the school community. For example, they engage in fewer extracurricular activities than their classmates do, and they're apt to express dissatisfaction with school in general.[245]

- **Increasing disinvolvement with school:** Dropping out isn't necessarily an all-or-none event. Many high school dropouts show lesser forms of "dropping out" many years before they officially leave school. Future dropouts are absent from school more frequently than their peers. They're also more likely to be occasionally suspended from school or to show a long-term pattern of dropping out, returning to school, and dropping out again.[246]

Students drop out for a variety of reasons. Some have little family and peer encouragement and support for school success. Others have extenuating life circumstances; perhaps they have medical problems, take a job to help support the family, or get pregnant. Many simply become dissatisfied with school: They may find the school environment unwelcoming or dangerous, be consistently victimized by bullies, perceive the curriculum to be boring and personally irrelevant, or doubt that they can pass high-stakes achievement tests on which graduation depends.[247] Sadly, teacher behaviors can enter into the picture as well. For example, a teacher might communicate low expectations for students' achievement either explicitly (e.g., by telling students that their chances of earning passing grades are slim) or implicitly (e.g., by brushing off their requests for assistance on assigned tasks). Students are more likely to drop out when they perceive their teachers to be uninterested in helping them succeed.[248]

Teachers may begin to see indicators of "dropping out," such as low school achievement and high absenteeism, as early as elementary school, and other common signs—low self-esteem, disruptive behavior, lack of involvement in school activities—may appear soon thereafter. So it's quite possible to identify potential dropouts early in their school careers and take steps to prevent or remediate academic difficulties before they become insurmountable. Research indicates clearly that for students at risk, prevention, early intervention, and long-term support are more effective than later, short-term efforts.[249]

---

[242] Boling & Evans, 2008; Rumberger, 2011; Slavin, 1989.

[243] Battin-Pearson et al., 2000; Brophy, 2002; Garnier, Stein, & Jacobs, 1997; Hattie, 2008; Rumberger, 2011.

[244] Battin-Pearson et al., 2000; Garnier et al., 1997; Suh, Suh, & Houston, 2007.

[245] Christenson & Thurlow, 2004; Hymel, Comfort, Schonert-Reichl, & McDougall, 1996; Rumberger, 2011.

[246] Christenson & Thurlow, 2004; Rumberger, 2011; Suh et al., 2007.

[247] Brayboy & Searle, 2007; Cornell, Gregory, Huang, & Fan, 2013; Hardré & Reeve, 2003; Hursh, 2007; Portes, 1996; Rumberger, 2011.

[248] Becker & Luthar, 2002; Rumberger, 2011; Suh et al., 2007.

[249] K. L. Alexander, Entwisle, & Dauber, 1995; Brooks-Gunn, 2003; Christenson & Thurlow, 2004; McCall & Plemons, 2001; Paris, Morrison, & Miller, 2006; Ramey & Ramey, 1998; Rumberger, 2011.

Encouraging and Supporting Students Who Are at Risk for Dropping Out

- **Make the curriculum relevant to students' lives and needs.**
  A math class in an inner-city middle school expresses concern about the 13 liquor stores located near the school and about the shady customers and drug dealers the stores attract. The students use yardsticks and maps to calculate the distance of each store from the school, gather information about zoning restrictions and other city government regulations, identify potential violations, meet with a local newspaper editor (who publishes an editorial describing the situation), and eventually meet with state legislators and the city council. As a result of students' efforts, city police monitor the liquor stores more closely, major violations are identified (leading to the closing of two stores), and the city council makes it illegal to consume alcohol within 600 feet of the school.

- **Pique students' interest with stimulating activities.**
  In a unit on the physics of sound, a junior high school science teacher shows students how basic principles of sound reveal themselves in rock music. On one occasion the teacher brings in a guitar and explains why holding down a string at different points along the neck of the guitar creates different frequencies and thus different notes.

- **Use students' strengths to promote a positive sense of self.**
  An elementary school in a low-income neighborhood forms a singing group (the Jazz Cats) for which students must try out. The group performs at a variety of community events, and the students enjoy considerable visibility for their talent. Group members exhibit increased self-esteem, improvement in other school subjects, and greater teamwork and leadership skills.

- **Through both words and actions, communicate optimism about students' chances for short-term and long-term personal and professional success.**
  A math teacher at a low-income, inner-city high school recruits students to participate in an intensive math program. The teacher and students work on evenings, Saturdays, and vacations, and many of them eventually pass the Advanced Placement calculus exam. (This real-life example is depicted in the 1988 film, *Stand and Deliver*, available on DVD.)

- **Provide extra support for academic success.**
  A middle school homework program meets every day after school in Room 103, where students find their homework assignments on a shelf. Students follow a particular sequence of steps to complete each assignment (assembling materials, having someone check their work, etc.) and use a checklist to make sure they don't skip any steps. Initially, a supervising teacher closely monitors what they do, but with time and practice, the students can do their homework with only minimal help and guidance.

- **Show students that they are personally responsible for their successes.**
  A teacher says to a student, "Your essay about recent hate crimes in the community is very powerful. You've given the topic considerable thought, and you've clearly mastered some of the techniques of persuasive writing that we've talked about this semester. I'd like you to think seriously about submitting your essay to the local paper for its editorial page. Can we spend some time during lunch tomorrow to fine-tune the grammar and spelling?"

- **Create peer support groups that enable students to provide mutual encouragement.**
  At a school that serves a large number of minority-group students who are at risk for academic failure, faculty and students create a Minority Achievement Committee (MAC) program designed to make academic achievement a high priority. Participation in the program is selective (i.e., students must show a commitment to academic improvement) and prestigious. In regular meetings, high-achieving 11th and 12th graders describe, model, and encourage many effective strategies, and they help younger students who are struggling with schoolwork.

- **Get students involved in extracurricular activities, especially those that involve making a long-term commitment to a group effort.**
  A teacher encourages a student with a strong throwing arm to go out for the school baseball team and introduces the student to the baseball coach. The coach, in turn, expresses his enthusiasm for having the student join the team and asks several current team members to help make him feel at home during team practices.

- **Involve students in school policy and management decisions.**
  At a high school that has historically had high drop-out rates, students and teachers hold regular "town meetings" to discuss issues of fairness and justice and establish rules for appropriate behavior. Meetings are democratic, with students and teachers alike having one vote apiece, and the will of the majority is binding.

Sources: J. P. Allen & Antonishak, 2008; L. W. Anderson & Pellicer, 1998; Belfiore & Hornyak, 1998 (homework program example); Christenson & Thurlow, 2004; Cosden, Morrison, Albanese, & Macias, 2001; Eccles, 2007; Feldman & Matjasko, 2005; Fuchs, Fuchs, et al., 2008; Higgins, 1995 (town meeting example); Jenlink, 1994 (Jazz Cats example); Knapp, Turnbull, & Shields, 1990; Ladson-Billings, 1994a; Lee-Pearce, Plowman, & Touchstone, 1998; Mathews, 1988 (inner-city math program example); McGovern, Davis, & Ogbu, 2008 (Minority Achievement Club example); Ramey & Ramey, 1998; Rumberger, 2011; Suh et al., 2007; Tate, 1995 (liquor store example); E. N. Walker, 2006; D. Wood, Larson, & Brown, 2009; Yeager & Dweck, 2012.

Students who are at risk for dropping out are a diverse group of individuals with a variety of needs, and there's probably no single strategy that can keep all of them in school until high school graduation. Nevertheless, effective teaching practices go a long way toward helping these students stay on the road to academic success and a high school diploma. The Classroom Strategies box "Encouraging and Supporting Students Who Are at Risk for Dropping Out" presents several strategies that researchers and experienced educators have found to be effective.

Above all, teachers who have high success rates with students at risk tend to be those who, through both words and deeds, communicate a genuine sense of caring, concern, and high regard for students as human beings. And in general, the most effective teaching strategies for students at risk are those that would be ideal for *any* student.

Teachers can make a significant difference in the lives of students who are at risk for poor long-term academic, social, or emotional outcomes. In the hotlinked Self-Check quiz and Application Exercise that follow, you can check and apply your understandings related to Big Idea 7.5:

Students who most need teachers' guidance and support are those who face exceptional personal or social challenges.

MyEdLab **Self-Check 7.5**

MyEdLab **Application Exercise 7.7.** In this activity, you can observe and analyze how a special education teacher provides explicit instruction in one important social skill.

7 SUMMARY

To summarize our discussions of personal, social, and moral development, we now return to the Big Ideas presented at the beginning of the chapter.

■ **7.1 Children's behaviors are the results of inherited traits, environmental conditions and contexts, and maturational changes in the brain, all of which gradually shape children's personalities and sense of self.** Children's and adolescents' personalities are the result of complex interactions between heredity (e.g., temperamental inclinations, genetically controlled brain maturation) and environment (e.g., home environments, cultural standards for behavior). Their personality characteristics lead them to behave somewhat consistently across situations, although distinctly different contexts can elicit distinctly different behaviors. For example, a child might be talkative with one or two close friends but shy and quiet in a large-group setting.

As children grow older, they construct increasingly complex and abstract understandings of who they are as people, and these understandings affect their actions and activity choices. They derive their self-perceptions, collectively known as *sense of self,* not only from their own prior successes and failures but also from the behaviors of others, from the achievements of groups to which they belong, and, often, from their schemas about appropriate behaviors for their gender. Ultimately, children and adolescents socialize *themselves* to a considerable degree, conforming to their own, self-constructed ideas about appropriate behavior.

■ **7.2 In order to benefit fully from their interactions with peers, children must have good social skills and be able to interpret and respond to various social situations and problems in productive ways.** Healthy peer relationships are critical for optimal personal and social development. Peers provide a testing ground for emerging social skills, help one another with challenging tasks, offer support and comfort in times of trouble or uncertainty, and are influential socialization agents. Furthermore, peers provide opportunities for young people to take others' perspectives, draw conclusions about others' motives and intentions, and develop workable solutions to interpersonal problems.

Children often form friendships even before they reach kindergarten or first grade. As they move through the school years, many of them form larger social groups (perhaps cliques, crowds,

or gangs), and some also form romantic relationships. Yet certain students are consistently rejected or neglected by their peers, and these students may need a good deal of teacher support.

Most children and adolescents actively try to make sense of their social world. With age, this *social cognition*—thinking about what other people might be thinking and feeling, and hypothesizing about how others might act and react in various situations—becomes increasingly complex and insightful, enabling effective interaction with adults and peers. But some young people have difficulty interpreting social cues in productive ways and may have few effective social skills. Such difficulties can occasionally lead to aggressive and potentially dangerous actions toward others.

Some types of aggression involve behaviors that might cause another person physical harm. But other forms—collectively known as *psychological aggression*—involve behaviors intended to inflict mental anguish or reduce self-esteem. An especially devastating form of psychological aggression is *cyberbullying,* in which someone uses a smartphone or the Internet to make embarrassing information or photographs available to a large number of peers.

■ **7.3 Some signs of moral reasoning and prosocial behavior emerge early in life, but key components of morality continue to evolve over the course of childhood and adolescence.** As children move through the grade levels, most acquire a clear sense of right and wrong, such that they behave in accordance with prosocial standards for behavior rather than acting solely out of self-interest. This developmental progression is the result of many things, including increasing capacities for empathy and abstract thought, an evolving appreciation for human rights and other people's welfare, and ongoing encounters with moral dilemmas and problems. Even at the high school level, however, students don't always take the moral high road, because personal needs and self-interests often enter into their moral decision making.

■ **7.4 Effective teachers accommodate individual differences in students' temperaments and personalities, help students acquire a healthy sense of self, and foster students' ongoing social and moral development.** Students are more likely to be academically successful and to acquire a positive sense of self when teachers accommodate their diverse temperaments and help them identify areas of particular talent. At the same time, teachers must communicate clear standards for behavior, explain why some behaviors are unacceptable, and, when possible, channel students' risk-taking tendencies into productive activities.

Most children and adolescents spend a good portion of their waking hours at school, making it an important environment in which to acquire good social skills and more advanced moral understandings. For example, teachers can help unpopular students acquire better social skills and more productive social information processing abilities, and they must actively discourage bullying behaviors of any sort. Often, too, teachers can take steps to encourage communication and interaction among students with diverse backgrounds and characteristics. And by engaging students in regular discussions about social and moral issues and getting students actively involved in community service, teachers can foster empathy and more advanced moral reasoning.

■ **7.5 Students who most need teachers' guidance and support are those who face exceptional personal or social challenges.** All students need ongoing teacher support and guidance, but supportive teachers are especially important for (a) students who face more than their fair share of challenges at home, (b) students who are homeless, (c) students who have little or no involvement in their peer group's social life, and (d) students with disabilities or emotional problems that adversely affect their social and psychological well-being. Some of these students—and certain other students as well—are at high risk for dropping out of school, perhaps because of chronically low academic achievement or perhaps because of a lack of emotional attachment to the school community. Teachers should remain optimistic that they *can* make a difference in getting many of these at-risk students on the road to greater academic and social success.

PRACTICE FOR YOUR LICENSURE EXAM

The Scarlet Letter

MyEdLab
Video Example 7.6.
You can observe Ms. Southam's class discussion in this video.

Ms. Southam's 11th-grade English class has been reading Nathaniel Hawthorne's *The Scarlet Letter.* Set in 17th-century Boston, the novel focuses largely on two characters who have been carrying on an illicit love affair: Hester Prynne, a young woman who has not seen or heard from her husband for the past 2 years, and the Reverend Arthur Dimmesdale, a pious and well-respected local preacher. When Hester becomes pregnant, she is imprisoned for adultery and eventually bears a child. The class is currently discussing Chapter 3, in which the governor and town leaders, including Dimmesdale, are urging Hester to name the baby's father.

> **Ms. Southam:** The father of the baby . . . how do you know it's Dimmesdale . . . the Reverend Arthur Dimmesdale? . . . What are the clues in the text in Chapter 3? . . . Nicole?
>
> **Nicole:** He acts very withdrawn. He doesn't even want to be involved with the situation. He wants the other guy to question her, because he doesn't want to look her in the face and ask her to name *him.*
>
> **Ms. Southam:** OK. Anything else? . . .
>
> **Student:** The baby.
>
> **Ms. Southam:** What about the baby?
>
> **Student:** She starts to cry, and her eyes follow him.
>
> **Ms. Southam:** That is one of my absolutely favorite little Hawthornisms.

Ms. Southam reads a paragraph about Dimmesdale and asks students to jot down their thoughts about him. She then walks around the room, monitoring what students are doing until they appear to have finished writing.

> **Ms. Southam:** What pictures do you have in your minds of this man . . . if you were directing a film of *The Scarlet Letter?*
>
> **Mike:** I don't have a person in mind, just characteristics. About five-foot-ten, short, well-groomed hair, well dressed. He looks really nervous and inexperienced. Guilty look on his face. Always nervous, shaking a lot.
>
> **Ms. Southam:** He's got a guilty look on his face. His lips always trembling, always shaking.
>
> **Mike:** He's very unsure about himself.
>
> **Matt:** Sweating really bad. Always going like this. (Matt shows how Dimmesdale might be wiping his forehead.) He does . . . he has his hanky. . . .
>
> **Ms. Southam:** Actually, we don't see him mopping his brow, but we do see him doing what? What's the action? Do you remember? If you go to the text, he's holding his hand over his heart, as though he's somehow suffering some pain.
>
> **Student:** Wire-framed glasses. . . . I don't know why. He's like. . . .
>
> **Mike:** He's kind of like a nerd-type guy. . . . Short pants. . . .
>
> **Ms. Southam:** But at the same time . . . I don't know if it was somebody in this class or somebody in another class. . . . he said, "Well, she was sure *worth* it." Worth risking your immortal soul for, you know? . . . Obviously she's sinned, but so has he, right? And if she was worth it, don't we also have to see him as somehow having been worthy of her risking *her* soul for this?

Student: Maybe he's got a good personality. . . .

Ms. Southam: He apparently is, you know, a spellbinding preacher. He really can grab the crowd.

Student: It's his eyes. Yeah, the eyes.

Ms. Southam: Those brown, melancholy eyes. Yeah, those brown, melancholy eyes. Absolutely.

1. Constructed-response question

In this classroom dialogue Ms. Southam and her students speculate about what the characters in the novel, especially Arthur Dimmesdale, might be thinking and feeling. In other words, they are engaging in social cognition.

A. Identify two examples of student statements that show social cognition.

B. For each example you identify, explain what it reveals about the speaker's social cognition.

2. Multiple-choice question

Ms. Southam does several things that are apt to enhance students' perspective-taking ability. Which one of the following is the best example?

a. She models enthusiasm for the novel ("That is one of my absolutely favorite little Hawthornisms").

b. She walks around the room as the students write down their thoughts about Dimmesdale.

c. She points out that Dimmesdale is "holding his hand over his heart, as though he's somehow suffering some pain."

d. She agrees with Mike's description of Dimmesdale as having a guilty look on his face.

MyEdLab **Licensure Exam 7.1**

Alexander Raths/Fotolia

8

Instructional Strategies

Big Ideas to Master in this Chapter

8.1 Effective teachers identify the knowledge and abilities they want students to acquire, and they plan instruction accordingly.

8.2 Sometimes instruction is most effective when it is teacher-directed—that is, when the teacher chooses the specific topics to be studied and the general course of a lesson.

8.3 Sometimes instruction is most effective when it is learner-directed—that is, when students have some control over the issues to be addressed and the ways in which to address them.

8.4 Different instructional strategies are appropriate for different instructional goals and objectives and for different students.

CASE STUDY: WESTWARD EXPANSION

Martin Quinn's sixth-grade class is studying the great westward expansion in North America during the middle 1800s. Today's lesson is about a typical journey west in a covered wagon. Mr. Quinn begins by projecting a 19th-century U.S. map on a screen at the front of the room. "Many people traveled by steamship up the Missouri River to the town of Independence," he says, and he uses a pointer to trace the route on the map. "Then they continued west in a covered wagon until they reached their final destination—maybe Colorado, Oregon, or California." He now shows several old photographs of people traveling in covered wagons and says, "A typical covered wagon was about 4 feet wide and maybe 10 or 12 feet long." He has two students use masking tape to mark a 4-by-10-foot rectangle on the classroom carpet. "How much room would a wagon with these dimensions give you for your family and supplies?" The students agree that people would have to be quite choosy about what they brought with them on the trip west.

"All right," Mr. Quinn continues, "let's think about the kinds of things you would need to pack in your wagon. Let's start with the kinds of food you'd want to bring and how much of each kind you should pack." He divides the students into groups of three or four members each and has them brainstorm what might seem to be a reasonable grocery list. After a few minutes, he writes each group's suggestions on the board.

At this point, Mr. Quinn clicks on an Internet link and projects an electronic copy of John Lyle Campbell's pamphlet *Idaho: Six Months in the New Gold Regions: The Emigrant's Guide*, published in 1864. "This pamphlet provided advice for a party of four men who might be traveling west to seek their fortunes in the quartz mining boom in Idaho." The pamphlet lists many things that the students haven't thought of and suggests much larger amounts than the students have estimated. For example, it recommends 12 sacks of flour, 400 pounds of bacon, 100 pounds of coffee, 15 gallons of vinegar, 50 pounds of lard, and "one good cow for milking purposes."

"What do you think about the list?" Mr. Quinn asks. "Does it make sense?" The students have varying opinions: "Fifty pounds of lard—eeuuww, gross! Isn't that stuff really bad for your arteries or something?" "We *way* underestimated our flour." "I don't understand why they needed to bring so much coffee." "The cow's a good idea, though."

Mr. Quinn's next question is, "*Why* did people need all of these things? Let's talk about that for a bit."

• What specific instructional strategies does Mr. Quinn use to engage and motivate his students? What strategies does he use to help them learn and remember the content of the lesson?

To engage and motivate his students, Mr. Quinn arouses their interest through a physical activity (students mark a "wagon" on the carpet), creates cognitive dissonance (the list in the pamphlet is quite different from the ones the students have generated), and makes the lesson a very social, interactive one. And he promotes learning and understanding, in part, by encouraging visual imagery and elaboration—for example, by making the subject matter concrete and vivid (through the old photographs and masking-tape wagon) and by asking students to speculate about why such things as lard and coffee might have been important to have.

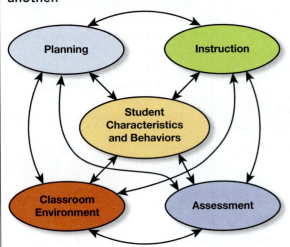

FIGURE 8.1 Planning, instruction, the classroom environment, classroom assessment practices, and student characteristics and behaviors are all interdependent and mutually influence one another.

Much of Mr. Quinn's lesson reflects **teacher-directed instruction**, in which the teacher calls most of the shots, choosing which topics will be addressed and carefully structuring students' activities. However, one of Mr. Quinn's strategies—having students develop grocery lists in small cooperative groups—reflects **learner-directed instruction**, in which students have some control regarding what they do and learn.[1] Decisions about whether to use teacher-directed or learner-directed strategies—or to combine both kinds of strategies into a single lesson, as Mr. Quinn does—should be based on the goals for instruction and on students' current knowledge and skill levels. And, in any case, the distinction we're making here is really a *continuum*—not an either–or situation—because instructional strategies can vary considerably in the degree to which teachers and students control the course of events.

In this chapter, we'll build on what we've learned about human learning and cognition, motivation, and child development to identify effective strategies for both planning and carrying out instruction. As you'll soon discover, planning and carrying out instruction are closely intertwined with two other essential elements of teaching—creating an effective classroom environment and assessing students' ongoing achievement levels—that we'll examine in Chapter 9 and Chapter 10, respectively. But at the heart of it all, *student characteristics and behaviors* must drive what teachers do in the classroom. To repeat a point made in Chapter 1, teachers' classroom strategies should be *learner centered* (see Figure 8.1). They should also encompass **evidence-based practices**—that is, they should be ones that research has consistently shown to be effective in helping students learn and achieve.

8.1 PLANNING INSTRUCTION

Big Idea 8.1 Effective teachers identify the knowledge and abilities they want students to acquire, and they plan instruction accordingly.

Good teachers engage in considerable advance planning: They identify the information and skills they want students to acquire, determine an appropriate sequence in which to teach the knowledge and skills, and develop classroom lessons and activities that will maximize learning and keep students motivated and on task. Ideally, teachers also coordinate their plans with one another—for example, by identifying common goals toward which everyone will strive or by developing interdisciplinary units that involve two or more classes and subject areas.

The following strategies are key elements of effective instructional planning.

Begin by identifying what students should ultimately know and be able to do.

An essential step in planning instruction is to identify the specific things students should accomplish during a lesson or unit, as well as the things they should accomplish over the course of the semester or school year. Educators use a variety of terms for such end results, including *goals, objectives, outcomes, targets, competencies, benchmarks,* and *standards.* In this book, we'll typically use the term **instructional goals** when referring to general, long-term outcomes of instruction. We'll use the term **instructional objectives** when referring to more specific outcomes of a particular lesson or unit.

Regardless of the terminologies they use, experts agree that the desired end results of instruction should influence what teachers teach, how they teach it, and how they assess students' learning and achievement. In fact, as a general rule, teachers should *begin* the planning process by

---

[1] Some educators instead use the terms *teacher-centered* and *learner-centered* in reference to this distinction. However, as pointed out in Chapter 1 and again in Figure 8.1, virtually all instructional strategies should focus (center) on what and how students are learning. The essential difference here lies in who *controls* the instructional activity.

determining what they ultimately want students to know and be able to do. One widely recommended approach is a **backward design**, in which teachers proceed through this sequence:[2]

1. Identify the desired end results in terms of knowledge and skills that students should attain—ideally including meaningful learning, conceptual understanding, and complex cognitive processes.

2. Determine acceptable evidence—in the form of performance on various classroom assessment tasks—to verify that students have achieved those results.

3. Plan learning experiences and instructional activities that enable students to master the knowledge and skills identified in Steps 1 and 2.

With such an approach, teachers essentially *begin at the end* and then choose assessment tasks and instructional strategies specifically related to that end (see Figure 8.2). For example, if the objective for a unit on addition is *rapid retrieval* of number facts, a teacher might create a timed quiz to assess students' ability to recall the facts quickly and easily and might employ gamelike computer software to enhance students' automaticity for the facts. But if the objective is *application* of number facts, a teacher may instead want to focus assessment methods and instructional strategies on word problems or, better still, on activities involving real objects and hands-on measurements.

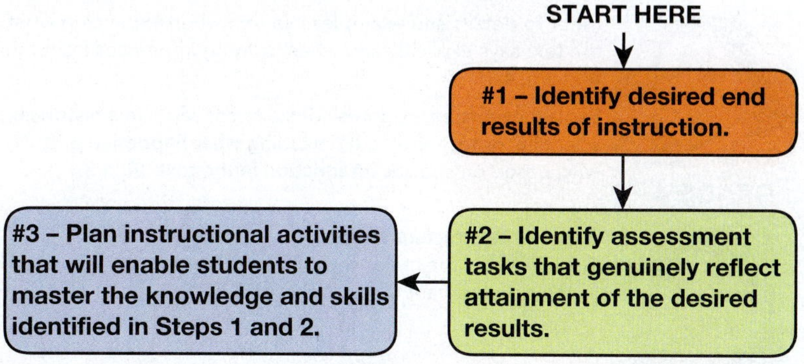

Knowing the desired final outcomes of instruction benefits not only teachers—who can then choose appropriate content, assessments, and instructional methods—but students as well. When students know what they need to accomplish, they can make more informed decisions about how to focus their efforts and allocate their study time, and they can more effectively monitor their comprehension as they read and study.[3] For example, if their teacher tells them that they should be able to apply science and math to everyday situations, they'll probably think about and study these subject areas very differently than if they somehow get the message that they should memorize definitions and formulas.

FIGURE 8.2 In a backward-design approach to instructional planning, a teacher begins with the desired end results and then mentally "travels" backward in time to identify appropriate assessments and instructional strategies.

START HERE

#1 – Identify desired end results of instruction.

#2 – Identify assessment tasks that genuinely reflect attainment of the desired results.

#3 – Plan instructional activities that will enable students to master the knowledge and skills identified in Steps 1 and 2.

Align long-term instructional goals with appropriate standards for various content domains.

Teachers don't pull their goals and objectives out of the blue, of course. One source of guidance comes from **content-area standards** identified by national and international discipline-specific professional groups (e.g., National Council for Geographic Education, National Association for Music Education). Such standards are typically in the form of general statements regarding the knowledge and skills that students should acquire at various grade levels in a particular content domain, as well as the characteristics that their students' accomplishments should reflect.

Also, in the United States, state departments of education have established comprehensive lists of standards in reading, writing, math, science, and social studies and sometimes in such domains as art, music, foreign languages, and physical education.[4] Many U.S. states have jointly adopted a set of **Common Core State Standards** in mathematics and English language arts, and some have signed on to the **Next Generation Science Standards**; you can find these standards on the Internet at corestandards.org and nextgenscience.org, respectively.[5] Table 8.1 presents examples of reading skills identified in the Common Core State Standards for English Language Arts,

---

[2] Tomlinson & McTighe, 2006; Wiggins & McTighe, 2011.

[3] Gronlund & Brookhart, 2009; McAshan, 1979.

[4] You can find many state standards online by typing "state educational standards" in an Internet search engine such as Google, Bing, or Yahoo!

[5] Notably, the Common Core standards are increasingly being adopted or adapted for use in schools outside of the United States—for example, in many English-speaking international schools around the world.

DEVELOPMENTAL TRENDS

TABLE 8.1 • Examples of How You Might Align Instructional Strategies with Common Core State Standards at Different Grade Levels

GRADE LEVEL	EXAMPLES OF COMMON CORE STATE STANDARDS FOR ENGLISH LANGUAGE ARTS	EXAMPLES OF INSTRUCTIONAL STRATEGIES THAT ADDRESS THESE STANDARDS
GRADE 2	Ask and answer such questions as *who, what, where, when, why,* and *how* to demonstrate understanding of key details in a text. (RL.2.1)[a]	During "settling down" time immediately after lunch each day, read a chapter of a high-interest children's novel, stopping frequently to ask questions that require students to go beyond the text itself (e.g., ask students to speculate about what a character might be feeling).
	Recount stories, including fables and folktales from diverse cultures, and determine their central message, lesson, or moral. (RL.2.2)	Have several students create props for and act out a story they have recently read, with other class members serving as the audience. Follow up with a class discussion of important lessons that one or more story characters might have learned from events or challenges they faced.
GRADE 4	Refer to details and examples in a text when explaining what the text says explicitly and when drawing inferences from the text. (RL.4.1).	As a reading group discusses Carl Hiaasen's *Hoot,* ask students to speculate about how the plot might progress and to identify clues in the text that support their predictions.
	Explain events, procedures, ideas, or concepts in a historical, scientific, or technical text, including what happened and why, based on specific information in the text. (RI.4.3)	When students are reading a chapter in their history textbook, ask *why* questions that encourage cause-and-effect connections (e.g., "Why did Columbus's crew want to sail back to Europe after several weeks on the open sea?").
GRADE 7	Analyze the structure an author uses to organize a text, including how the major sections contribute to the whole and to the development of the ideas. (RI.7.5)	Before students read a chapter in their science textbook, have them use its headings and subheadings to (1) create a general outline of the chapter and (2) generate questions they hope to answer as they read the chapter. Then, for homework, ask them to read and take notes on the chapter, using the outline and self-questions as guides for note taking.
	Trace and evaluate the argument and specific claims in a text, assessing whether the reasoning is sound and the evidence is relevant and sufficient to support the claims. (RI.7.8)	Give students an advertisement for a self-improvement product (e.g., a diet pill or exercise equipment); have them work in small cooperative learning groups to (1) identify the advertiser's motives and (2) evaluate the quality of evidence for the product's effectiveness.
GRADES 11–12	Analyze and evaluate the effectiveness of the structure an author uses in his or her position or argument, including whether the structure makes points clear, convincing, and engaging. (RI.11–12.5)	Describe common techniques in persuasive writing, and have students identify the various persuasive techniques used in newspaper editorials.
	Determine an author's point of view or purpose in a text in which the rhetoric is particularly effective, analyzing how style and content contribute to the power, persuasiveness or beauty of the text. (RI.11–12.6)	Ask students to identify the unstated assumptions underlying two news magazines' depictions of the same event (e.g., an assumption that one group is good or right, and another is bad or wrong).

[a] The letters "RL" indicate standards related to reading literature; the letters "RI" indicate standards related to reading informational text. The number or numbers before the period indicate the grade level; the number after the period indicates the particular standard for that grade level. For example, the first entry shown here, identified as "RL.2.1," is the first standard for grade 2 for reading literature.

Source: Excerpts from *Common Core State Standards.* © Copyright 2010. National Governors Association for Best Practices and Council of Chief State School Officers. Reprinted with permission. All rights reserved.

along with instructional strategies potentially useful in helping students acquire those skills. Notice that the two columns are in two different colors to help you remember that statements in the "Standards" column refer to things that *students* should be able to do, whereas statements in the "Strategies" column offer suggestions about what *teachers* might do.

Also notice that two of the examples presented in the rightmost column of Table 8.1 are suggestions for either science or history instruction. Teachers in *all* content domains must strive to enhance students' literacy skills. For example, we refer you to the supplementary standards "Grades 6–12 Literacy in History/Social Studies, Science, & Technical Subjects" described on the Common Core website (go to www.corestandards.org/ELA-Literacy).

In recent years, many teachers, parents, and policy makers have voiced major concerns—in some cases, downright paranoia—about the use of the Common Core standards in their states and local school districts. By and large, the concerns they've raised reflect a great deal of misinformation about the intent and implementation of these standards. In an effort to counter such misconceptions, we must stress a few basic facts about Common Core:

- Development of the standards was the joint initiative of many state governors and state commissioners of education in an effort to ensure that high school graduates in their states would be prepared for college and meaningful careers. The U.S. federal government was *not* involved in developing the standards, nor has it mandated their use in public schools.

- The standards do *not* prescribe particular instructional methods; in fact, the developers have emphatically stated that local schools and teachers should make their own decisions about how best to help students achieve the standards.

- The standards do *not* prescribe particular assessment tools for measuring students' achievement of the standards—for example, they do *not* require that students' achievement be assessed by one or more multiple-choice achievement tests. (Any tests that currently exist for this purpose have been developed by private companies and have *not* been endorsed by the developers of Common Core.)

The website corestandards.org addresses these and many other myths about Common Core; we authors strongly urge you to take a look at this website.

Keep in mind that existing content-area standards focus almost exclusively on what students should achieve in reading, writing, and various academic content domains. They largely overlook goals that lie *outside* particular content areas—for instance, goals related to technological literacy, effective study strategies, self-regulation techniques, and good social skills. The International Society for Technology in Education (ISTE) has developed standards that can help teachers enhance students' knowledge and skills related to using digital technologies and the Internet—for instance, how to create authentic technology-based products and how to evaluate and synthesize information available on Internet websites (go to iste.org/standards). But with an eye toward enhancing students' long-term academic and social success both at school and in the outside world, teachers should also formulate some of their *own* goals and objectives for instructional activities.

Include goals and objectives at varying levels of complexity and sophistication.

Notice that the standards presented in Table 8.1 focus largely on meaningful learning and complex cognitive processes—drawing inferences, analyzing and critically evaluating ideas, and so on. Such processes must be important components of teacher-developed goals and objectives as well. One simple tool that can help teachers broaden their view of what students should learn and be able to do is a 2001 revision of **Bloom's taxonomy**, a list of six general cognitive processes that vary in complexity:[6]

1. *Remember:* Recognizing or recalling information learned at an earlier time and stored in long-term memory
2. *Understand:* Constructing meaning from instructional materials and messages (e.g., drawing inferences, identifying new examples, summarizing)
3. *Apply:* Using knowledge in a familiar or new situation
4. *Analyze:* Breaking information into its constituent parts and perhaps also identifying interrelationships among the parts
5. *Evaluate:* Making judgments about information using certain criteria or standards
6. *Create:* Putting together knowledge, procedures, or both to form a coherent, structured, and possibly original whole

---

[6] Bloom's original taxonomy (B. S. Bloom, Englehart, Furst, Hill, & Krathwohl, 1956) uses nouns rather than verbs: *knowledge, comprehension, application, analysis, synthesis, evaluation.* In the revision shown here (L. W. Anderson & Krathwohl, 2001), *create* replaces and subsumes *synthesis,* and *evaluate* moves from sixth to fifth place.

Another helpful taxonomy can be found in *Understanding by Design,* a popular resource for guiding teachers through the backward-design process.[7] This taxonomy identifies six forms ("facets") that students' understanding of a topic might take:

1. *Explanation:* Integrating various bits of information into meaningful wholes (e.g., knowing the *hows* and *whys* of various facts and principles), drawing appropriate inferences, and possibly helping others understand the subject matter

2. *Interpretation:* Making sense of and identifying the underlying meanings of events, data, documents, and works of art and literature

3. *Application and adjustment:* Using acquired knowledge in new situations and diverse contexts

4. *Perspective:* Considering various points of view regarding an issue; trying to minimize bias in one's own analysis of the issue

5. *Empathy:* Looking at a situation or issue from a particular individual's or group's vantage point, perhaps based on the individual's or group's feelings or general worldviews

6. *Self-knowledge:* Identifying gaps in one's own understandings, as well as personal prejudices that might distort one's views and interpretations

Neither of the preceding taxonomies provides an exhaustive list of what students should be able to do while learning classroom subject matter; for example, neither taxonomy includes psychomotor skills. Nor do the particular sequences of items necessarily reflect progressions from simpler to more complex processes.[8] Even so, the taxonomies provide helpful reminders that there's much more to school learning and academic achievement than learning and recalling discrete facts.

The Classroom Strategies box "Identifying Goals and Objectives of Instruction" offers several suggestions that experienced educators have found to be helpful in guiding instruction and classroom assessment practices.

Ask students to identify some of their own goals for instruction.

With this suggestion, we're simply revisiting a recommendation made in Chapter 5: *Ask students to set some personal goals for learning and performance.* Naturally, student-chosen goals and objectives must be compatible with any mandated standards and with their teachers' goals and objectives. However, most school curricula do allow for some flexibility in what students focus on. For example, different students might choose different gymnastic skills to master, different art media to use, or different historical events to study in depth. By allowing students to identify some of their own goals and objectives, teachers encourage the *goal setting* that's an integral aspect of self-regulation (Chapter 3) and foster the sense of *autonomy* that's so important for motivation (Chapter 5).

Break complex tasks and topics into smaller pieces, identify a logical sequence for the pieces, and decide how best to teach each one.

Instructional planning also involves determining how best to break down complex topics and skills into manageable chunks. As examples, consider these four teachers:

- Ms. Begay, a third-grade teacher, plans to teach her students how to solve arithmetic word problems. She also wants to help them learn more effectively from reading materials.

- Mr. Marino, a middle school physical education teacher, wants his students to develop enough proficiency in basketball to feel comfortable playing either on organized basketball teams or in pick-up games in their neighborhoods.

- Mr. Wu, a junior high school music teacher, hopes to teach his new trumpet students how to play "Jingle Bell Rock" in time for the New Year's Day parade.

- Ms. Flores, a high school social studies teacher, is going to introduce her students to the intricacies of the federal judicial system.

All four teachers want to teach complex topics or skills. Accordingly, each of them should conduct a **task analysis**, identifying the essential behavioral or cognitive aspects of mastering a particular

---

[7] Wiggins & McTighe, 2005, 2011.
[8] L. W. Anderson & Krathwohl, 2001; Iran-Nejad & Stewart, 2010; Marzano & Kendall, 2007.

CLASSROOM STRATEGIES

Identifying Goals and Objectives of Instruction

- **Consult local, state, national, and international standards, but don't rely on them exclusively.**
  When identifying instructional goals for the year, a middle school science teacher takes into account the Next Generation Science Standards (nextgenscience.org), which her state has adopted as a framework for guiding public schools' science curricula. In addition, she identifies specific objectives related to two issues directly affecting many students in her inner-city school district: poor nutrition and air pollution.

- **Be realistic about what can be accomplished in a given time frame; allow time to pursue important topics in depth.**
  Rather than expect students to remember a lot of discrete facts in social studies, a second-grade teacher identifies several "Big Ideas" that students should master during the school year—for instance, the ideas that (1) all people have certain needs and desires that affect their behaviors and (2) different cultural groups may strive to satisfy those needs and desires in different ways.

- **Identify both short-term objectives and long-term goals.**
  A fourth-grade teacher wants students to learn how to spell 10 new words each week. He also wants them to write a coherent and grammatically correct short story by the end of the school year.

- **In addition to goals related to specific topics and content areas, identify goals related to students' general long-term academic success.**
  A middle school teacher knows that early adolescence is an important time for developing the learning and study strategies that students will need in high school and college. Throughout the school year, he continually introduces new strategies for learning and remembering classroom subject matter—for example, effective ways to organize class notes, mnemonic techniques for remembering important facts, and self-questions to answer while reading a textbook chapter—and regularly assesses students' progress in using these strategies.

- **Consider physical, social, motivational, and affective outcomes as well as cognitive outcomes.**
  A physical education teacher wants students to know the basic rules of basketball and to dribble and pass the ball appropriately. She also wants them to acquire a love of basketball, effective ways of working cooperatively with teammates, and a general desire to stay physically fit.

- **Describe goals and objectives not in terms of what the teacher will do during a lesson but in terms of what *students* should be able to do at the *end* of instruction— and, ideally, also in ways that point to appropriate assessment tasks.**
  A Spanish teacher knows that students often confuse the verbs *estar* and *ser* because both are translated into English as "to be." He identifies this objective for his students: "Students will correctly conjugate *estar* and *ser* in the present tense and use each one in appropriate contexts." He assesses students' ability to use the two verbs correctly through both paper–pencil quizzes and in-class conversations.

- **When formulating short-term objectives, identify specific behaviors that will reflect accomplishment of the objectives.**
  In a unit on the food pyramid, a health teacher identifies this objective for students: "Students will create menus for a breakfast, lunch, and dinner that, in combination, include all elements of the food pyramid in appropriate proportions."

- **When formulating long-term goals that involve complex topics or skills, list a few abstract outcomes and give examples of specific behaviors that reflect each one.**
  Faculty members at a junior high school identify this instructional goal for all students at their school: "Students will demonstrate effective listening skills, for example, by taking thorough and accurate notes, showing respect for diverse points of view, and seeking clarification when they don't understand."

Sources: Brophy, 2008; Brophy, Alleman, & Knighton, 2009; N. S. Cole, 1990; Gronlund & Brookhart, 2009; M. D. Miller, Linn, & Gronlund, 2009; Pellegrino, Chudowsky, & Glaser, 2001; Popham, 2014; Wiggins & McTighe, 2011.

topic or skill. The task analyses can then guide the teachers in their selections of appropriate methods and sequences in which to teach the subject matter.

Figure 8.3 illustrates three general approaches to task analysis:[9]

- **Behavioral analysis.** One way of analyzing a complex task is to identify the specific behaviors required to perform it. For example, Mr. Marino can identify the specific physical movements involved in dribbling, passing, and shooting a basketball. Similarly, Mr. Wu can identify key behaviors students must master in order to play a trumpet, such as how to correctly hold the instrument and how to blow into the mouthpiece.

- **Subject-matter analysis.** Another approach is to break down the subject matter into the specific topics, concepts, and principles it includes. For example, Ms. Flores can identify various aspects of the judicial system (concepts such as *innocent until proven guilty* and *reasonable doubt,* the roles that judges and juries play, etc.) and their interrelationships. And Mr. Wu can identify the basic elements of written music that his trumpet students must be able to interpret,

---

[9] R. E. Clark, Feldon, van Merriënboer, Yates, & Early, 2008; Jonassen, Hannum, & Tessmer, 1989.

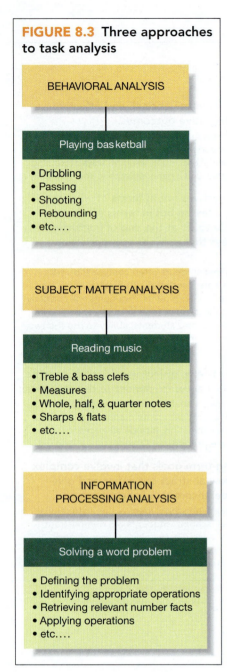

FIGURE 8.3 Three approaches to task analysis

BEHAVIORAL ANALYSIS

Playing basketball

- Dribbling
- Passing
- Shooting
- Rebounding
- etc....

SUBJECT MATTER ANALYSIS

Reading music

- Treble & bass clefs
- Measures
- Whole, half, & quarter notes
- Sharps & flats
- etc....

INFORMATION PROCESSING ANALYSIS

Solving a word problem

- Defining the problem
- Identifying appropriate operations
- Retrieving relevant number facts
- Applying operations
- etc....

such as the treble and bass clefs and whole, half, and quarter notes. Subject-matter analysis is especially important when the subject matter being taught includes many interrelated concepts and ideas that students should learn meaningfully and with conceptual understanding.

- **Information processing analysis.** A third approach is to specify the cognitive processes involved in a task. As an illustration, Ms. Begay can identify the mental processes involved in successfully solving an arithmetic word problem—for instance, correct encoding of the problem (e.g., determining whether it requires addition, subtraction, etc.) and rapid retrieval of basic number facts. Similarly, she can identify specific cognitive strategies useful in reading comprehension, such as finding main ideas, elaborating, and summarizing.

To get a taste of what a task analysis involves, try the following exercise.

SEE FOR YOURSELF

PEANUT BUTTER SANDWICH

Conduct a task analysis for the process of making a peanut butter sandwich:

1. Decide whether your approach should be a behavioral analysis, a subject-matter analysis, or an information processing analysis.
2. Using the approach you've selected, break the sandwich-making task into a number of small, teachable steps.
3. (Optional) If you're hungry and have the necessary materials close at hand, make an actual sandwich following the steps you've identified. Did your initial analysis omit any important steps?

Chances are good that you chose a behavioral analysis, because making a peanut butter sandwich is largely a behavioral rather than mental task. For example, you must know how to unscrew the peanut butter jar lid, get an appropriate amount of peanut butter on your knife, and spread the peanut butter gently enough that you don't tear the bread.

Conducting task analyses for complex skills and topics serves at least three important functions in instructional planning.[10] First, by identifying a task's specific components—whether behaviors, concepts and ideas, or cognitive processes—a teacher gains a better sense of what things students need to learn and the sequence in which to most effectively learn them. Second, a task analysis helps a teacher choose appropriate instructional strategies. For example, if one necessary component of solving arithmetic word problems is rapid retrieval of math facts from memory, repeated practice of the facts may be critical for developing automaticity. If another aspect of solving such problems is identifying the relevant operation to apply (addition, subtraction, etc.), then promoting a true understanding of mathematical concepts and principles (perhaps by using concrete manipulatives or authentic activities) is essential.

A third important function of a task analysis is determining what kind of *cognitive load* a new task might impose on students—in particular, whether or not certain aspects of a task might initially put a strain on students' limited working memory capacity. Sometimes the analysis will reveal that certain components of a task should be taught separately, one at a time. For instance, Mr. Wu may initially ask his beginning trumpet students to practice blowing into the mouthpiece correctly without worrying about the specific notes they produce. But on other occasions it might be both possible and desirable to teach the desired knowledge and behaviors entirely within the context of the overall task, in part because doing so makes the subject matter meaningful for students. For instance, Ms. Begay should almost certainly teach her students the processes involved in learning effectively from reading materials—elaborating, summarizing, and so on—primarily within the context of authentic reading activities.

Consider how you might best get and keep students actively engaged in instructional activities.

To truly benefit from classroom activities, students must be actively *engaged* in them—definitely cognitively engaged and ideally also physically and emotionally engaged in the subject matter at hand (recall the discussion of *academic engagement* in Chapter 5). At a minimum, students must

[10] Jonassen et al., 1989; R. E. Mayer, 2011a; Stokes, Luiselli, & Reed, 2010; van Merriënboer & Kester, 2008.

keep their attention focused on the verbal, visual, and behavioral aspects of lessons. But better still, students should *do something* with the subject matter, perhaps by drawing inferences, critically evaluating ideas, or applying what they're learning to solve new problems or create new products.[11]

In Chapter 5, we've previously identified many strategies for fostering and enhancing students' motivation. Here we're simply reminding our readers that effective planning involves identifying not only the information and skills that students need to acquire but also the kinds of tasks and activities that are likely to both (a) capture and keep students' interest and attention and (b) enhance their eagerness to persist in the face of academic challenges.

Develop step-by-step lesson plans.

After identifying goals for instruction and perhaps also conducting a task analysis, effective teachers develop one or more **lesson plans** to guide them during instruction. A lesson plan typically includes the following:

- The goal(s) or objective(s) of the lesson and, if applicable, relevant content-area standard(s)
- Instructional materials (e.g., textbooks, handouts, software programs) and equipment required
- Specific instructional strategies and the sequence in which they'll be used
- Assessment method(s) planned

Any lesson plan should also take into account the particular students who will be learning—their developmental levels, prior knowledge, cultural backgrounds, and (if applicable) disabilities and other special educational needs.

Many beginning teachers develop fairly detailed lesson plans that describe how they're going to help students learn the subject matter in question.[12] For instance, when we authors first began teaching, we spent many hours each week writing down the information, examples, questions, and student activities we wanted to use in class during the following week. But as teachers gain experience teaching certain topics, they learn which strategies work effectively and which do not, and they use some of the effective ones frequently enough that they can retrieve them quickly and easily from long-term memory. Thus, as time goes on, planning lessons becomes far less time consuming, and much of it becomes *mental* planning rather than planning on paper.

In planning lessons, teachers have many resources at their disposal, including experienced teachers' lesson plans in books and on the Internet. For example, the following websites offer lesson plans and related materials concerning a wide range of topics:

- Smithsonian Institution (smithsonianeducation.org)
- Educator's Reference Desk (eduref.org)
- Discovery Education (school.discoveryeducation.com)

In taking advantage of such resources, however, teachers must always keep in mind that *lessons should be closely tied to instructional goals and objectives.*

You should think of a lesson plan more as a guide than as a recipe—in other words, as a general plan of attack that can and should be adjusted as events unfold. For example, during the course of a lesson, a teacher may find it necessary to back up a bit and teach material that he or she had mistakenly assumed students had already mastered. Or, if students express considerable curiosity or have intriguing insights about a particular topic, a teacher might want to capitalize on this unique opportunity—this **teachable moment**—and spend more time exploring the topic than originally planned.

As the school year progresses, teachers' long-range plans may also change somewhat. For instance, teachers might find that initial task analyses of certain topics were overly simplistic or that previous expectations for students' achievement were either unrealistically high or

---

[11] For example, see M. T. H. Chi & Wylie, 2014.
[12] Calderhead, 1996; Corno, 2008; Sternberg & Horvath, 1995.

FIGURE 8.4 Opening screen of a class website for a sixth-grade humanities class

Source: Created by and used with permission from Jeffrey Scott Ormrod.

FIGURE 8.5 Example of how a class website can provide ongoing scaffolding for students' learning

Source: Created by and used with permission from Jeffrey Scott Ormrod.

unnecessarily low. Teachers must continually revise their plans as instruction proceeds and as classroom assessments reveal how well students are learning and achieving.

Create a class website to share goals and facilitate communication throughout the school year.

A traditional practice at the secondary and college levels has been to give students a printed syllabus that lists course topics, instructional goals, homework assignments, due dates, and scheduled assessments. But increasingly teachers at all levels are sharing such information—and much more—on class-specific Internet websites within their school's overall website. A variety of software packages are available to create such sites (e.g., see moodle.org). In the K–12 grades, students' parents typically have access to class websites as well.

As an example, Figure 8.4 shows the opening screen that teacher Jeff Ormrod created for one of his sixth-grade humanities classes. Notice that the course resources included two documents (a course outline and assessment criteria) that students could download. Scrolling further down on the website, students could learn about general goals for the class, get detailed information about various units and assignments, and find many downloadable documents.

As Jeff has gained experience as a teacher, he has increasingly used his class websites as means through which to scaffold students' learning, as illustrated in Figure 8.5. As part of a unit on early humans, his class had been reading Marjorie Cowley's *Dar and the Spear-Thrower*, and Jeff had regularly posted study guides that encouraged students to elaborate on what they were reading—for example, by posing such questions as "Why does Dar decide to leave his clan to find the stranger?" and "Explain how the 'wind was his enemy.'" The sidebar on the right provided links to various online resources (e.g., Merriam-Webster's online dictionary) and schoolwide blogs.

Class websites provide one easy way for teachers to communicate regularly with students and their parents. They can't be the *only* way, however. Not all students and parents have easy access to computers and the Internet at home. And some individuals—parents especially—may simply not have the technological literacy they need to access and navigate through an Internet website. Accordingly, teachers should also provide hard copies of assignments they want students to do as homework and of information they want parents to know.

As you have discovered, effective classroom instruction requires considerable advance planning. For one thing, teachers must take into account not only (a) any relevant content-area standards but also (b) students' individual and developmental characteristics and needs. Furthermore, instructional planning must be grounded in evidence-based practices and in general psychological principles of human learning, cognition, and motivation. In the hotlinked Self-Check quiz and Application Exercises that follow, you can check and apply your understandings related to Big Idea 8.1:

Effective teachers identify the knowledge and abilities they want students to acquire, and they plan instruction accordingly.

MyEdLab **Self-Check 8.1**

MyEdLab **Application Exercise 8.1.** In this exercise, you can practice using a backward design in lesson planning.

MyEdLab **Application Exercise 8.2.** In this exercise, you can see how one teacher aligned her instructional objectives for a lesson with some of the Common Core State Standards. You can also critique her effectiveness in communicating her objectives to her students.

8.2 CONDUCTING TEACHER-DIRECTED INSTRUCTION

Big Idea 8.2 Sometimes instruction is most effective when it is teacher-directed—that is, when the teacher chooses the specific topics to be studied and the general course of a lesson.

In the opening case study, Mr. Quinn directs the course of the lesson to a considerable degree. For example, he draws students' attention to materials projected on a screen at the front of the room, asks two students to mark the dimensions of a covered wagon on the floor, and has small student groups brainstorm supplies that pioneers might have needed for their journey. And through some of his questions (e.g., "*Why* did people need all of these things?") he nudges students toward the kinds of conclusions he wants them to draw about westward expansion in North America in the 1800s.

A good deal of teacher-directed instruction takes the form of **expository instruction**, in which information is presented (*exposed*) in more or less the same form that students are expected to learn it.[13] Mr. Quinn's lesson has several elements of expository instruction: He shows photographs of pioneer families and their temporary covered-wagon homes, describes the route that many pioneers took, and asks students to read an old pamphlet's recommendations about important food supplies for the long journey.

Some forms of expository instruction are exclusively one-way in nature, in that information goes only from teacher to learners. Examples are textbook reading assignments, educational videos, and most educational websites on the Internet. In each case, a "teacher" (e.g., a textbook author or video narrator) presents information without any possibility of getting information from students in return. Yet other forms can be quite interactive, with an ongoing exchange of information between teacher (or maybe a virtual "teacher," such as a computer) and students. For example, effective classroom lectures typically include opportunities for student input, perhaps in the form of answers to teacher questions, inquiries about ambiguous points, or reactions to certain ideas. In approaches such as *direct instruction* and *computer-based instruction*—both of which we'll consider shortly—student input is a frequent and essential ingredient despite the considerable control that the teacher or computer programmer has over the content and sequence of the lesson.

Strategies such as the following can enhance the effectiveness of teacher-directed instruction.

Begin with what students already know and believe.

Students are apt to engage in meaningful learning—to relate new material to things they already know—only if they have both the "new" and the "old" in working memory at the same time. Thus a strategy introduced in Chapter 2, *prior knowledge activation,* is an important first step in any teacher-directed instruction. In addition, asking students what they already know about a topic—or at least what they *think* they know about it—can uncover misconceptions that might wreak havoc with new learning and so must be vigorously addressed.

Encourage and support effective cognitive processes.

The effectiveness of teacher-directed instruction ultimately depends on the particular cognitive processes that instruction enables and encourages. To see this idea in action, try the following exercise.

──────────────── **SEE FOR YOURSELF** ────────────────
FINDING PEDAGOGY IN ONE OF YOUR TEXTBOOKS

1. Look at two or three chapters in this book or another textbook that you've recently read. Identify places where the authors have done specific things to help you learn and remember the material more effectively. What specific strategies did the authors use to facilitate effective cognitive processing?
2. In those same chapters, can you find places where you had trouble making sense of the ideas presented? If so, what might the authors have done differently in those instances?

───

[13] Some theorists use the term *expository instruction* only in reference to lectures and textbooks. Here we are using the term more broadly to refer to any approach that centers on the *transmission* of information from expert (e.g., classroom teacher, textbook writer, computer software designer) to student.

Table 8.2 • Enhancing Cognitive Processing in Teacher-Directed Instruction

GENERAL PRINCIPLE	EDUCATIONAL IMPLICATION	EXAMPLE
An **advance organizer**—a verbal or graphic introduction that lays out the general organizational framework of upcoming material—helps students make meaningful connections among the things they learn.	Introduce a new unit by describing the major ideas and concepts to be discussed and showing how they are interrelated.	Introduce a unit on vertebrates by saying something like this: "Vertebrates all have backbones. We'll be talking about five phyla of vertebrates—mammals, birds, reptiles, amphibians, and fish—that differ from one another in several ways, including whether their members are warm blooded or cold blooded; whether they have hair, scales, or feathers; and whether they lay eggs or bear live young."
Ongoing **connections to prior knowledge** help students learn classroom material more meaningfully, provided that students' existing understandings and beliefs are accurate.	Remind students of something they already know—that is, activate their prior knowledge—and point out how a new idea is related. Also, address any erroneous beliefs students have about the topic (see the discussion of *conceptual change* in Chapter 2).	Draw an analogy between *peristalsis* (muscular contractions that push food through the digestive tract) and the process of squeezing ketchup from a packet: "You squeeze the packet near one corner and run your fingers along the length of the packet toward an opening at the other corner. When you do this, you push the ketchup through the packet, in one direction, ahead of your fingers, until it comes out of the opening."
An **organized presentation** of material helps students make appropriate interconnections among ideas.	Help students organize material in a particular way by presenting the information using that same organizational structure.	Use a concept map to depict the main concepts and ideas of a topic and their interrelationships (see the discussion of *concept maps* in Chapter 3).
Various **signals** built into a presentation (e.g., italicized print, interspersed questions) can draw students' attention to important points.	Emphasize important ideas—for example, by writing them on the board, asking questions about them, or simply telling students what things are most important to learn.	When assigning a textbook chapter for homework, identify several questions that students should try to answer as they read the chapter.
Visual aids help students encode material visually as well as verbally.	Illustrate new material through pictures, photographs, diagrams, maps, physical models, and demonstrations.	When describing major battles of the American Civil War, present a map showing where each battle took place; point out that some battles were fought in especially strategic locations.
Appropriate **pacing** gives students adequate time to process information.	Pace a presentation slowly enough that students can draw inferences, form visual images, and in other ways engage in effective long-term memory storage processes.	Intersperse lengthy explanations with demonstrations or hands-on activities that illustrate some of the principles you're describing.
Summaries help students review and organize material and identify main ideas.	After a lecture or reading assignment, summarize the key points of the lesson.	At the end of a unit on poems by Emily Dickinson, summarize her work by describing the characteristics that made her poetry so unique and compelling.

Sources: Brophy et al., 2009; Bulgren, Deshler, Schumaker, & Lenz, 2000; Carney & Levin, 2002; Clement, 2008; Corkill, 1992; Dansereau, 1995; Edmonds et al., 2009; E. L. Ferguson & Hegarty, 1995; J. Hartley & Trueman, 1982; Ku, Chan, Wu, & Chen, 2008; Levin & Mayer, 1993; M. C. Linn & Eylon, 2011; Lorch, Lorch, & Inman, 1993; R. E. Mayer, 2010b; R. E. Mayer & Gallini, 1990; M. A. McDaniel & Einstein, 1989; Moreno, 2006; Newby, Ertmer, & Stepich, 1994, p. 4 (peristalsis example); R. E. Reynolds & Shirey, 1988; Scevak, Moore, & Kirby, 1993; M. Y. Small, Lovett, & Scher, 1993; Verdi & Kulhavy, 2002; Wade, 1992; P. T. Wilson & Anderson, 1986; Winn, 1991; Zook, 1991.

If you've chosen one or more chapters in this book, we authors are hoping that the See for Yourself exercises have helped you relate new topics to your own knowledge and experiences. We're hoping, too, that the case studies, videos, examples of students' work and teachers' strategies, and hotlinked Application Exercises have made abstract ideas more concrete for you. Perhaps some of the graphics, tables, and summaries have helped you organize concepts and principles. But if you've found certain parts of a chapter confusing or hard to understand, we encourage you to let us know.[14]

Researchers have identified several factors that improve the effectiveness of teacher-directed instruction through the cognitive processes they promote. Table 8.2 describes and illustrates these factors as general principles that teachers should keep in mind when, for whatever reason, they need to present information in a largely one-way fashion.

Intermingle explanations with examples and opportunities for practice.

By providing numerous examples of concepts and ideas, teachers make classroom topics more concrete for students and help them relate abstract subject matter to real-world objects and events (e.g., see Figure 8.6). And by providing many opportunities to practice new knowledge and skills, teachers

---

[14] You can reach us at jormrod@alumni.brown.edu and brettdjones@gmail.com.

foster automaticity and increase the likelihood that students will transfer what they've learned to real-world tasks and problems. For example, some high-interest video games can effectively help students practice and master basic math facts.[15]

An approach known as **direct instruction** makes considerable use of examples and practice opportunities to keep students actively engaged in learning and applying classroom subject matter. This approach involves small and carefully sequenced steps, fast pacing, and a great deal of teacher–student interaction. Each lesson typically involves most or all of the following components:[16]

1. **Review of previously learned material.** The teacher reviews relevant content from previous lessons, checks homework assignments involving that content, and reteaches any information or skills that students haven't yet mastered.

2. **Statement of the current lessons' objectives.** The teacher describes one or more concepts or skills that students should master in the new lesson.

3. **Presentation of new material in small, logically sequenced steps.** The teacher presents a small amount of information or a specific skill, perhaps through a verbal explanation, modeling, and one or more examples. The teacher may also provide an advance organizer, ask questions, or in other ways scaffold students' efforts to process and remember the material.

4. **Guided student practice and assessment after each step.** Students have frequent opportunities to practice what they're learning, perhaps by answering questions, solving problems, or performing modeled procedures. The teacher gives hints during students' early responses, provides immediate feedback about their performance, makes suggestions about how to improve, and provides additional instruction as needed. After students have completed guided practice, the teacher checks to be sure they've mastered the information or skill in question, perhaps by having them summarize what they've learned or answer a series of follow-up questions.

5. **Independent practice.** Once students have acquired some degree of competence, they engage in further practice either independently or in small cooperative groups. By doing so, they work toward achieving automaticity for the material in question.

6. **Frequent follow-up reviews.** Over the course of the school year, the teacher provides many opportunities for students to review previously learned material, perhaps through homework assignments, writing tasks, or quizzes.

The teacher moves back and forth among these components as necessary to ensure that all students are truly mastering the subject matter.

Direct instruction is most suitable for teaching information and skills that are clear-cut and best taught in a step-by-step sequence.[17] Because of the high degree of teacher–student interaction, it's often implemented more easily with small groups or in one-on-one tutoring sessions. Especially in such circumstances, it can lead to substantial gains in achievement.[18] Using direct instruction *exclusively* can be too much of a good thing, however, especially if teachers don't vary instructional methods to maintain students' interest and engagement—for instance, if they just present one drill-and-practice worksheet after another.[19]

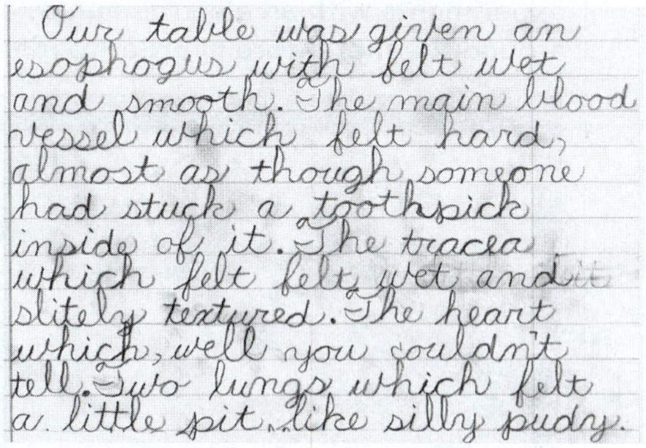

Take advantage of well-designed instructional software and Internet websites.

Many instructional software packages and Internet websites, collectively known as **computer-based instruction (CBI)**, are now available to either replace or supplement more traditional instructional methods. You can find some good examples at the following websites:

Discovery Education: www.discoveryeducation.com

Khan Academy: www.khanacademy.org

FIGURE 8.6 In a unit on anatomy, 10-year-old Berlinda and her classmates gained firsthand experience with components of the respiratory and circulatory systems.

Our table was given an esophogus with felt wet and smooth. The main blood vessel which felt hard, almost as though someone had stuck a toothpick inside of it. The tracea which felt felt, wet and slitely textured. The heart which, well you couldn't tell. Two lungs which felt a little pit. like silly pudy.

---

[15] Plass et al., 2013.

[16] Rosenshine, 2009; Rosenshine & Stevens, 1986.

[17] Rosenshine & Stevens, 1986; Spiro & DeSchryver, 2009.

[18] Rittle-Johnson, 2006; C. L. Watkins, 1997; Weinert & Helmke, 1995.

[19] Mac Iver, Reuman, & Main, 1995; Wasley, Hampel, & Clark, 1997.

FIGURE 8.7 In the intelligent tutoring system *My Science Tutor (MyST)*, elementary school students converse one on one with a virtual tutor, "Marni," who asks questions, "listens" to their answers, and tailors follow-up instruction accordingly. The screenshot on the left shows Marni asking a question about an animated electric circuit. The one on the right shows Marni "watching and listening" as a student experiments with an electromagnet, either increasing or decreasing the number of times the wire winds around the metal core in order to identify its possible effects on the magnet's strength.

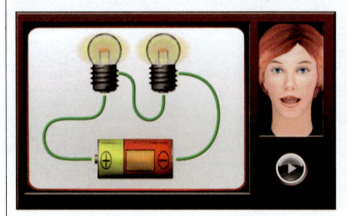 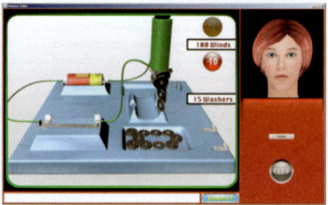

National Aeronautic and Space Administration: www.nasa.gov

National Museum of Natural History: www.mnh.si.edu

One especially noteworthy website in the preceding list is Khan Academy, which offers a large and growing collection of instructional videos on a wide variety of topics in math, science, economics, history, art, music, and computing.

Effective CBI programs incorporate principles of learning and cognition we've considered in earlier chapters. For example, they capture and hold students' attention with engaging tasks and graphics, encourage meaningful learning, and present diverse examples and practice exercises that encourage complex cognitive processes (e.g., problem solving, critical thinking, and scientific reasoning). Students tend to remain physically and cognitively engaged with such programs, in large part because they must continually respond to questions and problems and get regular feedback about how they're doing.

Some CBI programs provide drill and practice of basic knowledge and skills (e.g., math facts, typing, fundamentals of music), helping students develop automaticity in these areas. Others, known as **intelligent tutoring systems**, skillfully guide students through complex subject matter and can anticipate and address a wide variety of misconceptions and learning difficulties. Still others teach and scaffold complex study strategies, metacognitive skills, and self-regulation (e.g., look once again at the screenshot from *Betty's Brain* in Figure 3.11 of Chapter 3).

A good example of an intelligent tutoring system is *My Science Tutor*, or *MyST*, in which students in the upper elementary grades have one-on-one conversations with "Marni," a computer-animated woman who both talks to them and—through the software's voice recognition and language-processing components—also listens to and understands what they say in response to her questions.[20] Marni typically begins a conversation with a student by activating the student's prior knowledge about the topic, saying something such as "What have you been studying in science recently?" Then, after the topic of the lesson has been described, Marni presents a series of illustrations, animations, and interactive simulations and asks more specific questions—for instance, she might ask, "So, what's going on here?" or "What could you do to . . . ?"[21] She tailors subsequent instruction to the student's current understandings and addresses any misconceptions she virtually "thinks" the student might have. Figure 8.7 presents examples of what a student might see on the computer screen in lessons on electric circuits and electromagnetism, respectively.

think about it

Think about your own experiences with instructional software and Internet websites. In your view, what qualities enhance learning via computer-based instruction?

---

[20] W. Ward et al., 2013.

[21] W. Ward et al., 2013, pp. 1118–1119.

Well-designed CBI programs are often quite effective in helping students learn academic subject matter.[22] They can also be highly motivating, piquing situational interest and giving students the independence and frequent successes that can enhance their feelings of autonomy and competence.[23] But one caveat is in order here: Too *much* independence in choice-making in a program can lead students to flounder aimlessly and not make much progress in their learning. Good CBI programs provide considerable guidance about what students should do at various steps along the way.[24]

A downside of computer-based instruction is that it gives students few opportunities for social interaction and therefore does little to address their need for relatedness.[25] Yet it offers several advantages over more traditional, low-tech forms of expository instruction. For one thing, CBI programs can include animations, video clips, and spoken messages—components that aren't possible with traditional textbooks and other printed materials. Second, some programs can record and maintain ongoing data for every student, including such information as how far students have progressed in a program, how quickly they respond to questions, and how often they're right and wrong. With such data, teachers can monitor each student's progress and identify students who appear to be struggling with the material. And finally, a computer can be used to provide instruction when flesh-and-blood teachers aren't available. For example, CBI is often used in *distance learning,* a situation in which students receive instruction at a location physically separate from that of their instructor. Distance learning is becoming increasingly common in high schools, where part of students' courseloads might be online courses offered by universities or other accredited agencies.

At later points in the chapter, we'll explore additional uses of computer technology. Keep in mind, however, that using a computer or other digital technology is not, *in and of itself,* necessarily the key to better instruction.[26] New technologies can help students achieve at higher levels only when they provide instruction that teachers can't offer as easily or effectively in a low-tech manner. Little is gained when a student merely reads information on a computer screen rather than in a textbook.

Ask a lot of questions.

Virtually all effective teachers ask students a lot of questions. Some teacher questions are **lower-level questions** that call for information students have already studied. Such questions have several benefits:[27]

- They give teachers a good idea of what prior knowledge and misconceptions students have about a topic.
- They help keep students' attention on the lesson in progress, especially when *all* students must respond to each question in some way.
- They help teachers assess whether students are learning class material successfully or are confused about particular points. (Even very experienced teachers sometimes overestimate what students are actually learning during expository instruction.)
- They give students the opportunity to monitor their *own* comprehension—to determine whether they understand the information being presented or, instead, should ask for help or clarification.
- When students are asked questions about material they've studied earlier, they must review that material, which should promote greater recall later on.

---

[22] Azevedo & Witherspoon, 2009; Graesser, Li, & Forsyth, 2014; Kulik & Fletcher, 2016; Ma, Adesope, Nesbit, & Liu, 2014; Steenbergen-Hu & Cooper, 2014; Tamin, Bernard, Brokhovski, Abrami, & Schmid, 2011.

[23] Blumenfeld, Kempler, & Krajcik, 2006; Snir, Smith, & Raz, 2003.

[24] Kanar & Bell, 2013; Karich, Burns, & Maki, 2014; P. A. Kirschner & van Merriënboer, 2013.

[25] A. Collins & Halverson, 2009; Winn, 2002.

[26] R. E. Clark, Yates, Early, & Moulton, 2009; Moreno, 2006.

[27] Airasian, 1994; Brophy, 2006; F. W. Connolly & Eisenberg, 1990; P. W. Fox & LeCount, 1991; Lambert, Cartledge, Heward, & Lo, 2006; Wixson, 1984.

Following is an example of how one eighth-grade teacher promoted review of a lesson on ancient Egypt by asking questions:

Teacher: The Egyptians believed the body had to be preserved. What did they do to preserve the body in the earliest times?

Student: They dried them and stuffed them.

Teacher: I am talking about from the earliest times. What did they do? Carey.

Carey: They buried them in the hot sands.

Teacher: Right. They buried them in the hot sands. The sand was very dry, and the body was naturally preserved for many years. It would deteriorate more slowly. . . . What did they do later on after this time?

Student: They started taking out the vital organs.

Teacher: Right. What did they call the vital organs then?

Norm: Everything but the heart and brain.

Teacher: Right, the organs in the visceral cavity. The intestines, liver, and so on, which were the easiest parts to get at. Question?

Student: How far away from the Nile River was the burial of most kings?[28]

At the end of the dialogue, a *student* asks a question—one that requests additional information. The student is apparently trying to elaborate on the material, perhaps speculating that only land a fair distance from the Nile would be dry enough to preserve bodies for a lengthy period. Teachers can encourage such elaboration—and therefore also encourage new knowledge construction—by asking **higher-level questions** that require students to do something new with the information they've learned.[29] For instance, a higher-level question might ask students to generate their own examples of the concepts *alliteration* and *onomatopoeia* in creative writing, speculate about possible explanations for a cause-and-effect relationship in chemistry, or use a principle of economics to evaluate existing or proposed government policies.

Asking questions during a group lesson or as a follow-up to an independent reading assignment often enhances students' learning.[30] This is especially true when teachers ask higher-level questions that call for inferences, applications, justifications, or problem solving. Yet teachers must give students adequate time to respond to their questions. Just as students need time to process new information, they also need time to consider questions and retrieve knowledge relevant to possible answers. As previously noted in the discussion of *wait time* in Chapter 2, when teachers allow a few seconds to elapse after asking a question, a greater number of students will volunteer answers, and their responses will tend to be more sophisticated. Furthermore, as you'll learn in a Cultural Considerations box later in the chapter, students from some ethnic backgrounds often wait for several seconds before answering a question as a way of showing courtesy and respect for the speaker.

The Classroom Strategies box "Asking Questions to Promote and Assess Learning" presents examples of how teachers might use questions to foster effective cognitive processes and enhance students' learning.

Extend the school day with age-appropriate homework assignments.

Students can accomplish only so much during class time, and homework provides a means through which teachers can increase the length of the school day. On some occasions, teachers might use homework to give students extra practice with familiar information and procedures (perhaps as a way of promoting review and automaticity) or to introduce them to new yet simple material.[31]

MyEdLab
Video Example 8.1.
What purposes might questions be serving in the two lessons shown in this video—one in first-grade science and the other in middle school history?

---

[28] Aulls, 1998, p. 62.

[29] Brophy, 2006; Meece, 1994; Minstrell & Stimpson, 1996.

[30] Allington & Weber, 1993; Liu, 1990; Munro & Stephenson, 2009; Redfield & Rousseau, 1981.

[31] H. Cooper, 1989.

CLASSROOM STRATEGIES

Asking Questions to Promote and Assess Learning

- **Direct questions to the entire class, not just to a few students who seem eager to respond.**
  The girls in a high school science class rarely volunteer when their teacher asks questions. Although the teacher often calls on students who raise their hands, he occasionally calls on those who don't, and he makes sure that he calls on *every* student at least once a week.

- **When a question has only a few possible answers, have students vote on the particular answer they think is correct.**
  When beginning a lesson on dividing one fraction by another, a middle school math teacher writes this problem on the board:

  $$\tfrac{3}{4} \div \tfrac{1}{2} = ?$$

  She asks, "Before we talk about how we solve this problem, how many of you think the answer will be less than 1? How many think it will be greater than 1? How many think it will be *exactly* 1?" She tallies the number of hands that go up after each question and then says, "Hmmm, most of you think the answer will be less than 1. Let's look at how we solve a problem like this. Then each of you will know whether you were right or wrong."

- **Provide a means through which all students can write and show their answers.**
  A fourth-grade teacher gives each student a laminated board on which to write their answers to questions she asks during whole-class explanations. She finds that when all of her students can simultaneously answer her questions this way, they're more attentive and less disruptive during lessons.

- **Ask follow-up questions to probe students' reasoning.**
  In a geography lesson on Canada, a sixth-grade teacher points to the St. Lawrence River on a map and asks, "Which way does the water flow: toward the ocean or away from it?" When one student shouts out, "Away from it!" the teacher asks him, "Why do you think so?" The student's explanation reveals a common misconception: that rivers can flow only from north to south, never vice versa.

- **When students initially struggle with a question, provide sufficient scaffolding to enable them to answer correctly.**
  In a second-grade lesson on the food pyramid, a student incorrectly suggests that orange juice is a member of the "milk" group. His teacher nudges him in the right direction with these hints: "Everything in the milk group comes from a cow. What does orange juice come from? . . . Orange juice comes from oranges. If it comes from oranges, which group is oranges? . . . Is it fruit or bread?" The student acknowledges that oranges are fruit and that orange juice must therefore belong to the fruit group.

Sources: Brophy et al., 2009, p. 225 (food pyramid example); Lambert et al., 2006 (laminated board example).

In other situations, teachers might give homework assignments that ask students to apply classroom subject matter to their outside lives. For example, in a unit on lifestyle patterns, a teacher might ask second graders to compare their own homes with homes of earlier time periods (e.g., caves, log cabins) and to identify modern conveniences that make their lives easier and more comfortable.[32] On still other occasions, teachers might encourage students to bring items and ideas from home (e.g., small biological specimens from their neighborhood, information about family ancestry) and use them as the basis for in-class activities.[33] When teachers ask students to make connections between classroom material and the outside world through homework assignments, they are, of course, promoting *transfer*.

Doing homework appears to have a greater effect on achievement in the middle school and high school grades than in the elementary grades.[34] Although homework in elementary school may not enhance achievement very much, it can help students develop some of the study strategies and self-regulation skills they'll need in later years.[35] Undoubtedly the *quality* of assignments—for instance, whether they encourage rote memorization or meaningful learning, whether students find them boring or engaging—makes an appreciable difference both in what and how much students learn and in what kinds of learning and self-regulation strategies they develop.[36]

When assigning homework, teachers must remember that students differ considerably in the time and resources they have at home (e.g., reference books, computers, Internet access), in the amount and quality of assistance they can get from parents and other family members, and in the

MyEdLab
Video Example 8.2.

What specific concerns does 16-year-old Josh have about homework? What might teachers do to address some of his concerns?

---

[32] Alleman & Brophy, 1998.
[33] Alleman et al., 2010; Corno, 1996.
[34] H. Cooper, Robinson, & Patall, 2006.
[35] H. Cooper & Valentine, 2001; B. J. Zimmerman, 1998.
[36] Dettmers, Trautwein, Lüdtke, Kunter, & Baumert, 2010; Trautwein, Lüdtke, Kastens, & Köller, 2006.

extent to which they have the motivation and self-regulation strategies to keep themselves on task.[37] Teachers can maximize the benefits of homework by following a few simple guidelines:[38]

- Use assignments primarily for instructional and diagnostic purposes; minimize the degree to which homework is used to assess learning and determine final class grades.
- Make homework sufficiently intriguing and challenging that students *want* to complete it; for example, give it an authentic, real-world quality, but don't make it so difficult that it leaves students confused and frustrated.
- Provide the information and structure that students need to complete assignments with little or no assistance from others.
  - Give a mixture of required and voluntary assignments. (Voluntary ones should help give students a sense of autonomy and control, enhancing their intrinsic motivation.)
  - Discuss homework assignments in class the following day or as soon after that as possible.
  - When students have poor self-regulation skills or limited resources at home, establish supervised after-school homework programs.

Teachers must remember, too, that homework is appropriate only to help students achieve important educational goals—*never* to punish students for misbehavior.

Shoot for mastery of basic knowledge and skills.

When teachers move through lessons without making sure that all students master the content of each one, they may leave more and more students behind as they go along. For example, imagine that a class of 27 students, listed in Figure 8.8, is beginning a unit on fractions. The class progresses through several lessons as follows:

Lesson 1: The class studies the basic idea that a fraction represents a part of a whole: The denominator indicates the number of pieces into which the whole has been divided, and the numerator indicates how many of those pieces are present. By the end of the lesson, 23 children understand what a fraction is. But Sarah, Laura, Jason K., and Jason M. are either partly or totally confused.

Lesson 2: The class studies the process of reducing fractions to lowest terms (e.g., $\frac{12}{20}$ can be reduced to $\frac{3}{5}$). By the end of the lesson, 20 children understand this process. But Alison, Reggie, and Jason S. haven't mastered the idea that they need to divide both the numerator and denominator by the same number. Sarah, Laura, and the other two Jasons still don't understand what fractions *are* and so have trouble with this lesson as well.

Lesson 3: The class studies the process of adding two fractions, for now looking only at fractions with equal denominators (e.g., $\frac{1}{20} + \frac{11}{20} = \frac{12}{20}$). By the end of the lesson, 19 children can add fractions with the same denominator. Matt, Charlie, Maria F., and Maria W. keep adding the denominators together as well as the numerators (e.g., figuring that $\frac{2}{5} + \frac{2}{5} = \frac{4}{10}$). And Sarah, Laura, Jason K., and Jason M. continue to be puzzled about the general nature of fractions.

Lesson 4: The class combines the processes of adding fractions and reducing fractions to lowest terms. They must first add two fractions together and then, if necessary, reduce the sum to its lowest terms (e.g., after adding $\frac{1}{20} + \frac{11}{20}$, they must reduce the sum of $\frac{12}{20}$ to $\frac{3}{5}$). Here we lose Paul, Arla, and Karen because they keep forgetting to reduce the sum to

FIGURE 8.8 Sequential and hierarchical nature of knowledge about fractions

Students	Lesson 1: Concept of Fraction	Lesson 2: Reducing to Lowest Terms (Builds on Lesson 1)	Lesson 3: Adding Fractions with Same Denominators (Builds on Lesson 1)	Lesson 4: Adding Fractions & Reducing to Lowest Terms (Builds on Lessons 2 & 3)
Sarah	--→	--→	--→	--→
Laura	--→	--→	--→	--→
Jason K.	--→	--→	--→	--→
Jason M.	--→	--→	--→	--→
Alison	→	--→	→	--→
Reggie	→	--→	→	--→
Jason S.	→	--→	→	--→
Matt	→	→	--→	--→
Charlie	→	→	--→	--→
Maria F.	→	→	--→	--→
Maria W.	→	→	--→	--→
Paul	→	→	→	--→
Arla	→	→	→	--→
Karen	→	→	→	--→
Kevin	→	→	→	→
Nori	→	→	→	→
Marcy	→	→	→	→
Janelle	→	→	→	→
Joyce	→	→	→	→
Ming Tang	→	→	→	→
Georgette	→	→	→	→
LaVeda	→	→	→	→
Mark	→	→	→	→
Seth	→	→	→	→
Joanne	→	→	→	→
Rita	→	→	→	→
Shauna	→	→	→	→

--→ = nonmastery of subject matter
——→ = mastery of subject matter

[37] Dumont et al., 2012; Eilam, 2001; Fries, Dietz, & Schmid, 2008; Hoover-Dempsey et al., 2001; Xu, 2008.
[38] Alleman et al., 2010; Belfiore & Hornyak, 1998; H. Cooper, 1989; Cosden, Morrison, Albanese, & Macias, 2001; Dettmers et al., 2011; Garbe & Guy, 2006; Patall, Cooper, & Wynn, 2010; Trautwein et al., 2006; Trautwein, Niggli, Schnyder, & Lüdtke, 2009; Xu, 2008.

lowest terms. And of course, we've already lost Sarah, Laura, Alison, Reggie, Matt, Charlie, the two Marias, and the three Jasons on prerequisite skills. *We now have only 13 of our original 27 students understanding what they are doing—less than half the class!* (See the rightmost column of Figure 8.8.)

Mastery learning, in which students demonstrate competence in one topic before proceeding to the next, minimizes the likelihood of leaving some students behind as a class proceeds to increasingly challenging material.[39] This approach is based on three assumptions:

- Almost every student can learn a particular topic to mastery.
- Some students need more time to master a topic than others.
- Some students need more assistance than others.

As you can see, mastery learning represents a very optimistic approach to instruction. It assumes that most learners *can* learn school subject matter if given sufficient time and instruction. Furthermore, truly mastering a classroom topic increases the odds that students will be able to transfer what they've learned to new situations and problems and to think critically and creatively about it (recall the previous discussions of the *less-is-more* principle in Chapter 2 and Chapter 3).

A mastery learning approach to instruction looks a lot like direct instruction, in that the subject matter is broken into a series of small and logically sequenced steps, numerous opportunities for practice are provided, and learning is assessed after each step. But in addition, students move to the next step only after demonstrating mastery of the preceding one. Mastery is defined in specific, concrete terms—perhaps answering at least 90% of quiz items correctly. Students engaged in mastery learning often proceed through instructional units at their own pace, and thus different students may be studying different units at any given time.

Mastery learning has several advantages over nonmastery approaches to instruction. In particular, students tend to have a better attitude toward the subject matter, learn more, and perform at higher levels on classroom assessments. The benefits are especially striking for low-ability students.[40]

Mastery learning is most appropriate when the subject matter is hierarchical in nature—that is, when certain concepts and skills provide the foundation for future learning and genuine conceptual understanding. When instructional goals deal with such basics as word recognition, rules of grammar, arithmetic, or key scientific concepts, instruction designed to promote mastery learning may be in order. However, the very notion of mastery may be irrelevant to some long-term instructional goals. For example, skills related to critical thinking, scientific reasoning, and creative writing may continue to improve throughout childhood and adolescence without ever being completely mastered.

As a teacher, you are apt to find that teacher-directed strategies are sometimes the most effective way to help students accomplish important instructional goals. In the hotlinked Self-Check quiz and Application Exercises that follow, you can check and apply your understandings related to Big Idea 8.2:

Sometimes instruction is most effective when it is teacher-directed—that is, when the teacher chooses the specific topics to be studied and the general course of a lesson.

MyEdLab Self-Check 8.2

MyEdLab Application Exercise 8.3. In this exercise, you can apply what you have learned about direct instruction to a third-grade reading lesson.

MyEdLab Application Exercise 8.4. In this exercise, you can observe and evaluate a middle school geometry lesson that uses an instructional website to teach the concept of *tessellation*.

---

[39] For example, see B. S. Bloom, 1981; Fuchs et al., 2005; Guskey, 1985, 2010; B. J. Zimmerman & Didenedetto, 2008.

[40] Guskey, 2010; Hattie, 2009; C. C. Kulik, Kulik, & Bangert-Drowns, 1990; Shuell, 1996.

8.3 CONDUCTING LEARNER-DIRECTED INSTRUCTION

Big Idea 8.3 Sometimes instruction is most effective when it is learner-directed—that is, when students have some control over the issues to be addressed and the ways in which to address them.

At one point in the opening case study, students convene in small groups to brainstorm a possible grocery list for long-distance travel in the 1800s. As previously noted in Chapter 4, discussions with peers can enhance learning in numerous ways. For instance, when learners talk about and exchange ideas, they must elaborate on and organize their thoughts, can discover gaps and inconsistencies in their current understandings, and may encounter explanations that are more accurate and useful than their own. Not only can a group of learners engage in such *co-construction* of meaning, but they can also scaffold one another's learning efforts. Clearly, then, learners have a great deal to gain from interacting frequently not only with their teachers but also with one another.

Learner-directed instruction, in which students have considerable control over what and how they learn, often—although not always—involves interaction with classmates. The following strategies can enhance the effectiveness of learner-directed lessons and activities.

Have students discuss issues that lend themselves to multiple perspectives, explanations, or approaches.

Discussions of multifaceted and possibly controversial topics appear to have several benefits. Students are more likely to voice their opinions if they know there are multiple possible answers. They may, of their own accord, seek out new information that resolves seemingly contradictory data—in other words, they may be intrinsically motivated to resolve inconsistencies. They might reexamine and possibly revise their positions on issues. And they're more apt to develop a meaningful and well-integrated understanding of the subject matter they're studying.[41]

Student discussions can be fruitful in virtually any academic discipline. For example, in language arts, students might discuss various interpretations of classic works of literature, addressing questions with no easy or definitive right answers.[42] In history classes, students can read and discuss various documents related to a single historical event and, as a result, come to recognize that history isn't necessarily as cut-and-dried as traditional textbooks portray it.[43] (Recall the discussion of *epistemic beliefs* in Chapter 3.) In science classes, discussions of various and conflicting explanations of physical and biological phenomena can enhance scientific reasoning skills, promote conceptual change, and help students begin to understand that science is a dynamic and continually evolving set of concepts and principles rather than just a collection of discrete facts.[44] (This point, too, has implications for students' epistemic beliefs.) And in mathematics, discussions that focus on alternative approaches to solving a single problem can promote more complete understanding, more creative problem solving, and better transfer to new situations and problems.[45]

Students gain more from a class discussion when they participate actively in it.[46] And they're often more willing to speak openly when their audience is only two or three peers rather than the class as a whole, with the difference being especially noticeable for girls and for students with disabilities.[47] On some occasions, then, teachers may want to have students discuss an issue in small groups first—thereby giving them the chance to express and possibly gain support for their ideas in a relatively private context—before bringing them together for a whole-class discussion.[48]

---

[41] Jadallah et al., 2011; D. W. Johnson & Johnson, 2009b; Kuhn, 2015; Murphy, Wilkinson, Soter, Hennessey, & Alexander, 2009; Reznitskaya & Gregory, 2013; Sinatra & Mason, 2008.

[42] Applebee, Langer, Nystrand, & Gamoran, 2003; McGee, 1992; Wu, Anderson, Nguyen-Jahiel, & Miller, 2013.

[43] Leinhardt, 1994; vanSledright & Limón, 2006.

[44] Andriessen, 2006; Bell & Linn, 2002; K. Hogan, Nastasi, & Pressley, 2000; M. C. Linn, 2008.

[45] M. M. Chiu, 2008; Cobb et al., 1991; J. Hiebert & Wearne, 1996; Lampert, 1990; Webb et al., 2008.

[46] Lotan, 2006; A. M. O'Donnell, 1999; Webb, 1989.

[47] A.-M. Clark et al., 2003; Hattie & Gan, 2011; Théberge, 1994.

[48] D. W. Johnson & Johnson, 2009b; Minstrell & Stimpson, 1996.

Create a classroom atmosphere conducive to open debate and the constructive evaluation of ideas.

Students are more likely to share their ideas and opinions if their teacher is supportive of multiple viewpoints, if disagreeing with classmates is socially acceptable, and if students feel comfortable volunteering answers that turn out to be incorrect.[49] Strategies that can promote such an atmosphere include the following:[50]

- Communicate the message that understanding a topic at the end of a discussion is more important than having the correct answer (if there is one) at the beginning of the discussion.
- Communicate the beliefs that asking questions reflects curiosity, that differing perspectives on a controversial topic are both inevitable and healthy, and that changing one's opinion can be a sign of thoughtful reflection.
- Ask students to explain their reasoning and to try to understand one another's explanations.
- Help clarify a student's line of reasoning for classmates.
- Suggest that students build on one another's ideas whenever possible.
- Encourage students to be open in their agreement or disagreement with their classmates— that is, to "agree to disagree."
- Stress that although it's acceptable to critique ideas, it *isn't* acceptable to criticize people.
- When students' perspectives reflect misconceptions or errors in reasoning, gently guide them toward more productive understandings.
- Depersonalize challenges to a student's line of reasoning by framing questions in a third-person voice—for example, "What if someone were to respond to your claim by saying . . . ?"
- Occasionally ask students to defend a position that directly opposes what they actually believe.
- Require students to develop compromise solutions that take into account opposing perspectives.

Not only can such strategies promote more productive classroom discussions, but they also help to create a *sense of community* among students. We'll look at the benefits of creating a sense of community in Chapter 9.

When students become comfortable with disagreeing in a congenial way, they often find their interactions highly motivating, especially if they're emotionally involved in the topic under discussion (recall the concept of *hot cognition,* described in Chapter 5).[51] One fourth grader said this about her class's frequent small-group discussions:

> I like it when we get to argue, because I have a big mouth sometimes, and I like to talk out in class, and I get really tired of holding my hand up in the air. Besides, we only get to talk to each other when we go outside at recess, and this gives us a chance to argue in a nice way.[52]

Furthermore, students often acquire effective social skills during their class discussions. For example, when students meet in small, self-directed groups to discuss children's literature, they may develop and model for one another such skills as expressing agreement ("I agree with Kordell because . . ."), disagreeing tactfully ("Yeah, but they could see the fox sneak in"), justifying an opinion ("I think it shouldn't be allowed, because if he got to be king, who knows what he would do to the kingdom"), and seeking everyone's participation ("Ssshhh! Be quiet! Let Zeke talk!").[53]

---

[49] A.-M. Clark et al., 2003; Hadjioannou, 2007; E. M. Nussbaum, 2008.

[50] Hadjioannou, 2007; Hatano & Inagaki, 2003; Herrenkohl & Guerra, 1998; K. Hogan et al., 2000; D. W. Johnson & Johnson, 2009b; Lampert, Rittenhouse, & Crumbaugh, 1996; E. M. Nussbaum, 2008; Sinatra & Mason, 2008; Staples, 2007; Walshaw & Anthony, 2008; Webb et al., 2008.

[51] Hadjioannou, 2007; C. L. Smith, 2007.

[52] A.-M. Clark et al., 2003, p. 194.

[53] R. C. Anderson et al., 2001, pp. 16, 25; Certo, 2011.

Conduct activities in which students must depend on one another for their learning.

In the opening case study of Chapter 7, we had a situation in which students' success depended on their ability to work together on the annual eighth-grade class play. Cooperation with peers can enhance students' learning and achievement on smaller tasks as well. As an illustration, try the next exercise.

SEE FOR YOURSELF
PURPLE SATIN

Imagine yourself as a student in each of the three classrooms described here. How would you behave in each situation?

1. Mr. Alexander tells your class, "Let's find out which students can learn the most in this week's unit on the human digestive system. The three students getting the highest scores on Friday's quiz will get free tickets to the Purple Satin concert on Saturday." Purple Satin is a popular musical group you'd really like to see and hear in person, but the concert has been sold out for months.
2. Ms. Bernstein introduces her lesson this way: "I'm hoping that all of you will master the basics of human digestion this week. If you get a score of at least 90% on this Friday's quiz, I'll give you a free ticket to the Purple Satin concert."
3. Mr. Camacho begins the same lesson like this: "Beginning today, you'll be working in groups of three to study the human digestive system. On Friday, I'll give you a quiz to see how much you've learned. If all three members of your group score at least 90% on the quiz, your group will get free tickets to the Purple Satin concert."

In which class(es) are you likely to work hard to get free tickets to Purple Satin? How might you work *differently* in the three situations?

The first class (Mr. Alexander's) is obviously a very competitive one: Only the three best students are getting tickets to the concert. Will you try to earn one of those tickets? It all depends on what you think your chances are of being a top scorer on Friday's quiz. If you've been doing well on quizzes all year, you'll undoubtedly study harder than ever during this week's unit. If, instead, you've been doing poorly in class despite your best efforts, you probably won't work for something you're unlikely to get. But in either case, will you help your fellow students learn about the digestive system? Not if you want to go to the concert yourself!

In Ms. Bernstein's class, there's no competition for concert tickets. As long as you get a score of 90% or higher on the quiz, you'll get a ticket. But will you help your classmates understand what the pancreas does or learn the difference between the large and small intestines? Maybe—*if* you have the time and are feeling altruistic.

Now consider Mr. Camacho's class. Whether or not you get a concert ticket depends on how well you *and two other students* score on Friday's quiz. Are you going to help those two students learn about salivation and digestive enzymes? And can you expect them, in turn, to help you understand where the liver fits into the whole system? Absolutely!

In **cooperative learning**,[54] students work in small groups to achieve a common goal. Unlike an individualistic classroom such as Ms. Bernstein's (where one student's success is unrelated to peers' achievement) or a competitive classroom such as Mr. Alexander's (where one student's success partly depends on the *failure* of others), students in a cooperative learning environment such as Mr. Camacho's work together to achieve joint successes. When students engage in cooperative learning, they reap the many benefits of student dialogue, including greater comprehension and integration of the subject matter, recognition of inadequacies or misconceptions in understanding, and increased perspective-taking. Furthermore, when students cooperatively tackle a complex, challenging task, they can share the heavy cognitive load the task might involve and provide scaffolding for one another's efforts. Thus they're apt to have higher self-efficacy for accomplishing the task successfully.[55]

---

[54] Some theorists distinguish between *cooperative* learning and *collaborative* learning, with various theorists drawing the dividing line somewhat differently. Here we are using *cooperative learning* broadly to include collaborative approaches to learning.

[55] T. L. Good, McCaslin, & Reys, 1992; D. W. Johnson & Johnson, 2009a; F. Kirschner, Paas, & Kirschner, 2009; A. M. O'Donnell & O'Kelly, 1994; Webb & Palincsar, 1996.

When designed and structured appropriately, cooperative learning activities can promote high achievement in students of all ability levels, including many who have historically been at risk for academic failure.[56] Cooperative learning activities may also promote complex cognitive processes. Students essentially think aloud, modeling various learning and problem-solving strategies for one another and developing greater metacognitive awareness as a result.[57] An additional, nonacademic benefit is that students are more likely to believe that their classmates like them, and friendships across racial and ethnic groups and between students with and without disabilities are apt to form.[58]

Cooperative learning activities have potential pitfalls, however. Some students may be more interested in meeting social and performance goals (e.g., creating a good impression, getting an acceptable answer quickly) than they are in mastering the material, and thus their willingness to assist one another or ask for help may be compromised.[59] Students who do most of the work and most of the talking are likely to learn more than other group members.[60] Furthermore, students may occasionally agree to use an incorrect strategy or method that a particular group member has suggested, or they may share misconceptions about the topic they're studying.[61] And in some cases, students may simply not have the skills to cooperate and help one another learn.[62]

As you can see, cooperative learning isn't simply a process of putting students in groups and setting them loose to work together on an assignment. For a cooperative learning activity to be successful, teachers must structure it in such a way that cooperation is not only helpful for academic success but actually necessary for it.[63] The Classroom Strategies box "Enhancing the Effectiveness of Cooperative Learning" presents and illustrates several strategies for conducting effective cooperative group activities.

Have students conduct their own research about certain topics.

When we authors have used the term *research* in previous chapters, we've been referring to planned, systematic inquiry designed to acquire new knowledge for humankind in general. Here we mean it in a much looser sense: to find new information for *oneself* rather than having it spoon-fed. In some instances, such research may take the form of *discovery learning* or *inquiry learning* activities (e.g., see the Classroom Strategies box "Conducting Effective Discovery and Inquiry Learning Activities" in Chapter 6). But in many other cases, it involves finding information already available in books, magazines, newspapers, electronic databases, and elsewhere.

Increasingly, students are going to the Internet to find needed information. Internet search engines such as Google, Bing, and Yahoo! allow students to find websites on almost any topic. Alternatively, students might go directly to the online encyclopedia Wikipedia, which, as this book goes to press, has entries on more than 5 million topics written in English plus millions more written in other languages. Many Internet websites take the form of **hypermedia**, in which students can go from one electronic "page" to another one of their own choosing simply by clicking on a word, icon, or "button" on the screen.

An advantage of student-conducted research is that it enables students to pursue topics of personal interest and can enhance their sense of autonomy—hence it can foster intrinsic motivation for learning classroom subject matter. Keep in mind, however, that students don't always have the knowledge, self-regulation skills, and technological literacy they need to learn effectively as they explore the many resources the Internet offers, nor will they necessarily engage in elaboration or other cognitive processes that foster meaningful, enduring learning.[64] Furthermore, the Internet has no good quality-control mechanism to ensure that information is accurate, especially

MyEdLab
Video Example 8.3.
Watch this fifth-grade teacher conduct a class review of guidelines for cooperative group work. What particular benefits might his approach have?

---

[56] Ginsburg-Block, Rohrbeck, & Fantuzzo, 2006; Lou et al., 1996; Rohrbeck, Ginsburg-Block, Fantuzzo, & Miller, 2003; Slavin & Lake, 2008; S. M. Williams, 2010.

[57] T. L. Good et al., 1992; D. W. Johnson & Johnson, 2009a; A. King, 1999.

[58] Lou et al., 1996; J. H. Pfeifer, Brown, & Juvonen, 2007; Slavin, Hurley, & Chamberlain, 2003.

[59] Levy, Kaplan, & Patrick, 2000; Moje & Shepardson, 1998; Wentzel, 2009.

[60] Gayford, 1992; Lotan, 2006; Webb, 1989.

[61] T. L. Good et al., 1992; Stacey, 1992.

[62] Ladd, Kochenderfer-Ladd, Visconti, & Ettekal, 2012; Webb & Mastergeorge, 2003.

[63] D. W. Johnson & Johnson, 2009a; Slavin, 2011; van Drie, van Boxtel, & van der Linden, 2006.

[64] Arnesen, Elstad, Christophersen, & Vavik, 2014; Eysink & de Jong, 2012; P. A. Kirschner & van Merriënboer, 2013; C. N. Davidson, 2011; Winters, Greene, & Costich, 2008.

CLASSROOM STRATEGIES

Enhancing the Effectiveness of Cooperative Learning

- **Choose challenging tasks that students may have trouble accomplishing alone but *can* accomplish when several of them coordinate their efforts.**
  Although they haven't yet been taught how to divide by fractions, students in a fourth-grade class are asked to solve the following problem: *Mom makes small apple tarts, using three-quarters of an apple for each small tart. She has 20 apples. How many small apple tarts can she make?* They work in small groups to identify possible approaches to the problem. (An example of one group's discussion appears in the section "Social Interaction as Context" in Chapter 4.)

- **Form groups of students who are likely to work together productively and who each have unique knowledge and skills to offer.**
  An elementary school teacher divides his class into cooperative groups of three or four students each to design posters depicting significant events in their country's history. He makes sure that each group includes students of various ethnic backgrounds and students who will be able to contribute different skills to the task at hand. He also makes sure to split up students who don't work well together (e.g., close friends who get off task when they're together).

- **Provide clear goals toward which groups should work.**
  Students in a high school Spanish class work in small groups to create an episode of a soap opera (*telenovela*) spoken entirely in Spanish. Over the course of a 3-week period, each group (1) writes a short screenplay, (2) collects the necessary props and costumes, and (3) videotapes the episode so that their classmates can eventually watch it.

- **Structure tasks so that group members are dependent on one another for success.**
  A high school biology teacher asks cooperative groups to prepare for an upcoming class debate on the pros and cons of mosquito control in the community. She gives each group member a unique function. For example, one student acts as *reader* of information about the issue, another acts as *recorder* of group members' arguments, and a third acts as *checker* to determine whether all group members agree with each argument.

- **Provide clear guidelines about how to behave.**
  A seventh-grade math teacher forms cooperative groups in which students will work on a series of math problems. Before the students begin the task, the teacher has them brainstorm ground rules for working effectively in their groups. Students volunteer such ideas as "Talk quietly so you don't disturb other groups," "If you see someone in your group is in trouble, help them," and "Be patient with them."

- **Monitor group interactions.**
  A middle school social studies teacher asks cooperative groups to identify a possible plan for helping homeless people secure suitable housing. When he hears one student disparaging another because of a difference of opinion, he reminds the group that students should criticize ideas rather than people.

- **Provide critical information and insights when (but only when) a group is unlikely or unable to provide such information and insights for itself.**
  The same social studies teacher tells a group, "The solution you've developed assumes that most taxpayers would be willing to pay much higher taxes than they do now. Is that realistic?"

- **Make students individually accountable for their achievement.**
  An elementary school teacher has incorporated cooperative learning into a unit on calculating perimeters of squares, rectangles, and triangles. Later, she gives all students a quiz to assess their individual mastery of perimeters.

- **Reinforce group success.**
  The same elementary school teacher awards a few extra points to groups in which every member can demonstrate mastery of perimeters.

- **Ask students to evaluate their effectiveness in working as a group.**
  After cooperative groups have completed their assigned tasks, a teacher asks the groups to answer questions such as these: "Did all group members actively participate?" "Did they ask questions when they didn't understand one another?" "Did they criticize ideas rather than people?"

Sources: Blumenfeld, Marx, Soloway, & Krajcik, 1996; E. G. Cohen, 1994; Crook, 1995; Deutsch, 1993; Esmonde, 2009; J. D. Finn, Pannozzo, & Achilles, 2003; Gillies & Ashman, 1998; Ginsburg-Block et al., 2006; J. Hiebert et al., 1997, p. 118 (apple tarts problem); D. W. Johnson & Johnson, 1991, 2009b; Karau & Williams, 1995; Linnenbrink-Garcia, Rogat, & Koskey, 2011; Lotan, 2006; Lou et al., 1996; A. M. O'Donnell & O'Kelly, 1994; Slavin, 2011; van Drie et al., 2006; Webb & Farivar, 1999; Webb & Palincsar, 1996.

when posted by individuals rather than by government agencies or professional organizations. (For example, entries in Wikipedia, although generally accurate, occasionally include inaccuracies added by nonexperts, and some individuals may intentionally "rewrite" history or science to advance a particular personal or political agenda.) An additional concern is that some students may venture into unproductive domains, perhaps finding research papers they can pass off as their own (this is plagiarism), stumbling on sites that preach racist attitudes or offer pornographic images, or sharing personal information with people who might jeopardize their well-being.[65]

Clearly, then, students often need considerable scaffolding as they study a particular topic online, and their journeys into cyberspace should be closely monitored. Even in the secondary grades, students are likely to need considerable guidance about how to distinguish between helpful and unhelpful websites, sift through mountains of information in search of those tidbits most

---

[65] Nixon, 2005; Schofield, 2006.

relevant to their own purposes, critically evaluate the quality of the information they're finding, and synthesize what they discover into a cohesive, meaningful whole.[66]

One effective way to focus students' Internet searches is to post links to suitable websites on a class website. Alternatively, teachers might use or create a **webquest** activity, in which students can use a number of predetermined websites as they tackle an interesting and challenging task requiring higher-level thinking skills; WebQuest.org provides links to many examples. In using such strategies, teachers should give students explicit instructional objectives they need to accomplish as they conduct their Internet searches—for instance, by giving them specific questions to which they need to find answers.[67]

In addition, many school computer systems now include a *remote desktop* feature that can help teachers both scaffold and monitor students' use of the Internet. With this feature, a teacher can share his or her own computer screen with students and demonstrate how they should proceed with any online activity. The feature also allows a teacher to view every student's computer screen from afar. If a particular student goes astray, the teacher can lock the student's screen and send an appropriate message.

Have students teach one another.

Having some students provide instruction to other students—**peer tutoring**—can often be an effective learner-directed approach to teaching fundamental knowledge and skills. For example, a teacher might have students within a single class tutor one another. Alternatively, two or more collaborating teachers might have older students teach younger ones—for instance, by having fourth or fifth graders teach students in kindergarten or first grade.[68] The high school that one of us authors attended many years ago had a schoolwide tutoring program coordinated by the school's chapter of the National Honor Society.

Peer tutoring can lead to considerable gains in academic achievement.[69] One possible reason for its effectiveness is that it gets students actively and mentally engaged with the subject matter—something that doesn't necessarily happen in teacher-directed whole-class explanations. It also provides a context in which struggling students can ask questions when they don't understand something and can get regular feedback about their performance.[70]

Typically, peer tutoring sessions benefit tutors as well as those being tutored.[71] Students are more intrinsically motivated to learn something if they know they'll have to teach it to someone else, and they're apt to engage in considerable elaboration as they study and explain it.[72] Furthermore, in the process of directing and guiding other students' learning and problem solving, tutors may more fully internalize the cognitive strategies involved (recall the discussion of *internalization* in Chapter 6) and so become better able to direct and guide their *own* learning and problem solving. In other words, peer tutoring can foster greater self-regulation.[73] Peer tutoring has nonacademic benefits as well. Cooperation and other social skills improve, behavior problems diminish, and friendships form among students of different ethnic groups and between students with and without disabilities.[74]

Students don't always have the knowledge and skills that will enable them to become effective tutors, however, especially in the elementary grades.[75] In most cases, then, tutoring sessions

think about it

Have you personally benefited from being either the tutor or the learner in a peer-tutoring session? If so, in what way(s) did you benefit? If not, how might the session have been conducted differently?

---

[66] Afflerbach & Cho, 2010; P. A. Alexander & the Disciplined Reading and Learning Research Laboratory, 2012; P. A. Kirschner & van Merriënboer, 2013.

[67] Niederhauser, 2008.

[68] Inglis & Biemiller, 1997; Kermani & Moallem, 1997; D. R. Robinson, Schofield, & Steers-Wentzell, 2005; J. R. Sullivan & Conoley, 2004.

[69] Ginsburg-Block et al., 2006; Graesser, D'Mello, & Cade, 2011; K. C. Leung, 2015; D. R. Robinson et al., 2005; Roscoe & Chi, 2007.

[70] Graesser & Person, 1994; J. R. Sullivan & Conoley, 2004.

[71] Graesser et al., 2011; Inglis & Biemiller, 1997; K. C. Leung, 2015; D. R. Robinson et al., 2005.

[72] Benware & Deci, 1984; A. M. O'Donnell, 2006; Roscoe & Chi, 2007.

[73] Biemiller, Shany, Inglis, & Meichenbaum, 1998; Graesser et al., 2011.

[74] Cushing & Kennedy, 1997; DuPaul, Ervin, Hook, & McGoey, 1998; Greenwood, Carta, & Hall, 1988; D. R. Robinson et al., 2005.

[75] Graesser et al., 2011; Greenwood et al., 1988; Kermani & Moallem, 1997; D. Wood, Wood, Ainsworth, & O'Malley, 1995.

should be limited to subject matter that the tutors know well (we'll see an exception in just a moment). Training in effective tutoring skills is also helpful. For example, a teacher might show tutors how to establish a good relationship with the students they're tutoring, how to break a task into simple steps, and how and when to give feedback.[76]

Providing a structure for tutoring sessions often helps students facilitate their classmates' learning, especially in situations in which all students are novices with respect to the subject matter.[77] In one approach, students are given question "starters" that help them formulate higher-level questions to ask one another—for instance, "What is the difference between ___ and ___?" and "What do you think would happen to ___ if ___ happened?"[78] In the following dialogue, two seventh graders use question starters as they work together to learn more about muscles, a topic that neither of them has previously known much about:

Jon: How does the muscular system work, Kyle?

Kyle: Well . . . it retracts and contracts when you move.

Jon: Can you tell me more? . . . Um, why are muscles important, Kyle?

Kyle: They are important because if we didn't have them we couldn't move around.

Jon: But . . . how do muscles work? Explain it more.

Kyle: Um, muscles have tendons. Some muscles are called skeletal muscles. They are in the muscles that—like—in your arms—that have tendons that hold your muscles to your bones—to make them move and go back and forth. So you can walk and stuff.

Jon: Good. All right! How are the skeletal muscles and the cardiac muscles the same? . . .

Kyle: Well, they're both a muscle. And they're both pretty strong. And they hold things. I don't really think they have much in common.

Jon: Okay. Why don't you think they have much in common?

Kyle: Because the smooth muscle is—I mean the skeletal muscle is voluntary and the cardiac muscle is involuntary. Okay, I'll ask now. What do you think would happen if we didn't have smooth muscles?

Jon: We would have to be chewing harder. And so it would take a long time to digest food. We would have to think about digesting because the smooth muscles—like the intestines and stomach—are *in*voluntary. . . .

Kyle: Yeah, well—um—but, do you think it would *hurt* you if you didn't have smooth muscles?

Jon: Well, yeah—because you wouldn't have muscles to push the food along—in the stomach and intestines—you'd get plugged up! Maybe you'd hafta drink liquid—just liquid stuff. Yuk.[79]

Notice how the boys ask each other questions that encourage elaboration and metacognitive self-reflection (e.g., "Why don't you think they have much in common?" "Do you think it would hurt you if you didn't have smooth muscles?"). Through such structured interactions, students at the same grade and ability levels can provide valuable scaffolding for one another's learning efforts.[80]

Ideally, *all* students should have an opportunity to tutor others at one time or another. This is often easier said than done, because a few students may consistently achieve at a lower level than most of their peers. One strategy is to ask low-achieving students to tutor younger children or same-age classmates who have cognitive or physical disabilities.[81] Another possibility is to teach the students specific tasks or procedures they can share with their higher-achieving, but in this case uninformed, classmates.[82]

---

[76] Fueyo & Bushell, 1998; Inglis & Biemiller, 1997; Kermani & Moallem, 1997; D. R. Robinson et al., 2005.

[77] Fantuzzo, King, & Heller, 1992; Fuchs et al., 1996; Mathes, Torgesen, & Allor, 2001; Spörer & Brunstein, 2009.

[78] A. King, 1997, p. 230.

[79] A. King, Staffieri, & Adelgais, 1998, p. 141.

[80] A. King, 1998.

[81] Greenwood, 1991; J. R. Sullivan & Conoley, 2004.

[82] Cushing & Kennedy, 1997; Inglis & Biemiller, 1997; J. R. Sullivan & Conoley, 2004; Webb & Palincsar, 1996.

Use computer technology to enhance communication and collaboration.

Effective student interactions don't necessarily have to be face to face. Through such mechanisms as e-mail, chat software, electronic bulletin boards, Internet websites, and Skype (www.skype.com), computer technology enables students to communicate with their peers (either locally or around the world), exchange perspectives, brainstorm and build on one another's ideas, and occasionally pull experts into the conversation. Interactions of this nature are collectively known as **computer-supported collaborative learning (CSCL)**. Students must understand, however, that the rules for in-class discussions apply to electronic discussions as well. For example, students must accept that varying perspectives are both welcome and to be expected, and although they can certainly critique their classmates' ideas, they must do so respectfully and without ridicule.[83]

Software created at the University of Toronto provides an example of how technology can enhance student interaction and collaborative learning. The software, called Knowledge Forum (knowledgeforum.com), provides a multimedia database that enables students to jointly construct a body of shared knowledge about a particular topic, perhaps aerodynamics, optics, or the American Civil War. In this electronic environment, students post their work in the forms of reports, problem solutions, diagrams, flowcharts, short stories, and the like. Their classmates regularly respond, perhaps by giving feedback, building on ideas, offering alternative perspectives, or synthesizing what the group has collectively learned. The electronic nature of interactions gives students the time they may need to reflect on one another's ideas and may be especially welcoming for students who are shy or for other reasons feel uncomfortable communicating with peers more publicly. In essence, the software provides the foundation for a computer-based *community of learners* in which most students feel psychologically comfortable and "safe."[84]

Computer-supported collaborative learning appears to have several benefits. By making their findings and logical thinking processes clearly visible to one another, students can more easily reflect on and evaluate their own and others' ideas. Furthermore, students tend to focus on truly understanding classroom subject matter rather than on simply "getting things done" (i.e., they adopt mastery goals rather than performance goals), and as a result, they can better remember and apply classroom subject matter.[85] Furthermore, multinational student–student collaborations are an excellent way to get young learners thinking and acting as *global* citizens as well as citizens of a particular community and country.

Assign authentic real-world tasks and simulations, perhaps as group activities.

In Chapter 3 we noted the importance of *authentic activities*—activities similar to ones that students are apt to encounter in the outside world—as a means of promoting transfer of classroom subject matter to real-world situations. Complex tasks in the outside world must often be handled with little or no explicit guidance from others, and so growing children can best prepare for them by making many of their own decisions while completing similar tasks in the academic curriculum. Most authentic activities, then, should be more learner-directed than teacher-directed.

Some real-world tasks are easy to carry out within school walls. For example, students might bake a cake, write a newspaper article, conduct a scientific investigation, create a new entry for Wikipedia, or calculate the amount of carpet needed for an irregularly shaped room. Computer-based collaborative learning, too, can be brought into play here. For example, in the GLOBE Program (www.globe.gov), student groups around the world collaborate on inquiry-based projects related to environmental and earth sciences. Students in participating schools and classrooms collect and analyze data about various environmental topics (e.g., climate change, watershed dynamics), write reports, and share their findings with students and professional scientists elsewhere.

---

[83] Bellanca & Stirling, 2011; Kreijns, Kirschner, & Vermeulen, 2013.

[84] Hewitt & Scardamalia, 1998; Scardamalia & Bereiter, 2006, 2014.

[85] Bereiter & Scardamalia, 2006; Gehlbach et al., 2008; Greaves, Hayes, Wilson, Gielniak, & Peterson, 2012; Miyake, 2008; Scardamalia & Bereiter, 2006; Zhang, Scardamalia, Reeve, & Messina, 2009.

Other authentic tasks might take place in the outside community, perhaps even in the authentic *communities of practice* described in Chapter 4. For example, in **service learning**, students work on meaningful community service projects that are closely related to the classroom curriculum. To illustrate, children in the primary grades might regularly monitor the quantity of house pet "droppings" in an environmentally sensitive city park, and middle school students might gather information about liquor stores and possible zoning violations near school grounds.[86] In addition to the social, moral, and motivational benefits of community service projects (see Chapter 7), those that are closely tied to important instructional goals appear to enhance classroom learning.[87]

Yet not all real-world tasks are possible and practical to complete either in or outside of school, and in such instances *simulations* can provide a good alternative.[88] For example, students might conduct a mock trial of a historical figure (e.g., Alexander the Great, Adolf Hitler), role-play various characters in classic works of literature, or test the aerodynamic effectiveness of variously shaped paper airplanes.

When real-world tasks and simulations are impractical or impossible, consider using computer-based simulations and games.

Computer-based simulations can be highly effective. For example, children can learn a great deal about fractions with virtual "manipulatives" on a computer screen, and adolescents can systematically test various hypotheses that affect earthquakes or avalanches in a computer-simulated world. A particular advantage of simulations is that they can be designed in ways that keep students' cognitive load within reasonable bounds and appropriately scaffold students' efforts.[89]

Some computer-based simulations involve many students—they may even involve many schools—working together on common problems. For example, in an Internet-based simulation called GlobalEd (www.globaled.uconn.edu), middle school social studies classes become representatives for particular countries (e.g., one class might be France, another might be Nigeria), with different members of a class tackling different global issues (e.g., international conflicts, human rights, environmental issues). Students study their countries and issues and then electronically communicate with representatives from other "countries" (i.e., students in other schools) to share perspectives and negotiate treaties. Not only does the simulation enhance students' understanding of global issues, but it also enhances their perspective-taking ability and interest in social studies as a discipline.[90]

In another globally distributed simulation, Atlantis Remixed (ARX; atlantisremixed.org), students take on various roles (e.g., scientist, historian, mathematician) to tackle complex worldwide problems related to certain environmental or social issues, and they make decisions and take actions that have significant virtual "effects" on long-term outcomes.[91] As an example, Figure 8.9 shows a screenshot in ARX's series called World Games; in this particular simulation, students examine water quality in an effort to determine why fish populations are declining in a three-dimensional fictional world.

In some cases, computer-based simulations have a distinctly game-like nature. Despite their obvious element of play, some video games and other high-tech games can foster significant improvements in students' learning and achievement.[92] As an illustration, in an Internet-based game site called "Whyville" (www.whyville.net), older children and young adolescents become "citizens"

[86] Pickens, 2006; W.-M. Roth, 2011; Tate, 1995. The liquor-store example is described more fully in the Classroom Strategies box "Encouraging and Supporting Students at Risk for Dropping Out" in Chapter 7.

[87] Celio, Durlak, & Dymnicki, 2011; Dymond, Renzaglia, & Chun, 2007; Thapa, Cohen, Guffey, & Higgins-D'Alessandro, 2013.

[88] For example, see B. K. Lee, Patall, Cawthon, & Steingut, 2015.

[89] Baroody, Eiland, Purpura, & Reid, 2013; de Jong, 2011; Kafai & Dede, 2014; Kuhn & Pease, 2010; Sarama & Clements, 2009.

[90] Gehlbach et al., 2008.

[91] Barab, Gresalfi, & Arici, 2009; Barab et al., 2010.

[92] For in-depth discussions of this point, see Barab, Gresalfi, & Ingram-Goble, 2010; Squire, 2011; Tobias & Fletcher, 2011.

FIGURE 8.9   This screenshot from Atlantis Remixed illustrates a computer-based simulation activity in which students examine water quality in an effort to determine why fish populations are declining in a three-dimensional virtual world. For more information about the many simulations in Atlantis Remixed, go to atlantisremixed.org.

Source: Screenshot provided courtesy of Atlantis Remixed. Copyright © by Atlantis Remixed. Reprinted by permission.

who enter, explore, experiment, compete, and collaborate in a colorful, multifaceted virtual world with its own government, economy, and ecosystem. For example, after creating personal avatars, "Whyvillians" can earn "clams" (Whyville's virtual currency) and contribute to their community's collective knowledge and well-being by building energy-efficient homes, developing a new vaccine, creating a community recycling program, or identifying new species in a local coral reef (see Figure 8.10). In such a virtual environment, students not only learn and apply academic subject matter but also practice prosocial strategies and leadership skills.[93]

Provide sufficient scaffolding to ensure successful accomplishment of assigned tasks.

In discussions of various instructional strategies in this chapter, the word *scaffold* has often come up. Regardless of whether instruction is teacher-directed or learner-directed, students need enough structure and guidance that they know what they're supposed to do and can achieve some degree of success.[94] Yet teachers need to strike a happy medium here. They certainly don't want to structure classroom tasks to the point where only simple tasks and thought processes are required, with little room for students' independent decision making. Ultimately, teachers want students to develop and use complex cognitive processes—for example, to think analytically, critically, and creatively—and they must have classroom assignments and activities that promote such processes.

---

[93] Kafai & Fields, 2013; Tobias & Fletcher, 2011; Wouters, van Nimwegen, van Oostendorp, & van der Spek, 2013.

[94] Belland, Kim, & Hannafin, 2013; N. Carr, 2011; Jeong & Hmelo-Silver, 2016; van de Pol, Volman, & Beishuizen, 2010; Weinert & Helmke, 1995.

FIGURE 8.10 In this screenshot from Whyville, students' avatars encounter a variety of coral reef species as they SCUBA dive in a virtual coral reef. By identifying and counting these organisms, students learn about the reef ecosystem and keep track of the health of the reef. For more information, go to reef.whyville.net.

Source: Screenshot provided courtesy of Numedeon, Inc. the creators of Whyville. Copyright © by Numedeon, Inc. Reprinted by permission.

As a teacher, you will often find that learner-directed strategies are most appropriate for your instructional goals and objectives, especially when you want to promote such complex cognitive processes as transfer, problem solving, and critical thinking. In the hotlinked Self-Check quiz and Application Exercise that follow, you can check and apply your understandings related to Big Idea 8.3:

> *Sometimes instruction is most effective when it is learner-directed—that is, when students have some control over the issues to be addressed and the ways in which to address them.*

MyEdLab **Self-Check 8.3**

MyEdLab **Application Exercise 8.5.** In this exercise, you can explore various strategies for conducting a cooperative learning activity.

8.4 GENERAL INSTRUCTIONAL STRATEGIES

Big Idea 8.4 Different instructional strategies are appropriate for different instructional goals and objectives and for different students.

In planning and conducting lessons—whether they involve teacher-directed instruction, learner-directed instruction, or some combination of the two—many of the strategies we've identified in previous chapters are, of course, relevant. We authors suggest that some of the most critical ones are these:

- Regularly assess students' understandings. (Chapter 2)
- Guide and support self-regulated learning and behavior. (Chapter 3)

- Pursue topics in depth rather than superficially. (Chapter 3)
- Present challenges that students can realistically accomplish. (Chapter 5)
- Conduct interest-arousing lessons and activities. (Chapter 5)

The following strategies also apply across the board.

Take group differences into account.

Some instructional strategies are a better fit with students' cultural backgrounds than others. For example, students from cultures that especially value interpersonal cooperation (e.g., many Hispanic and Native American communities in the Western Hemisphere, Māori communities in New Zealand) are apt to achieve at higher levels in classrooms that have many interactive and collaborative activities. In contrast, recent immigrants from some Asian countries may be more accustomed to teacher-directed instruction than to learner-directed classroom activities; such may also be true for children in certain indigenous groups around the world.[95]

Culture-specific patterns of verbal interaction may also come into play, affecting the nature and amount of students' participation in whole-class discussions and question-answer sessions. The Cultural Considerations box "Cultural and Ethnic Differences in Verbal Interaction" gives some examples.

CULTURAL CONSIDERATIONS

Cultural and Ethnic Differences in Verbal Interaction

If you have grown up in mainstream Western culture, you've learned that there are certain ways of conversing with others that are socially acceptable and certain other ways that are definitely *not* acceptable. For example, if you're having lunch with a friend, the two of you will probably try to keep a conversation going throughout the meal. And if someone else is speaking—especially if that person is an authority figure—you probably know not to interrupt until the speaker has finished what he or she is saying. Once the speaker *is* finished, however, you can ask a question if you need further information.

Such social conventions are by no means universal. Here we look at cultural and ethnic differences in several aspects of verbal interaction: dialect, talkativeness, assertiveness, answering questions, and wait time.

DIALECT. Even if children speak English at home, they may use a form of English different from the Standard English typically considered acceptable at school. More specifically, they may speak in a different

dialect, a form of English (or, more generally, a form of any language) that includes some unique pronunciations, idioms, and grammatical structures. Dialects tend to be associated either with particular geographical regions or with particular ethnic and cultural groups. Perhaps the most widely studied ethnic dialect is African American English (you may also see the terms *Black English vernacular* and *Ebonics*). This dialect, which is actually a group of similar dialects, is used in many African American communities throughout the United States and is characterized by certain ways of speaking that are distinctly different from those of Standard English (e.g., "He got ten dollar," "Momma she mad," "He be talkin' ").[a] At one time many researchers believed that an African American dialect represented a less complex form of speech than Standard English, and so they urged educators to teach students to speak "properly" as quickly as possible. But most researchers now realize that African American dialects are, in fact, very complex languages with predictable sentence structures and that these dialects

promote communication and sophisticated thinking processes as readily as Standard English.[b]

When a local dialect is the language preferred by residents of a community, it's often the means through which people can most effectively connect with one another in day-to-day interactions. Furthermore, many children and adolescents view their native dialect as an integral part of their ethnic identity.[c] Nevertheless, lack of proficiency in Standard English can impede children's reading and writing development, and in later years, their use of a distinct regional or cultural dialect may lead other people to underestimate their ability levels.[d] For such reasons, many experts recommend that all students in English-speaking countries develop proficiency in Standard English.

Ultimately, children and adolescents function most effectively when they can use both their local dialect and Standard English in appropriate contexts. For example, although teachers may wish to encourage Standard English in most written work or in formal oral presentations, they might find other dialects

(continued)

---

[95] Castagno & Brayboy, 2008; Lillemyr, Søbstad, Marder, & Flowerday, 2011; Macfarlane, Webber Cookson-Cox, & McRae, 2014; Tyler et al., 2008.

quite appropriate in creative writing or informal class discussions.[e]

TALKATIVENESS. Relatively speaking, mainstream Western culture is a chatty one. People often say things to one another even when they have little to communicate, making small talk as a way of maintaining interpersonal relationships and filling awkward silences.[f] Furthermore, in some African American, Hawaiian, and Jewish cultures, adults and children alike may speak spontaneously and simultaneously, perhaps to show personal involvement in a conversation or perhaps to avoid being excluded from the conversation altogether.[g]

In certain other cultures, however, silence is golden. For example, in many parts of the world, children are expected to learn primarily by close, quiet observation of adults, rather than by asking questions or otherwise interrupting what adults are doing.[h] In fact, in some cultures—for instance, in many Mexican American and Southeast Asian communities, and in some African American communities—children learn very early in life that they should engage in conversation with adults only when their participation has been directly solicited.[i]

ASSERTIVENESS. Some talkative cultures are also assertive ones, in that people readily voice their opinions, perhaps even interrupting those who are speaking; for example, this is the case for many African Americans, European Americans, and Hawaiians. People from quieter cultures, such as many Asian

Americans, tend to be more subtle and tentative in expressing their opinions—for instance, they might begin a sentence by saying "I'm not sure, but perhaps . . . "—and they aren't as likely to reveal their emotions during conversations.[j]

ANSWERING QUESTIONS. A common interaction pattern in many Western classrooms is the **IRE cycle**: A teacher *initiates* an interaction by asking a question, a student *responds* to the question, and the teacher *evaluates* the response.[k] Similar interactions are often found in parent–child interactions in middle-income European American homes. For instance, when our own children were toddlers and preschoolers, we authors often asked them questions such as "How old are you?" and "What does a cow say?" and praised them when they answered correctly. But children who've grown up in certain other cultural groups aren't familiar with such question-and-answer sessions when they first come to school. Some of them may even be quite puzzled when a teacher asks questions to which he or she already knows the answers.[l]

WAIT TIME. After asking students a question, many teachers wait a second or less for them to respond (see Chapter 2). Not only does such a short wait time give many students insufficient time to retrieve relevant information and formulate an answer, but it's also incompatible with the interactional styles of some cultural groups. People from some cultures leave lengthy pauses before responding as a way of indicating respect,

as this statement by a Northern Cheyenne illustrates:

> Even if I had a quick answer to your question, I would never answer immediately. That would be saying that your question was not worth thinking about.[m]

Students from such cultures are more likely to participate in class and answer questions when given several seconds to respond.[n] An extended wait time both allows students to show respect and gives those with limited English proficiency some mental "translation" time.

[a] Hulit & Howard, 2006, p. 346; Owens, 1995, p. A-8.
[b] Alim & Baugh, 2007; Fairchild & Edwards-Evans, 1990; Hulit & Howard, 2006; Spears, 2007.
[c] Adger, Wolfram, & Christian, 2007; Godley & Escher, 2011; Ogbu, 2003.
[d] Adger et al., 2007; Charity, Scarborough, & Griffin, 2004; T. A. Roberts, 2005.
[e] Adger et al., 2007; DeBose, 2007; Ogbu, 2003.
[f] Gay, 2010; Trawick-Smith, 2003.
[g] Farber, Mindel, & Lazerwitz, 1988; Hale-Benson, 1986; Tharp, 1989; Gay, 2010; Tyler et al., 2008.
[h] Correa-Chávez, Rogoff, & Mejía Arauz, 2005; Gutiérrez & Rogoff, 2003; Kağıtçıbaşı, 2007; J. Li & Fischer, 2004.
[i] Delgado-Gaitan, 1994; C. A. Grant & Gomez, 2001; Ochs, 1982.
[j] Gay, 2010; Morelli & Rothbaum, 2007; Tyler et al., 2008; C. Ward, Bochner, & Furnham, 2001.
[k] Mehan, 1979.
[l] Adger et al., 2007; Crago, Annahatak, & Ningiuruvik, 1993; Heath, 1989; Rogoff, 2003, 2007.
[m] Gilliland, 1988, p. 27.
[n] Castagno & Brayboy, 2008; Gilliland, 1988; Mohatt & Erickson, 1981; Tharp, 1989.

Gender differences, too, must be taken into account. Many boys thrive on competition, and they can be fairly assertive in their efforts to achieve their goals.[96] In contrast, girls tend to do better when classroom activities involve cooperation rather than competition. Girls can be intimidated by whole-class discussions, however, and are more likely to participate when discussions and activities take place in small groups.[97] Because boys sometimes take charge of small-group activities, teachers may occasionally want to form all-female groups. By doing so, they're likely to increase girls' participation and encourage them to take leadership roles.[98]

Teachers' choices of instructional strategies may be especially critical in schools in low-income neighborhoods. Students in such schools often have more than their share of drill-and-practice work in basic skills—work that's hardly conducive to fostering excitement about academic subject matter.[99] Mastering basic knowledge and skills is essential, to be sure, but teachers can often incorporate these things into engaging lessons that ask students to apply what they're learning to individual interests and real-world contexts. For example, in a curriculum called "Kids Voting

---

[96] Benenson et al., 2002; Eisenberg, Martin, & Fabes, 1996; Maccoby, 2002.
[97] Théberge, 1994.
[98] Fennema, 1987; MacLean, Sasse, Keating, Steward, & Miller, 1995; Slavin et al., 2003.
[99] Duke, 2000; R. Ferguson, 1998; Pianta & Hamre, 2009; Portes, 1996.

USA," students at all grade levels have age-appropriate lessons about voting, political parties, and political issues, and they relate what they learn to local election campaigns.[100] Depending on the grade level, they might conduct their own mock elections, analyze candidates' attacks on opponents, or give speeches about particular propositions on a ballot. Students who participate in the program are more likely to attend regularly to media reports about an election, initiate discussions about the election with friends and family members, and be knowledgeable about candidates and election results. In fact, their knowledge and excitement about politics are contagious, because even their *parents* begin to pay more attention to the news, talk more frequently about politics, and gain greater knowledge about candidates and political issues.

It's important to remember, too, that students from low-income families may not have had as much access to and experience with computers and the Internet as their more economically advantaged peers have had. This is certainly *not* to say that teachers should avoid using technology with low-income students—quite the contrary!—but instead that teachers might need to provide more scaffolding for computer-related activities and assignments. And as noted earlier in the chapter, homework assignments should be technology-free unless it's clear that all students have equal access to any needed high-tech resources.

Consider how you might productively modify or supplement instructional strategies for the benefit of English language learners in your classroom.

Unless they have significant disabilities, virtually all children acquire proficiency in at least one language before they reach school age. That language may or may not be English. School-age children who are fluent in their native language but not in English are often referred to as **English language learners (ELLs)**. To the extent that elementary and secondary school students have limited knowledge of English, they're apt to have trouble with schoolwork in an English-based classroom.

The ideal situation for most English language learners is **bilingual education**, in which they receive intensive instruction in English while studying other academic subject areas in their native language, with the transition to English-only instruction occurring quite gradually over a period of several years.[101] Simple knowledge of basic conversational English—knowledge collectively known as **basic interpersonal communication skills (BICS)**—isn't enough for academic success in an English-only curriculum. Ultimately, students must have sufficient mastery of English vocabulary and syntax that they can easily understand and learn from English-based textbooks and lectures; in other words, they must have **cognitive academic language proficiency (CALP)**. Such mastery of English takes considerable time to achieve—often 5 to 7 years.[102]

It's obviously unreasonable to expect classroom teachers to be proficient in the native languages of all of their English language learners. Nevertheless, teachers can do many things to facilitate classroom learning and achievement for these students. The Classroom Strategies box "Working with English Language Learners" offers a few suggestions.

Also take developmental levels, individual differences, and special educational needs into account.

Instructional strategies must to some extent depend on students' ages and developmental levels. Strategies that involve teaching well-defined topics in a structured manner and giving students a lot of guidance and feedback (e.g., direct instruction, mastery learning) are often more appropriate for younger students than for older ones. Lectures (which are often somewhat abstract) and lengthy homework assignments tend to be more effective for older students—provided, of course, that they engage students' interest and attention and encourage meaningful learning.[103]

MyEdLab
Video Example 8.4.

In this video, an elementary school teacher explains how she tries to accommodate the needs of English language learners. What specific strategies does she use, and under what circumstances is each of them most likely to be effective?

[100] M. McDevitt & Chaffee, 1998, 2002; M. McDevitt & Kiousis, 2006; also see www.kidsvotingusa.org/

[101] Dixon et al., 2012; Garcia & Jensen, 2009; Marsh, Hau, & Kong, 2002; Tong, Lara-Alecio, Irby, Mathes, & Kwok, 2008.

[102] Carhill, Suárez-Orozco, & Páez, 2008; Cummins, 2000, 2008; Dixon et al., 2012; Padilla, 2006.

[103] Ausubel, Novak, & Hanesian, 1978; H. Cooper et al., 2006; Rosenshine & Stevens, 1986.

CLASSROOM STRATEGIES

Working with English Language Learners

- **If you don't speak a student's native language yourself, recruit and train parents, community volunteers, or other students to assist in providing instruction in that language.**
  A boy in a kindergarten class has grown up speaking Hmong, a language spoken in some Asian immigrant communities in the United States. His teacher recruits a fourth grader who can read an English picture book to the boy and translate it into Hmong. At one point the teacher points to a lily pad on a page of the book and asks the fourth grader to describe a lily pad in Hmong, as the boy has never encountered lily pads in his own life.

- **If possible, teach early reading skills in students' native languages.**
  When working with students whose families recently immigrated from Mexico, a first-grade teacher teaches basic letter–sound relationships and word decoding skills in Spanish (e.g., showing how the printed word *dos*, meaning "two," can be broken up into the sounds "duh," "oh," and "sss").

- **When using English to communicate, speak more slowly than you might otherwise, and clearly enunciate each word.**
  A middle school teacher is careful that he always says "going to" rather than "gonna" and "want to" rather than "wanna."

- **Use bilingual software.**
  Conducting a quick Google search using the key terms *bilingual*, *educational*, and *software*, a teacher finds many educational software programs with both English and Spanish options, including some free programs he can easily download to his classroom computers.

- **Use visual aids to supplement verbal explanations.**
  A high school history teacher uses photographs she has downloaded from the Internet to illustrate her verbal description of ancient Egypt. She also gives students a one-page outline that identifies the main ideas in her lesson.

- **During small-group learning activities, encourage same-language students to communicate with one another in their native language.**
  When a high school science teacher breaks students into cooperative groups to study the effects of weight, length, and amount of push on a pendulum's oscillation rate, she puts three native Chinese speakers in a single group. She suggests that they can talk in either English or Chinese as they conduct their experiments.

- **Have students work in pairs to make sense of textbook material.**
  As two middle school students read a section of their geography textbook, one reads aloud while the other listens and takes notes. They frequently stop to talk about what they've just read or to switch roles.

- **Encourage—but don't force—students to contribute to class discussions in English; be understanding of students who are initially reluctant to participate.**
  A high school social studies teacher often breaks his class into small groups to discuss controversial social and political issues. He intentionally places two recent immigrants with peers who are likely to be supportive as these English language learners struggle in their efforts to communicate.

Sources: Strategies are based on research and recommendations by Carhill et al., 2008; Comeau, Cormier, Grandmaison, & Lacroix, 1999; Duff, 2001; Egbert, 2009; Espinosa, 2007; Garcia, 1995; Herrell & Jordan, 2004; Igoa, 1995; Janzen, 2008; Krashen, 1996; McClelland, 2001; Padilla, 2006; Slavin & Cheung, 2005; Solórzano, 2008; Tong et al., 2008; Valdés, Bunch, Snow, & Lee, 2005.

The knowledge and skills that students bring to a lesson must also be a consideration.[104] Structured, teacher-directed approaches are usually most appropriate when students know little or nothing about the subject matter. But when students have mastered basic knowledge and skills, and particularly when they're self-regulating learners, they should begin directing some of their own learning, perhaps in small-group discussions, authentic activities, or independent research through hypermedia and the Internet.

Even when working with a single age-group, teachers must adjust their instructional goals and strategies to students' unique characteristics, and they must be especially flexible when working with students who have exceptional cognitive abilities or disabilities. Ideally, teachers individualize instruction for *every* student—a practice known as **differentiated instruction**. For example, to ensure that all students are working within their specific *zone of proximal development* (see Chapter 6), teachers may need to identify more basic goals for some students (e.g., those with intellectual disabilities) and provide especially challenging activities for certain other students. Strictly one-way expository instruction (e.g., a lecture, textbook chapter, or Internet website) can provide a quick and efficient means of introducing new ideas to students

---

[104] C. M. Connor et al., 2009; Corno, 2008; Kalyuga & Sweller, 2004.

who process information quickly and abstractly, yet it may be incomprehensible and overwhelming to students who have little background knowledge on which to build and to students who have learning disabilities. In contrast, direct instruction and mastery learning have been shown to be effective with students who have historically lagged behind their peers, but they may prevent rapid learners from progressing at a rate commensurate with their potential.[105] Also, many low-achieving students are apt to need considerable scaffolding during any note-taking activities; for example, students with learning disabilities or attention-deficit hyperactivity disorder (ADHD) can benefit from lesson-specific note-taking forms and frequent hints about what things they should include in their notes.[106]

Computer-based instructional strategies can be especially useful as a means of adapting instruction to students' unique ability levels. For example, intelligent tutoring systems are, by nature, designed to tailor instruction to individual students' knowledge levels and ongoing progress. Websites such as Khan Academy provide many short tutorials on specific topics in math, science, and other content domains. English-language tutorials and bilingual software for teaching basic skills are helpful when working with English language learners.[107] And certain tools within computer software programs, such as the spell-check and grammar-check functions in word processing programs, can provide the extra scaffolding that some students may need (e.g., see Figure 8.11).

FIGURE 8.11 Darren, a fifth grader who struggles with reading and writing, wrote this very cohesive paragraph with the help of a word processing program. A spell-checker enabled him to spell most, but not all, of the words correctly (he meant to use the words *very* and *sight*, not *vary* and *site*).

> When I was young it was almost impossible to read. One of my teachers told me I could learn to read if I worked hard. Learning to read was like climbing Mount Rushmore. It took a very long time but I finally got it. My Mom said she was vary proud. Reading was hard for me. It took five years for me to learn to read. Every day I would go to the learning center to learn my 400 site words. It was hard for me to learn these words but I did it. Reading is one of the most important things I have learned so far in my life.

An essential component of differentiated instruction is, of course, *regular assessment of students' progress*—just one example of the many ways in which instructional strategies and classroom assessment practices are intertwined. We'll explore this idea in depth in Chapter 10.

Combine several instructional approaches into a single lesson.

Throughout the 20th century and early 21st century, many educators have looked for—and in some cases decided that they've found—the single "best" way to teach children and adolescents. The result has been a series of movements in which educators advocate a particular instructional approach and then, a few years later, advocate a very different approach.[108] We authors have often wondered why the field of education is characterized by such pendulum swings, and we've developed several hypotheses. Perhaps some educators are looking for an *algorithm* for teaching—a specific procedure they can follow to guarantee high achievement. Perhaps they confuse theory with fact, thinking that the latest theoretical fad must inevitably be the one and only correct explanation of how children learn or develop, and thus conclude that the teaching implications they derive from the theory must also be correct. Or maybe they just have an overly simplistic view of what the goals of our educational system should be.

As should be clear by now, *there is no single best approach to classroom instruction.* Every instructional strategy has its merits, and each is useful in different situations. Table 8.3 lists several general instructional goals teachers are likely to have and suggests general instructional strategies that might be appropriate for each one. Notice that many of the strategies described in this chapter appear in two or more places in the table, reflecting the multiple purposes for which they might flexibly be used. A successful classroom—one in which students are acquiring and using school subject matter in truly meaningful ways—is undoubtedly a classroom in which a variety of approaches to instruction can be found.

---

[105] Arlin, 1984; Rosenshine & Stevens, 1986; Stein & Krishnan, 2007; Tomlinson & McTighe, 2006.

[106] J. R. Boyle, Forchelli, & Cariss, 2015.

[107] Egbert, 2009; Merrill et al., 1996.

[108] For example, see discussions by K. R. Harris & Alexander, 1998; Sfard, 1998.

Table 8.3 • Choosing an Instructional Strategy

WHEN YOUR GOAL IS TO HELP STUDENTS . . .	CONSIDER USING . . .
Master and review basic skills	• Direct instruction • Computer-based instruction (some programs) • Lower-level teacher questions • Mastery learning • Cooperative learning • Peer tutoring • Video games (some programs) • Homework assignments (those in which students practice skills they've previously learned at school)
Gain firsthand, concrete experience with a particular topic	• Discovery and inquiry learning (see Chapter 6) • Service learning • Simulations (e.g., through role-playing activities, instructional software programs, or Internet websites)
Gain an organized, relatively abstract body of knowledge about a topic	• Lectures • Textbooks and other assigned readings • Instructional websites • Intelligent tutoring systems
Connect school subject matter to real-world contexts and problems	• Authentic activities • Computer simulations • Inquiry learning • Computer-supported collaborative learning (either within a single classroom or in collaboration with students at other schools) • Appropriately designed and scaffolded homework assignments
Acquire advanced understandings about a topic and/or develop higher-level cognitive processes (e.g., problem solving, critical thinking, scientific reasoning)	• Higher-level teacher questions • Class discussions • Cooperative learning • Inquiry learning • Independent student research (using printed materials and/or the Internet) • Authentic activities • Computer simulations (some programs) • Computer-supported collaborative learning • Peer tutoring (which requires tutors to organize and elaborate on what they have previously learned)
Acquire increased metacognitive awareness and more effective reading and self-regulation strategies	• Computer-based instruction (some programs) • Reciprocal teaching (see Chapter 6) • Cooperative learning • Peer tutoring (which can enhance tutors' self-regulation skills) • Age-appropriate homework assignments (those that are scaffolded to foster independent study habits and such metacognitive processes as self-questioning and self-monitoring)
Acquire technological literacy skills	• Regular use of a class website • Computer-based instruction (e.g., intelligent tutoring systems) • Independent student research on the Internet • Webquests • Computer-supported collaborative learning • Computer simulations
Acquire effective strategies for interacting and working with others	• Class discussions • Reciprocal teaching • Small-group inquiry learning • Cooperative learning • Peer tutoring • Computer-supported collaborative learning • Multiplayer computer simulations and video games

In this chapter, you have learned about a wide variety of strategies for effectively planning and implementing instruction. In the hotlinked Self-Check quiz and Application Exercises that follow, you can check and apply your understandings related to Big Idea 8.4:

> *Different instructional strategies are appropriate for different instructional goals and objectives and for different students.*

MyEdLab **Self-Check 8.4**

MyEdLab **Application Exercise 8.6.** In this exercise, you can observe and analyze a bilingual lesson in high school history.

MyEdLab **Application Exercise 8.7.** In this exercise, you can apply what you have learned about planning and instruction to analyze an actual lesson plan.

8 SUMMARY

Two central roles of any teacher are planning and carrying out instruction. The four Big Ideas presented at the beginning of the chapter can help us summarize basic principles that should guide these activities.

■ **8.1: Effective teachers identify the knowledge and abilities they want students to acquire, and they plan instruction accordingly.** Good teachers engage in considerable advance planning. They identify the general instructional goals and more specific instructional objectives they would like students to accomplish. They align some of these goals and objectives with existing content-area standards, but they also include goals related to students' general academic and social development. In addition, good teachers conduct task analyses to break complex tasks into smaller and simpler components, consider how they can capture and keep students' interest and attention during instructional activities, and develop lesson plans that spell out the activities and assessments they'll use each day. Many teachers create class websites through which they can communicate detailed information about expectations and assignments and provide ongoing scaffolding for students' learning activities.

■ **8.2: Sometimes instruction is most effective when it is teacher-directed—that is, when the teacher chooses the specific topics to be studied and the general course of a lesson.** A good deal of teacher-directed instruction is expository in nature, presenting information in essentially the same form in which students are expected to learn it. In some cases (e.g., in textbook reading assignments and instructional websites), teacher-directed instruction is largely one-way in nature, with information going primarily from the teacher or some other expert to students. In other cases, it's more two-way, with information flowing regularly back and forth between the teacher (or perhaps a virtual "teacher," such as a computer) and students. For instance, direct instruction, intelligent tutoring systems, and mastery learning all involve many opportunities for student practice and teacher feedback. Teacher-directed instruction is,

like all instruction, most effective when it promotes effective cognitive processes—for instance, when it captures students' attention and encourages students to elaborate on and apply what they're learning.

■ **8.3: Sometimes instruction is most effective when it is learner-directed—that is, when students have some control over the issues to be addressed and the ways in which to address them.** To a considerable degree, students control the flow of events in class discussions, cooperative learning activities, independent research, peer tutoring, computer-supported collaborative learning, authentic activities, and multi-student simulations. Learner-directed instruction is most useful when topics and tasks lend themselves to multiple perspectives and approaches, when the teacher creates an atmosphere conducive to open debate, and when students have some ability to regulate their own learning and behavior. Even so, students may need some structure and guidance to help them accomplish assigned tasks successfully.

■ **8.4: Different instructional strategies are appropriate for different instructional goals and objectives and for different students.** For example, direct instruction or mastery learning is often advisable when students must learn basic skills to automaticity, whereas authentic and simulated activities are more appropriate when the goal is for students to apply those skills to real-world situations and problems. Small-group cooperative learning activities may be especially effective for girls, as well as for students whose cultural groups nurture and expect cooperation with others. Abstract lectures can sometimes be useful when working with high-achieving adolescents, whereas more concrete approaches (e.g., direct instruction) are often preferable for younger students, for students who have a history of low academic achievement, and for students who have little prior knowledge about the topic or skill in question. Truly effective teachers tailor their instructional strategies to their students' individual ability levels, predispositions, and needs.

PRACTICE FOR YOUR LICENSURE EXAM

Cooperative Learning Project

One Monday morning. Ms. Mihara begins the unit "Customs in Other Lands" in her fourth-grade class. She asks students to choose two or three students with whom they would like to work to study a particular country. After the students have assembled into six small groups, she assigns each group a country: Australia, Colombia, Ireland, Greece, Japan, or South Africa. She tells the students, "Today we'll go to the school library, where your group can find information on the customs of your country, print out relevant materials you find on the Internet, and check out books and magazines you think might be useful. Every day over the next 2 weeks, you'll have time to work with your group. A week from Friday, each group will give an oral report to the class."

During the next few class sessions, Ms. Mihara runs into many more problems than she anticipated. She realizes that the high achievers have gotten together to form one of the groups, and many socially oriented, "popular" students have flocked to two others. The remaining two groups are comprised of whichever students were left over. Some groups get to work immediately on their task, others spend their group time joking and sharing gossip, and still others are neither academically nor socially productive.

As the unit progresses, Ms. Mihara hears more and more complaints from students about their task: "Janet and I are doing all the work; Karen and Mary Kay aren't helping at all," "Eugene thinks he can boss the rest of us around because we're studying Ireland and he's Irish," "We're spending all this time but just can't seem to get anywhere!" And the group reports at the end of the unit differ markedly in quality: Some are carefully planned and informative, whereas others are disorganized and have little substance.

1. **Constructed-response question**

   Describe two things you might do to improve Ms. Mihara's cooperative learning activity. Base your improvements on research findings related to cooperative learning or on contemporary principles and theories of learning, development, or motivation.

2. **Multiple-choice question**

   Ms. Mihara never identifies an instructional objective for her unit "Customs in Other Lands." Which one of the following statements reflects recommended guidelines about how instructional goals and objectives should be formulated?

   a. "The teacher should expose students to many differences in behaviors and beliefs that exist in diverse cultures (e.g., eating habits, ceremonial practices, religious beliefs, moral values)."

   b. "The teacher should use a variety of instructional practices, including (but not limited to) lectures, direct instruction, textbook readings, and cooperative learning activities."

   c. "Students should study a variety of cultural behaviors and beliefs, including those of countries in diverse parts of the world."

   d. "Students should demonstrate knowledge of diverse cultural practices—for example, by describing three distinct ways in which another culture is different from their own."

   MyEdLab **Licensure Exam 8.1**

Monkey Business/Fotolia

9

Strategies for Creating Effective Classroom and School Environments

Big Ideas to Master in this Chapter

9.1 Effective teachers create a caring, respectful classroom environment in which students are consistently focused on accomplishing instructional goals and objectives.

9.2 Teachers are most effective when they coordinate their efforts with colleagues, outside agencies, and parents.

9.3 Effective interventions for reducing unproductive school behaviors are tailored to the circumstances, with students' long-term development and well-being as the ultimate goals.

9.4 Minimizing aggression and violence at school requires a three-tiered approach: (1) creating a respectful and supportive school environment, (2) intervening early for students at risk for social failure, and (3) providing intensive interventions for chronically aggressive students.

CASE STUDY: A CONTAGIOUS SITUATION

After receiving a teaching certificate in May, Ms. Cornell has accepted a position as a fifth-grade teacher. She has spent the summer identifying instructional goals for the year and planning lessons that should help students achieve those goals. Today, on the first day of school, she has jumped headlong into the curriculum she planned. But three problems quickly present themselves in the forms of Eli, Jake, and Vanessa.

These three students seem determined to disrupt the class at every possible opportunity. They move around the room without permission, intentionally annoying others as they walk to the pencil sharpener or wastebasket. They talk out of turn, often making disrespectful remarks to their teacher and peers. They rarely complete assignments, preferring instead to engage in horseplay or practical jokes. They seem especially prone to misbehavior during downtimes in the daily schedule—for example, at the beginning and end of the school day, before and after recess and lunch, and whenever Ms. Cornell is preoccupied with other students.

Ms. Cornell continues to follow her daily lesson plans, ignoring the problem students and hoping they'll eventually shape up. Yet the disruptive behavior continues, with the three of them delighting in one another's antics. Furthermore, the misbehavior begins to spread to other students. By the middle of October, Ms. Cornell's classroom is out of control, and the few students who are still interested in learning something are having a hard time doing so.

- In what ways has Ms. Cornell planned in advance for her classroom? In what ways has she *not* planned?

As a first-year teacher, Ms. Cornell is well prepared in some respects but not at all prepared in others. She has carefully identified her instructional goals and planned relevant lessons. But she has neglected to think about how she might keep students on task or how she might adjust lessons based on how students are progressing. And she hasn't considered how she might nip behavior problems in the bud before they begin to interfere with instruction and learning. In the absence of such planning, no curriculum can be very effective—not even one grounded firmly in sound principles of learning, motivation, and child development.

As we proceed through the chapter, we'll occasionally return to the opening case to identify reasons why Eli, Jake, and Vanessa are so disruptive and why their misbehaviors spread to other students. But we must make one point clear at the very beginning: The problem in Ms. Cornell's classroom is *not* one of too much noise and activity. Effective **classroom management**—creating and maintaining a class environment conducive to learning and achievement—has little to do with noise or activity level. A well-managed classroom is one in which students are consistently engaged in productive learning activities and in which students' behaviors rarely interfere with their own or others' achievement of instructional goals.

Creating and maintaining an environment in which students are continually engaged in productive activities can be a challenging task indeed. Teachers must tend to the unique needs of many students, must sometimes coordinate several activities at the same time, and must often make quick decisions about how to respond to unanticipated events. Furthermore, teachers must adjust their classroom management strategies to the particular instructional activities in progress—for example, cooperative learning activities call for different management strategies than direct instruction does. So it's not surprising that many beginning teachers mention classroom management as their number one concern.[1]

---

[1] Evertson & Weinstein, 2006; V. Jones, 2006.

MyEdLab
Video Example 9.1.
As this video illustrates, effective teachers communicate a genuine desire to support students' academic success and personal well-being. In what ways are the teacher's strategies similar to certain elements of authoritative parenting?

A good general model of effective classroom management is *authoritative parenting*, a parenting style described in Chapter 7.[2] As you may recall, authoritative parents:

- Provide a loving and supportive environment
- Hold high expectations and standards for children's behavior
- Explain why some behaviors are acceptable and others are not
- Consistently enforce rules for behavior
- Include children in decision making
- Provide age-appropriate opportunities for autonomy

As we explore classroom management strategies in the following sections, we'll often see one or more of these characteristics of authoritative parenting at work. We'll begin our discussion by looking at proactive, *preventive* strategies—those designed to establish a productive learning environment right from the start. Later we'll turn to strategies for addressing the unproductive behaviors that sometimes occur even in the best-managed classrooms.

9.1 CREATING AN ENVIRONMENT CONDUCIVE TO LEARNING

Big Idea 9.1 Effective teachers create a caring, respectful classroom environment in which students are consistently focused on accomplishing instructional goals and objectives.

When we talk about the classroom environment, to some extent we're talking about the actual physical setup—for instance, the arrangement of tables and chairs, the availability of tools and resources (painting supplies, computers, etc.), and the use of bulletin boards and other wall surfaces. But even more important is the psychological environment, or **classroom climate**.[3] The ideal classroom is one in which students feel safe and secure, make learning a high priority, and are willing to take chances and make mistakes as they tackle challenging new tasks. Such a climate is especially important for students who are at risk for academic failure and dropping out of school.[4]

The following recommendations summarize many strategies that researchers and experienced educators have identified for creating and maintaining an environment conducive to students' learning and academic achievement.

Arrange the classroom to maximize attention and minimize disruptions.

As teachers arrange furniture, identify places to put instructional materials and equipment, and determine where students will sit and work, they should consider the effects that various arrangements are likely to have on students' behavior. Here are several widely recommended strategies:[5]

- Arrange desks, tables, and chairs so that you and your students can easily interact and so that you can regularly survey the entire classroom for signs of possible confusion, frustration, or boredom.
- Establish traffic patterns that allow students to move around the classroom without disturbing one another.
- Liven up walls with some graphic displays, but don't create such a visually "busy" classroom that students are easily distracted from lessons.
- Keep intriguing materials out of sight and reach until they're needed.

---
[2] Gregory, Cornell, & Fan, 2011; J. M. T. Walker & Hoover-Dempsey, 2006.
[3] Hardré, Crowson, DeBacker, & White, 2007; Patrick, Ryan, & Kaplan, 2007; Reyes, Brackett, Rivers, White, & Salovey, 2012.
[4] Hamre & Pianta, 2005; V. E. Lee & Burkam, 2003; Rumberger, 2011.
[5] Bicard, Ervin, Bicard, & Baylot-Casey, 2012; K. Carter & Doyle, 2006; W. Doyle, 1986; Emmer & Evertson, 2009; A. V. Fisher, Godwin, & Seltman, 2014; Gettinger & Kohler, 2006.

- Split up friends who easily get off task when they're together (e.g., put them on opposite sides of the room).
- Place chronically misbehaving or uninvolved students close at hand.

Communicate caring and respect for every student.

As you should recall from Chapter 5, human beings seem to have a fundamental need to feel socially connected with others. In the classroom, this *need for relatedness* may reveal itself in a variety of ways. Some students might eagerly seek their teacher's approval for something they've done well. Other students might actually misbehave to gain their teacher's attention (this might possibly be true for Eli, Jake, and Vanessa in the opening case study). But in our own experiences, we authors have never met a child or adolescent who, deep down, didn't want positive, productive relationships with school faculty members.

To some extent, teachers can help meet students' need for relatedness by demonstrating, through the many little things they do, that they care about and respect students as people.[6] A smile and warm greeting at the beginning of the day, a compliment about a new haircut, and a concerned inquiry when a student comes to school angry or upset—all of these behaviors communicate caring and respect. One high school student described caring teachers this way:

> They show it. You might see them in the hallway and they ask how you're doing, how was your last report card, is there anything you need. Or, maybe one day you're looking a little upset. They'll pull you to the side and ask you what's wrong, is there anything I can do.[7]

It's important to establish one or more mechanisms through which students can communicate with their teacher *in private.* One option, especially for older students, is e-mail, perhaps through a class website. A low-tech alternative is a "What's Up?" form on which students might occasionally write and submit information about especially noteworthy or challenging events in their personal lives.[8] A third possibility is the use of two-way *dialogue journals,* in which individual students and their teacher both write one or more times each week. Figure 9.1 shows several entries in 6-year-old Matt's journal; each entry is followed by a response (indented) from his first-grade teacher. Notice that Matt feels comfortable enough with his teacher to engage in playful one-upmanship ("I can go fastr then you"). Although his writing skills are far from perfect—for instance, he writes *especially downhill skiing* as "spshal don hilscein"—they're certainly adequate to communicate his thoughts. Notice, too, that his teacher doesn't correct his misspellings. Her primary purposes are to encourage him to write and to open the lines of communication; giving negative feedback about spelling here might interfere with both of these goals.

think about it

How might the teacher adapt the journal assignment for students who can't yet read or write? (For examples of strategies, click **here**.)

FIGURE 9.1 Six-year-old Matt and his first-grade teacher communicate regularly through a two-way dialogue journal.

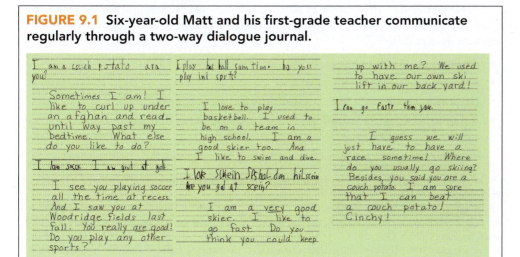

---

[6] Allday, Bush, Ticknor, & Walker, 2011; Certo, Cauley, & Chafin, 2002; J. Ellis, Fitzsimmons, & Small-McGinley, 2010; D. K. Meyer & Turner, 2006.

[7] Certo et al., 2002, p. 15.

[8] A. K. Smith, 2009.

MyEdLab
Interactive Case 9.1.

Good teacher–student relationships are one essential element of an effective classroom climate. You can explore several potentially effective strategies in this interactive simulation.

Yet it isn't enough simply to be "warm and fuzzy" with students. To show genuine caring and respect for them, teachers must also do these things:[9]

- Be well prepared for class and in other ways demonstrate a commitment to using effective teaching practices.
- Communicate high yet realistic expectations for performance and provide the support students need to meet those expectations.
- Include students in decision making and in evaluations of their work.
- Acknowledge that students can occasionally have an "off" day.

The quality of teacher–student relationships is one of the most influential factors affecting students' emotional well-being, motivation, and achievement at school. When students have positive, supportive relationships with teachers, they have higher self-efficacy and more intrinsic motivation to learn, engage in more self-regulated learning, are more likely to ask for help when they need it, are less apt to cheat on classroom assignments, and achieve at higher levels.[10]

Teacher affection, respect, and support are especially important for students who face exceptional hardships at home (e.g., extreme poverty, uninvolved or abusive parents, violent neighborhoods). When such students have one or more caring, trustworthy adults in their lives—and when they regularly come to a classroom that's warm, predictable, and dependable—they're more likely to have a strong sense of self-worth and to rise above their many challenges to succeed both in the classroom and in the outside world (recall the discussion of *resilient students* in Chapter 7).[11]

Work hard to improve relationships that have gotten off to a bad start.

Occasionally students come to school with an apparent chip on the shoulder, distrusting their teachers from day 1 because of previous hurtful relationships with parents or other adults. At other times teachers get relationships with certain students off to a bad start through their own actions—perhaps because they incorrectly attribute a student's low achievement to lack of effort rather than lack of skill or perhaps because they accuse a temperamentally high-energy child of being intentionally disobedient. Oftentimes students who have the poorest relationships with teachers are the ones most in need of *good* ones.[12]

Poor teacher–student relationships don't just undermine students' sense of relatedness and general well-being; they also undermine *teachers'* sense of relatedness and well-being. Furthermore, teachers may come to believe that they aren't able to achieve their goals for students' development and classroom performance and, as a result, may "burn out" and leave the teaching profession altogether.[13]

Regardless of the initial causes of poor teacher–student relationships, teachers must work hard to turn them into productive ones. The first step, of course, is to *identify* poor relationships using such signs as these:[14]

- A teacher has hostile feelings (e.g., dislike, anger) toward a student.
- A teacher rarely interacts with a student.
- A teacher's messages to a student usually involve criticism or faultfinding.
- A teacher has a sense of learned helplessness about his or her ability to work effectively with a student.

---

[9] L. H. Anderman, Patrick, Hruda, & Linnenbrink, 2002, p. 274; M.-L. Chang & Davis, 2009; H. A. Davis, 2003; H. A. Davis, Schutz, & Chambless, 2001; J. M. T. Walker & Hoover-Dempsey, 2006; Wentzel, Battle, Russell, & Looney, 2010.

[10] J. N. Hughes, Luo, Kwok, & Loyd, 2008; Kiuru et al., 2014; Marchand & Skinner, 2007; Murdock, Miller, & Kohlhardt, 2004; E. O'Connor, Dearing, & Collins, 2011; Pianta, Belsky, Vandergrift, Houts, & Morrison, 2008; Roorda, Koomen, Spilt, & Oort, 2011.

[11] Becker & Luthar, 2002; Juvonen, 2006; Masten, 2001; E. O'Connor & McCartney, 2007; D. A. O'Donnell, Schwab-Stone, & Muyeed, 2002; Werner & Smith, 2001.

[12] M.-L. Chang & Davis, 2009; Houts, Caspi, Pianta, Arseneault, & Moffitt, 2010; Juvonen, 2006; Keogh, 2003; Stipek & Miles, 2008; Wentzel, Donlan, Morrison, Russell, & Baker, 2009.

[13] Skaalvik & Skaalvik, 2008; Spilt, Koomen, & Thijs, 2011.

[14] M.-L. Chang & Davis, 2009; Hand, 2010; Pianta, 1999; Sutherland & Morgan, 2003.

Several strategies can help teachers repair these relationships. One is to think actively—perhaps in a brainstorming session with colleagues—about alternative hypotheses for why the student behaves as he or she does, being sure that the list of hypotheses offers potential solutions. Another is to meet one on one with the student to talk openly about the problem and possible ways to fix it (more on this point later in the chapter). Still another strategy—if school policy allows and parents give permission—is to spend some time with one or more students in a noncontrolling, recreational context that might allow more positive feelings to emerge.[15]

Create a sense of community and belongingness.

In Chapter 4, we described a *community of learners,* a class in which teacher and students consistently work together to help one another learn. Ultimately, teachers should also create a general **sense of community** in the classroom—a sense that they and their students share common goals, are mutually respectful and supportive of one another's efforts, and believe that everyone makes an important contribution to classroom learning.[16] Creating a sense of community engenders feelings of **belongingness**: Students see themselves as important and valued members of the classroom.[17]

When students share a sense of community, they're more likely to exhibit prosocial behavior, stay on task, express enthusiasm about classroom activities, and achieve at high levels. Furthermore, a sense of classroom community is associated with lower rates of emotional distress, disruptive classroom behavior, truancy, and dropping out.[18] And consistent experiences with caring and equitable classroom communities help students internalize attitudes essential for a successful democratic society, including a commitment to fairness and justice for everyone.[19]

The Classroom Strategies feature "Creating and Enhancing a Sense of Classroom Community" offers several strategies for helping students believe that they're valued members of the classroom. Perhaps the most important strategy is the first one: stressing that students must always treat one another with kindness and respect. Even when students must take issue with something that one of their classmates has said or done, they can do so tactfully and respectfully (e.g., see Figure 9.2).

FIGURE 9.2 Especially in the elementary grades, many students benefit from visual reminders about how to interact with classmates, as illustrated in these two posters displayed in a second-grade classroom.

Words to Use	Working with a Partner
I don't like it when ____.	Be polite.
Can you not do ____ ?	Help each other.
Can you please stop ____ ?	Share.
I need a break and then I'll come back to talk about it.	Listen to your partner.
	Be a good sport.
	Take turns.
	Talk about problems.
	Speak respectfully.

Posters courtesy of Christina Fox.

Create a goal-oriented and businesslike (but nonthreatening) atmosphere.

Although caring relationships with students are essential, teachers and students alike must recognize that they're at school to get certain things accomplished. Accordingly, a relatively businesslike atmosphere should prevail in the classroom most of the time. This isn't to say that class activities must be boring and tedious. On the contrary, they should be interesting and engaging, and they can sometimes be quite exciting. Entertainment and excitement shouldn't be thought of as goals in and of themselves, however. Rather, they're means to a more important goal: mastering academic subject matter.[20]

Despite this emphasis on business, the classroom atmosphere should never be uncomfortable or threatening. As noted in Chapter 5, students who are excessively anxious are unlikely to perform at their best. How can teachers be businesslike without being threatening? They can hold students accountable for achieving instructional objectives yet not place students under continual

---

[15] M.-L. Chang & Davis, 2009; Gehlbach, Brinkworth, & Harris, 2012; Pianta, 1999, 2006; Silverberg, 2003; Sutton & Wheatley, 2003.

[16] Ciani, Middleton, Summers, & Sheldon, 2010; Hamm, Hoffman, & Farmer, 2012; D. Kim, Solomon, & Roberts, 1995; Osterman, 2000.

[17] E. M. Anderman, 2002; J. Ellis et al., 2010.

[18] Hom & Battistich, 1995; Juvonen, 2006; Osterman, 2000; Patrick et al., 2007; Rumberger, 2011.

[19] C. A. Flanagan, Cumsille, Gill, & Gallay, 2007.

[20] Brophy, 2006; G. A. Davis & Thomas, 1989; Gettinger & Kohler, 2006.

CLASSROOM STRATEGIES

Creating and Enhancing a Sense of Classroom Community

- **Consistently communicate the message that *all* students deserve the kindness and respect of their classmates and are important members of the classroom community.**

  A middle school language arts class has three students with reading disabilities that are quite obvious in much of the students' oral and written work in class. The teacher doesn't publicly identify the students with disabilities, because doing so would violate their right to confidentiality about their conditions. However, she frequently communicates the message that students at any grade level vary widely in their reading abilities—usually through no fault of their own—and continually stresses that it is the class's responsibility to help *everyone* improve their literacy skills.

- **Create mechanisms through which students can all help to make the class run smoothly and efficiently.**

  A kindergarten teacher creates several "helper" roles (e.g., distributing art supplies, feeding the class goldfish) that he assigns to different students on a rotating basis.

- **Emphasize such prosocial values as sharing and cooperation, and provide opportunities for students to help one another.**

  As students work on in-class assignments each day, a seventh-grade math teacher sometimes asks, "Who has a problem that someone else might be able to help you solve?"

- **Make frequent use of interactive and collaborative teaching strategies.**

  In assigning students to cooperative learning groups, a high school social studies teacher usually puts a student with poor social skills (e.g., a student with Asperger syndrome) in a group with two or three more socially proficient students. Before the groups begin their work, the teacher reminds students of the class's rules for cooperative group work, such as "Listen to others politely and attentively" and "Address differences of opinion in respectful and constructive ways."

- **Solicit students' ideas and opinions, and incorporate them into class discussions and activities.**

  A first-grade teacher regularly has students vote on the storybook she should read during "settling-down" time after lunch each day. She first reads the book that gets the most votes, but she assures students who voted differently that she'll read their choices later in the week, saying, "It's important that everyone has a say in what we read."

- **Use competition only to create an occasional sense of playfulness in the class and only when all students have an equal chance of winning.**

  A high school Spanish teacher assigns a long-term cooperative group project in which students write and videotape Spanish soap operas (*telenovelas*). A few weeks later the teacher holds an "Academy Awards Banquet"—a potluck dinner for the students and their families. At the banquet, the teacher shows all the videos and then awards a variety of "Oscars." Although she gives only one group an Oscar for best telenovela, she gives every student an Oscar for some aspect of his or her performance.

- **Encourage students to be on the lookout for classmates on the periphery of ongoing activities—perhaps students with disabilities—and to ask these children to join in.**

  Teachers at an elementary school all adhere to and enforce the same *no-exclusion* policy on the playground: Any student who wants to be involved in a play activity *can* be involved.

- **Work on social skills with students whose interpersonal behaviors may victimize or alienate others.**

  A third grader often behaves aggressively toward classmates who have something she wants. For example, when waiting for her turn at the class computer, she may yell "*I* need to use it now!" or, instead, shove its current user out of the chair. In a private conference, her teacher points out the importance of patience and turn taking and suggests several ways she might politely make her needs known (e.g., "When might you be finished with the computer? Can I use it after you're done?") The teacher also has the student practice the strategies in various role-playing scenarios.

Sources: M.-L. Chang & Davis, 2009; Evertson & Emmer, 2009; Hamovitch, 2007; J. N. Hughes, 2012; D. Kim et al., 1995; Osterman, 2000; A. M. Ryan & Patrick, 2001; Sapon-Shevin, Dobbelaere, Corrigan, Goodman, & Mastin, 1998 (playground example); Stipek, 1996; Turnbull, Pereira, & Blue-Banning, 2000; M.-T. Wang & Holcombe, 2010; Wentzel, Donlan, & Morrison, 2012.

surveillance. They can point out errors without making students feel like failures. They can focus students' attention on personal progress rather than on how each one's performance compares to that of classmates. And they can admonish students for misbehavior but communicate that each new day is an opportunity for a fresh start.[21]

Establish reasonable rules and procedures.

In the opening case study, Ms. Cornell failed to provide guidelines about how students should behave—something she should have done the first week of school. A class without guidelines for appropriate behavior is apt to be chaotic and unproductive. Students must know that certain

---

[21] Dijkstra, Kuyper, van der Werf, Buunk, & van der Zee, 2008; K. L. Fletcher & Cassady, 2010; Patrick, Kaplan, & Ryan, 2011; C. R. Rogers, 1983; Spaulding, 1992.

FIGURE 9.3 Presenting classroom rules and procedures as information

Students are more likely to be intrinsically motivated to follow classroom rules and procedures if teachers present them as items of information rather than as forms of control.

A teacher might say this (information):

"You'll finish your independent assignments more quickly if you get right to work."

"As we practice for our fire drill, it's important to line up quickly and be quiet so we can hear the instructions we're given and will know what to do."

"This assignment is designed to help you develop the writing skills you'll need after you graduate. It's unfair to other authors to copy their work word for word, so we'll practice putting ideas into our own words and giving credit to authors whose ideas we borrow. Passing off another's writing and ideas as your own can lead to suspension in college or a lawsuit in the business world."

. . . rather than this (control):

"Please be quiet and do your own work."

"When the fire alarm sounds, line up quickly and quietly, and then wait for further instructions."

"Cheating and plagiarism are totally unacceptable in this classroom."

---

behaviors simply won't be tolerated, especially those that cause physical or psychological harm, damage other people's property, or interfere with classmates' learning and performance. Setting reasonable limits on classroom behavior not only fosters a more productive learning environment but also helps prepare students to become productive members of adult society (recall the discussion of *socialization* in Chapter 4).

Effective classroom managers establish and communicate certain rules and procedures right from the start.[22] They identify acceptable and unacceptable behaviors—not only about social interactions but also about punctuality and preparedness for each day's class. They develop consistent procedures and routines for such things as completing seatwork, asking for help, and turning in assignments. They have procedures in place for nonroutine events such as school assemblies, field trips, and fire drills. And in today's high-tech world, many teachers explicitly forbid cell phone use during class time, perhaps by having a box in which students deposit their phones at the beginning of class. Taking time to clarify rules and procedures—and periodically reviewing them—seems to be especially important in the early elementary grades, when students may not be familiar with how things are typically done at school.[23]

Students should understand that rules and procedures aren't merely the result of a teacher's personal whims but are designed to help the class run smoothly and efficiently. And despite restrictions on their behavior, students should have some sense of *autonomy* in the classroom (see Chapter 5). One strategy is to include students in decision making about the rules and procedures by which the class will operate—a strategy that's likely to enhance their sense of ownership of and adherence to those rules and procedures.[24]

Another strategy for preserving students' sense of autonomy is to present rules and requirements as *information*—for instance, as conditions that can help students accomplish classroom goals—rather than as mechanisms of *control* over students.[25] The left-hand side of Figure 9.3 presents three examples of rules and procedures presented in an informational manner; notice how each example provides one or more reasons for a teacher's request. The following scenario provides a simple illustration of how giving a reason can make a noticeable difference:

Gerard has little tolerance for frustration. Whenever he asks Ms. Donnelly for assistance, he wants it *now*. If she can't immediately help him, he screams, "You're no good!" or "You don't care!" and shoves other students' desks as he angrily walks back to his seat.

MyEdLab
Video Example 9.2.

Especially in the early elementary grades, good teachers periodically review expectations about appropriate classroom behaviors. What expectations does this first-grade teacher convey about how children should behave when they move to small-group learning centers?

---

[22] Borko & Putnam, 1996; W. Doyle, 1990; Emmer & Evertson, 2009; Gettinger & Kohler, 2006.

[23] K. Carter & Doyle, 2006; W. Doyle, 1990; Gettinger & Kohler, 2006; K. L. Lane, Menzies, Bruhn, & Crnobori, 2011.

[24] Evertson & Emmer, 2009; Nucci, 2009; M. Watson, 2008.

[25] Deci, 1992; Koestner, Ryan, Bernieri, & Holt, 1984; Reeve, 2009.

At one point during the school year, the class has a unit on interpersonal skills. One lesson addresses *timing*—the most appropriate and effective time to ask for someone's assistance. A week later, Gerard approaches Ms. Donnelly for help with a math problem. She is working with another student but briefly turns to Gerard and says, "Timing." She expects the usual screaming, but instead he responds, "Hey, Ms. D., I get it! I can ask you at another time!" He returns to his seat with a smile.[26]

Keep in mind that rules and procedures are easier to remember and therefore easier to follow if they're relatively simple and few in number.[27] Effective classroom managers tend to stress only the most important rules and procedures at the beginning of the school year and introduce additional rules and procedures as needed later on. Also keep in mind that although some order and predictability are essential for student productivity, *too much* order can make school a boring, routine place—one without an element of fun and spontaneity. Classrooms don't necessarily need rules and procedures for everything!

Enforce rules consistently and equitably.

Classroom rules are apt to be effective only if they're consistently enforced. For example, in the opening case study, Ms. Cornell imposes no consequences when Eli, Jake, and Vanessa misbehave. As we discovered in Chapter 4, imposing no adverse consequence for inappropriate behavior—especially when that consequence has been spelled out in advance—can actually be a form of *reinforcement* for the misbehavior. Not only do the three troublesome students continue to disrupt class, but other students start to behave similarly, reflecting the *peer-contagion* phenomenon described in Chapter 7. Students have essentially learned that "anything goes" in Ms. Cornell's classroom.

We'll consider guidelines for administering punishment later in the chapter, but for now, we should note that consistency in enforcing classroom rules should apply not only across occasions but also across *students*. Teachers almost invariably like some students more than others (e.g., they're apt to prefer high achievers), but they must keep their preferences to themselves. Students can be quite resentful of teachers who grant special favors to and overlook rule infractions of a few "pet" students.[28] And students who are unfairly accused or punished are, of course, even more resentful, as one high school student explains:

> Because like if you had a past record or whatever like in middle school if you got in trouble like at all, they would think that you're a slight trouble maker and if you got in trouble again, they would always . . . if you were anywhere that something bad happened or something against the rules or whatever, they pick you first because they think that you have a past. So they wouldn't like pick the kids that had never done anything.[29]

Thus consistency and equitable treatment for all students—or the lack thereof—is likely to have a significant effect on teacher–student relationships and overall classroom climate.[30]

Keep students productively engaged in worthwhile tasks.

As effective teachers plan lessons and classroom activities, they also plan specific ways of keeping students on task—something Ms. Cornell neglected to do in the opening case study. One strategy, of course, is to make the subject matter interesting and relevant to students' personal goals (see Chapter 5). Another is to incorporate variety into lessons, perhaps by using colorful audiovisual aids, conducting novel activities (e.g., small-group discussions, class debates), or occasionally moving to a different location (e.g., a computer lab or the school yard).[31] But above all else,

think about it

Thinking back to your years in elementary and secondary school, can you recall at least one student who was "teacher's pet"—someone who was clearly a favorite and had special privileges? Can you also recall a few students who were continually blamed for misdeeds, even when they weren't always the actual culprits?

[26] Based on an example described by Sullivan-DeCarlo, DeFalco, & Roberts, 1998, p. 81.

[27] W. Doyle, 1986; Emmer & Gerwels, 2006; K. L. Lane et al., 2011.

[28] Babad, 1995; Babad, Avni-Babad, & Rosenthal, 2003; J. Baker, 1999.

[29] Certo et al., 2002, p. 25.

[30] Babad et al., 2003; Peter & Dalbert, 2010; Wentzel et al., 2010.

[31] Brophy, Alleman, & Knighton, 2009; G. A. Davis & Thomas, 1989; Munn, Johnstone, & Chalmers, 1990.

effective teachers make sure students always have something to do. Thanks to their basic need for arousal, human beings have a hard time doing *nothing at all* for any length of time (again see Chapter 5). Students often misbehave when they have nothing to do or are bored with what they *are* doing.[32]

Effective classroom managers make sure there's little "empty" time in which nothing is going on. Following are several strategies for keeping students productively engaged:[33]

- Have something specific for students to do each day, even on the first day of class.
- Have materials organized and equipment set up before class.
- Conduct activities that ensure *all* students' involvement and participation.
- Maintain a brisk pace throughout each lesson (but not so fast that students can't keep up).
- Ensure that students' comments are relevant and helpful but not excessively long-winded. (For example, take chronic time-monopolizers aside for a private discussion about giving classmates a chance to speak.)
- Spend only short periods of class time assisting individual students unless other students are able to work independently and productively in the meantime.
- Ensure that students who finish an assigned task quickly have something else to do (e.g., reading a book or writing in a class journal).

Plan for transitions.

In the opening case study, Eli, Jake, and Vanessa often misbehave at the beginning and end of the school day, as well as before and after recess and lunch. Misbehaviors most frequently occur during transition times—as students end one activity and begin a second, or as they move from one classroom to another. Effective classroom managers take steps to ensure that transitions proceed quickly and without a loss of momentum.[34] For example, they establish procedures for moving from one activity to the next, and they ensure that there's little slack time in which students have nothing to do. And especially in the secondary grades, when students change classes every hour or so, effective classroom managers typically have a task for students to complete as soon as they enter the classroom. Consider these examples:

- An elementary school teacher has students follow the same procedure each day as lunchtime approaches: (1) Place completed assignments in the teacher's "In" basket, (2) put away supplies, (3) get out any home-packed lunches, and (4) line up quietly by the door.
- A middle school math teacher has students write down the next homework assignment as soon as they come to class.
- As students first enter the classroom, a middle school social studies teacher always hands them a short "Do It Now" assignment. For example, on one occasion he hands out a map of U.S. states and state capitals and instructs students to identify place names that might have Native American names and those that probably have European roots—a task that leads to a class discussion on the origins of place names.
- Before each class period begins, a ninth-grade creative writing teacher writes a topic or question on the board (e.g., "My biggest pet peeve"). Students know that when they come to class, they should immediately begin to write on the topic or question of the day.
- A high school physical education teacher has students begin each class session with five minutes of stretching exercises.

Although very different in nature, all of these strategies share the common goal of keeping students focused on productive activities.

---

[32] Gettinger & Kohler, 2006; J. Hunter & Csikszentmihalyi, 2003; Shernoff, Csikszentmihalyi, Schneider, & Shernoff, 2003.

[33] W. Doyle, 1986; Emmer & Evertson, 2009; Emmer & Gerwels, 2006; Gettinger, 1988; K. L. Lane et al., 2011; Munn et al., 1990.

[34] W. Doyle, 1984, 2006; Gettinger & Kohler, 2006. A phenomenon known as *behavioral momentum* is relevant here; for instance, see Ardoin, Martens, & Wolfe, 1999; Belfiore, Lee, Vargas, & Skinner, 1997; Mace et al., 1988.

MyEdLab
Interactive Case 9.2.

Effective teachers help students make smooth transitions from one activity to another. You can examine possible transitional strategies in this simulation.

Keep in mind that some students may have difficulty moving from one activity to another, especially if they're deeply engaged in what they're doing. Accordingly, it's often helpful to give students advance warning that a transition is coming, describe what the subsequent activity will be, and remind them of the usual procedures for switching from one task to another.[35]

Take individual and developmental differences into account.

Earlier we mentioned the importance of consistency and equity in enforcing classroom rules. But when it comes to *preventing* off-task behavior and encouraging more productive ones, optimal strategies may differ considerably from one student to the next. For example, during independent seatwork assignments, some students may work quite well with classmates close by, whereas others can be easily distracted unless they can work in a quiet spot, perhaps near a teacher's desk. And during small-group work, some groups may function quite effectively on their own, whereas others may need considerable guidance and supervision.

One important individual difference factor affecting classroom behavior is *temperament*, the extent to which a student is naturally inclined to be energetic, irritable, impulsive, and so on (see Chapter 7). To be truly effective classroom managers, teachers must realize that students' vastly different classroom behaviors may be due, in part, to biological predispositions that aren't entirely within students' control. Such a realization should influence teachers' beliefs about why students act as they do—that is, it should influence teachers' *attributions*—and these beliefs will, in turn, affect teachers' willingness to adapt classroom strategies to foster productive classroom behavior.[36]

Another individual difference variable that influences classroom behavior is ability level. Students are more likely to work diligently on their classwork when they have tasks and assignments appropriate for their current knowledge and skills. They're apt to misbehave when they're asked to do things that they perceive—either accurately or not—to be exceptionally difficult.[37] (Such may have been the case for Eli, Jake, and Vanessa in the opening case study.) We authors are *not* suggesting here that teachers assign tasks so easy that students learn nothing new in doing them (recall the discussion of *zone of proximal development* in Chapter 6). One workable strategy is to *begin* the school year with tasks students can easily complete. Such early tasks enable students to practice required routines and procedures and also give students a sense of confidence that they can succeed at assigned activities. Once a supportive classroom climate has been established and students are comfortable with classroom procedures, teachers can gradually introduce more challenging assignments.[38]

Developmental differences, too, must dictate classroom management strategies to some degree. Many children in the early elementary grades haven't had enough experience with formal education to know all the unspoken rules that govern classroom interactions—for instance, that students should remain silent when an adult is talking and that only the student who is called on should answer a question.[39] Children just beginning kindergarten or first grade may find their new school environment to be unsettling and anxiety arousing, as will many adolescents making the transition to middle school or high school (see Chapter 5). And, of course, children gain better social skills as they grow older, affecting their ability to interact effectively with their teacher and classmates (see Chapter 7). Table 9.1 presents these and other developmental considerations, along with examples of how teachers might accommodate them in classroom practice.

Continually monitor what students are doing.

Effective teachers communicate something called **withitness**: They know—and their students *know* that they know—what students are doing at all times. These teachers regularly scan the classroom, often move from one spot to another, and make frequent eye contact with individual

---

[35] K. Carter & Doyle, 2006; Emmer & Gerwels, 2006.
[36] W. Johnson, McGue, & Iacono, 2005; Keogh, 2003; A. Miller, 2006; Rothbart, 2011.
[37] Mac Iver, Reuman, & Main, 1995; Moore & Edwards, 2003; S. L. Robinson & Griesemer, 2006.
[38] W. Doyle, 1990; Emmer & Evertson, 2009.
[39] Mehan, 1979; Myles & Simpson, 2001; R. K. Payne, 2005.

DEVELOPMENTAL TRENDS
TABLE 9.1 • Effective Classroom Management at Different Grade Levels

GRADE LEVEL	AGE-TYPICAL CHARACTERISTICS	EXAMPLE	SUGGESTED STRATEGIES
K–2	• Anxiety about being in school, especially in the first few weeks and especially for students without preschool experience • Lack of familiarity with unspoken rules about appropriate classroom behavior • Short attention span and distractibility • Little self-regulation • Desire for teacher affection and approval • Considerable individual differences in social skills	Immediately after lunch on the first day of school, a first-grade teacher gathers her students at the front of the room for a storybook reading. Before she begins to read, she explains the importance of sitting quietly so that everyone can hear the story, and when students occasionally behave in ways that might distract others, she gently reminds them of appropriate school behaviors.	• Invite students and their parents to visit the classroom before the school year begins. • In the first week of the school year, place a high priority on establishing a warm, supportive relationship with every student. • Create a gathering place (e.g., a carpet) where students can sit close at hand for whole-class discussions. • Keep assignments relatively short and focused. • Create areas where students can work independently on tasks of their choosing (e.g., a reading center where students can listen to storybooks on tape or a computer). • Give students frequent opportunities to release pent-up energy. • Be explicit about acceptable classroom behavior; correct inappropriate behavior gently but consistently.
3–5	• Continuing desire for teacher approval, but with increasing concern about peer approval as well • Greater attentiveness to teachers who are emotionally expressive (e.g., teachers who often smile and show obvious concern in times of distress) • Increasing self-regulation skills • Gradually improving ability to reflect on one's own and others' thoughts and motives (i.e., increasing social cognition) • Increasing disengagement from school if students are consistently encountering academic or social failure	Nine-year-old Bailey is often disruptive and socially inappropriate—so much so that her classmates avoid her as much as possible. On several occasions her teacher takes her aside and respectfully requests more productive behavior. For example, on one occasion the teacher says, "Bailey, I'm very happy to have you in my class. But it would really help me—and I think it would help you, too—if you could raise your hand before you answer a question. That way, other kids also get a chance to answer questions."	• In both words and actions, consistently show students that you care about their academic progress and emotional well-being. • Provide increasing opportunities for independent work, but with enough structure to guide students' efforts. • Use two-way journals to communicate regularly with students about academic and personal issues. • In times of disagreement or conflict among classmates, ask students to reflect on one another's thoughts and feelings. • Make an extra effort to establish close, supportive relationships with students who appear to be academically and socially disengaged.
6–8	• Considerable anxiety about the transition to middle school, often as a result of more distant and less supportive relationships with teachers • Decrease in intrinsic motivation to learn academic subject matter • Increasing tendency to challenge traditional school norms for behavior—for instance, norms regarding clothing and hairstyle (for some students) • Increase in cheating behaviors; cheating less common if students think teachers respect them and are committed to helping them learn • Heightened concern about ability to fit in and be accepted by peers • Increase in bullying behaviors	The son of a neglectful single mother, 14-year-old D.J. has frequently moved from one relative's home to another. He is now spending a second year in seventh grade, where he's extremely disruptive and disrespectful. When he calls a classmate a "fag," his teacher takes him aside and says, "I won't tolerate that offensive word. But I know you're going through a lot at home, and I really want you to be successful here at school. How can I help?" D.J. admits that he has gay friends who wouldn't like the word he just used, and his teacher's obvious concern for his well-being soon leads to better behavior in class. Furthermore, he starts asking the teacher for help on assignments.	• Make an effort to interact with students outside of class (e.g., chat with them in the hallway, attend sporting events, chaperone school dances). • Plan lessons that are engaging and relevant to students' lives and needs. • Prohibit modes of dress that may threaten students' safety and well-being (e.g., gang insignia, racist T-shirts, sexually revealing attire), but otherwise give students some freedom of expression in what they wear. • Provide sufficient academic support that students have no reason to cheat; nevertheless, be on the lookout for possible cheating. • Do not tolerate bullying and other forms of aggression; address their underlying causes (see the discussion of aggression in Chapter 7). • Reach out to students who seem socially disconnected (e.g., invite them to join you for lunch in your classroom).

(continued)

GRADE LEVEL	AGE-TYPICAL CHARACTERISTICS	EXAMPLE	SUGGESTED STRATEGIES
 9–12	• Anxiety about the transition to high school, especially if seventh and eighth grades have been part of elementary school (as is true in some small school districts) • Social and romantic relationships often a source of distraction • Considerable self-regulation skills in some but not all students • High incidence of cheating, in part because peers communicate that cheating is acceptable • Disdain for classmates who work too hard for teacher approval (i.e., "brown-nosers") • Tendency for some adolescents to think that misbehavior will gain the admiration of classmates • Increase in violent behaviors, especially at schools in low-income neighborhoods	When a high school teacher sees 16-year-old Jerrod standing alone at a school dance, he approaches the boy to express empathy. "I remember my first school dance," the teacher tells him. "Boy, did I feel awkward! I was too shy to ask a girl to dance, and I was so afraid of making a fool of myself. What do you think we might do to make these events less intimidating?" Jerrod smiles and admits that he feels the same way his teacher once did, and they brainstorm ideas for helping students feel more comfortable at future dances.	• Remember that even in the high school grades, students achieve at higher levels when they have close, supportive relationships with teachers. • Regularly plan activities that involve social interaction; if possible, move desks and chairs to allow students to interact more easily. • Provide guidance and support for students who have few self-regulation skills to keep themselves on task. • Describe the various forms that cheating might take, and explain why cheating in *any* form is unacceptable. • Communicate approval privately rather than publicly. • Proactively address violence (see the section "Addressing Aggression and Violence at School" later in the chapter).

Sources: Some characteristics and suggestions based on Blanton & Burkley, 2008; Blugental, Lyon, Lin, McGrath, & Bimbela, 1999; K. Carter & Doyle, 2006; Castagno & Brayboy, 2008; Cizek, 2003; Emmer & Gerwels, 2006; Espinoza & Juvonen, 2011; Fingerhut & Christoffel, 2002; Hamre & Pianta, 2005; J. N. Hughes et al., 2008; Ladd, Herald-Brown, & Reiser, 2008; Mainhard, Brekelmans, den Brok, & Wubbels, 2011; Mehan, 1979; Murdock, Hale, & Weber, 2001; E. O'Connor & McCartney, 2007; Pellegrini, 2002; many other ideas derived from discussions in earlier chapters.

MyEdLab
Video Example 9.3.

Teacher *withitness* includes knowing which students are on task and which are not. In what ways does this teacher communicate withitness?

students. They know what misbehaviors are occurring *when* those misbehaviors occur, and they know who the perpetrators are.[40] Consider the following classroom example:

> In one second-grade classroom, an hour and a half of each morning is devoted to reading. Students spend part of this time with their teacher in small reading groups and the remainder of the time working on independent assignments tailored to their individual reading skills. As the teacher works with each reading group at the front of the classroom, she situates herself with her back to the wall so that she can simultaneously keep an eye on students working independently at their seats. She sends a quick and subtle signal—perhaps a stern expression, a finger to the lips, or a callout of a student's name—to any student who gets off task.

When teachers demonstrate such withitness, especially at the beginning of the school year, students are more likely to behave appropriately, stay on task, and achieve at high levels.[41]

Ideally, most classroom management strategies are *preventive* ones—that is, they set the stage for productive learning and behavior and minimize the likelihood of off-task behaviors and other behavioral problems. In the hotlinked Self-Check quiz and Application Exercises that follow, you can check and apply your understandings related to Big Idea 9.1:
> *Effective teachers create a caring, respectful classroom environment in which students are consistently focused on accomplishing instructional goals and objectives.*

MyEdLab **Self-Check 9.1**

MyEdLab **Application Exercise 9.1.** In this exercise, you can observe and analyze a teacher's strategies for arranging her classroom in ways that promote desired academic and social behaviors.

MyEdLab **Application Exercise 9.2.** In this exercise, you can observe and analyze a teacher's strategies for helping children learn and agree to a few basic rules for classroom behavior.

[40] Gettinger & Kohler, 2006; T. Hogan, Rabinowitz, & Craven, 2003; Kounin, 1970; K. L. Lane et al., 2011.
[41] W. Doyle, 1986; Gettinger & Kohler, 2006; Woolfolk & Brooks, 1985.

9.2 EXPANDING THE SENSE OF COMMUNITY BEYOND THE CLASSROOM

Big Idea 9.2 Teachers are most effective when they coordinate their efforts with colleagues, outside agencies, and parents.

Students' learning and development depend not only on what happens inside a particular classroom but also on what happens in other parts of the school building, in the neighborhood and community, and at home. Effective teachers coordinate their efforts with other influential individuals in students' lives—with other school faculty members, with professionals at community agencies, and especially with students' parents or other primary caregivers. Ideally, teachers should think of such joint efforts as *partnerships* in which everyone is working together to promote students' long-term development and learning. Following are several recommendations.

Collaborate with colleagues to create an overall sense of school community.

Teachers are far more effective if they coordinate their efforts with other faculty members through strategies such as these:[42]

- Identify common goals regarding what students should learn and achieve.
- Work together to identify and overcome obstacles to students' academic achievement.
- Establish a shared set of standards for students' behavior, along with systematic, schoolwide procedures for encouraging productive behaviors.
- Jointly and explicitly insist on respect for people with diverse backgrounds and needs— a strategy that translates into prohibitions against malicious teasing, derogatory rumor spreading, bullying, and other forms of peer harassment.

Thus, effective teachers not only create a sense of community within their individual classrooms but also create an overall **sense of school community**.[43] Students should consistently get two messages from teachers: (1) All faculty members are working together to help students become informed and productive citizens, and (2) students can and should *help and support one another.* A sense of school community involves close student–student relationships not only within individual classrooms but also across classrooms and grade levels. Cross-class peer tutoring, participation in extracurricular activities, student involvement in school decision making, frequent use of school mascots and other traditional school symbols—all of these help to create a sense that students are members of a mutually supportive school "family."[44]

When teachers and students share an overall sense of school community, students have more positive attitudes toward school, are more motivated to achieve at high levels, exhibit more prosocial behavior, and interact more often with peers from diverse backgrounds. Furthermore, when teachers collaborate in their efforts, they often have higher *collective self-efficacy*—a belief that by working as a team, they can definitely have an impact on students' learning and achievement (see Chapter 5)—and this collective self-confidence is correlated with students' academic performance.[45] Such a team spirit provides an additional advantage for beginning teachers: It provides the support structure (scaffolding) they sometimes need, especially when working with students who are at risk for school failure.[46]

---

[42] Battistich, Solomon, Watson, & Schaps, 1997; Espelage & Swearer, 2004; K. L. Lane, Kalberg, & Menzies, 2009; J. Lee & Shute, 2010; T. J. Lewis, Newcomer, Trussell, & Richter, 2006; O'Brennan, Waasdorp, & Bradshaw, 2014; M. Watson & Battistich, 2006.

[43] Battistich, Solomon, Kim, Watson, & Schaps, 1995; Battistich et al., 1997; M. Watson & Battistich, 2006.

[44] Juvonen, 2006; Nucci, 2009; D. R. Robinson, Schofield, & Steers-Wentzell, 2005.

[45] Goddard, Hoy, & Woolfolk Hoy, 2000; Hoy, Tarter, & Woolfolk Hoy, 2006; J. Lee & Shute, 2010.

[46] Chester & Beaudin, 1996.

Work cooperatively with other agencies that play key roles in students' lives.

Many students have regular contact with other institutions besides their schools—possibly with community recreation centers, social services, churches, hospitals, mental health clinics, or local judicial systems. Teachers are most effective if they think of themselves as part of a larger community team that promotes children's overall development and well-being. Thus, they should keep in contact with other people and institutions that play major roles in students' lives, coordinating efforts whenever possible.[47] Keep in mind, however, that school–agency cooperation regarding *individual* students—especially if it involves sharing potentially sensitive information—can typically occur only with written permission from students' parents.

Communicate regularly with parents and other primary caregivers.

Without a doubt, productive parent–teacher relationships enhance students' learning and achievement in the classroom, and ongoing communication between school and home is critical for these relationships.[48] At a minimum, teachers must stay in regular contact with parents and other primary caregivers about students' progress. Regular communication also provides a means through which families can give *teachers* information (e.g., about current circumstances at home or about effective motivational strategies). Following are several common mechanisms for enhancing school–family communication:

- **Parent–teacher conferences.** In most school districts, formal parent–teacher conferences are scheduled one or more times a year. Teachers sometimes include students in conferences (essentially making them parent–teacher–student conferences). Inviting other family members who share caregiving responsibilities (e.g., grandparents) can also be helpful.

- **Written communication.** Written communication can take a variety of forms, including (1) homework slips explaining each night's assignments, (2) informal notes acknowledging significant accomplishments, (3) teacher-constructed checklists that describe academic progress, and (4) general newsletters describing ongoing classroom activities.

- **Telephone conversations.** Telephone calls are useful when issues require immediate attention—for instance, when a student has won a prestigious award or, alternatively, has shown a sudden decline in performance for no apparent reason. In addition, telephone calls can be a good way of introducing oneself as a child's elementary school teacher for the coming school year.[49]

- **E-mail messages.** Obviously, e-mail is appropriate only when parents own computers, have both technological literacy skills and easy access to the Internet, and regularly check their e-mail in-boxes—things that are less likely to be true for low-income parents and for parents with only limited knowledge of English.

- **Class websites.** As noted in Chapter 8, many teachers now create class websites on which they post instructional goals, assignments, and the like. Typically such websites are available to parents as well as students, but, as is true for e-mail messages, they're most appropriate for parents who regularly use computers and the Internet.

As an example, Figure 9.4 shows one of the "weekly update" e-mail letters that a fourth-grade teacher regularly sends to her students' parents and other primary caregivers. Notice that, with students' diverse family structures in mind, she addresses the letter to "Families" rather than "Parents." Also notice how the letter simultaneously serves several purposes: to (1) request appropriate outdoor clothing, (2) remind family members about scheduled parent–teacher conferences and other upcoming events, (3) keep families in the loop about current academic lessons and projects, and (4) encourage families to contact her about any questions or concerns.

---

[47] J. L. Epstein, 1996; Kincheloe, 2009.

[48] P. A. Edwards & Turner, 2010; Gutman & McLoyd, 2000; J. Hughes & Kwok, 2007; Reschly & Christenson, 2009.

[49] Striepling-Goldstein, 2004.

FIGURE 9.4 In weekly e-mail messages like this one, a fourth-grade teacher in Virginia keeps in regular contact with her students' parents and other primary caregivers. "SOL" refers to the Standards of Learning tests, which are Virginia's statewide achievement tests administered near the end of each school year. Her "cumulative" classroom tests, which may include material from any previous point in the school year, are intended to encourage students to continue reviewing all of the topics and skills they have studied.

Families,

I hope everyone enjoyed a wonderful fall weekend! As the weather gets cooler, please remind your child to dress appropriately—we will go outside as long as the weather cooperates. So please send a coat, hat, etc.

This week is conference week. If you do not know your conference time, please let me know. I sent reminder forms home last week with most students. I really look forward to meeting with you all!

Here is what we have planned for this week:

Math: We will begin discussing place value. We will make and expand numbers, compare whole numbers, examine number lines, and look at numbers to the millions.

Language Arts: We will have word study this week. I have adjusted a few of the word study groups according to everyone's needs. We have begun the typing program in the computer lab. Although you do not have access to this at home, there is another typing program that is free: [the teacher includes a hotlink to the program]. This is a very important skill, so please encourage your child to type at home! We will be continuing to work on our Titanic projects and hope to have these finished by Friday. We will also begin a mystery mini-unit and will be reading quite a few short mysteries. We will also continue book club with *The Tale of Despereaux*. In writing. we will wrap up our personal narratives and begin brainstorming for each student's Winning Choices Essay. This essay is part of a contest sponsored by the Rotary Club and Montgomery County. We will be working on it together at school as our first major school writing project.

Science: We will continue to study weather. We will have a quick quiz tomorrow about weather tools. We have learned about types of clouds and will begin learning about temperature and air pressure this week.

History: We will wrap up our unit on First Virginians this week and have a test early next week. Just a reminder that all of our tests will be cumulative in an effort to continue to study for our end-of-the-year SOL test.

Important Dates:
10/24 - No school (conferences)
10/25 - PTA Fall Festival (6-8 PM)
11/1 - Early release
11/4 - Center for the Arts concert field trip (during school hours)
11/5 - No school (election day)
11/7 - End of grading period
11/14 - Field trip to BHS (during school hours—we will watch a Cinderella play)

As always, please let me know if you ever have questions or concerns.

Enjoy the week,

Ashleigh

When communicating with students' families, teachers don't necessarily have to limit themselves to what's going on in the classroom. Many parents welcome teachers' suggestions about how best to help their children at home. For instance, parents are often grateful for suggestions about how to assist with homework or how to foster their children's development more generally.[50] And they appreciate knowing what kinds of behaviors are and are not normal for a particular age-group.[51]

Invite families to participate in the academic and social life of the school.

In general, effective schools are *welcoming* schools that encourage not only students but also family members to participate in school activities.[52] Some parents are available on weekdays and are happy to assist with occasional field trips and class parties; a few may even be able to provide one-on-one tutoring for certain students. Many other parents are available in the evenings and can attend school open houses, school plays, band and choir performances, and fund-raising events. Some teachers have successfully used parent *coffee nights* during which they explain a new instructional strategy or *author teas* during which students read poems or short stories they've written.

In some instances, teachers or other faculty members might assemble a group of parents to discuss issues of mutual interest.[53] For example, they might use such a group as a sounding board when selecting topics to include in the classroom curriculum or thinking about assigning potentially controversial works of literature. Alternatively, teachers can use a discussion group as a mechanism through which teachers and parents alike can share ideas about how best to promote students' academic, personal, and social development on the home front.

Make an extra effort with seemingly "reluctant" parents.

Despite many opportunities to participate, some parents remain uninvolved in their children's education; for example, they may never attend scheduled parent–teacher conferences. Rather than jumping to the conclusion that these parents are also *uninterested* in their children's education, teachers must recognize several possible reasons that parents might be reluctant to make contact with their children's teachers. Some may have an exhausting work schedule or lack adequate child care. Others may know little English, have difficulty finding their way through the school system, or believe it's inappropriate to bother teachers with their concerns. Still others may have had such bad experiences when they themselves were students that they feel uncomfortable in a school building. And a few parents may be victims of mental illness or substance abuse, limiting their ability to support their children financially, academically, or otherwise.[54]

In some cases, a personal invitation can make a difference, as this parent's statement illustrates:

> The thing of it is, had someone not walked up to me and asked me specifically, I would not hold out my hand and say, "I'll do it." . . . You get parents here all the time, Black parents that are willing, but maybe a little on the shy side and wouldn't say I really want to serve on this subject. You may send me the form, I may never fill the form out. Or I'll think about it and not send it back. But you know if that principal, that teacher, my son's math teacher called and asked if I would. . . .[55]

---

[50] Not all parents use good judgment in their own, independent efforts to help their children with homework. Some parents' strategies can actually be counterproductive, especially if they create a source of conflict and stress in the family; see Dumont et al., 2012.

[51] C. Davis & Yang, 2005; J. M. T. Walker & Hoover-Dempsey, 2006.

[52] J. L. Epstein, 1996; N. E. Hill et al., 2004; G. R. López, 2001; Serpell, Baker, & Sonnenschein, 2005.

[53] J. L. Epstein, 1996; Fosnot, 1996; Rudman, 1993.

[54] Bornstein & Cote, 2010; Cazden, 2001; Dantas & Manyak, 2010; P. A. Edwards & Turner, 2010; C. L. Green, Walker, Hoover-Dempsey, & Sandler, 2007; J.-S. Lee & Bowen, 2006.

[55] A. A. Carr, 1997, p. 2.

Experienced educators have offered additional recommendations for getting seemingly reluctant parents more involved in their children's schooling:[56]

- Encourage parents to be assertive when they have questions or concerns.
- Invite other important family members to participate in school activities, especially if a student's cultural background places high value on extended families.
- Offer suggestions about learning activities that parents can easily do with their children at home.
- Find out what things certain family members do exceptionally well (e.g., carpentry, cooking), and ask them to share their talents with students.
- Provide opportunities for parents to volunteer for jobs that don't require them to leave home (e.g., to be someone whom students can call when unsure of homework assignments).
- Identify specific individuals (e.g., bilingual parents) who can translate for those who speak little or no English.
- Conduct parent–teacher conferences or parent discussions at times and locations convenient for families; make use of home visits *if* such visits are welcomed.
- Offer resources for parents at the school building (e.g., contacts with social and health services; classes in English, literacy, home repairs, arts and crafts).

Still another potentially effective strategy is to reinforce *parents* as well as students when the students do well at school. One administrator at a school serving many immigrant students put it this way:

> One of the things we do . . . is that we identify those students that had perfect attendance, those students that passed all areas of the [statewide achievement tests] and were successful. We don't honor the student, we honor the parents. We give parents a certificate. Because, we tell them, "through your efforts, and through your hard work, your child was able to accomplish this."[57]

A few parents may resist all efforts to get them involved. Especially in such circumstances, teachers must never penalize students for their parents' actions or inactions. Teachers must also realize that *they themselves* are apt to be among the most important academic and emotional resources in these students' lives.

As a traditional Nigerian proverb says, "It takes a village to raise a child." In the hot-linked Self-Check quiz and Application Exercise that follow, you can check and apply your understandings related to Big Idea 9.2:

Teachers are most effective when they coordinate their efforts with colleagues, outside agencies, and parents.

MyEdLab **Self-Check 9.2**

MyEdLab **Application Exercise 9.3.** This exercise will enable you to learn more about how schools can work effectively with parents.

9.3 REDUCING UNPRODUCTIVE BEHAVIORS

Big Idea 9.3 Effective interventions for reducing unproductive school behaviors are tailored to the circumstances, with students' long-term development and well-being as the ultimate goals.

Despite teachers' best efforts, students sometimes behave in ways that significantly disrupt classroom activities and interfere with learning. For purposes of our discussion, we'll define a **misbehavior** as any action that can potentially disrupt learning and planned classroom activities, puts

---

[56] Castagno & Brayboy, 2008; Dantas & Manyak, 2010; C. Davis & Yang, 2005; J. L. Epstein, 1996; Finders & Lewis, 1994; Hidalgo et al., 1995; G. R. López, 2001; Salend & Taylor, 1993; M. G. Sanders, 1996; J. M. T. Walker & Hoover-Dempsey, 2006.

[57] G. R. López, 2001, p. 273.

one or more students' physical safety or psychological well-being in jeopardy, or violates basic moral and ethical standards. Some misbehaviors are relatively minor and have little long-term impact on students' achievement and general well-being. Such behaviors as talking out of turn, writing brief notes to classmates during a teacher-directed lesson, and submitting homework assignments after their due date—especially if these behaviors occur infrequently—generally fall in this category. Other misbehaviors are far more serious, in that they definitely interfere with the learning or well-being of one or more students. For example, when students scream at their teachers, hit their classmates, or habitually refuse to participate in ongoing activities, then classroom learning—certainly that of the "guilty party" and sometimes that of other students as well—can be adversely affected, as can the overall classroom climate.

As is true in the opening case study, typically only a few students are responsible for the great majority of misbehaviors in any single classroom.[58] Such students are apt to be among teachers' greatest challenges, and it can be all too tempting to write them off as lost causes. Yet teachers must work vigorously to point these students in more productive directions. Without active interventions by teachers and other caring adults, students who are consistently disruptive or in other ways off task in the early grades may continue to show behavior problems later on.[59]

Teachers need to plan ahead about how they'll address students' misbehaviors. Although teachers must certainly be consistent in the consequences they impose for blatant rule infractions (recall our earlier discussion of consistency and equity), different strategies for reducing counterproductive behaviors over the long run may be more or less useful under different circumstances. Following are a number of possibilities.

Consider whether instructional strategies or classroom assignments might be partly to blame for off-task behaviors.

Principles of effective classroom management go hand in hand with principles of learning and motivation. When students are learning and achieving successfully and when they clearly want to pursue the class's instructional goals, they're apt to be busily engaged in productive activities for most of the school day. In contrast, when they have trouble understanding classroom subject matter or little interest in learning it, they're likely to exhibit the nonproductive or counterproductive classroom behaviors that result from frustration or boredom.[60]

When students misbehave, beginning teachers often think about what the students are doing wrong. In contrast, experienced teachers are more likely to think about what *they themselves* could do differently to keep students on task, and they modify their plans accordingly.[61] Here are several self-questions that can help a beginning teacher start thinking like an expert:

- How can I change my instructional strategies to pique students' interest?
- Are instructional materials so difficult or unstructured that students are getting frustrated? Or are they so easy or routine that students are bored?
- What are students really concerned about? For example, are they more concerned about interacting with peers than in gaining new knowledge and skills? How can I address students' motives and goals while simultaneously helping them achieve instructional classroom objectives?

Addressing such questions can help a teacher focus his or her efforts on the ultimate purpose of schooling: to help students *learn.*

Occasionally students are justifiably preoccupied with current events on the local or national scene—perhaps a tragic car accident involving classmates or a contentious political event—to the point that they can't focus on classroom subject matter. In such circumstances, teachers may want to abandon their lesson plans altogether, at least for a short time.

---

[58] W. Doyle, 2006.

[59] Dishion, Piehler, & Myers, 2008; Emmer & Gerwels, 2006; Vitaro, Brendgen, Larose, & Tremblay, 2005.

[60] Gettinger & Kohler, 2006; K. L. Lane et al., 2011; Metcalfe, Harvey, & Laws, 2013; Pekrun, Goetz, Daniels, Stupnisky, & Perry, 2010.

[61] Emmer & Stough, 2001; Sabers, Cushing, & Berliner, 1991; H. L. Swanson, O'Connor, & Cooney, 1990.

Consider whether cultural background might influence students' classroom behaviors.

As teachers determine which behaviors are truly unacceptable in their classrooms, they must keep in mind that some behaviors that their own culture deems inappropriate may be quite acceptable in another culture.[62] The following exercise presents three examples.

SEE FOR YOURSELF
IDENTIFYING MISBEHAVIORS

As you read each of the following scenarios, consider these questions:

- Would you classify the behavior as a *mis*behavior?
- What cultural group(s) might think that the behavior is acceptable?
- How might you deal with the behavior?

1. A student is frequently late for school, sometimes arriving more than an hour after the school bell has rung.
2. Two students are sharing answers as they take a quiz.
3. Several students are exchanging insults that become increasingly derogatory.

Tardiness (Example 1) interferes with learning because the student loses valuable instructional time; thus, it might reasonably be construed as a misbehavior. However, a student who is chronically tardy may live in a community that doesn't observe strict schedules and timelines—a pattern common in some Hispanic and Native American groups (see the Cultural Considerations box in Chapter 4). Furthermore, arrival time may not be entirely within the student's control. For instance, perhaps the student has household responsibilities or transportation issues that make punctuality difficult. A private conversation with the student, perhaps followed by a conference with family members, might be the most effective way to determine the root of the problem and identify potential solutions (more about such strategies shortly).

Sharing answers during a quiz (Example 2) is a misbehavior *if* students have been specifically instructed to do their own work. Because a quiz helps a teacher determine what students have and haven't learned, inaccurate quiz scores affect the teacher's instructional planning and so indirectly affect students' future learning. (Sharing answers can lower the *validity* of the quiz scores; we'll discuss this concept in Chapter 10.) Although the behavior represents cheating to many people, it might reflect the cooperative spirit and emphasis on group achievement evident in the cultures of many Native American, Mexican American, and Southeast Asian students (again see the Cultural Considerations box in Chapter 4). An adverse consequence is in order *if* a teacher has previously explained what cheating is in a way that students understand and *if* the teacher has clearly described situations in which collaboration is and isn't appropriate—in other words, if students know full well that their behavior violates classroom policy. A teacher who *hasn't* yet laid this groundwork must quickly do so in order to prevent such behavior from occurring again.

Exchanging insults (Example 3) might be psychologically harmful for the students involved and adversely affect the overall classroom climate. Alternatively, however, it might simply be an instance of *sounding,* a playful verbal interaction involving creative one-upmanship common in some African American communities (also known as *playing the dozens;* see the "Argument" exercise involving "Your momma" jokes in Chapter 4). How a teacher handles the situation must depend on the spirit in which students seem to view the exchange. Their body language—whether they're smiling or scowling, whether they seem relaxed or tense—can reveal a great deal. If the insults truly signal escalating hostilities, an immediate intervention is in order—perhaps separating the students, imposing an appropriate consequence, and following up with a private conference. If, instead, the insults reflect creative verbal play, a teacher may simply need to establish reasonable boundaries (e.g., racial and ethnic slurs are unacceptable).

MyEdLab
Video Example 9.5.
As the experienced teacher in this video explains, some students from diverse backgrounds may need explicit guidance about expected classroom behaviors. What concrete example does she give? What other expectations are hinted at in the classroom snippets shown in the video?

---

[62] For example, see Gay, 2006.

Ignore misbehaviors that are temporary, minor, and unlikely to be repeated or copied.

On some occasions, the best course of action is *no* action, at least nothing of a disciplinary nature. For example, consider these situations:

> Dimitra rarely breaks class rules. But one day, after you've just instructed students to work quietly and independently at their seats, you see her briefly whisper to the girl beside her. None of the other students seems to notice that Dimitra is temporarily disobeying your instructions.

> Herb is careless in chemistry lab and accidentally knocks over a small container of liquid—a harmless one, fortunately. He quickly apologizes and cleans up the mess.

Will these behaviors interfere with Dimitra's or Herb's academic achievement? Are they "contagious" behaviors that will spread to other students, as the horseplay does in Ms. Cornell's class in the opening case study? The answer to both questions is "Probably not."

Whenever a teacher stops an instructional activity to deal with a misbehavior, even for a few seconds, the teacher may disrupt the momentum of the activity and draw students' attention to the misbehaving classmate. Furthermore, by drawing class attention to a particular misbehavior, the teacher may unintentionally be reinforcing it.

Ignoring misbehavior is often reasonable in circumstances such as these:[63]

- When the behavior is a rare occurrence and probably won't be repeated
- When the behavior is unlikely to spread to other students
- When the behavior is the result of unusual and temporary conditions (e.g., the last day of school before a holiday, unsettling events in a student's personal life)
- When the behavior is typical for the age-group (e.g., kindergartners becoming restless after sitting for an extended time, sixth-grade boys and girls resisting holding hands during dance instruction)
- When the behavior's natural consequence is unpleasant enough to deter a student from doing it again
- When the behavior isn't seriously affecting classroom learning

Dimitra's behavior—briefly whispering to a classmate during independent seatwork—is unlikely to spread to her classmates (they don't see her do it) and probably isn't an instance of cheating (it occurs before she begins working on the assignment). Herb's behavior—knocking over a container of liquid in chemistry lab—has, in and of itself, resulted in an unpleasant consequence: He must clean up the mess. In both situations, then, ignoring the misbehavior is probably the best thing to do.

Give signals and reminders about what is and is not appropriate.

Some off-task behaviors, although not serious in nature, really do interfere with classroom learning and must be discouraged. Consider these situations as examples:

> As you're explaining a difficult concept, Marjorie is busily writing. At first, you think she's taking notes, but then you see her pass the paper across the aisle to Kang. A few minutes later Kang passes the same sheet back to Marjorie. It appears that the two students are writing personal notes when they should be attending to the lesson.

> You've separated your class into small groups for a cooperative learning activity. One group is frequently off task and probably won't complete its task if its members don't get down to business soon.

Effective classroom managers handle such minor behavior problems as unobtrusively as possible. They don't stop the lesson, distract other students, or call unnecessary attention to the

---

think about it

Can you relate *ignoring behavior* to a specific concept in operant conditioning? Why is ignoring *not* an effective strategy in Ms. Cornell's classroom? (See Chapter 4 if you need a refresher on negative reinforcement and its effects.) (For answers to these questions, click **here**.)

---

[63] G. A. Davis & Thomas, 1989; W. Doyle, 1986, 2006; Munn et al., 1990; Silberman & Wheelan, 1980; Wynne, 1990.

troublesome behavior.[64] In many cases they use *cueing*, a strategy introduced in Chapter 4. That is, they let students know, through a signal of one kind or another, that they're aware of the misbehavior and want it to cease.

Cueing takes a variety of forms. For instance, a teacher might use nonverbal cues, perhaps putting a finger to the lips to signal "Shhh" or perhaps moving close to a student and standing there until the problem behavior stops. When such nonverbal signals don't work, a brief verbal cue—stating a student's name, reminding students of correct behavior, or (if necessary) specifically describing an inappropriate behavior—may be in order. Ideally, a verbal cue should focus students' attention on what *should* be done rather than on what *isn't* being done.[65] For instance, instead of chastising students for being overly noisy during a cooperative group activity, a teacher might say, "As you exchange ideas, remember to use your *indoor voices* so that you don't distract other groups."

Some effective teachers use a bit of humor to take the sting out of verbal cues that might otherwise undermine productive teacher–student relationships.[66] For example, when a student comes into class late because he's been talking too long with friends in the hall, his teacher might teasingly tell him, "John, I know you have quite a fan club out there, but your fans in here—including *me*—are feeling a bit slighted that you don't want to spend time with us." Notice how this statement conveys that John has an admirable quality—he's a likeable guy—while also reminding him that punctuality is important.

Get students' perspectives about their behaviors.

Sometimes brief cues are insufficient to change a student's behavior. Consider these situations:

> Alonzo is almost always a few minutes late to your third-period algebra class. When he finally arrives, he takes several more minutes to pull his textbook and other class materials out of his backpack. You've often reminded him about the importance of coming to class on time, yet his tardiness continues.

> Trudy rarely completes class assignments. In fact, she often doesn't even *begin* them. On many previous occasions you've gently tried to get her on task, but usually without success. Today, when you look Trudy in the eye and ask her point blank to get to work, she defiantly responds, "I'm not going to do it. You can't make me!"

In such situations, talking privately with the student might be the next logical step. The discussion should be *private* for several reasons. First, as noted earlier, calling peers' attention to a problem behavior may actually reinforce the behavior rather than discourage it. Or, instead, the attention of classmates may cause a student to feel excessively embarrassed or humiliated—feelings that may make the student overly anxious about being in the classroom in the future. Finally, when a teacher spends too much class time dealing with a single misbehaving student, other students are apt to get off task.[67]

Private conversations with individual students give a teacher a chance to explain why certain behaviors are unacceptable and must stop. (Recall the discussion of *induction* in Chapter 7.) They also give students a chance to explain why they behave as they do. For instance, Alonzo might explain his chronic tardiness by revealing that he has diabetes and must check his blood sugar level between his second- and third-period classes. He can perform the procedure himself but would prefer to do it in the privacy of the school nurse's office on the other side of the building. Meanwhile, Trudy might reveal her long-standing frustration with subject matter and assignments she perceives as being impossible to make sense of. A boy with a reading disability once voiced such frustration in an interview with a researcher:

> They [teachers] used to hand us all our homework on Mondays. One day my teacher handed me a stack about an inch thick and as I was walking out of class there was a big trash can right there and

think about it
From a motivational standpoint, how might private discussions with students be helpful? (For potential benefits, click **here**.)

---

[64] K. Carter & Doyle, 2006; W. Doyle, 1990; Emmer, 1987.

[65] Evertson & Emmer, 2009; K. L. Lane et al., 2011.

[66] Henley, 2010.

[67] W. Doyle, 2006; Emmer & Gerwels, 2006; Scott & Bushell, 1974.

I'd, in front of everybody including the teacher, just drop it in the trash can and walk out. I did this because I couldn't read what she gave me. It was kind of a point that I wanted to get the teacher to realize. That while I'm doing it, inside it kind of like hurt because I really wanted to do it but I couldn't and just so it didn't look like I was goin' soft or anything like that I'd walk over to the trash and throw it in.[68]

Students' explanations often provide clues about how best to deal with their behavior over the long run. For example, given his need to go to the nurse's office between classes, Alonzo might always be a bit late; accordingly, his teacher might reassign him to a seat by the door so that he can join class unobtrusively when he arrives. Trudy's frustration with her schoolwork suggests that she needs additional scaffolding to help her succeed. It also hints at a possible undiagnosed learning disability that may warrant a referral to the school psychologist or another diagnostician. In some cases, conversations with students can reveal maladaptive interpretations of social situations. For instance, a chronically aggressive student may express the inaccurate belief that classmates "are always trying to pick a fight" (recall the discussion of *hostile attributional bias* in Chapter 7). In this instance, a teacher might consult with the school counselor about how to help the student interpret social interactions more productively.

Students won't always provide explanations that lead to such straightforward solutions, however. For example, it may be that Alonzo is chronically late to class simply because he sees no point in being punctual. Or perhaps Trudy says she doesn't want to do her assignments because, she says, "I'm sick and tired of other people always telling me what to do." In such circumstances, it's essential that teachers not get in a power struggle—a situation in which one person wins by dominating over the other in some way. Several strategies can minimize the likelihood of a power struggle:[69]

- Speak in a calm, matter-of-fact manner, describing the problem as you see it. ("You haven't turned in a single assignment in the past 3 weeks. You and I would both like for you to do well in my class, but that can't happen unless we work together to make it happen.")
- Present the problem as one involving unproductive behavior, *not* a personality flaw. ("You've come to class late almost every day this month.")
- Listen empathetically to what the student has to say, being openly accepting of the student's feelings and opinions. ("I get the impression that you don't enjoy classroom activities very much; I'd really like to hear what your concerns are.")
- Summarize what you think the student has told you, and seek clarification if necessary. ("It sounds as if you'd rather not let your classmates know how much trouble you're having with your schoolwork. Is that the problem, or is it something else?")
- Describe the effects of the problem behavior, including your personal reactions to it. ("When you come to class late each day, I worry that you're getting further and further behind. Sometimes I even feel a little hurt that you don't seem to value your time in my classroom.")
- Give the student a choice from among two or more acceptable options. ("Would you rather try to work quietly at your group's table, or would it be easier if you sat somewhere by yourself to complete your work?")
- Especially when working with an adolescent, try to identify a solution that enables the student to maintain credibility in the eyes of peers. ("I suspect you might be worrying that your friends will think less of you if you comply with my request. What could you and I do to address this problem?")

Ultimately, a teacher must communicate three things: (1) interest in the student's long-term school achievement, (2) concern that the misbehavior is interfering with that achievement, and (3) commitment to working cooperatively with the student to resolve the problem.

MyEdLab
Interactive Case 9.3.

Simple interventions can often be effective in reducing unproductive classroom behaviors. You can examine several strategies in this simulation.

---

[68] Zambo & Brem, 2004, p. 6.
[69] Colvin, Ainge, & Nelson, 1997; Emmer & Evertson, 2009; Henley, 2010; Keller & Tapasak, 2004; K. Lane, Falk, & Wehby, 2006.

Teach self-regulation techniques.

Sometimes students need one-on-one guidance in how they might better control their own behaviors. Consider these examples:

> Bradley's performance on assigned tasks is usually rather poor. You know he's capable of better work, because he occasionally submits assignments of exceptionally high quality. The root of Bradley's problem seems to be that he's off task most of the time—perhaps sketching pictures of sports cars, mindlessly fiddling with objects he's found on the floor, or simply daydreaming. Bradley would really like to improve his academic performance but doesn't seem to know how to do it.

> Georgia often talks without permission—for instance, blurting out answers to questions, interrupting classmates who are speaking, and initiating off-task conversations at inopportune times. On several occasions, you've spoken with Georgia about the problem, and she always promises to exercise more self-control in the future. Her behavior improves for a day or so, but after that, her mouth is off and running once again.

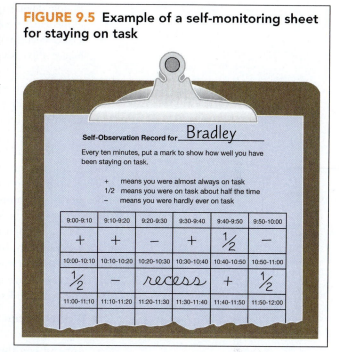

FIGURE 9.5 Example of a self-monitoring sheet for staying on task

Bradley's off-task behavior interferes with his own learning, and Georgia's excessive chattiness interferes with the learning of her classmates. Cueing and private discussions haven't led to any improvement. But both Bradley and Georgia have something going for them: They *want* to change their behavior.

In Chapter 3 we examined a variety of strategies for promoting self-regulated learning and behavior, and some of them might be helpful for Bradley and Georgia. *Self-monitoring* is especially useful when students need a reality check about the severity of a problem. For instance, Bradley may think he's on task far more often than he really is. To help him get a sense of how frequently he's *off* task, his teacher might give him a timer set to beep every 10 minutes and ask him to record whether he's been on task each time he hears a beep. (Figure 9.5 shows the kind of recording sheet he might use.) Similarly, Georgia may not realize how frequently she prevents her classmates from speaking. To alert her to the extent of the problem, her teacher might ask her to make a checkmark on a tally sheet every time she talks without permission.

If self-monitoring alone doesn't do the trick, *self-instructions* might help Georgia gain some self-restraint in classroom discussions:

1. *Button* my lips (by holding them tightly together).
2. *Raise* my hand.
3. *Wait* until I'm called on.

In addition, both students might use *self-imposed contingencies* to give themselves a motivational boost. For example, Bradley might award himself a point for each 10-minute period he's been on task. Georgia might give herself 5 points at the beginning of each school day and then subtract a point each time she speaks out of turn. By accumulating a certain number of points, the students could earn opportunities to engage in favorite activities.

Some students may initially need considerable scaffolding to help them learn to self-regulate their behaviors.[70] For example, in the first few days or weeks, a teacher might use one or more simple technological devices—perhaps a small buzzer the teacher can remotely activate from the other side of the room—to remind students of things they should be doing or give them feedback that they're doing something well.

Self-regulation strategies have several advantages. They help teachers avoid power struggles with students about who's in charge. They increase students' sense of autonomy and thus also

MyEdLab
Video Example 9.6.

Teacher-structured self-reinforcement contingencies can be quite effective in helping students with a history of classroom behavior problems. What kinds of structure does the teacher in this video provide?

---

[70] J. O. Cooper, Heron, & Heward, 2007; Duckworth, Gendler, & Gross, 2014; Meltzer, 2007.

increase students' motivation to learn and achieve in the classroom. Furthermore, self-regulation techniques benefit students over the long run, promoting productive behaviors that are likely to continue long after students have moved on from a particular classroom or school. And when students learn how to monitor and modify their own behavior, rather than depend on adults to do it for them, their teachers become free to do other things—for example, to teach!

When administering punishment, use only those consequences that have been shown to be effective in reducing problem behaviors.

In a well-managed classroom, reinforcement for productive behavior occurs far more often than punishment for inappropriate behavior. But consider the following scenarios:

> Bonnie doesn't handle frustration very well. Whenever she encounters an obstacle she can't immediately overcome, she responds by hitting, kicking, or breaking something. Once, during a class Valentine's Day party, she accidentally drops her cupcake. When she discovers that it's no longer edible, she throws her carton of milk across the room, hitting another child on the head.

> Two days before a high school football game against a cross-town rival, several members of the football team are caught spray-painting obscene words on the bleachers of the rival school's stadium.

Some misbehaviors interfere significantly with classroom learning or reflect a total disregard for other people's rights and welfare. These actions require an immediate remedy, and teachers or school administrators must impose consequences sufficiently unpleasant to discourage them. In other words, educators must occasionally use *punishment.* Punishment is especially useful when students appear to have little motivation to change their behavior.

As a general rule, teachers should use relatively mild forms of punishment in the classroom.[71] Severe punishment—for instance, something that lasts for several weeks or months, or something that seriously undermines students' sense of self-worth—can lead to such unwanted side effects as resentment, hostility, and truancy. Several forms of mild punishment are often effective in reducing undesirable classroom behaviors:

- **Verbal reprimands (scolding).** Although some students seem to thrive on teacher scolding because of the attention it brings, most students find verbal reprimands to be unpleasant and punishing, especially if given only infrequently. In general, reprimands are more effective when they're immediate, brief, and unemotional, and they should be given in private if at all possible. When scolded in front of peers, some students may relish the peer attention, and others may feel totally humiliated.[72]

- **Response cost.** Response cost involves the loss either of a previously earned reinforcer or of an opportunity to obtain reinforcement; in either case, it's a form of *removal punishment.* Response cost is especially effective when used in combination with reinforcement of appropriate behavior.[73] For example, when dealing with students who exhibit chronic behavior problems, teachers sometimes incorporate response cost into a point system or *token economy,* awarding points, plastic chips, or the like for good behavior (reinforcement) and taking away these things for inappropriate behavior (response cost). Students who accumulate a sufficient number of points or tokens can use them to "buy" objects, privileges, or enjoyable activities that are otherwise not available. (You may want to revisit the discussions of removal punishment and token economy in Chapter 4.)

- **Logical consequences.** A logical consequence is something that follows naturally or logically from a student's misbehavior; in other words, it's punishment that fits the crime. For example, if a student destroys a classmate's possession, a reasonable consequence is for the

[71] Landrum & Kauffman, 2006.

[72] M. L. Fuller, 2001; Landrum & Kauffman, 2006; Pfiffner & O'Leary, 1993; Van Houten, Nau, MacKenzie-Keating, Sameoto, & Colavecchia, 1982.

[73] Conyers et al., 2004; J. M. Donaldson, DeLeon, Fisher, & Kahng, 2014; Iwata & Bailey, 1974; Lentz, 1988.

student to replace it or pay for a new one. If two close friends talk so much that they aren't completing assignments, a reasonable consequence is that they be separated.[74]

- **Time-out.** A **time-out** is a specified period of time in which a student has no opportunity to receive the kinds of reinforcement to which other students have access. In a mild form, it might involve asking students to put their heads down on their desks or to sit away from other students, where they must quietly watch an enjoyable activity in which classmates are participating. For more significant infractions, it might involve placing a student for a short time in a separate place that's dull and boring—perhaps a remote corner of the classroom or playground.[75] Keep in mind, however, that a time-out is apt to be effective only if ongoing classroom activities are a source of pleasure and reinforcement for a student. If, instead, a time-out allows a student to escape difficult tasks or an overwhelming amount of noise and stimulation, it might actually be reinforcing and therefore might *increase* undesirable behavior.[76]

- **In-school suspension.** Like a time-out, **in-school suspension** involves removing a student from normal classroom activities. However, it often lasts one or more school days and involves close adult supervision in a separate room within the school building. Students receiving in-school suspension spend the day working on the same assignments that their nonsuspended peers do, enabling them to keep up with their schoolwork. But they have little or no opportunity for interaction with peers—an aspect of school that's reinforcing to most students. In-school suspension programs tend to be most effective when part of the suspension session is devoted to teaching appropriate behaviors and tutoring academic skills and when the supervising teacher acts as a supportive resource rather than punisher.[77]

Several other forms of punishment are typically *not* recommended. *Physical punishment* can, of course, lead to physical harm, and even mild forms (e.g., slapping a hand with a ruler) can lead to considerable resentment of the teacher and to such undesirable behaviors as inattention to school tasks, lying, aggression, vandalism, avoidance of school tasks, and truancy.[78] Any consequence that seriously threatens a student's sense of self-worth—*psychological punishment*—can lead to some of the same side effects as physical punishment (e.g., resentment, inattention to school tasks, truancy) and may possibly inflict long-term psychological harm.[79] *Assigning extra classwork* beyond that required for other students is inappropriate if done simply to punish a student's wrongdoing, in that it communicates the message that "schoolwork is unpleasant."[80] Nor is *giving low grades* appropriate; as we'll emphasize in Chapter 10, class grades should be based on students' academic achievements, not on their classroom behavior.[81] Finally, *out-of-school suspension* is rarely an effective means of changing a student's behavior. For one thing, suspension from school may be exactly what a student wants, in which case inappropriate behaviors are being reinforced rather than punished. Furthermore, out-of-school suspension involves a loss of valuable instructional time and interferes with any psychological attachment to school, thereby reducing low-achieving students' chances for academic and social success—sometimes to the point where they have little interest in returning to school.[82]

Two additional forms of punishment get mixed reviews regarding effectiveness. In some situations, *missing recess* is a logical consequence for students who fail to complete their schoolwork during regular class time because of off-task behavior. Yet research indicates that, especially at the elementary level, students can more effectively concentrate on school tasks if they have frequent

---

[74] Dreikurs, 1998; Landrum & Kauffman, 2006; Nucci, 2001.

[75] Historically, many time-outs involved putting students in a separate, isolated room designed specifically for time-outs. This practice has largely fallen out of favor in public schools except in cases of significant behavior problems, such as physical aggression (Alberto & Troutman, 2013).

[76] J. M. Donaldson & Vollmer, 2011; McClowry, 1998; Pfiffner, Barkley, & DuPaul, 2006; Rortvedt & Miltenberger, 1994; A. G. White & Bailey, 1990.

[77] Gootman, 1998; Pfiffner et al., 2006; Sheets, 1996; J. S. Sullivan, 1989.

[78] W. Doyle, 1990; Landrum & Kauffman, 2006; Nucci, 2006.

[79] Brendgen, Wanner, Vitaro, Bukowski, & Tremblay, 2007; J. Ellis et al., 2010; Hyman et al., 2006.

[80] H. Cooper, 1989; Corno, 1996.

[81] In addition to a problem with the validity of the grades (see Chapter 10), giving low grades as punishment for misbehavior can actually *increase* students' behavior problems (F. Zimmermann, Schütte, Taskinen, & Köller, 2013).

[82] American Psychological Association Zero Tolerance Task Force, 2008; Christenson & Thurlow, 2004; Gregory, Skiba, & Noguera, 2010; Osher, Bear, Sprague, & Doyle, 2010.

CLASSROOM STRATEGIES

Using Punishment Humanely and Effectively

- **Inform students ahead of time that certain behaviors are unacceptable, and explain how those behaviors will be punished.**

  A third-grade teacher makes one rule for recess perfectly clear: *Students must not do anything that might hurt someone else.* He gives his class several concrete examples, including throwing rocks, pulling hair, and pushing someone off the playground slide. "If you do anything that might hurt another child," he says, "you'll spend the next three recesses sitting on the bench just outside the classroom door—close enough that I can see you and make sure you're safe but far away from the other kids."

- **Help students understand why the punished behavior is unacceptable.**

  When several members of a high school football team are caught spray-painting obscenities on a rival school's stadium bleachers, three consequences are imposed: (1) The students will not be able to play in the upcoming game against the rival school, (2) they must visit the rival school's principal to make a formal apology and acknowledge that their actions showed poor sportsmanship and disregard for other people's property, and (3) they must repaint the affected areas of the bleachers, purchasing the paint with their own money.

- **Emphasize that it is the behavior—*not* the student—that is undesirable.**

  When a kindergartner angrily throws her carton of milk at a classmate, her teacher puts her in the "time-out corner" at the back of the room. "I like you a lot, Bonnie," the teacher tells her, "but I simply can't have you doing something that might hurt Susan. I like her just as much as I like you, and I want both of you to feel safe in my classroom."

- **Administer punishment privately, especially when other students are not aware of the transgression.**

  As a junior high school teacher walks down the hall, she overhears a student tell two friends a "knock-knock" joke that includes an insulting racial slur, and the friends laugh, clearly thinking that it's funny. The teacher pulls the three students aside and explains that she heard the joke and found it quite offensive. "Whether you told the joke or merely laughed at it," she says, "you were all showing disrespect for certain teachers and students at this school. Not only does your disrespect undermine our overall sense of school community, but it also violates school policy. The consequence of such behavior is one day of in-school suspension. I'll notify the principal's office that you'll be reporting for in-school suspension tomorrow. Be sure to bring your textbooks and class assignments so that you won't get behind in your schoolwork."

- **Simultaneously teach and reinforce desirable alternative behaviors.**

  In small-group discussions and cooperative learning activities, a middle school student often belittles other students' ideas. Her teacher takes her aside and reprimands her but also teaches her productive strategies for disagreeing with classmates. "One strategy," he suggests, "is to say something *good* about another person's idea but then to suggest an alternative that the group might consider. For example, you might say, 'I like how carefully you've thought about the problem, Jerry. Here's a different perspective I'd like the group to think about as well. . . .'" Later, when the teacher hears the student using the strategy during a small-group project, he catches her eye and gives her a "thumbs-up" sign.

Sources: Boyanton, 2010; Landrum & Kauffman, 2006; Lerman & Vorndran, 2002; Moles, 1990; Nucci, 2001; Parke, 1974; D. G. Perry & Perry, 1983; Ruef, Higgins, Glaeser, & Patnode, 1998.

breaks and opportunities to release pent-up energy.[83] And although *after-school detentions* are common practice at many schools, some students simply can't stay after school hours, perhaps because they have transportation issues, must take care of younger siblings at home, or are justifiably afraid to walk through certain neighborhoods after dark.[84]

A frequent criticism of punishment is that it's inhumane, or somehow cruel and barbaric. Indeed, certain forms of punishment, such as physical abuse and public humiliation, do constitute inhumane treatment.[85] Furthermore, physical punishment at school is illegal in many states. Teachers must be *extremely careful* in their use of punishment in the classroom. But when administered judiciously—and especially when administered within the context of a warm, supportive teacher–student relationship—some forms of mild punishment can lead to a rapid reduction in misbehavior without causing physical or psychological harm.[86] The Classroom Strategies feature "Using Punishment Humanely and Effectively" offers several guidelines for administering punishment in ways that will yield more productive student behaviors over the long run. As you'll notice, it includes possible consequences for the milk-carton-throwing and bleachers-spray-painting scenarios presented earlier.

---

[83] Owen et al., 2016; Pellegrini & Bohn, 2005; Pellegrini, Huberty, & Jones, 1995.

[84] Nichols, Ludwin, & Iadicola, 1999.

[85] For a good discussion of this point, see Hyman et al., 2004.

[86] Landrum & Kauffman, 2006; Nucci, 2001.

Confer with parents.

By and large, teachers' communications with parents should reflect the many positive, productive things going on in their classrooms. But sometimes teachers need to talk with students' parents or other primary caregivers about a serious or chronic behavior problem. Consider these situations:

> You give your students short homework assignments almost every night. Carolyn has turned in only about one-third of them. You're pretty sure she's capable of doing the work, and you know from previous parent–teacher conferences that her parents give her the time and support she needs to get assignments done. You've spoken with Carolyn several times about the problem, but she shrugs you off as if she doesn't really care whether she does well in your class.

> Students have often found things missing from their desks or personal storage bins after Roger has been in the vicinity. A few students have told you that they've seen Roger taking things that belong to others, and many of the missing objects have later turned up in Roger's possession. When you confront him about your suspicion that he's been stealing from classmates, he adamantly denies it. He says he has no idea how Cami's gloves or Marvin's new book ended up in his desk.

Conferring with parents is especially important when students' behavior problems show a pattern over time and have serious implications for students' long-term academic or social success. In some cases, a simple phone call may be sufficient. For example, Carolyn's parents may be unaware that she hasn't been doing her homework (she's been telling them she doesn't have any) and may be able to take the steps necessary to ensure that it gets done. In other instances, a school conference may be necessary. For example, a teacher might want to discuss Roger's suspected thefts with both Roger and his parent(s) together—something the teacher can do more effectively when everyone sits face to face in the same room.

Some ways of talking with parents are far more effective than others. Put yourself in a parent's shoes in the following exercise.

——— SEE FOR YOURSELF ———
PUTTING YOURSELF IN A PARENT'S SHOES

Imagine you're the parent of a seventh grader named Tommy. As you and Tommy are eating dinner one evening, you get a phone call.

> *You:* Hello?
> *Ms. J.:* This is Ms. Johnson, Tommy's teacher. May I talk with you for a few minutes?
> *You:* Of course. What can I do for you?
> *Ms. J.:* Well, I'm afraid I've been having some trouble with your son, and I thought you should know about it.
> *You:* Really? What's the problem?
> *Ms. J.:* Tommy hardly ever gets to class on time. When he does arrive, he spends most of his time horsing around with friends instead paying attention to lessons. It seems as if I have to speak to him three or four times every day about his behavior.
> *You:* How long has all this been going on?
> *Ms. J.:* For several weeks now. And the problem's getting worse rather than better. I'd really appreciate it if you'd talk with Tommy about the situation.
> *You:* Thank you for letting me know about this, Ms. Johnson.
> *Ms. J.:* You're most welcome. Good night.
> *You:* Good night, Ms. Johnson.

Take a few minutes to jot down some of the things that, as a parent, you might be thinking after this conversation.

You may have had a variety of thoughts, possibly including these:

- Why isn't Tommy taking his schoolwork more seriously?
- Isn't Tommy doing anything *right?*
- Has Ms. Johnson tried anything besides reprimanding Tommy for his behavior? Or is she laying all of this on *my* shoulders?

- Tommy's a good kid. I should know, because I raised him. For some reason, Ms. Johnson doesn't like him and so is finding fault with anything he does.

Only the first of these four reactions is likely to lead to a productive response on your part.

Notice how Ms. Johnson focused solely on the negative aspects of Tommy's classroom performance. As a result, you (as Tommy's parent) may possibly have felt anger toward your son or guilt about your ineffective parenting skills. Alternatively, if you remained confident about your son's scholastic abilities and your own ability as a parent, you may have begun to wonder about Ms. Johnson's ability to teach and motivate seventh graders. Sadly, too many teachers reach out to parents only to talk about students' weaknesses—never their strengths—as the following interview with Jamal illustrates:

Adult: Has your grandpa [Jamal's primary caregiver] come to school?

Jamal: Yup, when the teachers call him.

Adult: What did they call him for?

Jamal: The only time they call him is when I am being bad, the teacher will call him, he will come up here and have a meeting with the teacher.

Adult: If you are being good do the teachers call?

Jamal: No.[87]

Ideally, a teacher–parent discussion about problem behaviors is initiated within the context of an ongoing relationship characterized by mutual trust and respect and a shared concern for students' learning and well-being. For instance, a phone call to parents is most likely to yield productive results if teacher and parents already have a good working relationship and if the teacher is confident that parents won't overreact with harsh, excessive punishment of their child. Furthermore, when communicating with parents, teachers' overall messages about students should be positive and optimistic. For instance, a teacher might describe undesirable aspects of a student's classroom performance within the context of the many things the student does *well*. (Rather than starting out by complaining about Tommy's behavior, Ms. Johnson might have begun by saying that Tommy is a bright, capable young man with many friends and a good sense of humor.) And teachers must be clear about their commitment to working *together* with parents to help a student succeed in the classroom. The Classroom Strategies box "Talking with Parents about Students' Misbehaviors" presents several strategies for effectively approaching parents about a challenging behavior problem.

When talking with parents, teachers must keep in mind that different cultures have different perspectives on how best to address behavior problems (see the Cultural Considerations box "Cultural Differences in Parental Discipline"). Ultimately, teachers and parents must try to find common ground on which to develop strategies for helping children and adolescents thrive at school. At the same time, teachers must tactfully and sensitively help parents understand that certain consequences—for instance, severe physical and psychological punishments—are unlikely to be productive over the long run.

To address a chronic problem, plan and carry out a systematic intervention.

Sometimes problem behaviors are so disruptive and persistent that they require a systematic effort to change them. Consider these situations:

Tucker finds many reasons to roam about the room—he "has to" sharpen a pencil, "has to" get his homework out of his backpack, "has to" get a drink of water, and so on. As a result, Tucker gets very little work done and often distracts other students with his perpetual motion.

Janet's verbal abusiveness is getting out of hand. She frequently offends both you and her peers with sexually explicit language. You've tried praising her on occasions when she's pleasant to others, and she seems to appreciate your doing so, yet her abusive remarks continue.

---

[87] Dialogue from Kumar, Gheen, & Kaplan, 2002, p. 164.

CLASSROOM STRATEGIES

Talking with Parents about Students' Misbehaviors

- **Consult with parents if a collaborative effort might bring about a behavior change.**

  At a parent–teacher–student conference, a high school math teacher expresses concern that a student often falls asleep in class. Because the student has a computer and Wi-Fi in her room, her father speculates that she's surfing the Internet when she should be in bed. He looks at his daughter inquisitively, and her guilty facial confirms his suspicion. With the teacher's prompting, the father and the student identify an appropriate policy for home computer use—one that includes moving the computer to another room, where its use can be more closely monitored.

- **Begin with a description of a student's strengths.**

  In a phone conversation with a student's mother, a teacher describes several areas in which the student has made considerable progress and then asks for advice about strategies for helping the student stay on task and be more conscientious about completing his work.

- **Describe the problem in terms of inappropriate behaviors, *not* in terms of undesirable personality characteristics.**

  When describing a student's poor record of turning in homework assignments, her teacher says, "Carolyn has turned in only about a third of the homework I've assigned this year. Her attendance record is excellent, so I know she's been healthy, and she's certainly capable of doing the work." At no point does the teacher suggest that Carolyn is lazy, unmotivated, or stubborn.

- **Don't place blame; instead, acknowledge that raising children is rarely easy.**

  When conferring with the mother of a middle school student, a teacher mentions that the student seems to be more interested in talking to her friends than in getting her schoolwork done. The mother describes a similar problem at home: "Marnie's always been a much more social girl than I ever was. It's like pulling teeth just getting her off her phone to do her homework, and then we end up having a shouting match that gets us nowhere!" The teacher sympathetically responds, "Students seem to become especially concerned about social matters once they reach adolescence. How about if you, Marnie, and I meet some day after school to talk about the problem? Perhaps by putting our heads together the three of us can find a way to solve it."

- **Ask for information, and express your desire to work together to address the problem.**

  When a teacher finds that a student has regularly been taking items from classmates' personal storage bins, she sets up an appointment to meet with the student and his grandmother (the student's primary caregiver). "I like Roger a lot," the teacher says. "He has a great sense of humor, and his smile often lights up my day. I can't understand why he might want to 'borrow' items from other children without asking first. His actions have cost him several friendships. Do either of you have any ideas about how we might tackle the problem? I'd like to do whatever I can to help Roger repair his reputation with his classmates."

- **Agree on a strategy.**

  While reviewing a student's academic progress at a parent–teacher conference, an elementary teacher says, "Mark has a tendency to fiddle with things at his desk—he especially likes meticulously folding pieces of paper into little origami figures—when he should be getting his work done. As a result, he often doesn't complete his assignments." The student's father replies, "I've noticed the same thing when he works on his homework, but I bring a lot of paperwork home from the office every night and don't have time to constantly hound him to stay on task." The teacher and father talk more about the problem and agree that reinforcement for completed assignments might be helpful. Mark will earn points for high scores that will help him "buy" the new bicycle he's been asking his father for.

Sources: Christenson & Sheridan, 2001; C. Davis & Yang, 2005; Emmer & Evertson, 2009; Evertson & Emmer, 2009; A. Miller, 2006; Woolfolk Hoy, Davis, & Pape, 2006.

Imagine that both Tucker and Janet are in your class. You've already spoken with each of them about their unacceptable behavior, yet you've seen no improvement. You've suggested self-regulation techniques, but neither student seems interested in changing for the better. You've tried putting them in time-out for their actions, but Janet seems to enjoy the time away from her schoolwork, and Tucker sometimes has a valid reason for getting out of his seat. Although both students' parents are aware of and concerned about their children's classroom behaviors, their efforts at home haven't had an impact. And after all, these are largely *school* problems rather than home problems. So what do you do now?

When a serious misbehavior persists despite ongoing efforts to curtail it, a more intensive intervention is in order. Some interventions, known by such labels as **applied behavior analysis (ABA)**, *behavior therapy,* and *contingency management,* focus on changing stimulus conditions and response–consequence contingencies in a student's environment.[88] These approaches are based largely on certain principles presented in Chapter 4:

- Some stimuli tend to elicit certain kinds of behaviors.
- Learners are more likely to acquire behaviors that lead to desired consequences.
- Learners tend to steer clear of behaviors that lead to unpleasant consequences.

---

[88] For examples of such strategies, see Alberto & Troutman, 2013; Bradshaw, Zmuda, Kellam, & Ialongo, 2009; Ormrod, 2016.

CULTURAL CONSIDERATIONS

Cultural Differences in Parental Discipline

The vast majority of parents want what's best for their children and recognize the value of a good education for children's long-term success.[a] Yet parents from different cultural and ethnic groups sometimes have radically different ideas about which kinds of behaviors are problematic and require discipline. As an example, let's return to the opening case study in Chapter 4, which depicts a small slice of Navajo culture in the southwestern United States. Jack, a seventh grader, had been absent from school for an entire week. Not only were his parents seemingly unconcerned, but they didn't even go looking for him until they needed him at home to help with the family farm. Their attitudes and actions make sense only when we understand that they knew their son was probably safe with neighbors and believed that, as an adolescent, Jack was essentially an adult and responsible for his own decisions.[b] In contrast, many parents from Asian cultures expect children to immediately defer to and obey adult authority figures (e.g., parents

and teachers) and think that Western teachers are much too lenient with students.[c]

Disciplinary strategies also differ from culture to culture. In mainstream Western culture, praise is widely used as a strategy for encouraging good behavior, and reprimands and denial of privileges (e.g., "grounding") are often the consequences for unacceptable behavior. But such practices are hardly universal. Children in some cultures may be unaccustomed to direct praise for appropriate behavior and personal successes, perhaps because appropriate behavior is a social obligation (and thus not praiseworthy) or perhaps because adults express approval in other ways—for instance, by telling other people how skillful a child is.[d] And some cultural and religious groups use ostracism in an effort to keep children in line: If a child's misbehaviors are seen as bringing shame on the family or community, the child is ignored—for instance, given the "silent treatment"—for an extended time period.[e]

It's important to note that some cultural groups believe physical punishment to be

necessary for behavioral transgressions. When physical punishment is a common form of discipline in one's culture, children are more likely to accept *mild* physical punishment as appropriate and deserved. Even in such contexts, however, physical punishment is apt to have adverse effects on children's psychological well-being.[f] Accordingly, teachers should tactfully dissuade parents from using it, ideally by suggesting alternative consequences that can effectively reduce problem behaviors without causing harm.

[a]Dantas & Manyak, 2010; Gallimore & Goldenberg, 2001; Spera, 2005.
[b]Deyhle & LeCompte, 1999.
[c]Dien, 1998; Hidalgo, Siu, Bright, Swap, & Epstein, 1995; Kağitçibaşi, 2007; Tamis-Lemonda & McFadden, 2010.
[d]Greenfield et al., 2006; Kitayama, Duffy, & Uchida, 2007; Rogoff, 2003.
[e]Pang, 1995; K. D. Williams, 2001.
[f]Bornstein & Lansford, 2010; Lansford et al., 2005; Lansford, Deater-Decker, & Dodge, Bates, & Pettit, 2003.

With these principles in mind, effective teachers change the classroom environment to elicit more productive behaviors and establish more beneficial response–consequence contingencies. Thus they use strategies such as the following:

- Identify problem behaviors and desired behaviors in explicit (and ideally measurable) terms. Often the desired behaviors chosen are incompatible with problem behaviors—that is, it's impossible for a student to execute both kinds of behaviors at the same time.
- Identify reinforcers, punishments, or both that are truly effective for the student.
- Develop a specific intervention plan, which may involve reinforcement of desired behaviors, shaping, extinction, punishment, or some combination of these.
- Modify the classroom environment to minimize conditions that might elicit inappropriate behaviors.
- Collect data on the frequency of problem behaviors and desired behaviors both before and during the intervention.
- Monitor the program's effectiveness by observing how various behaviors change over time, and modify the program if necessary.
- Take steps to promote transfer of newly acquired behaviors (e.g., by having the student practice the behaviors in various realistic situations).
- Gradually phase out the intervention (e.g., through intermittent reinforcement) after desired behaviors are occurring regularly.

Often the strategies just listed are more effective when cognitive and motivational factors affecting students' behavior are also addressed—an approach known as *cognitive-behavioral therapy*. For example, teachers might also use one or more of the following strategies:

- Teach self-regulation skills.
- Teach effective social skills.

- Encourage better perspective taking and other aspects of social cognition.
- Make changes in the curriculum, instructional methods, or both to maximize the likelihood of academic success and high self-efficacy for school tasks.

How might a teacher use some of the preceding strategies to improve Tucker's classroom behavior? One approach would be to identify one or more effective reinforcers—given Tucker's constant fidgeting, opportunities for physical activity might be reinforcing—and then gradually shape more sedentary behavior. In addition, because some out-of-seat behaviors are quite appropriate (e.g., getting a reference book from the bookshelf, delivering a completed assignment to the teacher's "In" basket), the teacher might give Tucker a reasonable allotment of out-of-seat "tickets" he can use during the day. Tucker can probably also benefit from instruction and scaffolding regarding general organizational skills—in particular, assembling necessary supplies (notebooks, sharpened pencils, completed homework, etc.) before lessons begin.

A systematic intervention may be helpful with Janet as well. In this case, we might suspect that Janet lacks the social skills she needs to interact effectively with others. Her teacher or a school counselor might therefore need to begin by teaching her such skills through modeling, role-playing, and the like (see Chapter 7). Once Janet has gained some competence in interpersonal skills, her teacher can begin to reinforce her for using those skills. (Praise might be an effective reinforcer because she has responded positively to praise in the past.) Meanwhile, the teacher should also punish any relapses into old, abusive behavior patterns. (Time-outs haven't previously worked with Janet, but perhaps having her write apology notes to offended parties—a logical consequence—would help to drive home the message that some of her language is inappropriate.)

Determine whether certain undesirable behaviors might serve particular purposes for students.

Sometimes a student's misbehaviors, although maladaptive from a teacher's perspective, in one way or another help the student preserve a sense of well-being. Consider this example:

> Nine-year-old Samantha has been identified as having a mild form of autism and moderate speech disabilities. She frequently runs out of her third-grade classroom, damaging school property and classmates' belongings in her flight. When an adult tries to intervene, she fights back by biting, hitting, kicking, or pulling hair. On such occasions school personnel often ask her parents to take her home.
>
> By systematically collecting data on Samantha's classroom performance, a team of teachers and specialists discover that her misbehaviors typically occur when she either has been given or is expecting a difficult assignment. Departures from the regular schedule or the absence of favorite teachers further increase the frequency of misbehaviors.
>
> The team hypothesizes that Samantha's undesirable behaviors serve two purposes: They (1) help her escape unpleasant academic tasks and (2) enable her to gain the attention of valued adults. The team suspects, too, that Samantha feels as if she had little or no control over classroom activities and that she yearns for more social interaction with others.[89]

In trying to determine why Samantha misbehaves as she does, the team is taking an approach known as **functional analysis** (you may also see the term *functional behavior assessment*). Functional analysis identifies the specific stimulus conditions that exist both before and after Samantha makes inappropriate responses—the antecedents and consequences of particular behaviors—like so:

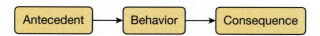

Antecedent → Behavior → Consequence

The team soon realizes that Samantha's behaviors are the result of *both* antecedent events (e.g., challenging tasks, changes in routine) and desirable consequences (e.g., getting attention, going home). In other words, Samantha's behaviors are serving certain *functions* for her: They get her attention from others (positive reinforcement) and enable her to escape things she doesn't want to

---

[89] DeVault, Krug, & Fake, 1996.

MyEdLab
Video Explanation 9.1.

This 19-minute video provides animated explanations of both ABA and functional analysis; it also provides concrete examples of how teachers might use these strategies in working with students who have chronic behavior problems.

MyEdLab
Video Example 9.7.

Notice how one girl in this video voluntarily removes herself from a small-group activity until "she's ready to come back," just as Samantha does when she goes to the relaxation room. In what ways does the teacher in the video encourage and support this self-regulation strategy?

do and places she doesn't want to be (escaping unpleasant things serves as negative reinforcement). Like Samantha, students with chronic behavior problems often misbehave when they're asked to do difficult or unpleasant tasks and when their misbehavior either helps them avoid these tasks or gains them the attention of others.[90]

Once a functional analysis has been completed, an approach known as **positive behavioral interventions and supports (PBIS)**[91] takes the process a step further. In particular, PBIS builds on knowledge about the functions of misbehaviors in order to encourage more productive behaviors. Following are typical strategies:[92]

- Teach behaviors that can serve the same purpose as—and can therefore replace—inappropriate behaviors.
- Modify the school environment to minimize conditions that might trigger inappropriate behaviors.
- Establish a predictable daily routine as a way of minimizing anxiety and making the student feel more comfortable and secure.
- Give the student opportunities to make choices; in this way, the student can often gain desired outcomes without having to resort to inappropriate behavior.
- Make changes in the curriculum, instruction, or both to maximize the likelihood of academic success (e.g., build on student interests, present material at a slower pace, or intersperse challenging tasks among easier and more enjoyable ones).
- Monitor the frequency of various behaviors to determine whether the intervention is working or, instead, requires modification.

For instance, after school faculty members have formed reasonable hypotheses regarding the roots of Samantha's inappropriate behaviors, they take several steps to help her acquire more productive ones:[93]

- Samantha is given a consistent and predictable daily schedule that includes frequent breaks from potentially challenging academic tasks and numerous opportunities to interact with others.
- Samantha is given "goal sheets" from which she can choose the academic tasks she'll work on, the length of time she'll work on them, and a reinforcer she'll receive for achieving each goal.
- Samantha is taught how to ask for help on challenging tasks.
- When Samantha feels she needs a break, she can ask to spend time in the "relaxation room," a quiet, private space where she can sit in a beanbag chair and listen to soothing audiotapes.
- If Samantha tries to leave the classroom, an adult immediately places her in the relaxation room, where she can calm down without a lot of adult attention.
- Samantha is given explicit instruction in how to interact appropriately with classmates. Initially, she earns points for appropriate social behaviors and can trade them for special treats (e.g., a family trip to Dairy Queen). Eventually, her new social skills lead to natural consequences—friendly interactions with peers—that make extrinsic reinforcers unnecessary.

Samantha's teachers and parents communicate regularly to coordinate their efforts. Her problem behaviors don't disappear overnight, but they show a dramatic decline over the next several months. By the time Samantha is 12 years old and in sixth grade, her grades consistently earn her a place on the honor roll, and she has a group of friends with whom she participates in several extracurricular activities.[94]

Let's return once again to Ms. Cornell's difficulties with Eli, Jake, and Vanessa in the opening case study. Here, too, a planned, systematic intervention, possibly including functional analysis and

[90] Greer et al., 2013; Mueller, Nkosi, & Hine, 2011; S. W. Payne & Dozier, 2013; Van Camp et al., 2000.

[91] Historically, this approach has been known as *positive behavior support* (PBS), but educators are increasingly using the term *positive behavioral interventions and supports* (PBIS), in part to avoid confusion with another "PBS"—the television network Public Broadcasting Service.

[92] For example, see Crone, Hawken, & Horner, 2015; Ruef, Higgins, Glaeser, & Patnode, 1998; Scheuermann & Hall, 2016; Wheeler & Richey, 2014. You can find additional suggestions at www.pbis.org, a website created and maintained by the U.S. Department of Education's Office of Special Education Programs (OSEP).

[93] DeVault et al., 1996.

[94] DeVault et al., 1996.

PBIS, might be in order. Reinforcing appropriate behaviors (if necessary, shaping such behaviors over a period of time) and punishing inappropriate behaviors are two obvious strategies. Furthermore, Ms. Cornell should make response–consequence contingencies clear, perhaps using contingency contracts (see Chapter 4). Ms. Cornell might also determine the purpose(s) that the students' misbehaviors serve (e.g., perhaps the three students crave attention, or perhaps they misbehave to avoid doing assignments for which they don't have adequate reading skills) and then either (1) identify more productive behaviors that can serve the same purpose(s) or (2) address academic or social problems that may be directly or indirectly contributing to the students' unproductive behaviors.

Table 9.2 summarizes the general approaches to addressing student misbehaviors described in the last few pages, and teachers are apt to use all of them at one time or another. Occasionally, however, chronic behavior problems involve not just a handful of students but an entire *school,* or at least a large subpopulation of a school's students (recall the opening case study "The School

Table 9.2 • Strategies for Addressing Undesirable Classroom Behaviors

STRATEGY	SITUATIONS IN WHICH IT'S APPROPRIATE	EXAMPLES
Ignoring the behavior	• The misbehavior is unlikely to be repeated. • The misbehavior is unlikely to spread to other students. • Unusual circumstances have only temporarily elicited the misbehavior. • The misbehavior doesn't seriously interfere with learning.	• One student discreetly passes a note to another student just before the end of class. • A student accidentally drops her books, startling other students and temporarily distracting them from their work. • An entire class is hyperactive on the last afternoon before spring break.
Cueing the student	• The misbehavior is a minor infraction but definitely interferes with students' learning. • The behavior is likely to improve with a subtle reminder.	• A student forgets to close his notebook at the beginning of a quiz. • Members of a cooperative learning group are talking so loudly that they distract other groups. • Several students are exchanging jokes during an independent seatwork assignment.
Discussing the problem privately with the student	• Cueing has been ineffective in changing the behavior. • The reasons for the misbehavior, if made clear, might suggest possible strategies for addressing it.	• A student is frequently late to class. • A student refuses to do certain kinds of assignments. • A student shows a sudden drop in motivation for no apparent reason.
Promoting self-regulation	• The student has a strong desire to improve his or her behavior.	• A student doesn't realize how frequently she interrupts her classmates. • A student seeks help in learning to control his anger. • A student acknowledges that her inability to stay on task is preventing her from earning the good grades she wants to get.
Punishment	• A behavior significantly interferes with classroom learning or reflects a blatant disregard for others' rights and welfare. • The student has little or no understanding or concern that the behavior is unacceptable.	• A student punches a classmate who inadvertently brushes past him. • A student tells a joke that insults people of a particular ethnic group. • A student vandalizes other students' lockers.
Conferring with parents	• A chronic behavior problem is likely to interfere with the student's long-term academic or social success. • The source of the problem may possibly lie outside school walls. • Parents are likely to work collaboratively with school faculty members to bring about a behavior change.	• A student does well in class but rarely turns in required homework assignments. • A student falls asleep in class almost every day. • A student is caught stealing classmates' lunches.
Conducting a planned, systematic intervention (e.g., applied behavior analysis, positive behavioral interventions and supports)	• The misbehavior has continued over a period of time and significantly interferes with one or more students' learning and achievement. • Other, less intensive approaches (e.g., cueing, private conferences, mild punishment) have been ineffective. • The student seems unwilling or unable to use self-regulation techniques. • The misbehavior may in some way enable a student to achieve desired outcomes.	• A student has unusual difficulty sitting still for age-appropriate time periods. • A member of the soccer team displays bursts of anger and aggression that are potentially dangerous to other players. • A student engages in disruptive behavior every time a difficult task is assigned.

Play" in Chapter 7). Perhaps most troubling is the prevalence of aggression and violence at some schools. Teachers play a key role in addressing widespread aggression and violence. In the final section of the chapter, we look at some strategies for doing so.

Even under the best of circumstances, teachers must occasionally deal with student misbehaviors. In the hotlinked Self-Check quiz and Application Exercises that follow, you can check and apply your understandings related to Big Idea 9.3:

> *Effective interventions for reducing unproductive school behaviors are tailored to the circumstances, with students' long-term development and well-being as the ultimate goals.*

MyEdLab **Self-Check 9.3**

MyEdLab **Application Exercise 9.4.** In this exercise, you can identify potentially effective strategies that teachers might use to address a variety of problem behaviors.

MyEdLab **Application Exercise 9.5.** In this exercise, you can observe and analyze one teacher's approach to dealing with a student conflict in his middle school classroom.

9.4 ADDRESSING AGGRESSION AND VIOLENCE AT SCHOOL

Big Idea 9.4 Minimizing aggression and violence at school requires a three-tiered approach: (1) creating a respectful and supportive school environment, (2) intervening early for students at risk for social failure, and (3) providing intensive interventions for chronically aggressive students.

In recent years the news media have focused considerable attention on violent school crime, and especially on school shootings, leading many people to believe that aggression in schools is on the rise. In reality, violent aggression involving serious injury or death is relatively rare on school grounds and, in the United States at least, has been *declining* rather than increasing. Most aggression at school involves minor physical injury, psychological harm (e.g., sexual or racial harassment), or destruction of property (e.g., vandalization of student lockers).[95]

If we consider *only* violent aggression that causes serious injury or death, then school is probably the safest place that young people can be.[96] But if we consider *all* forms of aggression—mild as well as severe, and psychological aggression as well as physical aggression—then aggression among children and adolescents occurs more frequently at school than in any other location, probably for two reasons. First, children and adolescents spend a great deal of time at school, more so than in any other place except home. Second, the sheer number of students attending even the smallest of schools makes some interpersonal conflict almost inevitable.

The roots of school aggression and violence are many and diverse. As we discovered in Chapter 7, a variety of cognitive factors (e.g., lack of perspective-taking, poor social problem-solving skills) predispose some students to aggressive behavior. Furthermore, some school- or neighborhood-specific cultures endorse the belief that defending one's reputation in the face of personal insults or indignities is a matter of "honor" that calls for aggressive action.[97] Developmental factors come into play as well. For example, many young children and a few adolescents have poor impulse control, and in early adolescence, the unsettling transition to middle school can lead some students to bully weaker age-mates as a way of gaining social status with peers.[98] Finally, aggression is a common reaction to frustration, and some students are repeatedly frustrated in their efforts to be academically and socially successful at school.[99]

---

[95] Borum, Cornell, Modzeleski, & Jimerson, 2010; Kupchik & Bracy, 2009; M. J. Mayer & Furlong, 2010; Robers, Zhang, Morgan, & Musu-Gillette, 2015.

[96] Robers et al., 2015.

[97] R. P. Brown, Osterman, & Barnes, 2009; K. M. Williams, 2001a.

[98] Bradshaw, 2015; Bronson, 2000; Espelage, Holt, & Henkel, 2003; Pellegrini, 2002.

[99] Bender, 2001; Casella, 2001b; Miles & Stipek, 2006.

Regardless of the roots of the behavior, educators must not tolerate *any* form of aggression or violence on school grounds. Students can learn and achieve at optimal levels only if they know that they're both physically and psychologically safe at school. Furthermore, if they *don't* feel safe, they're at increased risk for dropping out before high school graduation.[100] To be truly effective in combating aggression and violence, teachers and other school faculty members must attack these challenges on three levels, or *tiers,* depicted graphically in Figure 9.6.[101] The first three of the following four recommendations reflect these three tiers; the final one specifically addresses aggression that can result from hostilities among rival gangs on school grounds.

Make the creation of a nonviolent school environment a long-term effort.

One-shot "antiviolence" campaigns have little lasting effect on school aggression and violence. Instead, the key seems to be establishing and maintaining an overall **school climate** in which students feel physically and psychologically safe and are jointly committed to accomplishing important academic and personal goals. Creating a peaceful and productive school environment must be a long-term effort that includes many strategies:[102]

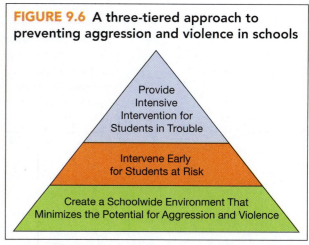

FIGURE 9.6 A three-tiered approach to preventing aggression and violence in schools

Provide Intensive Intervention for Students in Trouble

Intervene Early for Students at Risk

Create a Schoolwide Environment That Minimizes the Potential for Aggression and Violence

Based on a figure in *Safeguarding Our Children: An Action Guide* (p. 3), by K. Dwyer and D. Osher, 2000, Washington, DC: U.S. Departments of Education and Justice, American Institutes for Research.

- Make a schoolwide commitment to supporting *all* students' academic and social success.
- Provide a challenging and engaging curriculum.
- Form caring, trusting faculty–student relationships.
- Insist on genuine and equal respect—among students and faculty alike—for people of diverse backgrounds, races, and ethnic groups.
- Help students understand that other people's behaviors are *not* the result of enduring personality traits (e.g., general "meanness") but, instead, the result of certain beliefs and feelings that can change for the better.[103]
- Emphasize prosocial behaviors (e.g., sharing, helping, cooperating).
- Establish schoolwide policies and practices that foster appropriate behavior (e.g., give clear guidelines for behavior, consistently apply consequences for infractions, provide instruction in effective social interaction and problem-solving skills).
- Teach specific skills that students can use to intervene when they witness bullying.
- Provide mechanisms through which students can communicate their concerns about aggression and victimization openly and without fear of reprisal.
- Involve students in school decision making.
- Establish close working relationships with community agencies and families.
- Openly discuss safety issues.

Most of these strategies should look familiar, because they've surfaced at various places throughout this book. The final strategy on the list—openly discuss safety issues—encompasses a number of more specific strategies. For example, teachers should explain what bullying is and why it's unacceptable (see Chapter 7). Faculty members might also solicit students' input on potentially unsafe areas (perhaps an infrequently used restroom or back stairwell) that require more adult

---

[100] Filax, 2007; Rumberger, 2011.

[101] Dwyer & Osher, 2000; Hyman et al., 2006; Ihlo & Nantais, 2010; Osher et al., 2010; H. M. Walker et al., 1996. For a classic discussion of the three tiers, we urge you to read *Safeguarding Our Children: An Action Guide* by K. Dwyer and D. Osher (2000). You can download a copy from a variety of Internet websites, including www.ed.gov.

[102] Bradshaw, 2015; Burstyn & Stevens, 2001; Dwyer & Osher, 2000; L. M. Jones, Mitchell, & Turner, 2015; Learning First Alliance, 2001; Meehan, Hughes, & Cavell, 2003; G. M. Morrison, Furlong, D'Incau, & Morrison, 2004; Osher, Dwyer, & Jimerson, 2006; Pellegrini, 2002; S. W. Ross & Horner, 2009; Syvertsen, Flanagan, & Stout, 2009; Thapa, Cohen, Guffey, & Higgins-D'Alessandro, 2013; Warren et al., 2006; Yeager & Dweck, 2012.

[103] For an effective way of doing this (one in which students are taught about the malleability of the human brain), see Yeager & Dweck, 2012.

supervision. And a willingness to listen to students' concerns about troublesome and potentially dangerous classmates can provide important clues about which children and adolescents are most in need of assistance and intervention.

In recent years, many schools have successfully instituted **schoolwide positive behavioral interventions and supports (SWPBIS)** programs that encompass some of the same components previously described for applied behavior analysis and positive behavioral interventions and supports. These programs typically implement most or all of the following strategies for *all* students:

- Explicitly defining and teaching appropriate behaviors, including productive ways of getting desired outcomes (e.g., teacher attention)
- Designing a curriculum and implementing instructional practices tailored to students' current needs and ability levels
- Giving students opportunities to make choices
- Regularly reinforcing students for behaving appropriately, almost always with praise but often also with token reinforcers that can be traded for special prizes and privileges
- Providing considerable guidance and support (sometimes including individualized interventions) for students who need them
- Continually monitoring the program's effectiveness by examining office referrals, disciplinary actions, and other relevant data

Such steps often lead to dramatic changes in students' behavior and are especially helpful in schools that have historically had many discipline problems. Furthermore, teachers gain optimism that they can truly make a difference in improving students' classroom behavior and academic achievement.[104]

Intervene early for students at risk.

Perhaps 10 to 15% of students need some sort of intervention to help them interact effectively with peers, establish good working relationships with teachers, and become bona fide members of the school community.[105] Such intervention can't be a one-size-fits-all approach but must instead be tailored to students' particular strengths and needs. For some students, it might involve instruction in effective social skills. For other students, it might mean getting them actively involved in school clubs or extracurricular activities. For still others, it may require a well-planned, systematic effort to encourage and reinforce productive behaviors, perhaps through functional analysis and PBIS. But regardless of their nature, interventions are most effective when they occur *early* in the game—before students go too far down the path of antisocial behavior—and when they're developed and implemented by a multidisciplinary team of teachers and other professionals who bring various areas of expertise to the planning table.[106]

Provide intensive intervention for students in trouble.

For a variety of reasons, minor interventions aren't sufficient for a small percentage of students who are predisposed to be aggressive and violent. For example, some students have serious mental illnesses that interfere with their ability to think rationally, cope appropriately with everyday frustrations, and control impulses. Typically schools must work closely and collaboratively with other community agencies—perhaps mental health clinics, police and probation departments, and social services—to help students at high risk for aggression and violence.[107] Teachers are a vital component of this collaborative effort, offering insights about students' strengths and limitations, communicating with students' families about available services, and working with specialists to develop appropriate intervention strategies.

---

[104] Bradshaw, Mitchell, & Leaf, 2010; Ihlo & Nantais, 2010; T. J. Lewis et al., 2006; Osher et al., 2010; Warren et al., 2006.

[105] Ihlo & Nantais, 2010; K. L. Lane et al., 2011; Osher et al., 2006.

[106] Crone, Horner, & Hawken, 2004; Dwyer & Osher, 2000; Osher et al., 2010.

[107] Greenberg et al., 2003; Hyman et al., 2006; Rappaport, Osher, Garrison, Anderson-Ketchmark, & Dwyer, 2003.

FIGURE 9.7 Early warning signs of possible violent behavior

Experts have identified numerous warning signs that a student may possibly be contemplating violent actions against others. Any one of them alone is unlikely to signal a violent attack, but several of them *in combination* should lead a teacher to consult with school administrators and specially trained professionals about the student(s) of concern.

Social withdrawal. Over time, a student interacts less and less frequently with teachers and with all or most peers.

Excessive feelings of isolation, rejection, or persecution. A student may directly or indirectly express the belief that he or she is friendless, disliked, or unfairly picked on; such feelings are sometimes the result of long-term physical or psychological bullying by peers.

Rapid decline in academic performance. A student shows a dramatic change in academic performance and seems unconcerned about doing well. Cognitive and physical factors (e.g., learning disabilities, ineffective study skills, brain injury) have been ruled out as causes of the decline.

Poor coping skills. A student has little ability to deal effectively with frustration, takes the smallest affront personally, and has trouble bouncing back after minor disappointments.

Lack of anger control. A student frequently responds with uncontrolled anger to even the slightest injustice and may misdirect anger at innocent bystanders.

Apparent sense of superiority, self-centeredness, and lack of empathy. A student depicts himself or herself as smarter or in some other way better than peers, is preoccupied with his or her own needs, and has little regard for the needs of others. Underlying such characteristics may be low-esteem and depression.

Lengthy grudges. A student is unforgiving of others' transgressions, even after considerable time has elapsed.

Violent themes in drawings and written work. Violence predominates in a student's artwork, stories, or journal entries, and perhaps certain individuals (e.g., particular adults or peers) are regularly targeted in these fantasies. (Keep in mind that *occasional* violence in writing and art isn't unusual, especially for boys.)

Intolerance of individual and group differences. A student shows intense disdain and prejudice toward people of a certain race, ethnicity, gender, sexual orientation, religion, or disability.

History of violence, aggression, and other discipline problems. A student has a long record of seriously inappropriate behavior extending over several years.

Association with violent peers. A student associates regularly with a gang or other antisocial peer group.

Inappropriate role models. A student may speak with admiration about Satan, Adolf Hitler, Osama bin Laden, or some other malevolent figure.

Excessive alcohol or drug use. A student who abuses alcohol or drugs may have reduced self-control. In some cases, substance abuse signals significant mental illness.

Inappropriate access to firearms. A student has easy access to guns and ammunition and may regularly practice using them.

Threats of violence. A student has openly expressed an intent to harm someone else, perhaps in explicit terms or perhaps through ambiguous references to "something spectacular" happening at school on a particular day. *This warning sign alone requires immediate action.*

Sources: Dwyer, Osher, & Warger, 1998; O'Toole, 2000; U.S. Secret Service National Threat Assessment Center, 2000; M. W. Watson, Andreas, Fischer, & Smith, 2005.

Teachers' frequent interactions with students also put them in an ideal position to identify those children and adolescents most in need of intensive intervention to get them back on track for academic and social success. Especially after working with a particular age-group for a period of time, teachers acquire a good sense of what characteristics are and aren't normal for that age level. Teachers should also be on the lookout for the early warning signs of violence presented in Figure 9.7.

Although teachers must be ever vigilant for signals that a student might be planning to cause harm to others, it's essential to keep several points in mind. First, as mentioned earlier, extreme violence is *very rare* in schools. Unreasonable paranoia about potential school violence will prevent teachers from working effectively with students. Second, the great majority of students who exhibit one or a few of the warning signs listed in Figure 9.7 *won't* become violent.[108] And most importantly, teachers must *never* use the warning signs as a reason to unfairly accuse, isolate, or punish a student.[109] These signs provide a means of getting students the help they may need, not of excluding them from the education that all children and adolescents deserve.

Take additional measures to address gang violence.

A frequent source of aggression at some schools is gang-related hostilities. Although gangs are more prevalent in low-income, inner-city schools, they're sometimes found in suburban and rural schools as well. On an optimistic note, gang activity in schools has been *decreasing* in the last few years, at least in the United States.[110]

---

[108] U.S. Secret Service National Threat Assessment Center, 2000.
[109] Dwyer, Osher, & Warger, 1998.
[110] Howell & Lynch, 2000; Kodluboy, 2004; Robers et al., 2015.

The three-tiered approach to combating school aggression and violence just described can go a long way toward suppressing violent gang activities, but school faculty members often need to take additional measures as well. Recommended strategies include the following:[111]

- Identify the specific nature and scope of gang activity in the student population.
- Develop, communicate, and enforce clear-cut policies regarding potential threats to other students' safety.
- Forbid clothing, jewelry, and behaviors that signify membership in a particular gang (e.g., bandanas, shoelaces in gang colors, certain hand signs).[112]
- Actively mediate between-gang and within-gang disputes.

A case study at one middle school[113] illustrates just how effective the last of these strategies—mediation—can sometimes be in addressing gang-related aggression. Many students belonged to one of several gangs that seemed to "rule the school." Fights among rival gangs were common, and nongang members were frequent victims of harassment. Dress codes, counseling, and suspensions of chronic troublemakers had little impact on students' behavior. In desperation, two school counselors suggested that the school implement a mediation program, beginning with three large gangs that were responsible for most of the trouble. Interpersonal problems involving two or more gangs would be brought to a mediation team comprised of five school faculty members and three representatives from each of the three gangs. Team members had to abide by the following rules:

1. Really try to solve the problem.
2. No name-calling or put-downs.
3. No interrupting.
4. Be as honest as possible.
5. No weapons or acts of intimidation.
6. All sessions to be confidential until an agreement is reached or mediation is called off.[114]

To lay the groundwork for productive discussions, faculty members of the mediation team met separately with each of the three gangs to establish feelings of rapport and trust, explain how the mediation process would work, and gain students' cooperation with the plan.

In the first mediation session, common grievances were aired. Students agreed that they didn't like being insulted or intimated, that they worried about their physical safety, and that they all wanted one another's respect. In several additional meetings during the next two weeks, the team reached an agreement that a number of behaviors would be unacceptable at school: There would be no put-downs, name calling, hateful stares, threats, shoving, or gang graffiti. After the final meeting, each gang was separately called into the conference room. Its representatives on the mediation team explained the agreement, and other members of the gang were asked to sign it. Despite some skepticism, most members of all three gangs signed it.

A month later, it was clear that the process had been successful. Members of rival gangs nodded pleasantly to one another or gave one another a high-five sign as they passed in the hall. Gang members no longer felt compelled to hang out in groups for safety's sake. Members of two of the gangs were seen playing soccer together one afternoon. And there had been no gang-related fights all month.

As should be apparent from our discussion in this chapter, helping growing children and adolescents develop into successful, productive adults can occasionally be quite a challenge. Yet discovering that you actually *can* make a difference in students' lives—including the lives of some who are at risk for academic or social failure—is perhaps the most rewarding aspect of being a teacher.

---

[111] Kodluboy, 2004.

[112] A potential problem with this strategy is that it may violate students' civil liberties. For guidance on how to walk the line between ensuring students' safety and giving them reasonable freedom of expression, see Kodluboy, 2004; Rozalski & Yell, 2004.

[113] Sanchez & Anderson, 1990.

[114] Sanchez & Anderson, 1990, p. 54.

All school faculty members play key roles in creating an overall school climate in which students feel physically and psychologically safe. In the hotlinked Self-Check quiz and Application Exercise that follow, you can check and apply your understandings related to Big Idea 9.4:

> *Minimizing aggression and violence at school requires a three-tiered approach: (1) creating a respectful and supportive school environment, (2) intervening early for students at risk of social failure, and (3) providing intensive interventions for chronically aggressive students.*

MyEdLab **Self-Check 9.4**

MyEdLab **Application Exercise 9.6.** In this exercise, you can observe and analyze elements of a SWPBIS program in action.

9 SUMMARY

Effective classroom management involves both prevention and intervention, as reflected in the four Big Ideas presented at the beginning of the chapter.

■ **9.1: Effective teachers create a caring, respectful classroom environment in which students are consistently focused on accomplishing instructional goals and objectives.** Good teachers create a setting in which students are regularly engaged in planned tasks and activities and in which few student behaviors interfere with those tasks and activities. The physical arrangement of the classroom makes a difference, but more important is a psychological environment *(classroom climate)* in which students feel safe and secure, make learning a high priority, and are willing to take risks and make mistakes. Central to such a climate are (1) teacher–student relationships that communicate genuine caring and concern for every student and (2) an overall sense of community in the classroom—a sense that teachers and students have shared goals, are mutually respectful and supportive of one another's efforts, and believe that everyone makes an important contribution to classroom learning. At the same time, teachers must take charge to some extent, establishing rules and planning age-appropriate activities to ensure that students are continually working toward instructional goals and objectives.

■ **9.2: Teachers are most effective when they coordinate their efforts with colleagues, outside agencies, and parents.** Effective teachers work cooperatively with other faculty members, other institutions, and families to promote students' learning, development, and achievement. It's especially important that teachers stay in regular contact with parents and other primary caregivers, sharing information in both directions about the progress that students are making and coordinating efforts at school with those at home. Teachers may need to make an extra effort to establish productive working relationships with those parents who, on the surface, seem reluctant to become involved in their children's education.

■ **9.3: Effective interventions for reducing unproductive school behaviors are tailored to the circumstances, with students' long-term development and well-being as the**

ultimate goals. Despite teachers' best efforts, children and adolescents sometimes engage in behaviors that disrupt classroom learning, put one or more students' physical safety or psychological well-being in jeopardy, or violate basic moral and ethical standards. Some minor misbehaviors are usually best ignored, including those that probably won't be repeated, those that are unlikely to be imitated by other students, and those that occur only temporarily within the context of unusual circumstances. Other minor infractions can be dealt with simply and quickly by cueing students or by talking with them privately about their counterproductive behaviors. More serious and chronic behavior problems may require instruction in self-regulation strategies, punishment, consultation with parents, or intensive interventions that systematically combine a variety of strategies.

■ **9.4: Minimizing aggression and violence at school requires a three-tiered approach: (1) creating a respectful and supportive school environment, (2) intervening early for students at risk for social failure, and (3) providing intensive interventions for chronically aggressive students.** When certain students' behaviors seriously threaten others' sense of safety and well-being, and especially when aggression and violence are prevalent throughout the school building, a three-level approach may be necessary. First, faculty members must coordinate their efforts in creating a schoolwide environment that makes aggression and violence unlikely—for example, by establishing trusting teacher–student relationships, fostering a sense of mutual respect and understanding among students from diverse backgrounds, and providing mechanisms through which students can communicate their concerns without fear of reprisal. Second, faculty members must intervene early for students who are at risk for academic or social failure, providing them with the cognitive and social skills they need to be successful at school. Third, school personnel must seek intensive intervention for students who are especially prone to violence, show signs of significant mental illness, or in some other way are seriously troubled. Additional measures are sometimes needed to address incidents of aggression associated with intergang hostilities.

PRACTICE FOR YOUR LICENSURE EXAM

The Good Buddy

Mr. Schulak has wanted to be a teacher for as long as he can remember. In his many volunteer activities over the years—coaching a girls' basketball team, assisting with a Boy Scout troop, teaching Sunday school—he's discovered how much he enjoys working with children. Children obviously enjoy working with him as well. Many occasionally call or stop by his home to shoot baskets, talk over old times, or just say hello. Some of them even call him by his first name.

Now that Mr. Schulak has completed his college degree and obtained his teaching certificate, he's a first-year teacher at his hometown's junior high school. He's delighted to find that he already knows many of his students, and he spends the first few days of class renewing his friendships with them. But by the end of the week, he realizes that his classes have accomplished little of an academic nature.

The following Monday Mr. Schulak vows to get down to business. He begins each of his five class sessions by describing his instructional goals for the weeks to come and then introduces his first lesson. Unfortunately, many of his students are resistant to settling down and getting to work. They move from one seat to another, talk with friends, toss wadded-up paper "basketballs" across the room, and in general do anything *except* the academic tasks Mr. Schulak has in mind. In his second week as a new teacher, Mr. Schulak has already lost control of his classroom.

1. **Constructed-response question**

   Mr. Schulak is having considerable difficulty bringing his classes to order.

   A. Identify two critical things that Mr. Schulak has *not* done to get the school year off to a good start.

   B. Describe two strategies that Mr. Schulak might now use to remedy the situation.

2. **Multiple-choice question**

   Mr. Schulak is undoubtedly aware that good teachers show that they care about and respect their students. Which one of the following statements describes the kind of teacher–student relationship that is most likely to foster students' learning and achievement?

   a. The teacher communicates optimism about a student's potential for success and offers the support necessary for that success.

   b. The teacher spends a lot of time engaging in recreational activities with students after school and on weekends.

   c. The teacher focuses almost exclusively on what students do well and ignores or downplays what students do poorly.

   d. The teacher listens empathetically to students' concerns but reminds students that he or she alone must ultimately decide what transpires in the classroom.

   MyEdLab **Licensure Exam 9.1**

Blend Images/Alamy

10 Assessment Strategies

CASE STUDY: B IN HISTORY

Twelve-year-old Ellie is the highest achiever in Ms. Davidson's sixth-grade class. She eagerly engages in class discussions and activities, and she's conscientious about completing in-class assignments and homework. As a result of her consistent engagement and diligence in her schoolwork, she has earned straight As on report cards in previous years.

At the end of the school day one Friday, Ms. Davidson says, "As you all know, our first-quarter grading period ended last week. I'm handing out report cards for you to take home to your parents. I'm especially proud of one student who always puts forth her best effort, and her grades are almost perfect." She smiles affectionately at Ellie and hands her a report card. "Here you are. Just one B, Ellie, in history. I'm sure you'll be able to bring it up to an A next quarter."

Despite the praise, Ellie is devastated. The B has blindsided her; she had no idea it was coming. Embarrassed beyond words, she successfully fights back tears but looks down at her desk while Ms. Davidson distributes the other report cards. When the final school bell rings, Ellie quickly gathers her backpack and heads out the door, forgoing the usual after-school good-byes to her friends.

- What conclusions has Ms. Davidson drawn about Ellie, and on what kinds of information has she probably based each conclusion?
- Ellie's parents are unlikely to be concerned about her single B; they're more worried about her younger brother, who has shown significant delays in reading development. Why, then, might Ellie be so upset?
- Was it appropriate for Ms. Davidson to announce Ellie's grades to the class? Why or why not?

Obviously, Ms. Davidson has drawn conclusions about Ellie's achievement levels in various content domains, presumably based on Ellie's performance on assignments and quizzes and perhaps also based on day-to-day observations of what Ellie has said and done during class activities. In addition, Ms. Davidson has drawn a conclusion about Ellie's work habits (she "always puts forth her best effort"), perhaps after observing Ellie's regular on-task behavior at school and her consistency in completing homework.

In this chapter, we'll see that classroom assessments can take many different forms. The following definition sums up assessment's major features:

> **Assessment** is a process of observing a sample of a student's behavior and drawing inferences about the student's knowledge and abilities.

Several parts of this definition are important to note. First, assessment is an observation of students' *behavior*—including students' written responses to paper–pencil tasks—because it's impossible to look inside students' heads and see what knowledge and skills actually lurk there. Second, an assessment typically involves just a *sample* of behavior—teachers certainly can't observe and keep track of everything their students do during the school day. Finally, assessment involves drawing *inferences* from observed behaviors to make judgments about students' overall learning and achievement—or, in some cases, about their work habits, motives, attitudes, personality characteristics, or social skills. Such inference-drawing is a tricky business at best, and one that requires considerable thought about which behaviors can provide a reasonably accurate estimate of what students know, can do, and are likely to do.

Some assessments reflect **informal assessment**, in that they involve spontaneous, day-to-day observations of what students say and do at school. Others reflect **formal assessment**, in

FIGURE 10.1 In a backward-design approach, teachers begin by identifying the desired goals and objectives of instruction—which often reflect predetermined content-area standards—and then identify or create assessment tasks that should reflect attainment of those goals and objectives. Ideally, instructional planning occurs only *after* appropriate assessment tasks have been determined.

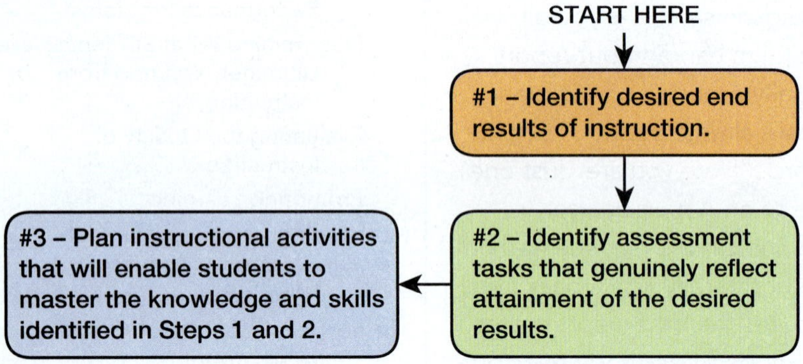

START HERE

#1 – Identify desired end results of instruction.

#2 – Identify assessment tasks that genuinely reflect attainment of the desired results.

#3 – Plan instructional activities that will enable students to master the knowledge and skills identified in Steps 1 and 2.

that they're planned in advance and used for a specific purpose—perhaps to determine what students have learned from an instructional unit or whether students can apply what they've learned to real-world problems. A formal assessment is *formal* in the sense that a particular time is set aside for it, students can prepare for it ahead of time, and it's intended to yield information about particular instructional objectives or content-area standards.

Classroom assessment practices are intertwined with virtually every other aspect of classroom functioning (look once again at Figure 8.1 at the beginning of Chapter 8). Teachers' instructional goals determine—or at least *should* determine—not only the content of classroom lessons but also the nature of assignments, tests, and other measures of students' achievement levels, as reflected in the **backward design** approach previously described in Chapter 8 and illustrated once again in Figure 10.1. Conversely, how students perform on ongoing assessments influences teachers' future planning, instructional methods, and classroom management strategies. Good classroom assessment practices also take into account students' existing characteristics and behaviors—attention spans, vocabulary levels, reading and writing skills, and so on.

But above all else, good assessment practices *enhance students' learning* over both the short and long run—something that's most likely to happen if students are in the loop about their academic progress. In the opening case study, Ellie clearly *hasn't* been in the loop about her progress in history. Although she undoubtedly knows that she has occasionally made errors on history assessment tasks, she hasn't been aware of how those errors might add up to a B rather than an A. And with her past straight-A record, she has set an extremely high standard for herself. Only perfection is good enough—an unrealistic standard held by some high-achieving sixth graders.[1] In addition, Ms. Davidson has announced Ellie's imperfection to the entire class. As a young adolescent, Ellie isn't sure which is worse: that her peers know she has earned the highest grades in the class or that they know she's *not* perfect in history. Not only does Ms. Davidson's announcement make Ellie extremely uncomfortable, but it also violates Ellie's right to confidentiality. In fact, as we'll discover later in the chapter, making a student's grades public, as Ms. Davidson does, is illegal, at least in the United States.

10.1 USING ASSESSMENTS FOR VARIOUS PURPOSES

Big Idea 10.1 Classroom assessments serve a variety of purposes, but in one way or another, they can all influence students' future learning and achievement.

You can best think of classroom assessments as *tools* that can guide teachers' decisions about how to help students learn and achieve and, later, their decisions about how to sum up what students have ultimately accomplished. Classroom assessments are rarely *perfect* tools, as we'll see in an upcoming section, but a critical first step in choosing the right ones is to determine the specific purpose(s) for which particular assessments are being used.

Classroom assessments can serve either—or in some cases both—of two general functions. **Formative assessment** involves determining what students know and can do *before or during instruction,* perhaps to identify students' existing strengths and interests, determine students' current knowledge and misconceptions about a topic, or ascertain students' progress midway through a unit or lesson. In contrast, **summative assessment** involves conducting an assessment *after instruction,* perhaps for the purpose of assigning final class grades or determining which students are ready for more advanced classes.

think about it

Be careful that you don't confuse the terms *formative assessment* and *formal assessment.* How are these two concepts different? (For key differences, click **here**.)

---

[1] Parker, 1997.

With these two basic kinds of assessment in mind, we'll now examine the roles that educational assessments can play in (1) guiding instructional decision making, (2) diagnosing learning and performance problems, (3) determining what students have learned at the end of instruction, (4) evaluating the quality of instruction, and (5) helping students learn *better*. The most important of these—helping students learn—is at the end of the list so that we can spend considerable time on it.

MyEdLab
Video Explanation 10.1.
This 5-minute video contrasts summative versus formative assessment and gives concrete examples to illustrate each one.

Guiding Instructional Decision Making

Certainly, formative assessments can help a teacher determine suitable points at which to begin instruction. Furthermore, conducting formative assessments throughout a lesson or unit can provide ongoing information about the appropriateness of current instructional goals and the effectiveness of current instructional strategies. For example, after finding that almost all students are completing assignments quickly and easily, a teacher might set instructional goals a bit higher. Alternatively, if many students struggle with concepts presented only through verbal explanations, a teacher might try a different instructional approach—perhaps a more concrete, hands-on one.

Yet summative assessments, too, must have an impact on instructional decision making. For example, any annual districtwide, statewide, provincial, or (for some countries) national achievement tests should guide teachers somewhat as they prioritize topics and skills on which to focus. In some cases, then, teachers must consider the nature of future summative assessments even *before* they conduct formative assessments (more about this issue in a later discussion of high-stakes tests).

Diagnosing Learning and Performance Problems

Why is Louis having trouble learning to read? Why does Gretel misbehave every time she faces a challenging assignment? Teachers ask such questions when they suspect that certain students might learn differently from their age-mates and may possibly require special educational services. Some assessment instruments are specifically designed to identify students' unique academic and personal needs. Most of these instruments require explicit training in their use and so are typically administered and interpreted by specialists (school psychologists, speech and language pathologists, etc.). Yet teachers' classroom assessments can provide considerable diagnostic information as well, especially when they reveal consistent error patterns and areas of difficulty (e.g., see Figure 10.2).[2]

FIGURE 10.2 In these and other work samples, 7-year-old Casey shows consistent difficulty in making connections between the sounds he hears and the sounds he represents in his writing—a difficulty that in his case reflects a learning disability known as *dyslexia*.

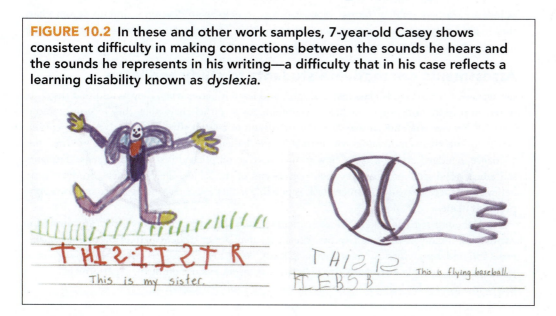

---

[2] You may sometimes see the term *diagnostic assessment* used in this context. The intent of diagnostic assessment is to acquire detailed information about students' current knowledge and abilities—through published tests and/or teacher-developed assessment tasks—in order to plan instruction that can maximize students' learning and achievement.

Many teachers now make regular use of short, formative assessments to determine whether certain students might have exceptional instructional needs. In this approach, known as **response to intervention (RTI)**, a teacher frequently assesses students' progress, keeping a lookout for students who have unusual difficulty acquiring certain basic skills despite teachers' evidence-based practices in both whole-class instruction and follow-up small-group work. Note the importance of *evidence-based practices* here: The teacher must have used instructional strategies that research has shown to be effective for most students. The RTI approach has gained particular popularity as a means of identifying students who have learning disabilities, but it's potentially useful for other students as well.[3]

Determining What Students Have Ultimately Learned from Instruction

In most instances, teachers should use formal assessments—rather than more casual, informal ones—to determine whether students have achieved instructional goals or met certain content-area standards. Formal summative assessments of achievement are important in any mastery-learning approach to instruction, and they're essential for assigning final grades. School counselors and administrators, too, may use summative assessment results to make placement decisions, such as deciding which students are most likely to do well in advanced classes and which might need additional coursework in basic skills.

Evaluating the Quality of Instruction

Final, summative measures of student achievement are also useful in evaluating how effective instruction has been. When most students perform poorly after an instructional unit, teachers should reflect not only on what students might have done differently but also on what *they themselves* might have done differently. For example, perhaps a teacher moved too quickly through material or provided insufficient opportunities to practice essential skills. In any event, consistently low assessment results for many or all students indicate that some modification of instruction is in order.

Promoting Learning

Whenever teachers conduct formative assessments to help them develop or modify lesson plans, they're obviously using assessment to enhance students' learning. Yet summative assessment can influence learning as well, as reflected in the following principles.

Assessments can motivate students to study and learn.

On average, students study class material more and learn it better when they're told that they'll be tested on it or in some other way held accountable for it, rather than when they're simply told to learn it.[4] Yet *how* students are assessed is as important as *whether* they're assessed. Assessments are especially effective as motivators when students are challenged to do their very best and their performance is judged on the basis of how well they've accomplished instructional goals.[5] Students' self-efficacy and attributions affect their perceptions of the "challenge," of course. Students must believe that success on an assessment task is possible if they exert reasonable effort and use appropriate strategies.

Although regular classroom assessments can be highly motivating, they are, in and of themselves, usually *extrinsic* motivators. Thus they may direct students' attention to performance goals and undermine intrinsic motivation to learn. Assessments are especially likely to encourage performance goals when students perceive them to be an evaluation of their performance rather than a mechanism for helping them master classroom subject matter.[6]

[3] T. A. Glover & Vaughn, 2010; Hoover, 2009; Mellard & Johnson, 2008.

[4] Dempster, 1991; N. Frederiksen, 1984b; Rohrer & Pashler, 2010.

[5] Mac Iver, Reuman, & Main, 1995; L. H. Meyer, Weir, McClure, & Walkey, 2008; Newstead, 2004.

[6] F. Danner, 2008; Grolnick & Ryan, 1987; Paris & Turner, 1994; Shernoff, 2013.

Assessments can influence students' cognitive processes as they study.

Students draw inferences about important instructional goals partly from the ways their learning is assessed. Thus, different assessment tasks can lead them to study and learn quite differently.[7] For example, students typically spend more time studying the things they think an assessment will address than the things they think the assessment won't cover. Furthermore, their expectations about the kinds of tasks they'll need to perform and the questions they'll need to answer influence whether they memorize isolated facts, on the one hand, or construct a meaningful, integrated body of knowledge, on the other.

As an example, look at the sixth-grade test about rocks shown in Figure 10.3. Part A (identifying rocks shown at the front of the room) may be assessing either basic knowledge or application (transfer), depending on whether the students have seen those particular rock specimens before. The rest of the test clearly focuses on memorized facts and so might encourage students to engage in rote learning as they study for future tests. For instance, consider the last item, "Every rock has a _____." Students can answer this item correctly *only* if they've learned the material verbatim: The missing word here is "story."

Classroom assessments can also influence students' views about the nature of various academic disciplines; that is, they can influence the *epistemic beliefs* described in Chapter 3. For example, if a teacher routinely gives quizzes that assess knowledge of specific facts, students are apt to conclude that a discipline is just that: a collection of undisputed facts. If, instead, a teacher asks students to take a position on a controversial issue and justify their position with evidence and logic, students get a very different message: that the discipline involves an integrated set of understandings that must be supported with reasoning and are subject to change over time.

FIGURE 10.3 Much of this sixth-grade geology test focuses on knowledge of specific facts and may encourage students to memorize, rather than understand, information about rocks.

A. Write whether each of the rocks shown at the front of the room is a sedimentary, igneous, or metamorphic rock.
1. _____
2. _____
3. _____

B. The following are various stages of the rock cycle. Number them from 1 to 9 to indicate the order in which they occur.
_____ Heat and pressure
_____ Crystallization and cooling
_____ Igneous rock forms
_____ Magma
_____ Weathering and erosion into sediments
_____ Melting
_____ Sedimentary rock forms
_____ Pressure and cementing
_____ Metamorphic rock forms

C. Write the letter for the correct definition of each rock group.
1. _____ Igneous   a. Formed when particles of eroded rock are deposited together and become cemented.
2. _____ Sedimentary   b. Produced by extreme pressures or high temperatures below the earth's surface.
3. _____ Metamorphic   c. Formed by the cooling of molten rock material from within the earth.

D. Fill in the blanks in each sentence.
1. The process of breaking down rock by the action of water, ice, plants, animals, and chemical changes is called _____.
2. All rocks are made of _____.
3. The hardness of rocks can be determined by a _____.
4. Continued weathering of rock will eventually produce _____.
5. Every rock has a _____.

[The test continues with several additional fill-in-the-blank and short-answer items.]

Assessment activities can be learning experiences in and of themselves.

In general, the very process of completing an assessment on classroom material helps students review the material and learn it better. Assessment tasks are especially valuable if they ask students to elaborate on or apply the material in a new way.[8] You've previously seen an example of such a task in Figure 3.10 in Chapter 3, and you'll see additional examples later in this chapter.

Assessments can provide feedback about learning progress.

It isn't terribly helpful to know only one's final scores on tests and assignments. To facilitate students' learning and achievement—and also to enhance students' self-efficacy for mastering school subject matter—assessment feedback must include specific information about where students have succeeded, where they've had difficulty, and how they might improve.[9]

---

[7] Carpenter, 2012; Corliss & Linn, 2011; N. Frederiksen, 1984b; Haertel, 2013.
[8] Dunlosky, Rawson, Marsh, Nathan, & Willingham, 2013; Corliss & Linn, 2011; Foos & Fisher, 1988; C. I. Johnson & Mayer, 2009; Rohrer & Pashler, 2010.
[9] Andrade & Cizek, 2010; Hattie & Gan, 2011; Shute, 2008; Wiliam, 2010.

One simple yet effective feedback strategy is to insert little nongraded "mini-tests" into lessons. For example, when an instructional strategy involves mostly *presenting* information without a lot of two-way teacher-student interaction—as can sometimes be true in a traditional lecture—occasionally interspersing a few multiple-choice or short-answer questions throughout the lesson can help students monitor their current understandings of the material being presented.[10]

Assessments can encourage intrinsic motivation and self-regulation *if* students play an active role in the assessment process.

As noted earlier, classroom assessments are typically extrinsic motivators that provide only externally imposed reasons for learning school subject matter. Yet students learn more effectively when they're *intrinsically* motivated, and they're more likely to be intrinsically motivated if they have some sense of autonomy about classroom activities (see Chapter 5). Furthermore, if students are to become self-regulating learners, they must acquire skills in self-monitoring and self-evaluation (see Chapter 3). For such reasons, students should be regular and active participants in the assessment of their own learning and performance (more on this point shortly). Ultimately, teachers should think of assessment as something they do *with* students rather than *to* them.[11]

Assessment isn't just something that accompanies instruction, then. In a very real sense, assessment *is* instruction: It gives students clear messages about what things are most important to accomplish and how best to accomplish them.

> Any single assessment might be simultaneously used for two or more purposes—for example, it might be used to (1) check on students' progress or mastery, (2) guide future instructional planning, and (3) provide signals about one or more students who may possibly require special educational services. As a teacher, then, you should try to think flexibly about the many things you could jointly accomplish with your classroom assessment tasks. In the hotlinked Self-Check quiz and Application Exercise that follow, you can check and apply your understandings related to Big Idea 10.1:
>
> *Classroom assessments serve a variety of purposes, but in one way or another, they can all influence students' future learning and achievement.*
>
> MyEdLab **Self-Check 10.1**
>
> MyEdLab **Application Exercise 10.1.** As you analyze a child's written numbers in this exercise, you can get a feel for the kinds of information that a simple assessment task might yield.

10.2 ENHANCING LEARNING THROUGH CLASSROOM ASSESSMENT PRACTICES

Big Idea 10.2 Effective teachers strategically use both formative and summative assessments to enhance students' learning.

As we've just seen, certain characteristics of classroom assessments are likely to have a significant impact on students' learning and achievement. Ideally, teachers should *intentionally* use assessments with students' long-term learning and development in mind. Following are several general recommendations.

Through both words and deeds, communicate that promoting learning and mastery—*not* passing judgment—is the ultimate goal.

Many students perceive classroom assessments to be evaluative judgments of their existing abilities, rather than mechanisms for helping them learn and achieve at high levels. Teachers can downplay the judgmental nature of assessments with strategies such as the following:[12]

---

[10] Glass & Sinha, 2013; Szpunar, Jing, & Schacter, 2014; Wiliam, 2011.

[11] Andrade, 2010; Panadero & Jonsson, 2013; Paris & Ayres, 1994; Reeve, Deci, & Ryan, 2004; Shepard, Hammerness, Darling-Hammond, & Rust, 2005.

[12] Andrade & Cizek, 2010; Black & Wiliam, 1998; Chappuis, 2009; Hattie & Gan, 2011; Panadero & Jonsson, 2013; Rohrer & Pashler, 2010; Szpunar et al., 2014.

- Describe the instructional goals and objectives being assessed in clear, understandable language.

- Assess students' progress frequently rather than infrequently, but *without* spending an inordinate time on assessment tasks that don't also enhance students' learning.

- When giving assessments, consistently convey a desire to enhance understanding and promote mastery, rather than to pass judgment.

- Help students recognize important (yet possibly subtle) differences between genuine mastery and more superficial knowledge.

- Engage students in constructive discussions of one another's work, with a focus on ideas for improvement.

- Give students opportunities to revise their work based on feedback they've received.

Such strategies can be especially important when working with students who are at risk for academic failure.[13]

Make assessment criteria explicit early in the instructional process.

Some assessment tasks yield clear-cut good and not-as-good responses; for example, assessments of typing speed and long division skills are usually pretty straightforward. But when a variety of behaviors and products might be equally good indicators of students' achievement levels related to a particular topic or skill—and especially when those behaviors and products can have varying degrees of quality—then explicit evaluation criteria are in order.

One simple strategy for making assessment criteria explicit is to create and distribute a **checklist** of characteristics that should be evident in students' work. For example, Figure 10.4 shows a checklist that one fourth-grade teacher has used for scoring students' performance on math word problems. Notice that the checklist includes both objectively scorable criteria (e.g., the correct answer) and more qualitative, subjectively scorable criteria (e.g., neatness of work, explanation of the problem solution).

When the focus of instruction is a complex, multifaceted topic or skill, a teacher might instead use a **rubric**—a two-dimensional matrix that identifies criteria for assessing different components of students' performance, along with concrete descriptions of various levels of performance relative to each component. As an example, Figure 10.5 shows a possible rubric for evaluating various qualities in students' nonfiction writing. The criteria aren't completely objective—for instance, what do the words *occasionally, a few,* and *many* mean?—but they can help a teacher pin down the kinds of supplementary instruction and activities that some students may need. Rubrics are probably most useful when they have the following characteristics:[14]

- They focus on only a few key attributes of skilled performance and describe these attributes in clear, concrete terms.

- They also focus on attributes that students can realistically acquire with appropriate instruction and practice.

- They are applicable to many tasks within the content domain.

Checklists and rubrics have at least three benefits. First, they give students clear targets toward which to shoot. Second, when well constructed, they enable teachers to evaluate students' performance consistently and with reasonable objectivity (more about this point in an upcoming

FIGURE 10.4 In this guide for scoring solutions to word problems in a fourth-grade class, both teacher and student evaluate various aspects of the student's performance.

Elements	Possible Points	Points Earned	
		Self	Teacher
1. You highlighted the question(s) to solve.	2	_____	_____
2. You picked an appropriate strategy.	2	_____	_____
3. Work is neat and organized.	2	_____	_____
4. Calculations are accurate.	2	_____	_____
5. Question(s) answered.	2	_____	_____
6. You have explained in words how you solved the problem.	5	_____	_____
TOTAL	_____	_____	_____

MyEdLab
Video Explanation 10.2.

This 15-minute video provides a good overview of effective formative assessments, along with illustrative examples of both rubrics and checklists.

[13] G. B. Hughes, 2010; Wiliam, 2011.
[14] Arter & Chappuis, 2006; Popham, 2006, 2014.

FIGURE 10.5 Possible rubric for evaluating students' nonfiction writing

Characteristic	Proficient	In Progress	Beginning to Develop
Correct spelling	Writer correctly spells all words.	Writer correctly spells most words.	Writer incorrectly spells many words.
Correct punctuation & capitalization	Writer uses punctuation marks and uppercase letters where, and only where, appropriate.	Writer occasionally (a) omits punctuation marks, (b) inappropriately uses punctuation marks, or (c) inappropriately uses uppercase/lowercase letters.	Writer makes many punctuation and/or capitalization errors.
Complete sentences	Writer uses complete sentences throughout, except when using an incomplete sentence for a clear stylistic purpose. Writing includes no run-on sentences.	Writer uses a few incomplete sentences that have no obvious stylistic purpose, or writer occasionally includes a run-on sentence.	Writer includes many incomplete sentences and/or run-on sentences; writer uses periods rarely or indiscriminately.
Clear focus	Writer clearly states main idea; sentences are all related to this idea and present a coherent message.	Writer only implies main idea; most sentences are related to this idea; a few sentences are unnecessary digressions.	Writer rambles, without a clear main idea; or writer frequently and unpredictably goes off topic.
Logical train of thought	Writer carefully leads the reader through his/her own line of thinking about the topic.	Writer shows some logical progression of ideas but occasionally omits a key point essential to the flow of ideas.	Writer presents ideas in no logical sequence.
Convincing statements/ arguments	Writer effectively persuades the reader with evidence or sound reasoning.	Writer includes some evidence or reasoning to support ideas/opinions, but a reader could easily offer counterarguments.	Writer offers ideas/opinions with little or no justification.

discussion of *reliability*). And third, they provide a means through which teachers can give students detailed feedback about the strengths and limitations of their performance—feedback that ideally can help students improve.

Ask students to evaluate their own performance.

Let's return to the opening case study, in which Ellie is blindsided by her B in history. Ms. Davidson has presumably been tracking Ellie's progress over time, but Ellie herself obviously hasn't been doing so.

Students become more skillful in self-assessment as they grow older,[15] but even students in the elementary grades have some ability to evaluate their own performance. Following are several strategies for including students in the assessment process and helping them develop important self-monitoring and self-evaluation skills:[16]

- Solicit students' ideas about assessment criteria and rubric design.
- Provide examples of good and not-as-good products—these should *not* come from current or recent students' work—and ask students to compare the examples on the basis of several criteria.
- Have students compare self-ratings of their performance with teacher ratings (e.g., notice the "Self" and "Teacher" columns in the word-problem scoring guide in Figure 10.4).
- Ask students to write practice questions similar to those they might see on an upcoming paper–pencil test.
- Have students keep ongoing records of their performance and chart their progress over time.

---

[15] van Kraayenoord & Paris, 1997.
[16] Andrade, 2010; A. L. Brown & Campione, 1996; Chappuis, 2009; McMillan, 2010; Paris & Ayres, 1994; Shepard, 2000; Stiggins & Chappuis, 2012.

- Have students reflect on their work in daily or weekly journal entries, where they can keep track of knowledge and skills they have and haven't mastered, as well as learning strategies that have and haven't been effective for them.
- Have students compile portfolios of their work, including self-reflective explanations of what various items reveal about their learning and achievement.
- Ask students to lead parent–teacher conferences.

It's important, too, that teachers encourage productive attributions; for instance, students should genuinely believe they can overcome their existing shortcomings with reasonable effort and good strategies.[17] And teachers should ask students to develop a follow-up action plan—to explicitly address the question *What do I need to do now?* based on their assessment results. Such an action plan might include identifying answers to more specific questions such as these:

- What specific things do I need to do to improve?
- What resources and assistance do I need to help me improve?
- How will I know when I have reached my goal?[18]

MyEdLab

Video Example 10.1.

What specific strategies does this first-grade teacher use to help students self-assess the quality of their own writing?

Assess students' ability to learn new things given varying levels of guidance and support.

One form of formative assessment is **dynamic assessment**, in which a teacher assesses students' ability to learn something new, typically in a one-on-one situation that includes instruction, assistance, or some other form of scaffolding.[19] Such an approach reflects Vygotsky's *zone of proximal development* and can reveal what students might be able to accomplish with appropriate structure and guidance. Dynamic assessment can provide a wealth of qualitative information about children's abilities, cognitive strategies, and approaches to learning. For example, it can give teachers insights into the following:[20]

- Students' readiness for instruction in particular topics and skills
- Students' motivational and affective patterns (e.g., self-efficacy, achievement goals, attributions, anxiety)
- Students' work habits (e.g., impulsiveness, persistence, reactions to frustration and failure)
- Potential obstacles to students' learning (e.g., distractibility, poor reading comprehension skills, lack of effective self-monitoring and self-evaluation skills)

Thus, dynamic assessment can yield information that teachers are unlikely to get through more traditional assessment strategies.

Take advantage of technology-based formative assessment tools.

Several Internet-based resources provide short formative assessments through which teachers can regularly monitor students' progress in literacy, math, or science. Following are four examples:

- Accelerated Reader (renaissance.com)
- AIMSweb (aimsweb.com)
- Diagnoser (diagnoser.com)
- DIBELS (Dynamic Indicators of Basic Early Literacy Skills; dibels.uoregon.edu)

Some of these resources provide means through which a teacher can immediately enter students' responses onto a handheld digital device, such as a tablet computer or personal digital assistant (PDA); others present short assessments that students themselves complete on a laptop or desktop computer. The programs keep track of students' performance over time and, at a teacher's request,

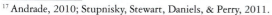

[17] Andrade, 2010; Stupnisky, Stewart, Daniels, & Perry, 2011.

[18] Questions based on Chappuis, 2009.

[19] For example, see Feuerstein, Feuerstein, & Falik, 2010; Fuchs, Compton, et al., 2008; Haywood & Lidz, 2007; Seethaler, Fuchs, Fuchs, & Compton, 2012; H. L. Swanson & Lussier, 2001.

[20] Feuerstein et al., 2010; Fuchs, Compton, et al., 2008; Hamers & Ruijssenaars, 1997; Haywood & Lidz, 2007; Tzuriel, 2000.

MyEdLab
Video Example 10.2.

Digital technologies offer many mechanisms for helping students assess their own performance and progress. What particular benefits does technology offer in this high school music lesson?

can quickly generate reports and graphs regarding both individual students and an entire class. Thus they're especially useful in *response-to-intervention* approaches to assessment (described earlier) and *curriculum-based measurement* (to be described a bit later in the section on validity).

Many computer software programs can help students *self-assess* their work. For instance, some Internet-based programs are specifically designed to help students evaluate qualities of their written work; an example is Latent Semantic Analysis (LSA; lsa.colorado.edu). Such programs can provide quick analyses of students' electronically written essays, short stories, and other compositions—whether students have used plausible word combinations, appropriate grammatical structures, and the like. Most word processing programs also provide this service to some degree through grammar checkers. Certainly, educators shouldn't let these programs replace human beings in evaluating students' written work; ultimately only *people* can reasonably evaluate the accuracy, organization, and logic of what students have written. However, when students use the programs for formative assessment purposes, they can gain substantive feedback that helps them improve the quality of their writing.[21]

Other digital technologies can enhance students' self-assessment abilities as well. For example, the class websites described in Chapter 8 provide a mechanism through which students can voluntarily upload early drafts of their work in order to get classmates' constructive feedback and suggestions. And in some cases, a teacher and students might use a video camera or a laptop computer to record students' actions or activities for subsequent analysis. For instance, a teacher might videotape a student's execution of a complex behavior and have the student apply certain criteria in self-evaluating the performance. At one middle school, students designed and built small models of wooden bridges, then videotaped their bridges as they placed a brick on top. Analyzing the videos frame by frame, they could detect possible flaws in their bridge designs.[22]

> As you've seen, a good classroom assessment strategy doesn't just *measure* students' existing achievement levels. It also *promotes* students' achievement—and, ideally, it also helps students become better able to self-evaluate their ongoing progress and eventual mastery of classroom subject matter. In the hotlinked Self-Check quiz and Application Exercise that follow, you can check and apply your understandings related to Big Idea 10.2:
>
> > *Effective teachers strategically use both formative and summative assessments to enhance students' learning.*
>
> **MyEdLab Self-Check 10.2**
>
> **MyEdLab Application Exercise 10.2.** In this exercise, you can observe and analyze the strategies a third-grade teacher uses to give a child concrete and constructive feedback about her writing.

10.3 IMPORTANT QUALITIES OF GOOD ASSESSMENT

Big Idea 10.3 Ideally, classroom assessments have four RSVP characteristics—reliability, standardization, validity, and practicality—with validity being the most important.

As a student, have you ever been assessed in a way you thought was unfair? If so, *why* was it unfair?

1. Did the teacher evaluate students' responses inconsistently?
2. Were some students assessed under more favorable conditions than others were?
3. Was the assessment a poor measure of what you had learned?
4. Was the assessment so time consuming that eventually you no longer cared how well you performed?

---

[21] Russell, 2010.
[22] Stokes, Luiselli, Reed, & Fleming, 2010; Warschauer, 2011.

In light of your experiences, what characteristics seem to be essential for good classroom assessment instruments and practices?

The four numbered questions just posed reflect, respectively, four *RSVP* characteristics of good classroom assessments: reliability, standardization, validity, and practicality. These characteristics are important considerations for any assessment activity, but they're especially important when educators use summative assessments to make potentially life-changing decisions—for instance, decisions about final class grades, placements in advanced classes, and appropriate services for students with disabilities.

A good assessment is reliable.

The reliability of an assessment instrument or procedure is the extent to which it yields consistent information about the knowledge, skills, or characteristics being assessed. To get a sense of what reliability involves, try the following exercise.

think about it
A quick review of a concept presented in Chapter 2: What purpose might *RSVP* serve in helping you remember the four important qualities of good assessment? (For an explanation, click **here**.)

SEE FOR YOURSELF
FOWL PLAY

Here is a sequence of events in the life of biology teacher Ms. Fowler:

- **Monday.** After completing a lesson on the bone structures of both birds and dinosaurs, Ms. Fowler asks students to write an essay explaining why many scientists believe that birds are descendants of dinosaurs. After school, she tosses the pile of essays on the back seat of her cluttered Chevrolet.
- **Tuesday.** Ms. Fowler looks high and low for the essays both at home and in her classroom, but she can't find them anywhere.
- **Wednesday.** Because Ms. Fowler wants to use the students' essays to determine what they've learned, she asks the class to write the same essay a second time.
- **Thursday.** Ms. Fowler finally finds Monday's essays on the back seat of her car.
- **Friday.** Ms. Fowler grades both sets of essays. She is surprised to find little consistency between them: Students who wrote the best essays on Monday didn't necessarily do well on Wednesday, and some of Monday's poorest performers did quite well on Wednesday.

Which results should Ms. Fowler use, Monday's or Wednesday's?

When teachers assess learning and achievement, they must be confident that their assessment results will be essentially the same regardless of whether they give the assessment Monday or Wednesday, whether the weather is sunny or rainy, and whether they evaluate students' responses while in a good mood or a foul frame of mind. Ms. Fowler's assessment task has poor reliability, because the results it yields are completely different from one day to another. So which day's results should she use? We've asked you a trick question here, because there's really no way to determine which set is more accurate.

Any single assessment task will rarely yield *exactly* the same results for the same student on two different occasions, even if the knowledge or ability being assessed remains the same. Many temporary conditions unrelated to the knowledge or ability being measured are apt to affect students' performance and almost inevitably lead to some fluctuation in assessment results. For instance, the inconsistencies in Ms. Fowler's two sets of student essays might have been due to one or more of the following temporary factors:

- **Day-to-day changes in students**—for example, changes in health, motivation, mood, and energy level

  A 24-hour flu was making the rounds among Ms. Fowler's students.

- **Variations in the physical environment**—for example, variations in room temperature, noise level, and outside distractions

  On Monday, students who sat by the window in Ms. Fowler's classroom enjoyed peace and quiet, but on Wednesday, they wrote their essays while noisy construction machinery was tearing up the pavement outside.

- **Variations in administration of the assessment**—for example, variations in instructions, timing, and the teacher's responses to students' questions

  On Monday, a few students wrote the essay after school because they had attended a rehearsal for the school play during class time. Ms. Fowler explained the task more clearly for them than she had during class, and she gave them as much time as they needed to finish. On Wednesday, a different group of students had to write the essay after school because of an across-town band concert during class time. Ms. Fowler explained the task very hurriedly and collected the essays before students had finished.

- **Characteristics of the assessment instrument**—for example, the length, clarity, and difficulty of tasks (e.g., ambiguous and very difficult tasks increase students' tendency to guess randomly)

  The essay topic, "Explain why many scientists believe that birds are descendants of dinosaurs," was an ambiguous one that students interpreted differently from one day to the next.

- **Subjectivity in scoring**—for example, judgments made on the basis of vague, imprecise criteria

  Ms. Fowler graded both sets of essays while watching *Chainsaw Murders at Central High* on television Friday night. She gave higher scores during kissing scenes, lower scores during stalking scenes.

When drawing conclusions about students' learning and achievement, teachers must be confident that the information on which they're basing their conclusions hasn't been overly distorted by temporary, irrelevant factors. Several strategies can increase the likelihood that an assessment yields reliable results:

- Include a variety of tasks, and look for consistency in students' performance on different tasks.
- Define each task clearly enough that students know exactly what they're being asked to do.
- Use a rubric that identifies specific, concrete criteria with which to evaluate students' performance.
- Try not to let expectations for students' performance influence judgments of *actual* performance.
- Avoid assessing students' achievement when they're unlikely to give their best performance—for instance, when they're sick.
- Administer the assessment in similar ways and under similar conditions for all students.

The last recommendation suggests that assessment procedures also be *standardized*, especially when—for whatever reason—students need to be compared to one another. We turn to this RSVP characteristic now.

A good assessment is standardized for most students.

The term **standardization** refers to the extent to which an assessment involves similar content and format and is administered and scored in the same way for everyone. In most situations, all students should get the same instructions, perform identical or similar tasks, have the same time limits, and work under the same constraints. Furthermore, all students' responses should be scored using the same criteria. For example, unless there are extenuating circumstances, a teacher shouldn't use tougher standards for one student than for another.

Many tests constructed and published by large-scale testing companies are called *standardized tests*. This label indicates that the tests have explicit procedures for administration and scoring that are consistently applied wherever the tests are used. (We'll look at standardized tests more closely later in the chapter.) Yet standardization is also important in teachers' own, self-constructed classroom assessments. Standardization increases the probability that any single assessment task will yield consistent results on different occasions—something that Ms. Fowler's essay question doesn't do.

Equity is an additional consideration. Especially if a summative assessment is being conducted, it's only fair to ask all students to be evaluated under similar conditions. We find an

think about it
Is this description of how standardized tests are administered consistent with your own experiences taking such tests?

exception in the assessment of students with special educational needs. In the United States, the Individuals with Disabilities Education Act (IDEA) mandates that schools make appropriate accommodations for students with physical, mental, social, or emotional disabilities. This mandate applies not only to instructional practices but to assessment practices as well. Specific modifications to assessment instruments and procedures must, of course, be tailored to students' particular disabilities. Following are examples:[23]

- Use computer technology to facilitate students' ability to perform reading and writing tasks—for instance, by presenting questions in enlarged font (e.g., for students with impaired vision) or allowing the use of spell checkers (e.g., for students with learning disabilities).

- Read paper–pencil test questions to students with limited reading skills (e.g., to students with dyslexia).

- Divide a lengthy assessment task into several shorter tasks for students who have limited attention spans (e.g., for students with ADHD).

- Administer an assessment in a quiet room with few distractions (e.g., for students with learning disabilities or ADHD).

- Give more time or frequent breaks during the assessment (e.g., for students who tire easily due to a chronic illness or traumatic brain injury).

- Construct individualized assessment instruments if some students are working toward instructional goals different from those of their classmates (e.g., as may often be the case for students with intellectual disabilities).

A good assessment has validity for its purpose.

Earlier you learned about *reliability*. Let's see whether you can apply (transfer) your understanding of reliability in the following exercise.

SEE FOR YOURSELF
FTOI

We authors have developed a test called the FTOI: the Fathead Test of Intelligence. It consists of only a tape measure and a *table of norms* that shows how children and adults of various ages typically perform on the test. Administration of the FTOI is quick and easy. You simply measure a person's head circumference just above the eyebrows (firmly but not too tightly) and compare your measurement to the average head circumference for the person's age-group. People with large heads (comparatively speaking) get high IQ scores. People with smaller heads get low scores.

Does the FTOI have high reliability? Answer the question before you read further.

No matter how often you measure a person's head, you're going to get similar scores from one time to the next. People with large heads will continue to be big-headed, and those with small heads will always have relatively small hat sizes. So the answer to our question is *yes:* The FTOI has high reliability because it yields consistent results. If you answered *no,* you were probably thinking that the FTOI doesn't really measure intelligence. But that's a problem with the FTOI's *validity,* not with its reliability.

The **validity** of an assessment is the extent to which it measures what it's intended to measure and allows us to draw appropriate inferences about the characteristic or ability in question. Does the FTOI measure intelligence? Are scores on a standardized, multiple-choice achievement test a good indication of whether students have mastered basic skills in reading and writing? Does students' performance at a school concert reflect what they've achieved in their instrumental music class? When assessments don't fulfill their intended purposes—when they're poor measures of students' knowledge and abilities—we have a validity problem.

As noted earlier, numerous irrelevant factors are apt to influence how well students perform in assessment situations. Some of these—such as students' health, classroom distractions,

---
[23] American Educational Research Association, American Psychological Association, & National Council on Measurement in Education, 1999; N. Gregg, 2009; Lovett, 2010.

and inconsistencies in scoring—are temporary conditions that lead to fluctuation in assessment results from one time to the next and thereby lower reliability. But other irrelevant factors are more stable—as reading ability and chronic test anxiety might be—and so their effects on assessment results will be relatively constant. For example, if Joe has poor reading skills, he may get consistently low scores on paper–pencil, multiple-choice achievement tests regardless of how much he has actually achieved in science, math, or social studies. When assessment results continue to be affected by the same irrelevant variables, the *validity* of the assessments is in doubt.

Psychologists distinguish among different kinds of validity, which are important in different situations. In some cases, we might be interested in *predictive validity*. That is, we might want to know how well scores on an assessment instrument predict performance in some future activity—for example, how well IQ scores predict students' future school achievement levels. At other times, we might be interested in *construct validity*. That is, we might want to know whether an assessment instrument measures a particular human trait or characteristic—for example, whether the FTOI test actually measures intelligence, or whether an alleged measure of personality actually measures one or more personality traits. In general, however, classroom teachers should be most concerned about **content validity**. That is, they need to be sure their assessment questions and tasks adequately represent the overall body of knowledge and skills—the content domain—being assessed.

As an illustration, Table 10.1 revisits the Common Core State Standards for English Language Arts (second column, in orange) and relevant instructional strategies (third column) first presented in Table 8.1 in Chapter 8. The table's right-most (fourth) column offers examples of informal and formal assessment strategies that might address those standards, and the instructional strategies in the third column provide additional opportunities for informal assessment. Some strategies in the table (e.g., having students write essays or create concept maps) involve **paper–pencil assessment**, whereby teachers present questions to answer, topics to address, or problems to solve, and students respond on paper—or, perhaps, an electronic equivalent, such as in a word processing document. But other examples (e.g., having students respond orally to questions or act out a story) reflect **performance assessment**, in which students show what they've learned by actively *doing* something rather than simply writing about it. As we'll discover later, paper–pencil and performance assessment tasks tend to be useful in different situations.

One strategy for ensuring content validity in *formative* assessments is **curriculum-based measurement (CBM)**, which is especially useful both in basic skills instruction and in a response-to-intervention approach to diagnosing persistent learning problems. In this approach teachers regularly administer assessments that each focus on a single, specific skill in the curriculum (e.g., word recognition in reading, addition of 2-digit numbers in math) as a means of tracking individual students' progress. Each assessment is typically quite short (perhaps only 1 to 4 minutes long) and yet can help teachers identify students who might need additional instruction in a certain skill in order to move forward. Many of the technology-based formative assessment tools described earlier enable teachers to take a CBM approach. For example, we refer you once again to AIMSweb (aimsweb.com) and DIBELS (dibels.uoregon.edu).

High content validity is *essential* whenever teachers conduct *summative* assessments—that is, when teachers want to assess students' final achievement levels in an instructional unit or course of study. A teacher maximizes content validity when assessment tasks are as similar as possible to the things students should ultimately be able to do. In other words, any assessment used in summative assessment should reflect instructional goals and objectives.

When a summative assessment is intended to encompass multiple topics, concepts, and skills—and possibly also multiple instructional goals—teachers can't always address each and every one of these things in the assessment. But taken as a whole, the things teachers ask students to do in the assessment should comprise a *representative* sample of the content domain being assessed. The most widely recommended strategy is to construct a blueprint that identifies the specific things a teacher wants to assess and the proportion of questions or tasks that should address each one. This blueprint frequently takes the form of a **table of specifications**, a two-way grid that indicates both what topics should be covered and what students should be able to *do* with each topic. Each cell of the grid indicates the relative importance of each topic–behavior combination, perhaps as a certain number or percentage of tasks or test items to be included in the

DEVELOPMENTAL TRENDS

TABLE 10.1 • Examples of How You Might Align Classroom Assessments with Common Core State Standards and Instruction at Different Grade Levels

GRADE LEVEL	EXAMPLES OF COMMON CORE STANDARDS FOR ENGLISH LANGUAGE ARTS	EXAMPLES OF INSTRUCTIONAL STRATEGIES THAT ADDRESS THESE STANDARDS *AND* PROVIDE A MEANS OF INFORMALLY ASSESSING STUDENTS' PROGRESS	EXAMPLES OF ASSESSMENTS THAT ALIGN WITH THE STANDARDS AND WITH CLASSROOM INSTRUCTION
GRADE 2	Ask and answer such questions as *who, what, where, when, why,* and *how* to demonstrate understanding of key details in a text. (RL.2.1)[a]	During "settling down" time immediately after lunch each day, read a chapter of a high-interest children's novel, stopping frequently to ask questions that require students to go beyond the text itself (e.g., ask students to speculate about what a character might be feeling).	Meet with students in small groups and ask each group member to describe a story in his or her own words. Follow up with questions such as "What happened next?" and "Why did [a character] do that?" to determine the extent to which each student has understood important elements of the story.
	Recount stories, including fables and folktales from diverse cultures, and determine their central message, lesson, or moral. (RL.2.2)	Have several students create props for and act out a story they have recently read, with other class members serving as the audience. Follow up with a class discussion of important lessons that one or more story characters might have learned from events or challenges they faced.	Give a reading group several age-appropriate Middle Eastern or Chinese folktales to read, and then ask the students, "What advice do you think this story is giving us?" Be sure that every group member answers the question, and communicate that there isn't necessarily a single right answer.
GRADE 4	Refer to details and examples in a text when explaining what the text says explicitly and when drawing inferences from the text. (RL.4.1)	As a reading group discusses Carl Hiaasen's *Hoot*, ask students to speculate about how the plot might progress and to identify clues in the text that support their predictions.	After students have read the first few chapters of Natalie Babbitt's *Tuck Everlasting* (in which the Tuck family has drunk from a well that gives everlasting life), ask them to write an essay speculating on problems the Tucks' immortality might create for them. Later, after they learn that Mae Tuck has killed someone, ask them to speculate about the implications of her arrest and to back up their predictions with clues in the text.
	Explain events, procedures, ideas, or concepts in a historical, scientific, or technical text, including what happened and why, based on specific information in the text. (RI.4.3)	When students are reading a chapter in their history textbook, ask *why* questions that encourage cause-and-effect connections (e.g., "Why did Columbus's crew want to sail back to Europe after several weeks on the open sea?").	Ask students to create concept maps that show interrelationships (including cause-and-effect relationships) among various events during a particular period in history.
GRADE 7	Analyze the structure an author uses to organize a text, including how the major sections contribute to the whole and to the development of the ideas. (RI.7.5)	Before students read a chapter in their science textbook, have them use its headings and subheadings to (1) create a general outline of the chapter and (2) generate questions they hope to answer as they read the chapter. Then, for homework, ask them to read and take notes on the chapter, using the outline and self-questions as guides for note taking.	Ask students to write a three-page summary of a chapter in their science book. Suggest that chapter headings and subheadings might help students organize their thoughts, but emphasize that their summaries should, first and foremost, focus on main ideas and a few supporting details.
	Trace and evaluate the argument and specific claims in a text, assessing whether the reasoning is sound and the evidence is relevant and sufficient to support the claims. (RI.7.8)	Give students an advertisement for a self-improvement product (e.g., a diet pill or exercise equipment); have them work in small cooperative learning groups to (1) identify the advertiser's motives and (2) evaluate the quality of evidence for the product's effectiveness.	Have students examine an Internet website that promotes an allegedly health-promoting product. Ask them to identify, either orally or in writing, possible flaws in the evidence and logic the website uses to convince people to purchase the product.

(continued)

GRADE LEVEL	EXAMPLES OF COMMON CORE STANDARDS FOR ENGLISH LANGUAGE ARTS	EXAMPLES OF INSTRUCTIONAL STRATEGIES THAT ADDRESS THESE STANDARDS *AND* PROVIDE A MEANS OF INFORMALLY ASSESSING STUDENTS' PROGRESS	EXAMPLES OF ASSESSMENTS THAT ALIGN WITH THE STANDARDS AND WITH CLASSROOM INSTRUCTION
GRADES 11–12	Analyze and evaluate the effectiveness of the structure an author uses in his or her position or argument, including whether the structure makes points clear, convincing, and engaging. (RI.11–12.5)	Describe common techniques in persuasive writing, and have students identify the various persuasive techniques used in newspaper editorials.	Ask students to (1) identify three specific persuasive techniques used in the U.S. Declaration of Independence of 1776 and (2) explain the particular purpose that each technique might have served in convincing people of the importance of gaining independence from England.
	Determine an author's point of view or purpose in a text in which the rhetoric is particularly effective, analyzing how style and content contribute to the power, persuasiveness or beauty of the text. (RI.11–12.6)	Ask students to identify the unstated assumptions underlying two news magazines' depictions of the same event (e.g., an assumption that one group is good or right and another is bad or wrong).	Give students a magazine article describing a recent event in the national or international news. Ask them to underline five sentences that reveal the author's cultural and/or political biases and to describe those biases in a two-page essay.

ᵃ The letters "RL" indicate standards related to reading literature; the letters "RI" indicate standards related to reading informational text. The number or numbers before the period indicate the grade level; the number after the period indicates the particular standard for that grade level. For example, the first entry shown here, identified as "RL.2.1," is the first standard for grade 2 for reading literature.

Source: Excerpts from *Common Core State Standards.* Copyright © 2010 by National Governors Association Center for Best Practices and Council of Chief State School Officers. Reprinted with permission. All rights reserved.

overall assessment. Figure 10.6 shows two examples. The table on the left, constructed for a 30-item paper–pencil quiz on addition, assigns different weights (i.e., different numbers of test items) to different topic–behavior combinations, with some combinations intentionally not being assessed at all. The table on the right, constructed for a high school physics unit on classical mechanics, instead uses percentages to identify the relative weights assigned to different topic–behavior combinations; the three behaviors it includes are based loosely on the first three processes in Bloom's taxonomy (*remember, understand, apply*; see Chapter 8). Both tables in Figure 10.6 intentionally place greater emphasis on some topic–behavior combinations than on others, but in other situations, equal weightings across the board might be quite appropriate.

FIGURE 10.6 Two examples of a table of specifications

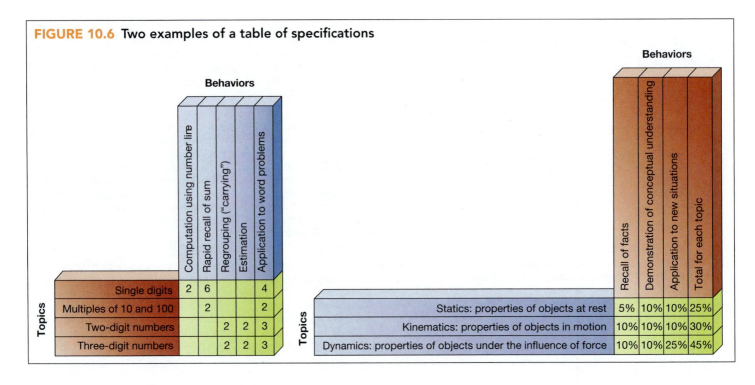

Topics	Computation using number line	Rapid recall of sum	Regrouping ("carrying")	Estimation	Application to word problems
Single digits	2	6			4
Multiples of 10 and 100		2			2
Two-digit numbers			2	2	3
Three-digit numbers			2	2	3

Topics	Recall of facts	Demonstration of conceptual understanding	Application to new situations	Total for each topic
Statics: properties of objects at rest	5%	10%	10%	25%
Kinematics: properties of objects in motion	10%	10%	10%	30%
Dynamics: properties of objects under the influence of force	10%	10%	25%	45%

A good assessment is practical.

The final RSVP characteristic is **practicality**—the extent to which assessment instruments and procedures are easy to use. Practicality encompasses issues such as these:

- How much time will it take to develop the questions and/or tasks to be used?
- Can the assessment be administered to many students at once, or is one-on-one administration required?
- Are expensive materials involved?
- How much time will the assessment take away from instructional activities?
- How quickly and easily can students' performance be evaluated?

There's often a trade-off between practicality and such other characteristics as validity and reliability. For example, a true–false test for a unit on tennis should be easy to construct and administer, but a performance assessment in which students actually demonstrate their tennis skills—even though it takes more time and energy—would undoubtedly be a more valid measure of how well students have mastered the game.

The four RSVP characteristics are summarized in Table 10.2. Of these, *validity is the most important*. Teachers must use assessment techniques that validly assess students' accomplishment of instructional goals and objectives. Yet it's important to note that *reliability is a necessary condition for validity*, especially when summative assessments are involved. Reliability doesn't guarantee validity, however, as our earlier Fathead Test of Intelligence exercise illustrated. Standardization is most relevant to summative assessments, especially those in which educators want to compare different students' performances (we'll identify reasons for occasionally doing so later in the chapter).

Table 10.2 • The RSVP Characteristics of Good Assessment

CHARACTERISTIC	DEFINITION	RELEVANT QUESTIONS TO CONSIDER
Reliability	The extent to which an assessment instrument or procedure yields consistent results for each student	• How much are students' scores affected by temporary conditions unrelated to the characteristic being assessed? • Do different people score students' performance similarly? • Do different parts of a single assessment instrument lead to similar conclusions about a student's achievement?
Standardization	The extent to which an assessment instrument or procedure is similar for all students	• Are all students assessed on identical or similar content? • Do all students have the same types of tasks to perform? • Is everyone given the same instructions? • Do all students have the same time limits? • Is everyone's performance evaluated using the same criteria?
Validity	The extent to which an assessment instrument or procedure measures what it is intended to measure and enables appropriate inferences to be made	• Does the assessment tap into a representative sample of the content domain being assessed (*content validity*)? • Do students' scores predict their later success in a domain (*predictive validity*)? • Does the instrument accurately measure a particular psychological or educational characteristic (*construct validity*)?
Practicality	The extent to which an assessment instrument or procedure is easy and inexpensive to use	• How much class time does the assessment take? • How quickly and easily can students' responses be scored? • Is special training required to administer or score the assessment? • Does the assessment require specialized materials that must be purchased?

Furthermore, standardization can enhance the reliability of assessment results and so can indirectly enhance their validity. Practicality should be a consideration only when validity isn't significantly jeopardized in the process.

Not only is it important for teachers to assess students' ongoing performance and progress, but it's also important for teachers to *assess their own assessment practices*. In the hotlinked Self-Check quiz and Application Exercise that follow, you can check and apply your understandings related to Big Idea 10.3:

Ideally, classroom assessments have four RSVP characteristics—reliability, standardization, validity, and practicality—with validity being the most important.

MyEdLab **Self-Check 10.3**

MyEdLab **Application Exercise 10.3.** In this exercise, you can practice using the four RSVP characteristics in evaluating a variety of classroom assessment strategies.

10.4 INFORMALLY AND FORMALLY ASSESSING STUDENTS' PROGRESS AND ACHIEVEMENTS

Big Idea 10.4 Spontaneous, informal assessments and preplanned formal assessments both have important roles to play in enhancing students' learning and achievement.

Now that we've examined desirable characteristics of any classroom assessment, we're in a good position to explore both informal and formal classroom assessment strategies. As we go along, we'll consider the goals and objectives for which various assessment strategies might be most appropriate and the RSVP characteristics of different approaches.

Conducting Informal Assessments

Teachers' spontaneous, unplanned assessments have several advantages. First and foremost, they provide continuing feedback about the effectiveness of ongoing instructional activities. Second, they can be easily adjusted at a moment's notice. For example, when students express misconceptions about a topic, a teacher's follow-up questions can probe their beliefs and reasoning processes. Third, informal assessments provide information that may either support or call into question the data obtained from more formal assessment tasks. Finally, regular observations of students' behaviors provide clues about social, emotional, and motivational factors affecting classroom performance and may often be the only practical means of assessing such instructional goals as "enjoys reading" or "shows courtesy."

Here we offer general strategies that can enhance the usefulness of informal assessments.

Observe both verbal and nonverbal behaviors.

Teachers can learn a lot both from what students *say* and from what they *do* during the school day. Following are examples of informal assessment strategies:

- Ask questions during a lesson (e.g., see the Classroom Strategies box "Asking Questions to Promote and Assess Learning" in Chapter 8).
- Listen to what and how much students contribute to whole-class and small-group discussions; make note of the kinds of questions they ask.
- Observe how quickly and proficiently students perform various physical tasks.
- Identify the kinds of activities in which students engage voluntarily (e.g., see Figure 10.7).
- Watch for body language that might reflect students' feelings about particular classroom tasks.

- Look at the relative frequency of on-task and off-task behaviors; also look for patterns in *when* students are off task (e.g., see the discussion of *functional analysis* in Chapter 9).
- Observe students' interactions with peers in class, at lunch, and on the playground.

By observing both verbal and nonverbal behaviors, teachers can acquire a lot of information not only about students' knowledge and misconceptions but also about students' study strategies, self-regulation skills, interests and priorities, feelings about classroom subject matter, and attributions for success and failure. For example, in the opening case study, Ellie's active engagement in class discussions and diligent completion of assignments have led Ms. Davidson to conclude that Ellie "always puts forth her best effort."

Ask yourself whether your existing beliefs and expectations might be biasing your judgments.

Let's return to a principle presented in Chapter 2: *Prior knowledge and beliefs affect new learning, usually for the better but sometimes for the worse.* This principle applies to teachers as well as to students. Like all human beings, teachers impose meanings on the things they see and hear, and those meanings are influenced by the things they already know or believe to be true. Teachers' existing beliefs about particular students, as well as their expectations for students' performance, inevitably affect teachers' ongoing informal assessments of students' behaviors.[24]

FIGURE 10.7 A recent in-depth psychoeducational evaluation has determined that despite IQ scores in the average range, 8-year-old Peter has exceptional difficulty with certain aspects of reading and math; he may also have a mild form of an autism spectrum disorder. As illustrated in this page from his "Going Back in Time" book, he appears to have a strong interest in drawing and writing about science fiction—an interest that his teachers might build on as they assign reading, writing, and math tasks.

Among the common sources of bias in teachers' informal assessments of student performance are their existing beliefs about students of different ethnic groups, genders, and socioeconomic groups.[25] A classic experiment with college students[26] provides an example. Students were told that they were participating in a study on teacher evaluation methods and then shown a video of a fourth grader named Hannah. Two versions of the video gave differing impressions about Hannah's socioeconomic status: Her clothing, the kind of playground on which she played, and information about her parents' occupations indirectly conveyed to some students that she was from a high socioeconomic background and to others that she was from a low socioeconomic background. All students watched Hannah taking an oral achievement test (one on which she performed at grade level) and were asked to rate her on several characteristics. Students who had been led to believe that Hannah came from a wealthy family rated her ability well above grade level, whereas students believing that she came from a poor family evaluated her as being below grade level. The two groups of students also rated Hannah's work habits, motivation, social skills, and general maturity differently.

Keep a written record of your observations.

Let's revisit another principle presented in Chapter 2: *Long-term memory isn't necessarily forever.* Teachers' memories of students' classroom behaviors can probably never be totally accurate, dependable records of what students have actually done and said. As normal human beings, teachers are

[24] Hattie, 2009; Ritts, Patterson, & Tubbs, 1992; Stiggins & Chappuis, 2012.

[25] Pellegrini, 2011; Ready & Wright, 2011; J. P. Robinson & Lubienski, 2011; van den Bergh, Denessen, Hornstra, Voeten, & Holland, 2010.

[26] Darley & Gross, 1983.

apt to remember some student behaviors but not others. When teachers must depend heavily on informal in-class observations of students' performance—and this will often be the case when working with young children who have limited reading and writing skills—they should keep ongoing, written records of what they see students do and what they hear students say, especially for students whose behaviors or comments aren't typical for their age-group.[27]

Don't take any single observation too seriously; instead, look for patterns over time.

The greatest strength of informal assessment is its practicality. It typically involves little or no teacher time either beforehand or after the fact (except for keeping written records of observations). Furthermore, it's flexible, in that teachers can adapt their assessment procedures on the spur of the moment, altering them as circumstances change.

Despite the practicality of informal assessment, its other RSVP characteristics are often questionable. For one thing, children and adolescents can behave inconsistently from one day to the next, or even within a single day or class period. Such inconsistency calls the reliability of informal assessments into question. A teacher who asks Mohamed a question in class may happen to ask him the *only* question for which he doesn't know the answer. A teacher who sees Naomi off task during an activity may happen to look at her during the *only* time she's off task. Furthermore, informal assessments are rarely, if ever, standardized for all students. Teachers ask different questions of different students, and they might observe one student in a context quite different from that of another student. Hence such assessments will definitely *not* yield the same kinds of information for all students.

Even when teachers see consistency in students' behavior over time, they don't always get accurate information about what students have learned. In other words, validity may be a problem. For example, Tom may intentionally answer questions incorrectly so that he doesn't come across as a know-it-all, and Margot may be reluctant to say anything because of a chronic stuttering problem. In general, when teachers use in-class questions to assess students' learning, they must be aware that some students—especially females and students from certain cultural groups—will be less eager to respond than others.[28]

When teachers use informal assessment to draw conclusions about what students know and can do, then, they should base their conclusions on many observations over a long period. Furthermore, they should treat any conclusions only as *hypotheses* that they must either confirm or disconfirm through other means. In the end, most teachers rely more heavily on formal assessment techniques to determine whether students have achieved instructional goals and objectives.

Designing and Giving Formal Assessments

Remember, formal classroom assessment tasks don't just *assess* students' learning, they also *have an impact on* students' learning. Furthermore, the conclusions teachers draw from assessment results—conclusions that affect final grades and decisions about promotion and graduation—can have a significant effect on students' future educational and career options. Accordingly, teachers must take their formal assessments very seriously, planning and designing them carefully, administering them under optimal conditions for student performance, and scoring them reliably and equitably.

Following are a number of recommendations that should increase the RSVP characteristics of formal classroom assessments.

Get as much information as possible within reasonable time limits.

On average, longer assessment instruments have greater validity and reliability. To see why this might be so, try the next exercise.

---

[27] M. D. Miller, Linn, & Gronlund, 2009; Stiggins & Chappuis, 2012.
[28] Castagno & Brayboy, 2008; Rogoff, 2003; Wentzel, 2009; also see the Cultural Considerations feature "Cultural and Ethnic Differences in Verbal Interaction" in Chapter 8.

—————————— **SEE FOR YOURSELF** ——————————
QUICK QUIZ

The following multiple-choice quiz is designed to assess what you learned about human motivation in Chapter 5. No peeking at the answers until you've answered both questions!

1. Which one of the following alternatives best illustrates *situated motivation?*
   a. Alexander has been interested in air travel and aerodynamics since he was a toddler, and he often sketches airplanes during his free time in class.
   b. When Barbara gets a lower grade on an assignment than she had anticipated, she says to her friends, "I deserved a much higher grade. Mr. Smith obviously doesn't like me very much."
   c. Colby is confident he'll do well on an upcoming history test because he has done well on other history tests throughout the semester.
   d. Although Donna has never been terribly interested in physical fitness, she eagerly learns an aerobic exercise routine her teacher has set to some of her favorite hip-hop music.

2. Which one of the following alternatives is the best example of *cognitive dissonance?*
   a. Alicia says to herself, "I don't really like math very much, but I'm taking it because it's important for getting into a good college."
   b. Bob is certain that metal always sinks, and so he's quite puzzled when he sees a large metal battleship floating in the harbor.
   c. Carly gets so anxious during an important test that she can hardly concentrate on the test items.
   d. David gets really angry when he reads about the mass genocides the Nazis carried out during World War II.

Now score your quiz. The correct answers are *d* and *b* for Items 1 and 2, respectively. If you answered both questions correctly, you earned an A (100%) on the quiz. If you answered only one question correctly, you earned an F (50%). And, of course, two incorrect answers also mean an F.

Unfortunately, the length of the quiz is problematic. First, we assessed your knowledge of only two concepts (situated motivation and cognitive dissonance) out of the many concepts presented in Chapter 5. Two concepts are hardly a representative sample of what you've learned about motivation, and so the quiz has questionable content validity. Second, if you interpreted one of the items differently than we authors intended for you to interpret it, you might have answered an item incorrectly despite having the knowledge to answer it correctly. For example, in Item 2, if you assumed that David had previously thought the Nazis were nice, tolerant people, you might reasonably have selected *d* as an example of cognitive dissonance. With this one slip-up, you would have gone from an A to an F. When a single misinterpretation moves a student from a very good grade to a very poor one—a misinterpretation that might occur on one occasion but not another—the reliability of the assessment is in doubt, and thus its validity is also questionable.

To some degree, then, longer is better when it comes to formal assessments. Ideally, a classroom assessment should include enough questions or tasks that (1) it adequately represents the content domain being assessed and (2) one or two errors due to irrelevant factors (such as misinterpretations of questions) don't seriously impact the final result. Teachers shouldn't go overboard, however. Students become very tired—and teachers have little time left for instruction—when tests and other assessment tasks take a great deal of time to complete.

When practical, use authentic tasks.

Historically, most educational assessment instruments have focused on measuring basic knowledge and skills in relative isolation from tasks typically found in the outside world. Spelling quizzes, math word problems, and physical fitness tests are examples of such traditional assessments. Yet ultimately students must be able to transfer their knowledge and skills to complex activities outside the classroom. The notion of **authentic assessment**—assessing students' knowledge and skills in an authentic, similar-to-real-life context—is gaining increasing prominence in today's schools.[29]

---

[29] For example, see E. L. Baker, 2007; R. L. Johnson, Penny, & Gordon, 2009; Quellmalz et al., 2013; Wiggins & McTighe, 2007.

FIGURE 10.8 In his aerial and side-view drawings of "Golden Boot Island," 12-year-old Francisco demonstrates what he has learned about depicting elevation and topography.

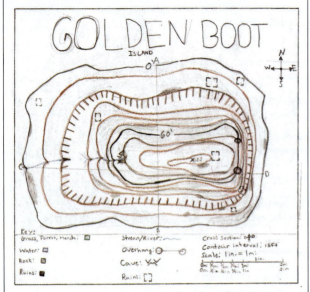

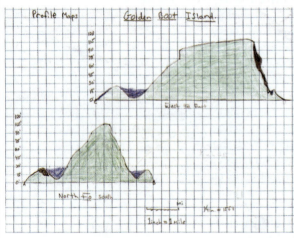

In some situations, an authentic assessment can involve paper and pencil. For example, a teacher might ask students to write a letter to a friend or submit articles to a school newspaper. At other times it involves performance tasks. For example, a teacher might ask students to converse in a foreign language, design and build a bookshelf, or successfully maneuver a car into a parallel parking space.[30] Occasionally authentic tasks have both paper–pencil and performance components. For example, a teacher might ask students to create and post new entries for Wikipedia or to write lab reports describing what they have done and discovered in a computer-simulated science experiment.

Whether they be paper–pencil, performance based, or some combination of the two, assessment tasks can be authentic to varying degrees. For instance, they might involve having students apply new skills to imagined or hypothetical—rather than truly real-world—situations. As an illustration, one seventh-grade social studies teacher asked students to apply their mapping skills in depicting an island with certain topographical features (e.g., a stream running into the ocean on the west shore) and contours of certain heights. Figure 10.8 shows 12-year-old Francisco's response to the assignment.

Use paper–pencil assessment tasks when they are consistent with instructional goals.

In some situations—for instance, when the desired outcome is simple recall of facts—a teacher might ask students to respond to multiple-choice or short-answer questions on a paper–pencil test. In other situations—for instance, when a teacher wants students to critique a literary work or use scientific evidence to back up a conclusion—essay tasks are often more appropriate. *If a teacher can truly assess knowledge of a domain by having students respond in writing, then a paper–pencil assessment is a good choice.*

Paper–pencil assessment is typically easier and faster, and thus has greater practicality, than performance assessment. Usually a paper–pencil task can be administered to all students at the same time and under the same conditions, so it's easily standardized. To the extent that a paper–pencil assessment has a large number of items that can be objectively scored—as is true for true–false and multiple-choice tests—it's also likely to be fairly reliable.

The RSVP characteristic of most concern in a paper–pencil assessment is its validity. When teachers ask questions that require only short, simple responses (e.g., true–false, multiple-choice, and matching questions), they can representatively sample students' knowledge about many topics within a relatively short time period. In this sense, then, such questions can yield high content validity. Yet these types of items may not accurately reflect important instructional goals. To assess students' ability to apply what they've learned to new situations, solve complex real-world problems, critically analyze the logic and evidence presented in a persuasive essay, or engage in other complex cognitive processes, teachers may sometimes need to be satisfied with a few tasks requiring lengthy responses.[31]

Unfortunately, many paper–pencil assessment instruments—especially teacher-created tests—focus primarily on basic skills and knowledge of discrete facts (e.g., look once again at Figure 10.3).[32] But with a little ingenuity, teachers can develop paper–pencil assessment tasks

---

[30] Educators are not in complete agreement in their use of the terms *performance assessment* and *authentic assessment,* and many treat the terms more or less as synonyms. We authors find it useful to consider separately whether an assessment involves *performance* (rather than paper and pencil) and whether it involves a complex, real-world *(authentic)* task. In the discussion here, then, we do *not* use the two terms interchangeably.

[31] Brookhart & Nitko, 2011; H.-S. Lee, Liu, & Linn, 2011; Marzano & Kendall, 2007.

[32] Bransford et al., 2006; Corliss & Linn, 2011; Nickerson, 1989; Poole, 1994; Shepard et al., 2005.

that require conceptual understanding and complex cognitive processes. You've already seen examples in Figure 3.11 (Chapter 3) and Figure 10.8. As another illustration, consider the following assessment task given to students who live an hour's drive from Rocky Mountain National Park, which has altitudes ranging from 1½ to more than 2 miles above sea level:

> A group of Girl Scouts went hiking in Rocky Mountain National Park. They noticed that it was harder to breathe when hiking in the mountains than when hiking in _____ [students' hometown]. During the hike, one girl opened a tube of suntan lotion that she bought in _____ [hometown]. When she opened it, a small squirt of air and lotion shot out.
>
> • Why did the girls have a hard time breathing?
> • Why did the air and lotion squirt out of the tube?[33]

Teachers can also assess complex cognitive processes with carefully constructed multiple-choice questions. In the "Quick Quiz" exercise you did earlier, you saw two multiple-choice questions that required you to transfer what you've learned about motivation to new situations. The last two items in the Classroom Strategies box "Constructing Multiple-Choice Items" are additional examples.

Use performance assessments when necessary to ensure validity.

In situations where paper–pencil tasks are clearly *not* a good reflection of what students have learned, teachers may need to sacrifice practicality to gain the greater validity that a performance assessment provides. Following are just a few of the many forms that performance tasks might take:

• Playing a musical instrument
• Conversing in a foreign language
• Engaging in a debate about social issues
• Fixing a malfunctioning machine
• Role-playing a job interview
• Presenting research findings to a group of teachers, peers, and community members

Performance assessment lends itself especially well to the assessment of complex achievements, such as those that involve simultaneous use of multiple skills. It can also be quite helpful in assessing problem solving, creativity, and critical thinking. Furthermore, performance tasks are often more meaningful, thought provoking, and authentic for students—and so often more motivating—than paper–pencil tasks.[34]

Some performance assessments focus on tangible *products* that students create—perhaps a sculpture, scientific invention, or poster display. In situations with no tangible product, teachers must instead look at the specific *processes and behaviors* that students exhibit—perhaps how they give an oral presentation, execute a forward roll, or play an instrumental solo. When teachers look at processes rather than products, they may in some instances probe students' *thinking processes*. For example, if a teacher who wants to determine whether students have acquired some of the concrete operational or formal operational abilities that Piaget described (e.g., conservation, separation and control of variables), the teacher might present tasks similar to those Piaget used and ask students to explain their reasoning (see Chapter 6). And a teacher can often determine how students reason about scientific phenomena by asking them to manipulate physical objects (e.g., chemicals in a chemistry lab, electrical circuit boards in a physics class), make predictions about what will happen under varying circumstances, and then explain their results.[35] The Classroom Strategies box "Developing Performance Assessments" offers several suggestions for using performance assessments for different age levels and content domains.

MyEdLab
Video Example 10.3.

This video shows a seventh-grade German teacher using computer technology for both instruction and performance assessment. Is the teacher conducting formative assessment or summative assessment?

think about it
Which topics and skills in the content domain(s) you will be teaching might be validly assessed with paper–pencil assessments? Which ones would require performance assessments?

---

[33] Pugh, Schmidt, & Russell, 2010, p. 9.

[34] Darling-Hammond, Ancess, & Falk, 1995; DiMartino & Castaneda, 2007; R. L. Johnson et al., 2009; Khattri & Sweet, 1996; Paris & Paris, 2001.

[35] De Corte, Greer, & Verschaffel, 1996; diSessa, 2007; Magnusson, Boyle, & Templin, 1994; Quellmalz & Hoskyn, 1997.

CLASSROOM STRATEGIES

Constructing Multiple-Choice Items

- **When assessing basic knowledge, rephrase ideas presented in class or in the textbook.**

  A middle school language arts teacher uses short multiple-choice quizzes to assess students' understanding of each week's new vocabulary words. The items never include the specific definitions students have been given. For instance, for the word *manacle*, students have been given this definition: "Device used to restrain a person's hands or wrists." But the item on the quiz is this one:

  Which one of the following words or phrases is closest in meaning to the word *manacle*?
  a. Insane
  b. Handcuffs
  c. Out of control
  d. Saltwater creature that clings to hard surfaces
  *(The correct answer is **b**.)*

- **Present incorrect alternatives that are clearly wrong to students who know the material but plausible to students who haven't mastered it.**

  After a unit on the seasons, a middle school science teacher asks this question:

  What is the *main* reason that it is colder in winter than in summer?
  a. Because the earth is in the part of its orbit farthest away from the sun
  b. Because wind is more likely to come from the north than from the south
  c. Because the sun's rays hit our part of the earth at more of an angle
  d. Because the snow on the ground reflects rather than absorbs the sun's heat
  *(The correct answer is **c**.)*

- **To assess complex cognitive processes, ask students to apply what they've learned to new situations.**

  A high school physics teacher includes the following question on a quiz designed to assess what students have learned about simple machines:

  An inventor has just designed a new device for cutting paper. Without knowing anything else about his invention, we can predict that it is probably which type of machine?

  a. A lever
  b. A movable pulley
  c. An inclined plane
  d. A wedge
  *(The correct answer is **d**.)*

- **Occasionally incorporate visual materials.**

  A high school geography teacher includes maps in some of his questions. Following is an example:

  Using the map below, choose the most logical explanation for why people living in the Middle East and people living in the Far East developed distinctly different languages.
  a. People in the Far East had little contact with those who lived in the Middle East.
  b. People who lived by the ocean had lifestyles very different from those who lived in the mountains.
  c. People who lived in southern climates had lifestyles very different from those of people who lived in northern climates.
  d. People in the two regions were constantly fighting over desirable farmland.
  *(The correct answer is **a**.)*

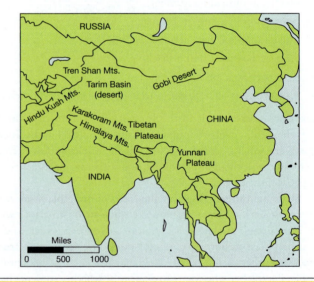

Although performance assessment tasks sometimes provide more valid indicators of students' accomplishments than paper–pencil tasks, students' responses to a *single* performance assessment task may be a poor indication of their overall achievement.[36] Content validity is at stake here. If time constraints allow students to perform only one or two complex tasks, those tasks may not be a representative sample of what students have learned and can do. In addition, teachers may have trouble standardizing assessment conditions for everyone and scoring students' performance consistently—problems that adversely affect reliability. And performance assessments are often less practical than more traditional paper–pencil assessments. Conducting a performance assessment can be quite time-consuming, especially when a teacher must observe students one by one or when a task requires students to spend considerable time in the outside community.

---

[36] Crehan, 2001; R. L. Johnson et al., 2009; S. Klassen, 2006; Stiggins & Chappuis, 2012.

CLASSROOM STRATEGIES

Developing Performance Assessments

- **Have students create products that reflect what they have learned.**

  A middle school science teacher asks students to make posters that summarize their projects for the school science fair. The teacher tells the students that the posters should include (1) a research question or hypothesis, (2) the method used to address the question or hypothesis, (3) results obtained, and (4) one or more conclusions.

- **When the assigned task doesn't yield a tangible product, observe students' behaviors and, if appropriate, probe their thinking processes.**

  After a unit on major and minor scales in an instrumental band class, a music teacher assesses students' understanding of natural minor scales by having them play three different ones on their instruments. If a student plays a scale incorrectly, the teacher asks the student to describe the structure of a minor scale (whole-step, half-step, whole-step, whole-step, half-step, whole-step, whole-step) and explain why the scale might not have sounded right.

- **Consider assigning complex, lengthy tasks as group projects.**

  In a unit on urban geography, a high school social studies teacher asks small cooperative groups to choose a 6- to 8-block neighborhood near their school and then (1) identify the neighborhood's types of housing, businesses, and public spaces and services; (2) also identify common modes of transportation (e.g., walking, driving, use of public transportation systems); (3) interview at least five residents and/or business owners in the neighborhood, asking about the things that these people think are "good" and "bad" about the neighborhood; (4) identify significant problems the neighborhood appears to have; and (5) write a report that both describes the group's findings and makes at least three recommendations for improving the neighborhood. In evaluating students' performance, the teacher considers each group's overall accomplishments plus individual students' contributions to the group effort.

- **Consider incorporating the assessment into normal instructional activities.**

  To assess students' understanding of simple graphs, a first-grade teacher distributes a table that lists the 12 months of the year. She asks her students to circulate around the room, gathering each class member's signature in a box beside his or her birthday month. In this way, students create graphs showing how many class members were born in each month. The graphs indicate that some but not all students have a general understanding of graphs. In the example shown here, many students (e.g., Cam, Sara, Kelsey, Adrienne, Spencer) have all written their names inside a single box in the table. However, a few students (Kristen, Jesse, Kristah, and Cameron) have used *two* cells to write their names, perhaps because they (1) haven't mastered the idea that one person equals one box in the table or (2) can't write small enough to fit their names inside a box and don't know how to solve this problem. The graph also shows that one child (Meg, who has a March birthday) hasn't yet learned to write words, including her name, in the traditional left-to-right manner.

Birthday Graph

Sources: Baxter, Elder, & Glaser, 1996; Boschee & Baron, 1993; DiMartino & Castaneda, 2007; Lester, Lambdin, & Preston, 1997; Newmann, 1997; Shavelson & Baxter, 1992; Stiggins & Chappuis, 2012.

As you can see, then, informal assessment, formal paper–pencil assessment, and formal performance assessment all have their strengths and weaknesses. Table 10.3 summarizes their RSVP characteristics and offers relevant suggestions. In the end, teachers may find that they can best assess students' achievement with a combination of paper–pencil and performance tasks and supplement their findings with informal observations of students' typical classroom behaviors.

Define tasks clearly, and give students some structure to guide their responses.

Contrary to what some teachers believe, there's usually little to be gained from assigning ambiguous tasks to assess students' learning and achievement. Whether or not students know how to respond to assessment tasks, they should at least understand what they're being asked to do. As an illustration, consider this essay question in a history class:

List the causes of the American Revolution.

Table 10.3 • Evaluating RSVP Characteristics of Different Kinds of Assessments				
KIND OF ASSESSMENT	**RELIABILITY**	**STANDARDIZATION**	**VALIDITY**	**PRACTICALITY**
Informal assessment	A single, brief assessment is not a reliable indicator of achievement. Teachers must look for consistency in a student's performance across time and in different contexts.	Informal observations are rarely, if ever, standardized. Accordingly, teachers should not compare one student to another on the basis of informal assessments alone.	Students' public behaviors in the classroom aren't always valid indicators of their achievement (e.g., some students may try to hide high achievement from peers, others may come from cultures that encourage listening more than talking).	Informal assessment is definitely practical: It's flexible and can occur spontaneously during instruction.
Formal paper–pencil assessment	Objectively scorable items are highly reliable. Teachers can enhance the reliability of subjectively scorable items by specifying scoring criteria in concrete terms.	In most instances paper–pencil tasks are easily standardized for all students. Giving students choices (e.g., regarding topics to write about or questions to answer) may increase motivation but reduces standardization.	Numerous questions requiring short, simple responses can provide a more representative sample of the content domain. But tasks requiring lengthy responses may sometimes more closely match instructional goals.	Paper–pencil assessment is usually practical: All students can be assessed at once, and no special materials are required.
Formal performance assessment	Performance assessment tasks are often difficult to score reliably. Teachers can enhance reliability by specifying scoring criteria in concrete terms (e.g., with a checklist or rubric).	Some performance assessment tasks are easily standardized, whereas others are not.	Performance tasks may sometimes be more consistent with instructional goals than paper–pencil tasks. However, a single performance task may not provide a representative sample of the content domain; several tasks may be necessary to ensure content validity.	Performance assessment is typically less practical than other approaches: It may involve special materials, and it can take a fair amount of class time, especially if students must be assessed one by one.

One student might take the word *list* literally and simply write "Stamp Act, Boston Massacre, Quartering Act." But another student might write several pages describing Britain's increasing demands for revenue from the American colonies, the colonists' resentment of taxation without representation, and King George III's apparent lack of concern about the colonists' welfare. Responses to unstructured tasks may go in so many different directions that scoring them consistently and reliably is virtually impossible. Especially in situations where a great deal of material is potentially relevant, students need guidance about the length and completeness of desired responses. For example, the previous essay task about the American Revolution might be rewritten like this:

> Identify three events or policies during the 1760s and/or 1770s that contributed to the outbreak of the American Revolution. For each one, explain in three to five sentences how it increased tension between England and the American colonies.

Performance assessment tasks, too, require a certain amount of structure, especially if they're used for summative (rather than formative) assessment. For instance, students should have detailed instructions about what they should accomplish, what materials and equipment they can use, and how much time they have to get the job done.[37] Such structure helps to standardize the assessment and so enables a teacher to evaluate students' performance more reliably. A *lot* of structure can decrease a performance task's validity, however. Especially when giving authentic assessments, teachers want assigned tasks to be similar to those in the outside world, and real-world

---

[37] Gronlund & Waugh, 2009; R. L. Johnson et al., 2009; Shepard et al., 2005.

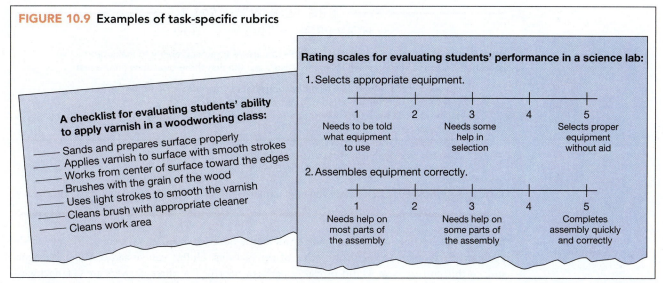

FIGURE 10.9 Examples of task-specific rubrics

Sources: Checklist from *Measurement and Assessment in Teaching,* 9th edition, by Robert L. Linn and M. David Miller. Copyright © 2005 by Pearson Education, Inc. Printed and electronically reproduced by permission of Pearson Education, Inc. Upper Saddle River, New Jersey. Scales from *Writing Instructional Objectives for Teaching and Assessment,* 7th edition, by Norman E. Gronlund. Copyright © 2011 by Pearson Education, Inc. Printed and electronically reproduced by permission of Pearson Education, Inc. Upper Saddle River, New Jersey.

tasks don't always have a lot of structure. Teachers must often seek a happy medium, providing enough structure to guide students in the right direction but not so much that students make few of their own decisions about how to proceed.

One obvious strategy for defining and structuring an assessment task is to give students a checklist or rubric by which their performance will be evaluated. You've previously seen examples for scoring fourth graders' word-problem solutions (Figure 10.4) and evaluating high school students' writing samples (Figure 10.5). If you look at those two figures once again, you'll notice that each one provides criteria that are applicable to a general *category* of tasks—solving word problems in one case and writing nonfiction in the other. Checklists and rubrics are most likely to impact students' long-term learning and development when they portray the desired qualities of virtually any product or performance in a particular domain—and especially when, through regular self-assessments, students begin to internalize and adopt those criteria as being important ones to meet time after time.[38]

Yet sometimes more task-specific checklists and rubrics are helpful as well. For example, Figure 10.9 presents a checklist for evaluating students' varnishing work in a woodworking class and two rating scales for evaluating students' preparatory activities in a science lab. Such scoring guides not only guide students in their efforts to meet particular instructional objectives but also help teachers evaluate students' performance consistently and reliably—thereby enhancing the validity of the assessment results.

Carefully scrutinize items and tasks for characteristics that might put some groups at an unfair disadvantage.

Earlier in the chapter, we spoke of the potential for teacher bias in judging students' behaviors in informal assessments. But bias can creep into more formal assessments as well. In particular, an assessment has **assessment bias** if any of its items either offend or unfairly penalize members of a particular group—perhaps students of a particular gender, family background, or socioeconomic status.[39] One well-known form of assessment bias is *cultural bias,* in which an assessment puts students from a particular cultural or ethnic group at a disadvantage for reasons that have nothing to do with the particular knowledge and skills being assessed. The next exercise provides an example.

---

[38] Arter & Chappuis, 2006; Popham, 2006.
[39] G. E. García & Pearson, 1994; R. L. Johnson et al., 2009; Popham, 2006.

SEE FOR YOURSELF
HOW PRODUCTIVE WILL YOU BE?

Imagine that you're taking a test designed to estimate your general ability to make productive contributions to the society in which you live. Here are the first three questions on the test:

1. When you enter a hogan, in which direction should you move around the fire?
2. Why is turquoise often attached to a baby's cradleboard?
3. If you need black wool for weaving a rug, which one of the following alternatives would give you the blackest color?
   a. Dye the wool with a mixture of sumac, ochre, and piñon gum.
   b. Dye the wool with a mixture of indigo, lichen, and mesquite.
   c. Use the undyed wool of specially bred black sheep.

Try to answer these questions before you read further.

Did you have trouble answering some or all of the questions? All three were written from the perspective of a particular culture—that of the Navajos. Unless you've had considerable exposure to this culture, you would probably perform poorly. The three answers are (1) clockwise, (2) to ward off evil, and (3) Alternative *a*—"Dye the wool with a mixture of sumac, ochre, and piñon gum."[40]

Is the test culturally biased? That depends. If the test is designed to assess your ability to succeed in a traditional Navajo community, the questions might be quite appropriate. But if it's designed to assess your ability to accomplish tasks for which knowledge of Navajo culture is irrelevant, the questions have cultural bias.

It's important to remember that an assessment has bias if it can potentially *offend* members of a particular group. For example, imagine a test question that implies that girls are more competent than boys, and imagine another question that includes a picture in which members of a particular ethnic or racial group are engaging in inappropriate behavior. Such questions exemplify assessment bias because some groups of students (boys in the first situation and members of the depicted group in the second) are likely to be offended by the questions and thus distracted from doing their best on the test. The Cultural Considerations box "Potential Sources of Assessment Bias" gives examples of things teachers should look for and think about.

When giving tests, encourage students to do their best, but don't arouse a lot of anxiety.

Most students get a little bit anxious about tests and other important assessments, and a small amount of anxiety can actually enhance performance (see Chapter 5). But some students become extremely anxious in test-taking situations—they have **test anxiety**—to the point where their scores significantly underestimate what they've learned.[41] Such students appear to be concerned primarily about the *evaluative* aspect of tests, worrying that someone will judge them as being "stupid" or in some other way inadequate. Excessive, debilitating test anxiety is especially common in girls, students from ethnic minority groups (recall the discussion of *stereotype threat* in Chapter 5), and students with disabilities.[42]

Test anxiety interferes not only with retrieval and performance at the time of an assessment but also with encoding and storage when learners are preparing for the assessment.[43] Thus highly test-anxious students don't just *test* poorly; they also *learn* poorly. Table 10.4 distinguishes between classroom assessment practices that are likely to lead to facilitating anxiety and those that may elicit debilitating anxiety.

---

[40] Gilpin, 1968; Nez, 2011.

[41] Cassady, 2010; Hembree, 1988; E. Hong, O'Neil, & Feldon, 2005; Lang & Lang, 2010.

[42] R. Carter, Williams, & Silverman, 2008; Cassady, 2010; Putwain, 2007; J. L. Smith, 2004; Steele, 1997; Whitaker Sena, Lowe, & Lee, 2007.

[43] Cassady, 2010; Zeidner & Matthews, 2005.

CULTURAL CONSIDERATIONS

Potential Sources of Assessment Bias

Consider these hypothetical assessment items, one for a math test and the other for a test of writing skills:

1. As a member of his high school baseball team this year, Mark has hit the ball 17 times in the 36 times he's been at bat. Of those hits, only 12 got him safely to base; the other 5 were either fly balls or sacrifice bunts that resulted in outs. And in three of Mark's at-bats, poor pitches enabled Mark to walk to first base. Based on this information, calculate Mark's batting average for the year so far.
2. Would you rather swim in an ocean, a lake, or a swimming pool? Write a two-page persuasive essay defending your choice.

Question 1 assumes a fair amount of knowledge about baseball—knowledge that some students, especially boys, are more likely to have than other students. Question 2 would obviously be difficult for students who haven't swum in all three situations and would be even more difficult for those who have never gone swimming at all; many students from low-income families might easily fall into one of these two categories. The items have assessment bias because some students will perform better than others because of differences in their background experiences, *not* because of differences in what they've learned in the classroom.

In considering possible sources of bias in classroom assessments, teachers must look not only at the content of their assessment tasks but also at how the tasks are being administered. For example, students who have recently immigrated and only begun to learn English—even those students with strong math skills—may do poorly on math word problems because most word problems require a good command of written English.[a] In such instances, a teacher might restate the problems in simpler English—or if possible, in students' native language—and perhaps draw pictures to help students understand the problem-solving tasks. And let's return to a point made in Chapter 4: Children from some cultural groups (e.g., those from some Native American communities) prefer to practice a skill privately until they attain reasonable mastery.[b] In such cases, a teacher might let students practice new skills away from the limelight and demonstrate their progress in private, one-on-one sessions.

An assessment instrument isn't necessarily biased just because one group of students gets higher scores than another group. It's biased only if the groups' scores are different when the knowledge and skills a teacher is trying to assess *aren't* different. In some cases, different groups have different backgrounds that affect their classroom learning and achievement as well as their performance on assessments. For example, the fact that, on average, boys have more mathematically oriented toys and experiences than girls may give them an advantage that affects both their ability to learn certain math concepts and processes *and* their ability to perform well on tasks assessing mastery of those concepts and processes.[c] Similarly, if students from low-income families have had few opportunities to venture beyond their immediate neighborhoods (fewer museum trips, less travel, etc.), their more limited exposure to diverse environments is likely to impact *both* their classroom achievement and their performance on assessments measuring that achievement.

[a] E. E. Garcia, 2005; J. P. Robinson, 2010; Solano-Flores, 2008.
[b] E. E. Garcia, 1994; Tyler et al., 2008.
[c] Jacobs, Davis-Kean, Bleeker, Eccles, & Malanchuk, 2005; Leaper & Friedman, 2007.

Establish conditions for the assessment that enable students to maximize their performance.

Administration procedures for an assessment can impact the validity of the results. For example, students are more likely to perform at their best when they complete an assessment in a comfortable environment with acceptable room temperature, adequate lighting, reasonable workspace, and minimal distractions. This comfort factor may be especially important for students who are easily distracted, unaccustomed to formal assessments, or uninterested in exerting much effort—for instance, students who are at risk for academic failure and dropping out of school.[44]

In addition, teachers should encourage students to ask questions whenever they're uncertain about what an assessment task is requiring them to do. (Even after many years of experience developing assignments and exams, we authors have occasionally had students interpreting and responding to tasks and questions in ways we didn't anticipate.) Without such encouragement, some students—including many from ethnic minority groups—may be reluctant to ask questions during formal assessments.[45]

---

[44] Popham, 2006; Shriner & Spicuzza, 1995.
[45] L. R. Cheng, 1987; C. A. Grant & Gomez, 2001; J. Li & Fischer, 2004.

Table 10.4 • Keeping Students' Anxiety at a Facilitative Level During Classroom Assessments

WHAT TO DO	WHAT *NOT* TO DO
Point out the value of the assessment as a feedback mechanism to improve learning; minimize use of the word *test* in describing the assessment.	Don't stress the fact that students' competence is being evaluated.
Administer one or more practice assessments or pretests—perhaps just a few quick items here and there—that give students an idea of what the final assessment will be like.	Don't keep the nature of the assessment a secret until the day it's administered.
Encourage students to do their best but not necessarily to expect perfection; for instance, say, "We're here to learn, and you can't do that without making mistakes."	Don't say or imply students that failing will have dire consequences.
Provide or allow the use of memory aids (e.g., a list of formulas or a single note card containing key facts) when instructional goals don't require students to commit information to memory.	Don't insist that students commit even trivial facts to memory.
Eliminate time limits unless speed is an important part of the skill being measured.	Don't give more questions or tasks than students can possibly respond to in the allotted time.
Continually survey the room, and be available to answer students' questions.	Don't hover over students, watching them closely as they complete the assessment.
Use unannounced ("pop") quizzes only for formative assessment (e.g., to determine an appropriate starting point for instruction).	Don't give occasional pop quizzes to motivate students to study regularly and to punish those who haven't kept up with assigned readings.
Use the results of numerous assessments to make important decisions (e.g., to assign grades).	Don't make important decisions on the basis of a single assessment.

Sources: Agarwal, D'Antonio, Roediger, McDermott, & McDaniel, 2014; Brophy, 1986, 2004 ("We're here to learn . . ." suggestion on p. 274); Cassady, 2010; Cizek, 2003; Gaudry & Bradshaw, 1970; K. T. Hill, 1984; K. T. Hill & Wigfield, 1984; Sieber, Kameya, & Paulson, 1970; Spaulding, 1992; Stipek, 2002b; Usher, 2009.

Take reasonable steps to discourage cheating.

When students cheat on assessments, their scores don't accurately reflect what they know and can do—hence the scores have little or no validity. Furthermore, cheating can be habit forming if students discover that it enables them to get good grades with minimal effort.[46] The best approach is prevention—making sure students don't cheat in the first place—through strategies such as these:

In the weeks or days before the assessment:

- Focus students' attention on mastery goals rather than on performance goals.
- Make success without cheating a realistic possibility.
- Use assessment tasks with obvious validity for important instructional goals and objectives.
- Create two or more assessment instruments that are equivalent in form and content but have different answers (e.g., for a test, use one form in class and another for make-ups, or use different forms for different class periods).
- Explain exactly what cheating is and why it's unacceptable (e.g., explain that cheating includes plagiarism, such as copying material word for word from the Internet without giving appropriate credit).[47]
- Explain what the consequence for cheating will be.

During the assessment (especially during a test or quiz):

- Insist that cell phones and other electronic devices be turned off and checked in at the classroom door.
- Have teacher-assigned seats during any assessments that require individual work rather than small-group work.
- Seat students as far away from one another as possible.
- Remain attentive to what students are doing throughout the assessment session, but without hovering over particular students.

---

[46] Cizek, 2003.

[47] Many middle school students erroneously believe that copying material verbatim from the Internet is appropriate and acceptable (Nixon, 2005).

Unfortunately, digital technologies now enable students to cheat in ways that weren't possible several decades ago. During quizzes, some ill-prepared students may try to communicate electronically to share answers (note the preceding recommendation about checking cell phones at the door). And when assignments require independent research in an unsupervised setting, a few students might try to pass off documents obtained on the Internet as being their own work. As teachers ourselves, we authors have found two strategies to be helpful in minimizing Internet-based plagiarism. First, we've designed assessment tasks that are so specific—and so tied to particular instructional goals—that documents found on the Internet don't meet the task requirements. Second, we've been vigilant for clues that point to questionable authorship—for example, sophisticated knowledge, vocabulary, and sentence structures that we don't typically see in our students' work.

If, despite reasonable precautions, cheating occurs and can be documented, teachers must administer whatever consequence they've previously described. This consequence should be severe enough to discourage a student from cheating again yet not so severe that the student's motivation and chances for academic success are significantly diminished over the long run. Having the student honestly redo the assessment task is one appropriate consequence; a teacher might also ask the student to write a paper about the moral implications and negative repercussions of academic dishonesty.[48] In general, teachers must remember that students' final grades should ultimately reflect *what they have learned* (more about this point a bit later). For this reason, many assessment experts recommend that the consequence for cheating *not* be a failing final grade if a student has, in other assessments, demonstrated mastery of the subject matter.[49]

Evaluating Students' Performance on Formal Assessments

As teachers evaluate students' performance on an assessment task, they must continue to be concerned about the four RSVP characteristics: reliability, standardization, validity, and practicality. Furthermore, they must keep in mind that their most important role is not to evaluate performance, but rather to *help students learn*. And for both pedagogical and legal reasons, they must preserve students' general sense of well-being and right to privacy. Each of the following strategies is valuable in achieving one or more of these ends.

After students have completed an assessment, review evaluation criteria to be sure they can adequately guide scoring.

Even the most experienced teachers can't always anticipate the many possible directions in which students might go in responding to classroom assessment tasks. As a general rule, teachers should use the criteria they've previously told students they would use. However, they may occasionally need to adjust (or perhaps add or eliminate) one or more criteria to accommodate unexpected responses and improve their ability to score the responses consistently, fairly, and reliably. Any adjustments should be made *before* a teacher begins scoring, rather than midway through the scoring process. For example, when grading written assessments, it's often helpful to skim a sample of students' papers first, looking for unusual responses and revising the criteria as needed.

Be as objective as possible.

A scoring checklist or rubric can certainly help teachers apply evaluation criteria objectively and consistently for all students, thereby increasing standardization, reliability, and validity. In addition, when assessments involve multiple tasks (e.g., several essay questions, or lab reports with several discrete sections), teachers can often evaluate students' responses more reliably by scoring everyone's response to the first task, then everyone's response to the second task, and so on. And covering students' names with small self-stick notes can help minimize the extent to which prior expectations for particular students influence judgments of students' actual performance levels.

---

[48] K. O'Connor, 2011.
[49] K. O'Connor, 2011; Stiggins & Chappuis, 2012.

Make note of any significant aspects of a student's performance that predetermined scoring criteria don't address.

Whenever teachers break down students' performance on a complex task into discrete behaviors, they can lose valuable information in the process.[50] In using rubrics for scoring, then, teachers may occasionally want to jot down other noteworthy characteristics of students' performance. This aspect of the scoring process will be neither standardized nor reliable, but it can sometimes be useful in identifying students' unique strengths and needs and can therefore be helpful in future instructional planning.

When determining overall scores, don't compare students to one another unless there is a compelling reason to do so.

Scores on tests and other assessments typically take one of three general forms. When teachers construct their own assessment instruments, they most often use a **raw score**, which is based solely on the number or percentage of points earned or items answered correctly. For example, a student who correctly answers 15 items on a 20-item multiple-choice test might get a score of 75%. A student who gets 3 points, 8 points, and 5 points on three essay questions, respectively, might get an overall score of 16. Raw scores are easy to calculate, and they appear to be easy to understand. But in fact, we sometimes have trouble knowing what raw scores really mean. Are scores of 75% and 16 good scores or bad ones? Without knowing what kinds of tasks an assessment includes, we have no easy way of interpreting a raw score.

A **criterion-referenced score** indicates what students have achieved in relation to specific instructional objectives or standards. Some criterion-referenced scores are either–or scores indicating that a student has passed or failed a unit, mastered or not mastered a skill, or met or not met an objective. Figure 10.10 illustrates this approach in a beginning swimming class. Other criterion-referenced scores indicate different levels of competence or achievement. For example, when using a rubric such as the one in Figure 10.5 to evaluate various characteristics of students' writing, a teacher might possibly assign a "3" to a *proficient* performance in, say, spelling or train of thought, with a "2" indicating an *in-progress* performance and a "1" indicating *beginning to develop*.

Adding various criterion-specific scores to get a single overall score can be problematic, however. For example, when using the writing rubric in Figure 10.5 to evaluate students' writing, we can't really say that *proficient* is worth three times as much as *beginning to develop* and that *in progress* is midway in quality between the two other levels; the numbers assigned to each level of performance are strictly arbitrary ones. Second, adding up all the scores to get a single score is based on the assumption that all criteria in the rubric are equally important—for instance, that using correct punctuation and capitalization is just as important as having a clear focus—when this assumption isn't necessarily correct. We authors have no immediate remedy for these two problems; we simply point out that it doesn't always make sense to use rubrics to obtain single criterion-referenced scores.[51]

Both raw scores and criterion-referenced scores are determined solely by looking at an individual student's performance. In contrast, a **norm-referenced score** is determined by comparing a student's performance with the performance of others—perhaps that of classmates or perhaps that of students in a nationwide *norm group*. A norm-referenced score tells us little about what a student specifically knows and can do. Instead, it tells us whether a student's performance is typical or unusual for the age or grade level.

Norm-referenced scores—in everyday lingo, those that result from "grading on the curve"—are often used in standardized tests (more about this point later). They're far less common in teacher-constructed classroom assessments. They may occasionally be necessary when designating

FIGURE 10.10 In this swimming class, students' accomplishments are reported in a criterion-referenced fashion.

> **Beginner Swimmer Class**
> **Springside Parks and Recreation Department**
>
> Students must demonstrate proficiency in each of the following:
>
> _____ Jump into chest-deep water
> _____ Hold breath under water for 8 seconds
> _____ Float in prone position for 10 seconds
> _____ Glide in prone position with flutter kick
> _____ Float on back for 10 seconds
> _____ Glide on back with flutter kick
> _____ Demonstrate crawl stroke and rhythmic breathing while standing in chest-deep water
> _____ Show knowledge of basic water safety rules

---

[50] Delandshere & Petrosky, 1998.

[51] Also see Humphry & Heldsinger, 2014; Reddy & Andrade, 2010.

"first chair" in an instrumental music class or choosing the best entries for a regional science fair. Teachers may also need to resort to a norm-referenced approach when assessing complex skills (e.g., poetry writing, advanced athletic skills, or critical analysis of literature) that are difficult to describe as "mastered." Teachers should probably *not* use norm-referenced scores on a regular basis, however. Such scores create a competitive situation in which students do well only if their performance surpasses that of their classmates. Thus norm-referenced scores can focus students' attention on performance goals rather than on mastery goals, and they may possibly encourage students to cheat on assessment tasks.[52] Furthermore, the competitive atmosphere that norm-referenced scores create is inconsistent with the *sense of community* discussed in Chapter 9.

Criterion-referenced scores communicate what teachers and students alike most need to know: whether instructional goals and objectives are being achieved. In doing so, they focus attention on mastery goals and, by showing improvement over time, can enhance students' self-efficacy for learning classroom subject matter. When criterion-referenced scores are hard to determine—perhaps because an assessment simultaneously addresses many instructional goals and objectives (something we authors don't generally recommend)—raw scores are usually the second best choice for teacher-constructed assessment tasks. But teachers must remember an important point about raw scores: They may provide very little information about the specific things students have and haven't learned.

Accompany any test scores with specific, constructive feedback.

We can't stress this point enough: The most important reason to assess students' current achievement levels is to help them learn and achieve *more*. Accordingly, teachers should provide detailed comments that tell students what they did well, where their weaknesses lie, and how they can improve.

Make allowances for risk taking and the occasional "bad day."

Students should feel comfortable enough about classroom assessments that they're willing to take risks and make mistakes. Only under these circumstances will they tackle the challenging tasks that can maximize their learning and cognitive development. Teachers encourage risk taking—and also decrease debilitating anxiety—not only when they communicate that mistakes are a normal part of learning but also when classroom assessment practices give students some leeway to be wrong without penalty.[53]

One strategy for encouraging risk taking is to *give frequent short assessments* rather than only a few very long ones that might each take an entire class period. Students who are assessed frequently are more likely to take occasional risks—and they have less test anxiety—because they know that no single assessment means "sudden death" if they get a low score. Frequent assessment has other benefits as well. It provides ongoing information to students and teachers alike about students' progress and about areas of weakness that need attention. It motivates students to study regularly, and with the pressure off to perform well on every single assignment and exam, students are less likely to cheat in order to get good grades. The bottom line is that students who are frequently assessed learn and achieve at higher levels than students who are assessed only after lengthy intervals.[54]

Another strategy is to *give students a chance to correct errors*. Especially when an assessment includes most or all of the content domain in question, students may learn as much—possibly even more—by correcting their errors on an assessment task. For example, in an approach known as *mastery reform*, some math teachers have students correct their errors as follows:

1. **Identification of the error.** Students describe in a short paragraph exactly what they don't yet know how to do.
2. **Statement of the process.** Using words rather than mathematical symbols, students explain the steps involved in the procedure they're trying to master.

---

[52] E. M. Anderman, Griesinger, & Westerfield, 1998; Mac Iver et al., 1995; Wentzel, Donlan, & Morrison, 2012.
[53] Clifford, 1990; N. E. Perry & Winne, 2004; Shepard et al., 2005.
[54] Crooks, 1988; E. D. Evans & Craig, 1990; McDaniel, Agarwal, Huelser, McDermott, & Roediger, 2011; Rohrer & Pashler, 2010.

3. **Practice.** Students demonstrate their mastery of the procedure with three new problems similar to the problem(s) they previously solved incorrectly.

4. **Statement of mastery.** Students state in a sentence or two that they have now mastered the procedure.

By completing these steps, students can replace a score on a previous assessment with the new, higher one. One high school math teacher has told one of us authors that this approach has a more general, long-term benefit as well: Many of his students eventually incorporate the four steps into their regular, internalized learning strategies.

Still another strategy is to *give retakes* when students perform poorly the first time around. As noted in the discussion of mastery learning in Chapter 8, some students need more time to master a topic than others and may therefore need to be assessed on the same material more than once. However, students who are allowed to redo the *same* test or assignment may work on the specific things the assessment covers without studying equally important but nonassessed material. (Remember, many classroom assessments can represent only small samples of the content in question.) Thus a teacher might construct two assessment instruments for the same content domain, using one as the initial assessment and the other for retakes. One of us authors has typically used this strategy when creating exams for her own students: She simultaneously constructs two exams using the same table of specifications, enabling her to have a first exam and a retake exam with similar content validities.

Respect students' right to privacy.

How would you feel if one of your instructors did the following?

- Returned test papers in the order of students' test scores, so that those with highest scores were handed out first, and you received yours *last?*
- Told your other instructors how poorly you had done on a test so that they could be on the lookout for other stupid things you might do?
- Looked through your school records and discovered that you scored 87 on an IQ test you took last year and that a personality test you unknowingly also took revealed some unusual sexual fantasies?

You'd probably be outraged that an instructor would do any of these things. Students' performance on assessment instruments should be somewhat confidential. But exactly *how* confidential? When should people know the results of students' assessments, and who should know them?

In the United States, teachers and other school faculty get legal guidance on these questions from the **Family Educational Rights and Privacy Act (FERPA)**, passed by the U.S. Congress in 1974. This legislation limits normal school testing practices primarily to the assessment of achievement and scholastic aptitude—two things that are clearly within the school's domain. Furthermore, it restricts access to students' assessment results to the few people who really need to know them: the students who earn them, their parents, and school personnel directly involved with students' education and well-being. Assessment results can be shared with other individuals (e.g., a family doctor or psychologist in private practice) *only* if the student (if at least 18 years old) or a parent gives written permission. Following are three implications of this legislative mandate for teachers' classroom practices:

- A teacher cannot ask students to reveal their political affiliation, sexual behavior or attitudes, illegal behaviors, potentially embarrassing psychological problems, or family income. (An exception: Questions about income are allowed if they're used only to ascertain eligibility for financial assistance—for example, to determine whether students qualify for a free-lunch program.)
- A teacher cannot post test scores in ways that allow students to learn one another's scores. For example, teachers can't post scores in alphabetical order or according to birthdays or social security numbers.
- A teacher cannot distribute papers in any way that allows students to observe one another's scores. For example, teachers can't let students search through a stack of scored papers to find their own.

Keeping students' assessment scores confidential makes educational as well as legal sense. Low scores can be a source of shame and embarrassment—especially if classmates know about them—and thus can increase students' anxiety levels about future assessments. Students with high scores can also suffer from having their scores made public. At many schools, it isn't cool to be smart, and high achievers may perform at lower levels to avoid risking peer rejection. And, of course, publicizing students' assessment results focuses students' attention on performance goals—that is, on making a good impression—rather than on mastering the subject matter.

In the opening case study, the teacher announces Ellie's grades to the entire class. The teacher's remarks violate FERPA, which applies to final grades as well as to individual assessment scores. Furthermore, making Ellie's grades public isn't in Ellie's best interest. Rather than motivate her to work harder (she's already highly motivated), it distresses her to the point that she no longer feels comfortable in her classroom.

Many educators initially interpreted FERPA as forbidding teachers to have students grade one another's test papers. In 2002, however, the U.S. Supreme Court ruled that this practice doesn't violate FERPA because the test scores obtained aren't yet a part of students' permanent school records.[55] Nevertheless, having students grade one another's classroom assessments—and thereby revealing some students' exceptionally high or low performance—can have adverse effects on students' sense of psychological well-being in the classroom. For this reason, we strongly urge teachers *not* to have students swap and grade one another's papers.

think about it
Reflecting on your own experiences as a student, can you recall situations in which FERPA was violated?

The preceding section and subsections have offered many strategies for effectively using informal assessments, paper–pencil assessments, and performance assessments to monitor and promote students' progress in and mastery of classroom subject matter. In the hotlinked Self-Check quiz and Application Exercises that follow, you can check and apply your understandings related to Big Idea 10.4:

> *Spontaneous, informal assessments and preplanned formal assessments both have important roles to play in enhancing students' learning and achievement.*

MyEdLab **Self-Check 10.4**

MyEdLab **Application Exercise 10.4.** In this exercise, you can identify possible developmental and motivational benefits of using checklists during cooperative performance assessment activities.

MyEdLab **Application Exercise 10.5.** In this exercise, you can apply what you've learned in the preceding section to evaluate various classroom assessment practices.

10.5 SUMMARIZING STUDENTS' ACHIEVEMENT WITH GRADES AND PORTFOLIOS

Big Idea 10.5 Final class grades provide only global, quantitative information about students' achievement levels; whenever possible, they should be supplemented with qualitative information, perhaps through student-constructed portfolios.

Teachers summarize students' achievement in a variety of ways. Some preschool and early elementary teachers use checklists to indicate specific accomplishments, and others write one- to two-page summaries describing students' strengths and areas needing improvement. Our focus here will be on the two most commonly used methods of summarizing achievement: grades and portfolios. Following are recommendations for using them.

---

[55] *Owasso Independent School District v. Falvo,* 534 U.S. 426.

Base final grades largely on final achievement levels and hard data.

Tempting as it might be to reward well-behaved, cooperative students with good grades and to punish chronic misbehavers with Ds or Fs, grades should ultimately reflect *how much students have learned*. Awarding good grades simply for good behavior or exceptional effort may lead students and their parents to overestimate the extent to which students have mastered classroom subject matter. And awarding low grades as punishment for disruptive or other undesirable behaviors can lead students to conclude (perhaps with good reason) that their teacher's grading system is arbitrary and meaningless—and in some cases can actually lead to an *increase* in student behavior problems.[56]

Also, although teachers certainly want to maximize students' improvement over the school year, assessment experts have made two good arguments against basing final grades on amount of improvement rather than on actual achievement levels. First, students who already show accomplishment of some of the year's instructional goals will have less room for improvement than their classmates. Second, when improvement is used as a criterion for grading, students trying to "beat the system" may quickly realize that they can achieve high grades simply by performing as poorly as possible when the school year begins.[57]

By and large, teachers should use hard data—such as the results of formal paper–pencil and performance assessments—when arriving at final conclusions about what students have achieved. For reasons we've previously identified, teachers' informal judgments of students' current achievement levels can easily be influenced by other things teachers know about students—for example, how often particular students misbehave in class and what their past achievement levels have been.[58]

Use many assessments to determine final grades, but don't count everything.

In the earlier discussion of risk taking, we identified several advantages of assessing students' learning and achievement frequently. In addition, using multiple assessments to determine final grades can help compensate for the imperfect reliability and validity of any single assessment. However, teachers probably don't want to consider *everything* students do. For instance, they may not want to include students' early efforts at new tasks, which are likely to involve considerable trial and error. And many assessments may be more appropriately used for formative assessment purposes—to guide instruction and help students learn—than for summative assessment.[59]

Share grading criteria with students, and keep students continually apprised of their progress.

To give students a sense that they have some control over their grades and other summaries of achievement (recall the discussion of *internal attributions* in Chapter 5), their teachers must tell them early in the semester or school year what the grading criteria will be. In addition, by providing concrete information about how grades will be assigned, teachers avoid unpleasant surprises when students actually receive their grades (recall Ellie's sense of devastation in the opening case study). If at some point teachers discover that initial grading criteria are overly stringent, they might need to lighten up in some way, perhaps by adjusting cutoffs or allowing retakes of critical assessments. But they must never change criteria midstream in a way that unfairly penalizes some students or imposes additional, unanticipated requirements.

Keep in mind that many students—younger ones especially—have limited self-monitoring skills. Furthermore, given the undependable nature of long-term memory (see Chapter 2), students may not have an accurate recollection of their various assessment scores over a period of several weeks or months. Thus it's often helpful to provide ongoing progress reports (e.g., see

[56] Brookhart, 2004; Cizek, 2003; Poorthuis et al., 2015; F. Zimmermann, Schütte, Taskinen, & Köller, 2013.

[57] Airasian, 1994; M. D. Miller, Linn, & Gronlund, 2009; Sax, 2010.

[58] Carbonneau & Selig, 2011; Hoge & Coladarci, 1989; J. P. Robinson & Lubienski, 2011.

[59] Andrade & Cizek, 2010; Brookhart, 2004; K. O'Connor, 2011; Shepard et al., 2005.

Figure 10.11) or teach students how to keep their own records. Once students gain sufficient computer literacy skills, *electronic gradebooks*—typically connected to a class website—provide an easy means by which teachers and students alike can track students' progress.

Keep parents in the loop.

Certainly parents don't need to be apprised of every score their child gets on a classroom assessment, but they have a right to know how their children are progressing. In fact, in the United States, an additional provision of FERPA is that parents have the right to review all of their children's test scores and other official school records. Furthermore, school personnel must present and interpret this information in a way that parents can understand.

In Chapter 9 we identified several strategies for keeping the lines of communication open with parents, and some of them—for instance, parent–teacher conferences and occasional notes or checklists sent home—are obviously useful for keeping parents in the loop about students' academic progress. What teachers must *not* do is use their communications with parents as punishment for insufficient student effort or other things they think students can control. As an example, let's look in on Ms. Ford's middle school math class. Ms. Ford has just handed back test papers with disappointing results, and the following class discussion ensues:

> *Ms. Ford:* When I corrected these papers, I was really, really shocked at some of the scores. And I think you will be too. I thought there were some that were so-so, and there were some that were devastating, in my opinion.
>
> *Student:* [Noise increasing.] Can we take them over?
>
> *Ms. Ford:* I am going to give them back to you. This is what I would like you to do: Every single math problem that you got wrong, for homework tonight and tomorrow, it is your responsibility to correct these problems and turn them in. In fact, I will say this, I want this sheet back to me by Wednesday at least. All our math problems that we got wrong I want returned to me with the correct answer.
>
> *Student:* Did anybody get 100?
>
> *Ms. Ford:* No.
>
> *Student:* Nobody got 100? [Groans]
>
> *Ms. Ford:* OK, boys and girls, shhh. I would say, on this test in particular, boys and girls, if you received a grade below 75 you definitely have to work on it. I do expect this quiz to be returned with Mom or Dad's signature on it. I want Mom and Dad to be aware of how we're doing.
>
> *Student:* No!
>
> *Student:* Do we have to show our parents? Is it a requirement to pass the class?
>
> *Ms. Ford:* If you do not return it with a signature, I will call home.[60]

Ms. Ford wants parents to know that their children aren't doing well in her class, but her approach has at least three drawbacks. First, many students may find it easier to forge an adultlike signature than to deliver bad news to a parent. Second, parents who do see their children's test papers won't have much information to help them interpret the results. (Are the low scores due to little effort? Poor study strategies? Poor instruction?) And third, Ms. Ford focuses entirely on the problem—low achievement—without offering suggestions for *solving* it.

Ultimately, teachers must think of themselves as working in cooperation with students and parents for something that everyone wants: students' academic success. Teachers' primary

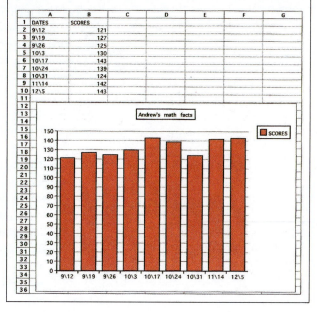

FIGURE 10.11 Computer spreadsheets and electronic gradebook software can help teachers and students keep track of students' performance on classroom assessments. Here we see a simple spreadsheet-based summary of 10-year-old Andrew's performance on math quizzes. Each quiz has been worth 150 points.

---

[60] J. C. Turner, Meyer, et al., 1998, pp. 740–741.

goal in communicating assessment results is to share information that will help achieve that end—something Ms. Ford neglects to do. Furthermore, because many students have done poorly on the test, Ms. Ford should consider whether something *she* has done—or not done—might account for the low scores. For instance, perhaps she allocated insufficient class time to certain concepts and skills, used ineffective strategies in teaching them, or constructed an exceptionally difficult test.

Accompany grades with descriptions of what the grades reflect.

As a general rule, final grades should reflect mastery of classroom subject matter and instructional goals—in other words, they should be criterion referenced to the degree possible.[61] When setting up a criterion-referenced grading system, teachers should determine as concretely as possible what they want each grade to communicate about students' achievement. For example, when assigning traditional letter grades, a teacher might use general descriptors such as the following:

Grade	Criteria
A	The student has a firm command of both basic and advanced knowledge and skills in the content domain. He or she is well prepared for future learning tasks.
B	The student has mastered all basic knowledge and skills. Mastery at a more advanced level is evident in some but not all areas. In most respects, he or she is ready for future learning tasks.
C	The student has mastered basic knowledge and skills but has difficulty with more advanced aspects of the subject matter. He or she lacks a few prerequisites critical for future learning tasks.
D	The student has mastered some but not all of the basics in the content domain. He or she lacks many prerequisites for future learning tasks.
F	The student shows little or no mastery of instructional objectives and cannot demonstrate the most elementary knowledge and skills. He or she lacks most of the prerequisites essential for success in future learning tasks.[62]

It's especially important to specify grading criteria when different students in the same classroom are working toward different instructional goals. For example, in the United States, the IDEA legislation stipulates that teachers and other school personnel identify appropriate instructional goals for individual children and adolescents who have special educational needs. Final evaluations of achievement, including final grades, should be based on students' accomplishment of those goals.[63]

Also accompany grades with qualitative information about students' performance.

Even when final grades are accompanied by descriptions of what they reflect, they are, at best, only general indicators of some *quantity* of what students have learned. Thus, it's often helpful to accompany grades with *qualitative* information—for instance, information about students' particular academic strengths, work habits, attitudes, social skills, and unique contributions to the classroom community. Students and parents alike often find such qualitative feedback quite informative and helpful. Comments should be fairly explicit, however. Feedback such as "a pleasure to have in class" communicates little or no new information.[64]

---

[61] For example, see K. O'Connor, 2011; Pattison, Grodsky, & Muller, 2013; Stiggins & Chappuis, 2012. Over the past several decades, teachers have gradually moved from norm-referenced grading (i.e., grading on the curve) to criterion-referenced grading. This focus on mastery of instructional goals and objectives, rather than on comparing students with one another, partly accounts for the increasing grade point averages ("grade inflation") about which some public figures complain.

[62] Based on criteria described by Frisbie & Waltman, 1992.

[63] For example, see Mastropieri & Scruggs, 2010; Venn, 2007.

[64] Brookhart, 2004, p. 183.

Use portfolios to show complex skills or improvements over time.

A **portfolio** is a collection of a student's work systematically collected over a lengthy time period. It might include writing samples, student-constructed objects (e.g., sculptures, inventions), photographs, audiotapes, video recordings, technology-based creations (e.g., PowerPoint presentations, student-created video games), or any combination of these. In most cases, *students* are the primary authors of their portfolios, albeit with developmentally appropriate teacher scaffolding. When students actively work to document their accomplishments in portfolios, they can gain a strong sense of ownership and autonomy regarding both their achievement levels and the evaluation process.

The samples of student work included in a portfolio are typically called *artifacts*. Most school portfolios also include student-written documentation that describes each artifact and a rationale for including it. For example, in Figure 10.12, 14-year-old Kurt describes and evaluates the writing samples he has included in a portfolio for his eighth-grade language arts class. As is true in Kurt's portfolio, many portfolios include two or more successive versions of a single item.

Portfolios take a variety of forms. Following are four types commonly used in school settings:[65]

- **Working portfolio**—Shows competencies up to the present time; is dynamic in content, with new artifacts that show increasing proficiency gradually replacing older, less skillful ones.
- **Developmental portfolio**—Includes several artifacts related to a particular set of skills; shows how a student has improved over time.
- **Course portfolio**—Includes assignments and reflections for a single course; typically also includes a summarizing reflection in which the student identifies his or her general accomplishments in the course.
- **Best-work portfolio**—Includes artifacts intended to showcase the student's particular achievements and unique talents.

These categories aren't necessarily mutually exclusive. For example, a course portfolio might have a developmental component, showing how a student has improved in one or more skills over the school year. And a best-work portfolio may be a work-in-progress for quite some time, thereby having the dynamic nature of a working portfolio.

MyEdLab
Video Example 10.4.

What specific guidance does this high school art teacher give his students as they create their best-work portfolios?

FIGURE 10.12 In this self-reflection, 14-year-old Kurt explains why he has chosen certain pieces to include in his eighth-grade language arts portfolio.

SELF-EVALUATION

The three pieces of writing in my portfolio that best represent who I am are: 1) "Author Ben Hoff," which is a story in the language of Ben Hoff; 2) "Quotes from *The Tao of Pooh*"; and 3) "Discrimination."

What "Author Ben Hoff" shows about me as a learner or a writer is that I am able to analyze and absorb the types and styles of an author and then transfer what I learn onto paper in a good final understandable piece of writing. This piece has good description, a good plot line, gets the point across, has a basic setting, and is understandable. I did not change too much of this piece from one draft to the next except punctuation, grammar and spelling. I did, however, add a quote from *The Tao of Pooh*.

"Quotes from *The Tao of Pooh*" shows that I am able to pull out good and significant quotes from a book, understand them, and put them into my own words. Then I can make them understandable to other people. This piece gets the point across well and is easy to understand. I really only corrected spelling and punctuation from one draft to the next.

"Discrimination" shows me that I am learning more about discrimination and how it might feel (even though I have never experienced really bad discrimination). I found I can get my ideas across through realistic writing. This piece has good description and was well written for the assignment. Besides correcting some punctuation and spelling, I changed some wording to make the story a little more clear.

For all three pieces, the mechanics of my writing tend to be fairly poor on my first draft, but that is because I am writing as thoughts come into my mind rather than focusing on details of grammar. Then my final drafts get better as I get comments and can turn my attention to details of writing.

The four most important things that I'm able to do as a writer are to: 1) get thoughts pulled into a story; 2) have that story understandable and the reader get something from it; 3) have the reader remember it was a good piece of writing; and 4) like the piece myself.

---

[65] R. S. Johnson, Mims-Cox, & Doyle-Nichols, 2006; Spandel, 1997.

The various kinds of portfolios are apt to be more or less suitable for different purposes. For example, developmental portfolios can show whether students are making reasonable progress toward long-term instructional goals; thus, they lend themselves well to formative assessment. Best-work portfolios are better suited for summative assessment; for instance, they might be used to communicate students' final accomplishments to parents, school administrators, college admissions officers, or potential employers. But regardless of whether they're used for formative or summative assessment, portfolios can, in general, have several benefits:[66]

- They capture the multifaceted nature of students' achievements, with a particular emphasis on complex skills.
- They can demonstrate students' performance on real-world, authentic assessment tasks (e.g., science experiments, service-learning projects).
- They provide practice in self-monitoring and self-evaluation, thereby enhancing students' self-regulation skills.
- They give students a sense of accomplishment and self-efficacy about areas that have been mastered, while possibly also alerting students to areas needing improvement.
- They provide a mechanism through which teachers can easily intertwine assessment with instruction: Students often include products that their teachers have assigned primarily for instructional purposes.
- Because the focus of portfolios is usually on complex skills, teachers are more likely to *teach* those skills.

RSVP characteristics can be a source of concern for portfolios, however, especially if they're used to evaluate—rather than simply communicate—students' learning and achievement.[67] When portfolios must be scored in some way, scoring is often unreliable, with different teachers rating them differently. In addition, there's an obvious standardization problem, because their contents can vary considerably from one student to another. Validity may or may not be an issue: Some portfolios may include enough artifacts to adequately represent what students have accomplished relative to instructional goals, but others may be unrepresentative. And because portfolios are likely to take a great deal of teacher time, they're less practical than other methods of summarizing achievement. All this is *not* to say that teachers should shy away from having students create portfolios, but they should be sure the potential benefits outweigh the disadvantages. And when using portfolios as summative assessments of what students have accomplished, teachers must identify explicit criteria for evaluating them.[68]

Creating a portfolio is typically a lengthy process that stretches out over several weeks or months; some best-work portfolios evolve over several years. So as not to overwhelm students by such a complex undertaking, it's often helpful to break the portfolio-construction process into a series of steps, scaffolding students' efforts at each step:[69]

1. **Planning:** Decide on the purpose(s) the portfolio will serve (e.g., which instructional goals and/or content-area standards it will address and whether it will be used primarily for formative or summative assessment); identify a preliminary plan of attack for creating the portfolio.

2. **Collection:** Save artifacts that demonstrate progress toward or achievement of particular goals and standards.

3. **Selection:** Review the saved artifacts, and choose those that best reflect achievement of the specified goals and standards.

4. **Reflection:** Write explanations and self-evaluations of each artifact; describe how the artifacts show current competencies and growth over time; relate achievements to previously identified goals and standards.

MyEdLab
Video Example 10.5.

What benefits might this portfolio conference have for 8-year-old Keenan and her teacher?

MyEdLab
Video Example 10.6.

In this video, two fifth-grade teachers prepare their classes for upcoming parent–teacher–student conferences in which students will present their portfolios to their parents. As you watch the video, identify several benefits that such student-led conferences might have.

[66] Banta, 2003; Darling-Hammond et al., 1995; DiMartino & Castaneda, 2007; R. S. Johnson et al., 2006; Paulson, Paulson, & Meyer, 1991; Popham, 2014; Spandel, 1997.

[67] Arter & Spandel, 1992; Banta, 2003; Popham, 2014; R. S. Johnson et al., 2006.

[68] See Darling-Hammond et al. (1995) for examples of criteria that schools have successfully used.

[69] Six steps based on R. S. Johnson et al., 2006.

5. **Projection:** Identify new goals toward which to strive.

6. **Presentation:** Share the portfolio with an appropriate audience (e.g., classmates, parents, college admissions personnel).

The Classroom Strategies box "Summarizing Students' Achievements with Portfolios" offers several suggestions for scaffolding students' efforts in creating portfolios.

Teachers must think carefully about how they—and in some cases also about how their students—can best summarize and communicate students' achievements over the course of a grading term, semester, or school year. In the hotlinked Self-Check quiz and Application Exercise that follow, you can check and apply your understandings related to Big Idea 10.5:

> *Final class grades provide only global, quantitative information about students' achievement levels; whenever possible, they should be supplemented with qualitative information, perhaps through student-constructed portfolios.*

MyEdLab **Self-Check 10.5**

MyEdLab **Application Exercise 10.6.** In this video case analysis, you can apply what you have learned about instructional strategies and human motivation to analyze the use of portfolios in a bilingual sixth-grade class.

CLASSROOM STRATEGIES

Summarizing Students' Achievements with Portfolios

- **Identify in advance the specific purpose(s) for which a portfolio will be used.**
  A third-grade teacher and her students agree to create portfolios that will show parents and other family members how much their writing skills improve over the school year. Throughout the year, students save their fiction and nonfiction, and eventually they choose pieces that best demonstrate mastery of some writing skills and progress on others. The children proudly present their portfolios at parent–teacher–student conferences at the end of the year.

- **Align portfolio contents with important instructional goals and/or content area standards.**
  At a high school in Ohio, 12th graders complete graduation portfolios with three components, each of which reflects one or more of the school's instructional goals for all graduates:
  - A *lifelong-learning skills* section shows mastery of a student's key skills in writing, math, science, and at least one other content domain.
  - A *democratic citizenship* section provides specific examples of how a student has been actively engaged in issues related to the local community or larger society (e.g., by contributing to a public service activity).
  - A *career-readiness* section contains a résumé, letters of recommendation from teachers or other adults, and other documents that show preparedness for postsecondary education or the workplace.

- **Ask students to select the contents of their portfolios; provide the scaffolding they need to make wise choices.**
  A fifth-grade teacher meets one on one with each of his students to help them choose artifacts that best reflect their achievements for the year. To give the students an idea of the kinds of things they might include, he shows them several portfolios that students have created in previous years. He shares only those portfolios that previous students and parents have given him permission to use in this way.

- **Identify specific criteria that should guide students' selections; possibly include students in the criteria identification process.**
  A middle school geography teacher leads his class in a discussion of criteria that students might use to identify artifacts for a course portfolio. After reviewing the instructional goals for the course, the class agrees that each portfolio should include at least one artifact demonstrating each of the following:
  - Map interpretation skills
  - Map construction skills
  - Understanding of interrelationships between physical environments and socioeconomic practices
  - Knowledge of cultural differences within the nation
  - Recognition that all cultures have many positive qualities

- **Have students include reflections on the products they include.**
  At the beginning of the school year, a ninth-grade journalism teacher tells students that they will be creating portfolios that show progress in journalistic writing during the semester. She asks them to save all of their drafts—"Even simple notes and outlines," she says. Later in the semester, as students begin to compile their portfolios, she asks them to look at their various drafts of each piece and to describe how the progression from one draft to the next shows their gradual mastery of journalism skills. She occasionally assigns these reflections

(continued)

as homework so that students spread the portfolio construction task over a 4-week period and therefore don't leave everything until the last minute.

- **Give students a general organizational scheme to follow.**
  When a high school requires students to complete portfolios as one of their graduation requirements, students get considerable guidance from their homeroom teachers. These teachers also provide a handout describing the elements each portfolio should include: title page, table of contents, introduction to the portfolio's contents and criteria guiding artifact selection, distinct sections for each content domain included, and final reflection that summarizes achievements.

- **Determine whether a physical format or electronic format is more suitable for the circumstances.**
  At a high school that places particular emphasis on visual and performing arts, students create electronic portfolios that showcase their talents in art, drama, dance, and/or instrumental music. They digitally photograph, videotape, or audiotape their projects and

performances, and they create word processing documents that describe and evaluate each one. They then divide their electronic documents into several logical categories, each of which they put in a separate electronic folder on an external storage device or password-protected website.

- **When using portfolios for summative assessments, develop a rubric to guide evaluation.**
  At a high school in New York City, a key instructional goal is for students to acquire certain dispositions and thinking processes—which the school collectively calls *habits of mind*—in their academic work. One of these habits of mind is the use of credible, convincing evidence to support statements and positions. The school develops a four-point rating scale to evaluate students' work on this criterion. A score of 4 is given to work that reflects "Generalizations and ideas supported by specific relevant and accurate information, which is developed in appropriate depth." At the other end of the scale, a score of 1 is given to work that reflects "Mostly general statements; little specific evidence relating to the topic."

Sources: Banta, 2003; Darling-Hammond et al., 1995, p. 39 (New York City high school example); DiMartino & Castaneda, 2007 (Ohio high school example); R. L. Johnson et al., 2009; R. S. Johnson et al., 2006; Paulson, Paulson, & Meyer, 1991; Popham, 2014; Spandel, 1997; Stiggins & Chappuis, 2012.

10.6 ASSESSING STUDENTS' ACHIEVEMENT AND ABILITIES WITH STANDARDIZED TESTS

Big Idea 10.6 Large-scale standardized tests can be helpful in estimating students' general achievement levels in particular domains, but educators should never use a single test score to make important decisions about individual students, nor should policy makers use average scores from a single test to evaluate teacher and school effectiveness.

MyEdLab
Video Example 10.7.

Standardized achievement test results can help teachers monitor students' progress, *provided that* they are closely aligned with important instructional goals and standards. What benefits and potential limitations of standards and standardized test scores do school administrators identify in this video? Also, what suggestion does principal Ron Wade offer for how his high school students might assist in promoting the achievement levels of students in the lower grades?

Final grades and portfolios are derived directly from things students do in the classroom. A different approach to summarizing what students know and can do is the **standardized test**, developed by test construction experts and published for use in many different schools and classrooms. The test is *standardized* in several ways: All students are given the same instructions and time limits, respond to the same (or very similar) questions or tasks, and have their responses evaluated relative to the same criteria. A test manual describes the instructions to give students, the time limits to impose, and the specific scoring criteria to use. Often the manual also provides information about test reliability for different populations and age-groups, as well as information from which teachers and school administrators can draw inferences about test validity for their own situation and purposes.

Some standardized tests are administered one on one. Such tests enable the examiner to observe a student's attention span, motivation, and other factors that may affect test performance. For this reason, individually administered tests are typically used when identifying cognitive disabilities and other special educational needs.

When circumstances call for giving *all* students a standardized test, testing them as a group is usually the only practical approach. Fortunately, computer technology can be helpful in two distinct ways. For one thing, computers are routinely used to electronically score a group paper–pencil test and generate reports about each student's performance. In addition, some tests come in computer-based rather than paper–pencil form. Computer-based standardized testing can provide several options that are either impractical or impossible with paper–pencil tests:

- It allows **adaptive assessment**, which adjusts the difficulty level of items as students proceed through a test and can thereby zero in on students' specific strengths and weaknesses fairly quickly.
- It can include animations, simulations, videos, and audiotaped messages—all of which can expand the kinds of knowledge and skills that test items assess.

- It enables assessment of how students approach specific problems and how quickly they accomplish specific tasks.
- It can provide on-the-spot scoring and analyses of students' performance.

Computer-based standardized tests tend to have reliability and validity levels similar to those of traditional paper–pencil tests. Their use should, of course, be limited to students who are familiar and comfortable with computers and have adequate keyboarding skills.

Table 10.5 describes four kinds of standardized tests that school districts use frequently: achievement tests, general scholastic aptitude tests, specific aptitude tests, and school readiness tests. Many of these tests yield norm-referenced scores. For example, if you look once again at the explanation of IQ scores in Chapter 6 (e.g., see Figure 6.10), you'll realize that IQ scores indicate *only* how children stack up against one another and so are norm-referenced. Norm-referenced scores take a variety of forms, and the computer-generated test results that schools and parents eventually receive can be quite detailed, sometimes to the point of being "TMI"—too much information. Appendix B, "Understanding and Interpreting Standardized Test Results," can help you make some sense of norm-referenced scores and computer-generated test reports.

Consistent with our emphasis on assessing students' learning and achievement in this chapter, our focus in the upcoming pages will be on standardized *achievement* tests. Such tests are useful in at least two ways. First, they enable teachers and school administrators to compare their own students' general achievement levels with the achievement of students elsewhere—information that may indirectly provide information about the effectiveness of the local curriculum and

Table 10.5 • Commonly Used Standardized Tests

KIND OF TEST	PURPOSE	GENERAL DESCRIPTION	SPECIAL CONSIDERATIONS
Achievement tests	To assess how much students have learned from what they have presumably been specifically taught	Test items are written to reflect the curriculum common to many schools. Test scores indicate achievement only in a broad and (often) norm-referenced sense: They estimate a student's general level of knowledge and skills in a particular domain relative to other students across the country.	• Most of these tests are more appropriate for measuring general levels of achievement than for determining specific information and skills that students have and have not acquired.
General scholastic aptitude and intelligence tests	To assess students' general capability to learn; to predict their general academic success over the short run	Test items typically focus on what and how much students have learned and deduced from their general, everyday experiences. For example, the tests may include items that ask students to define words, draw logical deductions, recognize analogies between seemingly unrelated topics, analyze geometric figures, or solve problems.	• Test scores should not be construed as an indication of learning potential over the long run. • Individually administered tests (in which the tester works one-on-one with a particular student) are preferable when students' verbal skills are limited or when exceptional giftedness or a significant disability is suspected.
Specific aptitude and ability tests	To predict how easily students are likely to learn in a specific content domain	Test items are similar to those in general scholastic aptitude tests, except that they focus on a specific domain (e.g., verbal skills, mathematical reasoning). Some aptitude tests, called *multiple-aptitude batteries*, yield subscores for a variety of domains simultaneously.	• Test scores should not be construed as an indication of learning potential over the long run. • Tests tend to have only limited ability to predict students' success in a particular domain and so should be used only in combination with other information about students.
School readiness tests	To determine whether young children have the prerequisite skills to be successful in a typical kindergarten or first-grade curriculum	Test items focus on basic knowledge and skills—for instance, recognition of colors and shapes, knowledge of numbers and letters, and ability to remember and follow directions.	• Test scores should be interpreted cautiously. Young children have shorter attention spans and less motivation to perform test-like tasks than older children do, leading to lower reliability and validity of test scores. • Tests should be used primarily for instructional planning purposes, *not* for deciding whether students are ready to begin formal schooling.*

*School readiness tests have become increasingly controversial, in part because the scores they yield typically correlate only moderately with children's academic performance even a year or so later. For various perspectives on these tests, see G. J. Duncan et al., 2007; Forget-Dubois et al., 2007; La Paro & Pianta, 2000; Pellegrini, 1998; C. E. Sanders, 1997; Stipek, 2002a.

instructional practices. Second, standardized achievement tests provide a means of tracking students' general progress over time and raising red flags about potential trouble spots. For example, imagine that Lucas has been getting average test scores year after year but then suddenly performs well below average in eighth grade, even though the test and comparative norm group are the same as in previous years. At this point, his teacher would want to ascertain whether the low performance was a temporary fluke (e.g., was Lucas sick on the test day?) or, instead, due to other, longer-term issues that require attention.

High-Stakes Tests and Accountability

In recent years a great deal of emphasis—entirely *too much* emphasis, in our opinion—has been placed on students' performance on standardized achievement tests. Many policy makers, business leaders, and other public figures have lamented students' low achievement test results and called for major overhauls of our educational system. Some of these reform-minded individuals equate high achievement with high scores on standardized tests and, conversely, low achievement with low test scores. Policy makers have put considerable pressure on teachers and educational administrators to get test scores up, and some threaten serious consequences for schools and faculty members who *don't* get the scores up. Here we're talking about both **high-stakes testing**—making major decisions on the basis of single assessments—and **accountability**—a mandated obligation of teachers, administrators, and other school personnel to accept responsibility for students' performance on those assessments.

In recent years, federal legislation in the United States has mandated both high-stakes testing and accountability in public elementary and secondary schools. Passed in 2001, the **No Child Left Behind Act**—sometimes known simply as **NCLB**—mandated that states establish challenging content-area standards in language arts, mathematics, and (a few years later) science. It further mandated that states annually assess students in grades 3 through 8 and at least once during the high school grades to determine whether students were making what the legislation called *adequate yearly progress* in meeting the state-determined standards, with progress being observed separately for students from diverse racial and socioeconomic groups. (Students with cognitive disabilities could be given alternative assessments but needed to show improvement commensurate with their ability levels.) Schools that demonstrated progress in all groups were to receive rewards, such as teacher bonuses or increased funding. In contrast, schools that didn't demonstrate progress were subject to sanctions and corrective actions (e.g., bad publicity, administrative restructuring, dismissal of staff members), and students had the option of attending a better public school at the school district's expense.

The No Child Left Behind Act was highly controversial—in part because many people perceived it to reflect too much federal control of individual states' educational policies—and in many respects it didn't bring about the changes it was intended to generate.[70] Furthermore, NCLB focused largely on standardized test scores—which didn't always have good content validity for local schools' curricula—as the means of determining whether students were making desired gains in achievement. Hence, in late 2015, NCLB was replaced by the **Every Student Succeeds Act (ESSA)**, which has given greater latitude to individual states for decision making regarding content-area standards, assessment techniques, and corrective actions for low-performing schools. Under this legislation, schools must continue to assess students' progress in language arts and math at least once each year in grades 3 through 8 and then at least one time during grades 9 through 12; schools must also assess students' achievement levels in science at least three times over the course of grades 3 through 12. However, schools can use other assessment tools to supplement standardized test scores as indicators of the quality of students' achievement levels and progress; for example, schools might consider performance assessments, portfolios, and indicators of such things as "student engagement . . . completion of advanced coursework . . . [and] postsecondary readiness." Also, ESSA places less emphasis on teacher and school accountability for students' achievement levels; thus, the regular assessments that it mandates don't have as much of a "high-stakes" nature as was true for NCLB.

---

[70] Forte, 2010; Mintrop & Sunderman, 2009; Polikoff, McEachin, Wrabel, & Duque, 2014.

In addition to teacher and school accountability, sometimes individual students are held accountable for their performance on statewide or schoolwide assessments. Some school districts have used students' performance on tests or other assessments as a basis for promotion to the next grade level or for awarding high school diplomas.[71] Typically, school personnel begin by identifying certain content-area standards (they sometimes use the word *competencies*) that students' final achievement should reflect. They then assess students' performance levels (sometimes known as *outcomes*) at the end of instruction, and only those students whose performance meets the predetermined standards and competencies move forward. Such a practice clearly calls for criterion-referenced rather than norm-referenced scores.

Systematic efforts to monitor schools' instructional effectiveness and students' academic progress are certainly well intentioned. Ideally, they can help schools determine whether instructional methods need revision and whether teachers need retooling. They can also help teachers identify students who aren't acquiring essential basic skills. However, current emphases on boosting students' test scores are fraught with difficulties in implementation. For example, teachers often spend a great deal of time teaching to the tests—a serious problem if the tests reflect only a few of the many instructional goals toward which students should be striving. And recall the teacher's dilemma in the opening case study ("Taking Over") in Chapter 3. In order to "cover" all the material on the eighth-grade math competency exam, Ms. Gaunt eventually abandons her efforts to help students master basic concepts and procedures, essentially throwing the *less-is-more* principle out the window.[72]

Using Standardized Achievement Tests Judiciously

In our final set of recommendations, we authors offer several suggestions for using standardized and high-stakes achievement tests in ways that maximize their usefulness.

When you have a choice in the test you use, choose one that has high validity for your curriculum and students.

Content validity is just as much a concern for standardized achievement tests as it is for teacher-constructed classroom assessments. Teachers and school administrators can best determine the content validity of a standardized achievement test by comparing a table of specifications for the test to their own curriculum.[73] School faculty members should also scrutinize the actual test items to see whether they predominantly address only basic knowledge and skills (as some tests do[74]) or, instead, also address conceptual understanding and complex cognitive processes. A test has high content validity for a particular school and classroom only if the topics and thinking skills emphasized in test items match local instructional goals and content-area standards.

Teach to the test if—but only if—it reflects important instructional goals.

When teachers are held accountable for their students' performance on a particular test, many of them understandably devote many class hours to the knowledge and skills the test assesses, and students may focus their studying efforts accordingly. The result is often that students perform at higher levels on a high-stakes test *without* improving their achievement and abilities more generally. If a test truly measures the things that are most important for students to learn—including such complex cognitive processes as transfer, problem solving, and critical thinking—then

---

[71] Such approaches go by a variety of names; *outcomes-based education* and *minimum competency testing* are two common ones.

[72] For various perspectives on the problems associated with high-stakes testing and NCLB, see W. Au, 2007; E. L. Baker, 2007; A. B. Brown & Clift, 2010; Duckworth, Quinn, & Tsukayama, 2012; A. S. Finn et al., 2014; Finnigan & Gross, 2007; Forte, 2010; B. Fuller, Wright, Gesicki, & Kang, 2007; M. G. Jones, Jones, & Hargrove, 2003; Polikoff, Porter, & Smithson, 2011; Solórzano, 2008.

[73] Test publishers typically construct a table of specifications and either include it in the test manual or make it available upon request. If a table isn't available, school personnel can construct one by tallying the number of items that tap into various topics and thinking skills.

[74] M. G. Jones et al., 2003; Mintrop & Sunderman, 2009; Polikoff et al., 2011.

focusing on those things is quite appropriate. If the test primarily assesses rote knowledge and basic skills, however, then such emphasis may undermine the improvements everyone wants to see in students' achievement.[75]

When preparing students for an upcoming standardized test, tell them what the test will be like and teach them good test-taking skills.

Teachers should typically prepare students ahead of time for a standardized test—for instance, by doing the following:

- Explain the general nature of the test and the tasks it involves (e.g., if applicable, mention that students aren't expected to know all the answers and that many students won't have enough time to respond to every item).
- Encourage students to do their best, but without describing the test as a life-or-death matter.
- Give students practice with the test's format and item types (e.g., demonstrate how to answer multiple-choice questions and fill in electronically scored answer sheets).
- Encourage students to get a full night's sleep and eat a good breakfast before taking the test.

To some degree, teachers can also help students prepare for standardized achievement tests by teaching them useful test-taking strategies, such as temporarily skipping difficult items, double-checking to be sure answers are marked in the correct spots, and the like. Teachers should keep in mind, however, that having effective test-taking skills—**testwiseness**—typically makes only a small difference in students' test scores. Furthermore, test-taking skills and student achievement are positively correlated: Students with many test-taking strategies tend to be higher achievers than students with few strategies. In other words, very few students get low test scores *only* because they're poor test takers. In most cases teachers better serve their students by teaching them the knowledge and skills that tests are designed to assess rather than spending an inordinate amount of time teaching them how to take tests.[76]

When administering the test, follow the directions closely and report any unusual circumstances.

Once the testing session begins, teachers should follow the test administration procedures to the letter, distributing test booklets as directed, asking students to complete any practice items provided, keeping time faithfully, and responding to students' questions in the prescribed manner. Remember, students in the test's norm group have taken the test under certain standardized conditions, and teachers must replicate those conditions as closely as possible. Occasionally teachers and students will face circumstances beyond their control (e.g., an unexpected power failure or exceptional outside noise). When such events significantly alter the conditions under which students are taking the test, they jeopardize the validity of the test results and must be reported. Teachers should also make note of any individual students who are behaving in ways unlikely to lead to maximum performance—for instance, students who appear exceptionally nervous, stare out the window for long periods, or seem to be marking answers haphazardly.[77]

Make appropriate accommodations for English language learners.

Without question, students' experience and facility with the English language affects their performance on English-based achievement tests, including high-stakes tests.[78] For instance, when children come to school after growing up in a non-English-speaking environment, it typically takes them considerable time—perhaps five to seven years—to gain sufficient proficiency in English to

---

[75] W. Au, 2007; E. L. Baker, 2007; M. G. Jones et al., 2003; Mintrop & Sunderman, 2009; Shepard et al., 2005; R. M. Thomas, 2005.

[76] J. R. Frederiksen & Collins, 1989; Geiger, 1997; Scruggs & Lifson, 1985; Shepard et al., 2005.

[77] M. D. Miller et al., 2009.

[78] Carhill, Suárez-Orozco, & Páez, 2008; Solórzano, 2008.

perform at their best in English-speaking classrooms.[79] Yet many school districts require these students to take high-stakes tests in English long before they achieve this proficiency, leading to test scores that significantly underestimate students' achievement levels.[80] Following are several recommended practices, provided that public policies and school district administrators allow for them (in the United States, ESSA allows some but not all of these practices):[81]

- Translate a test into a student's native language.
- Administer a test one on one, perhaps eliminating time limits, presenting questions orally, and allowing students to respond in their native language. (This practice reduces the second RSVP characteristic—standardization—but may be the only way to ensure the third RSVP characteristic—validity of the results.)
- Use alternative assessment methods (e.g., dynamic assessment, portfolios) to document achievement.
- Exclude English language learners' test scores when computing averages that reflect the overall achievement of a school or a particular subgroup within the school.

When interpreting test results, take students' ages and developmental levels into account.

Virtually any test score will be influenced by a variety of irrelevant factors that diminish the score's reliability and validity, including literacy skills, motivation, mood, energy level, and general health. Such factors are especially likely to influence the test results of young children, many of whom may have limited verbal skills, short attention spans, little motivation to do their best, and low tolerance for frustration. Furthermore, young children's erratic behaviors can make it difficult to maintain standardized testing conditions.[82]

In adolescence, other variables can affect the validity of scores on standardized tests. Although students may get a bit nervous about tests in the elementary grades (e.g., see Figure 10.13), test anxiety increases in the middle school and high school grades, sometimes to the point that it significantly interferes with students' concentration during a test. Furthermore, especially in high school, some students become quite cynical about the validity and usefulness of standardized tests. If students see little point to taking a test, they may read test items superficially, if at all, and a few may complete answer sheets simply by following a certain pattern (e.g., alternating between A and B) or filling in bubbles to make pictures or designs.[83] At *any* grade level, then, educators must be careful not to place too much stock in the specific scores that tests yield.

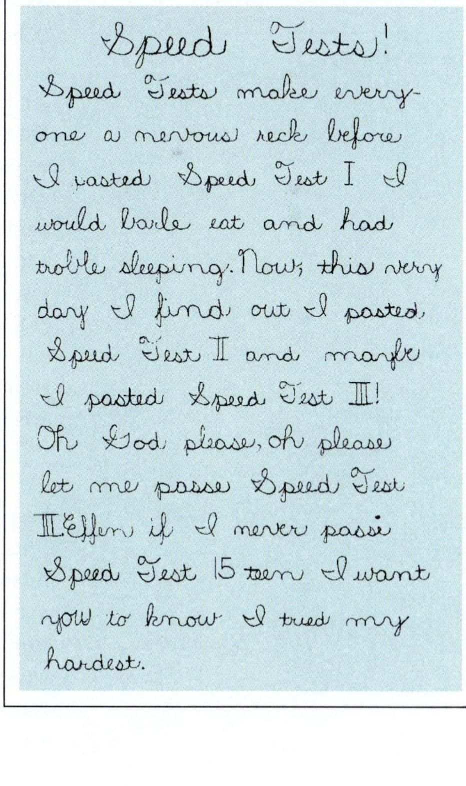

If tests are being used to measure teacher or school effectiveness, advocate for a focus on students' improvement over time rather than on age-group averages.

Assessing the degree to which each student makes progress during the school year may not be the best approach to assigning final grades (recall our earlier concerns about basing grades on improvement) but it is probably a reasonable approach to evaluating the effectiveness of teachers and schools. You may sometimes see the term **value-added assessment** used in reference to progress-based evaluation of teachers and schools.

Unfortunately, assessing students' improvement over a single school year isn't as easy as it might seem, especially when using standardized achievement test scores. We can't just find the difference between beginning-of-year and end-of-year test scores and say, "Hey, Mr. Black's students showed bigger gains than Ms. Brown's students did, so Mr. Black must be the better teacher." For one thing, if we calculate the mathematical

FIGURE 10.13 Eight-year-old Connie describes how overwhelming test anxiety can be.

> *Speed Tests!*
> *Speed Tests make everyone a nervous reck before I pasted Speed Test I I would barle eat and had troble sleeping. Now this very day I find out I pasted Speed Test II and maybe I pasted Speed Test III! Oh God please, oh please let me passe Speed Test II. Effen if I never passi Speed Test 15 teen I want you to know I tried my hardest.*

---

[79] Carhill et al., 2008; Cummins, 1984, 2008; Padilla, 2006.

[80] Solórzano, 2008; W. E. Wright, 2006.

[81] Haywood & Lidz, 2007; R. S. Johnson et al., 2006; Solórzano, 2008; W. E. Wright, 2006.

[82] Bracken & Walker, 1997; Carver, 2006; Fleege, Charlesworth, & Burts, 1992; Messick, 1983; Stipek, 2002a; Wodtke, Harper, & Schommer, 1989.

[83] Paris, Lawton, Turner, & Roth, 1991; W. E. Wright, 2006.

difference between two test scores with imperfect reliability and validity, the result will be a number with even *less* reliability and validity. Also, students can differ considerably in the *rates* at which they improve, with students from low-income families improving more slowly (on average) than their more economically advantaged peers. Furthermore, the particular school at which a teacher is working can have a major influence; for example, Mr. Black might be teaching at a newly built facility with many resources and a highly motivated student body, whereas Ms. Brown might be teaching in a dilapidated old school building with inadequate supplies and little or no sense of school community among students and faculty.

Statisticians have developed a variety of mathematical methods for taking such factors into account in calculating improvement scores, but none of them has yet emerged as a truly valid, dependable approach to measuring teacher or school effectiveness.[84] And statistical methods don't take into account an additional problem with improvement-based approaches to evaluating teacher and school effectiveness: Teachers may encourage students *not* to do well on assessments at the beginning of the school year so that students can maximize their so-called "improvement" during that year. As an illustration, when one sixth grader came home from school not too long ago, she explained to her parents that "My teachers told me not to try too hard on the first test. Otherwise, I wouldn't be able to improve as much when I took the test the next time."

So where does all of this leave us with respect to teacher accountability? At this point, we authors strongly urge educators and policy makers to move away from relying mainly on large-scale achievement tests as the primary indicators of student progress and teacher effectiveness. Ideally, decision makers should instead identify concrete, realistic instructional goals for students in a single school year—perhaps tailoring those goals to local students' strengths and needs and breaking them down into more specific and manageable short-term goals—and create reasonable criterion-referenced tasks to assess goal accomplishment.[85]

Never use a single test score to make important decisions about students.

What we authors have seen and heard in popular news media leads us to think that many politicians and other policy makers overestimate how much high-stakes and other standardized achievement tests can tell us: They assume that such instruments are highly accurate, comprehensive measures of students' academic achievement. True, these tests are often developed by experts with considerable training in test construction, but no test is completely reliable, and its validity will vary considerably depending on the context in which it's being used. Every test is fallible, and students do poorly on tests for a variety of reasons. Thus teachers, school administrators, parents, and others should never—and we do mean *never*—use a single assessment instrument or single test score to make important decisions about individual students. Nor should they use the results of a single test to make important decisions about large groups of students or about the teachers who teach them. It behooves everyone who has a personal or professional stake in children's education to be aware of the limitations of standardized tests and enlighten their fellow citizens accordingly.

Regardless of how students' learning and achievement are assessed, we must all continually keep one point in mind: *Tests and other educational assessments are useful but imperfect tools.* Standardized tests, teacher quizzes, classroom assignments, performance tasks, portfolios—all of these can tell us something about what students know and can do and what students still need to learn and master. The usefulness of any assessment strategy depends on how well matched it is to the situation in which it will be used and how reliable and valid it is for that situation. As a general rule, we should think of any educational assessment as a tool that, in combination with the other tools at teachers' disposal, can help improve classroom instruction and maximize students' learning and achievement over the long run.

---

[84] For example, see American Educational Research Association, 2015; American Statistical Association, 2014; E. M. Anderman, Gimbert, O'Connell, & Riegel, 2015; Ballou, Sanders, & Wright, 2004.

[85] American Educational Research Association, 2015; E. M. Anderman et al., 2015.

Teachers and school administrators must continually keep in mind the benefits and limitations of standardized tests, and to the extent that they can do so, they must advocate for appropriate use of standardized test scores in the evaluation of students' progress and teachers' and schools' effectiveness. In the hotlinked Self-Check quiz and Application Exercises that follow, you can check and apply your understandings related to Big Idea 10.6:

> Large-scale standardized tests can be helpful in estimating students' general achievement levels in particular domains, but educators should never use a single test score to make important decisions about individual students, nor should policy makers use average scores from a single test to evaluate teacher and school effectiveness.

MyEdLab Self-Check 10.6

MyEdLab Application Exercise 10.7. In this exercise, you can analyze how one sixth-grade teacher strategically prepares students for a high-stakes test.

MyEdLab Application Exercise 10.8. If you have read Appendix B as a supplement to this chapter, this exercise can give you practice in interpreting students' standardized achievement test scores.

10 SUMMARY

Regular assessments of students' learning and achievement are an essential component of effective classroom instruction. The Big Ideas presented at the beginning of the chapter can help us summarize key concepts and principles related to productive assessment practices.

■ **10.1: Classroom assessments serve a variety of purposes, but in one way or another, they can all influence students' future learning and achievement.** Assessment is a process of observing a sample of a student's behavior and drawing inferences about the student's knowledge and abilities. Some classroom assessments are used for formative assessment—that is, to guide future instruction and learning. Others are used for summative assessment—that is, to determine what students ultimately know and can do at the end of instruction. But regardless of a teacher's primary purposes in assessing students' knowledge and skills, the nature of the teacher's assessment instruments and practices gives students messages about what things are most important to learn and about how students should study and think about classroom subject matter.

■ **10.2: Effective teachers strategically use both formative and summative assessments to enhance students' learning.** Not only is assessment closely interconnected with instruction, then, but in a very real sense, it *is* instruction. Teachers can—and *should*—regularly and purposefully use classroom assessments to enhance students' ongoing progress and ultimate achievement levels. For example, they can (1) create checklists or rubrics that specify important qualities of good performance, (2) provide the scaffolding students need to evaluate their *own* performance, and (3) make use of formative assessment tools available on the Internet.

■ **10.3: Ideally, classroom assessments have four RSVP characteristics—reliability, standardization, validity, and practicality—with validity being the most important.** Teachers should keep four characteristics in mind when identifying assessment strategies and developing assessment instruments, especially those that will be used for summative evaluations of students' accomplishments. First, an assessment should be *reliable,* yielding consistent results regardless of the specific circumstances in which it is administered and scored. Second, it should be *standardized,* in that it has similar content and is administered and evaluated in a similar manner for everyone (some students with disabilities excepted). Third, it should be *valid,* being an accurate reflection of the knowledge and skills the teacher is trying to assess. Finally, it should be *practical,* staying within reasonable costs and time constraints.

■ **10.4: Spontaneous, informal assessments and preplanned formal assessments both have important roles to play in enhancing students' learning and achievement.** Teachers can sometimes assess students' characteristics and abilities informally, perhaps by simply observing what students do and listening to what they say in everyday activities. Informal assessment is flexible and practical and requires little or no advance planning. Unfortunately, it usually doesn't provide a representative sample of what students know and can do, and teachers' judgments are often biased by their beliefs and expectations regarding particular students.

When drawing firm conclusions about what students have and have not achieved—for example, when assigning final grades—teachers should base their conclusions largely on preplanned, formal assessments. Paper–pencil assessment tasks are usually the most practical ones, and so they're often preferable *if* they truly reflect instructional goals. Performance assessment tasks are often more appropriate for assessing complex achievements that require the integration of numerous skills, and accomplishment of some instructional objectives can be assessed *only* through direct observation of what students can do. Paper–pencil and performance assessments alike usually yield more useful information when tasks have some structure and when explicit, concrete scoring criteria are identified ahead of time.

Classroom assessment practices should allow leeway for students to take the risks so essential for the pursuit of challenging tasks—no single failure should seriously impact a student's long-term academic success. Furthermore, for both legal and educational reasons, teachers must keep students' assessment results confidential, communicating students' test scores, grades, and other information only to the students themselves, to their parents, and to school personnel directly involved in the students' education and well-being. And ultimately, teachers must remember that the ultimate purpose of *any* assessment is not to pass judgment, but rather to help students learn and achieve more effectively.

■ **10.5: Final class grades provide only global, quantitative information about students' achievement levels; whenever possible, they should be supplemented with qualitative information, perhaps through student-constructed portfolios.** Most teachers eventually need to boil down the results of classroom assessments into concise, general indicators of what students have learned. The most common procedure is to assign final grades that summarize what students have achieved during an academic term or school year. In most cases, final grades should reflect actual achievement levels and be based on hard data. The main problem with grades is that, by themselves, they communicate very little about what a student specifically

has learned and can do. Student portfolios, which can represent the multifaceted, complex nature of students' achievements, can often be an effective alternative or supplement to final class grades.

■ **10.6: Large-scale standardized tests can be helpful in estimating students' general achievement levels in particular domains, but educators should never use a single test score to make important decisions about individual students, nor should policy makers use average scores from a single test to evaluate teacher and school effectiveness.** Standardized achievement tests provide a means of tracking students' general progress over time and getting a rough idea of how students at a particular school compare to their peers elsewhere. In recent years standardized achievement tests have often been used to make important decisions about students and to hold school personnel accountable for students' achievement levels. Such *high-stakes testing* doesn't always promote higher student achievement levels—for example, it can lead some teachers to simply "teach to the test" and thereby give short shrift to important but non-tested instructional goals.

Standardized tests will undoubtedly continue to be used as important indicators of both (a) students' progress and (b) teacher and school quality, at least for the foreseeable future. Thus, teachers must become vocal advocates for reasonable and valid approaches to assessing students' overall achievement levels. For example, any high-stakes tests should be closely matched to important instructional goals, and students' ages, developmental levels, and proficiency in English must be accommodated in test design, administration, and interpretation. Also, influential policy makers must be made aware of the significant limitations of using students' achievement test scores as the sole indicators of teachers' and schools' overall effectiveness.

PRACTICE FOR YOUR LICENSURE EXAM

Two Science Quizzes

Knowing that frequent paper–pencil quizzes will encourage students to study and review class material regularly, Mr. Bloskas tells his ninth-grade science students that they'll have a quiz every Friday. As a first-year teacher, he has had little experience developing test questions, so he decides to use the questions in the test-item manual that accompanies the class textbook. The night before the first quiz, Mr. Bloskas types 30 multiple-choice and true–false items from the manual, making sure they cover the specific topics that he has addressed in class.

Mr. Bloskas's students complain that the questions are "picky." As he looks carefully at his quiz, he realizes that the students are right: The quiz measures nothing more than memorization of trivial details. So when he prepares the second quiz, he casts the test-item manual aside and writes two essay questions asking students to apply scientific principles they've studied to new, real-life situations.

The following Friday, students complain even more loudly about the second quiz: "This is too hard!" "We never studied this stuff!" "I liked the first quiz better!" Later, as Mr. Bloskas grades the essays, he is appalled to discover how poorly his students have performed.

1. **Constructed-response question**

   When identifying classroom assessment tasks, teachers must be sure that the tasks have validity, especially *content validity*.

   A. Compare Mr. Bloskas's two quizzes with respect to their content validity.

   B. Describe a reasonable approach Mr. Bloskas might use to create quizzes that have good content validity for his classes.

2. Multiple-choice question

The following alternatives present four possible explanations for the students' negative reactions to the second quiz. Drawing on contemporary theories of learning and motivation, choose the most likely explanation.

a. Multiple-choice and true–false items are more likely than essay questions to enhance students' sense of autonomy.

b. Learners are most likely to behave and study in ways that they expect will lead to reinforcement.

c. Multiple-choice and true–false items are apt to foster mastery goals, whereas essay questions are more likely to foster performance goals.

d. Multiple-choice and true–false items assess information in working (short-term) memory, whereas essay questions usually assess information in long-term memory.

MyEdLab **Licensure Exam 10.1**

Appendix A

Describing Associations with Correlation Coefficients

- Do students with high self-esteem perform better in school than students with low self-esteem?
- As students move through the grade levels, do they become more intrinsically motivated to learn classroom subject matter or, instead, *less* intrinsically motivated to learn it?
- When students are given two different tests of general cognitive ability in the same week, how similar are their scores on the two tests likely to be?
- Are children's emotional reactions to distressing circumstances related to their willingness to help the people in distress?

Each of these questions asks about an association between two variables—whether it be an association between self-esteem and school achievement, between grade level and intrinsic motivation, between two tests of general cognitive ability, or between emotional reactions and prosocial behavior. The nature of such associations is sometimes summarized by a statistic known as a **correlation coefficient**.

A correlation coefficient is a number between −1 and +1; most correlation coefficients are decimals (either positive or negative) somewhere between these two extremes. A correlation coefficient for two variables tells us about both the direction and the strength of the association between the variables.

Direction.   The direction of the association is indicated by the *sign* of the coefficient—in other words, by whether the number is positive or negative. A positive number indicates a *positive correlation:* As one variable increases, the other variable also increases. For example, there's a positive correlation between self-esteem and school achievement: Students with higher self-esteem achieve at higher levels.[1] In contrast, a negative number indicates a *negative correlation:* As one variable increases, the other variable decreases instead. For example, there's a negative correlation between grade level and intrinsic motivation: On average, students in the upper grades (e.g., in middle school and high school) have less intrinsic motivation to master classroom subject matter than younger students do.[2] Figure A.1 graphically depicts the two correlations just described.

Strength.   The strength of the association is indicated by the *size* of the coefficient. A number close to either +1 or −1 (e.g., +.89 or −.76) indicates a *strong* correlation: The two variables are closely related, so knowing the level of one variable allows us to predict the level of the other variable with considerable accuracy. For example, we often find a strong correlation between two tests of general cognitive ability given within a short time period: Students tend to get similar scores on both tests, especially if the tests cover similar kinds of content.[3] In contrast, a number close to 0 (e.g., +.08 or −.21) indicates a *weak* correlation: Knowing the level of one variable allows us to predict the level of the other variable but without much accuracy. For example, there's a weak association between young children's feelings of sadness and their prosocial behavior: On average, children who feel quite sad about a peer who needs help are more likely to provide the help than are less-sad children, but with many exceptions to this general rule (e.g., some sad children don't help at all).[4] Correlations in the middle range (e.g., those in the .40s and .50s, either positive or negative) indicate a *moderate* correlation.

---

[1]For example, see Marsh, Gerlach, Trautwein, Lüdtke, & Brettschneider, 2007.
[2]For example, see Gottfried, Fleming, & Gottfried, 2001.
[3]For example, see McGrew, Flanagan, Zeith, & Vanderwood, 1997.
[4]For example, see P. A. Miller, Eisenberg, Fabes, & Shell, 1996.

FIGURE A.1 Each face in these two graphs represents one student in a group of 50 students. The location of the face indicates the extent to which a student is high or low on the two characteristics indicated. There is a *positive correlation* between self-esteem and school achievement: Students with higher self-esteem tend to achieve at higher levels. There is a *negative correlation* between grade level and intrinsic motivation: Students in higher grades tend to have less intrinsic motivation to learn school subject matter than students in lower grades.

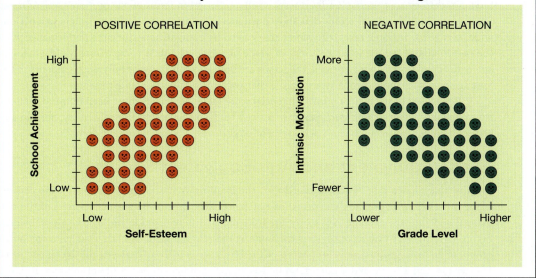

You may often encounter correlation coefficients in research articles in professional books and journals. For instance, you might read that students' visual–spatial thinking ability is positively correlated with their success in a math class or that there's a negative correlation between class size and students' achievement test scores. Whenever you see such evidence of correlation, you must remember one very important point: *Correlation does not necessarily indicate causation.* For example, based on correlations alone, we can't say that visual–spatial thinking ability specifically *leads to* greater mathematical ability, nor can we say that a large class size specifically *interferes with* classroom achievement. Each of these italicized phrases implies a causal relationship that doesn't necessarily exist. Only carefully designed experimental studies enable us to draw conclusions about the extent to which one thing causes or influences another.

Many calculators are now programmed to compute correlation coefficients. Alternatively, with an Internet browser such as Google or Bing, you can easily find websites that enable you to calculate correlations and other simple statistics. Computing a correlation coefficient by hand is complicated but certainly possible; you can find the formula through an Internet search or in most introductory statistics textbooks.

Appendix B

Understanding and Interpreting Standardized Test Results

Students' performance on standardized tests is often reported in terms of one or more *norm-referenced scores*—more specifically, as scores that show a student's performance relative to others in a nationwide *norm group*. In some cases, the scores are derived by comparing a student's performance with the performance of students at a variety of grade or age levels; such comparisons yield grade- or age-equivalent scores. In other cases, the scores are based on comparisons only with students of the *same* age or grade; these comparisons yield either percentile ranks or standard scores.

Regardless of the form a norm-referenced score takes, educators must keep in mind that *any test score reflects only a student's performance on a single test.* No test has perfect reliability, nor can any test score fully capture a student's achievement or abilities in a given content domain.

Grade-Equivalent and Age-Equivalent Scores

Imagine that Shawn takes a standardized test, the Reading Achievement Test (RAT). He gets 46 of the 60 test items correct; thus, 46 is his raw score. We turn to the norms reported in the test manual and find the average raw scores for students at different grade and age levels, shown in Figure B.1. Shawn's raw score of 46 is the same as the average score of 11th graders in the norm group, so he has a **grade-equivalent score** of 11. His score is halfway between the average score of 16-year-old and 17-year-old students, so he has an **age-equivalent score** of approximately 16½. Shawn is 13 years old and in eighth grade, so he has obviously done well on the RAT.

In general, grade- and age-equivalent scores are determined by matching a student's raw score to a particular grade or age level in the norm group. A student who performs as well as the average second grader on a reading test will get a grade-equivalent score of 2, regardless of the student's actual grade level. A student who gets the same raw score as the average 10-year-old on a physical fitness test will get an age-equivalent score of 10, regardless of whether that student is 5, 10, or 15 years old.

On the surface, grade- and age-equivalent scores seem so simple and straightforward. But they have a serious drawback: They give us no idea of the typical *range* of performance for students at a particular grade or age level. For example, a raw score of 34 on the RAT gives us a grade-equivalent score of 8, but obviously not all eighth graders will get raw scores of exactly 34. It's possible, and in fact quite likely, that many eighth graders will get raw scores several points above or below 34, thus getting grade-equivalent scores of 9 or 7 (perhaps even 10 or higher, or 6 or lower).

FIGURE B.1 Hypothetical norm-group data for the Reading Achievement Test (RAT)

Norms for Grade Levels		Norms for Age Levels	
Grade	Average Raw Score	Age	Average Raw Score
5	19	10	18
6	25	11	24
7	30	12	28
8	34	13	33
9	39	14	37
10	43	15	41
11	46	16	44
12	50	17	48

In previous decades, grade-equivalent scores were widely used to summarize students' performance on standardized achievement tests. Their use has declined in recent years because they are too often misinterpreted. For one thing, well-meaning policy makers have sometimes proposed that grade-equivalent scores should be a standard for performance—that *all* students should perform at grade level on an achievement test. Given the normal variability within most classrooms, this goal is unrealistic: It's mathematically impossible for everyone to be average or above-average. A second common misinterpretation is to conclude that grade-equivalent scores indicate the appropriate grade placement for a student—for example, concluding that a third grader who gets grade-equivalent scores of 5 or 6 in all subject areas should be immediately moved to fifth grade. Remember, a norm-referenced score reflects nothing more than a student's performance on a particular test at a particular time; it *doesn't* necessarily reflect a student's ability to handle the curriculum at a higher grade level. Furthermore, although advanced placements are occasionally quite appropriate, most students are more socially and emotionally comfortable with classmates of the same age. And, of course, good teachers tailor their instructional strategies to students' differing achievement levels.

Percentile Ranks

A **percentile rank** (sometimes simply called a **percentile**) is the percentage of people at the *same* age or grade level getting a raw score less than or equal to the student's raw score. To illustrate, let's once again consider Shawn's performance on the RAT. Because Shawn is in eighth grade, we would turn to the eighth-grade norms in the RAT test manual. If we discover that a raw score of 46 is at the 98th percentile for eighth graders, we know that Shawn has done as well as or better than 98% of eighth graders in the norm group. Similarly, a student getting a percentile rank of 25 has performed as well as or better than 25% of the norm group, and a student getting a score at the 60th percentile has done as well as or better than 60%. It's important to note that a percentile rank refers to a percentage of *people,* not to the percentage of correct items—a common misconception among teacher education students.

Percentile ranks are relatively simple to understand and therefore used frequently in reporting test results. But they too, have a significant drawback: They distort actual differences among students. As an illustration, consider the RAT percentile ranks of these four boys:

STUDENT	PERCENTILE RANK
Ernest	45
Frank	55
Giorgio	89
Wayne	99

In *actual achievement level* (as measured by the RAT), Ernest and Frank are probably very similar even though their percentile ranks are 10 points apart. However, a 10-point difference at the upper end of the scale probably reflects a substantial difference in achievement: Giorgio's percentile rank of 89 tells us that he knows quite a bit, but Wayne's percentile rank of 99 tells us that he knows an exceptional amount. In general, percentiles tend to *over*estimate differences in the middle range of the characteristic being measured: Scores a few points apart reflect similar achievement or ability levels. Meanwhile, percentiles *under*estimate differences at the upper and lower extremes: Scores only a few points apart often reflect substantial differences in achievement or ability. We avoid this problem when we use standard scores.

Standard Scores

The school nurse measures the heights of the 25 students in Ms. Oppenheimer's third-grade class, as shown on the left side of Figure B.2. The nurse then creates a graph of the children's heights, shown on the right side of Figure B.2. Notice that the graph is high in the middle and low on both ends. This shape tells us that most of Ms. Oppenheimer's students are more or less average in height, with only a few very short students (e.g., Pat, Amy, and Wil) and only a few very tall ones (e.g., Hal, Roy, and Jan).

Many psychologists believe that educational and psychological characteristics typically follow the same pattern we see for height: Most people are close to average, with fewer and fewer

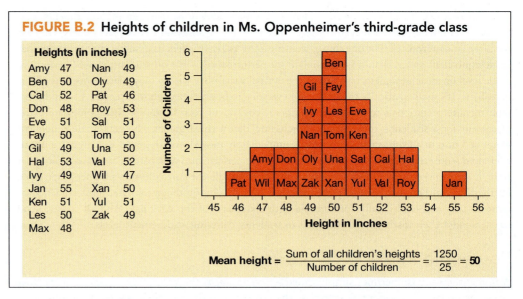

FIGURE B.2 Heights of children in Ms. Oppenheimer's third-grade class

Heights (in inches)

Amy	47	Nan	49
Ben	50	Oly	49
Cal	52	Pat	46
Don	48	Roy	53
Eve	51	Sal	51
Fay	50	Tom	50
Gil	49	Una	50
Hal	53	Val	52
Ivy	49	Wil	47
Jan	55	Xan	50
Ken	51	Yul	51
Les	50	Zak	49
Max	48		

$$\text{Mean height} = \frac{\text{Sum of all children's heights}}{\text{Number of children}} = \frac{1250}{25} = 50$$

people being counted as we move farther from the average. This theoretical pattern of educational and psychological characteristics, known as the **normal distribution (or normal curve)**, is shown in the margin. Standard scores reflect this normal distribution: Many students get scores in the middle range, and only a few get very high or very low scores.

Before we examine standard scores in detail, we need to understand two numbers used to derive them: the mean and standard deviation. The **mean (M)** is the average of a set of scores: We add all the scores together and divide by the total number of scores (or people). For example, if we add the heights of all 25 students in Ms. Oppenheimer's class and then divide by 25, we get a mean height of 50 inches (see the calculation at the bottom of Figure B.2).

The **standard deviation (SD)** indicates the *variability* of a set of scores. A small number tells us that, generally speaking, the scores are close together, and a large number tells us that they're spread far apart. For example, third graders tend to be more similar in height than eighth graders (some eighth graders are less than 5 feet tall; others may be almost 6 feet tall). The standard deviation for the heights of third graders is therefore smaller than the standard deviation for the heights of eighth graders. The formula for computing a standard deviation is fairly complex; fortunately, we don't need to know it in order to understand the role that a standard deviation plays in standard scores. Furthermore, the standard deviation for any published test is typically provided in the test manual. (If you're curious, you can find information about how to calculate standard deviations on Wikipedia and many other Internet websites.)

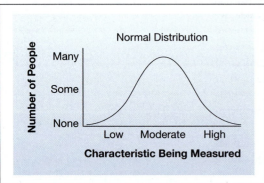

The mean and standard deviation can be used to divide the normal distribution into several parts, as shown in Figure B.3. The vertical line at the middle of the curve shows the mean; for a normal distribution, it's both the midpoint and the highest point of the curve. The thinner lines to either side reflect the standard deviation: We count out one standard deviation higher and lower than the mean and mark those two spots with vertical lines, and then we count another standard deviation to either side and draw two more lines. When we divide a normal distribution in this way, the percentages of students getting scores in each part are always the same. Approximately two-thirds (68%) get scores within one standard deviation of the mean (34% in each direction). As we go farther away from the mean, we find fewer and fewer students, with 28% lying between one and two standard deviations away (14% on each side) and only about 4% being more than two standard deviations away (2% at each end).

Now that we better understand the normal distribution and two statistics that describe it, let's return to standard scores. A **standard score** reflects a student's position in the normal distribution: It tells us how far

FIGURE B.3 Normal distribution divided by the mean and standard deviation

the student's performance is from the mean in terms of standard deviation units. Unfortunately, not all standard scores use the same scale: Scores used for various tests have different means and standard deviations. Five commonly used standard scores, depicted graphically in Figure B.4, are the following:

- **IQ scores** are frequently used to report students' performance on intelligence tests. They have a *mean of 100* and, for most tests, a *standard deviation of 15*. (If you look back at Figure 6.10 in Chapter 6, you'll see that we've broken up that curve by thirds of a standard deviation unit. The lines for 85 and 115 reflect one standard deviation from the mean score of 100. The lines for 70 and 130 reflect two SDs from the mean.)

- **ETS scores** are used on the SAT Reasoning Test, published by the Educational Testing Service (ETS). They have a *mean of 500* and a *standard deviation of 100*. However, no scores fall below 200 or above 800.

- **Stanines** (short for *standard nines*) are often used in reporting standardized achievement test results. They have a *mean of 5* and a *standard deviation of 2*. Because they're always reported as whole numbers, each score reflects a *range* of test performance, indicated by the shaded and nonshaded portions of the upper-right-hand curve in Figure B.4.

- **NCE scores** (short for *normal-curve-equivalent scores*) are increasingly being used in reporting standardized achievement test results. They have a *mean of 50* and a *standard deviation of 21.06*. However, it isn't possible to get a score of zero or below, nor is it possible to get a score of 100 or above.

- **z-scores** are the standard scores that statisticians most often use. They have a *mean of 0* and a *standard deviation of 1*.

The odd standard deviation for NCE scores (21.06) requires an explanation. It turns out that with this particular standard deviation, an NCE score of 1 is equivalent to a percentile score of 1 and, likewise, an NCE score of 99 is equivalent to a percentile score of 99. And, of course, an NCE score of 50 (being the mean and midpoint of the curve) is also a percentile score of 50. Thus NCE scores have the same general range as percentile ranks.[1]

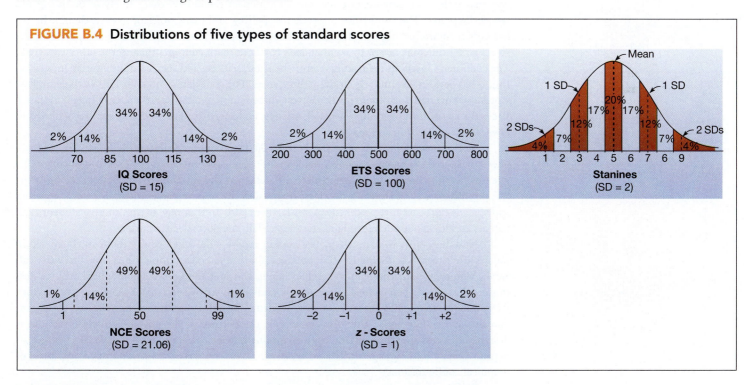

FIGURE B.4 Distributions of five types of standard scores

---

[1]Some educators find it helpful to calculate average test scores for a particular group of students (e.g., a particular class), and NCE scores allow us to do that. In contrast, percentile ranks *don't* allow calculation of averages: As noted earlier, they distort actual differences between students, making even the simplest mathematical calculations with them meaningless.

FIGURE B.5 Computer printout showing 12-year-old Ingrid's performance on a standardized achievement test

	STANINE	PERCENTILE	NATIONAL PERCENTILE BANDS
			WELL BELOW AVERAGE : BELOW : AVERAGE : ABOVE : WELL ABOVE AVERAGE
			1 5 10 20 30 40 50 60 70 80 90 95 99
READING COMPREHENSION	8	92	XXXXXXXXXXXXX
SPELLING	4	39	XXXXXXXXXXX
MATH COMPUTATION	4	37	XXXXXXXXXX
MATH CONCEPTS	5	57	XXXXXXXXXXX
SCIENCE	8	90	XXXXXXXXXXXXXX
SOCIAL STUDIES	7	84	XXXXXXXX
			1 5 10 20 30 40 50 60 70 80 90 95 99

Interpreting Computer-Generated Test Results: Two Examples

As test-analysis software programs have become more and more sophisticated, test publishers have been generating increasingly complex reports for teachers and parents. Some of these reports can be quite overwhelming. To help you make sense of them, we're starting with a report generated back in the "old days"—that is, in 1990. Although it's certainly outdated by today's standards, its simplicity makes it relatively easy to understand. Figure B.5 presents a computer printout of 12-year-old Ingrid's scores on various subtests of a national achievement test. Ingrid's percentile ranks and stanines have been computed by comparing her raw scores with those of a national norm group. On the basis of her test scores, Ingrid appears to have achieved at average to below-average levels in spelling and math computation, an average to above-average level in math concepts, and above-average to well-above-average levels in reading comprehension, science, and social studies.

The "national percentile bands" in Figure B.5 (i.e., the rows of Xs) are **confidence intervals** that reflect the amount of error (due to imperfect reliability) that's likely to be in Ingrid's percentile scores. The confidence intervals for spelling and math overlap, so even though Ingrid has gotten somewhat higher scores in math concepts than in spelling or math computation, the scores aren't different *enough* to say that she's better at math concepts than in the other two areas. The confidence intervals for reading comprehension, science, and social studies overlap as well, so Ingrid has performed similarly in these three areas. The confidence intervals for her three highest scores *don't* overlap with those for her lowest three scores. We can say, then, that Ingrid's relative strengths are in reading comprehension, science, and social studies, and that she has achieved at lower levels in spelling and math.

Notice how the numbers at the bottom of the computer printout (1, 5, 10, 20, etc.) are unevenly spaced. Remember a point made earlier about percentile ranks: They overestimate differences near the mean and underestimate differences at the extremes. The uneven spacing is the test publisher's way of showing this fact: It squishes the middle percentile scores closer together and spreads high and low percentile scores farther apart. In this way, it tries to give students and parents an idea about where students' test scores fall in a normal distribution.

Now let's turn to a much more detailed report—the kind you're more likely to see in today's high-tech world. Figure B.6 presents a hypothetical example for a student we'll call Sarah, who took both the Stanford Achievement Test and the Otis-Lennon School Ability Test in second grade. As you can see in the purple-and-white-striped section of the form, the Stanford Achievement Test yields scores related to students' overall achievement in a variety of content domains and subdomains. The Otis-Lennon (at the bottom of the purple-and-white section) is designed to assess students' general cognitive abilities with respect to both *verbal* tasks (those that depend heavily on language skills) and *nonverbal* tasks (those that involve numbers, pictures, or graphical configurations).

At first glance, the report can be quite daunting, but let's make sense of some of the data presented in the top section. The "Number Correct" columns are, of course, Sarah's raw scores on the overall tests and various subtests within them. The PR-S scores are really two separate scores: The first two digits indicate a percentile rank, and the digit after the hyphen is a stanine score.

FIGURE B.6 Hypothetical report for a second grader's performance on the Stanford Achievement Tests and Otis-Lennon School Ability Test

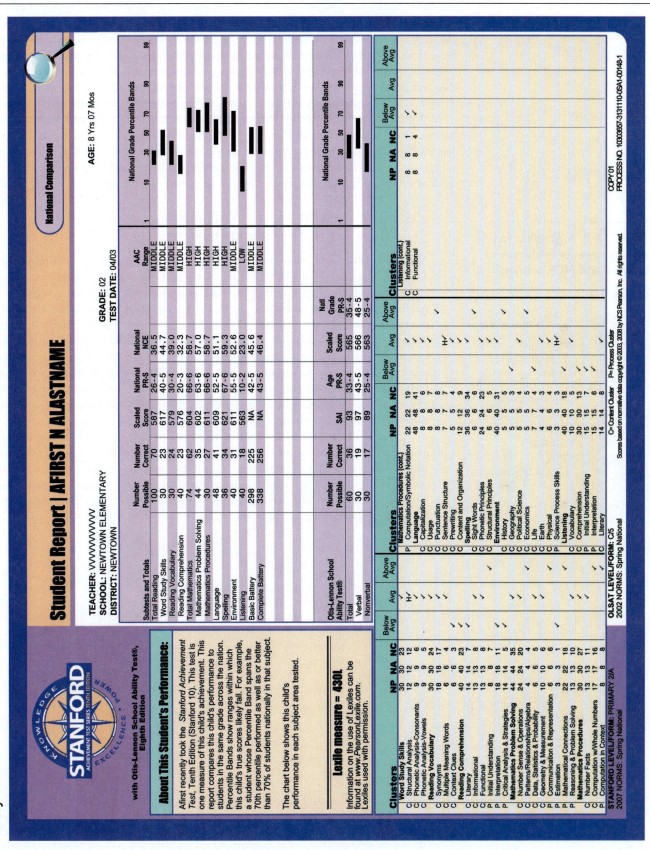

Source: From the Stanford Achievement Test Series, Tenth Edition (STANFORD 10); Copyright © 2003 by NCS Pearson, Inc. Reproduced with permission. All rights reserved.

The Stanford yields percentiles and stanines based on a national norm group of second graders; the Otis-Lennon yields two sets of percentiles and stanines, one set derived from the second-grade norms (the "Natl Grade PR-S") and the other derived from students in the norm group who are the same age as Sarah (the "Age PR-S"). We've previously explained the nature of NCE scores, and the SAI scores on the Otis-Lennon are based on the IQ-score scale we also described earlier ("SAI" refers to "School Ability Index"). We haven't specifically talked about scaled scores or what an AAC range might be, and we don't want to overwhelm our readers with too much information, so we're putting explanations of these columns in a footnote for readers who might be curious.[2]

Notice the "National Grade Percentile Bands" in the upper right part of the figure. These are confidence intervals intended to reflect the amount of error (and imperfect reliability) affecting Sarah's percentile scores. As is true in the simpler printout in Figure B.5, the graph squishes middle-range percentile ranks close together and spreads the high and low percentiles farther apart as a way of reflecting the scores' underlying normal distribution.

Helping Parents Understand Standardized Test Results

As noted in Chapter 10, one of the stipulations of the Family Educational Rights and Privacy Act (FERPA; passed by the U.S. Congress in 1974) is that school personnel must present and interpret test scores in a way that parents can understand. Given the complexity of most standardized test reports these days, that's a pretty tall order. Many parents are familiar with percentile ranks, and many others can easily grasp the notion of a percentile if it's explained to them. But we authors must say that, in our own experiences, explaining standard scores so that parents truly understand them can be a bit of a challenge, especially when the parents have little or no background in statistics. (And let's face it, most parents don't have such a background!) The simple graphic in Figure B.7 can help parents make better sense of stanines and NCE scores by seeing how these scores are related to simple percentages—in particular, to the relative proportions of students getting scores in different ranges.

Despite the considerable data that standardized tests can yield, educators and parents must remember that students' scores on these tests are, at best, only *imprecise estimates* of what students generally know and can do, and they may have little or no validity for certain students. We must all be *extremely cautious*—and occasionally downright skeptical—in our interpretations of students' standardized test results, and we mustn't place too much stock in the *exact* numbers we see in test reports.

FIGURE B.7 A graphic for helping parents understand stanines and NCE scores

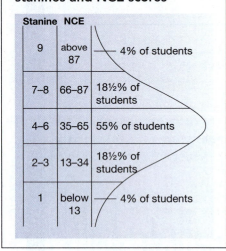

Stanine	NCE	
9	above 87	4% of students
7–8	66–87	18½% of students
4–6	35–65	55% of students
2–3	13–34	18½% of students
1	below 13	4% of students

---

[2]The "Scaled Scores" are statistical adjustments that reflect the difficulty level of a particular form of each test; they allow comparisons among students who've taken different forms of the tests, with some forms almost inevitably being slightly more difficult than others. "AAC Range" refers to "Ability–Achievement Comparison"; entries in this column indicate how Sarah's various achievement test scores compare with the Otis-Lennon's estimates of her general cognitive ability. For example, Sarah is "High" in her Math achievement scores, indicating that she has done better than have most students with Otis-Lennon scores similar to hers.

Glossary

academic engagement Extent of behavioral, cognitive, and emotional involvement in an academic activity.

accommodation Process of dealing with a new object or event by either modifying an existing scheme or forming a new one.

accountability Mandated obligation of teachers and other school personnel to accept responsibility for students' performance on high-stakes assessments.

action research Research conducted by teachers and other school personnel to address issues and problems in their own schools or classrooms.

adaptive assessment Assessment instrument in which students' performance on early items determines which items are presented subsequently; often administered via computer technology.

advance organizer Introduction to a lesson that provides an overall organizational scheme for the lesson.

affect Feelings, emotions, and moods that a learner brings to bear on a task.

African American English Dialect of some African American communities that is characterized by certain pronunciations, idioms, and grammatical constructions different from those of Standard English.

age-equivalent score Test score matching a particular student's performance with the average performance of students of a certain age.

algorithm Prescribed sequence of steps that guarantees a correct problem solution.

antecedent stimulus Stimulus that tends to evoke a particular kind of response.

anxiety Feeling of uneasiness and apprehension concerning a situation with an uncertain outcome.

APA style Rules and guidelines on referencing, editorial style, and manuscript format prescribed by the American Psychological Association.

applied behavior analysis (ABA) Systematic application of stimulus–response principles to address a chronic behavior problem.

apprenticeship Mentorship in which a novice works intensively with an expert to learn how to perform complex new skills.

assessment Process of observing a sample of a student's behavior and drawing inferences about the student's knowledge and abilities.

assessment bias Extent to which assessment tasks either offend or unfairly penalize some students because of their membership in a particular group (e.g., students of a particular gender or ethnic group).

assimilation Process of dealing with an object or event in a way that is consistent with an existing scheme.

assistive technology Any electronic or nonelectronic device that can enhance certain abilities or performance areas for students with disabilities.

astrocyte Star-shaped brain cell hypothesized to be involved in learning and memory; has chemically mediated connections with many other astrocytes and with neurons.

attention Focusing of mental processing on particular stimuli.

attention-deficit hyperactivity disorder (ADHD) Disorder marked by inattention, hyperactivity, impulsive behavior, or some combination of these characteristics.

attribution Self-constructed causal explanation for a personally experienced or observed event, such as one's own or another person's success or failure.

authentic activity Task or activity similar to one students might encounter in the outside world.

authentic assessment Assessment of students' knowledge and skills in a context similar to one that might be found in the outside world.

authoritarian parenting Parenting style characterized by rigid rules and expectations for behavior that children are asked to obey without question.

authoritative parenting Parenting style characterized by emotional warmth, high standards for behavior, explanation and consistent enforcement of rules, inclusion of children in decision making, and reasonable opportunities for autonomy.

autism spectrum disorders Disorders marked by impaired social cognition, social skills, and social interaction, presumably due to a brain abnormality; extreme forms often associated with significant cognitive and linguistic delays and highly unusual behaviors.

automaticity Ability to respond quickly and efficiently while mentally processing or physically performing a task.

backward design Approach to instructional planning in which a teacher first determines the desired end result of instruction (i.e., what knowledge and skills students should acquire), then identifies appropriate assessments, and finally determines appropriate instructional strategies.

basic interpersonal communication skills (BICS) Proficiency in English sufficient for day-to-day conversation with English speakers but *not* sufficient for academic success in an English-only curriculum.

behaviorism Theoretical perspective in which learning and behavior are described and explained in terms of stimulus–response relationships.

belongingness General sense that one is an important and valued member of the classroom.

bilingual education Second-language instruction in which students are instructed in academic subject areas in their native language while simultaneously being taught to speak and write in the second language.

Bloom's taxonomy Taxonomy of six cognitive processes, varying in complexity, that lessons might be designed to foster.

bully Person who frequently threatens, harasses, or causes injury to particular peers.

central executive Component of human memory that oversees the flow of information throughout the memory system.

checklist List of characteristics that good performance on an assessment task should have.

class inclusion Recognition that an object simultaneously belongs to a particular category and to one of its subcategories.

classroom climate Overall psychological atmosphere of the classroom.

classroom management Establishment and maintenance of a classroom environment conducive to students' learning and achievement.

clinical method Procedure in which an adult presents a task or problem and asks a child a series of questions about it, tailoring later questions to the child's responses to previous ones.

clique Moderately stable friendship group of perhaps four to eight members.

cognitive academic language proficiency (CALP) Mastery of English vocabulary and syntax sufficient for English language learners to achieve academic success in an English-only curriculum.

cognitive apprenticeship Mentorship in which an expert and novice work together on a challenging task, with the expert giving guidance about how to think about the task.

cognitive development Developmental changes in thinking, reasoning, and language.

cognitive dissonance Feeling of mental discomfort caused by new information that conflicts with current knowledge or beliefs.

cognitive load Cognitive burden that a particular learning activity places on working memory at any one time; includes both the amount of information learners must simultaneously think about and the specific cognitive processes learners must engage in to understand what they're studying.

cognitive process Particular way of thinking about and mentally responding to a certain event or piece of information.

cognitive psychology Theoretical perspective that focuses on the mental processes underlying learning and behavior; encompasses information processing theory, individual constructivism, and related perspectives.

cognitive style Characteristic way in which a learner tends to think about a task and process new information; typically comes into play automatically rather than by choice.

cognitive tool Concept, symbol, strategy, procedure, or other culturally constructed mechanism that helps people think about and respond to situations more effectively.

cognitive-developmental theory Theoretical perspective that characterizes human development as a sequence of qualitatively distinct stages; subsequent stages build on the acquisitions of preceding ones.

collective self-efficacy Shared belief of members of a group that they can be successful when they work together on a task.

Common Core State Standards Set of standards that most U.S. states have adopted to guide instruction and assessment in English-language arts and mathematics (see corestandards.org).

community of learners Class in which the teacher and students actively and collaboratively work to create a body of knowledge and to help one another learn.

community of practice Group of people who share common interests and goals and regularly interact and coordinate their efforts in pursuit of those interests and goals.

complex cognitive process Cognitive process that involves going well beyond information specifically learned (e.g., by analyzing, applying, or evaluating it).

comprehension monitoring Process of checking oneself to be sure one understands and can recall newly acquired information.

computer-supported collaborative learning (CSCL) Learner-directed approach to instruction in which students communicate and collaborate via computer technology and the Internet.

computer-supported instruction (CBI) Academic instruction provided by means of specially designed computer software and/or Internet websites.

concept Mental grouping of objects or events that have something in common.

concept map Diagram of concepts and their interrelationships; used to enhance learning and memory of a topic.

conceptual change Significant revision of one's existing beliefs about a topic, enabling new and discrepant information to be better understood and explained.

conceptual understanding Meaningfully learned and well-integrated knowledge about a topic, including many logical connections among specific concepts and ideas.

concrete operations stage Piaget's third stage of cognitive development, in which adultlike logic appears but is limited to concrete reality.

confidence interval Range around an assessment score reflecting the amount of error that might have influenced the student's performance on this particular occasion (reflecting imperfect reliability of the assessment instrument).

confirmation bias Tendency to seek information that confirms rather than discredits one's current beliefs.

conservation Realization that if nothing is added or taken away, amount stays the same regardless of alterations in shape or arrangement.

consolidation Neurological process in which newly acquired knowledge is firmed up in the brain; often takes several hours, sometimes even longer.

construction Mental process in which a learner takes many separate pieces of information and uses them to build an overall understanding or interpretation.

constructivism Theoretical perspective proposing that learners construct (rather than passively absorb) knowledge from their experiences.

content validity Extent to which an assessment includes a representative sample of tasks within the content domain being assessed.

content-area standards General statements regarding the knowledge and skills that students should gain and the characteristics that their accomplishments should reflect in a particular academic discipline.

contextual theory Theoretical perspective that focuses on how people's general physical, social, and/or cultural surroundings support their learning, development, and behavior.

contingency Situation in which one event (e.g., reinforcement) happens only after another event (e.g., a specific response) has already occurred; one event is *contingent* on the other's occurrence.

contingency contract Written agreement between teacher and student that identifies behaviors the student will exhibit and the reinforcers that will follow.

control group Group of people in a research study who are given either no intervention or a *placebo* treatment that is unlikely to have an effect on the dependent variable.

controversial student Student whom some peers strongly like and other peers strongly dislike.

conventional morality Uncritical acceptance of society's conventions regarding right and wrong behaviors.

conventional transgression Action that violates a culture's general expectations regarding socially appropriate behavior.

convergent thinking Process of pulling several pieces of information together to draw a conclusion or solve a problem.

cooperative learning Approach to instruction in which students work with a small group of peers to achieve a common goal and help one another learn.

core goal Long-term goal that drives much of what a learner does.

co-regulated learning Process through which an adult and child share responsibility for directing various aspects of the child's learning.

correlation Extent to which two variables are associated, such that when one variable increases, the other either increases or decreases somewhat predictably.

correlation coefficient Statistic that indicates the strength and direction of an association between two variables.

correlational study Research study that explores possible relationships among two or more variables.

cortex Upper and outer parts of the human brain, which are largely responsible for conscious and complex cognitive processes.

covert strategy Learning strategy that is strictly mental (rather than behavioral) in nature and thus cannot be directly observed by others.

creativity New and original behavior that yields a productive and culturally appropriate result.

criterion-referenced score Assessment score that specifically indicates what a student knows or can do.

critical thinking Process of evaluating the accuracy, credibility, and worth of information and lines of reasoning.

crowd Large, loose-knit social group that shares certain common interests and attitudes.

crystallized intelligence Knowledge and skills accumulated from prior experience, schooling, and culture.

cueing Use of simple signals to indicate that a certain behavior is desired or that a certain behavior should stop.

cultural mismatch Situation in which a child's home and school cultures hold conflicting expectations for the child's behavior.

culturally responsive teaching Use of instructional strategies that build on students' existing knowledge and skills and that accommodate their accustomed ways of behaving and learning.

culture Behaviors and belief systems that members of a long-standing social group share and pass along to successive generations.

culture of transfer Learning environment in which applying school subject matter to diverse situations and topics is both the expectation and the norm.

culture shock Sense of confusion when a student encounters a culture with behavioral expectations very different from those learned previously in other contexts.

curriculum-based measurement (CBM) Use of frequent assessments to track students' progress in acquiring basic skills; assessments are typically quite short (e.g., 1–4 minutes) and each focus on a specific skill.

cyberbullying Engaging in psychological aggression via wireless technologies or the Internet.

debilitating anxiety Anxiety of sufficient intensity that it interferes with performance.

decay Gradual weakening of information stored in long-term memory, especially if the information is used infrequently or not at all.

declarative knowledge Knowledge concerning the nature of how things are, were, or will be.

delay of gratification Ability to forego small, immediate reinforcers to obtain larger ones at a later time.

descriptive study Research study that enables researchers to draw conclusions about the current state of affairs regarding an issue but not about correlation or cause-and-effect relationships.

development Orderly, enduring changes that occur over the life span.

developmental milestone Appearance of a new, developmentally more advanced behavior.

dialect Form of a language that has certain unique pronunciations, idioms, and grammatical structures and is characteristic of a particular region or ethnic group.

differentiated instruction Practice of individualizing instructional methods—and possibly also individualizing specific content and instructional goals—to align with each student's existing knowledge, skills, and needs.

direct instruction Approach to instruction that uses a variety of techniques (e.g., explanations, questions, guided and independent practice) in a fairly structured manner to promote learning of fundamental knowledge and skills.

discovery learning Approach to instruction in which students construct their own knowledge about a topic through firsthand interaction with an aspect of their environment.

disequilibrium State of being unable to address new events with existing schemes; typically accompanied by mental discomfort.

disposition General inclination to approach and think about learning and problem-solving tasks in a particular way; typically has a motivational component in addition to cognitive components.

distributed cognition Enhancement of thinking and problem solving through the use of physical objects (e.g., technology), the cognitive tools of one's culture, and/or social collaboration and support; also known as *distributed intelligence*.

distributed intelligence Enhancement of thinking and problem solving through the use of physical objects (e.g., technology), the cognitive tools of one's culture, and/or social collaboration and support; also known as *distributed cognition*.

distributed knowledge Distribution of expertise across various members of a social group, such that group members must rely on one another to maximize their personal and collective success.

divergent thinking Process of generating many different ideas from a single starting point.

dynamic assessment Systematic examination of how easily and in what ways a student can acquire new knowledge or skills, perhaps within the context of instruction or scaffolding.

ecological systems theory Theoretical perspective emphasizing the various layers of a learner's social environment (family, community, etc.) and their interactive effects in influencing the learner's development.

educational psychology Academic discipline that (a) systematically studies the nature of human learning, development, motivation, and related topics and (b) applies its research findings to the identification and development of effective instructional practices.

effortful control General ability to inhibit immediate impulses in order to think and act productively; an aspect of temperament that is influenced by biology and brain maturation.

elaboration Cognitive process in which learners embellish on new information based on what they already know.

emotion regulation Process of keeping one's affective states and affect-related behaviors within productive, culturally desirable limits.

emotional and behavioral disorders Emotional states and behavior patterns that consistently and significantly disrupt academic learning and school success.

empathy Experience of sharing the same feelings as someone in unfortunate circumstances.

encoding Mentally changing the format of new information in order to remember it more easily.

English language learner (ELL) School-age child who is not fully fluent in English because of limited exposure to English prior to enrollment in an English-speaking school.

entity view of intelligence Belief that intelligence is a distinct ability that is relatively permanent and unchangeable.

epistemic belief Belief about the nature of knowledge or knowledge acquisition.

equilibration Movement from equilibrium to disequilibrium and back to equilibrium, a process that promotes the development of more complex thought and understandings.

equilibrium State of being able to address new events with existing schemes.

ethnic group People who have common historical roots, values, beliefs, and behaviors and who share a sense of interdependence.

ethnic identity Awareness of one's membership in a particular ethnic or cultural group, and willingness to adopt behaviors characteristic of the group.

ETS score Standard score with a mean of 500 and a standard deviation of 100.

Every Student Succeeds Act (ESSA) U.S. legislation passed in 2015 that continued the No Child Left Behind Act's mandates for frequent assessments of students' progress in reading, math, and science; however, it gave greater flexibility to individual states in terms of identifying appropriate standards, assessment techniques, and corrective actions for low-performing schools.

evidence-based practice Instructional method or other classroom strategy that research has consistently shown to bring about significant gains in students' development and/or academic achievement.

experimental study (experiment) Research study that involves both (a) the manipulation of one variable to determine its possible effect on another variable and (b) control of additional variables that might have an impact on the outcome; potentially allows conclusions about cause-and-effect relationships.

expertise Extensive and well-integrated knowledge of a topic that comes from many years of study and practice.

expository instruction Approach to instruction in which information is presented in essentially the same form in which students are expected to learn it.

externalizing behavior Symptom of an emotional or behavioral disorder that has a direct effect on other people (e.g., aggression, lack of self-control).

extinction Gradual disappearance of an acquired response; in the case of a response acquired through operant conditioning, it results from repeated lack of reinforcement for the response.

extrinsic motivation Motivation to engage in an activity because it leads to a desired reward or consequence.

extrinsic reinforcer Reinforcer that comes from the outside environment, rather than from within the learner.

facilitating anxiety Level of anxiety (usually relatively low) that enhances performance.

Family Educational Rights and Privacy Act (FERPA) U.S. legislation passed in 1974 that gives students and parents access to school records and limits other people's access to those records.

flow Intense form of intrinsic motivation, involving complete absorption in and concentration on a challenging activity.

fluid intelligence Ability to acquire knowledge quickly and adapt effectively to new situations.

formal assessment Preplanned, systematic attempt to ascertain what students have learned.

formal operations stage Piaget's fourth and final stage of cognitive development, in which logical reasoning processes are applied to abstract ideas as well as to concrete objects and more sophisticated scientific and mathematical reasoning processes emerge.

formative assessment Assessment conducted before or during instruction to facilitate instructional planning and enhance students' learning.

functional analysis Examination of inappropriate behavior and its antecedents and consequences to determine one or more purposes (functions) that the behavior might serve for the learner.

g Theoretical general factor in intelligence that influences one's ability to learn and perform in a wide variety of contexts.

gang Cohesive social group characterized by initiation rites, distinctive colors and symbols, territorial orientation, and feuds with rival groups.

gender schema Self-constructed, organized body of beliefs about characteristics and behaviors of males or females.

general transfer Instance of transfer in which the original learning task and the transfer task are different in both content and structure.

giftedness Unusually high ability in one or more areas, to such a degree that students require special educational services to help them meet their full potential.

goodness of fit Situation in which classroom conditions and expectations are compatible with students' temperaments and personality characteristics.

grade-equivalent score Test score matching a particular student's performance with the average performance of students at a certain grade level.

guided participation A child's performance, with guidance and support, of an activity in the adult world.

guilt Feeling of discomfort about having caused someone else pain or distress.

heuristic General strategy that facilitates problem solving or creativity but does not always yield a successful outcome.

higher-level question Question that requires students to use previously learned information in a new way—that is, to engage in one or more complex cognitive processes.

high-stakes testing Practice of using students' performance on a single assessment to make major decisions about students, school personnel, or overall school quality.

hostile attributional bias Tendency to interpret others' behaviors as reflecting hostile or aggressive intentions.

hot cognition Learning or cognitive processing that is emotionally charged.

hypermedia Collection of computer-based and electronically linked multimedia materials (e.g., text, pictures, sound, animations) that students can examine in a sequence of their own choosing.

identity Self-constructed definition of who one thinks one is and what things are important to accomplish in life.

ill-defined problem Problem in which the desired goal is unclear, some information needed to solve the problem is missing, and/or several possible solutions to the problem may exist.

illusion of knowing Thinking that one knows something that one actually does *not* know.

imaginary audience Belief that one is the center of attention in any social situation.

incentive Hoped-for, but not guaranteed, future consequence of behavior.

inclusion The practice of educating all students, including those with severe and multiple disabilities, in neighborhood schools and general education classrooms.

incompatible behaviors Two or more behaviors that cannot be performed simultaneously.

incremental view of intelligence Belief that intelligence can improve with effort and practice.

individual constructivism Theoretical perspective that focuses on how learners each construct their own idiosyncratic meanings from their experiences.

individual interest Long-term, relatively stable interest in a particular topic or activity.

Individuals with Disabilities Education Act (IDEA) U.S. legislation granting educational rights to people with cognitive, emotional, or physical disabilities from birth until age 21; initially passed in 1975, it has been amended and reauthorized several times and is now officially known as the Individuals with Disabilities Education Improvement Act.

induction Explanation of why a certain behavior is unacceptable, often with a focus on the pain or distress that someone has caused another.

informal assessment Assessment that results from a teacher's spontaneous, day-to-day observations of how students behave and perform at school.

information literacy Knowledge and skills that help a learner find, use, evaluate, organize, and use information about a particular topic.

information processing theory Theoretical perspective that focuses on the specific ways in which learners mentally think about, or process, new information and events.

inner speech Process of talking to and guiding oneself mentally rather than aloud.

inquiry learning Approach to instruction in which students apply complex reasoning skills in their examination and interpretation of new phenomena and data sources.

in-school suspension Consequence for misbehavior in which a student is placed in a quiet, boring room within the school building, typically to do schoolwork under close adult supervision.

instructional goal Desired long-term outcome of instruction.

instructional objective Desired outcome of a lesson or unit.

intellectual disability Disability characterized by significantly below-average general intelligence and deficits in adaptive behavior, both of which first appear in infancy or childhood; also known as *mental retardation.*

intelligence Ability to apply prior knowledge and experiences flexibly to accomplish challenging new tasks; involves many different mental processes and may vary in nature depending on one's culture.

intelligence test General measure of current cognitive functioning; often used to predict academic achievement over the short run.

intelligent tutoring system Computer software program that provides individually tailored instruction and practice, supplemented with ongoing guidance and feedback, related to a particular topic and set of skills.

interest Perception that an activity is intriguing and enjoyable; typically accompanied by both cognitive engagement and positive affect.

internalization Process through which a learner gradually incorporates socially based activities into his or her internal cognitive processes.

internalizing behavior Symptom of an emotional or behavioral disorder that adversely affects the student with the disorder but has little or no direct effect on other people (e.g., depression, social withdrawal).

intrinsic motivation Motivation to engage in an activity because it is enjoyable and interesting.

intrinsic reinforcer Reinforcer provided by oneself or inherent in a task being performed.

IQ Score on an intelligence test, determined by comparing a person's performance on the test with the performance of others in the same age-group; for most tests, it's a standard score with a mean of 100 and a standard deviation of 15.

IQ score Score on an intelligence test, determined by comparing a person's performance on the test with the performance of others in the same age-group; for most tests, it's a standard score with a mean of 100 and a standard deviation of 15.

IRE cycle Adult–child interaction marked by adult initiation (usually a question), child response, and adult evaluation.

keyword method Mnemonic technique in which a learner mentally connects two ideas by forming a visual image of one or more concrete objects (*keywords*) that either sound similar to, or symbolically represent, those ideas.

knowledge base A learner's existing knowledge about specific topics and the world in general.

learned helplessness General, fairly pervasive belief that one is incapable of accomplishing tasks and has little or no control over the environment.

learner-centered instruction Approach to teaching in which instructional strategies are chosen largely on the basis of students' existing abilities, predispositions, and needs.

learner-directed instruction Approach to instruction in which students have considerable control regarding the issues they address and the ways to address them.

learning Long-term change in mental representations or associations due to experience.

learning disability Deficiency in one or more specific cognitive processes despite relatively normal cognitive functioning in other areas.

learning strategy Intentional use of one or more specific cognitive processes for a particular learning task.

legitimate peripheral participation Initial involvement at the fringe of a community of practice as a way of gaining knowledge and skills related to the group's typical ways of doing things.

lesson plan Predetermined guide for a lesson that identifies instructional goals or objectives, necessary materials, instructional strategies, and one or more assessment methods.

logical consequence Unpleasant consequence that follows naturally or logically from a student's misbehavior.

long-term memory Component of memory that holds knowledge and skills for a relatively long time.

lower-level question Question that requires students to retrieve and recite what they have learned in essentially the same form they learned it.

mastery goal Desire to develop competence by acquiring new knowledge or mastering new skills.

mastery learning Approach to instruction in which students learn one topic thoroughly before moving to a subsequent one.

mastery orientation General, fairly pervasive belief that one is capable of accomplishing challenging tasks.

maturation A gradual, genetically driven acquisition of more advanced physical and neurological capabilities over the course of childhood and adolescence.

mean (M) Mathematical average of a set of scores.

meaningful learning Cognitive process in which a learner relates new information to prior knowledge.

mediated learning experience Social interaction in which an adult helps a child interpret a phenomenon or event in particular (usually culturally appropriate) ways.

memory Ability to save something (mentally) that has been previously learned; also, the mental "location" where such information is saved.

mental set Inclination to represent a problem or situation in a way that excludes potential solutions.

metacognition Knowledge and beliefs about one's own cognitive processes, as well as conscious attempts to engage in behaviors and thought processes that increase learning and memory.

mirror neuron Neuron in the brain that fires in either of two situations: (a) when a person is performing a particular behavior or (b) when the person sees someone else perform the behavior.

misbehavior Action that disrupts learning and planned classroom activities, puts students' physical safety or psychological well-being in jeopardy, or violates basic moral standards.

misconception Belief that is inconsistent with commonly accepted and well-validated explanations of certain phenomena or events.

mixed-methods research Research yielding information that includes both quantitative and qualitative findings.

mnemonic Memory aid or trick designed to help students learn and remember one or more specific pieces of information.

model Real or fictional individual who demonstrates a behavior that learners might emulate; alternatively, a set of instructions for successfully executing the behavior.

modeling Demonstrating a behavior for another person *or* observing and imitating another person's behavior.

moral dilemma Situation in which two or more people's rights or needs may be at odds and the morally correct action is not clear-cut.

moral transgression Action that causes harm or infringes on the needs or rights of others.

morality One's general standards regarding right and wrong behaviors.

motivation Inner state that energizes, directs, and sustains behavior.

multicultural education Instruction that integrates perspectives and experiences of numerous cultural groups throughout the curriculum.

multiple intelligences theory Theory that portrays intelligence as being comprised of three or more relatively independent abilities, with most people being stronger (more "intelligent") in some abilities than in others.

myelination Growth of a fatty coating (myelin) around neurons, enabling faster transmission of messages.

nativism Theoretical perspective proposing that the foundations of some behaviors and abilities are biologically built-in traits and possibly unique to the human species.

NCE score Standard score with a mean of 50 and a standard deviation of 21.06; an NCE score of 1 equals a percentile rank of 1, and an NCE score of 99 equals a percentile rank of 99.

need for arousal Ongoing need for either physical or cognitive stimulation.

need for autonomy Basic need to believe that one has some control regarding the course of one's life.

need for competence Basic need to believe that one can deal effectively with one's overall environment.

need for relatedness Basic need to feel socially connected to others and to secure others' love and respect.

negative reinforcement Phenomenon in which a response increases as a result of the removal (rather than presentation) of a stimulus.

negative transfer Phenomenon in which something learned at one time interferes with learning or performance at a later time.

neglected student Student about whom most peers have no strong feelings, either positive or negative.

neuron Cell in the brain or another part of the nervous system that specializes in transmitting information to other cells.

Next Generation Science Standards Set of standards that some U.S. states have adopted to guide instruction and assessment in science (see nextgenscience.org).

niche-picking Tendency for a learner to seek out environmental conditions that are a good match with his or her existing characteristics and behaviors.

No Child Left Behind Act (NCLB) U.S. legislation passed in 2001 that mandated regular standardized assessments of basic skills to determine whether students were making adequate yearly progress relative to state-determined standards in reading, math, and science; it also mandated that teachers and schools be held accountable for students' poor academic progress.

normal distribution (normal curve) Theoretical pattern of educational and psychological characteristics in which most individuals score somewhere in the middle range and only a few score at either extreme.

norm-referenced score Assessment score that indicates how a student's performance compares with the average performance of others.

operant conditioning Form of learning in which a response increases in frequency as a result of being followed by reinforcement.

organization Cognitive process in which a learner makes connections among new pieces of information (e.g., by forming categories, identifying hierarchies, determining cause-and-effect relationships).

overt strategy Learning strategy that is at least partially evident in the learner's behavior (e.g., taking notes during a lecture).

paper–pencil assessment Assessment in which students provide written responses to written items.

pedagogical content knowledge Knowledge about effective methods of teaching a specific topic or content area.

peer contagion Phenomenon in which certain behaviors, attitudes, and/or values spread from one child or adolescent to another, perhaps through modeling, peer reinforcement, social sanctions, or self-socialization.

peer mediation Approach to conflict resolution in which a student (acting as a mediator) asks peers in conflict to express their differing viewpoints and then work together to identify a reasonable resolution.

peer tutoring Approach to instruction in which one student provides instruction to help another student master a classroom topic.

percentile rank (percentile) Test score indicating the percentage of peers in the norm group getting a raw score less than or equal to a particular student's raw score.

performance assessment Assessment in which students demonstrate their knowledge and skills in a nonwritten fashion.

performance goal Desire to demonstrate competence and make a good impression.

performance-approach goal Desire to look good and receive favorable judgments from others.

performance-avoidance goal Desire not to look bad or receive unfavorable judgments from others.

personal fable Belief that one is completely unlike anyone else and so cannot be understood by others.

personal space Personally or culturally preferred distance between people during social interaction.

personality Characteristic ways in which a particular individual behaves, thinks, and feels in a wide range of circumstances.

perspective taking Ability to look at a situation from someone's else viewpoint.

physical aggression Action that can potentially cause bodily injury.

plasticity Ability to reorganize in order to adapt to changing circumstances; term often used in describing the human brain.

popular student Student whom many peers like and perceive to be kind and trustworthy.

portfolio Collection of a student's work compiled systematically over a lengthy time period.

positive behavioral interventions and supports (PBIS) Variation of traditional applied behavior analysis that involves identifying the purposes of undesirable behaviors and encouraging alternative behaviors that more appropriately accomplish those purposes.

positive reinforcement Phenomenon in which a response increases as a result of the presentation (rather than removal) of a stimulus.

positive transfer Phenomenon in which something learned at one time facilitates learning or performance at a later time.

postconventional morality Thinking in accordance with self-constructed, abstract principles regarding right and wrong behaviors.

practicality Extent to which an assessment instrument or procedure is inexpensive and easy to use and takes only a small amount of time to administer and score.

preconventional morality Lack of internalized standards about right and wrong behaviors; decision making based primarily on what seems best for oneself.

preoperational stage Piaget's second stage of cognitive development, in which children can think about objects and events beyond their immediate experience but do not yet reason in logical, adultlike ways.

presentation punishment Punishment involving presentation of a new stimulus, presumably one a learner finds unpleasant.

primary reinforcer Consequence that satisfies a built-in biological or psychological need.

principle Description of the specific effects of certain factors on other factors or outcomes, such as those related to learning or development.

prior knowledge activation Process of reminding learners of things they already know relative to a new topic.

proactive aggression Deliberate aggression against another as a means of obtaining a desired goal.

problem solving Using existing knowledge or skills to address an unanswered question or troubling situation.

problem-based learning Classroom activity in which students acquire new knowledge and skills while working on a complex problem similar to certain real-world problems.

procedural knowledge Knowledge concerning how to do something (e.g., a skill).

professional learning community Schoolwide collaborative effort in which teachers and administrators share a common vision for students' learning and achievement and work together to bring about desired student outcomes.

project-based learning Classroom activity in which students acquire new knowledge and skills while working on a complex, multifaceted project that yields a concrete end product.

prosocial behavior Behavior directed toward promoting the well-being of one or more other people rather than one's own well-being.

proximal goal Concrete goal that can be accomplished within a short time period; may be a steppingstone toward a longer-term goal.

psychodynamic theory Theoretical perspective that focuses on how early experiences affect personality development; some of these experiences may not be available for conscious recall and self-reflection.

psychological aggression Action intended to cause mental anguish or reduce self-esteem.

punishment Consequence that decreases the frequency of the response it follows.

qualitative research Research yielding information that cannot easily be reduced to numbers; typically involves an in-depth examination of a complex phenomenon.

quantitative research Research yielding information that is inherently numerical in nature or can easily be reduced to numbers.

quasi-experimental study Research study that involves the manipulation of one variable to determine its possible effect on another variable, but without total control of additional variables that might have an impact on the outcome.

raw score Assessment score based solely on the number or point value of correctly answered items.

reactive aggression Aggressive response to frustration or provocation.

reciprocal causation Mutual cause-and-effect relationships among environment, behavior, and personal variables as these three factors influence learning and development.

reciprocal teaching Approach to fostering reading and listening comprehension skills in which students take turns asking teacherlike questions of classmates.

reconstruction error Construction of a logical but incorrect "memory" by combining information retrieved from long-term memory with general knowledge and beliefs about the world.

recursive thinking Thinking about what other people may be thinking about oneself, possibly through multiple iterations.

reflective teaching Regular, ongoing examination and critique of one's assumptions and instructional strategies and revision of them as necessary to enhance students' learning and development.

rehearsal Cognitive process in which a learner repeats information over and over as a possible way of learning and remembering it.

reinforcer Consequence of a response that leads to increased frequency of the response; the act of following a response with a reinforcer is known as **reinforcement**.

rejected student Student whom many peers identify as being an undesirable social companion.

reliability Extent to which an assessment instrument yields consistent information about the knowledge, skills, or characteristics being assessed.

removal punishment Punishment involving removal of an existing stimulus, presumably one a learner finds desirable and doesn't want to lose.

resilient self-efficacy Belief that one can perform a task successfully even after experiencing setbacks.

resilient student Student who succeeds in school and in life despite exceptional hardships at home or in other important environmental contexts.

response Specific behavior that an individual exhibits.

response cost Loss either of a previously earned reinforcer or of an opportunity to obtain reinforcement.

response to intervention (RTI) Approach to diagnosing significant learning difficulties in which students are identified for in-depth assessment after failing to master certain basic skills despite evidence-based whole-class and small-group instructional practices.

retrieval Process of mentally "finding" information previously stored in memory.

retrieval cue Stimulus that provides guidance about where to "look" for a piece of information in long-term memory.

retrieval failure Inability to locate information that currently exists in long-term memory.

rote learning Cognitive process in which a learner tries to remember information in a relatively uninterpreted form, with little or no effort to make sense of or attach meaning to it.

rubric Two-dimensional table that includes two or more characteristics on one dimension and concrete criteria for rating them on the other dimension; useful in evaluating a multifaceted performance or product.

scaffolding Support mechanism that helps a learner successfully perform a challenging task.

schema Tightly organized set of facts about a specific concept or phenomenon.

scheme Organized group of similar actions or thoughts that are repeatedly used in response to the environment.

school climate Schoolwide atmosphere in which students feel physically and psychologically safe and also perceive a widespread commitment to everyone's academic progress and personal well-being.

schoolwide positive behavioral interventions and supports (SWPBIS) Systematic use of behaviorist principles to encourage and reinforce productive behaviors in all students; typically involves multiple layers of support in order to accommodate the varying needs and behavior patterns of different students.

script Schema that involves a predictable sequence of events related to a common activity.

secondary reinforcer Consequence that becomes reinforcing over time through its association with another reinforcer.

self-conscious emotion Affective state based on self-evaluations regarding the extent to which one's actions meet society's standards for appropriate and desirable behavior; examples are pride, guilt, and shame.

self-efficacy Belief that one is capable of executing certain behaviors or reaching certain goals.

self-evaluation Judgment of one's own performance or behavior.

self-fulfilling prophecy Expectation for an outcome that either directly or indirectly leads to the expected result.

self-handicapping Behavior that undermines one's own success as a way of protecting self-worth during potentially difficult tasks.

self-imposed contingency Self-reinforcement or self-punishment that follows a particular behavior.

self-instructions Instructions that one gives oneself while executing a complex task.

self-monitoring Observing and possibly recording one's own behavior to check progress toward a goal.

self-regulation Process of taking control of, monitoring, and evaluating one's own learning and behavior.

self-socialization Tendency to integrate personal observations and others' input into self-constructed standards for behavior and to choose actions consistent with those standards.

self-talk Process of talking to oneself as a way of guiding oneself through a task.

self-worth Belief about the extent to which one is generally a good, capable individual.

sense of community Shared belief that teacher and students have common goals, are mutually respectful and supportive, and all make important contributions to classroom learning.

sense of school community Shared belief that all faculty and students within a school are working together to help everyone learn and succeed.

sense of self Perceptions, beliefs, judgments, and feelings about oneself as a person; includes *self-concept* and *self-esteem*.

sensitive period Genetically determined age range during which a certain aspect of a child's development is especially susceptible to environmental conditions.

sensory register Component of memory that holds incoming information in an unanalyzed form for a very brief time (2 or 3 seconds at most, depending on the modality).

service learning Activity that promotes learning and development through participation in a meaningful community service project.

shame Feeling of embarrassment or humiliation after failing to meet certain standards for moral behavior.

shaping Process of reinforcing successively closer and closer approximations to a desired behavior.

situated learning and cognition Knowledge, behaviors, and thinking skills acquired and used primarily within certain contexts, with little or no retrieval and use in other contexts; sometimes involves dependence on physical or social support mechanisms available only in certain contexts.

situated motivation Motivation that emerges at least partly from conditions in a learner's immediate environment.

situational interest Interest evoked temporarily by something in the environment.

social cognition Process of thinking about how other people are likely to think, act, and react.

social cognitive theory Theoretical perspective that focuses on how people learn by observing others and how they eventually assume control over their own behavior.

social constructivism Theoretical perspective that focuses on people's collective efforts to impose meaning on their world.

social goal Desire related to establishing or maintaining relationships with other people.

social information processing Mental processes involved in making sense of and responding to social events.

socialization Process of molding a child's behavior and beliefs to be appropriate for his or her cultural group.

society Large, enduring social group that is socially and economically organized and has collective institutions and activities.

sociocultural theory Theoretical perspective emphasizing the importance of society and culture in promoting learning and development.

socioeconomic status (SES) One's general social and economic standing in society; encompasses family income, occupation, educational level, and related factors.

specific transfer Instance of transfer in which the original learning task and the transfer task overlap in some way.

stage theory Theory that depicts development as a series of relatively discrete periods (*stages*).

standard deviation (SD) Statistic indicating the amount of variability characterizing a set of scores.

Standard English Form of English generally considered acceptable at school, as reflected in textbooks and grammar instruction.

standard score Test score indicating how far a person's performance is from the mean with respect to standard deviation units.

standardization Extent to which assessments involve similar content and format and are administered and scored similarly for everyone.

standardized test Test developed by test construction experts and published for use in many different schools and classrooms.

stanine Standard score with a mean of 5 and a standard deviation of 2; always reported as a whole number.

stereotype Rigid, simplistic, and erroneous view of a particular group of people.

stereotype threat Awareness of a negative stereotype about one's own group and accompanying uneasiness that low performance will confirm the stereotype; leads (often unintentionally) to a reduction in performance.

stimulus (pl. stimuli) Specific object or event that influences an individual's learning or behavior.

storage Process of mentally "putting" new information into memory.

student at risk Student who is on a path toward undesirable long-term developmental outcomes (e.g., failure to graduate, criminal behavior, suicide).

student with special needs Student who is different enough from peers that he or she requires specially adapted instructional materials or practices.

subculture Group that resists the ways of the dominant culture and adopts its own norms for behavior.

summative assessment Assessment conducted after instruction to assess students' final achievement.

superimposed meaningful structure Familiar shape, word, sentence, poem, or story imposed on information in order to facilitate recall.

sympathy Feeling of sorrow for another person's distress, accompanied by concern for the person's well-being.

synapse Microscopic gap across which one neuron regularly communicates with another; reflects an ongoing but modifiable connection between the two neurons.

synaptic pruning Universal process in brain development in which many previously formed synapses wither away.

synaptogenesis Universal process in brain development (especially in the first few years) in which many new synapses spontaneously form.

table of specifications Two-way grid indicating the topics to be covered in an assessment and the things students should be able to do with those topics.

task analysis Process of identifying the specific behaviors, knowledge, or cognitive processes necessary to master a particular topic or skill.

teachable moment Situation or event (often unplanned) in which students might be especially predisposed to acquire particular knowledge or skills.

teacher-directed instruction Approach to instruction in which the teacher is largely in control of the content and course of the lesson.

technological literacy Knowledge and skills that a learner needs to effectively use digital technologies and media.

temperament Genetic predisposition to respond in particular ways to one's physical and social environments.

test anxiety Excessive anxiety about a particular test or about assessment in general.

testwiseness General test-taking know-how that enhances test performance.

theory Integrated set of concepts and principles developed to explain a particular phenomenon; may be constructed jointly by researchers over time (see Chapter 1) or individually by a single learner (see Chapter 2).

theory of mind Self-constructed understanding of one's own and other people's mental and psychological states (thoughts, feelings, etc.).

time-out Consequence for misbehavior in which a student cannot interact with others and has no opportunity to receive the kinds of reinforcement to which classmates have access.

token economy Classroom strategy in which desired behaviors are reinforced by small, insignificant items (tokens) that learners can use to "purchase" a variety of other, more desirable reinforcers.

transfer Phenomenon in which something a person has learned at one time affects how the person learns or performs in a later situation.

treatment group Group of people in a research study who are given a particular experimental intervention (e.g., a particular method of instruction).

universal (in development) Similar pattern in how children change and progress over time regardless of their specific environment.

validity Extent to which an assessment actually measures what it is intended to measure and allows appropriate inferences about the characteristic or ability in question.

value Belief that an activity has direct or indirect benefits.

value-added assessment Approach to evaluating teacher and school effectiveness based on students' academic progress rather than on absolute achievement levels.

verbal mediator Word or phrase that forms a logical connection, or mental "bridge," between two pieces of information.

vicarious punishment Phenomenon in which a response decreases in frequency when another person is observed being punished for that response.

vicarious reinforcement Phenomenon in which a response increases in frequency when another person is observed being reinforced for that response.

visual imagery Cognitive process in which a learner forms a mental picture of an object or idea.

wait time Length of time a teacher pauses, after either asking a question or hearing a student's comment, before saying something.

webquest Structured activity in which students use a number of teacher- or expert-chosen websites to tackle an engaging, challenging task that requires complex cognitive processes (e.g., problem solving, critical thinking).

well-defined problem Problem in which the goal is clearly stated, all the information needed to solve the problem is present, and only one correct answer exists.

withitness Classroom management strategy in which a teacher gives the impression of knowing what all students are doing at all times.

working memory Component of memory that holds and actively thinks about and processes a limited amount of information for a short time.

worldview General, culturally based set of assumptions about reality that influence understandings of a wide variety of phenomena.

zone of proximal development (ZPD) Range of tasks that a child can perform with the help and guidance of others but cannot yet perform independently.

z-**score** Standard score with a mean of 0 and a standard deviation of 1.

References

CHAPTER 1

Alexander, P. A. (2003). The development of expertise: The journey from acclimation to proficiency. *Educational Researcher, 32*(8), 10–14.

American Psychological Association (2010). *Publication manual of the American Psychological Association* (6th ed.). Washington, DC: Author.

Baumert, J., Kunter, M., Blum, W., Brunner, M., Voss, T., Jordan, A., . . . Tsai, Y.-M. (2010). Teachers' mathematical knowledge, cognitive activation in the classroom, and student progress. *American Educational Research Journal, 47,* 133–180.

Berliner, D. C. (2001). Learning about and learning from expert teachers. *International Journal of Educational Research, 35,* 463–483.

Blumberg, F. C. (Ed.). (2014). *Learning by playing: Video gaming in education.* New York, NY: Oxford University Press.

Borko, H., & Putnam, R. T. (1996). Learning to teach. In D. C. Berliner & R. C. Calfee (Eds.), *Handbook of educational psychology.* New York, NY: Macmillan.

Bransford, J., Darling-Hammond, L., & LePage, P. (2005). Introduction. In L. Darling-Hammond & J. Bransford (Eds.), *Preparing teachers for a changing world: What teachers should learn and be able to do* (pp. 1–39). San Francisco, CA: Jossey-Bass/Wiley.

Bransford, J., Derry, S., Berliner, D., & Hammerness, K. (with Beckett, K. L.) (2005). Theories of learning and their roles in teaching. In L. Darling-Hammond & J. Bransford (Eds.), *Preparing teachers for a changing world: What teachers should learn and be able to do* (pp. 40–87). San Francisco, CA: Jossey-Bass/Wiley.

Brouwer, N., & Korthagen, F. (2005). Can teacher education make a difference? *American Educational Research Journal, 42,* 153–224.

Castagno, A. E., & Brayboy, B. M. J. (2008). Culturally responsive schooling for Indigenous youth: A review of the literature. *Review of Educational Research, 78,* 941–993.

Clotfelter, C. T., Ladd, H. F., & Vigdor, J. (2007). Who teaches whom? Race and the distribution of novice teachers. *Economics of Education Review, 24,* 377–392.

Cochran, K. F., & Jones, L. L. (1998). The subject matter knowledge of preservice science teachers. In B. J. Fraser & K. G. Tobin (Eds.), *International handbook of science education* (Pt. II, pp. 707–718). Dordrecht, Netherlands: Kluwer.

Cook, B. G., Smith, G. J., & Tankersley, M. (2012). Evidence-based practices in education. In K. R. Harris, S. Graham, & T. Urdan (Eds.), *APA educational psychology handbook* (Vol. 1, pp. 495–527). Washington, DC: American Psychological Association.

Creswell, J. W. (2014). *Research design: Qualitative, quantitative, and mixed methods approaches* (4th ed.). Thousand Oaks, CA: Sage.

Darling-Hammond, L., & Bransford, J. (Eds.). (2005). *Preparing teachers for a changing world: What teachers should learn and be able to do.* San Francisco, CA: Jossey-Bass/Wiley.

Desimone, L. M. (2009). Improving impact studies of teachers' professional development: Toward better conceptualizations and measures. *Educational Researcher, 38,* 181–199.

DuFour, R., DuFour, R., & Eaker, R. (2008). *Revisiting professional learning communities at work: New insights for improving schools.* Bloomington, IN: Solution Tree.

Feldon, D. F. (2007). Cognitive load and classroom teaching: The double-edged sword of automaticity. *Educational Psychologist, 42,* 123–137.

Fives, H., & Gill, M. G. (Eds.). (2015). *International handbook of research on teachers' beliefs.* New York, NY: Routledge.

Gage, N. L. (1991). The obviousness of social and educational research results. *Educational Researcher, 20*(1), 10–16.

Goldstein, L. S., & Lake, V. E. (2000). "Love, love, and more love for children": Exploring preservice teachers' understanding of caring. *Teaching and Teacher Education, 16,* 861–872.

Graham, P., & Ferriter, W. M. (2009). *Building a professional learning community at work: A guide to the first year.* Bloomington, IN: Solution Tree.

Green, C. S. (2014). The perceptual and cognitive effects of action video game experience. In F. C. Blumberg (Ed.), *Learning by playing: Video gaming in education* (pp. 29–41). New York, NY: Oxford University Press.

Gregoire, M. (2003). Is it a challenge or a threat? A dual-process model of teachers' cognition and appraisal processes during conceptual change. *Educational Psychology Review, 15,* 147–179.

Guskey, T. R., & Sparks, D. (2002, April). *Linking professional development to improvements in student learning.* Paper presented at the annual meeting of the American Educational Research Association, New Orleans, LA.

Hammerness, K., Darling-Hammond, L., & Bransford, J. (with Berliner, D., Cochran-Smith, M., McDonald, M., & Zeichner, K.). (2005). How teachers learn and develop. In L. Darling-Hammond & J. Bransford (Eds.), *Preparing teachers for a changing world: What teachers should learn and be able to do* (pp. 358–389). San Francisco, CA: Jossey-Bass/Wiley.

Hamre, B. K., Pianta, R. C., Burchinal, M., Field, S., LoCasale-Crouch, J., Downer, J. T., . . . Scott-Little, C. (2012). A course on effective teacher–child interactions: Effects on teacher beliefs, knowledge, and observed practice. *American Educational Research Journal, 49,* 88–123.

Harris, K. R., Graham, S., & Urdan, T. (2012). Introduction. In K. R. Harris, S. Graham, & T. Urdan (Eds.), *APA educational psychology handbook* (Vol. 1, pp. xxi–xxx). Washington, DC: American Psychological Association.

Hattie, J. A. C. (2009). *Visible learning: A synthesis of over 800 meta-analyses relating to achievement.* London, England: Routledge.

Heck, A., Collins, J., & Peterson, L. (2001). Decreasing children's risk taking on the playground. *Journal of Applied Behavior Analysis, 34,* 349–352.

Henry, G. T., Bastian, K. C., & Fortner, C. K. (2011). Stayers and leavers: Early-career teacher effectiveness and attrition. *Educational Researcher, 40,* 271–280.

Hill, H. C., Blunk, M. L., Charalambous, C. Y., Lewis, J. M., Phelps, G. C., Sleep, L., & Ball, D. L. (2008). Mathematical knowledge for teaching and the mathematical quality of instruction: An exploratory study. *Cognition and Instruction, 26,* 430–511.

Hogan, T., Rabinowitz, M., & Craven, J. A., III (2003). Representation in teaching: Inferences from research of expert and novice teachers. *Educational Psychologist, 38,* 235–247.

Holt-Reynolds, D. (1992). Personal history-based beliefs as relevant prior knowledge in course work. *American Educational Research Journal, 29,* 325–349.

Holzberger, D., Philipp, A., & Kunter, M. (2013). How teachers' self-efficacy is related to instructional quality: A longitudinal analysis. *Journal of Educational Psychology, 105,* 774–786.

Kirschner, P. A., & van Merriënboer, J. J. G. (2013). Do learners really know best? Urban legends in education. *Educational Psychologist, 48,* 169–183.

Konstantopoulos, S., & Chung, V. (2011). The persistence of teacher effects in elementary grades. *American Educational Research Journal, 48,* 361–386.

Kozhevnikov, M., Evans, C., & Kosslyn, S. M. (2014). Cognitive style as environmentally sensitive individual differences in cognition: A modern synthesis and applications in education, business, and management. *Psychological Science in the Public Interest, 15,* 3–33.

Krätzig, G. P., & Arbuthnott, K. D. (2006). Perceptual learning style and learning proficiency: A test of the hypothesis. *Journal of Educational Psychology, 98,* 238–246.

Krauss, S., Brunner, M., Kunter, M., Baumert, J., Blum, W., Neubrand, M., & Jordan, A. (2008). Pedagogical content knowledge and content knowledge of secondary mathematics teachers. *Journal of Educational Psychology, 100,* 716–725.

Langer, J. A. (2000). Excellence in English in middle and high school: How teachers' professional lives support student achievement. *American Educational Research Journal, 37,* 397–439.

Larrivee, B. (2006). The convergence of reflective practice and effective classroom management. In C. M. Evertson & C. S. Weinstein (Eds.), *Handbook of classroom management: Research, practice, and contemporary issues* (pp. 983–1001). Mahwah, NJ: Erlbaum.

Mayer, R. E., & Massa, L. J. (2003). Three facets of visual and verbal learners: Cognitive ability, cognitive style, and learning preference. *Journal of Educational Psychology, 95,* 833–846.

McCombs, B. L. (Ed.). (2005). *Learner-centered principles: A framework for teaching.* Mahwah, NJ: Erlbaum.

McDevitt, T. M., & Ormrod, J. E. (2008). Fostering conceptual change about child development in prospective teachers and other college students. *Child Development Perspectives, 2,* 85–91.

McIntyre, E. (2010). Issues in funds of knowledge teaching and research: Key concepts from a study of Appalachian families and schooling. In M. L. Dantas & P. C. Manyak (Eds.), *Home–school connections in a multicultural society: Learning from and with culturally and linguistically diverse families* (pp. 201–217). New York, NY: Routledge.

Mills, G. E. (2014). *Action research: A guide for the teacher researcher* (5th ed.). Upper Saddle River, NJ: Pearson.

National Research Council. (2000). *How people learn: Brain, mind, experience, and school* (expanded ed.). Washington, DC: National Academies Press.

Ormrod, J. E. (2011). *Our minds, our memories: Enhancing thinking and learning at all ages.* Boston: Pearson.

Patrick, H., & Pintrich, P. R. (2001). Conceptual change in teachers' intuitive conceptions of learning, motivation, and instruction: The role of motivational and epistemological beliefs. In B. Torff & R. J. Sternberg (Eds.), *Understanding and teaching the intuitive mind: Student and teacher learning* (pp. 117–143). Mahwah, NJ: Erlbaum.

Raudenbush, S. W. (2009). The *Brown* legacy and the O'Connor challenge: Transforming schools in the images of children's potential. *Educational Researcher, 38,* 169–180.

Reynolds, W. M., & Miller, G. E. (2013). Volume preface. In W. M. Reynolds & G. E. Miller (Eds.), *Handbook of psychology, volume 7: Educational psychology* (pp. xv–xviii). Hoboken, NJ: Wiley.

Richardson, V. (2003). Preservice teachers' beliefs. In J. Raths & A. C. McAninch (Eds.), *Teacher beliefs and classroom performance: The impact of teacher education* (pp. 1–22). Greenwich, CT: Information Age.

Rogoff, B. (2003). *The cultural nature of human development.* Oxford, England: Oxford University Press.

Rothbart, M. K. (2011). *Becoming who we are: Temperament and personality in development.* New York, NY: Guilford.

Schlegel, A., Alexander, P., & Tse, P. U. (2016). Information processing in the mental workspace is fundamentally distributed. *Journal of Cognitive Neuroscience, 28*(2), 295–307. doi:10.1162/jocn_a_00899

Shulman, L. S. (1986). Those who understand: Knowledge growth in teaching. *Educational Researcher, 15*(2), 4–14.

Skaalvik, E. M., & Skaalvik, S. (2008). Teacher self-efficacy: Conceptual analysis and relations with teacher burnout and perceived school context. In H. W. Marsh, R. G. Craven, & D. M. McInerney (Eds.), *Self-processes, learning, and enabling human potential* (pp. 223–247). Charlotte, NC: Information Age.

Smith, A. K. (2009). *The art of possibility: Creating more successful learners.* Malibu, CA: Center for Collaborative Action Research, Pepperdine University. Retrieved from http://cadres.pepperdine.edu/ccar/projects.school.html

Smith, D. C., & Neale, D. C. (1991). The construction of subject-matter knowledge in primary science teaching. In J. Brophy (Ed.), *Advances in research on teaching: Vol. 2. Teachers' knowledge of subject matter as it relates to their teaching practice* (pp. 187–244). Greenwich, CT: JAI Press.

Squire, K. (2011). *Video games and learning: Teaching and participatory culture in the digital age.* New York, NY: Teachers College Press.

Tobias, S., & Fletcher, J. D. (Eds.) (2011). *Computer games and instruction.* Charlotte, NC: Information Age.

Waterhouse, L. (2006). Multiple intelligences, the Mozart effect, and emotional intelligence: A critical review. *Educational Psychologist, 41,* 207–225.

Windschitl, M. (2002). Framing constructivism in practice as the negotiation of dilemmas: An analysis of the conceptual, pedagogical, cultural, and political challenges facing teachers. *Review of Educational Research, 72,* 131–175.

Woolfolk Hoy, A., Davis, H., & Pape, S. J. (2006). Teacher knowledge and beliefs. In P. A. Alexander & P. H. Winne (Eds.), *Handbook of educational psychology* (2nd ed., pp. 715–737). Mahwah, NJ: Erlbaum.

CHAPTER 2

Abrahamson, D., & Lindgren, R. (2014). Embodiment and embodied design. In R. K. Sawyer (Ed.), *The Cambridge handbook of the learning sciences* (2nd ed., pp. 358–376). New York, NY: Cambridge University Press.

Alexander, P. A., & Jetton, T. L. (1996). The role of importance and interest in the processing of text. *Educational Psychology Review, 8,* 89–121.

Alexander, P. A., & Judy, J. E. (1988). The interaction of domain-specific and strategic knowledge in academic performance. *Review of Educational Research, 58,* 375–404.

Alexander, P. A., Kulikowich, J. M., & Schulze, S. K. (1994). How subject-matter knowledge affects recall and interest. *American Educational Research Journal, 31,* 313–337.

Alexander, P. A., Schallert, D. L., & Reynolds, R. E. (2009). What is learning anyway? A topographic perspective considered. *Educational Psychologist, 44,* 176–192.

Alibali, M. W., Spencer, R. C., Knox, L., & Kita, S. (2011). Spontaneous gestures influence strategy choices in problem solving. *Psychological Science, 22,* 1138–1144.

Alim, H. S. (2007). "The Whig party don't exist in my hood": Knowledge, reality, and education in the hip hop nation. In H. S. Alim & J. Baugh (Eds.), *Talkin Black talk: Language, education, and social change* (pp. 15–29). New York, NY: Teachers College Press.

Alloway, T. P, Gathercole, S. E., Kirkwood, H., & Elliott, J. (2009). The cognitive and behavioral characteristics of children with low working memory. *Child Development, 80,* 606–621.

Altmann, E. M., & Gray, W. D. (2002). Forgetting to remember: The functional relationship of decay and interference. *Psychological Science, 13,* 27–33.

Anderson, J. R. (1983). *The architecture of cognition.* Cambridge, MA: Harvard University Press.

Anderson, J. R. (1987). Skill acquisition: Compilation of weak-method problem solutions. *Psychological Review, 94,* 192–210.

Anderson, J. R. (2005). *Cognitive psychology and its implications* (6th ed.). New York, NY: Worth.

Anderson, J. R., Reder, L. M., & Simon, H. A. (1996). Situated learning and education. *Educational Researcher, 25*(4), 5–11.

Anderson, R. C., Reynolds, R. E., Schallert, D. L., & Goetz, E. T. (1977). Frameworks for comprehending discourse. *American Educational Research Journal, 14,* 367–381.

Aron, A. R. (2008). Progress in executive-function research: From tasks to functions to regions to networks. *Current Directions in Psychological Science, 17,* 124–129.

Aslin, R. N., & Newport, E. L. (2012). Statistical learning: From acquiring specific items to forming general rules. *Current Directions in Psychological Science, 21,* 170–176.

Atkins, S. M., Bunting, M. F., Bolger, D. J., & Dougherty, M. R. (2012). Training the adolescent brain: Neural plasticity and the acquisition of cognitive abilities. In V. F. Reyna, S. B. Chapman, M. R. Dougherty, & J. Confrey (Eds.), *The adolescent brain: Learning, reasoning, and decision making* (pp. 211–241). Washington, DC: American Psychological Association.

Atkinson, R. C., & Shiffrin, R. M. (1968). Human memory: A proposed system and its control processes. In K. W. Spence & J. T. Spence (Eds.), *The psychology of learning and motivation: Advances in research and theory* (Vol. 2). San Diego, CA: Academic Press.

Atkinson, R. K., Levin, J. R., Atkinson, L. A., Kiewra, K. A., Meyers, T., Kim, S. I., . . . Hwang, Y. (1999). Matrix and mnemonic text-processing adjuncts: Comparing and combining their components. *Journal of Educational Psychology, 91,* 342–357.

Ausubel, D. P., Novak, J. D., & Hanesian, H. (1978). *Educational psychology: A cognitive view* (2nd ed.). New York, NY: Holt, Rinehart & Winston.

Azano, A. (2011). The possibility of place: One teacher's use of place-based instruction for English students in a rural high school. *Journal of Research in Rural Education, 26*(10), 1–12.

Baddeley, A. (2012). Working memory: Theories, models, and controversies. *Annual Review of Psychology, 63,* 1–29.

Baddeley, A. D. (2001). Is working memory still working? *American Psychologist, 56,* 851–864.

Balch, W., Bowman, K., & Mohler, L. (1992). Music-dependent memory in immediate and delayed word recall. *Memory and Cognition, 20,* 21–28.

Banich, M. T. (2009). Executive function: The search for an integrated account. *Current Directions in Psychological Science, 18,* 89–94.

Barkley, R. A. (2006). *Attention-deficit hyperactivity disorder: A handbook for diagnosis and treatment* (3rd ed.). New York, NY: Guilford Press.

Barkley, R. A. (2010). School interventions. In G. S. Goodman (Ed.), *Educational psychology reader: The art and science of how people learn* (pp. 66–74). New York, NY: Peter Lang.

Baroody, A. J., Eiland, M. D., Purpura, D. J., & Reid, E. E. (2013). Can computer-assisted discovery learning foster first graders' fluency with the most basic addition combinations? *American Educational Research Journal, 50,* 533–573.

Barron, E., Riby, L. M., Greer, J., & Smallwood, J. (2011). Absorbed in thought: The effect of mind wandering on the processing of relevant and irrelevant events. *Psychological Science, 22,* 596–601.

Bartlett, F. C. (1932). *Remembering: A study in experimental and social psychology.* Cambridge, England: Cambridge University Press.

Bauer, P. J. (2002). Long-term recall memory: Behavioral and neuro-developmental changes in the first 2 years of life. *Current Directions in Psychological Science, 11,* 137–141.

Beck, D. M. (2010). The appeal of the brain in the popular press. *Perspectives on Psychological Science, 5,* 762–766.

Behrmann, M. (2000). The mind's eye mapped onto the brain's matter. *Current Directions in Psychological Science, 9,* 50–54.

Beilock, S. L., & Carr. T. H. (2004). From novice to expert performance: Memory, attention, and the control of complex sensorimotor skills. In A. M. Williams, N. J. Hodges, M. A. Scott, & M. L. J. Court (Eds.), *Skill acquisition in sport: Research, theory, and practice* (pp. 309–327). New York, NY: Routledge.

Ben-Yehudah, G., & Fiez, J. A. (2007). Development of verbal working memory. In D. Coch, K. W. Fischer, & G. Dawson (Eds.), *Human behavior, learning, and the developing brain: Typical development* (pp. 301–328). New York, NY: Guilford Press.

Berti, A. E., Toneatti, L., & Rosati, V. (2010). Children's conceptions about the origin of species: A study of Italian children's conceptions with and without instruction. *Journal of the Learning Sciences, 19,* 506–538.

Best, J. R., & Miller, P. H. (2010). A developmental perspective on executive function. *Child Development, 81,* 1641–1660.

Bjorklund, D. F., & Coyle, T. R. (1995). Utilization deficiencies in the development of memory strategies. In F. E. Weinert & W. Schneider (Eds.), *Research on memory development: State of the art and future directions* (pp. 161–180). Mahwah, NJ: Erlbaum.

Bjorklund, D. F., & Jacobs, J. W. (1985). Associative and categorical processes in children's memory: The role of automaticity in the development of organization in free recall. *Journal of Experimental Child Psychology, 39,* 599–617.

Bjorklund, D. F., Schneider, W., Cassel, W. S., & Ashley, E. (1994). Training and extension of a memory strategy: Evidence for utilization deficiencies in high- and low-IQ children. *Child Development, 65,* 951–965.

Bloom, L., & Tinker, E. (2001). The intentionality model and language acquisition. *Monographs of the Society for Research in Child Development, 66*(4, Serial No. 267).

Bower, G. H., Black, J. B., & Turner, T. J. (1979). Scripts in memory for text. *Cognitive Psychology, 11,* 177–220.

Bower, G. H., Karlin, M. B., & Dueck, A. (1975). Comprehension and memory for pictures. *Memory and Cognition, 3,* 216–220.

Brainerd, C. J., & Reyna, V. F. (2005). *The science of false memory.* Oxford, England: Oxford University Press.

Bransford, J. D., & Franks, J. J. (1971). The abstraction of linguistic ideas. *Cognitive Psychology, 2,* 331–350.

Brewer, W. F. (2008). Naive theories of observational astronomy: Review, analysis, and theoretical implications. In S. Vosniadou (Ed.), *International handbook of research on conceptual change* (pp. 155–204). New York, NY: Routledge.

Brigham, F. J., & Scruggs, T. E. (1995). Elaborative maps for enhanced learning of historical information: Uniting spatial, verbal, and imaginal information. *Journal of Special Education, 28,* 440.

Broekkamp, H., van Hout-Wolters, B. H. A. M., Rijlaarsdam, G., & van den Bergh, H. (2002). Importance in instructional text: Teachers' and students' perceptions of task demands. *Journal of Educational Psychology, 94,* 260–271.

Brophy, J. E., Alleman, J., & Knighton, B. (2009). *Inside the social studies classroom.* New York, NY: Routledge.

Brown, J. S., Collins, A., & Duguid, P. (1989). Situated cognition and the culture of learning. *Educational Researcher, 18*(1), 32–42.

Bruer, J. T., & Greenough, W. T. (2001). The subtle science of how experience affects the brain. In D. B. Bailey, Jr., J. T. Bruer, F. J. Symons, & J. W. Lichtman (Eds.), *Critical thinking about critical periods* (pp. 209–232). Baltimore, MD: Brookes.

Bulgren, J. A., Schumaker, J. B., & Deshler, D. D. (1994). The effects of a recall enhancement routine on the test performance of secondary students with and without learning disabilities. *Learning Disabilities Research and Practice, 9,* 2–11.

Butterworth, B., & Varma, S. (2014). Mathematical development. In D. Mareschal, B. Butterworth, & A. Tolmie (Eds.), *Educational neuroscience* (pp. 201– 236). West Sussex, UK: Wiley.

Byrnes, J. P. (2001). *Minds, brains, and learning: Understanding the psychological and educational relevance of neuroscientific research.* New York, NY: Guilford Press.

Byrnes, J. P. (2007). Some ways in which neuroscientific research can be relevant to education. In D. Coch, K. W. Fischer, & G. Dawson (Eds.), *Human behavior, learning, and the developing brain: Typical development* (pp. 30–49). New York, NY: Guilford Press.

Carey, S. (1986). Cognitive science and science education. *American Psychologist, 41,* 1123–1130.

Carlson, R., Chandler, P., & Sweller, J. (2003). Learning and understanding science instructional material. *Journal of Educational Psychology, 95,* 629–640.

Carr, M. (2010). The importance of metacognition for conceptual change and strategy use in mathematics. In H. S. Waters & W. Schneider (Eds.), *Metacognition, strategy use, and instruction* (pp. 176–197). New York, NY: Guilford Press.

Castagno, A. E., & Brayboy, B. M. J. (2008). Culturally responsive schooling for Indigenous youth: A review of the literature. *Review of Educational Research, 78,* 941–993.

Castelli, D. M., Hillman, C. H., Buck, S. M., & Erwin, H. E. (2007). Physical fitness and academic achievement in third- and fifth-grade students. *Journal of Sport & Exercise Psychology, 29,* 239–252.

Cepeda, N. J., Vul, E., Rohrer, D., Wixted, J. T., & Pashler, H. (2008). Spacing effects in learning: A temporal ridgeline of optimal retention. *Psychological Science, 19,* 1095–1102.

Chalmers, D. J. (1996). *The conscious mind: In search of a fundamental theory.* New York, NY: Oxford University Press.

Chambliss, M. J. (1994). Why do readers fail to change their beliefs after reading persuasive text? In R. Garner & P. A. Alexander (Eds.), *Beliefs about text and instruction with text* (pp. 76–89). Mahwah, NJ: Erlbaum.

Chan, C., Burtis, J., & Bereiter, C. (1997). Knowledge building as a mediator of conflict in conceptual change. *Cognition and Instruction, 15,* 1–40.

Cheng, P. W. (1985). Restructuring versus automaticity: Alternative accounts of skill acquisition. *Psychological Review, 92,* 414–423.

Chinn, C. A., & Brewer, W. F. (1993). The role of anomalous data in knowledge acquisition: A theoretical framework and implications for science instruction. *Review of Educational Research, 63,* 1–49.

Chinn, C. A., & Samarapungavan, A. (2009). Conceptual change—Multiple routes, multiple mechanisms: A commentary on Ohlsson (2009). *Educational Psychologist, 44,* 48–57.

Clark, D. B. (2006). Longitudinal conceptual change in students' understanding of thermal equilibrium: An examination of the process of conceptual restructuring. *Cognition and Instruction, 24,* 467–563.

Cohen, G. D. (2005). *The mature mind: The positive power of the aging brain.* New York, NY: Basic Books.

Cowan, N. (1995). *Attention and memory: An integrated framework.* New York, NY: Oxford University Press.

Cowan, N. (2007). What infants can tell us about working memory development. In L. M. Oakes & P. J. Bauer (Eds.), *Short- and long-term memory in infancy and early childhood: Taking the first steps toward remembering* (pp. 126–150). New York, NY: Oxford University Press.

Cowan, N. (2010). The magical mystery four: How is working memory capacity limited, and why? *Current Directions in Psychological Science, 19,* 51–57.

Cowan, N., Saults, J. S., & Morey, C. C. (2006). Development of working memory for verbal-spatial associations. *Journal of Memory and Language, 55,* 274–289.

Craik, F. I. M., & Watkins, M. J. (1973). The role of rehearsal in short-term memory. *Journal of Verbal Learning and Verbal Behavior, 12,* 598–607.

Cromley, J. G., & Azevedo, R. (2007). Testing and refining the direct and inferential mediation model of reading comprehension. *Journal of Educational Psychology, 99,* 311–325.

Croninger, R. G., & Valli, L. (2009). "Where is the action?" Challenges to studying the teaching of reading in elementary classrooms. *Educational Researcher, 38,* 100–108.

Crooks, T. J. (1988). The impact of classroom evaluation practices on students. *Review of Educational Research, 58,* 438–481.

Dahan, D. (2010). The time course of interpretation in speech comprehension. *Current Directions in Psychological Science, 19,* 121–126.

Darwin, C. J., Turvey, M. T., & Crowder, R. G. (1972). An auditory analogue of the Sperling partial report procedure: Evidence for brief auditory storage. *Cognitive Psychology, 3,* 255–267.

Das, J. P., Naglieri, J. A., & Kirby, J. R. (1994). *Assessment of cognitive processes.* Boston, MA: Allyn & Bacon.

Davachi, L., & Dobbins, I. G. (2008). Declarative memory. *Current Directions in Psychological Science, 17,* 112–118.

De Corte, E., Op't Eynde, P., Depaepe, F., & Verschaffel, L. (2010). The reflexive relation between students' mathematics-related beliefs and the mathematics classroom culture. In L. D. Bendixen & F. C. Feucht (Eds.), *Personal epistemology in the classroom: Theory, research, and implications for practice* (pp. 292–327). Cambridge, England: Cambridge University Press.

De La Paz, S., & McCutchen, D. (2011). Learning to write. In R. E. Mayer & P. A. Alexander (Eds.), *Handbook of research on learning and instruction* (pp. 32–54). New York, NY: Routledge.

DeLoache, J. S., & Todd, C. M. (1988). Young children's use of spatial categorization as a mnemonic strategy. *Journal of Experimental Child Psychology, 46,* 1–20.

DeMarie, D., & López, L. M. (2014). Memory in schools. In R. Fivush & P. J. Bauer (Eds.), *Wiley handbook on the development of human memory* (Vol. 2, pp. 836–864). New York, NY: Wiley.

Dempster, F. N. (1992). The rise and fall of the inhibitory mechanism: Toward a unified theory of cognitive development and aging. *Developmental Review, 12,* 45–75.

Dempster, F. N., & Corkill, A. J. (1999). Interference and inhibition in cognition and behavior: Unifying themes for educational psychology. *Educational Psychology Review, 11,* 1–88.

Deng, W., Aimone, J. B., & Gage, F. H. (2010). New neurons and new memories: How does adult hippocampal neurogenesis affect learning and memory? *Nature Reviews Neuroscience, 11,* 339–350.

Derry, S. J. (1996). Cognitive schema theory in the constructivist debate. *Educational Psychologist, 31,* 163–174.

Dinges, D. F., & Rogers, N. L. (2008). The future of human intelligence: Enhancing cognitive capability in a 24/7 world. In P. C. Kyllonen, R. D. Roberts, & L. Stankov (Eds.), *Extending intelligence: Enhancement and new constructs* (pp. 407–430). New York, NY: Erlbaum/Taylor & Francis.

diSessa, A. A. (2006). A history of conceptual change research. In R. K. Sawyer (Ed.), *The Cambridge handbook of the learning sciences* (pp. 265–281). Cambridge, England: Cambridge University Press.

Di Vesta, F. J., & Gray, S. G. (1972). Listening and notetaking. *Journal of Educational Psychology, 63,* 8–14.

Edens, K. M., & Potter, E. F. (2001). Promoting conceptual understanding through pictorial representation. *Studies in Art Education, 42,* 214–233.

Eilam, B. (2001). Primary strategies for promoting homework performance. *American Educational Research Journal, 38,* 691–725.

Einstein, G. O., & McDaniel, M. A. (2005). Prospective memory: Multiple retrieval processes. *Current Directions in Psychological Science, 14,* 286–290.

Ellis, E. S., & Friend, P. (1991). Adolescents with learning disabilities. In B. Y. L. Wong (Ed.), *Learning about learning disabilities.* San Diego, CA: Academic Press.

Ennis, C. D., & Chen, A. (2011). Learning motor skill in physical education. In R. E. Mayer & P. A. Alexander (Eds.), *Handbook of research on learning and instruction* (pp. 148–165). New York, NY: Routledge.

Ericsson, K. A. (1996). *The road to excellence: The acquisition of expert performance in the arts and science, sports, and games.* Mahwah, NJ: Erlbaum.

Ericsson, K. A. (2003). The acquisition of expert performance as problem solving. In J. E. Davidson & R. J. Sternberg (Eds.), *The psychology of problem solving* (pp. 31–83). Cambridge, England: Cambridge University Press.

Evans, G. W., & Schamberg, M. A. (2009). Childhood poverty, chronic stress, and adult working memory. *Proceedings of the National Academy of Sciences of the United States of America, 106,* 6545–6549.

Farkas, G. (2008). Quantitative studies of oppositional culture: Arguments and evidence. In J. U. Ogbu (Ed.), *Minority status, oppositional culture, and schooling* (pp. 312–347). New York, NY: Routledge.

Finn, B., & Roediger, H. L., III (2011). Enhancing retention through reconsolidation: Negative emotional arousal following retrieval enhances later recall. *Psychological Science, 22,* 781–786.

Fletcher, J. M., Lyon, G. R., Fuchs, L. S., & Barnes, M. A. (2007). *Learning disabilities: From identification to intervention.* New York, NY: Guilford Press.

Fox, E. (2009). The role of reader characteristics in processing and learning from informational text. *Review of Educational Research, 79,* 197–261.

Freedom Writers (with Gruwell, E.). (1999). *The Freedom Writers diary: How a teacher and 150 teens used writing to change themselves and the world around them.* New York, NY: Broadway Books.

Gardner, H. (2000b). *The disciplined mind: Beyond facts and standardized tests, the K–12 education that every child deserves.* New York, NY: Penguin Books.

Gaskins, I. W., & Pressley, M. (2007). Teaching metacognitive strategies that address executive function processes within a schoolwide curriculum. In L. Meltzer (Ed.), *Executive function in education: From theory to practice* (pp. 261–286). New York, NY: Guilford Press.

Gathercole, S. E., & Hitch, G. J. (1993). Developmental changes in short-term memory: A revised working memory perspective. In A. F. Collins, S. E. Gathercole, M. A. Conway, & P. E. Morris (Eds.), *Theories of memory* (pp. 189–209). Hove, England: Erlbaum.

Gathercole, S. E., Lamont, E., & Alloway, T. P. (2006). Working memory in the classroom. In S. Pickering (Ed.), *Working memory and education* (p. 219–240). New York, NY: Academic Press.

Geary, D. C. (2005). Folk knowledge and academic learning. In B. J. Ellis & D. F. Bjorklund (Eds.), *Origins of the social mind: Evolutionary psychology and child development* (pp. 493–519). New York, NY: Guilford Press.

Gelman, S. A. (2003). *The essential child: Origins of essentialism in everyday thought.* New York, NY: Oxford University Press.

Gelman, S. A., & Kalish, C. W. (2006). Conceptual development. In W. Damon & R. M. Lerner (Series Eds.), D. Kuhn & R. Siegler (Vol. Eds.), *Handbook of child psychology: Vol. 1. Cognition, perception, and language* (6th ed., 687–733). New York, NY: Wiley.

Ghetti, S., & Angelini, L. (2008). The development of recollection and familiarity in childhood and adolescence: Evidence from the dual-process signal detection model. *Child Development, 79,* 339–358.

Giaconia, R. M. (1988). Teacher questioning and wait-time (Doctoral dissertation, Stanford University, 1988). *Dissertation Abstracts International, 49,* 462A.

Goldenberg, C. (2001). Making schools work for low-income families in the 21st century. In S. B. Neuman & D. K. Dickinson (Eds.), *Handbook of early literacy research* (pp. 211–231). New York, NY: Guilford Press.

Goldin-Meadow, S., & Beilock, S. L. (2010). Action's influence on thought: The case of gesture. *Perspectives on Psychological Science, 5,* 664–674.

Goldstein, S. Naglieri, J. A., Princiotta, D., & Otero, T. M. (2014). Introduction: A history of executive functioning as a theoretical and clinical construct. In S. Goldstein & J. A. Naglieri (Eds.), *Handbook of Executive Functioning* (pp. 3–12). New York, NY: Springer Science+Business Media.

Gonsalves, B. D., & Cohen, N. J. (2010). Brain imaging, cognitive processes, and brain networks. *Perspectives on Psychological Science, 5,* 744–752.

Goodman, C. S., & Tessier-Lavigne, M. (1997). Molecular mechanisms of axon guidance and target recognition. In W. M. Cowan, T. M. Jessell, & S. L. Zipursky (Eds.), *Molecular and cellular approaches to neural development* (pp. 108–137). New York, NY: Oxford University Press.

Gould, E., Beylin, A., Tanapat, P., Reeves, A., & Shors, T. J. (1999). Learning enhances adult neurogenesis in the hippocampal formation. *Nature Neuroscience, 2,* 260–265.

Graham, S., Harris, K. R., & Fink, B. (2000). Is handwriting causally related to learning to write? Treatment of handwriting problems in beginning writers. *Journal of Educational Psychology, 92,* 620–633.

Greeno, J. G., & Engeström, Y. (2014). Learning in activity. In R. K. Sawyer (Ed.), *The Cambridge handbook of the learning sciences* (2nd ed., pp. 128–147). New York, NY: Cambridge University Press.

Greeno, J. G., Collins, A. M., & Resnick, L. B. (1996). Cognition and learning. In D. C. Berliner & R. C. Calfee (Eds.), *Handbook of educational psychology* (pp. 15–46). New York, NY: Macmillan.

Gregg, N. (2009). *Adolescents and adults with learning disabilities and ADHD: Assessment and accommodation.* New York, NY: Guilford Press.

Greif, M. L., Kemler Nelson, D. G., Keil, F. C., & Gutierrez, F. (2006). What do children want to know about animals and artifacts? Domain-specific requests for information. *Psychological Science, 17,* 455–459.

Hacker, D. J., Dunlosky, J., & Graesser, A. C. (2009a). A growing sense of "agency." In D. J. Hacker, J. Dunlosky, & A. C. Graesser (Eds.), *Handbook of metacognition in education* (pp. 1–4). New York, NY: Routledge.

Haier, R. J. (2001). PET studies of learning and individual differences. In J. L. McClelland & R. S. Siegler (Eds.), *Mechanisms of cognitive development: Behavioral and neural perspectives* (pp. 123–145). Mahwah, NJ: Erlbaum.

Halpern, D. F. (2006). Assessing gender gaps in learning and academic achievement. In P. A. Alexander & P. H. Winne (Eds.), *Handbook of educational psychology* (2nd ed., pp. 635–653). Mahwah, NJ: Erlbaum.

Halpern, D. F., & LaMay, M. L. (2000). The smarter sex: A critical review of sex differences in intelligence. *Educational Psychology Review, 12,* 229–246.

Han, X., Chen, M., Wang, F., Windrem, M., Wang, S., Shanz, S., . . . Nedergaard, M. (2013). Forebrain engraftment by human glial progenitor cells enhances synaptic plasticity and learning in adult mice. *Cell Stem Cell, 12,* 342–353.

Hatano, G., & Inagaki, K. (2003). When is conceptual change intended? A cognitive-sociocultural view. In G. M. Sinatra & P. R. Pintrich (Eds.), *Intentional conceptual change* (pp. 407–427). Mahwah, NJ: Erlbaum.

Hattie, J., & Timperley, H. (2007). The power of feedback. *Review of Educational Research, 77,* 81–112.

Haugwitz, M., Sumfleth, E., & Sandmann, A. (2010, April–May). *The influence of cognitive mapping on achievement in biology: Considering cognitive abilities as moderator.* Paper presented at the annual meeting of the American Educational Research Association, Denver, CO.

Healey, M. K., Campbell, K. L., Hasher, L., & Ossher, L. (2010). Direct evidence for the role of inhibition in resolving interference in memory. *Psychological Science, 21,* 1464–1470.

Heatherton, T. F., Macrae, C. N., & Kelley, W. M. (2004). What the social brain sciences can tell us about the self. *Current Directions in Psychological Science, 13,* 190–193.

Hecht, S. A., Close, L., & Santisi, M. (2003). Sources of individual differences in fraction skills. *Journal of Experimental Child Psychology, 86,* 277–302.

Hickey, D. J. (2011). Participation by design: Improving individual motivation by looking beyond it. In D. M. McInerney, R. A. Walker, & G. A. D. Liem (Eds.), *Sociocultural theories of learning and motivation: Looking back, looking forward* (pp. 137–161). Charlotte, NC: Information Age.

Holland, R. W., Hendriks, M., & Aarts, H. (2005). Smells like clean spirit: Nonconscious effects of scent on cognition and behavior. *Psychological Science, 16,* 689–693.

Horn, J. L. (2008). Spearman, g, expertise, and the nature of human cognitive capability. In P. C. Kyllonen, R. D. Roberts, & L. Stankov (Eds.), *Extending intelligence: Enhancement and new constructs* (pp. 185–230). New York, NY: Erlbaum/Taylor & Francis.

Huey, E. D., Krueger, F., & Grafman, J. (2006). Representations in the human prefrontal cortex. *Current Directions in Psychological Science, 15,* 167–171.

Hutchinson, J. B., Pak, S. S., & Turk-Browne, N. B. (2016). Biased competition during long-term memory formation. *Journal of Cognitive Neuroscience, 28*(1), 187–197. doi:10.1162/jocn_a_00889

Hynd, C. (1998a). Conceptual change in a high school physics class. In B. Guzzetti & C. Hynd (Eds.), *Perspectives on conceptual change: Multiple ways to understand knowing and learning in a complex world* (pp. 27–36). Mahwah, NJ: Erlbaum.

Hynd, C. (1998b). Observing learning from different perspectives: What does it mean for Barry and his understanding of gravity? In B. Guzzetti & C. Hynd (Eds.), *Perspectives on conceptual change: Multiple ways to understand knowing and learning in a complex world* (pp. 235–244). Mahwah, NJ: Erlbaum.

Immordino-Yang, M. H., Christodoulou, J. A., & Singh, V. (2012). Rest is not idleness: Implications of the brain's default mode for human development and education. *Perspectives on Psychological Science, 7,* 352–364.

Inagaki, K., & Hatano, G. (2006). Young children's conception of the biological world. *Current Directions in Psychological Science, 15,* 177–181.

Jegede, O. J., & Olajide, J. O. (1995). Wait-time, classroom discourse, and the influence of sociocultural factors in science teaching. *Science Education, 79,* 233–249.

Johnson-Glenberg, M. C. (2000). Training reading comprehension in adequate decoders/poor comprehenders: Verbal versus visual strategies. *Journal of Educational Psychology, 92,* 772–782.

Jones, M. S., Levin, M. E., Levin, J. R., & Beitzel, B. D. (2000). Can vocabulary-learning strategies and pair-learning formats be profitably combined? *Journal of Educational Psychology, 92,* 256–262.

Jung, R. E., & Haier, R. J. (2007). The parieto-frontal integration theory (P-FIT) of intelligence: Converging neuroimaging evidence. *Behavioral and Brain Sciences, 30,* 135–154.

Kail, R. V. (2007). Longitudinal evidence that increases in processing speed and working memory enhance children's reasoning. *Psychological Science, 18,* 312–313.

Kalyuga, S. (2010). Schema acquisition and sources of cognitive load. In J. L. Plass, R. Moreno, & R. Brünken (Eds.), *Cognitive Load Theory* (pp. 48–64). Cambridge, England: Cambridge University Press.

Karpicke, J. D. (2012). Retrieval-based learning: Active retrieval promotes meaningful learning. *Current Directions in Psychological Science, 21,* 157–163.

Keil, F. C. (1986). The acquisition of natural kind and artifact terms. In W. Demopolous & A. Marras (Eds.), *Language learning and concept acquisition* (pp. 133–153). Norwood, NJ: Ablex.

Keil, F. C. (1987). Conceptual development and category structure. In U. Neisser (Ed.), *Concepts and conceptual development: Ecological and intellectual factors in categorization* (pp. 175–200). Cambridge, England: Cambridge University Press.

Keil, F. C. (1989). *Concepts, kinds, and cognitive development.* Cambridge, MA: MIT Press.

Keil, F. C., & Newman, G. E. (2008). Two tales of conceptual change: What changes and what remains the same. In S. Vosniadou (Ed.), *International handbook on conceptual change* (pp. 83–101). New York, NY: Routledge.

Kelly, S. W., Burton, A. M., Kato, T., & Akamatsu, S. (2001). Incidental learning of real-world regularities. *Psychological Science, 12,* 86–89.

Kesebir, S., & Oishi, S. (2010). A spontaneous self-reference effect in memory: Why some birthdays are harder to remember than others. *Psychological Science, 21,* 1525–1531.

Kiewra, K. A. (1989). A review of note-taking: The encoding-storage paradigm and beyond. *Educational Psychology Review, 1,* 147–172.

Kihlstrom, J. F. (2013). Unconscious processes. In D. Reisberg (Ed.), *The Oxford handbook of cognitive psychology* (pp. 176–186). New York: Oxford University Press.

Killeen, P. R. (2001). The four causes of behavior. *Current Directions in Psychological Science, 10,* 136–140.

Kintsch, W. (2009). Learning and constructivism. In S. Tobias & T. M. Duffy (Eds.), *Constructivist instruction: Success or failure?* (pp. 223–241). New York, NY: Routledge.

Kirby, M., Maggi, S., & D'Angiulli, A. (2011). School start times and the sleep–wake cycle of adolescents: A review of critical evaluation of available evidence. *Educational Researcher, 40,* 56–61.

Kirschner, P. A., Sweller, J., & Clark, R. E. (2006). Why minimal guidance during instruction does not work: An analysis of the failure of constructivist, discovery, problem-based, experiential, and inquiry-based teaching. *Educational Psychologist, 41,* 75–86.

Konkle, T., Brady, T. F., Alvarez, G. A., & Oliva, A. (2010). Scene memory is more detailed than you think: The role of categories in visual long-term memory. *Psychological Science, 21,* 1551–1556.

Koob, A. (2009). *The root of thought.* Upper Saddle River, NJ: Pearson.

Kosslyn, S. M., Margolis, J. A., Barrett, A. M., Goldknopf, E. J., & Daly, P. F. (1990). Age differences in imagery ability. *Child Development, 61,* 995–1010.

Ku, Y.-M., Chan, W.-C., Wu, Y.-C., & Chen, Y.-H. (2008, March). *Improving children's comprehension of science text: Effects of adjunct questions and notetaking.* Paper presented at the annual meeting of the American Educational Research Association, New York, NY.

Kunzinger, E. L., III (1985). A short-term longitudinal study of memorial development during early grade school. *Developmental Psychology, 21,* 642–646.

Kyle, W. C., & Shymansky, J. A. (1989, April). Enhancing learning through conceptual change teaching. *NARST News, 31,* 7–8.

Langer, E. J. (2000). Mindful learning. *Current Directions in Psychological Science, 9,* 220–223.

Lee, V. R. (2010, April–May). *Misconstruals or more? The interactions of orbit diagrams and explanations of the seasons.* Paper presented at the annual meeting of the American Educational Research Association, Denver, CO.

LeFevre, J., Bisanz, J., & Mrkonjic, J. (1988). Cognitive arithmetic: Evidence for obligatory activation of arithmetic facts. *Memory and Cognition, 16,* 45–53.

Lehmann, M., & Hasselhorn, M. (2007). Variable memory strategy use in children's adaptive intratask learning behavior: Developmental changes and working memory influences in free recall. *Child Development, 78,* 1068–1082.

Lesgold, A. M. (2001). The nature and methods of learning by doing. *American Psychologist, 56,* 965–973.

Levstik, L. S. (2011). Learning history. In R. E. Mayer & P. A. Alexander (Eds.), *Handbook of research on learning and instruction* (pp. 108–126). New York, NY: Routledge.

Liben, L. S., & Myers, L. J. (2007). Developmental changes in children's understanding of maps: What, when, and how? In J. M. Plumert & J. P. Spencer (Eds.), *The emerging spatial mind* (pp. 193–218). New York, NY: Oxford University Press.

Lichtman, J. W. (2001). Developmental neurobiology overview: Synapses, circuits, and plasticity. In D. B. Bailey, Jr., J. T. Bruer, F. J. Symons, & J. W. Lichtman (Eds.), *Critical thinking about critical periods* (pp. 27–42). Baltimore, MD: Brookes.

Lien, M.-C., Ruthruff, E., & Johnston, J. C. (2006). Attentional limitations in doing two tasks at once: The search for exceptions. *Current Directions in Psychological Science, 15,* 89–93.

Light, P., & Butterworth, G. (Eds.). (1993). *Context and cognition: Ways of learning and knowing.* Mahwah, NJ: Erlbaum.

Limpo, T., & Alves, R. A. (2013). Modeling writing development: Contribution of transcription and self-regulation to Portuguese students' text generation quality. *Journal of Educational Psychology, 105*(2), 401–413.

Linn, M. C., & Eylon, B.-S. (2011). *Science learning and instruction: Taking advantage of technology to promote knowledge integration.* New York, NY: Routledge.

Loftus, E. F., & Loftus, G. R. (1980). On the permanence of stored information in the human brain. *American Psychologist, 35,* 409–420.

Logie, R. H. (2011). The functional organization and capacity limits of working memory. *Current Directions in Psychological Science, 20,* 240–245.

Lucariello, J., Kyratzis, A., & Nelson, K. (1992). Taxonomic knowledge: What kind and when? *Child Development, 63,* 978–998.

Macnamara, B. N., Hambrick, D. Z., & Oswald, F. L. (2014). Deliberate practice and performance in music, games, sports, education, and professions: A meta-analysis. *Psychological Science, 25,* 1608–1618.

Mandler, G. (2011). From association to organization. *Current Directions in Psychological Science, 20,* 232–235.

Mandler, J. M. (2007). On the origins of the conceptual system. *American Psychologist, 62,* 741–751.

Marcus, G. (2008). *Kluge: The haphazard construction of the human mind.* Boston, MA: Houghton Mifflin.

Mareschal, D., Johnson, M. H., Sirois, S., Spratling, M. W., Thomas, M. S. C., & Westermann, G. (2007). *Neuroconstructivism: Vol. 1. How the brain constructs cognition.* Oxford, England: Oxford University Press.

Maria, K. (1998). Self-confidence and the process of conceptual change. In B. Guzzetti & C. Hynd (Eds.), *Perspectives on conceptual change: Multiple ways to understand knowing and learning in a complex world* (pp. 7–16). Mahwah, NJ: Erlbaum.

Marley, S. C., Szabo, Z., Levin, J. R., & Glenberg, A. M. (2008, March). *Activity, observed activity, and children's recall of orally presented narrative passages.* Paper presented at the annual meeting of the American Educational Research Association, New York.

Marshall, H. H. (1992). *Redefining student learning: Roots of educational change.* Norwood, NJ: Ablex.

Martínez, P., Bannan-Ritland, B., Kitsantas, A., & Baek, J. Y. (2008, March). *The impact of an integrated science reading intervention on elementary children's misconceptions regarding slow geomorphological changes caused by water.* Paper presented at the annual meeting of the American Educational Research Association, New York, NY.

Mason, L., Gava, M., & Boldrin, A. (2008). On warm conceptual change: The interplay of text, epistemological beliefs, and topic interest. *Journal of Educational Psychology, 100,* 291–309.

Masten, A. S., Herbers, J. E., Desjardins, C. D., Cutuli, J. J., McCormick, C. M., Sapienza, J. K., . . . Zelazo, P. D. (2012). Executive function skills and school success in young children experiencing homelessness. *Educational Researcher, 41,* 375–384.

Mayer, R. E. (2010a). Fostering scientific reasoning with multimedia instruction. In H. S. Waters & W. Schneider (Eds.), *Metacognition, strategy use, and instruction* (pp. 160–175). New York, NY: Guilford.

Mayer, R. E. (2010b). Merlin C. Wittrock's enduring contributions to the science of learning. *Educational Psychologist, 45,* 46–50.

Mayer, R. E. (2011). Instruction based on visualizations. In R. E. Mayer & P. A. Alexander (Eds.), *Handbook of research on learning and instruction* (pp. 427–445). New York, NY: Routledge.

Mayer, R. E. (2012). Information processing. In K. R. Harris, S. Graham, & T. Urdan (Eds.), *APA educational psychology handbook* (Vol. 1, pp. 85–99). Washington, DC: American Psychological Association.

Mayer, R. E., & Wittrock, M. C. (1996). Problem-solving transfer. In D. C. Berliner & R. C. Calfee (Eds.), *Handbook of educational psychology* (pp. 47–62). New York, NY: Macmillan.

McCaslin, M., & Good, T. L. (1996). The informal curriculum. In D. C. Berliner & R. C. Calfee (Eds.), *Handbook of educational psychology* (pp. 622–670). New York, NY: Macmillan.

Meltzer, L. (Ed.). (2007). *Executive function in education: From theory to practice.* New York, NY: Guilford Press.

Merzenich, M. M. (2001). Cortical plasticity contributing to child development. In J. L. McClelland & R. S. Siegler (Eds.), *Mechanisms of cognitive development: Behavioral and neural perspectives* (pp. 67–95). Mahwah, NJ: Erlbaum.

Middleton, M. J., & Midgley, C. (2002). Beyond motivation: Middle school students' perceptions of press for understanding in math. *Contemporary Educational Psychology, 27,* 373–391.

Miller, G. A. (1956). The magical number seven, plus or minus two: Some limits on our capacity for processing information. *Psychological Review, 63,* 81–97.

Miller, G. A. (2010). Mistreating psychology in the decades of the brain. *Perspectives on Psychological Science, 5,* 716–743.

Minsky, M. (2006). *The emotion machine: Commonsense thinking, artificial intelligence, and the future of the human mind.* New York, NY: Simon and Schuster.

Minstrell, J., & Stimpson, V. (1996). A classroom environment for learning: Guiding students' reconstruction of understanding and reasoning. In L. Schauble & R. Glaser (Eds.), *Innovations in learning: New environments for education* (pp. 175–202). Mahwah, NJ: Erlbaum.

Miyake, A., & Friedman, N. P. (2012). The nature and organization of individual differences in executive functions: Four general conclusions. *Current Directions in Psychological Science, 21,* 8–14.

Miyake, N., & Kirschner, P. A. (2014). The social and interactive dimensions of collaborative learning. In R. K. Sawyer (Ed.), *The Cambridge handbook of the learning sciences* (2nd ed., pp. 418–438). New York, NY: Cambridge University Press.

Mohatt, G., & Erickson, F. (1981). Cultural differences in teaching styles in an Odawa school: A sociolinguistic approach. In H. T. Trueba, G. P. Guthrie, & K. H. Au (Eds.), *Culture and the bilingual classroom: Studies in classroom ethnography* (pp. 105–119). Rowley, MA: Newbury House.

Monfils, M.-H., Cowansage, K. K., Klann, E., & LeDoux, J. E. (2009). Extinction-reconsolidation boundaries: Key to persistent attenuation of fear memories. *Science, 324*(5929), 951–955.

Moreno, R. (2006). Learning in high-tech and multimedia environments. *Current Directions in Psychological Science, 15,* 63–67.

Murphy, P. K., & Mason, L. (2006). Changing knowledge and beliefs. In P. A. Alexander & P. H. Winne (Eds.), *Handbook of educational psychology* (2nd ed., pp. 305–324). Mahwah, NJ: Erlbaum.

Nee, D. E., Berman, M. G., Moore, K. S., & Jonides, J. (2008). Neuroscientific evidence about the distinction between short- and long-term memory. *Current Directions in Psychological Science, 17,* 102–106.

Neisser, U. (1967). *Cognitive psychology.* New York, NY: Appleton-Century-Crofts.

Nelson, C. A., III, Thomas, K. M., & de Haan, M. (2006). Neural bases of cognitive development. In W. Damon & R. M. Lerner (Series Eds.), D. Kuhn & R. Siegler (Vol. Eds.), *Handbook of child psychology. Vol. 2: Cognition, perception, and language* (6th ed., pp. 3–57). New York, NY: Wiley.

Nesbit, J. C., & Adesope, O. O. (2006). Learning with concept and knowledge maps: A meta-analysis. *Review of Educational Research, 76,* 413–448.

Newman, L. S. (1990). Intentional and unintentional memory in young children: Remembering vs. playing. *Journal of Experimental Child Psychology, 50,* 243–258.

Newstead, S. (2004). The purposes of assessment. *Psychology of Learning and Teaching, 3,* 97–101.

Nigg, J. T. (2010). Attention-deficit/hyperactivity disorder: Endophenotypes, structure, and etiological pathways. *Current Directions in Psychological Science, 19,* 24–29.

Noble, K. G., McCandliss, B. D., & Farah, M. J. (2007). Socioeconomic gradients predict individual differences in neurocognitive abilities. *Developmental Science, 10,* 464–460.

Nussbaum, J. (1985). The earth as a cosmic body. In R. Driver (Ed.), *Children's ideas of science.* Philadelphia, PA: Open University Press.

Oberauer, K., & Hein, L. (2012). Attention to information in working memory. *Current Directions in Psychological Science, 21,* 164–169.

Oberheim, N. A., Takano, T., Han, X., He, W., Lin, J. H. C., Wang, F., . . . Nedergaard, M. (2009). Uniquely hominid features of adult human astrocytes. *Journal of Neuroscience, 29,* 3276–3287.

Ornstein, P. A., Grammer, J. K., & Coffman, J. L. (2010). Teachers' "mnemonic style" and the development of skilled memory. In H. S. Waters & W. Schneider (Eds.), *Metacognition, strategy use, and instruction* (pp. 23–53). New York, NY: Guilford Press.

Ornstein, R. (1997). *The right mind: Making sense of the hemispheres.* San Diego, CA: Harcourt Brace.

Otero, T. M., & Barker, L. A. (2014). The frontal lobes and executive functioning. In S. Goldstein & J. A. Naglieri (Eds.), *Handbook of Executive Functioning* (pp. 29–44). New York, NY: Springer Science+Business Media.

Öztekin, I., Davachi, L., & McElree, B. (2010). Are representations in working memory distinct from representations in long-term memory? Neural evidence in support of a single store. *Psychological Science, 21,* 1123–1133.

Paxton, R. J. (1999). A deafening silence: History textbooks and the students who read them. *Review of Educational Research, 69,* 315–339.

Payne, J. D., & Kensinger, E. A. (2010). Sleep's role in the consolidation of emotional episodic memories. *Current Directions in Psychological Science, 19,* 290–295.

Pellegrini, A. D., & Bjorklund, D. F. (1997). The role of recess in children's cognitive performance. *Educational Psychologist, 32,* 35–40.

Pellegrini, A. D., & Bohn, C. M. (2005). The role of recess in children's cognitive performance and school adjustment. *Educational Researcher, 34*(1), 13–19.

Pereira, F., Detre, G., & Botvinick, M. (2011). Generating text from functional brain images. *Frontiers in Human Neuroscience, 5*(72). doi:10.3389/fnhum.2011.00072

Peterson, L. R., & Peterson, M. J. (1959). Short-term retention of individual items. *Journal of Experimental Psychology, 58,* 193–198.

Piaget, J. (1929). *The child's conception of the world.* New York, NY: Harcourt, Brace.

Pine, K. J., & Messer, D. J. (2000). The effect of explaining another's actions on children's implicit theories of balance. *Cognition and Instruction, 18,* 35–51.

Pintrich, P. R., Marx, R. W., & Boyle, R. A. (1993). Beyond cold conceptual change: The role of motivational beliefs and classroom contextual factors in the process of conceptual change. *Review of Educational Research, 63,* 167–199.

Plass, J. L., Moreno, R., & Brünken, R. (Eds.). (2010). *Cognitive Load Theory.* Cambridge, England: Cambridge University Press.

Plumert, J. M. (1994). Flexibility in children's use of spatial and categorical organizational strategies in recall. *Developmental Psychology, 30,* 738–747.

Porat, D. A. (2004). *It's not written here, but this is what happened:* Students' cultural comprehension of textbook narratives on the Israeli-Arab conflict. *American Educational Research Journal, 41,* 963–996.

Posner, M. I., & Rothbart, M. K. (2007). *Educating the human brain.* Washington, DC: American Psychological Association.

Prawat, R. S. (1993). The value of ideas: Problems versus possibilities in learning. *Educational Researcher, 22*(6), 5–16.

Pressley, M. (1982). Elaboration and memory development. *Child Development, 53,* 296–309.

Pressley, M., & Hilden, K. (2006). Cognitive strategies: Production deficiencies and successful strategy instruction everywhere. In W. Damon & R. M. Lerner (Series Eds.), D. Kuhn & R. Siegler (Vol. Eds.), *Handbook of child psychology: Vol. 2. Cognition, perception, and language* (6th ed., pp. 511–556). New York, NY: Wiley.

Pressley, M., Levin, J. R., & Delaney, H. D. (1982). The mnemonic keyword method. *Review of Educational Research, 52,* 61–91.

Pritchard, R. (1990). The effects of cultural schemata on reading processing strategies. *Reading Research Quarterly, 25,* 273–295.

Proctor, R. W., & Dutta, A. (1995). *Skill acquisition and human performance.* Thousand Oaks, CA: Sage.

Putnam, R. T. (1992). Thinking and authority in elementary-school mathematics tasks. In J. Brophy (Ed.), *Advances in research on teaching: Vol. 3. Planning and managing learning tasks and activities.* Greenwich, CT: JAI Press.

Pyc, M. A., & Rawson, K. A. (2009). Testing the retrieval effort hypothesis: Does greater difficulty correctly recalling information lead to higher levels of memory? *Journal of Memory and Language, 60,* 437–447.

Quinn, P. C. (2002). Category representation in young infants. *Current Directions in Psychological Science, 11,* 66–70.

Ranganath, C. (2010). Binding items and contexts: The cognitive neuroscience of episodic memory. *Current Directions in Psychological Science, 19,* 131–137.

Rasch, B., & Born, J. (2008). Reactivation and consolidation of memory during sleep. *Current Directions in Psychological Science, 17,* 188–192.

Reichle, E. D., Reineberg, A. E., & Schooler, J. W. (2010). Eye movements during mindless reading. *Psychological Science, 21,* 1300–1310.

Reiner, M., Slotta, J. D., Chi, M. T. H., & Resnick, L. B. (2000). Naive physics reasoning: A commitment to substance-based conceptions. *Cognition and Instruction, 18,* 1–34.

Reisberg, D. (1997). *Cognition: Exploring the science of the mind.* New York, NY: Norton.

Resnick, L. B. (1989). Developing mathematical knowledge. *American Psychologist, 44,* 162–169.

Roediger, H. L., III, & McDermott, K. B. (2000). Tricks of memory. *Current Directions in Psychological Science, 9,* 123–127.

Rogers, T. B., Kuiper, N. A., & Kirker, W. S. (1977). Self-reference and the encoding of personal information. *Journal of Personality and Social Psychology, 35,* 677–688.

Rohrer, D., & Pashler, H. (2007). Increasing retention without increasing study time. *Current Directions in Psychological Science, 16,* 183–186.

Rohrer, D., & Pashler, H. (2010). Recent research on human learning challenges conventional instructional strategies. *Educational Researcher, 39,* 406–412.

Roscoe, R. D., & Chi, M. T. H. (2007). Understanding tutor learning: Knowledge-building and knowledge-telling in peer tutors' explanations and questions. *Review of Educational Research, 77,* 534–574.

Rosen, G. D., Wang, Y., Fiondella, C. G., & LoTurco, J. J. (2009). The brain and developmental dyslexia: Genes, anatomy, and behavior. In K. Pugh & P. McCardle (Eds.), *How children learn to read: Current issues and new directions in the integration of cognition, neurobiology and genetics of reading and dyslexia research and practice* (pp. 21–42). New York, NY: Psychology Press.

Roth, K. J., & Anderson, C. (1988). Promoting conceptual change learning from science textbooks. In P. Ramsden (Ed.), *Improving learning: New perspectives* (pp. 109–141). London: Kogan Page.

Rowe, M. B. (1974). Wait-time and rewards as instructional variables, their influence on language, logic, and fate control: Part one—Wait time. *Journal of Research in Science Teaching, 11,* 81–94.

Rowe, M. B. (1987). Wait-time: Slowing down may be a way of speeding up. *American Educator, 11,* 38–43, 47.

Rumelhart, D. E., & Ortony, A. (1977). The representation of knowledge in memory. In R. C. Anderson, R. J. Spiro, & W. E. Montague (Eds.), *Schooling and the acquisition of knowledge* (pp. 99–136). Mahwah, NJ: Erlbaum.

Sadoski, M., & Paivio, A. (2001). *Imagery and text: A dual coding theory of reading and writing.* Mahwah, NJ: Erlbaum.

Säljö, R., & Wyndhamn, J. (1992). Solving everyday problems in the formal setting: An empirical study of the school as context for thought. In S. Chaiklin & J. Lave (Eds.), *Understanding practice* (pp. 327–342). New York, NY: Cambridge University Press.

Sapolsky, R. M. (1999). Glucocorticoids, stress, and their adverse neurological effects: Relevance to aging. *Experimental Gerontology, 34,* 721–732.

Schacter, D. L. (1999). The seven sins of memory: Insights from psychology and neuroscience. *American Psychologist, 54,* 182–203.

Scharfman, H. E., & Binder, D. K. (2013). Aquaporin-4 water channels and synaptic plasticity in the hippocampus. *Neurochemistry International, 63*(7), 702–711.

Schenck, J. (2011). *Teaching and the adolescent brain: An educator's guide.* New York, NY: W. W. Norton.

Schiller, D., Monfils, M.-H., Raio, C. M., Johnson, D. C., LeDoux, J. E., & Phelps, E. A. (2010). Preventing the return of fear in humans using reconsolidation update mechanisms. *Nature, 463*(7277), 49–53.

Schlegel, A., Prescott, A., & Tse, P. U. (2016). Information processing in the mental workspace is fundamentally distributed. *Journal of Cognitive Neuroscience, 28*(2), 295–307. doi:10.1162/jocn_a_00899

Schneider, W. (1993). Domain-specific knowledge and memory performance in children. *Educational Psychology Review, 5,* 257–273.

Schneider, W., & Pressley, M. (1989). *Memory development between 2 and 20.* New York, NY: Springer-Verlag.

Schraw, G. (2006). Knowledge: Structures and processes. In P. A. Alexander & P. H. Winne (Eds.), *Handbook of educational psychology* (2nd ed., pp. 245–263). Mahwah, NJ: Erlbaum.

Schwamborn, A., Mayer, R. E., Thillmann, H., Leopold, C., & Leutner, D. (2010). Drawing as a generative activity and drawing as a prognostic activity. *Journal of Educational Psychology, 102,* 872–879.

Scruggs, T. E., & Mastropieri, M. A. (1989). Mnemonic instruction of learning disabled students: A field-based evaluation. *Learning Disabilities Quarterly, 12,* 119–125.

Semb, G. B., & Ellis, J. A. (1994). Knowledge taught in school: What is remembered? *Review of Educational Research, 64,* 253–286.

Serpell, R., Baker, L., & Sonnenschein, S. (2005). *Becoming literate in the city: The Baltimore Early Childhood Project.* Cambridge, England: Cambridge University Press.

Shapiro, A. M. (2004). How including prior knowledge as a subject variable may change outcomes of learning research. *American Educational Research Journal, 41,* 159–189.

Shaywitz, S. E., Mody, M., & Shaywitz, B. A. (2006). Neural mechanisms in dyslexia. *Current Directions in Psychological Science, 15,* 278–281.

Shute, V. J. (2008). Focus on formative feedback. *Review of Educational Research, 78,* 153–189.

Siegel, D. J. (2012). *The developing mind: How relationships and the brain interact to shape who we are* (2nd ed.). New York, NY: Guilford Press.

Siegler, R. S. (2009). Improving the numerical understanding of children from low-income families. *Child Development Perspectives, 3,* 118–124.

Siegler, R. S., & Alibali, M. W. (2005). *Children's thinking* (4th ed.). Upper Saddle River, NJ: Prentice Hall.

Sinatra, G. M., & Pintrich, P. R. (Eds.). (2003). *Intentional conceptual change.* Mahwah, NJ: Erlbaum.

Sizer, T. R. (1992). *Horace's school: Redesigning the American high school.* Boston, MA: Houghton Mifflin.

Sizer, T. R. (2004). *Horace's compromise: The dilemma of the American high school.* Boston, MA: Houghton Mifflin.

Slavin, R. E., Hurley, E. A., & Chamberlain, A. (2003). Cooperative learning and achievement: Theory and research. In W. Reynolds & G. Miller (Eds.), *Handbook of psychology: Vol. 7. Educational psychology* (pp. 177–198). New York, NY: Wiley.

Slusher, M. P., & Anderson, C. A. (1996). Using causal persuasive arguments to change beliefs and teach new information: The mediating role of explanation availability and evaluation bias in the acceptance of knowledge. *Journal of Educational Psychology, 88,* 110–122.

Smith, C. L. (2007). Bootstrapping processes in the development of students' commonsense matter theories: Using analogical mappings, thought experiments, and learning to measure to promote conceptual restructuring. *Cognition and Instruction, 25,* 337–398.

Smith, C. L., Maclin, D., Grosslight, L., & Davis, H. (1997). Teaching for understanding: A study of students' preinstruction theories of matter and a comparison of the effectiveness of two approaches to teaching about matter and density. *Cognition and Instruction, 15,* 317–393.

Smith, E. E. (2000). Neural bases of human working memory. *Current Directions in Psychological Science, 9,* 45–49.

Sneider, C., & Pulos, S. (1983). Children's cosmographies: Understanding the earth's shape and gravity. *Science Education, 67,* 205–221.

Sperling, G. (1960). The information available in brief visual presentations. *Psychological Monographs, 74* (Whole No. 498).

Spunt, R. P., Falk, E. B., & Lieberman, M. D. (2010). Dissociable neural systems support retrieval of *how* and *why* action knowledge. *Psychological Science, 21,* 1593–1598.

Stepans, J. (1991). Developmental patterns in students' understanding of physics concepts. In S. M. Glynn, R. H. Yeany, & B. K. Britton (Eds.), *The psychology of learning science* (pp. 89–115). Mahwah, NJ: Erlbaum.

Strike, K. A., & Posner, G. J. (1992). A revisionist theory of conceptual change. In R. A. Duschl & R. J. Hamilton (Eds.), *Philosophy of science, cognitive psychology, and educational theory and practice* (pp. 147–176). New York, NY: State University of New York Press.

Sweller, J. (1988). Cognitive load during problem solving: Effects on learning. *Cognitive Science, 12,* 257–285.

Sweller, J. (1994). Cognitive load theory, learning difficulty, and instructional design. *Learning and Instruction, 4,* 295–312.

Sweller, J. (2008). Human cognitive architecture. In J. M. Spector, M. D. Merrill, J. van Merriënboer, & M. P. Driscoll (Eds.), *Handbook of research on educational communications and technology* (3rd ed., pp. 369–381). New York, NY: Erlbaum.

Szu, J. I., & Binder, D. K. (2016). The role of astrocytic aquaporin-4 in synaptic plasticity and learning and memory. *Frontiers in Integrative Neuroscience, 10*(8), 1–16. doi:10.3389/fnint.2016.00008

Tager-Flusberg, H. (2007). Evaluating the theory-of-mind hypothesis of autism. *Current Directions in Psychological Science, 16,* 311–315.

Tharp, R. G. (1989). Psychocultural variables and constants: Effects on teaching and learning in schools. *American Psychologist, 44,* 349–359.

Thomas, M. S. C., & Johnson, M. H. (2008). New advances in understanding sensitive periods in brain development. *Current Directions in Psychological Science, 17,* 1–5.

Tobin, K. (1987). The role of wait time in higher cognitive level learning. *Review of Educational Research, 57,* 69–95.

Tomporowski, P. D., Davis, C. L., Miller, P. H., & Naglieri, J. A. (2008). Exercise and children's intelligence, cognition, and academic achievement. *Educational Psychology Review, 20,* 111–131.

Torney-Purta, J. (1994). Dimensions of adolescents' reasoning about political and historical issues: Ontological switches, developmental processes, and situated learning. In M. Carretero & J. F. Voss (Eds.), *Cognitive and instructional processes in history and the social sciences* (pp. 103–122). Mahwah, NJ: Erlbaum.

Torrance, E. P. (1995). Insights about creativity: Questioned, rejected, ridiculed, ignored. *Educational Psychology Review, 7*, 313–322.

Tulving, E., & Thomson, D. M. (1973). Encoding specificity and retrieval processes in episodic memory. *Psychological Review, 80*, 352–373.

Urgolites, Z. J., & Wood, J. N. (2013). Visual long-term memory stores high-fidelity representations of observed actions. *Psychological Science, 24*, 403–411.

Van de Sande, C. C., & Greeno, J. G. (2012). Achieving alignment of perspectival framings in problem-solving this course. *Journal of the Learning Sciences, 21*, 1–44.

van der Veen, J. (2012). Draw your physics homework? Art as a path to understanding in physics teaching. *American Educational Research Journal, 49*, 356–407.

van Merriënboer, J. J. G., & Kester, L. (2008). Whole-task models in education. In J. M. Spector, M. D. Merrill, J. van Merriënboer, & M. P. Driscoll (Eds.), *Handbook of research on educational communications and technology* (3rd ed., pp. 441–456). New York, NY: Erlbaum.

Van Meter, P. (2001). Drawing construction as a strategy for learning from text. *Journal of Educational Psychology, 93*, 129–140.

Van Meter, P., & Garner, J. (2005). The promise and practice of learner-generated drawing: Literature review and synthesis. *Educational Psychology Review, 17*, 285–325.

VanSledright, B., & Brophy, J. (1992). Storytelling, imagination, and fanciful elaboration in children's historical reconstructions. *American Educational Research Journal, 29*, 837–859.

Varma, S., McCandliss, B. D., & Schwartz, D. L. (2008). Scientific and pragmatic challenges for bridging education and neuroscience. *Educational Researcher, 37*(3), 140–152.

Verdi, M. P., Kulhavy, R. W., Stock, W. A., Rittschof, K. A., & Johnson, J. T. (1996). Text learning using scientific diagrams: Implications for classroom use. *Contemporary Educational Psychology, 21*, 487–499.

Verghese, A., Garner, K. G., Mattingley, J. B., & Dux, P. E. (2016). Prefrontal cortex structure predicts training-induced improvements in multitasking performance. *The Journal of Neuroscience, 36*(9), 2638–2645.

Verkhratsky, A., & Butt, A. (2007). *Glial neurobiology*. Chichester, England: Wiley.

Vosniadou, S. (1994). Universal and culture-specific properties of children's mental models of the earth. In L. A. Hirschfeld & S. A. Gelman (Eds.), *Mapping the mind: Domain specificity in cognition and culture* (pp. 412–430). Cambridge, England: Cambridge University Press.

Vosniadou, S. (Ed.). (2008). *International handbook of research on conceptual change*. New York, NY: Routledge.

Vosniadou, S., & Brewer, W. F. (1987). Theories of knowledge restructuring in development. *Review of Educational Research, 57*, 51–67.

Vosniadou, S., Vamvakoussi, X., & Skopeliti, I. (2008). The framework theory approach to the problem of conceptual change. In S. Vosniadou (Ed.), *International handbook of research on conceptual change* (pp. 3–34). New York, NY: Routledge.

Walczyk, J. J., Wei, M., Griffith-Ross, D. A., Goubert, S. E., Cooper, A. L., & Zha, P. (2007). Development of the interplay between automatic processes and cognitive resources in reading. *Journal of Educational Psychology, 99*, 867–887.

Webb, N. M., Franke, M. L., Ing, M., Chan, A., De, T., Freund, D., & Battey, D. (2008). The role of teacher instructional practices in student collaboration. *Contemporary Educational Psychology, 33*, 360–381.

Wellman, H. M., & Gelman, S. A. (1998). Knowledge acquisition in foundational domains. In W. Damon (Series Ed.), D. Kuhn, & R. S. Siegler (Vol. Eds.), *Handbook of child psychology: Vol. 2. Cognition, perception, and language* (5th ed., pp. 523–573). New York, NY: Wiley.

White, J. J., & Rumsey, S. (1994). Teaching for understanding in a third-grade geography lesson. In J. Brophy (Ed.), *Advances in research on teaching: Vol. 4. Case studies of teaching and learning in social studies* (pp. 33–69). Greenwich, CT: JAI Press.

Wilder, A. A., & Williams, J. P. (2001). Students with severe learning disabilities can learn higher order comprehension skills. *Journal of Educational Psychology, 93*, 268–278.

Williams, R. F. (2012). Image schemas in clock-reading: Latent errors and emerging expertise. *The Journal of the Learning Sciences, 21*, 216–246.

Willingham, D. T. (2004). *Cognition: The thinking animal* (2nd ed.). Upper Saddle River, NJ: Prentice Hall.

Winn, W. (1991). Learning from maps and diagrams. *Educational Psychology Review, 3*, 211–247.

Wittrock, M. C. (1974). Learning as a generative process. *Educational Psychologist, 11*, 87–95.

Wixted, J. T. (2005). A theory about why we forget what we once knew. *Current Directions in Psychological Science, 14*, 6–9.

Wood, J. 2007). Visual working memory for observed actions. *Journal of Experimental Psychology: General, 136*, 639–652.

Zhang, W., & Luck, S. J. (2009). Sudden death and gradual decay in visual working memory. *Psychological Science, 20*, 423–428.

Zohar, A., & Aharon-Kraversky, S. (2005). Exploring the effects of cognitive conflict and direct teaching for students of different academic levels. *Journal of Research in Science Teaching, 42*, 829–855.

CHAPTER 3

Abrami, P. C., Bernard, R. M., Borokhovski, E., Wade, A., Surkes, M. A., Tamim, R., & Zhang, D. (2008). Instructional interventions affecting critical thinking skills and dispositions: A stage 1 meta-analysis. *Review of Educational Research, 78*, 1102–1134.

Afflerbach, P., & Cho, B.-Y. (2010). Determining and describing reading strategies: Internet and traditional forms of reading. In H. S. Waters & W. Schneider (Eds.), *Metacognition, strategy use, and instruction* (pp. 201–225). New York, NY: Guilford Press.

Alexander, J. M., Johnson, K. E., Scott, B., & Meyer, R. D. (2008). Stegosaurus and spoonbills: Mechanisms for transfer across biological domains. In M. F. Shaughnessy, M. V. E. Vennemann, & C. K. Kennedy (Eds.), *Metacognition: A recent review of research, theory, and perspectives* (pp. 63–83). Happauge, NY: Nova.

Allen, K. D. (1998). The use of an enhanced simplified habit-reversal procedure to reduce disruptive outbursts during athletic performance. *Journal of Applied Behavior Analysis, 31*, 489–492.

Amabile, T. M., & Hennessey, B. A. (1992). The motivation for creativity in children. In A. K. Boggiano & T. S. Pittman (Eds.), *Achievement and motivation: A social-developmental perspective* (pp. 54–76). Cambridge, England: Cambridge University Press.

Amsterlaw, J. (2006). Children's beliefs about everyday reasoning. *Child Development, 77*, 443–464.

Anderson, J. R., Reder, L. M., & Simon, H. A. (1996). Situated learning and education. *Educational Researcher, 25*(4), 5–11.

Anderson, L. W., & Pellicer, L. O. (1998). Toward an understanding of unusually successful programs for economically disadvantaged students. *Journal of Education for Students Placed at Risk, 3*, 237–263.

Andrade, H. L. (2010). Students as the definitive source of formative assessment: Academic self-assessment and the self-regulation of learning. In H. L. Andrade & G. G. Cizek (Eds.), *Handbook of formative assessment* (pp. 90–105). New York, NY: Routledge.

Andre, T., & Windschitl, M. (2003). Interest, epistemological belief, and intentional conceptual change. In G. M. Sinatra & P. R. Pintrich (Eds.), *Intentional conceptual change* (pp. 173–197). Mahwah, NJ: Erlbaum.

Astington, J. W., & Pelletier, J. (1996). The language of mind: Its role in teaching and learning. In D. R. Olson & N. Torrance (Eds.), *The handbook of education and human development: New models of learning, teaching, and schooling* (pp. 593–619). Cambridge, MA: Blackwell.

Atkinson, R. K., Levin, J. R., Atkinson, L. A., Kiewra, K. A., Meyers, T., Kim, S. I., . . . Hwang, Y. (1999). Matrix and mnemonic text-processing adjuncts: Comparing and combining their components. *Journal of Educational Psychology, 91*, 342–357.

Ausubel, D. P., Novak, J. D., & Hanesian, H. (1978). *Educational psychology: A cognitive view* (2nd ed.). New York, NY: Holt, Rinehart & Winston.

Azevedo, R. (2005a). Computer environments as metacognitive tools for enhancing learning. *Educational Psychologist, 40*, 193–197.

Azevedo, R. (2005b). Using hypermedia as a metacognitive tool for enhancing student learning? The role of self-regulated learning. *Educational Psychologist, 40*, 199–209.

Azevedo, R., & Witherspoon, A. M. (2009). Self-regulated learning with hypermedia. In D. J. Hacker, J. Dunlosky, & A. C. Graesser (Eds.), *Handbook of metacognition in education* (pp. 319–339). New York, NY: Routledge.

Baer, J., & Garrett, T. (2010). Teaching for creativity in an era of content standards and accountability. In R. A. Beghetto & J. C. Kaufman (Eds.), *Nurturing creativity in the classroom* (pp. 6–23). New York, NY: Cambridge University Press.

Baker, L. (1989). Metacognition, comprehension monitoring, and the adult reader. *Educational Psychology Review, 1*, 3–38.

Baker, L., & Brown, A. L. (1984). Metacognitive skills of reading. In D. Pearson (Ed.), *Handbook of reading research* (pp. 353–394). White Plains, NY: Longman.

Bandura, A. (1986). *Social foundations of thought and action: A social cognitive theory*. Upper Saddle River, NJ: Prentice Hall.

Bandura, A. (1989). Human agency in social cognitive theory. *American Psychologist, 44*, 1175–1184.

Bandura, A. (2008). Toward an agentic theory of the self. In H. W. Marsh, R. G. Craven, & D. M. McInerney (Eds.), *Self-processes, learning, and enabling human potential* (pp. 15–49). Charlotte, NC: Information Age.

Barab, S. A., Gresalfi, M., & Ingram-Goble, A. (2010). Transformational play: Using games to position person, content, and context. *Educational Researcher, 39*, 525–536.

Barnett, J. E. (2001, April). *Study strategies and preparing for exams: A survey of middle and high school students*. Paper presented at the annual meeting of the American Educational Research Association, Seattle, WA.

Barnett, M. (2005, April). *Engaging inner city students in learning through designing remote operated vehicles*. Paper presented at the annual meeting of the American Educational Research Association, Montreal, Canada.

Barnett, S. M., & Ceci, S. J. (2002). When and where do we apply what we learn? A taxonomy of far transfer. *Psychological Bulletin, 128*, 612–637.

Bassok, M. (2003). Analogical transfer in problem solving. In J. E. Davidson & R. J. Sternberg (Eds.), *The psychology of problem solving* (pp. 343–369). Cambridge, England: Cambridge University Press.

Beal, C. R., Arroyo, I., & Cohen, P. R. (2009, April). *Experimental evaluation of an intelligent tutoring system for middle school mathematics word problem solving*. Paper presented at the annual meeting of the American Educational Research Association, San Diego, CA.

Bear, P., Torgerson, C., & Dubois-Gerchak, K. (2010). A positive procedure to increase compliance in the general education classroom for a student with serious emotional disorders. In G. S. Goodman (Ed.), *Educational psychology reader: The art and science of how people learn* (pp. 75–87). New York, NY: Peter Lang.

Beghetto, R. A., & Kaufman, J. C. (Eds.) (2010). *Nurturing creativity in the classroom*. New York, NY: Cambridge University Press.

Belfiore, P. J., & Hornyak, R. S. (1998). Operant theory and application to self-monitoring in adolescents. In D. H. Schunk & B. J. Zimmerman (Eds.), *Self-regulated learning: From teaching to self-reflective practice* (pp. 184–202). New York, NY: Guilford Press.

Bendixen, L. D., & Feucht, F. C. (Eds.). (2010). *Personal epistemology in the classroom: Theory, research, and implications for practice*. Cambridge, England: Cambridge University Press.

Benton, S. L. (1997). Psychological foundations of elementary writing instruction. In G. D. Phye (Ed.), *Handbook of academic learning: Construction of knowledge* (pp. 235–264). San Diego, CA: Academic Press.

Bereiter, C. (1995). A dispositional view of transfer. In A. McKeough, J. Lupart, & A. Marini (Eds.), *Teaching for transfer: Fostering generalization in learning* (pp. 21–34). Mahwah, NJ: Erlbaum.

Beyer, B. K. (1985). Critical thinking: What is it? *Social Education, 49*, 270–276.

Black, J. B., Khan, S. A., & Huang, S. C. D. (2014). Video and computer games as grounding experiences for learning. In F. C. Blumberg (Ed.), *Learning by playing: Video gaming in education* (pp. 290–301). New York, NY: Oxford University Press.

Blair, C. (2002). School readiness: Integrating cognition and emotion in a neurobiological conceptualization of children's functioning at school entry. *American Psychologist, 57*, 111–127.

Bonney, C. R., & Sternberg, R. J. (2011). Learning to think critically. In R. E. Mayer & P. A. Alexander (Eds.), *Handbook of research on learning and instruction* (pp. 166–196). New York, NY: Routledge.

Bransford, J., Vye, N., Stevens, R., Kuhl, P., Schwartz, D., Bell, P., . . . Sabelli, N. (2006). Learning theories and education: Toward a decade of synergy. In P. A. Alexander & P. H. Winne (Eds.), *Handbook of educational psychology* (2nd ed., pp. 209–244). Mahwah, NJ: Erlbaum.

Bransford, J. D., Mosborg, S., Copland, M. A., Honig, M. A., Nelson, H. G., Gawel, D., . . . Vye, N. (2009). Adaptive people and adaptive systems: Issues of learning and design. In A. Hargreaves, A. Lieberman, M. Filan, & D. Hopkins (Eds.), *Second international handbook of educational change* (pp. 825–856). Dordrecht, Netherlands: Springer.

Bransford, J. D., & Schwartz, D. L. (1999). Rethinking transfer: A simple proposal with multiple implications. *Review of Research in Education, 24*, 61–100.

Bråten, I., Britt, M. A., Strømsø, H. I., & Rouet, J.-F. (2011). The role of epistemic beliefs in the comprehension of multiple expository texts: Toward an integrated model. *Educational Psychologist, 46,* 48–70.

Brenner, M. E., Mayer, R. E., Moseley, B., Brar, T., Durán, R., Reed, B. S., & Webb, D. (1997). Learning by understanding: The role of multiple representations in learning algebra. *American Educational Research Journal, 34,* 663–689.

Bromme, R., Kienhues, D., & Porsch, T. (2010). Who knows what and who can we believe? Epistemological beliefs are beliefs about knowledge (mostly) to be attained from others. In L. D. Bendixen & F. C. Feucht (Eds.), *Personal epistemology in the classroom: Theory, research, and implications for practice* (pp. 163–193). Cambridge, England: Cambridge University Press.

Bronson, M. B. (2000). *Self-regulation in early childhood: Nature and nurture.* New York, NY: Guilford Press.

Brooks, L. W., & Dansereau, D. F. (1987). Transfer of information: An instructional perspective. In S. M. Cormier & J. D. Hagman (Eds.), *Transfer of learning: Contemporary research and applications* (pp. 121–150). San Diego, CA: Academic Press.

Brophy, J. E., Alleman, J., & Knighton, B. (2009). *Inside the social studies classroom.* New York, NY: Routledge.

Brown, A. L., Campione, J., & Day, J. (1981). Learning to learn: On training students to learn from texts. *Educational Researcher, 10*(2), 14–21.

Brown, A. L., & Palincsar, A. S. (1987). Reciprocal teaching of comprehension strategies: A natural history of one program for enhancing learning. In J. Borkowski & J. D. Day (Eds.), *Cognition in special education: Comparative approaches to retardation, learning disabilities, and giftedness* (pp. 81–132). Norwood, NJ: Ablex.

Brunstein, J. C., & Glaser, C. (2011). Testing a path-analytic mediation model of how self-regulated writing strategies improve fourth graders' composition skills: A randomized controlled trial. *Journal of Educational Psychology, 103,* 922–938.

Buckley, M., & Saarni, C. (2009). Emotion regulation: Implications for positive youth development. In R. Gilman, E. S. Huebner, & M. J. Furlong (Eds.), *Handbook of positive psychology in schools* (pp. 107–118). New York, NY: Routledge.

Buehl, M. M., & Alexander, P. A. (2006). Examining the dual nature of epistemological beliefs. *International Journal of Educational Research, 45,* 28–42.

Bulgren, J. A., Marquis, J. G., Lenz, B. K., Deshler, D. D., & Schumaker, J. B. (2011). The effectiveness of a question-exploration routine for enhancing the content learning of secondary students. *Journal of Educational Psychology, 103,* 578–593.

Butler, D. L., & Winne, P. H. (1995). Feedback and self-regulated learning: A theoretical synthesis. *Review of Educational Research, 65,* 245–281.

Butler, R. (1998b). Determinants of help seeking: Relations between perceived reasons for classroom help-avoidance and help-seeking behaviors in an experimental context. *Journal of Educational Psychology, 90,* 630–644.

Carr, M. (2010). The importance of metacognition for conceptual change and strategy use in mathematics. In H. S. Waters & W. Schneider (Eds.), *Metacognition, strategy use, and instruction* (pp. 176–197). New York, NY: Guilford Press.

Chandler, M., Hallett, D., & Sokol, B. W. (2002). Competing claims about competing knowledge claims. In B. K. Hofer & P. R. Pintrich (Eds.), *Personal epistemology: The psychology of beliefs about knowledge and knowing* (pp. 145–168). Mahwah, NJ: Erlbaum.

Chi, M. T. H., Feltovich, P., & Glaser, R. (1981). Categorization and representation of physics problems by experts and novices. *Cognitive Science, 5,* 121–152.

Chinn, C. A. (2006). Learning to argue. In A. M. O'Donnell, C. E. Hmelo-Silver, & G. Erkens (Eds.), *Collaborative learning, reasoning, and technology* (pp. 355–383). Mahwah, NJ: Erlbaum.

Christenson, S. L., & Thurlow, M. L. (2004). School dropouts: Prevention, considerations, interventions, and challenges. *Current Directions in Psychological Science, 13,* 36–39.

Cognition and Technology Group at Vanderbilt. (1993). Anchored instruction and situated cognition revisited. *Educational Technology, 33*(3), 52–70.

Corker, K. S., & Donnellan, M. B. (2012). Setting lower limits high: The role of boundary goals in achievement motivation. *Journal of Educational Psychology, 104,* 138–149.

Corno, L., Cronbach, L. J., Kupermintz, H., Lohman, D. F., Mandinach, E. B., Porteus, A. W., & Talbert, J. E. (2002). *Remaking the concept of aptitude: Extending the legacy of Richard E. Snow.* Mahwah, NJ: Erlbaum.

Corno, L., & Mandinach, E. B. (2004). What we have learned about student engagement in the past twenty years. In D. M.

McInerney & S. Van Etten (Eds.), *Big theories revisited* (pp. 299–328). Greenwich, CT: Information Age.

Cosden, M., Morrison, G., Albanese, A. L., & Macias, S. (2001). When homework is not home work: After-school programs for homework assistance. *Educational Psychologist, 36,* 211–221.

Cox, B. D. (1997). The rediscovery of the active learner in adaptive contexts: A developmental-historical analysis of transfer of training. *Educational Psychologist, 32,* 41–55.

Csikszentmihalyi, M. (1996). *Creativity: Flow and the psychology of discovery and invention.* New York, NY: HarperCollins.

Dahlin, B., & Watkins, D. (2000). The role of repetition in the processes of memorizing and understanding: A comparison of the views of Western and Chinese secondary students in Hong Kong. *British Journal of Educational Psychology, 70,* 65–84.

Dai, D. Y., & Sternberg, R. J. (2004). Beyond cognitivism: Toward an integrated understanding of intellectual functioning and development. In D. Y. Dai & R. J. Sternberg (Eds.), *Motivation, emotion, and cognition: Integrative perspectives on intellectual functioning and development* (pp. 3–38). Mahwah, NJ: Erlbaum.

Damon, W. (1988). *The moral child: Nurturing children's natural moral growth.* New York, NY: Free Press.

Davidson, J. E., & Sternberg, R. J. (1998). Smart problem solving: How metacognition helps. In D. J. Hacker, J. Dunlosky, & A. C. Graesser (Eds.), *Metacognition in educational theory and practice* (pp. 47–68). Mahwah, NJ: Erlbaum.

Davidson, J. E., & Sternberg, R. J. (Eds.). (2003). *The psychology of problem solving.* Cambridge, England: Cambridge University Press.

Day, S. B., & Goldstone, R. L. (2012). The import of knowledge export: Connecting findings and theories of transfer of learning. *Educational Psychologist, 47,* 153–176.

De Corte, E. (2003). Transfer as the productive use of acquired knowledge, skills, and motivations. *Current Directions in Psychological Science, 12,* 142–146.

De Corte, E., Op't Eynde, P., Depaepe, F., & Verschaffel, L. (2010). The reflexive relation between students' mathematics-related beliefs and the mathematics classroom culture. In L. D. Bendixen & F. C. Feucht (Eds.), *Personal epistemology in the classroom: Theory, research, and implications for practice* (pp. 292–327). Cambridge, England: Cambridge University Press.

de Jong, T. (2011). Instruction based on computer simulations. In R. E. Mayer & P. A. Alexander (Eds.), *Handbook of research on learning and instruction* (pp. 446–466). New York, NY: Routledge.

De La Paz, S. (2005). Effects of historical reasoning instruction and writing strategy mastery in culturally and academically diverse middle school classrooms. *Journal of Educational Psychology, 97,* 139–156.

De La Paz, S., & Felton, M. K. (2010). Reading and writing from multiple source documents in history: Effects of strategy instruction with low to average high school writers. *Contemporary Educational Psychology, 35,* 174–192.

Dee-Lucas, D., & Larkin, J. H. (1991). Equations in scientific proofs: Effects on comprehension. *American Educational Research Journal, 28,* 661–682.

Demetriou, A., Christou, C., Spanoudis, G., & Platsidou, M. (2002). The development of mental processing: Efficiency, working memory, and thinking. *Monographs of the Society for Research in Child Development, 67*(1, Serial No. 268).

Derry, S. J., Levin, J. R., Osana, H. P., & Jones, M. S. (1998). Developing middle school students' statistical reasoning abilities through simulation gaming. In S. P. Lajoie (Ed.), *Reflections on statistics: Learning, teaching, and assessment in grades K–12* (pp. 175–195). Mahwah, NJ: Erlbaum.

Desoete, A., Roeyers, H., & De Clercq, A. (2003). Can offline metacognition enhance mathematical problem solving? *Journal of Educational Psychology, 95,* 188–200.

Di Vesta, F. J., & Gray, S. G. (1972). Listening and notetaking. *Journal of Educational Psychology, 63,* 8–14.

DiDonato, N. C. (2011, April). *Examining self- and co-regulated processes in a collaborative learning environment.* Paper presented at the annual meeting of the American Educational Research Association, New Orleans, LA.

Dole, J. A., Duffy, G. G., Roehler, L. R., & Pearson, P. D. (1991). Moving from the old to the new: Research on reading comprehension instruction. *Review of Educational Research, 61,* 239–264.

Dominowski, R. L. (1998). Verbalization and problem solving. In D. J. Hacker, J. Dunlosky, & A. C. Graesser (Eds.), *Metacognition in educational theory and practice* (pp. 25–45). Mahwah, NJ: Erlbaum.

Duckworth, A. L., & Seligman, M. E. P. (2005). Self-discipline outdoes IQ in predicting academic performance of adolescents. *Psychological Science, 16,* 939–944.

Duncker, K. (1945). On problem solving. *Psychological Monographs, 58* (Whole No. 270).

Dunlosky, J. (2013). Strengthening the student toolbox: Study strategies to boost learning. *American Educator, 37*(3), 12–21.

Dunlosky, J., & Lipko, A. R. (2007). Metacomprehension: A brief history and how to improve its accuracy. *Current Directions in Psychological Science, 16,* 228–232.

Dunning, D., Heath, C., & Suls, J. M. (2004). Flawed self-assessment: Implications for health, education, and the workplace. *Psychological Science in the Public Interest, 5,* 69–106.

Eason, S. H., Goldberg, L. F., Young, K. M., Geist, M. C., & Cutting, L. E. (2012). Reader–text interactions: How differential text and question types influence cognitive skills needed for reading comprehension. *Journal of Educational Psychology, 104,* 515–528.

Eccles, J. S., Wigfield, A., & Schiefele, U. (1998). Motivation to succeed. In W. Damon (Series Ed.) & N. Eisenberg (Vol. Ed.), *Handbook of child psychology: Vol. 3. Social, emotional, and personality development* (5th ed., pp. 1017–1095). New York, NY: Wiley.

Eilam, B. (2001). Primary strategies for promoting homework performance. *American Educational Research Journal, 38,* 691–725.

Elder, A. D. (2002). Characterizing fifth grade students' epistemological beliefs in science. In B. K. Hofer & P. R. Pintrich (Eds.), *Personal epistemology: The psychology of beliefs about knowledge and knowing* (pp. 347–363). Mahwah, NJ: Erlbaum.

Emmer, E. T. (1994, April). *Teacher emotions and classroom management.* Paper presented at the annual meeting of the American Educational Research Association, New Orleans, LA.

Engle, R. A. (2006). Framing interactions to foster generative learning: A situative explanation of transfer in a community of learners classroom. *Journal of the Learning Sciences, 15,* 451–498.

Engle, R. A., Lam, D. P., Meyer, X. S., & Nix, S. E. (2012). How does expansive framing promote transfer? Several proposed explanations and a research agenda for investigating them. *Educational Psychologist, 47,* 215–231.

Feldhusen, J. F., & Treffinger, D. J. (1980). *Creative thinking and problem solving in gifted education.* Dubuque, IA: Kendall/Hunt.

Feucht, F. C. (2010). Epistemic climate in elementary classrooms. In L. D. Bendixen & F. C. Feucht (Eds.), *Personal epistemology in the classroom: Theory, research, and implications for practice* (pp. 55–93). Cambridge, England: Cambridge University Press.

Fischer, K. W., & Daley, S. G. (2007). Connecting cognitive science and neuroscience to education: Potentials and pitfalls in inferring executive processes. In L. Meltzer (Ed.), *Executive function in education: From theory to practice* (pp. 55–72). New York, NY: Guilford Press.

Fitzsimmons, G. M., & Finkel, E. J. (2010). Interpersonal influences on self-regulation. *Current Directions in Psychological Science, 19,* 101–105.

Flavell, J. H., Friedrichs, A. G., & Hoyt, J. D. (1970). Developmental changes in memorization processes. *Cognitive Psychology, 1,* 324–340.

Flavell, J. H., Miller, P. H., & Miller, S. A. (2002). *Cognitive development* (4th ed.). Upper Saddle River, NJ: Prentice Hall.

Fletcher, K. L., & Cassady, J. C. (2010). Overcoming academic anxieties: Promoting effective coping and self-regulation strategies. In J. C. Cassady (Ed.), *Anxiety in schools: The causes, consequences, and solutions for academic anxieties* (pp. 177–200). New York, NY: Peter Lang.

Flum, H., & Kaplan, A. (2006). Exploratory orientation as an educational goal. *Educational Psychologist, 41,* 99–110.

Fonseca, B. A., & Chi, M. T. H. (2011). Instruction based on self-explanation. In R. E. Mayer & P. A. Alexander (Eds.), *Handbook of research on learning and instruction* (pp. 296–321). New York, NY: Routledge.

Frederiksen, N. (1984a). Implications of cognitive theory for instruction in problem-solving. *Review of Educational Research, 54,* 363–407.

Fries, S., Dietz, F., & Schmid, S. (2008). Motivational interference in learning: The impact of leisure alternatives on subsequent self-regulation. *Contemporary Educational Psychology, 33,* 119–133.

Gaskins, I. W., & Pressley, M. (2007). Teaching metacognitive strategies that address executive function processes within a schoolwide curriculum. In L. Meltzer (Ed.), *Executive function in education: From theory to practice* (pp. 261–286). New York, NY: Guilford Press.

Gaskins, I. W., Satlow, E., & Pressley, M. (2007). Executive control of reading comprehension in the elementary school. In L. Meltzer (Ed.), *Executive function in education: From theory to practice* (pp. 194–215). New York, NY: Guilford Press.

Gijbels, D., Dochy, F., Van den Bossche, P., & Segers, M. (2005). Effects of problem-based learning: A meta-analysis from the angle of assessment. *Review of Educational Research, 75,* 27–61.

Glass, A. L., Holyoak, K. J., & Santa, J. L. (1979). *Cognition.* Reading, MA: Addison-Wesley.

Glogger, I., Schwonke, R., Holzäpfel, L., Nückles, M., & Renkl, A. (2012). Learning strategies assessed by journal writing: Prediction of learning outcomes by quantity, quality, and combinations of learning strategies. *Journal of Educational Psychology, 104,* 452–468.

Glover, J. A., Ronning, R. R., & Reynolds, C. R. (Eds.). (1989). *Handbook of creativity.* New York, NY: Plenum Press.

Graham, S. (2006). Peer victimization in school: Exploring the ethnic context. *Current Directions in Psychological Science, 15,* 317–321.

Graham, S., & Harris, K. R. (1996). Addressing problems in attention, memory, and executive functioning. In G. R. Lyon & N. A. Krasnegor (Eds.), *Attention, memory, and executive function* (pp. 349–365). Baltimore, MD: Brookes.

Grant, H., & Dweck, C. (2001). Cross-cultural response to failure: Considering outcome attributions with different goals. In F. Salili & C. Chiu (Eds.), *Student motivation: The culture and context of learning* (pp. 203–219). Dordrecht, The Netherlands: Kluwer Academic.

Greene, J. A., & Azevedo, R. (2009). A macro-level analysis of SRL processes and their relations to the acquisition of a sophisticated mental model of a complex system. *Contemporary Educational Psychology, 34,* 18–29.

Gregg, M., & Leinhardt, G. (1994, April). *Constructing geography.* Paper presented at the annual meeting of the American Educational Research Association, New Orleans, LA.

Gresalfi, M. S., & Lester, F. (2009). What's worth knowing in mathematics? In S. Tobias & T. M. Duffy (Eds.), *Constructivist instruction: Success or failure?* (pp. 264–290). New York, NY: Routledge.

Griffin, M. M., & Griffin, B. W. (1994, April). *Some can get there from here: Situated learning, cognitive style, and map skills.* Paper presented at the annual meeting of the American Educational Research Association, New Orleans, LA.

Hacker, D. J., & Bol, L. (2004). Metacognitive theory: Considering the social-cognitive influences. In D. M. McNerney & S. Van Etten (Eds.), *Big theories revisited* (pp. 275–297). Greenwich, CT: Information Age.

Hacker, D. J., Dunlosky, J., & Graesser, A. C. (Eds.). (2009b). *Handbook of metacognition in education.* New York, NY: Routledge.

Haller, E. P., Child, D. A., & Walberg, H. J. (1988). Can comprehension be taught? A quantitative synthesis of "metacognitive" studies. *Educational Researcher, 17*(9), 5–8.

Halpern, D. F. (1997). *Critical thinking across the curriculum: A brief edition of thought and knowledge.* Mahwah, NJ: Erlbaum.

Halpern, D. F. (1998). Teaching critical thinking for transfer across domains. *American Psychologist, 53,* 449–455.

Halpern, D. F. (2008). Is intelligence critical thinking? Why we need a new definition of intelligence. In P. C. Kyllonen, R. D. Roberts, & L. Stankov (Eds.), *Extending intelligence: Enhancement and new constructs* (pp. 349–370). New York, NY: Erlbaum/Taylor & Francis.

Hambrick, D. Z., & Engle, R. W. (2003). The role of working memory in problem solving. In J. E. Davidson & R. J. Sternberg (Eds.), *The psychology of problem solving* (pp. 176–206). Cambridge, England: Cambridge University Press.

Hampson, S. E. (2008). Mechanisms by which childhood personality traits influence adult well-being. *Current Directions in Psychological Science, 17,* 264–268.

Harnishfeger, K. K. (1995). The development of cognitive inhibition: Theories, definitions, and research evidence. In F. N. Dempster & C. J. Brainerd (Eds.), *Interference and inhibition in cognition.* San Diego, CA: Academic Press.

Harris, K. R. (1986). Self-monitoring of attentional behavior versus self-monitoring of productivity: Effects of on-task behavior and academic response rate among learning disabled children. *Journal of Applied Behavior Analysis, 19,* 417–423.

Harris, K. R., Santangelo, T., & Graham, S. (2010). Metacognition and strategies instruction in writing. In H. S. Waters & W. Schneider (Eds.), *Metacognition, strategy use, and instruction* (pp. 226–256). New York, NY: Guilford Press.

Harris, R. J. (1977). Comprehension of pragmatic implications in advertising. *Journal of Applied Psychology, 62,* 603–608.

Harter, S. (1999). *The construction of the self: A developmental perspective.* New York, NY: Guilford Press.

Haskell, R. E. (2001). *Transfer of learning: Cognition, instruction, and reasoning.* San Diego, CA: Academic Press.

Hatano, G., & Inagaki, K. (2003). When is conceptual change intended? A cognitive-sociocultural view. In G. M. Sinatra & P. R. Pintrich (Eds.), *Intentional conceptual change* (pp. 407–427). Mahwah, NJ: Erlbaum.

Hattie, J., Biggs, J., & Purdie, N. (1996). Effects of learning skills interventions on student learning: A meta-analysis. *Review of Educational Research, 66,* 99–136.

Hattie, J. A. C. (2009). *Visible learning: A synthesis of over 800 meta-analyses relating to achievement.* London, England: Routledge.

Hatzigeorgiadis, A., Zourbanos, N., Galanis, E., & Theodorakis, Y. (2011). Self-talk and sports performance: A meta-analysis. *Perspectives on Psychological Science, 6,* 348–356.

Haugwitz, M., Sumfleth, E., & Sandmann, A. (2010, April–May). *The influence of cognitive mapping on achievement in biology: Considering cognitive abilities as moderator.* Paper presented at the annual meeting of the American Educational Research Association, Denver, CO.

Hecht, S. A., & Vagi, K. J. (2010). Sources of group and individual differences in emerging fraction skills. *Journal of Educational Psychology, 102,* 843–859.

Hewitt, J., Brett, C., Scardamalia, M., Frecker, K., & Webb, J. (1995, April). Supporting knowledge building through the synthesis of CSILE, FCL, & Jasper. In M. Lamon (Chair), *Schools for thought: Transforming classrooms into learning communities.* Symposium conducted at the annual meeting of the American Educational Research Association, San Francisco, CA.

Heyman, G. D. (2008). Children's critical thinking when learning from others. *Current Directions in Psychological Science, 17,* 344–347.

Hickey, D. J. (2011). Participation by design: Improving individual motivation by looking beyond it. In D. M. McInerney, R. A. Walker, & G. A. D. Liem (Eds.), *Sociocultural theories of learning and motivation: Looking back, looking forward* (pp. 137–161). Charlotte, NC: Information Age.

Hiebert, E. H., & Fisher, C. W. (1992). The tasks of school literacy: Trends and issues. In J. Brophy (Ed.), *Advances in research on teaching: Vol. 3. Planning and managing learning tasks and activities* (pp. 191–223). Greenwich, CT: JAI Press.

Hmelo-Silver, C. E. (2004). Problem-based learning: What and how do students learn? *Educational Psychology Review, 16,* 235–266.

Hmelo-Silver, C. E. (2006). Design principles for scaffolding technology-based inquiry. In A. M. O'Donnell, C. E. Hmelo-Silver, & G. Erkens (Eds.), *Collaborative learning, reasoning, and technology* (pp. 147–170). Mahwah, NJ: Erlbaum.

Hmelo-Silver, C. E., Duncan, R. G., & Chinn, C. A. (2007). Scaffolding and achievement in problem-based and inquiry learning: A response to Kirschner, Sweller, and Clark (2006). *Educational Psychologist, 42,* 99–107.

Ho, D. Y. F. (1994). Cognitive socialization in Confucian heritage cultures. In P. M. Greenfield & R. R. Cocking (Eds.), *Cross-cultural roots of minority child development.* Mahwah, NJ: Erlbaum.

Hofer, B. K., & Bendixen, L. D. (2012). Personal epistemology: Theory, research, and future directions. In K. R. Harris, S. Graham, & T. Urdan (Eds.), *APA Educational Psychology Handbook* (pp. 227–256). Washington, DC: American Psychological Association.

Hofer, B. K., & Pintrich, P. R. (1997). The development of epistemological theories: Beliefs about knowledge and knowing and their relation to learning. *Review of Educational Research, 67,* 88–140.

Hofer, B. K., & Pintrich, P. R. (Eds.). (2002). *Personal epistemology: The psychology of beliefs about knowledge and knowing.* Mahwah, NJ: Erlbaum.

Hofer, M. (2010). Adolescents' development of individual interests: A product of multiple goal regulation? *Educational Psychologist, 45,* 149–166.

Hung, W., Jonassen, D. H., & Liu, R. (2008). Problem-based learning. In J. M. Spector, M. D. Merrill, J. van Merriënboer, & M. P. Driscoll (Eds.), *Handbook of research on educational communications and technology* (3rd ed., pp. 485–506). New York, NY: Erlbaum.

Hursh, D. (2007). Assessing No Child Left Behind and the rise of neoliberal education policies. *American Educational Research Journal, 44,* 493–518.

Jacob, B. A. (2003). Accountability, incentives, and behavior: The impact of high-stakes testing in the Chicago Public Schools. *Education Next, 3*(1). Retrieved from www.educationnext.org/unabridged/20031/jacob.pdf

Jadallah, M., Anderson, R. C., Nguyen-Jahiel, K., Miller, B. W., Kim, I.-H., Kuo, L.-J., Wu, X. (2011). Influence of a teacher's scaffolding moves during child-led small-group discussions. *American Educational Research Journal, 48,* 194–230.

Johanning, D. I., D'Agostino, J. V., Steele, D. F., & Shumow, L. (1999, April). *Student writing, post-writing group collaboration, and learning in pre-algebra.* Paper presented at the annual meeting of the American Educational Research Association, Montreal, Canada.

Jones, M. G., Jones, B. D., & Hargrove, T. Y. (2003). *The unintended consequences of high-stakes testing.* Lanham, MD: Rowman & Littlefield.

Jones, M. H., Estell, D. B., & Alexander, J. M. (2008). Friends, classmates, and self-regulated learning: Discussions with peers inside and outside the classroom. *Metacognition Learning, 3,* 1–15.

Kağitçibaşi, Ç. (2007). *Family, self, and human development across cultures: Theory and applications* (2nd ed.). Mahwah, NJ: Erlbaum.

Kahl, B., & Woloshyn, V. E. (1994). Using elaborative interrogation to facilitate acquisition of factual information in cooperative learning settings: One good strategy deserves another. *Applied Cognitive Psychology, 8,* 465–478.

Kardash, C. A. M., & Amlund, J. T. (1991). Self-reported learning strategies and learning from expository text. *Contemporary Educational Psychology, 16,* 117–138.

Kardash, C. A. M., & Howell, K. L. (2000). Effects of epistemological beliefs and topic-specific beliefs on undergraduates' cognitive and strategic processing of dual-positional text. *Journal of Educational Psychology, 92,* 524–535.

Kardash, C. A. M., & Scholes, R. J. (1996). Effects of preexisting beliefs, epistemological beliefs, and need for cognition on interpretation of controversial issues. *Journal of Educational Psychology, 88,* 260–271.

Katayama, A. D., & Robinson, D. H. (2000). Getting students "partially" involved in note-taking using graphic organizers. *Journal of Experimental Education, 68,* 119–133.

Kester, L., Paas, F., & van Merriënboer, J. J. G. (2010). Instructional control of cognitive load in the design of complex learning environments. In J. L. Plass, R. Moreno, & R. Brünken (Eds.), *Cognitive Load Theory* (pp. 109–130). Cambridge, England: Cambridge University Press.

Kiewra, K. A. (1985). Investigating notetaking and review: A depth of processing alternative. *Educational Psychologist, 20,* 23–32.

Kiewra, K. A. (1989). A review of note-taking: The encoding-storage paradigm and beyond. *Educational Psychology Review, 1,* 147–172.

King, A. (1992). Comparison of self-questioning, summarizing, and notetaking-review as strategies for learning from lectures. *American Educational Research Journal, 29,* 303–323.

King, A. (1994). Guiding knowledge construction in the classroom: Effects of teaching children how to question and how to explain. *American Educational Research Journal, 31,* 338–368.

King, A. (1999). Discourse patterns for mediating peer learning. In A. M. O'Donnell & A. King (Eds.), *Cognitive perspectives on peer learning* (pp. 87–115). Mahwah, NJ: Erlbaum.

King, P. M., & Kitchener, K. S. (2002). The reflective judgment model: Twenty years of research on epistemic cognition. In B. K. Hofer & P. R. Pintrich (Eds.), *Personal epistemology: The psychology of beliefs about knowledge and knowing* (pp. 37–61). Mahwah, NJ: Erlbaum.

Kochanska, G., Gross, J. N., Lin, M.-H., & Nichols, K. E. (2002). Guilt in young children: Development, determinants, and relations with a broader system of standards. *Child Development, 73,* 461–482.

Koedinger, K., Aleven, V., Roll, I., & Baker, R. (2009). *In vivo* experiments on whether supporting metacognition in intelligent tutoring systems yields robust learning. In D. J. Hacker, J. Dunlosky, & A. C. Graesser (Eds.), *Handbook of metacognition in education* (pp. 383–412). New York, NY: Routledge.

Krajcik, J. S., & Blumenfeld, P. C. (2006). Project-based learning. In R. K. Sawyer (Ed.), *The Cambridge handbook of the learning sciences* (pp. 317–333). Cambridge, England: Cambridge University Press.

Kramarski, B., & Mevarech, Z. R. (2003). Enhancing mathematical reasoning in the classroom: The effects of cooperative learning and metacognitive training. *American Educational Research Journal, 40,* 281–310.

Ku, Y.-M., Chan, W.-C., Wu, Y.-C., & Chen, Y.-H. (2008, March). *Improving children's comprehension of science text: Effects of adjunct questions and notetaking.* Paper presented at the annual meeting of the American Educational Research Association, New York, NY.

Kuhn, D. (2001a). How do people know? *Psychological Science, 12,* 1–8.

Kuhn, D. (2001b). Why development does (and does not) occur: Evidence from the domain of inductive reasoning. In J. L. McClelland & R. S. Siegler (Eds.), *Mechanisms of cognitive development: Behavioral and neural perspectives* (pp. 221–249). Mahwah, NJ: Erlbaum.

Kuhn, D. (2006). Do cognitive changes accompany developments in the adolescent brain? *Perspectives on Psychological Science, 1,* 59–67.

Kuhn, D. (2009). The importance of learning about knowing: Creating a foundation for development of intellectual values. *Child Development Perspectives, 3,* 112–117.

Kuhn, D., & Crowell, A. (2011). Dialogic argumentation as a vehicle for developing young adolescents' thinking. *Psychological Science, 22,* 545–552.

Kuhn, D., Daniels, S., & Krishnan, A. (2003, April). *Epistemology and intellectual values as core metacognitive constructs.* Paper presented at the annual meeting of the American Educational Research Association, Chicago, IL.

Kuhn, D., & Franklin, S. (2006). The second decade: What develops (and how)? In W. Damon & R. M. Lerner (Series Eds.), D. Kuhn & R. Siegler (Vol. Eds.), *Handbook of child psychology: Vol. 1. Cognition, perception, and language* (6th ed., 953–993). New York, NY: Wiley.

Kuhn, D., Garcia-Mila, M., Zohar, A., & Andersen, C. (1995). Strategies of knowledge acquisition. *Monographs of the Society for Research in Child Development, 60* (Whole No. 245).

Kuhn, D., & Park, S.-H. (2005). Epistemological understanding and the development of intellectual values. *International Journal of Educational Research, 43,* 111–124.

Kuhn, D., & Pease, M. (2008). What needs to develop in the development of inquiry skills? *Cognition and Instruction, 26,* 512–599.

Kuhn, D., & Pease, M. (2010). The dual components of developing strategy use: Production and inhibition. In H. S. Waters & W. Schneider (Eds.), *Metacognition, strategy use, and instruction* (pp. 135–159). New York, NY: Guilford Press.

Kuhn, D., & Weinstock, M. (2002). What is epistemological thinking and why does it matter? In B. K. Hofer & P. R. Pintrich (Eds.), *Personal epistemology: The psychology of beliefs about knowledge and knowing* (pp. 121–144). Mahwah, NJ: Erlbaum.

Langer, E. J. (2000). Mindful learning. *Current Directions in Psychological Science, 9,* 220–223.

Lee, J., & Shute, V. J. (2010). Personal and social-contextual factors in K–12 academic performance: An integrative perspective on student learning. *Educational Psychologist, 45,* 185–202.

Lee, K., Ng, E. L., & Ng, S. F. (2009). The contributions of working memory and executive function to problem representation and solution generation in algebraic word problems. *Journal of Educational Psychology, 101,* 373–387.

Leelawong, K., & Biswas, G. (2008). Designing learning by teachable agents: The Betty's Brain system. *International Journal of Artificial Intelligence, 18*(3), 181–208.

Levstik, L. S. (2011). Learning history. In R. E. Mayer & P. A. Alexander (Eds.), *Handbook of research on learning and instruction* (pp. 108–126). New York, NY: Routledge.

Li, J. (2005). Mind or virtue: Western and Chinese beliefs about learning. *Current Directions in Psychological Science, 14,* 190–194.

Li, J., & Fischer, K. W. (2004). Thought and affect in American and Chinese learners' beliefs about learning. In D. Y. Dai & R. J. Sternberg (Eds.), *Motivation, emotion, and cognition: Integrative perspectives on intellectual functioning and development* (pp. 385–418). Mahwah, NJ: Erlbaum.

Liew, J., McTigue, E. M., Barrois, L., & Hughes, J. N. (2008). Adaptive and effortful control and academic self-efficacy beliefs on literacy and math achievement: A longitudinal study on 1st through 3rd graders. *Early Childhood Research Quarterly, 23,* 515–526.

Linn, M. C. (2008). Teaching for conceptual change: Distinguish or extinguish ideas. In S. Vosniadou (Ed.), *International handbook of research on conceptual change* (pp. 694–722). New York, NY: Routledge.

Linn, M. C., & Eylon, B.-S. (2011). *Science learning and instruction: Taking advantage of technology to promote knowledge integration.* New York, NY: Routledge.

Lodico, M. G., Ghatala, E. S., Levin, J. R., Pressley, M., & Bell, J. A. (1983). The effects of strategy monitoring training on children's selection of effective memory strategies. *Journal of Experimental Child Psychology, 35,* 273–277.

Loranger, A. L. (1994). The study strategies of successful and unsuccessful high school students. *Journal of Reading Behavior, 26,* 347–360.

Losh, S. C. (2003). On the application of social cognition and social location to creating causal explanatory structures. *Educational Research Quarterly, 26*(3), 17–33.

Lovett, S. B., & Flavell, J. H. (1990). Understanding and remembering: Children's knowledge about the differential effects of strategy and task variables on comprehension and memorization. *Child Development, 61,* 1842–1858.

Lubart, T. I., & Mouchiroud, C. (2003). Creativity: A source of difficulty in problem solving. In J. E. Davidson & R. J. Sternberg (Eds.), *The psychology of problem solving* (pp. 127–148). Cambridge, England: Cambridge University Press.

Luchins, A. S. (1942). Mechanization in problem solving: The effect of Einstellung. *Psychological Monographs, 54* (Whole No. 248).

Luciana, M., Conklin, H. M., Hooper, C. J., & Yarger, R. S. (2005). The development of nonverbal working memory and executive control processes in adolescents. *Child Development, 76,* 697–712.

MacDonald, S., Uesiliana, K., & Hayne, H. (2000). Cross-cultural and gender differences in childhood amnesia. *Memory, 8,* 365–376.

Mace, F. C., Belfiore, P. J., & Hutchinson, J. M. (2001). Operant theory and research on self-regulation. In B. Zimmerman & D. Schunk (Eds.), *Learning and academic achievement: Theoretical perspectives* (pp. 39–65). Mahwah, NJ: Erlbaum.

Manning, F. H., Lawless, K. A., Goldman, S. R., & Braasch, J. L. G. (2011, April). *Evaluating the usefulness of multiple sources with respect to an inquiry question: Middle school students' analysis and ranking of Internet search results.* Paper presented at the annual meeting of the American Educational Research Association, New Orleans, LA.

Marchand, G., & Skinner, E. A. (2007). Motivational dynamics of children's academic help-seeking and concealment. *Journal of Educational Psychology, 99,* 65–82.

Marcus, G. (2008). *Kluge: The haphazard construction of the human mind.* Boston, MA: Houghton Mifflin.

Marks, H. M. (2000). Student engagement in instructional activity: Patterns in the elementary, middle, and high school years. *American Educational Research Journal, 37,* 153–184.

Mason, L. (2010). Beliefs about knowledge and revision of knowledge: On the importance of epistemic beliefs for intentional conceptual change in elementary and middle school students. In L. D. Bendixen & F. C. Feucht (Eds.), *Personal epistemology in the classroom: Theory, research, and implications for practice* (pp. 258–291). Cambridge, England: Cambridge University Press.

Matthews, J. S., Ponitz, C. C., & Morrison, F. J. (2009). Early gender differences in self-regulation and academic achievement. *Journal of Educational Psychology, 101,* 689–704.

Mayer, R. E. (2010b). Merlin C. Wittrock's enduring contributions to the science of learning. *Educational Psychologist, 45,* 46–50.

Mayer, R. E. (2013). Problem solving. In D. Reisberg (Ed.), *The Oxford handbook of cognitive psychology* (pp. 769–778). New York, NY: Oxford University Press.

Mayer, R. E., & Wittrock, M. C. (1996). Problem-solving transfer. In D. C. Berliner & R. C. Calfee (Eds.), *Handbook of educational psychology.* New York, NY: Macmillan.

Mayer, R. E., & Wittrock, M. C. (2006). Problem solving. In P. A. Alexander & P. H. Winne (Eds.), *Handbook of educational psychology* (2nd ed., pp. 287–303). Mahwah, NJ: Erlbaum.

Mayfield, K. H., & Chase, P. N. (2002). The effects of cumulative practice on mathematics problem solving. *Journal of Applied Behavior Analysis, 35,* 105–123.

McCaslin, M., & Good, T. L. (1996). The informal curriculum. In D. C. Berliner & R. C. Calfee (Eds.), *Handbook of educational psychology.* New York, NY: Macmillan.

McCaslin, M., & Hickey, D. T. (2001). Self-regulated learning and academic achievement: A Vygotskian view. In B. Zimmerman & D. Schunk (Eds.), *Self-regulated learning and academic achievement: Theory, research, and practice* (2nd ed., pp. 227–252). Mahwah, NJ: Erlbaum.

McCrudden, M. T., & Schraw, G. (2007). Relevance and goal-focusing in text processing. *Educational Psychology Review, 19,* 113–139.

McDaniel, M. A., & Einstein, G. O. (1989). Material-appropriate processing: A contextualist approach to reading and studying strategies. *Educational Psychology Review, 1,* 113–145.

McKeown, M. G., & Beck, I. L. (2009). The role of metacognition in understanding and supporting reading comprehension. In D. J. Hacker, J. Dunlosky, & A. C. Graesser (Eds.), *Handbook of metacognition in education* (pp. 7–25). New York, NY: Routledge.

McMillan, J. H. (2010). The practical implications of educational aims and contexts for formative assessment. In H. L. Andrade & G. J. Cizek (Eds.), *Handbook of formative assessment* (pp. 41–58). New York, NY: Routledge.

McNamara, D. S., & Magliano, J. P. (2009). Self-explanation and metacognition: The dynamics of reading. In D. J. Hacker, J. Dunlosky, & A. C. Graesser (Eds.), *Handbook of metacognition in education* (pp. 60–81). New York, NY: Routledge.

Meichenbaum, D., & Goodman, J. (1971). Training impulsive children to talk to themselves: A means of developing self-control. *Journal of Abnormal Psychology, 77,* 115–126.

Meltzer, L. (Ed.). (2007). *Executive function in education: From theory to practice.* New York, NY: Guilford Press.

Meltzer, L., & Krishnan, K. (2007). Executive function difficulties and learning disabilities: Understandings and misunderstandings. In L. Meltzer (Ed.), *Executive function in education: From theory to practice* (pp. 77–105). New York, NY: Guilford Press.

Meltzer, L., Pollica, L. S., & Barzillai, M. (2007). Executive function in the classroom: Embedding strategy instruction into daily teaching practices. In L. Meltzer (Ed.), *Executive function in education: From theory to practice* (pp. 165–193). New York, NY: Guilford Press.

Mergendoller, J. R., Markham, T., Ravitz, J., & Larmer, J. (2006). Pervasive management of project based learning: Teachers as guides and facilitators. In C. M. Evertson & C. S. Weinstein (Eds.), *Handbook of classroom management: Research, practice, and contemporary issues* (pp. 583–615). Mahwah, NJ: Erlbaum.

Metzger, M. J., Flanagin, A. J., & Zwarun, L. (2003). College student Web use, perceptions of information credibility, and verification behavior. *Computers and Education, 41,* 271–290.

Miller, R. B., & Brickman, S. J. (2004). A model of future-oriented motivation and self-regulation. *Educational Psychology Review, 16,* 9–33.

Miller, S. D., Heafner, T., Massey, D., & Strahan, D. B. (2003, April). *Students' reactions to teachers' attempts to create the necessary conditions to promote the acquisition of self-regulation skills.* Paper presented at the annual meeting of the American Educational Research Association, Chicago, IL.

Minsky, M. (2006). *The emotion machine: Commonsense thinking, artificial intelligence, and the future of the human mind.* New York, NY: Simon and Schuster.

Mintzes, J. J., Wandersee, J. H., & Novak, J. D. (1997). Meaningful learning in science: The human constructivist perspective. In G. D. Phye (Ed.), *Handbook of academic learning: Construction of knowledge.* San Diego, CA: Academic Press.

Monte-Sano, C. (2008). Qualities of historical writing instruction: A comparative case study of two teachers' practices. *American Educational Research Journal, 45,* 1045–1079.

Moon, J. (2008). *Critical thinking: An exploration of theory and practice.* London, England: Routledge.

Morelli, G. A., & Rothbaum, F. (2007). Situating the child in context: Attachment relationships and self-regulation in different cultures. In S. Kitayama & D. Cohen (Eds.), *Handbook of cultural psychology* (pp. 500–527). New York, NY: Guilford Press.

Mueller, P. A., & Oppenheimer, D. M. (2014). The pen is mightier than the keyboard: Advantages of longhand over laptop note taking. *Psychological Science, 25,* 1159–1168.

Muis, K. R. (2004). Personal epistemology and mathematics: A critical review and synthesis of research. *Review of Educational Research, 74,* 317–377.

Muis, K. R. (2007). The role of epistemic beliefs in self-regulated learning. *Educational Psychologist, 42,* 173–190.

Muis, K. R., Bendixen, L. D., & Haerle, F. C. (2006). Domain-generality and domain-specificity in personal epistemology research: Philosophical and empirical reflections in the development of a theoretical framework. *Educational Psychology Review, 18,* 3–54.

Muis, K. R., & Duffy, M. C. (2013). Epistemic climate and epistemic change: Instruction designed to change students' beliefs and learning strategies and improve achievement. *Journal of Educational Psychology, 105,* 213–225.

Munakata, Y., Snyder, H. R., & Chatham, C. H. (2012). Developing cognitive control: Three key transitions. *Current Directions in Psychological Science, 21,* 71–77.

Murphy, P. K., & Mason, L. (2006). Changing knowledge and beliefs. In P. A. Alexander & P. H. Winne (Eds.), *Handbook of educational psychology* (2nd ed., pp. 305–324). Mahwah, NJ: Erlbaum.

Nesbit, J. C., & Adesope, O. O. (2006). Learning with concept and knowledge maps: A meta-analysis. *Review of Educational Research, 76,* 413–448.

Niu, W., & Zhou, Z. (2010). Creativity in mathematics teaching: A Chinese perspective. In R. A. Beghetto & J. C. Kaufman (Eds.), *Nurturing creativity in the classroom* (pp. 270–288). New York, NY: Cambridge University Press.

Nokes, J. D., & Dole, J. A. (2004). Helping adolescent readers through explicit strategy instruction. In T. L. Jetton & J. A. Dole (Eds.), *Adolescent literacy research and practice* (pp. 162–182). New York, NY: Guilford Press.

Novak, J. D. (1998). *Learning, creating, and using knowledge: Concept maps as facilitative tools in schools and corporations.* Mahwah, NJ: Erlbaum.

Nussbaum, E. M. (2008). Collaborative discourse, argumentation, and learning: Preface and literature review. *Contemporary Educational Psychology, 33,* 345–359.

Nussbaum, E. M., & Edwards, O. V. (2011). Critical questions and argument stratagems: A framework for enhancing and analyzing students' reasoning practices. *Journal of the Learning Sciences, 20,* 443–488.

O'Donnell, A. M., Hmelo-Silver, C. E., & Erkens, G. (Eds.). (2006). *Collaborative learning, reasoning, and technology.* Mahwah, NJ: Erlbaum.

Onosko, J. J., & Newmann, F. M. (1994). Creating more thoughtful learning environments. In J. N. Mangieri & C. C. Block (Eds.), *Advanced educational psychology: Enhancing mindfulness* (pp. 27–49). Fort Worth, TX: Harcourt Brace Jovanovich.

Ornstein, P. A., Grammer, J. K., & Coffman, J. L. (2010). Teachers' "mnemonic style" and the development of skilled memory. In H. S. Waters & W. Schneider (Eds.), *Metacognition, strategy use, and instruction* (pp. 23–53). New York, NY: Guilford Press.

Pajares, F. (2009). Toward a positive psychology of academic motivation: The role of self-efficacy beliefs. In R. Gilman, E. S. Huebner, & M. J. Furlong (Eds.), *Handbook of positive psychology in schools* (pp. 149–160). New York, NY: Routledge.

Paris, S. G., & Ayres, L. R. (1994). *Becoming reflective students and teachers with portfolios and authentic assessment.* Washington, DC: American Psychological Association.

Paris, S. G., & Paris, A. H. (2001). Classroom applications of research on self-regulated learning. *Educational Psychologist, 36*, 89–101.

Paxton, R. J. (1999). A deafening silence: History textbooks and the students who read them. *Review of Educational Research, 69*, 315–339.

Pea, R. D. (1987). Socializing the knowledge transfer problem. *International Journal of Educational Research, 11*, 639–663.

Perkins, D. N. (1990). The nature and nurture of creativity. In B. F. Jones & L. Idol (Eds.), *Dimensions of thinking and cognitive instruction* (pp. 415–443). Mahwah, NJ: Erlbaum.

Perkins, D. N. (1992). *Smart schools: From training memories to educating minds.* New York, NY: Free Press/Macmillan.

Perkins, D. N. (1995). *Outsmarting IQ: The emerging science of learnable intelligence.* New York, NY: Free Press.

Perkins, D., & Ritchhart, R. (2004). When is good thinking? In D. Y. Dai & R. J. Sternberg (Eds.), *Motivation, emotion, and cognition: Integrative perspectives on intellectual functioning and development* (pp. 351–384). Mahwah, NJ: Erlbaum.

Perkins, D. N., & Salomon, G. (2012). Knowledge to go: A motivational and dispositional view of transfer. *Educational Psychologist, 47*, 248–258.

Perkins, D. N., Tishman, S., Ritchhart, R., Donis, K., & Andrade, A. (2000). Intelligence in the wild: A dispositional view of intellectual traits. *Educational Psychology Review, 12*, 269–293.

Perry, M. (1991). Learning and transfer: Instructional conditions and conceptual change. *Cognitive Development, 6*, 449–468.

Perry, N. E. (1998). Young children's self-regulated learning and contexts that support it. *Journal of Educational Psychology, 90*, 715–729.

Perry, N. E., VandeKamp, K. O., Mercer, L. K., & Nordby, C. J. (2002). Investigating teacher-student interactions that foster self-regulated learning. *Educational Psychologist, 37*, 5–15.

Peverly, S. T., Brobst, K. E., Graham, M., & Shaw, R. (2003). College adults are not good at self-regulation: A study on the relationship of self-regulation, note taking, and test taking. *Journal of Educational Psychology, 95*, 335–346.

Pillow, B. H. (2002). Children's and adults' evaluation of the certainty of deductive inferences, inductive inferences, and guesses. *Child Development, 73*, 779–792.

Pintrich, P. R., & De Groot, E. V. (1990). Motivational and self-regulated learning components of classroom academic performance. *Journal of Educational Psychology, 82*, 33–40.

Plass, J. L., Kalyuga, S., & Leutner, D. (2010). Individual differences and Cognitive Load Theory. In J. L. Plass, R. Moreno, & R. Brünken (Eds.), *Cognitive Load Theory* (pp. 65–87). Cambridge, England: Cambridge University Press.

Polman, J. L. (2004). Dialogic activity structures for project-based learning environments. *Cognition and Instruction, 22*, 431–466.

Posner, M. I., & Rothbart, M. K. (2007). *Educating the human brain.* Washington, DC: American Psychological Association.

Prawat, R. S. (1989). Promoting access to knowledge, strategy, and disposition in students: A research synthesis. *Review of Educational Research, 59*, 1–41.

Pressley, M., El-Dinary, P. B., Marks, M. B., Brown, R., & Stein, S. (1992). Good strategy instruction is motivating and interesting. In K. A. Renninger, S. Hidi, & A. Krapp (Eds.), *The role of interest in learning and development* (pp. 333–358). Mahwah, NJ: Erlbaum.

Pressley, M., & Hilden, K. (2006). Cognitive strategies: Production deficiencies and successful strategy instruction everywhere. In W. Damon & R. M. Lerner (Series Eds.), D. Kuhn & R. Siegler (Vol. Eds.), *Handbook of child psychology: Vol. 2. Cognition, perception, and language* (6th ed., pp. 511–556). New York, NY: Wiley.

Pugh, K. J., & Bergin, D. A. (2006). Motivational influences on transfer. *Educational Psychologist, 41*, 147–160.

Pugh, K. J., Bergin, D. A., & Rocks, J. (2003, April). *Motivation and transfer: A critical review.* Paper presented at the annual meeting of the American Educational Research Association, Chicago, IL.

Purdie, N., & Hattie, J. (1996). Cultural differences in the use of strategies for self-regulated learning. *American Educational Research Journal, 33*, 845–871.

Qian, G., & Pan, J. (2002). A comparison of epistemological beliefs and learning from science text between American and Chinese high school students. In B. K. Hofer & P. R. Pintrich (Eds.), *Personal epistemology: The psychology of beliefs about knowledge and knowing* (pp. 365–385). Mahwah, NJ: Erlbaum.

Quintana, C., Zhang, M., & Krajcik, J. (2005). A framework for supporting metacognitive aspects of online inquiry through software-based scaffolding. *Educational Psychologist, 40*, 235–244.

Rawson, K. A., & Kintsch, W. (2005). Rereading effects depend on time of test. *Journal of Educational Psychology, 97*, 70–80.

Reid, R., Trout, A. L., & Schartz, M. (2005). Self-regulation interventions for children with attention deficit/hyperactivity disorder. *Exceptional Children, 71*, 361–377.

Reiter, S. N. (1994). Teaching dialogically: Its relationship to critical thinking in college students. In P. R. Pintrich, D. R. Brown, & C. E. Weinstein (Eds.), *Student motivation, cognition, and learning: Essays in honor of Wilbert J. McKeachie* (pp. 275-310). Mahwah, NJ: Erlbaum.

Renkl, A. (2011). Instruction based on examples. In R. E. Mayer & P. A. Alexander (Eds.), *Handbook of research on learning and instruction* (pp. 272–295). New York, NY: Routledge.

Renkl, A., Mandl, H., & Gruber, H. (1996). Inert knowledge: Analyses and remedies. *Educational Psychologist, 31*, 115–121.

Resnick, L. B. (1989). Developing mathematical knowledge. *American Psychologist, 44*, 162–169.

Reynolds, R. E., & Shirey, L. L. (1988). The role of attention in studying and learning. In C. E. Weinstein, E. T. Goetz, & P. A. Alexander (Eds.), *Learning and study strategies: Issues in assessment, instruction, and evaluation* (pp. 77–100). San Diego, CA: Academic Press.

Rittle-Johnson, B., Siegler, R. S., & Alibali, M. W. (2001). Developing conceptual understanding and procedural skill in mathematics: An iterative process. *Journal of Educational Psychology, 93*, 346–362.

Robinson, D. H., & Kiewra, K. A. (1995). Visual argument: Graphic organizers are superior to outlines in improving learning from text. *Journal of Educational Psychology, 87*, 455–467.

Roderick, M., & Camburn, E. (1999). Risk and recovery from course failure in the early years of high school. *American Educational Research Journal, 36*, 303–343.

Rogoff, B., Moore, L., Najafi, B., Dexter, A., Correa-Chávez, M., & Solís, J. (2007). Children's development of cultural repertoires through participation in everyday routines and practices. In J. E. Grusec & P. D. Hastings (Eds.), *Handbook of socialization: Theory and research* (pp. 490–515). New York, NY: Guilford Press.

Rohrer, D., & Pashler, H. (2010). Recent research on human learning challenges conventional instructional strategies. *Educational Researcher, 39*, 406–412.

Rosenshine, B., Meister, C., & Chapman, S. (1996). Teaching students to generate questions: A review of the intervention studies. *Review of Educational Research, 66*, 181–221.

Rothbart, M. K. (2011). *Becoming who we are: Temperament and personality in development.* New York, NY: Guilford Press.

Rule, D. C., & Bendixen, L. D. (2010). The integrative model of personal epistemology development: Theoretical underpinnings and implications for education. In L. D. Bendixen & F. C. Feucht (Eds.), *Personal epistemology in the classroom: Theory, research, and implications for practice* (pp. 94–123). Cambridge, England: Cambridge University Press.

Runco, M. A., & Chand, I. (1995). Cognition and creativity. *Educational Psychology Review, 7*, 243–267.

Ryan, A. M., Pintrich, P. R., & Midgley, C. (2001). Avoiding seeking help in the classroom: Who and why? *Educational Psychology Review, 13*, 93–114.

Ryan, R. M., & Brown, K. W. (2005). Legislating competence: High-stakes testing policies and their relations with psychological theories and research. In A. J. Elliot & C. S. Dweck (Eds.), *Handbook of competence and motivation* (pp. 354–372). New York, NY: Guilford Press.

Sandoval, W. A., Sodian, B., Koerber, S., & Wong, J. (2014). Developing children's early competencies to engage with science. *Educational Psychologist, 49*, 139–152.

Sarama, J., & Clements, D. H. (2009). "Concrete" computer manipulatives in mathematics education. *Child Development Perspectives, 3*, 145–150.

Schmidt, R. A., & Bjork, R. A. (1992). New conceptualizations of practice: Common principles in three paradigms suggest new concepts for training. *Psychological Science, 3*, 207–217.

Schneider, W. (2010). Metacognition and memory development in childhood and adolescence. In H. S. Waters & W. Schneider (Eds.), *Metacognition, strategy use, and instruction* (pp. 54–81). New York, NY: Guilford Press.

Schnittka, C. G., Brandt, C. B., Jones, B. D., & Evans, M. A. (2012). Informal engineering education after school: Employing the studio model for motivation and identification in STEM domains. *Advances in Engineering Education, 3*(2), 1–31.

Schoenfeld, A. H., & Hermann, D. J. (1982). Problem perception and knowledge structure in expert and novice mathematical problem solvers. *Journal of Experimental Psychology: Learning, Memory, and Cognition, 8*, 484–494.

Schommer, M. (1990). Effects of beliefs about the nature of knowledge on comprehension. *Journal of Educational Psychology, 82*, 498–504.

Schommer, M. (1994a). An emerging conceptualization of epistemological beliefs and their role in learning. In R. Garner & P. A. Alexander (Eds.), *Beliefs about text and instruction with text* (pp. 25–40). Mahwah, NJ: Erlbaum.

Schommer, M. (1994b). Synthesizing epistemological belief research: Tentative understandings and provocative confusions. *Educational Psychology Review, 6*, 293–319.

Schommer, M. (1997). The development of epistemological beliefs among secondary students: A longitudinal study. *Journal of Educational Psychology, 89*, 37–40.

Schommer, M., Calvert, C., Gariglietti, G., & Bajaj, A. (1997). The development of epistemological beliefs among secondary students: A longitudinal study. *Journal of Educational Psychology, 89*, 37–40.

Schommer-Aikins, M. (2002). An evolving theoretical framework for an epistemological belief system. In B. K. Hofer & P. R. Pintrich (Eds.), *Personal epistemology: The psychology of beliefs about knowledge and knowing* (pp. 103–118). Mahwah, NJ: Erlbaum.

Schommer-Aikins, M., Bird, M., & Bakken, L. (2010). Manifestations of an epistemological belief system in preschool to grade twelve classrooms. In L. D. Bendixen & F. C. Feucht (Eds.), *Personal epistemology in the classroom: Theory, research, and implications for practice* (pp. 31–54). Cambridge, England: Cambridge University Press.

Schraw, G., & Moshman, D. (1995). Metacognitive theories. *Educational Psychology Review, 7*, 351–371.

Schwartz, D. L., Chase, C. C., & Bransford, J. D. (2012). Resisting overzealous transfer: Coordinating previously successful routines with needs for new learning. *Educational Psychologist, 47*, 204–214.

Segedy, J. R., Kinnebrew, J. S., & Biswas, G. (2013). The effect of contextualized conversational feedback in a complex open-ended learning environment. *Educational Technology Research and Development, 61*(1), 71–89.

Shanahan, T. (2004). Overcoming the dominance of communication: Writing to think and to learn. In T. L. Jetton & J. A. Dole (Eds.), *Adolescent literacy research and practice* (pp. 59–74). New York, NY: Guilford Press.

Shepard, L., Hammerness, K., Darling-Hammond, L., & Rust, F. (with Snowden, J. B., Gordon, E., Gutierrez, C., & Pacheco, A.). (2005). Assessment. In L. Darling-Hammond & J. Bransford (Eds.), *Preparing teachers for a changing world: What teachers should learn and be able to do* (pp. 275–326). San Francisco, CA: Jossey-Bass/Wiley.

Short, E. J., Schatschneider, C. W., & Friebert, S. E. (1993). Relationship between memory and metamemory performance: A comparison of specific and general strategy knowledge. *Journal of Educational Psychology, 85*, 412–423.

Siegler, R. S., & Lin, X. (2010). Self-explanations promote children's learning. In H. S. Waters & W. Schneider (Eds.), *Metacognition, strategy use, and instruction* (pp. 85–112). New York, NY: Guilford Press.

Simonton, D. K. (2000). Creativity: Cognitive, personal, developmental, and social aspects. *American Psychologist, 55*, 151–158.

Sinatra, G. M., Kienhues, D., & Hofer, B. K. (2014). Addressing challenges to public understanding of science: Epistemic cognition, motivated reasoning, and conceptual change. *Educational Psychologist, 49*, 123–138.

Sinatra, G. M., & Pintrich, P. R. (Eds.). (2003). *Intentional conceptual change.* Mahwah, NJ: Erlbaum.

Smith, C. L., Maclin, D., Houghton, C., & Hennessey, M. G. (2000). Sixth-grade students' epistemologies of science: The impact of school science experiences on epistemological development. *Cognition and Instruction, 18*, 349–422.

Southerland, S. A., & Sinatra, G. M. (2003). Learning about biological evolution: A special case of intentional conceptual change. In G. M. Sinatra & P. R. Pintrich (Eds.), *Intentional conceptual change* (pp. 317–345). Mahwah, NJ: Erlbaum.

Spiro, R. J., & DeSchryver, M. (2009). Constructivism: When it's the wrong idea and when it's the only idea. In S. Tobias &

T. M. Duffy (Eds.), *Constructivist instruction: Success or failure?* (pp. 106–123). New York, NY: Routledge.

Squire, K. (2011). *Video games and learning: Teaching and participatory culture in the digital age.* New York, NY: Teachers College Press.

Stahl, S. A., & Shanahan, C. (2004). Learning to think like a historian: Disciplinary knowledge through critical analysis of multiple documents. In T. L. Jetton & J. A. Dole (Eds.), *Adolescent literacy research and practice* (pp. 94–115). New York, NY: Guilford Press.

Stanovich, K. E. (1999). *Who is rational? Studies of individual differences in reasoning.* Mahwah, NJ: Erlbaum.

Steinberg, L. (2009). Should the science of adolescent brain development inform public policy? *American Psychologist, 64,* 739–750.

Sternberg, R. J. (2010). Teaching for creativity. In R. A. Beghetto & J. C. Kaufman (Eds.), *Nurturing creativity in the classroom* (pp. 394–414). New York, NY: Cambridge University Press.

Stone, J. R., III, Alfeld, C., & Pearson, D. (2008). Rigor *and* relevance: Enhancing high school students' math skills through career and technical education. *American Educational Research Journal, 45,* 767–795.

Stone, N. J. (2000). Exploring the relationship between calibration and self-regulated learning. *Educational Psychology Review, 12,* 437–475.

Stright, A. D., Neitzel, C., Sears, K. G., & Hoke-Sinex, L. (2001). Instruction begins in the home: Relations between parental instruction and children's self-regulation in the classroom. *Journal of Educational Psychology, 93,* 456–466.

Sweller, J. (1994). Cognitive load theory, learning difficulty, and instructional design. *Learning and Instruction, 4,* 295–312.

Sweller, J. (2009a). Cognitive bases of human creativity. *Educational Psychology Review, 21,* 11–19.

Tate, W. F. (1995). Returning to the root: A culturally relevant approach to mathematics pedagogy. *Theory into Practice, 34,* 166–173.

Thomas, J. W. (1993). Expectations and effort: Course demands, students' study practices, and academic achievement. In T. M. Tomlinson (Ed.), *Motivating students to learn: Overcoming barriers to high achievement* (pp. 139–176). Berkeley, CA: McCutchan.

Torrance, E. P. (1970). *Encouraging creativity in the classroom.* Dubuque, IA: Wm. C. Brown.

Turner, J. C., Meyer, D. K., Cox, K. E., Logan, C., DiCintio, M., & Thomas, C. T. (1998). Creating contexts for involvement in mathematics. *Journal of Educational Psychology, 90,* 730–745.

Tyler, K. M., Uqdah, A. L., Dillihunt, M. L., Beatty-Hazelbaker, R., Connor, T., Gadson, N., . . . Stevens, R. (2008). Cultural discontinuity: Toward a quantitative investigation of a major hypothesis in education. *Educational Researcher, 37,* 280–297.

Usher, E. L. (2009). Sources of middle school students' self-efficacy in mathematics: A qualitative investigation. *American Educational Research Journal, 46,* 275–314.

Valiente, C., Lemery-Chalfant, K., & Swanson, J. (2010). Prediction of kindergartners' academic achievement from their effortful control and emotionality: Evidence for direct and moderated relations. *Journal of Educational Psychology, 102,* 550–560.

Valiente, C., Lemery-Chalfant, K., Swanson, J., & Reiser, M. (2008). Prediction of children's academic competence from their effortful control, relationships, and classroom participation. *Journal of Educational Psychology, 100,* 67–77.

VanSledright, B., & Limón, M. (2006). Learning and teaching social studies: A review of cognitive research in history and geography. In P. A. Alexander & P. H. Winne (Eds.), *Handbook of educational psychology* (2nd ed., pp. 545–570). Mahwah, NJ: Erlbaum.

Vaughn, S., Klingner, J. K., Swanson, E. A., Boardman, A. G., Roberts, G., Mohammed, S. S., & Stillman-Spisak, S. J. (2011). Efficacy of collaborative strategic reading with middle school students. *American Educational Research Journal, 48,* 938–964.

Veenman, M. V. J. (2011). Learning to self-monitor and self-regulate. In R. E. Mayer & P. A. Alexander (Eds.), *Handbook of research on learning and instruction* (pp. 197–218). New York, NY: Routledge.

Velanova, K., Wheeler, M. E., & Luna, B. (2008). Maturational changes in anterior cingulate and frontoparietal recruitment support the development of error processing and inhibitory control. *Cerebral Cortex, 18,* 2505–2522.

Vintere, P., Hemmes, N. S., Brown, B. L., & Poulson, C. L. (2004). Gross-motor skill acquisition by preschool dance students under self-instruction procedures. *Journal of Applied Behavior Analysis, 37,* 305–322.

Volet, S., Vaura, M., & Salonen, P. (2009). Self- and social regulation in learning contexts: An integrative perspective. *Educational Psychologist, 44,* 215–226.

Vosniadou, S. (1991). Conceptual development in astronomy. In S. M. Glynn, R. H. Yeany, & B. K. Britton (Eds.), *The psychology of learning science.* Hillsdale, NJ: Erlbaum.

Vye, N. J., Schwartz, D. L., Bransford, J. D., Barron, B. J., Zech, L., & The Cognition and Technology Group at Vanderbilt. (1998). SMART environments that support monitoring, reflection, and revision. In D. J. Hacker, J. Dunlosky, & A. C. Graesser (Eds.), *Metacognition in educational theory and practice* (pp. 305–346). Mahwah, NJ: Erlbaum.

Vygotsky, L. S. (1962). *Thought and language* (E. Haufmann & G. Vakar, Eds. and Trans.). Cambridge, MA: MIT Press.

Wade, S. E. (1992). How interest affects learning from text. In K. A. Renninger, S. Hidi, & A. Krapp (Eds.), *The role of interest in learning and development.* Mahwah, NJ: Erlbaum.

Wade-Stein, D., & Kintsch, E. (2004). Summary Street: Interactive computer support for writing. *Cognition and Instruction, 22,* 333–362.

Wagner, J. F. (2010). A transfer-in-pieces consideration of the perception of structure in the transfer of learning. *Journal of the Learning Sciences, 19,* 443–479.

Walkington, C., Sherman, M., & Petrosino, A. (2012). "Playing the game" of story problems: Coordinated situation-based reasoning with algebraic representation. *Journal of Mathematical Behavior, 31,* 174–195.

Wang, Q., & Ross, M. (2007). Culture and memory. In S. Kitayama & D. Cohen (Eds.), *Handbook of cultural psychology* (pp. 645–667). New York, NY: Guilford Press.

Wasley, P. A., Hampel, R. L., & Clark, R. W. (1997). *Kids and school reform.* San Francisco, CA: Jossey-Bass.

Webber, J., Scheuermann, B., McCall, C., & Coleman, M. (1993). Research on self-monitoring as a behavior management technique in special education classrooms: A descriptive review. *Remedial and Special Education, 14*(2), 38–56.

Wellman, H. M. (1985). The child's theory of mind: The development of conceptions of cognition. In S. R. Yussen (Ed.), *The growth of reflection in children.* San Diego, CA: Academic Press.

Wellman, H. M. (1990). *The child's theory of mind.* Cambridge, MA: MIT Press.

Wentzel, K. R., & Watkins, D. E. (2011). Instruction based on peer interactions. In R. E. Mayer & P. A. Alexander (Eds.), *Handbook of research on learning and instruction* (pp. 322–343). New York, NY: Routledge.

West, R. F., Toplak, M. E., & Stanovich, K. E. (2008). Heuristics and biases as measures of critical thinking: Associations with cognitive ability and thinking dispositions. *Journal of Educational Psychology, 100,* 930–941.

Wickelgren, W. A. (1974). *How to solve problems: Elements of a theory of problems and problem solving.* San Francisco, CA: Freeman.

Wiley, J., Goldman, S. R., Graesser, A. C., Sanchez, C. A., Ash, I. K., & Hemmerich, J. A. (2009). Source evaluation, comprehension, and learning in Internet science inquiry tasks. *American Educational Research Journal, 46,* 1060–1106.

Williams, J. P., Stafford, K. B., Lauer, K. D., Hall, K. M., & Pollini, S. (2009). Embedding reading comprehension training in content-area instruction. *Journal of Educational Psychology, 101,* 1–20.

Wilson, B. L., & Corbett, H. D. (2001). *Listening to urban kids: School reform and the teachers they want.* Albany, NY: State University of New York Press.

Winne, P. H. (1995). Inherent details in self-regulated learning. *Educational Psychologist, 30,* 173–187.

Winne, P. H., & Hadwin, A. F. (1998). Studying as self-regulated learning. In D. J. Hacker, J. Dunlosky, & A. C. Graesser (Eds.), *Metacognition in educational theory and practice* (pp. 277–304). Mahwah, NJ: Erlbaum.

Winters, F. I., Greene, J. A., & Costich, C. M. (2008). Self-regulation of learning within computer-based learning environments: A critical analysis. *Educational Psychology Review, 20,* 429–444.

Wirkala, C., & Kuhn, D. (2011). Problem-based learning in K–12 education: Is it effective and how does it achieve its effects? *American Educational Research Journal, 48,* 1157–1186.

Wolters, C. A. (2003). Regulation of motivation: Evaluating an underemphasized aspect of self-regulated learning. *Educational Psychologist, 38,* 189–205.

Wolters, C. A., & Rosenthal, H. (2000). The relation between students' motivational beliefs and their use of motivational regulation strategies. *International Journal of Educational Research, 33,* 801–820.

Wong, B. Y. L. (1985). Self-questioning instructional research: A review. *Review of Educational Research, 55,* 227–268.

Wood, E., Willoughby, T., McDermott, C., Motz, M., Kaspar, V., & Ducharme, M. J. (1999). Developmental differences in study behavior. *Journal of Educational Psychology, 91,* 527–536.

Yang, F.-Y., & Tsai, C.-C. (2010). An epistemic framework for scientific reasoning in informal contexts. In L. D. Bendixen & F. C. Feucht (Eds.), *Personal epistemology in the classroom: Theory, research, and implications for practice* (pp. 124–162). Cambridge, England: Cambridge University Press.

Zhong, C.-B., Dijksterhuis, A., & Galinsky, A. D. (2008). The merits of unconscious thought in creativity. *Psychological Science, 19,* 912–918.

Zimmerman, B. J. (1998). Developing self-fulfilling cycles of academic regulation: An analysis of exemplary instructional models. In D. H. Schunk & B. J. Zimmerman (Eds.), *Self-regulated learning: From teaching to self-reflective practice* (pp. 1–19). New York, NY: Guilford Press.

Zimmerman, B. J. (2004). Sociocultural influence and students' development of academic self-regulation: A social-cognitive perspective. In D. M. McInerney & S. Van Etten (Eds.), *Big theories revisited* (pp. 139–164). Greenwich, CT: Information Age.

Zimmerman, B. J., & Cleary, T. J. (2009). Motives to self-regulate learning: A social cognitive account. In K. R. Wentzel & A. Wigfield (Eds.), *Handbook of motivation at school* (pp. 247–264). New York, NY: Routledge.

Zimmerman, B. J., & Kitsantas, A. (2005). The hidden dimension of personal competence: Self-regulated learning and practice. In A. J. Elliot & C. S. Dweck (Eds.), *Handbook of competence and motivation* (pp. 509–526). New York, NY: Guilford Press.

Zimmerman, B. J., & Moylan, A. R. (2009). Self-regulation: Where metacognition and motivation intersect. In D. J. Hacker, J. Dunlosky, & A. C. Graesser (Eds.), *Handbook of metacognition in education* (pp. 299–315). New York, NY: Routledge.

Zimmerman, B. J., & Risemberg, R. (1997). Self-regulatory dimensions of academic learning and motivation. In G. D. Phye (Ed.), *Handbook of academic learning: Construction of knowledge* (pp. 105–125). San Diego, CA: Academic Press.

Zimmerman, B. J., & Schunk, D. H. (2004). Self-regulating intellectual processes and outcomes; A social cognitive perspective. In D. Y. Dai & R. J. Sternberg (Eds.), *Motivation, emotion, and cognition: Integrative perspectives on intellectual functioning and development* (pp. 323–349). Mahwah, NJ: Erlbaum.

Zohar, A., & Aharon-Kraversky, S. (2005). Exploring the effects of cognitive conflict and direct teaching for students of different academic levels. *Journal of Research in Science Teaching, 42,* 829–855.

Zusho, A., & Barnett, P. A. (2011). Personal and contextual determinants of ethnically diverse female high school students' patterns of academic help seeking and help avoidance in English and mathematics. *Contemporary Educational Psychology, 36,* 152–164.

CHAPTER 4

Achterberg, M., Peper, J. S., van Duijvenvoorde, A. C. K., Mandl, R. C. W., & Crone, E. A. (2016). Frontostriatal white matter integrity predicts development of delay of gratification: A longitudinal study. *The Journal of Neuroscience, 36*(6), 1954–1961.

Adger, C. T., Wolfram, W., & Christian, D. (2007). *Dialects in schools and communities* (2nd ed.). New York, NY: Routledge.

Afflerbach, P., & Cho, B.-Y. (2010). Determining and describing reading strategies: Internet and traditional forms of reading. In H. S. Waters & W. Schneider (Eds.), *Metacognition, strategy use, and instruction* (pp. 201–225). New York, NY: Guilford Press.

Aikens, N. L., & Barbarin, O. (2008). Socioeconomic differences in reading trajectories: The contribution of family, neighborhood, and school contexts. *Journal of Educational Psychology, 100,* 235–251.

Allison, K. W. (1998). Stress and oppressed social category membership. In J. Swim & C. Stangor (Eds.), *Prejudice: The target's perspective* (pp. 149–170). San Diego, CA: Academic Press.

Anderman, E. M., & Mueller, C. E. (2010). Middle school transitions and adolescent development. In J. Meece & J. Eccles (Eds.), *Handbook of research on schools, schooling, and human development* (pp. 198–215). Mahwah, NJ: Erlbaum.

Anderman, L. H., Patrick, H., Hruda, L. Z., & Linnenbrink, E. A. (2002). Observing classroom goal structures to clarify and expand goal theory. In C. Midgley (Ed.), *Goals, goal structures, and patterns of adaptive learning* (pp. 243–278). Mahwah, NJ: Erlbaum.

Anderson, C. A., Berkowitz, L., Donnerstein, E., Huesmann, L. R., Johnson, J. D., Linz, D., . . . Wartella, E. (2003). The influence of media violence on youth. *Psychological Science in the Public Interest, 4,* 81–110.

Anderson, L. H. (1999). *Speak.* New York, NY: Puffin Books.

Andriessen, J. (2006). Arguing to learn. In R. K. Sawyer (Ed.), *The Cambridge handbook of the learning sciences* (pp. 443–459). Cambridge, England: Cambridge University Press.

Arbib, M. (Ed.) (2005). *Action to language via the mirror neuron system.* New York, NY: Cambridge University Press.

Ash, D. (2002). Negotiations of thematic conversations about biology. In G. Leinhardt, K. Crowley, & K. Knutson (Eds.), *Learning conversations in museums* (pp. 357–400). Mahwah, NJ: Erlbaum.

Ashiabi, G. S., & O'Neal, K. K. (2008). A framework for understanding the association between food insecurity and children's developmental outcomes. *Child Development Perspectives, 2,* 71–77.

Astuti, R., Solomon, G. E. A., & Carey, S. (2004). Constraints on conceptual development. *Monographs of the Society for Research in Child Development, 69*(3, Serial No. 277).

Atance, C. M. (2008). Future thinking in young children. *Current Directions in Psychological Science, 17,* 295–298.

Atran, S., Medin, D. L., & Ross, N. O. (2005). The cultural mind: Environmental decision making and cultural modeling within and across populations. *Psychological Review, 112,* 744–776.

Au, K. H. (1980). Participation structures in a reading lesson with Hawaiian children: Analysis of a culturally appropriate instructional event. *Anthropology and Education Quarterly, 11,* 91–115.

Bandura, A. (1977). *Social learning theory.* Englewood Cliffs, NJ: Prentice Hall.

Bandura, A. (1986). *Social foundations of thought and action: A social cognitive theory.* Upper Saddle River, NJ: Prentice Hall.

Bandura, A. (1989). Human agency in social cognitive theory. *American Psychologist, 44,* 1175–1184.

Bandura, A. (2006). Toward a psychology of human agency. *Perspectives on Psychological Science, 1,* 164–180.

Bandura, A. (2008). Toward an agentic theory of the self. In H. W. Marsh, R. G. Craven, & D. M. McInerney (Eds.), *Self-processes, learning, and enabling human potential* (pp. 15–49). Charlotte, NC: Information Age.

Banks, J. A., & Banks, C. A. M. (Eds.). (1995). *Handbook of research on multicultural education.* New York, NY: Macmillan.

Banks, J., Cochran-Smith, M., Moll, L., Richert, A., Zeichner, K., LePage, P., Darling-Hammond, L., & Duffy, H. (with McDonald, M.). (2005). Teaching diverse learners. In L. Darling-Hammond & J. Bransford (Eds.), *Preparing teachers for a changing world: What teachers should learn and be able to do* (pp. 232–274). San Francisco, CA: Jossey-Bass/Wiley.

Barab, S. A., & Dodge, T. (2008). Strategies for designing embodied curriculum. In J. M. Spector, M. D. Merrill, J. van Merriënboer, & M. P. Driscoll (Eds.), *Handbook of research on educational communications and technology* (3rd ed., pp. 97–110). New York, NY: Erlbaum.

Barbarin, O., Mercado, M., & Jigjidsuren, D. (2010). Development for tolerance and respect for diversity in the context of immigration. In E. L. Grigorenko & R. Takanishi (Eds.), *Immigration, diversity, and education* (pp. 276–288). New York, NY: Routledge.

Barron, B. (2006). Interest and self-sustained learning as catalysts of development: A learning ecologies perspective. *Human Development, 49,* 193–224.

Bay-Hinitz, A. K., Peterson, R. F., & Quilitch, H. R. (1994). Cooperative games: A way to modify aggressive and cooperative behaviors in young children. *Journal of Applied Behavior Analysis, 27,* 435–446.

Becker, B. E., & Luthar, S. S. (2002). Social-emotional factors affecting achievement outcomes among disadvantaged students: Closing the achievement gap. *Educational Psychologist, 37,* 197–214.

Bendixen, L. D., & Rule, D. C. (2004). An integrative approach to personal epistemology: A guiding model. *Educational Psychologist, 39,* 69–80.

Benton, D. (2008). Nutrition and intellectual development. In P. C. Kyllonen, R. D. Roberts, & L. Stankov (Eds.), *Extending intelligence: Enhancement and new constructs* (pp. 373–394). New York, NY: Erlbaum/Taylor & Francis.

Bereiter, C., & Scardamalia, M. (2006). Education for the Knowledge Age: Design-centered models of teaching and instruction. In P. A. Alexander & P. H. Winne (Eds.), *Handbook of educational psychology* (2nd ed., pp. 695–713). Mahwah, NJ: Erlbaum.

Berg, W. K., Wacker, D. P., Cigrand, K., Merkle, S., Wade J., Henry, K., & Wang, Y.-C. (2007). Comparing functional

analysis and paired-choice assessment results in classroom settings. *Journal of Applied Behavior Analysis, 40,* 545–552.

Berliner, D. C. (2005, April). *Ignoring the forest, blaming the trees: Our impoverished view of educational reform.* Paper presented at the annual meeting of the American Educational Research Association, Montreal, Canada.

Berti, A. E., Toneatti, L., & Rosati, V. (2010). Children's conceptions about the origin of species: A study of Italian children's conceptions with and without instruction. *Journal of the Learning Sciences, 19,* 506–538.

Bielaczyc, K., & Collins, A. (2006). Fostering knowledge-creating communities. In A. M. O'Donnell, C. E. Hmelo-Silver, & G. Erkens (Eds.), *Collaborative learning, reasoning, and technology* (pp. 37–60). Mahwah, NJ: Erlbaum.

Bigler, R. S., & Liben, L. S. (2007). Developmental intergroup theory: Explaining and reducing children's social stereotyping and prejudice. *Current Directions in Psychological Science, 16,* 162–166.

Bondy, J. M., & Pennington, L. K. (2016): Illegal aliens, criminals, and hypersexual spitfires: Latin@ youth and pedagogies of citizenship in media texts. *The Social Studies.* Advance online publication. doi: 10.1080/00377996.2016.1149045

Bornstein, M. H., & Cote, L. R. (2010). Immigration and acculturation. In M. H. Bornstein (Ed.), *Handbook of cultural developmental science* (pp. 531–552). New York, NY: Psychology Press.

Boutte, G. S., & McCormick, C. B. (1992). Authentic multicultural activities: Avoiding pseudomulticulturalism. *Childhood Education, 68,* 140–144.

Bowman, L. G., Piazza, C. C., Fisher, W. W., Hagopian, L. P., & Kogan, J. S. (1997). Assessment of preference for varied versus constant reinforcers. *Journal of Applied Behavior Analysis, 30,* 451–458.

Boyanton, D. (2010). Behaviorism and its effect upon learning in the schools. In G. S. Goodman (Ed.), *Educational psychology reader: The art and science of how people learn* (pp. 49–65). New York, NY: Peter Lang.

Boyer, E., Miltenberger, R. G., Batsche, C., & Fogel, V. (2009). Video modeling by experts with video feedback to enhance gymnastics skills. *Journal of Applied Behavior Analysis, 42,* 855–860.

Braaksma, M. A. H., Rijlaarsdam, G., & van den Bergh, H. (2002). Observational learning and the effects of model-observer similarity. *Journal of Educational Psychology, 94,* 405–415.

Branch, C. (1999). Race and human development. In R. H. Sheets & E. R. Hollins (Eds.), *Racial and ethnic identity in school practices: Aspects of human development* (pp. 7–28). Mahwah, NJ: Erlbaum.

Braun, L. J. (1998). *The cat who saw stars.* New York, NY: G. P. Putnam's Sons.

Brayboy, B. M. J., & Searle, K. A. (2007). Thanksgiving and serial killers: Representations of American Indians in schools. In S. Books (Ed.), *Invisible children in the society and its schools* (3rd ed., pp. 173–192). Mahwah, NJ: Erlbaum.

Brody, G. H., Chen, Y.-F., Murry, V. M., Ge, X., Simons, R. L., Gibbons, F. X., . . . Cutrona, C. E. (2006). Perceived discrimination and the adjustment of African American youths: A five-year longitudinal analysis with contextual moderation effects. *Child Development, 77,* 1170–1189.

Bromme, R., Kienhues, D., & Porsch, T. (2010). Who knows what and who can we believe? Epistemological beliefs are beliefs about knowledge (mostly) to be attained from others. In L. D. Bendixen & F. C. Feucht (Eds.), *Personal epistemology in the classroom: Theory, research, and implications for practice* (pp. 163–193). Cambridge, England: Cambridge University Press.

Bronfenbrenner, U. (1989). Ecological systems theory. In R. Vasta (Ed.), *Annals of child development* (Vol. 6, pp. 187–251). Greenwich, CT: JAI Press.

Bronfenbrenner, U. (2005). *Making human beings human: Bioecological perspectives on human development.* Thousand Oaks, CA: Sage.

Bronfenbrenner, U., & Morris, P. A. (1998). The ecology of developmental processes. In W. Damon (Series Ed.) & R. M. Lerner (Vol. Ed.), *Handbook of child psychology: Vol. 1. Theoretical models of human development* (5th ed., pp. 993–1028). New York, NY: Wiley.

Brooks-Gunn, J., Linver, M. R., & Fauth, R. C. (2005). Children's competence and socioeconomic status in the family and neighborhood. In A. J. Elliot & C. S. Dweck (Eds.), *Handbook of competence and motivation* (pp. 414–435). New York, NY: Guilford Press.

Brophy, J. E., Alleman, J., & Knighton, B. (2009). *Inside the social studies classroom.* New York, NY: Routledge.

Brown, A. L., & Campione, J. C. (1994). Guided discovery in a community of learners. In K. McGilly (Ed.), *Classroom lessons:*

Integrating cognitive theory and classroom practice (pp. 229–270). Cambridge, MA: MIT Press.

Brown, J. S., Collins, A., & Duguid, P. (1989). Situated cognition and the culture of learning. *Educational Researcher, 18*(1), 32–42.

Brown, W. H., Fox, J. J., & Brady, M. P. (1987). Effects of spatial density on 3- and 4-year-old children's socially directed behavior during freeplay: An investigation of a setting factor. *Education and Treatment of Children, 10,* 247–258.

Bryan, J. H. (1975). Children's cooperation and helping behaviors. In E. M. Hetherington (Ed.), *Review of child development research* (Vol. 5, pp. 127–181). Chicago: University of Chicago Press.

Butler, D. L., & Winne, P. H. (1995). Feedback and self-regulated learning: A theoretical synthesis. *Review of Educational Research, 65,* 245–281.

Byrnes, J. P. (2003). Factors predictive of mathematics achievement in White, Black, and Hispanic 12th graders. *Journal of Educational Psychology, 95,* 316–326.

Cameron, L., Rutland, A., Brown, R., & Douch, R. (2006). Changing children's intergroup attitudes toward refugees: Testing different models of extended contact. *Child Development, 77,* 1208–1219.

Campione, J. C., Shapiro, A. M., & Brown, A. L. (1995). Forms of transfer in a community of learners: Flexible learning and understanding. In A. McKeough, J. Lupart, & A. Marini (Eds.), *Teaching for transfer: Fostering generalization in learning* (pp. 35–68). Mahwah, NJ: Erlbaum.

Carnagey, N. L., Anderson, C. A., & Bartholow, B. D. (2007). Media violence and social neuroscience: New questions and new opportunities. *Current Directions in Psychological Science, 16,* 178–182.

Castagno, A. E., & Brayboy, B. M. J. (2008). Culturally responsive schooling for Indigenous youth: A review of the literature. *Review of Educational Research, 78,* 941–993.

Chen, X., & Wang, L. (2010). China. In M. H. Bornstein (Ed.), *Handbook of cultural developmental science* (pp. 429–444). New York, NY: Psychology Press.

Chinn, C. A. (2006). Learning to argue. In A. M. O'Donnell, C. E. Hmelo-Silver, & G. Erkens (Eds.), *Collaborative learning, reasoning, and technology* (pp. 355–383). Mahwah, NJ: Erlbaum.

Chisholm, J. S. (1996). Learning "respect for everything": Navajo images of development. In C. P. Hwant, M. E. Lamb, & I. E. Sigel (Eds.), *Images of childhood* (pp. 167–183). Mahwah, NJ: Erlbaum.

Cizek, G. J. (2003). *Detecting and preventing classroom cheating: Promoting integrity in assessment.* Thousand Oaks, CA: Corwin.

Cohen, A. B. (2009). Many forms of culture. *American Psychologist, 64,* 194–204.

Cole, M. (2006). Culture and cognitive development in phylogenetic, historical and ontogenetic perspective. In W. Damon & R. M. Lerner (Series Eds.), D. Kuhn & R. Siegler (Vol. Eds.), *Handbook of child psychology: Vol. 2. Cognition, perception, and language* (6th ed., pp. 636–683). New York, NY: Wiley.

Cole, M., & Hatano, G. (2007). Cultural-historical activity theory: Integrating phylogeny, cultural history, and ontogenesis in cultural psychology. In S. Kitayama & D. Cohen (Eds.), *Handbook of cultural psychology* (pp. 109–135). New York, NY: Guilford Press.

Collins, A. (2006). Cognitive apprenticeship. In R. K. Sawyer (Ed.), *The Cambridge handbook of the learning sciences* (pp. 47–60). Cambridge, England: Cambridge University Press.

Conyers, C., Miltenberger, R., Maki, A., Barenz, R., Jurgens, M., Sailer, A., . . . Kopp, B. (2004). A comparison of response cost and differential reinforcement of other behavior to reduce disruptive behavior in a preschool classroom. *Journal of Applied Behavior Analysis, 37,* 411–415.

Cooney, C. (1997). *Wanted.* New York, NY: Scholastic.

Costa, A. L. (2008). *Meditative environments: Creating conditions for intellectual growth.* Thousand Oaks, CA: Corwin.

Craft, M. A., Alberg, S. R., & Heward, W. L. (1998). Teaching elementary students with developmental disabilities to recruit teacher attention in a general education classroom: Effects on teacher praise and academic productivity. *Journal of Applied Behavior Analysis, 31,* 399–415.

Croninger, R. G., & Valli, L. (2009). "Where is the action?" Challenges to studying the teaching of reading in elementary classrooms. *Educational Researcher, 38,* 100–108.

Cross, W. E., Jr., Strauss, L., & Fhagen-Smith, P. (1999). African American identity development across the life span: Educational implications. In R. H. Sheets & E. R. Hollins (Eds.), *Racial and ethnic identity in school practices: Aspects of human development* (pp. 29–47). Mahwah, NJ: Erlbaum.

Davis, O. S. P., Haworth, C. M. A., & Plomin, R. (2009). Dramatic increase in heritability of cognitive development from early to middle childhood: An 8-year longitudinal study of 8,700 pairs of twins. *Psychological Science, 20,* 1301–1308.

Decety, J., & Cacioppo, J. (2010). Frontiers in human neuroscience: The golden triangle and beyond. *Perspectives on Psychological Science, 5,* 767–771.

Dehaene, S. (2007). A few steps toward a science of mental life. *Mind, Brain, and Education, 1*(1), 28–47.

Deyhle, D., & LeCompte, M. (1999). Cultural differences in child development: Navajo adolescents in middle schools. In R. H. Sheets & E. R. Hollins (Eds.), *Racial and ethnic identity in school practices: Aspects of human development* (pp. 123–139). Mahwah, NJ: Erlbaum.

Deyhle, D., & Margonis, F. (1995). Navajo mothers and daughters: Schools, jobs, and the family. *Anthropology and Education Quarterly, 26,* 135–167.

Dilworth, J. E., & Moore, C. F. (2006). Mercy mercy me: Social injustice and the prevention of environmental pollutant exposures among ethnic minority and poor children. *Child Development, 77,* 247–265.

Dolezal, D. N., & Kurtz, P. F. (2010). Evaluation of combined-antecedent variables on functional analysis results and treatment of problem behavior in a school setting. *Journal of Applied Behavior Analysis, 43,* 309–314.

Dovidio, J. F., & Gaertner, S. L. (1999). Reducing prejudice: Combating intergroup biases. *Current Directions in Psychological Science, 8,* 101–105.

Duncan, G. J., & Magnuson, K. A. (2005). Can family socioeconomic resources account for racial and ethnic test score gaps? *The Future of Children, 15*(1), 35–54.

Eisenberg, M. B., & Berkowitz, R. E. (2011). *The Big6 workshop handbook: Implementation and impact* (4th ed.). Worthington, OH: Linworth.

Ellis, J., Fitzsimmons, S., & Small-McGinley, J. (2010). Encouraging the discouraged: Students' views for elementary classrooms. In G. S. Goodman (Ed.), *Educational psychology reader: The art and science of how people learn* (pp. 251–272). New York, NY: Peter Lang.

Engle, R. A. (2006). Framing interactions to foster generative learning: A situative explanation of transfer in a community of learners classroom. *Journal of the Learning Sciences, 15,* 451–498.

Engle, R. A., & Conant, F. R. (2002). Guiding principles for fostering productive disciplinary engagement: Explaining an emergent argument in a community of learners classroom. *Cognition and Instruction, 20,* 399–483.

Eriks-Brophy, A., & Crago, M. B. (1994). Transforming classroom discourse: An Inuit example. *Language and Education, 8*(3), 105–122.

Evans, E. M. (2008). Conceptual change and evolutionary biology: A developmental analysis. In S. Vosniadou (Ed.), *International handbook of research on conceptual change* (pp. 263–294). New York, NY: Routledge.

Evans, G. W. (2004). The environment of childhood poverty. *American Psychologist, 59,* 77–92.

Evans, G. W., & Kim, P. (2007). Childhood poverty and health: Cumulative risk exposure and stress dysregulation. *Psychological Science, 18,* 953–957.

Evans-Winters, V., & Ivie, C. (2009). Lost in the shuffle: Recalling a critical pedagogy for urban girls. In S. R. Steinberg (Ed.), *Diversity and multiculturalism: A reader* (pp. 411–421). New York, NY: Peter Lang.

Farkas, G. (2008). Quantitative studies of oppositional culture: Arguments and evidence. In J. U. Ogbu (Ed.), *Minority status, oppositional culture, and schooling* (pp. 312–347). New York, NY: Routledge.

Feinberg, M., & Willer, R. (2011). Apocalypse soon? Dire messages reduce belief in global warming by contradicting just-world beliefs. *Psychological Science, 22,* 34–38.

Feltz, D. L., Chase, M. A., Moritz, S. E., & Sullivan, P. J. (1999). A conceptual model of coaching efficacy: Preliminary investigation and instrument development. *Journal of Educational Psychology, 91,* 765–776.

Feuerstein, R, Feuerstein, R. S., & Falik, L. H. (2010). *Beyond smarter: Mediated learning and the brain's capacity for change.* New York, NY: Teachers College Press.

Fisher, W. W., & Mazur, J. E. (1997). Basic and applied research on choice responding. *Journal of Applied Behavior Analysis, 30,* 387–410.

Fletcher, J. M., Lyon, G. R., Fuchs, L. S., & Barnes, M. A. (2007). *Learning disabilities: From identification to intervention.* New York, NY: Guilford Press.

Flynn, J. R. (2003). Movies about intelligence: The limitations of *g. Current Directions in Psychological Science, 12,* 95–99.

Fonseca, B. A., & Chi, M. T. H. (2011). Instruction based on self-explanation. In R. E. Mayer & P. A. Alexander (Eds.), *Handbook of research on learning and instruction* (pp. 296–321). New York, NY: Routledge.

Fowler, S. A., & Baer, D. M. (1981). "Do I have to be good all day?" The timing of delayed reinforcement as a factor in generalization. *Journal of Applied Behavior Analysis, 14,* 13–24.

Frost, J. L., Shin, D., & Jacobs, P. J. (1998). Physical environments and children's play. In O. N. Saracho & B. Spodek (Eds.), *Multiple perspectives on play in early childhood education* (pp. 255–294). Albany: State University of New York Press.

Fuligni, A. J. (1998). The adjustment of children from immigrant families. *Current Directions in Psychological Science, 7,* 99–103.

Furnham, A. (2003). Belief in a just world: Research progress over the past decade. *Personality and Individual Differences, 34,* 795–817.

Gallese, V., Gernsbacher, M. A., Heyes, C., Hickok, G., & Iacoboni, M. (2011). Mirror neuron forum. *Perspectives on Psychological Science, 6,* 369–407.

Garcia, E. E. (1994). *Understanding and meeting the challenge of student cultural diversity.* Boston, MA: Houghton Mifflin.

Gauvain, M. (2001). *The social context of cognitive development.* New York, NY: Guilford Press.

Geiger, K. B., LeBlanc, L. A., Dillon, C. M., & Bates, S. L. (2010). An evaluation of preference for video and in vivo modeling. *Journal of Applied Behavior Analysis, 43,* 279–283.

Gerard, J. M., & Buehler, C. (2004). Cumulative environmental risk and youth maladjustment: The role of youth attributes. *Child Development, 75,* 1832–1849.

Gershoff, E. T., Aber, J. L., Raver, C. C., & Lennon, M. C. (2007). Income is not enough: Incorporating material hardship into models of income associations with parenting and child development. *Child Development, 78,* 70–95.

Gerst, M. S. (1971). Symbolic coding processes in observational learning. *Journal of Personality and Social Psychology, 19,* 7–17.

Gil, L., Bråten, I., Vidal-Abarca, E., & Strømsø, H. I. (2010). Summary versus argument tasks when working with multiple documents: Which is better for whom? *Contemporary Educational Psychology, 35,* 157–173.

Gilliland, H. (1988). Discovering and emphasizing the positive aspects of the culture. In H. Gilliland & J. Reyhner (Eds.), *Teaching the Native American* (pp. 21–36). Dubuque, IA: Kendall/Hunt.

Goldenberg, C. (2001). Making schools work for low-income families in the 21st century. In S. B. Neuman & D. K. Dickinson (Eds.), *Handbook of early literacy research* (pp. 211–231). New York, NY: Guilford Press.

Goldstein, N. E., Arnold, D. H., Rosenberg, J. L., Stowe, R. M., & Ortiz, C. (2001). Contagion of aggression in day care classrooms as a function of peer and teacher responses. *Journal of Educational Psychology, 93,* 708–719.

Gollnick, D. M., & Chinn, P. C. (2009). *Multicultural education in a pluralistic society* (8th ed.). Upper Saddle River, NJ: Merrill/Pearson.

Goodnow, J. J. (2010). Culture. In M. H. Bornstein (Ed.), *Handbook of cultural developmental science* (pp. 3–19). New York, NY: Psychology Press.

Grace, D. M., David, B. J., & Ryan, M. K. (2008). Investigating preschoolers' categorical thinking about gender through imitation, attention, and the use of self-categories. *Child Development, 79,* 1928–1941.

Green, L., Fry, A. F., & Myerson, J. (1994). Discounting of delayed rewards: A life-span comparison. *Psychological Science, 5,* 33–36.

Greenfield, P. M., Trumbull, E., Keller, H., Rothstein-Fisch, C., Suzuki, L. K., & Quiroz, B. (2006). Cultural conceptions of learning and development. In P. A. Alexander & P. H. Winne (Eds.), *Handbook of educational psychology* (2nd ed., pp. 675–692). Mahwah, NJ: Erlbaum.

Greeno, J. G., Collins, A. M., & Resnick, L. B. (1996). Cognition and learning. In D. C. Berliner & R. C. Calfee (Eds.), *Handbook of educational psychology* (pp. 15–46). New York, NY: Macmillan.

Griffin, S. A., Case, R., & Capodilupo, A. (1995). Teaching for understanding: The importance of the central conceptual structures in the elementary mathematics curriculum. In A. McKeough, J. Lupart, & A. Marini (Eds.), *Teaching for transfer: Fostering generalization in learning* (pp. 123–151). Mahwah, NJ: Erlbaum.

Grissmer, D. W., Williamson, S., Kirby, S. N., & Berends, M. (1998). Exploring the rapid rise in Black achievement scores in the United States (1970–1990). In U. Neisser (Ed.), *The rising curve: Long-term gains in IQ and related measures* (pp. 251–285). Washington, DC: American Psychological Association.

Gruman, D. H., Harachi, T. W., Abbott, R. D., Catalano, R. F., & Fleming, C. B. (2008). Longitudinal effects of student mobility on three dimensions of elementary school engagement. *Child Development, 79,* 1833–1852.

Guerra, N. G., Huesmann, L. R., & Spindler, A. (2003). Community violence exposure, social cognition, and aggression among urban elementary school children. *Child Development, 74,* 1561–1576.

Gutiérrez, K. D., & Rogoff, B. (2003). Cultural ways of learning: Individual traits or repertoires of practice. *Educational Researcher, 32*(5), 19–25.

Haden, C. A., Ornstein, P. A., Eckerman, C. O., & Didow, S. M. (2001). Mother-child conversational interactions as events unfold: Linkages to subsequent remembering. *Child Development, 72,* 1016–1031.

Hall, R. V., Axelrod, S., Foundopoulos, M., Shellman, J., Campbell, R. A., & Cranston, S. S. (1971). The effective use of punishment to modify behavior in the classroom. *Educational Technology, 11*(4), 24–26. Reprinted in K. D. O'Leary & S. O'Leary (Eds.). (1972). *Classroom management: The successful use of behavior modification.* New York, NY: Pergamon.

Halpern, D. F., & LaMay, M. L. (2000). The smarter sex: A critical review of sex differences in intelligence. *Educational Psychology Review, 12,* 229–246.

Harlow, H. F., & Zimmerman, R. R. (1959). Affectional responses in the infant monkey. *Science, 130,* 421–432.

Harris, K. R., Santangelo, T., & Graham, S. (2010). Metacognition and strategies instruction in writing. In H. S. Waters & W. Schneider (Eds.), *Metacognition, strategy use, and instruction* (pp. 226–256). New York, NY: Guilford Press.

Harrison, A. M., & Pyles, D. A. (2013). The effects of verbal instruction and shaping to improve tackling by high school football players. *Journal of Applied Behavior Analysis, 46,* 518–522.

Hartley, K., & Bendixen, L. D. (2001). Educational research in the Internet age: Examining the role of individual characteristics. *Educational Researcher, 30*(9), 22–26.

Hatano, G., & Inagaki, K. (2003). When is conceptual change intended? A cognitive-sociocultural view. In G. M. Sinatra & P. R. Pintrich (Eds.), *Intentional conceptual change* (pp. 407–427). Mahwah, NJ: Erlbaum.

Hattie, J. (2009). *Visible learning: A synthesis of over 800 meta-analyses relating to achievement.* London: Routledge.

Hattie, J., & Gan, M. (2011). Instruction based on feedback. In R. E. Mayer & P. A. Alexander (Eds.), *Handbook of research on learning and instruction* (pp. 249–271). New York, NY: Routledge.

Hattie, J., & Timperley, H. (2007). The power of feedback. *Review of Educational Research, 77,* 81–112.

Hearold, S. (1986). A synthesis of 1,043 effects of television on social behavior. In G. Comstock (Ed.), *Public communication and behavior* (Vol. 1, pp. 65–133). New York, NY: Academic Press.

Helton, G. B., & Oakland, T. D. (1977). Teachers' attitudinal responses to differing characteristics of elementary school students. *Journal of Educational Psychology, 69,* 261–266.

Hemphill, L., & Snow, C. (1996). Language and literacy development: Discontinuities and differences. In D. R. Olson & N. Torrance (Eds.), *The handbook of education and human development: New models of learning, teaching, and schooling* (pp. 173–201). Cambridge, MA: Blackwell.

Hernandez, D. J., Denton, N. A., & Macartney, S. E. (2008). Children in immigrant families: Looking to America's future. *Social Policy Report, 22*(3) (Society for Research in Child Development).

Hess, R. D., & Holloway, S. D. (1984). Family and school as educational institutions. In R. D. Parke, R. N. Emde, H. P. McAdoo, & G. P. Sackett (Eds.), *Review of child development research* (Vol. 7, pp. 179–222). Chicago: University of Chicago Press.

Hewitt, J., Brett, C., Scardamalia, M., Frecker, K., & Webb, J. (1995, April). Supporting knowledge building through the synthesis of CSILE, FCL, & Jasper. In M. Lamon (Chair), *Schools for thought: Transforming classrooms into learning communities.* Symposium conducted at the annual meeting of the American Educational Research Association, San Francisco, CA.

Hewitt, J., & Scardamalia, M. (1998). Design principles for distributed knowledge building processes. *Educational Psychology Review, 10,* 75–96.

Hiebert, E. H., & Raphael, T. E. (1996). Psychological perspectives on literacy and extensions to educational practice. In D. C. Berliner & R. C. Calfee (Eds.), *Handbook of educational psychology* (pp. 550–602). New York, NY: Macmillan.

Hiebert, J., Carpenter, T. P., Fennema, E., Fuson, K. C., Wearne, D., Murray, H., . . . Human, P. (1997). *Making sense: Teaching and learning mathematics with understanding.* Portsmouth, NH: Heinemann.

Hill, N. E., Bush, K. R., & Roosa, M. W. (2003). Parenting and family socialization strategies and children's mental health: Low-income Mexican-American and Euro-American mothers and children. *Child Development, 74*, 189–204.

Hine, P., & Fraser, B. J. (2002, April). *Combining qualitative and quantitative methods in a study of Australian students' transition from elementary to high school.* Paper presented at the annual meeting of the American Educational Research Association, New Orleans, LA.

Hogan, K., Nastasi, B. K., & Pressley, M. (2000). Discourse patterns and collaborative scientific reasoning in peer and teacher-guided discussions. *Cognition and Instruction, 17*, 379–432.

Hollins, E. R. (1996). *Culture in school learning: Revealing the deep meaning.* Mahwah, NJ: Erlbaum.

Hong, Y., Morris, M. W., Chiu, C., & Benet-Martínez, V. (2000). Multicultural minds: A dynamic constructivist approach to culture and cognition. *American Psychologist, 55*, 709–720.

Hubbs-Tait, L., Nation, J. R., Krebs, N. F., & Bellinger, D. C. (2005). Neurotoxicants, micronutrients, and social environments: Individual and combined effects on children's development. *Psychological Science in the Public Interest, 6*, 57–121.

Hughes, J. M., Bigler, R. S., & Levy, S. R. (2007). Consequences of learning about historical racism among European American and African American children. *Child Development, 78*, 1689–1705.

Hunt, P., & Goetz, L. (1997). Research on inclusive educational programs, practices, and outcomes for students with severe disabilities. *Journal of Special Education, 31*, 3–29.

Hynd, C. (1998b). Observing learning from different perspectives: What does it mean for Barry and his understanding of gravity? In B. Guzzetti & C. Hynd (Eds.), *Perspectives on conceptual change: Multiple ways to understand knowing and learning in a complex world* (pp. 235–244). Mahwah, NJ: Erlbaum.

Igoa, C. (1995). *The inner world of the immigrant child.* Mahwah, NJ: Erlbaum.

Irujo, S. (1988). An introduction to intercultural differences and similarities in nonverbal communication. In J. S. Wurzel (Ed.), *Toward multiculturalism: A reader in multicultural education* (pp. 114–138). Yarmouth, ME: Intercultural Press.

Ito, M., Baumer, S., Bittanti, M., Boyd, D., Cody, R., Herr-Stephenson, B., . . . Tripp, L. (2009). *Hanging out, messing around, geeking out: Kids living and learning with new media.* Cambridge, MA: MIT Press.

Jansen, B. A. (2007). *The Big6 in middle school: Teaching information and communication technology skills.* Columbus, OH: Linworth.

Jansen, B. A. (2009). *The Big6 goes primary: Teaching information and communication technology skills in the K–3 curriculum.* Columbus, OH: Linworth.

Jiang, B. (2010). English language learners: Understanding their needs. In G. S. Goodman (Ed.), *Educational psychology reader: The art and science of how people learn* (pp. 179–194). New York, NY: Peter Lang.

Johnson, D. W., & Johnson, R. T. (2009b). Energizing learning: The instructional power of conflict. *Educational Researcher, 38*, 37–51.

John-Steiner, V., & Mahn, H. (1996). Sociocultural approaches to learning and development: A Vygotskian framework. *Educational Psychologist, 31*, 191–206.

Jordan, N. C., Glutting, J., Dyson, N., Hassinger-Das, B., & Irwin, C. (2012). Building kindergartners' number sense: A randomized controlled study. *Journal of Educational Psychology, 104*, 647–660.

Kağitçibaşi, Ç. (2007). *Family, self, and human development across cultures: Theory and applications* (2nd ed.). Mahwah, NJ: Erlbaum.

Katzir, T., & Paré-Blagoev, J. (2006). Applying cognitive neuroscience research to education: The case of literacy. *Educational Psychologist, 41*, 53–74.

Keil, F. C., & Newman, G. E. (2008). Two tales of conceptual change: What changes and what remains the same. In S. Vosniadou (Ed.), *International handbook on conceptual change* (pp. 83–101). New York, NY: Routledge.

Kelemen, D. (2004). Are children "intuitive theists"?: Reasoning about purpose and design in nature. *Psychological Science, 15*, 295–301.

Killen, M. (2007). Children's social and moral reasoning about exclusion. *Current Directions in Psychological Science, 16*, 32–36.

Kim, J. (2011). Is it bigger than hip-hop? Examining the problems and potential of hip-hop in the curriculum. In V. Kinloch (Ed.), *Urban literacies: Critical perspectives on language, learning, and community* (pp. 160–176). New York, NY: Teachers College Press.

Kincheloe, J. L. (2009). No short cuts in urban education: Metropedagogy and diversity. In S. R. Steinberg (Ed.),

Diversity and multiculturalism: A reader (pp. 379–409). New York, NY: Peter Lang.

King, A. (1999). Discourse patterns for mediating peer learning. In A. M. O'Donnell & A. King (Eds.), *Cognitive perspectives on peer learning* (pp. 87–115). Mahwah, NJ: Erlbaum.

Kirschenbaum, R. J. (1989). Identification of the gifted and talented American Indian student. In C. J. Maker & S. W. Schiever (Eds.), *Critical issues in gifted education: Vol. 2. Defensible programs for cultural and ethnic minorities* (pp. 91-101). Austin, TX: Pro-Ed.

Kitayama, S. (2002). Culture and basic psychological processes—Toward a system view of culture: Comment on Oyserman et al. (2002). *Psychological Bulletin, 128*, 89–96.

Kitayama, S., Duffy, S., & Uchida, Y. (2007). Self as cultural mode of being. In S. Kitayama & D. Cohen (Eds.), *Handbook of cultural psychology* (pp. 136–174). New York, NY: Guilford Press.

Koltko-Rivera, M. E. (2004). The psychology of worldviews. *Review of General Psychology, 8*, 3–58.

Krumboltz, J. D., & Krumboltz, H. B. (1972). *Changing children's behavior.* Upper Saddle River, NJ: Prentice Hall.

Kuhn, D. (2015). Thinking together and alone. *Educational Researcher, 44*, 46–53.

Kuhn, D., & Crowell, A. (2011). Dialogic argumentation as a vehicle for developing young adolescents' thinking. *Psychological Science, 22*, 545–552.

Kumar, R., Gheen, M. H., & Kaplan, A. (2002). Goal structures in the learning environment and students' disaffection from learning and schooling. In C. Midgley (Ed.), *Goals, goal structures, and patterns of adaptive learning* (pp. 143–173). Mahwah, NJ: Erlbaum.

Ladson-Billings, G. (1995a). But that's just good teaching! The case for culturally relevant pedagogy. *Theory into Practice, 34*, 159–165.

Ladson-Billings, G. (1995b). Toward a theory of culturally relevant pedagogy. *American Educational Research Journal, 32*, 465–491.

LaFromboise, T., Coleman, H. L. K., & Gerton, J. (1993). Psychological impact of biculturalism: Evidence and theory. *Psychological Bulletin, 114*, 395–412.

Lampert, M., Rittenhouse, P., & Crumbaugh, C. (1996). Agreeing to disagree: Developing sociable mathematical discourse. In D. R. Olson & N. Torrance (Eds.), *The handbook of education and human development: New models of learning, teaching, and schooling* (pp. 731–764). Cambridge, MA: Blackwell.

Landrum, T. J., & Kauffman, J. M. (2006). Behavioral approaches to classroom management. In C. M. Evertson & C. S. Weinstein (Eds.), *Handbook of classroom management: Research, practice, and contemporary issues* (pp. 47–71). Mahwah, NJ: Erlbaum.

Lane, K. L., Menzies, H. M., Bruhn, A. L., & Crnobori, M. (2011). *Managing challenging behaviors in schools: Research-based strategies that work.* New York, NY: Guilford Press.

Langer, J. A. (2011). *Envisioning knowledge: Building literacy in the academic disciplines.* New York, NY: Teachers College Press.

Lave, J. (1991). Situating learning in communities of practice. In L. B. Resnick, J. M. Levine, & S. D. Teasley (Eds.), *Perspectives on socially shared cognition* (pp. 63–82). Washington, DC: American Psychological Association.

Lave, J., & Wenger, E. (1991). *Situated learning: Legitimate peripheral participation.* Cambridge, England: Cambridge University Press.

Lee, C. D. (2010). Soaring above the clouds, delving the ocean's depths: Understanding the ecologies of human learning and the challenge for education science. *Educational Researcher, 39*, 643–655.

Lee, J.-S., & Bowen, N. K. (2006). Parent involvement, cultural capital, and the achievement gap among elementary school children. *American Educational Research Journal, 43*, 193–218.

Lejuez, C. W., Schaal, D. W., & O'Donnell, J. (1998). Behavioral pharmacology and the treatment of substance abuse. In J. J. Plaud & G. H. Eifert (Eds.), *From behavior theory to behavior therapy* (pp. 116–135). Boston, MA: Allyn & Bacon.

Leu, D. J., O'Byrne, W. I., Zawilinski, L., McVerry, J. G., & Everett-Cacopardo, H. (2009). Expanding the new literacies conversation. *Educational Researcher, 38*, 264–269.

Levstik, L. S. (2011). Learning history. In R. E. Mayer & P. A. Alexander (Eds.), *Handbook of research on learning and instruction* (pp. 108–126). New York, NY: Routledge.

Liben, L. S., & Myers, L. J. (2007). Developmental changes in children's understanding of maps: What, when, and how? In J. M. Plumert & J. P. Spencer (Eds.), *The emerging spatial mind* (pp. 193–218). New York, NY: Oxford University Press.

Light, P., & Butterworth, G. (Eds.). (1993). *Context and cognition: Ways of learning and knowing.* Mahwah, NJ: Erlbaum.

Lipka, J., Yanez, E., Andrew-Ihrke, D., & Adam, S. (2009). A two-way process for developing effective culturally based

math: Examples from math in a cultural context. In B. Greer, S. Mukhopadhyay, A. B. Powell, & S. Nelson-Barber (Eds.), *Culturally responsive mathematics education* (pp. 257–280). New York, NY: Routledge.

Lomawaima, K. T. (1995). Educating Native Americans. In J. A. Banks & C. A. M. Banks (Eds.), *Handbook of research on multicultural education.* New York, NY: Macmillan.

Long, M. C., Conger, D., & Iatarole, P. (2012). Effects of high school course-taking on secondary and post-secondary success. *American Educational Research Journal, 49*, 285–322.

Lopez, A. M. (2003). Mixed-race school-age children: A summary of census 2000 data. *Educational Researcher, 32*(6), 25–37.

Losh, S. C. (2003). On the application of social cognition and social location to creating causal explanatory structures. *Educational Research Quarterly, 26*(3), 17–33.

Mac Iver, D. J., Reuman, D. A., & Main, S. R. (1995). Social structuring of the school: Studying what is, illuminating what could be. In J. T. Spence, J. M. Darley, & D. J. Foss (Eds.), *Annual review of psychology* (Vol. 46, pp. 375–400). Palo Alto, CA: Annual Review.

Magill, R. A. (1993). Modeling and verbal feedback influences on skill learning. *International Journal of Sport Psychology, 24*, 358–369.

Manning, F. H., Lawless, K. A., Goldman, S. R., & Braasch, J. L. G. (2011, April). *Evaluating the usefulness of multiple sources with respect to an inquiry question: Middle school students' analysis and ranking of Internet search results.* Paper presented at the annual meeting of the American Educational Research Association, New Orleans, LA.

Manning, M. L., & Baruth, L. G. (2009). *Multicultural education of children and adolescents* (5th ed.). Boston, MA: Allyn & Bacon/Pearson.

Mantzicopoulos, P. Y., Knutson, D. J. (2000). Head Start children: School mobility and achievement in the early grades. *Journal of Educational Research, 93*, 305–311.

Markus, H. R., & Hamedani, M. G. (2007). Sociocultural psychology: The dynamic interdependence among self systems and social systems. In S. Kitayama & D. Cohen (Eds.), *Handbook of cultural psychology* (pp. 3–39). New York, NY: Guilford Press.

Martin, C. L., & Ruble, D. (2004). Children's search for gender cues: Cognitive perspectives on gender development. *Current Directions in Psychological Science, 13*, 67–70.

Martin, S. S., Brady, M. P., & Williams, R. E. (1991). Effects of toys on the social behavior of preschool children in integrated and nonintegrated groups: Investigation of a setting event. *Journal of Early Intervention, 15*, 153–161.

Matute-Bianchi, M. E. (2008). Situational ethnicity and patterns of school performance among immigrant and nonimmigrant Mexican-descent students. In J. U. Ogbu (Ed.), *Minority status, oppositional culture, and schooling* (pp. 398–432). New York, NY: Routledge.

McBrien, J. L. (2005). *Discrimination and academic motivation in adolescent refugee girls.* Unpublished doctoral dissertation, Emory University, Atlanta, GA.

McCarthy, A., Lee, K., Itakura, S., & Muir, D. W. (2006). Cultural display rules drive eye gaze during thinking. *Journal of Cultural Psychology, 37*, 717–722.

McComas, J. J., Thompson, A., & Johnson, L. (2003). The effects of presession attention on problem behavior maintained by different reinforcers. *Journal of Applied Behavior Analysis, 36*, 297–307.

McDaniel, L. (1997). *For better, for worse, forever.* New York, NY: Bantam.

McIntyre, E. (2010). Issues in funds of knowledge teaching and research: Key concepts from a study of Appalachian families and schooling. In M. L. Dantas & P. C. Manyak (Eds.), *Home–school connections in a multicultural society: Learning from and with culturally and linguistically diverse families* (pp. 201–217). New York, NY: Routledge.

McLoyd, V. C. (1998). Socioeconomic disadvantage and child development. *American Psychologist, 53*, 185–204.

Medin, D. L. (2005, August). *Role of culture and expertise in cognition.* Invited address presented at the annual meeting of the American Psychological Association, Washington, DC.

Mejía-Arauz, R., Rogoff, B., Dexter, A., & Najafi, B. (2007). Cultural variation in children's social organization. *Child Development, 78*, 1001–1014.

Meyer, K. A. (1999). Functional analysis and treatment of problem behavior exhibited by elementary school children. *Journal of Applied Behavior Analysis, 32*, 229–232.

Miller, D. L., & Kelley, M. L. (1994). The use of goal setting and contingency contracting for improving children's homework performance. *Journal of Applied Behavior Analysis, 27*, 73–84.

Miller, L. S. (1995). *An American imperative: Accelerating minority educational advancement*. New Haven, CT: Yale University Press.

Miller, P. M. (2011). A critical analysis of the research on student homelessness. *Review of Educational Research, 81,* 308–337.

Mohan, E. (2009). Putting multiethnic students on the radar: A case for greater consideration of our multiethnic students. In S. R. Steinberg (Ed.), *Diversity and multiculturalism: A reader* (pp.132–141). New York, NY: Peter Lang.

Moje, E. B., & Hinchman, K. (2004). Culturally responsive practices for youth literacy learning. In T. L. Jetton & J. A. Dole (Eds.), *Adolescent literacy research and practice* (pp. 321–350). New York, NY: Guilford Press.

Monzó, L. D. (2010). Fostering academic identities among Latino immigrant students: Contextualizing parents' roles. In M. L. Dantas & P. C. Manyak (Eds.), *Home–school connections in a multicultural society: Learning from and with culturally and linguistically diverse families* (pp. 112–130). New York, NY: Routledge.

Moore, J. W., & Edwards, R. P. (2003). An analysis of aversive stimuli in classroom demand contexts. *Journal of Applied Behavior Analysis, 36,* 339–348.

Mueller, M. M., Nkosi, A., & Hine, J. F. (2011). Functional analysis in public schools: A summary of 90 functional analyses. *Journal of Applied Behavior Analysis, 44,* 807–818.

Murdock, T. B. (2000). Incorporating economic context into educational psychology: Methodological and conceptual challenges. *Educational Psychologist, 35,* 113–124.

Murphy, P. K., Wilkinson, I. A. G., & Soter, A. O. (2011). Instruction based on discussion. In R. E. Mayer & P. A. Alexander (Eds.), *Handbook of research on learning and instruction* (pp. 382–407). New York, NY: Routledge.

Murphy, P. K., Wilkinson, I. A. G., Soter, A. O., Hennessey, M. N., & Alexander, J. F. (2009). Examining the effects of classroom discussion on students' comprehension of text: A meta-analysis. *Journal of Educational Psychology, 101,* 740–764.

Narciss, S. (2008). Feedback strategies for interactive learning tasks. In J. M. Spector, M. D. Merrill, J. van Merriënboer, & M. P. Driscoll (Eds.), *Handbook of research on educational communications and technology* (3rd ed., pp. 125–143). New York, NY: Erlbaum.

NCSS Task Force on Ethnic Studies Curriculum Guidelines. (1992). Curriculum guidelines for multicultural education. *Social Education, 56,* 274–294.

Nelson, K. (1993). The psychological and social origins of autobiographical memory. *Psychological Science, 4,* 7–14.

Nelson, K. (1996). *Language in cognitive development: The emergence of the mediated mind.* Cambridge, England: Cambridge University Press.

Nesdale, D., Maass, A., Durkin, K., & Griffiths, J. (2005). Group norms, threat, and children's racial prejudice. *Child Development, 76,* 652–663.

Nettles, S. M., Caughy, M. O., & O'Campo, P. J. (2008). School adjustment in the early grades: Toward an integrated model of neighborhood, parental, and child processes. *Review of Educational Research, 78,* 3–32.

Nielsen, M., & Tomaselli, K. (2010). Overimitation in Kalahari bushman children and the origins of human cultural cognition. *Psychological Science, 21,* 729–736.

Noble, K. G., Tottenham, N., & Casey, B. J. (2005). Neuroscience perspectives on disparities in school readiness and cognitive achievement. *The Future of Children, 15*(1), 71–89.

Nolen, S. B. (2011). Motivation, engagement, and identity: Opening a conversation. In D. M. McInerney, R. A. Walker, & G. A. D. Liem (Eds.), *Sociocultural theories of learning and motivation: Looking back, looking forward* (pp. 109–135). Charlotte, NC: Information Age.

Norton, E. S., Kovelman, I., & Pettito, L.-A. (2007). Are there separate neural systems for spelling? New insights into the role of rules and memory in spelling from functional magnetic resonance imaging. *Mind, Brain, and Behavior, 1*(1), 48–59.

Nussbaum, E. M. (2008). Collaborative discourse, argumentation, and learning: Preface and literature review. *Contemporary Educational Psychology, 33,* 345–359.

Ogbu, J. U. (2008a). Collective identity and the burden of "acting White" in Black history, community, and education. In J. U. Ogbu (Ed.), *Minority status, oppositional culture, and schooling* (pp. 29–63). New York, NY: Routledge.

Oskamp, S. (Ed.). (2000). *Reducing prejudice and discrimination.* Mahwah, NJ: Erlbaum.

Padilla, A. M. (1994). Bicultural development: A theoretical and empirical examination. In R. G. Malgady & O. Rodriguez (Eds.), *Theoretical and conceptual issues in Hispanic mental health* (pp. 20–51). Malabar, FL: Krieger.

Palincsar, A. S., & Herrenkohl, L. R. (1999). Designing collaborative contexts: Lessons from three research programs. In A. M. O'Donnell & A. King (Eds.), *Cognitive perspectives on peer learning* (pp. 151–177). Mahwah, NJ: Erlbaum.

Paradise, R., & Robles, A. (2016). Two Mazahua (Mexican) communities: Introducing a collective orientation into everyday school life. *European Journal of Psychology of Education, 31,* 61–77. doi:10.1007/s10212-015-0262-9

Pea, R. D. (1993). Practices of distributed intelligence and designs for education. In G. Salomon (Ed.), *Distributed cognitions: Psychological and educational considerations* (pp. 47–87). Cambridge, England: Cambridge University Press.

Pearce, R. R. (2006). Effects of cultural and social structural factors on the achievement of White and Chinese American students at school transition points. *American Educational Research Journal, 43,* 75–101.

Pelphrey, K. A., & Carter, E. J. (2007). Brain mechanisms underlying social perception deficits in autism. In D. Coch, G. Dawson, & K. W. Fischer (Eds.), *Human behavior, learning, and the developing brain: Atypical development* (pp. 56–86). New York, NY: Guilford Press.

Pfeifer, J. H., Brown, C. S., & Juvonen, J. (2007). Teaching tolerance in schools: Lessons learned since *Brown v. Board of Education* about the development and reduction of children's prejudice. *Social Policy Report, 21*(2), 3–13, 16–17, 20–23.

Phalet, K., Andriessen, I., & Lens, W. (2004). How future goals enhance motivation and learning in multicultural classrooms. *Educational Psychology Review, 16,* 59–89.

Phelan, P., Davidson, A. L., & Cao, H. T. (1991). Students' multiple worlds: Negotiating the boundaries of family, peer, and school cultures. *Anthropology and Education Quarterly, 22,* 224–250.

Phillips, G., McNaughton, S., & MacDonald, S. (2004). Managing the mismatch: Enhancing early literacy progress for children with diverse language and cultural identities in mainstream urban schools in New Zealand. *Journal of Educational Psychology, 96,* 309–323.

Pianta, R. C., & Hamre, B. K. (2009). Conceptualization, measurement, and improvement of classroom processes: Standardized observation can leverage capacity. *Educational Researcher, 38,* 109–119.

Pitner, R. O., Astor, R. A., Benbenishty, R., Haj-Yahia, M. M., & Zeira, A. (2003). The effects of group stereotypes on adolescents' reasoning about peer retribution. *Child Development, 74,* 413–425.

Plumert, J. M., & Spencer, J. P. (Eds.). (2007). *The emerging spatial mind.* Oxford, England: Oxford University Press.

Porat, D. A. (2004). It's not written here, but this is what happened: Students' cultural comprehension of textbook narratives on the Israeli-Arab conflict. *American Educational Research Journal, 41,* 963–996.

Posner, M. I., & Rothbart, M. K. (2007). *Educating the human brain.* Washington, DC: American Psychological Association.

Powers, L. E., Sowers, J. A., & Stevens, T. (1995). An exploratory, randomized study of the impact of mentoring on the self-efficacy and community-based knowledge of adolescents with severe physical challenges. *Journal of Rehabilitation, 61*(1), 33–41.

Premack, D. (1959). Toward empirical behavior laws: I. Positive reinforcement. *Psychological Review, 66,* 219–233.

Premack, D. (1963). Rate differential reinforcement in monkey manipulation. *Journal of Experimental Analysis of Behavior, 6,* 81–89.

Quintana, S. M., Aboud, F. E., Chao, R. K., Contreras-Grau, J., Cross, W. E., Jr., Hudley, C., . . . Vietze, D. L. (2006). Race, ethnicity, and culture in child development: Contemporary research and future directions. *Child Development, 77,* 1129–1141.

Radziszewska, B., & Rogoff, B. (1988). Influence of adult and peer collaborators on children's planning skills. *Developmental Psychology, 24,* 840–848.

Raudenbush, S. W. (2009). The *Brown* legacy and the O'Connor challenge: Transforming schools in the images of children's potential. *Educational Researcher, 38,* 169–180.

Reynolds, R. E., Taylor, M. A., Steffensen, M. S., Shirey, L. L., & Anderson, R. C. (1982). Cultural schemata and reading comprehension. *Reading Research Quarterly, 17,* 353–366.

Reznitskaya, A., & Gregory, M. (2013). Student thought and classroom language: Examining the mechanisms of change in dialogic teaching. *Educational Psychologist, 48,* 114–133.

Robbins, P., & Aydede, M. (Eds.). (2009). *The Cambridge handbook of situated cognition.* Cambridge, England: Cambridge University Press.

Robinson, S. L., & Griesemer, S. M. R. (2006). Helping individual students with problem behavior. In C. M. Evertson

& C. S. Weinstein (Eds.), *Handbook of classroom management: Research, practice, and contemporary issues* (pp. 787–802). Mahwah, NJ: Erlbaum.

Rogoff, B. (1994, April). *Developing understanding of the idea of communities of learners.* Paper presented at the annual meeting of the American Educational Research Association, New Orleans, LA.

Rogoff, B. (2003). *The cultural nature of human development.* Oxford, England: Oxford University Press.

Rogoff, B., Matusov, E., & White, C. (1996). Models of teaching and learning: Participation in a community of learners. In D. R. Olson & N. Torrance (Eds.), *The handbook of education and human development: New models of learning, teaching, and schooling* (pp. 388–414). Cambridge, MA: Blackwell.

Root, M. P. P. (1999). The biracial baby boom: Understanding ecological constructions of racial identity in the 21st century. In R. H. Sheets & E. R. Hollins (Eds.), *Racial and ethnic identity in school practices: Aspects of human development* (pp. 67–89). Mahwah, NJ: Erlbaum.

Rosenthal, T. L., Alford, G. S., & Rasp, L. M. (1972). Concept attainment, generalization, and retention through observation and verbal coding. *Journal of Experimental Child Psychology, 13,* 183–194.

Rothstein-Fisch, C., & Trumbull, E. (2008). *Managing diverse classrooms: How to build on students' strengths.* Alexandria, VA: Association for Supervision and Curriculum Development.

Rumberger, R. W. (2011). *Dropping out: Why students drop out of high school and what can be done about it.* Cambridge, MA: Harvard University Press.

Rushton, J. P. (1980). *Altruism, socialization, and society.* Upper Saddle River, NJ: Prentice Hall.

Säljö, R., & Wyndhamn, J. (1992). Solving everyday problems in the formal setting: An empirical study of the school as context for thought. In S. Chaiklin & J. Lave (Eds.), *Understanding practice* (pp. 327–342). New York, NY: Cambridge University Press.

Salomon, G. (1993). No distribution without individuals' cognition: A dynamic interactional view. In G. Salomon (Ed.), *Distributed cognitions: Psychological and educational considerations* (pp. 111–138). Cambridge, England: Cambridge University Press.

Sanders, M. G. (1996). Action teams in action: Interviews and observations in three schools in the Baltimore School–Family–Community Partnership Program. *Journal of Education for Students Placed at Risk, 1,* 249–262.

Sasso, G. M., & Rude, H. A. (1987). Unprogrammed effects of training high-status peers to interact with severely handicapped children. *Journal of Applied Behavior Analysis, 20,* 35–44.

Sawyer, R. J., Graham, S., & Harris, K. R. (1992). Direct teaching, strategy instruction, and strategy instruction with explicit self-regulation: Effects on the composition skills and self-efficacy of students with learning disabilities. *Journal of Educational Psychology, 84,* 340–352.

Sawyer, R. K., & Greeno, J. G. (2009). Situativity and learning. In P. Robbins & M. Aydede (Eds.), *The Cambridge handbook of situated cognition* (pp. 347–367). Cambridge, England: Cambridge University Press.

Scardamalia, M., & Bereiter, C. (2006). Knowledge building: Theory, pedagogy, and technology. In R. K. Sawyer (Ed.), *The Cambridge handbook of the learning sciences* (pp. 97–115). Cambridge, England: Cambridge University Press.

Scarr, S., & McCartney, K. (1983). How people make their own environments: A theory of genotype environment effects. *Child Development, 54,* 424–435.

Schank, R. C., & Abelson, R. P. (1995). Knowledge and memory: The real story. In R. S. Wyer, Jr. (Ed.), *Advances in social cognition: Vol. 8. Knowledge and memory: The real story* (pp. 1–85). Mahwah, NJ: Erlbaum.

Schultz, K., Buck, P., & Niesz, T. (2000). Democratizing conversations: Racialized talk in a post-desegregated middle school. *American Educational Research Journal, 37,* 33–65.

Schunk, D. H. (1981). Modeling and attributional effects on children's achievement: A self-efficacy analysis. *Journal of Educational Psychology, 73,* 93–105.

Schunk, D. H. (1998). Teaching elementary students to self-regulate practice of mathematical skills with modeling. In D. H. Schunk & B. J. Zimmerman (Eds.), *Self-regulated learning: From teaching to self-reflective practice* (pp. 137–159). New York, NY: Guilford Press.

Schunk, D. H., & Hanson, A. R. (1985). Peer models: Influence on children's self-efficacy and achievement. *Journal of Educational Psychology, 77,* 313–322.

Schunk, D. H., & Swartz, C. W. (1993). Goals and progress feedback: Effects on self-efficacy and writing achievement. *Contemporary Educational Psychology, 18,* 337–354.

Schwartz, S. J., Unger, J. B., Zamboanga, B. L., & Szapocznik, J. (2010). Rethinking the concept of acculturation: Implications for theory and research. *American Psychologist, 65,* 237–251.

Schwarz, B. B., Neuman, Y., & Biezuner, S. (2000). Two wrongs may make a right . . . if they argue together! *Cognition and Instruction, 18,* 461–494.

Scruggs, T. E., & Mastropieri, M. A. (1994). Successful mainstreaming in elementary science classes: A qualitative study of three reputational cases. *American Educational Research Journal, 31,* 785–811.

Sharples, M., & Pea, R. (2014). Mobile learning. In R. K. Sawyer (Ed.), *The Cambridge handbook of the learning sciences* (2nd ed., pp. 501–521). New York, NY: Cambridge University Press.

Shute, V. J. (2008). Focus on formative feedback. *Review of Educational Research, 78,* 153–189.

Siegler, R. S. (2009). Improving the numerical understanding of children from low-income families. *Child Development Perspectives, 3,* 118–124.

Sigman, M., & Whaley, S. E. (1998). The role of nutrition in the development of intelligence. In U. Neisser (Ed.), *The rising curve: Long-term gains in IQ and related measures* (pp. 155–182). Washington, DC: American Psychological Association.

Sinatra, G. M., & Pintrich, P. R. (Eds.). (2003). *Intentional conceptual change.* Mahwah, NJ: Erlbaum.

Sirin, S. R. (2005). Socioeconomic status and academic achievement: A meta-analytic review of research. *Review of Educational Research, 75,* 417–453.

Sirin, S. R., & Ryce, P. (2010). Cultural incongruence between teachers and families: Implications for immigrant students. In E. L. Grigorenko & R. Takanishi (Eds.), *Immigration, diversity, and education* (pp. 151–169). New York, NY: Routledge.

Skinner, B. F. (1953). *Science and human behavior.* New York, NY: Macmillan.

Skinner, B. F. (1954). The science of learning and the art of teaching. *Harvard Educational Review, 24,* 86–97.

Skinner, B. F. (1968). *The technology of teaching.* New York, NY: Appleton-Century-Crofts.

Slavin, R. E. (1987). Ability grouping and student achievement in elementary schools: A best-evidence synthesis. *Review of Educational Research, 57,* 293–336.

Slonim, M. B. (1991). *Children, culture, ethnicity: Evaluating and understanding the impact.* New York, NY: Garland.

Smith, C. L. (2007). Bootstrapping processes in the development of students' commonsense matter theories: Using analogical mappings, thought experiments, and learning to measure to promote conceptual restructuring. *Cognition and Instruction, 25,* 337–398.

Smith, E. R., & Conrey, F. R. (2009). The social context of cognition. In P. Robbins & M. Aydede (Eds.), *The Cambridge handbook of situated cognition* (pp. 454–466). Cambridge, England: Cambridge University Press.

Smith, H. L. (1998). Literacy and instruction in African American communities: Shall we overcome? In B. Pérez (Ed.), *Sociocultural contexts of language and literacy* (pp. 189– 222). Mahwah, NJ: Erlbaum.

Smitherman, G. (1998). Black English/Ebonics: What it be like? In T. Perry & L. Delpit (Eds.), *The real Ebonics debate: Power, language, and the education of African-American children* (pp. 29–37). Boston, MA: Beacon Press.

Soodak, L. C., & McCarthy, M. R. (2006). Classroom management in inclusive settings. In C. M. Evertson & C. S. Weinstein (Eds.), *Handbook of classroom management: Research, practice, and contemporary issues* (pp. 461–489). Mahwah, NJ: Erlbaum.

Southerland, S. A., & Sinatra, G. M. (2003). Learning about biological evolution: A special case of intentional conceptual change. In G. M. Sinatra & P. R. Pintrich (Eds.), *Intentional conceptual change* (pp. 317–345). Mahwah, NJ: Erlbaum.

Spera, C. (2005). A review of the relationship among parenting practices, parenting styles, and adolescent school achievement. *Educational Psychology Review, 17,* 125–146.

Spiro, R. J., & DeSchryver, M. (2009). Constructivism: When it's the wrong idea and when it's the only idea. In S. Tobias & T. M. Duffy (Eds.), *Constructivist instruction: Success or failure?* (pp. 106–123). New York, NY: Routledge.

Stack, C. B., & Burton, L. M. (1993). Kinscripts. *Journal of Comparative Family Studies, 24,* 157–170.

Stahl, G., Koschmann, T., & Suthers, D. D. (2006). Computer-supported collaborative learning. In R. K. Sawyer (Ed.), *The Cambridge handbook of the learning sciences* (pp. 409–425). Cambridge, England: Cambridge University Press.

Stainback, S., & Stainback, W. (1992). Schools as inclusive communities. In W. Stainback & S. Stainback (Eds.), *Controversial issues confronting special education: Divergent perspectives* (pp. 29–43). Boston, MA: Allyn & Bacon.

Steinberg, L., Graham, S., O'Brien, L., Woolard, J., Cauffman, E., & Banich, M. (2009). Age differences in future orientation and delay discounting. *Child Development, 80,* 28–44.

Stokes, J. V., Luiselli, J. K., & Reed, D. D. (2010). A behavioral intervention for teaching tackling skills to high school football athletes. *Journal of Applied Behavior Analysis, 43,* 509–512.

Stokes, J. V., Luiselli, J. K., Reed, D. D., & Fleming, R. K. (2010). Behavioral coaching to improve offensive line pass-blocking skills of high school football athletes. *Journal of Applied Behavior Analysis, 43,* 463–472.

Suina, J. H., & Smolkin, L. B. (1994). From natal culture to school culture to dominant society culture: Supporting transitions for Pueblo Indian students. In P. M. Greenfield & R. R. Cocking (Eds.), *Cross-cultural roots of minority child development* (pp. 115–130). Mahwah, NJ: Erlbaum.

Tamis-Lemonda, C. S., & McFadden, K. E. (2010). The United States of America. In M. H. Bornstein (Ed.), *Handbook of cultural developmental science* (pp. 299–322). New York, NY: Psychology Press.

Tatum, B. D. (1997). *"Why are all the black kids sitting together in the cafeteria?" and other conversations about race.* New York, NY: Basic Books.

Tessler, M., & Nelson, K. (1994). Making memories: The influence of joint encoding on later recall by young children. *Consciousness and Cognition, 3,* 307–326.

Thelen, E., & Smith, L. B. (1998). Dynamic systems theories. In W. Damon (Ed.-in-chief) and R. M. Lerner (Vol. Ed.), *Handbook of child psychology: Vol. 1. Theoretical models of human development* (5th ed., pp. 563–634). New York, NY: Wiley.

Theobald, P., & Herley, W. (2009). Rurality, locality, and the diversity question. In S. R. Steinberg (Ed.), *Diversity and multiculturalism: A reader* (pp. 423–434). New York, NY: Peter Lang.

Thompson, R. A., & Nelson, C. A. (2001). Developmental science and the media: Early brain development. *American Psychologist, 56,* 5–15.

Trawick-Smith, J. (2003). *Early childhood development: A multicultural perspective* (3rd ed.). Upper Saddle River, NJ: Merrill/Prentice Hall.

Tunstall, P., & Gipps, C. (1996). Teacher feedback to young children in formative assessment: A typology. *British Educational Research Journal, 22,* 389–404.

Turkanis, C. G. (2001). Creating curriculum with children. In B. Rogoff, C. G. Turkanis, & L. Bartlett (Eds.), *Learning together: Children and adults in a school community* (pp. 91–102). New York, NY: Oxford University Press.

Tyler, K. M., Uqdah, A. L., Dillihunt, M. L., Beatty-Hazelbaker, R., Connor, T., Gadson, N., . . . Stevens, R. (2008). Cultural discontinuity: Toward a quantitative investigation of a major hypothesis in education. *Educational Researcher, 37,* 280–297.

Ulichny, P. (1996). Cultures in conflict. *Anthropology and Education Quarterly, 27,* 331–364.

Ulke-Kurcuoglu, B., & Kircaali-Iftar, G. (2010). A comparison of the effects of providing activity and material choice to children with autism spectrum disorders. *Journal of Applied Behavior Analysis, 43,* 717–721.

Valkenburg, P. M., & Peter, J. (2007). Preadolescents' and adolescents' online communication and their closeness to friends. *Developmental Psychology, 43,* 267–277.

Van Camp, C. M., Lerman, D. C., Kelley, M. E., Roane, H. S., Contrucci, S. A., & Vorndran, C. M. (2000). Further analysis of idiosyncratic antecedent influences during the assessment and treatment of problem behavior. *Journal of Applied Behavior Analysis, 33,* 207–221.

van den Bergh, L., Denessen, E., Hornstra, L., Voeten, M., & Holland, R. W. (2010). The implicit prejudiced attitudes of teachers: Relations to teacher expectations and the ethnic achievement gap. *American Educational Research Journal, 47,* 497–527.

Vang, C. (2010). The psycho-social dimensions of multicultural education. In G. S. Goodman (Ed.), *Educational psychology reader: The art and science of how people learn* (pp. 195–208). New York, NY: Peter Lang.

Varnum, M. E. W., Grossmann, I., Kitayama, S., & Nisbett, R. E. (2010). The origin of cultural differences in cognition: The social orientation hypothesis. *Current Directions in Psychological Science, 19,* 9–13.

Vasquez, J. A. (1988). Contexts of learning for minority students. *Educational Forum, 6,* 243–253.

Vintere, P., Hemmes, N. S., Brown, B. L., & Poulson, C. L. (2004). Gross-motor skill acquisition by preschool dance students under self-instruction procedures. *Journal of Applied Behavior Analysis, 37,* 305–322.

Vollmer, T. R., & Hackenberg, T. D. (2001). Reinforcement contingencies and social reinforcement: Some reciprocal relations between basic and applied research. *Journal of Applied Behavior Analysis, 34,* 241–253.

Vygotsky, L. S. (1962). *Thought and language* (E. Haufmann & G. Vakar, Eds. and Trans.). Cambridge, MA: MIT Press.

Vygotsky, L. S. (1978). *Mind in society: The development of higher psychological processes.* Cambridge, MA: Harvard University Press.

Walshaw, M., & Anthony, G. (2008). The teacher's role in classroom discourse: A review of recent research into mathematics classrooms. *Review of Educational Research, 78,* 516–551.

Walters, G. C., & Grusec, J. E. (1977). *Punishment.* San Francisco, CA: Freeman.

Wang, M.-T., & Holcombe, R. (2010). Adolescents' perceptions of school environment, engagement, and academic achievement in middle school. *American Educational Research Journal, 47,* 633–662.

Ward, C., Bochner, S., & Furnham, A. (2001). *The psychology of culture shock* (2nd ed.). London, England: Routledge.

Warschauer, M. (2011). *Learning in the cloud: How (and why) to transform schools with digital media.* New York, NY: Teachers College Press.

Weatherford, J. (1988). *Indian givers: How the Indians of the Americas transformed the world.* New York, NY: Crown.

Webb, N. M., & Palincsar, A. S. (1996). Group processes in the classroom. In D. C. Berliner & R. C. Calfee (Eds.), *Handbook of educational psychology* (pp. 841–873). New York, NY: Macmillan.

Wenger, E. (1998). *Communities of practice: Learning, meaning, and identity.* Cambridge, England: Cambridge University Press.

Wentzel, K. R., & Looney, L. (2007). Socialization in school settings. In J. E. Grusec & P. D. Hastings (Eds.), *Handbook of socialization: Theory and research* (pp. 382–403). New York, NY: Guilford Press.

Wentzel, K. R., & Watkins, D. E. (2011). Instruction based on peer interactions. In R. E. Mayer & P. A. Alexander (Eds.), *Handbook of research on learning and instruction* (pp. 322–343). New York, NY: Routledge.

White, T., & Pea, R. (2011). Distributed by design: On the promises and pitfalls of collaborative learning with multiple representations. *Journal of the Learning Sciences, 20,* 489–547.

Wiley, J., & Bailey, J. (2006). Effects of collaboration and argumentation on learning from Web pages. In A. M. O'Donnell, C. E. Hmelo-Silver, & G. Erkens (Eds.), *Collaborative learning, reasoning, and technology* (pp. 297–321). Mahwah, NJ: Erlbaum.

Wiley, J., Goldman, S. R., Graesser, A. C., Sanchez, C. A., Ash, I. K., & Hemmerich, J. A. (2009). Source evaluation, comprehension, and learning in Internet science inquiry tasks. *American Educational Research Journal, 46,* 1060–1106.

Williams, T., & Williams, K. (2010). Self-efficacy and performance in mathematics: Reciprocal determinism in 33 nations. *Journal of Educational Psychology, 102,* 453–456.

Wise, A. F., & O'Neill, K. (2009). Beyond more versus less: A reframing of the debate on instructional guidance. In S. Tobias & T. M. Duffy (Eds.), *Constructivist instruction: Success or failure?* (pp. 82–105). New York, NY: Routledge.

Wood, D., Bruner, J. S., & Ross, G. (1976). The role of tutoring in problem-solving. *Journal of Child Psychology and Psychiatry, 17,* 89–100.

Wright, M. O., & Masten, A. S. (2006). Resilience processes in development: Fostering positive adaptation in the context of adversity. In S. Goldstein & R. B. Brooks (Eds.), *Handbook of resilience in children* (pp. 17–37). New York, NY: Springer.

Yoshikawa, H., Aber, J. L., & Beardslee, W. R. (2012). The effects of poverty on the mental, emotional, and behavioral health of children and youth: Implications for prevention. *American Psychologist, 67,* 272–284.

Zambo, D., & Brem, S. K. (2004). Emotion and cognition in students who struggle to read: New insights and ideas. *Reading Psychology, 25,* 1–16.

Zhang, J., Scardamalia, M., Reeve, R., & Messina, R. (2009). Designs for collective cognitive responsibility in knowledge-building communities. *Journal of the Learning Sciences, 18,* 7–44.

Zimmerman, B. J., & Kitsantas, A. (1999). Acquiring writing revision skill: Shifting from process to outcome self-regulatory goals. *Journal of Educational Psychology, 91,* 241–250.

CHAPTER 5

Ackerman, B. P., Izard, C. E., Kobak, R., Brown, E. D., & Smith, C. (2007). Relation between reading problems and internalizing behavior in school for preadolescent children from economically disadvantaged families. *Child Development, 78,* 581–596.

Adolphs, R., & Damasio, A. R. (2001). The interaction of affect and cognition: A neurobiological perspective. In J. P. Forgas (Ed.), *Handbook of affect and social cognition* (pp. 27–49). Mahwah, NJ: Erlbaum.

Ahmed, W., Werf, G., Kuyper, H., & Minnaert, A. (2013). Emotions, self-regulated learning, and achievement in mathematics: A growth curve analysis. *Journal of Educational Psychology, 105*(1), 150–161.

Ainley, M. (2006). Connecting with learning: Motivation, affect, and cognition in interest processes. *Educational Psychology Review, 18*, 391–405.

Ainley, M., & Ainley, J. (2011). Student engagement with science in early adolescence: The contribution of enjoyment to students' continuing interest in learning about science. *Contemporary Educational Psychology, 36*, 4–12.

Ainley, M., & Ainley, J. (2015). Early science learning experiences: Triggered and maintained interest. In K. A. Renninger, M. Nieswandt, & S. Hidi (Eds.), *Interest in mathematics and science learning* (pp. 17–31). Washington, DC: American Educational Research Association.

Alderman, M. K. (1990). Motivation for at-risk students. *Educational Leadership, 48*(1), 27–30.

Alexander, E. S. (2006, April). *Beyond S.M.A.R.T.? Integrating hopeful thinking into goal setting for adolescents at-risk of dropping out of high school.* Paper presented at the annual meeting of the American Educational Research Association, San Francisco, CA.

Alexander, J. M., Johnson, K. E., Leibham, M. E., & Kelley, K. (2008). The development of conceptual interests in young children. *Cognitive Development, 23*, 324–334.

Alexander, P. A. (1997). Mapping the multidimensional nature of domain learning: The interplay of cognitive, motivational, and strategic forces. In P. R. Pintrich & M. L. Maehr (Eds.), *Advances in motivation and achievement* (Vol. 10). Greenwich, CT: JAI Press.

Alexander, P. A., Kulikowich, J. M., & Schulze, S. K. (1994). How subject-matter knowledge affects recall and interest. *American Educational Research Journal, 31*, 313–337.

Alim, H. S. (2007). "The Whig party don't exist in my hood": Knowledge, reality, and education in the hip hop nation. In H. S. Alim & J. Baugh (Eds.), *Talkin Black talk: Language, education, and social change* (pp. 15–29). New York: Teachers College Press.

Amabile, T. M., & Hennessey, B. A. (1992). The motivation for creativity in children. In A. K. Boggiano & T. S. Pittman (Eds.), *Achievement and motivation: A social-developmental perspective.* Cambridge, England: Cambridge University Press.

Ames, C. (1984). Competitive, cooperative, and individualistic goal structures: A cognitive-motivational analysis. In R. Ames & C. Ames (Eds.), *Research on motivation in education: Vol. 1. Student motivation* (pp. 177–207). San Diego, CA: Academic Press.

Ames, C. (1992). Classrooms: Goals, structures, and student motivation. *Journal of Educational Psychology, 84*, 261–271.

Ames, C., & Archer, J. (1988). Achievement goals in the classroom: Students' learning strategies and motivation processes. *Journal of Educational Psychology, 80*, 260–267.

Ames, R. (1983). Help-seeking and achievement orientation: Perspectives from attribution theory. In A. Nadler, J. Fisher, & B. DePaulo (Eds.), *New directions in helping* (Vol. 2, pp. 165–186). New York, NY: Academic Press.

Anderman, E. M., Griesinger, T., & Westerfield, G. (1998). Motivation and cheating during early adolescence. *Journal of Educational Psychology, 90*, 84–93.

Anderman, E. M., & Maehr, M. L. (1994). Motivation and schooling in the middle grades. *Review of Educational Research, 64*, 287–309.

Anderman, E. M., Noar, S., Zimmerman, R. S., & Donohew, L. (2004). The need for sensation as a prerequisite for motivation to engage in academic tasks. In M. L. Maehr & P. Pintrich (Eds.), *Advances in motivation and achievement: Motivating students, improving schools: The legacy of Carol Midgley* (Vol. 13, pp. 1–26). Greenwich: JAI Press.

Anderman, E. M., & Wolters, C. A. (2006). Goals, values, and affect: Influences on student motivation. In P. A. Alexander & P. H. Winne (Eds.), *Handbook of educational psychology* (2nd ed., pp. 369–389). Mahwah, NJ: Erlbaum.

Anderman, L. H., & Anderman, E. M. (1999). Social predictors of changes in students' achievement goal orientation. *Contemporary Educational Psychology, 25*, 21–37.

Anderman, L. H., & Anderman, E. M. (2009). Oriented towards mastery: Promoting positive motivational goals for students. In R. Gilman, E. S. Huebner, & M. J. Furlong (Eds.), *Handbook of positive psychology in schools* (pp. 161–173). New York, NY: Routledge.

Anderman, L. H., Andrzejewski, C. E., & Allen, J. (2011). How do teachers support students' motivation and learning in their classrooms? *Teachers College Record, 113*(5), 969–1003.

Anderman, L. H., Patrick, H., Hruda, L. Z., & Linnenbrink, E. A. (2002). Observing classroom goal structures to clarify and expand goal theory. In C. Midgley (Ed.), *Goals, goal structures, and patterns of adaptive learning* (pp. 243–278). Mahwah, NJ: Erlbaum.

Andre, T., & Windschitl, M. (2003). Interest, epistemological belief, and intentional conceptual change. In G. M. Sinatra & P. R. Pintrich (Eds.), *Intentional conceptual change* (pp. 173–197). Mahwah, NJ: Erlbaum.

Arnett, J. (1999). Adolescent storm and stress, reconsidered. *American Psychologist, 54*, 317–326.

Aronson, J., Lustina, M. J., Good, C., Keough, K., Steele, C. M., & Brown, J. (1999). When white men can't do math: Necessary and sufficient factors in stereotype threat. *Journal of Experimental Social Psychology, 35*, 29–46.

Aronson, J., & Steele, C. M. (2005). Stereotypes and the fragility of academic competence, motivation, and self-concept. In A. J. Elliot & C. S. Dweck (Eds.), *Handbook of competence and motivation* (pp. 436–456). New York, NY: Guilford Press.

Ashcraft, M. H. (2002). Math anxiety: Personal, educational, and cognitive consequences. *Current Directions in Psychological Science, 11*, 181–184.

Assor, A., & Connell, J. P. (1992). The validity of students' self-reports as measures of performance affecting self-appraisals. In D. H. Schunk & J. L. Meece (Eds.), *Student perceptions in the classroom* (pp. 25–50). Mahwah, NJ: Erlbaum.

Assor, A., Vansteenkiste, M., & Kaplan, A. (2009). Identified versus introjected approach and introjected avoidance motivations in school and in sports: The limited benefits of self-worth strivings. *Journal of Educational Psychology, 101*, 482–497.

Babad, E. (1993). Teachers' differential behavior. *Educational Psychology Review, 5*, 347–376.

Bandura, A. (1986). *Social foundations of thought and action: A social cognitive theory.* Upper Saddle River, NJ: Prentice Hall.

Bandura, A. (1994). Self-efficacy. In V. S. Ramachaudran (Ed.), *Encyclopedia of human behavior* (Vol. 4, pp. 71-81). New York: Academic Press.

Bandura, A. (1997). *Self-efficacy: The exercise of control.* New York, NY: Freeman.

Bandura, A. (2000). Exercise of human agency through collective efficacy. *Current Directions in Psychological Science, 9*, 75–78.

Bandura, A. (2006). Toward a psychology of human agency. *Perspectives on Psychological Science, 1*, 164–180.

Bandura, A. (2008). Toward an agentic theory of the self. In H. W. Marsh, R. G. Craven, & D. M. McInerney (Eds.), *Self-processes, learning, and enabling human potential* (pp. 15–49). Charlotte, NC: Information Age.

Banks, J. A., & Banks, C. A. M. (Eds.). (1995). *Handbook of research on multicultural education.* New York, NY: Macmillan.

Bao, X., & Lam, S. (2008). Who makes the choice? Rethinking the role of autonomy and relatedness in Chinese children's motivation. *Child Development, 79*, 269–283.

Barkley, R. A. (1996). Linkages between attention and executive functions. In G. R. Lyon & N. A. Krasnegor (Eds.), *Attention, memory, and executive function.* Baltimore, MD: Brookes.

Battistich, V., Solomon, D., Kim, D., Watson, M., & Schaps, E. (1995). Schools as communities, poverty levels of student populations, and students' attitudes, motives, and performance: A multilevel analysis. *American Educational Research Journal, 32*, 627–658.

Beike, S. M., & Zentall, S. S. (2012). "The snake raised its head": Content novelty alters the reading performance of students at risk for reading disabilities and ADHD. *Journal of Educational Psychology, 104*(3), 529–540.

Beilock, S. L. (2008). Math performance in stressful situations. *Current Directions in Psychological Science, 17*, 339–343.

Bembenutty, H., & Karabenick, S. A. (2004). Inherent association between academic delay of gratification, future time perspective, and self-regulated learning. *Educational Psychology Review, 16*, 35–57.

Benes, F. M. (2007). Corticolimbic circuitry and psychopathology: Development of the corticolimbic system. In D. Coch, G. Dawson, & K. W. Fischer (Eds.), *Human behavior, learning, and the developing brain: Atypical development* (pp. 331–361). New York, NY: Guilford Press.

Benner, A. D., & Graham, S. (2009). The transition to high school as a developmental process among multiethnic urban youth. *Child Development, 80*, 356–376.

Ben-Zeev, T., Carrasquillo, C. M., Ching, A. M. L., Kliengklom, T. J., McDonald, K. L., Newhall, D. C., . . . Fein, S. (2005). "Math is hard!" (Barbie™, 1994): Responses of threat vs.

challenge-mediated arousal to stereotypes alleging intellectual inferiority. In A. M. Gallagher & J. C. Kaufman (Eds.), *Gender differences in mathematics: An integrative psychological approach* (pp. 189–206). Cambridge, England: Cambridge University Press.

Bergin, C., & Bergin, D. (2009). Attachment in the classroom. *Educational Psychology Review, 21*, 141–170.

Berkowitz, L. (1989). Frustration-aggression hypothesis: Examination and reformulation. *Psychological Bulletin, 106*, 59–73.

Berlyne, D. E. (1960). *Conflict, arousal, and curiosity.* New York, NY: McGraw-Hill.

Blackwell, L. S., Trzesniewski, K. H., & Dweck, C. S. (2007). Implicit theories of intelligence predict achievement across an adolescent transition: A longitudinal study and an intervention. *Child Development, 78*, 246–263.

Blumenfeld, P. C., Kempler, T. M., & Krajcik, J. S. (2006). Motivation and cognitive engagement in learning environments. In R. K. Sawyer (Ed.), *The Cambridge handbook of the learning sciences* (pp. 475–488). Cambridge, England: Cambridge University Press.

Boaler, J. (2002). *Experiencing school mathematics: Traditional and reform approaches to teaching and their impact on student learning.* Mahwah, NJ: Erlbaum.

Boekaerts, M., de Koning, E., & Vedder, P. (2006). Goal-directed behavior and contextual factors in the classroom: An innovative approach to the study of multiple goals. *Educational Psychologist, 41*, 33–51.

Boggiano, A. K., & Pittman, T. S. (Eds.). (1992). *Achievement and motivation: A social-developmental perspective.* Cambridge, England: Cambridge University Press.

Bong, M. (2001). Between- and within-domain relations of academic motivation among middle and high school students: Self-efficacy, task-value, and achievement goals. *Journal of Educational Psychology, 93*, 23–34.

Bong, M. (2009). Age-related differences in achievement goal differentiation. *Journal of Educational Psychology, 101*, 879–896.

Bong, M., & Skaalvik, E. M. (2003). Academic self-concept and self-efficacy: How different are they really? *Educational Psychology Review, 15*, 1–40.

Bower, G. H. (1994). Some relations between emotions and memory. In P. Ekman & R. J. Davidson (Eds.), *The nature of emotion: Fundamental questions.* New York, NY: Oxford University Press.

Bower, G. H., & Forgas, J. P. (2001). Mood and social memory. In J. P. Forgas (Ed.), *Handbook of affect and social cognition* (pp. 95–120). Mahwah, NJ: Erlbaum.

Bower, J. E., Moskowitz, J. T., & Epel, E. (2009). Is benefit finding good for your health? Pathways linking positive life changes after stress and physical health outcomes. *Current Directions in Psychological Science, 18*, 337–341.

Brayboy, B. M. J., & Searle, K. A. (2007). Thanksgiving and serial killers: Representations of American Indians in schools. In S. Books (Ed.), *Invisible children in the society and its schools* (3rd ed., pp. 173–192). Mahwah, NJ: Erlbaum.

Brophy, J. E. (1986). *On motivating students* (Occasional Paper No. 101). East Lansing: Michigan State University, Institute for Research on Teaching.

Brophy, J. E. (1987). Synthesis of research on strategies for motivating students to learn. *Educational Leadership, 45*(2), 40–48.

Brophy, J. E. (2004). *Motivating students to learn* (2nd ed.). Mahwah, NJ: Erlbaum.

Brophy, J. E. (2006). Observational research on generic aspects of classroom teaching. In P. A. Alexander & P. H. Winne (Eds.), *Handbook of educational psychology* (2nd ed., pp. 755–780). Mahwah, NJ: Erlbaum.

Brophy, J. (2008). Developing students' appreciation for what is taught in school. *Educational Psychologist, 43*, 132–141.

Brophy, J. E., & Alleman, J. (1992). Planning and managing learning activities: Basic principles. In J. Brophy (Ed.), *Advances in research on teaching: Vol. 3. Planning and managing learning tasks and activities* (pp. 1–46). Greenwich, CT: JAI Press.

Brophy, J. E., Alleman, J., & Knighton, B. (2009). *Inside the social studies classroom.* New York, NY: Routledge.

Brown, B. B. (1990). Peer groups. In S. Feldman & G. Elliott (Eds.), *At the threshold: The developing adolescent* (pp. 171–196). Cambridge, MA: Harvard University Press.

Brown, B. B., Eicher, S. A., & Petrie, S. (1986). The importance of peer group ("crowd") affiliation in adolescence. *Journal of Adolescence, 9*, 73–96.

Burhans, K. K., & Dweck, C. S. (1995). Helplessness in early childhood: The role of contingent worth. *Child Development, 66*, 1719–1738.

Butler, R. (1989). Mastery versus ability appraisal: A developmental study of children's observations of peers' work. *Child Development, 60,* 1350–1361.

Butler, R. (1994). Teacher communication and student interpretations: Effects of teacher responses to failing students on attributional inferences in two age groups. *British Journal of Educational Psychology, 64,* 277–294.

Butler, R. (1998a). Age trends in the use of social and temporal comparison for self-evaluation: Examination of a novel developmental hypothesis. *Child Development, 69,* 1054–1073.

Butler, R. (2008). Evaluating competence and maintaining self-worth between early and middle childhood: Blissful ignorance or the construction of knowledge and strategies in context? In H. W. Marsh, R. G. Craven, & D. M. McInerney (Eds.), *Self-processes, learning, and enabling human potential* (pp. 193–222). Charlotte, NC: Information Age.

Cacioppo, J. T., Petty, R. E., Feinstein, J. A., & Jarvis, W. B. G. (1996). Dispositional differences in cognitive motivation: The life and times of individuals varying in need for cognition. *Psychological Bulletin, 119,* 197–253.

Cameron, J. (2001). Negative effects of reward on intrinsic motivation—A limited phenomenon: Comment on Deci, Koestner, and Ryan (2001). *Review of Educational Research, 71,* 29–42.

Camras, L. A., Chen, Y., Bakeman, R., Norris, K., & Cain, T. R. (2006). Culture, ethnicity, and children's facial expressions: A study of European American, Mainland Chinese, Chinese American, and adopted Chinese girls. *Emotion, 6,* 103–114.

Carrasco, R. L. (1981). Expanded awareness of student performance: A case study in applied ethnographic monitoring in a bilingual classroom. In H. T. Trueba, G. P. Guthrie, & K. H. Au (Eds.), *Culture and the bilingual classroom: Studies in classroom ethnography* (pp. 153–177). Rowley, MA: Newbury House.

Carver, C. S., & Scheier, M. F. (1990). Origins and functions of positive and negative affect: A control-process view. *Psychological Review, 97,* 19–35.

Cassady, J. C. (2004). The influence of cognitive test anxiety across the learning-testing cycle. *Learning and Instruction, 14,* 569–592.

Chabrán, M. (2003). Listening to talk from and about students on accountability. In M. Carnoy, R. Elmore, & L. S. Siskin (Eds.), *The new accountability: High schools and high-stakes testing* (pp. 129–145). New York, NY: RoutledgeFalmer.

Chinn, C. A. (2006). Learning to argue. In A. M. O'Donnell, C. E. Hmelo-Silver, & G. Erkens (Eds.), *Collaborative learning, reasoning, and technology* (pp. 355–383). Mahwah, NJ: Erlbaum.

Chittum, J. R., & Jones, B. D. (2015). Motivating students to engage during reading instruction: Intentionally designing instruction using a model of academic motivation. *Ohio Reading Teacher, 45*(1), 29–40.

Chiu, C.-Y., & Hong, Y.-Y. (2005). Cultural competence: Dynamic processes. In A. J. Elliot & C. S. Dweck (Eds.), *Handbook of competence and motivation* (pp. 489–505). New York, NY: Guilford Press.

Christenson, S. L., Reschly, A. L., & Wylie, C. (2012). Epilogue. In S. L. Christenson, A. L. Reschly, & C. Wylie (Eds.), *Handbook of research on student engagement* (pp. 813–817). New York, NY: Springer.

Church, M. A., Elliot, A. J., & Gable, S. L. (2001). Perceptions of classroom environment, achievement goals, and achievement outcomes. *Journal of Educational Psychology, 93,* 43–54.

Cizek, G. J. (2003). *Detecting and preventing classroom cheating: Promoting integrity in assessment.* Thousand Oaks, CA: Corwin.

Cleveland, M. J., Gibbons, F. X., Gerrard, M., Pomery, E. A., & Brody, G. H. (2005). The impact of parenting on risk cognitions and risk behavior: A study of mediation and moderation in a panel of African American adolescents. *Child Development, 76,* 900–916.

Clifford, M. M. (1990). Students need challenge, not easy success. *Educational Leadership, 48*(1), 22–26.

Cohen, G. L., & Garcia, J. (2008). Identity, belonging, and achievement: A model, interventions, implications. *Current Directions in Psychological Science, 17,* 365–369.

Cole, P. M., Bruschi, C. J., & Tamang, B. L. (2002). Cultural differences in children's emotional reactions to difficult situations. *Child Development, 73,* 983–996.

Cole, P. M., Tamang, B. L., & Shrestha, S. (2006). Cultural variations in the socialization of young children's anger and shame. *Child Development, 77,* 1237–1251.

Cole, P. M., & Tan, P. Z. (2007). Emotion socialization from a cultural perspective. In J. E. Grusec & P. D. Hastings (Eds.), *Handbook of socialization: Theory and research* (pp. 516–542). New York, NY: Guilford Press.

Collins, W. A. (2005, April). *A "new look" in social development? Re-framing and extending the canon.* Invited address at the Developmental Science Teaching Institute at the biennial meeting of the Society for Research in Child Development, Atlanta, GA.

Combs, A. W., Richards, A. C., & Richards, F. (1976). *Perceptual psychology.* New York, NY: Harper & Row.

Connell, J. P., & Wellborn, J. G. (1991). Competence, autonomy, and relatedness: A motivational analysis of self-system processes. In M. R. Gunnar & L. A. Sroufe (Eds.), *Self processes and development: The Minnesota Symposia on Child Psychology* (Vol. 23, pp. 43–77). Mahwah, NJ: Erlbaum.

Cook, P. J., & Ludwig, J. (2008). The burden of "acting White": Do Black adolescents disparage academic achievement? In J. U. Ogbu (Ed.), *Minority status, oppositional culture, and schooling* (pp. 275–297). New York, NY: Routledge.

Corno, L., & Rohrkemper, M. M. (1985). The intrinsic motivation to learn in classrooms. In C. Ames & R. Ames (Eds.), *Research on motivation in education: Vol. 2. The classroom milieu* (pp. 53–90). San Diego, CA: Academic Press.

Corpus, J. H., McClintic-Gilbert, M. S., & Hayenga, A. O. (2009). Within-year changes in children's intrinsic and extrinsic motivational orientations: Contextual predictors and academic outcomes. *Contemporary Educational Psychology, 34,* 154–166.

Covington, M. V. (1987). Achievement motivation, self-attributions, and the exceptional learner. In J. D. Day & J. G. Borkowski (Eds.), *Intelligence and exceptionality* (pp. 355–389). Norwood, NJ: Ablex.

Covington, M. V. (1992). *Making the grade: A self-worth perspective on motivation and school reform.* Cambridge, England: Cambridge University Press.

Covington, M. V. (2000). Intrinsic versus extrinsic motivation in schools: A reconciliation. *Current Directions in Psychological Science, 9,* 22–25.

Covington, M. V., & Müeller, K. J. (2001). Intrinsic versus extrinsic motivation: An approach/avoidance reformulation. *Educational Psychology Review, 13,* 157–176.

Crocker, J., & Knight, K. M. (2005). Contingencies of self-worth. *Current Directions in Psychological Science, 14,* 200–203.

Csikszentmihalyi, M. (1990). *Flow: The psychology of optimal experience.* New York, NY: HarperPerennial.

Csikszentmihalyi, M., Abuhamdeh, S., & Nakamura, J. (2005). Flow. In A. J. Elliot & C. S. Dweck (Eds.), *Handbook of competence and motivation* (pp. 598–608). New York, NY: Guilford Press.

Csikszentmihalyi, M., & Nakamura, J. (1989). The dynamics of intrinsic motivation: A study of adolescents. In C. Ames & R. Ames (Eds.), *Research on motivation in education: Vol. 3. Goals and cognitions* (pp. 45–71). San Diego, CA: Academic Press.

Curtis, K. A. (1992). Altering beliefs about the importance of strategy: An attributional intervention. *Journal of Applied Social Psychology, 22,* 953–972.

d'Ailly, H. (2003). Children's autonomy and perceived control in learning: A model of motivation and achievement in Taiwan. *Journal of Educational Psychology, 95,* 84–96.

Damasio, A. R. (1994). *Descartes' error: Emotion, reason, and the human brain.* New York, NY: Avon Books.

Danner, F. (2008, March). *The effects of perceptions of classroom assessment practices and academic press on classroom mastery goals and high school students' self-reported cheating.* Paper presented at the annual meeting of the American Educational Research Association, New York, NY.

Davies, P. G., & Spencer, S. J. (2005). The gender-gap artifact: Women's underperformance in quantitative domains through the lens of stereotype threat. In A. M. Gallagher & J. C. Kaufman (Eds.), *Gender differences in mathematics: An integrative psychological approach* (pp. 172–188). Cambridge, England: Cambridge University Press.

Davis, H. A. (2003). Conceptualizing the role and influence of student-teacher relationships on children's social and cognitive development. *Educational Psychologist, 38,* 207–234.

Davis, L. E., Ajzen, I., Saunders, J., & Williams, T. (2002). The decision of African American students to complete high school: An application of the theory of planned behavior. *Journal of Educational Psychology, 94,* 810–819.

Davis-Kean, P. E., Huesmann, R., Jager, J., Collins, W. A., Bates, J. E., & Lansford, J. E. (2008). Changes in the relation of self-efficacy beliefs and behaviors across development. *Child Development, 79,* 1257–1269.

deCharms, R. (1972). Personal causation training in the schools. *Journal of Applied Social Psychology, 2,* 95–113.

Deci, E. L. (1992). The relation of interest to the motivation of behavior: A self-determination theory perspective. In K. A. Renninger, S. Hidi, & A. Krapp (Eds.), *The role of interest in learning and development* (pp. 43–47). Mahwah, NJ: Erlbaum.

Deci, E. L., Koestner, R., & Ryan, R. M. (1999). A meta-analytic review of experiments examining the effects of extrinsic rewards on intrinsic motivation. *Psychological Bulletin, 125*(6), 627–668.

Deci, E. L., Koestner, R., & Ryan, R. M. (2001). Extrinsic rewards and intrinsic motivation in education: Reconsidered once again. *Review of Educational Research, 71,* 1–27.

Deci, E. L., & Moller, A. C. (2005). The concept of competence: A starting place for understanding intrinsic motivation and self-determined extrinsic motivation. In A. J. Elliot & C. S. Dweck (Eds.), *Handbook of competence and motivation* (pp. 579–597). New York, NY: Guilford Press.

Deci, E. L., & Ryan, R. M. (1985). *Intrinsic motivation and self-determination in human behavior.* New York, NY: Plenum Press.

Deci, E. L., & Ryan, R. M. (1992). The initiation and regulation of intrinsically motivated learning and achievement. In A. K. Boggiano & T. S. Pittman (Eds.), *Achievement and motivation: A social-developmental perspective* (pp. 3–36). Cambridge, England: Cambridge University Press.

Deci, E. L., & Ryan, R. M. (1995). Human autonomy: The basis for true self-esteem. In M. H. Kernis (Ed.), *Efficacy, agency, and self-esteem* (pp. 31–49). New York, NY: Plenum Press.

Deci, E. L., & Ryan, R. M. (2012). Motivation, personality, and development within embedded social contexts: An overview of self-determination theory. In R. M. Ryan (Ed.), *The Oxford handbook of human motivation* (pp. 85–107). New York, NY: Oxford University Press.

Deyhle, D., & LeCompte, M. (1999). Cultural differences in child development: Navajo adolescents in middle schools. In R. H. Sheets & E. R. Hollins (Eds.), *Racial and ethnic identity in school practices: Aspects of human development* (pp. 123–139). Mahwah, NJ: Erlbaum.

Dien, T. (1998). Language and literacy in Vietnamese American communities. In B. Pérez (Ed.), *Sociocultural contexts of language and literacy* (pp. 137–177). Mahwah, NJ: Erlbaum.

Dijkstra, P., Kuyper, H., van der Werf, G., Buunk, A. P., & van der Zee, Y. G. (2008). Social comparison in the classroom: A review. *Review of Educational Research, 78,* 828–879.

Dodge, K. A., Asher, S. R., & Parkhurst, J. T. (1989). Social life as a goal-coordination task. In C. Ames & R. Ames (Eds.), *Research on motivation in education: Vol. 3. Goals and cognitions* (pp. 107–135). San Diego, CA: Academic Press.

Dotterer, A. M., McHale, S. M., & Crouter, A. C. (2009). The development and correlates of academic interests from childhood through adolescence. *Journal of Educational Psychology, 101,* 509–519.

Dowson, M., & McInerney, D. M. (2001). Psychological parameters of students' social and work avoidance goals: A qualitative investigation. *Journal of Educational Psychology, 93,* 35–42.

Doyle, W. (1986a). Classroom organization and management. In M. C. Wittrock (Ed.), *Handbook of research on teaching* (3rd ed., pp. 392–431). New York, NY: Macmillan.

DuBois, D. L., Burk-Braxton, C., Swenson, L. P., Tevendale, H. D., & Hardesty, J. L. (2002). Race and gender influences on adjustment in early adolescence: Investigation of an integrative model. *Child Development, 73,* 1573–1592.

Duckworth, A. L., Peterson, C., Matthews, M. D., & Kelly, D. R. (2007). Grit: perseverance and passion for long-term goals. *Journal of Personality and Social Psychology, 92*(6), 1087–1101.

Dunlap, G., dePerczel, M., Clarke, S., Wilson, D., Wright, S., White, R., & Gomez, A. (1994). Choice making to promote adaptive behavior for students with emotional and behavioral challenges. *Journal of Applied Behavior Analysis, 27,* 505–518.

Durik, A. M., & Harackiewicz, J. M. (2007). Different strokes for different folks: How individual interest moderates the effects of situational factors on task interest. *Journal of Educational Psychology, 99,* 597–610.

Durik, A. M., Vida, M., & Eccles, J. S. (2006). Task values and ability beliefs as predictors of high school literacy choices: A developmental analysis. *Journal of Educational Psychology, 98,* 382–393.

Dweck, C. S. (1978). Achievement. In M. E. Lamb (Ed.), *Social and personality development.* New York, NY: Holt, Rinehart & Winston.

Dweck, C. S. (1986). Motivational processes affecting learning. *American Psychologist, 41,* 1040–1048.

Dweck, C. S. (2000). *Self-theories: Their role in motivation, personality, and development.* Philadelphia, PA: Psychology Press.

Dweck, C. S. (2006). *Mindset: The new psychology of success.* New York, NY: Random House.

Dweck, C. S. (2009). Foreword. In F. D. Horowitz, R. F. Subotnik, & D. J. Matthews (Eds.), *The development of giftedness and talent across the life span* (pp. xi–xiv). Washington, DC: American Psychological Association.

Dweck, C. S., & Elliott, E. S. (1983). Achievement motivation. In E. M. Hetherington (Ed.), *Handbook of child psychology: Vol. 4. Socialization, personality, and social development* (4th ed., pp. 643–691). New York, NY: Wiley.

Dweck, C. S., & Leggett, E. L. (1988). A social-cognitive approach to motivation and personality. *Psychological Review, 95*, 256–273.

Dweck, C. S., Mangels, J. A., & Good, C. (2004). Motivational effects on attention, cognition, and performance. In D. Y. Dai & R. J. Sternberg (Eds.), *Motivation, emotion, and cognition: Integrative perspectives on intellectual functioning and development* (pp. 41–55). Mahwah, NJ: Erlbaum.

Dweck, C. S., & Molden, D. C. (2005). Self-theories: Their impact on competence motivation and acquisition. In A. J. Elliot & C. S. Dweck (Eds.), *Handbook of competence and motivation* (pp. 122–140). New York, NY: Guilford Press.

Eccles, J. S. (2005). Subjective task value and the Eccles et al. model of achievement-related choices. In A. J. Elliot & C. S. Dweck (Eds.), *Handbook of competence and motivation* (pp. 105–121). New York, NY: Guilford Press.

Eccles, J. S. (2007). Families, schools, and developing achievement-related motivations and engagement. In J. E. Grusec & P. D. Hastings (Eds.), *Handbook of socialization: Theory and research* (pp. 665–691). New York, NY: Guilford Press.

Eccles, J. (2009). Who am I and what am I going to do with my life? Personal and collective identities as motivators of action. *Educational Psychologist, 44*, 78–89.

Eccles, J. S., Jacobs, J. E., & Harold, R. D. (1990). Gender role stereotypes, expectancy effects, and parents' socialization of gender differences. *Journal of Social Issues, 46*, 183–201. doi:10.1111/j.1540-4560.1990.tb01929.x.

Eccles, J. S., & Midgley, C. (1989). Stage-environment fit: Developmentally appropriate classrooms for young adolescents. In C. Ames & R. Ames (Eds.), *Research on motivation in education: Vol. 3. Goals and cognitions* (pp. 139–186). San Diego, CA: Academic Press.

Eccles, J. S., Wigfield, A., & Schiefele, U. (1998). Motivation to succeed. In W. Damon (Series Ed.) & N. Eisenberg (Vol. Ed.), *Handbook of child psychology: Vol. 3. Social, emotional, and personality development* (5th ed., pp. 1017–1095). New York, NY: Wiley.

Eccles [Parsons], J. S., Adler, T. F., Futterman, R., Goff, S. B., Kaczala, C. M., Meece, J. L., & Midgley, C. (1983). Expectancies, values, and academic behaviors. In J. T. Spence (Ed.), *Achievement and achievement motivation* (pp. 75–146). San Francisco, CA: Freeman.

Eid, M., & Diener, E. (2001). Norms for experiencing emotions in different cultures: Inter- and intranational differences. *Journal of Personality and Social Psychology, 81*, 869–885.

Elkind, D. (1981). *Children and adolescents: Interpretive essays on Jean Piaget* (3rd ed.). New York, NY: Oxford University Press.

Elliot, A. J. (2005). A conceptual history of the achievement goal construct. In A. J. Elliot & C. S. Dweck (Eds.), *Handbook of competence and motivation* (pp. 52–72). New York, NY: Guilford Press.

Elliot, A. J., & Dweck, C. S. (2005a). Competence and motivation: Competence as the core of achievement motivation. In A. J. Elliot & C. S. Dweck (Eds.), *Handbook of competence and motivation* (pp. 3–12). New York, NY: Guilford Press.

Elliot, A. J., & Dweck, C. S. (Eds.). (2005b). *Handbook of competence and motivation*. New York, NY: Guilford Press.

Elliot, A. J., & McGregor, H. A. (2000, April). Approach and avoidance goals and autonomous-controlled regulation: Empirical and conceptual relations. In A. Assor (Chair), *Self-determination theory and achievement goal theory: Convergences, divergences, and educational implications.* Symposium conducted at the annual meeting of the American Educational Research Association, New Orleans, LA.

Elliot, A. J., Shell, M. M., Henry, K. B., & Maier, M. A. (2005). Achievement goals, performance contingencies, and performance attainment: An experimental test. *Journal of Educational Psychology, 97*, 630–640.

Epstein, J. L. (1989). Family structures and student motivation. In R. E. Ames & C. Ames (Eds.), *Research on motivation in education: Vol. 3. Goals and cognitions* (pp. 259–295). New York, NY: Academic Press.

Eysenck, M. W. (1992). *Anxiety: The cognitive perspective.* Hove, England: Erlbaum.

Feather, N. T. (1982). *Expectations and actions: Expectancy-value models in psychology.* Mahwah, NJ: Erlbaum.

Ferrari, M., & Elik, N. (2003). Influences on intentional conceptual change. In G. M. Sinatra & P. R. Pintrich (Eds.), *Intentional conceptual change* (pp. 21–54). Mahwah, NJ: Erlbaum.

Fiske, A. P., & Fiske, S. T. (2007). Social relationships in our species and cultures. In S. Kitayama & D. Cohen (Eds.),

Handbook of cultural psychology (pp. 283–306). New York, NY: Guilford Press.

Flum, H., & Kaplan, A. (2006). Exploratory orientation as an educational goal. *Educational Psychologist, 41*, 99–110.

Ford, D. Y. (1996). *Reversing underachievement among gifted black students.* New York, NY: Teachers College Press.

Ford, M. E., & Nichols, C. W. (1991). Using goal assessments to identify motivational patterns and facilitate behavioral regulation and achievement. In M. Maehr & P. R. Pintrich (Eds.), *Advances in motivation and achievement: Vol. 7. Goals and self-regulatory processes* (pp. 51–84). Greenwich, CT: JAI Press.

Ford, M. E., & Smith, P. R. (2007). Thriving with social purpose: An integrative approach to the development of optimal human functioning. *Educational Psychologist, 42*, 153–171.

Försterling, F., & Morgenstern, M. (2002). Accuracy of self-assessment and task performance: Does it pay to know the truth? *Journal of Educational Psychology, 94*, 576–585.

Fredricks, J. A., Blumenfeld, P. C., & Paris, A. H. (2004). School engagement: Potential of the concept, state of the evidence. *Review of Educational Research, 74*(1), 59–109.

Fredrickson, B. (2009). *Positivity: Groundbreaking research reveals how to embrace the hidden strength of positive emotions, overcome negativity, and thrive.* New York, NY: Crown Publishing.

Freeman, K. E., Gutman, L. M., & Midgley, C. (2002). Can achievement goal theory enhance our understanding of the motivation and performance of African American young adolescents? In C. Midgley (Ed.), *Goals, goal structures, and patterns of adaptive learning* (pp. 175–204). Mahwah, NJ: Erlbaum.

Frenzel, A. C., Goetz, T., Lüdtke, O., Pekrun, R., & Sutton, R. E. (2009). Emotional transmission in the classroom: Exploring the relationship between teacher and student enjoyment. *Journal of Educational Psychology, 101*, 705–716.

Fuchs, L. S., Fuchs, D., Karns, K., Hamlett, C. L., Katzaroff, M., & Dutka, S. (1997). Effects of task-focused goals on low-achieving students with and without learning disabilities. *American Educational Research Journal, 34*, 513–543.

Fuligni, A. J., & Hardway, C. (2004). Preparing diverse adolescents for the transition to adulthood. *The Future of Children, 14*(2), 99–119.

Furrer, C., & Skinner, E. (2003). Sense of relatedness as a factor in children's academic engagement and performance. *Journal of Educational Psychology, 95*, 148–162.

Gabriele, A. J. (2007). The influence of achievement goals on the constructive activity of low achievers during collaborative problem solving. *British Journal of Educational Psychology, 77*, 121–141.

Garner, R., Brown, R., Sanders, S., & Menke, D. J. (1992). "Seductive details" and learning from text. In K. A. Renninger, S. Hidi, & A. Krapp (Eds.), *The role of interest in learning and development* (pp. 239–254). Mahwah, NJ: Erlbaum.

Gaskill, P. J. (2001, April). *Differential effects of reinforcement feedback and attributional feedback on second-graders' self-efficacy.* Paper presented at the annual meeting of the American Educational Research Association, Seattle, WA.

Gentry, M., Gable, R. K., & Rizza, M. G. (2002). Students' perceptions of classroom activities: Are there grade-level and gender differences? *Journal of Educational Psychology, 94*, 539–544.

Goetz, T., Frenzel, A. C., Hall, N. C., & Pekrun, R. (2008). Antecedents of academic emotions: Testing the internal/external frame of reference model for academic enjoyment. *Contemporary Educational Psychology, 33*, 9–33.

Goldenberg, C. (1992–1993). Instructional conversations: Promoting comprehension through discussion. *The Reading Teacher, 46*(4), 316–326.

Gollwitzer, P. M., & Bargh, J. A. (2005). Automaticity in goal pursuit. In A. J. Elliot & C. S. Dweck (Eds.), *Handbook of competence and motivation* (pp. 624–646). New York, NY: Guilford Press.

Good, C., Aronson, J., & Inzlicht, M. (2003). Improving adolescents' standardized test performance: An intervention to reduce the effects of stereotype threat. *Journal of Applied Developmental Psychology, 24*, 645–662.

Good, T. L., & Brophy, J. E. (1994). *Looking in classrooms* (6th ed.). New York, NY: HarperCollins.

Good, T. L., & Nichols, S. L. (2001). Expectancy effects in the classroom: A special focus on improving the reading performance of minority students in first-grade classrooms. *Educational Psychologist, 36*, 113–126.

Goodenow, C. (1993). The psychological sense of school membership among adolescents: Scale development and educational correlates. *Psychology in the Schools, 30*(1), 79–90.

Goodman, G. S., Ghetti, S., Quas, J. A., Edelstein, R. S., Alexander, K. W., Redlich, A. D., . . . Jones, D. P. (2003).

A prospective study of memory for child sexual abuse: New findings relevant to the repressed-memory controversy. *Psychological Science, 14*, 113–118.

Gottfried, A. E. (1990). Academic intrinsic motivation in young elementary school children. *Journal of Educational Psychology, 82*, 525–538.

Graham, S. (1989). Motivation in Afro-Americans. In G. L. Berry & J. K. Asamen (Eds.), *Black students: Psychosocial issues and academic achievement* (pp. 40–68). Newbury Park, CA: Sage.

Graham, S. (1990). Communicating low ability in the classroom: Bad things good teachers sometimes do. In S. Graham & V. S. Folkes (Eds.), *Attribution theory: Applications to achievement, mental health, and interpersonal conflict* (pp. 17–36). Mahwah, NJ: Erlbaum.

Graham, S., & Golen, S. (1991). Motivational influences on cognition: Task involvement, ego involvement, and depth of information processing. *Journal of Educational Psychology, 83*, 187–194.

Graham, S., & Weiner, B. (1996). Theories and principles of motivation. In D. C. Berliner & R. C. Calfee (Eds.), *Handbook of educational psychology* (pp. 63–84). New York, NY: Macmillan.

Grant, H., & Dweck, C. (2001). Cross-cultural response to failure: Considering outcome attributions with different goals. In F. Salili & C. Chiu (Eds.), *Student motivation: The culture and context of learning* (pp. 203–219). Dordrecht, The Netherlands: Kluwer Academic.

Gunderson, E. A., Ramirez, G., Levine, S. C., & Beilock, S. L. (2012). The role of parents and teachers in the development of gender-related math attitudes. *Sex Roles, 66*(3), 153–166.

Hagger, M. S., Chatzisarantis, N. L. D., Barkoukis, V., Wang, C. K. J., & Baranowski, J. (2005). Perceived autonomy support in physical education and leisure-time physical activity: A cross-cultural evaluation of the trans-contextual model. *Journal of Educational Psychology, 97*, 376–390.

Hall, N. C., Goetz, T., Haynes, T. L., Stupnisky, R. H., & Chipperfield, J. G. (2006, April). *Self-regulation of primary and secondary control: Optimizing control striving in an academic achievement setting.* Paper presented at the annual meeting of the American Educational Research Association, San Francisco, CA.

Hardré, P. L., & Reeve, J. (2003). A motivational model of rural students' intentions to persist in, versus drop out of, high school. *Journal of Educational Psychology, 95*, 347–356.

Hardré, P. L., Crowson, H. M., DeBacker, T. K., & White, D. (2007). Predicting the motivation of rural high school students. *Journal of Experimental Education, 75*, 247–269.

Hareli, S., & Weiner, B. (2002). Social emotions and personality inferences: A scaffold for a new direction in the study of achievement motivation. *Educational Psychologist, 37*, 183–193.

Harmon-Jones, E. (2001). The role of affect in cognitive-dissonance processes. In J. P. Forgas (Ed.), *Handbook of affect and social cognition* (pp. 237–255). Mahwah, NJ: Erlbaum.

Harter, S. (1992). The relationship between perceived competence, affect, and motivational orientation within the classroom: Processes and patterns of change. In A. K. Boggiano & T. S. Pittman (Eds.), *Achievement and motivation: A social-developmental perspective* (pp. 77–114). Cambridge, England: Cambridge University Press.

Harter, S. (1999). *The construction of the self: A developmental perspective.* New York, NY: Guilford Press.

Hattie, J. (2008). Processes of integrating, developing, and processing self information. In H. W. Marsh, R. G. Craven, & D. M. McInerney (Eds.), *Self-processes, learning, and enabling human potential* (pp. 51–85). Charlotte, NC: Information Age.

Hattie, J. A. C. (2009). *Visible learning: A synthesis of over 800 meta-analyses relating to achievement.* London: Routledge.

Hattie, J., & Timperley, H. (2007). The power of feedback. *Review of Educational Research, 77*, 81–112.

Hawkins, F. P. L. (1997). *Journey with children: The autobiography of a teacher.* Niwot: University Press of Colorado.

Hawley, C. A. (2005). Saint or sinner? Teacher perceptions of a child with traumatic brain injury. *Pediatric Rehabilitation, 8*, 117–129.

Hayenga, A. O., & Corpus, J. H. (2010). Profiles of intrinsic and extrinsic motivations: A person-centered approach to motivation and achievement in middle school. *Motivation and Emotion, 34*(4), 371–383.

Heine, S. J. (2007). Culture and motivation: What motivates people to act in the ways that they do? In S. Kitayama & D. Cohen (Eds.), *Handbook of cultural psychology* (pp. 714–733). New York, NY: Guilford Press.

Hembree, R. (1988). Correlates, causes, effects, and treatment of test anxiety. *Review of Educational Research, 58*, 47–77.

Hennessey, B. A. (1995). Social, environmental, and developmental issues and creativity. *Educational Psychology Review, 7*, 163–183.

Heron, W. (1957). The pathology of boredom. *Scientific American, 196*(1), 52–56.

Hess, R. D., & Azuma, M. (1991). Cultural support for learning: Contrasts between Japan and the United States. *Educational Researcher, 29*(9), 2–8.

Hess, R. D., Chih-Mei, C., & McDevitt, T. M. (1987). Cultural variations in family beliefs about children's performance in mathematics: Comparisons among People's Republic of China, Chinese-American, and Caucasian-American families. *Journal of Educational Psychology, 79*, 179–188.

Heuer, F., & Reisberg, D. (1992). Emotion, arousal, and memory for detail. In S. Christianson (Ed.), *Handbook of emotion and memory* (pp. 151–180). Hillsdale, NJ: Erlbaum.

Hidi, S., & Harackiewicz, J. M. (2000). Motivating the academically unmotivated: A critical issue for the 21st century. *Review of Educational Research, 70*, 151–179.

Hidi, S., & McLaren, J. (1990). The effect of topic and theme interestingness on the production of school expositions. In H. Mandl, E. De Corte, N. Bennett, & H. F. Friedrich (Eds.), *Learning and instruction in an international context* (pp. 295–308). Oxford, England: Pergamon Press.

Hidi, S., & Renninger, K. A. (2006). The four-phase model of interest development. *Educational Psychologist, 41*, 111–127.

Hidi, S., Renninger, K. A., & Krapp, A. (2004). Interest, a motivational variable that combines affecting and cognitive functioning. In D. Y. Dai & R. J. Sternberg (Eds.), *Motivation, emotion, and cognition: Integrative perspectives on intellectual functioning and development* (pp. 89–115). Mahwah, NJ: Erlbaum.

Hill, K. T., & Sarason, S. B. (1966). The relation of test anxiety and defensiveness to test and school performance over the elementary school years: A further longitudinal study. *Monographs for the Society of Research in Child Development, 31*(2, Serial No. 104).

Hine, P., & Fraser, B. J. (2002, April). *Combining qualitative and quantitative methods in a study of Australian students' transition from elementary to high school.* Paper presented at the annual meeting of the American Educational Research Association, New Orleans, LA.

Hinkley, J. W., McInerney, D. M., & Marsh, H. W. (2001, April). *The multi-faceted structure of school achievement motivation: A case for social goals.* Paper presented at the annual meeting of the American Educational Research Association, Seattle, WA.

Hinnant, J. B., O'Brien, M., & Ghazarian, S. R. (2009). The longitudinal relations of teacher expectations to achievement in the early school years. *Journal of Educational Psychology, 101*, 662–670.

Hofer, M. (2010). Adolescents' development of individual interests: A product of multiple goal regulation? *Educational Psychologist, 45*, 149–166.

Holliday, B. G. (1985). Towards a model of teacher-child transactional processes affecting black children's academic achievement. In M. B. Spencer, G. K. Brookins, & W. R. Allen (Eds.), *Beginnings: The social and affective development of black children* (pp. 117–131). Mahwah, NJ: Erlbaum.

Hong, Y., Chiu, C., & Dweck, C. S. (1995). Implicit theories of intelligence: Reconsidering the role of confidence in achievement motivation. In M. H. Kernis (Ed.), *Efficacy, agency, and self-esteem* (pp. 197–216). New York, NY: Plenum Press.

Hufton, N., Elliott, J., & Illushin, L. (2002). Achievement motivation across cultures: Some puzzles and their implications for future research. *New Directions for Child and Adolescent Development, 96*, 65–85.

Hughes, J. N., Luo, W., Kwok, O.-M., & Loyd, L. K. (2008). Teacher-student support, effortful engagement, and achievement: A 3-year longitudinal study. *Journal of Educational Psychology, 100*, 1–14.

Huguet, P., & Régner, I. (2007). Stereotype threat among schoolgirls in quasi-ordinary classroom circumstances. *Journal of Educational Psychology, 99*, 545–560.

Husman, J., & Freeman, B. (1999, April). *The effect of perceptions of instrumentality on intrinsic motivation.* Paper presented at the annual meeting of the American Educational Research Association, Montreal, Canada.

Hymel, S., Comfort, C., Schonert-Reichl, K., & McDougall, P. (1996). Academic failure and school dropout: The influence of peers. In J. Juvonen & K. R. Wentzel (Eds.), *Social motivation: Understanding children's school adjustment* (pp. 313–345). Cambridge, England: Cambridge University Press.

Hynd, C. (2003). Conceptual change in response to persuasive messages. In G. M. Sinatra & P. R. Pintrich (Eds.), *Intentional conceptual change* (pp. 291–315). Mahwah, NJ: Erlbaum.

Igoa, C. (1995). *The inner world of the immigrant child.* Mahwah, NJ: Erlbaum.

Inglehart, M., Brown, D. R., & Vida, M. (1994). Competition, achievement, and gender: A stress theoretical analysis. In P. R. Pintrich, D. R. Brown, & C. E. Weinstein (Eds.), *Student motivation, cognition, and learning: Essays in honor of Wilbert J. McKeachie* (pp. 311–329). Mahwah, NJ: Erlbaum.

Iyengar, S. S., & Lepper, M. R. (1999). Rethinking the value of choice: A cultural perspective on intrinsic motivation. *Journal of Personality and Social Psychology, 76*, 349–366.

Jacobs, J. E. (1991). Influence of gender stereotypes on parent and child mathematics attitudes. *Journal of Educational Psychology, 83*, 518–527. doi:10.1037//0022-0663.83.4.518.

Jacobs, J. E., Davis-Kean, P., Bleeker, M., Eccles, J. S., & Malanchuk, O. (2005). "I can, but I don't want to": The impact of parents, interests, and activities on gender differences in math. In A. M. Gallagher & J. C. Kaufman (Eds.), *Gender differences in mathematics: An integrative psychological approach* (pp. 246–263). Cambridge, England: Cambridge University Press.

Jacobs, J. E., Lanza, S., Osgood, D. W., Eccles, J. S., & Wigfield, A. (2002). Changes in children's self-competence and values: Gender and domain differences across grades one through twelve. *Child Development, 73*, 509–527.

Jagacinski, C. M., & Nicholls, J. G. (1984). Conceptions of ability and related affects in task involvement and ego involvement. *Journal of Educational Psychology, 76*, 909–919.

Jagacinski, C. M., & Nicholls, J. G. (1987). Competence and affect in task involvement and ego involvement: The impact of social comparison information. *Journal of Educational Psychology, 79*, 107–114.

Jang, H., Kim, E. J., & Reeve, J. (2012). Longitudinal test of self-determination theory's motivation mediation model in a naturally occurring classroom context. *Journal of Educational Psychology, 104*(4), 1175–1188.

Johnson, D. W., & Johnson, R. T. (2009a). An educational psychology success story: Social interdependence theory and cooperative learning. *Educational Researcher, 38*, 365–379.

Jones, B. D. (2009). Motivating students to engage in learning: The MUSIC Model of Academic Motivation. *International Journal of Teaching and Learning in Higher Education, 21*(2), 272–285.

Jones, B. D. (2015). *Motivating students by design: Practical strategies for professors*. Charleston, SC: CreateSpace.

Jones, B. D. (2016). *User guide for assessing the components of the MUSIC Model of Academic Motivation*. Retrieved from http://www.theMUSICmodel.com

Jones, B. D., Byrd, C. N., & Lusk, D. L. (2009). High school students' beliefs about intelligence. *Research in the Schools, 16*(2), 1–14.

Jones, B. D., Ruff, C., & Osborne, J. W. (2015). Fostering students' identification with mathematics and science. In K. A. Renninger, M. Nieswandt, & S. Hidi (Eds.), *Interest in mathematics and science learning* (pp. 331–352). Washington, DC: American Educational Research Association.

Jones, B. D., Wilkins, J. L. M., Long, M. H., & Wang, F. (2012). Testing a motivational model of achievement: How students' mathematical beliefs and interests are related to their achievement. *European Journal of Psychology of Education, 27*(1), 1–20.

Jones, E. E., & Berglas, S. (1978). Control of attributions about the self through self-handicapping strategies: The appeal of alcohol and the role of underachievement. *Personality and Social Psychology Bulletin, 4*, 200–206.

Jussim, L., Eccles, J., & Madon, S. (1996). Social perception, social stereotypes, and teacher expectations: Accuracy and the quest for the powerful self-fulfilling prophecy. In L. Berkowitz (Ed.), *Advances in experimental social psychology* (pp. 281–388). New York, NY: Academic Press.

Juvonen, J. (2000). The social functions of attributional face-saving tactics among early adolescents. *Educational Psychology Review, 12*, 15–32.

Juvonen, J. (2006). Sense of belonging, social bonds, and school functioning. In P. A. Alexander & P. H. Winne (Eds.), *Handbook of educational psychology* (2nd ed., pp. 655–674). Mahwah, NJ: Erlbaum.

Kagan, J. (2010). Emotions and temperament. In M. H. Bornstein (Ed.), *Handbook of cultural developmental science* (pp. 175–194). New York, NY: Psychology Press.

Kağitçibaşi, Ç. (2007). *Family, self, and human development across cultures: Theory and applications* (2nd ed.). Mahwah, NJ: Erlbaum.

Kaplan, A. (1998, April). *Task goal orientation and adaptive social interaction among students of diverse cultural backgrounds.* Paper presented at the annual meeting of the American Educational Research Association, San Diego, CA.

Kaplan, A., & Midgley, C. (1997). The effect of achievement goals: Does level of perceived academic competence make a difference? *Contemporary Educational Psychology, 22*, 415–435.

Kaplan, A., & Midgley, C. (1999). The relationship between perceptions of the classroom goal structure and early adolescents' affect in school: The mediating role of coping strategies. *Learning and Individual Differences, 11*, 187–212.

Katz, L. (1993). All about me: Are we developing our children's self-esteem or their narcissism? *American Educator, 17*(2), 18–23.

Kerger, S., Martin, R., & Brunner, M. (2011). How can we enhance girls' interest in scientific topics? *British Journal of Educational Psychology, 81*, 606–628.

Kerns, L. L., & Lieberman, A. B. (1993). *Helping your depressed child.* Rocklin, CA: Prima.

Kim, H. S., Sherman, D. K., & Taylor, S. E. (2008). Culture and social support. *American Psychologist, 63*, 518–526.

King, N. J., & Ollendick, T. H. (1989). Children's anxiety and phobic disorders in school settings: Classification, assessment, and intervention issues. *Review of Educational Research, 59*, 431–470.

Kirkland, M. C. (1971). The effect of tests on students and schools. *Review of Educational Research, 41*, 303–350.

Klassen, R. (2002). Writing in early adolescence: A review of the role of self-efficacy beliefs. *Educational Psychology Review, 14*, 173–203.

Klassen, R. M., & Lynch, S. L. (2007). Self-efficacy from the perspective of adolescents with LD and their specialist teachers. *Journal of Learning Disabilities, 40*, 494–507.

Koestner, R., Ryan, R. M., Bernieri, F., & Holt, K. (1984). Setting limits in children's behavior: The differential effects of controlling versus informational styles on intrinsic motivation and creativity. *Journal of Personality, 52*, 233–248.

Krampen, G. (1987). Differential effects of teacher comments. *Journal of Educational Psychology, 79*, 137–146.

Kuhl, J., & Kraska, K. (1989). Self-regulation and metamotivation: Computational mechanisms, development, and assessment. In R. Kanfer, P. L. Ackerman, & R. Cudeck (Eds.), *Abilities, motivation, and methodology: The Minnesota Symposium on Learning and Individual Differences* (pp. 343–374). Mahwah, NJ: Erlbaum.

Kuhbandner, C., Spitzer, B., & Pekrun, R. (2011). Read-out of emotional information from iconic memory: The longevity of threatening stimuli. *Psychological Science, 22*, 695–700.

Kuhn, D., & Park, S.-H. (2005). Epistemological understanding and the development of intellectual values. *International Journal of Educational Research, 43*, 111–124.

Kuklinski, M. R., & Weinstein, R. S. (2001). Classroom and developmental differences in a path model of teacher expectancy effects. *Child Development, 72*, 1554–1578.

Kumar, R., Gheen, M. H., & Kaplan, A. (2002). Goal structures in the learning environment and students' disaffection from learning and schooling. In C. Midgley (Ed.), *Goals, goal structures, and patterns of adaptive learning* (pp. 143–173). Mahwah, NJ: Erlbaum.

La Guardia, J. G., (2009). Developing who I am: A self-determination theory approach to the establishment of healthy identities. *Educational Psychologist, 44*, 90–104.

Labouvie-Vief, G., & González, M. M. (2004). Dynamic integration: Affect optimization and differentiation in development. In D. Y. Dai & R. J. Sternberg (Eds.), *Motivation, emotion, and cognition: Integrative perspectives on intellectual functioning and development* (pp. 237–272). Mahwah, NJ: Erlbaum.

Lackaye, T. D., & Margalit, M. (2006). Comparisons of achievement, effort, and self-perceptions among students with learning disabilities and their peers from different achievement groups. *Journal of Learning Disabilities, 39*, 432–446.

Lam, S.-F., Jimerson, S., Shin, H., Cefai, C., Veiga, F. H., Hatzichristou, C., . . . Zollneritsch, J. (2016). Cultural universality and specificity of student engagement in school: The results of an international study from 12 countries. *British Journal of Educational Psychology, 86*, 137–153.

Lam, S.-F., Yim, P.-S., & Ng, Y.-L. (2008). Is effort praise motivational? The role of beliefs in the effort-ability relationship. *Contemporary Educational Psychology, 33*, 694–710.

Landers, D. M. (2007). The arousal-performance relationship revisited. In D. Smith (Ed.), *Essential readings in sport and exercise psychology* (pp. 211–218). Champaign, IL: Human Kinetics.

Lane, K., Falk, K., & Wehby, J. (2006). Classroom management in special education classrooms and resource rooms. In C. M. Evertson & C. S. Weinstein (Eds.), *Handbook of classroom management: Research, practice, and contemporary issues* (pp. 439–460). Mahwah, NJ: Erlbaum.

Langer, E. J. (1997). *The power of mindful learning.* Reading, MA: Addison-Wesley.

Langer, J. A. (2000). Excellence in English in middle and high school: How teachers' professional lives support student achievement. *American Educational Research Journal, 37*, 397–439.

Lapsley, D. K. (1993). Toward an integrated theory of adolescent ego development: The "new look" at adolescent egocentrism. *American Journal of Orthopsychiatry, 63,* 562–571.

Larson, R. W. (2000). Toward a psychology of positive youth development. *American Psychologist, 55,* 170–183.

Larson, R. W., & Brown, J. R. (2007). Emotional development in adolescence: What can be learned from a high school theater program? *Child Development, 78,* 1083–1099.

Larson, R. W., Moneta, G., Richards, M. H., & Wilson, S. (2002). Continuity, stability, and change in daily emotional experience across adolescence. *Child Development, 73,* 1151–1165.

Lau, S., & Nie, Y. (2008). Interplay between personal goals and classroom goal structures in predicting student outcomes: A multilevel analysis of person-context interactions. *Journal of Educational Psychology, 100,* 15–29.

Lens, W., Simons, J., & Dewitte, S. (2002). From duty to desire: The role of students' future time perspective and instrumentality perceptions for study motivation and self-regulation. In F. Pajares & T. Urdan (Eds.), *Adolescence and education: Vol. 2. Academic motivation of adolescents* (pp. 221–245). Greenwich, CT: Information Age.

Lepper, M. R., Corpus, J. H., & Iyengar, S. S. (2005). Intrinsic and extrinsic motivational orientations in the classroom: Age differences and academic correlates. *Journal of Educational Psychology, 97,* 184–196.

Lepper, M. R., & Hodell, M. (1989). Intrinsic motivation in the classroom. In C. Ames & R. Ames (Eds.), *Research on motivation in education: Vol. 3. Goals and cognitions* (pp. 73–105). San Diego, CA: Academic Press.

Lewis, M., & Sullivan, M. W. (2005). The development of self-conscious emotions. In A. J. Elliot & C. S. Dweck (Eds.), *Handbook of competence and motivation* (pp. 185–201). New York, NY: Guilford Press.

Li, J. (2005). Mind or virtue: Western and Chinese beliefs about learning. *Current Directions in Psychological Science, 14,* 190–194.

Li, J. (2006). Self in learning: Chinese adolescents' goals and sense of agency. *Child Development, 77,* 482–501.

Li, J., & Fischer, K. W. (2004). Thought and affect in American and Chinese learners' beliefs about learning. In D. Y. Dai & R. J. Sternberg (Eds.), *Motivation, emotion, and cognition: Integrative perspectives on intellectual functioning and development* (pp. 385–418). Mahwah, NJ: Erlbaum.

Liem, A. D., Lau, S., & Nie, Y. (2008). The role of self-efficacy, task value, and achievement goals in predicting learning strategies, task disengagement, peer relationship, and achievement outcome. *Contemporary Educational Psychology, 33,* 486–512.

Liem, G. A. D. (2016). Academic and social achievement goals: Their additive, interactive, and specialized effects on school functioning. *British Journal of Educational Psychology, 86,* 37–56.

Linnenbrink, E. A. (2005). The dilemma of performance-approach goals: The use of multiple goal contexts to promote students' motivation and learning. *Journal of Educational Psychology, 97,* 197–213.

Linnenbrink, E. A., & Pintrich, P. R. (2002). Achievement goal theory and affect: An asymmetrical bidirectional model. *Educational Psychologist, 37,* 69–78.

Linnenbrink, E. A., & Pintrich, P. R. (2003). Achievement goals and intentional conceptual change. In G. M. Sinatra & P. R. Pintrich (Eds.), *Intentional conceptual change* (pp. 347–374). Mahwah, NJ: Erlbaum.

Linnenbrink, E. A., & Pintrich, P. R. (2004). Role of affect in cognitive processing in academic contexts. In D. Y. Dai & R. J. Sternberg (Eds.), *Motivation, emotion, and cognition: Integrative perspectives on intellectual functioning and development* (pp. 57–87). Mahwah, NJ: Erlbaum.

Locke, E. A., & Latham, G. P. (2002). Building a practically useful theory of goal setting and task motivation: A 35-year odyssey. *American Psychologist, 57,* 705–717.

Locke, E. A., & Latham, G. P. (2006). New directions in goal-setting theory. *Current Directions in Psychological Science, 15,* 265–268.

Lockhart, K. L., Chang, B., & Story, T. (2002). Young children's beliefs about the stability of traits: Protective optimism? *Child Development, 73,* 1408–1430.

Lodewyk, K. R., & Winne, P. H. (2005). Relations among the structure of learning tasks, achievement, and changes in self-efficacy in secondary students. *Journal of Educational Psychology, 97,* 3–12.

Mac Iver, D. J., Stipek, D. J., & Daniels, D. H. (1991). Explaining within-semester changes in student effort in junior high school and senior high school courses. *Journal of Educational Psychology, 83,* 201–211.

Maehr, M. L. (1984). Meaning and motivation: Toward a theory of personal investment. In R. Ames & C. Ames (Eds.), *Research on motivation in education: Vol. 1. Student motivation* (pp. 115–144). San Diego, CA: Academic Press.

Maehr, M. L., & Anderman, E. M. (1993). Reinventing schools for early adolescents: Emphasizing task goals. *Elementary School Journal, 93,* 593–610.

Marachi, R., Friedel, J., & Midgley, C. (2001, April). *"I sometimes annoy my teacher during math": Relations between student perceptions of the teacher and disruptive behavior in the classroom.* Paper presented at the annual meeting of the American Educational Research Association, Seattle, WA.

Marcus, G. (2008). *Kluge: The haphazard construction of the human mind.* Boston, MA: Houghton Mifflin.

Marsh, H. W., & Craven, R. (1997). Academic self-concept: Beyond the dustbowl. In G. D. Phye (Ed.), *Handbook of classroom assessment: Learning, achievement, and adjustment* (pp. 131–198). San Diego, CA: Academic Press.

Martin, A. J. (2008). Enhancing student motivation and engagement: The effects of a multidimensional intervention. *Contemporary Educational Psychology, 33,* 239–269.

Martin, A. J., & Dowson, M. (2009). Interpersonal relationships, motivation, engagement, and achievement: Yields for theory, current issues, and educational practice. *Review of Educational Research, 79,* 327–365.

Martin, A. J., Marsh, H. W., & Debus, R. L. (2001). A quadripolar need achievement representation of self-handicapping and defensive pessimism. *American Educational Research Journal, 38,* 583–610.

Martin, A. J., Marsh, H. W., Williamson, A., & Debus, R. L. (2003). Self-handicapping, defensive pessimism, and goal orientation: A qualitative study of university students. *Journal of Educational Psychology, 95,* 617–628.

Maslow, A. H. (1973). Theory of human motivation. In R. J. Lowry (Ed.), *Dominance, self-esteem, self-actualization: Germinal papers of A. H. Maslow* (pp. 153–173). Monterey, CA: Brooks/Cole.

Maslow, A. H. (1987). *Motivation and personality* (3rd ed.). New York, NY: Harper & Row.

Mason, L., Gava, M., & Boldrin, A. (2008). On warm conceptual change: The interplay of text, epistemological beliefs, and topic interest. *Journal of Educational Psychology, 100,* 291–309.

Matthews, G., Zeidner, M., & Roberts, R. D. (2006). Models of personality and affect for education: A review and synthesis. In P. A. Alexander & P. H. Winne (Eds.), *Handbook of educational psychology* (2nd ed., pp. 163–186). Mahwah, NJ: Erlbaum.

McCombs, B. L. (1988). Motivational skills training: Combining metacognitive, cognitive, and affective learning strategies. In C. E. Weinstein, E. T. Goetz, & P. A. Alexander (Eds.), *Learning and study strategies: Issues in assessment, instruction, and evaluation* (pp. 11–24). San Diego, CA: Harcourt Brace Jovanovich.

McCombs, B. L. (1996). Alternative perspectives for motivation. In L. Baker, P. Afflerbach, & D. Reinking (Eds.), *Developing engaged readers in school and home communities* (pp. 67–87). Hillsdale, NJ: Erlbaum.

McCourt, F. (2005). *Teacher man: A memoir.* New York, NY: Scribner.

McGaugh, J. L. (2015). Consolidating memories. *Annual Review of Psychology, 66,* 1–24.

McGregor, H. A., & Elliot, A. J. (2002). Achievement goals as predictors of achievement-relevant processes prior to task engagement. *Journal of Educational Psychology, 94,* 381–395.

McKown, C., & Weinstein, R. S. (2003). The development and consequences of stereotype consciousness in middle childhood. *Child Development, 74,* 498–515.

McLeod, D. B., & Adams, V. M. (Eds.). (1989). *Affect and mathematical problem solving: A new perspective.* New York, NY: Springer-Verlag.

McLoyd, V. C. (1998). Socioeconomic disadvantage and child development. *American Psychologist, 53,* 185–204.

McMillan, J. H., Singh, J., & Simonetta, L. G. (1994). The tyranny of self-oriented self-esteem. *Educational Horizons, 72*(3), 141–145.

McNally, R. J., & Geraerts, E. (2009). A new solution to the recovered memory debate. *Perspectives on Psychological Science, 4,* 126–134.

McNeil, N. M., & Alibali, M. W. (2000). Learning mathematics from procedural instruction: Externally imposed goals influence what is learned. *Journal of Educational Psychology, 92,* 734–744.

Meece, J. L. (1994). The role of motivation in self-regulated learning. In D. H. Schunk & B. J. Zimmerman (Eds.),

Self-regulation of learning and performance: Issues and educational applications (pp. 25–44). Mahwah, NJ: Erlbaum.

Meece, J. L., & Holt, K. (1993). A pattern analysis of students' achievement goals. *Journal of Educational Psychology, 85,* 582–590.

Meehan, B. T., Hughes, J. N., & Cavell, T. A. (2003). Teacher-student relationships as compensatory resources for aggressive children. *Child Development, 74,* 1145–1157.

Mellers, B. A., & McGraw, A. P. (2001). Anticipated emotions as guides to choice. *Current Directions in Psychological Science, 10,* 210–214.

Mesquita, B., & Leu, J. (2007). The cultural psychology of emotion. In S. Kitayama & D. Cohen (Eds.), *Handbook of cultural psychology* (pp. 734–759). New York, NY: Guilford Press.

Meyer, D. K., & Turner, J. C. (2002). Discovering emotion in classroom motivation research. *Educational Psychologist, 37,* 107–114.

Meyer, L. H., Weir, K. F., McClure, J., & Walkey, F. (2008, March). *The relationship of motivation orientations to future achievement in secondary school.* Paper presented at the annual meeting of the American Educational Research Association, New York, NY.

Middleton, M. J., & Midgley, C. (1997). Avoiding the demonstration of lack of ability: An under-explored aspect of goal theory. *Journal of Educational Psychology, 89,* 710–718.

Middleton, M. J., & Midgley, C. (2002). Beyond motivation: Middle school students' perceptions of press for understanding in math. *Contemporary Educational Psychology, 27,* 373–391.

Midgley, C. (Ed.) (2002). *Goals, goal structures, and patterns of adaptive learning.* Mahwah, NJ: Erlbaum.

Midgley, C., Kaplan, A., & Middleton, M. (2001). Performance-approach goals: Good for what, for whom, under what circumstances, and at what cost? *Journal of Educational Psychology, 93,* 77–86.

Midgley, C., Kaplan, A., Middleton, M., Maehr, M., Urdan, T., Anderman, L. H., . . . Roeser, R. (1998). The development and validation of scales assessing students' achievement goal orientations. *Contemporary Educational Psychology, 23,* 113–131.

Midgley, C., Middleton, M. J., Gheen, M. H., & Kumar, R. (2002). Stage-environment fit revisited: A goal theory approach to examining school transitions. In C. Midgley (Ed.), *Goals, goal structures, and patterns of adaptive learning* (pp. 109–142). Mahwah, NJ: Erlbaum.

Miller, S. D., & Meece, J. L. (1997). Enhancing elementary students' motivation to read and write: A classroom intervention study. *Journal of Educational Research, 90,* 286–300.

Milner, H. R. (2006). Classroom management in urban classrooms. In C. M. Evertson & C. S. Weinstein (Eds.), *Handbook of classroom management: Research, practice, and contemporary issues* (pp. 491–522). Mahwah, NJ: Erlbaum.

Mitchell, M. (1993). Situational interest: Its multifaceted structure in the secondary school mathematics classroom. *Journal of Educational Psychology, 85,* 424–436.

Morelli, G. A., & Rothbaum, F. (2007). Situating the child in context: Attachment relationships and self-regulation in different cultures. In S. Kitayama & D. Cohen (Eds.), *Handbook of cultural psychology* (pp. 500–527). New York, NY: Guilford Press.

Murdock, T. B. (1999). The social context of risk: Status and motivational predictors of alienation in middle school. *Journal of Educational Psychology, 91,* 62–75.

Murphy, P. K., & Alexander, P. A. (2000). A motivated exploration of motivation terminology. *Contemporary Educational Psychology, 25,* 3–53.

Newman, R. S., & Schwager, M. T. (1995). Students' help seeking during problem solving: Effects of grade, goal, and prior achievement. *American Educational Research Journal, 32,* 352–376.

Nicholls, J. G. (1984). Conceptions of ability and achievement motivation. In R. Ames & C. Ames (Eds.), *Research on motivation in education: Vol. 1. Student motivation* (pp. 39–73). San Diego, CA: Academic Press.

Nicholls, J. G. (1990). What is ability and why are we mindful of it? A developmental perspective. In R. J. Sternberg & J. Kolligian (Eds.), *Competence considered* (pp. 11–40). New Haven, CT: Yale University Press.

Nisbett, R. E. (2009). *Intelligence and how to get it.* New York, NY: Norton.

Nolen, S. B. (1996). Why study? How reasons for learning influence strategy selection. *Educational Psychology Review, 8,* 335–355.

Nolen, S. B. (2007). Young children's motivation to read and write: Development in social contexts. *Cognition and Instruction, 25,* 219–270.

Nolen, S. B., Horn, I. S., Ward, C. J. (2015). Situating motivation. *Educational Psychologist, 50*(3), 234–247.

Norenzayan, A., Choi, I., & Peng, K. (2007). Perception and cognition. In S. Kitayama & D. Cohen (Eds.), *Handbook of cultural psychology* (pp. 569–594). New York, NY: Guilford Press.

Oakes, J., & Guiton, G. (1995). Matchmaking: The dynamics of high school tracking decisions. *American Educational Research Journal, 32*, 3–33.

Ogbu, J. U. (2003). *Black American students in an affluent suburb: A study of academic disengagement.* Mahwah, NJ: Erlbaum.

Öhman, A., & Mineka, S. (2003). The malicious serpent: Snakes as a prototypical stimulus for an evolved module of fear. *Current Directions in Psychological Science, 12,* 5–9.

Osborne, J. W. (2007). Linking stereotype threat and anxiety. *Educational Psychology, 27*(1), 135–154.

Osborne, J. W., & Jones, B. D. (2011). Identification with academics and motivation to achieve in school: How the structure of the self influences academic outcomes. *Educational Psychology Review, 23*(1), 131–158.

Otis, N., Grouzet, F. M. E., & Pelletier, L. G. (2005). Latent motivational change in an academic setting: A 3-year longitudinal study. *Journal of Educational Psychology, 97*, 170–183.

Page-Voth, V., & Graham, S. (1999). Effects of goal setting and strategy use on the writing performance and self-efficacy of students with writing and learning problems. *Journal of Educational Psychology, 91*, 230–240.

Pajares, F. (2005). Gender differences in mathematics self-efficacy beliefs. In A. M. Gallagher & J. C. Kaufman (Eds.), *Gender differences in mathematics: An integrative psychological approach* (pp. 294–315). Cambridge, England: Cambridge University Press.

Paley, V. G. (1984). *Boys and girls: Superheroes in the doll corner.* Chicago, IL: University of Chicago Press.

Palmer, D. J., & Goetz, E. T. (1988). Selection and use of study strategies: The role of the studier's beliefs about self and strategies. In C. E. Weinstein, E. T. Goetz, & P. A. Alexander (Eds.), *Learning and study strategies: Issues in assessment, instruction, and evaluation* (pp. 41–61). San Diego, CA: Academic Press.

Pang, V. O. (1995). Asian Pacific American students: A diverse and complex population. In J. A. Banks & C. A. M. Banks (Eds.), *Handbook of research on multicultural education* (pp. 412–426). New York, NY: Macmillan.

Paris, S. G., & Byrnes, J. P. (1989). The constructivist approach to self-regulation and learning in the classroom. In B. J. Zimmerman & D. H. Schunk (Eds.), *Self-regulated learning and academic achievement: Theory, research, and practice* (pp. 169–200). New York, NY: Springer-Verlag.

Paris, S. G., & Cunningham, A. E. (1996). Children becoming students. In D. C. Berliner & R. C. Calfee (Eds.), *Handbook of educational psychology* (pp. 117–147). New York, NY: Macmillan.

Paris, S. G., & Turner, J. C. (1994). Situated motivation. In P. R. Pintrich, D. R. Brown, & C. E. Weinstein (Eds.), *Student motivation, cognition, and learning: Essays in honor of Wilbert J. McKeachie* (pp. 213–237). Mahwah, NJ: Erlbaum.

Parkes, K., Jones, B. D., & Wilkins, J. (2015). Assessing music students' motivation using the MUSIC Model of Academic Motivation Inventory. *UPDATE: Applications of Research in Music Education.* Advance online publication. doi:10.1177/8755123315620835

Patall, E. A., Cooper, H., & Wynn, S. R. (2010). The effectiveness and relative importance of choice in the classroom. *Journal of Educational Psychology, 102*(4), 896–915.

Patrick, H., Anderman, L. H., & Ryan, A. M. (2002). Social motivation and the classroom social environment. In C. Midgley (Ed.), *Goals, goal structures, and patterns of adaptive learning* (pp. 85–108). Mahwah, NJ: Erlbaum.

Patrick, H., Mantzicopoulos, Y., & Samarapungavan, A. (2009). Motivation for learning science in kindergarten: Is there a gender gap and does integrated inquiry and literacy instruction make a difference? *Journal of Research in Science Teaching, 46,* 166–191.

Patrick, H., Ryan, A. M., Anderman, L. H., Middleton, M. J., Linnenbrink, L., Hruda, L. Z., . . . Midgley, C. (1997). *Observing Patterns of Adaptive Learning (OPAL): A scheme for classroom observations.* Ann Arbor, MI: The University of Michigan.

Pekrun, R. (2006). The control-value theory of achievement emotions: Assumptions, corollaries, and implications for educational research and practice. *Educational Psychology Review, 18,* 315–341.

Pekrun, R., Elliot, A., & Maier, M. A. (2006). Achievement goals and discrete achievement emotions: A theoretical model and prospective test. *Journal of Educational Psychology, 98*, 583–597.

Pekrun, R., Goetz, T., Titz, W., & Perry, R. P. (2002). Academic emotions in students' self-regulated learning and achievement: A program of qualitative and quantitative research. *Educational Psychologist, 37*, 91–105.

Pellegrini, A. D., & Long, J. D. (2004). Part of the solution and part of the problem: The role of peers in bullying, dominance, and victimization during the transition from primary school through secondary school. In D. L. Espelage & S. M. Swearer (Eds.), *Bullying in American schools: A social-ecological perspective on prevention and intervention* (pp. 107–117). Mahwah, NJ: Erlbaum.

Peng, K., & Nisbett, R. E. (1999). Culture, dialecticism, and reasoning about contradiction. *American Psychologist, 54,* 741–754.

Perry, N. E., Turner, J. C., & Meyer, D. K. (2006). Classrooms as contexts for motivating learning. In P. A. Alexander & P. H. Winne (Eds.), *Handbook of educational psychology* (2nd ed., pp. 327–348). Mahwah, NJ: Erlbaum.

Peterson, C. (1990). Explanatory style in the classroom and on the playing field. In S. Graham & V. S. Folkes (Eds.), *Attribution theory: Applications to achievement, mental health, and interpersonal conflict* (pp. 53–75). Mahwah, NJ: Erlbaum.

Peterson, C. (2006). *A primer in positive psychology.* New York, NY: Oxford University Press.

Peterson, C., Maier, S., & Seligman, M. (1993). *Learned helplessness: A theory for the age of personal control.* New York, NY: Oxford University Press.

Phalet, K., Andriessen, I., & Lens, W. (2004). How future goals enhance motivation and learning in multicultural classrooms. *Educational Psychology Review, 16*, 59–89.

Phelan, P., Davidson, A. L., & Cao, H. T. (1991). Students' multiple worlds: Negotiating the boundaries of family, peer, and school cultures. *Anthropology and Education Quarterly, 22,* 224–250.

Phelan, P., Yu, H. C., & Davidson, A. L. (1994). Navigating the psychosocial pressures of adolescence: The voices and experiences of high school youth. *American Educational Research Journal, 31,* 415–447.

Phelps, E. A., & Sharot, T. (2008). How (and why) emotion enhances the subjective sense of recollection. *Current Directions in Psychological Science, 17,* 147–152.

Pianta, R. C., Belsky, J., Vandergrift, N., Houts, R., & Morrison, F. J. (2008). Classroom effects on children's achievement trajectories in elementary school. *American Educational Research Journal, 45,* 365–397.

Pintrich, P. R. (2003). Motivation and classroom learning. In W. M. Reynolds, G. E. Miller (Vol. Eds.), & I. B. Weiner (Editor-in-Chief), *Handbook of psychology: Vol. 7. Educational psychology* (pp. 103–122). New York, NY: Wiley.

Pintrich, P. R., Marx, R. W., & Boyle, R. A. (1993). Beyond cold conceptual change: The role of motivational beliefs and classroom contextual factors in the process of conceptual change. *Review of Educational Research, 63*, 167–199.

Pintrich, P. R., & Schrauben, B. (1992). Students' motivational beliefs and their cognitive engagement in academic tasks. In D. Schunk & J. Meece (Eds.), *Students' perceptions in the classroom: Causes and consequences* (pp. 149–183). Mahwah, NJ: Erlbaum.

Pintrich, P. R., & Schunk, D. H. (2002). *Motivation in education: Theory, research, and applications* (2nd ed.). Upper Saddle River, NJ: Merrill/Prentice Hall.

Pomerantz, E. M., & Saxon, J. L. (2001). Conceptions of ability as stable and self-evaluative processes: A longitudinal examination. *Child Development, 72,* 152–173.

Posner, M. I., & Rothbart, M. K. (2007). *Educating the human brain.* Washington, DC: American Psychological Association.

Powell, S., & Nelson, B. (1997). Effects of choosing academic assignments on a student with attention deficit hyperactivity disorder. *Journal of Applied Behavior Analysis, 30*, 181–183.

Preckel, F., Holling, H., & Vock, M. (2006). Academic underachievement: Relationship with cognitive motivation, achievement motivation, and conscientiousness. *Psychology in the Schools, 43,* 401–411.

Pressley, M., Borkowski, J. G., & Schneider, W. (1987). Cognitive strategies: Good strategy users coordinate metacognition and knowledge. In R. Vasta (Ed.), *Annals of child development* (Vol. 4, pp. 80–129). Greenwich, CT: JAI Press.

Pugh, K. J., & Bergin, D. A. (2006). Motivational influences on transfer. *Educational Psychologist, 41*, 147–160.

Pulfrey, C., & Darnon, C., & Butera, F. (2013). Autonomy and task performance: Explaining the impact of grades on intrinsic motivation. *Journal of Educational Psychology, 105*(1), 39–57.

Qian, G., & Pan, J. (2002). A comparison of epistemological beliefs and learning from science text between American and Chinese high school students. In B. K. Hofer & P. R. Pintrich (Eds.), *Personal epistemology: The psychology of beliefs about knowledge and knowing* (pp. 365–385). Mahwah, NJ: Erlbaum.

Qin, L., Pomerantz, E. M., & Wang, Q. (2009). Are gains in decision-making autonomy during early adolescence beneficial for emotional functioning? The case of the United States and China. *Child Development, 80,* 1705–1721.

Raine, A., Reynolds, C., & Venables, P. H. (2002). Stimulation seeking and intelligence: A prospective longitudinal study. *Journal of Personality and Social Psychology, 82,* 663–674.

Ratelle, C. F., Guay, F., Vallerand, R. J., Larose, S., & Senécal, C. (2007). Autonomous, controlled, and amotivated types of academic motivation: A person-oriented analysis. *Journal of Educational Psychology, 99,* 734–746.

Raudenbush, S. W. (1984). Magnitude of teacher expectancy effects on pupil IQ as a function of credibility induction: A synthesis of findings from 18 experiments. *Journal of Educational Psychology, 76,* 85–97.

Raufelder, D., Sahabandu, D., Martínez, G. S., & Escobar, V. (2015). The mediating role of social relationships in the association of adolescents' individual school self-concept and their school engagement, belonging and helplessness in school. *Educational Psychology, 35*(2), 137–157.

Rawsthorne, L. J., & Elliot, A. J. (1999). Achievement goals and intrinsic motivation: A meta-analytic review. *Personality and Social Psychology Review, 3,* 326–344.

Reed, J. H., Schallert, D. L., Beth, A. D., & Woodruff, A. L. (2004). Motivated reader, engaged writer: The role of motivation in the literate acts of adolescents. In T. L. Jetton & J. A. Dole (Eds.), *Adolescent literacy research and practice* (pp. 251–282). New York, NY: Guilford Press.

Reeve, J. (2006). Teachers as facilitators: What autonomy-supportive teachers do and why their students benefit. *The Elementary School Journal, 106*(3), 225–236.

Reeve, J. (2009a). *Understanding motivation and emotion* (5th ed.). Hoboken, NJ: Wiley.

Reeve, J. (2009b). Why teachers adopt a controlling motivating style toward students and how they can become more autonomy supportive. *Educational Psychologist, 44,* 159–175.

Reeve, J., Bolt, E., & Cai, Y. (1999). Autonomy-supportive teachers: How they teach and motivate students. *Journal of Educational Psychology, 91,* 537–548.

Reeve, J., Deci, E. L., & Ryan, R. M. (2004). Self-determination theory: A dialectical framework for understanding sociocultural influences on student motivation. In D. M. McInerney & S. Van Etten (Eds.), *Big theories revisited* (pp. 31–60). Greenwich, CT: Information Age.

Régner, I., Escribe, C., & Dupeyrat, C. (2007). Evidence of social comparison in mastery goals in natural academic settings. *Journal of Educational Psychology, 99,* 575–583.

Reisberg, D., & Heuer, F. (1992). Remembering the details of emotional events. In E. Winograd & U. Neisser (Eds.), *Affect and accuracy in recall: Studies of "flashbulb" memories* (pp. 162–189). Cambridge, England: Cambridge University Press.

Renninger, K. A. (2009). Interest and identity development in instruction: An inductive model. *Educational Psychologist, 44,* 105–118.

Renninger, K. A., & Hidi, S. (2011). Revisiting the conceptualization, measurement, and generation of interest. *Educational Psychologist, 46*(3), 168–184.

Renninger, K. A., Hidi, S., & Krapp, A. (Eds.). (1992). *The role of interest in learning and development.* Mahwah, NJ: Erlbaum.

Renninger, K. A., Nieswandt, M., & Hidi, S. (2015). Introduction: On the power of interest. In K. A. Renninger, M. Nieswandt, & S. Hidi (Eds.), *Interest in mathematics and science learning* (pp. 1–14). Washington, DC: American Educational Research Association.

Reyes, M. R., Brackett, M. A., Rivers, S. E., White, M., & Salovey, P. (2012). Classroom emotional climate, student engagement, and academic achievement. *Journal of Educational Psychology, 104*(3), 700–712.

Reyna, C. (2000). Lazy, dumb, or industrious: When stereotypes convey attribution information in the classroom. *Educational Psychology Review, 12,* 85–110.

Reyna, C., & Weiner, B. (2001). Justice and utility in the classroom: An attributional analysis of the goals of teachers' punishment and intervention strategies. *Journal of Educational Psychology, 93,* 309–319.

Reyna, V. F., & Farley, F. (2006). Risk and rationality in adolescent decision making: Implications for theory, practice, and public policy. *Psychological Science in the Public Interest, 7*(1), 1–44.

Rhodewalt, F., & Vohs, K. D. (2005). Defensive strategies, motivation, and the self: A self-regulatory process view. In

A. J. Elliot & C. S. Dweck (Eds.), *Handbook of competence and motivation* (pp. 548–565). New York, NY: Guilford Press.

Richards, J. M. (2004). The cognitive consequences of concealing feelings. *Current Directions in Psychological Science, 13,* 131–134.

Riggs, J. M. (1992). Self-handicapping and achievement. In A. K. Boggiano & T. S. Pittman (Eds.), *Achievement and motivation: A social-developmental perspective* (pp. 244–267). Cambridge, England: Cambridge University Press.

Rimm-Kaufman, S. E., Baroody, A. E., Larsen, R. A. A., Curby, T. W., & Abry, T. (2014). To what extent do teacher-student interaction quality and student gender contribute to fifth graders' engagement in mathematics learning? *Journal of Educational Psychology, 107*(1), 170–185.

Roberts, G. C., Treasure, D. C., & Kavussanu, M. (1997). Motivation in physical activity contexts: An achievement goal perspective. *Advances in Motivation and Achievement, 10,* 413–447.

Roderick, M., & Camburn, E. (1999). Risk and recovery from course failure in the early years of high school. *American Educational Research Journal, 36,* 303–343.

Roeser, R. W., Marachi, R., & Gehlbach, H. (2002). A goal theory perspective on teachers' professional identities and the contexts of teaching. In C. Midgley (Ed.), *Goals, goal structures, and patterns of adaptive learning* (pp. 205–241). Mahwah, NJ: Erlbaum.

Rogoff, B. (2003). *The cultural nature of human development.* Oxford, England: Oxford University Press.

Rolland, R. G. (2012). Synthesizing the evidence on classroom goal structures in middle and secondary schools: A meta-analysis and narrative review. *Review of Educational Research, 82*(4), 396–435.

Roorda, D. L., Koomen, H. M. Y., Spilt, J. L., & Oort, F. J. (2011). The influence of affective teacher-student relationships on students' school engagement and achievement: A meta-analytic approach. *Review of Educational Research, 81,* 493–529.

Rose, A. J. (2002). Co-rumination in the friendship of girls and boys. *Child Development, 73,* 1830–1843.

Rosenthal, R. (1994). Interpersonal expectancy effects: A 30-year perspective. *Current Directions in Psychological Science, 3,* 176–179.

Rosenthal, R., & Jacobson, L. (1968). *Pygmalion in the classroom: Teacher expectation and pupils' intellectual development.* New York, NY: Holt, Rinehart & Winston.

Ross, J. A. (1988). Controlling variables: A meta-analysis of training studies. *Review of Educational Research, 58,* 405–437.

Rothbaum, F., Weisz, J. R., & Snyder, S. S. (1982). Changing the world and changing the self: A two-process model of perceived control. *Journal of Personality and Social Psychology, 42,* 5–37.

Rovee-Collier, C. (1999). The development of infant memory. *Current Directions in Psychological Science, 8,* 80–85.

Rudolph, K. D., Caldwell, M. S., & Conley, C. S. (2005). Need for approval and children's well-being. *Child Development, 76,* 309–323.

Rudolph, K. D., Lambert, S. F., Clark, A. G., & Kurlakowsky, K. D. (2001). Negotiating the transition to middle school: The role of self-regulatory processes. *Child Development, 72,* 929–946.

Rueda, R., & Moll, L. C. (1994). A sociocultural perspective on motivation. In H. F. O'Neil, Jr., & M. Drillings (Eds.), *Motivation: Theory and research* (pp. 117–137). Mahwah, NJ: Erlbaum.

Ryan, A. M., Hicks, L., & Midgley, C. (1997). Social goals, academic goals, and avoiding help seeking in the classroom. *Journal of Early Adolescence, 17,* 152–171.

Ryan, A. M., & Patrick, H. (2001). The classroom social environment and changes in adolescents' motivation and engagement during middle school. *American Educational Research Journal, 38,* 437–460.

Ryan, A. M., Pintrich, P. R., & Midgley, C. (2001). Avoiding seeking help in the classroom: Who and why? *Educational Psychology Review, 13,* 93–114.

Ryan, K. E., & Ryan, A. M. (2005). Psychological processes underlying stereotype threat and standardized math test performance. *Educational Psychologist, 40,* 53–63.

Ryan, K. E., Ryan, A. M., Arbuthnot, K., & Samuels, M. (2007). Students' motivation for standardized math exams: Insights from students. *Educational Researcher, 36*(1), 5–13.

Ryan, R. M., Connell, J. P., & Grolnick, W. S. (1992). When achievement is *not* intrinsically motivated: A theory of internalization and self-regulation in school. In A. K. Boggiano & T. S. Pittman (Eds.), *Achievement and motivation: A social-developmental perspective* (pp. 167–188). Cambridge, England: Cambridge University Press.

Ryan, R. M., & Deci, E. L. (2000). Self-determination theory and the facilitation of intrinsic motivation, social development, and well-being. *American Psychologist, 55,* 68–78.

Ryan, R. M., Mims, V., & Koestner, R. (1983). Relation of reward contingency and interpersonal context to intrinsic motivation: A review and test using cognitive evaluation theory. *Journal of Personality and Social Psychology, 45,* 736–750.

Sarason, I. G. (Ed.). (1980). *Test anxiety: Theory, research, and applications.* Mahwah, NJ: Erlbaum.

Schacter, D. L. (1999). The seven sins of memory: Insights from psychology and neuroscience. *American Psychologist, 54,* 182–203.

Schank, R. C. (1979). Interestingness: Controlling inferences. *Artificial Intelligence, 12,* 273–297.

Scheier, M. F., & Carver, C. S. (1992). Effects of optimism on psychological and physical well-being: Theoretical overview and empirical update. *Cognitive Therapy and Research, 16,* 201–228.

Schiefele, U. (1991). Interest, learning, and motivation. *Educational Psychologist, 26,* 299–323.

Schiefele, U. (1992). Topic interest and levels of text comprehension. In K. A. Renninger, S. Hidi, & A. Krapp (Eds.), *The role of interest in learning and development* (pp. 151–182). Mahwah, NJ: Erlbaum.

Schiefele, U. (1998). Individual interest and learning: What we know and what we don't know. In L. Hoffman, A. Krapp, K. Renninger, & J. Baumert (Eds.), *Interest and learning: Proceedings of the Seeon Conference on Interest and Gender* (pp. 91–104). Kiel, Germany: IPN.

Schmidt, A. C., Hanley, G. P., & Layer, S. A. (2009). A further analysis of the value of choice: Controlling for illusory discriminative stimuli and evaluating the effects of less preferred items. *Journal of Applied Behavior Analysis, 42,* 711–716.

Schraw, G., & Lehman, S. (2001). Situational interest: A review of the literature and directions for future research. *Educational Psychology Review, 13,* 23–52.

Schultheiss, O. C., & Brunstein, J. C. (2005). An implicit motive perspective on competence. In A. J. Elliot & C. S. Dweck (Eds.), *Handbook of competence and motivation* (pp. 31–51). New York, NY: Guilford Press.

Schunk, D. H. (1983). Developing children's self-efficacy and skills: The roles of social comparative information and goal setting. *Contemporary Educational Psychology, 8,* 76–86.

Schunk, D. H. (1990, April). *Socialization and the development of self-regulated learning: The role of attributions.* Paper presented at the annual meeting of the American Educational Research Association, Boston, MA.

Schunk, D. H., Meece, J. L., & Pintrich, P. R. (2014). *Motivation in education: Theory, research, and applications.* Upper Saddle River, NJ: Pearson.

Schunk, D. H., & Pajares, F. (2004). Self-efficacy in education revisited: Empirical and applied evidence. In D. M. McInerney & S. Van Etten (Eds.), *Big theories revisited* (pp. 115–138). Greenwich, CT: Information Age.

Schunk, D. H., & Pajares, F. (2005). Competence perceptions and academic functioning. In A. J. Elliot & C. S. Dweck (Eds.), *Handbook of competence and motivation* (pp. 85–104). New York, NY: Guilford Press.

Schunk, D. H., & Usher, E. L. (2012). Social cognitive theory and motivation. In R. M. Ryan (Ed.), *The Oxford Handbook of Human Motivation* (pp. 13–27). New York, NY: Oxford University Press.

Schunk, D. H., & Zimmerman, B. J. (2006). Competence and control beliefs: Distinguishing the means and ends. In P. A. Alexander & P. H. Winne (Eds.), *Handbook of educational psychology* (2nd ed., pp. 349–367). Mahwah, NJ: Erlbaum.

Schutz, P. A. (1994). Goals as the transactive point between motivation and cognition. In P. R. Pintrich, D. R. Brown, & C. E. Weinstein (Eds.), *Student motivation, cognition, and learning: Essays in honor of Wilbert J. McKeachie* (pp. 135–166). Mahwah, NJ: Erlbaum.

Schwinger, M., & Wild, E. (2012). Prevalence, stability, and functionality of achievement goal profiles in mathematics from third to seventh grade. *Contemporary Educational Psychology, 37,* 1–13.

Sedikides, C., & Gregg, A. P. (2008). Self-enhancement: Food for thought. *Perspectives on Psychological Science, 3,* 102–116.

Seligman, M. E. P. (1991). *Learned optimism.* New York, NY: Knopf.

Sherman, D. K., & Cohen, G. L. (2002). Accepting threatening information: Self-affirmation and the reduction of defensive biases. *Current Directions in Psychological Science, 11,* 119–123.

Shernoff, D. J., Knauth, S., & Makris, E. (2000). The quality of classroom experiences. In M. Csikszentmihalyi & B. Schneider, *Becoming adult: How teenagers prepare for the world of work* (pp. 141–164). New York, NY: Basic Books.

Shim, S. S., & Ryan, A. M. (2006, April). *The nature and the consequences of changes in achievement goals during early adolescence.* Paper presented at the annual meeting of the American Educational Research Association, San Francisco, CA.

Shim, S. S., Ryan, A. M., & Anderson, C. J. (2008). Achievement goals and achievement during early adolescence: Examining time-varying predictor and outcome variables in growth-curve analysis. *Journal of Educational Psychology, 100,* 655–671.

Shipman, S., & Shipman, V. C. (1985). Cognitive styles: Some conceptual, methodological, and applied issues. In E. W. Gordon (Ed.), *Review of research in education* (Vol. 12, pp. 229–291). Washington, DC: American Educational Research Association.

Shores, M., & Shannon, D. (2007). The effects of self-regulation, motivation, anxiety, and attributions on mathematics achievement for fifth and sixth grade students. *School Science and Mathematics, 107*(6), 225–236.

Shute, V. J. (2008). Focus on formative feedback. *Review of Educational Research, 78,* 153–189.

Sideridis, G. D. (2005). Goal orientation, academic achievement, and depression: Evidence in favor of a revised goal theory framework. *Journal of Educational Psychology, 97,* 366–375.

Sinatra, G. M., & Mason, L. (2008). Beyond knowledge: Learner characteristics influencing conceptual change. In S. Vosniadou (Ed.), *International handbook of research on conceptual change* (pp. 560–582). New York, NY: Routledge.

Sins, P. H. M., van Joolingen, W. R., Savelsbergh, E. R., & van Hout-Wolters, B. (2008). Motivation and performance within a collaborative computer-based modeling task: Relations between students' achievement goal orientation, self-efficacy, cognitive processing, and achievement. *Contemporary Educational Psychology, 33,* 58–77.

Skaalvik, E. (1997). Self-enhancing and self-defeating ego orientation: Relations with task avoidance orientation, achievement, self-perceptions, and anxiety. *Journal of Educational Psychology, 89,* 71–81.

Skaalvik, E. M., & Skaalvik, S. (2008). Teacher self-efficacy: Conceptual analysis and relations with teacher burnout and perceived school context. In H. W. Marsh, R. G. Craven, & D. M. McInerney (Eds.), *Self-processes, learning, and enabling human potential* (pp. 223–247). Charlotte, NC: Information Age.

Skinner, E., Furrer, C., Marchand, G., & Kindermann, T. (2008). Engagement and disaffection in the classroom: Part of a larger motivational dynamic? *Journal of Educational Psychology, 100,* 765–781.

Skinner, E. A., & Pitzer, J. R. (2012). Developmental dynamics of student engagement, coping, and everyday resilience. In S. L. Christenson, A. L. Reschly, & C. Wylie (Eds.), *Handbook of research on student engagement* (pp. 21–44). New York, NY: Springer.

Smith, J. L. (2004). Understanding the process of stereotype threat: A review of mediational variables and new performance goal directions. *Educational Psychology Review, 16,* 177–206.

Snow, R. E., Corno, L., & Jackson, D., III (1996). Individual differences in affective and conative functions. In D. C. Berliner & R. C. Calfee (Eds.), *Handbook of educational psychology* (pp. 243–310). New York, NY: Macmillan.

Snyder, C. R. (1994). *The psychology of hope: You can get there from here.* New York, NY: Free Press.

Snyder, C. R. (2002). Hope theory: Rainbows in the mind. *Psychological Inquiry, 13,* 249–275.

Soenens, B., Sierens, E., Vansteenkiste, M., Dochy, F., & Goossens, L. (2011). Psychologically controlling teaching: Examining outcomes, antecedents, and mediators. *Journal of Educational Psychology, 104*(1), 108–120.

Solomon, R. C. (1984). Getting angry: The Jamesian theory of emotion in anthropology. In R. Shweder & R. A. Levine (Eds.), *Culture theory: Essays on mind, self, and emotion* (pp. 238–256). Cambridge, England: Cambridge University Press.

Southerland, S. A., & Sinatra, G. M. (2003). Learning about biological evolution: A special case of intentional conceptual change. In G. M. Sinatra & P. R. Pintrich (Eds.), *Intentional conceptual change* (pp. 317–345). Mahwah, NJ: Erlbaum.

Spaulding, C. L. (1992). *Motivation in the classroom.* New York, NY: McGraw-Hill.

Spear, L. P. (2000). Neurobehavioral changes in adolescence. *Current Directions in Psychological Science, 9,* 11–114.

Spera, C. (2005). A review of the relationship among parenting practices, parenting styles, and adolescent school achievement. *Educational Psychology Review, 17,* 125–146.

Standage, M., Duda, J. L., & Ntoumanis, N. (2003). A model of contextual motivation in physical education: Using constructs from self-determination and achievement goal theories to predict physical activity intentions. *Journal of Educational Psychology, 95*, 97–110.

Steele, C. M. (1997). A threat in the air: How stereotypes shape intellectual identity and performance. *American Psychologist, 52*, 613–629.

Steinberg, L. (1996). *Beyond the classroom: Why school reform has failed and what parents need to do*. New York, NY: Touchstone.

Stipek, D. J. (1993). *Motivation to learn: From theory to practice* (2nd ed.). Boston, MA: Allyn & Bacon.

Stipek, D. J. (1996). Motivation and instruction. In D. C. Berliner & R. C. Calfee (Eds.), *Handbook of educational psychology* (pp. 85–113). New York, NY: Macmillan.

Stipek, D. J. (2002). *Motivation to learn: Integrating theory and practice* (4th ed.). Boston, MA: Allyn & Bacon.

Stodolsky, S. S., Salk, S., & Glaessner, B. (1991). Student views about learning math and social studies. *American Educational Research Journal, 28*, 89–116.

Sue, S., & Chin, R. (1983). The mental health of Chinese-American children: Stressors and resources. In G. J. Powell (Ed.), *The psychosocial development of minority children* (pp. 385–397). New York, NY: Brunner/Mazel.

Suina, J. H., & Smolkin, L. B. (1994). From natal culture to school culture to dominant society culture: Supporting transitions for Pueblo Indian students. In P. M. Greenfield & R. R. Cocking (Eds.), *Cross-cultural roots of minority child development* (pp. 47–55). Mahwah, NJ: Erlbaum.

Swann, W. B., Jr., Chang-Schneider, C., & McClarty, K. L. (2007). Do people's self-views matter? Self-concept and self-esteem in everyday life. *American Psychologist, 62*, 84–94.

Tabachnick, S. E., Miller, R. B., & Relyea, G. E. (2008). The relationships among students' future-oriented goals and subgoals, perceived task instrumentality, and task-oriented self-regulation strategies in an academic environment. *Journal of Educational Psychology, 100*(3), 629–642.

Tamis-Lemonda, C. S., & McFadden, K. E. (2010). The United States of America. In M. H. Bornstein (Ed.), *Handbook of cultural developmental science* (pp. 299–322). New York, NY: Psychology Press.

Thomas, S., & Oldfather, P. (1997). Intrinsic motivations, literacy, and assessment practices: "That's my grade. That's me." *Educational Psychologist, 32*, 107–123.

Thorndike-Christ, T. (2008, March). *Profiles in failure: The etiology of maladaptive beliefs about mathematics.* Paper presented at the annual meeting of the American Educational Research Association, New York, NY.

Timm, P., & Borman, K. (1997). The soup pot don't stretch that far no more: Intergenerational patterns of school leaving in an urban Appalachian neighborhood. In M. Sellter & L. Weis (Eds.), *Beyond black and white: New faces and voices in U.S. schools* (pp. 257–282). Albany, NY: State University of New York Press.

Tobias, S. (1994). Interest, prior knowledge, and learning. *Review of Educational Research, 64*, 37–54.

Tomback, R. M., Williams, A. Y., & Wentzel, K. R. (2005, April). *Young adolescents' concerns about the transition to high school.* Poster presented at the annual meeting of the American Educational Research Association, Montreal, Canada.

Tsai, J. L. (2007). Ideal affect: Cultural causes and behavioral consequences. *Perspectives on Psychological Science, 2*, 242–259.

Tsai, J. L., & Chentsova-Dutton, Y. (2003). Variation among European Americans in emotional facial expression. *Journal of Cross Cultural Psychology, 34*, 650–657.

Tsai, Y.-M., Kunter, M., Lüdtke, O., Trautwein, U., & Ryan, R. M. (2008). What makes lessons interesting? The role of situational and individual factors in three school subjects. *Journal of Educational Psychology, 100*, 460–472.

Tucker, V. G., & Anderman, L. H. (1999, April). *Cycles of learning: Demonstrating the interplay between motivation, self-regulation, and cognition.* Paper presented at the annual meeting of the American Educational Research Association, Montreal, Canada.

Turner, J. C. (1995). The influence of classroom contexts on young children's motivation for literacy. *Reading Research Quarterly, 30*, 410–441.

Turner, J. C., Meyer, D. K., Cox, K. E., Logan, C., DiCintio, M., & Thomas, C. T. (1998). Creating contexts for involvement in mathematics. *Journal of Educational Psychology, 90*, 730–745.

Turner, J. C., & Patrick, H. (2008). How does motivation develop and why does it change? Reframing motivation research. *Educational Psychologist, 43*, 119–131.

Turner, J. C., Thorpe, P. K., & Meyer, D. K. (1998). Students' reports of motivation and negative affect: A theoretical and empirical analysis. *Journal of Educational Psychology, 90*, 758–771.

Turner, J. E., Husman, J., & Schallert, D. L. (2002). The importance of students' goals in their emotional experience of academic failure: Investigating the precursors and consequences of shame. *Educational Psychologist, 37*, 79–89.

Tyler, K. M., Uqdah, A. L., Dillihunt, M. L., Beatty-Hazelbaker, R., Connor, T., Gadson, N., . . . Stevens, R. (2008). Cultural discontinuity: Toward a quantitative investigation of a major hypothesis in education. *Educational Researcher, 37*, 280–297.

Urdan, T. C. (1997). Achievement goal theory: Past results, future directions. In M. L. Maehr & P. R. Pintrich (Eds.), *Advances in motivation and achievement* (Vol. 10, pp. 99–141). Greenwich, CT: JAI Press.

Urdan, T. C., & Maehr, M. L. (1995). Beyond a two-goal theory of motivation and achievement: A case for social goals. *Review of Educational Research, 65*, 213–243.

Urdan, T., & Mestas, M. (2006). The goals behind performance goals. *Journal of Educational Psychology, 98*, 354–365.

Urdan, T., & Midgley, C. (2001). Academic self-handicapping: What we know, what more there is to learn. *Educational Psychology Review, 13*, 115–138.

Urdan, T. C., Midgley, C., & Anderman, E. M. (1998). The role of classroom goal structure in students' use of self-handicapping strategies. *American Educational Research Journal, 35*, 101–122.

Urdan, T., Ryan, A. M., Anderman, E. M., & Gheen, M. H. (2002). Goals, goal structures, and avoidance behaviors. In C. Midgley (Ed.), *Goals, goal structures, and patterns of adaptive learning* (pp. 55–83). Mahwah, NJ: Erlbaum.

Urdan, T., & Turner, J. C. (2005). Competence motivation in the classroom. In A. J. Elliot & C. S. Dweck (Eds.), *Handbook of competence and motivation* (pp. 297–317). New York, NY: Guilford Press.

Usher, E. L. (2009). Sources of middle school students' self-efficacy in mathematics: A qualitative investigation. *American Educational Research Journal, 46*, 275–314.

Usher, E. L., & Pajares, F. (2008). Sources of self-efficacy in school: Critical review of the literature and future directions. *Review of Educational Research, 78*, 751–796.

Usher, E. L., & Pajares, F. (2009). Sources of self-efficacy in mathematics: A validation study. *Contemporary Educational Psychology, 34*, 89–101.

Valentine, J. C., Cooper, H., Bettencourt, B. A., & DuBois, D. L. (2002). Out-of-school activities and academic achievement: The mediating role of self-beliefs. *Educational Psychologist, 37*, 245–256.

Vallerand, R. J., Fortier, M. S., & Guay, F. (1997). Self-determination and persistence in a real-life setting: Toward a motivational model of high school dropout. *Journal of Personality and Social Psychology, 72*, 1161–1176.

van Laar, C. (2000). The paradox of low academic achievement but high self-esteem in African American students: An attributional account. *Educational Psychology Review, 12*, 33–61.

Vansteenkiste, M., Lens, W., & Deci, E. L. (2006). Intrinsic versus extrinsic goal contents in self-determination theory: Another look at the quality of academic motivation. *Educational Psychologist, 41*, 19–31.

Vansteenkiste, M., Zhou, M., Lens, W., & Soenens, B. (2005). Experiences of autonomy and control among Chinese learners: Vitalizing or immobilizing? *Journal of Educational Psychology, 97*, 468–483.

Vaughn, B. J., & Horner, R. H. (1997). Identifying instructional tasks that occasion problem behaviors and assessing the effects of student versus teacher choice among these tasks. *Journal of Applied Behavior Analysis, 30*, 299–312.

Voss, J. F., & Schauble, L. (1992). Is interest educationally interesting? An interest-related model of learning. In K. A. Renninger, S. Hidi, & A. Krapp (Eds.), *The role of interest in learning and development* (pp. 101–120). Mahwah, NJ: Erlbaum.

Wade, S. E. (1992). How interest affects learning from text. In K. A. Renninger, S. Hidi, & A. Krapp (Eds.), *The role of interest in learning and development* (pp. 255–277). Mahwah, NJ: Erlbaum.

Walls, T. A., & Little, T. D. (2005). Relations among personal agency, motivation, and school adjustment in early adolescence. *Journal of Educational Psychology, 97*, 23–31.

Walton, G. M., & Spencer, S. J. (2009). Latent ability: Grades and test scores systematically underestimate intellectual ability of negatively stereotyped students. *Psychological Science, 20*, 1132–1139.

Wang, J., & Lin, E. (2005). Comparative studies on U.S. and Chinese mathematics learning and the implications for standards-based mathematics teaching reform. *Educational Researcher, 34*(5), 3–13.

Watt, H. M. G. (2004). Development of adolescents' self-perceptions, values, and task perceptions according to gender and domain in 7th- through 11th grade Australian students. *Child Development, 75*, 1556–1574.

Weiner, B. (1984). Principles for a theory of student motivation and their application within an attributional framework. In R. Ames & C. Ames (Eds.), *Research on motivation in education: Vol. 1. Student motivation* (pp. 78–108). San Diego, CA: Academic Press.

Weiner, B. (1986). *An attributional theory of motivation and emotion.* New York, NY: Springer-Verlag.

Weiner, B. (2000). Intrapersonal and interpersonal theories of motivation from an attributional perspective. *Educational Psychology Review, 12*, 1–14.

Weiner, B. (2004). Attribution theory revisited: Transforming cultural plurality into theoretical unity. In D. M. McInerney & S. Van Etten (Eds.), *Big theories revisited* (pp. 13–29). Greenwich, CT: Information Age.

Weiner, B. (2005). Motivation from an attribution perspective and the social psychology of perceived competence. In A. J. Elliot & C. S. Dweck (Eds.), *Handbook of competence and motivation* (pp. 73–84). New York, NY: Guilford Press.

Weiner, B. (2010). The development of an attribution-based theory of motivation: A history of ideas. *Educational Psychologist, 45*(1), 28–36.

Weinstein, R. S. (2002). *Reaching higher: The power of expectations in schooling.* Cambridge, MA: Harvard University Press.

Weinstein, R. S., Madison, S. M., & Kuklinski, M. R. (1995). Raising expectations in schooling: Obstacles and opportunities for change. *American Educational Research Journal, 32*, 121–159.

Wentzel, K. R. (1997). Student motivation in middle school: The role of perceived pedagogical caring. *Journal of Educational Psychology, 89*(3), 411–419.

Wentzel, K. R. (1999). Social-motivational processes and interpersonal relationships: Implications for understanding motivation at school. *Journal of Educational Psychology, 91*, 76–97.

Wentzel, K. R., Filisetti, L., & Looney, L. (2007). Adolescent prosocial behavior: The role of self-processes and contextual cues. *Child Development, 78*, 895–910.

Wentzel, K. R., & Wigfield, A. (1998). Academic and social motivational influences on students' academic performance. *Educational Psychology Review, 10*, 155–175.

White, R. (1959). Motivation reconsidered: The concept of competence. *Psychological Review, 66*, 297–333.

Whitley, B. E., Jr., & Frieze, I. H. (1985). Children's causal attributions for success and failure in achievement settings: A meta-analysis. *Journal of Educational Psychology, 77*, 608–616.

Wigfield, A. (1994). Expectancy-value theory of achievement motivation: A developmental perspective. *Educational Psychology Review, 6*, 49–78.

Wigfield, A., Byrnes, J. P., & Eccles, J. S. (2006). Development during early and middle adolescence. In P. A. Alexander & P. H. Winne (Eds.), *Handbook of educational psychology* (2nd ed., pp. 87–113). Mahwah, NJ: Erlbaum.

Wigfield, A., & Eccles, J. (1992). The development of achievement task values: A theoretical analysis. *Developmental Review, 12*, 265–310.

Wigfield, A., & Eccles, J. (2000). Expectancy-value theory of achievement motivation. *Contemporary Educational Psychology, 25*, 68–81.

Wigfield, A., & Eccles, J. (2002). The development of competence beliefs, expectancies for success, and achievement values from childhood to adolescence. In A. Wigfield & J. Eccles (Eds.), *Development of achievement motivation* (pp. 91–120). San Diego, CA: Academic Press.

Wigfield, A., Eccles, J., Mac Iver, D., Reuman, D., & Midgley, C. (1991). Transitions at early adolescence: Changes in children's domain-specific self-perceptions and general self-esteem across the transition to junior high school. *Developmental Psychology, 27*, 552–565.

Wigfield, A., Eccles, J. S., & Pintrich, P. R. (1996). Development between the ages of 11 and 25. In D. C. Berliner & R. C. Calfee (Eds.), *Handbook of educational psychology* (pp. 148–185). New York, NY: Macmillan.

Wigfield, A., & Meece, J. L. (1988). Math anxiety in elementary and secondary school students. *Journal of Educational Psychology, 80*, 210–216.

Wigfield, A., & Wagner, A. L. (2005). Competence, motivation, and identity development during adolescence. In A. J. Elliot & C. S. Dweck (Eds.), *Handbook of competence and motivation* (pp. 222–239). New York, NY: Guilford Press.

Wijnia, L., Loyens, S. M. M., Derous, E., & Schmidt, H. G. (2015). How important are student-selected versus instructor-selected literature resources for students' learning and motivation in problem-based learning? *Instructional Science, 43*(1), 39–58.

Wiles, J., & Bondi, J. (2001). *The new American middle school: Educating preadolescents in an era of change.* Upper Saddle River, NJ: Merrill/Prentice Hall.

Williams, A. W. (2013). *An action research study using the MUSIC Model of Academic Motivation to increase reading motivation in a fourth-grade classroom.* Unpublished doctoral dissertation, Virginia Tech, Blacksburg, VA.

Williams, K. M. (2001a). "Frontin' it": Schooling, violence, and relationships in the 'hood. In J. N. Burstyn, G. Bender, R. Casella, H. W. Gordon, D. P. Guerra, K. V. Luschen, et al., *Preventing violence in schools: A challenge to American democracy* (pp. 95–108). Mahwah, NJ: Erlbaum.

Williams, T., & Williams, K. (2010). Self-efficacy and performance in mathematics: Reciprocal determinism in 33 nations. *Journal of Educational Psychology, 102*, 453–466.

Wilson, B. L., & Corbett, H. D. (2001). *Listening to urban kids: School reform and the teachers they want.* Albany: State University of New York Press.

Wisner Fries, A. B., & Pollak, S. D. (2007). Emotion processing and the developing brain. In D. Coch, K. W. Fischer, & G. Dawson (Eds.), *Human behavior, learning, and the developing brain: Typical development* (pp. 329–361). New York, NY: Guilford Press.

Witkow, M. R., & Fuligni, A. J. (2007). Achievement goals and daily school experiences among adolescents with Asian, Latino, and European American backgrounds. *Journal of Educational Psychology, 99,* 584–596.

Wlodkowski, R. J., & Ginsberg, M. B. (1995). *Diversity and motivation: Culturally responsive teaching.* San Francisco, CA: Jossey-Bass.

Yeager, D. S., & Dweck, C. S. (2012). Mindsets that promote resilience: When students believe that personal characteristics can be developed. *Educational Psychologist, 47*(4), 302–314.

Young, J. R., & Young, J. L. (2015). Anxious for answers: A meta-analysis of the effects of anxiety on African American K–12 students' mathematics achievement. *Journal of Mathematics Education at Teachers College, 6*(2), 1–8.

Youniss, J., & Yates, M. (1999). Youth service and moral-civic identity: A case for everyday morality. *Educational Psychology Review*, *11*, 361–376.

Zahn-Waxler, C., Friedman, R. J., Cole, P., Mizuta, I., & Hiruma, N. (1996). Japanese and United States preschool children's responses to conflict and distress. *Child Development*, *67*, 2462–2477.

Zahorik, J. A. (1994, April). *Making things interesting.* Paper presented at the annual meeting of the American Educational Research Association, New Orleans, LA.

Zajonc, R. B. (1980). Feeling and thinking: Preferences need no inferences. *American Psychologist*, *35*, 151–175.

Zeelenberg, R., Wagenmakers, E.-J., & Rotteveel, M. (2006). The impact of emotion on perception: Bias or enhanced processing? *Psychological Science, 17,* 287–291.

Zeidner, M. (1998). *Test anxiety: The state of the art.* New York, NY: Plenum Press.

Zeidner, M., & Matthews, G. (2005). Evaluation anxiety: Current theory and research. In A. J. Elliot & C. S. Dweck (Eds.), *Handbook of competence and motivation* (pp. 141–163). New York, NY: Guilford Press.

Zeldin, A. L., & Pajares, F. (2000). Against the odds: Self-efficacy beliefs of women in mathematical, scientific, and technological careers. *American Educational Research Journal*, *37*, 215–246.

Ziegert, D. I., Kistner, J. A., Castro, R., & Robertson, B. (2001). Longitudinal study of young children's responses to challenging achievement situations. *Child Development*, *72*, 609–624.

Zimmerman, B. J. (1998). Developing self-fulfilling cycles of academic regulation: An analysis of exemplary instructional models. In D. H. Schunk & B. J. Zimmerman (Eds.), *Self-regulated learning: From teaching to self-reflective practice* (pp. 1–19). New York, NY: Guilford Press.

Zimmerman, B. J., Bandura, A., & Martinez-Pons, M. (1992). Self-motivation for academic attainment: The role of self-efficacy beliefs and personal goal setting. *American Educational Research Journal*, *29*, 663–676.

Zimmerman, B. J., & Kitsantas, A. (2005). The hidden dimension of personal competence: Self-regulated learning and practice. In A. J. Elliot & C. S. Dweck (Eds.), *Handbook of competence and motivation* (pp. 509–526). New York, NY: Guilford Press.

CHAPTER 6

Ackerman, P. L., & Lohman, D. F. (2006). Individual differences in cognitive functions. In P. A. Alexander & P. H. Winne (Eds.), *Handbook of educational psychology* (2nd ed., pp. 139–161). Mahwah, NJ: Erlbaum.

Alexander, J. M., Johnson, K. E., Albano, J., Freygang, T., & Scott, B. (2006). Relations between intelligence and the development of metaconceptual knowledge. *Metacognition and Learning*, *1*, 51–67.

Alexander, J. M., Johnson, K. E., Leibham, M. E., & Kelley, K. (2008). The development of conceptual interests in young children. *Cognitive Development, 23,* 324–334.

Alexander, P. A. (1997). Mapping the multidimensional nature of domain learning: The interplay of cognitive, motivational, and strategic forces. In P. R. Pintrich & M. L. Maehr (Eds.), *Advances in motivation and achievement* (Vol. 10, pp. 213–250). Greenwich, CT: JAI Press.

Alexander, P. A. (1998). Positioning conceptual change within a model of domain literacy. In B. Guzzetti & C. Hynd (Eds.), *Perspectives on conceptual change: Multiple ways to understand knowing and learning in a complex world* (pp. 55–76). Mahwah, NJ: Erlbaum.

Alexander, P. A. (2004). A model of domain learning: Reinterpreting expertise as a multidimensional, multistage process. In D. Y. Dai & R. J. Sternberg (Eds.), *Motivation, emotion, and cognition: Integrative perspectives on intellectual functioning and development* (pp. 273–298). Mahwah, NJ: Erlbaum.

Alexander, P. A., & Judy, J. E. (1988). The interaction of domain-specific and strategic knowledge in academic performance. *Review of Educational Research, 58,* 375–404.

Alfassi, M. (2004). Reading to learn: Effects of combined strategy instruction on high school students. *Journal of Educational Research, 97,* 171–184.

Alfieri, L., Brooks, P. J., Aldrich, N. J., & Tenenbaum, H. R. (2011). Does discovery-based instruction enhance learning? *Journal of Educational Psychology, 103,* 1–18.

Ambrose, D., Allen, J., & Huntley, S. B. (1994). Mentorship of the highly creative. *Roeper Review*, *17*, 131–133.

Applebee, A. N., Langer, J. A., Nystrand, M., & Gamoran, A. (2003). Discussion-based approaches to developing understanding: Classroom instruction and student performance in middle and high school English. *American Educational Research Journal, 40*, 685–730.

Barab, S. A., & Plucker, J. A. (2002). Smart people or smart contexts? Cognition, ability, and talent development in an age of situated approaches to knowing and learning. *Educational Psychologist*, *37*, 165–182.

Barchfeld, P., Sodian, B., Thoermer, C., & Bullock, M. (2005, April). *The development of experiment generation abilities from primary school to late adolescence.* Poster presented at the biennial meeting of the Society for Research in Child Development, Atlanta, GA.

Bartholomew, D. J. (2004). *Measuring intelligence: Facts and fallacies.* Cambridge, England: Cambridge University Press.

Barton, K. C., & Levstik, L. S. (1996). "Back when God was around and everything": Elementary children's understanding of historical time. *American Educational Research Journal*, *33*, 419–454.

Batshaw, M. L., & Shapiro, B. K. (2002). Mental retardation. In M. L. Batshaw (Ed.), *Children with disabilities* (5th ed., 287–306). Baltimore, MD: Brookes.

Baumeister, A. A. (1989). Mental retardation. In C. G. Lask & M. Hersen (Eds.), *Handbook of child psychiatric diagnosis* (pp. 61–94). New York, NY: Wiley.

Bebko, J. M., Burke, L., Craven, J., & Sarlo, N. (1992). The importance of motor activity in sensorimotor development: A perspective from children with physical handicaps. *Human Development*, *35*, 226–240.

Beck, S. R., Robinson, E. J., Carroll, D. J., & Apperly, I. A. (2006). Children's thinking about counterfactuals and future hypotheticals as possibilities. *Child Development*, *77*, 413–426.

Bédard, J., & Chi, M. T. H. (1992). Expertise. *Current Directions in Psychological Science*, *1*, 135–139.

Beirne-Smith, M., Ittenbach, R. F., & Patton, J. R. (2002). *Mental retardation* (6th ed.). Upper Saddle River, NJ: Merrill/Prentice Hall.

Belsky, J., Bakermans-Kranenburg, M. J., & van IJzendoorn, M. H. (2007). For better *and* for worse: Differential susceptibility to environmental influences. *Current Directions in Psychological Science, 16,* 300–304.

Benton, D. (2008). Nutrition and intellectual development. In P. C. Kyllonen, R. D. Roberts, & L. Stankov (Eds.), *Extending intelligence: Enhancement and new constructs* (pp. 373–394). New York, NY: Erlbaum/Taylor & Francis.

Ben-Yehudah, G., & Fiez, J. A. (2007). Development of verbal working memory. In D. Coch, K. W. Fischer, & G. Dawson (Eds.), *Human behavior, learning, and the developing brain: Typical development* (pp. 301–328). New York, NY: Guilford Press.

Berk, L. E. (1994). Why children talk to themselves. *Scientific American*, *271*, 78–83.

Bialystok, E. (1994). Representation and ways of knowing: Three issues in second language acquisition. In N. C. Ellis (Ed.), *Implicit and explicit learning of languages* (pp. 549–569). London, England: Academic Press.

Biemiller, A., Shany, M., Inglis, A., & Meichenbaum, D. (1998). Factors influencing children's acquisition and demonstration of self-regulation on academic tasks. In D. H. Schunk & B. J. Zimmerman (Eds.), *Self-regulated learning: From teaching to self-reflective practice* (pp. 203–224). New York, NY: Guilford Press.

Bjorklund, D. F. (1987). How age changes in knowledge base contribute to the development of children's memory: An interpretive review. *Developmental Review*, *7*, 93–130.

Blakemore, S.-J., & Choudhury, S. (2006). Brain development during puberty: State of the science. *Developmental Science, 9*(1), 11–14.

Bornstein, M. H., Hahn, C.-S., Bell, C., Haynes, O. M., Slater, A., Golding, J., . . . ALSPAC Study Team (2006). Stability in cognition across early childhood: A developmental cascade. *Psychological Science*, *17*, 151–158.

Bortfeld, H., & Whitehurst, G. J. (2001). Sensitive periods in first language acquisition. In D. B. Bailey, Jr., J. T. Bruer, F. J. Symons, & J. W. Lichtman (Eds.), *Critical thinking about critical periods* (pp. 173–192). Baltimore, MD: Brookes.

Boxerman, J. Z. (2009, April). *Students' understanding of erosion.* Paper presented at the annual meeting of the American Educational Research Association, San Diego, CA.

Bracken, B. A., McCallum, R. S., & Shaughnessy, M. F. (1999). An interview with Bruce A. Bracken and R. Steve McCallum, authors of the Universal Nonverbal Intelligence Test (UNIT). *North American Journal of Psychology*, *1*, 277–288.

Brainerd, C. J. (2003). Jean Piaget, learning research, and American education. In B. J. Zimmerman & D. H. Schunk (Eds.), *Educational psychology: A century of contributions* (pp. 251–287). Mahwah, NJ: Erlbaum.

Bransford, J., D., Mosborg, S., Copland, M. A., Honig, M. A., Nelson, H. G., Gawel, D., . . . Vye, N. (2009). Adaptive people and adaptive systems: Issues of learning and design. In A. Hargreaves, A. Lieberman, M. Filan, & D. Hopkins (Eds.), *Second international handbook of educational change* (pp. 825–856). Dordrecht, Netherlands: Springer.

Brody, N. (1992). *Intelligence* (2nd ed.). San Diego, CA: Academic Press.

Brody, N. (1997). Intelligence, schooling, and society. *American Psychologist*, *52*, 1046–1050.

Brody, N. (2008). Does education influence intelligence? In P. C. Kyllonen, R. D. Roberts, & L. Stankov (Eds.), *Extending intelligence: Enhancement and new constructs* (pp. 85–92). New York, NY: Erlbaum/Taylor & Francis.

Brown, A. L., & Palincsar, A. S. (1987). Reciprocal teaching of comprehension strategies: A natural history of one program for enhancing learning. In J. Borkowski & J. D. Day (Eds.), *Cognition in special education: Comparative approaches to retardation, learning disabilities, and giftedness* (pp. 81–132). Norwood, NJ: Ablex.

Brown, J. S., Collins, A., & Duguid, P. (1989). Situated cognition and the culture of learning. *Educational Researcher*, *18*(1), 32–42.

Brown, M. C., McNeil, N. M., & Glenberg, A. M. (2009). Using concreteness in education: Real problems, potential solutions. *Child Development Perspectives, 3,* 160–164.

Bruer, J. T. (1999). *The myth of the first three years: A new understanding of early brain development and lifelong learning.* New York, NY: Free Press.

Bruer, J. T., & Greenough, W. T. (2001). The subtle science of how experience affects the brain. In D. B. Bailey, Jr., J. T. Bruer, F. J. Symons, & J. W. Lichtman (Eds.), *Critical thinking about critical periods* (pp. 209–232). Baltimore, MD: Brookes.

Bruner, J. S. (1966). *Toward a theory of instruction*. Cambridge, MA: Harvard University Press.

Bryck, R. L., & Fisher, P. A. (2012). Training the brain: Practical applications of neural plasticity from the intersection of cognitive neuroscience, developmental psychology, and prevention science. *American Psychologist, 67,* 87–100.

Burgaleta, M., Johnson, W., Waber, D. P., Colom, R., & Karama, S. (2014). Cognitive ability changes and dynamics of cortical thickness development in healthy children and adolescents. *NeuroImage, 84*, 810–819.

Butterfield, E. C., & Ferretti, R. P. (1987). Toward a theoretical integration of cognitive hypotheses about intellectual differences among children. In J. G. Borkowski & J. D. Day (Eds.), *Cognition in special children: Approaches to retardation, learning disabilities, and giftedness* (pp. 195–223). Norwood, NJ: Ablex.

Byrnes, J. P. (1988). Formal operations: A systematic reformulation. *Developmental Review*, *8*, 66–87.

Byrnes, J. P. (2001). *Minds, brains, and learning: Understanding the psychological and educational relevance of neuroscientific research.* New York, NY: Guilford Press.

Byrnes, J. P., & Fox, N. A. (1998). The educational relevance of research in cognitive neuroscience. *Educational Psychology Review, 10*, 297–342.

Cacioppo, J. T., Petty, R. E., Feinstein, J. A., & Jarvis, W. B. G. (1996). Dispositional differences in cognitive motivation: The life and times of individuals varying in need for cognition. *Psychological Bulletin, 119*, 197–253.

Carey, S. (1985). *Conceptual change in childhood.* Cambridge, MA: MIT Press.

Carrasco, R. L. (1981). Expanded awareness of student performance: A case study in applied ethnographic monitoring in a bilingual classroom. In H. T. Trueba, G. P. Guthrie, & K. H. Au (Eds.), *Culture and the bilingual classroom: Studies in classroom ethnography* (pp. 153–177). Rowley, MA: Newbury House.

Carroll, J. B. (1993) *Human cognitive abilities: A survey of factor-analytic studies.* New York, NY: Cambridge University Press.

Carroll, J. B. (2003). The higher stratum structure of cognitive abilities: Current evidence supports *g* and about ten broad factors. In H. Nyborg (Ed.), *The scientific study of general intelligence* (pp. 5–22). New York, NY: Pergamon.

Case, R., & Okamoto, Y., in collaboration with Griffin, S., McKeough, A., Bleiker, C., Henderson, B., & Stephenson, K. M. (1996). The role of central conceptual structures in the development of children's thought. *Monographs of the Society for Research in Child Development, 61*(1, Serial No. 246).

Cassidy, S. (2004). Learning styles: An overview of theories, models, and measures. *Educational Psychology, 24*, 419–444.

Cattell, R. B. (1963). Theory of fluid and crystallized intelligence: A critical experiment. *Journal of Educational Psychology, 54*, 1–22.

Cattell, R. B. (1987). *Intelligence: Its structure, growth, and action.* Amsterdam: North-Holland.

Ceci, S. J. (2003). Cast in six ponds and you'll reel in something: Looking back on 25 years of research. *American Psychologist, 58*, 855–864.

Chapman, D. A., Scott, K. G., & Mason, C. A. (2002). Early risk factors for mental retardation: Role of maternal age and maternal education. *American Journal on Mental Retardation, 107*, 46–59.

Chein, J. M., & Schneider, W. (2012). The brain's learning and control architecture. *Current Directions in Psychological Science, 21*, 78–84.

Chi, M. T. H. (1978). Knowledge structures and memory development. In R. S. Siegler (Ed.), *Children's thinking: What develops?* (pp. 73–96). Mahwah, NJ: Erlbaum.

Chi, M. T. H., Glaser, R., & Rees, E. (1982). Expertise in problem solving. In R. J. Sternberg (Ed.), *Advances in the psychology of human intelligence* (Vol. 1, pp. 7–75). Hillsdale, NJ: Erlbaum.

Clark, A.-M., Anderson, R. C., Kuo, L., Kim, I., Archodidou, A., & Nguyen-Jahiel, K. (2003). Collaborative reasoning: Expanding ways for children to talk and think in school. *Educational Psychology Review, 15*, 181–198.

Cole, M. (1990). Cognitive development and formal schooling: The evidence from cross-cultural research. In L. C. Moll (Ed.), *Vygotsky and education* (pp. 89–110). New York, NY: Cambridge University Press.

Cole, M. (2006). Culture and cognitive development in phylogenetic, historical and ontogenetic perspective. In W. Damon & R. M. Lerner (Series Eds.), D. Kuhn & R. Siegler (Vol. Eds.), *Handbook of child psychology: Vol. 2. Cognition, perception, and language* (6th ed., pp. 636–686). New York, NY: Wiley.

Cole, S. W. (2009). Social regulation of human gene expression. *Current Directions in Psychological Science, 18*, 133–137.

Collins, A. (2006). Cognitive apprenticeship. In R. K. Sawyer (Ed.), *The Cambridge handbook of the learning sciences* (pp. 47–60). Cambridge, England: Cambridge University Press.

Collins, A., Brown, J. S., & Newman, S. E. (1989). Cognitive apprenticeship: Teaching the crafts of reading, writing, and mathematics. In L. B. Resnick (Ed.), *Knowing, learning, and instruction: Essays in honor of Robert Glaser* (pp. 453–494). Mahwah, NJ: Erlbaum.

Coplan, R. J., & Arbeau, K. A. (2009). Peer interactions and play in early childhood. In K. H. Rubin, W. M. Bukowski, & B. Laursen (Eds.), *Handbook of peer interactions, relationships, and groups* (pp. 143–161). New York, NY: Guilford Press.

Cornell, D. G., Pelton, G. M., Bassin, L. E., Landrum, M., Ramsay, S. G., Cooley, M. R., . . . Hamrick, E. (1990). Self-concept and peer status among gifted program youth. *Journal of Educational Psychology, 82*, 456–463.

Corno, L., Cronbach, L. J., Kupermintz, H., Lohman, D. F., Mandinach, E. B., Porteus, A. W., & Talbert, J. E. (2002). *Remaking the concept of aptitude: Extending the legacy of Richard E. Snow.* Mahwah, NJ: Erlbaum.

Cornoldi, C. (2010). Metacognition, intelligence, and academic performance. In H. S. Waters & W. Schneider (Eds.), *Metacognition, strategy use, and instruction* (pp. 257–277). New York, NY: Guilford Press.

Cowan, N., Ricker, T. J., Clark, K. M., Hinrichs, G. A., & Glass, B. A. (2015). Knowledge cannot explain the developmental growth of working memory capacity. *Developmental Science, 18*(1), 132–145.

Coyle, T. R., Pillow, D. R., Snyder, A. C., & Kochunov, P. (2011). Processing speed mediates the development of general intelligence *(g)* in adolescence. *Psychological Science, 22*, 1265–1269.

Crago, M. B. (1988). *Cultural context in the communicative interaction of young Inuit children.* Unpublished doctoral dissertation, McGill University, Montreal, Canada.

Curry, L. (1990). A critique of the research on learning styles. *Educational Leadership, 47*(2), 50–56.

Dai, D. Y. (2010). *The nature and nurture of giftedness: A new framework for understanding gifted education.* New York, NY: Teachers College Press.

Dai, D. Y., & Sternberg, R. J. (2004). Beyond cognitivism: Toward an integrated understanding of intellectual functioning and development. In D. Y. Dai & R. J. Sternberg (Eds.), *Motivation, emotion, and cognition: Integrative perspectives on intellectual functioning and development* (pp. 3–38). Mahwah, NJ: Erlbaum.

Dai, D. Y., & Wang, X. (2007). The role of need for cognition and reader beliefs in text comprehension and interest development. *Contemporary Educational Psychology, 32*, 332–347.

Daley, T. C., Whaley, S. E., Sigman, M. D., Espinosa, M. P., & Neumann, C. (2003). IQ on the rise: The Flynn effect in rural Kenyan children. *Psychological Science, 14*, 215–219.

D'Amato, R. C., Chitooran, M. M., & Whitten, J. D. (1992). Neuropsychological consequences of malnutrition. In D. I. Templer, L. C. Hartlage, & W. G. Cannon (Eds.), *Preventable brain damage: Brain vulnerability and brain health* (pp. 193–213). New York, NY: Springer.

Davis, O. S. P., Haworth, C. M. A., & Plomin, R. (2009). Dramatic increase in heritability of cognitive development from early to middle childhood: An 8-year longitudinal study of 8,700 pairs of twins. *Psychological Science, 20*, 1301–1308.

De Corte, E., Greer, B., & Verschaffel, L. (1996). Mathematics teaching and learning. In D. C. Berliner & R. C. Calfee (Eds.), *Handbook of educational psychology* (pp. 491–549). New York, NY: Macmillan.

de Jong, T. (2011). Instruction based on computer simulations. In R. E. Mayer & P. A. Alexander (Eds.), *Handbook of research on learning and instruction* (pp. 446–466). New York, NY: Routledge.

de Jong, T., & van Joolingen, W. R. (1998). Scientific discovery learning with computer simulations of conceptual domains. *Review of Educational Research, 68*, 179–201.

Deary, I. J., Strand, S., Smith, P., & Fernandez, C. (2007). Intelligence and educational achievement. *Intelligence, 35*, 13–21.

DeBacker, T. K., & Crowson, H. M. (2009). The influence of need for closure on learning and teaching. *Educational Psychology Review, 21*, 303–323.

Deng, W., Aimone, J. B., & Gage, F. H. (2010). New neurons and new memories: How does adult hippocampal neurogenesis affect learning and memory? *Nature Reviews Neuroscience, 11*, 339–350.

Dennen, V. P., & Burner, K. J. (2008). The cognitive apprenticeship model in educational practice. In J. M. Spector, M. D. Merrill, J. van Merriënboer, & M. P. Driscoll (Eds.), *Handbook of research on educational communications and technology* (3rd ed., pp. 425–439). New York, NY: Erlbaum.

Diamond, A., Barnett, W. S., Thomas, J., & Munro, S. (2007). Preschool program improves cognitive control. *Science, 318*, 1387–1338.

Diamond, M., & Hopson, J. (1998). *Magic trees of the mind.* New York, NY: Dutton.

diSessa, A. A. (2007). An interactional analysis of clinical interviewing. *Cognition and Instruction, 25*, 523–565.

Donaldson, M. (1978). *Children's minds*. New York, NY: Norton.

Dorris, M. (1989). *The broken cord.* New York, NY: Harper & Row.

Duckworth, A. L., & Seligman, M. E. P. (2005). Self-discipline outdoes IQ in predicting academic performance of adolescents. *Psychological Science, 16*, 939–944.

Duyme, M., Dumaret, A., & Tomkiewicz, S. (1999). How can we boost IQs of "dull" children? A late adoption study. *Proceedings of the National Academy of Sciences, USA, 96*, 8790–8794.

Dweck, C. S. (2009). Foreword. In F. D. Horowitz, R. F. Subotnik, & D. J. Matthews (Eds.), *The development of giftedness and talent across the life span* (pp. xi–xiv). Washington, DC: American Psychological Association.

Elkind, D. (1981). *Children and adolescents: Interpretive essays on Jean Piaget* (3rd ed.). New York, NY: Oxford University Press.

Elliott, D. J. (1995). *Music matters: A new philosophy of music education.* New York, NY: Oxford University Press.

Empson, S. B. (1999). Equal sharing and shared meaning: The development of fraction concepts in a first-grade classroom. *Cognition and Instruction, 17*, 283–342.

Ericsson, K. A. (2003). The acquisition of expert performance as problem solving. In J. E. Davidson & R. J. Sternberg (Eds.), *The psychology of problem solving* (pp. 31–83). Cambridge, England: Cambridge University Press.

Evans, J. J., Floyd, R. G., McGrew, K. S., & Leforgee, M. H. (2001). The relations between measures of Cattell-Horn-Carroll (CHC) cognitive abilities and reading achievement during childhood and adolescence. *School Psychology Review, 31*, 246–262.

Eysink, T. H. S., de Jong, T., Berthold, K., Kolloffel, B., Opfermann, M., & Wouters, P. (2009). Learner performance in multimedia learning arrangements: An analysis across instructional approaches. *American Educational Research Journal, 46*, 1107–1149.

Fahrmeier, E. D. (1978). The development of concrete operations among the Hausa. *Journal of Cross-Cultural Psychology, 9*, 23–44.

Feuerstein, R, Feuerstein, R. S., & Falik, L. H. (2010). *Beyond smarter: Mediated learning and the brain's capacity for change.* New York, NY: Teachers College Press.

Fischer, K. W., & Immordino-Yang, M. H. (2002). Cognitive development and education: From dynamic general structure to specific learning and teaching. In E. Lagemann (Ed.), *Traditions of scholarship in education* (pp. 1–55). Chicago, IL: Spencer Foundation.

Fischer, K. W., Knight, C. C., & Van Parys, M. (1993). Analyzing diversity in developmental pathways: Methods and concepts. In R. Case & W. Edelstein (Eds.), *The new structuralism in cognitive development: Theory and research on individual pathways* (pp. 33–56). Basel, Switzerland: Karger.

Flanagan, D. P., & Ortiz, S. O. (2001). *Essentials of cross-battery assessment.* New York, NY: Wiley.

Flavell, J. H. (1963). *The developmental psychology of Jean Piaget*. New York, NY: Van Nostrand Reinhold.

Flavell, J. H. (1994). Cognitive development: Past, present, and future. In R. D. Parke, P. A. Ornstein, J. J. Rieser, & C. Zahn-Waxler (Eds.), *A century of developmental psychology* (pp. 569–587). Washington, DC: American Psychological Association.

Flavell, J. H., Miller, P. H., & Miller, S. A. (2002). *Cognitive development* (4th ed.). Upper Saddle River, NJ: Prentice Hall.

Fletcher, K. L., & Bray, N. W. (1995). External and verbal strategies in children with and without mild mental retardation. *American Journal on Mental Retardation, 99*, 363–475.

Flieller, A. (1999). Comparison of the development of formal thought in adolescent cohorts aged 10 to 15 years (1967–1996 and 1972–1993). *Developmental Psychology, 35*, 1048–1058.

Flum, H., & Kaplan, A. (2006). Exploratory orientation as an educational goal. *Educational Psychologist, 41*, 99–110.

Flynn, J. R. (2003). Movies about intelligence: The limitations of *g*. *Current Directions in Psychological Science, 12*, 95–99.

Flynn, J. R. (2007). *What is intelligence? Beyond the Flynn effect.* New York, NY: Cambridge University Press.

Frazier, B. N., Gelman, S. A., & Wellman, H. M. (2009). Preschoolers' search for explanatory information within adult–child conversation. *Child Development, 80*, 1592–1611.

Frederiksen, N. (1984a). Implications of cognitive theory for instruction in problem-solving. *Review of Educational Research, 54*, 363–407.

Fujimura, N. (2001). Facilitating children's proportional reasoning: A model of reasoning processes and effects of intervention on strategy change. *Journal of Educational Psychology, 93*, 589–603.

Ganea, P. A. Shutts, K., Spelke, E. S., & DeLoache, J. S. (2007). Thinking of things unseen: Infants' use of language to update mental representations. *Psychological Science, 18*, 734–739.

Gardner, H. (1983). *Frames of mind: The theory of multiple intelligences*. New York, NY: Basic Books.

Gardner, H. (1998, April). *Where to draw the line: The perils of new paradigms.* Paper presented at the annual meeting of the American Educational Research Association, San Diego, CA.

Gardner, H. (1999). *Intelligence reframed: Multiple intelligences for the 21st century.* New York, NY: Basic Books.

Gardner, H. (2000a). A case against spiritual intelligence. *International Journal for the Psychology of Religion, 10*(1), 27–34.

Gardner, H. (2003, April). *Multiple intelligences after twenty years.* Paper presented at the annual meeting of the American Educational Research Association, Chicago, IL.

Geary, D. C. (1998). What is the function of mind and brain? *Educational Psychology Review, 10,* 377–387.

Geary, D. C. (2008). An evolutionarily informed education science. *Educational Psychologist, 43,* 179–195.

Gelman, S. A. (2003). *The essential child: Origins of essentialism in everyday thought.* New York, NY: Oxford University Press.

Gershkoff-Stowe, L., & Thelen, E. (2004). U-shaped changes in behavior: A dynamic systems perspective. *Journal of Cognition and Development, 1*(5), 11–36.

Giedd, J. N., Blumenthal, J., Jeffries, N. O., Castellanos, F. X., Liu, H., Zijdenbos, A., . . . Rapoport, J. L. (1999). Brain development during childhood and adolescence: A longitudinal MRI study. *Nature Neuroscience, 2,* 861–863.

Giedd, J. N., Stockman, M., Weddle, C., Liverpool, M., Wallace, G. L., Lee, N. R., . . . Lenroot, R. K. (2012). Anatomic magnetic resonance imaging of the developing child and adolescent brain. In V. F. Reyna, S. B. Chapman, M. R. Dougherty, & J. Confrey (Eds.), *The adolescent brain: Learning, reasoning, and decision making* (pp. 15–35). Washington, DC: American Psychological Association.

Ginsburg, H. P., Cannon, J., Eisenband, J., & Pappas, S. (2006). Mathematical thinking and learning. In K. McCartney & D. Phillips (Eds.), *Blackwell handbook of early childhood development* (pp. 208–229). Malden, MA: Blackwell.

Girotto, V., & Light, P. (1993). The pragmatic bases of children's reasoning. In P. Light & G. Butterworth (Eds.), *Context and cognition: Ways of learning and knowing* (pp. 134–156). Mahwah, NJ: Erlbaum.

Graesser, A. C., D'Mello, S., & Cade, W. (2011). Instruction based on tutoring. In R. E. Mayer & P. A. Alexander (Eds.), *Handbook of research on learning and instruction* (pp. 408–426). New York, NY: Routledge.

Greenfield, P. M., Trumbull, E., Keller, H., Rothstein-Fisch, C., Suzuki, L. K., & Quiroz, B. (2006). Cultural conceptions of learning and development. In P. A. Alexander & P. H. Winne (Eds.), *Handbook of educational psychology* (2nd ed., pp. 675–692). Mahwah, NJ: Erlbaum.

Gresalfi, M. S. (2009). Taking up opportunities to learn: Constructing dispositions in mathematics classrooms. *Journal of the Learning Sciences, 18,* 327–369.

Gustafsson, J. (2008). Schooling and intelligence: Effects of track of study on level and profile of cognitive abilities. In P. C. Kyllonen, R. D. Roberts, & L. Stankov (Eds.), *Extending intelligence: Enhancement and new constructs* (pp. 37–59). New York, NY: Erlbaum/Taylor & Francis.

Gustafsson, J., & Undheim, J. O. (1996). Individual differences in cognitive functions. In D. C. Berliner & R. C. Calfee (Eds.), *Handbook of educational psychology* (pp. 186–242). New York, NY: Macmillan.

Haier, R. J. (2003). Positron emission tomography studies of intelligence: From psychometrics to neurobiology. In H. Nyborg (Ed.), *The scientific study of general intelligence* (pp. 41–51). New York, NY: Pergamon.

Halford, G. S., & Andrews, G. (2006). Reasoning and problem solving. In W. Damon & R. M. Lerner (Series Eds.), D. Kuhn & R. Siegler (Vol. Eds.), *Handbook of child psychology: Vol. 2. Cognition, perception, and language* (6th ed., 00. 557–608). New York, NY: Wiley.

Hallahan, D. P., Kauffman, J. M., & Pullen, P. C. (2009). *Exceptional learners: An introduction to special education* (11th ed.). Boston, MA: Allyn & Bacon.

Halpern, D. F. (1998). Teaching critical thinking for transfer across domains. *American Psychologist, 53,* 449–455.

Halpern, D. F. (2008). Is intelligence critical thinking? Why we need a new definition of intelligence. In P. C. Kyllonen, R. D. Roberts, & L. Stankov (Eds.), *Extending intelligence: Enhancement and new constructs* (pp. 349–370). New York, NY: Erlbaum/Taylor & Francis.

Hampson, S. E. (2008). Mechanisms by which childhood personality traits influence adult well-being. *Current Directions in Psychological Science, 17,* 264–268.

Hardy, I., Jonen, A., Möller, K., & Stern, E. (2006). Effects of instructional support within constructivist learning environments for elementary school students' understanding of "floating and sinking." *Journal of Educational Psychology, 98,* 307–326.

Hart, E. R., & Speece, D. L. (1998). Reciprocal teaching goes to college: Effects for postsecondary students at risk for academic failure. *Journal of Educational Psychology, 90,* 670–681.

Hattie, J. A. C. (2009). *Visible learning: A synthesis of over 800 meta-analyses relating to achievement.* London: Routledge.

Hayslip, B., Jr. (1994). Stability of intelligence. In R. J. Sternberg (Ed.), *Encyclopedia of human intelligence* (Vol. 2, pp. 1019–1026). New York, NY: Macmillan.

Haywood, H. C., & Lidz, C. S. (2007). *Dynamic assessment in practice: Clinical and educational applications.* Cambridge, England: Cambridge University Press.

Heward, W. L. (2009). *Exceptional children: An introduction to special education* (9th ed.). Upper Saddle River, NJ: Merrill/Pearson Education.

Hmelo-Silver, C. E. (2006). Design principles for scaffolding technology-based inquiry. In A. M. O'Donnell, C. E. Hmelo-Silver, & G. Erkens (Eds.), *Collaborative learning, reasoning, and technology* (pp. 147–170). Mahwah, NJ: Erlbaum.

Horn, J. L. (2008). Spearman, g, expertise, and the nature of human cognitive capability. In P. C. Kyllonen, R. D. Roberts, & L. Stankov (Eds.), *Extending intelligence: Enhancement and new constructs* (pp. 185–230). New York, NY: Erlbaum/Taylor & Francis.

Hunt, E. (2008). Improving intelligence: What's the difference from education? In P. C. Kyllonen, R. D. Roberts, & L. Stankov (Eds.), *Extending intelligence: Enhancement and new constructs* (pp. 15–35). New York, NY: Erlbaum/Taylor & Francis.

Hutchins, E. (1995). *Cognition in the wild.* Cambridge, MA: MIT Press.

Huttenlocher, P. R., & Dabholkar, A. S. (1997). Regional differences in synaptogenesis in human cerebral cortex. *Journal of Comparative Neurology, 387,* 167–178.

Inhelder, B., & Piaget, J. (1958). *The growth of logical thinking from childhood to adolescence* (A. Parsons & S. Milgram, Trans.). New York, NY: Basic Books.

Johnson, M. H., & de Haan, M. (2001). Developing cortical specialization for visual-cognitive function: The case of face recognition. In J. L. McClelland & R. S. Siegler (Eds.), *Mechanisms of cognitive development: Behavioral and neural perspectives* (pp. 253–270). Mahwah, NJ: Erlbaum.

Johnson, W. (2010). Understanding the genetics of intelligence: Can height help? Can corn oil? *Current Perspectives in Psychological Science, 19,* 177–182.

Johnson-Glenberg, M. C. (2000). Training reading comprehension in adequate decoders/poor comprehenders: Verbal versus visual strategies. *Journal of Educational Psychology, 92,* 772–782.

Jung, R. E., & Haier, R. J. (2007). The parieto-frontal integration theory (P-FIT) of intelligence: Converging neuroimaging evidence. *Behavioral and Brain Sciences, 30,* 135–154.

Kağitçibaşi, Ç. (2007). *Family, self, and human development across cultures: Theory and applications* (2nd ed.). Mahwah, NJ: Erlbaum.

Kail, R. V. (1990). *The development of memory in children* (3rd ed.). New York, NY: Freeman.

Kail, R. V. (1998). *Children and their development.* Upper Saddle River, NJ: Prentice Hall.

Kail, R. V. (2007). Longitudinal evidence that increases in processing speed and working memory enhance children's reasoning. *Psychological Science, 18,* 312–313.

Kardash, C. A. M., & Scholes, R. J. (1996). Effects of preexisting beliefs, epistemological beliefs, and need for cognition on interpretation of controversial issues. *Journal of Educational Psychology, 88,* 260–271.

Karplus, R., Pulos, S., & Stage, E. K. (1983). Proportional reasoning of early adolescents. In R. Lesh & M. Landau (Eds.), *Acquisition of mathematics concepts and processes* (pp. 45–90). San Diego, CA: Academic Press.

Karpov, Y. V., & Haywood, H. C. (1998). Two ways to elaborate Vygotsky's concept of mediation: Implications for instruction. *American Psychologist, 53,* 27–36.

Kemler Nelson, D. G., Egan, L. C., & Holt, M. B. (2004). When children ask, "What is it?" what do they want to know about artifacts? *Psychological Science, 15,* 384–389.

Keogh, B. K., & MacMillan, D. L. (1996). Exceptionality. In D. C. Berliner & R. C. Calfee (Eds.), *Handbook of educational psychology* (pp. 311–330). New York, NY: Macmillan.

Kharitonova, M., Winter, W., & Sheridan, M. A. (2015). As working memory grows: A developmental account of neural bases of working memory capacity in 5- to 8-year old children and adults. *Journal of Cognitive Neuroscience, 27*(9), 1775–1788.

King, P. M., & Kitchener, K. S. (2002). The reflective judgment model: Twenty years of research on epistemic cognition. In B. K. Hofer & P. R. Pintrich (Eds.), *Personal epistemology: The psychology of beliefs about knowledge and knowing* (pp. 37–61). Mahwah, NJ: Erlbaum.

Kirschner, P. A., Sweller, J., & Clark, R. E. (2006). Why minimal guidance during instruction does not work: An analysis of the failure of constructivist, discovery, problem-based, experiential, and inquiry-based teaching. *Educational Psychologist, 41,* 75–86.

Klaczynski, P. A. (2001). Analytic and heuristic processing influences on adolescent reasoning and decision-making. *Child Development, 72,* 844–861.

Klahr, D. (2009). "To every thing there is a season, and a time to every purpose under the heavens": What about direct instruction? In S. Tobias & T. M. Duffy (Eds.), *Constructivist instruction: Success or failure?* (pp. 291–310). New York, NY: Routledge.

Kolb, B., Gibb, R., & Robinson, T. E. (2003). Brain plasticity and behavior. *Current Directions in Psychological Science, 12,* 1–5.

Kovas, Y., Malykh, S., & Petrill, S. A. (2014). Genetics for education. In D. Mareschal, B. Butterworth, & A. Tolmie (Eds.), *Educational neuroscience* (pp. 77–109). West Sussex, UK: Wiley.

Kovas, Y., Petrill, S. A., & Plomin, R. (2007). The origins of diverse domains of mathematics: Generalist genes but specialist environments. *Journal of Educational Psychology, 99,* 128–139.

Kovas, Y., & Plomin, R. (2007). Learning abilities and disabilities: Generalist genes, specialist environments. *Current Directions in Psychological Science, 16,* 284–288.

Krätzig, G. P., & Arbuthnott, K. D. (2006). Perceptual learning style and learning proficiency: A test of the hypothesis. *Journal of Educational Psychology, 98,* 238–246.

Kuhn, D. (2001a). How do people know? *Psychological Science, 12,* 1–8.

Kuhn, D. (2001b). Why development does (and does not) occur: Evidence from the domain of inductive reasoning. In J. L. McClelland & R. S. Siegler (Eds.), *Mechanisms of cognitive development: Behavioral and neural perspectives* (pp. 221–249). Mahwah, NJ: Erlbaum.

Kuhn, D. (2006). Do cognitive changes accompany developments in the adolescent brain? *Perspectives on Psychological Science, 1,* 59–67.

Kuhn, D., & Franklin, S. (2006). The second decade: What develops (and how)? In W. Damon & R. M. Lerner (Series Eds.), D. Kuhn & R. Siegler (Vol. Eds.), *Handbook of child psychology: Vol. 1. Cognition, perception, and language* (6th ed., pp. 953–993). New York, NY: Wiley.

Kuhn, D., Garcia-Mila, M., Zohar, A., & Andersen, C. (1995). Strategies of knowledge acquisition. *Monographs of the Society for Research in Child Development, 60* (Whole No. 245).

Kuhn, D., & Pease, M. (2008). What needs to develop in the development of inquiry skills? *Cognition and Instruction, 26,* 512–599.

Kuhn, D., & Pease, M. (2010). The dual components of developing strategy use: Production and inhibition. In H. S. Waters & W. Schneider (Eds.), *Metacognition, strategy use, and instruction* (pp. 135–159). New York, NY: Guilford Press.

Kulik, J. A., & Kulik, C. C. (1997). Ability grouping. In N. Colangelo & G. Davis (Eds.), *Handbook of gifted education* (2nd ed., pp. 230–242). Boston, MA: Allyn & Bacon.

Lajoie, S. P., & Derry, S. J. (Eds.). (1993). *Computers as cognitive tools.* Mahwah, NJ: Erlbaum.

Landesman, S., & Ramey, C. (1989). Developmental psychology and mental retardation: Integrating scientific principles with treatment practices. *American Psychologist, 44,* 409–415.

Lave, J., & Wenger, E. (1991). *Situated learning: Legitimate peripheral participation.* Cambridge, England: Cambridge University Press.

Leach, J. T., & Scott, P. H. (2008). Teaching for conceptual understanding: An approach drawing on individual and sociocultural perspectives. In S. Vosniadou (Ed.), *International handbook on conceptual change* (pp. 647–675). New York, NY: Routledge.

Lenroot, R. K., & Giedd, J. N. (2007). The structural development of the human brain as measured longitudinally with magnetic resonance imaging. In D. Coch, K. W. Fischer, & G. Dawson (Eds.), *Human behavior, learning, and the developing brain: Typical development* (pp. 50–73). New York, NY: Guilford Press.

Lerner, R. M. (2002). *Adolescence: Development, diversity, context, and application.* Upper Saddle River, NJ: Prentice Hall.

Lerner, R. M., Liben, L. S., & Mueller, U. (Eds.). (2015). *Handbook of child psychology and developmental science: Volume 2, cognitive processes* (7th ed.). Hoboken, NJ: Wiley.

Li, J., & Fischer, K. W. (2004). Thought and affect in American and Chinese learners' beliefs about learning. In D. Y. Dai & R. J. Sternberg (Eds.), *Motivation, emotion, and cognition: Integrative perspectives on intellectual functioning and development* (pp. 385–418). Mahwah, NJ: Erlbaum.

Liben, L. S., & Myers, L. J. (2007). Developmental changes in children's understanding of maps: What, when, and how? In J. M. Plumert & J. P. Spencer (Eds.), *The emerging spatial mind* (pp. 193–218). New York, NY: Oxford University Press.

Lickliter, R. (2013). Biological development: Theoretical approaches, techniques, and key findings. In P. D. Zelazo (Ed.), *The Oxford handbook of developmental psychology: Vol.*

1. Body and mind (pp. 65– 90). New York, NY: Oxford University Press.

Linn, M. C., Clement, C., Pulos, S., & Sullivan, P. (1989). Scientific reasoning during adolescence: The influence of instruction in science knowledge and reasoning strategies. *Journal of Research in Science Teaching, 26,* 171–187.

Linn, M. C., & Eylon, B.-S. (2011). *Science learning and instruction: Taking advantage of technology to promote knowledge integration.* New York, NY: Routledge.

Lodewyk, K. R., & Winne, P. H. (2005). Relations among the structure of learning tasks, achievement, and changes in self-efficacy in secondary students. *Journal of Educational Psychology, 97,* 3–12.

Lorch, R. F., Jr., Lorch, E. P., Calderhead, W. J., Dunlap, E. E., Hodell, E. C., & Freer, B. D. (2010). Learning the control of variables strategy in higher and lower achieving classrooms: Contributions of explicit instruction and experimentation. *Journal of Educational Psychology, 102,* 90–101.

Losh, S. C. (2003). On the application of social cognition and social location to creating causal explanatory structures. *Educational Research Quarterly, 26*(3), 17–33.

Lovell, K. (1979). Intellectual growth and the school curriculum. In F. B. Murray (Ed.), *The impact of Piagetian theory: On education, philosophy, psychiatry, and psychology* (pp. 191–208). Baltimore, MD: University Park Press.

Lubinski, D., & Bleske-Rechek, A. (2008). Enhancing development in intellectually talented populations. In P. C. Kyllonen, R. D. Roberts, & L. Stankov (Eds.), *Extending intelligence: Enhancement and new constructs* (pp. 109–132). New York, NY: Erlbaum/Taylor & Francis.

Luciana, M., Conklin, H. M., Hooper, C. J., & Yarger, R. S. (2005). The development of nonverbal working memory and executive control processes in adolescents. *Child Development, 76,* 697–712.

Luckasson, R., Borthwick-Duffy, S., Buntinx, W. H. E., Coulter, D. L., Craig, E. M., Reeve, A., . . . Tasse, M. J. (Eds.). (2002). *Mental retardation: Definition, classification, and systems of supports* (10th ed.). Washington, DC: American Association on Mental Retardation.

Lupart, J. L. (1995). Exceptional learners and teaching for transfer. In A. McKeough, J. Lupart, & A. Marini (Eds.), *Teaching for transfer: Fostering generalization in learning* (pp. 215–228). Mahwah, NJ: Erlbaum.

Maker, C. J., & Schiever, S. W. (Eds.). (1989). *Critical issues in gifted education: Vol. 2. Defensible programs for cultural and ethnic minorities.* Austin, TX: Pro-Ed.

Mandler, J. M. (2007). On the origins of the conceptual system. *American Psychologist, 62,* 741–751.

Mareschal, D., Johnson, M. H., Sirois, S., Spratling, M. W., Thomas, M. S. C., & Westermann, G. (2007). *Neuroconstructivism: Vol. 1. How the brain constructs cognition.* Oxford, England: Oxford University Press.

Martin, T. (2009). A theory of physically distributed learning: How external environments and internal states interact in mathematics learning. *Child Development Perspectives, 3,* 140–144.

Mason, L. (2003). Personal epistemologies and intentional conceptual change. In G. M. Sinatra & P. R. Pintrich (Eds.), *Intentional conceptual change* (pp. 199–236). Mahwah, NJ: Erlbaum.

Matthews, D. J. (2009). Developmental transitions in giftedness and talent: Childhood into adolescence. In F. D. Horowitz, R. F. Subotnik, & D. J. Matthews (Eds.), *The development of giftedness and talent across the life span* (pp. 89–107). Washington, DC: American Psychological Association.

Matthews, G., Zeidner, M., & Roberts, R. D. (2006). Models of personality and affect for education: A review and synthesis. In P. A. Alexander & P. H. Winne (Eds.), *Handbook of educational psychology* (2nd ed., pp. 163–186). Mahwah, NJ: Erlbaum.

Mayer, R. E., & Massa, L. J. (2003). Three facets of visual and verbal learners: Cognitive ability, cognitive style, and learning preference. *Journal of Educational Psychology, 95,* 833–846.

McDevitt, T. M., & Ormrod, J. E. (2016). *Child development and education* (6th ed.). Upper Saddle River, NJ: Pearson.

McGee, K. D., Knight, S. L., & Boudah, D. J. (2001, April). *Using reciprocal teaching in secondary inclusive English classroom instruction.* Paper presented at the annual meeting of the American Educational Research Association, Seattle, WA.

McGrew, K. S., Flanagan, D. P., Zeith, T. Z., & Vanderwood, M. (1997). Beyond g: The impact of *Gf-Gc* specific cognitive abilities research on the future use and interpretation of intelligence tests in the schools. *School Psychology Review, 26,* 189–210.

McLane, J. B., & McNamee, G. D. (1990). *Early literacy.* Cambridge, MA: Harvard University Press.

McLoyd, V. C. (1998). Socioeconomic disadvantage and child development. *American Psychologist, 53,* 185–204.

McNeil, N. M., & Uttal, D. H. (2009). Rethinking the use of concrete materials in learning: Perspectives from development and education. *Child Development Perspectives, 3,* 137–139.

Meinz, E. J., & Hambrick, D. Z. (2010). Deliberate practice is necessary but not sufficient to explain individual differences in piano sight-reading skill: The role of working memory capacity. *Psychological Science, 21,* 914–919.

Mendaglio, S. (2010). Anxiety in gifted students. In J. C. Cassady (Ed.), *Anxiety in schools: The causes, consequences, and solutions for academic anxieties* (pp. 153–173). New York, NY: Peter Lang.

Merrill, P. F., Hammons, K., Vincent, B. R., Reynolds, P. L., Christensen, L., & Tolman, M. N. (1996). *Computers in education* (3rd ed.). Boston, MA: Allyn & Bacon.

Messick, S. (1994b). The matter of style: Manifestations of personality in cognition, learning, and testing. *Educational Psychologist, 29,* 121–136.

Metz, K. E. (1995). Reassessment of developmental constraints on children's science instruction. *Review of Educational Research, 65,* 93–127.

Miller, J. G. (1997). A cultural-psychology perspective on intelligence. In R. J. Sternberg & E. L. Grigorenko (Eds.), *Intelligence, heredity, and environment* (pp. 269–302). Cambridge, England: Cambridge University Press.

Minami, M., & McCabe, A. (1996). Compressed collections of experiences: Some Asian American traditions. In A. McCabe (Ed.), *Chameleon readers: Some problems cultural differences in narrative structure pose for multicultural literacy programs* (pp. 72–97). New York, NY: McGraw-Hill.

Minstrell, J., & Stimpson, V. (1996). A classroom environment for learning: Guiding students' reconstruction of understanding and reasoning. In L. Schauble & R. Glaser (Eds.), *Innovations in learning: New environments for education* (pp. 175–202). Mahwah, NJ: Erlbaum.

Monte-Sano, C. (2008). Qualities of historical writing instruction: A comparative case study of two teachers' practices. *American Educational Research Journal, 45,* 1045–1079.

Moore, D. S. (2013). Behavioral genetics, genetics, and epigenetics. In P. D. Zelazo (Ed.), *The Oxford Handbook of Developmental Psychology: Vol. 1. Body and mind* (pp. 91– 128). New York, NY: Oxford University Press.

Moran, S., & Gardner, H. (2006). Extraordinary achievements: A developmental and systems analysis. In W. Damon & R. M. Lerner (Series Eds.), D. Kuhn & R. Siegler (Vol. Eds.), *Handbook of child psychology: Vol. 2. Cognition, perception, and language* (6th ed., pp. 905–949). New York, NY: Wiley.

Moreno, R. (2006). Learning in high-tech and multimedia environments. *Current Directions in Psychological Science, 15,* 63–67.

Morra, S., Gobbo, C., Marini, Z., & Sheese, R. (2008). *Cognitive development: Neo-Piagetian perspectives.* New York, NY: Erlbaum.

Murphy, P. K., & Mason, L. (2006). Changing knowledge and beliefs. In P. A. Alexander & P. H. Winne (Eds.), *Handbook of educational psychology* (2nd ed., pp. 305–324). Mahwah, NJ: Erlbaum.

Neisser, U. (1998a). Introduction: Rising test scores and what they mean. In U. Neisser (Ed.), *The rising curve: Long-term gains in IQ and related measures* (pp. 3–22). Washington, DC: American Psychological Association.

Neisser, U. (Ed.). (1998b). *The rising curve: Long-term gains in IQ and related measures.* Washington, DC: American Psychological Association.

Neisser, U., Boodoo, G., Bouchard, T. J., Boykin, A. W., Brody, N., Ceci, S. J., . . . Urbina, S. (1996). Intelligence: Knowns and unknowns. *American Psychologist, 51,* 77–101.

Nelson, C. A., III, Thomas, K. M., & de Haan, M. (2006). Neural bases of cognitive development. In W. Damon & R. M. Lerner (Series Eds.), D. Kuhn & R. Siegler (Vol. Eds.), *Handbook of child psychology: Vol. 2: Cognition, perception, and language* (6th ed., pp. 3–57). New York, NY: Wiley.

Nelson, K., & Fivush, R. (2004). The emergence of autobiographical memory: A social cultural developmental theory. *Psychological Review, 111,* 486–511.

Newcombe, N., & Huttenlocher, J. (1992). Children's early ability to solve perspective-taking problems. *Developmental Psychology, 28,* 635–643.

Nieto, S., & Bode, P. (2008). *Affirming diversity: The sociopolitical context of multicultural education* (5th ed.). Boston, MA: Allyn & Bacon.

Nisbett, R. E. (2009). *Intelligence and how to get it.* New York, NY: Norton.

Nisbett, R. E., Aronson, J., Blair, C., Dickens, W., Flynn, J., Halpern, D. F., & Turkheimer, E. (2012). Intelligence: New findings and theoretical developments. *American Psychologist, 67,* 130–159.

Norenzayan, A., Choi, I., & Peng, K. (2007). Perception and cognition. In S. Kitayama & D. Cohen (Eds.), *Handbook of cultural psychology* (pp. 569–594). New York, NY: Guilford Press.

Ogbu, J. U. (1994). From cultural differences to differences in cultural frame of reference. In P. M. Greenfield & R. R. Cocking (Eds.), *Cross-cultural roots of minority child development* (pp. 365–391). Mahwah, NJ: Erlbaum.

Ogbu, J. U. (2008a). Collective identity and the burden of "acting White" in Black history, community, and education. In J. U. Ogbu (Ed.), *Minority status, oppositional culture, and schooling* (pp. 29–63). New York, NY: Routledge.

Ormrod, J. E., & McGuire, D. J. (2007). *Case studies: Applying educational psychology* (2nd ed.). Upper Saddle River, NJ: Merrill/Prentice Hall.

Otero, T. M., & Barker, L. A. (2014). The frontal lobes and executive functioning. In S. Goldstein & J. A. Naglieri (Eds.), *Handbook of Executive Functioning* (pp. 29–44). New York, NY: Springer Science+Business Media.

Owens, R. E., Jr. (1996). *Language development* (4th ed.). Boston, MA: Allyn & Bacon.

Palincsar, A. S., & Brown, A. L. (1984). Reciprocal teaching of comprehension-fostering and comprehension-monitoring activities. *Cognition and Instruction, 1,* 117–175.

Palincsar, A. S., & Brown, A. L. (1989). Classroom dialogues to promote self-regulated comprehension. In J. Brophy (Ed.), *Advances in research on teaching* (Vol. 1, pp. 35–71). Greenwich, CT: JAI Press.

Palincsar, A. S., & Herrenkohl, L. R. (1999). Designing collaborative contexts: Lessons from three research programs. In A. M. O'Donnell & A. King (Eds.), *Cognitive perspectives on peer learning* (pp. 151–177). Mahwah, NJ: Erlbaum.

Palmer, E. L. (1965). Accelerating the child's cognitive attainments through the inducement of cognitive conflict: An interpretation of the Piagetian position. *Journal of Research in Science Teaching, 3,* 324.

Park, D. C., & Huang, C.-M. (2010). Culture wires the brain: A cognitive neuroscience perspective. *Perspectives on Psychological Science, 5,* 391–400.

Parker, W. D. (1997). An empirical typology of perfectionism in academically talented children. *American Educational Research Journal, 34,* 545–562.

Pashler, H., McDaniel, M., Rohrer, D., & Bjork, R. (2009). Learning styles: Concepts and evidence. *Psychological Science in the Public Interest, 9,* 105–119.

Patton, J. R., Blackbourn, J. M., & Fad, K. S. (1996). *Exceptional individuals in focus* (6th ed.). Upper Saddle River, NJ: Merrill/Prentice Hall.

Paus, T., Zijdenbos, A., Worsley, K., Collins, D. L., Blumenthal, J., Giedd, J. N., . . . Evans, A. C. (1999). Structural maturation of neural pathways in children and adolescents: In vivo study. *Science, 283,* 1908–1911.

Pea, R. D. (1993). Practices of distributed intelligence and designs for education. In G. Salomon (Ed.), *Distributed cognitions: Psychological and educational considerations* (pp. 47–87). Cambridge, England: Cambridge University Press.

Pea, R. D., & Maldonado, H. (2006). WILD for learning: Interacting through new computing devices anytime, anywhere. In R. K. Sawyer (Ed.), *The Cambridge handbook of the learning sciences* (pp. 427–441). Cambridge, England: Cambridge University Press.

Pellegrini, A. D. (2009). Research and policy on children's play. *Child Development Perspectives, 3,* 131–136.

Perkins, D. N. (1995). *Outsmarting IQ: The emerging science of learnable intelligence.* New York, NY: Free Press.

Perkins, D., & Ritchhart, R. (2004). When is good thinking? In D. Y. Dai & R. J. Sternberg (Eds.), *Motivation, emotion, and cognition: Integrative perspectives on intellectual functioning and development* (pp. 351–384). Mahwah, NJ: Erlbaum.

Perkins, D. N., Tishman, S., Ritchhart, R., Donis, K., & Andrade, A. (2000). Intelligence in the wild: A dispositional view of intellectual traits. *Educational Psychology Review, 12,* 269–293.

Phelps, L., McGrew, K. S., Knopik, S. N., & Ford, L. (2005). The general (g), broad, and narrow CHC stratum characteristics of the WJ III and WISC-III tests: A confirmatory cross-battery investigation. *School Psychology Quarterly, 20,* 66–88.

Piaget, J. (1928). *Judgment and reasoning in the child* (M. Warden, Trans.). New York, NY: Harcourt, Brace.

Piaget, J. (1952a). *The child's conception of number* (C. Gattegno & F. M. Hodgson, Trans.). London: Routledge & Kegan Paul.

Piaget, J. (1952b). *The origins of intelligence in children* (M. Cook, Trans.). New York, NY: Norton.

Piaget, J. (1959). *The language and thought of the child* (3rd ed.; M. Gabain, Trans.). London: Routledge & Kegan Paul.

Piaget, J. (1970). Piaget's theory. In P. H. Mussen (Ed.), *Carmichael's manual of psychology* (pp. 703–732). New York, NY: Wiley.

Piaget, J. (1980). *Adaptation and intelligence: Organic selection and phenocopy* (S. Eames, Trans.). Chicago: University of Chicago Press.

Piirto, J. (1999). *Talented children and adults: Their development and education* (2nd ed.). Upper Saddle River, NJ: Merrill/Prentice Hall.

Pinker, S. (2007). *The stuff of thought: Language as a window into human nature.* New York, NY: Viking.

Plass, J. L., Kalyuga, S., & Leutner, D. (2010). Individual differences and Cognitive Load Theory. In J. L. Plass, R. Moreno, & R. Brünken (Eds.), *Cognitive Load Theory* (pp. 65–87). Cambridge, England: Cambridge University Press.

Plomin, R., & Spinath, F. M. (2004). Intelligence: Genetics, genes, and genomics. *Journal of Personality and Social Psychology, 86,* 112–129.

Pribram, K. H. (1997). The work in working memory: Implications for development. In N. A. Krasnegor, G. R. Lyon, & P. S. Goldman-Rakic (Eds.), *Development of the prefrontal cortex: Evolution, neurobiology, and behavior* (pp. 359–378). Baltimore, MD: Brookes.

Price-Williams, D. R., Gordon, W., & Ramirez, M. (1969). Skill and conservation. *Developmental Psychology, 1,* 769.

Proctor, B. E., Floyd, R. G., & Shaver, R. B. (2005). Cattell-Horn-Carroll broad cognitive ability profiles of low math achievers. *Psychology in the Schools, 42*(1), 1–12.

Proctor, R. W., & Dutta, A. (1995). *Skill acquisition and human performance.* Thousand Oaks, CA: Sage.

Prout, H. T. (2009). Positive psychology and students with intellectual disabilities. In R. Gilman, E. S. Huebner, & M. J. Furlong (Eds.), *Handbook of positive psychology in schools* (pp. 371–381). New York, NY: Routledge.

Pulos, S., & Linn, M. C. (1981). Generality of the controlling variables scheme in early adolescence. *Journal of Early Adolescence, 1,* 26–37.

Quinn, P. C. (2007). On the infant's prelinguistic conception of spatial relations: Three developmental trends and their implications for spatial language learning. In J. M. Plumert & J. P. Spencer (Eds.), *The emerging spatial mind* (pp. 117–141). New York, NY: Oxford University Press.

Rabinowitz, M., & Glaser, R. (1985). Cognitive structure and process in highly competent performance. In F. D. Horowitz & M. O'Brien (Eds.), *The gifted and the talented: Developmental perspectives* (pp. 75–98). Washington, DC: American Psychological Association.

Raine, A., Reynolds, C., & Venables, P. H. (2002). Stimulation seeking and intelligence: A prospective longitudinal study. *Journal of Personality and Social Psychology, 82,* 663–674.

Raudenbush, S. W. (2009). The *Brown* legacy and the O'Connor challenge: Transforming schools in the images of children's potential. *Educational Researcher, 38,* 169–180.

Reinking, D., & Leu, D. J. (Chairs) (2008, March). *Understanding Internet reading comprehension and its development among adolescents at risk of dropping out of school.* Poster session presented at the annual meeting of the American Educational Research Association, New York, NY.

Renzulli, J. S. (2002). Emerging conceptions of giftedness: Building a bridge to the new century. *Exceptionality, 10*(2), 67–75.

Rhodes, B. (2008). Challenges and opportunities for intelligence augmentation. In P. C. Kyllonen, R. D. Roberts, & L. Stankov (Eds.), *Extending intelligence: Enhancement and new constructs* (pp. 395–405). New York, NY: Erlbaum/Taylor & Francis.

Ricciuti, H. N. (1993). Nutrition and mental development. *Current Directions in Psychological Science, 2,* 43–46.

Riding, R. J., & Cheema, I. (1991). Cognitive styles—An overview and integration. *Educational Psychology, 11,* 193–215.

Rizzi, T. S., & Posthuma, D. (2013). Genes and intelligence. In D. Reisberg (Ed.), *The Oxford handbook of cognitive psychology* (pp. 823–841). New York, NY: Oxford University Press.

Roberts, R. D., & Lipnevich, A. A. (2012). From general intelligence to multiple intelligences: Meanings, models, and measures. In K. R. Harris, S. Graham, & T. Urdan (Eds.), *APA educational psychology handbook* (Vol. 2, pp. 33–57). Washington, D.C.: American Psychological Association.

Rogoff, B. (1990). *Apprenticeship in thinking: Cognitive development in social context.* New York, NY: Oxford University Press.

Rogoff, B. (1991). Social interaction as apprenticeship in thinking: Guidance and participation in spatial planning. In L. B.

Resnick, J. M. Levine, & S. D. Teasley (Eds.), *Perspectives on socially shared cognition* (pp. 349–364). Washington, DC: American Psychological Association.

Rogoff, B. (2003). *The cultural nature of human development.* Oxford, England: Oxford University Press.

Rosenshine, B., & Meister, C. (1992). The use of scaffolds for teaching higher-level cognitive strategies. *Educational Leadership, 49*(7), 26–33.

Rosenshine, B., & Meister, C. (1994). Reciprocal teaching: A review of the research. *Review of Educational Research, 64,* 479–530.

Rosser, R. (1994). *Cognitive development: Psychological and biological perspectives.* Boston, MA: Allyn & Bacon.

Roth, W., & Bowen, G. M. (1995). Knowing and interacting: A study of culture, practices, and resources in a grade 8 open-inquiry science classroom guided by a cognitive apprenticeship metaphor. *Cognition and Instruction, 13,* 73–128.

Rothbart, M. K. (2007). Temperament, development, and personality. *Current Directions in Psychological Science, 16,* 207–212.

Salomon, G. (1993). No distribution without individuals' cognition: A dynamic interactional view. In G. Salomon (Ed.), *Distributed cognitions: Psychological and educational considerations* (pp. 111–138). Cambridge, England: Cambridge University Press.

Sarama, J., & Clements, D. H. (2009). "Concrete" computer manipulatives in mathematics education. *Child Development Perspectives, 3,* 145–150.

Sattler, J. M. (2001). *Assessment of children: Cognitive applications* (4th ed.). San Diego, CA: Author.

Scarr, S., & McCartney, K. (1983). How people make their own environments: A theory of genotype environment effects. *Child Development, 54,* 424–435.

Scarr, S., & Weinberg, R. A. (1976). IQ test performance of black children adopted by white families. *American Psychologist, 31,* 726–739.

Schauble, L. (1990). Belief revision in children: The role of prior knowledge and strategies for generating evidence. *Journal of Experimental Child Psychology, 49,* 31–57.

Schliemann, A. D., & Carraher, D. W. (1993). Proportional reasoning in and out of school. In P. Light & G. Butterworth (Eds.), *Context and cognition: Ways of learning and knowing* (pp. 47–73). Mahwah, NJ: Erlbaum.

Schwartz, D. L., & Martin, T. (2004). Inventing to prepare for future learning: The hidden efficiency of encouraging original student production in statistics instruction. *Cognition and Instruction, 22,* 129–184.

Shavinina, L. V., & Ferrari, M. (2004). Extracognitive facets of developing high ability: Introduction to some important issues. In L. V. Shavinina & M. Ferrari (Eds.), *Beyond knowledge: Extracognitive aspects of developing high ability* (pp. 3–13). Mahwah, NJ: Erlbaum.

Shaw, P., Greenstein, D., Lerch, J., Clasen, L., Lenroot, R., Gogtay, N., . . . Giedd, J. (2006). Intellectual ability and cortical development in children and adolescents. *Nature, 440,* 676–679.

Shen, H., Sabaliauskas, N., Sherpa, A., Fenton, A. A., Stelzer, A., Aoki, C., & Smith, S. S. (2010). A critical role for $\alpha 4\beta\delta$ GABA$_A$ receptors in shaping learning deficits at puberty in mice. *Science, 327*(5972), 1515–1518.

Sherman, J., & Bisanz, J. (2009). Equivalence in symbolic and nonsymbolic contexts: Benefits of solving problems with manipulatives. *Journal of Educational Psychology, 101,* 88–100.

Siegler, R. S. (2009). Improving the numerical understanding of children from low-income families. *Child Development Perspectives, 3,* 118–124.

Siegler, R. S., & Alibali, M. W. (2005). *Children's thinking* (4th ed.). Upper Saddle River, NJ: Prentice Hall.

Siegler, R. S., & Lin, X. (2010). Self-explanations promote children's learning. In H. S. Waters & W. Schneider (Eds.), *Metacognition, strategy use, and instruction* (pp. 85–112). New York, NY: Guilford Press.

Siegler, R. S., & Svetina, M. (2006). What leads children to adopt new strategies? A microgenetic/cross-sectional study of class inclusion. *Child Development, 77,* 997–1015.

Sigman, M., & Whaley, S. E. (1998). The role of nutrition in the development of intelligence. In U. Neisser (Ed.), *The rising curve: Long-term gains in IQ and related measures* (pp. 155–182). Washington, DC: American Psychological Association.

Simonton, D. K. (2001). Talent development as a multidimensional, multiplicative, and dynamic process. *Current Directions in Psychological Science, 10,* 39–42.

Slater, W. H. (2004). Teaching English from a literacy perspective: The goal of high literacy for all students. In T. L. Jetton & J. A. Dole (Eds.), *Adolescent literacy research and practice* (pp. 40–58). New York, NY: Guilford Press.

Slavin, R. E., Lake, C., Chambers, B., Cheung, A., & Davis, S. (2009). Effective reading programs for the elementary grades: A best-evidence synthesis. *Review of Educational Research, 79,* 1391–1466.

Smith, C. L., Maclin, D., Grosslight, L., & Davis, H. (1997). Teaching for understanding: A study of students' preinstruction theories of matter and a comparison of the effectiveness of two approaches to teaching about matter and density. *Cognition and Instruction, 15,* 317–393.

Smith, H. L. (1998). Literacy and instruction in African American communities: Shall we overcome? In B. Pérez (Ed.), *Sociocultural contexts of language and literacy* (pp. 189–222). Mahwah, NJ: Erlbaum.

Southerland, S. A., & Sinatra, G. M. (2003). Learning about biological evolution: A special case of intentional conceptual change. In G. M. Sinatra & P. R. Pintrich (Eds.), *Intentional conceptual change* (pp. 317–345). Mahwah, NJ: Erlbaum.

Sowell, E. R., & Jernigan, T. L. (1998). Further MRI evidence of late brain maturation: Limbic volume increases and changing asymmetries during childhood and adolescence. *Developmental Neuropsychology, 14,* 599–617.

Sowell, E. R., Thompson, P. M., Holmes, C. J., Jernigan, T. L., & Toga, A. W. (1999). *In vivo* evidence for post-adolescent brain maturation in frontal and striatal regions. *Nature Neuroscience, 2,* 859–861.

Spear, L. P. (2007). Brain development and adolescent behavior. In D. Coch, K. W. Fischer, & G. Dawson (Eds.), *Human behavior, learning, and the developing brain: Typical development* (pp. 362–396). New York, NY: Guilford Press.

Spearman, C. (1904). General intelligence, objectively determined and measured. *American Journal of Psychology, 15,* 201–293.

Spearman, C. (1927). *The abilities of man: Their nature and measurement.* New York, NY: Macmillan.

Spencer, J. P., Blumberg, M. S., McMurray, B., Robinson, S. R., Samuelson, L. K., & Tomblin, J. B. (2009). Short arms and talking eggs: Why we should no longer abide the nativist–empiricist debate. *Child Development Perspectives, 3,* 79–87.

Spörer, N., & Brunstein, J. C. (2009). Fostering the reading comprehension of secondary school students through peer-assisted learning: Effects on strategy knowledge, strategy use, and task performance. *Contemporary Educational Psychology, 34,* 289–297.

Sroufe, L. A., Cooper, R. G., DeHart, G., & Bronfenbrenner, U. (1992). *Child development: Its nature and course* (2nd ed.). New York, NY: McGraw-Hill.

Stanovich, K. E. (1999). *Who is rational? Studies of individual differences in reasoning.* Mahwah, NJ: Erlbaum.

Stanovich, K. (2009). *What intelligence tests miss: The psychology of rational thought.* New Haven, CT: Yale University Press.

Steinberg, L. (2009). Should the science of adolescent brain development inform public policy? *American Psychologist, 64,* 739–750.

Steiner, H. H., & Carr, M. (2003). Cognitive development in gifted children: Toward a more precise understanding of emerging differences in intelligence. *Educational Psychology Review, 15,* 215–246.

Sternberg, R. J. (1998). Teaching triarchically improves school achievement. *Journal of Educational Psychology, 90,* 374–384.

Sternberg, R. J. (2003). *Wisdom, intelligence, and creativity synthesized.* Cambridge, England: Cambridge University Press.

Sternberg, R. J. (2004). Culture and intelligence. *American Psychologist, 59,* 325–338.

Sternberg, R. J. (2005). Intelligence, competence, and expertise. In A. J. Elliot & C. S. Dweck (Eds.), *Handbook of competence and motivation* (pp. 15–30). New York, NY: Guilford Press.

Sternberg, R. J. (2007). Intelligence and culture. In S. Kitayama & D. Cohen (Eds.), *Handbook of cultural psychology* (pp. 547–568). New York, NY: Guilford Press.

Sternberg, R. J., Forsythe, G. B., Hedlund, J., Horvath, J. A., Wagner, R. K., Williams, W. M., . . . Grigorenko, E. L. (2000). *Practical intelligence in everyday life.* Cambridge, England: Cambridge University Press.

Subotnik, R. F., Olszewski-Kubilus, P., & Worrell, F. C. (2011). Rethinking giftedness and gifted education: A proposed direction forward base on psychological science. *Psychological Science in the Public Interest, 12,* 3–54.

Swanson, H. L. (2008). Working memory and intelligence in children: What develops? *Journal of Educational Psychology, 100,* 581–602.

Sweller, J. (2010). Cognitive Load Theory: Recent theoretical advances. In J. L. Plass, R. Moreno, & R. Brünken (Eds.), *Cognitive Load Theory* (pp. 29–47). Cambridge, England: Cambridge University Press.

Tamburrini, J. (1982). Some educational implications of Piaget's theory. In S. Modgil & C. Modgil (Eds.), *Jean Piaget: Consensus and controversy* (pp. 309–325). New York, NY: Praeger.

Tanner, J. M., & Inhelder, B. (Eds.). (1960). *Discussions of child development: A consideration of the biological, psychological, and cultural approaches to the understanding of human development and behavior: Vol. 4. The proceedings of the fourth meeting of the World Health Organization Study Group on the Psychobiological Development of the Child, Geneva, 1956.* New York, NY: International Universities Press.

Terry, A. W. (2003). Effects of service learning on young, gifted adolescents and their community. *Gifted Child Quarterly, 47,* 295–308.

Terry, A. W. (2008). Student voices, global echoes: Service-learning and the gifted. *Roeper Review, 30,* 45–51.

Thomas, M. S. C., & Johnson, M. H. (2008). New advances in understanding sensitive periods in brain development. *Current Directions in Psychological Science, 17,* 1–5.

Thurstone, L. L. (1938). *Primary mental abilities.* Chicago, IL: University of Chicago Press.

Tourniaire, F., & Pulos, S. (1985). Proportional reasoning: A review of the literature. *Educational Studies in Mathematics, 16,* 181–204.

Trautwein, U., Lüdtke, O., Schnyder, I., & Niggli, A. (2006). Predicting homework effort: Support for a domain-specific, multilevel homework model. *Journal of Educational Psychology, 98,* 438–456.

Turkheimer, E., Haley, A., Waldron, M., D'Onofrio, B., & Gottesman, I. I. (2003). Socioeconomic status modifies heritability of IQ in young children. *Psychological Science, 14,* 623–628.

Turnbull, A., Turnbull, R., & Wehmeyer, M. L. (2010). *Exceptional lives: Special education in today's schools* (6th ed.). Upper Saddle River, NJ: Merrill.

Van Dooren, W., De Bock, D., Hessels, A., Janssens, D., & Verschaffel, L. (2005). Not everything is proportional: Effects of age and problem type on propensities for overgeneralization. *Cognition and Instruction, 23,* 57–86.

van IJzendoorn, M. H., Juffer, F., & Klein Poelhuis, C. W. (2005). Adoption and cognitive development: A meta-analytic comparison of adopted and nonadopted children's IQ and school performance. *Psychological Bulletin, 131,* 301–316.

Van Leijenhorst, L., Crone, E. A., & Van der Molen, M. W. (2007). Developmental trends for object and spatial working memory: A psychophysiological analysis. *Child Development, 78,* 987–1000.

van Merriënboer, J. J. G., & Sweller, J. (2005). Cognitive load theory and complex learning: Recent developments and future directions. *Educational Psychology Review, 17,* 147–177.

VanSledright, B., & Limón, M. (2006). Learning and teaching social studies: A review of cognitive research in history and geography. In P. A. Alexander & P. H. Winne (Eds.), *Handbook of educational psychology* (2nd ed., pp. 545–570). Mahwah, NJ: Erlbaum.

Varnum, M. E. W., Grossmann, I., Kitayama, S., & Nisbett, R. E. (2010). The origin of cultural differences in cognition: The social orientation hypothesis. *Current Directions in Psychological Science, 19,* 9–13.

Voss, J. F., Greene, T. R., Post, T. A., & Penner, B. D. (1983). Problem-solving skill in the social sciences. In G. H. Bower (Ed.), *The psychology of learning and motivation* (Vol. 17, pp. 165–213). San Diego, CA: Academic Press.

Vygotsky, L. S. (1962). *Thought and language* (E. Haufmann & G. Vakar, Eds. and Trans.). Cambridge, MA: MIT Press.

Vygotsky, L. S. (1978). *Mind in society: The development of higher psychological processes.* Cambridge, MA: Harvard University Press.

Vygotsky, L. S. (1987). *The collected works of L. S. Vygotsky* (Vol. 3; R. W. Rieber & A. S. Carton, Eds.). New York, NY: Plenum Press.

Vygotsky, L. S. (1997). *Educational psychology* (R. Silverman, Trans.). Boca Raton, FL: St. Lucie Press.

Walker, E. F. (2002). Adolescent neurodevelopment and psychopathology. *Current Directions in Psychological Science, 11,* 24–28.

Walton, G. M., & Spencer, S. J. (2009). Latent ability: Grades and test scores systematically underestimate intellectual ability of negatively stereotyped students. *Psychological Science, 20,* 1132–1139.

Wang, Q., & Ross, M. (2007). Culture and memory. In S. Kitayama & D. Cohen (Eds.), *Handbook of cultural psychology* (pp. 645–667). New York, NY: Guilford Press.

Waterhouse, L. (2006). Multiple intelligences, the Mozart effect, and emotional intelligence: A critical review. *Educational Psychologist, 41,* 207–225.

West, R. F., Toplak, M. E., & Stanovich, K. E. (2008). Heuristics and biases as measures of critical thinking: Associations with cognitive ability and thinking dispositions. *Journal of Educational Psychology, 100,* 930–941.

White, B. Y., & Frederiksen, J. R. (1998). Inquiry, modeling, and metacognition: Making science accessible to all students. *Cognition and Instruction, 16,* 3–118.

White, B. Y., & Frederiksen, J. (2005). A theoretical framework and approach for fostering metacognitive development. *Educational Psychologist, 40,* 211–223.

White, B., Frederiksen, J., & Collins, A. (2009). The interplay of scientific inquiry and metacognition: More than a marriage of convenience. In D. J. Hacker, J. Dunlosky, & A. C. Graesser (Eds.), *Handbook of metacognition in education* (pp. 175–205). New York, NY: Routledge.

Winner, E. (1988). *The point of words.* Cambridge, MA: Harvard University Press.

Winner, E. (2000a). Giftedness: Current theory and research. *Current Directions in Psychological Science, 9,* 153–156.

Winner, E. (2000b). The origins and ends of giftedness. *American Psychologist, 55,* 159–169.

Winsler, A., & Naglieri, J. (2003). Overt and covert verbal problem-solving strategies: Developmental trends in use, awareness, and relations with task performance in children aged 5 to 17. *Child Development, 74,* 659–678.

Wiser, M., & Smith, C. L. (2008). Learning and teaching about matter in grades K–8: When should the atomic–molecular theory be introduced? In S. Vosniadou (Ed.), *International handbook of research on conceptual change* (pp. 205–231). New York, NY: Routledge.

Wolf, M., Gottwald, S., Galante, W., Norton, E., & Miller, L. (2009). How the origins of the reading brain instruct our knowledge of reading intervention. In K. Pugh & P. McCardle (Eds.), *How children learn to read: Current issues and new directions in the integration of cognition, neurobiology and genetics of reading and dyslexia research and practice* (pp. 289–299). New York, NY: Psychology Press.

Wood, D., Bruner, J. S., & Ross, G. (1976). The role of tutoring in problem-solving. *Journal of Child Psychology and Psychiatry, 17,* 89–100.

Yokota, S., Takeuchi, H., Hashimoto, T., Hashizume, H., Asano, K., Asano, M., . . . Kawashima, R. (2015). Individual differences in cognitive performance and brain structure in typically developing children. *Developmental Cognitive Neuroscience, 14,* 1–7.

Zelazo, P. D. (2013). Developmental psychology: A new synthesis. In P. D. Zelazo (Ed.), *The Oxford Handbook of Developmental Psychology: Vol. 1. Body and mind* (pp. 3–12). New York, NY: Oxford University Press.

Zhang, L.-F., & Sternberg, R. J. (2006). *The nature of intellectual styles.* Mahwah, NJ: Erlbaum.

Zigler, E. F., & Finn-Stevenson, M. (1992). Applied developmental psychology. In M. H. Bornstein & M. E. Lamb (Eds.), *Developmental psychology: An advanced textbook* (pp. 677–729). Mahwah, NJ: Erlbaum.

Zohar, A., & Aharon-Kraversky, S. (2005). Exploring the effects of cognitive conflict and direct teaching for students of different academic levels. *Journal of Research in Science Teaching, 42,* 829–855.

CHAPTER 7

Adalbjarnardottir, S., & Selman, R. L. (1997). "I feel I have received a new vision": An analysis of teachers' professional development as they work with students on interpersonal issues. *Teaching and Teacher Education, 13,* 409–428.

Ahn, J. (2005, April). *Young immigrant children's cultural transition and self-transformation.* Paper presented at the annual meeting of the American Educational Research Association, Montreal, Quebec, Canada.

Aikins, J. W., & Litwack, S. D. (2011). Prosocial skills, social competence, and popularity. In A. H. N. Cillessen, D. Schwartz, & L. Mayeux (Eds.), *Popularity in the peer system* (pp. 140–162). New York, NY: Guilford Press.

Alapack, R. (1991). The adolescent first kiss. *Humanistic Psychologist, 19,* 48–67.

Albert, D., Chein, J., & Steinberg, L. (2013). The teenage brain: Peer influences on adolescent decision making. *Current Directions in Psychological Science, 22,* 114–120.

Alemán, A. M. M., & Vartman, K. L. (2009). *Online social networking on campus: Understanding what matters in student culture.* New York, NY: Routledge.

Alexander, K. L., Entwisle, D. R., & Dauber, S. L. (1995). *On the success of failure.* New York, NY: Cambridge University Press.

Allen, J. P., & Antonishak, J. (2008). Adolescent peer influences: Beyond the dark side. In M. J. Prinstein & K. A. Dodge (Eds.), *Understanding peer influence in children and adolescents* (pp. 141–160). New York, NY: Guilford Press.

Allen, L., & Aber, J. L. (2006). The development of ethnic identity during adolescence. *Developmental Psychology, 42,* 1–10.

Altermatt, E. R. (2012). Children's achievement-related discourse with peers: Uncovering the processes of peer influence. In A. M. Ryan & G. W. Ladd (Eds.), *Peer relationships and adjustment at school* (pp. 109–134). Charlotte, NC: Information Age.

Altschul, I., Oyserman, D., & Bybee, D. (2006). Racial-ethnic identity in mid-adolescence: Content and change as predictors of academic achievement. *Child Development, 77,* 1155–1169.

Anderman, E. M., Griesinger, T., & Westerfield, G. (1998). Motivation and cheating during early adolescence. *Journal of Educational Psychology, 90,* 84–93.

Anderman, L. H., Freeman, T. M., & Mueller, C. E. (2007). The "social" side of social context: Interpersonal affiliative dimensions of students' experiences and academic dishonesty. In E. M. Anderman & T. B. Murdock (Eds.), *The psychology of academic cheating* (pp. 203–228). San Diego, CA: Elsevier.

Anderson, L. W., & Pellicer, L. O. (1998). Toward an understanding of unusually successful programs for economically disadvantaged students. *Journal of Education for Students Placed at Risk, 3,* 237–263.

Angold, A., Worthman, C., & Costello, E. J. (2003). Puberty and depression. In C. Hayward (Ed.), *Gender differences at puberty* (pp. 137–164). Cambridge, England: Cambridge University Press.

Ansary, N. S., Elias, M. J., Greene, M. B., & Green, S. (2015). Guidance for schools selecting antibullying approaches: Translating evidence-base strategies to contemporary implementation realities. *Educational Researcher, 44,* 27–36.

Arens, A. K., Yeung, A. S., Craven, R. G., & Hasselhorn, M. (2011). The twofold multidimensionality of academic self-concept: Domain specificity and separation between competence and affect components. *Journal of Educational Psychology, 103,* 970–981.

Arnold, M. L. (2000). Stage, sequence, and sequels: Changing conceptions of morality, post-Kohlberg. *Educational Psychology Review, 12,* 365–383.

Arsenio, W. F., & Lemerise, E. A. (2004). Aggression and moral development: Integrating social information processing and moral domain models. *Child Development, 75,* 987–1002.

Asher, S. R., & McDonald, K. A. (2009). The behavioral basis of acceptance, rejection, and perceived popularity. In K. H. Rubin, W. M. Bukowski, & B. Laursen (Eds.), *Handbook of peer interactions, relationships, and groups* (pp. 232–248). New York, NY: Guilford Press.

Asher, S. R., & Paquette, J. A. (2003). Loneliness and peer relations in childhood. *Current Directions in Psychological Science, 12,* 75–78.

Asher, S. R., & Renshaw, P. D. (1981). Children without friends: Social knowledge and social skill training. In S. R. Asher & J. M. Gottman (Eds.), *The development of children's friendships* (pp. 273–296). New York, NY: Cambridge University Press.

Assor, A., & Connell, J. P. (1992). The validity of students' self-reports as measures of performance affecting self-appraisals. In D. H. Schunk & J. L. Meece (Eds.), *Student perceptions in the classroom* (pp. 22–50). Mahwah, NJ: Erlbaum.

Banks, J. A., & Banks, C. A. M. (Eds.). (1995). *Handbook of research on multicultural education.* New York, NY: Macmillan.

Barber, B. K., Stolz, H. E., & Olsen, J. A. (2005). Parental support, psychological control, and behavioral control: Assessing relevance across time, culture, and method. *Monographs of the Society for Research in Child Development, 70*(4, Serial No. 282).

Bates, J. E., & Pettit, G. S. (2007). Temperament, parenting, and socialization. In J. E. Grusec & P. D. Hastings (Eds.), *Handbook of socialization: Theory and research* (pp. 153–177). New York, NY: Guilford Press.

Batson, C. D. (1991). *The altruism question: Toward a social-psychological answer.* Hillsdale, NJ: Erlbaum.

Batson, C. D., & Thompson, E. R. (2001). Why don't moral people act morally? Motivational considerations. *Current Directions in Psychological Science, 10,* 54–57.

Battin-Pearson, S., Newcomb, M. D., Abbott, R. D., Hill, K. G., Catalano, R. F., & Hawkins, J. D. (2000). Predictors of early high school dropout: A test of five theories. *Journal of Educational Psychology, 92,* 568–582.

Baumeister, R. F., Campbell, J. D., Krueger, J. I., & Vohs, K. D. (2003). Does high self-esteem cause better performance, interpersonal success, happiness, or healthier lifestyles? *Psychological Science in the Public Interest, 4,* 1–44.

Baumeister, R. F., Smart, L., & Boden, J. M. (1996). Relation of threatened egotism to violence and aggression: The dark side of high self-esteem. *Psychological Review, 103,* 5–33.

Baumrind, D. (1989). Rearing competent children. In W. Damon (Ed.), *Child development today and tomorrow* (pp. 349–378). San Francisco, CA: Jossey-Bass.

Baumrind, D. (1991). Parenting styles and adolescent development. In R. M. Lerner, A. C. Petersen, & J. Brooks-Gunn

(Eds.), *Encyclopedia of adolescence* (pp. 746–748). New York, NY: Garland.

Becker, B. E., & Luthar, S. S. (2002). Social-emotional factors affecting achievement outcomes among disadvantaged students: Closing the achievement gap. *Educational Psychologist, 37*, 197–214.

Belfiore, P. J., & Hornyak, R. S. (1998). Operant theory and application to self-monitoring in adolescents. In D. H. Schunk & B. J. Zimmerman (Eds.), *Self-regulated learning: From teaching to self-reflective practice* (pp. 184–202). New York, NY: Guilford Press.

Bellanca, J. A., & Stirling, T. (2011). *Classrooms without borders: Using Internet projects to teach communication and collaboration.* New York, NY: Teachers College Press.

Bellmore, A. (2011). Peer rejection and unpopularity: Associations with GPAs across the transition to middle school. *Journal of Educational Psychology, 103*, 282–295.

Belsky, J., & Pluess, M. (2009). The nature (and nurture?) of plasticity in early human development. *Perspectives on Psychological Science, 4*, 345–351.

Bem, S. L. (1981). Gender schema theory: A cognitive account of sex typing. *Psychological Review, 88*, 354–364.

Benenson, J. F., Maiese, R., Dolenszky, E., Dolensky, N., Sinclair, N., & Simpson, A. (2002). Group size regulates self-assertive versus self-deprecating responses to interpersonal competition. *Child Development, 73*, 1818–1829.

Bergamo, M., & Evans, M. A. (2005, April). *Rules of surviving peer relationships: Advice from middle school students.* Poster presented at the annual meeting of the American Educational Research Association, Montreal, Quebec, Canada.

Bergin, D. A., & Cooks, H. C. (2008). High school students of color talk about accusations of "acting White." In J. U. Ogbu (Ed.), *Minority status, oppositional culture, and schooling* (pp. 145–166). New York, NY: Routledge.

Berzonsky, M. D., & Kuk, L. S. (2000). Identity status, identity processing style, and the transition to university. *Journal of Adolescent Research, 15*, 81–98.

Best, D. L. (2010). Gender. In M. H. Bornstein (Ed.), *Handbook of cultural developmental science* (pp. 209–222). New York, NY: Psychology Press.

Bierman, K. L., Miller, C. L., & Stabb, S. D. (1987). Improving the social behavior and peer acceptance of rejected boys: Effect of social skill training with instructions and prohibitions. *Journal of Consulting and Clinical Psychology, 55*, 194–200.

Bierman, K. L., & Powers, C. J. (2009). Social skills training to improve peer relations. In K. H. Rubin, W. M. Bukowski, & B. Laursen (Eds.), *Handbook of peer interactions, relationships, and groups* (pp. 603–621). New York, NY: Guilford Press.

Bigler, R. S., Brown, C. S., & Markell, M. (2001). When groups are not created equal: Effects of group status on the formation of intergroup attitudes in children. *Child Development, 72*, 1151–1162.

Black-Gutman, D., & Hickson, F. (1996). The relationship between racial attitudes and social-cognitive development in children: An Australian study. *Developmental Psychology, 32*, 448–456.

Blair, C., & Razza, R. P. (2007). Relating effortful control, executive function, and false belief understanding to emerging math and literacy ability in kindergarten. *Child Development, 78*, 647–663.

Blanton, H., & Burkley, M. (2008). Deviance regulation theory: Applications to adolescent social influence. In M. J. Prinstein & K. A. Dodge (Eds.), *Understanding peer influence in children and adolescents* (pp. 94–121). New York, NY: Guilford Press.

Blasi, A. (1980). Bridging moral cognition and moral action: A critical review of the literature. *Psychological Bulletin, 88*, 593–637.

Blasi, A. (1995). Moral understanding and the moral personality: The process of moral integration. In W. M. Kurtines & J. L. Gewirtz (Eds.), *Moral development: An introduction* (pp. 229–253). Boston, MA: Allyn & Bacon.

Block, J. H. (1983). Differential premises arising from differential socialization of the sexes: Some conjectures. *Child Development, 54*, 1335–1354.

Boling, C. J., & Evans, W. H. (2008). Reading success in the secondary classroom. *Preventing School Failure, 52*(2), 59–66.

Bong, M., & Skaalvik, E. M. (2003). Academic self-concept and self-efficacy: How different are they really? *Educational Psychology Review, 15*, 1–40.

Boom, J., Brugman, D., & van der Heijden, P. G. M. (2001). Hierarchical structure of moral stages assessed by a sorting task. *Child Development, 72*, 535–548.

Bornstein, M. H., & Lansford, J. E. (2010). Parenting. In M. H. Bornstein (Ed.), *Handbook of cultural developmental science* (pp. 259–277). New York, NY: Psychology Press.

Bosacki, S. L. (2000). Theory of mind and self-concept in preadolescents: Links with gender and language. *Journal of Educational Psychology, 92*, 709–717.

Bracken, B. (2009). Positive self-concepts. In R. Gilman, E. S. Huebner, & M. J. Furlong (Eds.), *Handbook of positive psychology in schools* (pp. 89–106). New York, NY: Routledge.

Bradley, R. H. (2010). The HOME environment. In M. H. Bornstein (Ed.), *Handbook of cultural developmental science* (pp. 505–530). New York, NY: Psychology Press.

Bradshaw, C. P. (2015). Translating research to practice in bullying prevention. *American Psychologist, 70*, 322–332.

Brayboy, B. M. J., & Searle, K. A. (2007). Thanksgiving and serial killers: Representations of American Indians in schools. In S. Books (Ed.), *Invisible children in the society and its schools* (3rd ed., pp. 173–192). Mahwah, NJ: Erlbaum.

Brendgen, M., Boivin, M., Vitaro, F., Bukowski, W. M., Dionne, G., Tremblay, R. E., & Pérusse, D. (2008). Linkages between children's and their friends' social and physical aggression: Evidence for a gene-environment interaction? *Child Development, 79*, 13–29.

Brewer, M. B., & Yuki, M. (2007). Culture and social identity. In S. Kitayama & D. Cohen (Eds.), *Handbook of cultural psychology* (pp. 307–322). New York, NY: Guilford Press.

Brody, G. H., & Shaffer, D. R. (1982). Contributions of parents and peers to children's moral socialization. *Developmental Review, 2*, 31–75.

Brooks-Gunn, J. (2003). Do you believe in magic?: What we can expect from early childhood intervention programs. *Social Policy Report of the Society for Research in Child Development, 17*(1), 3–14.

Brooks-Gunn, J., Linver, M. R., & Fauth, R. C. (2005). Children's competence and socioeconomic status in the family and neighborhood. In A. J. Elliot & C. S. Dweck (Eds.), *Handbook of competence and motivation* (pp. 414–435). New York, NY: Guilford Press.

Brooks-Gunn, J., & Paikoff, R. L. (1993). "Sex is a gamble, kissing is a game": Adolescent sexuality and health promotion. In S. G. Millstein, A. C. Petersen, & E. O. Nightingale (Eds.), *Promoting the health of adolescents: New directions for the twenty-first century* (pp. 180–208). New York, NY: Oxford University Press.

Brophy, J. E. (2002). Social promotion. In J. Guthrie (Ed.), *Encyclopedia of education* (2nd ed., Vol. 6, pp. 2262–2265). New York, NY: Macmillan.

Brophy, J. E., Alleman, J., & Knighton, B. (2009). *Inside the social studies classroom.* New York, NY: Routledge.

Brown, B. B. (1990). Peer groups. In S. Feldman & G. Elliott (Eds.), *At the threshold: The developing adolescent* (pp. 171–196). Cambridge, MA: Harvard University Press.

Brown, B. B. (1993). School culture, social politics, and the academic motivation of U.S. students. In T. M. Tomlinson (Ed.), *Motivating students to learn: Overcoming barriers to high achievement* (pp. 63–98). Berkeley, CA: McCutchan.

Brown, B. B. (1999). "You're going out with *who?*" Peer group influences on adolescent romantic relationships. In W. Furman, B. B. Brown, & C. Feiring (Eds.), *The development of romantic relationships in adolescence* (pp. 291–329). Cambridge, England: Cambridge University Press.

Brown, B. B. (2011). Popularity in peer group perspective: The role of status in adolescent peer systems. In A. H. N. Cillessen, D. Schwartz, & L. Mayeux (Eds.), *Popularity in the peer system* (pp. 165–192). New York, NY: Guilford Press.

Brown, B. B., Bakken, J. P., Ameringer, S. W., & Mahon, S. D. (2008). A comprehensive conceptualization of the peer influence process in adolescence. In M. J. Prinstein & K. A. Dodge (Eds.), *Understanding peer influence in children and adolescents* (pp. 17–44). New York, NY: Guilford Press.

Brown, B. B., Feiring, C., & Furman, W. (1999). Missing the love boat: Why researchers have shied away from adolescent romance. In W. Furman, B. B. Brown, & C. Feiring (Eds.), *The development of romantic relationships in adolescence* (pp. 1–16). Cambridge, England: Cambridge University Press.

Brown, B. B., Herman, M., Hamm, J. V., & Heck, D. J. (2008). Ethnicity and image: Correlates of crowd affiliation among ethnic minority youth. *Child Development, 79*, 529–546.

Brown, R. P., Osterman, L. L., & Barnes, C. D. (2009). School violence and the culture of honor. *Psychological Science, 20*, 1400–1405.

Bukowski, W. M., Brendgen, M., & Vitaro, F. (2007). Peers and socialization: Effects on externalizing and internalizing problems. In J. E. Grusec & P. D. Hastings (Eds.), *Handbook of socialization: Theory and research* (pp. 355–381). New York, NY: Guilford Press.

Bukowski, W. M., Motzoi, C., & Meyer, F. (2009). Friendship as process, function, and outcome. In K. H. Rubin, W. M. Bukowski, & B. Laursen (Eds.), *Handbook of peer interactions, relationships, and groups* (pp. 217–231). New York, NY: Guilford Press.

Bukowski, W. M., Velasquez, A. M., & Brendgen, M. (2008). Variation in patterns of peer influence: Considerations of self and other. In M. J. Prinstein & K. A. Dodge (Eds.), *Understanding peer influence in children and adolescents* (pp. 125–140). New York, NY: Guilford Press.

Butler, R. (2008). Evaluating competence and maintaining self-worth between early and middle childhood: Blissful ignorance or the construction of knowledge and strategies in context? In H. W. Marsh, R. G. Craven, & D. M. McInerney (Eds.), *Self-processes, learning, and enabling human potential* (pp. 193–222). Charlotte, NC: Information Age.

Byrne, B. M. (2002). Validating the measurement and structure of self-concept: Snapshots of past, present, and future research. *American Psychologist, 57*, 897–909.

Caldwell, M. S., Rudolph, K. D., Troop-Gordon, W., & Kim, D. (2004). Reciprocal influences among relational self-views, social disengagement, and peer stress during early adolescence. *Child Development, 75*, 1140–1154.

Campbell, C. G., Parker, J. G., & Kollat, S. H. (2007, March). *The influence of contingent self-esteem and appearance.* Paper presented at the biennial meeting of the Society for Research in Child Development, Boston, MA.

Caprara, G. V., Barbaranelli, C., Pastorelli, C., Bandura, A., & Zimbardo, P. G. (2000). Prosocial foundations of children's academic achievement. *Psychological Science, 11*, 302–306.

Caprara, G. V., Dodge, K. A., Pastorelli, C., & Zelli, A. (2007). How marginal deviations sometimes grow into serious aggression. *Child Development Perspectives, 1*, 33–39.

Card, N. A., Stucky, B. D., Sawalani, G. M., & Little T. D. (2008). Direct and indirect aggression during childhood and adolescence: A meta-analytic review of gender differences, intercorrelations, and relations to maladjustment. *Child Development, 79*, 1185–1229.

Carr, N. (2011). *The shallows: What the Internet is doing to our brains.* New York, NY: W. W. Norton.

Casella, R. (2001a). The cultural foundations of peer mediation: Beyond a behaviorist model of urban school conflict. In J. N. Burstyn, G. Bender, R. Casella, H. W. Gordon, D. P. Guerra, K. V. Luschen, . . . Williams, K. M., *Preventing violence in schools: A challenge to American democracy* (pp. 159–179). Mahwah, NJ: Erlbaum

Caspi, A. (1998). Personality development across the life course. In W. Damon (Series Ed.) & N. Eisenberg (Vol. Ed.), *Handbook of child psychology: Vol. 3. Social, emotional, and personality development* (5th ed., pp. 311–388). New York, NY: Wiley.

Cauce, A. M., Mason, C., Gonzales, N., Hiraga, Y., & Liu, G. (1994). Social support during adolescence: Methodological and theoretical considerations. In F. Nestemann & K. Hurrelmann (Eds.), *Social networks and social support in childhood and adolescence* (pp. 89–110). Berlin, Germany: Aldine de Gruyter.

Celio, C. I., Durlak, J., & Dymnicki, A. (2011). A meta-analysis of the impact of service-learning on students. *Journal of Experiential Education, 34*, 164–181.

Certo, J. (2011). Social skills and leadership abilities among children in small group literature discussions. *Journal of Research in Childhood Education, 25*(1), 62–81.

Champagne, F. A., & Mashoodh, R. (2009). Genes in context: Gene–environment interplay and the origins of individual differences in behavior. *Current Directions in Psychological Science, 18*, 127–131.

Chan, J. M., & O'Reilly, M. F. (2008). A Social Stories™ intervention package for students with autism in inclusive classroom settings. *Journal of Applied Behavior Analysis, 41*, 405–409.

Chang, L. (2003). Variable effects of children's aggression, social withdrawal, and prosocial leadership as functions of teacher beliefs and behaviors. *Child Development, 74*, 535–548.

Chang, L., Liu, H., Wen, Z., Fung, K. Y., Wang, Y, & Xu, Y. (2004). Mediating teacher liking and moderating authoritative teachering on Chinese adolescents' perceptions of antisocial and prosocial behaviors. *Journal of Educational Psychology, 96*, 369–380.

Chang, L., Mak, M. C. K., Li, T. Wu, B. P., Chen, B. B., & Hui, J. L. (2011). Cultural adaptations to environmental variability: An evolutionary account of East–West differences. *Educational Psychology Review, 23*, 99–129.

Chang, M.-L., & Davis, H. A. (2009). Understanding the role of teacher appraisals in shaping the dynamics of their relationships with students: Deconstructing teachers' judgments of disruptive behavior/students. In P. Schutz & M. Zembylas (Eds.), *Advances in teacher emotion research: The impact of teachers' lives* (pp. 95–125). New York, NY: Springer.

Chapman, J. W., Tunmer, W. E., & Prochnow, J. E. (2000). Early reading-related skills and performance, reading self-concept, and the development of academic self-concept: A longitudinal study. *Journal of Educational Psychology, 92*, 703–708.

Chavous, T. M., Bernat, D. H., Schmeelk-Cone, K., Caldwell, C. H., Kohn-Wood, L., & Zimmerman, M. A. (2003). Racial identity and academic attainment among African American adolescents. *Child Development, 74*, 1076–1090.

Chen, E. (2012). Protective factors for health among low-socioeconomic-status individuals. *Current Directions in Psychological Science, 21*, 189–193.

Chen, E., Langer, D. A., Raphaelson, Y. E., & Matthews, K. A. (2004). Socioeconomic status and health in adolescents: The role of stress interpretations. *Child Development, 75*, 1039–1052.

Chen, X., Chung, J., & Hsiao, C. (2009). Peer interactions and relationships from a cross-cultural perspective. In K. H. Rubin, W. M. Bukowski, & B. Laursen (Eds.), *Handbook of peer interactions, relationships, and groups* (pp. 432–451). New York, NY: Guilford Press.

Chen, X., & Wang, L. (2010). China. In M. H. Bornstein (Ed.), *Handbook of cultural developmental science* (pp. 429–444). New York, NY: Psychology Press.

Chiu, M.-S. (2012). The internal/external frame of reference model, big-fish-little-pond effect, and combined model for mathematics and science. *Journal of Educational Psychology, 104*, 87–107.

Christenson, S. L., & Thurlow, M. L. (2004). School dropouts: Prevention, considerations, interventions, and challenges. *Current Directions in Psychological Science, 13*, 36–39.

Cillessen, A. H. N., & Rose, A. J. (2005). Understanding popularity in the peer system. *Current Directions in Psychological Science, 14*, 102–105.

Cillessen, A. H. N., Schwartz, D., & Mayeux, L. (Eds.). (2011). *Popularity in the peer system.* New York, NY: Guilford Press.

Cillessen, A. H. N., & van den Berg, Y. H. M. (2012). Popularity and school adjustment. In A. M. Ryan & G. W. Ladd (Eds.), *Peer relationships and adjustment at school* (pp. 135–164). Charlotte, NC: Information Age.

Cizek, G. J. (2003). *Detecting and preventing classroom cheating: Promoting integrity in assessment.* Thousand Oaks, CA: Corwin.

Clarke, S., Dunlap, G., Foster-Johnson, L., Childs, K. E., Wilson, D., White, R., & Vera, A. (1995). Improving the conduct of students with behavioral disorders by incorporating student interests into curricular areas. *Behavioral Disorders, 20*, 221–237.

Cohen, G. L., & Garcia, J. (2008). Identity, belonging, and achievement: A model, interventions, implications. *Current Directions in Psychological Science, 17*, 365–369.

Coie, J. D., & Cillessen, A. H. N. (1993). Peer rejection: Origins and effects on children's development. *Current Directions in Psychological Science, 2*, 89–92.

Coie, J. D., & Dodge, K. A. (1998). Aggression and antisocial behavior. In W. Damon (Series Ed.) & N. Eisenberg (Vol. Ed.), *Handbook of child psychology: Vol. 3. Social, emotional, and personality development* (5th ed., pp. 779–862). New York, NY: Wiley.

Colby, A., & Kohlberg, L. (1984). Invariant sequence and internal consistency in moral judgment stages. In W. M. Kurtines & J. L. Gewirtz (Eds.), *Morality, moral behavior, and moral development* (pp. 41–51). New York, NY: Wiley.

Colby, A., Kohlberg, L., Gibbs, J., & Lieberman, M. (1983). A longitudinal study of moral judgment. *Monographs of the Society for Research in Child Development, 48*(1–2, Serial No. 200).

Cole, D. A., Maxwell, S. E., Martin, J. M., Peeke, L. G., Seroczynski, A. D., Tram, J. M., . . . Maschman, T. (2001). The development of multiple domains of child and adolescent self-concept: A cohort sequential longitudinal design. *Child Development, 72*, 1723–1746.

Cole, P. M., & Tan, P. Z. (2007). Emotion socialization from a cultural perspective. In J. E. Grusec & P. D. Hastings (Eds.), *Handbook of socialization: Theory and research* (pp. 516–542). New York, NY: Guilford Press.

Collins, W. A., Maccoby, E. E., Steinberg, L., Hetherington, E. M., & Bornstein, M. H. (2000). Contemporary research on parenting: The case for nature and nurture. *American Psychologist, 55*, 218–232.

Connolly, J., & Goldberg, A. (1999). Romantic relationships in adolescence: The role of friends and peers in their emergence and development. In W. Furman, B. B. Brown, & C. Feiring (Eds.), *The development of romantic relationships in adolescence* (pp. 266–290). Cambridge, England: Cambridge University Press.

Connor, D. J., & Baglieri, S. (2009). Tipping the scales: Disabilities studies ask "How much diversity can you take?" In S. R. Steinberg (Ed.), *Diversity and multiculturalism: A reader* (pp. 341–361). New York, NY: Peter Lang.

Cook, P. J., & Ludwig, J. (2008). The burden of "acting White": Do Black adolescents disparage academic achievement? In J. U. Ogbu (Ed.), *Minority status, oppositional culture, and schooling* (pp. 275–297). New York, NY: Routledge.

Coplan, R. J., & Arbeau, K. A. (2009). Peer interactions and play in early childhood. In K. H. Rubin, W. M. Bukowski, & B. Laursen (Eds.), *Handbook of peer interactions, relationships, and groups* (pp. 143–161). New York, NY: Guilford Press.

Cornell, D., Gregory, A., Huang, F., & Fan, X. (2013). Perceived prevalence of teasing and bullying predicts high school dropout rates. *Journal of Educational Psychology, 105*, 138–149.

Cosden, M., Morrison, G., Albanese, A. L., & Macias, S. (2001). When homework is not home work: After-school programs for homework assistance. *Educational Psychologist, 36*, 211–221.

Creasey, G. L., Jarvis, P. A., & Berk, L. E. (1998). Play and social competence. In O. N. Saracho & B. Spodek (Eds.), *Multiple perspectives on play in early childhood education.* Albany, NY: State University of New York Press.

Crick, N. R., & Dodge, K. A. (1996). Social information-processing mechanisms in reactive and proactive aggression. *Child Development, 67*, 993–1002.

Crick, N. R., Grotpeter, J. K., & Bigbee, M. A. (2002). Relationally and physically aggressive children's intent attributions and feelings of distress for relational and instrumental peer provocation. *Child Development, 73*, 1134–1142.

Crick, N. R., Murray-Close, D., Marks, P. E. L., & Mohajeri-Nelson, N. (2009). Aggression and peer relationships in school-age children: Relational and physical aggression in group and dyadic contexts. In K. H. Rubin, W. M. Bukowski, & B. Laursen (Eds.), *Handbook of peer interactions, relationships, and groups* (pp. 287–302). New York, NY: Guilford Press.

Crocker, J., & Knight, K. M. (2005). Contingencies of self-worth. *Current Directions in Psychological Science, 14*, 200–203.

Crosnoe, R. (2011). *Fitting in, standing out: Navigating the social challenge of high school to get an education.* Cambridge, England: Cambridge University Press.

Cross, W. E., Jr., Strauss, L., & Fhagen-Smith, P. (1999). African American identity development across the life span: Educational implications. In R. H. Sheets & E. R. Hollins (Eds.), *Racial and ethnic identity in school practices: Aspects of human development* (pp. 29–47). Mahwah, NJ: Erlbaum.

Crosson-Tower, C. (2010). *Understanding child abuse and neglect* (8th ed.). Boston, MA: Allyn & Bacon.

Crouter, A. C., Whiteman, S. D., McHale, S. M., & Osgood, D. W. (2007). Development of gender attitude traditionality across middle childhood and adolescence. *Child Development, 78*, 911–926.

Cummings, E. M., Schermerhorn, A. C., Davies, P. T., Goeke-Morey, M. C., & Cummings, J. S. (2006). Interparental discord and child adjustment: Prospective investigations of emotional security as an explanatory mechanism. *Child Development, 77*, 132–152.

Cunningham, C. E., & Cunningham, L. J. (2006). Student-mediated conflict resolution programs. In R. A. Barkley, *Attention-deficit hyperactivity disorder: A handbook for diagnosis and treatment* (3rd ed., pp. 590–607). New York, NY: Guilford.

Dalrymple, N. J. (1995). Environmental supports to develop flexibility and independence. In K. A. Quill (Ed.), *Teaching children with autism: Strategies to enhance communication and socialization.* New York, NY: Delmar.

Damon, W. (1988). *The moral child: Nurturing children's natural moral growth.* New York, NY: Free Press.

Damon, W., & Hart, D. (1988). *Self-understanding from childhood and adolescence.* New York, NY: Cambridge University Press.

Danner, F. (2008, March). *The effects of perceptions of classroom assessment practices and academic press on classroom mastery goals and high school students' self-reported cheating.* Paper presented at the annual meeting of the American Educational Research Association, New York, NY.

Darwich, L., Hymel, S., & Waterhouse, T. (2012). School avoidance and substance use among lesbian, gay, bisexual, and questioning youths: The impact of peer victimization and adult support. *Journal of Educational Psychology, 104*, 381–392.

Davies, P. T., & Woitach, M. J. (2008). Children's emotional security in the interparental relationship. *Current Directions in Psychological Science, 17*, 269–274.

Davila, J. (2008). Depressive symptoms and adolescent romance: Theory, research, and implications. *Child Development Perspectives, 2*(1), 26–31.

Davis-Kean, P. E., Huesmann, R., Jager, J., Collins, W. A., Bates, J. E., & Lansford, J. E. (2008). Changes in the relation of self-efficacy beliefs and behaviors across development. *Child Development, 79*, 1257–1269.

Davis-Kean, P. E., & Sandler, H. M. (2001). A meta-analysis of measures of self-esteem for young children: A framework for future measures. *Child Development, 72*, 887–906.

Davison, M. (2011, April). *Are you standing in my shoes? How affective and cognitive teaching sequences influence historical empathy.* Paper presented at the annual meeting of the American Educational Research Association, New Orleans, LA.

Deaux, K. (1984). From individual differences to social categories: Analysis of a decade's research on gender. *American Psychologist, 39*, 105–116.

Decety, J., & Cowell, J. M. (2014). Friends or foes: Is empathy necessary for moral behavior? *Perspectives on Psychological Science, 9*, 525–537.

DeRidder, L. M. (1993). Teenage pregnancy: Etiology and educational interventions. *Educational Psychology Review, 5*, 87–107.

Deutsch, M. (1993). Educating for a peaceful world. *American Psychologist, 48*, 510–517.

DeVries, R., & Zan, B. (1996). A constructivist perspective on the role of the sociomoral atmosphere in promoting children's development. In C. T. Fosnot (Ed.), *Constructivism: Theory, perspectives, and practice* (pp. 103–119). New York, NY: Teachers College Press.

DeYoung, C. G., Hirsh, J. B., Shane, M. S., Papademetris, X., Rajeevan, N., & Gray, J. R. (2010). Testing predictions from personality neuroscience: Brain structure and the Big Five. *Psychological Science, 21*, 820–828.

Dijkstra, P., Kuyper, H., van der Werf, G., Buunk, A. P., & van der Zee, Y. G. (2008). Social comparison in the classroom: A review. *Review of Educational Research, 78*, 828–879.

Dilg, M. (2010). *Our worlds in our words: Exploring race, class, gender, and sexual orientation in multicultural classrooms.* New York, NY: Teachers College Press.

Dishion, T. J., Piehler, T. F., & Myers, M. W. (2008). Dynamics and ecology of adolescent peer influence. In M. J. Prinstein & K. A. Dodge (Eds.), *Understanding peer influence in children and adolescents* (pp. 72–93). New York, NY: Guilford Press.

Dodge, K. A. (1986). A social information processing model of social competence in children. In M. Perlmutter (Ed.), *Minnesota Symposia on Child Psychology: Vol. 18. Cognitive perspectives in children's social and behavioral development* (pp. 77–126). Mahwah, NJ: Erlbaum.

Dodge, K. A. (2009). Mechanisms of gene–environment interaction effects in the development of conduct disorder. *Perspectives on Psychological Science, 4*, 408–414.

Dodge, K. A., Godwin, J., & The Conduct Problems Prevention Research Group (2013). Social-information-processing patterns mediate the impact of preventive intervention on adolescent antisocial behavior. *Psychological Science, 24*, 456–465.

Dodge, K. A., Lansford, J. E., Burks, V. S., Bates, J. E., Pettit, G. S., Fontaine, R., & Price, J. M. (2003). Peer rejection and social information-processing factors in the development of aggressive behavior problems in children. *Child Development, 74*, 374–393.

Dodge, K. A., Malone, P. S., Lansford, J. E., Miller, S., Pettit, G. S., & Bates, J. E. (2009). A dynamic cascade model of the development of substance-use onset. *Monographs of the Society for Research in Child Development, 74*(3, Serial No. 294), 1–119.

Donaldson, S. K., & Westerman, M. A. (1986). Development of children's understanding of ambivalence and causal theories of emotion. *Developmental Psychology, 22*, 655–662.

Dovidio, J. F., & Gaertner, S. L. (1999). Reducing prejudice: Combating intergroup biases. *Current Directions in Psychological Science, 8*, 101–105.

Dowson, M., & McInerney, D. M. (2001). Psychological parameters of students' social and work avoidance goals: A qualitative investigation. *Journal of Educational Psychology, 93*, 35–42.

DuBois, D. L., Portillo, N., Rhodes, J. E., Silverthorn, N., & Valentine, J. C. (2011). How effective are mentoring programs for youth? A systematic assessment of the evidence. *Psychological Science in the Public Interest, 12*, 57–91.

Dubow, E. F., Huesmann, L. R., & Greenwood, D. (2007). Media and youth socialization: Underlying processes and moderators of effects. In J. E. Grusec & P. D. Hastings (Eds.), *Handbook of socialization: Theory and research* (pp. 404–430). New York, NY: Guilford Press.

Duffy, F. H., Shankardass, A., McAnulty, G. B., & Als, H. (2013, July 31). The relationship of Asperger's syndrome to autism: A preliminary EEG coherence study. *BMC Medicine, 11*: 175. doi:10.1186/1741-7015-11-175.

Dunham, Y., Baron, A. S., & Banaji, M. R. (2006). From American city to Japanese village: A cross-cultural investigation of implicit race attitudes. *Child Development*, *77*, 1268–1281.

Dweck, C. S. (2000). *Self-theories: Their role in motivation, personality, and development.* Philadelphia, PA: Psychology Press.

Dweck, C. S. (2008). Can personality be changed? The role of beliefs in personality and change. *Current Directions in Psychological Science, 17,* 391–394.

Eccles, J. S. (2007). Families, schools, and developing achievement-related motivations and engagement. In J. E. Grusec & P. D. Hastings (Eds.), *Handbook of socialization: Theory and research* (pp. 665–691). New York, NY: Guilford Press.

Eccles, J. (2009). Who am I and what am I going to do with my life? Personal and collective identities as motivators of action. *Educational Psychologist, 44,* 78–89.

Eckert, P. (1989). *Jocks and burnouts: Social categories and identity in the high school.* New York, NY: Teachers College Press.

Eisenberg, N. (1982). The development of reasoning regarding prosocial behavior. In N. Eisenberg (Ed.), *The development of prosocial behavior* (pp. 219–249). San Diego, CA: Academic Press.

Eisenberg, N. (1995). Prosocial development: A multifaceted model. In W. M. Kurtines & J. L. Gewirtz (Eds.), *Moral development: An introduction* (pp. 401–429). Boston, MA: Allyn & Bacon.

Eisenberg, N., Carlo, G., Murphy, B., & Van Court, N. (1995). Prosocial development in late adolescence: A longitudinal study. *Child Development*, *66*, 1179–1197.

Eisenberg, N., & Fabes, R. A. (1998). Prosocial development. In W. Damon (Series Ed.) & N. Eisenberg (Vol. Ed.), *Handbook of child psychology: Vol. 3. Social, emotional, and personality development* (5th ed., pp. 701–778). New York, NY: Wiley.

Eisenberg, N., Martin, C. L., & Fabes, R. A. (1996). Gender development and gender effects. In D. C. Berliner & R. C. Calfee (Eds.), *Handbook of educational psychology* (pp. 358–396). New York, NY: Macmillan.

Eisenberg, N., Zhou, Q., & Köller, S. (2001). Brazilian adolescents' prosocial moral judgment and behavior: Relations to sympathy, perspective taking, gender-role orientation, and demographic characteristics. *Child Development*, *72*, 518–534.

Elkind, D. (1981). *Children and adolescents: Interpretive essays on Jean Piaget* (3rd ed.). New York, NY: Oxford University Press.

Elliott, S. N., & Busse, R. T. (1991). Social skills assessment and intervention with children and adolescents. *School Psychology International*, *12*, 63–83.

Ellis, W. E., & Zarbatany, L. (2007). Peer group status as a moderator of group influence on children's deviant, aggressive, and prosocial behavior. *Child Development*, *78*, 1240–1254.

Ellison, N. B., Steinfield, C., & Lampe, C. (2007). The benefits of *Facebook* "friends": Social capital and college students' use of online social network sites. *Journal of Computer-Mediated Communication*, *12*, 1143–1168.

Elmore, K. C., & Oyserman, D. (2012). If 'we' can succeed, 'I' can too: Identity-based motivation and gender in the classroom. *Contemporary Educational Psychology, 37,* 176–185.

El-Sheikh, M., Kouros, C. D., Erath, S., Cummings, E. M., Keller, P., & Staton, L. (2009). Marital conflict and children's externalizing behavior: Interactions between parasympathetic and sympathetic nervous system activity. *Monographs of the Society for Research in Child Development, 74*(1, Serial No. 292), 1–78.

Epstein, J. S. (1998). Introduction: Generation X, youth culture, and identity. In J. S. Epstein (Ed.), *Youth culture: Identity in a postmodern world* (pp. 1–23). Malden, MA: Blackwell.

Espelage, D. L., & Swearer, S. M. (Eds.). (2004). *Bullying in American schools: A social-ecological perspective on prevention and intervention.* Mahwah, NJ: Erlbaum.

Evans, E. D., & Craig, D. (1990). Teacher and student perceptions of academic cheating in middle and senior high schools. *Journal of Educational Research*, *84*(1), 44–52.

Evans, G. W., & Kim, P. (2007). Childhood poverty and health: Cumulative risk exposure and stress dysregulation. *Psychological Science, 18,* 953–957.

Evertson, C. M., & Weinstein, C. S. (Eds.). (2006). *Handbook of classroom management: Research, practice, and contemporary issues.* Mahwah, NJ: Erlbaum.

Faircloth, B. S. (2012). "Wearing a mask" vs. connecting identity with learning. *Contemporary Educational Psychology, 37,* 186–194.

Fantuzzo, J. W., LeBoeuf, W. A., Chen, C.-C., Rouse, H. L., & Culhane, D. P. (2012). The unique and combined effects of homelessness and school mobility on the educational outcomes of young children. *Educational Researcher, 41,* 393–402.

Farver, J. A. M., & Branstetter, W. H. (1994). Preschoolers' prosocial responses to their peers' distress. *Developmental Psychology*, *30*, 334–341.

Feddes, A. R., Noack, P., & Rutland, A. (2009). Direct and extended friendship effects on minority and majority children's interethnic attitudes: A longitudinal study. *Child Development, 80,* 377–390.

Feldman, A. F., & Matjasko, J. L. (2005). The role of school-based extracurricular activities in adolescent development: A comprehensive review and future directions. *Review of Educational Research*, *75*, 159–210.

Figner, B., & Weber, E. U. (2011). Who takes risks when and why? Determinants of risk taking. *Current Directions in Psychological Science, 20,* 211–216.

Filax, G. (2007). Queer in/visibility: The case of Ellen, Michel, and Oscar. In S. Books (Ed.), *Invisible children in the society and its schools* (3rd ed., pp. 213–234). Mahwah, NJ: Erlbaum.

Flanagan, C. A., & Faison, N. (2001). Youth civic development: Implications of research for social policy and programs. *Social Policy Report of the Society for Research in Child Development, 15*(1), 1–14.

Flanagan, C. A., & Tucker, C. J. (1999). Adolescents' explanations for political issues: Concordance with their views of self and society. *Developmental Psychology*, *35*, 1198–1209.

Flavell, J. H. (2000). Development of children's knowledge about the mental world. *International Journal of Behavioral Development*, *24*(1), 15–23.

Flavell, J. H., Green, F. L., & Flavell, E. R. (1995). Young children's knowledge about thinking. *Monographs of the Society for Research in Child Development*, *60*(1, Serial No. 243).

Flavell, J. H., & Miller, P. H. (1998). Social cognition. In W. Damon (Series Ed.), D. Kuhn & R. S. Siegler (Vol. Eds.), *Handbook of child psychology: Vol. 2. Cognition, perception, and language* (5th ed., pp. 851–898). New York, NY: Wiley.

Flavell, J. H., Miller, P. H., & Miller, S. A. (2002). *Cognitive development* (4th ed.). Upper Saddle River, NJ: Prentice Hall.

Fontaine, R. G., Yang, C., Dodge, K. A., Bates, J. E., & Pettit, G. S. (2008). Testing an individual systems model of response evaluation and decision (RED) and antisocial behavior across adolescence. *Child Development, 79,* 462–475.

Fox, N. A., Henderson, H. A., Rubin, K. H., Calkins, S. D., & Schmidt, L. A. (2001). Continuity and discontinuity of behavioral inhibition and exuberance: Psychophysical and behavioral influences across the first four years of life. *Child Development*, *72*, 1–21.

Frankenberger, K. D. (2000). Adolescent egocentrism: A comparison among adolescents and adults. *Journal of Adolescence*, *23*, 343–354.

The Freedom Writers (with Gruwell, E.) (1999). *The Freedom Writers diary: How a teacher and 150 teens used writing to change themselves and the world around them.* New York, NY: Broadway Books.

Frey, K. S., Hirschstein, M. K., Edstrom, L. V., & Snell, J. L. (2009). Observed reductions in school bullying, nonbullying aggression, and destructive bystander behavior: A longitudinal evaluation. *Journal of Educational Psychology, 101,* 466–481.

Fuchs, L. S., Fuchs, D., Craddock, C., Hollenbeck, K. N., Hamlett, C. L., & Schatschneider, C. (2008). Effects of small-group tutoring with and without validated classroom instruction on at-risk, students' math problem solving: Are two tiers of prevention better than one? *Journal of Educational Psychology, 100,* 491–509.

Furman, W., Brown, B. B., & Feiring, C. (Eds.). (1999). *The development of romantic relationships in adolescence.* Cambridge, England: Cambridge University Press.

Furman, W., & Buhrmester, D. (1992). Age and sex differences in perceptions of networks and personal relationships. *Child Development*, *63*, 103–115.

Furman, W., & Collins, W. A. (2009). Adolescent romantic relationships and experiences. In K. H. Rubin, W. M. Bukowski, & B. Laursen (Eds.), *Handbook of peer interactions, relationships, and groups* (pp. 341–360). New York, NY: Guilford Press.

Furman, W., & Simon, V. A. (2008). Homophily in adolescent romantic relationships. In M. J. Prinstein & K. A. Dodge (Eds.), *Understanding peer influence in children and adolescents* (pp. 203–224). New York, NY: Guilford Press.

Galambos, N. L., Barker, E. T., & Almeida, D. M. (2003). Parents *do* matter: Trajectories of change in externalizing and internalizing problems in early adolescence. *Child Development*, *74*, 578–594.

Gallese, V., Gernsbacher, M. A., Heyes, C., Hickok, G., & Iacoboni, M. (2011). Mirror neuron forum. *Perspectives on Psychological Science, 6,* 369–407.

Galván, A. (2012). Risky behavior in adolescents: The role of the developing brain. In V. F. Reyna, S. B. Chapman, M. R. Dougherty, & J. Confrey (Eds.), *The adolescent brain: Learning, reasoning, and decision making* (pp. 267–289). Washington, DC: American Psychological Association.

Gardiner, H. W., & Kosmitzki, C. (2008). *Lives across cultures: Cross-cultural human development* (4th ed.). Boston, MA: Allyn & Bacon.

Garnier, H. E., Stein, J. A., & Jacobs, J. K. (1997). The process of dropping out of high school: A 19-year perspective. *American Educational Research Journal*, *34*, 395–419.

Gavin, L. A., & Fuhrman, W. (1989). Age differences in adolescents' perceptions of their peer groups. *Developmental Psychology*, *25*, 827–834.

Gazelle, H., & Ladd, G. W. (2003). Anxious solitude and peer exclusion: A diathesis-stress model of internalizing trajectories in childhood. *Child Development*, *74*, 257–278.

Gehlbach, H., Brinkworth, M. E., & Harris, A. D. (2012). Changes in teacher–student relationships. *British Journal of Educational Psychology, 82,* 690–704.

Gehlbach, H., Brown, S. W., Ioannou, A., Boyer, M. A., Hudson, N., Niv-Solomon, A., . . . Janik, L. (2008). Increasing interest in social studies: Social perspective taking and self-efficacy in stimulating stimulations. *Contemporary Educational Psychology, 33,* 894–914.

Genova, W. J., & Walberg, H. J. (1984). Enhancing integration in urban high schools. In D. E. Bartz & M. L. Maehr (Eds.), *Advances in motivation and achievement: Vol. 1. The effects of school desegregation on motivation and achievement.* Greenwich, CT: JAI Press.

Gest, S. D., Domitrovich, C. E., & Welsh, J. A. (2005). Peer academic reputation in elementary school: Associations with changes in self-concept and academic skills. *Journal of Educational Psychology, 97,* 337–346.

Gibbs, J. C. (1995). The cognitive developmental perspective. In W. M. Kurtines & J. L. Gewirtz (Eds.), *Moral development: An introduction* (pp. 27–48). Boston, MA: Allyn & Bacon.

Gilligan, C. F. (1982). *In a different voice.* Cambridge, MA: Harvard University Press.

Gilligan, C. F. (1987). Moral orientation and moral development. In E. F. Kittay & D. T. Meyers (Eds.), *Women and moral theory* (pp. 19–33). Totowa, NJ: Rowman & Littlefield.

Glaser, D. (2000). Child abuse and neglect and the brain: A review. *Journal of Child Psychology and Psychiatry and Allied Disciplines*, *41*, 97–116.

Gnepp, J. (1989). Children's use of personal information to understand other people's feelings. In C. Saarni & P. L. Harris (Eds.), *Children's understanding of emotion* (pp. 151–177). Cambridge, England: Cambridge University Press.

Gniewosz, B., & Noack, P. (2012). What you see is what you get: The role of early adolescents' perceptions in the intergenerational transmission of academic values. *Contemporary Educational Psychology, 37,* 70–79.

Goldstein, S., & Brooks, R. B. (Eds.). (2006). *Handbook of resilience in children.* New York, NY: Springer.

Goldston, D. B., Molock, S. D., Whitbeck, L. B., Murakami, J. L., Zayas, L. H., & Nagayama Hall, G. C. (2008). Cultural considerations in adolescent suicide prevention and psychosocial treatment. *American Psychologist, 63,* 14–31.

Goodnow, J. J. (2010). Culture. In M. H. Bornstein (Ed.), *Handbook of cultural developmental science* (pp. 3–19). New York, NY: Psychology Press.

Goodwin, M. H. (2006). *The hidden life of girls: Games of stance, status, and exclusion.* Malden, MA: Blackwell.

Gopnik, A., & Meltzoff, A. N. (1997). *Words, thoughts, and theories.* Cambridge, MA: MIT Press.

Gottman, J. M. (1986). The world of coordinated play: Same- and cross-sex friendship in young children. In J. M. Gottman & J. G. Parker (Eds.), *Conversations of friends: Speculations on affective development* (pp. 139–191). Cambridge, England: Cambridge University Press.

Graham, S., & Hudley, C. (2005). Race and ethnicity in the study of motivation and competence. In A. J. Elliot & C. S. Dweck (Eds.), *Handbook of competence and motivation* (pp. 392–413). New York, NY: Guilford Press.

Granic, I., Lobel, A., & Engels, R. C. M. E. (2014). The benefits of playing video games. *American Psychologist, 69,* 66–78.

Gray, M. R., & Steinberg, L. (1999). Unpacking authoritative parenting: Reassessing a multidimensional concept. *Journal of Marriage and the Family*, *61*, 574–587.

Greenfield, P. M. (1994). Independence and interdependence as developmental scripts: Implications for theory, research, and practice. In P. M. Greenfield & R. R. Cocking (Eds.), *Cross-cultural roots of minority child development* (pp. 1–37). Mahwah, NJ: Erlbaum.

Greenhoot, A. F., Tsethlikai, M., & Wagoner, B. J. (2006). The relations between children's past experiences, social knowledge, and memories for social situations. *Journal of Cognition and Development, 7,* 313–340.

Greenhow, C., Robelia, B., & Hughes, J. E. (2009). Web 2.0 and classroom research: What path should we take now? *Educational Researcher, 38,* 246–259.

Greitemeyer, T. (2011). Effects of prosocial media on social behavior: When and why does media exposure affect helping and aggression? *Current Directions in Psychological Science, 20,* 251–255.

Grimes, N. (2002). *Bronx masquerade.* New York, NY: Penguin.

Gross, E. F. (2009). Logging on, bouncing back: An experimental investigation of online communication following social exclusion. *Developmental Psychology, 45,* 1787–1793.

Gross, E. F., Juvonen, J., & Gable, S. L. (2002). Internet use and well-being in adolescence. *Journal of Social Issues, 58,* 75–90.

Guay, F., Boivin, M., & Hodges, E. V. E. (1999). Social comparison processes and academic achievement: The dependence of the development of self-evaluations on friends' performance. *Journal of Educational Psychology, 91,* 564–568.

Gummerum, M., Keller, M., Takezawa, M., & Mata, J. (2008). To give or not to give: Children's and adolescents' sharing and moral negotiations in economic decision situations. *Child Development, 79,* 562–576.

Guthrie, P. (2001). "Catching sense" and the meaning of belonging on a South Carolina Sea island. In S. S. Walker (Ed.), *African roots/American cultures: Africa in the creation of the Americas* (pp. 275–283). Lanham, MD: Rowman & Littlefield.

Haidt, J. (2012). *The righteous mind: Why good people are divided by politics and religion.* New York, NY: Random House.

Halgunseth, L. C., Ispa, J. M., & Rudy, D. (2006). Parental control in Latino families: An integrated review of the literature. *Child Development, 77,* 1282–1297.

Hamlin, J. K. (2013). Moral judgment and action in preverbal infants and toddlers: Evidence for an innate moral core. *Current Directions in Psychological Science, 22,* 186–193.

Hamlin, J. K., & Wynn, K. (2011). Young infants prefer prosocial to antisocial others. *Cognitive Development, 26,* 30–39.

Hamm, J. V., Hoffman, A., & Farmer, T. W. (2012). Peer cultures of academic effort and achievement in adolescence. In A. M. Ryan & G. W. Ladd (Eds.), *Peer relationships and adjustment at school* (pp. 219–250). Charlotte, NC: Information Age.

Hamovitch, B. (2007). Hoping for the best: "Inclusion" and stigmatization in a middle school. In S. Books (Ed.), *Invisible children in the society and its schools* (3rd ed., pp. 263–281). Mahwah, NJ: Erlbaum.

Hampson, S. E. (2008). Mechanisms by which childhood personality traits influence adult well-being. *Current Directions in Psychological Science, 17,* 264–268.

Hardré, P. L., & Reeve, J. (2003). A motivational model of rural students' intentions to persist in, versus drop out of, high school. *Journal of Educational Psychology, 95,* 347–356.

Harris, J. R. (1998). *The nurture assumption: Why children turn out the way they do.* New York, NY: Free Press.

Harris, K. R. (1982). Cognitive-behavior modification: Application with exceptional students. *Focus on Exceptional Children, 15,* 1–16.

Harris, M. B. (1997). Preface: Images of the invisible minority. In M. B. Harris (Ed.), *School experiences of gay and lesbian youth: The invisible minority* (pp. xiv–xxii). Binghamton, NY: Harrington Park Press.

Harris, M. J., & Rosenthal, R. (1985). Mediation of interpersonal expectancy effects: 31 meta-analyses. *Psychological Bulletin, 97,* 363–386.

Harris, P. L. (2006). Social cognition. In W. Damon & R. M. Lerner (Series Eds.), D. Kuhn & R. Siegler (Vol. Eds.), *Handbook of child psychology: Vol. 2. Cognition, perception, and language* (6th ed., pp. 811–858). New York, NY: Wiley.

Hart, D. (1988). The adolescent self-concept in social context. In D. K. Lapsley & F. C. Power (Eds.), *Self, ego, and identity: Integrative approaches* (pp. 71–90). New York, NY: Springer-Verlag.

Hart, D., & Fegley, S. (1995). Prosocial behavior and caring in adolescence: Relations to self-understanding and social judgment. *Child Development, 66,* 1346–1359.

Harter, S. (1983). Children's understanding of multiple emotions: A cognitive-developmental approach. In W. F. Overton (Ed.), *The relationship between social and cognitive development* (pp. 147–194). Mahwah, NJ: Erlbaum.

Harter, S. (1999). *The construction of the self: A developmental perspective.* New York, NY: Guilford Press.

Harter, S., & Whitesell, N. R. (1989). Developmental changes in children's understanding of single, multiple, and blended emotion concepts. In C. Saarni & P. Harris (Eds.), *Children's understanding of emotion* (pp. 81–116). Cambridge, England: Cambridge University Press.

Hartl, A. C., Laursen, B., & Cillessen, A. H. N. (2015). A survival analysis of adolescent friendships: The downside of dissimilarity. *Psychological Science, 26,* 1304–1315.

Hastings, P. D., Utendale, W. T., & Sullivan, C. (2007). The socialization of prosocial development. In J. E. Grusec & P. D. Hastings (Eds.), *Handbook of socialization: Theory and research* (pp. 638–664). New York, NY: Guilford Press.

Hattie, J. (2008). Processes of integrating, developing, and processing self information. In H. W. Marsh, R. G. Craven, & D. M. McInerney (Eds.), *Self-processes, learning, and enabling human potential* (pp. 51–85). Charlotte, NC: Information Age.

Hattie, J. A. C. (2009). *Visible learning: A synthesis of over 800 meta-analyses relating to achievement.* London, England: Routledge.

Hawley, P. H. (2014). The duality of human nature: Coercion and prosociality in youths' hierarchy ascension and social success. *Psychological Science, 23,* 433–438.

Helwig, C. C., & Jasiobedzka, U. (2001). The relation between law and morality: Children's reasoning about socially beneficial and unjust laws. *Child Development, 72,* 1382–1393.

Helwig, C. C., Zelazo, P. D., & Wilson, M. (2001). Children's judgments of psychological harm in normal and noncanonical situations. *Child Development, 72,* 66–81.

Hemmings, A. B. (2004). *Coming of age in U.S. high schools: Economic, kinship, religious, and political crosscurrents.* Mahwah, NJ: Erlbaum.

Herbers, J. E., Cutuli, J. J., Supkoff, L. M. Heistad, D., Chan, C.-K., Hinz, E., & Masten, A. S. (2012). Early reading skills and academic achievement trajectories of students facing poverty, homelessness, and high residential mobility. *Educational Researcher, 41,* 366–374.

Herbert, J., & Stipek, D. (2005). The emergence of gender differences in children's perceptions of their academic competence. *Journal of Applied Developmental Psychology, 26,* 276–295.

Hertel, P. T., & Mathews, A. (2011). Cognitive bias modification: Past perspectives, current findings, and future applications. *Perspectives on Psychological Science, 6,* 521–536.

Higgins, A. (1995). Educating for justice and community: Lawrence Kohlberg's vision of moral education. In W. M. Kurtines & J. L. Gewirtz (Eds.), *Moral development: An introduction.* Boston, MA: Allyn & Bacon.

Hill, P. L., & Roberts, B. W. (2010). Propositions for the study of moral personality development. *Current Directions in Psychological Science, 19,* 380–383.

Hitlin, S., Brown, J. S., & Elder, G. H., Jr. (2006). Racial self-categorization in adolescence: Multiracial development and social pathways. *Child Development, 77,* 1298–1308.

Hobson, P. (2004). *The cradle of thought: Exploring the origins of thinking.* Oxford, England: Oxford University Press.

Hoffman, M. L. (1991). Empathy, social cognition, and moral action. In W. M. Kurtines & J. L. Gewirtz (Eds.), *Moral behavior and development: Vol. 1. Theory* (pp. 275–301). Mahwah, NJ: Erlbaum.

Hoffman, M. L. (2000). *Empathy and moral development: Implications for caring and justice.* New York, NY: Cambridge University Press.

Hoglund, W. L. G. (2007). School functioning in early adolescence: Gender-linked responses to peer victimization. *Journal of Educational Psychology, 99,* 683–699.

Hollenstein, T., & Lougheed, J. P. (2013). Beyond storm and stress: Typicality, transactions, timing, and temperament to account for adolescent change. *American Psychologist, 68,* 444–454.

Holt, M. K., & Keyes, M. A. (2004). Teachers' attitudes toward bullying. In D. L. Espelage & S. M. Swearer (Eds.), *Bullying in American schools: A social-ecological perspective on prevention and intervention* (pp. 121–139). Mahwah, NJ: Erlbaum.

Hong, Y., Wan, C., No, S., & Chiu, C.-Y. (2007). Multicultural identities. In S. Kitayama & D. Cohen (Eds.), *Handbook of cultural psychology* (pp. 323–345). New York, NY: Guilford Press.

Honz, K., Kiewra, K. A., & Yang, Y.-S. (2010). Cheating perceptions and prevalence across academic settings. *Mid-Western Educational Researcher, 23,* 10–17.

Horne, A. M., Orpinas, P., Newman-Carlson, D., & Bartolomucci, C. L. (2004). Elementary school Bully Busters Program: Understanding why children bully and what to do about it. In D. L. Espelage & S. M. Swearer (Eds.), *Bullying in American schools: A social-ecological perspective on prevention and intervention* (pp. 297–325). Mahwah, NJ: Erlbaum.

Hudley, C., & Graham, S. (1993). An attributional intervention to reduce peer-directed aggression among African American boys. *Child Development, 64,* 124–138.

Huntsinger, C. S., & Jose, P. E. (2006). A longitudinal investigation of personality and social adjustment among Chinese

American and European American adolescents. *Child Development, 77,* 1309–1324.

Hursh, D. (2007). Assessing No Child Left Behind and the rise of neoliberal education policies. *American Educational Research Journal, 44,* 493–518.

Hyde, J. S. (2007). New directions in the study of gender similarities and differences. *Current Directions in Psychological Science, 16,* 259–263.

Hyde, J. S., Lindberg, S. M., Linn, M. C., Ellis, A. B., & Williams, C. C. (2008). Gender similarities characterize math performance. *Science, 321*(5888), 494–495.

Hyman, I., Kay, B., Tabori, A., Weber, M., Mahon, M., & Cohen, I. (2006). Bullying: Theory, research, and interventions. In C. M. Evertson & C. S. Weinstein (Eds.), *Handbook of classroom management: Research, practice, and contemporary issues* (pp. 855–884). Mahwah, NJ: Erlbaum.

Hymel, S. (1986). Interpretations of peer behavior: Affective bias in childhood and adolescence. *Child Development, 57,* 431–445.

Hymel, S., Comfort, C., Schonert-Reichl, K., & McDougall, P. (1996). Academic failure and school dropout: The influence of peers. In J. Juvonen & K. R. Wentzel (Eds.), *Social motivation: Understanding children's school adjustment* (pp. 313–345). Cambridge, England: Cambridge University Press.

Igoa, C. (2007). Immigrant children: Art as a second language. In S. Books (Ed.), *Invisible children in the society and its schools* (3rd ed., pp. 117–140). Mahwah, NJ: Erlbaum.

Izard, C., Fine, S., Schultz, D., Mostow, A., Ackerman, B., & Youngstrom, E. (2001). Emotion knowledge as a predictor of social behavior and academic competence in children at risk. *Psychological Science, 12,* 18–23.

Jacobs, J. E., & Klaczynski, P. A. (2002). The development of judgment and decision making during childhood and adolescence. *Current Directions in Psychological Science, 11,* 145–149.

Jaffee, S. R., Hanscombe, K. B., Haworth, C. M. A., Davis, O. S. P., & Plomin, R. (2012). Chaotic homes and children's disruptive behavior: A longitudinal cross-lagged twin study. *Psychological Science, 23,* 643–650.

Jenlink, C. L. (1994, April). *Music: A lifeline for the self-esteem of at-risk students.* Paper presented at the annual meeting of the American Educational Research Association, New Orleans, LA.

Johnson, D. W., & Johnson, R. T. (1996). Conflict resolution and peer mediation programs in elementary and secondary schools: A review of the research. *Review of Educational Research, 66,* 459–506.

Johnson, D. W., & Johnson, R. T. (2006). Conflict resolution, peer mediation, and peacemaking. In C. M. Evertson & C. S. Weinstein (Eds.), *Handbook of classroom management: Research, practice, and contemporary issues* (pp. 803–832). Mahwah, NJ: Erlbaum.

Johnson, D. W., Johnson, R., Dudley, B., Ward, M., & Magnuson, D. (1995). The impact of peer mediation training on the management of school and home conflicts. *American Educational Research Journal, 32,* 829–844.

Johnson, H. C., & Friesen, B. (1993). Etiologies of mental and emotional disorders in children. In H. Johnson (Ed.), *Child mental health in the 1990s: Curricula for graduate and undergraduate* (pp. 27–46). Washington, DC: U.S. Department of Health and Human Services.

Jones, L. M., Mitchell, K. J., & Turner, H. A. (2015). Victim reports of bystander reactions to in-person and online peer harassment: A national survey of adolescents. *Journal of Youth and Adolescence, 44,* 2308–2320.

Jonkmann, K., Trautwein, U., & Lüdtke, O. (2009). Social dominance in adolescence: The moderating role of the classroom context and behavioral heterogeneity. *Child Development, 80,* 338–355.

Juvonen, J. (2006). Sense of belonging, social bonds, and school functioning. In P. A. Alexander & P. H. Winne (Eds.), *Handbook of educational psychology* (2nd ed., pp. 655–674). Mahwah, NJ: Erlbaum.

Juvonen, J., & Cadigan, R. J. (2002). Social determinants of public behavior of middle school youth: Perceived peer norms and need to be accepted. In F. Pajares & T. Urdan (Eds.), *Adolescence and education, Vol. 2: Academic motivation of adolescents* (pp. 277–297). Greenwich, CT: Information Age.

Juvonen, J., & Galván, A. (2008). Peer influence in involuntary social groups. In M. J. Prinstein & K. A. Dodge (Eds.), *Understanding peer influence in children and adolescents* (pp. 225–244). New York, NY: Guilford.

Juvonen, J., & Hiner, M. (1991, April). *Perceived responsibility and annoyance as mediators of negative peer reactions.* Paper presented at the annual meeting of the American Educational Research Association, Chicago, IL.

Juvonen, J., & Weiner, B. (1993). An attributional analysis of students' interactions: The social consequences of perceived responsibility. *Educational Psychology Review, 5*, 325–345.

Kagan, J. (2010). Emotions and temperament. In M. H. Bornstein (Ed.), *Handbook of cultural developmental science* (pp. 175–194). New York, NY: Psychology Press.

Kagan, J., Snidman, N., Kahn, V., & Towsley, S. (2007). The preservation of two infant temperaments into adolescence. *Monographs of the Society for Research in Child Development, 72*(2, Serial No. 287).

Kağitçibaşi, Ç. (2007). *Family, self, and human development across cultures: Theory and applications* (2nd ed.). Mahwah, NJ: Erlbaum.

Kahne, J. E., & Sporte, S. E. (2008). Developing citizens: The impact of civic learning opportunities on students' commitment to civic participation. *American Educational Research Journal, 45*, 738–766.

Katchadourian, H. (1990). Sexuality. In S. S. Feldman & G. R. Elliott (Eds.), *At the threshold: The developing adolescent* (pp. 330–351). Cambridge, MA: Harvard University Press.

Keogh, B. K. (2003). *Temperament in the classroom.* Baltimore, MD: Brookes.

Kerns, L. L., & Lieberman, A. B. (1993). *Helping your depressed child.* Rocklin, CA: Prima.

Killen, M., & Smetana, J. (2008). Moral judgment and moral neuroscience: Intersections, definitions, and issues. *Child Development Perspectives, 2*(1), 1–6.

Kim, J., & Cicchetti, D. (2006). Longitudinal trajectories of self-system processes and depressive symptoms among maltreated and nonmaltreated children. *Child Development, 77*, 624–639.

Kim-Cohen, J., & Gold, A. L. (2009). Measured gene-environment interactions and mechanisms promoting resilient development. *Current Directions in Psychological Science, 18*, 138–142.

Kindermann, T. A., McCollam, T., & Gibson, E. (1996). Peer networks and students' classroom engagement during childhood and adolescence. In J. Juvonen & K. Wentzel (Eds.), *Social motivation: Understanding children's school adjustment* (pp. 279–312). Cambridge, England: Cambridge University Press.

Kinney, D. (1993). From "nerds" to "normals": Adolescent identity recovery within a changing social system. *Sociology of Education, 66*, 21–40.

Knapp, M. S., Turnbull, B. J., & Shields, P. M. (1990). New directions for educating the children of poverty. *Educational Leadership, 48*(1), 4–9.

Knoll, L. J., Magis-Weinberg, L., Speekenbrink, M., & Blakemore, S. (2015). Social influence on risk perception during adolescence. *Psychological Science, 26*, 583–592.

Kochanska, G., Gross, J. N., Lin, M.-H., & Nichols, K. E. (2002). Guilt in young children: Development, determinants, and relations with a broader system of standards. *Child Development, 73*, 461–482.

Kodluboy, D. W. (2004). Gang-oriented interventions. In J. C. Conoley & A. P. Goldstein (Eds.), *School violence intervention* (2nd ed., pp. 194–232). New York, NY: Guilford Press.

Kohlberg, L. (1976). Moral stages and moralization: The cognitive-developmental approach. In T. Lickona (Ed.), *Moral development and behavior: Theory, research, and social issues* (pp. 31–55). New York, NY: Holt, Rinehart & Winston.

Kohlberg, L. (1984). *The psychology of moral development: The nature and validity of moral stages*. San Francisco, CA: Harper & Row.

Kohlberg, L. (1986). A current statement on some theoretical issues. In S. Modgil & C. Modgil (Eds.), *Lawrence Kohlberg: Consensus and controversy* (pp. 485–456). Philadelphia, PA: Falmer Press.

Köller, O., Zeinz, H., & Trautwein, U. (2008). Class-average achievement, marks, and academic self-concept in German primary schools. In H. W. Marsh, R. G. Craven, & D. M. McInerney (Eds.), *Self-processes, learning, and enabling human potential* (pp. 331–352). Charlotte, NC: Information Age.

Konishi, C., Saewyc, E., & Smith, A. (2011, April). *Fostering respect for sexual diversity: Social and emotional health among sexual minority youth.* Poster presented at the annual meeting of the American Educational Research Association, New Orleans, LA.

Kowalski, R. M., & Limber, S. P. (2007). Electronic bullying among middle school students. *Journal of Adolescent Health, 41*, S22–S30.

Krebs, D. L. (2008). Morality: An evolutionary account. *Perspectives on Psychological Science, 3*, 149–172.

Krebs, D. L., & Van Hesteren, F. (1994). The development of altruism: Toward an integrative model. *Developmental Review, 14*, 103–158.

Kroger, J. (2007). *Identity development: Adolescence through adulthood* (2nd ed.). Thousand Oaks, CA: Sage.

Kurtines, W. M., Berman, S. L., Ittel, A., & Williamson, S. (1995). Moral development: A co-constructivist perspective. In W. M. Kurtines & J. L. Gewirtz (Eds.), *Moral development: An introduction* (pp. 633–656). Boston, MA: Allyn & Bacon.

Ladd, G. W., Kochenderfer-Ladd, B., Visconti, K. J., & Ettekal, I. (2012). Classroom peer relations and children's social and scholastic development. In A. M. Ryan & G. W. Ladd (Eds.), *Peer relationships and adjustment at school* (pp. 11–49). Charlotte, NC: Information Age.

Ladson-Billings, G. (1994a). *The dreamkeepers: Successful teachers of African American children.* San Francisco, CA: Jossey-Bass.

LaFontana, K. M., & Cillessen, A. H. N. (2010). Developmental changes in the priority of perceived status in childhood and adolescence. *Social Development, 19*, 130–147.

Lane, K. L., Menzies, H. M., Bruhn, A. L., & Crnobori, M. (2011). *Managing challenging behaviors in schools: Research-based strategies that work.* New York, NY: Guilford Press.

Lapsley, D. K. (1993). Toward an integrated theory of adolescent ego development: The "new look" at adolescent egocentrism. *American Journal of Orthopsychiatry, 63*, 562–571.

Larson, R. W., Clore, G. L., & Wood, G. A. (1999). The emotions of romantic relationships: Do they wreak havoc on adolescents? In W. Furman, B. B. Brown, & C. Feiring (Eds.), *The development of romantic relationships in adolescence* (pp. 19–49). Cambridge, England: Cambridge University Press.

Laupa, M., & Turiel, E. (1995). Social domain theory. In W. M. Kurtines & J. L. Gewirtz (Eds.), *Moral development: An introduction* (pp. 455–473). Boston, MA: Allyn & Bacon.

Laursen, B., Bukowski, W. M., Aunola, K., & Nurmi, J.-E. (2007). Friendship moderates prospective associations between social isolation and adjustment problems in young children. *Child Development, 78*, 1395–1404.

Leadbeater, B. J., & Hoglund, W. L. G. (2009). The effects of peer victimization and physical aggression on changes in internalizing from first to third grade. *Child Development, 80*, 843–859.

Leaf, J. B., Oppenheim-Leaf, M. L., Call, N. A., Sheldon, J. B., Sherman, J. A., Taubman, M., . . . Leaf, R. (2012). Comparing the teaching interaction procedure to social stories for people with autism. *Journal of Applied Behavior Analysis, 45*, 281–298.

Leaper, C., & Friedman, C. K. (2007). The socialization of gender. In J. E. Grusec & P. D. Hastings (Eds.), *Handbook of socialization: Theory and research* (pp. 561–587). New York, NY: Guilford Press.

Lee, K., Talwar, V., McCarthy, A., Ross, I., Evans, A., & Arruda, C. (2014). Can classic moral stories promote honesty in children? *Psychological Science, 25*, 1630–1636.

Lee, P., & Ashby, R. (2001). Empathy, perspective taking, and rational understanding. In O. L. Davis, E. A. Yeager, & S. J. Foster (Eds.), *Historical empathy and perspective taking in the social studies* (pp. 21–50). Lanham, MD: Rowman & Littlefield.

Lee-Pearce, M. L., Plowman, T. S., & Touchstone, D. (1998). Starbase-Atlantis, a school without walls: A comparative study of an innovative science program for at-risk urban elementary students. *Journal of Education for Students Placed at Risk, 3*, 223–235.

Lenski, A., Husemann, N., Trautwein, U., & Lüdtke, O. (2010, April–May). *Academic cheating: A multidimensional point of view.* Paper presented at the annual meeting of the American Educational Research Association, Denver, CO.

Levitt, M. J., Guacci-Franco, N., & Levitt, J. L. (1993). Convoys of social support in childhood and early adolescence: Structure and function. *Developmental Psychology, 29*, 811–818.

Lewis, M., & Sullivan, M. W. (2005). The development of self-conscious emotions. In A. J. Elliot & C. S. Dweck (Eds.), *Handbook of competence and motivation* (pp. 185–201). New York, NY: Guilford Press.

Li, Y., Anderson, R. C., Nguyen-Jahiel, K., Dong, T., Archodidou, A., Kim, I.-H., . . . Miller, B. (2007). Emergent leadership in children's discussion groups. *Cognition and Instruction, 25*, 75–111.

Liben, L. S., & Bigler, R. S. (2002). The developmental course of gender differentiation: Conceptualizing, measuring, and evaluating constructs and pathways. *Monographs of the Society for Research in Child Development, 67*(2, Serial No. 269).

Liem, G. A. D., Marsh, H. W., Martin, A. J., McInerney, D. M., & Yeung, A. S. (2013). The big-fish-little-pond effect and a national policy of within-school ability streaming: Alternative frames of reference. *American Educational Research Journal, 50*, 326–370.

Liew, J., McTigue, E., Barrois, L., & Hughes, J. N. (2008, March). *I am, therefore I think: Effortful control, academic self-efficacy, and achievement in early grade school.* Paper presented at the annual meeting of the American Educational Research Association, New York, NY.

Lippa, R. A. (2002). *Gender, nature, and nurture.* Mahwah, NJ: Erlbaum.

Liu, D., Sabbagh, M. A., Gehring, W. J., & Wellman, H. M. (2009). Neural correlates of children's theory of mind development. *Child Development, 80*, 318–326.

Lockhart, K. L., Chang, B., & Story, T. (2002). Young children's beliefs about the stability of traits: Protective optimism? *Child Development, 73*, 1408–1430.

Loose, F., Régner, I., Morin, A. J. S., & Dumas, F. (2012). Are academic discounting and devaluing double-edged swords? Their relations to global self-esteem, achievement goals, and performance among stigmatized students. *Journal of Educational Psychology, 104*, 713–725.

Lord, C. E. (2010). Autism: From research to practice. *American Psychologist, 65*, 815–826.

Luna, B., Paulsen, D. J., Padmanabhan, A., & Geier, C. (2013). The teenage brain: Cognitive control and motivation. *Current Directions in Psychological Science, 22*, 94–100.

Lundeberg, M., & Mohan, L. (2009). Context matters: Gender and cross-cultural differences in confidence. In D. J. Hacker, J. Dunlosky, & A. C. Graesser (Eds.), *Handbook of metacognition in education* (pp. 221–239). New York, NY: Routledge.

Luyckx, K., Schwartz, S. J., Berzonsky, M. D., Soenens, B., Vansteenkiste, M., Smits, I., & Goossens, L. (2008). Capturing ruminative exploration: Extending the four-dimensional model of identity formation in late adolescence. *Journal of Research in Personality, 42*, 58–82.

Ma, X., & Kishor, N. (1997). Attitude toward self, social factors, and achievement in mathematics: A meta-analytic review. *Educational Psychology Review, 9*, 89–120.

Maccoby, E. E. (2002). Gender and group process: A developmental perspective. *Current Directions in Psychological Science, 11*, 54–58.

Maccoby, E. E. (2007). Historical overview of socialization research and theory. In J. E. Grusec & P. D. Hastings (Eds.), *Handbook of socialization: Theory and research* (pp. 13–41). New York, NY: Guilford Press.

Macfarlane, A., Webber, M., Cookson-Cox, C., & McRae, H. (2014). *Ka Awatea: An iwi case study of Māori students' success* (Report to Ngā Pae o te Māramatanga). Christchurch, New Zealand: Māori Research Laboratory, University of Canterbury.

MacMaster, K., Donovan, L. A., & MacIntyre, P. D. (2002). The effects of being diagnosed with a learning disability on children's self-esteem. *Child Study Journal, 32*, 101–108.

Mahoney, J. L., Cairns, B. D., & Farmer, T. W. (2003). Promoting interpersonal competence and educational success through extracurricular activity participation. *Journal of Educational Psychology, 95*, 409–418.

Maikovich, A. K., Jaffee, S. R., Odgers, C. L., & Gallop, R. (2008). Effects of family violence on psychopathology symptoms in children previously exposed to maltreatment. *Child Development, 79*, 1498–1512.

Malti, T., Gummerum, M., Keller, M., & Buchman, M. (2009). Children's moral motivation, sympathy, and prosocial behavior. *Child Development, 80*, 442–460.

Mandara, J., Gaylord-Harden, N. K., Richards, M. H., & Ragsdale, B. L. (2009). The effects of changes in racial identity and self-esteem on changes in African American adolescents' mental health. *Child Development, 80*, 1660–1675.

Marcia, J. E. (1980). Identity in adolescence. In J. Adelson (Ed.), *Handbook of adolescent psychology* (pp. 159–187). New York, NY: Wiley.

Marcia, J. (1991). Identity and self-development. In R. M. Lerner, A. C. Petersen, & J. Brooks-Gunn (Eds.), *Encyclopedia of adolescence* (Vol. 1, pp. 529–533). New York, NY: Garland.

Marcus, R. F. (1980). Empathy and popularity of preschool children. *Child Study Journal, 10*, 133–145.

Marsh, H. W., & Craven, R. G. (2006). Reciprocal effects of self-concept and performance from a multidimensional perspective: Beyond seductive pleasure and unidimensional perspectives. *Perspectives on Psychological Science, 1*, 133–163.

Marsh, H. W., Gerlach, E., Trautwein, U., Lüdtke, O., & Brettschneider, W.-D. (2007). Longitudinal study of preadolescent sport self-concept and performance: Reciprocal effects and causal ordering. *Child Development, 78*, 1640–1656.

Marsh, H. W., & O'Mara, A. J. (2008). Self-concept is as multidisciplinary as it is multidimensional: A review of theory, measurement, and practice in self-concept research. In H. W. Marsh, R. G. Craven, & D. M. McInerney (Eds.), *Self-processes, learning, and enabling human potential* (pp. 87–115). Charlotte, NC: Information Age.

Martin, A., & Olson, K. R. (2015). Beyond good and evil: What motivations underlie children's prosocial behavior? *Perspectives on Psychological Science, 10*, 159–175.

Martin, A. J., & Dowson, M. (2009). Interpersonal relationships, motivation, engagement, and achievement: Yields for theory, current issues, and educational practice. *Review of Educational Research, 79,* 327–365.

Martinez-Torteya, C., Bogat, G. A., von Eye, A., & Levendosky, A. A. (2009). Resilience among children exposed to domestic violence: The role of risk and protective factors. *Child Development, 80,* 562–577.

Masten, A. S., & Coatsworth, J. D. (1998). The development of competence in favorable and unfavorable environments. *American Psychologist, 53,* 205–220.

Mathews, J. (1988). *Escalante: The best teacher in America.* New York, NY: Henry Holt.

Matthews, G., Zeidner, M., & Roberts, R. D. (2006). Models of personality and affect for education: A review and synthesis. In P. A. Alexander & P. H. Winne (Eds.), *Handbook of educational psychology* (2nd ed., pp. 163–186). Mahwah, NJ: Erlbaum.

Mayer, J. D., Salovey, P., & Caruso, D. R. (2008). Emotional intelligence: New ability or eclectic traits? *American Psychologist, 63,* 503–517.

Mayer, M. J., & Furlong, M. J. (2010). How safe are our schools? *Educational Researcher, 39,* 16–26.

Mayeux, L., Houser, J. J., & Dyches, K. D. (2011). Social acceptance and popularity: Two distinct forms of peer status. In A. H. N. Cillessen, D. Schwartz, & L. Mayeux (Eds.), *Popularity in the peer system* (pp. 79–102). New York, NY: Guilford.

McBrien, J. L. (2005). *Discrimination and academic motivation in adolescent refugee girls.* Unpublished doctoral dissertation, Emory University, Atlanta, GA.

McCall, R. B., & Plemons, B. W. (2001). The concept of critical periods and their implications for early childhood services. In D. B. Bailey, Jr., J. T. Bruer, F. J. Symons, & J. W. Lichtman (Eds.), *Critical thinking about critical periods* (pp. 267–287). Baltimore, MD: Brookes.

McDevitt, T. M., & Ormrod, J. E. (2007). *Child development and education* (3rd ed.). Upper Saddle River, NJ: Merrill/Prentice Hall.

McDougall, P., & Vaillancourt, T. (2015). Long-term adult outcomes of peer victimization in childhood and adolescence: Pathways to adjustment and maladjustment. *American Psychologist, 70,* 300–310.

McElhaney, K. B., Antonishak, J., & Allen, J. P. (2008). "They like me, they like me not": Popularity and adolescents' perceptions of acceptance predicting social functioning over time. *Child Development, 79,* 720–731.

McFarland, S., Brown, D., & Webb, M. (2013). Identification with all humanity as a moral concept and psychological construct. *Current Directions in Psychological Science, 22,* 194–198.

McGovern, M. L., Davis, A., & Ogbu, J. U. (2008). The Minority Achievement Committee: Students leading students to greater success in school. In J. U. Ogbu (Ed.), *Minority status, oppositional culture, and schooling* (pp. 560–573). New York, NY: Routledge.

McInerney, D. M., Marsh, H. W., & Craven, R. (2008). Self-processes, learning, and enabling human potential. In H. W. Marsh, R. G. Craven, & D. M. McInerney (Eds.), *Self-processes, learning, and enabling human potential* (pp. 3–11). Charlotte, NC: Information Age.

McLoyd, V. C. (1998). Socioeconomic disadvantage and child development. *American Psychologist, 53,* 185–204.

Meichenbaum, D. (1977). *Cognitive-behavior modification: An integrative approach.* New York, NY: Plenum Press.

Mendoza-Denton, R., & Mischel, W. (2007). Integrating system approaches to culture and personality: The cultural cognitive-affective processing system. In S. Kitayama & D. Cohen (Eds.), *Handbook of cultural psychology* (pp. 175–195). New York, NY: Guilford Press.

Menon, M., Tobin, D. D., Corby, B. C., Menon, M., Hodges, E. V. E., & Perry, D. G. (2007). The developmental costs of high self-esteem for antisocial children. *Child Development, 78,* 1627–1639.

Meyer, E. J. (2009). Creating schools that value sexual diversity. In S. R. Steinberg (Ed.), *Diversity and multiculturalism: A reader* (pp. 173–192). New York, NY: Peter Lang.

Miller, B. C., & Benson, B. (1999). Romantic and sexual relationship development during adolescence. In W. Furman, B. B. Brown, & C. Feiring (Eds.), *The development of romantic relationships in adolescence* (pp. 99–121). Cambridge, England: Cambridge University Press.

Miller, J. G. (2007). Cultural psychology of moral development. In S. Kitayama & D. Cohen (Eds.), *Handbook of cultural psychology* (pp. 477–499). New York, NY: Guilford Press.

Miller, J. G., Kahle, S., & Hastings, P. D. (2015). Roots and benefits of costly giving: Children who are more altruistic have greater autonomic flexibility and less family wealth. *Psychological Science, 26,* 1038–1045.

Miller, P. M. (2011). A critical analysis of the research on student homelessness. *Review of Educational Research, 81,* 308–337.

Mills, B., Reyna, V. F., & Estrada, S. (2008). Explaining contradictory relations between risk perception and risk taking. *Psychological Science, 19,* 429–433.

Moll, J., de Oliveira-Souza, R., Garrido, G. J., Bramati, I. E., Caparelli-Daquer, E. M., Paiva, M. L., . . . Grafman, J. (2007). The self as a moral agent: Linking the neural bases of social agency and moral sensitivity. *Social Neuroscience, 2,* 336–352.

Moore, S., & Rosenthal, D. (2006). *Sexuality in adolescence: Current trends.* London, England: Routledge.

Murdock, T. B., & Anderman, E. M. (2006). Motivational perspectives on student cheating: Toward an integrated model of academic dishonesty. *Educational Psychologist, 41,* 129–145.

Murdock, T. B., Miller, A., & Kohlhardt, J. (2004). Effects of classroom context variables on high school students' judgments of the acceptability and likelihood of cheating. *Journal of Educational Psychology, 96,* 765–777.

Myles, B. S., & Simpson, R. L. (2001). Understanding the hidden curriculum: An essential social skill for children and youth with Asperger syndrome. *Intervention in School and Clinic, 36,* 279–286.

Narváez, D., & Rest, J. (1995). The four components of acting morally. In W. M. Kurtines & J. L. Gewirtz (Eds.), *Moral development: An introduction* (pp. 385–400). Boston, MA: Allyn & Bacon.

Nasir, N. S., McLaughlin, M. W., & Jones, A. (2009). What does it mean to be African American? Constructions of race and academic identity in an urban public high school. *American Educational Research Journal, 46,* 73–114.

Neel, R. S., Jenkins, Z. N., & Meadows, N. (1990). Social problem-solving behaviors and aggression in young children: A descriptive observational study. *Behavioral Disorders, 16,* 39–51.

Nell, V. (2002). Why young men drive dangerously: Implications for injury prevention. *Current Directions in Psychological Science, 11,* 75–79.

Nesdale, D., Maass, A., Durkin, K., & Griffiths, J. (2005). Group norms, threat, and children's racial prejudice. *Child Development, 76,* 652–663.

Nestemann, F., & Hurrelmann, K. (Eds.). (1994). *Social networks and social support in childhood and adolescence.* Berlin, Germany: Aldine de Gruyter.

Newgent, R. A., Cavell, T. A., Johnson, C. A., & Stegman, C. E. (2008, March). *Impact of a lunch buddy mentoring program on potential victims of peer harassment.* Paper presented at the annual meeting of the American Educational Research Association, New York, NY.

Newman, R. S. (2008). Adaptive and nonadaptive help seeking with peer harassment: An integrative perspective of coping and self-regulation. *Educational Psychologist, 43,* 1–15.

Newman, R. S., & Murray, B. J. (2005). How students and teachers view the seriousness of peer harassment: When is it appropriate to seek help? *Journal of Educational Psychology, 97,* 347–365.

Nucci, L. (2001). *Education in the moral domain.* Cambridge, England: Cambridge University Press.

Nucci, L. (2006). Classroom management for moral and social development. In C. M. Evertson & C. S. Weinstein (Eds.), *Handbook of classroom management: Research, practice, and contemporary issues* (pp. 711–731). Mahwah, NJ: Erlbaum.

Nucci, L. (2009). *Nice is not enough: Facilitating moral development.* Upper Saddle River, NJ: Merrill/Pearson.

Nucci, L. P., & Nucci, M. S. (1982). Children's social interactions in the context of moral and conventional transgressions. *Child Development, 53,* 403–412.

Nucci, L. P., & Weber, E. K. (1995). Social interactions in the home and the development of young children's conceptions of the personal. *Child Development, 66,* 1438–1452.

Nuemi, J.-W. (2008). Self and socialization: How do young people navigate through adolescence? In H. W. Marsh, R. G. Craven, & D. M. McInerney (Eds.), *Self-processes, learning, and enabling human potential* (pp. 305–327). Charlotte, NC: Information Age.

O'Connor, C., Mueller, J., Lewis, R. L., Rivas-Drake, D., & Rosenberg, S. (2011). "Being" Black and strategizing for excellence in a racially stratified academic hierarchy. *American Educational Research Journal, 48,* 1232–1257.

O'Donnell, D. A., Schwab-Stone, M. E., & Muyeed, A. Z. (2002). Multidimensional resilience in urban children exposed to community violence. *Child Development, 73,* 1265–1282.

Ogbu, J. U. (2008a). Collective identity and the burden of "acting White" in Black history, community, and education. In J. U. Ogbu (Ed.), *Minority status, oppositional culture, and schooling* (pp. 29–63). New York, NY: Routledge.

Ogbu, J. U. (2008b). Multiple sources of peer pressures among African American students. In J. U. Ogbu (Ed.), *Minority status, oppositional culture, and schooling* (pp. 89–111). New York, NY: Routledge.

Olneck, M. R. (1995). Immigrants and education. In J. A. Banks & C. A. M. Banks (Eds.), *Handbook of research on multicultural education* (pp. 310–327). New York, NY: Macmillan.

O'Mara, A. J., Marsh, H. W., Craven, R. G., & Debus, R. L. (2006). Do self-concept interventions make a difference? A synergistic blend of construct validation and meta-analysis. *Educational Psychologist, 41,* 181–206.

Oppenheimer, L. (1986). Development of recursive thinking: Procedural variations. *International Journal of Behavioral Development, 9,* 401–411.

Orenstein, P. (1994). *Schoolgirls: Young women, self-esteem, and the confidence gap.* New York, NY: Doubleday.

Oskamp, S. (Ed.). (2000). *Reducing prejudice and discrimination.* Mahwah, NJ: Erlbaum.

Paciello, M., Fida, R., Tramontano, C., Lupinetti, C., & Caprara, G. V. (2008). Stability and change of moral disengagement and its impact on aggression and violence in late adolescence. *Child Development, 79,* 1288–1309.

Paget, K. F., Kritt, D., & Bergemann, L. (1984). Understanding strategic interactions in television commercials: A developmental study. *Journal of Applied Developmental Psychology, 5,* 145–161.

Pahl, K., & Way, N. (2006). Longitudinal trajectories of ethnic identity among urban Black and Latino adolescents. *Child Development, 77,* 1403–1415.

Pajares, F. (2005). Gender differences in mathematics self-efficacy beliefs. In A. M. Gallagher & J. C. Kaufman (Eds.), *Gender differences in mathematics: An integrative psychological approach* (pp. 294–315). Cambridge, England: Cambridge University Press.

Pajares, F. (2009). Toward a positive psychology of academic motivation: The role of self-efficacy beliefs. In R. Gilman, E. S. Huebner, & M. J. Furlong (Eds.), *Handbook of positive psychology in schools* (pp. 149–160). New York, NY: Routledge.

Parada, R. H., Craven, R. G., & Marsh, H. W. (2008). The Beyond Bullying Secondary Program: An innovative program empowering teachers to counteract bullying in schools. In H. W. Marsh, R. G. Craven, & D. M. McInerney (Eds.), *Self-processes, learning, and enabling human potential* (pp. 373–395). Charlotte, NC: Information Age.

Paris, S. G., Morrison, F. J., & Miller, K. F. (2006). Academic pathways from preschool through elementary school. In P. A. Alexander & P. H. Winne (Eds.), *Handbook of educational psychology* (2nd ed., pp. 61–85). Mahwah, NJ: Erlbaum.

Park, N., & Peterson, C. (2009). Strengths of character in schools. In R. Gilman, E. S. Huebner, & M. J. Furlong (Eds.), *Handbook of positive psychology in schools* (pp. 65–76). New York, NY: Routledge.

Pawlas, G. E. (1994). Homeless students at the school door. *Educational Leadership, 51*(8), 79–82.

Pedersen, S., Vitaro, F., Barker, E. D., & Borge, A. I. H. (2007). The timing of middle-childhood peer rejection and friendship: Linking early behavior to early-adolescent adjustment. *Child Development, 78,* 1037–1051.

Pellegrini, A. D. (2002). Bullying, victimization, and sexual harassment during the transition to middle school. *Educational Psychologist, 37,* 151–163.

Pellegrini, A. D. (2011). "In the eye of the beholder": Sex bias in observations and ratings of children's aggression. *Educational Researcher, 40,* 281–286.

Pellegrini, A. D., & Bartini, M. (2000). A longitudinal study of bullying, victimization, and peer affiliation during the transition from primary school to middle school. *American Educational Research Journal, 37,* 699–725.

Pellegrini, A. D., & Bohn, C. M. (2005). The role of recess in children's cognitive performance and school adjustment. *Educational Researcher, 34*(1), 13–19.

Pellegrini, A. D., Kato, K., Blatchford, P., & Baines, E. (2002). A short-term longitudinal study of children's playground games across the first year of school: Implications for social competence and adjustment to school. *American Educational Research Journal, 39,* 991–1015.

Pellegrini, A. D., Roseth, C. J., Van Ryzin, M. J., & Solberg, D. W. (2011). Popularity as a form of social dominance: An evolutionary perspective. In A. H. N. Cillessen, D. Schwartz, & L. Mayeux (Eds.), *Popularity in the peer system* (pp. 123–139). New York, NY: Guilford.

Pelphrey, K. A., & Carter, E. J. (2007). Brain mechanisms underlying social perception deficits in autism. In D. Coch, G. Dawson, & K. W. Fischer (Eds.), *Human behavior, learning, and the developing brain: Atypical development* (pp. 56–86). New York, NY: Guilford Press.

Pepler, D., Jiang, D., Craig, W., & Connolly, J. (2008). Developmental trajectories of bullying and associated factors. *Child Development, 79,* 325–338.

Pérez, B. (1998). *Sociocultural contexts of language and literacy.* Mahwah, NJ: Erlbaum.

Perkins, S. A., & Turiel, E. (2007). To lie or not to lie: To whom and under what circumstances. *Child Development, 78,* 609–621.

Perner, J., & Wimmer, H. (1985). "John *thinks* that Mary *thinks* that . . ." Attribution of second-order beliefs by 5- to 10-year-old children. *Journal of Experimental Child Psychology, 39,* 437–471.

Petersen, R. D. (2004). *Understanding contemporary gangs in America: An interdisciplinary approach.* Upper Saddle River, NJ: Prentice Hall.

Pfeifer, J. H., Brown, C. S., & Juvonen, J. (2007). Teaching tolerance in schools: Lessons learned since *Brown v. Board of Education* about the development and reduction of children's prejudice. *Social Policy Report, 21*(2), 3–13, 16–17, 20–23. Ann Arbor, MI: Society for Research in Child Development.

Pfeifer, M., Goldsmith, H. H., Davidson, R. J., & Rickman, M. (2002). Continuity and change in inhibited and uninhibited children. *Child Development, 73,* 1474–1485.

Phelan, P., Yu, H. C., & Davidson, A. L. (1994). Navigating the psychosocial pressures of adolescence: The voices and experiences of high school youth. *American Educational Research Journal, 31,* 415–447.

Piaget, J. (1960). *The moral judgment of the child* (M. Gabain, Trans.). Glencoe, IL: Free Press. (First published in 1932)

Polakow, V. (2007). In the shadows of the ownership society: Homeless children and their families. In S. Books (Ed.), *Invisible children in the society and its schools* (3rd ed., pp. 39–62). Mahwah, NJ: Erlbaum.

Pollack, W. S. (2006). Sustaining and reframing vulnerability and connection: Creating genuine resilience in boys and young males. In. S. Goldstein & R. B. Brooks (Eds.), *Handbook of resilience in children* (pp. 65–77). New York, NY: Springer.

Portes, P. R. (1996). Ethnicity and culture in educational psychology. In D. C. Berliner & R. C. Calfee (Eds.), *Handbook of educational psychology* (pp. 331–355). New York, NY: Macmillan.

Poulin, F., & Boivin, M. (1999). Proactive and reactive aggression and boys' friendship quality in mainstream classrooms. *Journal of Emotional and Behavioral Disorders, 7,* 168–177.

Power, F. C., Higgins, A., & Kohlberg, L. (1989). *Lawrence Kohlberg's approach to moral education.* New York, NY: Columbia University Press.

Prinstein, M. J., & Dodge, K. A. (2008a). Current issues in peer influence research. In M. J. Prinstein & K. A. Dodge (Eds.), *Understanding peer influence in children and adolescents* (pp. 3–13). New York, NY: Guilford Press.

Prinstein, M. J., & Dodge, K. A. (Eds.). (2008b). *Understanding peer influence in children and adolescents.* New York, NY: Guilford Press.

Raine, A. (2008). From genes to brain to antisocial behavior. *Current Directions in Psychological Science, 17,* 323–328.

Ramey, C. T., & Ramey, S. L. (1998). Early intervention and early experience. *American Psychologist, 53,* 109–120.

Ramiah, A. A., & Hewstone, M. (2013). Intergroup contact as a tool for reducing, resolving, and preventing intergroup conflict: Evidence, limitations, and potential. *American Psychologist, 68,* 527–542.

Raskauskas, J. (2010). Text-bullying: Associations with traditional bullying and depression among New Zealand adolescents. *Journal of School Violence, 9,* 74–97.

Reimer, J., Paolitto, D. P., & Hersh, R. H. (1983). *Promoting moral growth: From Piaget to Kohlberg* (2nd ed.). White Plains, NY: Longman.

Rest, J., Narvaez, D., Bebeau, M., & Thoma, S. (1999). A neo-Kohlbergian approach: The DIT and schema theory. *Educational Psychology Review, 11,* 291–324.

Reyna, V. F., Chapman, S. B., Dougherty, M. R., & Confrey, J. (Eds.). (2012). *The adolescent brain: Learning, reasoning, and decision making.* Washington, DC: American Psychological Association.

Reyna, V. F., & Farley, F. (2006). Risk and rationality in adolescent decision making: Implications for theory, practice, and public policy. *Psychological Science in the Public Interest, 7*(1), 1–44.

Rhodes, M., & Gelman, S. A. (2008). Categories influence predictions about individual consistency. *Child Development, 79,* 1270–1287.

Rivers, I., Chesney, T., & Coyne, I. (2011). Cyberbullying. In C. P. Monks & I. Coyne (Eds.), *Bullying in different contexts* (pp. 211–230). Cambridge, England: Cambridge University Press.

Rivers, I., Poteat, V. P., Noret, N., & Ashurst, N. (2009). Observing bullying at school: The mental health implications of witness status. *School Psychology Quarterly,* 24(4), 211–223.

Rizzolatti, G., & Sinigaglia, C. (2008). *Mirrors in the brain—How our minds share actions and emotions* (F. Anderson, Trans.). Oxford, England: Oxford University Press.

Robbins, E., & Rochat, P. (2011). Emerging signs of strong reciprocity in human ontogeny. *Frontiers in Psychology, 2,* Article 353. doi:10.3389/fpsyg.2011.00353

Robins, R. W., & Trzesniewski, K. H. (2005). Self-esteem development across the lifespan. *Current Directions in Psychological Science, 14,* 158–162.

Robinson, J. P., & Espelage, D. L. (2011). Inequities in educational and psychological outcomes between LGBTQ and straight students in middle and high school. *Educational Researcher, 40,* 315–330.

Rodkin, P. C., Espelage, D. L., & Hanish, L. D. (2015). A relational framework for understanding bullying: Developmental antecedents and outcomes. *American Psychologist, 70,* 311–321.

Rogoff, B. (2003). *The cultural nature of human development.* Oxford, England: Oxford University Press.

Rose, A. J. (2002). Co-rumination in the friendship of girls and boys. *Child Development, 73,* 1830–1843.

Rose, A. J., & Smith, R. L. (2009). Sex differences in peer relationships. In K. H. Rubin, W. M. Bukowski, & B. Laursen (Eds.), *Handbook of peer interactions, relationships, and groups* (pp. 379–393). New York, NY: Guilford Press.

Ross, M., & Wang, Q. (2010). Why we remember and what we remember: Culture and autobiographical memory. *Perspectives on Psychological Science, 5,* 401–409.

Ross, S. W, & Horner, R. H. (2009). Bully prevention in positive behavior support. *Journal of Applied Behavior Analysis, 42,* 747–759.

Roth, W.-M. (2011). Object/motives and emotion: A cultural-historical activity theoretic approach to motivation in learning and work. In D. M. McInerney, R. A. Walker, & G. A. D. Liem (Eds.), *Sociocultural theories of learning and motivation: Looking back, looking forward* (pp. 43–63). Charlotte, NC: Information Age.

Rothbart, M. K. (2007). Temperament, development, and personality. *Current Directions in Psychological Science, 16,* 207–212.

Rothbart, M. K. (2011). *Becoming who we are: Temperament and personality in development.* New York, NY: Guilford.

Rothbart, M. K., Sheese, B. E., & Posner, M. I. (2007). Executive attention and effortful control: Linking temperament, brain networks, and genes. *Child Development Perspectives, 1,* 2–7.

Rothbaum, F., & Trommsdorff, G. (2007). Do roots and wings complement or oppose one another? The socialization of relatedness and autonomy in cultural context. In J. E. Grusec & P. D. Hastings (Eds.), *Handbook of socialization: Theory and research* (pp. 461–489). New York, NY: Guilford Press.

Rubin, K. H. (1982). Nonsocial play in preschoolers: Necessarily evil? *Child Development, 53,* 651–657.

Rubin, K. H., Cheah, C., & Menzer, M. M. (2010). Peers. In M. H. Bornstein (Ed.), *Handbook of cultural developmental science* (pp. 223–237). New York, NY: Psychology Press.

Ruble, D. N., Martin, C. L., & Berebaum, S. A. (2006). Gender development. In W. Damon & R. M. Lerner (Series Eds.) & N. Eisenberg (Vol. Ed.), *Handbook of child psychology: Vol. 3. Social, emotional, and personality development* (6th ed., pp. 858–932). Hoboken, NJ: Wiley.

Rudolph, K. D., Caldwell, M. S., & Conley, C. S. (2005). Need for approval and children's well-being. *Child Development, 76,* 309–323.

Ruffman, T., Slade, L., & Crowe, E. (2002). The relation between children's and mothers' mental state language and theory-of-mind understanding. *Child Development, 73,* 734–751.

Rumberger, R. W. (2011). *Dropping out: Why students drop out of high school and what can be done about it.* Cambridge, MA: Harvard University Press.

Rushton, J. P. (1980). *Altruism, socialization, and society.* Upper Saddle River, NJ: Prentice Hall.

Ryan, A. M. (2000). Peer groups as a context for the socialization of adolescents' motivation, engagement, and achievement in school. *Educational Psychologist, 35,* 101–111.

Ryan, A. M. (2001). The peer group as a context for the development of young adolescent motivation and achievement. *Child Development, 72,* 1135–1150.

Ryan, A. M., Jamison, R. S., Shin, H., & Thompson, G. N. (2012). Social achievement goals and adjustment at school during early adolescence. In A. M. Ryan & G. W. Ladd (Eds.), *Peer relationships and adjustment at school* (pp. 165–186). Charlotte, NC: Information Age.

Ryan, A. M., & Shim, S. S. (2008). An exploration of young adolescents' social achievement goals and social adjustment in middle school. *Journal of Educational Psychology, 100,* 672–687.

Ryan, R. M., & Kuczkowski, R. (1994). The imaginary audience, self-consciousness, and public individuation in adolescence. *Journal of Personality, 62,* 219–237.

Saarni, C., Campos, J. J., Camras, L. A., & Witherington, D. (2006). Emotional development: Action, communication, and understanding. In W. Damon & R. M. Lerner (Eds. in Chief) & N. Eisenberg (Vol. Ed.), *Handbook of child psychology, Vol. 3. Social, emotional, and personality development* (6th ed., pp. 226–299). Hoboken, NJ: Wiley.

Salmivalli, C., & Peets, K. (2009). Bullies, victims, and bully–victim relationships in middle childhood and early adolescence. In K. H. Rubin, W. M. Bukowski, & B. Laursen (Eds.), *Handbook of peer interactions, relationships, and groups* (pp. 322–340). New York, NY: Guilford Press.

Sandstrom, M. J. (2011). The power of popularity: Influence processes in childhood and adolescence. In A. H. N. Cillessen, D. Schwartz, & L. Mayeux (Eds.), *Popularity in the peer system* (pp. 219–244). New York, NY: Guilford Press.

Saudino, K. J., & Plomin, R. (2007). Why are hyperactivity and academic achievement related? *Child Development, 78,* 972–986.

Savin-Williams, R. C. (2008). Then and now: Recruitment, definition, diversity, and positive attributes of same-sex populations. *Developmental Psychology, 44,* 135–138.

Scarr, S. (1992). Developmental theories for the 1990s: Development and individual differences. *Child Development, 63,* 1–19.

Scarr, S. (1993). Biological and cultural diversity: The legacy of Darwin for development. *Child Development, 64,* 1333–1353.

Schlaefli, A., Rest, J. R., & Thoma, S. J. (1985). Does moral education improve moral judgment? A meta-analysis of intervention studies using the defining issues test. *Review of Educational Research, 55,* 319–352.

Schmidt, M. F. H., & Tomasello, M. (2012). Young children enforce social norms. *Current Directions in Psychological Science, 21,* 232–236.

Schofield, J. W. (1995). Improving intergroup relations among students. In J. A. Banks & C. A. M. Banks (Eds.), *Handbook of research on multicultural education.* New York, NY: Macmillan.

Schoon, I. (2006). *Risk and resilience: Adaptations in changing times.* Cambridge, England: Cambridge University Press.

Schult, C. A. (2002). Children's understanding of the distinction between intentions and desires. *Child Development, 73,* 1727–1747.

Schultz, K., Buck, P., & Niesz, T. (2000). Democratizing conversations: Racialized talk in a post-desegregated middle school. *American Educational Research Journal, 37,* 33–65.

Schunk, D. H., & Pajares, F. (2004). Self-efficacy in education revisited: Empirical and applied evidence. In D. M. McInerney & S. Van Etten (Eds.), *Big theories revisited* (pp. 115–138). Greenwich, CT: Information Age.

Schwartz, D., Dodge, K. A., Coie, J. D., Hubbard, J. A., Cillessen, A. H., Lemerise, E. A., & Bateman, H. (1998). Social-cognitive and behavioral correlates of aggression and victimization in boys' play groups. *Journal of Abnormal Child Psychology, 26,* 431–440.

Schwartz, D., & Gorman, A. H. (2011). The high price of high status: Popularity as a mechanism of risk. In A. H. N. Cillessen, D. Schwartz, & L. Mayeux (Eds.), *Popularity in the peer system* (pp. 245–270). New York, NY: Guilford.

Seaton, M., Marsh, H. W., & Craven, R. G. (2010). Big-fish-little-pond effect: Generalizability and moderation—Two sides of the same coin. *American Educational Research Journal, 47,* 390–433.

Seaton, E. K., Scottham, K. M., & Sellers, R. M. (2006). The status model of racial identity development in African American adolescents: Evidence of structure, trajectories, and well-being. *Child Development, 77,* 1416–1426.

Selman, R. L. (1980). *The growth of interpersonal understanding.* San Diego, CA: Academic Press.

Serbin, L., & Karp, J. (2003). Intergenerational studies of parenting and the transfer of risk from parent to child. *Current Directions in Psychological Science, 12,* 138–142.

Shariff, S. (2008). *Cyber-bullying: Issues and solutions for the school, the classroom and the home.* London, England: Routledge.

Shulman, E. P., Smith, A. R., Silva, K., Icenogle, G., Duell, N., Chein, J., & Steinberg, L. (2016). The dual systems model: Review, reappraisal, and reaffirmation. *Developmental Cognitive Neuroscience, 17,* 103–117.

Shure, M. B., & Aberson, B. (2006). Enhancing the process of resilience through effective thinking. In. S. Goldstein & R. B.

Brooks (Eds.), *Handbook of resilience in children* (pp. 373–394). New York, NY: Springer.

Simons, R. L., Whitbeck, L. B., Conger, R. D., & Conger, K. J. (1991). Parenting factors, social skills, and value commitments as precursors to school failure, involvement with deviant peers, and delinquent behavior. *Journal of Youth and Adolescence, 20*, 645–664.

Sinai, M., Kaplan, A., & Flum, H. (2012). Promoting identity exploration within the school curriculum: A design-based study in a junior high literature lesson in Israel. *Contemporary Educational Psychology, 37*, 195–205.

Slavin, R. E. (1989). Students at risk of school failure: The problem and its dimensions. In R. E. Slavin, N. L. Karweit, & N. A. Madden (Eds.), *Effective programs for students at risk* (pp. 206–231). Boston, MA: Allyn & Bacon.

Sleeter, C. E., & Grant, C. A. (1999). *Making choices for multicultural education: Five approaches to race, class, and gender* (3rd ed.). Upper Saddle River, NJ: Merrill/Prentice Hall.

Smetana, J. G. (1981). Preschool children's conceptions of moral and social rules. *Child Development, 52*, 1333–1336.

Smetana, J. G. (2005). Adolescent-parent conflict: Resistance and subversion as developmental process. In L. Nucci (Ed.), *Conflict, contradiction, and contrarian elements in moral development and education* (pp. 69–91). Mahwah, NJ: Erlbaum.

Smetana, J. G. (2006). Social cognitive domain theory: Consistencies and variations in children's moral and social judgments. In M. Killen & J. Smetana (Eds.), *Handbook of moral development* (pp. 119–154). Mahwah, NJ: Erlbaum.

Smetana, J. G., & Braeges, J. L. (1990). The development of toddlers' moral and conventional judgments. *Merrill-Palmer Quarterly, 36*, 329–346.

Smith, E. R., & Semin, G. R. (2007). Situated social cognition. *Current Directions in Psychological Science, 16*, 132–135.

Smith, P. K. (2011). Bullying in schools: Thirty years of research. In C. P. Monks & I. Coyne (Eds.), *Bullying in different contexts* (pp. 36–60). Cambridge, England: Cambridge University Press.

Smokowski, P., Buchanan, R. L., & Bacalleo, M, L. (2009). Acculturation and adjustment in Latino adolescents: How cultural risk factors and assets influence multiple domains of adolescent mental health. *Journal of Primary Prevention, 30*, 371–393.

Snarey, J. (1995). In a communitarian voice: The sociological expansion of Kohlbergian theory, research, and practice. In W. M. Kurtines & J. L. Gewirtz (Eds.), *Moral development: An introduction* (pp. 109–133). Boston, MA: Allyn & Bacon.

Somerville, L. H. (2013). The teenage brain: Sensitivity to social evaluation. *Current Directions in Psychological Science, 22*, 121–127.

Somerville, L. H., Jones, R. M., & Casey, B. J. (2010). A time of change: Behavioral and neural correlates of adolescent sensitivity to appetitive and aversive environmental cues. *Brain and Cognition, 72*, 124–133.

Somerville, L. H., Jones, R. M., Ruberry, E. J., Dyke, J. P., Glover, G., & Casey, B. J. (2013). The medial prefrontal cortex and the emergence of self-conscious emotion in adolescence. *Psychological Science, 24*, 1554–1562.

Spear, L. P. (2007). Brain development and adolescent behavior. In D. Coch, K. W. Fischer, & G. Dawson (Eds.), *Human behavior, learning, and the developing brain: Typical development* (pp. 362–396). New York, NY: Guilford Press.

Spinrad, T. L., & Eisenberg, N. (2009). Empathy, prosocial behavior, and positive development in schools. In R. Gilman, E. S. Huebner, & M. J. Furlong (Eds.), *Handbook of positive psychology in schools* (pp. 119–129). New York, NY: Routledge.

Spunt, R. P., & Lieberman, M. D. (2013). The busy social brain: Evidence for automaticity and control in the neural systems supporting social cognition and action understanding. *Psychological Science, 24*, 80–86.

Steinberg, L. (1996). *Beyond the classroom: Why school reform has failed and what parents need to do.* New York, NY: Touchstone.

Steinberg, L. (2005). Cognitive and affective development in adolescence. *Trends in Cognitive Sciences, 9*(2), 69–74.

Steinberg, L. (2009). Should the science of adolescent brain development inform public policy? *American Psychologist, 64*, 739–750.

Steuer, G., & Dresel, M. (2011, April). *Dealing with errors in mathematics classrooms: The relevance of error climate and personal achievement motivation.* Paper presented at the annual meeting of the American Educational Research Association, New Orleans, LA.

Stewart, L., & Pascual-Leone, J. (1992). Mental capacity constraints and the development of moral reasoning. *Journal of Experimental Child Psychology, 54*, 251–287.

Stice, E. (2003). Puberty and body image. In C. Hayward (Ed.), *Gender differences at puberty* (pp. 61–76). Cambridge, England: Cambridge University Press.

Stright, A. D., Gallagher, K. C., & Kelley, K. (2008). Infant temperament moderates relations between maternal parenting in early childhood and children's adjustment in first grade. *Child Development, 79*, 186–200.

Suh, S., Suh, J., & Houston, I. (2007). Predictors of categorical at-risk high school dropouts. *Journal of Counseling & Development, 85*, 196–203.

Sullivan, A. L., & Simonson, G. R. (2016). A systematic review of school-based social-emotional interventions for refugees and war-traumatized youth. *Review of Educational Research, 86*, 503–530.

Sullivan, J. R., & Conoley, J. C. (2004). Academic and instructional interventions with aggressive students. In J. C. Conoley & A. P. Goldstein (Eds.), *School violence intervention* (2nd ed., pp. 235–255). New York, NY: Guilford.

Swearer, S. M., Espelage, D. L., Vaillancourt, T., & Hymel, S. (2010). What can be done about school bullying? Linking research to educational practice. *Educational Researcher, 39*, 38–47.

Tager-Flusberg, H. (2007). Evaluating the theory-of-mind hypothesis of autism. *Current Directions in Psychological Science, 16*, 311–315.

Tamis-Lemonda, C. S., & McFadden, K. E. (2010). The United States of America. In M. H. Bornstein (Ed.), *Handbook of cultural developmental science* (pp. 299–322). New York, NY: Psychology Press.

Tate, W. F. (1995). Returning to the root: A culturally relevant approach to mathematics pedagogy. *Theory into Practice, 34*, 166–173.

Tatum, B. D. (1997). *"Why are all the Black kids sitting together in the cafeteria?" and other conversations about race.* New York, NY: Basic Books.

Themann, K. S., & Goldstein, H. (2001). Social stories, written text cues, and video feedback: Effects on social communication of children with autism. *Journal of Applied Behavior Analysis, 34*, 425–446.

Thomaes, S., Bushman, B. J., Stegge, H., & Olthof, T. (2008). Trumping shame by blasts of noise: Narcissism, self-esteem, shame, and aggression in young adolescents. *Child Development, 79*, 1792–1801.

Thomaes, S., Reijntjes, A., Orobio de Castro, B., & Bushman, B. J. (2009). Reality bites—Or does it? Realistic self-views buffer negative mood following social threat. *Psychological Science, 20*, 1079–1083.

Thomas, A., & Chess, S. (1977). *Temperament and development.* New York, NY: Brunner/Mazel.

Thompson, M., & Grace, C. O. (with Cohen, L. J.). (2001). *Best friends, worst enemies: Understanding the social lives of children.* New York, NY: Ballantine.

Thompson, R. A., & Wyatt, J. M. (1999). Current research on child maltreatment: Implications for educators. *Educational Psychology Review, 11*, 173–201.

Thorkildsen, T. A. (1995). Conceptions of social justice. In W. M. Kurtines & J. L. Gewirtz (Eds.), *Moral development: An introduction* (pp. 511–533). Boston, MA: Allyn & Bacon.

Thorkildsen, T. A., Golant, C. J., & Cambray-Engstrom, E. (2008). Essential solidarities for understanding Latino adolescents' moral and academic engagement. In C. Hudley & A. E. Gottfried (Eds.), *Academic motivation and the culture of school in childhood and adolescence* (pp. 73–98). New York, NY: Oxford University Press.

Tisak, M. (1993). Preschool children's judgments of moral and personal events involving physical harm and property damage. *Merrill-Palmer Quarterly, 39*, 375–390.

Tobias, S., Fletcher, J. D., Dai, D. Y., & Wind, A. P. (2011). Review of research on computer games. In S. Tobias & J. D. Fletcher (Eds.), *Computer games and instruction* (pp. 127–221). Charlotte, NC: Information Age.

Trautwein, U., Gerlach, E., & Lüdtke, O. (2008). Athletic classmates, physical self-concept, and free-time physical activity: A longitudinal study of frame of reference effects. *Journal of Educational Psychology, 100*, 988–1001.

Triandis, H. C. (1995). *Individualism and collectivism.* Boulder, CO: Westview Press.

Troop-Gordon, W., & Asher, S. R. (2005). Modification in children's goals when encountering obstacles in conflict resolution. *Child Development, 76*, 568–582.

Tsethlikai, M., & Greenhoot, A. F. (2006). The influence of another's perspective on children's recall of previously misconstrued events. *Developmental Psychology, 42*, 732–745.

Tsethlikai, M., Guthrie-Fulbright, Y., & Loera, S. (2007, March). *Social perspective coordination ability and children's recall of mutual*

conflict. Paper presented at the biennial meeting of the Society for Research in Child Development, Boston, MA.

Turiel, E. (1983). *The development of social knowledge: Morality and convention.* Cambridge, England: Cambridge University Press.

Turiel, E. (1998). The development of morality. In W. Damon (Series Ed.) & N. Eisenberg (Vol. Ed.), *Handbook of child psychology: Vol. 3. Social, emotional, and personality development* (5th ed., pp. 863–932). New York, NY: Wiley.

Turiel, E. (2002). *The culture of morality: Social development, context, and conflict.* Cambridge, England: Cambridge University Press.

Turiel, E. (2006). The development of morality. In W. Damon & R. M. Lerner (Eds. in Chief) & N. Eisenberg (Vol. Ed.), *Handbook of child psychology, Vol. 3. Social, emotional, and personality development* (6th ed., pp. 789–857). Hoboken, NJ: Wiley.

Turiel, E., Smetana, J. G., & Killen, M. (1991). Social contexts in social cognitive development. In W. M. Kurtines & J. L. Gewirtz (Eds.), *Moral behavior and development: Vol. 2. Research* (pp. 307–332). Mahwah, NJ: Erlbaum.

Turnbull, A., Turnbull, R., & Wehmeyer, M. L. (2010). *Exceptional lives: Special education in today's schools* (6th ed.). Upper Saddle River, NJ: Merrill.

Vadeboncoeur, J. A., Vellos, R. E., & Goessling, K. P. (2011). Learning as (one part) identity construction. In D. M. McInerney, R. A. Walker, & G. A. D. Liem (Eds.), *Sociocultural theories of learning and motivation: Looking back, looking forward* (pp. 223–251). Charlotte, NC: Information Age.

Valentine, J. C., Cooper, H., Bettencourt, B. A., & DuBois, D. L. (2002). Out-of-school activities and academic achievement: The mediating role of self-beliefs. *Educational Psychologist, 37*, 245–256.

Valentine, J. C., DuBois, D. L., & Cooper, H. (2004). The relation between self-beliefs and academic achievement: A meta-analytic review. *Educational Psychologist, 39*, 111–133.

Valiente, C., Lemery-Calfant, K., Swanson, J., & Reiser, M. (2008). Prediction of children's academic competence from their effortful control, relationships, and classroom participation. *Journal of Educational Psychology, 100*, 67–77.

Valkenburg, P. M., & Peter, J. (2009). Social consequences of the Internet for adolescents: A decade of research. *Current Directions in Psychological Science, 18*, 1–5.

van den Berg, Y. H. M., Seters, E., & Cillessen, A. H. N. (2012). Changing peer perceptions and victimization through classroom arrangements: A field experiment. *Journal of Abnormal Child Psychology, 40*, 403–412.

van Goozen, S. H. M., Fairchild, G., & Harold, G. T. (2008). The role of neurobiological deficits in childhood antisocial behavior. *Current Directions in Psychological Science, 17*, 224–228.

Vaughn, S. (1991). Social skills enhancement in students with learning disabilities. In B. Y. L. Wong (Ed.), *Learning about learning disabilities* (pp. 407–440). San Diego, CA: Academic Press.

Vitaro, F., Gendreau, P. L., Tremblay, R. E., & Oligny, P. (1998). Reactive and proactive aggression differentially predict later conduct problems. *Journal of Child Psychology and Psychiatry and Allied Disciplines, 39*, 377–385.

Wainryb, C., Brehl, B. A., & Matwin, S. (2005). Being hurt and hurting others: Children's narrative accounts and moral judgments of their own interpersonal conflicts. *Monographs of the Society for Research in Child Development, 70* (3; Serial No. 281).

Walker, E. N. (2006). Urban high school students' academic communities and their effects on mathematics success. *American Educational Research Journal, 43*, 43–73.

Walker, J. M. T., & Hoover-Dempsey, K. V. (2006). Why research on parental involvement is important to classroom management. In C. M. Evertson & C. S. Weinstein (Eds.), *Handbook of classroom management: Research, practice, and contemporary issues* (pp. 665–684). Mahwah, NJ: Erlbaum.

Waterhouse, L. (2006). Multiple intelligences, the Mozart effect, and emotional intelligence: A critical review. *Educational Psychologist, 41*, 207–225.

Watkins, D. E., & Wentzel, K. R. (2008). Training boys with ADHD to work collaboratively: Social and learning outcomes. *Contemporary Educational Psychology, 33*, 625–646.

Watson, M. W., Andreas, J. B., Fischer, K. W., & Smith, K. (2005). Patterns of risk factors leading to victimization and aggression in children and adolescents. In K. A. Kendall-Tackett & S. M. Giacomoni (Eds.), *Child victimization: Maltreatment, bullying and dating violence, prevention and intervention* (pp. 12.1–12.23). Kingston, NJ: Civic Research Institute.

Way, N. (1998). *Everyday courage: The lives and stories of urban teenagers.* New York, NY: New York University Press.

Webb, N. M., & Farivar, S. (1994). Promoting helping behavior in cooperative small groups in middle school mathematics. *American Educational Research Journal*, *31*, 369–395.

Weichold, K., Silbereisen, R. K., & Schmitt-Rodermund, E. (2003). Short-term and long-term consequences of early versus late physical maturation in adolescents. In C. Hayward (Ed.), *Gender differences at puberty* (pp. 241–276). Cambridge, England: Cambridge University Press.

Weiss, L. H., & Schwarz, J. C. (1996). The relationship between parenting types and older adolescents' personality, academic achievement, adjustment, and substance use. *Child Development*, *67*, 2101–2114.

Weissberg, R. P. (1985). Designing effective social problem-solving programs for the classroom. In B. H. Schneider, K. H. Rubin, & J. E. Ledingham (Eds.), *Children's peer relations: Issues in assessment and intervention* (pp. 225–242). New York, NY: Springer-Verlag.

Wellman, H. M. (1990). *The child's theory of mind.* Cambridge, MA: MIT Press.

Wellman, H. M., & Gelman, S. A. (1998). Knowledge acquisition in foundational domains. In W. Damon (Series Ed.), D. Kuhn, & R. S. Siegler (Vol. Eds.), *Handbook of child psychology: Vol. 2. Cognition, perception, and language* (5th ed., pp. 523–573). New York, NY: Wiley.

Wellman, H. M., Phillips, A. T., & Rodriguez, T. (2000). Young children's understanding of perception, desire, and emotion. *Child Development*, *71*, 895–912.

Wentzel, K. R. (2009). Peers and academic functioning at school. In K. H. Rubin, W. M. Bukowski, & B. Laursen (Eds.), *Handbook of peer interactions, relationships, and groups* (pp. 531–547). New York, NY: Guilford Press.

Wentzel, K., Baker, S., & Russell, S. (2009). Peer relationships and positive adjustment at school. In R. Gilman, E. S. Huebner, & M. J. Furlong (Eds.), *Handbook of positive psychology in schools* (pp. 229–243). New York, NY: Routledge.

Wentzel, K. R., Donlan, A. E., Morrison, D. A., Russell, S. L., & Baker, S. A. (2009, April). *Adolescent non-compliance: A social ecological perspective.* Paper presented at the annual meeting of the American Educational Research Association, San Diego, CA.

Wentzel, K. R., Filisetti, L., & Looney, L. (2007). Adolescent prosocial behavior: The role of self-processes and contextual cues. *Child Development*, *78*, 895–910.

Wentzel, K. R., & Watkins, D. E. (2011). Instruction based on peer interactions. In R. E. Mayer & P. A. Alexander (Eds.), *Handbook of research on learning and instruction* (pp. 322–343). New York, NY: Routledge.

Werner, E. E., & Smith, R. S. (2001). *Journeys from childhood to midlife: Risk, resilience, and recovery.* Ithaca, NY: Cornell University Press.

White, R., & Cunningham, A. M. (1991). *Ryan White: My own story.* New York, NY: Signet.

Whitesell, N. R., Mitchell, C. M., Kaufman, C. E., Spicer, P., & the Voices of Indian Teens Project Team. (2006). Developmental trajectories of personal and collective self-concept among American Indian adolescents. *Child Development*, *77*, 1487–1503.

Wigfield, A., Byrnes, J. P., & Eccles, J. S. (2006). Development during early and middle adolescence. In P. A. Alexander & P. H. Winne (Eds.), *Handbook of educational psychology* (2nd ed., pp. 87–113). Mahwah, NJ: Erlbaum.

Wiles, J., & Bondi, J. (2001). *The new American middle school: Educating preadolescents in an era of change.* Upper Saddle River, NJ: Merrill/Prentice Hall.

Willard, N. E. (2007). *Cyberbullying and cyberthreats: Responding to the challenge of online social aggression, threats, and distress.* Champaign, IL: Research Press.

Williams, K. M. (2001a). "Frontin' it": Schooling, violence, and relationships in the 'hood. In J. N. Burstyn, G. Bender, R. Casella, H. W. Gordon, D. P. Guerra, K. V. Luschen, . . . Williams, K. M., *Preventing violence in schools: A challenge to American democracy* (pp. 95–108). Mahwah, NJ: Erlbaum.

Williams, K. M. (2001b). What derails peer mediation? In J. N. Burstyn, G. Bender, R. Casella, H. W. Gordon, D. P. Guerra, K. V. Luschen, . . . Williams, K. M., *Preventing violence in schools: A challenge to American democracy* (pp. 199–208). Mahwah, NJ: Erlbaum.

Williams, T., & Williams, K. (2010). Self-efficacy and performance in mathematics: Reciprocal determinism in 33 nations. *Journal of Educational Psychology, 102,* 453–456.

Wolak, J., Finkelhor, D., Mitchell, K. J., & Ybarra, M. L. (2008). Online "predators" and their victims: Myths, realities, and implications for prevention and treatment. *American Psychologist, 63,* 111–128.

Wood, D., Larson, R. W., & Brown, J. R. (2009). How adolescents come to see themselves as more responsible through participation in youth programs. *Child Development, 80,* 285–309.

Woolfe, T., Want, S. C., & Siegal, M. (2002). Signposts to development: Theory of mind in deaf children. *Child Development*, *73*, 768–778.

Wright, E. J. (2007, March). *The negative self-focus trap: Emerging self-focused emotion regulation and increased depression risk.* Paper presented at the biennial meeting of the Society for Research in Child Development, Boston, MA.

Xu, Y., Farver, J., Chang, L, Yu, L., & Zhang, Z. (2006). Culture, family context, and children's coping strategies in peer interactions. In X. Chen, D. French, & B. H. Schneider (Eds.), *Peer relationships in cultural context* (pp. 264–280). New York, NY: Cambridge University Press.

Yang, C., & Brown, B. B. (2013). Motives for using Facebook, patterns of Facebook activities, and late adolescents' social adjustment to college. *Journal of Youth and Adolescence, 42,* 403–416.

Yates, M., & Youniss, J. (1996). A developmental perspective on community service in adolescence. *Social Development*, *5*, 85–111.

Yau, J., & Smetana, J. G. (2003). Conceptions of moral, social-conventional, and personal events among Chinese preschoolers in Hong Kong. *Child Development*, *74*, 647–658.

Yeager, D. S., & Dweck, C. S. (2012). Mindsets that promote resilience: When students believe that personal characteristics can be developed. *Educational Psychologist, 47,* 302–314.

Yeager, D. S., Johnson, R., Spitzer, B. J., Trzesniewski, K. H., Powers, J., & Dweck, C. S. (2014). The far-reaching effects of believing people can change: Implicit theories of personality shape stress, health, and achievement during adolescence. *Journal of Personality and Social Psychology, 106,* 867–884.

Yell, M. L., Robinson, T. R., & Drasgow, E. (2001). Cognitive behavior modification. In T. J. Zirpoli & K. J. Melloy, *Behavior management: Applications for teachers* (3rd ed., pp. 200–246). Upper Saddle River, NJ: Merrill/Prentice Hall.

Yeung, R. S., & Leadbeater, B. J. (2007, March). *Peer victimization and emotional and behavioral problems in adolescence: The moderating effect of adult emotional support.* Paper presented at the biennial meeting of the Society for Research in Child Development, Boston, MA.

Yip, T., & Fuligni, A. J. (2002). Daily variation in ethnic identity, ethnic behaviors, and psychological well-being among American adolescents of Chinese descent. *Child Development*, *73*, 1557–1572.

Young, L., & Saxe, R. (2009). Innocent intentions: A correlation between forgiveness for accidental harm and neural activity. *Neuropsychologia, 47,* 2065–2072.

Youniss, J., & Yates, M. (1999). Youth service and moral-civic identity: A case for everyday morality. *Educational Psychology Review*, *11*, 361–376.

Yuker, H. E. (Ed.). (1988). *Attitudes toward persons with disabilities.* New York, NY: Springer.

Yun, C., Farran, D. C., Lipsey, M. W., & Bilbrey, C. (2010, April–May). *Academic self-concept and achievement in young children.* Poster presented at the annual meeting of the American Educational Research Association, Denver, CO.

Zahn-Waxler, C., Radke-Yarrow, M., Wagner, E., & Chapman, M. (1992). Development of concern for others. *Developmental Psychology*, *28*, 126–136.

Zambo, D. (2003, April). *Thinking about reading: Talking to children with learning disabilities.* Paper presented at the annual meeting of the American Educational Research Association, Chicago, IL.

Zeidner, M., Roberts, R. D., & Matthews, G. (2002). Can emotional intelligence be schooled? A critical review. *Educational Psychologist*, *37*, 215–231.

Zhou, Q., Wang, Y., Deng, X., Eisenberg, N., Wolchik, S. A., & Tein, J.-Y. (2008). Relations of parenting and temperament to Chinese children's experience of negative life events, coping efficacy, and externalizing problems. *Child Development, 79,* 493–513.

Zimmer-Gembeck, M. J., & Helfand, M. (2008). Ten years of longitudinal research on U.S. adolescent sexual behavior: Developmental correlates of sexual intercourse and the importance of age, gender and ethnic background. *Developmental Review, 28,* 153–224.

Zimmerman, B. J., & Moylan, A. R. (2009). Self-regulation: Where metacognition and motivation intersect. In D. J. Hacker, J. Dunlosky, & A. C. Graesser (Eds.), *Handbook of metacognition in education* (pp. 299–315). New York, NY: Routledge.

CHAPTER 8

Adger, C. T., Wolfram, W., & Christian, D. (2007). *Dialects in schools and communities* (2nd ed.). New York, NY: Routledge.

Afflerbach, P., & Cho, B.-Y. (2010). Determining and describing reading strategies: Internet and traditional forms of reading. In H. S. Waters & W. Schneider (Eds.), *Metacognition, strategy use, and instruction* (pp. 201–225). New York, NY: Guilford Press.

Airasian, P. W. (1994). *Classroom assessment* (2nd ed.). New York, NY: McGraw-Hill.

Alexander, P. A., & the Disciplined Reading and Learning Research Laboratory (2012). Reading into the future: Competence for the 21st century. *Educational Psychologist, 47,* 259–280.

Alim, H. S., & Baugh, J. (Eds.). (2007). *Talkin Black talk: Language, education, and social change.* New York, NY: Teachers College Press.

Alleman, J., & Brophy, J. (1998). Strategic learning opportunities during out-of-school hours. *Social Studies and the Young Learner, 10*(4), 10–13.

Alleman, J., Knighton, B., Botwinski, B., Brophy, J., Ley, R., & Middlestead, S. (2010). *Homework done right: Powerful learning in real-life situations.* Thousand Oaks, CA: Corwin.

Allington, R. L., & Weber, R. (1993). Questioning questions in teaching and learning from texts. In B. K. Britton, A. Woodward, & M. Binkley (Eds.), *Learning from textbooks: Theory and practice* (pp. 47–68). Mahwah, NJ: Erlbaum.

Anderson, L. W., & Krathwohl, D. R. (Eds.). (2001). *A taxonomy for learning, teaching, and assessing: A revision of Bloom's taxonomy of educational objectives.* New York, NY: Longman.

Anderson, R. C., Nguyen-Jahiel, K., McNurlen, B., Archodidou, A., Kim, S.-Y., Reznitskaya, A., . . . Gilbert, L. (2001). The snowball phenomenon: Spread of ways of talking and ways of thinking across groups of children. *Cognition and Instruction, 19,* 1–46.

Andriessen, J. (2006). Arguing to learn. In R. K. Sawyer (Ed.), *The Cambridge handbook of the learning sciences* (pp. 443–459). Cambridge, England: Cambridge University Press.

Applebee, A. N., Langer, J. A., Nystrand, M., & Gamoran, A. (2003). Discussion-based approaches to developing understanding: Classroom instruction and student performance in middle and high school English. *American Educational Research Journal, 40,* 685–730.

Arlin, M. (1984). Time, equality, and mastery learning. *Review of Educational Research, 54,* 65–86.

Arnesen, T., Elstad, E., Christophersen, K.-A., & Vavik, L. (2014, April). *What significance does students' access to Internet in school have for their perseverance in academic work? An empirical analysis based on Nordic students.* Poster presented at the annual meeting of the American Educational Research Association, Philadelphia, PA.

Aulls, M. W. (1998). Contributions of classroom discourse to what content students learn during curriculum enactment. *Journal of Educational Psychology, 90,* 56–69.

Ausubel, D. P., Novak, J. D., & Hanesian, H. (1978). *Educational psychology: A cognitive view* (2nd ed.). New York, NY: Holt, Rinehart & Winston.

Azevedo, R., & Witherspoon, A. M. (2009). Self-regulated learning with hypermedia. In D. J. Hacker, J. Dunlosky, & A. C. Graesser (Eds.), *Handbook of metacognition in education* (pp. 319–339). New York, NY: Routledge.

Barab, S. A., Gresalfi, M., & Arici, A. (2009). Why educators should care about games. *Teaching for the 21st Century, 67*(1), 76–80.

Barab, S. A., Gresalfi, M., & Ingram-Goble, A. (2010). Transformational play: Using games to position person, content, and context. *Educational Researcher, 39,* 525–536.

Baroody, A. J., Eiland, M. D., Purpura, D. J., & Reid, E. E. (2013). Can computer-assisted discovery learning foster first graders' fluency with the most basic addition combinations? *American Educational Research Journal, 50,* 533–573.

Belfiore, P. J., & Hornyak, R. S. (1998). Operant theory and application to self-monitoring in adolescents. In D. H. Schunk & B. J. Zimmerman (Eds.), *Self-regulated learning: From teaching to self-reflective practice* (pp. 184–202). New York, NY: Guilford.

Bell, P., & Linn, M. C. (2002). Beliefs about science: How does science instruction contribute? In B. K. Hofer & P. R. Pintrich (Eds.), *Personal epistemology: The psychology of beliefs about knowledge and knowing* (pp. 321–346). Mahwah, NJ: Erlbaum.

Bellanca, J. A., & Stirling, T. (2011). *Classrooms without borders: Using Internet projects to teach communication and collaboration.* New York, NY: Teachers College Press.

Belland, B. R., Kim, C., & Hannafin, M. J. (2013). A framework for designing scaffolds that improve motivation and cognition. *Educational Psychologist, 48,* 243–270.

Benenson, J. F., Maiese, R., Dolenszky, E., Dolensky, N., Sinclair, N., & Simpson, A. (2002). Group size regulates self-assertive versus self-deprecating responses to interpersonal competition. *Child Development, 73,* 1818–1829.

Benware, C., & Deci, E. L. (1984). Quality of learning with an active versus passive motivational set. *American Educational Research Journal, 21,* 755–765.

Bereiter, C., & Scardamalia, M. (2006). Education for the Knowledge Age: Design-centered models of teaching and instruction. In P. A. Alexander & P. H. Winne (Eds.), *Handbook of educational psychology* (2nd ed., pp. 695–713). Mahwah, NJ: Erlbaum.

Biemiller, A., Shany, M., Inglis, A., & Meichenbaum, D. (1998). Factors influencing children's acquisition and demonstration of self-regulation on academic tasks. In D. H. Schunk & B. J. Zimmerman (Eds.), *Self-regulated learning: From teaching to self-reflective practice* (pp. 203–224). New York, NY: Guilford Press.

Bloom, B. S. (1981). *All our children learning.* New York, NY: McGraw-Hill.

Bloom, B. S., Englehart, M. D., Furst, E. J., Hill, W. H., & Krathwohl, D. R. (1956). *Taxonomy of educational objectives. The classification of educational goals: Handbook I. Cognitive domain.* New York, NY: David McKay.

Blumenfeld, P. C., Kempler, T. M., & Krajcik, J. S. (2006). Motivation and cognitive engagement in learning environments. In R. K. Sawyer (Ed.), *The Cambridge handbook of the learning sciences* (pp. 475–488). Cambridge, England: Cambridge University Press.

Blumenfeld, P. C., Marx, R. W., Soloway, E., & Krajcik, J. (1996). Learning with peers: From small group cooperation to collaborative communities. *Educational Researcher, 25*(8), 37–40.

Boyle, J. R., Forchelli, G. A., & Cariss, K. (2015). Note-taking interventions to assist students with disabilities in content area classes. *Preventing School Failure, 59,* 186–195.

Brophy, J. E. (2006). Observational research on generic aspects of classroom teaching. In P. A. Alexander & P. H. Winne (Eds.), *Handbook of educational psychology* (2nd ed., pp. 755–780). Mahwah, NJ: Erlbaum.

Brophy, J. (2008). Developing students' appreciation for what is taught in school. *Educational Psychologist, 43,* 132–141.

Brophy, J. E., Alleman, J., & Knighton, B. (2009). *Inside the social studies classroom.* New York, NY: Routledge.

Bulgren, J. A., Deshler, D. D., Schumaker, J. B., & Lenz, B. K. (2000). The use and effectiveness of analogical instruction in diverse secondary content classrooms. *Journal of Educational Psychology, 92,* 426–441.

Calderhead, J. (1996). Teachers: Beliefs and knowledge. In D. C. Berliner & R. C. Calfee (Eds.), *Handbook of educational psychology* (pp. 709–725). New York, NY: Macmillan.

Carhill, A., Suárez-Orozco, C., & Páez, M. (2008). Explaining English language proficiency among adolescent immigrant students. *American Educational Research Journal, 45,* 1045–1079.

Carney, R. N., & Levin, J. R. (2002). Pictorial illustrations *still* improve students' learning from text. *Educational Psychology Review, 14,* 5–26.

Carr, N. (2011). *The shallows: What the Internet is doing to our brains.* New York, NY: W. W. Norton.

Castagno, A. E., & Brayboy, B. M. J. (2008). Culturally responsive schooling for Indigenous youth: A review of the literature. *Review of Educational Research, 78,* 941–993.

Celio, C. I., Durlak, J., & Dymnicki, A. (2011). A meta-analysis of the impact of service-learning on students. *Journal of Experiential Education, 34,* 164–181.

Certo, J. (2011). Social skills and leadership abilities among children in small group literature discussions. *Journal of Research in Childhood Education, 25*(1), 62–81.

Charity, A. H., Scarborough, H. S., & Griffin, D. M. (2004). Familiarity with school English in African American children and its relation to early reading achievement. *Child Development, 75,* 1340–1356.

Chi, M. T. H., & Wylie, R. (2014). The ICAP framework: Linking cognitive engagement to active learning outcomes. *Educational Psychologist, 49,* 219–243.

Chiu, M. M. (2008). Effects of argumentation on group microcreativity: Statistical discourse analyses of algebra students' collaborative problem solving. *Contemporary Educational Psychology, 33,* 382–402.

Clark, A.-M., Anderson, R. C., Kuo, L., Kim, I., Archodidou, A., & Nguyen-Jahiel, K. (2003). Collaborative reasoning: Expanding ways for children to talk and think in school. *Educational Psychology Review, 15,* 181–198.

Clark, R. E., Feldon, D. F., van Merriënboer, J. J. G., Yates, K. A., & Early, S. (2008). Cognitive task analysis. In J. M. Spector, M. D. Merrill, J. van Merriënboer, & M. P. Driscoll (Eds.), *Handbook of research on educational communications and technology* (3rd ed., pp. 577–593). New York, NY: Routledge.

Clark, R. E., Yates, K., Early, S., & Moulton, K. (2009). An analysis of the failure of electronic media and discovery-based learning: Evidence for the performance benefits of guided training methods. In K. H. Silber & R. Foshay (Eds.), *Handbook of training and improving workplace performance: Vol. 1. Instructional design and training delivery* (pp. 263–297). New York, NY: Wiley.

Clement, J. (2008). The role of explanatory models in teaching for conceptual change. In S. Vosniadou (Ed.), *International handbook of research on conceptual change* (pp. 417–452). New York, NY: Routledge.

Cobb, P., Wood, T., Yackel, E., Nicholls, J., Wheatley, G., Trigatti, B., & Perlwitz, M. (1991). Assessment of a problem centered second-grade mathematics project. *Journal for Research in Mathematics Education, 22,* 3–29.

Cohen, E. G. (1994). Restructuring the classroom: Conditions for productive small groups. *Review of Educational Research, 64,* 1–35.

Cole, N. S. (1990). Conceptions of educational achievement. *Educational Researcher, 19*(3), 2–7.

Collins, A., & Halverson, R. (2009). *Rethinking education in the age of technology: The digital revolution and schooling in America.* New York, NY: Teachers College Press.

Comeau, L., Cormier, P., Grandmaison, É., & Lacroix, D. (1999). A longitudinal study of phonological processing skills in children learning to read in a second language. *Journal of Educational Psychology, 91,* 29–43.

Connolly, F. W., & Eisenberg, T. E. (1990). The feedback classroom: Teaching's silent friend. *T.H.E. Journal, 17*(5), 75–77.

Connor, C. M., Piasta, S. B., Fishman, B., Glasney, S., Schatschneider, C., Crowe, E., . . . Morrison, F. J. (2009). Individualizing student instruction precisely: Effects of child X instruction interactions on first graders' literacy development. *Child Development, 80,* 77–100.

Cooper, H. (1989). Synthesis of research on homework. *Educational Leadership, 47*(3), 85–91.

Cooper, H., Robinson, J. C., & Patall, E. A. (2006). Does homework improve academic achievement? A synthesis of research, 1987–2003. *Review of Educational Research, 76,* 1–62.

Cooper, H., & Valentine, J. C. (2001). Using research to answer practical questions about homework. *Educational Psychologist, 36,* 143–153.

Corkill, A. J. (1992). Advance organizers: Facilitators of recall. *Educational Psychology Review, 4,* 33–67.

Corno, L. (1996). Homework is a complicated thing. *Educational Researcher, 25*(8), 27–30.

Corno, L. (2008). On teaching adaptively. *Educational Psychologist, 43,* 161–173.

Correa-Chávez, M., Rogoff, B., & Mejía Arauz, R. (2005). Cultural patterns in attending to two events at once. *Child Development, 76,* 664–678.

Cosden, M., Morrison, G., Albanese, A. L., & Macias, S. (2001). When homework is not home work: After-school programs for homework assistance. *Educational Psychologist, 36,* 211–221.

Crago, M. B., Annahatak, B., & Ningiuruvik, L. (1993). Changing patterns of language socialization in Inuit homes. *Anthropology and Education Quarterly, 24,* 205–223.

Crook, C. (1995). On resourcing a concern for collaboration within peer interactions. *Cognition and Instruction, 13,* 541–547.

Cummins, J. (2000). *Language, power, and pedagogy: Bilingual children in the crossfire.* Clevedon, England: Multilingual Matters.

Cummins, J. (2008). BICS and CALP: Empirical and theoretical status of the distinction. In B. Street & N. H. Hornberger (Eds.), *Encyclopedia of language and education* (2nd ed., Vol. 2, pp. 71–83). New York, NY: Springer.

Cushing, L. S., & Kennedy, C. H. (1997). Academic effects of providing peer support in general education classrooms on students without disabilities. *Journal of Applied Behavior Analysis, 30,* 139–151.

Dansereau, D. F. (1995). Derived structural schemas and the transfer of knowledge. In A. McKeough, J. Lupart, & A. Marini (Eds.), *Teaching for transfer: Fostering generalization in learning* (pp. 93–122). Mahwah, NJ: Erlbaum.

Davidson, C. N. (2011). *Now you see it: How the brain science of attention will transform the way we live, work, and learn.* New York, NY: Viking.

de Jong, T. (2011). Instruction based on computer simulations. In R. E. Mayer & P. A. Alexander (Eds.), *Handbook of research on learning and instruction* (pp. 446–466). New York, NY: Routledge.

DeBose, C. E. (2007). The Ebonics phenomenon, language planning, and the hegemony of Standard English. In H. S. Alim & J. Baugh (Eds.), *Talkin Black talk: Language, education, and social change* (pp. 30–42). New York, NY: Teachers College Press.

Delgado-Gaitan, C. (1994). Socializing young children in Mexican-American families: An intergenerational perspective. In P. M. Greenfield & R. R. Cocking (Eds.), *Cross-cultural roots of minority child development* (pp. 55–86). Mahwah, NJ: Erlbaum.

Dettmers, S., Trautwein, U., Lüdtke, O., Goetz, T., Frenzel, A. C., & Pekrun, R. (2011). Students' emotions during homework in mathematics: Testing a theoretical model of antecedents and achievement outcomes. *Contemporary Educational Psychology, 36,* 25–35.

Dettmers, S., Trautwein, U., Lüktke, O., Kunter, M., & Baumert, J. (2010). Homework works if homework quality is high: Using multilevel modeling to predict the development of achievement in mathematics. *Journal of Educational Psychology, 102,* 467–482.

Deutsch, M. (1993). Educating for a peaceful world. *American Psychologist, 48,* 510–517.

Dixon, L. Q., Zhao, J., Shin, J.-Y., Wu, S., Su, J.-H., Burgess-Brigham, R., . . . Snow, C. (2012). What we know about second language acquisition: A synthesis from four perspectives. *Review of Educational Research, 82,* 5–60.

Duff, P. A. (2001). Language, literacy, content, and (pop) culture: Challenges for ESL students in mainstream courses. *Canadian Modern Language Review, 58*(1), 103–132.

Duke, N. K. (2000). For the rich it's richer: Print experiences and environments offered to children in very low- and very high-socioeconomic status first-grade classrooms. *American Educational Research Journal, 37,* 441–478.

Dumont, H., Trautwein, U., Lüdtke, O., Neumann, M., Niggli, A., & Schnyder, I. (2012). Does parental homework involvement mediate the relationship between family background and educational outcomes? *Contemporary Educational Psychology, 55–69.*

DuPaul, G. J., Ervin, R. A., Hook, C. L., & McGoey, K. E. (1998). Peer tutoring for children with attention deficit hyperactivity disorder: Effects on classroom behavior and academic performance. *Journal of Applied Behavior Analysis, 31,* 579–592.

Dymond, S. K., Renzaglia, A., & Chun, E. (2007). Elements of effective high school service learning programs that include students with and without disabilities. *Remedial and Special Education, 28,* 227–243.

Edmonds, M. S., Vaughn, S., Wexler, J., Reutebuch, C., Cable, A., Tackett, K. K., & Schnakenberg, J. W. (2009). A synthesis of reading interventions and effects of reading comprehension outcomes for older struggling students. *Review of Educational Research, 79,* 262–300.

Egbert, J. (2009). *Supporting learning with technology: Essentials of classroom practice.* Upper Saddle River, NJ: Pearson/Merrill Prentice Hall.

Eilam, B. (2001). Primary strategies for promoting homework performance. *American Educational Research Journal, 38,* 691–725.

Eisenberg, N., Martin, C. L., & Fabes, R. A. (1996). Gender development and gender effects. In D. C. Berliner & R. C. Calfee (Eds.), *Handbook of educational psychology* (pp. 358–396). New York, NY: Macmillan.

Esmonde, I. (2009). Ideas and identities: Supporting equity in cooperative mathematics learning. *Review of Educational Research, 79,* 1008–1043.

Espinosa, L. (2007). English-language learners as they enter school. In R. Pianta, M. Cox, & K. Snow (Eds.), *School readiness and the transition to kindergarten in the era of accountability* (pp. 175–196). Baltimore, MD: Brookes.

Eysink, T. H. S., & de Jong, T. (2012). Does instructional approach matter? How elaboration plays a crucial role in multimedia learning. *Journal of the Learning Sciences, 21,* 583–625.

Fairchild, H. H., & Edwards-Evans, S. (1990). African American dialects and schooling: A review. In A. M. Padilla, H. H. Fairchild, & C. M. Valadez (Eds.), *Bilingual education: Issues and strategies* (pp. 75–85). Newbury Park, CA: Sage.

Fantuzzo, J. W., King, J., & Heller, L. R. (1992). Effects of reciprocal peer tutoring on mathematics and school adjustment: A component analysis. *Journal of Educational Psychology, 84,* 331–339.

Farber, B., Mindel, C. H., & Lazerwitz, B. (1988). The Jewish American family. In C. H. Mindel, R. W. Habenstein, & R. Wright (Eds.), *Ethnic families in America: Patterns and variations* (pp. 350–385). New York, NY: Elsevier.

Fennema, E. (1987). Sex-related differences in education: Myths, realities, and interventions. In V. Richardson-Koehler (Ed.), *Educators' handbook: A research perspective* (pp. 329–347). White Plains, NY: Longman.

Ferguson, E. L., & Hegarty, M. (1995). Learning with real machines or diagrams: Application of knowledge to real-world problems. *Cognition and Instruction, 13*, 129–160.

Ferguson, R. (1998). Can schools narrow the Black-White test score gap? In C. Jencks & M. Phillips (Eds.), *The Black-White test score gap* (pp. 318–374). Washington, DC: Brookings Institute.

Finn, J. D., Pannozzo, G. M., & Achilles, C. M. (2003). The "why's" of class size: Student behavior in small classes. *Review of Educational Research, 73*, 321–368.

Fox, P. W., & LeCount, J. (1991, April). *When more is less: Faculty misestimation of student learning.* Paper presented at the annual meeting of the American Educational Research Association, Chicago, IL.

Fries, S., Dietz, F., & Schmid, S. (2008). Motivational interference in learning: The impact of leisure alternatives on subsequent self-regulation. *Contemporary Educational Psychology, 33,* 119–133.

Fuchs, L. S., Compton, D. L., Fuchs, D., Paulsen, K., Bryant, J. D., & Hamlett, C. L. (2005). The prevention, identification, and cognitive determinants of math difficulty. *Journal of Educational Psychology, 97*, 493–513.

Fuchs, L. S., Fuchs, D., Karns, K., Hamlett, C. L., Dutka, S., & Katzaroff, M. (1996). The relation between student ability and the quality and effectiveness of explanations. *American Educational Research Journal, 33*, 631–664.

Fueyo, V., & Bushell, D., Jr. (1998). Using number line procedures and peer tutoring to improve the mathematics computation of low-performing first graders. *Journal of Applied Behavior Analysis, 31*, 417–430.

Garbe, G., & Guy, D. (2006, Summer). No homework left behind. *Educational Leadership* (online issue). Retrieved from the Association for Supervision and Curriculum Development website: http://www.ascd.org/portal/site/ascd/menuitem.459dee008f99653fb85516f762108a0c

Garcia, E. E. (1995). Educating Mexican American students: Past treatment and recent developments in theory, research, policy, and practice. In J. A. Banks & C. A. M. Banks (Eds.), *Handbook of research on multicultural education* (pp. 372–387). New York, NY: Macmillan.

Garcia, E. E., & Jensen, B. (2009). Early educational opportunities for children of Hispanic origins. *Social Policy Report, 23*(2), 3–19.

Gay, G. (2010). *Culturally responsive teaching: Theory, research, and practice* (2nd ed.). New York, NY: Teachers College Press.

Gayford, C. (1992). Patterns of group behavior in open-ended problem solving in science classes of 15-year-old students in England. *International Journal of Science Education, 14*, 41–49.

Gehlbach, H., Brown, S. W., Ioannou, A., Boyer, M. A., Hudson, N., Niv-Solomon, A., . . . Janik, L. (2008). Increasing interest in social studies: Social perspective taking and self-efficacy in stimulating stimulations. *Contemporary Educational Psychology, 33,* 894–914.

Gillies, R. M., & Ashman, A. D. (1998). Behavior and interactions of children in cooperative groups in lower and middle elementary grades. *Journal of Educational Psychology, 90*, 746–757.

Gilliland, H. (1988). Discovering and emphasizing the positive aspects of the culture. In H. Gilliland & J. Reyhner (Eds.), *Teaching the Native American* (pp. 21–36). Dubuque, IA: Kendall/Hunt.

Ginsburg-Block, M. D., Rohrbeck, C. A., & Fantuzzo, J. W. (2006). A meta-analytic review of social, self-concept, and behavioral outcomes of peer-assisted learning. *Journal of Educational Psychology, 98*, 732–749.

Godley, A., & Escher, A. (2011, April). *Bidialectical African-American students' views on code-switching in and out of school.* Paper presented at the annual meeting of the American Educational Research Association, New Orleans, LA.

Good, T. L., McCaslin, M. M., & Reys, B. J. (1992). Investigating work groups to promote problem solving in mathematics. In J. Brophy (Ed.), *Advances in research on teaching: Vol. 3. Planning and managing learning tasks and activities* (pp. 115–160). Greenwich, CT: JAI.

Graesser, A., D'Mello, S., & Cade, W. (2011). Instruction based on tutoring. In R. E. Mayer & P. A. Alexander (Eds.), *Handbook of research on learning and instruction* (pp. 408–426). New York, NY: Routledge.

Graesser, A. C., Li, H., & Forsyth, C. (2014). Learning by communicating in natural language with conversational agents. *Current Directions in Psychological Science, 23,* 374–380.

Graesser, A., & Person, N. K. (1994). Question asking during tutoring. *American Educational Research Journal, 31*, 104–137.

Grant, C. A., & Gomez, M. L. (2001). *Campus and classroom: Making schooling multicultural* (2nd ed.). Upper Saddle River, NJ: Merrill/Prentice Hall.

Greaves, T. W., Hayes, J., Wilson, L., Gielniak, M., & Peterson, E. L. (2012). *Revolutionizing education through technology: The Project RED roadmap for transformation.* Eugene, OR: International Society for Technology in Education.

Greenwood, C. R. (1991). Classwide peer tutoring: Longitudinal effects on the reading, language, and mathematics achievement of at-risk students. *Journal of Reading, Writing, and Learning Disabilities International*, 7(2), 105–123.

Greenwood, C. R., Carta, J. J., & Hall, R. V. (1988). The use of peer tutoring strategies in classroom management and educational instruction. *School Psychology Review, 17*, 258–275.

Gronlund, N. E., & Brookhart, S. M. (2009). *Writing instructional objectives* (8th ed.). Upper Saddle River, NJ: Merrill/Pearson.

Guskey, T. R. (1985). *Implementing mastery learning.* Belmont, CA: Wadsworth.

Guskey, T. R. (2010). Formative assessment: The contributions of Benjamin S. Bloom. In H. L. Andrade & G. J. Cizek (Eds.), *Handbook of formative assessment* (pp. 106–124). New York, NY: Routledge.

Gutiérrez, K. D., & Rogoff, B. (2003). Cultural ways of learning: Individual traits or repertoires of practice. *Educational Researcher, 32*(5), 19–25.

Hadjioannou, X. (2007). Bringing the background to the foreground: What do classroom environments that support authentic discussions look like? *American Educational Research Journal, 44*, 370–399.

Hale-Benson, J. E. (1986). *Black children: Their roots, culture, and learning styles.* Baltimore, MD: Johns Hopkins University Press.

Harris, K. R., & Alexander, P. A. (1998). Integrated, constructivist education: Challenge and reality. *Educational Psychology Review, 10*, 115–127.

Hartley, J., & Trueman, M. (1982). The effects of summaries on the recall of information from prose: Five experimental studies. *Human Learning, 1*, 63–82.

Hatano, G., & Inagaki, K. (2003). When is conceptual change intended? A cognitive-sociocultural view. In G. M. Sinatra & P. R. Pintrich (Eds.), *Intentional conceptual change* (pp. 407–427). Mahwah, NJ: Erlbaum.

Hattie, J. A. C. (2009). *Visible learning: A synthesis of over 800 meta-analyses relating to achievement.* London, England: Routledge.

Hattie, J. A. C., & Gan, M. (2011). Instruction based on feedback. In R. E. Mayer & P. A. Alexander (Eds.), *Handbook of research on learning and instruction* (pp. 249–271). New York, NY: Routledge.

Heath, S. B. (1989). Oral and literate traditions among Black Americans living in poverty. *American Psychologist, 44*, 367–373.

Herrell, A., & Jordan, M. (2004). *Fifty strategies for teaching English language learners* (2nd ed.). Upper Saddle River, NJ: Merrill/Prentice Hall.

Herrenkohl, L. R., & Guerra, M. R. (1998). Participant structures, scientific discourse, and student engagement in fourth grade. *Cognition and Instruction, 16*, 431–473.

Hewitt, J., & Scardamalia, M. (1998). Design principles for distributed knowledge building processes. *Educational Psychology Review, 10*, 75–96.

Hiebert, J., Carpenter, T. P., Fennema, E., Fuson, K. C., Wearne, D., Murray, H., . . . Human, P. (1997). *Making sense: Teaching and learning mathematics with understanding.* Portsmouth, NH: Heinemann.

Hiebert, J., & Wearne, D. (1996). Instruction, understanding, and skill in multidigit addition and subtraction. *Cognition and Instruction, 14*, 251–283.

Hogan, K., Nastasi, B. K., & Pressley, M. (2000). Discourse patterns and collaborative scientific reasoning in peer and teacher-guided discussions. *Cognition and Instruction, 17*, 379–432.

Hoover-Dempsey, K. V., Battiato, A. C., Walker, J. M. T., Reed, R. P., DeJong, J. M., & Jones, K. P. (2001). Parental involvement in homework. *Educational Psychologist, 36*, 195–209.

Hulit, L. M., & Howard, M. R. (2006). *Born to talk* (4th ed.). Boston, MA: Allyn & Bacon.

Igoa, C. (1995). *The inner world of the immigrant child.* Mahwah, NJ: Erlbaum.

Inglis, A., & Biemiller, A. (1997, March). *Fostering self-direction in mathematics: A cross-age tutoring program that enhances math problem solving.* Paper presented at the annual meeting of the American Educational Research Association, Chicago, IL.

Iran-Nejad, A., & Stewart, W. (2010). Understanding as an educational objective: From seeking and playing with taxonomies to discovering and reflecting on revelations. *Research in the Schools, 17,* 64–76.

Jadallah, M., Anderson, R. C., Nguyen-Jahiel, K., Miller, B. W., Kim, I.-H., Kuo, L.-J., . . . Wu, X. (2011). Influence of a teacher's scaffolding moves during child-led small-group discussions. *American Educational Research Journal, 48,* 194–230.

Janzen, J. (2008). Teaching English language learners in the content areas. *Review of Educational Research, 78,* 1010–1038.

Jeong, H., & Hmelo-Silver, C. E. (2016). Seven affordances of computer-supported collaborative learning: How to support collaborative learning? How can technologies help? *Educational Psychologist, 51,* 247–265.

Johnson, D. W., & Johnson, R. T. (1991). *Learning together and alone: Cooperative, competitive, and individualistic learning* (3rd ed.). Upper Saddle River, NJ: Prentice Hall.

Johnson, D. W., & Johnson, R. T. (2009a). An educational psychology success story: Social interdependence theory and cooperative learning. *Educational Researcher, 38,* 365–379.

Johnson, D. W., & Johnson, R. T. (2009b). Energizing learning: The instructional power of conflict. *Educational Researcher, 38,* 37–51.

Jonassen, D. H., Hannum, W. H., & Tessmer, M. (1989). *Handbook of task analysis procedures.* New York, NY: Praeger.

Kafai, Y. B., & Dede, C. (2014). Learning in virtual worlds. In R. K. Sawyer (Ed.), *The Cambridge handbook of the learning sciences* (2nd ed., pp. 522–542). New York, NY: Cambridge University Press.

Kafai, Y. B., & Fields, D. A. (2013). *Connected play: Tweens in a virtual world.* Cambridge, MA: MIT Press.

Kağitçibaşi, Ç. (2007). *Family, self, and human development across cultures: Theory and applications* (2nd ed.). Mahwah, NJ: Erlbaum.

Kalyuga, S., & Sweller, J. (2004). Measuring knowledge to optimize cognitive load factors during instruction. *Journal of Educational Psychology, 96*, 558–568.

Kanar, A. M., & Bell, B. S. (2013). Guiding learners through technology-based instruction: The effects of adaptive guidance design and individual differences on learning over time. *Journal of Educational Psychology, 105,* 1067–1081.

Karau, S. J., & Williams, K. D. (1995). Social loafing: Research findings, implications, and future directions. *Current Directions in Psychological Science, 4*, 134–140.

Karich, A. C., Burns, M. K., & Maki, K. E. (2014). Updated meta-analysis of learner control within educational technology. *Review of Educational Research, 84,* 392–410.

Kermani, H., & Moallem, M. (1997, March). *Cross-age tutoring: Exploring features and processes of peer-mediated learning.* Paper presented at the annual meeting of the American Educational Research Association, Chicago, IL.

King, A. (1997). ASK to THINK—TEL WHY®©: A model of transactive peer tutoring for scaffolding higher level complex learning. *Educational Psychologist, 32*, 221–235.

King, A. (1998). Transactive peer tutoring: Distributing cognition and metacognition. *Educational Psychology Review, 10*, 57–74

King, A. (1999). Discourse patterns for mediating peer learning. In A. M. O'Donnell & A. King (Eds.), *Cognitive perspectives on peer learning* (pp. 87–115). Mahwah, NJ: Erlbaum.

King, A., Staffieri, A., & Adelgais, A. (1998). Mutual peer tutoring: Effects of structuring tutorial interaction to scaffold peer learning. *Journal of Educational Psychology, 90*, 134–152.

Kirschner, F., Paas, F., & Kirschner, P. A. (2009). A cognitive load approach to collaborative learning: United brains for complex tasks. *Educational Psychology Review, 21,* 31–42.

Kirschner, P. A., & van Merriënboer, J. J. G. (2013). Do learners really know best? Urban legends in education. *Educational Psychologist, 48,* 169–183.

Krashen, S. D. (1996). *Under attack: The case against bilingual education.* Culver City, CA: Language Education Associates.

Kreijns, K., Kirschner, P. A., & Vermeulen, M. (2013). Social aspects of CSCL environments: A research framework. *Educational Psychologist, 48,* 229–242.

Ku, Y.-M., Chan, W.-C., Wu, Y.-C., & Chen, Y.-H. (2008, March). *Improving children's comprehension of science text: Effects of adjunct questions and notetaking.* Paper presented at the annual meeting of the American Educational Research Association, New York, NY.

Kuhn, D. (2015). Thinking together and alone. *Educational Researcher, 44,* 46–53.

Kuhn, D., & Pease, M. (2008). What needs to develop in the development of inquiry skills? *Cognition and Instruction, 26,* 512–599.

Kulik, C. C., Kulik, J. A., & Bangert-Drowns, R. L. (1990). Effectiveness of mastery learning programs: A meta-analysis. *Review of Educational Research, 60*, 265–299.

Kulik, J. A., & Fletcher, J. D. (2016). Effectiveness of intelligent tutoring systems: A meta-analytic review. *Review of Educational Research, 86,* 42–78.

Ladd, G. W., Kochenderfer-Ladd, B., Visconti, K. J., & Ettekal, I. (2012). Classroom peer relations and children's social and scholastic development. In A. M. Ryan & G. W. Ladd (Eds.), *Peer relationships and adjustment at school* (pp. 11–49). Charlotte, NC: Information Age.

Lambert, M. C., Cartledge, G., Heward, W. L., & Lo, Y.-Y. (2006). Effects of response cards on disruptive behavior and academic responding during math lessons by fourth-grade urban students. *Journal of Positive Behavioral Interventions, 8,* 88–99.

Lampert, M. (1990). When the problem is not the question and the solution is not the answer: Mathematical knowing and teaching. *American Educational Research Journal, 27,* 29–63.

Lampert, M., Rittenhouse, P., & Crumbaugh, C. (1996). Agreeing to disagree: Developing sociable mathematical discourse. In D. R. Olson & N. Torrance (Eds.), *The handbook of education and human development: New models of learning, teaching, and schooling* (pp. 731–764). Cambridge, MA: Blackwell.

Lee, B. K., Patall, E. A., Cawthon, S. W., & Steingut, R. R. (2015). The effect of drama-based pedagogy on preK–16 outcomes: A meta-analysis of research from 1985 to 2012. *Review of Educational Research, 85,* 3–49.

Leinhardt, G. (1994). History: A time to be mindful. In G. Leinhardt, I. L. Beck, & C. Stainton (Eds.), *Teaching and learning in history* (pp. 209–255). Mahwah, NJ: Erlbaum.

Leung, K. C. (2015). Preliminary empirical model of crucial determinants of best practice for peer tutoring on academic achievement. *Journal of Educational Psychology, 107,* 558–579.

Levin, J. R., & Mayer, R. E. (1993). Understanding illustrations in text. In B. K. Britton, A. Woodward, & M. Binkley (Eds.), *Learning from textbooks: Theory and practice* (pp. 95–113). Mahwah, NJ: Erlbaum.

Levy, I., Kaplan, A., & Patrick, H. (2000, April). *Early adolescents' achievement goals, intergroup processes, and attitudes towards collaboration.* Paper presented at the annual meeting of the American Educational Research Association, New Orleans, LA.

Li, J., & Fischer, K. W. (2004). Thought and affect in American and Chinese learners' beliefs about learning. In D. Y. Dai & R. J. Sternberg (Eds.), *Motivation, emotion, and cognition: Integrative perspectives on intellectual functioning and development* (pp. 385–418). Mahwah, NJ: Erlbaum.

Lillemyr, O. F., Søbstad, F., Marder, K., & Flowerday, T. (2010). Indigenous and non-Indigenous primary school students' attitudes on play, humour, learning and self-concept: A comparative perspective. *European Early Childhood Education Research Journal, 18,* 243–267.

Linn, M. C. (2008). Teaching for conceptual change: Distinguish or extinguish ideas. In S. Vosniadou (Ed.), *International handbook on conceptual change* (pp. 694–722). New York, NY: Routledge.

Linn, M. C., & Eylon, B.-S. (2011). *Science learning and instruction: Taking advantage of technology to promote knowledge integration.* New York, NY: Routledge.

Linnenbrink-Garcia, L., Rogat, T. K., & Koskey, K. L. K. (2011). Affect and engagement during small group instruction. *Contemporary Educational Psychology, 36,* 13–24.

Liu, L. G. (1990, April). *The use of causal questioning to promote narrative comprehension and memory.* Paper presented at the annual meeting of the American Educational Research Association, Boston, MA.

Lorch, R. F., Jr., Lorch, E. P., & Inman, W. E. (1993). Effects of signaling topic structure on text recall. *Journal of Educational Psychology, 85,* 281–290.

Lotan, R. A. (2006). Managing groupwork in heterogeneous classrooms. In C. M. Evertson & C. S. Weinstein (Eds.), *Handbook of classroom management: Research, practice, and contemporary issues* (pp. 525–539). Mahwah, NJ: Erlbaum.

Lou, Y., Abrami, P. C., Spence, J. C., Poulsen, C., Chambers, B., & d'Apollonia, S. (1996). Within-class grouping: A meta-analysis. *Review of Educational Research, 66,* 423–458.

Ma, W., Adesope, O. O., Nesbit, J. C., & Liu, Q. (2014). Intelligent tutoring systems and learning outcomes: A meta-analysis. *Journal of Educational Psychology, 106,* 901–918.

Mac Iver, D. J., Reuman, D. A., & Main, S. R. (1995). Social structuring of the school: Studying what is, illuminating what could be. In J. T. Spence, J. M. Darley, & D. J. Foss (Eds.), *Annual review of psychology* (Vol. 46, pp. 375–400). Palo Alto, CA: Annual Review.

Maccoby, E. E. (2002). Gender and group process: A developmental perspective. *Current Directions in Psychological Science, 11,* 54–58.

Macfarlane, A., Webber, M., Cookson-Cox, C., & McRae, H. (2014). *Ka Awatea: An iwi case study of Māori students' success* (Report to Ngā Pae o te Māramatanga). Christchurch, New Zealand: Māori Research Laboratory, University of Canterbury.

MacLean, D. J., Sasse, D. K., Keating, D. P., Stewart, B. E., & Miller, F. K. (1995, April). *All-girls' mathematics and science instruction in early adolescence: Longitudinal effects.* Paper presented at the annual meeting of the American Educational Research Association, San Francisco, CA.

Marsh, H. W., Hau, K.-T., & Kong, C.-K. (2002). Multilevel causal ordering of academic self-concept and achievement: Influence of language of instruction (English compared with Chinese) for Hong Kong students. *American Educational Research Journal, 39,* 727–763.

Marzano, R. J., & Kendall, J. S. (2007). *The new taxonomy of educational objectives* (2nd ed.). Thousand Oaks, CA: Corwin.

Mathes, P. G., Torgesen, J. K., & Allor, J. H. (2001). The effects of peer-assisted literacy strategies for first-grade readers with and without additional computer-assisted instruction. *American Educational Research Journal, 38,* 371–410.

Mayer, R. E. (2010b). Merlin C. Wittrock's enduring contributions to the science of learning. *Educational Psychologist, 45,* 46–50.

Mayer, R. E. (2011a). *Applying the science of learning.* Boston, MA: Allyn and Bacon.

Mayer, R. E., & Gallini, J. (1990). When is an illustration worth ten thousand words? *Journal of Educational Psychology, 82,* 715–726.

McAshan, H. H. (1979). *Competency-based education and behavioral objectives.* Englewood Cliffs, NJ: Educational Technology.

McClelland, J. L. (2001). Failures to learn and their remediation: A Hebbian account. In J. L. McClelland & R. S. Siegler (Eds.), *Mechanisms of cognitive development: Behavioral and neural perspectives* (pp. 97–121). Mahwah, NJ: Erlbaum.

McDaniel, M. A., & Einstein, G. O. (1989). Material-appropriate processing: A contextualist approach to reading and studying strategies. *Educational Psychology Review, 1,* 113–145.

McDevitt, M., & Chaffee, S. H. (1998). Second chance political socialization: "Trickle-up" effects of children on parents. In T. J. Johnson, C. E. Hays, & S. P. Hays (Eds.), *Engaging the public: How government and the media can reinvigorate American democracy* (pp. 57–66). Lanham, MD: Rowman & Littlefield.

McDevitt, M., & Chaffee, S. H. (2002). From top-down to trickle-up influence: Revisiting assumptions about the family in political socialization. *Political Communication, 19,* 281–301.

McDevitt, M., & Kiousis, S. (2006). Deliberative learning: An evaluative approach to interactive civic education. *Communication Education, 55,* 247–264.

McGee, L. M. (1992). An exploration of meaning construction in first graders' grand conversations. In C. K. Kinzer & D. J. Leu (Eds.), *Literacy research, theory, and practice: Views from many perspectives* (pp. 177–186). Chicago, IL: National Reading Conference.

Meece, J. L. (1994). The role of motivation in self-regulated learning. In D. H. Schunk & B. J. Zimmerman (Eds.), *Self-regulation of learning and performance: Issues and educational applications* (pp. 25–44). Mahwah, NJ: Erlbaum.

Mehan, H. (1979). *Social organization in the classroom.* Cambridge, MA: Harvard University Press.

Merrill, P. F., Hammons, K., Vincent, B. R., Reynolds, P. L., Christensen, L., & Tolman, M. N. (1996). *Computers in education* (3rd ed.). Boston, MA: Allyn & Bacon.

Miller, M. D., Linn, R. L., & Gronlund, N. E. (2009). *Measurement and assessment in teaching* (10th ed.). Upper Saddle River, NJ: Merrill/Pearson.

Minstrell, J., & Stimpson, V. (1996). A classroom environment for learning: Guiding students' reconstruction of understanding and reasoning. In L. Schauble & R. Glaser (Eds.), *Innovations in learning: New environments for education* (pp. 175–202). Mahwah, NJ: Erlbaum.

Miyake, N. (2008). Conceptual change through collaboration. In S. Vosniadou (Ed.), *International handbook of research on conceptual change* (pp. 453–478). New York, NY: Routledge.

Mohatt, G., & Erickson, F. (1981). Cultural differences in teaching styles in an Odawa school: A sociolinguistic approach. In H. T. Trueba, G. P. Guthrie, & K. H. Au (Eds.), *Culture and the bilingual classroom: Studies in classroom ethnography* (pp. 105–119). Rowley, MA: Newbury House.

Moje, E. B., & Shepardson, D. P. (1998). Social interactions and children's changing understanding of electric circuits: Exploring unequal power relations in "peer"-learning groups. In B. Guzzetti & C. Hynd (Eds.), *Perspectives on conceptual change: Multiple ways to understand knowing and learning in a complex world* (pp. 225–234). Mahwah, NJ: Erlbaum.

Morelli, G. A., & Rothbaum, F. (2007). Situating the child in context: Attachment relationships and self-regulation in different cultures. In S. Kitayama & D. Cohen (Eds.), *Handbook of cultural psychology* (pp. 500–527). New York, NY: Guilford Press.

Moreno, R. (2006). Learning in high-tech and multimedia environments. *Current Directions in Psychological Science, 15,* 63–67.

Munro, D. W., & Stephenson, J. (2009). The effects of response cards on student and teacher behavior during vocabulary instruction. *Journal of Applied Behavior Analysis, 42,* 795–800.

Murphy, P. K., Wilkinson, I. A. G., Soter, A. O., Hennessey, M. N., & Alexander, J. F. (2009). Examining the effects of classroom discussion on students' comprehension of text: A meta-analysis. *Journal of Educational Psychology, 101,* 740–764.

Newby, T. J., Ertmer, P. A., & Stepich, D. A. (1994, April). *Instructional analogies and the learning of concepts.* Paper presented at the annual meeting of the American Educational Research Association, New Orleans, LA.

Niederhauser, D. S. (2008). Educational hypertext. In J. M. Spector, M. D. Merrill, J. van Merriënboer, & M. P. Driscoll (Eds.), *Handbook of research on educational communications and technology* (3rd ed., pp. 199–210). New York, NY: Erlbaum.

Nixon, A. S. (2005, April). *Moral reasoning in the digital age: How students, teachers, and parents judge appropriate computer uses.* Paper presented at the annual meeting of the American Educational Research Association, Montreal, Quebec, Canada.

Nussbaum, E. M. (2008). Collaborative discourse, argumentation, and learning: Preface and literature review. *Contemporary Educational Psychology, 33,* 345–359.

Ochs, E. (1982). Talking to children in western Samoa. *Language and Society, 11,* 77–104.

O'Donnell, A. M. (1999). Structuring dyadic interaction through scripted cooperation. In A. M. O'Donnell & A. King (Eds.), *Cognitive perspectives on peer learning* (pp. 179–196). Mahwah, NJ: Erlbaum.

O'Donnell, A. M. (2006). The role of peers and group learning. In P. A. Alexander & P. H. Winne (Eds.), *Handbook of educational psychology* (2nd ed., pp. 781–802). Mahwah, NJ: Erlbaum.

O'Donnell, A. M., & O'Kelly, J. (1994). Learning from peers: Beyond the rhetoric of positive results. *Educational Psychology Review, 6,* 321–349.

Ogbu, J. U. (2003). *Black American students in an affluent suburb: A study of academic disengagement.* Mahwah, NJ: Erlbaum.

Owens, R. E., Jr. (1995). *Language disorders: A functional approach to assessment and intervention* (2nd ed.). Boston, MA: Allyn & Bacon.

Padilla, A. M. (2006). Second language learning: Issues in research and teaching. In P. A. Alexander & P. H. Winne (Eds.), *Handbook of educational psychology* (2nd ed., pp. 571–591). Mahwah, NJ: Erlbaum.

Patall, E. A., Cooper, H., & Wynn, S. R. (2010). The effectiveness and relative importance of choice in the classroom. *Journal of Educational Psychology, 102,* 896–915.

Pellegrino, J. W., Chudowsky, N., & Glaser, R. (Eds.). (2001). *Knowing what students know: The science and design of educational assessment.* Washington DC: National Academy Press.

Pfeifer, J. H., Brown, C. S., & Juvonen, J. (2007). Teaching tolerance in schools: Lessons learned since *Brown v. Board of Education* about the development and reduction of children's prejudice. *Social Policy Report, 21*(2), 3–13, 16–17, 20–23. Ann Arbor, MI: Society for Research in Child Development.

Pianta, R. C., & Hamre, B. K. (2009). Conceptualization, measurement, and improvement of classroom processes: Standardized observation can leverage capacity. *Educational Researcher, 38,* 109–119.

Pickens, J. (2006, Winter). "Poop study" engages primary students. *Volunteer Monitor* (National Newsletter of Volunteer Watershed Monitoring), *18*(1), 13, 21.

Plass, J. L., O'Keefe, P. A., Homer, B. D., Case, J., Hayward, E. O., Stein, M., & Perlin, K. (2013). The impact of individual, competitive, and collaborative mathematics game play on learning, performance, and motivation. *Journal of Educational Psychology, 105,* 1050–1066.

Popham, W. J. (1995). *Classroom assessment: What teachers need to know.* Boston, MA: Allyn & Bacon.

Portes, P. R. (1996). Ethnicity and culture in educational psychology. In D. C. Berliner & R. C. Calfee (Eds.), *Handbook of educational psychology* (pp. 331–357). New York, NY: Macmillan.

Redfield, D. L., & Rousseau, E. W. (1981). A meta-analysis of experimental research on teacher questioning behavior. *Review of Educational Research, 51,* 237–245.

Reynolds, R. E., & Shirey, L. L. (1988). The role of attention in studying and learning. In C. E. Weinstein, E. T. Goetz, & P. A. Alexander (Eds.), *Learning and study strategies: Issues in assessment, instruction, and evaluation* (pp. 77–100). San Diego, CA: Academic Press.

Reznitskaya, A., & Gregory, M. (2013). Student thought and classroom language: Examining the mechanisms of change in dialogic teaching. *Educational Psychologist, 48,* 114–133.

Rittle-Johnson, B. (2006). Promoting transfer: Effects of self-explanation and direct instruction. *Child Development*, *77*, 1–15.

Roberts, T. A. (2005). Articulation accuracy and vocabulary size contributions to phonemic awareness and word reading in English language learners. *Journal of Educational Psychology, 97,* 601–616.

Robinson, D. R., Schofield, J. W., & Steers-Wentzell, K. L. (2005). Peer and cross-age tutoring in math: Outcomes and their design implications. *Educational Psychology Review*, *17*, 327–362.

Rogoff, B. (2003). *The cultural nature of human development.* Oxford, England: Oxford University Press.

Rogoff, B. (2007, March). Cultural perspectives help us see developmental processes. In M. Gauvain & R. L. Munroe (Chairs), *Contributions of socio-historical theory and cross-cultural research to the study of child development.* Symposium conducted at the biennial meeting of the Society for Research in Child Development, Boston, MA.

Rohrbeck, C. A., Ginsburg-Block, M. D., Fantuzzo, J. W., & Miller, T. R. (2003). Peer-assisted learning interventions with elementary school students: A meta-analytic review. *Journal of Educational Psychology*, *95*, 240–257.

Roscoe, R. D., & Chi, M. T. H. (2007). Understanding tutor learning: Knowledge-building and knowledge-telling in peer tutors' explanations and questions. *Review of Educational Research, 77,* 534–574.

Rosenshine, B. (2009). The empirical support for direct instruction. In S. Tobias & T. M. Duffy (Eds.), *Constructivist instruction: Success or failure?* (pp. 201–220). New York, NY: Routledge.

Rosenshine, B., & Stevens, R. (1986). Teaching functions. In M. C. Wittrock (Ed.), *Handbook of research on teaching* (3rd ed., pp. 376–391). New York, NY: Macmillan.

Roth, W.-M. (2011). Object/motives and emotion: A cultural-historical activity theoretic approach to motivation in learning and work. In D. M. McInerney, R. A. Walker, & G. A. D. Liem (Eds.), *Sociocultural theories of learning and motivation: Looking back, looking forward* (pp. 43–63). Charlotte, NC: Information Age.

Sarama, J., & Clements, D. H. (2009). "Concrete" computer manipulatives in mathematics education. *Child Development Perspectives, 3,* 145–150.

Scardamalia, M., & Bereiter, C. (2006). Knowledge building: Theory, pedagogy, and technology. In R. K. Sawyer (Ed.), *The Cambridge handbook of the learning sciences* (pp. 97–115). New York, NY: Cambridge University Press.

Scardamalia, M., & Bereiter, C. (2014). Knowledge building and creation: Theory, pedagogy, and technology. In R. K. Sawyer (Ed.), *The Cambridge handbook of the learning sciences* (2nd ed., pp. 397–417). New York, NY: Cambridge University Press.

Scevak, J. J., Moore, P. J., & Kirby, J. R. (1993). Training students to use maps to increase text recall. *Contemporary Educational Psychology*, *18*, 401–413.

Schofield, J. W. (2006). Internet use in schools: Promise and problems. In R. K. Sawyer (Ed.), *The Cambridge handbook of the learning sciences* (pp. 521–534). Cambridge, England: Cambridge University Press.

Sfard, A. (1998). On two metaphors for learning and the dangers of choosing just one. *Educational Researcher*, *27*(2), 4–13.

Shuell, T. J. (1996). Teaching and learning in a classroom context. In D. C. Berliner & R. C. Calfee (Eds.), *Handbook of educational psychology* (pp. 726–764). New York, NY: Macmillan.

Sinatra, G. M., & Mason, L. (2008). Beyond knowledge: Learner characteristics influencing conceptual change. In S. Vosniadou (Ed.), *International handbook of research on conceptual change* (pp. 560–582). New York, NY: Routledge.

Slavin, R. E. (2011). Instruction based on cooperative learning. In R. E. Mayer & P. A. Alexander (Eds.), *Handbook of research on learning and instruction* (pp. 344–360). New York, NY: Routledge.

Slavin, R. E., & Cheung, A. (2005). A synthesis of research on language of reading instruction for English language learners. *Review of Educational Research, 75,* 247–284.

Slavin, R. E., Hurley, E. A., & Chamberlain, A. (2003). Cooperative learning and achievement: Theory and research. In W. Reynolds & G. Miller (Eds.), *Handbook of psychology: Vol. 7. Educational psychology* (pp. 177–198). New York, NY: Wiley.

Slavin, R. E., & Lake, C. (2008). Effective programs in elementary mathematics: A best-evidence synthesis. *Review of Educational Research, 78,* 427–515.

Small, M. Y., Lovett, S. B., & Scher, M. S. (1993). Pictures facilitate children's recall of unillustrated expository prose. *Journal of Educational Psychology*, *85*, 520–528.

Smith, C. L. (2007). Bootstrapping processes in the development of students' commonsense matter theories: Using analogical mappings, thought experiments, and learning to measure to promote conceptual restructuring. *Cognition and Instruction, 25,* 337–398.

Snir, J., Smith, C. L., & Raz, G. (2003). Linking phenomena with competing underlying models: A software tool for introducing students to the particulate model of matter. *Science Education*, *87*, 794–830.

Solórzano, R. W. (2008). High stakes testing: Issues, implications, and remedies for English language learners. *Educational Researcher, 78,* 260–329.

Spears, A. K. (2007). Improvisation, semantic license, and augmentation. In H. S. Alim & J. Baugh (Eds.), *Talkin Black talk: Language, education, and social change* (pp. 100–111). New York, NY: Teachers College Press.

Spiro, R. J., & DeSchryver, M. (2009). Constructivism: When it's the wrong idea and when it's the only idea. In S. Tobias & T. M. Duffy (Eds.), *Constructivist instruction: Success or failure?* (pp. 106–123). New York, NY: Routledge.

Spörer, N., & Brunstein, J. C. (2009). Fostering the reading comprehension of secondary school students through peer-assisted learning: Effects on strategy knowledge, strategy use, and task performance. *Contemporary Educational Psychology, 34,* 289–297.

Squire, K. (2011). *Video games and learning: Teaching and participatory culture in the digital age.* New York, NY: Teachers College Press.

Stacey, K. (1992). Mathematical problem solving in groups: Are two heads better than one? *Journal of Mathematical Behavior*, *11*, 261–275.

Staples, M. (2007). Supporting whole-class collaborative inquiry in a secondary mathematics classroom. *Cognition and Instruction*, *25*, 161–217.

Steenbergen-Hu, S., & Cooper, H. (2014). A meta-analysis of the effectiveness of intelligent tutoring systems on college students' academic learning. *Journal of Educational Psychology, 106,* 331–347.

Stein, J. A., & Krishnan, K. (2007). Nonverbal learning disabilities and executive function: The challenges of effective assessment and teaching. In L. Meltzer (Ed.), *Executive function in education: From theory to practice* (pp. 106–132). New York, NY: Guilford.

Sternberg, R. J., & Horvath, J. A. (1995). A prototype view of expert teaching. *Educational Researcher*, *24*(6), 9–17.

Stokes, J. V., Luiselli, J. K., & Reed, D. D. (2010). A behavioral intervention for teaching tackling skills to high school football athletes. *Journal of Applied Behavior Analysis, 43,* 509–512.

Sullivan, J. R., & Conoley, J. C. (2004). Academic and instructional interventions with aggressive students. In J. C. Conoley & A. P. Goldstein (Eds.), *School violence intervention* (2nd ed., pp. 235–255). New York, NY: Guilford Press.

Tamin, R. M., Bernard, R. M., Borokhovski, E., Abrami, P. C., & Schmid, R. F. (2011). What forty years of research says about the impact of technology on learning: A second-order meta-analysis and validation study. *Review of Educational Research, 81,* 4–28.

Tate, W. F. (1995). Returning to the root: A culturally relevant approach to mathematics pedagogy. *Theory into Practice*, *34*, 166–173.

Thapa, A., Cohen, J., Guffey, S., & Higgins-D'Alessandro, A. (2013). A review of school climate research. *Review of Educational Research, 83,* 357–385.

Tharp, R. G. (1989). Psychocultural variables and constants: Effects on teaching and learning in schools. *American Psychologist*, *44*, 349–359.

Théberge, C. L. (1994, April). *Small-group vs. whole-class discussion: Gaining the floor in science lessons.* Paper presented at the annual meeting of the American Educational Research Association, New Orleans, LA.

Tobias, S., & Fletcher, J. D. (Eds.). (2011). *Computer games and instruction.* Charlotte, NC: Information Age.

Tomlinson, C. A., & McTighe, J. (2006). *Integrating Differentiated Instruction and Understanding by Design.* Alexandria, VA: Association for Supervision and Curriculum Development.

Tong, F., Lara-Alecio, R., Irby, B., Mathes, P., & Kwok, O.-M. (2008). Accelerating early academic oral English development in transitional bilingual and structured English immersion programs. *American Educational Research Journal, 45,* 1011–1044.

Trautwein, U., Lüdtke, O., Kastens, C., & Köller, O. (2006). Effort on homework in grades 5–9: Development, motivational antecedents, and the association with effort on classwork. *Child Development, 77,* 1094–1111.

Trautwein, U., Niggli, A., Schnyder, I., & Lüdtke, O. (2009). Between-teacher differences in homework assignments and the development of students' homework effort, homework emotions, and achievement. *Journal of Educational Psychology, 101,* 176–189.

Trawick-Smith, J. (2003). *Early childhood development: A multicultural perspective* (3rd ed.). Upper Saddle River, NJ: Merrill/Prentice Hall.

Tyler, K. M., Uqdah, A. L., Dillihunt, M. L., Beatty-Hazelbaker, R., Connor, T., Gadson, N., . . . Stevens, R. (2008). Cultural discontinuity: Toward a quantitative investigation of a major hypothesis in education. *Educational Researcher, 37,* 280–297.

Valdés, G., Bunch, G., Snow, C., & Lee, C. (with Matos, L.). (2005). Enhancing the development of students' language(s). In L. Darling-Hammond & J. Bransford (Eds.), *Preparing teachers for a changing world: What teachers should learn and be able to do* (pp. 126–168). San Francisco, CA: Jossey-Bass/Wiley.

van de Pol, J., Volman, M., & Beishuizen, J. (2010). Scaffolding in teacher–student interaction: A decade of research. *Educational Psychology Review, 22,* 271–296.

van Drie, J., van Boxtel, C., & van der Linden, J. (2006). Historical reasoning in a computer-supported collaborative learning environment. In A. M. O'Donnell, C. E. Hmelo-Silver, & G. Erkens (Eds.), *Collaborative learning, reasoning, and technology* (pp. 265–296). Mahwah, NJ: Erlbaum.

van Merriënboer, J. J. G., & Kester, L. (2008). Whole-task models in education. In J. M. Spector, M. D. Merrill, J. van Merriënboer, & M. P. Driscoll (Eds.), *Handbook of research on educational communications and technology* (3rd ed., pp. 441–456). New York, NY: Erlbaum.

vanSledright, B., & Limón, M. (2006). Learning and teaching social studies: A review of cognitive research in history and geography. In P. A. Alexander & P. H. Winne (Eds.), *Handbook of educational psychology* (2nd ed., pp. 545–570). Mahwah, NJ: Erlbaum.

Verdi, M. P., & Kulhavy, R. W. (2002). Learning with maps and texts: An overview. *Educational Psychology Review*, *14*, 27–46.

Wade, S. E. (1992). How interest affects learning from text. In K. A. Renninger, S. Hidi, & A. Krapp (Eds.), *The role of interest in learning and development* (pp. 255–277). Mahwah, NJ: Erlbaum.

Walshaw, M., & Anthony, G. (2008). The teacher's role in classroom discourse: A review of recent research into mathematics classrooms. *Review of Educational Research, 78,* 516–551.

Ward, C., Bochner, S., & Furnham, A. (2001). *The psychology of culture shock* (2nd ed.). London, England: Routledge.

Ward, W., Cole, R., Bolaños, D., Buchenroth-Martin, C., Svirsky, E., & Weston, T. (2013). My Science Tutor: A conversational multimedia virtual tutor. *Journal of Educational Psychology, 105,* 1115–1125.

Wasley, P. A., Hampel, R. L., & Clark, R. W. (1997). *Kids and school reform.* San Francisco, CA: Jossey-Bass.

Watkins, C. L. (1997). *Project Follow Through: A case study of contingencies influencing instructional practices of the educational establishment.* Cambridge, MA: Cambridge Center for Behavioral Studies.

Webb, N. M. (1989). Peer interaction and learning in small groups. *International Journal of Educational Research*, *13*, 21–39.

Webb, N. M., & Farivar, S. (1999). Developing productive group interaction in middle school mathematics. In A. M. O'Donnell & A. King (Eds.), *Cognitive perspectives on peer learning* (pp. 117–149). Mahwah, NJ: Erlbaum.

Webb, N. M., Franke, M. L., Ing, M., Chan, A., De, T., Freund, D., & Battey, D. (2008). The role of teacher instructional practices in student collaboration. *Contemporary Educational Psychology, 33,* 360–381.

Webb, N. M., & Mastergeorge, A. M. (2003). The development of students' helping behavior and learning in peer-directed small groups. *Cognition and Instruction, 21,* 361–428.

Webb, N. M., & Palincsar, A. S. (1996). Group processes in the classroom. In D. C. Berliner & R. C. Calfee (Eds.), *Handbook of educational psychology* (pp. 841–873). New York, NY: Macmillan.

Weinert, F. E., & Helmke, A. (1995). Learning from wise Mother Nature or Big Brother Instructor: The wrong choice as seen from an educational perspective. *Educational Psychologist, 30*, 135–142.

Wentzel, K. R. (2009). Peers and academic functioning at school. In K. H. Rubin, W. M. Bukowski, & B. Laursen (Eds.), *Handbook of peer interactions, relationships, and groups* (pp. 531–547). New York, NY: Guilford Press.

Wiggins, G., & McTighe, J. (2005). *Understanding by Design* (expanded 2nd ed.). Alexandria, VA: Association for Supervision and Curriculum Development.

Wiggins, G., & McTighe, J. (2011). *The Understanding by Design guide to creating high-quality units.* Alexandria, VA: Association for Supervision and Curriculum Development.

Williams, S. M. (2010, April–May). *The impact of collaborative, scaffolded learning in K–12 schools: A meta-analysis.* Paper presented at the annual meeting of the American Educational Research Association, Denver, CO.

Wilson, P. T., & Anderson, R. C. (1986). What they don't know will hurt them: The role of prior knowledge in comprehension. In J. Orasanu (Ed.), *Reading comprehension: From research to practice* (pp. 31–48). Mahwah, NJ: Erlbaum.

Winn, W. (1991). Learning from maps and diagrams. *Educational Psychology Review, 3*, 211–247.

Winn, W. (2002). Current trends in educational technology research: The study of learning environments. *Educational Psychology Review, 14*, 331–351.

Winters, F. I., Greene, J. A., & Costich, C. M. (2008). Self-regulation of learning within computer-based learning environments: A critical analysis. *Educational Psychology Review, 20*, 429–444.

Wixson, K. K. (1984). Level of importance of post-questions and children's learning from text. *American Educational Research Journal, 21*, 419–433.

Wood, D., Wood, H., Ainsworth, S., & O'Malley, C. (1995). On becoming a tutor: Toward an ontogenetic model. *Cognition and Instruction, 13*, 565–581.

Wouters, P., van Nimwegen, C., van Oostendorp, H., & van der Spek, E. D. (2013). A meta-analysis of the cognitive and motivational effects of serious games. *Journal of Educational Psychology, 105*, 249–265.

Wu, X., Anderson, R. C., Nguyen-Jahiel, K., & Miller, B. (2013). Enhancing motivation and engagement through collaborative discussion. *Journal of Educational Psychology, 105*, 622–632.

Xu, J. (2008). Models of secondary school students' interest in homework: A multilevel analysis. *American Educational Research Journal, 45*, 1180–1205.

Zhang, J., Scardamalia, M., Reeve, R., & Messina, R. (2009). Designs for collective cognitive responsibility in knowledge-building communities. *Journal of the Learning Sciences, 18*(1), 7–44.

Zimmerman, B. J. (1998). Developing self-fulfilling cycles of academic regulation: An analysis of exemplary instructional models. In D. H. Schunk & B. J. Zimmerman (Eds.), *Self-regulated learning: From teaching to self-reflective practice* (pp. 1–19). New York, NY: Guilford Press.

Zimmerman, B. J., & Didenedetto, M. K. (2008). Mastery learning and assessment: Implications for students and teachers in an era of high-stakes testing. *Psychology in the Schools, 45*, 206–216.

Zook, K. B. (1991). Effects of analogical processes on learning and misrepresentation. *Educational Psychology Review, 3*, 41–72.

CHAPTER 9

Alberto, P. A., & Troutman, A. C. (2013). *Applied behavior analysis for teachers* (9th ed.). Columbus, OH: Pearson.

Allday, R. A., Bush, M., Ticknor, N., & Walker, L. (2011). Using teacher greetings to increase speed to task engagement. *Journal of Applied Behavior Analysis, 44*, 393–396.

American Psychological Association Zero Tolerance Task Force (2008). Are zero tolerance policies effective in the schools? An evidentiary review and recommendations. *American Psychologist, 63*, 852–862.

Anderman, E. M. (2002). School effects on psychological outcomes during adolescence. *Journal of Educational Psychology, 94*, 795–809.

Anderman, L. H., Patrick, H., Hruda, L. Z., & Linnenbrink, E. A. (2002). Observing classroom goal structures to clarify and expand goal theory. In C. Midgley (Ed.), *Goals, goal structures, and patterns of adaptive learning* (pp. 243–278). Mahwah, NJ: Erlbaum.

Ardoin, S. P., Martens, B. K., & Wolfe, L. A. (1999). Using high-probability instructional sequences with fading to increase student compliance during transitions. *Journal of Applied Behavior Analysis, 32*, 339–351.

Babad, E. (1995). The "teacher's pet phenomenon," students' perceptions of teachers' differential behavior, and students' morale. *Journal of Educational Psychology, 87*, 361–374.

Babad, E., Avni-Babad, D., & Rosenthal, R. (2003). Teachers' brief nonverbal behaviors in defined instructional situations can predict students' evaluations. *Journal of Educational Psychology, 95*, 553–562.

Baker, J. (1999). Teacher-student interaction in urban at-risk classrooms: Differential behavior, relationship quality, and student satisfaction with school. *The Elementary School Journal, 100*, 57–70.

Battistich, V., Solomon, D., Kim, D., Watson, M., & Schaps, E. (1995). Schools as communities, poverty levels of student populations, and students' attitudes, motives, and performance: A multilevel analysis. *American Educational Research Journal, 32*, 627–658.

Battistich, V., Solomon, D., Watson, M., & Schaps, E. (1997). Caring school communities. *Educational Psychologist, 32*, 137–151.

Becker, B. E., & Luthar, S. S. (2002). Social-emotional factors affecting achievement outcomes among disadvantaged students: Closing the achievement gap. *Educational Psychologist, 37*, 197–214.

Belfiore, P. J., Lee, D. L., Vargas, A. U., & Skinner, C. H. (1997). Effects of high-preference single-digit mathematics problem completion on multiple-digit mathematics problem performance. *Journal of Applied Behavior Analysis, 30*, 327–330.

Bender, G. (2001). Resisting dominance? The study of a marginalized masculinity and its construction within high school walls. In J. N. Burstyn, G. Bender, R. Casella, H. W. Gordon, D. P. Guerra, K. V. Luschen, . . . Williams, K. M. *Preventing violence in schools: A challenge to American democracy* (pp. 61–77). Mahwah, NJ: Erlbaum.

Bicard, D. F., Ervin, A., Bicard, S. C., & Baylot-Casey, L. (2012). Differential effects of seating arrangements on disruptive behavior of fifth grade students during independent seatwork. *Journal of Applied Behavior Analysis, 45*, 407–411.

Blanton, H., & Burkley, M. (2008). Deviance regulation theory: Applications to adolescent social influence. In M. J. Prinstein & K. A. Dodge (Eds.), *Understanding peer influence in children and adolescents* (pp. 94–121). New York, NY: Guilford Press.

Blugental, D. B., Lyon, J. E., Lin, E. K., McGrath, E. P., & Bimbela, A. (1999). Children "tune out" to the ambiguous communication style of powerless adults. *Child Development, 70*, 214–230.

Borko, H., & Putnam, R. T. (1996). Learning to teach. In D. C. Berliner & R. C. Calfee (Eds.), *Handbook of educational psychology* (pp. 673–708). New York, NY: Macmillan.

Bornstein, M. H., & Cote, L. R. (2010). Immigration and acculturation. In M. H. Bornstein (Ed.), *Handbook of cultural developmental science* (pp. 531–552). New York, NY: Psychology Press.

Bornstein, M. H., & Lansford, J. E. (2010). Parenting. In M. H. Bornstein (Ed.), *Handbook of cultural developmental science* (pp. 259–277). New York, NY: Psychology Press.

Borum, R., Cornell, D. G., Modzeleski, W., & Jimerson, S. R. (2010). What can be done about school shootings? A review of the evidence. *Educational Researcher, 39*, 27–37.

Boyanton, D. (2010). Behaviorism and its effect upon learning in the schools. In G. S. Goodman (Ed.), *Educational psychology reader: The art and science of how people learn* (pp. 49–65). New York, NY: Peter Lang.

Bradshaw, C. P. (2015). Translating research to practice in bullying prevention. *American Psychologist, 70*, 322–332.

Bradshaw, C. P., Mitchell, M. M., & Leaf, P. J. (2010). Examining the effects of schoolwide behavioral interventions and supports on student outcomes. *Journal of Positive Behavior Interventions, 12*(3), 133–148.

Bradshaw, C. P., Zmuda, J. H., Kellam, S. G., & Ialongo, N. S. (2009). Longitudinal impact of two universal preventive interventions in first grade on educational outcomes in high school. *Journal of Educational Psychology, 101*, 926–937.

Brendgen, M., Wanner, G., Vitaro, F., Bukowski, W. M., & Tremblay, R. E. (2007). Verbal abuse by the teacher during childhood and academic, behavioral, and emotional adjustment in young adulthood. *Journal of Educational Psychology, 99*, 26–38.

Bronson, M. B. (2000). *Self-regulation in early childhood: Nature and nurture.* New York, NY: Guilford Press.

Brophy, J. E. (2006). Observational research on generic aspects of classroom teaching. In P. A. Alexander & P. H. Winne (Eds.), *Handbook of educational psychology* (2nd ed., pp. 755–780). Mahwah, NJ: Erlbaum.

Brophy, J. E., Alleman, J., & Knighton, B. (2009). *Inside the social studies classroom.* New York, NY: Routledge.

Brown, R. P., Osterman, L. L., & Barnes, C. D. (2009). School violence and the culture of honor. *Psychological Science, 20*, 1400–1405.

Burstyn, J. N., & Stevens, R. (2001). Involving the whole school in violence prevention. In J. N. Burstyn, G. Bender, R. Casella, H. W. Gordon, D. P. Guerra, K. V. Luschen, . . . Williams, K. M. *Preventing violence in schools: A challenge to American democracy* (pp. 139–158). Mahwah, NJ: Erlbaum.

Carr, A. A. (1997, March). *The participation "race": Kentucky's site based decision teams.* Paper presented at the annual meeting of the American Educational Research Association, Chicago, IL.

Carter, K., & Doyle, W. (2006). Classroom management in early childhood and elementary classrooms. In C. M. Evertson & C. S. Weinstein (Eds.), *Handbook of classroom management: Research, practice, and contemporary issues* (pp. 373–406). Mahwah, NJ: Erlbaum.

Casella, R. (2001b). What is violent about "school violence"? The nature of violence in a city high school. In J. N. Burstyn, G. Bender, R. Casella, H. W. Gordon, D. P. Guerra, K. V. Luschen, . . . Williams, K. M. *Preventing violence in schools: A challenge to American democracy* (pp. 15–46). Mahwah, NJ: Erlbaum.

Castagno, A. E., & Brayboy, B. M. J. (2008). Culturally responsive schooling for Indigenous youth: A review of the literature. *Review of Educational Research, 78*, 941–993.

Cazden, C. B. (2001). *Classroom discourse: The language of teaching and learning* (2nd ed.). Portsmouth, NH: Heinemann.

Certo, J. L., Cauley, K. M., & Chafin, C. (2002, April). *Students' perspectives on their high school experience.* Paper presented at the annual meeting of the American Educational Research Association, New Orleans, LA.

Chang, M.-L., & Davis, H. A. (2009). Understanding the role of teacher appraisals in shaping the dynamics of their relationships with students: Deconstructing teachers' judgments of disruptive behavior/students. In P. Schutz & M. Zembylas (Eds.), *Advances in teacher emotion research: The impact of teachers' lives* (pp. 95–125). New York, NY: Springer.

Chester, M. D., & Beaudin, B. Q. (1996). Efficacy beliefs of newly hired teachers in urban schools. *American Educational Research Journal, 33*, 233–257.

Christenson, S. L., & Sheridan, S. M. (2001). *Schools and families: Creating essential connections for learning.* New York, NY: Guilford Press.

Christenson, S. L., & Thurlow, M. L. (2004). School dropouts: Prevention, considerations, interventions, and challenges. *Current Directions in Psychological Science, 13*, 36–39.

Ciani, K. D., Middleton, M. J., Summers, J. J., & Sheldon, K. M. (2010). Buffering against performance classroom goal structures: The importance of autonomy support and classroom community. *Contemporary Educational Psychology, 35*, 88–99.

Cizek, G. J. (2003). *Detecting and preventing classroom cheating: Promoting integrity in assessment.* Thousand Oaks, CA: Corwin.

Colvin, G., Ainge, D., & Nelson, R. (1997). How to defuse defiance, threats, challenges, confrontations. *Teaching Exceptional Children, 29*(6), 47–51.

Conyers, C., Miltenberger, R., Maki, A., Barenz, R., Jurgens, M., Sailer, A., . . . Kopp, B. (2004). A comparison of response cost and differential reinforcement of other behavior to reduce disruptive behavior in a preschool classroom. *Journal of Applied Behavior Analysis, 37*, 411–415.

Cooper, H. (1989). Synthesis of research on homework. *Educational Leadership, 47*(3), 85–91.

Cooper, J. O., Heron, T. E., & Heward, W. I. (2007). *Applied behavior analysis* (2nd ed.). Upper Saddle River, NJ: Merrill/Prentice Hall.

Corno, L. (1996). Homework is a complicated thing. *Educational Researcher, 25*(8), 27–30.

Crone, D. A., Hawken, L. S., & Horner, R. H. (2015). *Building positive behavior support systems in schools: Functional behavioral assessment* (2nd ed.). New York, NY: Guilford Press.

Crone, D. A., Horner, R. H., & Hawken, L. S. (2004). *Responding to problem behavior in schools: The behavior education program.* New York, NY: Guilford Press.

Dantas, M. L., & Manyak, P. C. (Eds.). (2010). *Home–school connections in a multicultural society: Learning from and with culturally and linguistically diverse families.* New York, NY: Routledge.

Davis, C., & Yang, A. (2005). *Parents and teachers working together.* Turners Falls, MA: Northeast Foundation for Children.

Davis, G. A., & Thomas, M. A. (1989). *Effective schools and effective teachers.* Boston, MA: Allyn & Bacon.

Davis, H. A. (2003). Conceptualizing the role and influence of student-teacher relationships on children's social and cognitive development. *Educational Psychologist, 38*, 207–234.

Davis, H. A., Schutz, P. A., & Chambless, C. B. (2001, April). *Uncovering the impact of social relationships in the classroom: Viewing relationships with teachers from different lenses.* Paper presented at the annual meeting of the American Educational Research Association, Seattle, WA.

Deci, E. L. (1992). The relation of interest to the motivation of behavior: A self-determination theory perspective. In K. A. Renninger, S. Hidi, & A. Krapp (Eds.), *The role of interest in learning and development* (pp. 43–70). Mahwah, NJ: Erlbaum.

DeVault, G., Krug, C., & Fake, S. (1996, September). Why does Samantha act that way: Positive behavioral support leads to successful inclusion. *Exceptional Parent,* 43–47.

Deyhle, D., & LeCompte, M. (1999). Cultural differences in child development: Navajo adolescents in middle schools. In R. H. Sheets & E. R. Hollins (Eds.), *Racial and ethnic identity in school practices: Aspects of human development* (pp. 123–139). Mahwah, NJ: Erlbaum.

Dien, T. (1998). Language and literacy in Vietnamese American communities. In B. Pérez (Ed.), *Sociocultural contexts of language and literacy* (pp. 123–162). Mahwah, NJ: Erlbaum.

Dijkstra, P., Kuyper, H., van der Werf, G., Buunk, A. P., & van der Zee, Y. G. (2008). Social comparison in the classroom: A review. *Review of Educational Research, 78,* 828–879.

Dishion, T. J., Piehler, T. F., & Myers, M. W. (2008). Dynamics and ecology of adolescent peer influence. In M. J. Prinstein & K. A. Dodge (Eds.), *Understanding peer influence in children and adolescents* (pp. 72–93). New York, NY: Guilford Press.

Donaldson, J. M., & Vollmer, T. R. (2012). A procedure for thinning the schedule of time-out. *Journal of Applied Behavior Analysis, 45,* 625–630.

Donaldson, J. M., DeLeon, I. G., Fisher, A. B., & Kahng, S. (2014). Effects of and preference for conditions of token earned versus token loss. *Journal of Applied Behavior Analysis, 47,* 537–548.

Doyle, W. (1984). How order is achieved in classrooms: An interim report. *Journal of Curriculum Studies, 16,* 259–277.

Doyle, W. (1986). Classroom organization and management. In M. C. Wittrock (Ed.), *Handbook of research on teaching* (3rd ed., pp. 392–431). New York, NY: Macmillan.

Doyle, W. (1990). Classroom management techniques. In O. C. Moles (Ed.), *Student discipline strategies: Research and practice* (pp. 113–129). Albany, NY: State University of New York Press.

Doyle, W. (2006). Ecological approaches to classroom management. In C. M. Evertson & C. S. Weinstein (Eds.), *Handbook of classroom management: Research, practice, and contemporary issues* (pp. 97–125). Mahwah, NJ: Erlbaum.

Dreikurs, R. (1998). *Maintaining sanity in the classroom: Classroom management techniques* (2nd ed.). Bristol, PA: Hemisphere.

Duckworth, A. L., Gendler, T. S., & Gross, J. J. (2014). Self-control in school-age children. *Educational Psychologist, 49,* 199–217.

Dumont, H., Trautwein, U., Lüdtke, O., Neumann, M., Niggli, A., & Schnyder, I. (2012). Does parental homework involvement mediate the relationship between family background and educational outcomes? *Contemporary Educational Psychology, 55*–69.

Dwyer, K., & Osher, D. (2000). *Safeguarding our children: An action guide.* Washington, DC: U.S. Departments of Education and Justice, American Institutes for Research. Retrieved from http://www.ed.gov/pubs/edpubs.html

Dwyer, K., Osher, D., & Warger, C. (1998). *Early warning, timely response: A guide to safe schools.* Washington, DC: U.S. Department of Education. Retrieved from http://www2.ed.gov

Edwards, P. A., & Turner, J. D. (2010). Do you hear what I hear? Using the parent story approach to listen and learn from African American parents. In M. L. Dantas & P. C. Manyak (Eds.), *Home–school connections in a multicultural society: Learning from and with culturally and linguistically diverse families* (pp. 137–155). New York, NY: Routledge.

Ellis, J., Fitzsimmons, S., & Small-McGinley, J. (2010). Encouraging the discouraged: Students' views for elementary classrooms. In G. S. Goodman (Ed.), *Educational psychology reader: The art and science of how people learn* (pp. 251–272). New York, NY: Peter Lang.

Emmer, E. T. (1987). Classroom management and discipline. In V. Richardson-Koehler (Ed.), *Educators' handbook: A research perspective* (pp. 23–258). White Plains, NY: Longman.

Emmer, E. T., & Evertson, C. M. (2009). *Classroom management for middle and high school teachers* (8th ed.). Upper Saddle River, NJ: Pearson.

Emmer, E. T., & Gerwels, M. C. (2006). Classroom management in middle and high school classrooms. In C. M. Evertson & C. S. Weinstein (Eds.), *Handbook of classroom management: Research, practice, and contemporary issues* (pp. 407–437). Mahwah, NJ: Erlbaum.

Emmer, E. T., & Stough, L. M. (2001). Classroom management: A critical part of educational psychology, with implications for teacher education. *Educational Psychologist, 36,* 103–112.

Epstein, J. L. (1996). Perspectives and previews on research and policy for school, family, and community partnerships. In A. Booth & J. F. Dunn (Eds.), *Family-school links: How do they affect educational outcomes?* (pp. 209–246). Mahwah, NJ: Erlbaum.

Espelage, D. L., Holt, M. K., & Henkel, R. R. (2003). Examination of peer-group contextual effects on aggression during early adolescence. *Child Development, 74,* 205–220.

Espelage, D. L., & Swearer, S. M. (Eds.). (2004). *Bullying in American schools: A social-ecological perspective on prevention and intervention.* Mahwah, NJ: Erlbaum.

Espinoza, G., & Juvonen, J. (2011). Perceptions of the school social context across the transition to middle school: Heightened sensitivity among Latino students? *Journal of Educational Psychology, 103,* 749–758.

Evertson, C. M., & Emmer, E. T. (2009). *Classroom management for elementary teachers* (8th ed.). Upper Saddle River, NJ: Pearson.

Evertson, C. M., & Weinstein, C. S. (Eds.). (2006). *Handbook of classroom management: Research, practice, and contemporary issues.* Mahwah, NJ: Erlbaum.

Filax, G. (2007). Queer in/visibility: The case of Ellen, Michel, and Oscar. In S. Books (Ed.), *Invisible children in the society and its schools* (3rd ed., pp. 213–234). Mahwah, NJ: Erlbaum.

Finders, M., & Lewis, C. (1994). Why some parents don't come to school. *Educational Leadership, 51*(8), 50–54.

Fingerhut, L. A., & Christoffel, K. K. (2002). Firearm-related death and injury among children and adolescents. *The Future of Children, 12*(2), 25–37.

Fisher, A. V., Godwin, K. E., & Seltman, H. (2014). Visual environment, attention allocation, and learning in young children: When too much of a good thing may be bad. *Psychological Science, 25,* 1362–1370.

Flanagan, C. A., Cumsille, P., Gill, S., & Gallay, L. S. (2007). School and community climates and civic commitments: Patterns for ethnic minority and majority students. *Journal of Educational Psychology, 99,* 421–431.

Fletcher, K. L., & Cassady, J. C. (2010). Overcoming academic anxieties: Promoting effective coping and self-regulation strategies. In J. C. Cassady (Ed.), *Anxiety in schools: The causes, consequences, and solutions for academic anxieties* (pp. 177–200). New York, NY: Peter Lang.

Fosnot, C. T. (1996). Constructivism: A psychological theory of learning. In C. T. Fosnot (Ed.), *Constructivism: Theory, perspectives, and practice* (pp. 8–33). New York, NY: Teachers College Press.

Fuller, M. L. (2001). Multicultural concerns and classroom management. In C. A. Grant & M. L. Gomez, *Campus and classroom: Making schooling multicultural* (2nd ed., pp. 109–134). Upper Saddle River, NJ: Merrill/Prentice Hall.

Gallimore, R., & Goldenberg, C. (2001). Analyzing cultural models and settings to connect minority achievement and school improvement research. *Educational Psychologist, 36,* 45–56.

Gay, G. (2006). Connections between classroom management and culturally responsive teaching. In C. M. Evertson & C. S. Weinstein (Eds.), *Handbook of classroom management: Research, practice, and contemporary issues* (pp. 343–370). Mahwah, NJ: Erlbaum.

Gehlbach, H., Brinkworth, M. E., & Harris, A. D. (2012). Changes in teacher–student relationships. *British Journal of Educational Psychology, 82,* 690–704.

Gettinger, M. (1988). Methods of proactive classroom management. *School Psychology Review, 17,* 227–242.

Gettinger, M., & Kohler, K. M. (2006). Process-outcome approaches to classroom management and effective teaching. In C. M. Evertson & C. S. Weinstein (Eds.), *Handbook of classroom management: Research, practice, and contemporary issues* (pp. 73–95). Mahwah, NJ: Erlbaum.

Goddard, R. D., Hoy, W. K., & Woolfolk Hoy, A. (2000). Collective teacher efficacy: Its meaning, measure, and impact on student achievement. *American Educational Research Journal, 37,* 479–507.

Gootman, M. E. (1998). Effective in-house suspension. *Educational Leadership, 56*(1), 39–41.

Green, C. L., Walker, J. M. T., Hoover-Dempsey, K. V., & Sandler, H. M. (2007). Parents' motivation for involvement in children's education: An empirical test of a theoretical model of parental involvement. *Journal of Educational Psychology, 99,* 532–544.

Greenberg, M. T., Weissberg, R. P., O'Brien, M. U., Zins, J. E., Fredericks, L., Resnik, H., & Elias, M. J. (2003). Enhancing school-based prevention and youth development through coordinated social, emotional, and academic learning. *American Psychologist, 58,* 466–474.

Greenfield, P. M., Trumbull, E., Keller, H., Rothstein-Fisch, C., Suzuki, L. K., & Quiroz, B. (2006). Cultural conceptions of learning and development. In P. A. Alexander & P. H. Winne (Eds.), *Handbook of educational psychology* (2nd ed., pp. 675–692). Mahwah, NJ: Erlbaum.

Greer, B. D., Neidert, P. L., Dozier, C. L., Payne, S. W., Zonneveld, K. L. M., & Harper, A. M. (2013). Functional analysis and treatment of problem behavior in early education classes. *Journal of Applied Behavior Analysis, 46,* 289–295.

Gregory, A., Cornell, D., & Fan, X. (2011). The relationship of school structure and support to suspension rates for Black and White high school students. *American Educational Research Journal, 48,* 904–934.

Gregory, A., Skiba, R. J., & Noguera, P. A. (2010). The achievement gap and the discipline gap: Two sides of the same coin? *Educational Researcher, 39,* 59–68.

Gutman, L. M., & McLoyd, V. C. (2000). Parents' management of their children's education within the home, at school, and in the community: An examination of African-American families living in poverty. *Urban Review, 32*(1), 1–24.

Hamm, J. V., Hoffman, A., & Farmer, T. W. (2012). Peer cultures of academic effort and achievement in adolescence. In A. M. Ryan & G. W. Ladd (Eds.), *Peer relationships and adjustment at school* (pp. 219–250). Charlotte, NC: Information Age.

Hamovitch, B. (2007). Hoping for the best: "Inclusion" and stigmatization in a middle school. In S. Books (Ed.), *Invisible children in the society and its schools* (3rd ed., pp. 263–281). Mahwah, NJ: Erlbaum.

Hamre, B. K., & Pianta, R. C. (2005). Can instructional and emotional support in the first-grade classroom make a difference for children at risk of school failure? *Child Development, 76,* 949–967.

Hand, V. M. (2010). The co-construction of opposition in a low-track mathematics classroom. *American Educational Research Journal, 47,* 97–132.

Hardré, P. L., Crowson, H. M., DeBacker, T. K., & White, D. (2007). Predicting the motivation of rural high school students. *Journal of Experimental Education, 75,* 247–269.

Henley, M. (2010). *Classroom management: A proactive approach* (2nd ed.). Columbus, OH: Pearson.

Hidalgo, N. M., Siu, S., Bright, J. A., Swap, S. M., & Epstein, J. L. (1995). Research on families, schools, and communities: A multicultural perspective. In J. A. Banks & C. A. M. Banks (Eds.), *Handbook of research on multicultural education* (pp. 498–524). New York, NY: Macmillan.

Hill, N. E., Castellino, D. R., Lansford, J. E., Nowlin, P., Dodge, K. A., Bates, J. E., & Pettit, G. S. (2004). Parent academic involvement as related to school behavior, achievement, and aspirations: Demographic variations across adolescence. *Child Development, 75,* 1491–1509.

Hogan, T., Rabinowitz, M., & Craven, J. A., III. (2003). Representation in teaching: Inferences from research of expert and novice teachers. *Educational Psychologist, 38,* 235–247.

Hom, A., & Battistich, V. (1995, April). *Students' sense of school community as a factor in reducing drug use and delinquency.* Paper presented at the annual meeting of the American Educational Research Association, San Francisco, CA.

Houts, R. M., Caspi, A., Pianta, R. C., Arseneault, L., & Moffitt, T. E. (2010). The challenging pupil in the classroom: The effect of the child on the teacher. *Psychological Science, 21,* 1802–1810.

Howell, J. C., & Lynch, J. P. (2000, August). Youth gangs in schools. *Juvenile Justice Bulletin* (OJJDP Publication NCJ-183015). Washington, DC: U.S. Department of Justice, Office of Juvenile Justice and Delinquency Prevention.

Hoy, W. K., Tarter, C. J., & Woolfolk Hoy, A. (2006). Academic optimism of schools: A force for student achievement. *American Educational Research Journal, 43,* 425–446.

Hughes, J. N. (2012). Teachers as managers of students' peer context. In A. M. Ryan & G. W. Ladd (Eds.), *Peer relationships and adjustment at school* (pp. 189–218). Charlotte, NC: Information Age.

Hughes, J. N., & Kwok, O. (2007). Influence of student-teacher and parent-teacher relationships on lower achieving readers' engagement and achievement in the primary grades. *Journal of Educational Psychology, 99,* 39–51.

Hughes, J. N., Luo, W., Kwok, O.-M., & Loyd, L. K. (2008). Teacher-student support, effortful engagement, and achievement: A 3-year longitudinal study. *Journal of Educational Psychology, 100,* 1–14.

Hunter, J., & Csikszentmihalyi, M. (2003). The positive psychology of interested adolescents. *Journal of Youth and Adolescence, 32*, 27–35.

Hyman, I., Kay, B., Tabori, A., Weber, M., Mahon, M., & Cohen, I. (2006). Bullying: Theory, research, and interventions. In C. M. Evertson & C. S. Weinstein (Eds.), *Handbook of classroom management: Research, practice, and contemporary issues* (pp. 855–884). Mahwah, NJ: Erlbaum.

Hyman, I., Mahon, M., Cohen, I., Snook, P., Britton, G., & Lurkis, L. (2004). Student alienation syndrome: The other side of school violence. In J. C. Conoley & A. P. Goldstein (Eds.), *School violence intervention* (2nd ed., pp. 483–506). New York, NY: Guilford Press.

Ihlo, T., & Nantais, M. (2010). Evidence-based interventions within a multi-tier framework for positive behavioral supports. In T. A. Glover & S. Vaughn (Eds.), *The promise of response to intervention: Evaluating current science and practice* (pp. 239–266). New York, NY: Guilford Press.

Iwata, B. A., & Bailey, J. S. (1974). Reward versus cost token systems: An analysis of the effects on students and teacher. *Journal of Applied Behavior Analysis, 7*, 567–576.

Johnson, W., McGue, M., & Iacono, W. G. (2005). Disruptive behavior and school grades: Genetic and environmental relations in 11-year-olds. *Journal of Educational Psychology, 97*, 391–405.

Jones, L. M., Mitchell, K. J., & Turner, H. A. (2015). Victim reports of bystander reactions to in-person and online peer harassment: A national survey of adolescents. *Journal of Youth and Adolescence, 44*, 2308–2330.

Jones, V. (1996). Classroom management. In J. Sikula, T. J. Buttery, & E. Guyton (Eds.), *Handbook of research on teacher education* (2nd ed., pp. 503–521). New York, NY: Macmillan.

Juvonen, J. (2006). Sense of belonging, social bonds, and school functioning. In P. A. Alexander & P. H. Winne (Eds.), *Handbook of educational psychology* (2nd ed., pp. 655–674). Mahwah, NJ: Erlbaum.

Kağitçibaşi, Ç. (2007). *Family, self, and human development across cultures: Theory and applications* (2nd ed.). Mahwah, NJ: Erlbaum.

Keller, H. R., & Tapasak, R. C. (2004). Classroom-based approaches. In J. C. Conoley & A. P. Goldstein (Eds.), *School violence intervention* (2nd ed., pp. 103–130). New York, NY: Guilford Press.

Keogh, B. K. (2003). *Temperament in the classroom.* Baltimore, MD: Brookes.

Kim, D., Solomon, D., & Roberts, W. (1995, April). *Classroom practices that enhance students' sense of community.* Paper presented at the annual meeting of the American Educational Research Association, San Francisco, CA.

Kincheloe, J. L. (2009). No short cuts in urban education: Metropedagogy and diversity. In S. R. Steinberg (Ed.), *Diversity and multiculturalism: A reader* (pp. 379–409). New York, NY: Peter Lang.

Kitayama, S., Duffy, S., & Uchida, Y. (2007). Self as cultural mode of being. In S. Kitayama & D. Cohen (Eds.), *Handbook of cultural psychology* (pp. 136–174). New York, NY: Guilford Press.

Kiuru, N., Pakarinen, E., Vasalampi, K., Silinskas, G., Aunola, K., Poikkeus, A.-M., . . . Nurmi, J.-E. (2014). Task-focused behavior mediates the associations between supportive interpersonal environments and students' academic performance. *Psychological Science, 25*, 1018–1024.

Kodluboy, D. W. (2004). Gang-oriented interventions. In J. C. Conoley & A. P. Goldstein (Eds.), *School violence intervention* (2nd ed., pp. 194–232). New York, NY: Guilford Press.

Koestner, R., Ryan, R. M., Bernieri, F., & Holt, K. (1984). Setting limits in children's behavior: The differential effects of controlling versus informational styles on intrinsic motivation and creativity. *Journal of Personality, 52*, 233–248.

Kounin, J. S. (1970). *Discipline and group management in classrooms.* New York, NY: Holt, Rinehart & Winston.

Kumar, R., Gheen, M. H., & Kaplan, A. (2002). Goal structures in the learning environment and students' disaffection from learning and schooling. In C. Midgley (Ed.), *Goals, goal structures, and patterns of adaptive learning* (pp. 143–173). Mahwah, NJ: Erlbaum.

Kupchik, A., & Bracy, N. L. (2009). The news media on school crime and violence: Constructing dangerousness and fueling fear. *Youth Violence and Juvenile Justice, 7*, 136–155.

Ladd, G. W., Herald-Brown, S. L., & Reiser, M. (2008). Does chronic classroom peer rejection predict the development of children's classroom participation during the grade school years? *Child Development, 79*, 1001–1015.

Landrum, T. J., & Kauffman, J. M. (2006). Behavioral approaches to classroom management. In C. M. Evertson & C. S. Weinstein (Eds.), *Handbook of classroom management: Research, practice, and contemporary issues* (pp. 47–71). Mahwah, NJ: Erlbaum.

Lane, K., Falk, K., & Wehby, J. (2006). Classroom management in special education classrooms and resource rooms. In C. M. Evertson & C. S. Weinstein (Eds.), *Handbook of classroom management: Research, practice, and contemporary issues* (pp. 439–460). Mahwah, NJ: Erlbaum.

Lane, K. L., Kalberg, J. R., & Menzies, H. M. (2009). *Developing schoolwide programs to prevent and manage problem behaviors: A step-by-step approach.* New York, NY: Guilford Press.

Lane, K. L., Menzies, H. M., Bruhn, A. L., & Crnobori, M. (2011). *Managing challenging behaviors in schools: Research-based strategies that work.* New York, NY: Guilford Press.

Lansford, J. E., Chang, L., Dodge, K. A., Malone, P. S., Oburu, P., Palmérus, K., . . . Quinn, N. (2005). Physical discipline and children's adjustment: Cultural normativeness as a moderator. *Child Development, 76*, 1234–1246.

Lansford, J. E., Deater-Decker, K., Dodge, K. A., Bates, J. E., & Pettit, G. S. (2003). Ethnic differences in the link between physical discipline and later adolescent externalizing behaviors. *Journal of Child Psychology and Psychiatry, 44*, 1–13.

Learning First Alliance. (2001). *Every child learning: Safe and supportive schools.* Washington, DC: Association for Supervision and Curriculum Development.

Lee, J., & Shute, V. J. (2010). Personal and social-contextual factors in K–12 academic performance: An integrative perspective on student learning. *Educational Psychologist, 45*, 185–202.

Lee, J.-S., & Bowen, N. K. (2006). Parent involvement, cultural capital, and the achievement gap among elementary school children. *American Educational Research Journal, 43*, 193–218.

Lee, V. E., & Burkam, D. T. (2003). Dropping out of high school: The role of school organization and structure. *American Educational Research Journal, 40*, 353–393.

Lentz, F. E. (1988). Reductive procedures. In J. C. Witt, S. N. Elliott, & F. M. Gresham (Eds.), *Handbook of behavior therapy in education.* New York, NY: Plenum Press.

Lerman, D. C., & Vorndran, C. M. (2002). On the status of knowledge for using punishment: Implications for treating behavior disorders. *Journal of Applied Behavior Analysis, 35*, 431–464.

Lewis, T. J., Newcomer, L. L., Trussell, R., & Richter, M. (2006). Schoolwide positive behavior support: Building systems to develop and maintain appropriate social behavior. In C. M. Evertson & C. S. Weinstein (Eds.), *Handbook of classroom management: Research, practice, and contemporary issues* (pp. 833–854). Mahwah, NJ: Erlbaum.

López, G. R. (2001). Redefining parental involvement: Lessons from high-performing migrant-impacted schools. *American Educational Research Journal, 38*, 253–288.

Mac Iver, D. J., Reuman, D. A., & Main, S. R. (1995). Social structuring of the school: Studying what is, illuminating what could be. In J. T. Spence, J. M. Darley, & D. J. Foss (Eds.), *Annual review of psychology* (Vol. 46, pp. 375–400). Palo Alto, CA: Annual Review.

Mace, F. C., Hock, M. L., Lalli, J. S., West, B. J., Belfiore, P., Pinter, E., & Brown, D. K. (1988). Behavioral momentum in the treatment of noncompliance. *Journal of Applied Behavior Analysis, 21*, 123–141.

Mainhard, M. T., Brekelmans, M., den Brok, P., & Wubbels, T. (2011). The development of the classroom social climate during the first months of the school year. *Contemporary Educational Psychology, 36*, 190–200.

Marchand, G., & Skinner, E. A. (2007). Motivational dynamics of children's academic help-seeking and concealment. *Journal of Educational Psychology, 99*, 65–82.

Masten, A. S. (2001). Ordinary magic: Resilience processes in development. *American Psychologist, 56*, 227–238.

Mayer, M. J., & Furlong, M. J. (2010). How safe are our schools? *Educational Researcher, 39*, 16–26.

McClowry, S. G. (1998). The science and art of using temperament as the basis for intervention. *School Psychology Review, 27*, 551–563.

Meehan, B. T., Hughes, J. N., & Cavell, T. A. (2003). Teacher-student relationships as compensatory resources for aggressive children. *Child Development, 74*, 1145–1157.

Mehan, H. (1979). *Social organization in the classroom.* Cambridge, MA: Harvard University Press.

Meltzer, L. (Ed.). (2007). *Executive function in education: From theory to practice.* New York, NY: Guilford Press.

Metcalfe, L. A., Harvey, E. A., & Laws, H. B. (2013). The longitudinal relation between academic/cognitive skills and externalizing behavior problems in preschool children. *Journal of Educational Psychology, 105*, 881–894.

Meyer, D. K., & Turner, J. C. (2002). Discovering emotion in classroom motivation research. *Educational Psychologist, 37*, 107–114.

Miles, S. B., & Stipek, D. (2006). Contemporaneous and longitudinal associations between social behavior and literacy achievement in a sample of low-income elementary school children. *Child Development, 77*, 103–117.

Miller, A. (2006). Contexts and attributions for difficult behavior in English classrooms. In C. M. Evertson & C. S. Weinstein (Eds.), *Handbook of classroom management: Research, practice, and contemporary issues* (pp. 1093–1120). Mahwah, NJ: Erlbaum.

Moles, O. C. (Ed.). (1990). *Student discipline strategies: Research and practice.* Albany, NY: State University of New York Press.

Moore, J. W., & Edwards, R. P. (2003). An analysis of aversive stimuli in classroom demand contexts. *Journal of Applied Behavior Analysis, 36*, 339–348.

Morrison, G. M., Furlong, M. J., D'Incau, B., & Morrison, R. L. (2004). The safe school: Integrating the school reform agenda to prevent disruption and violence at school. In J. C. Conoley & A. P. Goldstein (Eds.), *School violence intervention* (2nd ed., pp. 256–296). New York, NY: Guilford Press.

Mueller, M. M., Nkosi, A., & Hine, J. F. (2011). Functional analysis in public schools: A summary of 90 functional analyses. *Journal of Applied Behavior Analysis, 44*, 807–818.

Munn, P., Johnstone, M., & Chalmers, V. (1990, April). *How do teachers talk about maintaining effective discipline in their classrooms?* Paper presented at the annual meeting of the American Educational Research Association, Boston, MA.

Murdock, T. B., Hale, N. M., & Weber, M. J. (2001). Predictors of cheating among early adolescents: Academic and social motivations. *Contemporary Educational Psychology, 26*, 96–115.

Murdock, T. B., Miller, A., & Kohlhardt, J. (2004). Effects of classroom context variables on high school students' judgments of the acceptability and likelihood of cheating. *Journal of Educational Psychology, 96*, 765–777.

Myles, B. S., & Simpson, R. L. (2001). Understanding the hidden curriculum: An essential social skill for children and youth with Asperger syndrome. *Intervention in School and Clinic, 36*, 279–286.

Nichols, J. D., Ludwin, W. G., & Iadicola, P. (1999). A darker shade of gray: A year-end analysis of discipline and suspension data. *Equity and Excellence in Education, 32*(1), 43–55.

Nucci, L. P. (2001). *Education in the moral domain.* Cambridge, England: Cambridge University Press.

Nucci, L. P. (2006). Classroom management for moral and social development. In C. M. Evertson & C. S. Weinstein (Eds.), *Handbook of classroom management: Research, practice, and contemporary issues* (pp. 711–731). Mahwah, NJ: Erlbaum.

Nucci, L. (2009). *Nice is not enough: Facilitating moral development.* Upper Saddle River, NJ: Merrill/Pearson.

O'Brennan, L. M., Waasdorp, T. E., & Bradshaw, C. P. (2014). Strengthening bullying prevention through school staff connectedness. *Journal of Educational Psychology, 106*, 870–880.

O'Connor, E., Dearing, E., & Collins, B. A. (2011). Teacher–child relationship and behavior problem trajectories in elementary school. *American Educational Research Journal, 48*, 120–162.

O'Connor, E., & McCartney, K. (2007). Examining teacher–child relationships and achievement as part of an ecological model of development. *American Educational Research Journal, 44*, 340–369.

O'Donnell, D. A., Schwab-Stone, M. E., & Muyeed, A. Z. (2002). Multidimensional resilience in urban children exposed to community violence. *Child Development, 73*, 1265–1282.

Ormrod, J. E. (2016). *Human learning* (7th ed.). Columbus, OH: Pearson.

Osher, D., Bear, G. G., Sprague, J. R., & Doyle, W. (2010). How can we improve school discipline? *Educational Researcher, 39*, 48–58.

Osher, D., Dwyer, K., & Jimerson, S. R. (2006). Safe, supportive, and effective schools: Promoting school success to reduce school violence. In S. R. Jimerson & M. Furlong (Eds.), *Handbook of school violence and school safety: From research to practice* (pp. 51–71). Mahwah, NJ: Erlbaum.

Osterman, K. F. (2000). Students' need for belonging in the school community. *Review of Educational Research, 70*, 323–367.

O'Toole, M. E. (2000). *The school shooter: A threat assessment perspective.* Quantico, VA: Federal Bureau of Investigation. Retrieved from http://www.fbi.gov/publications/school/school2.pdf

Owen, K. B., Parker, P. D., Van Zanden, B., MacMillan, F., Astell-Burt, T., & Lonsdale, C. (2016). Physical activity and school engagement in youth: A systematic review and meta-analysis. *Educational Psychologist, 51*, 129–145.

Pang, V. O. (1995). Asian Pacific American students: A diverse and complex population. In J. A. Banks & C. A. M. Banks (Eds.), *Handbook of research on multicultural education* (pp. 412–426). New York, NY: Macmillan.

Parke, R. D. (1974). Rules, roles, and resistance to deviation: Explorations in punishment, discipline, and self-control. In A. Pick (Ed.), *Minnesota Symposia on Child Psychology* (Vol. 8, pp. 111–143). Minneapolis, MN: University of Minnesota Press.

Patrick, H., Kaplan, A., & Ryan, A. M. (2011). Positive classroom motivational environments: Convergence between mastery goal structure and classroom social climate. *Journal of Educational Psychology, 103,* 367–382.

Patrick, H., Ryan, A. M., & Kaplan, A. M. (2007). Early adolescents' perceptions of the classroom social environment, motivational beliefs, and engagement. *Journal of Educational Psychology, 99,* 83–98.

Payne, R. K. (2005). *A framework for understanding poverty* (4th rev. ed.). Highlands, TX: aha! Process.

Payne, S. W., & Dozier, C. L. (2013). Positive reinforcement as treatment for problem behavior maintained by negative reinforcement. *Journal of Applied Behavior Analysis, 46,* 699–703.

Pekrun, R., Goetz, T., Daniels, L. M., Stupnisky, R. H., & Perry, R. P. (2010). Boredom in achievement settings: Exploring control–value antecedents and performance outcomes of a neglected emotion. *Journal of Educational Psychology, 102,* 531–549.

Pellegrini, A. D. (2002). Bullying, victimization, and sexual harassment during the transition to middle school. *Educational Psychologist, 37,* 151–163.

Pellegrini, A. D., & Bohn, C. M. (2005). The role of recess in children's cognitive performance and school adjustment. *Educational Researcher, 34*(1), 13–19.

Pellegrini, A. D., Huberty, P. D., & Jones, I. (1995). The effects of recess timing on children's playground and classroom behaviors. *American Educational Research Journal, 32,* 845–864.

Perry, D. G., & Perry, L. C. (1983). Social learning, causal attribution, and moral internalization. In J. Bisanz, G. L. Bisanz, & R. Kail (Eds.), *Learning in children: Progress in cognitive development research* (pp. 105–136). New York, NY: Springer-Verlag.

Peter, F., & Dalbert, C. (2010). Do my teachers treat me justly? Implications of students' justice experience for class climate experience. *Contemporary Educational Psychology, 35,* 297–305.

Pfiffner, L. J., Barkley, R. A., & DuPaul, G. J. (2006). Treatment of ADHD in school settings. In R. A. Barkley, *Attention-deficit hyperactivity disorder: A handbook for diagnosis and treatment* (3rd ed., pp. 547–589). New York, NY: Guilford Press.

Pfiffner, L. J., & O'Leary, S. G. (1993). School-based psychological treatments. In J. L. Matson (Ed.), *Handbook of hyperactivity in children* (pp. 234–255). Boston, MA: Allyn & Bacon.

Pianta, R. C. (1999). *Enhancing relationships between children and teachers.* Washington, DC: American Psychological Association.

Pianta, R. C. (2006). Classroom management and relationships between children and teachers: Implications for research and practice. In C. M. Evertson & C. S. Weinstein (Eds.), *Handbook of classroom management: Research, practice, and contemporary issues* (pp. 685–709). Mahwah, NJ: Erlbaum.

Pianta, R. C., Belsky, J., Vandergrift, N., Houts, R., & Morrison, F. J. (2008). Classroom effects on children's achievement trajectories in elementary school. *American Educational Research Journal, 45,* 365–397.

Rappaport, N., Osher, D., Garrison, E. G., Anderson-Ketchmark, C., & Dwyer, K. (2003). Enhancing collaboration within and across disciplines to advance mental health in schools. In M. D. Weist, S. W. Evans, & N. A. Lever (Eds.), *Handbook of school mental health: Advancing practice and research* (pp. 107–118). New York, NY: Kluwer Academic Press.

Reeve, J. (2009). Why teachers adopt a controlling motivating style toward students and how they can become more autonomy supportive. *Educational Psychologist, 44,* 159–175.

Reschly, A. L., & Christenson, S. L. (2009). Parents as essential partners for fostering students' learning outcomes. In R. Gilman, E. S. Huebner, & M. J. Furlong (Eds.), *Handbook of positive psychology in schools* (pp. 257–272). New York, NY: Routledge.

Reyes, M. R., Brackett, M. A., Rivers, S. E., White, M., & Salovey, P. (2012). Classroom emotional climate, student engagement, and academic achievement. *Journal of Educational Psychology, 104,* 700–712.

Robers, S., Zhang, J., Morgan, R. E., & Musu-Gillette, L. (2015). *Indicators of school crime and safety: 2014* (NCES 2015-070/NCJ 248036). Washington, DC: National Center for Education Statistics, U.S. Department of Education, and Bureau of Justice Statistics, Office of Justice Programs, U.S. Department of Justice. Retrieved from http://nces.ed.gov/pubs2015/2015072.pdf

Robinson, D. R., Schofield, J. W., & Steers-Wentzell, K. L. (2005). Peer and cross-age tutoring in math: Outcomes and

their design implications. *Educational Psychology Review, 17,* 327–362.

Robinson, S. L., & Griesemer, S. M. R. (2006). Helping individual students with problem behavior. In C. M. Evertson & C. S. Weinstein (Eds.), *Handbook of classroom management: Research, practice, and contemporary issues* (pp. 787–802). Mahwah, NJ: Erlbaum.

Rogers, C. R. (1983). *Freedom to learn for the 80's.* Upper Saddle River, NJ: Merrill/Prentice Hall.

Rogoff, B. (2003). *The cultural nature of human development.* Oxford, England: Oxford University Press.

Roorda, D. L., Koomen, H. M. Y., Spilt, J. L., & Oort, F. J. (2011). The influence of affective teacher–student relationships on students' school engagement and achievement: A meta-analytic approach. *Review of Educational Research, 81,* 493–529.

Rortvedt, A. K., & Miltenberger, R. G. (1994). Analysis of a high-probability instructional sequence and time-out in the treatment of child noncompliance. *Journal of Applied Behavior Analysis, 27,* 327–330.

Ross, S. W., & Horner, R. H. (2009). Bully prevention in positive behavior support. *Journal of Applied Behavior Analysis, 42,* 747–759.

Rothbart, M. K. (2011). *Becoming who we are: Temperament and personality in development.* New York, NY: Guilford Press.

Rozalski, M. E., & Yell, M. L. (2004). Law and school safety. In J. C. Conoley & A. P. Goldstein (Eds.), *School violence intervention* (2nd ed., pp. 507–523). New York, NY: Guilford Press.

Rudman, M. K. (1993). Multicultural children's literature: The search for universals. In M. K. Rudman (Ed.), *Children's literature: Resource for the classroom* (2nd ed., pp. 113–145). Norwood, MA: Christopher-Gordon.

Ruef, M. B., Higgins, C., Glaeser, B., & Patnode, M. (1998). Positive behavioral support: Strategies for teachers. *Intervention in School and Clinic, 34*(1), 21–32.

Rumberger, R. W. (2011). *Dropping out: Why students drop out of high school and what can be done about it.* Cambridge, MA: Harvard University Press.

Ryan, A. M., & Patrick, H. (2001). The classroom social environment and changes in adolescents' motivation and engagement during middle school. *American Educational Research Journal, 38,* 437–460.

Sabers, D. S., Cushing, K. S., & Berliner, D. C. (1991). Differences among teachers in a task characterized by simultaneity, multidimensionality, and immediacy. *American Educational Research Journal, 28,* 63–88.

Salend, S. J., & Taylor, L. (1993). Working with families: A cross-cultural perspective. *Remedial and Special Education, 14*(5), 25–32, 39.

Sanchez, F., & Anderson, M. L. (1990). Gang mediation: A process that works. *Principal, 69*(4), 54–56.

Sanders, M. G. (1996). Action teams in action: Interviews and observations in three schools in the Baltimore School–Family–Community Partnership Program. *Journal of Education for Students Placed at Risk, 1,* 249–262.

Sapon-Shevin, M., Dobbelaere, A., Corrigan, C., Goodman, K., & Mastin, M. (1998). Everyone here can play. *Educational Leadership, 56*(1), 42–45.

Scheuermann, B. K., & Hall, J. A. (2016). *Positive behavioral supports for the classroom* (3rd ed.). Columbus, OH: Pearson.

Scott, J., & Bushell, D. (1974). The length of teacher contacts and students' off-task behavior. *Journal of Applied Behavior Analysis, 7,* 39–44.

Serpell, R., Baker, L., & Sonnenschein, S. (2005). *Becoming literate in the city: The Baltimore Early Childhood Project.* Cambridge, England: Cambridge University Press.

Sheets, J. (1996). Designing an effective in-school suspension program to change student behavior. *NASSP Bulletin, 80*(579), 86–90.

Shernoff, D., Csikszentmihalyi, M., Schneider, B., & Shernoff, E. (2003). Student engagement in high school classrooms from the perspective of flow theory. *School Psychology Quarterly, 18,* 158–176.

Silberman, M. L., & Wheelan, S. A. (1980). *How to discipline without feeling guilty: Assertive relationships with children.* Champaign, IL: Research Press.

Silverberg, R. P. (2003, April). *Developing relational space: Teachers who came to understand themselves and their students as learners.* Paper presented at the annual meeting of the American Educational Research Association, Chicago, IL.

Skaalvik, E. M., & Skaalvik, S. (2008). Teacher self-efficacy: Conceptual analysis and relations with teacher burnout and

perceived school context. In H. W. Marsh, R. G. Craven, & D. M. McInerney (Eds.), *Self-processes, learning, and enabling human potential* (pp. 223–247). Charlotte, NC: Information Age.

Smith, A. K. (2009). *The art of possibility: Creating more successful learners.* Malibu, CA: Center for Collaborative Action Research, Pepperdine University. Retrieved from http://cadres.pepperdine.edu/ccar/projects.school.html

Spaulding, C. L. (1992). *Motivation in the classroom.* New York, NY: McGraw-Hill.

Spera, C. (2005). A review of the relationship among parenting practices, parenting styles, and adolescent school achievement. *Educational Psychology Review, 17,* 125–146.

Spilt, J. L., Koomen, H. M. Y., & Thijs, J. T. (2011). Teacher wellbeing: The importance of teacher–student relationships. *Educational Psychology Review, 23,* 457–477.

Stipek, D. J. (1996). Motivation and instruction. In D. C. Berliner & R. C. Calfee (Eds.), *Handbook of educational psychology* (pp. 85–113). New York, NY: Macmillan.

Stipek, D. J., & Miles, S. (2008). Effects of aggression on achievement: Does conflict with the teacher make it worse? *Child Development, 79,* 1721–1735.

Striepling-Goldstein, S. H. (2004). The low-aggression classroom: A teacher's view. In J. C. Conoley & A. P. Goldstein (Eds.), *School violence intervention* (2nd ed., pp. 23–53). New York, NY: Guilford Press.

Sullivan, J. S. (1989). Planning, implementing, and maintaining an effective in-school suspension program. *Clearing House, 62,* 409–410.

Sullivan-DeCarlo, C., DeFalco, K., & Roberts, V. (1998). Helping students avoid risky behavior. *Educational Leadership, 56*(1), 80–82.

Sutherland, K. S., & Morgan, P. L. (2003). Implications of transactional processes in classrooms for students with emotional/behavioral disorders. *Preventing School Failure, 48*(6), 32–45.

Sutton, R. E., & Wheatley, K. F. (2003). Teachers' emotions and teaching: A review of the literature and directions for future research. *Educational Psychology Review, 15,* 327–358.

Swanson, H. L., O'Connor, J. E., & Cooney, J. B. (1990). An information processing analysis of expert and novice teachers' problem solving. *American Educational Research Journal, 27,* 533–556.

Syvertsen, A. K., Flanagan, C. A., & Stout, M. D. (2009). Code of silence: Students' perceptions of school climate and willingness to intervene in a peer's dangerous plan. *Journal of Educational Psychology, 101,* 219–232.

Tamis-Lemonda, C. S., & McFadden, K. E. (2010). The United States of America. In M. H. Bornstein (Ed.), *Handbook of cultural developmental science* (pp. 299–322). New York, NY: Psychology Press.

Thapa, A., Cohen, J., Guffey, S., & Higgins-D'Alessandro, A. (2013). A review of school climate research. *Review of Educational Research, 83,* 357–385.

Turnbull, A. P., Pereira, L., & Blue-Banning, M. (2000). Teachers as friendship facilitators. *Teaching Exceptional Children, 32*(5), 66–70.

U.S. Secret Service National Threat Assessment Center, in collaboration with the U.S. Department of Education (2000, October). *Safe school initiative: An interim report on the prevention of targeted violence in schools.* Washington, DC: Author.

Van Camp, C. M., Lerman, D. C., Kelley, M. E., Roane, H. S., Contrucci, S. A., & Vorndran, C. M. (2000). Further analysis of idiosyncratic antecedent influences during the assessment and treatment of problem behavior. *Journal of Applied Behavior Analysis, 33,* 207–221.

Van Houten, R., Nau, P., MacKenzie-Keating, S., Sameoto, D., & Colavecchia, B. (1982). An analysis of some variables influencing the effectiveness of reprimands. *Journal of Applied Behavior Analysis, 15,* 65–83.

Vitaro, F., Brendgen, M., Larose, S., & Tremblay, R. E. (2005). Kindergarten disruptive behaviors, protective factors, and educational achievement by early adulthood. *Journal of Educational Psychology, 97,* 617–629.

Walker, H. M., Horner, R. H., Sugai, G., Bullis, M., Sprague, J. R., Bricker, D., & Kaufman, M. J. (1996). Integrated approaches to preventing antisocial behavior patterns among school-age children and youth. *Journal of Emotional and Behavioral Disorders, 4,* 194–209.

Walker, J. M. T., & Hoover-Dempsey, K. V. (2006). Why research on parental involvement is important to classroom management. In C. M. Evertson & C. S. Weinstein (Eds.), *Handbook of classroom management: Research, practice, and contemporary issues* (pp. 665–684). Mahwah, NJ: Erlbaum.

Wang, M.-T., & Holcombe, R. (2010). Adolescents' perceptions of school environment, engagement, and academic achievement in middle school. *American Educational Research Journal, 47,* 633–662.

Warren, J. S., Bohanon-Edmonson, H. M., Turnbull, A. P., Sailor, W., Wickham, D., Griggs, P., & Beech, S. E. (2006). School-wide positive behavior support: Addressing behavior problems that impeded student learning. *Educational Psychology Review, 18,* 187–198.

Watson, M. (2008). Developmental discipline and moral education. In L. Nucci & D. Narvaez (Eds.), *Handbook of moral and character education* (pp. 175–203). New York, NY: Routledge.

Watson, M., & Battistich, V. (2006). Building and sustaining caring communities. In C. M. Evertson & C. S. Weinstein (Eds.), *Handbook of classroom management: Research, practice, and contemporary issues* (pp. 253–279). Mahwah, NJ: Erlbaum.

Watson, M. W., Andreas, J. B., Fischer, K. W., & Smith, K. (2005). Patterns of risk factors leading to victimization and aggression in children and adolescents. In K. A. Kendall-Tackett & S. M. Giacomoni (Eds.), *Child victimization: Maltreatment, bullying and dating violence, prevention and intervention* (pp. 12.1–12.23). Kingston, NJ: Civic Research Institute.

Wentzel, K. R., Battle, A., Russell, S. L., & Looney, L. B. (2010). Social supports from teachers and peers as predictors of academic and social motivation. *Contemporary Educational Psychology, 35,* 193–202.

Wentzel, K. R., Donlan, A., & Morrison, D. (2012). Peer relationships and social motivational processes. In A. M. Ryan & G. W. Ladd (Eds.), *Peer relationships and adjustment at school* (pp. 79–107). Charlotte, NC: Information Age.

Wentzel, K. R., Donlan, A. E., Morrison, D. A., Russell, S. L., & Baker, S. A. (2009, April). *Adolescent non-compliance: A social ecological perspective.* Paper presented at the annual meeting of the American Educational Research Association, San Diego, CA.

Werner, E. E., & Smith, R. S. (2001). *Journeys from childhood to midlife: Risk, resilience, and recovery.* Ithaca, NY: Cornell University Press.

Wheeler, J. J., & Richey, D. D. (2014). *Behavior management: Principles and practice of positive behavioral supports* (3rd ed.). Columbus, OH: Pearson.

White, A. G., & Bailey, J. S. (1990). Reducing disruptive behaviors of elementary physical education students with sit and watch. *Journal of Applied Behavior Analysis, 23,* 353–359.

Williams, K. D. (2001). *Ostracism: The power of silence.* New York, NY: Guilford Press.

Williams, K. M. (2001a). "Frontin' it": Schooling, violence, and relationships in the 'hood. In J. N. Burstyn, G. Bender, R. Casella, H. W. Gordon, D. P. Guerra, K. V. Luschen, . . . Williams, K. M. *Preventing violence in schools: A challenge to American democracy* (pp. 95–108). Mahwah, NJ: Erlbaum.

Woolfolk, A. E., & Brooks, D. M. (1985). The influence of teachers' nonverbal behaviors on students' perceptions and performances. *Elementary School Journal, 85,* 513–528.

Woolfolk Hoy, A., Davis, H., & Pape, S. J. (2006). Teacher knowledge and beliefs. In P. A. Alexander & P. H. Winne (Eds.), *Handbook of educational psychology* (2nd ed., pp. 715–737). Mahwah, NJ: Erlbaum.

Wynne, E. A. (1990). Improving pupil discipline and character. In O. C. Moles (Ed.), *Student discipline strategies: Research and practice* (pp. 167–190). Albany, NY: State University of New York Press.

Yeager, D. S., & Dweck, C. S. (2012). Mindsets that promote resilience: When students believe that personal characteristics can be developed. *Educational Psychologist, 47,* 302–314.

Zambo, D., & Brem, S. K. (2004). Emotion and cognition in students who struggle to read: New insights and ideas. *Reading Psychology, 25,* 1–16.

Zimmermann, F., Schütte, K., Taskinen, P., & Köller, O. (2013). Reciprocal effects between adolescent externalizing problems and measures of achievement. *Journal of Educational Psychology, 105,* 747–761.

CHAPTER 10

Agarwal, P. K., D'Antonio, L., Roediger, H. L., III, McDermott, K. B., & McDaniel, M. A. (2014). Classroom-based programs of retrieval practice reduce middle school and high school students' test anxiety. *Journal of Applied Research in Memory and Cognition, 3,* 131–139.

Airasian, P. W. (1994). *Classroom assessment* (2nd ed.). New York, NY: McGraw-Hill.

American Educational Research Association (2015). AERA statement on use of value-added models (VAM) for the evaluation of educators and educator preparation programs. *Educational Researcher, 44,* 448–452.

American Educational Research Association, American Psychological Association, & National Council on Measurement in Education. (1999). *Standards for educational and psychological testing* (2nd ed.). Washington, DC: American Educational Research Association.

American Statistical Association (2014). *ASA statement on using value-added models for educational assessment.* Alexandria, VA: Author. Retrieved from https://www.amstat.org/policy/pdfs/ASA_VAM_Statement.pdf

Anderman, E. M., Gimbert, B., O'Connell, A., & Riegel, L. (2015). Approaches to academic growth assessment. *British Journal of Educational Psychology, 85,* 138–153.

Anderman, E. M., Griesinger, T., & Westerfield, G. (1998). Motivation and cheating during early adolescence. *Journal of Educational Psychology, 90,* 84–93.

Andrade, H. L. (2010). Students as the definitive source of formative assessment: Academic self-assessment and the self-regulation of learning. In H. L. Andrade & G. G. Cizek (Eds.), *Handbook of formative assessment* (pp. 90–105). New York, NY: Routledge.

Andrade, H. L., & Cizek, G. J. (Eds.). (2010). *Handbook of formative assessment.* New York, NY: Routledge.

Arter, J. A., & Chappuis, J. (2006). *Creating and recognizing quality rubrics.* Columbus, OH: Pearson.

Arter, J. A., & Spandel, V. (1992). Using portfolios of student work in instruction and assessment. *Educational Measurement: Issues and Practice, 11*(1), 36–44.

Au, W. (2007). High-stakes testing and curricular control: A qualitative metasynthesis. *Educational Researcher, 36*(5), 258–267.

Baker, E. L. (2007). The end(s) of testing. *Educational Researcher, 36,* 309–317.

Ballou, D., Sanders, W., & Wright, P. (2004). Controlling for student background in value-added assessment of teachers. *Journal of Educational and Behavioral Statistics, 29,* 37–65.

Banta, T. W. (Ed.). (2003). *Portfolio assessment: Uses, cases, scoring, and impact.* San Francisco, CA: Jossey-Bass.

Baxter, G. P., Elder, A. D., & Glaser, R. (1996). Knowledge-based cognition and performance assessment in the science classroom. *Educational Psychologist, 31,* 133–140.

Black, P., & Wiliam, D. (1998). Assessment and classroom learning. *Assessment in Education, 5*(1), 7–74.

Boschee, F., & Baron, M. A. (1993). *Outcome-based education: Developing programs through strategic planning.* Lancaster, PA: Technomic.

Bracken, B. A., & Walker, K. C. (1997). The utility of intelligence tests for preschool children. In D. P. Flanagan, J. L. Genshaft, & P. L. Harrison (Eds.), *Contemporary intellectual assessment: Theories, tests, and issues* (pp. 484–502). New York, NY: Guilford Press.

Bransford, J., Vye, N., Stevens, R., Kuhl, P., Schwartz, D., Bell, P., . . . Sabelli, N. (2006). Learning theories and education: Toward a decade of synergy. In P. A. Alexander & P. H. Winne (Eds.), *Handbook of educational psychology* (2nd ed., pp. 209–244). Mahwah, NJ: Erlbaum.

Brookhart, S. M. (2004). *Grading.* Upper Saddle River, NJ: Merrill/Prentice Hall.

Brookhart, S. M., & Nitko, A. J. (2011). Strategies for constructing assessment of higher order thinking skills. In G. Schraw & D. R. Robinson (Eds.), *Assessment of higher order thinking skills* (pp. 327–359). Charlotte, NC: Information Age.

Brophy, J. E. (1986). *On motivating students* (Occasional Paper No. 101). East Lansing, MI: Michigan State University, Institute for Research on Teaching.

Brophy, J. E. (2004). *Motivating students to learn* (2nd ed.). Mahwah, NJ: Erlbaum.

Brown, A. B., & Clift, J. W. (2010). The unequal effect of adequate yearly progress: Evidence from school visits. *American Educational Research Journal, 47,* 774–798.

Brown, A. L., & Campione, J. C. (1996). Psychological theory and the design of innovative learning environments: On procedures, principles, and systems. In L. Schauble & R. Glaser (Eds.), *Innovations in learning: New environments for education* (pp. 289–325). Mahwah, NJ: Erlbaum.

Carbonneau, K. J., & Selig, J. P. (2011, April). *Teacher judgments of student mathematics achievement: The moderating role of student–teacher conflict.* Paper presented at the annual meeting of the American Educational Research Association, New Orleans, LA.

Carhill, A., Suárez-Orozco, C., & Páez, M. (2008). Explaining English language proficiency among adolescent immigrant students. *American Educational Research Journal, 45,* 1045–1079.

Carpenter, S. K. (2012). Testing enhances the transfer of learning. *Current Directions in Psychological Science, 21,* 279–283.

Carter, R., Williams, S., & Silverman, W. K. (2008). Cognitive and emotional facets of test anxiety in African American school children. *Cognition and Emotion, 22,* 539–551.

Carver, S. M. (2006). Assessing for deep understanding. In R. K. Sawyer (Ed.), *The Cambridge handbook of the learning sciences* (pp. 205–221). Cambridge, England: Cambridge University Press.

Cassady, J. C. (2010). Test anxiety: Contemporary theories and implications for learning. In J. C. Cassady (Ed.), *Anxiety in schools: The causes, consequences, and solutions for academic anxieties* (pp. 7–26). New York, NY: Peter Lang.

Castagno, A. E., & Brayboy, B. M. J. (2008). Culturally responsive schooling for Indigenous youth: A review of the literature. *Review of Educational Research, 78,* 941–993.

Chappuis, J. (2009). *Seven strategies of assessment for learning.* Boston, MA: Pearson Assessment Training Institute.

Cheng, L. R. (1987). *Assessing Asian language performance.* Rockville, MD: Aspen.

Cizek, G. J. (2003). *Detecting and preventing classroom cheating: Promoting integrity in assessment.* Thousand Oaks, CA: Corwin.

Clifford, M. M. (1990). Students need challenge, not easy success. *Educational Leadership, 48*(1), 22–26.

Corliss, S. B., & Linn, M. C. (2011). Assessing learning from inquiry science instruction. In G. Schraw & D. R. Robinson (Eds.), *Assessment of higher order thinking skills* (pp. 219–243). Charlotte, NC: Information Age.

Crehan, K. D. (2001). An investigation of the validity of scores on locally developed performance measures in a school assessment program. *Educational and Psychological Measurement, 61,* 841–848.

Crooks, T. J. (1988). The impact of classroom evaluation practices on students. *Review of Educational Research, 58,* 438–481.

Cummins, J. (1984). *Bilingualism and special education: Issues in assessment and pedagogy.* Clevedon, England: Multilingual Matters.

Cummins, J. (2008). BICS and CALP: Empirical and theoretical status of the distinction. In B. Street & N. H. Hornberger (Eds.), *Encyclopedia of language and education* (2nd ed., Vol. 2, pp. 71–83). New York, NY: Springer.

Danner, F. (2008, March). *The effects of perceptions of classroom assessment practices and academic press on classroom mastery goals and high school students' self-reported cheating.* Paper presented at the annual meeting of the American Educational Research Association, New York, NY.

Darley, J. M., & Gross, P. H. (1983). A hypothesis-confirming bias in labeling effects. *Journal of Personality and Social Psychology, 44,* 20–33.

Darling-Hammond, L., Ancess, J., & Falk, B. (1995). *Authentic assessment in action: Studies of schools and students at work.* New York, NY: Teachers College Press.

De Corte, E., Greer, B., & Verschaffel, L. (1996). Mathematics teaching and learning. In D. C. Berliner & R. C. Calfee (Eds.), *Handbook of educational psychology* (pp. 491–549). New York, NY: Macmillan.

Delandshere, G., & Petrosky, A. R. (1998). Assessment of complex performances: Limitations of key measurement assumptions. *Educational Researcher, 27*(2), 14–24.

Dempster, F. N. (1991). Synthesis of research on reviews and tests. *Educational Leadership, 48*(7), 71–76.

DiMartino, J., & Castaneda, A. (2007). Assessing applied skills. *Educational Leadership, 64,* 38–42.

diSessa, A. A. (2007). An interactional analysis of clinical interviewing. *Cognition and Instruction, 25,* 523–565.

Duckworth, A. L., Quinn, P. D., & Tsukayama, E. (2012). What No Child Left Behind leaves behind: The roles of IQ and self-control in predicting standardized achievement test scores and report card grades. *Journal of Educational Psychology, 104,* 439–451.

Duncan, G. J., Dowsett, C. J., Claessens, A., Magnuson, K., Huston, A. C., Klevanov, P., . . . Japel, C. (2007). School readiness and later achievement. *Developmental Psychology, 43,* 1428–1446.

Dunlosky, J., Rawson, K. A., Marsh, E. J., Nathan, M. J., & Willingham, D. T. (2013). Improving students' learning with effective learning techniques: Promising directions from cognitive and educational psychology. *Psychological Science in the Public Interest, 14,* 4–58.

Evans, E. D., & Craig, D. (1990). Teacher and student perceptions of academic cheating in middle and senior high schools. *Journal of Educational Research, 84*(1), 44–52.

Feuerstein, R, Feuerstein, R. S., & Falik, L. H. (2010). *Beyond smarter: Mediated learning and the brain's capacity for change.* New York, NY: Teachers College Press.

Finn, A. S., Kraft, M. A., West, M. R., Leonard, J. A., Bish, C. E., Martin, R. E., . . . Gabrieli, J. D. E. (2014). Cognitive skills, student achievement tests, and schools. *Psychological Science, 25,* 736–744.

Finnigan, K. S., & Gross, B. (2007). Do accountability policy sanctions influence teacher motivation? Lessons from Chicago's low-performing schools. *American Educational Research Journal, 44,* 594–629.

Fleege, P. O., Charlesworth, R., & Burts, D. C. (1992). Stress begins in kindergarten: A look at behavior during standardized testing. *Journal of Research in Childhood Education, 7*(1), 20–26.

Foos, P. W., & Fisher, R. P. (1988). Using tests as learning opportunities. *Journal of Educational Psychology, 80,* 179–183.

Forget-Dubois, N., Lemelin, J.-P., Bolvin, M., Dionne, G., Séguin, J. R., Vitaro, F., & Tremblay, R. E. (2007). Predicting early school achievement with the EDI: A longitudinal population-based study. *Early Education and Development. Special Issue: The Early Development Instrument, 18,* 405–426.

Forte, E. (2010). Examining the assumptions underlying the NCLB federal accountability policy on school improvement. *Journal of Educational Psychology, 102,* 76–88.

Frederiksen, J. R., & Collins, A. (1989). A systems approach to educational testing. *Educational Researcher, 18*(9), 27–32.

Frederiksen, N. (1984b). The real test bias: Influences of testing on teaching and learning. *American Psychologist, 39,* 193–202.

Frisbie, D. A., & Waltman, K. K. (1992). Developing a personal grading plan. *Educational Measurement: Issues and Practice, 11*(3), 35–42. Reprinted in K. M. Cauley, F. Linder, & J. H. McMillan (Eds.), 1994, *Educational psychology 94/95.* Guilford, CT: Dushkin.

Fuchs, L. S., Compton, D. L., Fuchs, D., Hollenbeck, K. N., Craddock, C. F., & Hamlett, C. L. (2008). Dynamic assessment of algebraic learning in predicting third graders' development of mathematical problem solving. *Journal of Educational Psychology, 100,* 829–850.

Fuller, B., Wright, J., Gesicki, K., & Kang, E. (2007). Gauging growth: How to judge No Child Left Behind. *Educational Researcher, 36*(5), 268–278.

Garcia, E. E. (1994). *Understanding and meeting the challenge of student cultural diversity.* Boston, MA: Houghton Mifflin.

Garcia, E. E. (2005, April). *Any test in English is a test of English: Implications for high stakes testing.* Paper presented at the annual meeting of the American Educational Research Association, Montreal, Quebec, Canada.

García, G. E., & Pearson, P. D. (1994). Assessment and diversity. In L. Darling-Hammond (Ed.), *Review of research in education* (Vol. 20, pp. 337–391). Washington, DC: American Educational Research Association.

Gaudry, E., & Bradshaw, G. D. (1970). The differential effect of anxiety on performance in progressive and terminal school examinations. *Australian Journal of Psychology, 22*(1), 1–4.

Geiger, M. A. (1997). An examination of the relationship between answer changing, testwiseness and examination performance. *Journal of Experimental Education, 66,* 49–60.

Gilpin, L. (1968). *The enduring Navaho.* Austin, TX: University of Texas Press.

Glass, A. L., & Sinha, N. (2013). Multiple-choice questioning is an efficient instructional methodology that may be widely implemented in academic courses to improve exam performance. *Current Directions in Psychological Science, 22,* 471–477.

Glover, T. A., & Vaughn, S. (Eds.). (2010). *The promise of response to intervention: Evaluating current science and practice.* New York, NY: Guilford.

Grant, C. A., & Gomez, M. L. (2001). *Campus and classroom: Making schooling multicultural* (2nd ed.). Upper Saddle River, NJ: Merrill/Prentice Hall.

Gregg, N. (2009). *Adolescents and adults with learning disabilities and ADHD: Assessment and accommodation.* New York, NY: Guilford.

Grolnick, W. S., & Ryan, R. M. (1987). Autonomy in children's learning: An experimental and individual difference investigation. *Journal of Personality and Social Psychology, 52,* 890–898.

Gronlund, N. E., & Waugh, C. K. (2009). *Assessment of student achievement* (9th ed.). Columbus, OH: Pearson.

Haertel, E. (2013). How is testing supposed to improve schooling? *Measurement: Interdisciplinary Research and Perspectives, 11*(1–2), 1–18.

Hamers, J. H. M., & Ruijssenaars, A. J. J. M. (1997). Assessing classroom learning potential. In G. D. Phye (Ed.), *Handbook of academic learning: Construction of knowledge* (pp. 550–571). San Diego, CA: Academic Press.

Hattie, J. A. C. (2009). *Visible learning: A synthesis of over 800 meta-analyses relating to achievement.* London, England: Routledge.

Hattie, J., & Gan, M. (2011). Instruction based on feedback. In R. E. Mayer & P. A. Alexander (Eds.), *Handbook of research on learning and instruction* (pp. 249–271). New York, NY: Routledge.

Haywood, H. C., & Lidz, C. S. (2007). *Dynamic assessment in practice: Clinical and educational applications.* Cambridge, England: Cambridge University Press.

Hembree, R. (1988). Correlates, causes, effects, and treatment of test anxiety. *Review of Educational Research, 58,* 47–77.

Hill, K. T. (1984). Debilitating motivation and testing: A major educational problem, possible solutions, and policy applications. In R. Ames & C. Ames (Eds.), *Research on motivation in education: Vol. 1. Student motivation* (pp. 245–274). San Diego, CA: Academic Press.

Hill, K. T., & Wigfield, A. (1984). Test anxiety: A major educational problem and what can be done about it. *Elementary School Journal, 85,* 105–126.

Hoge, R. D., & Coladarci, T. (1989). Teacher-based judgments of academic achievement: A review of literature. *Review of Educational Research, 59,* 297–313.

Hong, E., O'Neil, H. F., & Feldon, D. (2005). Gender effects on mathematics achievement: Mediating role of state and trait self-regulation. In A. M. Gallagher & J. C. Kaufman (Eds.), *Gender differences in mathematics: An integrative psychological approach* (pp. 264–293). Cambridge, England: Cambridge University Press.

Hoover, J. J. (2009). *RTI assessment essentials for struggling learners.* Thousand Oaks, CA: Corwin.

Hughes, G. B. (2010). Formative assessment practices that maximize learning for students at risk. In H. L. Andrade & G. J. Cizek (Eds.), *Handbook of formative assessment* (pp. 212–232). New York, NY: Routledge.

Humphry, S. M., & Heldsinger, S. A. (2014). Common structural design features of rubrics can represent a threat to validity. *Educational Researcher, 43,* 253–263.

Jacobs, J. E., Davis-Kean, P., Bleeker, M., Eccles, J. S., & Malanchuk, O. (2005). "I can, but I don't want to": The impact of parents, interests, and activities on gender differences in math. In A. M. Gallagher & J. C. Kaufman (Eds.), *Gender differences in mathematics: An integrative psychological approach* (pp. 246–263). Cambridge, England: Cambridge University Press.

Johnson, C. I., & Mayer, R. E. (2009). A testing effect with multimedia learning. *Journal of Educational Psychology, 101,* 621–629.

Johnson, R. L., Penny, J. A., & Gordon, B. (2009). *Assessing performance: Designing, scoring, and validating performance tasks.* New York, NY: Guilford Press.

Johnson, R. S., Mims-Cox, J. S., & Doyle-Nichols, A. (2006). *Developing portfolios in education: A guide to reflection, inquiry, and assessment.* Thousand Oaks, CA: Sage.

Jones, M. G., Jones, B. D., & Hargrove, T. Y. (2003). *The unintended consequences of high-stakes testing.* Lanham, MD: Rowman & Littlefield.

Khattri, N., & Sweet, D. (1996). Assessment reform: Promises and challenges. In M. B. Kane & R. Mitchell (Eds.), *Implementing performance assessment: Promises, problems, and challenges* (pp. 1–21). Mahwah, NJ: Erlbaum.

Klassen, S. (2006). Contextual assessment in science education: Background, issues, and policy. *Science Education, 90,* 820–851.

La Paro, K. M., & Pianta, R. C. (2000). Predicting children's competence in the early school years: A meta-analytic review. *Review of Educational Research, 70,* 443–484.

Lang, J. W. B., & Lang, J. (2010). Priming competence diminishes the link between cognitive test anxiety and test performance: Implications for the interpretation of test scores. *Psychological Science, 21,* 811–819.

Leaper, C., & Friedman, C. K. (2007). The socialization of gender. In J. E. Grusec & P. D. Hastings (Eds.), *Handbook of socialization: Theory and research* (pp. 561–587). New York, NY: Guilford Press.

Lee, H.-S., Liu, O. L., & Linn, M. C. (2011). Validating measurement of knowledge integration in science using multiple-choice and explanation items. *Applied Measurement in Education, 24,* 115–136.

Lester, F. K., Jr., Lambdin, D. V., & Preston, R. V. (1997). A new vision of the nature and purposes of assessment in the mathematics classroom. In G. D. Phye (Ed.), *Handbook of classroom assessment: Learning, achievement, and adjustment* (pp. 287–319). San Diego, CA: Academic Press.

Li, J., & Fischer, K. W. (2004). Thought and affect in American and Chinese learners' beliefs about learning. In D. Y. Dai & R. J. Sternberg (Eds.), *Motivation, emotion, and cognition:*

Integrative perspectives on intellectual functioning and development (pp. 385–418). Mahwah, NJ: Erlbaum.

Lovett, B. J. (2010). Extended time testing accommodations for students with disabilities: Answers to five fundamental questions. *Review of Educational Research, 80,* 611–638.

Mac Iver, D. J., Reuman, D. A., & Main, S. R. (1995). Social structuring of the school: Studying what is, illuminating what could be. In J. T. Spence, J. M. Darley, & D. J. Foss (Eds.), *Annual review of psychology* (Vol. 46, pp. 375–400). Palo Alto, CA: Annual Review.

Magnusson, S. J., Boyle, R. A., & Templin, M. (1994, April). *Conceptual development: Re-examining knowledge construction in science.* Paper presented at the annual meeting of the American Educational Research Association, New Orleans, LA.

Marzano, R. J., & Kendall, J. S. (2007). *The new taxonomy of educational objectives* (2nd ed.). Thousand Oaks, CA: Corwin Press.

Mastropieri, M. A., & Scruggs, T. E. (2010). *The inclusive classroom: Strategies for effective instruction* (4th ed.) Columbus, OH: Pearson.

McDaniel, M. A., Agarwal, P. K., Huelser, B. J., McDermott, K. B., & Roediger, H. L., III (2011). Test-enhanced learning in a middle school science classroom: The effects of quiz frequency and placement. *Journal of Educational Psychology, 103,* 399–414.

McMillan, J. H. (2010). The practical implications of educational aims and contexts for formative assessment. In H. L. Andrade & G. J. Cizek (Eds.), *Handbook of formative assessment* (pp. 41–58). New York, NY: Routledge.

Mellard, D. F., & Johnson, E. (2008). *RTI: A practitioner's guide to implementing response to intervention.* Thousand Oaks, CA: Corwin.

Messick, S. (1983). Assessment of children. In W. Kessen (Ed.), *Handbook of child psychology* (Vol. 1, pp. 477–526). New York, NY: Wiley.

Meyer, L. H., Weir, K. F., McClure, J., & Walkey, F. (2008, March). *The relationship of motivation orientations to future achievement in secondary school.* Paper presented at the annual meeting of the American Educational Research Association, New York, NY.

Miller, M. D., Linn, R. L., & Gronlund, N. E. (2009). *Measurement and assessment in teaching* (10th ed.). Upper Saddle River, NJ: Merrill/Pearson.

Mintrop, H., & Sunderman, G. L. (2009). Predictable failure of federal sanctions-driven accountability for school improvement—And why we may retain it anyway. *Educational Researcher, 38,* 353–364.

Newmann, F. M. (1997). Authentic assessment in social studies: Standards and examples. In G. D. Phye (Ed.), *Handbook of classroom assessment: Learning, achievement, and adjustment* (pp. 360–380). San Diego, CA: Academic Press.

Newstead, S. (2004). The purposes of assessment. *Psychology of Learning and Teaching, 3,* 97–101.

Nez, C., with Avila, J. S. (2011). *Code talker.* New York, NY: Berkley.

Nickerson, R. S. (1989). New directions in educational assessment. *Educational Researcher, 18*(9), 3–7.

Nixon, A. S. (2005, April). *Moral reasoning in the digital age: How students, teachers, and parents judge appropriate computer uses.* Paper presented at the annual meeting of the American Educational Research Association, Montreal, Quebec, Canada.

O'Connor, K. (2011). *A repair kit for grading: 15 fixes for broken grades* (2nd ed.). Boston, MA: Pearson Assessment Training Institute.

Padilla, A. M. (2006). Second language learning: Issues in research and teaching. In P. A. Alexander & P. H. Winne (Eds.), *Handbook of educational psychology* (2nd ed., pp. 571–591). Mahwah, NJ: Erlbaum.

Panadero, E., & Jonsson, A. (2013). The use of scoring rubrics for formative assessment purposes revisited: A review. *Educational Research Review, 9,* 129–144.

Paris, S. G., & Ayres, L. R. (1994). *Becoming reflective students and teachers with portfolios and authentic assessment.* Washington, DC: American Psychological Association.

Paris, S. G., Lawton, T. A., Turner, J. C., & Roth, J. L. (1991). A developmental perspective on standardized achievement testing. *Educational Researcher, 20*(5), 12–20, 40.

Paris, S. G., & Paris, A. H. (2001). Classroom applications of research on self-regulated learning. *Educational Psychologist, 36,* 89–101.

Paris, S. G., & Turner, J. C. (1994). Situated motivation. In P. R. Pintrich, D. R. Brown, & C. E. Weinstein (Eds.), *Student motivation, cognition, and learning: Essays in honor of Wilbert J. McKeachie* (pp. 213–238). Mahwah, NJ: Erlbaum.

Parker, W. D. (1997). An empirical typology of perfectionism in academically talented children. *American Educational Research Journal, 34,* 545–562.

Pattison, E., Grodsky, E., & Muller, C. (2013). Is the sky falling? Grade inflation and the signaling power of grades. *Educational Researcher, 42,* 259–265.

Paulson, F. L., Paulson, P. R., & Meyer, C. A. (1991). What makes a portfolio a portfolio? *Educational Leadership, 49*(5), 60–63.

Pellegrini, A. D. (1998). Play and the assessment of young children. In O. N. Saracho & B. Spodek (Eds.), *Multiple perspectives on play in early childhood education* (pp. 220–239). Albany: State University of New York Press.

Pellegrini, A. D. (2011). "In the eye of the beholder": Sex bias in observations and ratings of children's aggression. *Educational Researcher, 40,* 281–286.

Perry, N. E., & Winne, P. H. (2004). Motivational messages from home and school: How do they influence young children's engagement in learning? In D. M. McNerney & S. Van Etten (Eds.), *Big theories revisited* (pp. 199–222). Greenwich, CT: Information Age.

Polikoff, M. S., McEachin, A. J., Wrabel, S. L., & Duque, M. (2014). The waive of the future? School accountability in the waiver era. *Educational Researcher, 43,* 45–54.

Polikoff, M. S., Porter, A. C., & Smithson, J. (2011). How well aligned are state assessments of student achievement with state content standards? *American Educational Research Journal, 48,* 965–995.

Poole, D. (1994). Routine testing practices and the linguistic construction of knowledge. *Cognition and Instruction, 12,* 125–150.

Poorthuis, A. M. G., Juvonen, J., Thomaes, S., Denissen, J. J. A., Orobio de Castro, B., & van Aken, M. A. G. (2015). Do grades shape students' school engagement? The psychological consequences of report card grades at the beginning of secondary school. *Journal of Educational Psychology, 107,* 842–854.

Popham, W. J. (2006). *Assessment for educational leaders.* Boston, MA: Pearson/Allyn & Bacon.

Popham, W. J. (2014). *Classroom assessment: What teachers need to know* (7th ed.). Columbus, OH: Pearson.

Pugh, K. J., Schmidt, K., & Russell, C. (2010, May). *Fostering transformative experiences in science: A design-based study.* Paper presented at the annual meeting of the American Educational Research Association, Denver, CO.

Putwain, D. W. (2007). Test anxiety in UK schoolchildren: Prevalence and demographic patterns. *British Journal of Educational Psychology, 77,* 579–593.

Quellmalz, E. S., Davenport, J. L., Timms, M. J., DeBoer, G. E., Jordan, K. A., Huang, C.-W., & Buckley, B. C. (2013). Next-generation environments for assessing and promoting complex science learning. *Journal of Educational Psychology, 105,* 1100–1114.

Quellmalz, E., & Hoskyn, J. (1997). Classroom assessment of reading strategies. In G. D. Phye (Ed.), *Handbook of classroom assessment: Learning, achievement, and adjustment* (pp. 103–130). San Diego, CA: Academic Press.

Ready, D. D., & Wright, D. L. (2011). Accuracy and inaccuracy in teachers' perceptions of young children's cognitive abilities: The role of child background and classroom context. *American Educational Research Journal, 48,* 335–360.

Reddy, Y. M., & Andrade, H. (2010). A review of rubric use in higher education. *Assessment and Evaluation in Higher Education, 35,* 435–448.

Reeve, J., Deci, E. L., & Ryan, R. M. (2004). Self-determination theory: A dialectical framework for understanding sociocultural influences on student motivation. In D. M. McInerney & S. Van Etten (Eds.), *Big theories revisited* (pp. 31–60). Greenwich, CT: Information Age.

Ritts, V., Patterson, M. L., & Tubbs, M. E. (1992). Expectations, impressions, and judgments of physically attractive students: A review. *Review of Educational Research, 62,* 413–426.

Robinson, J. P. (2010). The effects of test translation on young English learners' mathematics performance. *Educational Researcher, 39,* 582–590.

Robinson, J. P., & Lubienski, S. T. (2011). The development of gender achievement gaps in mathematics and reading during elementary and middle school: Examining direct cognitive assessments and teacher ratings. *American Educational Research Journal, 48,* 268–302.

Rogoff, B. (2003). *The cultural nature of human development.* Oxford, England: Oxford University Press.

Rohrer, D., & Pashler, H. (2010). Recent research on human learning challenges conventional instructional strategies. *Educational Researcher, 39,* 406–412.

Russell, M. K. (2010). Technology-aided formative assessment of learning: New developments and applications. In H. L. Andrade & G. J. Cizek (Eds.), *Handbook of formative assessment* (pp. 125–138). New York, NY: Routledge.

Sanders, C. E. (1997). Assessment during the preschool years. In G. D. Phye (Ed.), *Handbook of classroom assessment: Learning, achievement, and adjustment* (pp. 227–264). San Diego, CA: Academic Press.

Sax, G. (2010). *Principles of educational and psychological measurement and evaluation* (4th ed.). Belmont, CA: Wadsworth.

Scruggs, T. E., & Lifson, S. A. (1985). Current conceptions of test-wiseness: Myths and realities. *School Psychology Review, 14,* 339–350.

Seethaler, P. M. Fuchs, L. S., Fuchs, D., & Compton, D. L. (2012). Predicting first graders' development of calculation versus word-problem performance: The role of dynamic assessment. *Journal of Educational Psychology, 104,* 224–234.

Shavelson, R. J., & Baxter, G. P. (1992). What we've learned about assessing hands-on science. *Educational Leadership, 49*(8), 20–25.

Shepard, L. A. (2000). The role of assessment in a learning culture. *Educational Researcher, 29*(7), 4–14.

Shepard, L. A., Hammerness, K., Darling-Hammond, L., & Rust, F. (with Snowden, J. B., Gordon, E., Gutierrez, C., & Pacheco, A.). (2005). Assessment. In L. Darling-Hammond & J. Bransford (Eds.), *Preparing teachers for a changing world: What teachers should learn and be able to do* (pp. 275–326). San Francisco, CA: Jossey-Bass/Wiley.

Shernoff, D. (2013). *Optimal learning environments to promote student engagement.* New York, NY: Springer.

Shriner, J. G., & Spicuzza, R. J. (1995). Procedural considerations in the assessment of students at risk for school failure. *Preventing School Failure, 39*(2), 33–38.

Shute, V. J. (2008). Focus on formative feedback. *Review of Educational Research, 78,* 153–189.

Sieber, J. E., Kameya, L. I., & Paulson, F. L. (1970). Effect of memory support on the problem-solving ability of test-anxious children. *Journal of Educational Psychology, 61,* 159–168.

Smith, J. L. (2004). Understanding the process of stereotype threat: A review of mediational variables and new performance goal directions. *Educational Psychology Review, 16,* 177–206.

Solano-Flores, G. (2008). Who is given tests in what language by whom, when, and where? The need for probabilistic views of language in the testing of English language learners. *Educational Researcher, 37,* 189–199.

Solórzano, R. W. (2008). High stakes testing: Issues, implications, and remedies for English language learners. *Educational Researcher, 78,* 260–329.

Spandel, V. (1997). Reflections on portfolios. In G. D. Phye (Ed.), *Handbook of academic learning: Construction of knowledge* (pp. 573–591). San Diego, CA: Academic Press.

Spaulding, C. L. (1992). *Motivation in the classroom.* New York, NY: McGraw-Hill.

Steele, C. M. (1997). A threat in the air: How stereotypes shape intellectual identity and performance. *American Psychologist, 52,* 613–629.

Stiggins, R. J., & Chappuis, J. (2012). *An introduction to student-involved assessment FOR learning* (6th ed.). Boston, MA: Pearson Assessment Training Institute.

Stipek, D. J. (2002a). At what age should children enter kindergarten? A question for policy makers and parents. *Social Policy Report of the Society for Research in Child Development, 16*(2), 3–16.

Stipek, D. J. (2002b). *Motivation to learn: From theory to practice* (4th ed.). Boston, MA: Allyn & Bacon.

Stokes, J. V., Luiselli, J. K., Reed, D. D., & Fleming, R. K. (2010). Behavioral coaching to improve offensive line pass-blocking skills of high school football athletes. *Journal of Applied Behavior Analysis, 43,* 463–472.

Stupnisky, R. H., Stewart, T. L., Daniels, L. M., & Perry, R. P. (2011). When do students ask why? Examining the precursors and outcomes of causal search among first-year college students. *Contemporary Educational Psychology, 36,* 201–211.

Swanson, H. L., & Lussier, C. M. (2001). A selective synthesis of the experimental literature on dynamic assessment. *Review of Educational Research, 71,* 321–363.

Szpunar, K. K., Jing, H. G., & Schacter, D. L. (2014). Overcoming overconfidence in learning from video-recorded lectures: Implications of interpolated testing for online education. *Journal of Applied Research in Memory and Cognition, 3,* 161–164.

Thomas, R. M. (2005). *High-stakes testing: Coping with collateral damage.* Mahwah, NJ: Erlbaum.

Turner, J. C., Meyer, D. K., Cox, K. E., Logan, C., DiCintio, M., & Thomas, C. T. (1998). Creating contexts for involvement in mathematics. *Journal of Educational Psychology, 90,* 730–745.

Tyler, K. M., Uqdah, A. L., Dillihunt, M. L., Beatty-Hazelbaker, R., Connor, T., Gadson, N., . . . Stevens, R. (2008). Cultural discontinuity: Toward a quantitative investigation of a major hypothesis in education. *Educational Researcher, 37,* 280–297.

Tzuriel, D. (2000). Dynamic assessment of young children: Educational and intervention perspectives. *Educational Psychology Review, 12,* 385–435.

Usher, E. L. (2009). Sources of middle school students' self-efficacy in mathematics: A qualitative investigation. *American Educational Research Journal, 46,* 275–314.

van den Bergh, L., Denessen, E., Hornstra, L., Voeten, M., & Holland, R. W. (2010). The implicit prejudiced attitudes of teachers: Relations to teacher expectations and the ethnic achievement gap. *American Educational Research Journal, 47,* 497–527.

van Kraayenoord, C. E., & Paris, S. G. (1997). Australian students' self-appraisal of their work samples and academic progress. *Elementary School Journal, 97,* 523–537.

Venn, J. J. (2007). *Assessing students with special needs* (4th ed.). Upper Saddle River, NJ: Pearson.

Warschauer, M. (2011). *Learning in the cloud: How (and why) to transform schools with digital media.* New York, NY: Teachers College Press.

Wentzel, K. R. (2009). Peers and academic functioning at school. In K. H. Rubin, W. M. Bukowski, & B. Laursen (Eds.), *Handbook of peer interactions, relationships, and groups* (pp. 531–547). New York, NY: Guilford Press.

Wentzel, K. R., Donlan, A., & Morrison, D. (2012). Peer relationships and social motivational processes. In A. M. Ryan & G. W. Ladd (Eds.), *Peer relationships and adjustment at school* (pp. 79–107). Charlotte, NC: Information Age.

Whitaker Sena, J. D., Lowe, P. A., & Lee, S. W. (2007). Significant predictors of test anxiety among students with and without learning disabilities. *Journal of Learning Disabilities, 40,* 360–376.

Wiggins, G., & McTighe, J. (2007). *Schooling by design.* Alexandria, VA: Association of Supervision and Curriculum Development.

Wiliam, D. (2010). An integrative summary of the research literature and implications for a new theory of formative assessment. In H. L. Andrade & G. J. Cizek (Eds.), *Handbook of formative assessment* (pp. 18–40). New York, NY: Routledge.

Wiliam, D. (2011). *Embedded formative assessment.* Bloomington, IN: Solution Tree.

Wodtke, K. H., Harper, F., & Schommer, M. (1989). How standardized is school testing? An exploratory observational study of standardized group testing in kindergarten. *Educational Evaluation and Policy Analysis, 11,* 223–235.

Wright, W. E. (2006). A catch-22 for language learners. *Educational Leadership, 64*(3), 22–27.

Zeidner, M., & Matthews, G. (2005). Evaluation anxiety: Current theory and research. In A. J. Elliot & C. S. Dweck (Eds.), *Handbook of competence and motivation* (pp. 141–163). New York, NY: Guilford Press.

Zimmermann, F., Schütte, K., Taskinen, P., & Köller, O. (2013). Reciprocal effects between adolescent externalizing problems and measures of achievement. *Journal of Educational Psychology, 105,* 747–761.

APPENDIX A

Gottfried, A. E., Fleming, J. S., & Gottfried, A. W. (1994). Role of parental motivational practices in children's academic intrinsic motivation and achievement. *Journal of Educational Psychology, 86,* 104–113.

Marsh, H. W., Gerlach, E., Trautwein, U., Lüdtke, O., & Brettschneider, W.-D. (2007). Longitudinal study of preadolescent sport self-concept and performance reciprocal effects and causal ordering. *Child Development, 78,* 1640–1656.

McGrew, K. S., Flanagan, D. P., Zeith, T. Z., & Vanderwood, M. (1997). Beyond g: The impact of *Gf-Gc* specific cognitive abilities research on the future use and interpretation of intelligence tests in the schools. *School Psychology Review, 26,* 189–210.

Miller, P. A., Eisenberg, N., Fabes, R. A., & Shell, R. (1996). Relations of moral reasoning and vicarious emotion to young children's prosocial behavior toward peers and adults. *Developmental Psychology, 32,* 210–219.

Name Index

Subject Index